MICROECONOMICS

The McGraw-Hill Economics Series

SURVEY OF ECONOMICS

Brue, McConnell, and Flynn
Essentials of Economics
Fourth Edition

Mandel
M: Economics—The Basics
Fourth Edition

Schiller and Gebhardt
Essentials of Economics
Eleventh Edition

PRINCIPLES OF ECONOMICS

Asarta and Butters
Connect Master: Economics
Second Edition

Colander
Economics, Microeconomics, and Macroeconomics
Eleventh Edition

Frank, Bernanke, Antonovics, and Heffetz
Principles of Economics, Principles of Microeconomics, Principles of Macroeconomics
Seventh Edition

Frank, Bernanke, Antonovics, and Heffetz
Streamlined Editions: Principles of Economics, Principles of Microeconomics, Principles of Macroeconomics
Third Edition

Karlan and Morduch
Economics, Microeconomics, Macroeconomics
Third Edition

McConnell, Brue, and Flynn
Economics, Microeconomics, Macroeconomics
Twenty-Second Edition

Samuelson and Nordhaus
Economics, Microeconomics, and Macroeconomics
Nineteenth Edition

Schiller and Gebhardt
The Economy Today, The Micro Economy Today, and The Macro Economy Today
Fifteenth Edition

Slavin
Economics, Microeconomics, and Macroeconomics
Twelfth Edition

ECONOMICS OF SOCIAL ISSUES

Guell
Issues in Economics Today
Ninth Edition

Register and Grimes
Economics of Social Issues
Twenty-First Edition

ECONOMETRICS AND DATA ANALYTICS

Hilmer and Hilmer
Practical Econometrics
First Edition

Prince
Predictive Analytics for Business Strategy
First Edition

MANAGERIAL ECONOMICS

Baye and Prince
Managerial Economics and Business Strategy
Ninth Edition

Brickley, Smith, and Zimmerman
Managerial Economics and Organizational Architecture
Sixth Edition

Thomas and Maurice
Managerial Economics
Thirteenth Edition

INTERMEDIATE ECONOMICS

Bernheim and Whinston
Microeconomics
Second Edition

Dornbusch, Fischer, and Startz
Macroeconomics
Thirteenth Edition

Frank
Microeconomics and Behavior
Ninth Edition

ADVANCED ECONOMICS

Romer
Advanced Macroeconomics
Fifth Edition

MONEY AND BANKING

Cecchetti and Schoenholtz
Money, Banking, and Financial Markets
Sixth Edition

URBAN ECONOMICS

O'Sullivan
Urban Economics
Ninth Edition

LABOR ECONOMICS

Borjas
Labor Economics
Eighth Edition

McConnell, Brue, and Macpherson
Contemporary Labor Economics
Eleventh Edition

PUBLIC FINANCE

Rosen and Gayer
Public Finance
Tenth Edition

ENVIRONMENTAL ECONOMICS

Field and Field
Environmental Economics: An Introduction
Seventh Edition

INTERNATIONAL ECONOMICS

Appleyard and Field
International Economics
Ninth Edition

Pugel
International Economics
Seventeenth Edition

MICROECONOMICS

Improve Your World

THIRD EDITION

Dean Karlan

Northwestern University and Innovations for Poverty Action

Jonathan Morduch

New York University

MICROECONOMICS: IMPROVE YOUR WORLD, THIRD EDITION

1 2 3 4 5 6 7 8 9 LWI 24 23 22 21 20

ISBN 978-1-260-52107-8 (bound edition)
MHID 1-260-52107-9 (bound edition)
ISBN 978-1-260-52097-2 (loose-leaf edition)
MHID 1-260-52097-8 (loose-leaf edition)

Portfolio Director: *Anke Weekes*
Senior Product Developer: *Christina Kouvelis*
Marketing Manager: *Bobby Pearson*
Senior Project Manager, Core Content: *Kathryn D. Wright*
Senior Project Manager, Assessment Content: *Keri Johnson*
Project Manager, Media Content: *Karen Jozefowicz*
Senior Buyer: *Laura Fuller*
Senior Designer: *Matt Diamond*
Content Licensing Specialist: *Lorraine Buczek*
Cover Image: *©Sashkin/Shutterstock*
Compositor: *SPi Global*

Library of Congress Cataloging-in-Publication Data

Names: Karlan, Dean S., author. | Morduch, Jonathan, author.
Title: Microeconomics / Dean Karlan, Northwestern University and Innovations for
    Poverty Action, Jonathan Morduch, New York University.
Description: Third Edition. | New York, NY : McGraw-Hill Education, [2020]
Identifiers: LCCN 2019033378 | ISBN 9781260521078 (hardcover)
Subjects: LCSH: Microeconomics.
Classification: LCC HB172 .K36 2020 | DDC 338.5—dc23
LC record available at https://lccn.loc.gov/2019033378

dedication

We dedicate this book to our families.

—Dean and Jonathan

about the authors

Dean Karlan

©Dean Karlan

Dean Karlan is the Frederic Esser Nemmers Distinguished Professor of Economics and Finance at the Kellogg School of Management at Northwestern University and President and Founder of Innovations for Poverty Action (IPA). Dean started IPA in 2002 with two aims: to help learn what works and what does not in the fight against poverty and other social problems around the world, and then to implement successful ideas at scale. IPA has worked in over 50 countries, with 1,000 employees around the world. Dean's personal research focuses on using field experiments to learn more about the effectiveness of financial services for low-income households, with a focus on using behavioral economics approaches to improve financial products and services as well as build sustainable sources of income. His research includes related areas, such as charitable fund-raising, voting, health, and education. Dean is also cofounder of stickK.com, a start-up that helps people use commitment contracts to achieve personal goals, such as losing weight or completing a problem set on time, and in 2015 he cofounded ImpactMatters, an organization that produces ratings of charities based on impact estimates. Dean is a Sloan Foundation Research Fellow, a Guggenheim Fellow, and an Executive Committee member of the Board of the MIT Jameel Poverty Action Lab. In 2007 he was awarded a Presidential Early Career Award for Scientists and Engineers. He is coeditor of the *Journal of Development Economics*. He holds a BA from University of Virginia, an MPP and MBA from University of Chicago, and a PhD in Economics from MIT. He has coauthored *The Goldilocks Challenge* (2018), *Failing in the Field* (2016), and *More Than Good Intentions: Improving the Ways the World's Poor Borrow, Save, Farm, Learn, and Stay Healthy* (2011).

Jonathan Morduch

©Jonathan Morduch

Jonathan Morduch is Professor of Public Policy and Economics at New York University's Wagner Graduate School of Public Service. Jonathan focuses on innovations that expand the frontiers of finance and how financial markets shape economic growth and inequality. Jonathan has lived and worked in Asia, but his newest book, *The Financial Diaries: How American Families Cope in a World of Uncertainty* (written with Rachel Schneider and published by Princeton University Press, 2017), follows families in California, Mississippi, Ohio, Kentucky, and New York as they cope with economic ups and downs over a year. The new work jumps off from ideas in *Portfolios of the Poor: How the World's Poor Live on $2 a Day* (Princeton University Press, 2009), which Jonathan coauthored and which describes how families in Bangladesh, India, and South Africa devise ways to make it through a year living on $2 a day or less. Jonathan's research on financial markets is collected in *The Economics of Microfinance* and *Banking the World*, both published by MIT Press. At NYU, Jonathan is executive director of the Financial Access Initiative, a center that supports research on extending access to finance in low-income communities. Jonathan's ideas have also shaped policy through work with the United Nations, World Bank, and other international organizations. In 2009, the Free University of Brussels awarded Jonathan an honorary doctorate to recognize his work on microfinance. He holds a BA from Brown and a PhD from Harvard, both in Economics.

Karlan and **Morduch** first met in 2001 and have been friends and colleagues ever since. Before writing this text, they collaborated on research on financial institutions. Together, they've written about new directions in financial access for the middle class and poor, and in Peru they set up a laboratory to study incentives in financial contracts for loans to women to start small enterprises. In 2006, together with Sendhil Mullainathan, they started the Financial Access Initiative, a center dedicated to expanding knowledge about financial solutions for the 40 percent of the world's adults who lack access to banks. This text reflects their shared passion for using economics as a tool to improve one's own life and to promote better business and public policies in the broader world.

brief contents

Thinking Like an Economist

Part 1 The Power of Economics 1
1 Economics and Life 3
2 Specialization and Exchange 25

Part 2 Supply and Demand 47
3 Markets 49
4 Elasticity 79
5 Efficiency 103
6 Government Intervention 129

Microeconomics: Thinking Like a Microeconomist

Part 3 Individual Decisions 163
7 Consumer Behavior 165
8 Behavioral Economics: A Closer Look at Decision Making 189
9 Game Theory and Strategic Thinking 203
10 Information 229
11 Time and Uncertainty 245

Part 4 Firm Decisions 265
12 The Costs of Production 267
13 Perfect Competition 293
14 Monopoly 323
15 Monopolistic Competition and Oligopoly 353
16 The Factors of Production 383
17 International Trade 419

Part 5 Public Economics 449
18 Externalities 451
19 Public Goods and Common Resources 477
20 Taxation and the Public Budget 497
21 Poverty, Inequality, and Discrimination 525
22 Political Choices 563
23 Public Policy and Choice Architecture 585

The field and practice of economics has changed a lot. Most textbooks haven't. This one is different.

Economics is now much more empirical, even compared to 15 years ago. The incredible data and computing power available today have transformed research on economic inequality, mobility, health care, trade, the environment, media, finance, macro mechanisms, and—well, you name it. Almost every part of economics is being reshaped by new evidence. Topics often not thought of as "economics," such as love, happiness, sports, and social networks, are now regularly analyzed through economic frameworks.

We've found that **incorporating new research and evidence makes teaching and learning easier, not harder,** by connecting to what students see in everyday life. The new economics of inequality, for example, shows students that the field is not single-mindedly concerned with overall growth of an economy but also with whether and why some are left out of that growth (and what to do about it). Similarly, new work on international trade shows that economists are deeply engaged by who's winning and who's losing as markets expand. Increasingly, **economic research is also leading to new, practical ideas to improve lives.**

In our own work, for example, we show how financial innovations inspired by behavioral economics can help people save and invest more effectively, and we've worked these insights into the text where appropriate. For example, a box in Chapter 21, based on recent financial-diary research, illustrates, through a description of one family's financial struggle, the problem of income instability.

Another transformation in economics is happening as the field attracts **new voices.** Younger economists have taken a broad view of economics. They come from a wider variety of backgrounds, and they are more likely to be women, compared to scholars a generation ago. This edition brings their voices more fully into the intro course.

- In Chapter 4, we describe an experiment by Pascaline Dupas and Jessica Cohen that shows how elasticities shape policies to prevent communicable disease.
- In Chapter 22, we draw on Thomas Fujiwara's study showing how new voting technologies expanded voting and led to an increase in the provision of public goods.

The work of these economists has inspired us, and we hope that examples of their work will help students find new connections—and maybe even some new role models—in economics.

Throughout the text, we have worked hard to **inspire students.** Students' impressions of economics sometimes are right: The field can be dry and technical—and thus often harder to learn. But it doesn't have to be that way.

We've aimed at a casual tone, imagining that we're having a conversation with students, with **down-to-earth situations and personal examples that resonate with student readers.** For example:

- How understanding price elasticity can help you spend less money on plane tickets.
- Whether the cost of college is worth it. (Spoiler: It probably is.)

Teachers know the value of a good story, one that connects economic principles to ideas and issues in the world. In our text, **we weave real stories into the presentation**—at the start of every chapter and as recurring examples and in boxes throughout the chapters. For example, Chapter 2 uses the cell phone market to illustrate supply and demand, and Chapter 4 uses the price of a latte to demonstrate elasticity. **We employ economic tools as a way of explaining real people and their decisions.**

We then layer policy implications into the discussion of economic ideas and principles. For example, in Chapter 1, the idea of opportunity cost is first framed as a personal example of whether to spend the evening having dinner with friends. We next broaden the idea to the opportunity cost of an unpaid internship, and later in the chapter broaden the idea still further with a box that asks students to compare the cost of an iPad to charitable giving as a way to think about opportunity costs in a global context.

Our goal in this third edition is to help close the gap between economics in the classroom and the economic world that students see around them. **Our aim is not just to bring students up to date, but to demonstrate the idea that "Economics can improve your world."**

Who are we? Why did we write this text?

Microeconomics draws on our own experiences as academic economists, teachers, and policy advisors. We are based at large research universities and often work with and advise nonprofit organizations, governments, international agencies, donors, and private firms. Much of our research involves figuring out **how to improve the way real markets function.** Working with partners in the United States and on six continents, we are involved in testing new economic ideas. *Microeconomics* draws on the spirit of that work, as well as similar research, taking students through the process of engaging with real problems, using analytical tools to devise solutions, and ultimately showing what works and why.

One of the best parts of writing this text, promoting its first edition, and revising for the second and third editions has been the opportunity to spend time with instructors across the country. We've been inspired by their creativity and passion and have learned from their pedagogical ideas. One of the questions we often ask fellow instructors is why they originally became interested in economics. A common response—one we share—is an attraction to the logic and power of economics as a social science. We also often hear instructors describe something slightly different: the way that economics appealed to them as **a tool for making sense of life's complexities,** whether in business, politics, or daily life. We wrote this text to give instructors a way to share with their students both of those ways that economics matters.

We also are grateful to the many adopters and near-adopters of the first two editions who provided many helpful suggestions for ways to make the third edition an even better resource for instructors and students. As you'll see in the list of chapter-by-chapter changes that starts on page xxiii, we've worked hard to fulfill your expectations and meet that goal.

We hope to inspire students to continue their studies in economics, and we promise this text will give them something useful to take away even if they choose other areas of study.

Finally, we hope that, in ways small and large, the tools they learn in these pages and this course will help them to think critically about their environment, to live better lives, and to make an impact on their world. Our underlying motive throughout has been to demonstrate—through stories, examples, research, and policy discussions—**the good that economics can do to "improve your world."**

Dean Karlan
Northwestern University

Jonathan Morduch
New York University

Karlan/Morduch connects with students—from its consistent data-driven and impact-based approach to a wide variety of examples and case studies, demonstrating how questions can be used to address real issues. By **teaching the *right questions to ask,*** the text provides students with a method for working through decisions they'll face as consumers, employees, entrepreneurs, and voters. Here are the four questions:

- **Question 1: *What are the wants and constraints of those involved?*** This question introduces the concept of *scarcity.* It asks students to think critically about the preferences and resources driving decision making in a given situation. It links into discussions of utility functions, budget constraints, strategic behavior, and new ideas that expand our thinking about rationality and behavioral economics.

- **Question 2: *What are the trade-offs?*** This question focuses on *opportunity cost.* It asks students to understand trade-offs in any decision, including factors that might go beyond the immediate financial costs and benefits. Consideration of trade-offs takes us to discussions of marginal decision making, sunk costs, nonmonetary costs, and discounting.

- **Question 3: *How will others respond?*** This question asks students to focus on *incentives,* both their incentives and the incentives of others. Students consider how individual choices aggregate in both expected and unexpected ways, and what happens when incentives change. The question links into understanding supply and demand, elasticity, competition, taxation, game theory, and monetary and fiscal policy.

- **Question 4: *Are resources being allocated in the best way possible?*** This question relates to *efficiency.* It asks students to start from an assumption that markets work to provide desired goods and services, and then to think carefully about why something that seems like a good idea isn't already being done. We encourage students to revisit their answers to the previous three questions, to see whether they missed something about the trade-offs, incentives, or other forces at work, or are looking at a genuine market failure. When we consider allocations, we also ask who's winning and who's losing through economic changes. This fourth question links topics such as public goods, externalities, information gaps, monopoly, arbitrage, and how the economy operates in the long run versus the short run.

Engaging pedagogical features

Compelling examples and stories open each chapter and are woven throughout the narrative. These include such examples as eBay, gifts of ugly holiday sweaters, how to curb littering, the cost of prescription medicines, why diamonds are expensive, the music-recording industry, why MLB pitchers are paid more than farm workers, why politicians haven't enacted a carbon tax, how a jar of peanut butter relates to the size of the U.S. economy, the Great Recession and the housing bubble, cigarette money in World War II, and the iPhone as an import. Through these stories, we introduce to students issues that consumers, voters, businesspeople, and family members face in their lives.

Additionally, the following **features add interesting real-world details:**

- **Economics in Action** boxes, originally titled Real Life, describe a short case or policy question, findings from history or academic studies, and anecdotes from the field.

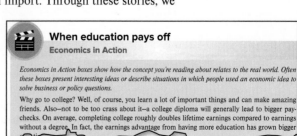

When education pays off
Economics in Action

Economics in Action boxes show how the concept you're reading about relates to the real world. Often these boxes present interesting ideas or describe situations in which people used an economic idea to solve business or policy questions.

Why go to college? Well, of course, you learn a lot of important things and can make amazing friends. Also—not to be too crass about it—a college diploma will generally lead to bigger paychecks. On average, completing college roughly doubles lifetime earnings compared to earnings without a degree. In fact, the earnings advantage of having more education has grown bigger

Does ice cream cause polio?
From Another Angle

From Another Angle boxes show you a completely different way of looking at an economic concept. We find that a little bit of weirdness goes a long way in helping us to remember things.

Polio is a disease that once crippled or killed thousands of children in the United States every year. Before the cause of polio was known, doctors noticed that polio infections seemed to be more common ~~children who had been~~ ~~ing lots of ice cream. Observing this *correlation* led~~

The opportunity cost of a life
What Do You Think?

What Do You Think? present questions that require you to combine facts and economic analysis with values and moral reasoning. There can be many "correct" answers, depending on your values and goals.

The philosopher Peter Singer writes that opportunity costs can be a matter of life or death. Imagine you are a salesperson, and on your way to a meeting on a hot summer day, you drive by a lake. Suddenly, you notice that a child who has been swimming in the lake is drowning. No one else is in sight.

You have a choice. If ~~you~~ ~~car an~~ ~~into the lake to save t~~ ~~child, you will be late~~

Finding a travel bargain
Econ and YOU

Econ and YOU boxes show tips, strategies, and other ways that economics can inform choices—big and small—in your own life.

Are you fantasizing about traveling someplace warm for spring break? Taking a trip to see family or friends? If you've looked at airline prices, you'll know that some tickets can be really expensive and some much ~~cheaper~~—even on the same routes. Why?

- **From Another Angle** boxes show a different way of looking at an economic concept—a different way of thinking about a situation, a humorous story, or sometimes just an unusual application of a standard idea.

- **What Do You Think?** boxes offer a longer case study, with implications for public policy and student-related issues. They present relevant data or historical evidence and ask students to employ both economic analysis and normative arguments to defend a position. We leave the student with open-ended questions, which professors can assign as homework or use for classroom discussion. Many of these boxes are current ideas: the $15 minimum wage, who should be able to buy assault rifles, payday lending, preventive health care, immigration, the estate tax, affirmative action in college admission, and more.

- **Econ and YOU** boxes are **new to this edition** and have been created to show students how they might apply economics in their personal decisions. Topics included in this new boxed feature include personal finance, raising a family, unpaid internships, among others. We weave these everyday scenarios with economic principles to help students develop economic intuition.

In this edition, we've added numerous new stories across the four categories of boxed examples, and we've updated many more with fresh data. Throughout, our approach is to offer a **positive outlook** that can be achieved through the application of economic principles to real-world problems.

Our voice throughout the text is casual and (we think, and hope!) fun to read. We've tried to include examples, products, issues, and problems that students will find of interest. In addition, where terminology or ideas are potentially confusing, we've built in two additional features to help clarify:

⚠ CAUTION: COMMON MISTAKE

You may notice that these five factors include price-related issues such as the price of relat~~ed~~ goods and expectations about future prices. So why do we refer to them as *nonprice determinan~~ts~~*? We do so in order to differentiate them from the effect of the *current price* of the good demand for that good.

- **Caution: Common Mistake** and **Take Note**—offer in-depth explanations of a concept or use of terminology. These boxes call attention to common misunderstandings or provide further explanation of tricky concepts. Students appreciate that rather than smoothing over confusing ideas and language, we offer the support they need to understand economic language and reasoning on a deeper level.

Throughout this text, every chapter contains built-in review tools and study devices for student use:

- **Test Yourself questions tied to learning objectives** appear at the end of each major section and prompt students to make sure they understand the topics covered before moving on.

TAKE NOTE... ✎

- Remember that the elasticity of *demand* is calculated by dividing a positive number by a negative number, or by dividing a negative number by a positive number, so the answer is always negative.

- The elasticity of *supply*, on the other hand, is calculated by dividing either a positive ~~number by a~~ ~~positiv~~ ~~er~~

- **Conclusions** at the end of each chapter sum up the overall lessons learned and look ahead to how the topic just presented will be used in other chapters.

- **Key Terms** provide a convenient list of the economic terminology introduced and defined in the chapter.

- **Summaries** give a deeper synopsis of what each learning objective covered.

Also located at the end of each chapter and smoothly integrated with the chapter text, are questions and problems for each learning objective:

- **Review Questions** guide students through review and application of the concepts covered in the chapter. These range from straightforward questions about theories or formulas to more open-ended narrative questions.
- High-quality **Problems and Applications** problem sets provide quantitative homework opportunities.

Both sets of content, plus **additional Extra Practice Questions**, are **fully integrated with Connect®**, enabling online assignments and grading.

Unique coverage

Microeconomics presents the *core principles* of economics but also seeks to present some of the **new ideas that are expanding the basics of economic theory**. The sequence of chapters follows a fairly traditional route through the core principles. In a departure from the norm, we present the chapters on individual decision making (Part 3) before firm decisions (Part 4). We believe that by thinking first about the choices faced by individuals, students become better prepared to understand the choices of firms, groups, and governments. The text proceeds step-by-step from the personal to the public, allowing students to build toward an understanding of aggregate decisions on a solid foundation of individual decision making.

Microeconomics offers several stand-alone chapters focused on new ideas that are expanding economic theory, which can add nuance and depth to the core principles curriculum: **behavioral economics, game theory, information, time and uncertainty, political choices, and choice architecture.**

In addition, because students need reinforcement with the math requirements of the course, *Microeconomics* contains seven unique math appendixes that explain math topics important to understanding economics. **McGraw-Hill Connect®** also offers a math preparedness assignment for those needing a refresher.

The Karlan and Morduch product was built "from the ground up" with the expectation of *complete digital integration* of the text and related hands-on learning materials. All content in the chapter and online is tagged to the chapter learning objectives. Further, this text comes with a robust line-up of learning and teaching products, built for simple and reliable usability. See below for the highlights of our digital offer within **McGraw-Hill Connect®**.

McGraw-Hill Connect

SmartBook adaptive reading, assignable end-of-chapter exercises, additional problem sets, interactive graphing practice, assignable video resources, math remediation, and more! See pages xx–xxi for more information.

Instructor resources

All supplements accompany this text in a completely seamless integration. The following ancillaries are available for quick download and convenient access via the instructor resource site available through McGraw-Hill Connect. Instructor resources are password protected for security.

- **Test bank**: Thousands of quality static and new algorithmic questions have been thoroughly accuracy checked and are tagged with the corresponding learning objective, level of difficulty, economic concept, AACSB learning category, and Bloom's Taxonomy objective for easy filtering.
- **PowerPoint presentations**: Each presentation covers crucial information and supplies animated figures that are identical to those in the book. The presentations also contain sample exercises, instructor notes, and more.
- **Instructor guide**: This resource provides a wealth of resources to help organize and enrich the course. Elements include: learning objectives, chapter outline, beyond the lecture, and clicker questions.
- **Solutions manual**: Answers to all end-of-chapter review questions and problems have been separated for the instructor guide for quick access.

Your book, your way

McGraw-Hill Create™ enables you to select and arrange the combination of traditional and unique chapters and appendixes that will be perfect for *your* course, at an affordable price for *your* students. Visit www.mheducation.com/highered/learning-solutions/create.html for more information.

Assurance of learning ready

Many educational institutions today are focused on the notion of *assurance of learning,* an important element of some accreditation standards. Karlan and Morduch's *Microeconomics* is designed specifically to support your assurance of learning initiatives with a simple, yet powerful solution. Each test bank question for *Microeconomics* maps to a specific chapter learning outcome/objective listed in the text. You can use our test bank software or Connect to easily query for learning outcomes/objectives that directly relate to the learning objectives for your course. You can then use the reporting features to aggregate student results in similar fashion, making the collection and presentation of assurance of learning data simple and easy.

AACSB statement

McGraw-Hill Education is a proud corporate member of AACSB International. Understanding the importance and value of AACSB accreditation, Karlan and Morduch's *Microeconomics* recognizes the curricula guidelines detailed in the AACSB standards for business accreditation by connecting selected questions in the text and the test bank to the general knowledge and skill guidelines in the AACSB standards.

The statements contained in *Microeconomics* are provided only as a guide for the users of this textbook. The AACSB leaves content coverage and assessment within the purview of individual schools, the mission of the school, and the faculty. While *Microeconomics* and the teaching package make no claim of any specific AACSB qualification or evaluation, we have within *Microeconomics* labeled selected questions according to the general knowledge and skills areas.

McGraw-Hill customer care contact information

At McGraw-Hill, we understand that getting the most from new technology can be challenging. That's why our services don't stop after you purchase our products. You can reach our Product Specialists 24 hours a day to get product training online. Or you can search our knowledge bank of Frequently Asked Questions on our support website. For Customer Support, call **800-331-5094,** or visit www.mheducation.com/highered/contact.html. One of our Technical Support Analysts will be able to assist you in a timely fashion.

McGraw Hill — Connect Economics

As a learning science company, we create interactive learning content that supports higher order thinking skills. Read below to learn how each of our market-leading Connect assets take students higher and drives a deeper level of content understanding. Elevate your Economics course!

SmartBook 2.0

SmartBook 2.0 makes study time as productive and efficient as possible. Students move between reading and practice modes to learn the content within the chapter. As they progress, the adaptive engine identifies knowledge gaps and offers up content to reinforce areas of weakness.

Videos

Tutorial videos provide engaging explanations to help students grasp challenging concepts. Application videos bring economics to life with relevant, real world examples. All videos include closed captioning for accessibility and are assignable with assessment questions for improved retention.

Interactive Graphs

Interactive Graphs provide visual displays of real data and economic concepts for students to manipulate. All graphs are accompanied by assignable assessment questions and feedback to guide students through the experience of learning to read and interpret graphs and data.

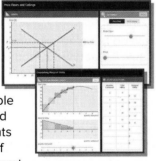

Math Preparedness

Math Preparedness assignments help students refresh important prerequisite topics necessary to be successful in economics. Tutorial videos are included to help illustrate math concepts to students visually.

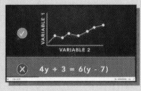

Graphing Exercises

Graphing tools within Connect provide opportunities for students to draw, interact with, manipulate, and analyze graphs in their online auto-graded assignments. The Connect graphing tool is easy to use and helps students apply and practice important economic ideas.

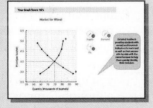

Homework Problems

End-of-chapter homework problems reinforce chapter content through a variety of question types including questions that make use of the graphing tool. Problems with algorithmic variations and auto-grading are also available.

For more information, please visit **www.mheducation.com/highered/economics**

FOR INSTRUCTORS

You're in the driver's seat.

Want to build your own course? No problem. Prefer to use our turnkey, prebuilt course? Easy. Want to make changes throughout the semester? Sure. And you'll save time with Connect's auto-grading too.

65%
Less Time Grading

They'll thank you for it.

Adaptive study resources like SmartBook® 2.0 help your students be better prepared in less time. You can transform your class time from dull definitions to dynamic debates. Find out more about the powerful personalized learning experience available in SmartBook 2.0 at **www.mheducation.com/highered/connect/smartbook**

Make it simple, make it affordable.

Connect makes it easy with seamless integration using any of the major Learning Management Systems—Blackboard®, Canvas, and D2L, among others—to let you organize your course in one convenient location. Give your students access to digital materials at a discount with our inclusive access program. Ask your McGraw-Hill representative for more information.

Solutions for your challenges.

A product isn't a solution. Real solutions are affordable, reliable, and come with training and ongoing support when you need it and how you want it. Our Customer Experience Group can also help you troubleshoot tech problems—although Connect's 99% uptime means you might not need to call them. See for yourself at **status. mheducation.com**

Effective, efficient studying.

Connect helps you be more productive with your study time and get better grades using tools like SmartBook 2.0, which highlights key concepts and creates a personalized study plan. Connect sets you up for success, so you walk into class with confidence and walk out with better grades.

Study anytime, anywhere.

Download the free ReadAnywhere app and access your online eBook or SmartBook 2.0 assignments when it's convenient, even if you're offline. And since the app automatically syncs with your eBook and SmartBook 2.0 assignments in Connect, all of your work is available every time you open it. Find out more at **www.mheducation.com/readanywhere**

> *"I really liked this app—it made it easy to study when you don't have your text-book in front of you."*
>
> - Jordan Cunningham, Eastern Washington University

No surprises.

The Connect Calendar and Reports tools keep you on track with the work you need to get done and your assignment scores. Life gets busy; Connect tools help you keep learning through it all.

Calendar: owattaphotos/Getty Images

Learning for everyone.

McGraw-Hill works directly with Accessibility Services Departments and faculty to meet the learning needs of all students. Please contact your Accessibility Services office and ask them to email accessibility@mheducation.com, or visit **www.mheducation.com/about/accessibility** for more information.

detailed content changes

We've made numerous changes to the third edition of this text, prompted by users, reviewers, and developing ideas in economics. This section provides a detailed list of changes.

In all chapters

In all chapters, the authors have made the following changes:

- Updated real-world data in text, figures, and tables.
- Added a **new category of boxed insert, "Econ and YOU,"** that offers examples of economics at play in personal decisions large and small. Topics include personal finance, raising a family, and unpaid internships, among others.
- Added new boxes (see details in the chapter lists below).
- Freshened existing boxes either by updating or by substituting new box topics for old ones, as detailed below. In addition, we've retitled the "Real Life" boxes as "Economics in Action."
- Reformatted long discussions into smaller bites of content, to further sharpen the text's already-strong readability and student interest.
- Added more female names and examples throughout. Added more non-Western names in end-of-chapter materials.
- Added photos in some boxes, for greater student interest.

The following list does not repeat these text-wide changes but, rather, details specific changes made to each chapter.

Chapter 1: Economics and Life

- Changed the fourth economist's question from "Why isn't someone already doing it?" to "Are resources being allocated in the best way possible?" to clarify the idea of efficiency. Revised the associated text section on efficiency, with discussion of the practical implications of efficiency.
- Clarified the opportunity cost example—changed from going on a road trip to having dinner with friends. Added example of unpaid internship.
- Added "Marginal decision making" subheading.
- New Figure 1-1 (showing total revenue generated by bowling alleys correlated with per capita consumption of sour cream) illustrates the need to differentiate between correlation and causation.
- Replaced the box about Malthus's model with a new Economics in Action box, titled *When education pays off,* about Goldin & Katz's model explaining gains from education.

Chapter 2: Specialization and Exchange

- Slightly revised and shortened the From Another Angle box about Babe Ruth as an example of absolute and comparative advantage.
- Replaced Bill Gates as a text example of specialization with Stacy Brown-Philpot, CEO of TaskRabbit.
- Replaced the Economics in Action *Is self-sufficiency a virtue?* box with a new box *Winners and losers;* the new box describes the closing of an Ohio factory as a way to show how

international trade results in some winners and some losers (suggesting that getting the benefits of trade can depend on compensating those who lose out from trade).

- Moved from online-only into the print product the Economics in Action box *Comparative advantage: The good, the bad, and the ugly* that discusses whether a country's loss of comparative advantage at producing a particular good is something to worry about.

Appendix A: Math Essentials: Understanding Graphs and Slopes

- Revised Figures A-1 and A-3 with new data.
- Replaced Figure A-2 with data showing market share for domestic and imported vehicle types.

Chapter 3: Markets

- Replaced the Real Life *The Prius shortage of 2003* box with a new Economics in Action box, *The great Elmo shortage.*
- Revised the Economics in Action *Give a man a fish* box to clarify the findings of economist Robert Jensen's research on how cell phones changed the market for fish in Kerala, India.

Chapter 4: Elasticity

- Revised the Economics in Action *Does charging for bednets decrease malaria?* box to clarify and better highlight the work of Jessica Cohen and Pascaline Dupas on the price elasticity of demand for bednets in Kenya.
- Updated the What Do You Think? *Should entrance fees at national parks be raised?* box to include the 2017 proposal to increase fees in national parks.
- Removed the Where Can It Take You? *Pricing analyst* box and replaced it with a new Econ and YOU *Finding a travel bargain* box that discusses how understanding price elasticity can help when you buy airline tickets.

Chapter 5: Efficiency

- In the "Willingness to sell and the supply curve" subsection, revised the example (and related figures) by changing Seller #1 from a comic book collector to a college student wanting money to see a favorite band.
- Changed the Real Life *Haggling and bluffing* box to an Econ and YOU *It pays to negotiate* box that discusses salary negotiations as a common version of price negotiation. The new box references recent research by Marianne Bertrand; Hannah Riley Bowles, Linda Babcock, and Lei Lai; Andres Leibbrandt and John List; and Ellen Pao on gender differences in negotiation.

Chapter 6: Government Intervention

- Revised the What Do You Think? *Put a cap on payday lending?* box (including questions) to make it more personal (a broken-down car).
- Revised the data in the "Buyers pay more" example in Figure 6-10.
- Removed the Where Can It Take You? *Public economics* box and replaced it with a new Econ and YOU *Out of sight, out of mind* box that looks at research by Raj Chetty, Adam Looney, and Kory Kroft to test whether grocery-store shoppers "forget" about sales tax when they look at price tags.
- Replaced the What Do You Think? *Farm subsidies* box with a new *Fight for $15* box that looks at the debate and economic research about a $15 federal minimum wage.

Chapter 7: Consumer Behavior

- Revised the Real Life *The science of happiness* box. Repurposed as an Econ and YOU box titled *Spending your way to happiness?*, it now looks at the idea of utility to understand what makes people happy and includes research by Tamas Hajdu and Gabor Hajdu from a survey tracking the overall life satisfaction and spending habits of 10,000 people in Hungary.
- Fixed text references to points in panels A and B of Figure 7-1, and added a point B to panel B of Figure 7-1.
- Repurposed the What Do You Think? *Choosing a league* box to Econ and YOU.
- Shortened the Economics in Action *Why we give* box.

Appendix E: Using Indifference Curves

- Changed the gender in the example used throughout the appendix from male (Malik) to female (Laila), to further differentiate the related examples used in the body of Chapter 7 and in this appendix.

Chapter 8: Behavioral Economics

- Added a new Econ and YOU *Is a dollar a dollar?* box about the method-of-payment effect.

Chapter 9: Game Theory and Strategic Thinking

- In the "Prisoners' dilemma" subsection, changed the text references from the Bush and Kerry 2004 campaign to more-generic *Party A* and *Party B*.
- Revised the colors used in the decision matrixes in the chapter to make them more lively.
- Repurposed the From Another Angle *Tit-for-tat and human emotions* box to an Econ and YOU *Can game theory explain why you feel guilt?* box; the box looks at how emotions may have promoted cooperation in hunter-gatherer societies.
- Revised the Real Life *Dr. Strangelove. . .* box to an Economics in Action box titled *Totally MAD* that focuses on the story of Soviet Commander Stanislav Petrov who used his understanding of game theory, and his intuition, to decide *not* to launch a missile attack against the United States in 1983.

Chapter 10: Information

- Replaced the Where Can It Take You? *Risk management* box with a new Econ and YOU *Is college worth it?* box that discusses the financial return on a college degree and introduces Bryan Caplan's idea of a degree as a signaling device.
- Deleted the Real Life *Dress for success* box.
- Revised the What Do You Think? *From spray paint to auto insurance* box, retitled *Should teenagers be able to buy assault rifles?* to focus on a more current and controversial issue of statistical discrimination.
- Moved from online-only into the print product the What Do You Think? box *How much information is too much?* for a health-related look at adverse selection.

Chapter 11: Time and Uncertainty

- Added a new Econ and YOU *The rule of 70* box about how to estimate compounding of both savings and debt over time.
- Repurposed the From Another Angle *Hindsight is 20/20* box to an Econ and YOU *Are extended warranties worth it?* box that looks at the costs and benefits of such insurance.

Appendix F: Math Essentials: Compounding

Shortened the discussion of the rule of 70 in this appendix and elaborated on it in the body of Chapter 11 instead.

Chapter 12: The Costs of Production

- Revised the chapter-opening feature story to discuss EpiPen pricing (instead of Lipitor).
- Repurposed the From Another Angle *The "production" of kids* box to an Econ and YOU *The quarter-million dollar kid* box, updated with USDA estimates.
- Revised the From Another Angle *Beyond the bottom line* box for greater clarity about the goals of social enterprises.
- Revised Figure 12-2 by changing the axes to flatten out the total production curve.
- Revised Figure 12-3 by changing the axes to flatten out the average and marginal product curves.
- Added new subheadings "Graphing total cost" and "Graphing average cost" to present the discussion of total and average costs in smaller bites.
- Revised Figure 12-4 by changing the axes and showing data points, for better student understanding.
- Revised Figure 12-5 by changing the axes and showing data points, with call-out labels to differentiate between the lowest points on the AVC and ATC curves, for better student understanding.
- Revised Figure 12-6 by changing the axes and showing data points to correct the shape of the marginal cost curve.
- Revised Figure 12-7 by changing the axes and showing data points to correct the shape of the marginal cost curve and its intersection with the average total cost curve.
- Revised Figure 12-9 to make the long-run ATC curve more U-shaped and highlight that the long-run ATC curve represents the lowest point of all short-run ATC curves.
- Updated the Economics in Action *Walmart and economies of scale* box with a comparison of economies of scale for Walmart and Amazon.
- Updated and shortened the What Do You Think? *The profit motive and "orphan" drugs* box, retitled *Should drug companies care about neglected diseases?* to focus on the ethical issues surrounding drug development.

Chapter 13: Perfect Competition

- Revised the Real Life *Bazaar competition* box and retitled it Economics in Action *Why does the "Motor Mile" exist?* to discuss why we often see many businesses of the same type clustered near each other.
- Revised Figure 13-1 to show a more traditional marginal cost curve.
- Added a new From Another Angle *Who wants competition?* box, discussing that the amount of competition in a market can make or break a contestant's hopes on the ABC television show *Shark Tank.*

Chapter 14: Monopoly

- Made slight revisions to the discussion of natural monopolies, to clarify.
- Revised the From Another Angle *Poor monopolists* box for greater clarity and retitled it *Phone ladies.*
- Updated the text examples of recent big mergers (e.g., Amazon and Whole Foods).
- Added a new From Another Angle *The origins of Monopoly* box, discussing the original economic message and intent of the now-familiar board game.

Chapter 15: Monopolistic Competition and Oligopoly

- Updated Figure 15-1 with revised data showing market share in the music business.
- Added a new Econ and YOU *Fight the (market) power!* box about market power and its economic effects.
- In the "Oligopolies in competition" subsection, added subheadings for "Two firms (duopoly)" and "Three or more firms," to break down text into smaller discrete bites.

Chapter 16: The Factors of Production

- Replaced the featured player (Clayton Kershaw) in the chapter-opening story with Mike Trout.
- Expanded the discussion of the income and price effects of a wage increase with additional explanation of the fact that individual labor supply curves are not always linear and so the effect of a change in wages on hours worked may depend on where an individual is on the labor supply curve.
- Corrected the text statement in the discussion of Figure 16-7, which said (incorrectly) that demand shifted to the right, rather than to the left.
- Updated Figure 16-8, to show immigration through 2017.
- Revised the What Do You Think *Should the United States be a country of immigrants?* box to expand the discussion and to include mention of H-1B visas.
- Updated Figure 16-11, showing the factor distribution of income.
- In the subsection on "minimum wages and efficiency wages," expanded the text discussion of the effects of minimum-wage laws.
- Revised the online-only box on monopsony in baseball with a new Economics in Action *Have noncompete clauses gone too far?* box that explores how the idea of monopsony applies in today's labor market.
- Updated with a new paragraph on the 2018 Supreme Court ruling that public-sector unions can't force all employees to join the union and pay union dues.

Chapter 17: International Trade

- Replaced the chapter-opening feature story with one titled *A New Meaning to "Made in the USA"* that focuses on U.S.–China trade.
- Repurposed the old chapter-opening feature story about the garment business in Lesotho to a new in-chapter Economics in Action *Made in Lesotho. But why?* box to show that trade agreements can sometimes be more important than natural resources and climate in producing comparative advantage.
- In both the "Becoming a net importer" and "Becoming a net exporter" sections, expanded the text a bit to acknowledge that though the outcome of competition in world trade might be efficient, trade forces uncomfortable economic adjustments and has real political consequences.
- Clarified the callout labels in Figure 17-6.
- Revised the price data in Figure 17-7.
- Deleted the subsection "Selective exemptions from quotas and tariffs."
- In the "WTO and trade mediation" section, added a paragraph about the most-favored-nation provision. Also added a short discussion about 2018 trade negotiations between the United States and China.
- Revised the From Another Angle *Are environmental regulations bad for the environment?* box to address the idea of *pollution displacement* enabled by international trade and trade agreements.
- Retitled the subheading "Fair(ly) free trade" to "Pocketbook activism."
- Deleted the What Do You Think? *Lift the embargo on Cuba?* box.

Chapter 18: Externalities

- Added clarifying text statements about the terminology *marginal social cost* curve and the *marginal social benefit* curve.
- Replaced the Real Life *The fight over cap-and-trade legislation* box with a new Economics in Action *Why not tax ourselves?* box about the difficulties of imposing taxes on external costs like contributions to greenhouse-gas emissions.

Chapter 19: Public Goods and Common Resources

- Slightly revised examples in Figure 19-1 showing four categories of goods.
- Added as key terms *private goods* and *artificially scarce goods.*
- Added a new Economics in Action *Artificially scarce music* box about how streaming services like Spotify and Pandora make music excludable, creating an artificially scarce good that enables the services to charge a price above marginal cost.
- Replaced the text paragraph about Elinor Ostrom's research with a new Economics in Action *It's not necessarily a tragedy* box that looks in more depth at Ostrom's research into how social norms can sometimes be powerful enough for commonly held property to be managed extremely well.
- Moved from online-only into the print product the Economics in Action *Why the Colorado River no longer reaches the ocean* box that illustrates some mistakes in the management of a very important common resource, water.
- Deleted the Real Life *North American fisheries learn from failure* box.

Chapter 20: Taxation and the Public Budget

- Updated the tax data in the chapter's text, figures, and tables.
- Shortened the From Another Angle *Love the sinner, love the sin tax* box, now retitled *Can some taxes make people happier?* and refocused on the purpose and effects of "sin taxes," particularly in helping people curb consumption of cigarettes or alcohol.
- Added subheadings under the "Personal income tax" subheading for smaller bites of content and to differentiate between calculating personal income tax and the topic of capital gains tax.
- In the section on "Other taxes," added a paragraph about Internet sales tax collection, with reference to the 2018 Supreme Court ruling.
- Retitled the What Do You Think? *Death, taxes, and "death taxes"* box as *Death and taxes.*
- Revised the term *nondiscretionary spending* to *mandatory spending* and made it a key term.
- Added a short paragraph about voluntary gifts to the U.S. Treasury.

Chapter 21: Poverty, Inequality, and Discrimination

- Updated poverty data in the chapter's text, figures, and tables.
- Replaced the Real Life *What if your $2 a day doesn't come every day?* box with a related Economics in Action box, *Up and down in America* that focuses on Jonathan Morduch's U.S. financial diaries research.
- Slightly broadened LO 21-2 to address factors that contribute to poverty.
- Revised and shortened the Economics in Action *Getting out of the neighborhood* box.
- Revised the discussion of the Gini coefficient to use 100 (rather than 1) to indicate perfectly unequal income distribution, to reflect data found in typical Gini-coefficient resources.
- The revised Figure 21-5 now shows Gini coefficients for 30 countries.
- Added a new From Another Angle *Just give money* box about universal basic income (UBI). The new box replaces the online-only From Another Angle *Paying people to help themselves* box.

acknowledgments

Many people helped us create this text. It's said that "it takes a village," but it often felt like we had the benefit of an entire town.

We thank Meredith Startz, Ted Barnett, and Andrew Wright for the foundational work they contributed to the first edition, which still shines through in this edition. Thanks, too, to Victor Matheson (College of the Holy Cross), Diana Beck (New York University), Amanda Freeman (Kansas State University), and John Kane (SUNY–Oswego) for their contributions to and thoughts about early drafts of chapters.

An energetic group of collaborators helped us shape second-edition content in ways that are relevant and engaging for a student audience: David "Dukes" Love (Williams College) steered us through the writing of the macro chapters, helping us revamp our treatment of the aggregate expenditure model and how it leads into the aggregate demand and aggregate supply model. Erin Moody (University of Maryland) applied her extensive classroom experience as an essential contributor throughout the micro chapters, ensuring that we addressed the many suggestions we received from users and reviewers of our text. Camille Soltau Nelson (Oregon State University) analyzed Chapter 18, "Externalities," and made immeasurable improvements. Our IPA team of researchers, Radhika Lokur and Noor Sethi, brought a recent-student perspective to the text and helped us update many of our examples and figures with the most current data.

Many other talented individuals have contributed to previous editions. We thank Bob Schwab, Kevin Stanley, Ross vanWassenhove, and James Peyton for closely reviewing a draft of our revised Chapter 18 and helping guide us toward a final version. We thank John Neri and Murat Doral for providing detailed feedback on all the macro chapters of the text. We appreciate Jodi Begg's help in providing a base to work from for Chapter 28, "Aggregate Expenditure." We thank Chiuping Chen, Ashley Hodgson, Michael Machiorlatti, and Germain Pichop for reviewing said chapter in its draft stages to ensure we were on the right track.

We thank Peggy Dalton (Frostburg State University) and Erin Moody (University of Maryland) for their many and varied contributions to end-of-chapter and test bank content, both in the text and in Connect. We are very appreciative of the extensive work done by Katrina Babb (Indiana State University) and Susan Bell (Seminole State College) in accuracy-checking this content. In addition, we thank Greg Gilpin (Montana State University) for authoring the PowerPoint Presentation and Russell Kellogg (University of Colorado Denver) for authoring the LearnSmart content.

Ted Barnett played an essential role in this edition, helping us introduce new material and new ways of describing economic ideas. We are grateful for his creativity and knowledge of pedagogy and economics. He also made improvements to the test bank content. We thank Dick Startz for sharing his insights about new approaches in macroeconomics and for his feedback. Fatima Khan led the efforts to update the data and figures throughout the text.

We also want to share our appreciation to the following people at McGraw-Hill for the hard work they put into creating the product you see before you: Anke Weekes, Portfolio Director, helped us communicate the overarching vision and promoted our revision. Bobby Pearson, Marketing Manager, guided us in visiting schools and working with the sales team. Ann Torbert, Content Developer, has been an exemplary editor, improving the exposition on each page and keeping attention on both the big picture and key details. We feel lucky to have had her partnership on all three editions. Christina Kouvelis, Senior Product Developer, managed innumerable and indispensable details—reviews, manuscript, and the many aspects of the digital products and overall package. Kathryn Wright, Senior Core Content Project Manager, helped turn our manuscript into the finished, polished product you see before you. Keri Johnson, Senior Assessment Content Project Manager, skillfully guided the digital plan. Thanks, too, to Douglas Ruby, Senior Director of Digital Content, for his careful shepherding of the digital materials that accompany the text.

Thank You!

Creating the third edition of a book is a daunting task. We wanted to do everything we could to improve upon the previous editions, and we couldn't have done this without professors who told us honestly what they thought we could do better. To everyone who helped shape this edition, we thank you for sharing your insights and recommendations.

Symposia

Luca Bossi
University of Pennsylvania

Regina Cassady
Valencia College

June Charles
North Lake College

Monica Cherry
St. John Fisher College and State University of New York at Buffalo

George Chikhladze
University of Missouri-Columbia

Patrick Crowley
Texas A&M University-Corpus Christi

Attila Cseh
Valdosta State University

Susan Doty
University of Texas at Tyler

Irene Foster
George Washington University

Don Holley
Boise State University

Ricot Jean
Valencia College

Sarah Jenyk
Youngstown State University

Stephanie Jozefowicz
Indiana University of Pennsylvania

Nkongolo Kalala
Bluegrass Community and Technical College

Carrie Kerekes
Florida Gulf Coast University

Brandon Koford
Weber State University

Soloman Kone
City University of New York

W. J. Lane
University of New Orleans

Jose Lopez-Calleja
Miami Dade College

Erika Martinez
University of South Florida-Tampa

Geri Mason
Seattle Pacific University

ABM Nasir
North Carolina Central University

Eric Nielsen
Saint Louis Community College

Rich Numrich
College of Southern Nevada

Michael Polcen
Northern Virginia Community College

Martin Sabo
Community College of Denver

Latisha Settlage
University of Arkansas-Fort Smith

Mark Showalter
Brigham Young University

Warren Smith
Palm Beach State College

Kay Strong
Baldwin Wallace University

Ryan Umbeck
Ivy Tech Community College

Ross vanWassenhove
University of Houston

Terry Von Ende
Texas Tech University

Jennifer Wissink
Cornell University

Focus Groups

Siddiq Abdullah
University of Massachusetts-Boston

Seemi Ahmad
Dutchess Community College

Nurul Aman
University of Massachusetts-Boston

Aimee Chin
University of Houston

Can Erbil
Boston College

Varun Gupta
Wharton County Junior College

Moon Han
North Shore Community College

Hilaire Jean-Gilles
Bunker Hill Community College

Jennifer Lehman
Wharton County Junior College

Mikko Manner,
Dutchess Community College

Nara Mijid
Central Connecticut State University

Shahruz Mohtadi
Suffolk University

Victor Moussoki
Lone Star College

Kevin Nguyen
Lone Star College

Jan Palmer
Ohio University

Julia Paxton
Ohio University

Tracy Regan
Boston College

Christina Robinson
Central Connecticut State University

Rosemary Rossiter
Ohio University

Sara Saderion
Houston Community College

Reviews

Steve Abid
Grand Rapids Community College

Eric Abrams
McKendree University

Richard Ugunzi Agesa
Marshall University

Seemi Ahmad
Dutchess Community College

Jason A. Aimone
Baylor University

Donald L. Alexander
Western Michigan University

Ricky Ascher
Broward College and Palm Beach State College

Shannon Aucoin
University of Louisiana at Lafayette

Gyanendra Baral
Oklahoma City Community College

Klaus Becker
Texas Tech University

Pedro Bento
West Virginia University

Jennifer Bossard
Doane College

Kristen Broady
Fort Valley State University

Gregory Brock
Georgia Southern University

Giuliana Andreopoulos Campanelli
William Paterson University

Paul Chambers
University of Central Missouri

Sewin Chan
New York University

Joni Charles
Texas State University

Chiuping Chen
American River College

Tom Creahan
Morehead State University

Nicholas Dadzie
Bowling Green State University

Can Dogan
North American University

Brandon Dupont
Western Washington University

Matthew J. Easton
Pueblo Community College

Jennifer Elias
Radford University

Linda K. English
Baylor University

Irene R. Foster
George Washington University

Alka Gandhi
Northern Virginia Community College

Soma Ghosh
Albright College

Gregory Gilpin
Montana State University

Lisa Workman Gloege
Grand Rapids Community College

Cynthia Harter
Eastern Kentucky University

Darcy Hartman
Ohio State University

Ashley Hodgson
St. Olaf College

Don Holley
Boise State University

Yuri Hupka
Oklahoma State University

Harvey James
University of Missouri

Sarah Jenyk
Youngstown State University

Allison Kaminaga
Bryant University

Mina Kamouie
Ohio University

Russell Kellogg
University of Colorado Denver

Melissa Knox
University of Washington

Benjamin Kwitek
Pueblo Community College

Greg Lindeblom
Broward College

Michael Machiorlatti
Oklahoma City Community College

Rita Madarassy
Santa Clara University

Edouard Mafoua
State University of New York at Canton

C. Lucy Malakar
Lorain County Community College

Geri Mason
Seattle Pacific University

Katherine McClain
University of Georgia

Bruce McClung
Texas State University

Robin McCutcheon
Marshall University

Tia M. McDonald
Ohio University

William McLean
Oklahoma State University

Jennifer Meredith
Seattle Pacific University

John Min
Northern Virginia Community College

Sam Mirmirani
Bryant University

Ida A. Mirzaie
Ohio State University

Franklin G. Mixon Jr.
Columbus State University

Erin Moody
University of Maryland

Barbara Moore
University of Central Florida

Christopher Mushrush
Illinois State University

Charles Myrick
Oklahoma City Community College

Camille Nelson
Oregon State University

Per Norander
University of North Carolina-Charlotte

Ronald Oertel
Western Washington University

Constantin Ogloblin
Georgia Southern University

Alex Olbrecht
Ramapo College of New Jersey

Beau Olen
Oregon State University

Tomi Ovaska
Youngstown State University

Jan Palmer
Ohio University

Julia Paxton
Ohio University

James Peyton
Highline College

Germain Pichop
Oklahoma City Community College

Brennan Platt
Brigham Young University

Elizabeth Porter
University of North Carolina-Asheville

Mathew Price
Oklahoma City Community College

Christina Robinson
Central Connecticut State University

Matthew Roelofs
Western Washington University

Randall R. Rojas
University of California-Los Angeles

John Rykowski
Kalamazoo Valley Community College

Robert M. Schwab
University of Maryland

Gasper Sekelj
Clarkson University

James K. Self
Indiana University

Michael Scott
Pueblo Community College

Mark Showalter
Brigham Young University

Kevin Stanley
Highline College

Steve Trost
Virginia Polytechnic Institute and State University

Ross S. vanWassenhove
University of Houston

Allison Witman
University of North Carolina-Wilimington

In addition, we continue to be grateful to the first-edition contributors, who over the course of several years of development attended focus groups or symposia or provided content reviews. Thanks to the following, whose insights, recommendations, and feedback helped immeasurably as the project took shape.

Mark Abajian
San Diego Mesa College

Tom Adamson
Midland University

Richard Agesa
Marshall University

Rashid Al-Hmoud
Texas Tech University

Frank Albritton
Seminole State College-Sanford

Terence Alexander
Iowa State University

Clifford Althoff
Joliet Junior College

Diane Anstine
North Central College

Michael Applegate
Oklahoma State University-Stillwater Campus

Ali Ataiifar
Delaware County Community College

Roberto Ayala
California State Polytechnic University-Pomona

Jim Barbour
Elon University

Gary Benson
Southwest Community College

Laura Jean Bhadra
Northern Virginia Community College-Manassas

Prasun Bhattacharjee
East Tennessee State University-Johnson City

Radha Bhattacharya
California State University-Fullerton

Michael Bonnal
University of Tennessee-Chattanooga

Camelia Bouzerdan
Middlesex Community College

Dale Bremmer
Rose-Hulman Institute of Technology

Anne Bresnock
University of California-Los Angeles

Bruce Brown
California State Polytechnic University-Pomona

Ken Brown
University of Northern Iowa

Laura Bucila
Texas Christian University

Andrew Cassey
Washington State University

Kalyan Chakraborty
Emporia State University

Catherine Chambers
University of Central Missouri

Britton Chapman
State College of Florida-Manatee

Sanjukta Chaudhuri
University of Wisconsin-Eau Claire

Chiuping Chen
American River College

Ron Cheung
Oberlin College

Young Back Choi
Saint John's University

Dmitriy Chulkov
Indiana University-Kokomo

Cindy Clement
University of Maryland-College Park

Howard Cochran
Belmont University

Jim Cox
Georgia Perimeter College

Matt Critcher
University of Arkansas Community College-Batesville

Chifeng Dai
Southern Illinois University-Carbondale

Thomas Davidson
Principia College

Rafael Donoso
Lone State College-North Harris

Floyd Duncan
Virginia Military Institute

David Eaton
Murray State University

Eric Eide
Brigham Young University-Provo

Marwan El Nasser
State University of New York-Fredonia

Harry Ellis
University of North Texas

Maxwell Eseonu
Virginia State University

Brent Evans
Mississippi State University

Russell Evans
Oklahoma State University

Fidelis Ezeala-Harrison
Jackson State University

Chris Fant
Spartanburg Community College

Michael Fenick
Broward College

Abdollah Ferdowsi
Ferris State University

Tawni Ferrarini
Northern Michigan University

Herbert Flaig
Milwaukee Area Technical College

Irene Foster
George Washington University

Joseph Franklin
Newberry College

Shelby Frost
Georgia State University

Fran Lara Garib
San Jacinto College

Deborah Gaspard
Southeast Community College

Karen Gebhardt
Colorado State University

Juan Alejandro Gelves
Midwestern State University

Kirk Gifford
Brigham Young University-Idaho

Otis Gilley
Louisiana Technical University

Gregory Gilpin
Montana State University-Bozeman

Bill (Wayne) Goffe
State University of New York-Oswego

Michael Gootzeit
University of Memphis

George Greenlee
St. Petersburg College

Galina Hale
Federal Reserve Bank of San Francisco

Oskar Harmon
University of Connecticut-Stamford

David Hedrick
Central Washington University-Ellensburg

Dennis Heiner
College of Southern Idaho

Andrew Helms
Washington College

David Hickman
Frederick Community College

Ashley Hodgson
Saint Olaf College

Vanessa Holmes
Pennsylvania State University-Scranton

Scott Houser
Colorado School of Mines

Gregrey Hunter
California Polytechnic University-Pomona

Kyle Hurst
University of Colorado-Denver

Jonathan Ikoba
Scott Community College

Onur Ince
Appalachian State University

Dennis Jansen
Texas A&M University

Shuyi Jiang
Emmanuel College

Barbara Heroy John
University of Dayton

James Johnson
*University of Arkansas Community
College-Batesville*

Mahbubul Kabir
Lyon College

Ahmad Kader
University of Nevada-Las Vegas

John Kane
State University of New York-Oswego

Tsvetanka Karagyozova
Lawrence University

Joel Kazy
State Fair Community College

Daniel Kuester
Kansas State University

Gary Langer
Roosevelt University

Daniel Lawson
Oakland Community College

Richard Le
Cosumnes River College

Jim Lee
Texas A&M University-Corpus Christi

Willis Lewis
Winthrop University

Qing Li
College of the Mainland

Tin-Chun Lin
Indiana University Northwest-Gary

Delwin Long
San Jacinto College

Katie Lotz
Lake Land College

Karla Lynch
North Central Texas College

Arindam Mandal
Siena College

Daniel Marburger
Arkansas State University-Jonesboro

Geri Mason
Seattle Pacific University

Victor Matheson
College of the Holy Cross

Bryan McCannon
Saint Bonaventure University

Michael McIlhon
Century Community and Technical College

Hannah McKinney
Kalamazoo College

Al Mickens
*State University of New York-Old
Westbury*

Nara Mijid
Central Connecticut State University

Martin Milkman
Murray State University

Douglas Miller
University of Missouri-Columbia

Gregory Miller
Wallace Community College-Selma

Edward Millner
Virginia Commonwealth University

Mitch Mitchell
Bladen Community College

Daniel Morvey
Piedmont Technical College

Rebecca Moryl
Emmanuel College

Tina Mosleh
Ohlone College

Thaddaeus Mounkurai
Daytona State College-Daytona Beach

Chris Mushrush
Illinois State University

Muhammad Mustafa
South Carolina State University

Tony Mutsune
Iowa Wesleyan College

Max Grunbaum Nagiel
Daytona State College-Daytona Beach

John Nordstrom
College of Western Idaho

Emlyn Norman
Texas Southern University

Christian Nsiah
Black Hills State University

Jan Ojdana
University of Cincinnati

Ronald O'Neal
Camden County College

Serkan Ozbeklik
Claremont McKenna College

Debashis Pal
University of Cincinnati-Cincinnati

Robert Pennington
University of Central Florida-Orlando

Andrew Perumal
University of Massachusetts-Boston

Steven Peterson
University of Idaho

Brennan Platt
Brigham Young University

Sanela Porca
University of South Carolina-Aiken

Gregory Pratt
Mesa Community College

William Prosser
Cayuga Community College

Gregory Randolph
Southern New Hampshire University

Mitchell Redlo
Monroe Community College

Timothy Reynolds
Alvin Community College

Michael Rolleigh
Williams College

Amanda Ross
West Virginia University-Morgantown

Jason Rudbeck
University of Georgia

Michael Ryan
Gainesville State College

Robert Rycroft
University of Mary Washington

Michael Salemi
University of North Carolina-Chapel Hill

Gregory Saltzman
Albion College

Ravi Samitamana
Daytona State College

Saied Sarkarat
West Virginia University-Parkersburg

Naveen Sarna
Northern Virginia Community College-Alexandria

Jesse Schwartz
Kennesaw State University

Abdelkhalik Shabayek
Lane College

Mark Showalter
Brigham Young University

Cheri Sides
Lane College

Megan Silbert
Salem College

Sovathana Sokhom
Loyola Marymount University

Souren Soumbatiants
Franklin University

Marilyn Spencer
Texas A&M University-Corpus Christi

Brad Stamm
Cornerstone University

Karl Strauss
Saint Bonaventure University

Chuck Stull
Kalamazoo College

Abdulhamid Sukar
Cameron University

Albert Sumell
Youngstown State University

Philip Isak Szmedra
Georgia Southwestern State University

Christine Tarasevich
Del Mar College

Noreen Templin
Butler Community College

Darryl Thorne
Valencia College East

Kiril Tochkov
Texas Christian University

Demetri Tsanacas
Ferrum College

George Tvelia
Suffolk County Community College

Nora Underwood
University of Central Florida

Jose Vazquez
University of Illinois-Champaign

Marieta Velikova
Belmont University

Jeffery Vicek
Parkland College

Jennifer Vincent
Champlain College

Terry von Ende
Texas Tech University

Craig Walker
Oklahoma Baptist University

Jennifer Ward-Batts
Wayne State University

Tarteashia Williams
Valencia College-West Campus

Melissa Wiseman
Houston Baptist University

Jim Wollscheid
University of Arkansas-Fort Smith

Jeff Woods
University of Indianapolis

Ranita Wyatt
Pasco-Hernando Community College-West Campus

Suthathip Yaisawarng
Union College

Jim Yates
Darton College

Daehyun Yoo
Elon University

Ceren Ertan Yoruk
Sage College of Albany

Chuck Zalonka
Oklahoma State University-Oklahoma City

Finally, thanks to the following instructors, and their students, who class-tested chapters of the first edition before publication. Their engagement with the content and their feedback from the "test drive" made this a better product.

Richard Agesa
Marshall University

Anne Bresnock
University of California-Los Angeles

Chiuping Chen
American River College

John Kane
State University of New York-Oswego

Jim Lee
Texas A&M University-Corpus Christi

Martin Milkman
Murray State University

Kolleen Rask
College of the Holy Cross

Jesse Schwartz
Kennesaw State University

Jennifer Vincent
Champlain College

detailed contents

Part 1
The Power of Economics 1
Chapter 1
Economics and Life 3

Making an Impact with Small Loans 3

The Basic Insights of Economics 4
    Scarcity 5
    Opportunity cost and marginal decision making 6
    Incentives 9
    Efficiency 10
An Economist's Problem-Solving Toolbox 12
    Correlation and causation 13
    Models 15
    Positive and normative analysis 17
Conclusion 19

Chapter 2
Specialization and Exchange 25

The Origins of a T-Shirt 25

Production Possibilities 27
    Drawing the production possibilities frontier 27
    Choosing among production possibilities 30
    Shifting the production possibilities frontier 31
Absolute and Comparative Advantage 33
    Absolute advantage 33
    Comparative advantage 33
Why Trade? 35
    Specialization 35
    Gains from trade 37
    Comparative advantage over time 40
Conclusion 42

APPENDIX A Math Essentials: Understanding Graphs and Slope 46A
Creating a Graph 46A
    Graphs of one variable 46A
    Graphs of two variables 46C
Slope 46F
    Calculating slope 46G
    The direction of a slope 46H
    The steepness of a slope 46I

Part 2
Supply and Demand 47
Chapter 3
Markets 49

Mobiles Go Global 49

Markets 50
    What is a market? 50
    What is a competitive market? 50
Demand 52
    The demand curve 53
    Determinants of demand 53
    Shifts in the demand curve 57
Supply 59
    The supply curve 60
    Determinants of supply 60
    Shifts in the supply curve 62
Market Equilibrium 63
    Reaching equilibrium 64
    Changes in equilibrium 65
Conclusion 72

APPENDIX B Math Essentials: Working with Linear Equations 78A
Interpreting the Equation of a Line 78A
    Turning a graph into an equation 78B
    Turning an equation into a graph 78B
    Equations with x and y reversed 78D
Shifts and Pivots 78E
Solving for Equilibrium 78H

Chapter 4
Elasticity 79

Coffee Becomes Chic 79

What Is Elasticity? 80
Price Elasticity of Demand 81
    Calculating price elasticity of demand 81
    Determinants of price elasticity of demand 84
    Using price elasticity of demand 85
Price Elasticity of Supply 92
    Calculating price elasticity of supply 92
    Determinants of price elasticity of supply 93

Other Elasticities 94
  Cross-price elasticity of demand 94
  Income elasticity of demand 95
Conclusion 98

APPENDIX C Math Essentials: Calculating Percentage Change, Slope, and Elasticity 102A
Percentage Change 102A
Slope and Elasticity 102B
  X over Y, or Y over X? 102D
  Elasticity changes along lines with constant slope 102D

Chapter 5
Efficiency 103

A Broken Laser Pointer Starts an Internet Revolution 103

Willingness to Pay and Sell 104
  Willingness to pay and the demand curve 105
  Willingness to sell and the supply curve 107
Measuring Surplus 109
  Consumer surplus 110
  Producer surplus 112
  Total surplus 113
Using Surplus to Compare Alternatives 115
  Market equilibrium and efficiency 115
  Changing the distribution of total surplus 117
  Deadweight loss 118
  Missing markets 119
Conclusion 121

APPENDIX D Math Essentials: The Area under a Linear Curve 128A
The Area under a Linear Curve 128A

Chapter 6
Government Intervention 129

Feeding the World, One Price Control at a Time 129

Why Intervene? 130
  Three reasons to intervene 130
  Four real-world interventions 131
Price Controls 132
  Price ceilings 132
  Price floors 136
Taxes and Subsidies 139
  Taxes 140
  Subsidies 146
Evaluating Government Interventions 150
  How big is the effect of a tax or subsidy? 151
  Short-run versus long-run impact 153
Conclusion 156

Part 3
Individual Decisions 163
Chapter 7
Consumer Behavior 165

The Season for Giving 165

The Basic Idea of Utility 166
  Utility and decision making 167
  Revealed preference 168
  Utility functions 169
Marginal Utility 170
  Maximizing utility within constraints 172
Responding to Changes in Income and Prices 175
  Changes in income 175
  Changes in prices 177
Utility and Society 180
  Utility and status 180
  Utility and altruism 182
  Utility and reciprocity 183
Conclusion 184

APPENDIX E Using Indifference Curves 188A
Representing Preferences Graphically 188A
  Consumption bundles and indifference curves 188A
  Properties of indifference curves 188C
  Perfect substitutes and perfect complements 188D
Understanding Consumer Choice 188E
  Equalizing the marginal utility of the last purchase 188E
  Finding the highest indifference curve 188G
How Consumers Respond to Change 188H
  Responding to a change in income 188I
  Responding to a change in prices 188I
  Deriving the demand curve using indifference curves 188K
Conclusion 188L

Chapter 8
Behavioral Economics:
A Closer Look at Decision Making 189

When Is $20 Not Quite $20? 189

Dealing with Temptation and Procrastination 191
  Time inconsistency, competing selves, and commitment 191
Thinking Irrationally about Costs 194
  The sunk-cost fallacy 194
  Undervaluing opportunity costs 195
Forgetting about Fungibility 196
  Creating mental categories for money 196
Conclusion 199

Chapter 9
Game Theory and Strategic Thinking 203

Litterbugs Beware 203

Games and Strategic Behavior 204
  Rules, strategies, and payoffs 205
One-Time Games and the Prisoners' Dilemma 205
  Prisoners' dilemma 205
  Finding the dominant strategy 207
  Reaching equilibrium 208
  Avoiding competition through commitment 209
  Promoting competition in the public interest 210
Repeated Play in the Prisoners' Dilemma 212
  The tit-for-tat strategy 212
Sequential Games 214
  Think forward, work backward 215
  Deterring market entry: A sequential game 215
  First-mover advantage in sequential games 218
  Repeated sequential games 218
  Commitment in sequential games 219
Conclusion 221

Chapter 10
Information 229

A Solution for Student Loans? 229

Information: Knowledge Is Power 230
  Information asymmetry 231
  Adverse selection and the lemons problem 231
  Principal–agent problems and moral hazard 233
  Moral hazard and adverse selection—avoiding confusion 234
Solving Information Problems 235
  Screening 235
  Signaling 236
  Reputation 237
  Statistical discrimination 237
  Regulation and education 239
Conclusion 241

Chapter 11
Time and Uncertainty 245

Is College Worth It? 245

Value over Time 246
  Timing matters 246
  Interest rates 247
  Compounding 248
  Present value 249
Risk and Uncertainty 251
  What is risk? 251

  Expected value 252
  Propensity for risk 253
Insurance and Managing Risk 254
  The market for insurance 254
  Pooling and diversifying risk 254
  Problems with insurance 258
Conclusion 260

APPENDIX F Math Essentials:
Compounding 264A
Compounding and Future Value 264A
  The rule of 70 264C

Part 4
Firm Decisions 265

Chapter 12
The Costs of Production 267

What Are You Paying for in That Prescription? 267

The Building Blocks of Business: Revenues,
  Costs, and Profits 268
  Profit is revenue minus costs 269
  Fixed and variable costs 269
  Explicit and implicit costs 271
  Economic and accounting profit 272
Production Functions 274
  Marginal product 274
Cost Curves 277
  Total, average, and marginal costs 277
Production in the Short Run and the Long Run 283
  Costs in the long run 283
  Economies and diseconomies of scale 283
Conclusion 287

Chapter 13
Perfect Competition 293

Trainside Variety 293

A Competitive Market 294
  Characteristics of a competitive market 294
  Revenues in a perfectly competitive market 298
Profits and Production Decisions 300
  Deciding how much to produce 300
  Deciding when to operate 303
Behind the Supply Curve 307
  Short-run supply 307
  Long-run supply 308
  *Why the long-run market supply curve shouldn't slope upward,
    but does 313*
  Responding to shifts in demand 315
Conclusion 316

Chapter 14
Monopoly 323

Diamonds Weren't Always Forever 323

Why Do Monopolies Exist? 324
    Barriers to entry 325
How Monopolies Work 327
    Monopolists and the demand curve 327
    Monopoly revenue 329
Problems with Monopoly and Public Policy Solutions 333
    The welfare costs of monopoly 334
    Public policy responses 336
Market Power and Price Discrimination 341
    What is price discrimination? 341
Conclusion 346

Chapter 15
**Monopolistic Competition and
Oligopoly 353**

Which One of These Is Just Like the Others? 353

What Sort of Market? 354
    Oligopoly and monopolistic competition 355
Monopolistic Competition 356
    Monopolistic competition in the short run 357
    Monopolistic competition in the long run 358
    The welfare costs of monopolistic competition 361
    Product differentiation, advertising, and branding 362
Oligopoly 367
    Oligopolies in competition 368
    *Compete or collude? Using game theory to analyze
        oligopolies 371*
    Oligopoly and public policy 374
Conclusion 376

Chapter 16
The Factors of Production 383

The Fields of California 383

The Factors of Production: Land, Labor, and Capital 384
    Derived demand 385
    Marginal productivity 385
    Picking the right combination of inputs 385
Labor Markets and Wages 386
    Demand for labor 387
    Supply of labor 389
    Reaching equilibrium 393
    Shifts in labor supply and labor demand 394
    What's missing? Human capital 399

Land and Capital 401
    Capitalists: Who are they? 401
    Markets for land and capital 401
    The factor distribution of income 403
Real-World Labor Markets 405
    Minimum wages and efficiency wages 405
    Company towns, unions, and labor laws 407
    Changing demographics 409
Conclusion 411

Chapter 17
International Trade 419

A New Meaning to "Made in the USA" 419

Why Trade? A Review 420
    Comparative advantage 420
    Gains from trade 421
    The roots of comparative advantage 422
    Incomplete specialization 424
From Autarky to Free Trade 425
    Becoming a net-importer 426
    Becoming a net-exporter 428
    Big economy, small economy 430
Restrictions on Trade 433
    Why restrict trade? 433
    Tariffs 433
    Quotas 435
Trade Agreements 437
    International labor and capital 437
    The WTO and trade mediation 438
    Labor and environmental standards 439
    Embargoes: Trade as foreign policy 441
Conclusion 442

Part 5
Public Economics 449
Chapter 18
Externalities 451

The Costs of Car Culture 451

What Are Externalities? 452
    External costs and benefits 453
    Negative externalities and the problem of "too much" 455
    Positive externalities and the problem of "too little" 457
Private Solutions to Externalities 459
Public Solutions to Externalities 463
    Taxes and subsidies 464

Other policy options: Quotas and tradable allowances 467

Targeting externalities with public policy 469

Conclusion 469

Chapter 19
Public Goods and Common Resources 477

A New Tragedy of the Commons 477

Characteristics of Goods 478

Excludable goods 479

Rival-in-consumption goods 479

Four categories of goods 480

Public Goods 481

The free-rider problem 481

Solutions to the free-rider problem 484

Common Resources 486

The tragedy of the commons 486

Solutions to the tragedy of the commons 487

Conclusion 492

Chapter 20
Taxation and the Public Budget 497

Happy to Pay Taxes? 497

Why Tax? 498

Principles of Taxation 500

Efficiency: How much (extra) will the tax cost? 500

Revenue: How much money will the tax raise? 503

Incidence: Who ultimately pays the tax? 505

A Taxonomy of Taxes 508

Personal income tax 508

Capital gains tax 511

Payroll tax 511

Corporate income tax 512

Other taxes 512

The Public Budget 514

Balancing the budget 516

Conclusion 519

Chapter 21
Poverty, Inequality, and Discrimination 525

Striking It Richer 525

Poverty 526

Measuring poverty 527

Why are people poor? 533

Inequality 536

Measuring inequality 536

Income inequality versus income mobility 542

Policies to Reduce Poverty and Inequality 543

Public policy goals 543

The welfare state 545

Trade-offs between equity and efficiency 548

Discrimination 549

Measuring discrimination in the labor market 550

Do free markets reduce discrimination? 552

Long-term effects of discrimination 552

Conclusion 554

Chapter 22
Political Choices 563

Global Warming Hot Potato 563

The Economics of Elections 564

Stick to the middle: Median-voter theorem 565

The elusive perfect voting system 567

Political participation and the myth of the "rational voter" 572

The Economics of Policy-Making 574

Diffuse costs, concentrated benefits 574

Corruption and rent-seeking 576

The system matters: How political structure affects outcomes 577

Conclusion 579

Chapter 23
Public Policy and Choice Architecture 585

Saving more for Tomorrow 585

Choice Architecture and Nudges 587

Why nudge? 587

Mistakes people make 590

Tools of Choice Architecture 592

Commitment devices 592

Information campaigns and disclosure rules 593

Default rules 595

Framing choices 597

Conclusion 598

Guide to Data Sources GU-1

Glossary GL-1

Indexes IN-1

feature boxes

ECONOMICS IN ACTION

When education pays off 17

Specialization sauce 37

Winners and losers 39

Comparative advantage: The good, the bad, and the ugly 41

Can instant noodle sales predict a recession? 56

The great Elmo shortage 66

Give a man a fish 71

Does charging for bednets decrease malaria? 87

The unintended consequences of biofuel subsidies 150

Why we give 183

Give more tomorrow 192

Take out a contract on yourself 193

What do price-matching guarantees guarantee? 213

Totally MAD 220

The weather can't cheat 234

Walmart and economies of scale 285

Why does the "Motor Mile" exist? 297

How Ford changed the world 313

Rockers vs. Ticketmaster 337

What really sells loans? 364

Have noncompete clauses gone too far? 407

Made in Lesotho. But why? 423

Why not tax ourselves? 468

Artificially scarce music 480

It's not necessarily a tragedy 487

Why the Colorado River no longer reaches the ocean 491

The insecure future of Social Security 518

Up and down in America 532

Getting out of the neighborhood 534

Are Emily and Greg more employable than Lakisha and Jamal? 551

The rise of Donald Trump 566

Ranked-choice takes the Golden ticket to Washington 571

Face value—May the best-looking politician win 573

Enfranchising the poor helps the poor 578

It's all about timing 588

Who doesn't want to be an organ donor? 595

FROM ANOTHER ANGLE

Does ice cream cause polio? 14

Babe Ruth, star pitcher 34

How much would you pay to keep the Internet from disappearing? 110

Beyond the bottom line 273

Who wants competition? 309

Phone ladies 336

The origins of Monopoly 340

Rickshaw rides: Price discrimination and asymmetric information 346

Coke, Pepsi, and the not-so-secret formula 366

Are environmental regulations bad for the environment? 440

Does no-fault divorce law increase the divorce rate? 463

Why does Wikipedia work? 483

Can some taxes make people happier? 499

"Just give money" 546

Turn down the AC for a smiley face 597

ECON AND YOU

Finding a travel bargain 97

It pays to negotiate 108

Out of sight, out of mind 152

Spending your way to happiness? 168

Choosing a league 181

Why we give 183

Is a dollar a dollar? 198

Can game theory explain why you feel guilt? 214

Is college worth it? 236

The rule of 70 249

Are extended warranties worth it? 257

The quarter-million dollar kid 271

Fight the (market) power! 362

Is payday lending predatory? 594

WHAT DO YOU THINK?

The opportunity cost of a life 7

The cost of college cash 18

Should entrance fees at national parks be raised? 91

Kidneys for sale 120

Put a cap on payday lending? 135

Fight for $15 154

Credit-card categories: More realistic or more confusing? 197

Surviving with strategic thinking 217

Should teenagers be able to buy assault rifles? 238

How much information is too much? 240

Who should bear the risk that a college degree doesn't pay off? 255

Should health insurance include preventive care? 259

Should drug companies care about neglected diseases? 286

Should the United States be a country of immigrants? 397

Work, wages, and social value 404

Population policy and the wealth of nations 410

Reclining transactions 461

Should conservationists be principled or pragmatic? 489

Death and taxes 513

The super-wealthy 540

Affirmative action in college admissions 553

The Power of Economics

PART ONE

The two chapters in Part 1 will introduce you to . . .

the tools and intuition essential to the study of economics. Chapter 1, "Economics and Life," presents four questions that introduce the fundamental concepts of economic problem solving. We also describe how economists think about data and analyze policies: You'll see that we typically separate how one *wants* the world to look ("normative" analysis) from how the world *actually* works ("positive" analysis).

Chapter 2, "Specialization and Exchange," presents the ideas of absolute and comparative advantage, to explain how people (and countries) can most effectively use their resources and talents. Should you hire a plumber or fix the pipes yourself? Should you become a pop star or an economist? We develop these ideas to show how trade can make everyone better off, on both a personal and a national level.

This is just a start. Throughout the book, we'll use these tools to gain a deeper understanding of how people interact and manage their resources, which in turn gives insight into tough problems of all sorts. Economic ideas weave a common thread through many subjects, from the purely economic to political, environmental, and cultural issues, as well as personal decisions encountered in everyday life. Economics is much more than just the study of money, and we hope you'll find that what you learn here will shed light far beyond your economics classes.

Economics and Life

Making an Impact with Small Loans

On the morning of October 13, 2006, Bangladeshi economist Muhammad Yunus received an unexpected telephone call from Oslo, Norway. Later that day, the Nobel committee announced that Yunus and the Grameen Bank, which he founded in 1976, would share the 2006 Nobel Peace Prize. Past recipients of the Nobel Peace Prize include Mother Teresa, who spent over 50 years ministering to beggars and lepers; Martin Luther King Jr., who used peaceful protest to oppose racial segregation; and the Dalai Lama, an exiled Tibetan Buddhist leader who symbolizes the struggle for religious and cultural tolerance. What were an economist and his bank doing in such company?

Grameen is not a typical bank. Yes, it makes loans and offers savings accounts, charging customers for its services, just like other banks. But it serves some of the poorest people in the poorest villages in one of the poorest countries in the world. It makes loans so small that it's hard for people in wealthy countries to imagine what good they can do: The first group of loans Yunus made totaled only $27. Before Grameen came along, other banks had been unwilling to work in these poor communities. They

©lev radin/Shutterstock

believed it wasn't worth bothering to lend such small amounts; many believed the poor could not be counted on to repay their loans.

Yunus disagreed. He was convinced that even small loans would allow poor villagers to expand their small businesses—maybe buying a sewing machine or a cow to produce milk for the local market—and earn more money. Or perhaps a villager wouldn't expand a small business but would instead use the money to pay for a health emergency or to buy food when faced with hunger. Regardless of the way the loans were used, villagers' lives would be more comfortable and secure, and their children would have a better future. Yunus claimed that they would be able to repay the loans and that his new bank would earn a profit.

Muhammad Yunus was trained as an economist. He earned a PhD at Vanderbilt University in Nashville and then taught in Tennessee before becoming a professor in Bangladesh. When a devastating famine struck Bangladesh, Yunus became disillusioned with teaching. What did abstract equations and stylized graphs have to do with the suffering he saw around him?

Ultimately, Yunus realized that economic thinking holds the key to solving hard problems that truly matter. The genius of Grameen Bank is that it is neither a traditional charity nor a traditional bank. Instead, it is a business that harnesses basic economic insights to make the world a better place.

LEARNING OBJECTIVES

LO 1.1 Explain the economic concept of scarcity.

LO 1.2 Explain the economic concepts of opportunity cost and marginal decision making.

LO 1.3 Explain the economic concept of incentives.

LO 1.4 Explain the economic concept of efficiency.

LO 1.5 Distinguish between correlation and causation.

LO 1.6 List the characteristics of a good economic model.

LO 1.7 Distinguish between positive and normative analysis.

In this book, we'll introduce you to the tools economists are using to tackle some of the world's biggest challenges, from health care reform, to climate change, to lifting people out of poverty. Of course, these tools are not just for taking on causes worthy of Nobel Prizes. Economics can also help you become a savvier consumer, successfully launch a new cell phone app, or simply make smarter decisions about how to spend your time and money. Throughout this book, we promise we'll ask you not just to memorize theories, but also to apply the ideas you read about to the everyday decisions you face in your own life. Text discussions will spotlight such decisions as will boxed inserts such as those titled "Econ and YOU."

The Basic Insights of Economics

When people think of economics, they often think of the stock market, the unemployment rate, or media reports saying things like "the Federal Reserve has raised its target for the federal funds rate." Although economics does include these topics, its reach is much broader.

economics
the study of how people, individually and collectively, manage resources

Economics is the study of how people manage resources. Decisions about how to allocate resources can be made by individuals, but also by groups of people in families, firms, governments, and other organizations. In economics, *resources* are not just physical things like cash and gold mines. They are also intangible things, such as time, ideas, technology, job experience, and even personal relationships.

microeconomics
the study of how individuals and firms manage resources

Traditionally, economics has been divided into two broad fields: microeconomics and macroeconomics. **Microeconomics** is the study of how individuals and firms manage resources. **Macroeconomics** is the study of the economy as a whole, and how policy-makers manage the growth and behavior of the overall economy. Microeconomics and macroeconomics are highly related and interdependent; we need both to fully understand how economies work.

macroeconomics
the study of the economy as a whole, and how policy-makers manage the growth and behavior of the overall economy

Economics starts with the idea that people compare the choices available to them and purposefully behave in the way that will best achieve their goals. As human beings, we have ambitions and we make plans to realize them. We strategize. We marshal our resources. When people make choices to achieve their goals in the most effective way possible given the resources they have, economists say they are exhibiting **rational behavior**. The assumption that people behave rationally isn't perfect. As we'll see later in the text, people can sometimes be short-sighted or swayed merely by the way choices are presented. Nevertheless, the assumption of rational behavior helps to explain a lot about the world.

People use economics every day, from Wall Street to Walmart, from state capitol buildings to Bangladeshi villages. They apply economic ideas to everything from shoe shopping to baseball, from running a hospital to running for political office. What ties these topics together is a common approach to problem solving. Economists tend to approach problems by asking four questions:

1. What are the wants and constraints of those involved?
2. What are the trade-offs?
3. How will others respond?
4. Are resources being allocated in the best way possible?

rational behavior making choices to achieve goals in the most effective way possible

Underneath these questions are some important economics concepts, which we will begin to explore in this chapter. The questions and the underlying concepts are based on just a few common-sense assumptions about how people behave, yet they offer a surprising amount of insight into tough problems of all sorts. They are so important to economic problem solving that they will come up again and again in this text. In this chapter we'll take a bird's-eye view of economics, focusing on the fundamental concepts and skimming over the details. Later in the text, we'll return to each question in more depth.

Scarcity

Question 1: What are the wants and constraints of those involved?

For the most part, people make decisions that are aimed at getting the things they want. Of course, you can't always get what you want. People want a lot of things, but they are *constrained* by limited resources. Economists define **scarcity** as the condition of wanting more than we can get with available resources.

Scarcity is a fact of life. You have only so much time and only so much money. You can arrange your resources in a lot of different ways—studying or watching TV, buying a car, or traveling to Las Vegas—but at any given time, you have a fixed range of possibilities. Scarcity also describes the world on a collective level: As a society, we can produce only so many things, and we have to decide how those things are divided among many people.

On the other hand, some things are not restricted by resources. Consider, for example, knowledge. The total quantity of available knowledge does not diminish as more and more people acquire it. Similarly, sunlight and air can also be considered nonscarce goods. In economic terms, however, it is safe to say that most goods are considered to be scarce.

The first question to ask in untangling a complex economic problem is, "What are the wants and constraints of those involved?" Given both rational behavior and scarcity, we can expect people to try to get what they want but to be constrained by the limited resources available to them. Suppose you *want* to spend as much time as possible this summer taking road trips around the country. You are *constrained* by the available time (three months of summer vacation) and by the amount of money you have available to pay for gas, food, and places to stay. Behaving rationally, you might choose to work double shifts for two months to earn enough to spend one month on the road. Since you are now *constrained* by having only one month to travel, you'll have to prioritize your time, activities, and expenses.

Now put yourself in Muhammad Yunus's shoes, back in 1976. He sees extremely poor but entrepreneurial Bangladeshi villagers and thinks they could improve their lives with access to loans. Why aren't banks providing financial services for these people? We can apply the first of the economists' questions to start to untangle this puzzle: *What are the wants and constraints of those involved?* In this case, those involved are traditional Bangladeshi banks and poor Bangladeshi villagers.

Let's look at both:

- The banks *want* to make profits by lending money to people who will pay them back with interest. The banks are *constrained* by having limited funds available to lend and

LO 1.1 Explain the economic concept of scarcity.

scarcity the condition of wanting more than we can get with available resources

needing to pay employees and branch expenses. We can therefore expect banks to prioritize making large loans to customers they believe are likely to pay them back. Before 1976, that meant wealthier, urban Bangladeshis, not the very poor in remote rural villages.

- The villagers *want* the chance to increase their incomes. They have energy and business ideas but are *constrained* in their ability to borrow money because banks believe they are too poor to repay loans.

Analyzing the wants and constraints of those involved gives us some valuable information about why poor Bangladeshis didn't have access to loans. Banks *wanted* to earn profits and managed their *constrained* funds to prioritize those they thought would be profitable customers. Bangladeshi villagers *wanted* to increase their incomes but couldn't follow up on business opportunities due to *constrained* start-up money.

That's good information, but we haven't yet come up with the solution that Dr. Yunus was looking for. To take the next step in solving the puzzle, we turn to another question economists often ask.

Opportunity cost and marginal decision making

Question 2: *What are the trade-offs?*

Every decision in life involves weighing the *trade-off* between costs and benefits. We look at our options and decide whether it is worth giving up one in order to get the other. We choose to do things only when we think the benefits will be greater than the costs. The potential *benefit* of taking an action is often easy to see: Having dinner with friends would be fun. Taking a loan from a bank would help pay emergency expenses that occur. The *costs* of a decision, on the other hand, are not always clear.

You might think it *is* clear—that the cost of a meal with friends is simply the amount of money you spend on dinner. But something is missing from that way of thinking. The true cost of something is not just the amount you have to pay for it. Rather, the cost also includes the *opportunity you must now give up for something that you might have enjoyed otherwise.* Suppose, if you hadn't gone out for dinner, your second choice would have been to spend that night watching a newly released movie. The true cost of going out for dinner includes passing up the enjoyment you would have had at the movie. Behaving rationally, you should go out to dinner only if it will be more valuable to you than the best alternative use for your time and money. This is a matter of personal preference. Because people have different alternatives and place different values on things like a dinner or a movie, they will make different decisions.

opportunity cost
the value to you of what you have to give up in order to get something; the value you could have gained by choosing the next-best alternative

Opportunity costs   Economists call this true cost of your choice the **opportunity cost**. It is equal to the value to you of what you have to give up in order to get something. Put another way, opportunity cost is the value you could have gained by choosing your next-best alternative—the "opportunity" you have to pass up in order to take your first choice.

Let's return to the dinner. Say you're going with a friend and her plan B would have been staying home to catch up on homework. The opportunity cost of her dinner is different from yours. For her, the opportunity cost is the satisfaction she would have had from finally catching up on her work. If she's behaving rationally, she will join you for dinner only if she believes it will be more valuable than staying home with her assignments.

Opportunity cost helps us think more clearly about trade-offs. If someone asked you how much your dinner cost and you responded by adding up the cost of your appetizer, main course, and a drink, you would be failing to capture some of the most important and interesting aspects of the trade-offs you made. Opportunity cost helps us to see why, for example, a self-employed consultant and a factory worker earning the same amount of money may face truly different trade-offs when they dream about taking the same vacation for the same price. The self-employed consultant likely forgoes earning income in order to take the time off for a vacation. The factory worker likely gets paid vacation days. The opportunity cost for the consultant includes the value of what he or she would buy with the money earned by working instead of taking the vacation. The opportunity cost for the factory worker includes the benefit she would get from taking a different vacation. Thus the opportunity cost of a vacation for the consultant is much higher than it is for the factory worker. That difference makes it more expensive for the consultant to take a vacation than the factory worker.

Economists often express opportunity cost as a dollar value. Suppose you're offered a part-time job that pays $100 a week for four months (or $1,600 in total). Alternatively, you have the chance to take an internship for four months that offers useful career-related experience but no pay. Your time is tight, so you have to choose between the offers.

What are the opportunity costs of the choices? The opportunity cost of the unpaid internship is the $1,600 that you would have earned if you had instead chosen the paid job. The opportunity cost of the paid job is a bit trickier. It's what you would give up by not taking the internship. Part of the value of the internship is that you expect the experience to contribute to your career. It may be hard to put an exact number on the expected value to your career, but you may be able to predict whether the expected contribution of the internship is bigger or smaller than $1,600. The internship would be appealing if the expected gain to your career substantially exceeds $1,600. Otherwise, the paid job could make more financial sense.

Of course, we're simplifying a lot here. You might need the money now, rather than at a later date—which would push you toward the paid job. Also, you may be looking for gains that are not purely financial—like having interesting experiences and meeting new people. Either way, thinking about opportunity costs is a critical part of making good decisions of all kinds.

Once you start to think about opportunity costs, you see them everywhere. For an application of opportunity cost to a serious moral question, read the What Do You Think? box "The opportunity cost of a life."

The opportunity cost of a life
What Do You Think?

What Do You Think? boxes present questions that require you to combine facts and economic analysis with values and moral reasoning. There can be many "correct" answers, depending on your values and goals.

The philosopher Peter Singer writes that opportunity costs can be a matter of life or death. Imagine you are a salesperson, and on your way to a meeting on a hot summer day, you drive by a lake. Suddenly, you notice that a child who has been swimming in the lake is drowning. No one else is in sight.

You have a choice. If you stop the car and dive into the lake to save the child, you will be late for your meeting, miss out on making a sale, and lose $1,500. The *opportunity cost* of saving the child's life is $1,500.

Alternatively, if you continue on to your meeting, you earn the $1,500, but you lose the opportunity to dive into the lake and save the child's life. The *opportunity cost* of going to the meeting is one child's life.

What would you do? Most people don't hesitate. They immediately say they would stop the car, dive into the lake, and save the drowning child. After all, a child's life is worth more than $1,500.

(continued)

Now suppose you're thinking about spending $1,500 on a new MacBook. That $1,500 could instead have been used for some charitable purpose, such as immunizing a group of children in another country against yellow fever. Suppose that for every $1,500 donated, an average of one child's life ends up being saved. What is the opportunity cost of buying a MacBook? According to Peter Singer, it is the same as the opportunity cost of going straight to the meeting: a child's life.

These two situations are not exactly the same, of course, but why does the first choice (jump in the lake) seem so obvious to most people, while the second seems much less obvious?

WHAT DO YOU THINK?

1. In what ways do the two situations presented by Singer—the sales meeting and the drowning child versus the MacBook and the unvaccinated child—differ?
2. Singer argues that even something like buying a MacBook is a surprisingly serious moral decision. Do you agree? What sort of opportunity costs do you typically consider when making such a decision?
3. What might be missing from Singer's analysis of the trade-offs people face when making a decision about how to spend money?

Marginal decision making   Another important principle for understanding trade-offs is the idea that rational people make decisions *at the margin*. **Marginal decision making** describes the idea that rational people compare the *additional* benefits of a choice against the *additional* costs, without considering related benefits and costs of past choices.

marginal decision making
comparison of additional benefits of a choice against the additional costs it would bring, without considering related benefits and costs of past choices

For example, suppose an amusement park has a $20 admission price and charges $2 per ride. If you are standing outside the park, the cost of the first ride is $22: You will have to pay the admission price and buy a ticket for the ride. Once you are inside the park, the *marginal* cost of each additional ride is $2. When deciding whether to go on the roller coaster a second or third time, you should compare only the benefit or enjoyment you will get from one more ride to the opportunity cost of that additional ride.

This may sound obvious, but in practice, many people don't make decisions on the margin. Suppose you get into the amusement park and start to feel sick shortly thereafter. If doing something else with your $2 and your time would bring you more enjoyment than another roller coaster ride while feeling sick, the rational thing to do would be to leave. The relevant trade-off is between the *additional* benefits that going on another ride would bring versus the additional costs. You cannot get back the $20 admission fee or any of the other money you've already spent on rides.

sunk cost
a cost that has already been incurred and cannot be recovered or refunded

Economists call a cost that has already been incurred and cannot be recovered a **sunk cost**. Sunk costs should not have any bearing on your *marginal* decision about what to do next. But many people feel the need to go on a few more rides to psychologically justify the $20 admission.

Trade-offs play a crucial role in businesses' decisions about what goods and services to produce. Let's return to the example that started this chapter and apply the idea to a bank in Bangladesh: *What are the trade-offs involved in making a small loan?*

- For traditional banks, the opportunity cost of making small loans to the poor was the money that the bank could have earned by making loans to wealthier clients instead.
- For poor borrowers, the opportunity cost of borrowing was whatever else they would have done with the time they spent traveling to the bank and with the money they would pay in fees and interest on the loan. The benefit, of course, was whatever the loan would enable them to do that they could not have done otherwise, such as starting a small business or buying food or livestock.

Based on this analysis of trade-offs, we can see why traditional banks made few loans to poor Bangladeshis. Banks perceived the poor to be risky clients. The opportunity cost of making small loans to the poor seemed to outweigh the benefits—unless the banks charged very high fees. From the perspective of poor rural villagers, high fees meant that the opportunity cost of borrowing was higher than the benefits; they chose not to borrow under the terms offered by banks.

Notice that the answer to this question built off the answer to the first: We had to know the wants and constraints of each party before we could assess the trade-offs they faced. Now that we understand the motivations and the trade-offs that led to the situation Dr. Yunus observed, we can turn to a third question he might have asked himself when considering what would happen when he founded the Grameen Bank.

Incentives

Question 3: How will others respond?

You're in the mood for pizza, so you decide to go to a favorite neighborhood restaurant that has a short menu: pizza and spaghetti. When you get there, you discover that the prices have changed. Both used to cost $15, which made your decision relatively easy: which food were you in the mood for that night? Tonight you discover that pizza now costs $50, instead of $15.

What will you do? You could leave, but you're already here, are hungry, and feel committed to stay. Unless you can easily afford $50 for a pizza or you just really hate spaghetti, you'll order spaghetti. We're sure that you can think of ways to spend $35 that are worth more to you than your preference for pizza over spaghetti. But what if the prices had changed less drastically—say, $18 for pizza? That might be a tougher call.

As the trade-offs change, so will the choices people make. When the restaurant owner considers how much to charge for each dish, she must consider *how others will respond* to changing prices. If she knows the pizza is popular, she might be tempted to try charging more to boost her profits. But as she increases the price, fewer diners will decide to order it.

If a trade-off faced by a lot of people changes, even by a small amount, the combined change in behavior by everyone involved can add up to a big shift. Asking "How will others respond?" to a trade-off that affects a lot of people gives us a complete picture of how a particular decision affects the world. The collective reaction to a changing trade-off is a central idea in economics; it will come up in almost every chapter of this book. You'll see it in questions such as

- What happens when prices change?
- What happens when the government implements a new policy?
- What happens when a company introduces a new product?

Answering any of these questions requires us to consider a large-scale reaction, rather than the behavior of just one person, company, or policy-maker.

In answering this question about trade-offs, economists commonly make two assumptions. The first is that people respond to incentives. An **incentive** is something that causes people to behave in a certain way by changing the trade-offs they face. Incentives can be positive or negative:

- A *positive* incentive (sometimes just called an *incentive*) makes people *more likely* to do something. For example, lowering the price of spaghetti creates a positive incentive for people to order it because it lowers the opportunity cost: When you pay less for spaghetti, you give up fewer other things you could have spent the money on.
- A *negative* incentive (sometimes called a *disincentive*) makes them *less likely* to do it. Charging people more for pizza is a negative incentive to buy pizza because they now have to give up more alternative purchases.

The second assumption economists make about trade-offs is that nothing happens in a vacuum. That is, you can't change just one thing in the world without eliciting a response from others. If you change your behavior—even if only in a small way—that action will change the incentives of the people around you, causing them to change their behavior in response. If you invent a new

LO 1.3 Explain the economic concept of incentives.

incentive something that causes people to behave in a certain way by changing the trade-offs they face

product, competitors will copy it. If you raise prices, consumers will buy less. If you tax a good or service, people will produce less of it.

Asking *how others will respond* can help prevent bad decisions by predicting the undesirable side effects of a change in prices or policies. The question can also be used to design changes that elicit positive responses. When Muhammad Yunus was setting up Grameen Bank, he had to think carefully about the incentives that both rural villagers and traditional banks faced; he considered how those incentives could be changed without incurring negative side effects.

One reason banks saw rural villagers as risky customers is that they were too poor to have collateral to offer the bank. *Collateral* is a possession, like a house or a car, pledged by a borrower to a lender. If the borrower cannot repay the loan, the lender keeps the collateral. The threat of losing the collateral increases the cost of choosing to not repay the loan; collateral gives the borrower a positive incentive to repay. When traditional banks thought about lending to poor Bangladeshis, they believed that without the threat of losing collateral, the villagers would be unlikely to repay their loans.

Yunus needed to think up a different way of creating a positive incentive for poor customers to repay their loans. His best-known solution was to require borrowers to apply for loans in five-person groups. Every person in the group would have a stake in the success of the other members. If one person didn't repay a loan, no one else in the group could borrow from the bank again.

Yunus's idea, called *group responsibility*, was simple but hugely significant. Yunus concluded that borrowers would have a strong incentive to repay their loans: They wouldn't want to ruin relationships with other members of the group—their fellow villagers, with whom they live every day and rely on for mutual support in hard times. This incentive, in turn, changed the trade-off faced by banks; they responded by being more willing to lend to the poor. By asking himself how villagers would respond to the new kind of loan and how banks in turn would respond to the villagers' response, Yunus was able to predict that his idea could be the key to spreading banking services to the poor.

Dr. Yunus's predictions proved to be correct. Seeing that poor villagers nearly always repaid their loans under Grameen's system gave other banks confidence that small borrowers could be reliable customers. Banks offering microloans, savings accounts, and other services to the very poor have spread around the world. As a result of Yunus's creativity and thoughtfulness about incentives, the poor have better access to financial services, and banks earn money from providing them. Today, other ideas have proved even more effective in providing the right incentives for small borrowers, continuing in the tradition of experimentation and innovation pioneered by Yunus and Grameen Bank.

Throughout this book, you will see many examples of how the power of incentives can be harnessed to accomplish everything from increasing a company's profits to protecting the environment. But before we get carried away with brilliant economic innovations, we have to ask ourselves one more question, the final test for any ideas that come out of our problem-solving process.

Efficiency

Question 4: Are resources being allocated in the best way possible?

LO 1.4 Explain the economic concept of efficiency.

efficiency
use of resources to ensure that people get what they most want and need given the available resources

Once you've considered needs, incentives, and trade-offs, it's natural to ask whether resources are being used in the best way possible. Of course, there are many ways to define "in the best way possible."

One way is to ask whether outcomes are fair or ethical. Of course, people debate what's fair or ethical, and we'll stop regularly to consider the fairness of economic outcomes too (especially in "What do you think?" boxes).

Here, we focus on a separate concept: efficiency. It's one of the building blocks of economic thinking, and it has a specific meaning that differs from the everyday usage of the word. For economists, **efficiency** is not just about maximizing productivity, it is also about ensuring that people get what they most want and need given the available resources.

Efficiency doesn't mean that outcomes are necessarily fair or ethical, but it reflects an important idea about economic outcomes. As described later in the text, when the economy is efficient, there is no way to reorganize things to make anyone better off *without someone else becoming worse off.*

A *resource* is anything that can be used to make something of value, from natural resources (such as water and trees) to human resources (such as talents and knowledge). When the economy is efficient, resources are being used to create the greatest *total* economic value to society. (We'll take a broad view for now: Something is *valuable* if someone wants it.)

Practical implications of efficiency   Let's turn to a practical implication. There are millions of businesses in the world, each trying to make a profit. When consumers want a good or service, businesses have incentives to earn money by providing it. When you think you see a big, unexploited opportunity—a new product, policy, technology, or business model that could change the world or earn you millions of dollars—stop for a moment. Ask yourself: If it's such a great idea, *why isn't someone doing it?*

One possible answer is simply that nobody has thought of it before. That's possible. Perhaps you *have* seen an efficient way to allocate resources in a way that produces economic value for society. But if *you* have seen the opportunity, doesn't it seem likely that at least one of the billions of other smart, rational people in the world will have seen it too?

This leads to our final claim: *Under normal circumstances, individuals and firms will act to provide the things people want.* If a genuine profit-making opportunity exists, someone will take advantage of it, and usually sooner rather than later.

Don't get us wrong: We're not saying there is never an opportunity to do something new in the world. Great new ideas happen all the time—they drive progress. But there's a strong possibility that other people have already thought about the idea, and if they chose not to take advantage of it, that's a hint that you might be missing something. In that case, the first thing to do is backtrack to the first three economists' questions:

- Have you misjudged people's wants and constraints?
- Have you miscalculated the trade-offs they face?
- Have you misunderstood how people will respond to incentives?

If you think back through those questions and still think you're on to something, here are some more possibilities to consider. We said that *under normal circumstances*, the economy is operating efficiently and individuals or firms provide the things people want. What are some ways in which circumstances might not be normal?

- *Innovation:* Innovation is the explanation you're hoping is correct. Maybe your idea has not been used yet because it is too new. If you have come up with a truly new idea, whether it is new technology or a new business model, people cannot have taken advantage of it yet because it didn't exist before.

- *Market failure:* Market failures are an important cause of inefficiency. Sometimes people and firms fail to take advantage of opportunities because something prevents them from capturing the benefits of the opportunity or imposes additional costs on them. For instance, maybe your great new idea won't work because it would be impossible to prevent others from quickly copying it. Or perhaps your great new idea won't work because a few big companies already have the market for it sewn up. Economists call such situations *market failures.* We will discuss market failures in much greater depth later in the text.

- *Intervention:* If a powerful force—often the government—intervenes in the economy, transactions cannot take place the way they normally would. We'll see later in the text that many government economic policies intentionally or unintentionally interfere with people's ability to take advantage of profit-making opportunities.

- *Unprofitable idea:* Maybe your idea won't produce a profit. Individuals and governments have goals other than profit, of course—for example, creating great art or promoting social justice. But if your idea doesn't also generate a profit, then it is less surprising that no one has taken advantage of it.

When Muhammad Yunus asked himself the question, "Why isn't someone already lending to the poor?" he first identified a market failure involving lack of collateral. Understanding the market-failure problem enabled him to come up with the idea of group responsibility to fix it. But then he had to ask himself, "Why aren't other banks already using the group responsibility idea?"

Maybe there was another market failure Yunus hadn't spotted. Maybe some government policy prevented it. Maybe traditional banks had considered it and decided it still wouldn't generate a profit. Yunus wasn't primarily interested in making a profit, of course—he was interested in helping the poor. But if microloans weren't going to earn a profit for the banks even with group responsibility, then that would explain why no one was already doing it.

Fortunately, none of those answers were correct. This was a case in which the answer to *why isn't someone already doing it?* was that the idea was *genuinely new.* Grameen Bank was able to help very poor people in Bangladesh by lending them money, while making enough profit to expand and serve more customers. Today, over 20 million people in Bangladesh can get small loans from Grameen Bank and other organizations. Around the world, over 200 million low-income customers enjoy the same opportunity. Sometimes, something that seems like a great new idea really *is* exactly that.

✓ TEST YOURSELF

In every chapter of this book you will find a few Test Yourself quizzes. These questions test your understanding of the concepts presented in the preceding section. If you have trouble answering any of the questions, go back and review the section. Don't move forward until you understand these ideas.

- ☐ How do constraints affect decision making? **[LO 1.1]**
- ☐ What do opportunity costs represent? **[LO 1.2]**
- ☐ What is the name for something that changes the trade-offs that people face when making a decision? **[LO 1.3]**
- ☐ Give four reasons that might explain why a product isn't already in the market. **[LO 1.4]**

An Economist's Problem-Solving Toolbox

The four questions we've just discussed are some of the fundamental insights of economics. Using them to understand how the world *might* work is only half the battle. Understanding when and how to apply them is the other half. In this second part of this chapter, we will describe some tools economists use to apply these insights to real situations.

Accurately spotting the fundamental economic concepts at work in the world is sometimes less obvious than you might think. Throughout history, people have observed the world around them and drawn conclusions that have proved hilariously—or sometimes tragically—wrong. We now know that the sun doesn't revolve around the earth. Droughts are not caused by witches giving people the evil eye. Yet, intelligent people once believed these things. It's human nature to draw meaning from the patterns we observe around us, but our conclusions are not always correct.

Economic analysis requires us to combine theory with observations and to subject both to tough scrutiny before drawing conclusions. In this section we will see how to put together theories and facts to determine what causes what. We will also distinguish between the way things *are* and the way we think they *should be.* You can apply these tools to all sorts of situations, from personal life choices to business decisions and policy analysis.

Correlation and causation

A die-hard sports fan may wear a particular jersey while watching his or her team win the NBA finals or Super Bowl, and then forever insist that jersey is lucky. This is an exaggerated example of a common human tendency: When we see that two events occur together, we tend to assume that one causes the other. Economists, however, try to be particularly careful about what causes what.

To differentiate between two variables that move together and two variables that have a cause-and-effect relationship, we use two different terms. For the instance in which two variables have a consistent relationship, we say there is a **correlation** between them. Correlation can be positive or negative:

- If both variables tend to move in the same direction, we say they are *positively correlated*. For example, wearing raincoats is positively correlated with rain.
- When two variables move in opposite directions, we say they are *negatively correlated*. High temperatures are negatively correlated with people wearing down jackets.

If there is no consistent relationship between two variables, we say they are *uncorrelated*.

Correlation differs from causation. **Causation** means that one variable causes the other. As the preceding examples show, causation and correlation often go together. Weather and clothing are often correlated because weather *causes* people to make certain choices about the clothing they wear.

Correlation and causation do not *always* go together in a straightforward way, as Figure 1-1 humorously shows. Correlation and causation can be confused in three major ways: coincidence, omitted variables, and reverse causation.

Coincidence   Does the result of the Super Bowl predict the performance of the stock market? A few years ago, some people thought it might. The Super Bowl pits the top team from the American Football Conference against the top team from the National Football Conference. For a long time, when a team from the AFC won, the stock market had a bad year; when a team from the NFC won, the stock market had a great year. In fact, this pattern held true nearly 80 percent of the time between 1967 and 2017.

Would it have been a good idea to base your investment strategy on the results of the Super Bowl? We think not. There is no plausible cause-and-effect relationship here. Stock market outcomes happened to be *correlated with* Super Bowl outcomes for a number of years, but there is no

LO 1.5 Distinguish between correlation and causation.

correlation
a consistently observed relationship between two variables

causation
a relationship between two events in which one brings about the other

---

FIGURE 1-1

Total revenue generated by bowling alleys correlates with per capita consumption of sour cream   The graph shows the relationship between X and Y. Obviously, there's no connection between X and Y, but if you took these data at face value, you might think otherwise.

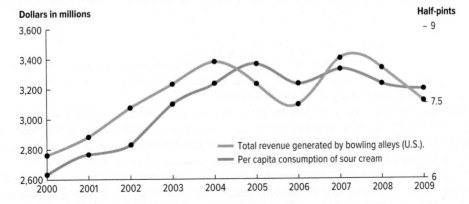

Source: www.tylervigen.com/view_correlation?id=28797

logical way they could be *caused by* them. If you search long enough for odd coincidences, you will eventually find some.

Omitted variables   Consider the following statement: There is a positive correlation between the presence of firefighters and people with serious burn injuries. Does this statement mean that firefighters cause burn injuries? Of course not. We know that firefighters are not burning people; they're trying to save them. Instead, there must be some common underlying variable behind both observed outcomes—fires, in this case.

Sometimes, two events that are correlated occur together because both are caused by the same underlying factor. Each has a causal relationship with a third factor, but not with each other. The underlying factor is called an *omitted variable*—despite the fact that it is an important part of the cause-and-effect story, it has been left out of the analysis. The From Another Angle box "Does ice cream cause polio?" tells the story of an omitted variable that convinced some doctors to mistakenly campaign against a staple of summer fun: ice cream.

Does ice cream cause polio?
From Another Angle

From Another Angle boxes show you a completely different way of looking at an economic concept. We find that a little bit of weirdness goes a long way in helping us to remember things.

Polio is a disease that once crippled or killed thousands of children in the United States every year. Before the cause of polio was known, doctors noticed that polio infections seemed to be more common in children who had been eating lots of ice cream. Observing this *correlation* led some people to assume that there was a *causal* relationship between the two. Some doctors recommended that kids stop eating ice cream, and many fearful parents understandably took their advice.

We now know that ice cream is safe. Polio is caused by a virus that spreads from one person to another. The virus is transmitted through contaminated food and water—for example, dirty swimming pools or water fountains. It has nothing to do with ice cream.

The ice cream confusion was caused by an *omitted variable*: warm weather. In warm weather, children are more likely to use swimming pools and water fountains. And in warm weather, children are also more likely to eat ice cream. Polio was therefore *correlated* with eating ice cream, but it certainly wasn't *caused* by it.

Happily, in 1952 a scientist named Jonas Salk developed a vaccine that made polio a rare disease. One unintended benefit was that doctors, and parents, stopped telling kids to stay away from ice cream.

Source: Steve Lohr, "For Today's Graduate, Just One Word: Statistics," *New York Times*, August 5, 2009.

Reverse causation   A third common source of confusion between correlation and causation is *reverse causation*: Did A cause B, or did B cause A? When two events always happen together, it can be hard to say which caused the other.

Let's return to the correlation between rain and raincoats. If we knew nothing about rain, we might observe that it often appears together with raincoats; we might conclude that wearing a raincoat (A) causes rain (B). In this case, we all know that the causation goes the other way, but observation alone does not tell us that.

Looking at the timing of two correlated events can sometimes provide clues. Often, if A happens before B, it hints that A causes B rather than vice versa. But grabbing a raincoat as you leave home in the morning frequently happens *before* it rains in the afternoon. The timing notwithstanding, taking your raincoat with you in the morning clearly does not *cause* rain later in the day. In this case, your *anticipation* of B causes A to happen.

An important lesson for economists and noneconomists alike is never to take observations at face value. Always make sure you can explain *why* two events are related. To do so, you need another tool in the economist's toolbox: a model.

Models

A **model** is a simplified representation of a complicated situation. In economics, models show how people, firms, and governments make decisions about managing resources and how their decisions interact. An economic model can represent a situation as basic as how people decide what car to buy or as complex as what causes a global recession.

Because models simplify complex problems, they allow us to focus our attention on the most important parts. Models rarely include every detail of a given situation, but that is a good thing. If we had to describe the entire world with perfect accuracy before solving a problem, we'd be so overwhelmed with details that we'd never get the answer. By carefully simplifying the situation to its essentials, we can get useful answers that are *approximately* right.

One of the most basic models of the economy is the **circular flow model**. The economy involves billions of transactions every day, and the circular flow model helps show how all of those transactions work together. The model slashes through complexity to show important patterns. Figure 1-2 shows the circular flow of economic transactions in a graphic format called the *circular flow diagram*.

The first simplification of the circular flow model is to narrow our focus to the two most important types of actors in the economy, households and firms:

- *Households* are vital in two ways. First, they supply land and labor to firms and invest capital in firms. (Land, labor, and capital are called the *factors of production*.) Second, they buy the goods and services that firms produce.
- *Firms* too are vital but do the opposite of households: They buy or rent the land, labor, and capital supplied by households, and they produce and sell goods and services.

The circular flow model shows that firms and households are tightly connected through both production and consumption.

LO 1.6 List the characteristics of a good economic model.

model
a simplified representation of the important parts of a complicated situation

circular flow model
a simplified representation of how the economy's transactions work together

FIGURE 1-2

Circular flow diagram

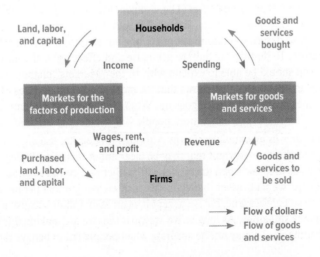

In another helpful simplification, the circular flow model narrows the focus to two markets that connect households and firms:

- The *market for goods and services* is exactly what it sounds: It reflects all of the activity involved in the buying and selling of goods and services. In this market, households spend their wages from labor and their income from land and capital, and firms earn revenue from selling their goods and services.
- The second market is the *market for the factors of production*. Here, households supply land, labor, and capital, and firms hire and purchase or rent these inputs.

The model puts all of this together. The transactions we have described are part of two loops:

- One is a loop of inputs and outputs as they travel throughout the economy. The *inputs* are the land, labor, and capital firms use to produce goods. The *outputs* are the goods and services that firms produce using the factors of production.
- Another loop represents the flow of dollars. Households buy goods and services using the money they get from firms for using their factors of production. Firms get revenues from selling these goods and services—and, in turn, firms can then use the money to buy or rent factors of production.

You might be a little dizzy at this point, with everything spinning in loops. To help straighten things out, let's follow $5 from your wallet as it flows through the economy. You could spend this $5 in any number of ways. As you're walking down the street, you see a box of donuts sitting in the window of your local bakery. You head in and give the baker your $5, a transaction in the market for goods. The money represents revenue for the baker and spending by you. The donuts are an output of the bakery.

The story of your $5 is not over, though. In order to make more donuts, the baker puts that $5 toward buying inputs in the market for the factors of production. This might include paying rent for the bakery or paying wages for an assistant. The baker's spending represents income for the households that provide the labor in the bakery or rent out the space. Once the baker pays wages or rent with that $5, it has made it through a cycle in the circular flow.

As the circular flow model shows, an economic model approximates what happens in the real economy. Later in the text, we'll discuss other models that focus on specific questions—like how much gasoline prices will go up when the government raises taxes or how fast the economy is likely to grow in the next decade.

The best models lead us to clearer answers about complicated questions. What makes a good economic model? We have already said that good models can leave out details that are not crucial, and they focus on the important aspects of a situation. To be useful, a model *should* also do three things:

1. *A good model predicts cause and effect.* The circular flow model gives a useful description of the basics of the economy. Often, though, we want to go further. Many times we want a model not only to describe economic connections but also to predict how things will happen in the future. To do that, we have to get cause and effect right. If your model says that A causes B, you should be able to explain why. In the "Markets" chapter we'll learn about a central model in economics that shows that for most goods and services, the quantity people want to buy goes down as the price goes up. Why? As the cost of an item rises, but the benefit of owning it remains the same, more people will decide that the trade-off is not worth it.

2. *A good model states its assumptions clearly.* Although models are usually too simple to fit the real world perfectly, it's important that they be clear about their simplifying assumptions. Doing so helps us to know when the model will predict real events accurately and when it will not. For example, we said earlier that economists often assume that people behave rationally. We know that isn't always true, but we accept it as an assumption because it is *approximately* accurate in many situations. As long as we are clear that we are making this assumption, we will know that the model may not be accurate when people fail to behave rationally.

3. *A good model describes the real world accurately.* If a model does not describe what actually happens in the real world, something about the model is wrong. We've admitted that models are not perfectly accurate because they are intentionally simpler than the real world. But if a model predicts things that are not usually or approximately true, it is not useful. How do we tell if a model is realistic? Economists test their models by observing what happens in the real world and collecting data, which they use to verify or reject the model. In the Economics in Action box "When education pays off," take a look at a model that explains the returns that people experience when investing in a college education.

When education pays off
Economics in Action

Economics in Action boxes show how the concept you're reading about relates to the real world. Often these boxes present interesting ideas or describe situations in which people used an economic idea to solve business or policy questions.

Why go to college? Well, of course, you learn a lot of important things and can make amazing friends. Also—not to be too crass about it—a college diploma will generally lead to bigger paychecks. On average, completing college roughly doubles lifetime earnings compared to earnings without a degree. In fact, the earnings advantage from having more education has grown bigger over time.

What drives those gains to education? To answer that question, Claudia Goldin and Lawrence Katz, economists at Harvard University, pieced together a century of data on wages in the United States. Two models helped them explain the patterns over time.

The first model predicts that education boosts earnings because it allows workers to take advantage of technical innovations that increase productivity. The greater the pace of technical innovation, the bigger will be the wage gains from education. Goldin and Katz's data showed a century-long steady increase in technology (starting well before the latest mobile phones, office technologies, and self-driving cars), which helped sustain wage growth for educated workers.

But Goldin and Katz argue that the story doesn't end there. Their second model focuses on the number of people getting educated. The second model predicts that when opportunities created by new technology increase much faster than education rates, there's more competition for educated workers. To attract workers, firms offer higher wages, and wages grow even faster than predicted by the education rate alone.

So, why are the gains to education continuing at a high rate, and even growing over time? It turns out that college *completion rates* have been slowing in the United States in recent decades. Students are starting school, but many are leaving before getting degrees. Overall, nearly a third of students who started college in 2011 had not finished or were no longer enrolled six years later. One consequence is a bigger *relative gain* for those who ultimately do get diplomas—and a wider gap in earnings between those who finish college and those who don't.

Sources: Brad Hershbein and Melissa Kearney, "Major Decisions: What Graduates Earn Over Their Lifetimes," *Hamilton Project,* September 2014; Claudia Goldin and Lawrence F. Katz, "The Future of Inequality: The Other Reason Education Matters So Much," *Milken Institute Review,* Third Quarter, 2009.

Positive and normative analysis

Economics is a field of study in which people frequently confuse facts with judgments that are based on beliefs. Think about the following example:

- *Statement #1:* Income taxes reduce the number of hours that people want to work.
- *Statement #2:* Income taxes should be reduced or abolished.

LO 1.7 Distinguish between positive and normative analysis.

positive statement
a factual claim about how the world actually works

normative statement
a claim about how the world should be

A famous quote makes this point nicely: "Everyone has a right to their own opinion, but not to their own facts." If you search the internet for this quote, you'll see that it has been attributed to many people.
Source: Karen Glasbergen, used with permission.

Many people have trouble separating these two statements. Some feel that the second statement flows logically from the first. Others disagree with the second statement, so they assume the first can't possibly be true.

If you read carefully, however, you'll see that the first sentence is a statement about cause and effect. Thus, it can be proved true or false by data and evidence. A statement that makes a factual claim about how the world *actually* works is called a **positive statement**.

The second sentence, on the other hand, cannot be proved true or false. Instead, it indicates what *should be* done—but only if we share certain goals, understandings, and moral beliefs. A statement that makes a claim about how the world *should be* is called a **normative statement**.

To see how important the distinction between positive and normative statements can be, consider two claims that a physicist might make:

- *Positive statement:* A nuclear weapon with the explosive power of 10 kilotons of TNT will have a fallout radius of up to six miles.
- *Normative statement:* The United States was right to use nuclear weapons in World War II.

Although people could disagree about both of these statements, the first is a question of scientific fact; the second depends heavily on a person's ethical and political beliefs. The first statement may inform your opinion of the second, but you can still agree with one and not the other.

Earlier in this chapter, we introduced a feature called "What Do You Think?" that asks for your opinion about an important policy or life decision. From this point forward, you can use your understanding of the differences between normative and positive analysis to untangle the questions asked in these boxes and combine the two kinds of analysis to arrive at a conclusion. Begin trying your hand at this with the What Do You Think? box "The cost of college cash."

Throughout this text, remember that *you don't have to buy into a particular moral or political outlook in order for economics to be useful to you.* Our goal is to provide you with a toolbox of economic concepts that you can use

"You're certainly entitled to your opinion."

? The cost of college cash
What Do You Think?

In 2014–2015, the average yearly cost of a college education ranged from $16,188 at public universities to $37,424 at private universities. Students have a number of options for paying the bill. They can take out federal loans, private loans, or a combination of the two to defer payments until later, or they can use savings or earnings to foot the bill.

Students who qualify for federal loans enjoy benefits such as limits on the interest rate they can be charged or the total payments they can be expected to make. They also have the possibility of loan forgiveness if they enter certain fields after graduation.

Lending to students is a controversial topic. Some people argue for more controls on private lending institutions, such as interest-rate caps and greater protection for students who default. They reason that lending programs should support students who would not otherwise be able to afford college. Furthermore, they argue, graduating with a lot of debt discourages students from going into lower-paid public service jobs.

Other people maintain that the existing lending system is fine. Getting a college degree, they argue, increases a person's future earning power so much that graduates should be able to handle the debt, even at high interest rates. They worry that overregulation will discourage private lenders from offering student loans, defeating the purpose of giving students better access to financial assistance.

WHAT DO YOU THINK?

Use the four basic questions economists ask to break down the problem. Remember that your answer can draw on both positive analysis (what *will* happen if a certain policy is followed) and normative analysis (what *should* be done, given your values and goals). You should be able to say which parts of your answers fall into each category.

1. What motivations and constraints apply to students who are considering different schools and loan options? What motivations and constraints apply to private lenders?
2. What opportunity costs do students face when deciding how to pay for college? Should they avoid loans by skipping college altogether or by working their way through college?
3. How would prospective students respond to government limits on the interest rate on student loans? How would private banks that offer student loans respond?
4. Why do you think the federal government has not yet implemented interest-rate caps on private student loans? Do you anticipate any unintended side-effects of that policy?
5. Consider your arguments in response to questions 1 through 4. Which parts were based on normative statements and which on positive statements?

Sources: "Trends in college pricing," *National Center for Education Statistics,* http://nces.ed.gov/fastfacts/display .asp?id=76; "How much student debt is too much?" http://roomfordebate.blogs.nytimes.com/2009/06/14/ how-much-student-debt-is-too-much/?scp=1&sq=student%20loans&st=cse.

to engage in positive analysis. We will also highlight important decisions you may face that will require you to engage in normative thinking, informed by economic analysis. You will find that economics can help you to make better decisions and identify the most effective policies, regardless of your goals and beliefs.

✓ TEST YOURSELF

☐ What does it mean when two variables are positively correlated? **[LO 1.5]**
☐ What are the characteristics of a good economic model? **[LO 1.6]**
☐ What is the difference between a positive statement and a normative statement? **[LO 1.7]**

Conclusion

Economists approach problems differently from many other people. A basic principle of human behavior underlies economics—the idea that people typically make choices to achieve their goals in the most effective way possible, subject to the constraints they face.

In this chapter we have introduced the basic concepts economists use, as well as four questions they ask to break down problems. Throughout this book, you will see these concepts and questions over and over again:

1. Scarcity: *What are the wants and constraints of those involved?*
2. Opportunity cost: *What are the trade-offs?*
3. Incentives: *How will others respond?*
4. Efficiency: *Are resources being allocated in the best way possible?*

In later chapters, as we progress to more complicated problems, try using these four questions to break down problems into manageable pieces. Then you can tackle those smaller pieces using the four fundamental concepts presented in this chapter.

Key Terms

economics, p. 4

microeconomics, p. 4

macroeconomics, p. 4

rational behavior, p. 4

scarcity, p. 5

opportunity cost, p. 6

marginal decision making, p. 8

sunk costs, p. 8

incentive, p. 9

efficiency, p. 10

correlation, p. 13

causation, p. 13

model, p. 15

circular flow model, p. 15

positive statement, p. 18

normative statement, p. 18

Summary

LO 1.1 Explain the economic concept of scarcity.

Economists usually assume that people behave rationally and live within a condition of scarcity. Answering the question *What are the wants and constraints of those involved?* tells you what to expect from each player in the situation you are analyzing. Given rational behavior and scarcity, you can expect people to work to get what they want (their motivations) using the limited resources at their disposal (their constraints).

LO 1.2 Explain the economic concepts of opportunity cost and marginal decision making.

Trade-offs arise when you must give up something to get something else. Answering *What are the trade-offs?* will tell you about the costs and benefits associated with a decision. The full cost of doing something is its *opportunity cost*—the value to you of what you have to give up in order to get something, or the value you could have gained by choosing the next-best alternative.

Economists assume that rational people make decisions "at the margin," by comparing any additional benefits of a choice to the extra costs it brings. If people are behaving rationally when they face trade-offs, they will always choose to do something if the marginal benefit is greater than the opportunity cost. They will never do it if the opportunity cost is greater than the marginal benefit.

LO 1.3 Explain the economic concept of incentives.

The collective reaction to changing trade-offs is a central idea in economics. Asking *How will others respond?* will give you a complete picture of how a particular decision affects the world. You can assume that any action will bring a response because people react to changes in their incentives.

LO 1.4 Explain the economic concept of efficiency.

In economics, efficiency is the use of resources to ensure that people get what they most want and need given the available resources. Under normal circumstances, markets are efficient.

So, when you see what seems to be unexploited opportunity, you should ask: If it's such a great idea, *why isn't someone already doing it?* Markets usually allocate resources efficiently. When they don't, other explanations might be in play: a market failure may have occurred; government may have intervened in the economy; there may be goals other than profit involved; or there may be a genuine opportunity for innovation.

LO 1.5 Distinguish between correlation and causation.

When there is a consistently observed relationship between two variables, we say they are *correlated*. This is different from a *causal* relationship, in which one variable brings about the other. Three common ways in which correlation and causation are confused are coincidence, omitted variables, and reverse causation.

LO 1.6 List the characteristics of a good economic model.

A model is a simplified representation of the important parts of a complicated situation. In economics, models usually show how people, firms, and governments make decisions about managing resources and how their decisions interact. The *circular flow model* is a representation of how the transactions of households and firms flow through the economy.

A good economic model should predict cause and effect, describe the world accurately, and state its assumptions clearly. Economists test their models by observing what happens in the world and collecting data that can be used to support or reject their models.

LO 1.7 Distinguish between positive and normative analysis.

A statement that makes a factual claim about how the world actually works is called a *positive* statement. A statement that makes a claim about how the world should be is called a *normative* statement. Economics is a field in which people frequently confuse positive statements with normative statements. You do not have to adopt a particular moral or political point of view to use economic concepts and models.

Review Questions

1. Suppose you are shopping for new clothes to wear to job interviews, but you're on a tight budget. In this situation, what are your wants and constraints? What does it mean to behave rationally in the face of scarcity? **[LO 1.1]**

2. You are a student with a demanding schedule of classes. You also work part time and your supervisor allows you to determine your schedule. In this situation, what is your scarce resource? How do you decide how many hours to work? **[LO 1.1]**

3. Think about the definition of scarcity that you learned in this chapter. Name three ways that you confront scarcity in your own life. **[LO 1.1]**

4. When shopping for your interview clothes, what are some trade-offs you face? What is the opportunity cost of buying new clothes? What are the benefits? How do you balance the two? **[LO 1.2]**

5. You have an 8:30 class this morning, but you are feeling extremely tired. How do you decide whether to get some extra sleep or go to class? **[LO 1.2]**

6. It's Friday night. You already have a ticket to a concert, which cost you $30. A friend invites you to go out for a game of paintball instead. Admission would cost you $25, and you think you'd get $25 worth of enjoyment out of it. Your concert ticket is nonrefundable. What is your opportunity cost (in dollars) of playing paintball? **[LO 1.2]**

7. Suppose you have two job offers and are considering the trade-offs between them. Job A pays $45,000 per year; it includes health insurance and two weeks of paid vacation. Job B pays $30,000 per year; it includes four weeks of paid vacation but no health insurance. **[LO 1.2]**

   a. List the benefits of Job A and the benefits of Job B.

   b. List the opportunity cost of Job A and the opportunity cost of Job B.

8. Your former neighbors gave you their lawnmower when they moved. You are thinking of using this gift to mow lawns in your neighborhood this summer for extra cash. As you think about what to charge your neighbors and whether this idea is worth your effort, what opportunity costs do you need to consider? **[LO 1.2]**

9. Think of a few examples of incentives in your daily life. How do you respond to those incentives? **[LO 1.3]**

10. You supervise a team of salespeople. Your employees already receive a company discount. Suggest a positive incentive and a negative incentive you could use to improve their productivity. **[LO 1.3]**

11. Your boss decides to pair workers in teams and offer bonuses to the most productive team. Why might your boss offer team bonuses instead of individual bonuses? **[LO 1.3]**

12. Think of a public policy–a local or national law, tax, or public service–that offers an incentive for a particular behavior. Explain what the incentive is, who is offering it, and what they are trying to encourage or discourage. Does the incentive work? **[LO 1.3]**

13. Why do individuals or firms usually provide the goods and services people want? **[LO 1.4]**

14. You may have seen TV advertisements for products or programs that claim to teach a sure-fire way to make millions on the stock market. Apply the *Why isn't someone already doing it?* test to this situation. Do you believe the ads? Why or why not? **[LO 1.4]**

15. Describe an innovation in technology, business, or culture that had a major economic impact in your lifetime. **[LO 1.4]**

16. Why do people confuse correlation with causation? **[LO 1.5]**

17. Name two things that are positively correlated and two things that are negatively correlated. **[LO 1.5]**

18. Why is it important for a good economic model to predict cause and effect? **[LO 1.6]**

19. Why is it important for a good economic model to make clear assumptions? **[LO 1.6]**

20. What is the difference between disagreeing about a positive statement and disagreeing about a normative statement? **[LO 1.7]**

21. Would a good economic model be more likely to address a positive statement or a normative statement? Why? **[LO 1.7]**

22. Write a positive statement and a normative statement about your favorite hobby. **[LO 1.7]**

Problems and Applications

1. Think about how and why goods and resources are scarce. Goods and resources can be scarce for reasons that are inherent to their nature at all times, that are temporary or seasonal, or that are artificially created. Separate the goods listed below into two groups; indicate which (if any) are artificially scarce (AS) and which (if any) are inherently scarce (IS). **[LO 1.1]**

   a. Air of any quality _____

   b. Land _____

   c. Patented goods _____

   d. Original Picasso paintings _____

2. You are looking for a new apartment in Manhattan. Your income is $4,000 per month, and you know that you should not spend more than 25 percent of your income on rent. You have come across the listings for one-bedroom apartments shown in Table 1P-1. You are indifferent about location, and transportation costs are the same to each neighborhood. **[LO 1.1]**

TABLE 1P-1

Location	Monthly Rent
Chelsea	$1,200
Battery Park	2,200
Delancey	950
Midtown	1,500

a. Which apartments fall within your budget?

b. Suppose that you adhere to the 25 percent guideline but also receive a $1,000 cost-of-living supplement because you are living and working in Manhattan. Which apartments fall within your budget now?

3. Suppose the price of a sweater is $26. Jaylen's benefit from purchasing each additional sweater is given in Table 1P-2. He gets the most benefit from the first sweater and less benefit from each additional sweater. If Jaylen is behaving rationally, how many sweaters will he purchase? **[LO 1.2]**

TABLE 1P-2

	Marginal benefit ($)
1st sweater	60
2nd sweater	45
3rd sweater	40
4th sweater	33
5th sweater	22
6th sweater	18

4. Sweaters sell for $15 at the crafts fair. Allie knits sweaters; her marginal costs are given in Table 1P-3. Allie's costs increase with each additional sweater. If Allie is behaving rationally, how many sweaters will she sell? **[LO 1.2]**

TABLE 1P-3

	Marginal cost ($)
1st sweater	5
2nd sweater	8
3rd sweater	12
4th sweater	18
5th sweater	25
6th sweater	32

5. Last year, you estimated you would earn $5 million in sales revenues from developing a new product. So far, you have spent $3 million developing the product, but it is not yet complete. Meanwhile, this year you have new sales projections that show expected revenues from the new product will actually be only $4 million. How much should you be willing to spend to complete the product development? **[LO 1.2]**

a. $0.

b. Up to $1 million.

c. Up to $4 million.

d. Whatever it takes.

6. Consider the following examples. For each one, say whether the incentive is positive or negative. **[LO 1.3]**

a. Bosses who offer time-and-a-half for working on national holidays.

b. Mandatory minimum sentencing for drug offenses.

c. Fines for littering.

d. Parents who offer their children extra allowance money for good grades.

7. Consider the events that change prices as described in Table 1P-4. For each one, say whether the opportunity cost of consuming the affected good increases or decreases. **[LO 1.3]**

TABLE 1P-4

		Affected good
a.	A local movie theater offers a student discount.	Movie tickets
b.	A tax on soft drinks passes in your state.	Soft drinks
c.	Subsidies on corn are cut in half.	Corn subsidies
d.	Your student health center begins offering flu shots for free.	Flu shots

8. Your best friend has an idea for a drive-through bar. Indicate the best explanation for why others have not taken advantage of her idea: true innovation, market failure, government intervention, or unprofitability. **[LO 1.4]**

9. Your best friend has an idea for a long-distance car service to drive people across the country. Indicate the best explanation for why others have not taken advantage of her idea: true innovation, market failure, intervention, or unprofitability. **[LO 1.4]**

10. Determine whether each of the following questionable statements is best explained by coincidence, an omitted variable, or reverse causation. **[LO 1.5]**
    a. In cities that have more police, crime rates are higher.
    b. Many retired people live in states where everyone uses air conditioning during the summer.
    c. More people come down with the flu during the Winter Olympics than during the Summer Olympics.
    d. For the last five years, Punxsutawney Phil has seen his shadow on Groundhog Day, and spring has come late.

11. For each of the pairs below, determine whether they are positively correlated, negatively correlated, or uncorrelated. **[LO 1.5]**
    a. Time spent studying and test scores.
    b. Vaccination and illness.
    c. Soft drink preference and music preference.
    d. Income and education.

12. Each statement below is part of an economic model. Indicate whether the statement is a prediction of cause and effect or an assumption. **[LO 1.6]**
    a. People behave rationally.
    b. If the price of a good falls, people will consume more of that good.

c. Mass starvation will occur as population outgrows the food supply.
    d. Firms want to maximize profits.

13. From the list below, select the characteristics that describe a good economic model. **[LO 1.6]**
    a. Includes every detail of a given situation.
    b. Predicts that A causes B.
    c. Makes approximately accurate assumptions.
    d. Fits the real world perfectly.
    e. Predicts things that are usually true.

14. Determine whether each of the following statements is positive or normative. (Remember that a positive statement isn't necessarily *correct*; it just makes a factual claim rather than a moral judgment.) **[LO 1.7]**
    a. People who pay their bills on time are less likely than others to get into debt.
    b. Hard work is a virtue.
    c. Everyone should pay his or her bills on time.
    d. China has a bigger population than any other country in the world.
    e. China's One-Child Policy (which limits families to one child each) helped to spur the country's rapid economic growth.
    f. Lower taxes are good for the country.

15. You just received your midterm exam results and your professor wrote the following note: "You received a 70 on this exam, the average score. If you want to improve your grade, you should study more." Evaluate your professor's note. **[LO 1.7]**
    a. Is the first sentence positive or normative?
    b. Is the second sentence positive or normative?

Specialization and Exchange

The Origins of a T-Shirt

How can we get the most out of available resources? It's one of the most basic economic questions. (Remember the efficiency question in Chapter 1.) Factory managers ask it when looking for ways to increase production. National leaders ask it as they design economic policy. Activists ask it when they look for ways to reduce poverty or conserve the environment. And, in a different way, it's a question we all ask ourselves when thinking about what to do in life and how to make sure that we're taking full advantage of our talents.

To get a handle on this question, we start by thinking about resources at the highest level: the logic of international trade and the specialization of production between countries. By the end of the chapter, we hope that you'll see how the same ideas apply to decisions at any scale, right down to whether it makes more sense to fix your own computer or pay a specialist to do it for you.

We'll start with what seems to be a simple question: Where did your T-shirt come from? Look at the tag. We're betting it was made in a place you've never been to, and maybe never thought of visiting. Bangladesh? Honduras? Malaysia? Sri Lanka?

That "made in" label tells only part of the story. Chances are that your shirt's history spans other parts of the globe. Consider a standard T-shirt: The cotton might have been grown in Mali and then shipped to Pakistan, where it was spun into yarn. The yarn might have been sent to Bangladesh, where it was woven into cloth, cut into pieces, and assembled into a shirt. That shirt might then have traveled all the way to the United States, where it was shipped to a store near you. A couple of

©igor kisselev/Alamy

years from now, when you are cleaning out your closet, you may donate the shirt to a charity, which may ship it to a second-hand clothing vendor in Mali—right back where your shirt's travels began.

Of course, this is not only the story of shirts. It is remarkably similar to the story of shoes, computers, phones, and cars, among many other manufactured goods. Today, the products and services most of us take for granted come to us through an incredibly complex global network of farms, mines, factories, traders, and stores. Why is the production of even a simple T-shirt spread across the world? Why is the cotton grown in Mali and the sewing done in Bangladesh, rather than vice versa? Why isn't the whole shirt made in the United States, so that it doesn't have to travel so far to reach you?

LEARNING OBJECTIVES

LO 2.1 Construct a production possibilities graph, and describe what causes shifts in production possibilities curves.

LO 2.2 Define absolute and comparative advantage.

LO 2.3 Explain why people specialize.

LO 2.4 Explain how the gains from trade follow from comparative advantage.

This chapter addresses fundamental economic questions about who produces which goods and why. The fact that millions of people and firms around the globe coordinate their activities to provide consumers with the right combination of goods and services seems like magic.

This feat of coordination doesn't happen by chance, nor does a superplanner tell everyone where to go and what to do. Instead, the global production line is a natural outcome of people everywhere acting in their own self-interest to improve their own lives. Economists call this coordination mechanism the *invisible hand*, an idea that was first suggested by the eighteenth-century economic thinker Adam Smith.

To get some insight into the *who* and *why* of production, consider how the story of shirts has changed over the last few centuries. For most of the 1800s, Americans wore shirts made in the United States. Today, however, most shirts are made in Bangladesh, China, and other countries where factory wages are low. Have American workers become worse at making shirts over the last two centuries? Definitely not. In fact, as we'll see in this chapter, it doesn't even mean that Bangladeshi workers are better than American workers at making shirts. Instead, each good tends to be produced by the country, company, or person with the lowest opportunity cost for producing that good.

Countries and firms *specialize* in making goods for which they have the lowest opportunity cost. They then trade with one another to get the combination of goods they want to consume. Although the resulting *gains from trade* can be shared such that everyone ends up better off, finding the right policies to help workers and industries affected by trade can be difficult in practice.

The concepts in this chapter apply not just to the wealth of nations and international trade. They also illuminate the daily choices most people face: Who should cook which dishes at Thanksgiving dinner? Should you hire a plumber or fix the pipes yourself? Should you become a rock star or an economist? The concepts these questions raise can be subtle and are sometimes misunderstood. We hope this chapter will provide insights that will help you become a better resource manager in all areas of your life.

Production Possibilities

In Chapter 1, "Economics and Life," we talked about economic models. Good models help us understand complex situations through simplifying assumptions that allow us to zero in on the important aspects. The story of why Bangladesh now produces shirts for Americans that Americans themselves were producing 200 years ago is a complex one, as you'd expect. But by simplifying it into a model, we can reach useful insights.

Let's assume the United States and Bangladesh produce only two things—shirts and, say, bushels of wheat. (In reality, of course, they produce many things, but we're trying not to get bogged down in details right now.) The model uses "wheat" to stand in for "stuff other than shirts," allowing us to focus on what we're really interested in—shirts.

Using this model we'll perform a thought experiment about production using a tool called the *production possibilities frontier*. This tool is used in other contexts as well, many of which have no connection to international trade. Here we use it to show what has changed over the last couple of centuries to explain why Americans now buy shirts from Bangladesh.

LO 2.1 Construct a production possibilities graph, and describe what causes shifts in production possibilities curves.

Drawing the production possibilities frontier

Let's step back in time to the United States in 1800. In our simple model, there are 2 million American workers, and they have two choices of where to work: shirt factories or wheat farms. In shirt factories, each worker produces 1 shirt per day. On wheat farms, each worker produces 2 bushels of wheat per day.

What would happen if everyone worked on a wheat farm? The United States would produce 4 million bushels of wheat per day (2 bushels of wheat per worker × 2 million workers). This is one "production possibility." Alternatively, what would happen if everyone went to work in a shirt factory? The United States would produce 2 million shirts per day (1 shirt per worker × 2 million workers). Those production possibilities are represented as entries A and E (the top and bottom rows) in panel A of Figure 2-1.

Of course, the United States wouldn't want just shirts or just wheat—and there is no reason that all workers have to produce the same thing. There are many different combinations of shirts and wheat that American workers could produce. Some of these are shown as rows B, C, and D in panel A of Figure 2-1. For example, if one-quarter of the workers go to the shirt factory, they can make 500,000 (0.5 million) shirts (1 shirt per worker × 500,000 workers); the remaining workers can produce 3 million bushels of wheat (2 bushels per worker × 1.5 million workers). This production possibility is represented by row B. Or maybe 1 million workers would make shirts (1 million shirts) and 1 million would produce wheat (2 million bushels). That's row C.

For a graphic look at the production possibilities, we can plot them as points on a graph, as shown in panel B of Figure 2-1. If we fill in enough points, we create the solid green line shown in Figure 2-2. This is the **production possibilities frontier (PPF)**. It is a line or curve that shows all the possible combinations of outputs that can be produced using all available resources. In this case, the frontier plots all combinations of shirts and wheat that can be produced using all available workers in the United States. Points inside the frontier (such as point T) are achievable but don't make full use of all available resources.

The production possibilities frontier helps us answer the first of the economists' questions discussed in Chapter 1, "Economics and Life": *What are the wants and constraints of those involved?* People in the United States *want* to consume shirts and wheat (and other things, of course; remember, we're simplifying). The production possibilities frontier gives us a way to represent the *constraints* on production. The United States cannot produce combinations of shirts

production possibilities frontier (PPF) a line or curve that shows all the possible combinations of two outputs that can be produced using all available resources

FIGURE 2-1

Possible production combinations

(A)

Production possibilities	Bushels of wheat (millions)	Shirts (millions)
A	4	0
B	3	0.5
C	2	1.0
D	1	1.5
E	0	2.0

(B)

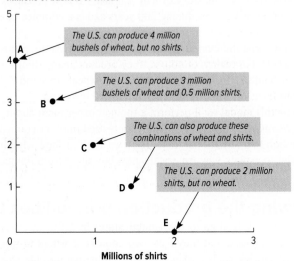

The United States can produce the maximum number of shirts or the maximum amount of wheat by devoting all its resources to one good or the other. But by allocating some resources to the production of each good, the United States can also produce many different combinations of wheat and shirts.

FIGURE 2-2

Production possibilities frontier

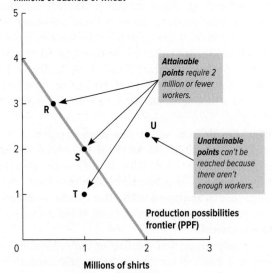

Points on or below the production possibilities frontier, such as R, S, and T, represent combinations of goods that the United States can produce with available resources. Points outside the frontier, such as U, are unattainable because there aren't enough resources.

and wheat that lie outside the frontier—such as point U in Figure 2-2. There just aren't enough workers or hours in the day to produce at point U, no matter how workers are allocated between shirts and wheat.

The production possibilities frontier also addresses the second economists' question: *What are the trade-offs?* Each worker can make *either* 1 shirt *or* 2 bushels of wheat per day. In other words, there is a trade-off between the quantity of wheat produced and the quantity of shirts produced. If we want an extra shirt, one worker has to stop producing bushels of wheat for a day. Therefore, the opportunity cost of 1 shirt is 2 bushels of wheat. Each bushel of wheat takes one worker half a day, so the opportunity cost of a bushel of wheat is half a shirt.

This opportunity cost is represented graphically by the *slope* of the production possibilities frontier. Moving up the frontier means getting more wheat at the cost of fewer shirts. Moving down the frontier means less wheat and more shirts. Looking at Figure 2-2, you'll notice that the slope of the line is −2. This is the same as saying that the opportunity cost of 1 shirt is always 2 bushels of wheat.

For a refresher on calculating and interpreting slopes, see Appendix A, "Math Essentials: Understanding Graphs and Slope," which follows this chapter.

Production possibilities frontiers when opportunity costs differ   So far, we've made the assumption that all workers are able to make the same amount of each good. In reality, some workers will probably be nimble-fingered and great at making shirts; others will be more naturally gifted at farming. What happens if we adjust our simple model to reflect this reality?

Let's start off with all workers producing wheat and nobody making shirts. If we reallocate the workers who are best at making shirts, we can get a lot of shirts without giving up too much wheat. In other words, the opportunity cost of making the first few shirts is quite low.

Now imagine almost all workers are making shirts, so that only the best farmers are left producing wheat. If we reallocate most of the remaining workers to shirt making, we give up a lot of wheat to get only a few extra shirts. The opportunity cost of getting those last few shirts is very high.

We can add a little more nuance to the model, to include land and machinery as resources also needed for production. We would find that the same pattern holds: As more of each resource is allocated to production, the opportunity cost of producing an additional unit of a good typically increases. This happens because we expect producers to always produce as efficiently as they can, which means, all else equal, using the resources with the lowest opportunity cost.

Let's start with everyone producing wheat. With wheat production pushed to the maximum, some farmers probably have to work on land that isn't well-suited to producing wheat. It could be that the land is swampy, or the soil has been overfarmed and depleted of nutrients. When farmers who had been working on this poor land switch over to making shirts, the economy will lose only a little wheat and gain many shirts in return. In contrast, if only a small amount of wheat is being grown using only the best, most fertile land, reallocating the last few farmers will cause a relatively large decrease in wheat production for each additional shirt.

Returning to the simplest model where workers are the only input to production, we can translate this increasing opportunity cost into the production possibilities frontier. Doing so, we get a curve that bows out (a concave curve) instead of a straight line, as shown in Figure 2-3. Panel A shows what happens if we have just three types of workers:

- For every bushel of wheat, some can make 1 shirt; they're the workers between points C_1 and C_2.
- For every bushel of wheat, some can make only $\frac{1}{2}$ of a shirt (between points C_2 and C_3).
- For every bushel of wheat, some can make only $\frac{1}{4}$ of a shirt (between points C_3 and C_4).

In other words, as we go down the curve, we move from those who are better at making shirts to those who are better at producing wheat. As we do so, the opportunity cost of making shirts in terms of producing wheat increases. As that happens, the slope of the curve gets steeper (−1 between C_1 and C_2, −2 between C_2 and C_3, and −4 between C_3 and C_4).

FIGURE 2-3

Bowed-out (concave) production possibilities frontier

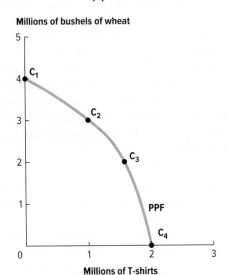

(A) Constructing the PPF

Millions of bushels of wheat

1. Giving up 1 million bushels of wheat results in a gain of 1 million shirts.
Slope = −1

2. Giving up 1 million bushels of wheat gains only 1/2 million shirts.
Slope = −2

3. Giving up 1 million bushels of wheat gains only 1/4 million shirts.
Slope = −4

PPF

Millions of T-shirts

At point C_1, all workers produce wheat, and switching the best sewers to making shirts will result in a big gain in the quantity of shirts. As more and better farmers switch to making shirts, however, the gain in shirts produced decreases relative to the loss in the quantity of wheat. As a result the slope of the PPF is steeper from C_2 to C_3, and again from C_3 to C_4.

(B) The PPF

Millions of bushels of wheat

PPF

Millions of T-shirts

In reality, each worker has slightly different skills and therefore a slightly different opportunity cost of making shirts in terms of wheat. As a result, we get a smoothly curved production possibilities frontier.

In reality there aren't just three types of workers—each of the 2 million workers will have slightly different skills. The many possibilities will result in a curve that looks smooth, as in panel B of Figure 2-3. At each point of the curved production possibilities frontier, the slope represents the opportunity cost of getting more wheat or more shirts, based on the skills of the next worker who could switch.

Choosing among production possibilities

What can the production possibilities frontier tell us about what combination of goods an economy will choose to produce? Earlier, we noted that economies can produce at points inside the frontier, as well as points on it. However, choosing a production point *inside* the frontier means a country could get more wheat, more shirts, or both, just by using all available workers. For instance, in Figure 2-4, the United States can get more wheat without giving up any shirts, by moving from point B_1 to point B_2. It can do the same by moving from point B_2 to B_3.

But once at the frontier, the United States will have to give up some of one good to get more of the other. Points like B_3 that lie *on* the frontier are called **efficient** because they squeeze the most output possible from all available resources. Points *within* (inside) the frontier are *inefficient* because they do not use all available resources.

In the real world, economies aren't always efficient. A variety of problems can cause some workers to be unemployed or other resources to be left idle. We'll return to these issues in detail in future chapters. For now, we'll assume that production is always efficient. People and firms usually try to squeeze as much value as they can out of the resources available to them, so efficiency is a reasonable starting assumption.

efficient points
combinations of production possibilities that squeeze the most output possible from all available resources

FIGURE 2-4
Choosing an efficient production combination

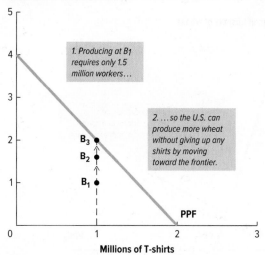

Millions of bushels of wheat

1. Producing at B_1 requires only 1.5 million workers…

2. …so the U.S. can produce more wheat without giving up any shirts by moving toward the frontier.

B_3

B_2

B_1

PPF

Millions of T-shirts

The United States needs only 1.5 million workers to reach point B_1. If the country employs more workers, it can reach point B_2 and get more wheat without giving up any shirts. The country can keep employing more workers until it reaches point B_3 (or any other point on the frontier) and there are no more workers left. Once the frontier is reached, getting more of one good requires giving up some of the other.

FIGURE 2-5
Choosing between efficient combinations

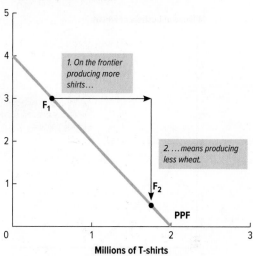

Millions of bushels of wheat

1. On the frontier producing more shirts…

F_1

2. …means producing less wheat.

F_2

PPF

Millions of T-shirts

At all points on the production possibilities frontier, the United States employs the entire workforce. Because the country uses all its resources fully at each point, choosing between points on the frontier is a matter of preference when there is no trade with other countries. The United States may choose to produce more wheat and fewer shirts (point F_1) or more shirts and less wheat (point F_2), depending on what its consumers want.

Based on the assumption of efficiency, we can predict that an economy will choose to produce at a point *on* the frontier rather than inside it. What the production possibilities frontier cannot tell us is *which* point on the frontier that will be. Will it be F_1 in Figure 2-5, for example? Or will the United States choose to move down the curve to F_2, producing more shirts at the expense of less wheat? We can't say whether point F_1 or F_2 is better without knowing more about the situation. If the U.S. economy is completely self-sufficient, the decision depends on what combination of shirts and wheat people in the United States want to consume. If trade with other countries is possible, it also depends on consumers and production possibilities in those countries, as we'll see later in the chapter.

Shifting the production possibilities frontier

Thus far, we've built a simple model that tells us what combinations of T-shirts and wheat the United States could produce in 1800. However, a lot of things have changed since 1800, including incredible improvements in technology that improve production possibilities. The production possibilities frontier is a useful tool for illustrating this change and understanding how it affects the constraints and trade-offs the country faces. Two main factors drive the change in U.S. production possibilities: the number of workers and changes in technology.

First, there are more workers. The U.S. population now is about 60 times larger than it was in 1800. Having more workers means more people available to produce shirts and wheat. Graphically, we can represent this change by shifting the entire frontier outward. Panel A of Figure 2-6 shows what happens to the frontier when the U.S. population doubles, with each worker still able to produce 1 shirt or 2 bushels of wheat per day.

FIGURE 2-6

Shifting the production possibilities frontier

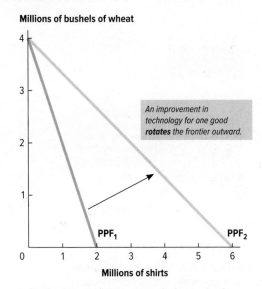

(A) Change in resources: Population growth

Millions of bushels of wheat

*An increase in available resources **shifts** the entire frontier outward.*

PPF₁   PPF₂

Millions of shirts

Production possibilities expand when resources increase. If the working population grows, the country can make more of everything by producing at the same rate as before. *This causes the frontier to shift outward.* If the population doubled, so would the maximum possible quantities of shirts and wheat.

(B) Change in technology: Invention of the power loom

Millions of bushels of wheat

*An improvement in technology for one good **rotates** the frontier outward.*

PPF₁   PPF₂

Millions of shirts

Production possibilities expand when technology improves. If the textile industry adopts the power loom, workers can make more shirts in the same amount of time. *This causes the frontier to rotate outward.* The rate of wheat production remains constant while the rate of shirt production increases, so the slope of the frontier changes.

The real magic of expanded productive capacity lies in the incredible technological advances that have taken place. In 1810, a businessman from Boston named Francis Cabot Lowell traveled to England to learn about British textile factories and to copy their superior technology. He brought back the power loom, which enabled workers to weave much more cotton fabric every day than they could before.[1]

We can model this change in technology through the production possibilities frontier by changing the rate of shirt production from 1 to 3 shirts per day, as shown in panel B of Figure 2-6. As the rate of shirt production increases, while the rate of wheat production remains the same, the shape of the curve changes. In this case, it pivots outward along the *x*-axis: This pivot indicates that for any given number of workers assigned to shirt-making, more shirts are produced than before. At every point except one (where all workers are producing wheat), the country can produce more with the same number of workers, thanks to improved technology.

For a refresher about shifts and pivots in graphs, see Appendix B, "Math Essentials: Working with Linear Equations," which follows Chapter 3, "Markets."

✓ TEST YOURSELF

☐ Could a person or country ever produce a combination of goods that lies outside the production possibilities frontier? Why or why not? **[LO 2.1]**

☐ Would an increase in productivity as a result of a new technology shift a production possibilities frontier inward or outward? **[LO 2.1]**

Absolute and Comparative Advantage

The United States used to be the world's biggest clothing manufacturer. In the 1800s, it had the technology and scale to be a leader in producing cotton shirts. Since then, the U.S. population has grown larger, and manufacturing technology has improved even more. So, why do less than 5 percent of global clothing exports come from the United States?[2]

Up to now, we have worked with a very simple model of production to highlight the key trade-offs faced by individual producers. If there is no trade between countries, then the United States can consume only those goods that it produces on its own. In the real world, however, goods are made all over the world. If Americans want to buy more shirts than the United States produces, they can get them from somewhere else. Under these conditions, how can we predict which countries will produce which goods?

Understanding how resources are allocated among multiple producers is a step toward understanding why big firms work with specialized suppliers. It also helps explain why a wealthy, productive country like the United States trades with much poorer, less-productive countries. In this section we will see that trade actually increases total production, which can benefit everyone involved. To see why, let's turn to the question of why many T-shirts sold in the United States today are made in Bangladesh.

Absolute advantage

Suppose that taking into account all the improvements in shirt-making and wheat-growing technology since 1800, an American worker can now make 50 shirts or grow 200 bushels of wheat per day.[3] A Bangladeshi worker, in comparison, can produce 25 shirts or 50 bushels of wheat. (Why the differences? Perhaps U.S. workers use faster cloth-cutting technology, or maybe because U.S. farmers use fertilizers, pesticides, and irrigation systems that farmers in Bangladesh don't.) In other words, given the same number of workers, the United States can produce twice as many shirts or four times as much wheat as Bangladesh.

If a producer can generate more output than others with a given amount of resources, that producer has an **absolute advantage**. In our simplified model, the United States has an absolute advantage over Bangladesh at producing both shirts and wheat because it can make more of both products than Bangladesh can per worker.

Comparative advantage

Absolute advantage is not the end of the story, though. If it were, the United States would still be producing the world's shirts. The problem is that for every T-shirt the United States produces, it uses resources that could otherwise be spent growing wheat. Of course, the same could be said of Bangladesh. But in our model of T-shirt and wheat production, the opportunity cost of making 1 shirt in the United States is 4 bushels of wheat (200 bushels ÷ 50 shirts = 4 bushels per shirt). The opportunity cost of making 1 shirt in Bangladesh is only 2 bushels of wheat (50 bushels ÷ 25 shirts = 2 bushels per shirt). The United States has to give up more to make a shirt than Bangladesh does.

When a producer can make a good at a lower opportunity cost than other producers, we say it has a **comparative advantage** at producing that good. In our model, Bangladesh has a comparative advantage over the United States at shirt-making: Its opportunity cost of producing a shirt is only 2 bushels of wheat, compared to 4 bushels of wheat for the United States.

The United States, on the other hand, has a comparative advantage over Bangladesh at producing wheat: Each time the United States produces a bushel of wheat, it gives up the opportunity to produce one-quarter of a shirt (50 shirts ÷ 200 bushels = $\frac{1}{4}$ shirt per bushel). For Bangladesh, however, the opportunity cost of producing a bushel of wheat is larger: it's one-half of a shirt (25 shirts ÷ 50 bushels = $\frac{1}{2}$ shirt per bushel). The United States has a lower opportunity cost for producing wheat than Bangladesh ($\frac{1}{4}$ shirt is less than $\frac{1}{2}$ shirt). Therefore, we say the United States has a comparative advantage over Bangladesh at wheat production.

LO 2.2 Define absolute and comparative advantage.

absolute advantage the ability to produce more of a good or service than others can with a given amount of resources

comparative advantage the ability to produce a good or service at a lower opportunity cost than others

A country can have a comparative advantage without having an absolute advantage. In our scenario, the United States has an absolute advantage over Bangladesh at producing both shirts and wheat, but it has a bigger advantage at producing wheat than at making shirts. It can make four times as much wheat per worker as Bangladesh (200 versus 50 bushels) but only twice as many shirts per worker (50 versus 25). It's better at both—but it's "more better," so to speak, at producing wheat. (We know that "more better" is not good grammar, but it nicely expresses the idea.) Likewise, Bangladesh has a comparative advantage at the good it is "less worse" at (producing shirts), even though it does not have an absolute advantage at either compared to the United States.

You may have noticed that for each country, the opportunity cost of growing wheat is the *inverse* of the opportunity cost of producing shirts. (For the United States, $\frac{1}{4}$ is the inverse of 4; for Bangladesh, $\frac{1}{2}$ is the inverse of 2.) Mathematically, this means that it is impossible for one country to have a comparative advantage at producing both goods. Each producer's opportunity cost depends on its *relative* ability at producing different goods. Logic tells us that you can't be better at A than at B and also better at B than at A. (And mathematically, if X is bigger than Y, then $\frac{1}{X}$ will be smaller than $\frac{1}{Y}$.) The United States can't be better at producing wheat than shirts relative to Bangladesh and at the same time be better at producing shirts than wheat relative to Bangladesh. As a result, no producer has a comparative advantage at everything, and each producer has a comparative advantage at something.

We can check this international trade scenario against an example closer to home. When your family makes Thanksgiving dinner, does the best cook make everything? If you have a small family, maybe one person *can* make the whole dinner. But if your family is anything like our families, you will need several cooks. Grandma is by far the most experienced cook, yet the potato peeling always gets outsourced to the kids. Is that because the grandchildren are better potato peelers than Grandma? We think that's probably not the case. Grandma has an absolute advantage at everything having to do with Thanksgiving dinner. Still, the kids may have a *comparative* advantage at potato peeling, which frees up Grandma to make those tricky pie crusts.

We can find applications of comparative advantage everywhere in life. Sports is no exception. Look at the From Another Angle box "Babe Ruth, star pitcher" for another example.

Babe Ruth, star pitcher
From Another Angle

Babe Ruth had an absolute advantage at both pitching and hitting, but his comparative advantage at hitting made him one of the best hitters of all time.
Source: Library of Congress Prints & Photographs Division [LC-DIG-npcc-02009]

New York Yankees manager Miller Huggins faced a tough choice. It was 1920, and his baseball team had acquired the baseball legend Babe Ruth. Everyone knew that Babe Ruth was an amazing hitter. In 1920 he hit 54 home runs. That year, only one other baseball *team* collectively hit as many home runs as Ruth *alone* did.

But Babe Ruth was also an amazing pitcher. In 1918 he had set a record for the most consecutive scoreless innings pitched in the World Series—a record that was not broken until 1961. He could easily have become one of the best pitchers of his generation.

Huggins had to determine the right role for Babe Ruth. The problem was that Babe Ruth was both the best pitcher *and* the best hitter on the team. From a practical point of view, Ruth couldn't do both (pitching takes too much energy).

What does a manager do when one player has an absolute advantage at multiple positions? One answer is to turn to comparative advantage.

Although Ruth had an *absolute* advantage at both pitching and hitting, he had a *comparative* advantage as a hitter. The opportunity cost of having Ruth pitch was the number of games the Yankees would win by having him bat instead. Huggins decided the opportunity cost of Ruth's pitching was higher than the opportunity cost of his batting. The team would do relatively better when Ruth was hitting. Huggins' decision worked out well: Babe Ruth is now known as one of the greatest hitters of all time.

Source: 2016 Family of Babe Ruth and Babe Ruth League c/o *Luminary Group LLC*.

✓ TEST YOURSELF

☐ What does it mean to have an absolute advantage at producing a good? **[LO 2.2]**

☐ What does it mean to have a comparative advantage at producing a good? **[LO 2.2]**

☐ Can more than one producer have an absolute advantage at producing the same good? Why or why not? **[LO 2.2]**

Why Trade?

The United States is perfectly capable of producing its own shirts and its own wheat. In fact, in our simple model, it has an absolute advantage at producing both goods. So, why buy shirts from Bangladesh? We are about to see that both countries are actually able to consume more when they specialize in producing the good for which they have a comparative advantage and then trade with one another.

Specialization

If you lived 200 years ago, your everyday life would have been full of tasks that probably never even cross your mind today. You might have milked a cow, hauled water from a well, split wood, cured meat, mended a hole in a sock, and repaired a roof.

LO 2.3 Explain why people specialize.

Contrast that with life today. Almost everything we use comes from someone who specializes in providing a particular good or service. We bet you don't churn the butter you put on your toast. You probably wouldn't begin to know how to construct the parts in your smartphone. We are guessing you don't usually sew your own clothes or grow your own wheat. In today's world, all of us are dependent on one another for the things we need on a daily basis.

In our model, when the United States and Bangladesh work in isolation, each produces some shirts and some wheat—each in the combinations that its consumers prefer. Suppose the United States has 150 million workers and Bangladesh has 80 million. As before,

- each U.S. worker can make 50 shirts or 200 bushels of wheat and
- each Bangladeshi worker can make 25 shirts or 50 bushels of wheat.

Now, suppose these production combinations occur:

- Based on U.S. consumers' preferences, U.S. workers are split so that they produce 1 billion shirts and 26 billion bushels of wheat.
- In Bangladesh, workers are allocated to produce 0.5 billion shirts and 3 billion bushels of wheat.

TABLE 2-1

Production with and without specialization

When Bangladesh and the United States each specializes in the production of one good, the two countries can produce an extra 0.5 billion T-shirts and 1 billion bushels of wheat using the same number of workers and the same technology.

	Country	Wheat (billions of bushels)	T-shirts (billions)
Without specialization	United States	26	1
	Bangladesh	3	0.5
	Total	**29**	**1.5**
With specialization	United States	30	0
	Bangladesh	0	2
	Total	**30**	**2**

Even though Bangladesh's productivity per worker is lower, it has a large number of workers and so is able to produce a large total quantity of goods. (The quantities of shirts and wheat are unrealistically large because we are assuming they are the only goods being produced. In reality, of course, countries produce many different goods, but this simplifying assumption helps us to zero in on a real-world truth.)

We have seen that if the United States and Bangladesh are self-sufficient (each producing what its people want to consume), then together the two countries can make 1.5 billion T-shirts and 29 billion bushels of wheat, as shown at the top of Table 2-1 ("without specialization"). What would happen if, instead, Bangladesh put all its resources into making shirts and the United States put all its resources into producing wheat?

If each country focuses on producing the good for which it has a comparative advantage, total production increases. Focusing in this way is called **specialization**. It's the practice of spending all of your resources producing a particular good. When each country specializes in making a particular good according to its comparative advantage, total production possibilities are greater than if each produced the exact combination of goods its own consumers want.

The bottom section of Table 2-1 ("with specialization") shows us:

specialization
spending all of your time producing a particular good

United States

200 bushels per worker × 150 million workers = 30 billion bushels

Bangladesh

25 shirts per worker × 80 million workers = 2 billion shirts

By specializing, the two countries together can produce 1 billion bushels of wheat more than before, *plus* 0.5 billion more shirts. Specialization increases total production, using the same number of workers and the same technology.

This rule applies to all sorts of goods and services. It explains why dentists hire roofers to fix a roof leak and why roofers hire dentists to fill a cavity. See the Economics in Action box "Specialization sauce" for an example of the power of specialization in a setting you are probably somewhat familiar with—McDonald's.

Specialization sauce
Economics in Action

Pizza Hut, Wendy's, and other fast-food chains serve food that's pretty fast and pretty cheap. On any given day, about one-third of U.S. kids and teens eat fast food. But fast food didn't always exist. Fast food as we know it was created in 1948 by Dick and Mac McDonald, the founders of McDonald's. The McDonald brothers were inspired by the way workers specialized on particular tasks when making cars on factory assembly lines. The McDonalds decided to use the same idea when running a restaurant. Instead of assigning employees to general food preparation, they split each order into parts, dividing the steps required to prepare a meal. One employee became the grilling specialist; another added mustard and ketchup. A different employee operated the potato fryer, and yet another mixed the milkshakes.

Specialization resulted in efficiency that created the fast-food business.
©WR Publishing/Alamy

Any single employee could almost certainly learn how to grill a burger, add condiments, make fries, *and* mix a milkshake. And in each restaurant, one particularly skilled employee may well have been the fastest at every step in making a meal.

Even so, specialization was far more efficient when employing a team of workers. By assigning only one specific task to each worker, the founders of McDonald's revolutionized the speed and quantity of food preparation. Harnessing the power of specialization allowed them to grill more burgers, fry more potatoes, and feed more hungry customers.

Source: Eric Schlosser, *Fast Food Nation* (Boston: Houghton Mifflin, 2002), pp. 19–20.

Gains from trade

When countries specialize in producing the goods for which they have a comparative advantage, total production increases. The problem with specialization is that each producer ends up with only one good—in our model, wheat in the United States, T-shirts in Bangladesh. If Americans want to wear T-shirts and Bangladeshis want to enjoy wheat, they must trade.

Suppose that Bangladesh and the United States agree to trade 3.5 billion bushels of wheat for 1.5 billion T-shirts. As a result, each country ends up with an additional 0.5 billion bushels of wheat, and the United States also has 0.5 billion more shirts than before. The improvement in outcomes that occurs when specialized producers exchange goods and services is called the **gains from trade**.

Figure 2-7 shows how the gains from trade affect a country's consumption. Before the trade, it was impossible for the United States and Bangladesh to consume any combination of goods outside their production possibilities frontiers. After the trade between the two specialized producers, each country's consumption increases to a point that was previously unachievable. If Bangladesh consumes the same amount of shirts as before and trades the remaining, both countries are able to consume 0.5 billion bushels more wheat after opening up to trade.

In Figure 2-7, the gains from the U.S.–Bangladesh trade are distributed equally: 0.5 billion bushels more wheat for the United States and 0.5 billion bushels more wheat for Bangladesh. In reality, the distribution can vary. The gains do not have to be equal for the trading arrangement to benefit everyone. If Bangladesh takes an extra 0.25 billion bushels of wheat and the United States an extra 0.75 billion (or vice versa), both countries will still be better off than if they worked alone.

Overall, there is room for trade as long as two things occur: (1) the two countries differ in their opportunity costs to produce a good and (2) they set a favorable trading price. A favorable trading

LO 2.4 Explain how the gains from trade follow from comparative advantage.

gains from trade
the improvement in outcomes that occurs when producers specialize and exchange goods and services

FIGURE 2-7

Specialization and gains from trade

(A) United States' gains from trade

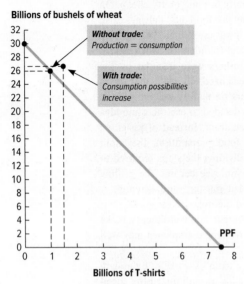

(B) Bangladesh's gains from trade

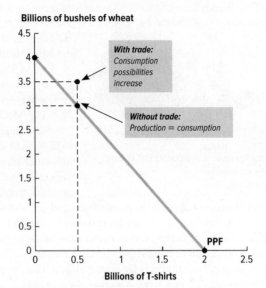

If a country does not specialize and trade, its production and consumption are both limited to points along its production possibilities frontier. By specializing and achieving gains from trading, the United States gains 0.5 million T-shirts and 0.5 billion bushels of wheat.

By opening up to trade, Bangladesh also gains 0.5 billion bushels of wheat compared to what it could produce on its production possibilities frontier.

price needs to benefit both parties. If T-shirts from Bangladesh are too expensive, the United States will refuse to buy them. Similarly, if U.S. wheat is too expensive, Bangladesh will not buy it. If the United States agrees to trade 3.5 billion bushels of wheat for 1.5 billion T-shirts, it must be because the United States values 3.5 billion bushels of wheat less than 1.5 billion T-shirts.

To see how much each country values a good, we must look at its opportunity costs. Recall that the opportunity cost of 1 T-shirt for Bangladesh is 2 bushels of wheat. In other words, the value of 1 T-shirt for Bangladesh is at least 2 bushels of wheat. If the United States offered to trade 1 bushel of wheat in exchange for 1 T-shirt, Bangladesh would refuse such a trade; Bangladesh could simply produce the wheat itself. Bangladesh needs to receive at least 2 bushels of wheat in exchange for 1 T-shirt.

To see how many bushels of wheat the United States is willing to give up in exchange for 1 T-shirt, we can look at the United States' opportunity cost. The opportunity cost of 1 T-shirt for the United States is 4 bushels of wheat. Thus, the United States will only trade up to 4 bushels of wheat in exchange for 1 T-shirt. More than 4 bushels of wheat would be worth more than 1 T-shirt. If Bangladesh tries to charge a price greater than the United States' opportunity cost, the United States will choose to make the T-shirts itself. In order for trade to benefit both countries, the trade price of 1 T-shirt must be at least 2 bushels of wheat but less than 4 bushels of wheat.

In general, two countries will benefit from a trade price that falls between their opportunity costs. In our example, the price at which Bangladesh and the United States are willing to trade T-shirts must fall between Bangladesh's opportunity cost for producing T-shirts and the

United States' opportunity cost for producing T-shirts. If Bangladesh is the country that has specialized in T-shirts, it cannot charge a price greater than the United States' opportunity cost. If it does, the United States will simply make the T-shirts itself. Conversely, Bangladesh must receive a price that covers its opportunity costs for making T-shirts or it will not be willing to trade.

What's true about countries is also true about individuals who specialize (and then pay for what they need). For example, consider Stacy Brown-Philpot, the chief executive officer of Task-Rabbit. The company's business is all about creating gains from specialization and trade by running a global online marketplace that connects freelance workers to people needing jobs done. The same principles of specialization and trade guide Stacy Brown-Philpot in her own work. She hires many managers to help run TaskRabbit, but she is likely a better manager than most of them (after all, she very successfully ran TaskRabbit's day-to-day operations before becoming chief executive). Let's say Brown-Philpot can resolve a key operational issue in an hour, but for every hour she's distracted from leading TaskRabbit, the company's profits go down by $1,000. The less-experienced manager earns only $50 an hour, so even if he takes two to three times to resolve the problem, it's still worth it for Brown-Philpot to hire him and spend her own time keeping up TaskRabbit's productivity. Brown-Philpot may have an absolute advantage at managing day-to-day problems, but the opportunity cost in lost profits means the less-experienced manager has a comparative advantage. (Brown-Philpot's comparative advantage is at developing the business strategy for TaskRabbit.) Here, everyone can end up better off if they specialize in their jobs.

In spite of the gains from specializing and trading, not everyone considers this an obvious choice in every circumstance. We've seen that international trade can bring gains to countries, and specialization in jobs can bring gains to individuals. But it's not true that all citizens necessarily gain from international trade. In the example above, T-shirt businesses (and their employees) in the United States lose from international trade. Their well-being depends on their ability to shift into other, similar jobs and lines of business. They might also get help from the government. It may be hard to find similar jobs, however, and government help is not guaranteed. Thus, in practice, international trade policy can be controversial despite its many advantages. For some examples, see the Economics in Action box "Winners and losers."

Winners and losers

Economics in Action

Trade can bring big gains to economies, but that doesn't mean that everyone wins.

Tracy Warner knows that first-hand. She worked at the Maytag factory in Galesburg, Illinois, until 2004, when Maytag shut down the plant and shifted jobs to other countries where wages are lower. The refrigerator factory had employed 1,600 workers in Galesburg, and Warner was earning $37,000 a year. After the factory closed, she found a job as a teacher's assistant and worked nights as a janitor, taking home about $21,000 a year in total.

Other people in town had more positive benefits from trade:

- One of Warner's neighbors saw his paychecks triple. He's a foreman at the railroad, and increased trade keeps the trains busy, giving him ample opportunities to work overtime.
- The owner of the local appliance store happily reported a boom in sales of inexpensive high-quality televisions, thanks to trade with Asia.
- Customers of the local appliance store spent a lot less money on televisions and used that extra money to buy better food, go to more movies, and get more presents for their children.

The exact trade-offs created by trade—gains together with losses—are now being recognized thanks to data analysis and rigorous economic research. On the downside, the increase in

(continued)

imports from China was responsible for about one-quarter of the decline in manufacturing jobs in the United States between 1990 and 2007. On the upside, researchers estimate that access to cheaper goods has increased the purchasing power of middle-income Americans by 37 percent.

The U.S. government offers a patchwork of programs and benefits to help workers who have lost their jobs. Workers who can prove their jobs were lost to foreign competition can get an extra six months of unemployment insurance and enroll in job training programs. Workers over 50 years old can earn wage insurance worth up to $12,000 over two years.

These government programs help workers cope with job losses, but they require that workers be flexible. When Tracy Warner lost her job, she was able to use training money from the federal government to complete her degree in communications. However, she couldn't find a job in Galesburg that used her new credentials and had to find low-wage work.

A big question about trade, then, is not just whether it's good for the economy overall. (Most often it is.) The question is also about whether those who suffer initially can then adjust to the new economy.

Sources: Binyamim Appelbaum, "Towns Decline Illustrates Perils of Trade Deals," *New York Times*, May 18, 2015, p. A1; David Autor, David Dorn, and Gordon Hanson, "The China Syndrome: Local Labor Market Effects of Import Competition in the United States," *American Economic Review* 2013, 103(6): 2121–2168; Pablo D. Fajgelbaum and Amit K. Khandelwal, "Measuring the Unequal Gains to Trade," *Quarterly Journal of Economics* 131, no. 3 (August 1, 2016), pp. 1113–1180, https://doi.org/10.1093/qje/qjw01.

Comparative advantage over time

Our simplified model of production possibilities and trade helps us to understand why Americans now buy shirts from other countries. But we noted at the beginning of the chapter that this wasn't always the case: 200 years ago, the United States was selling shirts to the rest of the world. To understand this change, we can apply our model to shifts in comparative advantage over time. These shifts have caused significant changes in different countries' economies and trade patterns.

When the Industrial Revolution began, Great Britain led the world in clothing manufacturing. In the nineteenth century, the United States snatched the comparative advantage through a combination of new technology (which led to higher productivity) and cheap labor (which led to lower production costs). Gradually, the comparative advantage in clothing shifted away from the United States to other countries. Clothing manufacturing moved from country to country, searching for ever-lower costs:

- By the 1930s, 40 percent of the world's cotton goods were made in Japan, where workers from the countryside were willing to work long hours for low wages.
- In the mid-1970s, clothing manufacturing moved to Hong Kong, Taiwan, and Korea, where wages were even lower than those in Japan.
- The textile industry then moved to China in the early 1990s, when millions of young women left their farms to work for wages as much as 90 percent lower than those in Hong Kong. Similar changes happened in Bangladesh.

There's an upside to the progressive relocation of this industry and its jobs: Eventually high-wage jobs replaced low-wage jobs, and these countries experienced considerable economic growth.

Losing a comparative advantage in clothing production sounds like a bad thing at first. But as we know from our model, you can't lose comparative advantage in one thing without gaining it in another. Changes in clothing manufacturing were driven by workers in each country getting more skilled at industries that paid better than making clothes—such as making cars, or programming computers, or providing financial services. This meant the opportunity cost of making clothes increased. The comparative advantage in clothing production shifted to countries where the workers lacked skills in better-paying industries and so were willing to work in textile factories for lower wages.

Most historians would agree that it wasn't a sign of failure when countries lost their comparative advantage in clothing production—it was a sign of success. Former textile producers like Great Britain, the United States, Japan, Korea, and Hong Kong are all much wealthier now than they were when they were centers of clothing manufacturing.

However, these changes probably didn't look or feel like success at the time, especially for workers in textile factories who saw their jobs disappearing overseas. This same tension is arising today in other industries as companies "outsource" tasks that can be done more cheaply in other countries.

The Economics in Action box "Comparative advantage: The good, the bad, and the ugly" considers whether a country's loss of comparative advantage at producing a particular good is something to worry about.

Comparative advantage: The good, the bad, and the ugly
Economics in Action

You may have noticed that when you call the customer service line for many large companies, you are likely to end up speaking with someone in India or the Philippines. Thirty years ago, that was not the case—call centers for American customers were almost all located in the United States.

The United States has not become "worse" at running call centers. In fact, it may still have an absolute advantage at it. Over time, though, technology has improved the quality and lowered the cost of international phone calls. At the same time, higher education and fluency in English have become more common in other countries. As a result, the comparative advantage at running call centers has shifted, and many U.S. companies find it more profitable to move them offshore.

When jobs move overseas, people worry that the country is sliding down a slippery slope of economic decline. They ask, "Is something wrong with our schools? Have our companies lost their competitive edge?" Sometimes people mistakenly refer to this phenomenon as the United States "losing its comparative advantage." Based on what you have learned in this chapter, you know that cannot be the case. Everyone has a comparative advantage at something. If the United States no longer has a comparative advantage at running call centers, its comparative advantage has shifted to some other industry.

There are valid reasons to be concerned about shifts in comparative advantage. One is the disruptive effects on people who were employed in the industry that is in decline. They may find they do not have the right skills to find new jobs in industries that are growing. Retraining is often possible, but not always easy.

Comparative advantage has no moral compass. Sometimes high productivity in an industry is driven by factors we feel proud of, like hard work, innovative technology, or savvy business practices. At other times, it is driven by things of which we are now ashamed. The success of nineteenth-century cotton growers in the American South owed as much to the huge pool of cheap labor provided by the evil of slavery as it did to inventions like the cotton gin.

For a more recent example, consider the differences in regulations between wealthy and poor countries today. Factories in developing nations can often produce at lower cost than those in industrialized ones. In part, this advantage is due to the fact that they do not have to pay minimum wages, provide a safe workplace, or clean up the pollution they cause. Is that fair? That normative question is up for debate. Comparative advantage is not a matter of morals; it is simply a matter of fact.

☐ Why do people or countries specialize? **[LO 2.3]**

☐ How do two countries benefit from trading with each other? **[LO 2.4]**

☐ Is it possible to not have a comparative advantage at anything? Why or why not? **[LO 2.4]**

Conclusion

Specialization and trade can make everyone better off. It is not surprising, then, that in an economy driven by individuals seeking to make a profit or improve their communities, people specialize so as to exploit their comparative advantages. That principle is as true for countries, like the United States and Bangladesh, as it is for individuals picking their careers.

No government intervention is required to coordinate production. The great economic thinker Adam Smith suggested the term *invisible hand* to describe this coordinating mechanism:

> It is not from the benevolence of the butcher, the brewer, or the baker that we expect our dinner, but from their regard to their [self-interest]. . . . he intends only his own gain, and he is in this, as in many other cases, led by an invisible hand to promote an end which was no part of his intention.[4]

The functioning of the invisible hand depends on a lot of other assumptions, such as free competition and full information. Later in the text we will discuss these assumptions, and will note when they work and when they do not.

Most people take for granted the prevalence of specialization and trade in their everyday lives. Few stop to think about the benefits and where they come from. In this chapter we tried to dig down to the bottom of the assumptions people make and expose the logic behind the gains from trade. We also noted the costs from trade. Even when a country, as a whole, gains from trade, some workers and businesses may lose out as they face more competition. As we proceed—especially when we return to topics like international trade and government intervention in the markets—try to remember the winners and losers, together with the possibility of broad gains when people interact with one another in economic exchanges.

Key Terms

production possibilities frontier (PPF), p. 27

efficient points, p. 30

absolute advantage, p. 33

comparative advantage, p. 33

specialization, p. 36

gains from trade, p. 37

Summary

LO 2.1 Construct a production possibilities graph, and describe what causes shifts in production possibilities curves.

A production possibilities graph shows all the combinations of two goods that a person or an economy can produce with a given amount of time, resources, and technology. The production possibilities frontier is a line on that graph that shows all the maximum attainable combinations of goods. Producers of goods and services are not likely to choose a combination of goods inside the production possibilities frontier because they could achieve a higher production level with the same amount of resources. They cannot choose points outside the frontier, which would require more than the available resources. The choice between combinations on the production possibilities frontier is a matter of preference.

Shifts in the production possibilities frontier can be caused by changes in technology, as well as changes in population and other resources. Increases in technological capabilities and population will shift the PPF outward; decreases in these factors will shift the PPF inward.

> **LO 2.2** Define absolute and comparative advantage.

Producers have an absolute advantage at making a good when they can produce more output than others with a given amount of resources. If you put two people or countries to work making the same good, the person or country that is more productive has an absolute advantage.

People or countries have a comparative advantage when they are better at producing one good than they are at producing other goods, relative to other producers. Everyone has a comparative advantage at something, whether or not they have an absolute advantage at anything.

> **LO 2.3** Explain why people specialize.

Specialization means spending all or much of your time producing a particular good. Production is highest when people or countries specialize in producing the good for which they have a comparative advantage. Specialization increases total production, using the same number of workers and the same technology.

> **LO 2.4** Explain how the gains from trade follow from comparative advantage.

The increase in total production that occurs from specialization and exchange is called the gains from trade. With specialization and trade, two parties can increase production and consumption, and each ends up better off.

Shifts in comparative advantage over time have caused significant changes in different countries' economies and trade patterns. These changes signal general economic success, although they can be painful for the individual workers and industries involved. Even when a country as a whole gains from trade, some workers and businesses may lose out as they face more competition.

Review Questions

1. You've been put in charge of a bake sale for a local charity, at which you are planning to sell cookies and cupcakes. What would a production possibilities graph of this situation show? **[LO 2.1]**

2. You manage two employees at a pet salon. Your employees perform two tasks, giving flea baths and grooming animals. If you constructed a single production possibilities frontier for flea baths and grooming that combined both of your employees' work efforts, would you expect the production possibilities frontier to be linear (a straight line)? Explain why or why not. **[LO 2.1]**

3. You and another volunteer are in charge of a bake sale for a local charity, at which you are planning to sell cookies and cupcakes. **[LO 2.2]**

   a. What would it mean for one of you to have an absolute advantage at baking cookies or cupcakes? Could one of you have an absolute advantage at baking both items?

   b. What would it mean for you or the other volunteer to have a comparative advantage at baking cookies or cupcakes? Could one of you have a comparative advantage at baking both items?

4. You and another volunteer are in charge of a bake sale for a local charity, at which you are planning to sell cookies and cupcakes. Suppose you have a comparative advantage at baking cookies, and the other volunteer has a comparative advantage at baking cupcakes. Make a proposal to the volunteer about how to split up the baking. Explain how you can both gain from specializing, and why. **[LO 2.3]**

5. At the flower shop, where you manage two employees, your employees perform two tasks: caring for the displays of cut flowers and making flower arrangements to fill customer orders. Explain how you would approach organizing your employees and assigning them tasks. **[LO 2.3]**

6. Suppose two countries produce the same two goods and have identical production possibilities frontiers. Do you expect these countries to trade? Explain why or why not. **[LO 2.4]**

7. Brazil is the largest coffee producer in the world, and coffee is one of Brazil's major export goods. Suppose that in 20 years, Brazil no longer produces much coffee and imports most of its coffee instead. Explain why Brazil might change its trade pattern over time. **[LO 2.4]**

Problems and Applications

1. Your friend Sam owns a catering business and has been asked to prepare appetizers for a university reception during homecoming weekend. She has an unlimited amount of ingredients but only six hours to prepare them. Sam can make 300 mini-sandwiches or 150 servings of melon slices topped with smoked salmon and a dab of sauce per hour. **[LO 2.1]**

   a. Draw Sam's production possibilities frontier.

   b. Now suppose that the university decides to postpone the reception until after the big game, so

Sam has an extra four hours to prepare. Redraw her production possibilities frontier to show the impact of this increase in resources.

c. Now, in addition to the extra time to prepare, suppose Sam's friend Chris helps by preparing the melon slices. Sam can now make 300 mini-sandwiches or 300 melon appetizers per hour. Redraw Sam's production possibilities frontier to show the impact of increased productivity in making melon appetizers.

2. Your friend Sam has been asked to prepare appetizers for the university reception. She has an unlimited amount of ingredients and six hours in which to prepare them. Sam can make 400 mini-sandwiches or 200 servings of melon slices topped with smoked salmon and a dab of sauce per hour. **[LO 2.1]**

   a. What is Sam's opportunity cost of making one mini-sandwich?

   b. What is Sam's opportunity cost of making one melon appetizer?

   c. Suppose the reception has been postponed, so Sam has an extra four hours to prepare. What is the opportunity cost of making one mini-sandwich now?

   d. Suppose the reception has been postponed, so Sam has an extra four hours to prepare. What is the opportunity cost of making one melon appetizer now?

   e. Suppose Sam's friend Chris helps by preparing the melon slices, increasing Sam's productivity to 400 mini-sandwiches or 400 melon appetizers per hour. What is the opportunity cost of making one mini-sandwich now?

   f. Suppose Sam's friend Chris helps by preparing the melon slices, increasing Sam's productivity to 400 mini-sandwiches or 400 melon appetizers per hour. What is the opportunity cost of making one melon appetizer now?

3. Suppose that Canada produces two goods: lumber and fish. It has 18 million workers, each of whom can cut 10 feet of lumber or catch 20 fish each day. **[LO 2.1]**

   a. What is the maximum amount of lumber Canada could produce in a day?

   b. What is the maximum amount of fish it could produce in a day?

   c. Draw Canada's production possibilities frontier.

   d. Use your graph to determine how many fish can be caught if 60 million feet of lumber are cut.

4. The graph in Figure 2P-1 shows Tanya's weekly production possibilities frontier for doing homework (writing papers and doing problem sets). **[LO 2.1]**

FIGURE 2P-1

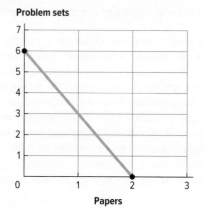

a. What is the slope of the production possibilities frontier?

b. What is the opportunity cost of doing one problem set?

c. What is the opportunity cost of writing one paper?

5. Use the production possibilities frontier in Figure 2P-2 to answer the following questions. **[LO 2.1]**

FIGURE 2P-2

Screwdrivers

a. What is the slope of the PPF between point A and point B?

b. What is the slope of the PPF between point B and point C?

c. Is the opportunity cost of producing hammers higher between points A and B or between points B and C?

d. Is the opportunity cost of producing screwdrivers higher between points A and B or between points B and C?

6. For each point on the PPF in Figure 2P-3, note whether the point is attainable and efficient, attainable and inefficient, or unattainable. **[LO 2.1]**

FIGURE 2P-3

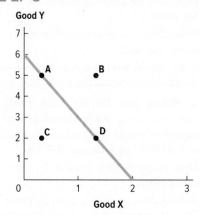
Good Y

7. For each point on the PPF in Figure 2P-4, note whether the point is attainable and efficient, attainable and inefficient, or unattainable. **[LO 2.1]**

FIGURE 2P-4

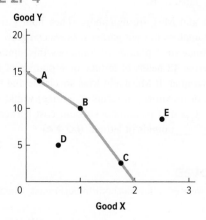
Good Y

8. The Red Cross and the WIC (Women, Infants, and Children) program both provide emergency food packages and first-aid kits to New York City homeless shelters. Table 2P-1 shows their weekly production possibilities in providing emergency goods to NYC homeless shelters. NYC homeless shelters need a total of 20 first-aid kits per week. Currently, they get 10 kits from the Red Cross and 10 kits from WIC. With their remaining resources, how many food packages can each organization provide to NYC homeless shelters? **[LO 2.1]**

TABLE 2P-1

	Red Cross	WIC
Food packages	300	200
First-aid kits	50	20

9. Suppose that three volunteers are preparing cookies and cupcakes for a bake sale. Diana can make 26 cookies or 19 cupcakes per hour; Andy can make 24 cookies or 18 cupcakes; and Sam can make 9 cookies or 13 cupcakes. **[LO 2.2]**

   a. Who has the absolute advantage at making cookies?

   b. Who has the absolute advantage at making cupcakes?

10. Paula and Carlo are coworkers. Their production possibilities frontiers for counseling clients and writing memos are given in Figure 2P-5. **[LO 2.2]**

FIGURE 2P-5

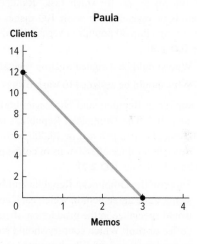
Paula

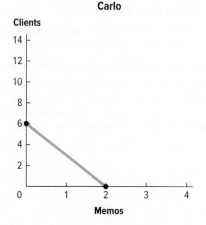
Carlo

a. Which worker has an absolute advantage in counseling clients?

b. Which worker has a comparative advantage in counseling clients?

c. Which worker has an absolute advantage in writing memos?

d. Which worker has a comparative advantage in writing memos?

11. Two students are assigned to work together on a project that requires both writing and an oral presentation. Steve can write 1 page or prepare 4 minutes of a presentation each day. Anna can write 3 pages or prepare 2 minutes of a presentation each day. **[LO 2.2]**

   a. Who has a comparative advantage at writing?

   b. Suppose that Steve goes to a writing tutor and learns some tricks that enable him to write 4 pages each day. Now who has a comparative advantage at writing?

12. Suppose that the manager of a restaurant has two new employees, Rahul and Henriette, and is trying to decide which one to assign to which task. Rahul can chop 20 pounds of vegetables or wash 100 dishes per hour. Henriette can chop 30 pounds of vegetables or wash 120 dishes. **[LO 2.3]**

   a. Who should be assigned to chop vegetables?

   b. Who should be assigned to wash dishes?

13. The Dominican Republic and Nicaragua both produce coffee and rum. The Dominican Republic can produce 20,000 tons of coffee per year or 10,000 barrels of rum. Nicaragua can produce 30,000 tons of coffee per year or 5,000 barrels of rum. **[LO 2.3]**

   a. Suppose the Dominican Republic and Nicaragua sign a trade agreement in which each country would specialize in the production of either coffee or rum. Which country should specialize in producing coffee? Which country should specialize in producing rum?

   b. What are the minimum and maximum prices at which these countries will trade coffee?

14. Eleanor and her little brother Josh are responsible for two chores on their family's farm, gathering eggs and collecting milk. Eleanor can gather 9 dozen eggs or collect 3 gallons of milk per week. Josh can gather 2 dozen eggs or collect 2 gallons of milk per week. **[LO 2.3]**

a. The family wants 2 gallons of milk per week and as many eggs as the siblings can gather. Currently, Eleanor and Josh collect one gallon of milk each and as many eggs as they can. How many dozens of eggs does the family have per week?

b. If the siblings were to specialize, which should collect the milk?

c. If the siblings were to specialize, how many dozens of eggs would the family have per week?

15. Suppose Russia and Sweden each produces only paper and cars. Russia can produce 8 tons of paper or 4 million cars each year. Sweden can produce 25 tons of paper or 5 million cars each year. **[LO 2.4]**

   a. Draw the production possibilities frontier for each country.

   b. Both countries want 2 million cars each year and as much paper as they can produce along with 2 million cars. Find this point on each production possibilities frontier and label it "A."

   c. Suppose the countries specialize. Which country will produce cars?

   d. Once they specialize, suppose they work out a trade of 2 million cars for 6 tons of paper. Find the new *consumption* point for each country and label it "B."

16. Maya and Max are neighbors. They both grow lettuce and tomatoes in their gardens. Maya can grow 45 heads of lettuce or 9 pounds of tomatoes this summer. Max can grow 42 heads of lettuce or 6 pounds of tomatoes this summer. If Maya and Max specialize and trade, the price of tomatoes (in terms of lettuce) would be as follows: 1 pound of tomatoes would cost between _____ and _____ pounds of lettuce. **[LO 2.4]**

Endnotes

1. http://www.encyclopedia.com/topic/Francis_Cabot_Lowell.aspx

2. http://www.economist.com/news/leaders/21646204-asias-dominance-manufacturing-will-endure-will-make-development-harder-others-made

3. http://www.agclassroom.org/gan/timeline/farm_tech.htm

4. Adam Smith, *An Inquiry into the Nature and Causes of the Wealth of Nations*, 1776.

Math Essentials: Understanding Graphs and Slope

Graphing is an essential component of economics. We touched on graphs in Chapter 2, "Specialization and Exchange," and we'll only see more graphs from here on out in the course. In order to truly understand the concepts of economics, you'll need to understand the basics of graphing. In this appendix, we'll discuss how to create and interpret different types of graphs.

Creating a Graph

A graph is one way to visually represent data. In this text, we use graphs to describe and interpret economic relationships. For example, we use a graph called a production possibilities frontier to explore opportunity costs and trade-offs in production. We use graphs of average, variable, and marginal costs to explore production decisions facing a firm. And—the favorite of economists everywhere—we use graphs to show supply and demand and the resulting relationship between price and quantity.

Graphs of one variable

Graphs of a single variable come in three main forms: the bar chart, the pie chart, and the line graph. In school, you've probably made all three and plastered them on science-fair posters and presentations or used them in reports. These graphs are versatile; they can be used to present all sorts of information. Throughout economics, and in this text, you'll come across these graphs frequently.

Probably the most common single-variable graph is the *bar graph*, an example of which is shown in Figure A-1. The bar graph shows the size or frequency of a variable using bars—hence the name. The size of the bar on the *y*-axis shows the value of the variable, while the *x*-axis contains the categories of the variables. In Figure A-1, for example, the bar graph shows the number of monthly average users (in billions) of the top five

LEARNING OBJECTIVES

LO A.1 Create four quadrants using *x*- and *y*-axes and plot points on a graph.

LO A.2 Use data to calculate slope.

LO A.3 Interpret what the direction and steepness of slope indicate about a line.

LO A.1 Create four quadrants using *x*- and *y*-axes and plot points on a graph.

FIGURE A-1

Top five social networking websites

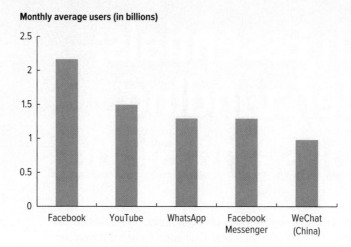

Monthly average users (in billions)

Source: "Most famous social network sites worldwide as of January 2018, ranked by number of active users (in millions)," *Statista*, https://www.statista.com/statistics/272014/global-social-networks-ranked-by-number-of-users/, accessed March 18, 2018.

major social media platforms as of January 2018. Since the bars stack up next to each other, a bar graph makes it clear exactly where each news site stands in comparison to the others. As you can see, the larger bars for Facebook and YouTube mean that these sites get more visits than WhatsApp.

In general, bar graphs are versatile. You can show the distribution of letter grades in a class or the average monthly high and low temperatures in your city. Any time the size of a variable is important, you are generally going to want to use a bar graph.

Pie graphs (or pie charts) are generally used to show how much of certain components make up a whole. Pie graphs are usually a circle, cut into wedges that represent how much each makes up of the whole. Figure A-2 shows the market share of domestic and imported vehicle types (as of March 2018). The wedges show that trucks make up a much larger share of the market than cars, that domestic truck producers hold a much larger share of truck sales than car sales, and that imported cars have a larger market share than domestic-made cars.

The most common use of pie graphs is for budgeting. You'll often see government and business income and expenses broken down in a pie graph. Also, come election time, you'll see pie graphs all over the news media, representing the percentage of votes in an election each candidate receives.

A final type of graph is called a *line* (or *time-series*) *graph*. This type of graph is helpful when you are trying to emphasize the trend of a single variable. In economics, the most common usage of line graphs is to show the value of a variable over time. Inflation rates, GDP, and government debt over decades are all prime candidates to be presented on a line graph.

Figure A-3 shows the GDP growth rate in Mexico since 1960 on a time-series graph. Presenting the data this way makes it clear that Mexico's GDP growth was strong during the 1960s and 70s (anything above 4 percent growth is very good), dipped below zero in 2009, and rose into positive territory in 2010 and beyond.

Ultimately, single-variable graphs can take us only so far. In order to get at some of the most fundamental issues of economics, we need to be able to plot the values of two variables (such as price and quantity) simultaneously.

FIGURE A-2

Market share of domestic and imported vehicle types

This pie graph shows the market share of different types of vehicles in the U.S. market—the larger the wedge, the larger the market share. As the chart shows, trucks make up a much larger share of the market than cars. However, domestic producers hold a much larger share of truck sales than car sales.

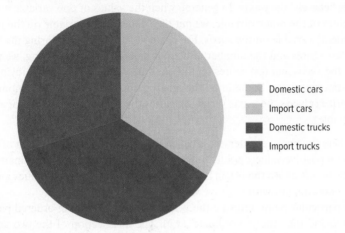

Domestic cars
Import cars
Domestic trucks
Import trucks

Source: *WSJ* Markets Data Center, www.wsj.com/mdc/public/page/2_3022-autosales.html.

FIGURE A-3

GDP growth in Mexico

A line graph commonly shows a variable over a range of time. This allows the trend in the variable to be clear. In this case, you can see that GDP growth in Mexico has been highly variable, but overall, GDP growth was higher on average before 1980.

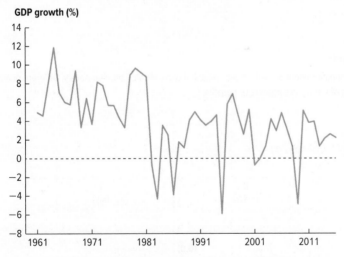

Source: World Bank World Development Indicators.

Graphs of two variables

In order to present two or more variables on a graph, we need something called the *Cartesian coordinate system*. With only two dimensions, this graphing system consists of two axes: the *x* (horizontal) axis and the *y* (vertical) axis. We can give these axes other names, depending on what economic variables we want to represent, such as price and quantity, or inputs and outputs.

In some cases, it doesn't matter which variable we put on each axis. At other times, logic or convention will determine the axes. There are two common conventions in economics that it will be useful for you to remember:

1. **Price on the *y*-axis, quantity on the *x*-axis:** When we graph the relationship between price and quantity in economics, price is always on the *y*-axis and quantity is always on the *x*-axis.
2. **The *x*-axis "causes" the *y*-axis:** In general, when the values of one variable are dependent on the values of the other variable, we put the "dependent" variable on the *y*-axis and the "independent" variable on the *x*-axis. For example, if we were exploring the relationship between test scores and the number of hours a student spends studying, we would place hours on the *x*-axis and test scores on the *y*-axis because hours spent studying affect scores, generally not vice versa. Sometimes, though, the opposite is true. In economics, we often say that price (always the *y*-axis variable) causes the quantity demanded of a good (the *x*-axis variable).

The point where the two axes intersect is called the *origin*. Points to the right of the origin have *x*-coordinates with positive values; points to the left of the origin have *x*-coordinates with negative values. Similarly, points above the origin have *y*-coordinates with positive values and points below the origin have *y*-coordinates with negative values.

To specify a particular point, indicate the *x*- and *y*-coordinates in an ordered pair. Indicate the *x*-coordinate first, and then the *y*-coordinate: (*x*,*y*). The intersection of the two axes creates four quadrants, as shown in Figure A-4.

Quadrant I: (*x*,*y*) The *x*- and *y*- coordinates are both positive.

Quadrant II: (−*x*,*y*) The *x*-coordinate is negative and the *y*-coordinate is positive.

Quadrant III: (−*x*,−*y*) The *x*- and *y*-coordinates are both negative.

Quadrant IV: (*x*,−*y*) The *x*-coordinate is positive and the *y*-coordinate is negative.

Origin: (0,0) The *x*- and *y*-coordinates are both zero at the origin.

FIGURE A-4

The four quadrants

The Cartesian coordinate system is a way to plot values of two variables simultaneously. Different quadrants reflect whether the values of *x* and *y* are positive or negative.

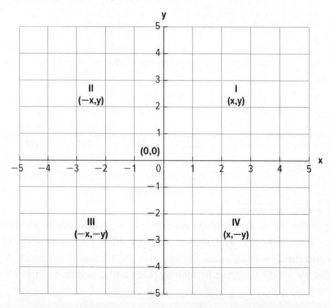

FIGURE A-5

Plotting points on a graph

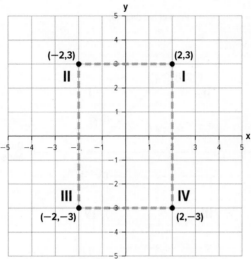

Each set of ordered pairs corresponds to a place on the Cartesian coordinate system.

Figure A-5 shows the following points plotted on a graph.

Quadrant I: (2,3)

Quadrant II: (−2,3)

Quadrant III: (−2,−3)

Quadrant IV: (2,−3)

In economics, we often isolate quadrant I when graphing. This is because there are many economic variables for which negative values do not make sense. For example, one important graph we use in economics is the relationship between the price of a good and the quantity of that good demanded or supplied. Since it doesn't make sense to consider negative prices and quantities, we show only quadrant I when graphing supply and demand.

Figure A-6 shows a line in quadrant I that represents the relationship between the price of hot dogs at the ballpark and the quantity of hot dogs that a family wants to buy. Price is on the *y*-axis and the quantity of hot dogs the family demands is on the *x*-axis. For instance, one coordinate pair on this line is (3,2), meaning that if the price of hot dogs is $2, the family will want to buy 3 of them.

We could extend this demand curve in ways that make sense graphically but that don't represent logical price-quantity combinations in the real world. For instance, if we extend the demand curve into quadrant II, we have points such as (−2,7). If we extend the demand curve into quadrant IV, we have points such as (6,−1). However, it doesn't make sense to talk about someone demanding negative 2 hot dogs, nor does it make sense to think about a price of negative $1.

Remember that we are not just graphing arbitrary points. Rather, we are illustrating a real relationship between variables that has meaning in the real world. Both (−2,7) and (6,−1) are points that are consistent with the equation for this demand curve, but neither point makes sense to include in our analysis. For graphing this price-quantity relationship, we would limit our graph to quadrant I.

However, some variables you will study (such as revenue) may have negative values that make sense. When this is the case, graphs will show multiple quadrants.

FIGURE A-6

Thinking about the logic behind graphs

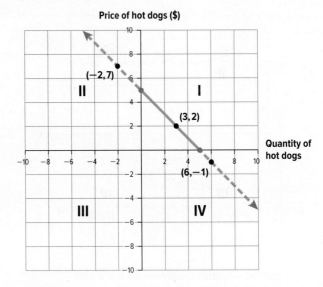

Plotting points in the four quadrants on a graph gives a line.

Slope

Both the table and the graph in Figure A-7 represent a particular relationship between two variables, *x* and *y*. For every *x*, there is a corresponding *y*. When we plot the points in the table, we see that there is a consistent relationship between the value of *x* and the value of *y*. In this case, we can see at a glance that whenever the *x* value increases by 1, the *y* value increases by 0.5. We can describe this relationship as the *slope* of the line.

FIGURE A-7

The slope of a line

X	Y
−4	2
−2	3
0	4
2	5
4	6

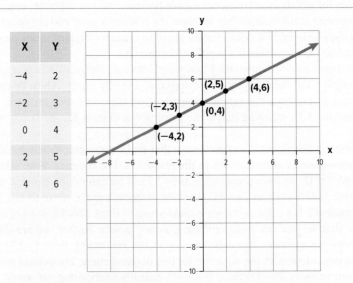

Slope refers to the shape of the line and is determined by the change in *y* and *x*.

Slope is a ratio of vertical distance (change in y) to horizontal distance (change in x). We begin to calculate slope by labeling one point along the line Point 1, which we denote (x_1, y_1), and another point along the line Point 2, which we denote (x_2, y_2). We can then calculate the horizontal distance by subtracting x_1 from x_2. We calculate vertical distance by subtracting y_1 from y_2.

slope
the ratio of vertical distance (change in y) to horizontal distance (change in x)

EQUATION A-1
$$\text{Horizontal distance} = \Delta x = (x_2 - x_1)$$
$$\text{Vertical distance} = \Delta y = (y_2 - y_1)$$

The vertical distance is sometimes referred to as the **rise**, while the horizontal distance is known as the **run**. "Rise over run" is an easy way to remember how to calculate slope.

rise
vertical distance; calculated as the change in y

EQUATION A-2
$$\text{Slope} = \frac{\text{Rise}}{\text{Run}} = \frac{\Delta y}{\Delta x} = \frac{(y_2 - y_1)}{(x_2 - x_1)}$$

run
horizontal distance; calculated as the change in x

When the relationship between x and y is linear (which means that it forms a straight line), the slope is constant. That is, for each one-unit change in the x-variable, the corresponding y-variable always changes by the same amount. Therefore, we can use any two points to calculate the slope of the line—it doesn't matter which ones we pick because the slope is the same everywhere on the line.

Slope gives us important information about the relationship between our two variables. As you'll see, slope tells us something about both the direction of the relationship between two variables (whether they move in the same direction) and the magnitude of the relationship (how much y changes in response to a change in x).

Calculating slope

In Figure A-8, the rise, or vertical distance between point (2,3) and point (4,5), is 5 minus 3, which equals 2. The run, or horizontal distance, is 4 minus 2, which equals 2. Therefore, the slope of the line in Figure A-8 is calculated as:

LO A.2 Use data to calculate slope.

$$\text{Slope} = \frac{(y_2 - y_1)}{(x_2 - x_1)} = \frac{(5 - 3)}{(4 - 2)} = \frac{2}{2} = 1$$

Let's return to Figure A-7 and apply this same calculation. Because the relationship between x and y is linear, we can use any two points to calculate the slope. Let's pick the point (2,5) to be point 1, which we call (x_1, y_1). Then, pick the point (4,6) to be point 2, which we call (x_2, y_2).

$$\frac{(y_2 - y_1)}{(x_2 - x_1)} = \frac{(6 - 5)}{(4 - 2)} = \frac{1}{2} = 0.5$$

Note that it doesn't matter which point we pick as point 1 and which as point 2. We could have chosen 5 as y_2 and 6 as y_1 rather than vice versa. All that matters is that y_1 is from the same ordered pair as x_1 and y_2 from the same pair as x_2. To prove that this is true, let's calculate slope again using (2,5) as point 2. The slope still comes out to 0.5:

$$\frac{(y_2 - y_1)}{(x_2 - x_1)} = \frac{(5 - 6)}{(2 - 4)} = \frac{(-1)}{(-2)} = \frac{1}{2} = 0.5$$

Use two different points from the table in Figure A-7 to calculate slope again. Try using the points $(-4, 2)$ and $(0, 4)$. Do you get 0.5 as your answer?

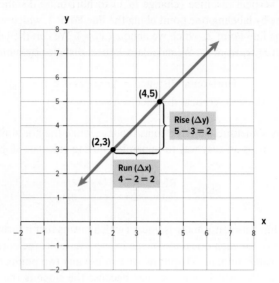

You can calculate the slope by dividing the change in the *y* value over the change in *x*—the rise over the run.

The direction of a slope

LO A.3 Interpret what the direction and steepness of slope indicate about a line.

The direction of a slope tells us something meaningful about the relationship between the two variables we are representing. For instance, when children get older, they grow taller. If we represented this relationship in a graph, we would see an upward-sloping line, telling us that height increases as age increases, rather than decreasing. Of course, it is common knowledge that children get taller, not shorter, as they get older. But if we were looking at a graph of a relationship we did not already understand, the slope of the line would show us at a glance how the two variables relate to one another.

To see how we can learn from the direction of a slope and how to calculate it, look at the graphs in panels A and B of Figure A-9.

In panel A, we can see that when *x* increases from 1 to 2, *y* also increases, from 2 to 4. If we move the other direction down the line, we see that when *x* decreases from 2 to 1, *y* also decreases, from 4 to 2. In other words, *x* and *y* move in the same direction. Therefore, *x* and *y* are said to have a *positive relationship*. Not surprisingly, this means that the slope of the line is a positive number:

$$\text{Slope} = \frac{\Delta y}{\Delta x} = \frac{2}{1} = 2$$

When the slope of a line is positive, we know that *y* increases as *x* increases, and *y* decreases as *x* decreases. If a line leans upward, then its slope is positive.

Now, turn to the graph in panel B. In this case, when *x* increases from 1 to 2, *y* decreases from 4 to 2. Reading from the other direction, when *x* decreases from 2 to 1, *y* increases from 2 to 4. Therefore, *x* and *y* move in opposite directions and are said to have a *negative relationship*. The slope of the line is a negative number:

$$\text{Slope} = \frac{\Delta y}{\Delta x} = \frac{-2}{1} = -2$$

FIGURE A-9

The direction of a slope

(A) Positive relationship

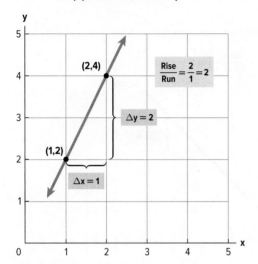

(B) Negative relationship

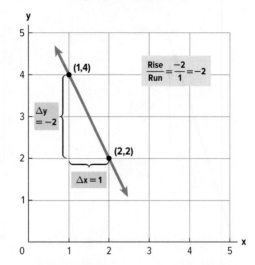

If a line slopes upward, its slope is positive; *y* increases as *x* increases, or *y* decreases as *x* decreases.

If a line slopes downward, its slope is negative: *y* decreases as *x* increases, or *y* increases as *x* decreases.

When the slope of a line is negative, we know that *y* decreases as *x* increases, and *y* increases as *x* decreases. If a line leans downward, then its slope is negative.

In Chapter 3, "Markets," you will see applications of these positive and negative relationships between the variables price and quantity. Here's a preview:

- You will see a positive relationship between price and quantity when you encounter a *supply curve*. You will learn the meaning of that positive relationship: As the price of a good increases, suppliers are willing to supply a larger quantity to markets. Supply curves, therefore, are upward-sloping.

- You will see a negative relationship between price and quantity when you encounter a *demand curve*. You will learn the meaning of that negative relationship: As the price of a good increases, consumers are willing to purchase a smaller quantity. Demand curves are downward-sloping.

From these examples, you can see that two variables (such as price and quantity) may have more than one relationship with each other, depending on whose choices they represent and under what circumstances.

The steepness of a slope

In addition to the *direction* of the relationship between variables, the *steepness* of the slope also gives us important information. It tells us how much *y* changes for a given change in *x*.

In both panels of Figure A-10, the relationship between *x* and *y* is positive (upward-sloping), and the distance between the *x* values, Δ*x*, is the same. However, the change in *y* that results from a one-unit change in *x* is greater in panel A than it is in panel B. In other words, the slope is *steeper* in panel A and *flatter* in panel B.

FIGURE A-10

The steepness of a slope

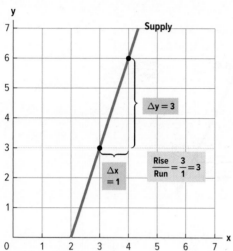

(A) Steeper slope

The larger the number representing slope is, the steeper the curve will be. The slope in panel A is steeper than the slope in panel B.

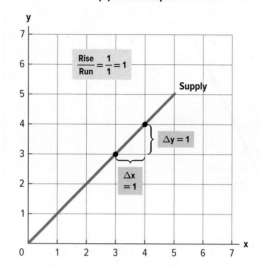

(B) Flatter slope

The closer the slope is to zero, the flatter the curve will be. The slope in panel B is flatter than the slope in panel A.

Numerically, the closer the number representing the slope is to zero, the flatter the curve will be. Remember that both positive and negative numbers can be close to zero. So, a slope of −1 is equally steep as a slope of 1, although one slopes downward and the other upward. Correspondingly, a line with a slope of −5 is steeper than a line with a slope of −1 or one with a slope of 1.

In general, slope is used to describe how much y changes in response to a one-unit change in x. In economics, we are sometimes interested in how much x changes in response to a one-unit change in y. For example, in Chapter 4, "Elasticity," you will see how quantity (on the x-axis) responds to a change in price (on the y-axis).

Key Terms

slope, p. 46G

rise, p. 46G

run, p. 46G

Problems and Applications

1. Create four quadrants using x- and y-axes. Use your graph to plot the following points. **[LO A.1]**
   a. (1,4)   c. (−3,−3)
   b. (−2,1)   d. (3,−2)

2. Create four quadrants using x- and y-axes. Use your graph to plot the following points. **[LO A.1]**
   a. (0,4)   c. (1,0)
   b. (0,−2)   d. (−3,0)

3. Use the curve labeled "Demand" in Figure AP-1 to create a table (schedule) that shows Price in one column and Quantity in another. What is the slope of the curve labeled "Demand"? [**LO A.2**]

FIGURE AP-1

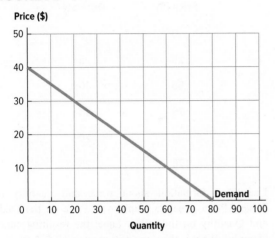

4. Use the curve labeled "Demand" in Figure AP-2 to create a table (schedule) that shows Price in one column and Quantity in another. What is the slope of the curve labeled "Demand"? [**LO A.2**]

FIGURE AP-2

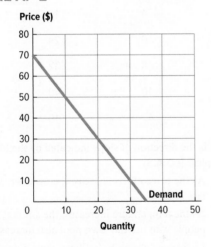

5. Use the information about price and quantity in Table AP-1 to create a graph, with Price on the *y*-axis and Quantity on the *x*-axis. Label the resulting curve "Demand." What is the slope of that curve? [**LO A.2**]

TABLE AP-1

Price ($)	Quantity
0	120
2	100
4	80
6	60
8	40
10	20
12	0

6. Use the information about price and quantity in Table AP-2 to create a graph, with Price on the *y*-axis and Quantity on the *x*-axis. Label the resulting curve "Demand." What is the slope of that curve? [**LO A.2**]

TABLE AP-2

Price ($)	Quantity
0	5
5	4
10	3
15	2
20	1
25	0

7. Use the curve labeled "Supply" in Figure AP-3 to create a table (schedule) that shows Price in one column and Quantity in another. What is the slope of the curve labeled "Supply"? **[LO A.2]**

FIGURE AP-3

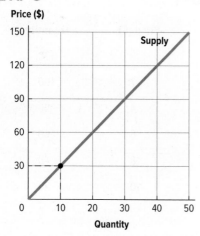

8. Use the curve labeled "Supply" in Figure AP-4 to create a table (schedule) that shows Price in one column and Quantity in another. What is the slope of the curve labeled "Supply"? **[LO A.2]**

FIGURE AP-4

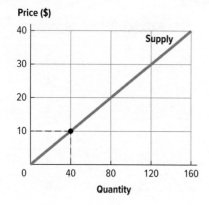

9. Use the information about price and quantity in Table AP-3 to create a graph, with Price on the y-axis and Quantity on the x-axis. Label the resulting curve "Supply." What is the slope of that curve? **[LO A.2]**

TABLE AP-3

Price ($)	Quantity
0	0
25	5
50	10
75	15
100	20
125	25

10. Use the information about price and quantity in Table AP-4 to create a graph, with Price on the y-axis and Quantity on the x-axis. Label the resulting curve "Supply." What is the slope of that curve? **[LO A.2]**

TABLE AP-4

Price ($)	Quantity
0	0
2	8
4	16
6	24
8	32
10	40
12	48

11. What is the direction of slope indicated by the following examples? **[LO A.3]**

    a. As the price of rice increases, consumers want less of it.

    b. As the temperature increases, the amount of people who use the town pool also increases.

    c. As farmers use more fertilizer, their output of tomatoes increases.

12. Rank the following equations by the steepness of their slope from lowest to highest. **[LO A.3]**

    a. $y = -3x + 9$

    b. $y = 4x + 2$

    c. $y = -0.5x + 4$

Supply and Demand

PART TWO

The four chapters in Part 2 will introduce you to . . .

the basics of markets, which form the baseline for most economic analysis. Chapter 3, "Markets," introduces supply and demand. Any time we go into the store and decide to buy something, we act on our demand for that good. On the other side, the store figured out that it made sense for them to supply that good to us. The interaction between the forces of demand and supply determines the price we pay and how much gets bought and sold.

Chapters 4, 5, and 6 ("Elasticity," "Efficiency," and "Government Intervention") will use demand and supply to answer a variety of questions: Why do people rush to the store when Apple slashes the price of an iPhone? Why would the government ever want to set limits on prices in the market?

Together with Part 1, the chapters in this part introduce the basic concepts of economic problem solving. To start, we've stripped down these ideas to their simplest form. These same concepts will return throughout the text, and we will build on them as we turn to different problems.

Markets

Mobiles Go Global

For many people, a cell phone is on the list of things never to leave the house without, right up there with a wallet and keys. For better or worse, cell phones have become a fixture of everyday life.

It's hard to believe that as recently as the late 1990s, cell phones were a luxury that only a third of Americans enjoyed. Before that, in the 1980s, they were big, heavy devices, seldom bought for personal use at all. In less than a quarter of a century, this expensive sci-fi technology became a relatively cheap, universal convenience. Today 95 percent of Americans own a cellphone. In fact, around two-thirds of the world's 7.4 billion people have a cell phone subscription.[1] For instance, 44 percent of Africa's 1.2 billion citizens now have service.[2] This phenomenal growth makes it easier to keep up with friends and family. It also connects small-town merchants to businesses in distant cities, opening up new economic possibilities.

©WAYHOME studio/Shutterstock

How does a product move from expensive to cheap, from rare to commonplace, so quickly? The answer partly lies in the relationship between supply and demand. This chapter shows how the forces of supply and demand interact to determine the quantities and prices of goods that are bought and sold in competitive markets.

The basic story of how a new product takes hold is a familiar one. In the beginning, cell phones were expensive and rare. Over time, the technology improved, the price dropped, the product caught on, and sales took off. Throughout this process of change, markets allow for ongoing communication between buyers and producers, using prices as a signal. The up-and-down movement of prices ensures that the quantity of a product that is available stays in balance with the quantity consumers want to buy.

To explain the leap in usage that cell phones have made over time, however, we need to go further than just price signals. Outside forces that influence supply and demand, such as changes in technology, fashion trends, and economic ups and downs, have driven that transformation. Markets have the remarkable ability to adjust to these changes without falling out of balance.

LEARNING OBJECTIVES

LO 3.1 Identify the defining characteristics of a competitive market.

LO 3.2 Draw a demand curve, and describe the external factors that determine demand.

LO 3.3 Distinguish between a shift in and a movement along the demand curve.

LO 3.4 Draw a supply curve and describe the external factors that determine supply.

LO 3.5 Distinguish between a shift in and a movement along the supply curve.

LO 3.6 Explain how supply and demand interact to drive markets to equilibrium.

LO 3.7 Evaluate the effect of changes in supply and demand on the equilibrium price and quantity.

In this chapter, we'll step into the shoes of consumers and producers to examine the trade-offs they face. We'll see that the issues that drive supply and demand in the cell phone industry are not unique. In fact, the functioning of markets, as summarized in the theory of supply and demand, is the bedrock of almost everything in this text. Mastering this theory will help you to solve all kinds of problems, from what price to sell your product for as a businessperson, to how to find the cheapest gasoline, to the causes of holiday toy shortages.

Markets

In Chapter 2, "Specialization and Exchange," we discussed the power of the "invisible hand" to coordinate complex economic interactions. The key feature of an economy organized by the invisible hand is that private individuals, rather than a centralized planning authority, make the decisions. Such an economy is often referred to as a **market economy**.

What is a market?

What do we mean by a *market?* The word might make you think of a physical location where buyers and sellers come together face-to-face—like a farmers' market or a mall. But people do not have to be physically near each other to make an exchange. For example, think of online retailers like Amazon.com or of fruit that is grown in South America but sold all over the world. The term **market** actually refers to the buyers and sellers who trade a particular good or service, not to a physical location.

Which buyers and sellers are included in the market depends on the context. The manager of a clothing store at your local mall might think about the market for T-shirts in terms of people who live locally and the other places they could buy T-shirts, like competing stores, garage sales, or online retailers. The CEO of a major clothing brand, on the other hand, might include garment factories in Bangladesh and the fashion preferences of customers living all over the world in her idea of a market. Which boundaries are relevant depends on the scope of trades that are being made.

What is a competitive market?

Making simplifying assumptions can help us zero in on important ideas. In this chapter, we will make a big simplifying assumption—that markets are *competitive*. A **competitive market** is one in which fully informed, price-taking buyers and sellers easily trade a standardized good or service. Let's unpack this multipart definition: Imagine you're driving up to an intersection where there is a gas station on each corner. This scenario demonstrates the four defining characteristics of a perfectly competitive market.

market economy
an economy in which private individuals, rather than a centralized planning authority, make the decisions

market
buyers and sellers who trade a particular good or service

LO 3.1 Identify the defining characteristics of a competitive market.

50

First, we bet you'd find that a gallon of gas costs almost the same in each station at the intersection. Why? Recall the third economists' question from Chapter 1, "Economics and Life": If one station tries to raise its price, *how will others respond?* Assuming the stations are offering standardized gallons of gas, customers should be indifferent between buying from one station or another at a given price. If one raises its price, all the drivers will simply go to a cheaper station instead. The gas station that raised prices will end up losing customers. For this reason, no individual seller has the power to change the market price. In economic terminology, a buyer or seller who cannot affect the market price is called a **price taker**.

The drivers going by are also price takers. If you try to negotiate a discount at one of the gas stations before filling your tank, you won't get far—the owner would rather wait and sell to other customers who will pay more. The price is the price; your choice is to take it or leave it. In competitive markets, both buyers and sellers are price takers.

Second, the gas sold by each station is the same—your car will run equally well regardless of *which* brand you buy. This means that the gas being sold is a **standardized good**—a good or service for which any two units of it have the same features and are interchangeable. In a competitive market, the good being bought and sold is standardized.

Third, the price at each gas station is prominently displayed on a big sign. As you drive by, you can immediately see how much a gallon of each type of gas costs at each station. In a competitive market, you have *full information* about the price and features of the good being bought and sold.

Finally, it's easy for you to choose any of the four gas stations at the intersection. The stations are very near each other, and you don't have to have special equipment to fill up your tank or pay an entrance fee to get into the station. In competitive markets, there are no **transaction costs**—the costs incurred by buyer and seller in agreeing to and executing a sale of goods or services. Thus, in competitive markets, you don't have to pay anything for the privilege of buying or selling in the market. You can easily do business in this four-station market for gasoline.

By thinking about the gas stations at a single intersection, you have learned the four characteristics of perfectly competitive markets. Table 3-1 summarizes the four characteristics of a perfectly competitive market: price-taking participants, a standardized good, full information, and no transaction costs.

In reality, few markets are truly *perfectly* competitive. Even gas stations at the same intersection might not be: Maybe one can charge a few cents more per gallon because it uses gas with less ethanol or offers regular customers an attractive loyalty scheme or has a Dunkin' Donuts to entice hungry drivers. In future chapters, we'll spend a lot of time thinking about the different ways that markets in the real world are structured and why it matters when they fall short of perfect competition.

The market for cell phones is not perfectly competitive either. Cell phones are not standardized goods—some models look cooler, or have better cameras, or have access to different apps or calling plans. You're unlikely to be completely indifferent between two different cell phones at the same price, as you are between two gallons of gas. Furthermore, the fact that there are a limited number of service providers means that sellers aren't always price takers. If only one network has

competitive market
a market in which fully informed, price-taking buyers and sellers easily trade a standardized good or service

price taker
a buyer or seller who cannot affect the market price. In a perfectly competitive market, firms are price takers as a consequence of many sellers selling standardized goods

standardized good
a good for which any two units have the same features and are interchangeable

transaction costs
the costs incurred by buyer and seller in agreeing to and executing a sale of goods or services

TABLE 3-1

Four characteristics of perfectly competitive markets

Characteristic	Description
Participants are price takers	Neither buyers nor sellers have the power to affect the market price.
Standardized good	Any two units of the good have the same features and are interchangeable.
Full information	Market participants know everything about the price and features of the good.
No transaction costs	There is no cost to participate in exchanges in the market.

good coverage in your area or has an exclusive deal with a popular type of phone, it can get away with charging a premium.

So, why do we *assume* perfect competition if markets in the real world are rarely perfectly competitive? The answer is that the simple model of competitive markets we will develop in this chapter leads us to useful insights, even in markets that aren't perfectly competitive. Taking the time now to make sure you understand perfect competition, inside and out, will better prepare you to understand why it matters when markets aren't perfectly competitive. As we go through this chapter, we'll note some ways in which the real cell phone market departs from perfect competition. By the end of the chapter, we hope you'll agree that the simple model of perfect competition tells us a lot, if not everything, about how the real cell phone market works.

✓ TEST YOURSELF

☐ What is a market? What are the characteristics of a competitive market? **[LO 3.1]**
☐ Why are participants in competitive markets called *price takers*? **[LO 3.1]**

Demand

Demand describes how much of something people are willing and able to buy under certain circumstances. Suppose someone approached you and asked if you would like a new cell phone. What would you answer? You might think, "Sure," but as a savvy person, you would probably first ask, "For how much?" Whether you want something (or how much of it you want) depends on how much you have to pay for it.

These days most people in the United States have cell phones, but that hasn't been the case for very long. Let's assume for the sake of our model that cell phones are standardized—one model, with given features and calling plans. Now, put yourself in the position of a consumer in the mid-1990s (maybe a relative of yours, for example). You face purchasing decisions at different prices:

- Maybe you've seen cell phones advertised at $499 and think it's not worth it to you.
- As the price goes down over time to $399, and $299, you're still not tempted to buy it.
- At $199, you start to consider it.
- Then, the first time you see a cell phone advertised for less than $125, you decide to buy.

Different people bought their first cell phone at different prices: At any given time, with any given price, some people in the population are willing and able to buy a phone and others aren't. If we add up all of these individual choices, we get overall *market demand*. The amount of a particular good that buyers in a market will purchase at a given price during a specified period is called the **quantity demanded**. For almost all goods, the lower the price goes, the higher the quantity demanded.

This inverse relationship between price and quantity demanded is so important that economists refer to it as the **law of demand**. The first requirement for the law of demand is the idea sometimes known as *ceteris paribus*, the Latin term for "all other things being the same." In other words, the law of demand says that, when all else is held equal (when all other factors remain the same), quantity demanded rises as price falls.

Economists frequently rely on the idea of *ceteris paribus* to isolate the expected effect of a single change in the economy. For example, suppose you want to predict what would happen next year to cell phone sales if cell phone prices go down. The law of demand tells us that if cell phone prices go down, *holding all else equal*, quantity demanded will go up.

But what if the economy is not doing well next year and consumers hold back on buying new cell phones? In this instance, we *cannot* say in general that "if cell phone prices go down, quantity demanded will go up" because not everything else has been held the same. Instead, the negative impact of the weak economy may offset the positive impact of the reduction in price. We need to

quantity demanded
the amount of a particular good that buyers will purchase at a given price during a specified period

law of demand
a fundamental characteristic of demand that states that, all else equal, quantity demanded rises as price falls

be more specific. So, it is critical to "hold all else equal" in order to make clear statements about what we can predict.

The law of demand isn't a made-up law that economists have imposed on markets. Rather, it holds true because it describes the underlying reality of individual people's decisions. The key is to think about the *trade-offs* that people face when making the decision to buy.

What happens when the price of something falls? First, the benefit that you get from purchasing it remains the same because the item itself is unchanged. But the opportunity cost has fallen: When the price goes down, you don't have to give up as many other purchases in order to get the item. When benefits stay the same and opportunity cost goes down, this trade-off suddenly starts to look a lot better. When the trade-off between costs and benefits tips toward benefits, more people will want to buy the good.

Of course, falling prices will not have been the only consideration in people's decisions to buy their first cell phone. Some might have decided to buy one when they got a pay raise at work. Others might have bought one at the point when most of their friends owned one. Incomes, expectations, and tastes all play a role; economists call these factors *nonprice determinants* of demand. We'll discuss their potential effects later in this chapter. First, let's focus on the relationship between price and quantity demanded.

The demand curve

The law of demand says that the quantity of cell phones demanded will be different at every price level. For this reason, it is often useful to represent demand as a table, called a **demand schedule**. A demand schedule shows the quantities of a particular good or service that consumers are willing and able to purchase (demand) at various prices. Panel A of Figure 3-1 shows a hypothetical annual demand schedule for cell phones in the United States. (Remember, we're assuming that cell phones are a standardized good. This isn't quite right, but the basic principle holds true: When cell phone prices are lower, you're more likely to buy a new one.) The demand schedule assumes that factors other than price remain the same.

Panel B of Figure 3-1 shows another way to represent demand, by drawing each price-quantity combination from the demand schedule as a point on a graph. That graph, called a **demand curve**, visually displays the demand schedule. That is, it is a graph that shows the quantities of a particular good or service that consumers will demand at various prices. The demand curve also represents consumers' *willingness to buy:* It shows the highest amount consumers will pay for any given quantity.

On the demand curve, quantity goes on the *x*-axis (the horizontal axis) and price on the *y*-axis (the vertical axis). The result is a downward-sloping line that reflects the inverse relationship between price and quantity. The demand curve in Figure 3-1 represents exactly the same information as the demand schedule.

Determinants of demand

The demand curve represents the relationship between price and quantity demanded *with everything else held constant*. If everything else is *not* held constant—that is, if one of the nonprice factors that determines demand changes—the curve will shift.

The downward-sloping demand curve reflects the trade-offs that people face between (1) the benefit they expect to receive from a good and (2) the opportunity cost they face for buying it. Therefore, any factor that changes this balance at a given price will change people's willingness to buy, and thus their purchasing decisions.

The nonprice determinants of demand can be divided into five major categories:

- Consumer preferences.
- The prices of related goods.
- Income of the consumers.
- Expectations of future prices.
- The number of buyers in the market.

LO 3.2 Draw a demand curve, and describe the external factors that determine demand.

demand schedule
a table that shows the quantities of a particular good or service that consumers are willing and able to purchase (demand) at various prices

demand curve
a graph that shows the quantities of a particular good or service that consumers will demand at various prices

Since demand curves and other material in this chapter make extensive use of lines and linear equations, you may want to review those concepts in Appendix B, "Math Essentials: Working with Linear Equations," which follows this chapter.

FIGURE 3-1

Demand schedule and the demand curve

(A) Demand schedule

Cell phones (millions)	Price ($)
30	180
60	160
90	140
120	120
150	100
180	80
210	60
240	40
270	20

This demand schedule shows the quantity of cell phones demanded each year at various prices. As prices decrease, consumers want to purchase more cell phones.

(B) Demand curve

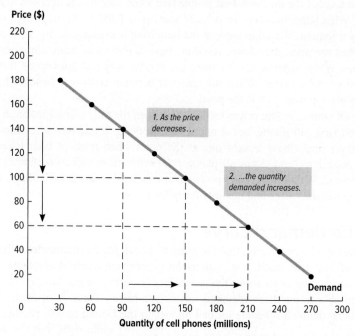

1. As the price decreases...

2. ...the quantity demanded increases.

This demand curve is a graphic representation of the demand schedule for cell phones in the United States. Each entry in the demand schedule is plotted on this curve.

Table 3-2 summarizes the impact of each factor on demand. Each of these nonprice determinants affects either the benefits or the opportunity cost of buying a good, even if the price of the good itself remains the same.

 CAUTION: COMMON MISTAKE

You may notice that these five factors include price-related issues such as the price of related goods and expectations about future prices. So why do we refer to them as *nonprice determinants*? We do so in order to differentiate them from the effect of the *current price* of the good on demand for that good.

Consumer preferences   Consumer preferences are the personal likes and dislikes that make buyers more or less inclined to purchase a good. We don't need to know *why* people like what they like or to agree with their preferences; we just need to know that these likes and dislikes influence their purchases. At any given price, some consumers will get more enjoyment (i.e., benefits) out of a cell phone than do others. That enjoyment may be based simply on how much they like talking to friends, or whether they use their phones for work, or any number of other personal preferences.

TABLE 3-2

Determinants of demand

Determinant	Examples of an increase in demand	Examples of a decrease in demand
Consumer preferences	A "Buy American" ad campaign appeals to national pride, increasing the demand for U.S.-made sneakers.	An outbreak of *E. coli* decreases the demand for spinach.
Prices of related goods	A decrease in the price of hot dogs increases the demand for relish, a complementary good.	A decrease in taxi fares decreases the demand for subway rides, a substitute good.
Incomes	An economic downturn lowers incomes, increasing the demand for ground beef, an inferior good.	An economic downturn lowers incomes, decreasing the demand for steak, a normal good.
Expectations	A hurricane destroys part of the world papaya crop, causing expectations that prices will rise and increasing the current demand for papayas.	An announcement that a new smartphone soon will be released decreases the demand for the current model.
Number of buyers	An increase in life expectancy increases the demand for nursing homes and medical care.	A falling birthrate decreases the demand for diapers.

Some consumer preferences are fairly constant across time, such as those that arise from personality traits or cultural attitudes and beliefs. For example, a recluse may have little desire for a cell phone; an on-the-go executive may find a cell phone (or two) to be essential. Other preferences will change over time, in response to external events or fads. For instance, it's more useful to own a cell phone when all your friends already have one. And more people may demand cell phones after a national disaster, knowing they want to be able to reach their families in emergencies.

Prices of related goods   Another factor that affects the demand for a particular good is the prices of related goods. There are two kinds of related goods: substitutes and complements.

We say that goods are **substitutes** when they serve similar-enough purposes that a consumer might purchase one in place of the other—for example, rice and pasta. If the price of rice doubles while the price of pasta stays the same, demand for pasta will increase. That's because the *opportunity cost* of pasta has decreased: You can buy less rice for the same amount of money, so you give up less potential rice when you buy pasta. If the two goods are quite similar, we call them *close substitutes*. Similar fishes, such as salmon and trout, might be considered close substitutes.

For many Americans deciding whether to buy their first cell phone, the nearest substitute would have been a landline phone. Cell phones and landlines are not very close substitutes: You can use them for the same purposes at home or the office, but only one of them can go for a walk with you. Still, if the price of U.S. landline phone service had suddenly skyrocketed, we can be sure that change would have increased the demand for cell phones.

In fact, the very high cost of landline phone services in many developing countries is one reason why cell phones spread very quickly. In the United States, almost every household had a landline phone before it had a cell phone. In many poor countries, landlines are so expensive that very few people can afford one. That's why cell phones are often called a *leapfrog technology:* People go straight from no phone to cell phone, hopping over an entire stage of older technology.

Related goods that are consumed together, so that purchasing one will make a consumer more likely to purchase the other, are called **complements**. Peanut butter and jelly, cereal and milk, cars and gasoline are all complements. If the price of one of the two goods increases, demand for the other will likely decrease. Why? As consumers purchase less of the first good, they will want less

substitutes
goods that serve a similar-enough purpose that a consumer might purchase one in place of the other

complements
goods that are consumed together, so that purchasing one will make consumers more likely to purchase the other

of the other to go with it. Conversely, if the price of one of the two goods declines, demand for the other will likely increase. For example, when the prices of new cell phones fall, consumers will be more likely to buy new accessories to go with them.

Incomes   Not surprisingly, the amount of income people earn affects their demand for goods and services: The bigger your paycheck, the more money you can afford to spend on the things you want. The smaller your paycheck, the more you have to cut back.

normal goods
goods for which demand increases as income increases

Most goods are **normal goods**, meaning that an increase in income causes an increase in demand. Likewise, for normal goods, a decrease in income causes a decrease in demand. For most people, cell phones are a normal good. If someone cannot currently afford a cell phone, she's more likely to buy one when her income rises. If someone already has a cell phone, she's more likely to upgrade to a newer, fancier cell phone when her income rises.

inferior goods
goods for which demand decreases as income increases

For some goods, called **inferior goods**, the opposite relationship holds: As income increases, demand decreases. Typically, people replace inferior goods with more expensive and appealing substitutes when their incomes rise. For many people, inexpensive grocery items like instant noodles, some canned foods, and generic store brands might be inferior goods. When their incomes rise, people replace these goods with fresher, more expensive ingredients. Decreases in income occur for many people during economic downturns; thus, the demand for inferior goods reflects the overall health of the economy. For an example, see the Economics in Action box "Can instant noodle sales predict a recession?"

Can instant noodle sales predict a recession?
Economics in Action

If you were to open a typical college student's kitchen cupboard, what would you find? Many students rely on a decidedly unglamorous food item: ramen instant noodles. Packed with cheap calories, this tasty snack is famously inexpensive.

Ramen noodles are an example of an inferior good. When people's budgets are tight (as are those of most students), these noodles sell well. When incomes rise, ramen sales drop and more expensive foods replace them.

In Thailand, ramen noodles have even been used as an indicator of overall economic health. The Mama Noodles Index tracks sales of a popular brand of instant ramen noodles. Because the demand for inferior goods increases when incomes go down, an increase in ramen sales could signal a downturn in incomes and an oncoming recession. In fact, observers of the Thai economy say that the Mama Noodles Index does a pretty good job of reflecting changing economic conditions.

Even the demand for inferior goods may decrease during severe economic downturns, however. Although the Mama Noodles Index has risen as expected when the Thai economy falters, the index unexpectedly dropped 15 percent during the deep recession of early 2009.

So are instant noodles an inferior good or a normal good? In Thailand, the answer may depend on who you are or how severely your income has dropped. For the middle class, who choose between ramen and more expensive

When budgets are tight, ramen noodles tend to sell well. When incomes rise, ramen sales tend to drop.
©Alexander Alexeev/123RF

Markets ■ Chapter 3   **57**

foods, ramen may indeed be an inferior good. For the poor, whose choice more likely is whether or not they will get enough to eat, ramen may be a normal good. When their incomes rise, they may buy more ramen; when their incomes fall, even noodles may be a luxury.

Sources: "Using their noodles," *Associated Press,* September 5, 2005, www.theage.com.au/news/world/using-their-noodles/2005/09/04/1125772407287.html.; Kwanchai Rungfapaisarn, "Downturn bites into instant-noodle market as customers tighten belts," *The Nation,* March 20, 2009, www.nationmultimedia.com/business/Downturn-bites-into-instant-noodle-market-as-custo-30098402.html.

Expectations   Changes in consumers' expectations about the future—especially future prices—can also affect demand. If consumers expect prices to fall in the future, they may postpone a purchase until a later date, causing current demand to decrease. If you think cell phones will go on sale in a few months, you might put off your purchase until then. Or you might delay upgrading your smartphone in the hope that when the next model releases, the current model will drop in price. When prices are expected to drop in the future, demand decreases.

Conversely, if consumers expect prices to rise in the future, they may wish to purchase a good immediately to avoid a higher price. This reasoning often occurs in speculative markets, like the stock market or sometimes the housing market. Buyers purchase stock or a house expecting prices to rise, so they can sell at a profit. In these markets, then, demand increases when prices are low and are expected to rise.

Number of buyers   The demand curve represents the demand of a particular number of potential buyers. In general, an increase in the number of potential buyers in a market will increase demand. A decrease in the number of buyers will decrease it. Major population shifts, like an increase in immigration or a drop in the birthrate, can create nationwide changes in demand. As the number of teenagers and college students increases, the demand for cell phones increases too.

Shifts in the demand curve

What happens to the demand curve when one of the five nonprice determinants of demand changes? The entire demand curve shifts, either to the right or to the left. The shift is horizontal rather than vertical because nonprice determinants affect the quantity demanded at *each* price. When the quantity demanded at a given price is now higher, the point on the curve corresponding to that price is now further right. When the quantity demanded at a given price is lower, the point on the curve corresponding to that price is now further left.

Consider what happens, for example, when the economy is growing and people's incomes are rising. Let's assume the price of cell phones does not change ("all else held equal"). But with rising incomes, more people will choose to buy a new cell phone at any given price, causing quantity demanded to be higher at every possible price. Panel A of Figure 3-2 shows the resulting shift of the demand curve to the right, from D_A to D_B. In contrast, if the economy falls into a recession and people begin pinching pennies, quantity demanded will decrease at every price, and the curve will shift to the left, from D_A to D_C.

It is important to distinguish between these *shifts* in demand, which move the entire curve, and *movements along* a given demand curve. Remember this key point: *Shifts in the demand curve are caused by changes in the nonprice determinants of demand.* A recession, for example, would lower incomes and move the whole demand curve left. When we say "demand decreases," this is what we are talking about.

In contrast, suppose that the price of phones increases but everything else stays the same— that is, there is no change in the nonprice determinants of demand. Because the demand curve describes the quantity consumers will demand at any possible price, not just the current market price, we don't have to shift the curve to figure out what happens when the price goes up. Instead,

LO 3.3 Distinguish between a shift in and a movement along the demand curve.

FIGURE 3-2

Shifts in the demand curve versus movement along the demand curve

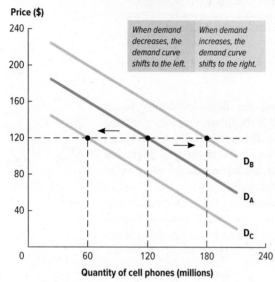

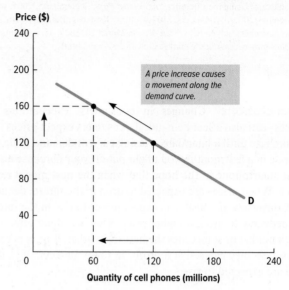

Changes in external factors cause the entire demand curve to shift. The shift from D_A to D_B represents an increase in demand, meaning that consumers want to buy more cell phones at each price. The shift from D_A to D_C represents a decrease in demand, meaning that consumers want to buy fewer cell phones at each price.

A price change causes a movement along the demand curve, but the curve itself remains constant.

we simply look at a different point on the curve to describe what is actually happening in the market right now.

To find the quantity that consumers will want to purchase at this new price, we move along the existing demand curve from the old price to the new one. If, for instance, the price of cell phones increases, we find the new quantity demanded by moving up along the demand curve to the new price point, as shown in panel B of Figure 3-2. The price change does not shift the curve itself because the curve already describes what consumers will do at any price.

To summarize, panel A of Figure 3-2 shows a *shift in demand* as the result of a change in the nonprice determinants; panel B shows a *movement along the demand curve* as the result of a change in price.

Economists use very specific terminology to distinguish between a shift in the demand curve and movement along the demand curve:

- We say that a change in one of the nonprice determinants of demand causes an "increase in demand" or "decrease in demand"—that is, a *shift* of the entire demand curve.

- To distinguish this from *movement along* the demand curve, we say that a change in price causes an "increase in the quantity demanded" or "decrease in the quantity demanded."

Just keep in mind that a "change in demand" is different from a "change in the quantity demanded." Observing this seemingly small difference in terminology prevents a great deal of confusion.

Understanding the effects of changes in both price and the nonprice determinants of demand is a key tool for businesspeople and policy-makers. Suppose you are in charge of an industry group whose members want to spur demand for cell phones. One idea might be to start an advertising campaign to increase the real or perceived benefits of owning a cell phone. If you understand the determinants of demand, you know that the advertising campaign would change consumer preferences. In other words, a successful advertising campaign would shift the demand curve for cell phones to the right. Similarly, if you are a congressional representative who is considering a tax cut to stimulate the economy, you know that a tax cut increases consumers' disposable incomes, increasing the demand for all normal goods. In other words, you are hoping that the resulting increase in incomes will shift the demand curve for cell phones to the right.

✓ TEST YOURSELF

☐ What are the five nonprice determinants of demand? **[LO 3.2]**

☐ What is the difference between a change in demand and a change in quantity demanded? **[LO 3.3]**

Supply

We've discussed the factors that determine how many phones consumers want to buy at a given price. But are cell phone producers necessarily willing to sell that many? The concept of *supply* describes how much of a good or service producers will offer for sale under given circumstances. The **quantity supplied** is the amount of a particular good or service that producers will offer for sale at a given price during a specified period.

As with demand, we can find overall *market supply* by adding up the individual decisions of each producer. Imagine you own a factory that can produce cell phones or other consumer electronics. You face production decisions at different prices:

- If the price of cell phones is $110, you might decide there's good money to be made and use your entire factory space to produce cell phones.
- If the price is only $80, you might produce some cell phones but decide it will be more profitable to devote part of your factory to producing laptop computers.
- If the cell phone price drops to $55, you might decide you'd make more money by producing only laptops.

Each producer will have a different price point at which it decides it's worthwhile to supply cell phones. This rule—all else held equal, quantity supplied increases as price increases—is called the **law of supply**.

(In reality, it's costly to switch a factory from making cell phones to laptops or other goods. However, the simple version illustrates a basic truth: The higher the price of a good, the more of that good producers will want to supply. Similarly, the lower the price of a good, the less of that good producers will want to supply.)

As with demand, supply varies with price because the decision to produce a good is about the *trade-off* between the benefit the producer will receive from selling the good and the opportunity cost of the time and resources that go into producing it. When the market price goes up and all other factors remain constant, the benefit of production increases relative to the opportunity cost, and the trade-off involved in production makes it more favorable to produce more.

For instance, if the price of phones goes up and the prices of raw materials stay the same, existing phone producers may open new factories, and new companies may start looking to enter the cell phone market. The same holds true across other industries. If air travelers seem willing to pay higher prices, airlines will increase the frequency of flights, add new routes, and buy new planes so they can carry more passengers. When prices drop, they cut back their flight schedules and cancel their orders for new planes.

quantity supplied
the amount of a particular good or service that producers will offer for sale at a given price during a specified period

law of supply
a fundamental characteristic of supply that states that, all else equal, quantity supplied rises as price rises

The supply curve

LO 3.4 Draw a
supply curve and
describe the external
factors that deter-
mine supply.

Like demand, supply can be represented as a table or a graph. A **supply schedule** is a table that shows the quantities of a particular good or service that producers will supply at various prices. Panel A of Figure 3-3 shows a hypothetical supply schedule for U.S. cell phone providers.

A **supply curve** is a graph of the information in the supply schedule. Just as the demand curve showed consumers' willingness to buy, so the supply curve shows producers' *willingness to sell:* It shows the minimum price producers must receive to supply any given quantity. Panel B of Figure 3-3 shows the supply curve of U.S. cell phone providers—visually representing the supply schedule.

supply schedule
a table that shows the
quantities of a particular
good or service that
producers will supply at
various prices

Determinants of supply

The law of supply describes how the quantity that producers are willing to supply changes as price changes. But what determines the quantity supplied at any given price? As with demand, a number of *nonprice factors* determine the opportunity cost of production and therefore producers' willingness to supply a good or service. *When a nonprice determinant of supply changes, the entire supply curve will shift.* Such shifts reflect a change in the quantity of goods supplied at *every* price.

The nonprice determinants of supply can be divided into five major categories:

supply curve
a graph that shows the
quantities of a particular
good or service that
producers will supply at
various prices

- Prices of related goods.
- Technology.
- Prices of inputs.

- Expectations.
- The number of sellers.

FIGURE 3-3

Supply schedule and the supply curve

(A) Supply schedule

Cell phones (millions)	Price ($)
270	180
240	160
210	140
180	120
150	100
120	80
90	60
60	40
30	20

This supply schedule shows the quantity of cell phones supplied each year at various prices. As prices decrease, suppliers want to produce fewer cell phones.

(B) Supply curve

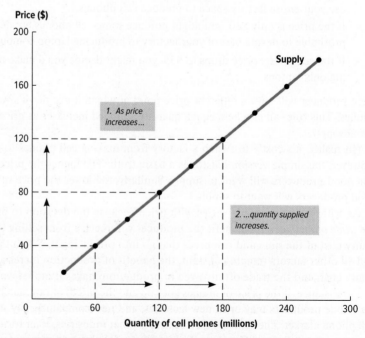

This supply curve is a graphic representation of the supply schedule for cell phones in the United States. It shows the quantity of cell phones that suppliers will produce at various prices.

TABLE 3-3

Determinants of supply

Determinant	Examples of an increase in supply	Examples of a decrease in supply
Price of related goods	The price of gas rises, so an automaker increases its production of smaller, more fuel-efficient cars.	The price of clean energy production falls, so the power company reduces the amount of power it supplies using coal power plants.
Technology	The installation of robots increases productivity and lowers costs; the supply of goods increases.	New technology allows corn to be made into ethanol, so farmers plant more corn and fewer soybeans; the supply of soybeans decreases.
Prices of inputs	A drop in the price of tomatoes decreases the production cost of salsa; the supply of salsa increases.	An increase in the minimum wage increases labor costs at food factories; the supply of processed food decreases.
Expectations	New research points to the health benefits of eating papayas, leading to expectations that the demand for papayas will rise. More farmers plant papayas, increasing the supply.	Housing prices are expected to rise, so builders hold back on new construction projects today (in order to build later when housing prices are higher), decreasing the supply of homes in the near future.
Number of sellers	Subsidies make the production of corn more profitable, so more farmers plant corn; the supply of corn increases.	New licensing fees make operating a restaurant more expensive; some small restaurants close, decreasing the supply of restaurants.

Each of these factors determines the opportunity cost of production relative to a given benefit (i.e., the price) and therefore the trade-off that producers face. Table 3-3 shows how the supply of various products responds to changes in each determinant.

Prices of related goods   Return to your factory, where you can produce either cell phones or laptops. Just as you chose to produce more laptops and fewer cell phones when the price of cell phones dropped, you would do the same if the price of laptops increased while the price of cell phones stayed constant.

The price of related goods determines supply because it affects the opportunity cost of production. When you choose to produce cell phones, you forgo the profits you would have earned from producing something else. If the price of that something else increases, the amount you forgo in profits also increases. For instance, imagine you can grow wheat or corn (or other crops, for that matter) on your land. If the price of corn increases, the quantity of wheat (the substitute crop) you are willing to grow falls. Why? Because each acre you devote to wheat is one fewer acre you can use to grow corn.

Technology

Improved technology enables firms to produce more efficiently, using fewer resources to make a given product. Doing so lowers production costs, increasing the quantity producers are willing to supply at each price.

Improved technology has played a huge role in the changing popularity of cell phones. As technological innovation in the construction of screens, batteries, and mobile networks and in the processing of electronic data has leapt forward, the cost of producing a useful, consumer-friendly cell phone has plummeted. As a result, producers are now willing to supply more cell phones at lower prices.

In 1980, this cutting-edge technology cost $4,000.
©Rubberball/Duston Todd/Getty Images

Prices of inputs   The prices of the inputs used to produce a good are an important part of its cost. When the prices of inputs increase, production costs rise, and the quantity of the product that producers are willing to supply at any given price decreases.

Small amounts of silver and gold are used inside cell phones, for example. When the prices of these precious metals rise, the cost of manufacturing each cell phone increases, and the total number of units that producers collectively are willing to make at any given price goes down. Conversely, when input prices fall, supply increases.

Expectations   Suppliers' expectations about prices in the future also affect quantity supplied. For example, when the price of real estate is expected to rise in the future, more real estate developers will wait to embark on construction projects, decreasing the supply of houses in the near future. When expectations change and real estate prices are projected to fall in the future, many of those projects will be rushed to completion, causing the supply of houses to rise.

Number of sellers   The market supply curve represents the quantities of a product that a particular number of producers will supply at various prices in a given market. This means that the number of sellers in the market is considered to be one of the fixed parts of the supply curve. We've already seen that the sellers in the market will decide to supply more if the price of a good is higher. This does not mean that the number of sellers will change based on price in the short run.

There are, however, nonprice factors that cause the number of sellers to change in a market and move the supply curve. For example, suppose cell phone producers must meet strict licensing requirements. If those licensing requirements are dropped, more companies may enter the market, willing to supply a certain number of cell phones at each price. These additional phones must be added to the number of cell phones existing producers are already willing to supply at each price point.

Shifts in the supply curve

LO 3.5 Distinguish between a shift in and a movement along the supply curve.

Just as with demand, changes in price cause suppliers to move to a different point on the same supply curve, while changes in the nonprice determinants of supply shift the supply curve itself. A change in a nonprice determinant increases or decreases *supply*. A change in price increases or decreases the *quantity supplied*.

A change in one of the nonprice determinants increases or decreases the supply at any given price. These shifts are shown in panel A of Figure 3-4. An increase in supply shifts the curve to the right. A decrease in supply shifts the curve to the left. For instance, an improvement in battery technology that decreases the cost of producing cell phones will shift the entire supply curve to the right, from S_A to S_B; the quantity of phones supplied at every price is higher than before. Conversely, an increase in the price of the gold needed for cell phones raises production costs, shifting the supply curve to the left, from S_A to S_C.

As with demand, we differentiate these shifts in the supply curve from a movement along the supply curve, which is shown in panel B of Figure 3-4. If the price of cell phones changes, but the nonprice determinants of supply stay the same, we find the new quantity supplied by moving along the supply curve to the new price point.

Also, as with demand, economists use very specific terminology to distinguish between a shift in the supply curve and movement along the supply curve:

- We say that a change in one of the nonprice determinants of supply causes an "increase in supply" or "decrease in supply"—that is, a *shift* of the entire supply curve.
- To distinguish this from *movement along* the supply curve, we say that a change in price causes an "increase in the quantity supplied" or "decrease in the quantity supplied."

FIGURE 3-4

Shifts in the supply curve versus movement along the supply curve

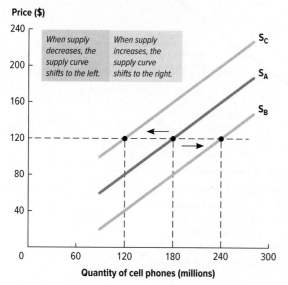

(A) Shifts in the supply curve

When supply decreases, the supply curve shifts to the left. When supply increases, the supply curve shifts to the right.

Changes in external factors cause the entire supply curve to shift. The shift from S_A to S_B represents an increase in supply, meaning that producers are willing to supply more cell phones at each price. The shift from S_A to S_C represents a decrease in supply, meaning that producers are willing to supply fewer cell phones at each price.

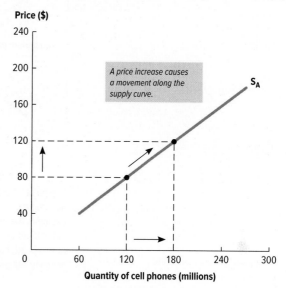

(B) Movement along the supply curve

A price increase causes a movement along the supply curve.

A price change causes a movement along the supply curve, but the curve itself remains constant.

✓ TEST YOURSELF

☐ What does the law of supply say about the relationship between price and quantity supplied? **[LO 3.4]**

☐ In which direction does the supply curve shift when the price of inputs increases? **[LO 3.5]**

Market Equilibrium

We've discussed the factors that influence the quantities supplied and demanded by producers and consumers. To find out what actually happens in the market, however, we need to combine these concepts. The prices and quantities of the goods that are exchanged in the real world depend on the *interaction* of supply with demand.

Graphically, this convergence of supply with demand happens at the point where the demand curve intersects the supply curve, a point called the market **equilibrium**. The price at this point is called the **equilibrium price** and the quantity at this point is called the **equilibrium quantity**.

Bear with us for a moment as we point out the obvious: There is no sale without a purchase. You can't sell something unless someone buys it. Although this point may be obvious, the implication for markets is profound. When markets work well, the quantity supplied exactly equals the quantity demanded.

We can think of this intersection, where quantity supplied equals quantity demanded, as the point at which buyers and sellers "agree" on the quantity of a good they are willing to exchange at a given price. At higher prices, sellers want to sell more than buyers want to buy. At lower prices,

equilibrium
the situation in a market when the quantity supplied equals the quantity demanded; graphically, this convergence happens where the demand curve intersects the supply curve

equilibrium price
the price at which the quantity supplied equals the quantity demanded

equilibrium quantity
the quantity that is supplied and demanded at the equilibrium price

FIGURE 3-5

Market equilibrium in the U.S. market for cell phones

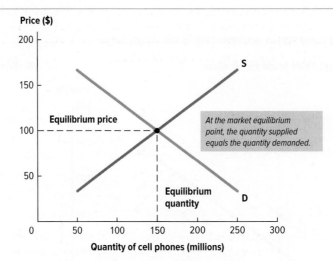

The point where the supply curve intersects the demand curve is called the equilibrium point. In this example, the equilibrium price is $100, and the equilibrium quantity is 150 million cell phones. At this point, consumers are willing to buy exactly as many cell phones as producers are willing to sell.

buyers want to buy more than sellers are willing to sell. Because every seller finds a buyer at the equilibrium price and quantity, and no one is left standing around with extra goods or an empty shopping cart, the equilibrium price is sometimes called the *market-clearing price*.

In reality, things don't always work so smoothly: Short-run "friction" sometimes slows the process of reaching equilibrium, even in well-functioning markets. As a result, smart businesspeople may hold some inventory for future sale, and consumers may need to shop around for specific items. On the whole, though, the concept of equilibrium is incredibly accurate (and important) in describing how markets function.

Figure 3-5 shows the market equilibrium for cell phones in the United States. It was constructed by combining the market supply and demand curves shown in Figures 3-1 and 3-3. In this market, the equilibrium price is $100, and the equilibrium quantity supplied and demanded is 150 million phones.

Reaching equilibrium

LO 3.6 Explain how supply and demand interact to drive markets to equilibrium.

How does a market reach equilibrium? Do sellers know intuitively what price to charge? No. Instead, they tend to set prices by trial and error, by past experience with customers, or by thinking through their costs and adding in a bit of profit. Irrespective of the firm's pricing process, typically the incentives buyers and sellers face naturally drive the market toward an equilibrium price and quantity.

Figure 3-6 shows two graphs, one in which the starting price is above the equilibrium price and the other in which it is below the equilibrium price. In panel A, we imagine that cell phone suppliers think they'll be able to charge $160 for a cell phone, so they produce 240 million phones. They find, though, that consumers will buy only 60 million. (We can read those quantities demanded and supplied at a price of $160 from the demand and supply curves.) When the quantity supplied is higher than the quantity demanded, we say that there is a **surplus** of phones, or an **excess supply**. Manufacturers are stuck holding extra phones in their warehouses; they want to sell that stock and must reduce the price to attract more customers. They have an incentive to keep lowering the price until quantity demanded increases to reach quantity supplied.

surplus

(excess supply)

a situation in which the quantity of a good that is supplied is higher than the quantity demanded

FIGURE 3-6

Reaching equilibrium in the market for cell phones

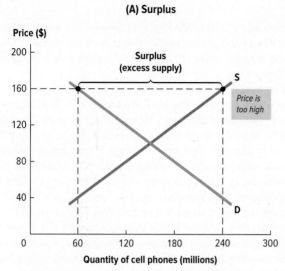

(A) Surplus

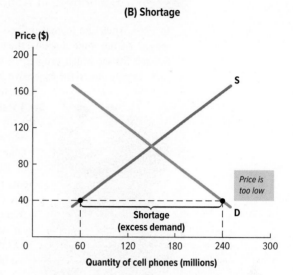

(B) Shortage

When the initial price for cell phones is above the equilibrium point, producers want to supply more cell phones than consumers want to buy. The gap between the quantity supplied and the quantity demanded is called a surplus, or excess supply.

When the initial price for cell phones is below the equilibrium point, consumers want to buy more cell phones than sellers want to produce. The distance between the quantity demanded and the quantity supplied is called a shortage, or excess demand.

In panel B of Figure 3-6, we imagine that cell phone producers make the opposite mistake—they think they'll be able to charge only $40 per phone. They make only 60 million cell phones, but consumers actually are willing to buy 240 million cell phones at that price. When the quantity demanded is higher than the quantity supplied, we say there is a **shortage**, or **excess demand**. Producers will see long lines of people waiting to buy the few available cell phones; they will quickly realize that they could make more money by charging a higher price. They have an incentive to increase the price until quantity demanded decreases to equal quantity supplied, and no one is left standing in line.

Thus, at any price above or below the equilibrium price, sellers face an incentive to raise or lower prices. No one needs to engineer the market equilibrium or share secret information about what price to charge. Instead, money-making incentives drive the market toward the equilibrium price, at which there is neither a surplus nor a shortage. The Economics in Action box "The great Elmo shortage" describes a case in which a producer started out charging the wrong price, but the market solved the problem.

shortage (excess demand) a situation in which the quantity of a good that is demanded is higher than the quantity supplied

Changes in equilibrium

We've seen what happens to the supply and demand curves when a nonprice factor changes. Because the equilibrium price and quantity are determined by the interaction of supply and demand, a shift in either curve will also change the market equilibrium. Some changes will cause only the demand curve to shift; some, only the supply curve. Some changes will affect both the supply and demand curves.

LO 3.7 Evaluate the effect of changes in supply and demand on the equilibrium price and quantity.

The great Elmo shortage
Economics in Action

In 1996, American toymaker Tyco introduced "Tickle Me Elmo" in time for the winter holiday season. As the name suggests, the toy was a plush version of the famous furry red character from Sesame Street, which erupted in wild laughter when "tickled." Tyco expected only moderate sales, largely due to the expensive $30 price tag.

In October, though, actor Rosie O'Donnell plugged the new toy on her TV show, and sales of Tickle Me Elmo took off. By Thanksgiving, the toy was so popular that many stores ran out of stock. Tyco did its best to meet the surge in demand, even flying inventory from China in private jets. That wasn't enough. Faced with a shortage of Elmos, shoppers started taking drastic (and sometimes violent) measures. In Canada, a store employee was severely injured when a group of 300 shoppers noticed he was holding a Tickle Me Elmo and stampeded to get it. The *New York Times* even reported a story involving a Toys-"R"-Us store in Queens, NY, a case of Elmos, and a suspicious late-night shopping spree by members of a famous crime family. An Elmo even went missing from a New York City Police Station.

People offered to sell Elmos for hundreds or even thousands more than the $30 retail price. (That is exactly the economic result we'd expect when there is a shortage of a good.) Enterprising organizations and charities started raffling off Elmos; a radio station in Wichita, Kansas, solicited donations by threatening to destroy an Elmo along with a condemned building.

While it may seem a bit excessive, these types of "crazes" are often part of toy sales at the holidays. Unfortunately for producers and consumers, predicting the hot toy of the season is nearly impossible. If, like Tyco, they guess wrong, factories often can't catch up to surging demand, resulting in long lines, inflated prices, frustrated parents, and disappointed kids. However, the story of Tickle Me Elmo also shows that the "perfect" holiday gift will always be available to those who are willing and able to pay the price.

The shortage of Tickle Me Elmo dolls one holiday season demonstrated what happens to price in the case of excess demand.
©Meeyoung Son/Alamy

Sources: Dan Berry, "A Christmas Tale of the Gottis and Tickle Me Elmo," *The New York Times,* December 18, 1996, www.nytimes.com/1996/12/18/nyregion/a-christmas-tale-of-the-gottis-and-tickle-me-elmo.html; E.S. Huffman, "How 'Tickle Me Elmo' Caused Holiday Hysteria in 1996," *Uproxx,* December 16, 2015, https://uproxx.com/life/tickle-me-elmo-craze-history/; Jake Rossen, "Oral History: Tickle Me Elmo Turns 21," *Mental Floss,* November 16, 2017, http://mentalfloss.com/article/83563/oral-history-tickle-me-elmo-turns-20.

To determine the effect on market equilibrium of a change in a nonprice factor, ask yourself a few questions:

1. Does the change affect demand? If so, does demand increase or decrease?
2. Does the change affect supply? If so, does supply increase or decrease?
3. How does the combination of changes in supply and demand affect the equilibrium price and quantity?

Shifts in demand   We suggested earlier that landline service is a *substitute* for cell phones and that if the price of landline service suddenly skyrockets, then demand for cell phones increases.

In other words, the demand curve shifts to the right. The price of landline service probably doesn't affect the supply of cell phones because it doesn't change the costs or expectations that cell phone manufacturers face. So the supply curve stays put.

Figure 3-7 shows the effect of the increase in landline price on the market equilibrium for cell phones. Because the new demand curve intersects the supply curve at a different point, the equilibrium price and quantity change. The new equilibrium price is $120, and the new equilibrium quantity is 180 million.

We can summarize this effect in terms of the three questions to ask following a change in a nonprice factor:

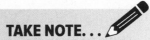

TAKE NOTE...

Remember, when we say that supply or demand increases or decreases, we're referring to a *shift in the entire curve*. A change in quantity demanded or supplied would be a *movement* along the curve.

1. *Does demand increase or decrease?* Yes, the change in the price of landline phone service increases demand for cell phones at every price.

2. *Does supply increase or decrease?* No, the change in the price of landline phone service does not affect any of the nonprice determinants of supply. The supply curve stays where it is.

3. *How does the combination of changes in supply and demand affect equilibrium price and quantity?* The increase in demand shifts the demand curve to the right, pushing the equilibrium to a higher point on the stationary supply curve. The new point at which supply and demand "agree" represents a price of $120 and a quantity of 180 million phones.

Shifts in supply What would happen if a breakthrough in battery technology enabled cell phone manufacturers to construct phones with the same battery life for less money? Once again, asking *How will others respond?* helps us predict the market response. We can see that the new

---

FIGURE 3-7

Shift in the demand for cell phones

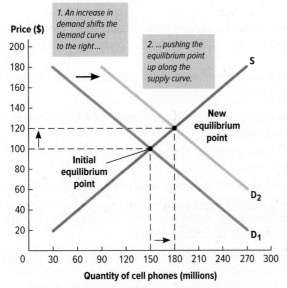

When an external factor increases the demand for cell phones at all prices, the demand curve shifts to the right. This increase in demand results in a new equilibrium point. Consumers purchase more cell phones at a higher price.

FIGURE 3-8

Shift in the supply of cell phones

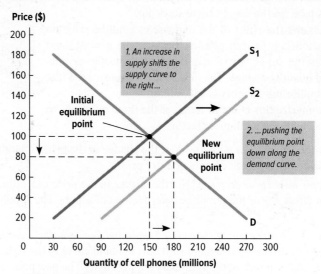

When an external factor affects the supply of cell phones at all prices, the supply curve shifts. In this example, supply increases and the market reaches a new equilibrium point. Consumers purchase more phones at a lower price.

technology does not have much impact on demand: Customers probably have no idea how much the batteries in their phones cost to make, nor will they care as long as battery life stays the same. However, cheaper batteries definitely decrease production costs, increasing the number of phones manufacturers are willing to supply at any given price. So the demand curve stays where it is, and the supply curve shifts to the right.

Figure 3-8 shows the shift in supply and the new equilibrium point. The new supply curve intersects the demand curve at a new equilibrium point, representing a price of $80 and a quantity of 180 million phones.

Once again, we can analyze the effect of the change in battery technology on the market for cell phones in three steps:

1. *Does demand increase or decrease?* No, the nonprice determinants of demand are not affected by battery technology.

2. *Does supply increase or decrease?* Yes, supply increases because the new battery technology lowers production costs.

3. *How does the combination of changes in supply and demand affect equilibrium price and quantity?* The increase in supply shifts the supply curve to the right, pushing the equilibrium to a lower point on the stationary demand curve. The new equilibrium price and quantity are $80 and 180 million phones.

Table 3-4 summarizes the effect of some other changes in demand or supply on the equilibrium price and quantity.

Shifts in both demand and supply   In our discussion so far, we've covered examples in which only demand or supply shifted. However, it's possible that factors that shift demand and supply in the market for cell phones could coincidentally happen at the same time. For example, an increase in landline cost (a demand factor) could occur simultaneously with an improvement

TABLE 3-4

Effect of changes in demand or supply on the equilibrium price and quantity

Example of change in demand or supply	Effect on equilibrium price and quantity	Shift in curve
A successful "Buy American" advertising campaign increases the demand for Fords.	The demand curve shifts to the right. The equilibrium price and quantity increase.	
An outbreak of *E. coli* reduces the demand for spinach.	The demand curve shifts to the left. The equilibrium price and quantity decrease.	
The use of robots decreases production costs.	The supply curve shifts to the right. The equilibrium price decreases and the equilibrium quantity increases.	
An increase in the minimum wage increases labor costs.	The supply curve shifts to the left. The equilibrium price increases and the equilibrium quantity decreases.	

in battery technology (a supply factor). It's also possible that a single change could affect both supply and demand.

For instance, suppose that in addition to reducing the cost of production, the new battery technology makes cell phone batteries last longer. We already know that cheaper batteries will increase supply. As we saw before with increases in supply, price decreases while the quantity increases. Asking *how consumers will respond* allows us to see that the improvement in battery life will also increase demand: Longer-lasting batteries will make a cell phone more valuable to consumers at any given price. As a result, both the demand curve and the supply curve shift to the right. Panels A and B of Figure 3-9 both show that the effect of a double change is a new equilibrium point at a higher price and a higher quantity.

Even without looking at a graph, we could have predicted that in this case the equilibrium *quantity* would rise. Increases in demand and increases in supply both independently lead to a higher equilibrium quantity—and the combination will certainly do so as well.

Without more information, however, we cannot predict the change in equilibrium *price*. Holding all else equal, an increase in demand leads to an increase in price, but an increase in supply leads to a decrease in price. To find the net effect on equilibrium price, we would have to know whether the shift in demand outweighs the shift in supply shown in panel A of Figure 3-9, or vice versa, which is shown in panel B.

FIGURE 3-9

Shifts in both demand and supply

An increase in supply and demand shifts both curves to the right, resulting in a higher quantity traded. However, the direction of the price shift depends on whether supply or demand increases more.

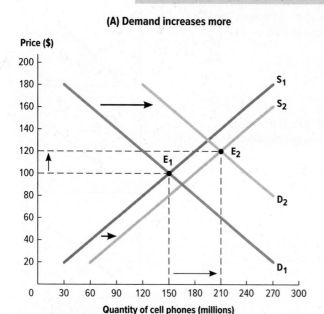

(A) Demand increases more

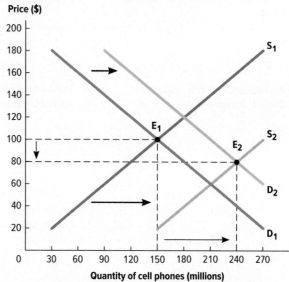

(B) Supply increases more

Sometimes, supply and demand shift together. In this example, both curves shift to the right, but demand increases more. At the new equilibrium point, E₂, consumers purchase more cell phones at a higher price.

Sometimes, supply and demand shift together. In this example, both curves shift to the right, but supply increases more. At the new equilibrium point, E₂, consumers purchase more cell phones at a lower price.

We can state this idea more generally: When supply and demand shift together, it is possible to predict *either* the direction of the change in quantity *or* the direction of the change in price without knowing how much the curves shift. Table 3-5 shows some rules you can use to predict the outcome of these shifts in supply and demand. These rules are:

- When supply and demand shift in the *same* direction, we can predict the direction of the change in quantity but not the direction of the change in price.
- When supply and demand shift in *opposite* directions, the change in price is predictable, but not the change in quantity.

Thinking about the intuition behind these rules may help you to remember them. Any time you are considering a situation in which supply and demand shift at the same time, ask yourself,

TABLE 3-5

Predicting changes in price and quantity when supply and demand change simultaneously

Supply change	Demand change	Price change	Quantity change
Decrease	Decrease	?	↓
Decrease	Increase	↑	?
Increase	Increase	?	↑
Increase	Decrease	↓	?

"What do buyers and sellers agree on?" For instance, when both supply and demand increase, buyers and sellers "agree" that at any given price, the quantity they are willing to exchange is higher. The reverse is true when both supply and demand decrease: Buyers and sellers agree that at a given price, the quantity they are willing to exchange is lower.

Applying this reasoning to opposite shifts in supply and demand—when one increases but the other decreases—is trickier. To find out what buyers and sellers "agree" on, try rephrasing what it means for demand to increase. One way to say it is that consumers are willing to buy a *higher* quantity at the *same* price. Another way to say it is that consumers are willing to pay a *higher* price to buy the *same* quantity. So, when demand increases and supply decreases, buyers are willing to pay more for the same quantity; also, sellers are willing to supply the same quantity only if they receive a higher price. In other words, they can "agree" on a higher price at any given quantity. We can therefore predict that the equilibrium price will increase.

The opposite is true when demand decreases and supply increases. Buyers are willing to buy the same quantity as before only if the price is lower, and sellers are willing to supply the same quantity at a lower price. Because the two groups can "agree" on a lower price at any given quantity, we can predict that the price will decrease.

Of course, you can always work out the effect of simultaneous shifts in demand and supply by working through the three questions described in the previous section. Draw the shifts in each curve on a graph, as is done in two cases in panels A and B of Figure 3-9, and find the new equilibrium.

Before you finish this chapter, read the Economics in Action box "Give a man a fish" for some information about how cell phones affected supply and demand in one developing country.

Give a man a fish
Economics in Action

Cell phones can do many things: They can help you find the perfect restaurant, get directions, make new friends, or even manage your money. What if they could also help markets operate more efficiently?

That's what economist Robert Jensen found when he studied the market for fish in Kerala, a state on India's southern coast. Kerala is famous for its palm-lined beaches, and, not surprisingly, fishing is an important economic activity.

Initially, Jensen noticed that prices varied widely across different markets along the coast. Like most goods, these prices were governed by the laws of supply and demand. For example, if the fishing boats from one town had a great day and brought in huge hauls of fish, fish prices would plummet in that town. On the other hand, a special holiday in one town could inspire people to buy more fish, jacking up the price.

This variance in price created quite a problem for fishermen. Without information about the prices in other markets along the coast, fishermen had no way of knowing if it would be worth the time and extra fuel to check on prices somewhere else. The result was that fishermen usually sold at the going rate (if they could find buyers) in their home port, regardless of the price. On days of really bad luck, they would have to throw away fish because they were not be able to find a buyer at any price.

Jensen found that the fishermen solved this problem once cell phone service was introduced. While out on the ocean fishing, they could communicate with one another, and with people on land, and were able to find out where their catches would be most profitable that day. They used that information to travel to the right town to sell their fish. Supply began to better match the demand in each town, and prices became more uniform across towns.

(continued)

Access to the right information allowed the market for fish to reach an efficient equilibrium. Sellers earned an average of 8 percent more in profits (due to fewer fish being thrown away), and buyers paid an average of 4 percent less for their fish. Fishermen increased their incomes, and consumers stretched their incomes further.

As the saying goes, "Give a man a fish and he will eat for a day. Teach a man to fish and he will eat for a lifetime." To this wisdom, we might add, "Give people cell phones, and they might earn an 8 percent increase in profits."

Source: R. Jensen, "Give a Man a Fish, " *The Quarterly Journal of Economics* 122, no. 3 (2007).

✓ TEST YOURSELF

☐ What is the market equilibrium? **[LO 3.6]**

☐ What happens to the equilibrium price and quantity if the supply curve shifts right but the demand curve stays put? **[LO 3.7]**

Conclusion

By the time you reach the end of this course, you'll be quite familiar with the words *supply* and *demand*. We take our time on this subject for good reason: An understanding of supply and demand is the foundation of economic problem solving. You'll be hard-pressed to make wise economic choices without it.

Although markets are not always perfectly competitive, you may be surprised at how accurately many real-world phenomena can be described using the simple rules of supply and demand. In the next chapters we'll use these rules to explain how consumers and producers respond to price changes and government policies.

Key Terms

market economy, p. 50

market, p. 50

competitive market, p. 50

price taker, p. 51

standardized good, p. 51

transaction costs, p. 51

quantity demanded, p. 52

law of demand, p. 52

demand schedule, p. 53

demand curve, p. 53

substitutes, p. 55

complements, p. 55

normal goods, p. 56

inferior goods, p. 56

quantity supplied, p. 59

law of supply, p. 59

supply schedule, p. 60

supply curve, p. 60

equilibrium, p. 63

equilibrium price, p. 63

equilibrium quantity, p. 63

surplus (excess supply), p. 64

shortage (excess demand), p. 65

Summary

LO 3.1 Identify the defining characteristics of a competitive market.

A market is the group of buyers and sellers who trade a particular good or service. In competitive markets, a large number of buyers and sellers trade standardized goods and services. They have full information about the goods, and there is no cost to participate in exchanges in the market. Participants in competitive markets are called price takers because they can't affect the prevailing price for a good.

LO 3.2 Draw a demand curve, and describe the external factors that determine demand.

A demand curve is a graph that shows the quantities of a particular good or service that consumers will demand at various prices. It also shows consumers' highest willingness to pay for a given quantity. The law of demand states that for almost all goods, the quantity demanded increases as the price decreases. This relationship results in a downward-sloping demand curve.

Several nonprice factors contribute to consumers' demand for a good at a given price: Consumer preferences, the prices of related goods, incomes, and expectations about the future all affect demand. On a marketwide level, the number of buyers also can increase or decrease total demand. When one of these underlying factors changes, the demand curve will shift to the left or the right.

LO 3.3 Distinguish between a shift in and a movement along the demand curve.

When one of the nonprice factors that drives demand changes, the entire curve *shifts* to the left or the right. With this shift, the quantity demanded at any given price changes. When demand increases, the curve shifts to the right; when demand decreases, it shifts to the left.

When the nonprice determinants of demand stay the same, a change in the price of a good leads to a *movement along* the curve, rather than a shift in the curve.

LO 3.4 Draw a supply curve and describe the external factors that determine supply.

A supply curve is a graph that shows the quantities of a particular good or service that producers will supply at various prices. It shows the minimum price producers must receive to supply any given quantity. The law of supply states that the quantity supplied increases as the price increases, resulting in an upward-sloping supply curve.

Several nonprice factors determine the supply of a good at any given price: They include the prices of related goods, technology, prices of inputs, expectations about the future, and the number of sellers in the market. If one of these underlying factors changes, the supply curve will shift to the left or the right.

LO 3.5 Distinguish between a shift in and a movement along the supply curve.

Just as with demand, a change in the nonprice determinants of supply will cause the entire supply curve to shift to the left or the right. As a result, the quantity supplied is higher or lower at any given price than it was before. When supply increases, the curve shifts to the right; when supply decreases, it shifts to the left.

A shift in the supply curve differs from movement along the supply curve. A movement along the curve happens when the price of a good increases but the nonprice determinants of supply stay the same.

LO 3.6 Explain how supply and demand interact to drive markets to equilibrium.

When a market is in equilibrium, the quantity supplied equals the quantity demanded. The incentives that individual buyers and sellers face drive a competitive market toward equilibrium. If the prevailing price is too high, a surplus will result, and sellers will lower their prices to get rid of the excess supply. If the prevailing price is too low, a shortage will result, and buyers will bid up the price until the excess demand disappears.

LO 3.7 Evaluate the effect of changes in supply and demand on the equilibrium price and quantity.

When one or more of the underlying factors that determine supply or demand change, one or both curves will shift, leading to a new market equilibrium price and quantity.

To calculate the change in the equilibrium price and quantity, you must first determine whether a change affects demand, and, if so, in which direction the curve will shift. Then you must determine whether the change also affects supply, and, if so, in which direction that curve will shift. Finally, you must determine the new equilibrium point where the two curves intersect.

Review Questions

1. Think about a competitive market in which you participate regularly. For each of the characteristics of a competitive market, explain how your market meets these requirements. **[LO 3.1]**

2. Think about a noncompetitive market in which you participate regularly. Explain which characteristic(s) of competitive markets your market does not meet. **[LO 3.1]**

3. Explain why a demand curve slopes downward. **[LO 3.2]**

4. In each of the following examples, name the factor that affects demand and describe its impact on your demand for a new cell phone. **[LO 3.2]**
   a. You hear a rumor that a new and improved model of the phone you want is coming out next year.
   b. Your grandparents give you $500.
   c. A cellular network announces a holiday sale on a data package that includes the purchase of a new smartphone.
   d. A friend tells you how great his new phone is and suggests that you get one, too.

5. Consider the following events:
   a. The price of cell phones goes down by 25 percent during a sale.
   b. You get a 25 percent raise at your job.

Which event represents a shift in the demand curve? Which represents a movement along the curve? What is the difference? **[LO 3.3]**

6. What is the difference between a change in demand and a change in quantity demanded? **[LO 3.3]**

7. Explain why a supply curve slopes upward. **[LO 3.4]**

8. In each of the following examples, name the factor that affects supply and describe its impact on the supply of cell phones. **[LO 3.4]**

    a. Economic forecasts suggest that the demand for cell phones will increase in the future.

    b. The price of plastic goes up.

    c. A new screen technology reduces the cost of making cell phones.

9. Consider the following events:

    a. A fruitworm infestation ruins a large number of apple orchards in Washington state.

    b. Demand for apples goes down, causing the price to fall.

    Which event represents a shift in the supply curve? Which represents a movement along the curve? What is the difference? **[LO 3.5]**

10. What is the difference between a change in supply and a change in quantity supplied? **[LO 3.5]**

11. What is the relationship between supply and demand when a market is in equilibrium? Explain how the incentives facing cell phone companies and consumers cause the market for cell phones to reach equilibrium. **[LO 3.6]**

12. Explain why the equilibrium price is often called the market-clearing price. **[LO 3.6]**

13. Suppose an economic boom causes incomes to increase. Explain what will happen to the demand and supply of phones, and predict the direction of the change in the equilibrium price and quantity. **[LO 3.7]**

14. Suppose an economic boom drives up wages for the sales representatives who work for cell phone companies. Explain what will happen to the demand and supply of phones, and predict the direction of the change in the equilibrium price and quantity. **[LO 3.7]**

15. Suppose an economic boom causes incomes to increase and at the same time drives up wages for the sales representatives who work for cell phone companies. Explain what will happen to the demand for and supply of phones and predict the direction of the change in the equilibrium price and quantity. **[LO 3.7]**

Problems and Applications

1. Consider shopping for cucumbers in a farmers' market. For each statement below, note which characteristic of competitive markets the statement describes. *Choose from:* standardized good, full information, no transaction costs, and participants are price takers. **[LO 3.1]**

    a. All of the farmers have their prices posted prominently in front of their stalls.

    b. Cucumbers are the same price at each stall.

    c. There is no difficulty moving around between stalls as you shop and choosing between farmers.

    d. You and the other customers all seem indifferent about which cucumbers to buy.

2. Suppose two artists are selling paintings for the same price in adjacent booths at an art fair. By the end of the day, one artist has nearly sold out of her paintings while the other artist has sold nothing. Which characteristic of competitive markets has not been met and best explains this outcome? **[LO 3.1]**

    a. Standardized good.

    b. Full information.

    c. No transaction costs.

    d. Participants are price takers.

3. Using the demand schedule in Table 3P-1, draw the daily demand curve for slices of pizza in a college town. **[LO 3.2]**

TABLE 3P-1

Price ($)	Quantity demanded (slices)
0.00	350
0.50	300
1.00	250
1.50	200
2.00	150
2.50	100
3.00	50
3.50	0

4. Consider the market for cars. Which determinant of demand is affected by each of the following events? *Choose from:* consumer preferences, prices of related goods, incomes, expectations, and the number of buyers. **[LO 3.2]**

    a. Environmentalists launch a successful One Family, One Car campaign.

    b. A baby boom occurred 16 years ago.

    c. Layoffs increase as the economy sheds millions of jobs.

d. An oil shortage causes the price of gasoline to soar.

e. The government offers tax rebates in return for the purchase of commuter rail tickets.

f. The government announces a massive plan to bail out the auto industry and subsidize production costs.

5. If a decrease in the price of laptops causes the demand for tablets to increase, are laptops and tablets substitutes or complements? **[LO 3.2]**

6. If rising incomes cause the demand for beer to decrease, is beer a normal or inferior good? **[LO 3.2]**

7. Consider the market for corn. Say whether each of the following events will cause a shift in the demand curve or a movement along the curve. If it will cause a shift, specify the direction. **[LO 3.3]**

   a. A drought hits corn-growing regions, cutting the supply of corn.

   b. The government announces a new subsidy for biofuels made from corn.

   c. A global recession reduces the incomes of consumers in poor countries, who rely on corn as a staple food.

   d. A new hybrid variety of corn seed causes a 15 percent increase in the yield of corn per acre.

   e. An advertising campaign by the beef producers' association highlights the health benefits of corn-fed beef.

8. The demand curve in Figure 3P-1 shows the monthly market for sweaters at a local clothing store. For each of the following events, draw the new outcome. **[LO 3.3]**

FIGURE 3P-1

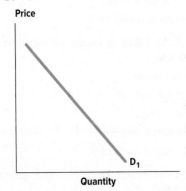

Price

D₁

Quantity

   a. Sweaters fall out of fashion.

   b. There is a shortage of wool.

   c. The winter is particularly long and cold this year.

   d. Sweater vendors offer a sale.

9. Using the supply schedule found in Table 3P-2, draw the daily supply curve for slices of pizza in a college town. **[LO 3.4]**

TABLE 3P-2

Price ($)	Quantity supplied (slices)
0.00	0
0.50	50
1.00	100
1.50	150
2.00	200
2.50	250
3.00	300
3.50	350

10. Consider the market for cars. Which determinant of supply is affected by each of the following events? *Choose from:* prices of related goods, technology, prices of inputs, expectations, and the number of sellers in the market. **[LO 3.4]**

    a. A steel tariff increases the price of steel.

    b. Improvements in robotics increase efficiency and reduce costs.

    c. Factories close because of an economic downturn.

    d. The government announces a plan to offer tax rebates for the purchase of commuter rail tickets.

    e. The price of trucks falls, so factories produce more cars.

    f. The government announces that it will dramatically rewrite efficiency standards, making it much harder for automakers to produce their cars.

11. Consider the market for corn. Say whether each of the following events will cause a shift in the supply curve or a movement along the curve. If it will cause a shift, specify the direction. **[LO 3.5]**

    a. A drought hits corn-growing regions.

    b. The government announces a new subsidy for biofuels made from corn.

    c. A global recession reduces the incomes of consumers in poor countries, who rely on corn as a staple food.

    d. A new hybrid variety of corn seed causes a 15 percent increase in the yield of corn per acre.

    e. An advertising campaign by the beef producers' association highlights the health benefits of corn-fed beef.

12. The supply curve in Figure 3P-2 shows the monthly market for sweaters at a local craft market. For each of the following events, draw the new outcome. [LO 3.5]

FIGURE 3P-2

a. The price of wool increases.
b. Demand for sweaters decreases.
c. A particularly cold winter is expected to begin next month.
d. Demand for sweaters increases.

13. Refer to the demand and supply schedule shown in Table 3P-3. [LO 3.6]

TABLE 3P-3

Price ($)	Quantity demanded (slices)	Quantity supplied (slices)
0.00	350	0
0.50	300	50
1.00	250	100
1.50	200	150
2.00	150	200
2.50	100	250
3.00	50	300
3.50	0	350

a. If pizza parlors charge $3.50 per slice, will there be excess supply or excess demand? What is the amount of excess supply or excess demand at that price?

b. If pizza parlors charge $1.00 per slice, will there be excess supply or excess demand? What is the amount of excess supply or excess demand at that price?

c. What are the equilibrium price and quantity in this market?

The graph in Figure 3P-3 shows the weekly market for pizzas in a small town. Use this graph to answer Problems 14–16.

FIGURE 3P-3

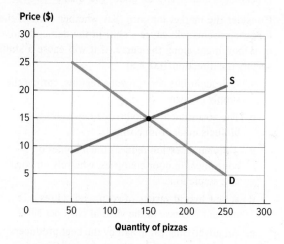

14. Which of the following events will occur at a price of $20? [LO 3.6]
    a. Equilibrium.
    b. Excess demand.
    c. Excess supply.
    d. No pizzas supplied.
    e. No pizzas demanded.

15. Which of the following events will occur at a price of $10? [LO 3.6]
    a. Equilibrium.
    b. Excess demand.
    c. Excess supply.
    d. No pizzas supplied.
    e. No pizzas demanded.

16. What are the equilibrium price and quantity of pizzas? [LO 3.6]

17. The graph in Figure 3P-4 shows supply and demand in the market for automobiles. For each of the following events, draw the new market outcome and say whether the equilibrium price and quantity will increase or decrease. **[LO 3.7]**

FIGURE 3P-4

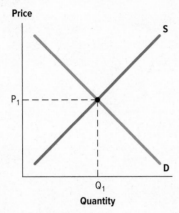

a. Environmentalists launch a successful One Family, One Car campaign.
b. A steel tariff increases the price of steel.
c. A baby boom occurred 16 years ago.

d. An oil shortage causes the price of gasoline to soar.
e. Improvements in robotics increase efficiency and reduce costs.
f. The government offers a tax rebate for the purchase of commuter rail tickets.

18. Say whether each of the following changes will increase or decrease the equilibrium price and quantity, or whether the effect cannot be predicted. **[LO 3.7]**
    a. Demand increases; supply remains constant.
    b. Supply increases; demand remains constant.
    c. Demand decreases; supply remains constant.
    d. Supply decreases; demand remains constant.
    e. Demand increases; supply increases.
    f. Demand decreases; supply decreases.
    g. Demand increases; supply decreases.
    h. Demand decreases; supply increases.

Endnotes

1. http://www.gsmamobileeconomy.com/GSMA_Global_Mobile_Economy_Report_2015.pdf
2. http://www.ngrguardiannews.com/2015/06/africas-mobile-phone-penetration-now-67/

Math Essentials: Working with Linear Equations

Relationships between variables can be represented with algebraic equations, as well as graphs and tables. You should be comfortable moving among all three representations. We addressed graphs in Appendix A, "Math Essentials: Understanding Graphs and Slope"; if you didn't read it then, you might want to do so now.

Interpreting the Equation of a Line

If the relationship between two variables is linear, it can be represented by the equation for a line, which is commonly written as:

EQUATION B-1 $$y = mx + b$$

In this form, called the *slope intercept form*, m is the slope of the line and b is the y-intercept.

All linear equations provide information about the slope and y-intercept of the line. From our discussion in Appendix A, "Math Essentials: Understanding Graphs and Slope," we already know that slope is the ratio of vertical distance (change in y) to horizontal distance (change in x). So what does the y-intercept tell us? It is the point at which the line crosses the y-axis. Put another way, it is the value of y when x is 0. Knowing these values is useful in turning an equation into a graph. Also, as we'll see, they can allow us to get information about the real economic relationship being represented without even having to graph it.

Although you might see the equation for a line rearranged in several different forms, just remember that if y is on the left-hand side of the equation, whatever number is multiplying x (known as the *coefficient of x*) is your slope. If you don't see a number in front of x, the slope is 1. The number being added to or subtracted from a multiple of x is a constant that represents the y-intercept. If you don't see this number, you know that the y-intercept is zero. Take a look at a few examples in Table B-1.

LEARNING OBJECTIVES

LO B.1 Use linear equations to interpret the equation of a line.

LO B.2 Use linear equations to explain shifts and pivots.

LO B.3 Use linear equations to solve for equilibrium.

LO B.1 Use linear equations to interpret the equation of a line.

Equation	Slope	y-intercept
$y = 6x + 4$	6	4
$y = -x - 2$	-1	-2
$y = 10 - 2x$	-2	10
$y = -4x$	-4	0

Turning a graph into an equation

To see how to translate a graph into an algebraic equation, look at Figure B-1. What is the equation that represents this relationship? To derive this equation, we need to find the values of the slope and the y-intercept. We can calculate the slope at any point along the line:

$$\text{Slope} = \frac{\Delta y}{\Delta x} = \frac{(y_2 - y_1)}{(x_2 - x_1)}$$

$$= \frac{(6 - 5)}{(4 - 2)} = \frac{1}{2} = 0.5$$

By looking at the graph to see where the line intersects the y-axis, we can tell that the y-intercept is 4. Therefore, if we write the equation in the form $y = mx + b$, we get $y = 0.5x + 4$. Our table, graph, and equation all give us the same information about the relationship between x and y.

Turning an equation into a graph

Let's work in the opposite direction now, starting with an equation and seeing what information it gives us. The following equation takes the form $y = mx + b$, with P and Q substituted for y and x, respectively.

$$P = -5Q + 25$$

We know from looking at this equation that it represents a line with a slope of -5 and a y-intercept of 25. Suppose that we know this equation represents supply or demand, but we're not sure which. How can we tell whether this is a demand equation or a supply equation? Easy. The slope is negative. We don't need a graph to tell us that the relationship between P and Q is negative and the line will be downward-sloping. Therefore, the equation must represent demand rather than supply.

Because the y-intercept in our equation is 25, we know that the demand curve will cross the y-axis at 25. This tells us that when price is 25, quantity demanded is 0. In order for consumers to demand a positive quantity, price must be lower than 25.

If we need to know more about the relationship represented by the equation, we can graph the demand curve. Since we know that 25 is the y-intercept, we can use the point $(0,25)$ to begin plotting our graph as shown in Figure B-2.

It takes only two points to define a line, and we already have one from the y-intercept. To find a second point, we can plug in any value of Q and solve for the corresponding P (or vice versa). For example, if we let $Q = 2$ and solve for P, we get:

$$P = -5(2) + 25$$
$$P = -10 + 25$$
$$P = 15$$

We can now plot the point $(2,15)$ and connect it to the y-intercept at $(0,25)$.

FIGURE B-1

Translating a graph into an algebraic equation

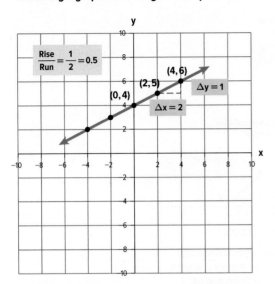

By using information provided on a graph, you can easily construct an equation of the line in the form $y = mx + b$. The slope, m, is calculated by taking the rise of a line over its run. The value of the y-intercept provides the b part of the equation.

FIGURE B-2

Translating an algebraic equation into a graph

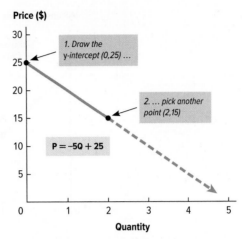

The first step in graphing the equation of a line in the form $y = mx + b$ is to plot the y intercept, given by b. Then pick another point by choosing any value of x or y, and solving the equation for the other variable to get an ordered pair that represents another point on the line. Connecting these two points gives the line.

Rather than plugging in random points, though, it is often useful to know the x-intercept as well as the y-intercept. On a demand curve, this will tell us what quantity is demanded when price is 0. To find this intercept, we can let P = 0 and solve for Q:

$$0 = -5Q + 25$$
$$-25 = -5Q$$
$$5 = Q$$

We can now plot the point (5,0) and connect it to (0,25) to graph the demand curve.

Finding intercepts is useful for interpreting other types of graphs as well. In a production possibilities frontier, the intercepts tell you how much of one good will be produced if all resources are used to produce that good and none are used to produce the other good. In the production possibilities frontier shown in Figure B-3, for example, we can find the y-intercept to see that by devoting all workers to making shirts and none to producing wheat, 2 million T-shirts can be produced. Alternatively, we can find the x-intercept to see that if all workers grow wheat and none make shirts, 4 million bushels of wheat can be produced.

We saw in Chapter 2, "Specialization and Exchange," that the slope of the frontier represents the trade-off between producing two goods. We can use our intercepts as the two points we need to calculate the slope.

$$\text{Slope} = \frac{\Delta y}{\Delta x} = \frac{(4 \text{ million} - 0)}{(0 - 2 \text{ million})} = \frac{4}{-2} = -2$$

You know that the slope of the frontier will be negative because it represents a trade-off: You can't make more wheat without giving up some shirts. Because an increase in wheat means a decrease in shirts, the two variables move in opposite directions and have a negative

Using intercepts to interpret a production possibilities frontier

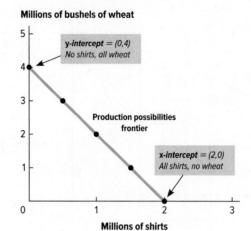

Millions of bushels of wheat

y-intercept = (0,4)
No shirts, all wheat

Production possibilities frontier

x-intercept = (2,0)
All shirts, no wheat

Millions of shirts

The intercepts of a production possibilities frontier give the maximum amount of a good a country can produce by dedicating all resources in the economy to the production of that good. In this case, with all workers dedicated to the production of one good or the other, the economy can make either 4 million bushels of wheat or 2 million shirts.

relationship. This frontier has a constant slope, which means that the trade-off between the two goods—which we can also think of as the opportunity cost of producing shirts in terms of wheat—is also constant.

Equations with *x* and *y* reversed

Thus far, we have represented demand and supply equations with P (or *y*) isolated on the left side of the equation. For example, our demand equation was given as P = −5Q + 25. You may find, however, that in some places, demand and supply equations are given with Q (or *x*) isolated on the left side of the equation instead.

When you see this, you cannot read the equation as giving you the slope and the *y*-intercept. Instead, when an equation is in this form, you have the inverse of slope and the *x*-intercept.

Look at our demand equation again. If we rearrange the equation to solve for Q, we have an equation of the form *x* = *ny* + *a*:

$$P = -5Q + 25$$

$$P - 25 = -5Q$$

$$-\frac{1}{5}P + 5 = Q \quad \text{or} \quad Q = -\frac{1}{5}P + 5$$

We know that the starting equation represents the same underlying relationship as the final equation. For instance, we know that our slope is −5, but in the rearranged form where we have solved for Q, the coefficient multiplying P is the inverse of slope, or $-\frac{1}{5}$. We can generalize this observation to say that when we have an equation of the form *x* = *ny* + a, $n = \frac{1}{m}$, where *m* is the slope of the line from the same equation expressed in the form *y* = *mx* + *b*. We also know that 25 is the

FIGURE B-4

Same line, different equation forms

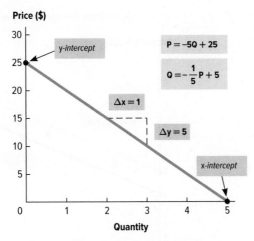

Regardless of whether you solve an equation
for P or Q, the resulting line is the same.

y-intercept. But in our rearranged form, a represents the x-intercept, which is 5. The graph in Figure B-4 shows that these two equations represent different aspects of the same line.

Keep in mind that $P = -5Q + 25$ is the same equation as $Q = -\frac{1}{5}P + 5$; we have simply rearranged it to solve for Q instead of P.

Shifts and Pivots

Imagine that your campus cafeteria has a deli with a salad bar and that the price of a salad depends on the number of ingredients you add to it. This relationship is represented by the following equation:

$$y = 0.5x + 4$$

where

y = total price of the salad

x = number of added ingredients

Because our variables are the price of a salad and the number of ingredients, negative quantities do not make sense: You can't have negative carrots in your salad, and we doubt that the cafeteria is paying you to buy salads. Therefore, we can isolate the graph of this equation to the first quadrant, as shown in panel A of Figure B-5.

Our y-intercept of 4 represents the price of a salad if you add zero ingredients. In other words, a plain bowl of lettuce costs $4. The slope of 0.5 represents the cost of adding ingredients to the salad. Each additional ingredient costs 50 cents. The fact that (2,5) is a point along the line shows that the price of a salad with two added ingredients is $5.

How much is a salad with six added ingredients?

$$y = 0.5(6) + 4$$
$$y = 3 + 4$$
$$y = 7$$

A salad with six added ingredients is $7, and (6,7) is another point on the graph.

FIGURE B-5

Shifting a line to change the intercept

(A) Restrict the graph to Quadrant I

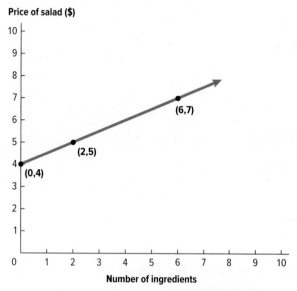

(B) Shift the line upward by moving the intercept

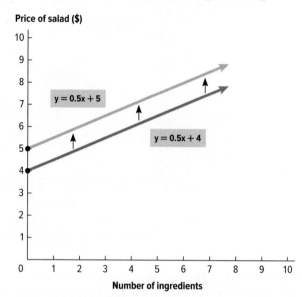

In order to easily change the intercept, first restrict the line to values in the first quadrant. This will clearly show the *y*-intercept of the line.

Once the *y*-intercept is clear, you can shift the line to the new intercept indicated by the equation of the line.

Now, let's see what happens to our graph when the baseline price of a bowl of lettuce without additional ingredients increases to $5. This baseline price is represented by the *y*-intercept, which changes from 4 to 5. The slope of the graph does not change because each additional ingredient still costs 50 cents.

Thus, our equation changes to $y = 0.5x + 5$. Rather than regraphing this new question from scratch, we can simply *shift* the original line to account for the change in the *y*-intercept, as shown in panel B of Figure B-5.

Suppose, instead, that the price of lettuce remains at $4, but the price of additional ingredients increases to $1 each. How will this change the graph and equation?

If the price of lettuce with zero additional ingredients remains at $4, the *y*-intercept will also stay the same. However, the slope will change, increasing from 50 cents to $1. Figure B-6 shows that this change of slope will *pivot* the line in our graph.

Our equation changes as well. This time, we substitute 1 in place of 0.5 for the slope. Thus, $y = x + 4$. (Remember that no coefficient on *x* indicates that the slope is 1.)

What happens if the baseline price of lettuce goes up to $5 *and* the price of toppings goes up to $1? We have to both *shift and pivot* the line to represent the change in the intercept and the slope. (Sounds like a fitness routine, doesn't it?) Figure B-7 shows both changes.

You will need to shift and pivot lines in many places throughout this book to represent changes in the relationship between two variables. For instance, we saw in Chapter 3, "Markets," that when a nonprice determinant of demand changes, you need to *shift* the demand curve to show that people demand a higher or lower quantity of a good at any given price. When consumers

FIGURE B-6

Pivoting a line to change the slope

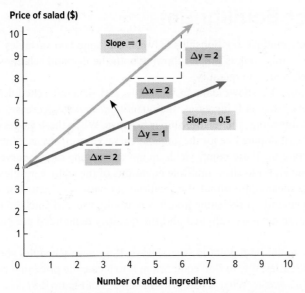

Changes in slope will pivot the equation of a line. Increases
in slope will rotate the line upward; decreases in slope will
rotate the line downward.

FIGURE B-7

Shift and pivot

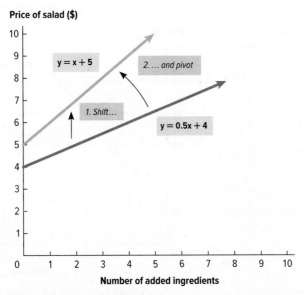

In order to handle a change in slope and intercept, you first
shift the line to the new intercept and then pivot the line to
reflect the new slope.

become more or less sensitive to changes in price, you need to *pivot* the demand curve to represent a change in slope.

Solving for Equilibrium

LO B.3 Use linear equations to solve for equilibrium.

One graph can show multiple relationships between the same two variables. The most frequent case we encounter in this book is graphs showing both the demand relationship and the supply relationship between price and quantity.

Panel A of Figure B-8 shows data from supply and demand schedules. Remember from Chapter 3, "Markets," that as P increases, the quantity *demanded* decreases. Since P and Q are moving in opposite directions, the relationship is negative. When these values are plotted in panel B, we have a downward-sloping line for the demand curve. Conversely, as P increases, the quantity *supplied* increases. Plotting these points yields an upward-sloping supply curve.

When we use one graph to show multiple equations of the same variables, we do so in order to show something meaningful about the relationship between them. For instance, when we show supply and demand on the same graph, we usually want to find the equilibrium point—the point at which the quantity supplied and the quantity demanded are equal to one another at the same price.

We can find the equilibrium point in several ways. If we have schedules showing both demand and supply data, the easiest way to find equilibrium is to locate the price that corresponds to *equal supply and demand quantities*. What is that price in panel A of Figure B-8? At a price of 80, Q is 60 in the demand schedule as well as in the supply schedule.

We can also find the equilibrium point easily by looking at a graph showing both supply and demand. The one-and-only point where the two lines intersect is the equilibrium.

FIGURE B-8

Graphing the supply and demand schedules

(A) Supply and demand schedules

Price ($)	Q$_{demand}$	Q$_{supply}$
20	180	0
30	160	10
40	140	20
50	120	30
80	60	60
90	40	70
100	20	80
110	0	90

The supply and demand schedules show the quantities demanded and supplied for a given price.

(B) Graphing the schedules

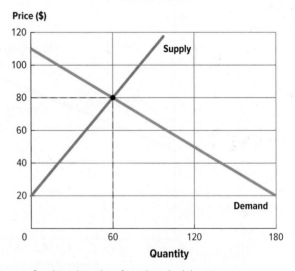

Graphing the values from the schedules gives a downward-sloping demand curve and an upward-sloping supply curve.

Sometimes, however, it is useful to find equilibrium from equations alone, without having to graph them or to calculate a whole schedule of points by plugging in different prices. Usually you'll want to use this method when you are given equations but no graph or schedule. However, just for practice, let's first derive the supply and demand equations from Figure B-8 and then figure out the equilibrium point.

We want to start by representing supply and demand as equations of the form $y = mx + b$. Let y = price and x = quantity. We need to determine the slope (m) and the y-intercept (b) for each equation.

First, the demand equation: What is the y-intercept? It is the value of y when x is 0. Looking at panel A in Figure B-8, we can see that when Q is zero, P is 110. The y-intercept of the demand equation is 110. Now we need the slope. Because this is a linear relationship and the slope is constant, we can determine the slope using any two points. Let's use the points (180,20) and (160,30).

$$\frac{\Delta y}{\Delta x} = \frac{(P_2 - P_1)}{(Q_2 - Q_1)} = \frac{(20 - 30)}{(180 - 160)} = \frac{-10}{20} = -0.5$$

Thus, our demand equation is: $P = -0.5Q + 110$.

We'll use the same procedure to derive the supply equation. Looking at the supply schedule, we can see that when Q is zero, P is 20. The y-intercept is 20. To determine slope, let's use the points (0,20) and (10,30).

$$\frac{\Delta y}{\Delta x} = \frac{(P_2 - P_1)}{(Q_2 - Q_1)} = \frac{(20 - 30)}{(0 - 10)} = \frac{-10}{-10} = 1$$

Thus, our supply equation is: $P = Q + 20$.

Now that we have our equations, we can use them to solve for equilibrium. Equilibrium represents a point that is on both the demand and supply curves; graphically, it is where the two curves intersect. This means that P on the demand curve must equal P on the supply curve, and the same for Q. Therefore, it makes sense that we find this point by setting the two equations equal to each other.

$$P_D = -0.5Q + 110$$
$$P_S = Q + 20$$
$$P_D = P_S$$

therefore,

$$-0.5Q + 110 = Q + 20$$

This allows us to solve for a numeric value for Q.

$$1.5Q + 20 = 110$$
$$1.5Q = 90$$
$$Q = 60$$

Now that we have a value for Q, we can plug it in either the supply or demand equation to get the value for P. Let's use our supply equation.

$$P = 20 + Q$$
$$P = 20 + 60$$
$$P = 80$$

Solving for equilibrium using the equations gives us the same point we found using the demand and supply schedules: Q = 60 and P = 80 (60,80).

Problems and Applications

1. Use the demand curve in Figure BP-1 to derive a demand equation. **[LO B.1]**

FIGURE BP-1

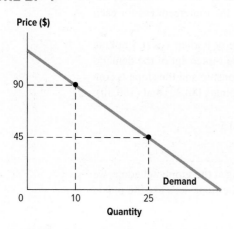

2. Use the demand schedule in Table BP-1 to derive a demand equation. **[LO B.1]**

TABLE BP-1

Price ($)	Quantity
0	320
10	280
20	240
30	200
40	160
50	120
60	80
70	40
80	0

3. Use the supply curve in Figure BP-2 to derive a supply equation. **[LO B.1]**

FIGURE BP-2

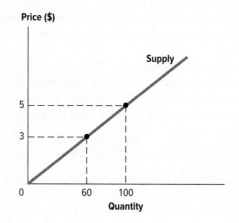

4. Use the supply schedule in Table BP-2 to derive a supply equation. **[LO B.1]**

TABLE BP-2

Price ($)	Quantity
100	0
200	25
300	50
400	75
500	100
600	125

5. Graph the equation $P = 2Q + 3$. Is this a supply curve or a demand curve? **[LO B.1]**

6. Graph the equation $P = -8Q + 10$. Is this a supply curve or a demand curve? **[LO B.1]**

7. Rearrange the equation $Q = 5 - 0.25P$ and sketch the graph. Is this a supply curve or a demand curve? **[LO B.1]**

8. Rearrange the equation $Q = 0.2P$ and sketch the graph. Is this a supply curve or a demand curve? **[LO B.1]**

9. The entrance fee at your local amusement park is $20 for the day. The entrance fee includes all rides except roller coasters. Roller coasters cost an extra $2 per ride. **[LO B.2]**

   a. Write an equation that represents how much money you will spend on rides as a function of the number of rides you go on: S = total spending on rides; Q = the quantity of roller coaster rides.

   b. What is your total spending on rides if you ride 4 roller coasters?

   c. Draw a graph of the relationship between total spending on rides and the number of roller coaster rides.

   d. Redraw the graph from part (c) to show what changes if the entrance fee increases to $25.

   e. Rewrite the equation from part (a) to incorporate the increased entrance fee of $25.

   f. After the entrance fee increases to $25, what is your total spending on rides if you ride 4 roller coasters?

10. Use the following two equations: **[LO B.3]**

    $(1)\ P = 12 - 2Q$

    $(2)\ P = 3 + Q$

    a. Find the equilibrium price and quantity.

    b. Graph the demand and supply equations. Illustrate the equilibrium point.

11. With reference to Table BP-3: **[LO B.3]**

TABLE BP-3

Price ($)	Quantity demanded	Quantity supplied
0	12	0
20	10	4
40	8	8
60	6	12
80	4	16
100	2	20
120	0	24

a. Use the information from the table to create the demand and supply equations.

b. Use your demand and supply equations to solve for equilibrium.

c. Graph supply and demand curves. Illustrate the equilibrium point.

Elasticity

Coffee Becomes Chic

In the 1990s, a coffeehouse craze rippled through middle-class communities in the United States, as a strong economy bolstered sales of high-priced espresso drinks. Soon, Americans were making daily pilgrimages to a place called Starbucks, where a cup of coffee had been transformed into the "Starbucks' experience," complete with soundtrack, mints, and charity-themed water bottles. For 15 years the Starbucks' business model was highly successful. From 1992 through 2007, the company expanded by over 15,000 stores.

When the U.S. economy stumbled in 2008, however, Starbucks's growth rate dropped to an all-time low. Competitors and customers began to ask, "How much is too much for a cup of coffee?" Presumably, Starbucks' executives had asked themselves that very question over the course of more than a decade. Given the company's phenomenal rate of expansion, they must have had the right answer—at least until the economy started having problems.

©amenic181/123RF

How do businesses like Starbucks make pricing decisions? How do they anticipate and react to changing circumstances? We learned in the prior chapter that when price changes, quantity demanded changes. If Starbucks raised the price of its lattes—perhaps due to a coffee supply shortage caused by poor weather in Ethiopia—that change would reduce the quantity demanded by consumers. This chapter introduces the idea of elasticity, which describes *how much* this change in prices will affect consumers.

Like the market for cell phones, the market for gourmet coffee is not perfectly competitive. Managers of a big company like Starbucks have some ability to set prices, and they try to choose prices that will earn the largest profits. They also try to respond to changing market conditions: How much will sales fall if the price of coffee beans drives up the cost of a latte? How much will people decrease their coffee consumption during a recession? How many customers will be lost if competitors like Dunkin' Donuts and McDonald's offer less-expensive coffee? Even in perfectly competitive markets, producers want to predict how their profits will change in response to economic conditions and changes in the market price.

Nonprofit service providers also often need to think about price elasticity. For instance, a nonprofit hospital wants to set the price of care so as to cover costs without driving away too many patients. Similarly, colleges and universities want to cover costs and keep education affordable for students.

The ability to address issues like these is critical for any public or private organization. Understanding how to price a Starbucks' latte requires the same kind of thinking as figuring out whether to raise entrance fees to national parks to cover the costs of maintaining the wilderness. Solving these challenges relies on a tool called *elasticity*, a measure of how much supply and demand will respond to changes in price and income.

LEARNING OBJECTIVES

LO 4.1 Calculate price elasticity of demand using the mid-point method.

LO 4.2 Explain how the determinants of price elasticity of demand affect the degree of elasticity.

LO 4.3 Calculate price elasticity of supply using the mid-point method.

LO 4.4 Explain how the determinants of price elasticity of supply affect the degree of elasticity.

LO 4.5 Calculate cross-price elasticity of demand, and interpret the sign of the elasticity.

LO 4.6 Calculate income elasticity of demand, and interpret the sign of the elasticity.

In this chapter, you will learn how to calculate the effect of a price change on the quantity supplied or demanded. You will become familiar with some rules that businesses and policy-makers follow when they cannot measure elasticity exactly. Using what you know about supply and demand, you will be able to categorize different types of goods by noting whether their elasticities are positive or negative. You will also learn how to use a rough approximation of price elasticity to tell whether raising prices will raise or lower an organization's total revenue.

What Is Elasticity?

If Starbucks raises the price of a latte, we can expect the quantity of lattes demanded to fall. But by how much? Although we saw in Chapter 3, "Markets," that price increases cause the quantity demanded to fall in a competitive market, we have not yet been able to say *how big* that movement will be. That question is the subject of this chapter.

Elasticity is a measure of how much consumers and producers will respond to a change in market conditions. The concept can be applied to supply or demand. Also, it can be used to measure responses to a change in the price of a good, a change in the price of a related good, or a change in income.

The concept of elasticity allows economic decision makers to anticipate *how others will respond* to changes in market conditions. Whether you are a business owner trying to sell cars or a public official trying to set sales taxes, you need to know how much a change in prices will affect consumers' willingness to buy.

There are several measures of elasticity:

- The most commonly used measures of elasticity are *price elasticity of demand* and *price elasticity of supply*. These two concepts describe how much the quantity demanded and the quantity supplied change when the price of a good changes.

elasticity
a measure of how much consumers and producers will respond to a change in market conditions

- The *cross-price elasticity of demand* describes how much the demand curve shifts when the price of another good changes. It tells us how much the quantity of coffee demanded changes, for example, when the price of tea increases.
- Another helpful measure, *income elasticity of demand*, measures how much the demand curve shifts when consumers' incomes change.

We'll examine these four elasticity concepts in this chapter. Let's begin with price elasticity of demand.

Price Elasticity of Demand

Price elasticity of demand describes the size of the change in the quantity demanded of a good or service when its price changes. We showed in Chapter 3, "Markets" that quantity demanded generally decreases when the price increases, but so far we have not been able to say *how much* it decreases. Price elasticity of demand fills this gap in our understanding of supply and demand.

Another way to think about price elasticity of demand is as a measure of consumers' sensitivity to price changes. Sensitivity to price changes is measured as more or less elastic:

- When consumers' buying decisions are highly influenced by price, we say that their demand is *more elastic*. By that, we mean that a small change in price causes a large change in the quantity demanded.
- When consumers are not very sensitive to price changes—that is, when they will buy approximately the same quantity, regardless of the price—we say that their demand is *more inelastic*.

price elasticity of demand
the size of the change in the quantity demanded of a good or service when its price changes

Calculating price elasticity of demand

Consider the challenge Starbucks faced in shoring up falling sales during the recession. In this situation, a business might lower its prices by offering a sale. But would a sale work? How much could Starbucks's managers expect purchases to increase as a result of the sale? In other words, *How will customers respond* to a sale? The ability to answer this question is a critical tool for businesses. To do so, we need to know the price elasticity of demand for Starbucks coffee.

Let's say that Starbucks usually charges $2 for a cup of coffee. What might happen if it offers a special sale price of $1.50? Suppose that before the sale, Starbucks sold 10 million cups of coffee each day. Now, say that consumers react to the sale by increasing the quantity demanded to 15 million cups per day. Figure 4-1 shows the quantity demanded before and after the sale as two points on the demand curve for coffee. Based on the results of this sale, what can we say about consumers' sensitivity to the price of coffee at Starbucks?

Mathematically, price elasticity is the percentage change in the quantity of a good that is demanded in response to a given percentage change in price. The basic formula looks like Equation 4-1.

LO 4.1 Calculate price elasticity of demand using the mid-point method.

EQUATION 4-1 $$\text{Price elasticity of demand} = \frac{\% \text{ change in Q demanded}}{\% \text{ change in P}}$$

To calculate percentage change, we will be using the **mid-point method**. The mid-point method measures the percentage change relative to a point *midway between the two points*. The mid-point method can be used to calculate the percentage change in quantity demanded, for example (the numerator in Equation 4-1). We do that by dividing the change in quantity demanded by the mid-point (average) quantity, as shown in Equation 4-2.

mid-point method
method that measures percentage change in quantity demanded (or quantity supplied) relative to a point midway between two points on a curve; used to estimate elasticity

EQUATION 4-2 $$\% \text{ change in Q demanded} = \frac{Q_2 - Q_1}{\text{Average of Q}} = \frac{Q_2 - Q_1}{\left(\frac{Q_2 + Q_1}{2}\right)}$$

FIGURE 4-1

Elasticity of the demand for coffee

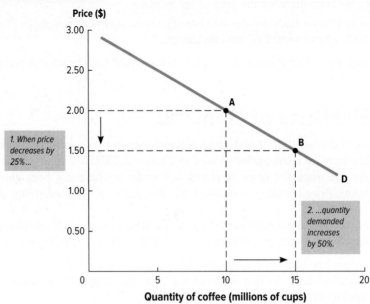

When the price of coffee is $2 a cup, consumers demand
10 million cups. If the price falls to $1.50 per cup, the
quantity demanded increases to 15 million cups.

In the denominator of this expression, the mid-point (average) quantity is equal to the sum of the two quantities divided by 2.

We can find the percentage change in price (the denominator of Equation 4-1) in the same way, as shown in Equation 4-3.

EQUATION 4-3

$$\% \text{ change in P} = \frac{P_2 - P_1}{\text{Average of P}} = \frac{P_2 - P_1}{\left(\dfrac{P_2 + P_1}{2}\right)}$$

Putting Equation 4-2 and Equation 4-3 together, we get Equation 4-4, which is the mid-point method for calculating the price elasticity of demand. This is a fully fleshed-out version of Equation 4-1.

EQUATION 4-4

$$\text{Price elasticity of demand} = \frac{(Q_2 - Q_1)/[(Q_2 + Q_1)/2]}{(P_2 - P_1)/[(P_2 + P_1)/2]}$$

Looking at our example, we find that the demand for coffee went from 10 million cups at $2 to 15 million cups at $1.50. So the average (mid-point) quantity demanded was 12.5 million cups. The average (mid-point) price was $1.75. If we plug the original and sale quantities and prices into Equation 4-4, what do we find? The price was cut by 29 percent and the quantity demanded rose by 40 percent. That tells us that the price elasticity of demand is −1.38.

$$\text{Price elasticity of demand} = \frac{\left(\dfrac{15 \text{ million} - 10 \text{ million}}{12.5 \text{ million}}\right)}{\left(\dfrac{1.50 - 2.00}{1.75}\right)} = \frac{0.40}{-0.29} = -1.38$$

CAUTION: COMMON MISTAKE

Another way of calculating *percentage change* is to divide the difference between the starting and ending levels by the starting level. Using this method, the percentage change in quantity demanded would be expressed as:

$$\% \text{ change in quantity demanded} = \left[\frac{(Q_2 - Q_1)}{Q_1} \right]$$

Notice that the denominator of this expression is simply the starting value of quantity demanded. While you may have used this method before, this method causes a measurement problem when we use it to calculate elasticity: The elasticity changes depending on which direction we move along the demand curve. To avoid this problem, we will be using the mid-point method for calculating percentage change in this chapter.

What does it mean for the price elasticity of demand to be −1.38? Remember that the elasticity describes the size of the change in the quantity demanded of a good when its price changes. A measure of −1.38 price elasticity of demand for cups of coffee means that a 1 percent decrease in the price of coffee will lead to a 1.38 percent increase in the quantity of coffee cups demanded. (Alternatively, we could also say that a 1 percent *increase* in the price of coffee will lead to a 1.38 percent *decrease* in the quantity of coffee cups demanded.)

The *price elasticity of demand will always be a negative number*. Why? Because price and quantity demanded *move in opposite directions*:

- A positive change in price will cause a negative change in the quantity demanded.
- A negative change in price will cause a positive change in the quantity demanded.

In our example, the price of coffee decreased and the quantity demanded increased.

However, be aware that economists often drop the negative sign and express the price elasticity of demand as a positive number, just for the sake of convenience. Don't be fooled! Under normal circumstances, price elasticity of demand is always negative, whether or not the negative sign is printed.

 CAUTION: COMMON MISTAKE

Some texts include the negative sign, and others drop the negative sign. Another way to think of an elasticity measure is as an absolute value. The *absolute value* of a number is its distance from zero, or its numerical value without regard to its sign. For example, the absolute values of 4 and −4 are both 4. The absolute value of elasticity measures the "size" of the response, while the sign measures its direction. Sometimes only the absolute value will be printed, when it is assumed that you know the direction of the change.

You might be wondering why we work with percentages in calculating elasticity. Why not just compare the change in the quantity demanded to the change in price? The answer is that percentages allow us to avoid some practical problems. Think about what would happen if one person measured coffee in 12-ounce cups, while another measured it by the pot or the gallon. Without percentages, we would have several different measures of price elasticity, depending on which unit of measurement we used. To avoid this problem, economists use the *percentage change* in quantity rather than the *absolute change* in quantity. That way, the elasticity of demand for coffee is the same whether we measure the quantity in cups, pots, or gallons.

LO 4.2 Explain how the determinants of price elasticity of demand affect the degree of elasticity.

Determinants of price elasticity of demand

How would the quantity demanded of lattes (or your drink of choice) change if the price fell from $3 to $1.50? Now, how much would the quantity demanded of cotton socks change if the price fell from $10 per pack to $5? Although both represent a 50 percent price reduction, we suspect that the former might change your buying habits more than the latter. Socks are socks, and $5 savings probably won't make you rush out and buy twice as many. To state this more formally, we would say that the demand for lattes is more elastic than the demand for socks.

The underlying idea here is that consumers are more sensitive to price changes for some goods and services than for others. As said earlier, we can classify the degree of sensitivity to price changes by labeling the demand for a particular good as elastic or inelastic. More rigorous definitions of these terms will be given later, but for now remember this: When consumers are very responsive to price changes for a particular good, we say that the demand for that good is *more elastic*. When consumers are not very responsive to price changes for a particular good, we say the demand for that good is *more inelastic*.

Why isn't price elasticity of demand the same for all goods and services? Many factors determine consumers' responsiveness to price changes. The availability of substitutes, relative need and relative cost, and the time needed to adjust to price changes all affect price elasticity of demand.

Availability of substitutes   Recall from Chapter 3, "Markets," that substitutes are goods that are distinguishable from one another but have similar uses. When the price of a good with a close substitute increases, consumers will buy the substitute instead. If close substitutes are available for a particular good, then the demand for that good will be *more elastic* than if only distant substitutes are available. For example, the price elasticity of demand for cranberry juice is likely to be relatively elastic; if the price gets too high, many consumers may switch to grape juice.

Degree of necessity   When a good is a basic necessity, people will buy it even if its price rises. The demand for socks probably is not very elastic, nor is the demand for home heating during the winter. Although people may not like it when the prices of these goods rise, they will buy them to maintain a basic level of comfort. And when prices fall, they probably won't buy vastly more socks or make their homes a lot hotter.

In comparison, the demand for luxuries like vacations, expensive cars, and jewelry is likely to be much more elastic. Most people can easily do without these goods when their prices rise. Note, however, that the definition of a necessity depends on your standards and circumstances. In Florida, air conditioning may be a necessity and heating a luxury; the opposite is likely to be true in Alaska.

Cost relative to income   All else held equal, if consumers spend a very small share of their incomes on a good, their demand for the good will be less elastic than otherwise. For instance, most people can get a year's supply of ballpoint pens for just a few dollars. Even if the price doubled, a year's supply would still cost less than $10, so consumers probably would not bother to adjust their consumption of ballpoint pens.

The opposite is also true: If a good costs a very large proportion of a person's income, like going on a luxury three-week vacation to the beach, the demand for the good will be more elastic. If the price of rooms at high-end beachfront hotels doubles, then a lot of people will decide to do something else with their vacations.

Adjustment time   Goods often have much more elastic demand over the long run than over the short run. Often, adjusting to price changes takes some time. Consider how you might react to an increase in the price of gasoline. In the short run, you might cancel a weekend road trip, but you would still have to do the same amount of driving as usual to school, work, or the grocery store. Over a year, however, you could consider other choices that would further reduce your consumption of gas, such as buying a bus pass or a bicycle, getting a more fuel-efficient car, or moving closer to work or school.

Scope of the market A major caveat to the determinants just described is that each depends on how you define the market for a good or service. The price elasticity of demand for bananas might be high, but the price elasticity of demand for *fruit* could still be low because there are more substitutes for bananas than for the broader category of fruit. Similarly, although water might have a very low price elasticity of demand as a basic necessity, the demand for *bottled* water could be extremely elastic.

Using price elasticity of demand

When we make decisions in the real world, we often don't know the exact price elasticity of demand. But we don't always need to estimate elasticity precisely to know that consumers will react differently to price changes for lattes than for socks. Instead, businesses and other decision makers often know something general about the shape of the demand curve they are facing. Being able to place goods into several broad categories of elasticity can facilitate real pricing decisions in situations without full information.

At the extremes, demand can be perfectly elastic or perfectly inelastic. When demand is **perfectly elastic**, the quantity demanded drops to zero when the price increases even a minuscule amount. Thus, a perfectly elastic demand curve is horizontal, as shown in panel A of Figure 4-2. This graph indicates that consumers are very sensitive to price. When demand is **perfectly inelastic**, the quantity demanded is the same no matter what the price. Thus, the demand curve is vertical, as shown in panel B of Figure 4-2. These two extremes rarely occur in real life.

perfectly elastic demand
demand for which any increase in price will cause quantity demanded to drop to zero; represented by a perfectly horizontal line

perfectly inelastic demand
demand for which quantity demanded remains the same regardless of price; represented by a perfectly vertical line

FIGURE 4-2

Perfectly elastic and perfectly inelastic demand

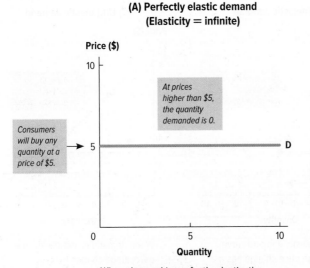

(A) Perfectly elastic demand (Elasticity = infinite)

At prices higher than $5, the quantity demanded is 0.

Consumers will buy any quantity at a price of $5.

When demand is perfectly elastic, the demand curve is horizontal. At prices above $5, consumers will not buy any quantity of the good.

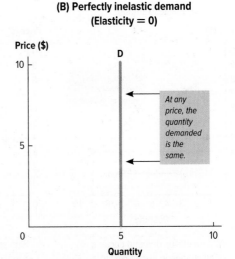

(B) Perfectly inelastic demand (Elasticity = 0)

At any price, the quantity demanded is the same.

When demand is perfectly inelastic, the demand curve is vertical. Consumers will always demand the same quantity of a good, regardless of the price.

elastic
demand that has an
absolute value of
elasticity greater than 1

Between these two extremes, elasticity is commonly divided into three quantifiable categories: elastic, inelastic, and unit-elastic. When the absolute value of the price elasticity of demand is greater than 1, we call the associated quantity demanded **elastic**. With elastic demand, a given percentage change in the price of a good will cause an even larger percentage change in the quantity demanded. For example, panel A of Figure 4-3 shows that for elastic demand, an 80 percent change in price could lead to a 150 percent change in the quantity demanded. Remember, we are using the mid-point method to calculate the percentage change here.

inelastic
demand that has an
absolute value of
elasticity less than 1

When the absolute value of the price elasticity of demand is less than 1, we say that demand is **inelastic**. With inelastic demand, a given percentage change in price will cause a smaller percentage change in the quantity demanded. Panel B of Figure 4-3 illustrates that for inelastic demand, an 80 percent change in price might lead to a 50 percent change in the quantity demanded.

unit-elastic
demand that has an
absolute value of
elasticity exactly
equal to 1

If the absolute value of elasticity is exactly 1—that is, if a percentage change in price causes the same percentage change in the quantity demanded—then we say that demand is **unit-elastic**. Panel C of Figure 4-3 illustrates that for unit-elastic demand, an 80 percent change in price leads to an 80 percent change in the quantity demanded.

The concept of elasticity is not merely a theoretical tool. Businesses and policy decisions often depend on the value of particular elasticities. Table 4-1 displays actual estimates of price elasticities for a selection of goods. You can ask yourself why some price elasticities are larger than others. Why is the quantity demanded of air travel more elastic for leisure travel than business travel? Why is the quantity demanded of gasoline more elastic in the long run than the short run?

As we'll see later in this chapter, the terms *elastic*, *inelastic*, and *unit-elastic* can be used to describe any sort of elasticity, not just the price elasticity of demand. Although these categories may sound academic, they can have serious implications for real-world business and policy decisions. The Economics in Action box "Does charging for bednets decrease malaria?" describes a case in which knowing whether the price elasticity of demand is elastic or inelastic is a matter of life and death.

FIGURE 4-3

Elastic, inelastic, and unit-elastic demand

1. After price decreases by 80% under...

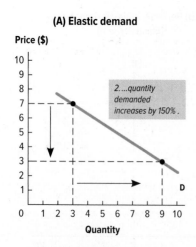

(A) Elastic demand

2. ...quantity demanded increases by 150%.

With an elastic demand curve, a small change in price leads to a big change in the quantity demanded. As a result, the price elasticity of demand is greater than 1.

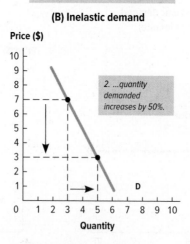

(B) Inelastic demand

2. ...quantity demanded increases by 50%.

With an inelastic demand curve, even a large price change has a small effect on the quantity demanded. As a result, the price elasticity of demand is less than 1.

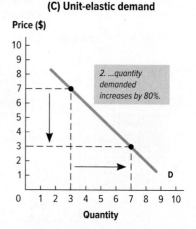

(C) Unit-elastic demand

2. ...quantity demanded increases by 80%.

When demand is unit-elastic, the percentage change in price equals the percentage change in quantity, so that the price elasticity of demand is exactly 1.

TABLE 4-1
Estimated price elasticities of demand

Good	Estimated elasticities
Oil in the short run	−0.02
Eggs	−0.27
Gasoline in the short run	−0.05 to −0.6
Water (residential)	−0.41
Alcoholic drinks	−0.44
Gasoline in the long run	−0.25 to −0.7
Electricity	−0.38 to −0.61
Soft drinks	−0.7 to −0.8
Heroin	−0.8
Business air travel	−0.8
Leisure air travel	−1.6
NFL ticket resales	−2.94

Sources: T. Andreyeva, M. W. Long, and K. D. Brownell, "The impact of food prices on consumption: A systematic review of research on the price elasticity of demand for food," *American Journal of Public Health* 100, no. 2 (2010), p. 216; T. Helbling et al., "Oil scarcity, growth, and global imbalances," *in* International Monetary Fund, *World Economic Outlook,* April 2011, ch. 3, www.imf.org/external/pubs/ft/weo/2011/01/pdf/c3.pdf; S. M. Olmstead and R. N. Stavins, "Comparing price and nonprice approaches to urban water conservation," *Water Resources Research* 45, no. 4 (2009); T. A. Olmstead, S. M. Alessi, B. Kline, R. L. Pacula, and N. M. Petry, "The price elasticity of demand for heroin: Matched longitudinal and experimental evidence," *Journal of Health Economics* 41 (2015), pp. 59–71; P. Belobaba, A. Odoni, and C. Barnhart, eds., *The Global Airline Industry* (New York: Wiley & Sons, 2015), p. 61; M. A. Diehl, J. G. Maxcy, and J. Drayer, "Price elasticity of demand in the secondary market: Evidence from the National Football League," *Journal of Sports Economics* 16, no. 6 (August 2015), pp. 557–75; A. J. Ros, "An econometric assessment of electricity demand in the United States using panel data and the impact of retail competition on prices," *Insight in Economics,* June 9, 2015, www.nera.com/content/dam/nera/publications/2015/PUB_Econometric_Assessment_Elec_Demand_US_0615.pdf; P. Krugman, "Prices and gasoline demand," *The New York Times,* May 9, 2008, http://krugman.blogs.nytimes.com/2008/05/09/prices-and-gasoline-demand/?_r=0; L. Levin, M. S. Lewis, and F. A. Wolak, "High frequency evidence on the demand for gasoline," April 12, 2013, http://web.stanford.edu/group/fwolak/cgi-bin/sites/default/files/files/Levin_Lewis_Wolak_demand.pdf.

Does charging for bednets decrease malaria?
Economics in Action

It's hard to sleep when mosquitoes are buzzing. Most of the time, though, the worst outcome is waking up tired, dotted with a few itchy bites. But in some parts of the world, mosquitoes spread diseases like malaria that kill millions of young people every year.

Jessica Cohen and Pascaline Dupas, economics researchers working on a project in Kenya, saw some good news: The most dangerous mosquitoes come out only at night, and risks are cut sharply by sleeping under a bednet. The bad news is that many people, especially the poorest, don't have bednets.

Cohen and Dupas wanted to promote use of bednets, so they set up an organization to turn ideas into action (www.tamtamafrica.org). They faced a big, practical question: Should bednets be handed out for free? Or should providers sell them, perhaps at a discounted price?

(continued)

One argument for selling bednets is that customers who buy them will probably value them more (and thus use them more) compared to people who get nets for free. If organizations sell bednets, they may also be able to distribute more of them.

On the other hand, the law of demand states that the quantity demanded falls at higher prices. Charging for nets might dissuade some people—particularly, the very poorest families—from getting nets.

As economists, Cohen and Dupas realized their practical question was: What's the price elasticity of the demand for bednets? To measure the elasticity, the two professors set up an experiment in western Kenya. Some people were offered bednets for free; others were offered bednets at a range of different prices. Cohen and Dupas found that charging a fee sharply reduced the quantity of the nets demanded. When the price increased from zero to just $0.75, the number of people wanting bednets dropped by 75 percent! Furthermore, the people who bought bednets did not use them more effectively than those who received them for free.

If profit were the goal in this campaign, a few bednets sold at $0.75 would generate more revenue than a lot of bednets given away for free. But the goal was to help save lives, not to make a profit. Based on the high price elasticity, Cohen and Dupas concluded that for organizations with a social mission, free distribution of bednets beat charging a fee.

Sources: J. Cohen and P. Dupas, "Free distribution or cost sharing? Evidence from a randomized malaria prevention experiment," *Quarterly Journal of Economics* 125, no. 1 (February 2010), pp. 1–45; T. Ogden, *Experimental Conversations: Perspectives on Randomized Trials in Development Economics* (Cambridge, MA: MIT Press, 2017).

Knowing whether the demand for a good is elastic or inelastic is extremely useful in business. That information allows a manager to determine whether a price increase will cause total revenue to rise or fall. **Total revenue** is the amount that a firm receives from the sale of goods and services, calculated as the quantity sold multiplied by the price paid for each unit. This number is important for an obvious reason: It tells us how much money sellers receive when they sell something.

An increase in price affects total revenue in two ways:

total revenue
the amount that a firm receives from the sale of goods and services; calculated as the quantity sold multiplied by the price paid for each unit

- It causes a *quantity effect*, or a decrease in total revenue that results from selling fewer units of the good.

- It causes a *price effect*, or an increase in total revenue that results from receiving a higher price for each unit sold.

Figure 4-4 shows both the quantity effect and the price effect. When the quantity effect outweighs the price effect, a price increase will cause a drop in total revenue, as it does in Figure 4-4. When the price effect outweighs the quantity effect, a price increase will raise total revenue.

When demand is elastic, a price increase causes total revenue to fall. We already know that when demand is elastic, a change in price will cause a larger percentage change in quantity demanded. Another way of saying this is that the quantity effect outweighs the price effect. So when demand is elastic, a price increase causes a proportionally larger decrease in the quantity demanded, and total revenue falls.

Conversely, when demand is inelastic, the percentage change in price is larger than the percentage change in quantity demanded. The price effect outweighs the quantity effect, and total revenue increases. With inelastic demand, then, consumers will purchase less of a good when its price rises, but the change in the quantity demanded will be proportionally less than the change in price.

Figure 4-5 shows this trade-off between the price and quantity effects. As you can see, panel A shows an elastic demand in which a $1 change in price causes the quantity demanded to increase by 4,000. With the inelastic demand curve in panel B, a $2 decrease in price increases quantity demanded by only 1,000.

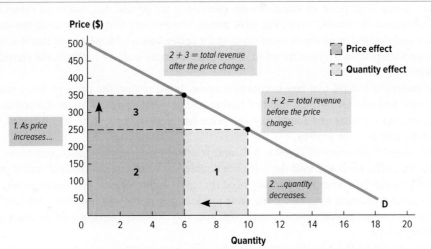

FIGURE 4-4

Effect of a price increase on total revenue

The colored rectangles represent total revenue at two different prices. As the price increases from $250 to $350, total revenue is affected in two ways. The blue rectangle represents the increase in revenue received for each unit sold (the price effect). The yellow rectangle represents the decrease in total revenue as the number of units sold drops (the quantity effect). The elasticity of demand determines which effect is larger. In this case, the yellow area is larger than the blue area, meaning that the quantity effect outweighs the price effect, and total revenue decreases.

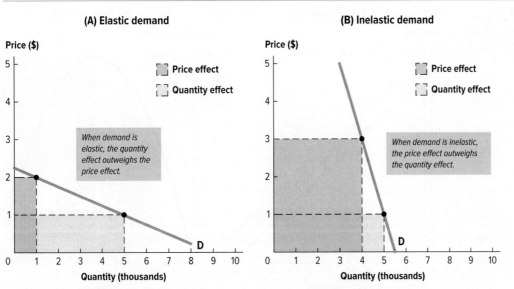

FIGURE 4-5

Elasticity and changes in total revenue

In this market, demand is elastic. At a price of $1, 5,000 units are sold for a total revenue of $5,000. If the price increases to $2, only 1,000 units are sold for a total revenue of only $2,000. The quantity effect outweighs the price effect.

In this market, demand is inelastic. At a price of $1, 5,000 units are sold for a total revenue of $5,000. If the price increases to $3, the number of units sold drops by only 1,000, to 4,000 units. Because the price effect outweighs the quantity effect, total revenue climbs to $12,000, an increase of $7,000.

There is one final point to make. So far, everything we've said has described elasticity *at a particular spot on the demand curve*. For most goods, however, elasticity varies along the curve. So when we said that the price elasticity of demand for coffee was -1.38, we meant that it was -1.38 for a price change from \$1.50 to \$2 a cup. If the price changes from \$2 to \$2.50, the elasticity will be different.

The reasoning behind this fact is common sense. Imagine that the price of lattes plummets to 10 cents, and you get into the habit of buying one every morning. What would you do if you showed up one morning and found that the price had doubled overnight, to 20 cents? We bet you'd shrug and buy one anyway.

Now, imagine the price of lattes is \$10, and you buy them only as occasional treats. If you arrive at the coffee shop and find the price has doubled to \$20, what will you do? You'd probably consider very carefully whether you really need that latte. In both cases, you would be responding to a 100 percent increase in price for the same product, but you would react very differently. This makes perfect sense: In one case, the latte costs you only 10 more cents, but in the other, it costs an additional \$10.

Your reactions to the latte illustrate a general rule: *Demand tends to be more elastic when price is high and more inelastic when price is low.* This brings us to an important caveat about the three graphs shown in Figure 4-3. Although the example of an elastic demand curve in panel A has a steeper *slope* than the inelastic demand curve in panel B, we now know that slope is not the same as elasticity.

In fact, the elasticity of demand is different at different points along a linear demand curve. The reasoning is nonintuitive, but straightforward when you think about it graphically. Look at Figure 4-6. The line in panel B has a constant slope, but the percentage changes in price and

FIGURE 4-6

Changes in elasticity along the demand curve

(A) Demand and revenue schedule

Price ($)	Quantity	Total revenue ($)
50	0	0
45	1	45
40	2	80
35	3	105
30	4	120
25	5	125
20	6	120
15	7	105
10	8	80
5	9	45
0	10	0

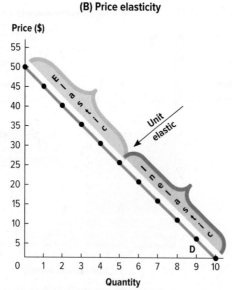

(B) Price elasticity

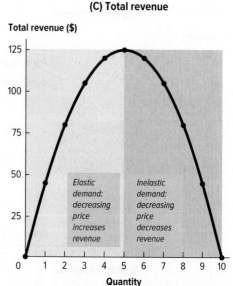

(C) Total revenue

This table lists the data shown in the graphs in panels A and B. Quantity demanded always increases as price falls. Total revenue rises until the price falls to \$25, then falls at lower prices.

Price elasticity of demand varies along the demand curve. Above a certain price, demand is elastic; below it, demand is inelastic.

This graph shows total revenue along the demand curve shown above. Total revenue first rises, but then begins to fall as demand moves from elastic to inelastic.

quantity are very different at either end of the curve. For instance, going from $45 to $40 is a much smaller difference (in percentage terms) than from $10 to $5, but the slope of the curve is the same between both sets of points.

The result is that as we move along a linear demand curve starting from a price equal to zero, revenue first increases as the price increases, and then decreases with higher prices. (You can see this result in the "Total revenue" column in panel A.) The maximum revenue occurs where demand is unit-elastic.

Panel C of Figure 4-6 graphs out the total revenue curve associated with the demand curve in panel B, using calculations from the schedule in Panel A. Note that when the price is high, lowering the price will increase revenue. For example, when the price decreases from $45 to $40 (see the schedule), total revenue almost doubles, from $45 to $80. When the price is low, however, lowering it further decreases total revenue. Moving from $10 to $5, for example, decreases total revenue from $80 to $45.

Price elasticity of demand has all sorts of real-world applications. See, for example, the issue discussed in the What Do You Think? box "Should entrance fees at national parks be raised?"

Should entrance fees at national parks be raised?
What Do You Think?

America boasts 58 national parks spread across 84 million acres of the country's most famous natural spaces, including Yellowstone, the Grand Canyon, and the Florida Everglades. In 2017, 84 million people visited the parks—the most on record. These parks are feeling the strain; roads, trails, docks, and concessions at parks across the country need serious repairs. The U.S. Department of the Interior estimates that fully funding these fixes would cost $12 billion.

In October 2017, Interior Secretary Ryan Zinke proposed fee increases at 17 of the most popular national parks, including Zion, Joshua Tree, and Grand Canyon. During peak season, entrance fees for these parks would double to $70 per car, $50 per motorcycle, $30 per person. (For comparison, a ticket at Magic Kingdom in Orlando costs $129 on a "peak" day.) The Department of the Interior estimates that these increases could raise revenue at those parks by $70 million, a 34 percent increase.

During a 30-day public comment period, supporters and opponents of the plan weighed in on the issue. Many of these comments went straight to the bottom line: "This price hike is just too much. Having to pay $70 just to get in would definitely make me consider other options for our family vacation." Others noted that the price increases might make the parks unaffordable for families and individuals with low incomes.

The potential for a sharp decrease in overall visitors is especially concerning for business owners in areas around these parks. In 2015, visitors to national parks spent nearly $17 billion at businesses within 60 miles of park borders, supporting 295,000 jobs.

On the flip side, some commenters noted that facilities and ecosystems would get a much needed breather if fewer people visited. For example, Zion National Park, which received 4.3 million visitors in 2016, is often packed with tour buses in the summer, and rangers have found trails cut through sensitive environments. The problem has reached the point where the park has considered making a reservation system to allocate park visits.

After reviewing the comments, the U.S. Department of the Interior scrapped its original plan and is instead considering smaller rate increases and fees targeted at foreign visitors. Because parks need more revenue, the question isn't *if* rates will go up. Instead, the Department of the Interior is trying to balance the need for more revenue against the desire to keep wild areas accessible and local economies healthy.

(continued)

For a refresher on slope versus elasticity, see Appendix C, "Math Essentials: Calculating Percentage Change, Slope, and Elasticity," which follows this chapter.

✓ TEST YOURSELF

☐ What is the formula for calculating the price elasticity of demand? **[LO 4.1]**
☐ Why should you use the mid-point method to calculate the price elasticity of demand? **[LO 4.1]**
☐ If demand is inelastic, will an increase in price lead to more, less, or the same amount of revenue **[LO 4.2]**
☐ If demand is elastic, will an increase in price lead to more, less, or the same amount of revenue? **[LO 4.2]**
☐ If demand is unit-elastic, will an increase in price lead to more, less, or the same amount of revenue? **[LO 4.2]**

Price Elasticity of Supply

What happens when an increase in coffee consumption drives up the price of coffee beans? *How will the coffee market respond* to the price change? We can predict, based on the law of supply, that coffee growers will respond to an increase in price by increasing their production. But by how much will they increase production? The concept of price elasticity of supply can help us answer that question.

price elasticity of supply
the size of the change in the quantity supplied of a good or service when its price changes

Price elasticity of supply is the size of the change in the quantity supplied of a good or service when its price changes. Price elasticity of supply measures producers' responsiveness to a change in price, just as price elasticity of demand measures consumers' responsiveness to a change in price.

Chapter 3, "Markets," showed that when prices rise, producers supply larger quantities of a good; when prices fall, they supply smaller quantities. Just as the price elasticity of demand for a good tells us how much the quantity demanded changes as we move along the demand curve, the price elasticity of supply tells us how much the quantity supplied changes as we move along the supply curve.

Calculating price elasticity of supply

LO 4.3 Calculate price elasticity of supply using the mid-point method.

Price elasticity of supply, shown in Equation 4-5, is measured in the same way as price elasticity of demand: as the percentage change in quantity divided by the percentage change in price.

EQUATION 4-5

$$\text{Price elasticity of supply} = \frac{\%\text{ change in quantity supplied}}{\%\text{ change in price}}$$

To ensure that elasticity will be the same whether you move up or down the supply curve, you should use the mid-point method, as in Equation 4-6.

EQUATION 4-6 $$\text{Price elasticity of supply} = \frac{(Q_2 - Q_1)/[(Q_1 + Q_2)/2]}{(P_2 - P_1)/[(P_1 + P_2)/2]}$$

Suppose that when the price of coffee beans goes from \$1 to \$1.20 per pound, production increases from 90 million pounds of coffee beans per year to 100 million pounds. Using the mid-point method, the percentage change in quantity supplied would be:

$$\text{\% change in quantity supplied} = \frac{(100 \text{ million} - 90 \text{ million})}{95 \text{ million}} = 11\%$$

The percentage change in price would be:

$$\text{\% change in price} = \frac{1.2 - 1}{1.1} = 18\%$$

So the price elasticity of supply at this point on the supply curve is:

$$\text{Price elasticity of supply} = \frac{11\%}{18\%} = 0.6$$

As with the price elasticity of demand, we can describe the price elasticity of supply using three categories:

- *Elastic*, if it has an absolute value greater than 1.
- *Inelastic*, if it has an absolute value less than 1.
- *Unit-elastic*, if it has an absolute value of exactly 1.

We can also describe the extreme cases: Supply is *perfectly elastic* if the quantity supplied could be anything at a given price, and is zero at any other price. At the other extreme, supply is *perfectly inelastic* if the quantity supplied is the same, regardless of the price.

Going back to our example, an elasticity of 0.6 tells us that the supply of coffee beans is relatively inelastic, at least in the short run. Does this result make sense? As it turns out, coffee takes a long time to grow. Coffee plants don't produce a full yield for four to six years after they are planted. Because coffee growers can't increase production quickly, it makes sense that the supply of coffee would be inelastic. (What if prices had fallen from \$1.20 to \$1, instead of rising from \$1 to \$1.20? Using the mid-point method, the elasticity would be the same.)

There is one important difference between the elasticities of supply and demand: The price elasticity of demand is always negative and the price elasticity of supply is always positive. The reason is simple: The quantity demanded always moves in the *opposite direction* from the price, but the quantity supplied moves in the *same direction* as the price.

TAKE NOTE... 🖉

- Remember that the elasticity of *demand* is calculated by dividing a positive number by a negative number, or by dividing a negative number by a positive number, so the answer is always negative.

- The elasticity of *supply*, on the other hand, is calculated by dividing either a positive number by another positive number or a negative number by another negative number. In either case, the answer is always positive.

Remembering this rule can help you to check your arithmetic.

Determinants of price elasticity of supply

Whether supply is elastic or inelastic depends on the supplier's ability to change the quantity produced in response to price changes. Three factors affect a supplier's ability to expand production: the availability of inputs, the flexibility of the production process, and the time needed to adjust to changes in price. Recall that this last factor—time—is also a determinant of the elasticity of demand. Just as consumers take time to change their habits, suppliers need time to ramp up production.

LO 4.4 Explain how the determinants of price elasticity of supply affect the degree of elasticity.

Availability of inputs   The production of some goods can be expanded easily, just by adding extra inputs. For example, a bakery can easily buy extra flour and yeast to produce more bread, probably at the same cost per loaf. Increasing the supply of other goods is more difficult, however, and sometimes is impossible. If the price of Frida Khalo paintings goes up, there isn't much anyone can do to produce more of them.

In other words, the elasticity of supply depends on the elasticity of the supply of inputs. If producing more of a good will cost a lot more than the initial quantity did because the extra inputs will be harder to find or more costly, then the producer will be reluctant to increase the quantity supplied. Higher and higher prices will be needed to convince the producer to go to the extra expense.

Flexibility of the production process   The easiest way for producers to adjust the quantity supplied of a particular good is to draw production capacity away from other goods when its price rises, or to reassign capacity to other goods when its price falls. Farmers may find this sort of substitution relatively simple: When corn prices are high, they will plant more acres with corn; when corn prices are low, they will reassign acres to more profitable crops. Other producers have much less flexibility. If you own a company that manufactures specialized parts for Toyota, you might need to buy new machinery to begin making parts for Ford, let alone switch to another type of product entirely.

Adjustment time   As with demand, supply is more elastic over long periods than over short periods. That is, producers can make more adjustments in the long run than in the short run. In the short run, the number of hotel rooms at Disneyland is fixed; in the medium and long run, old rooms can be renovated and new hotels can be built. Production capacity can also increase or decrease over time as new firms start up or old ones shut down.

✓ **TEST YOURSELF**

☐ How would you calculate the price elasticity of supply? **[LO 4.3]**
☐ What are the three determinants of the price elasticity of supply? **[LO 4.4]**

Other Elasticities

The demand for a good is sensitive to more than just the price of the good. Because people are clever, flexible, and always on the lookout for ways to make the most of opportunities, demand also responds to changing circumstances, such as the prices of other goods and the incomes consumers earn. Let's consider two other demand elasticities, the *cross-price elasticity of demand* and the *income elasticity of demand*.

Cross-price elasticity of demand

LO 4.5 Calculate cross-price elasticity of demand, and interpret the sign of the elasticity.

Earlier we noted that price elasticities are affected by the availability of alternative options. For example, we might expect a Starbucks latte to have relatively price-elastic demand because some people will shift to buying coffee from Dunkin' Donuts when the price of a Starbucks latte rises. Once again, recalling the four economists' questions we presented in Chapter 1, "Economics and Life," asking *How will others respond?* is the key to understanding the situation.

What happens if the price of Dunkin' Donuts regular coffee falls but the price of a Starbucks latte stays the same? **Cross-price elasticity of demand** describes how much demand changes when the price of a *different* good changes. For example, because lattes and regular coffee are substitutes, we expect the demand for lattes to decrease when the price of regular coffee falls (as some people switch from lattes to coffee). The reverse also holds: If the price of a cup of

Dunkin' Donuts coffee rises, while the price of a Starbucks latte remains the same, we expect the demand for lattes to increase (as some people switch from coffee to the relatively cheaper latte). Equation 4-7 gives the formula for the cross-price elasticity of demand.

EQUATION 4-7

$$\text{Cross-price elasticity of demand between A and B} = \frac{\%\text{ change in quantity of A demanded}}{\%\text{ change in price of B}}$$

Remember that nonprice determinants (like income or tastes) will shift a demand curve. In the case of cross-price elasticity, the price of a substitute or a complement is a nonprice determinant. Thus, the entire demand curve shifts. However, we still measure this change in demand by observing the change in the quantity demanded. But in this case, the initial quantity demanded is on one demand curve and the final quantity demanded is on another demand curve.

When two goods are substitutes, we expect their cross-price elasticity of demand to be positive. That is, an increase in the price of one will cause an increase in the quantity demanded of the other. On the other hand, a decrease in the price of one good will cause a decrease in the quantity demanded of the other. Just how elastic the demand is depends on how close the two substitutes are: If they are very close substitutes, a change in the price of one will cause a large change in the quantity demanded of the other, so that cross-price elasticity will be high. If they are not close substitutes, cross-price elasticity will be low.

Cross-price elasticity can also be negative. We saw that the price elasticity of demand is always negative and can be expressed as an absolute value. In contrast, cross-price elasticity can be positive or negative. Its sign tells us about the relationship between two goods:

- When two goods are substitutes, their cross-price elasticity will be positive.
- When two goods are complements (that is, when they are consumed together), cross-price elasticity will be negative.

For example, when people drink more coffee, they want more cream to go with it. Coffee and cream are complements, not substitutes. So when the demand for coffee increases, the demand for cream will increase, all else held equal. When two goods are linked in this way, their cross-price elasticity will be negative: an increase in the price of one good will decrease the quantity demanded of both goods. Again, the relative size of the elasticity tells us how strongly the two goods are linked. If the two goods are strong complements, their cross-price elasticity will be a large negative number. If the two goods are loosely linked, their cross-price elasticity will be negative but not far below zero.

Income elasticity of demand

People buy some goods in roughly the same amounts, no matter how wealthy they are. Salt, toothpaste, and toilet paper are three examples. These are not the sort of products people rush out to buy when they get a raise at work. Other goods, though, are very sensitive to changes in income. If you got a raise, you might splurge on new clothes or a meal at a fancy restaurant.

The **income elasticity of demand** for a good describes how much demand changes in response to a change in consumers' incomes. Similar to cross-price elasticity, a change in income causes the demand curve to shift. We measure this change in demand by observing the change in the quantity demanded. As Equation 4-8 shows, the income elasticity of demand is expressed as the ratio of the percentage change in the quantity demanded to the percentage change in income:

EQUATION 4-8

$$\text{Income elasticity of demand} = \frac{\%\text{ change in quantity demanded}}{\%\text{ change in income}}$$

Recall from Chapter 3, "Markets," that increases in income raise the demand for normal goods and lower the demand for inferior goods. Income elasticity tells us how much the demand for these goods changes.

cross-price elasticity of demand
a measure of how the demand for one good changes when the price of a different good changes

LO 4.6 Calculate income elasticity of demand, and interpret the sign of the elasticity.

income elasticity of demand
a measure of how much the demand for a good changes in response to a change in consumers' incomes

For example, a Starbucks Frappuccino® is a normal good that might be fairly responsive to changes in income. When people become wealthier, they will buy more of a small luxury item like this. Therefore, we would guess that the income elasticity of demand for fancy iced coffee drinks is positive (because the drink is a normal good) and relatively large (because the drink is a non-necessity that has many cheaper substitutes).

Regular coffee is also generally a normal good, so its income elasticity should be positive. However, we might guess that it will be less elastic than a Frappuccino's. Many people consider their standard cup of coffee every day before work to be more of a necessity than a luxury and will buy it regardless of their incomes. Another way to put it is that the demand for Frappuccinos is income-elastic, while the demand for plain coffee is relatively income-inelastic.

For normal goods like these, income elasticity is positive because as incomes rise, demand increases. This then leads to an increase in quantity demanded. Both necessities and luxuries are normal goods, and although their income elasticities are positive, their sizes vary:

- If the good is a necessity, income elasticity of demand will be positive and less than 1.
- If the good is a luxury, income elasticity will be positive and greater than 1.

As with the cross-price elasticity of demand, the income elasticity of demand can be negative as well as positive. The income elasticity of demand is negative for inferior goods because quantity demanded decreases as incomes increase.

In 2009 Starbucks introduced a new retail product, VIA® Ready instant coffee. Although some coffee enthusiasts sneered, others thought it was a shrewd move at a time of economic hardship. Instant coffee mix may be an inferior good in some places: As incomes increase, people will drink more expensive beverages and *decrease* their consumption of instant coffee. During a recession, however, budgets tighten and people may increase their consumption of instant coffee as they cut back on more expensive drinks. At least, that is what Starbucks was hoping. In this scenario, the income elasticity of instant coffee would be small and negative. A less-appealing inferior good that people quickly abandon as they grow richer would have a large, negative income elasticity.

Once again, the sign and size of a good's elasticity tell us a lot about the good. Table 4-2 summarizes what we have learned about the four types of elasticity.

TABLE 4-2

Four measures of elasticity

Measure	Equation	Negative	Positive	More elastic	Less elastic
Price elasticity of demand	% change in quantity demanded / % change in price	Always	Never	Over time, for substitutable goods and luxury items	In the short run, for unique and necessary items
Price elasticity of supply	% change in quantity supplied / % change in price	Never	Always	Over time, with flexible production	In the short run, with production constraints
Cross-price elasticity	% change in quantity demanded of A / % change in price of B	For complements	For substitutes	For near-perfect substitutes and strong complements	For loosely related goods
Income elasticity	% change in quantity demanded / % change in income	For inferior goods	For normal goods	For luxury items with close substitutes	For unique and necessary items

If you find this discussion of price elasticity particularly interesting, you might want to consider work as a pricing analyst. In the near term, though, you can apply your knowledge about price elasticity when you buy airline tickets. You can read more about this in the Econ and YOU box "Finding a travel bargain."

Finding a travel bargain

Econ and YOU

Econ and YOU boxes show tips, strategies, and other ways that economics can inform choices—big and small—in your own life.

Are you fantasizing about traveling someplace warm for spring break? Taking a trip to see family or friends? If you've looked at airline prices, you'll know that some tickets can be really expensive and some much cheaper—even on the same routes. Why?

Airline prices are, of course, partly determined by the cost of getting you from point A to point B. If you fly from, say, Atlanta to Los Angeles, you'll pay more than when flying from Atlanta to Miami—simply because the cost of jet fuel and the time spent by pilots and flight attendants increase with distance. But even on the Atlanta to LA flight, you will pay different ticket prices depending on where you sit on the plane. When we checked the website of a major airline, for example, sitting in business class cost twice as much as sitting in economy because it costs the airline more to give you extra room and extra service.

But cost is not the whole story. Airlines know that different customers have different price elasticities. People traveling for business, for example, tend to have low price elasticities: they are less sensitive to cost than other fliers, especially when they need to get to important meetings and events. Airlines take advantage of that knowledge by raising prices for business travelers. (Similar principles apply to train travel and car rentals.)

In contrast, travelers who are flexible and on tight budgets, including many college students, tend to be sensitive to price. Their price elasticities for airline tickets are high, and they will make alternative plans if prices rise too much.

Airlines make the most profits when they can sort out which customers have high price elasticities, which have low elasticities, and which are in between. They do this by devising restrictions (no flexibility in seat choice for basic economy, for example) and amenities (more legroom in business class) that appeal to customers with different price elasticities. Cut-price airlines like Frontier, Spirit, Southwest, and JetBlue built their entire business models around serving customers with high price elasticities. On these airlines even the most basic amenities (carry-on bags, seat selection, and snacks and drinks) often cost extra. (The airlines also likely make money on people's being overly optimistic, when they make their reservations, that they will not spend money on the extra amenities, but then, as the day of the flight approaches, they do.)

On airlines with a wider variety of ticket options, finding a cheaper ticket may require signaling that you have a high price elasticity. That means making choices that are *not* typical for

©kasto/123RF

low-elasticity customers like business travelers. Staying over on Saturday night often signals low elasticity (since business travelers tend to head home for the weekend). Or buying tickets early (some say seven weeks is the sweet spot). Or accepting the restrictions, such as limited overhead bin access and restrictions on changing your ticket, that come with "basic economy" tickets. You might find that these trade-offs are worth it, but sometimes they can turn a great deal into a headache, with lots of extra fees for flight changes and baggage fees.

✓ TEST YOURSELF

☐ Why is the cross-price elasticity of demand positive for substitutes? **[LO 4.5]**

☐ Why does the income-elasticity of demand depend on whether a good is normal or inferior? **[LO 4.6]**

Conclusion

Supply and *demand* may be the most common words in economics, but applying these concepts to the real world requires a bit of elaboration. Elasticity is the first of several concepts we will study that will help you to apply the concepts of supply and demand to business and policy questions. In this chapter we saw how elasticity can be used to predict how price changes will influence revenue. In the coming chapters we will use elasticity to predict the effects of government intervention in the market, and we will dig deeper into the consumer and producer choices that drive elasticity.

Key Terms

elasticity, p. 80

price elasticity of demand, p. 81

mid-point method, p. 81

perfectly elastic demand, p. 85

perfectly inelastic demand, p. 85

elastic, p. 86

inelastic, p. 86

unit-elastic, p. 86

total revenue, p. 88

price elasticity of supply, p. 92

cross-price elasticity of demand, p. 94

income elasticity of demand, p. 95

Summary

LO 4.1 Calculate price elasticity of demand using the mid-point method.

Elasticity is a measure of consumers' and producers' responsiveness to a change in market conditions. Understanding the elasticity for a good or service allows economic decision makers to anticipate the outcome of changes in market conditions and to calibrate prices so as to maximize revenues.

Price elasticity of demand is the size of the change in the quantity demanded of a good or service when its price changes. Elasticity should be calculated as a percentage using the mid-point method to avoid problems with conflicting units of measurement and with the direction of a change.

Price elasticity of demand is almost always negative because the quantity demanded falls as the price rises. It is usually represented as an absolute value, without the negative sign.

LO 4.2 Explain how the determinants of price elasticity of demand affect the degree of elasticity.

In general, demand is inelastic for goods that have no close substitutes, are basic necessities, or cost a relatively small proportion of consumers' income. Demand

is also inelastic over short periods and for broadly defined markets.

When demand is elastic, a percentage change in the price of a good will cause a larger percentage change in the quantity demanded; the absolute value of the elasticity will be greater than 1. When demand is inelastic, a percentage change in price will cause a smaller percentage change in the quantity demanded; the absolute value of the elasticity will be less than 1. When demand is unit-elastic, the percentage changes in price and quantity will be equal, and the elasticity will be exactly 1.

LO 4.3 Calculate price elasticity of supply using the mid-point method.

Price elasticity of supply is the size of the change in the quantity supplied of a good or service when its price changes. Price elasticity of supply is almost always positive because the quantity supplied increases as the price increases.

LO 4.4 Explain how the determinants of price elasticity of supply affect the degree of elasticity.

Supply is generally inelastic when additional inputs to the production process are difficult to get and the production process is inflexible. Supply is also inelastic over short periods.

Supply is considered elastic when the absolute value of its price elasticity is greater than 1, inelastic when the absolute value is less than 1, and unit-elastic when it is exactly 1.

> **LO 4.5** Calculate cross-price elasticity of demand, and interpret the sign of the elasticity.

Cross-price elasticity of demand is the percentage change in the quantity demanded in response to a given percentage change in the price of a *different* good. The cross-price elasticity of demand between two goods will be positive if they are substitutes and negative if they are complements.

> **LO 4.6** Calculate income elasticity of demand, and interpret the sign of the elasticity.

Income elasticity of demand is the percentage change in the quantity of a good demanded in response to a given percentage change in income. Income elasticity of demand will be positive for normal goods and negative for inferior goods.

Review Questions

1. You are advising a coffee shop manager who wants to estimate how much sales will change if the price of a latte rises. You tell her that she should measure the change in sales using the percentage change in quantity of coffee sold rather than the number of cups of coffee or the total ounces of coffee sold. Similarly, you tell her that she should measure the price increase in percentage terms rather than in terms of absolute dollars. Explain why she should measure elasticity in percentage terms rather than in terms of dollars and cups. **[LO 4.1]**

2. Explain why the coffee shop manager should calculate elasticity using the mid-point method. **[LO 4.1]**

3. You are working as a private math tutor to raise money for a trip during spring break. First explain why the price elasticity of demand for math tutoring might be elastic. Then explain why the price elasticity of demand for math tutoring might be inelastic. **[LO 4.2]**

4. You are working as a private math tutor to raise money for a trip during spring break. You want to earn as much money as possible, and you think the demand for math tutors is currently inelastic. Should you increase or decrease the price you charge? Explain. **[LO 4.2]**

5. You have been hired by the government of Kenya, which produces a lot of coffee, to examine the supply of gourmet coffee beans. Suppose you discover that the

price elasticity of supply is 0.85. Explain this number to the Kenyan government. **[LO 4.3]**

6. You have noticed that the price of tickets to your university's basketball games keeps increasing, but the supply of tickets remains the same. Why might supply be unresponsive to changes in price? **[LO 4.3]**

7. Which will have a more price-elastic supply over six months: real estate in downtown Manhattan or real estate in rural Oklahoma? Explain your reasoning. **[LO 4.4]**

8. Certain skilled labor, such as hair cutting, requires licensing or certification, which is costly and takes a long time to acquire. Explain what would happen to the price elasticity of supply for haircuts if this licensing requirement were removed. **[LO 4.4]**

9. Although we could describe both the cross-price elasticity of demand between paper coffee cups and plastic coffee lids and the cross-price elasticity of demand between sugar and artificial sweeteners as highly elastic, the first cross-price elasticity is negative and the second is positive. What is the reason for this? **[LO 4.5]**

10. Name two related goods you consume that would have a positive cross-price elasticity. What happens to your consumption of the second good if the price of the first good increases? **[LO 4.5]**

11. Name two related goods you consume that would have a negative cross-price elasticity. What happens to your consumption of the second good if the price of the first good increases? **[LO 4.5]**

12. In France, where cheese is an important and traditional part of people's meals, people eat about six times as much cheese per person as in the United States. In which country do you think the demand for cheese will be more income-elastic? Why? **[LO 4.6]**

13. Name a good you consume for which your income elasticity of demand is positive. What happens when your income increases? **[LO 4.6]**

14. Name a good you consume for which your income elasticity of demand is negative. What happens when your income increases? **[LO 4.6]**

Problems and Applications

1. When the price of a bar of chocolate is $1, the quantity demanded is 100,000 bars. When the price rises to $1.50, the quantity demanded falls to 60,000 bars. Calculate the price elasticity of demand using the mid-point method. **[LO 4.1]**

   a. Suppose the price increases from $1 to $1.50. Calculate the price elasticity of demand.

   b. Suppose the price decreases from $1.50 to $1. Calculate the price elasticity of demand.

2. If the price elasticity of demand for used cars priced between $4,000 and $6,000 is −1.2 (using the mid-point method), what will be the percent change in quantity demanded when the price of a used car falls from $6,000 to $4,000? **[LO 4.1]**

3. Three points are identified on the graph in Figure 4P-1. **[LO 4.2]**

FIGURE 4P-1

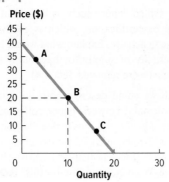

a. At point A, is demand inelastic, elastic, or unit-elastic?

b. At point B, is demand inelastic, elastic, or unit-elastic?

c. At point C, is demand inelastic, elastic, or unit-elastic?

4. Which of the following has a more elastic demand in the short run? **[LO 4.2]**

a. Pomegranate juice or drinking water?

b. Cereal or Rice Krispies®?

c. Speedboats or gourmet chocolate?

5. In each of the following instances, determine whether demand is elastic, inelastic, or unit-elastic. **[LO 4.2]**

a. If price increases by 10 percent and quantity demanded decreases by 15 percent, demand is _____.

b. If price decreases by 10 percent and quantity demanded increases by 5 percent, demand is _____.

6. In each of the following instances, determine whether quantity demanded will increase or decrease, and by how much. **[LO 4.2]**

a. If price elasticity of demand is −1.3 and price increases by 2 percent, quantity demanded will _____ by _____ percent.

b. If price elasticity of demand is −0.3 percent and price decreases by 2 percent, quantity demanded will _____ by _____ percent.

Problems 7 and 8 refer to the demand schedule shown in Table 4P-1. For each price change, say whether demand is **elastic, unit-elastic,** *or* **inelastic,** *and say whether total revenue* **increases, decreases,** *or* **stays the same.**

TABLE 4P-1

Price ($)	Quantity demanded
80	0
70	50
60	100
50	150
40	200
30	250
20	300
10	350
0	400

7. Consider each of the following price increase scenarios. **[LO 4.2]**

a. Price increases from $10 to $20. Demand is _____ and total revenue _____.

b. Price increases from $30 to $40. Demand is _____ and total revenue _____.

c. Price increases from $50 to $60. Demand is _____ and total revenue _____.

8. Price decreases from $60 to $50. Demand is _____ and total revenue _____. **[LO 4.2]**

Problems 9–12 refer to Figure 4P-2.

FIGURE 4P-2

9. Draw the price effect and the quantity effect for a price change from $60 to $50. Which effect is larger? Does total revenue increase or decrease? No calculation is necessary. **[LO 4.2]**

10. Draw the price effect and the quantity effect for a price change from $30 to $20. Which effect is larger? Does total revenue increase or decrease? No calculation is necessary. **[LO 4.2]**

11. Draw the price effect and the quantity effect for a price change from $60 to $70. Which effect is larger? Does total revenue increase or decrease? No calculation is necessary. **[LO 4.2]**

12. Draw the price effect and the quantity effect for a price change from $10 to $20. Which effect is larger? Does total revenue increase or decrease? No calculation is necessary. **[LO 4.2]**

13. Use the graph in Figure 4P-3 to calculate the price elasticity of supply between points A and B using the midpoint method. **[LO 4.3]**

FIGURE 4P-3

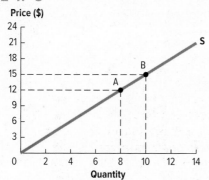

14. If the price of a haircut is $15, the number of haircuts provided is 125. If the price rises to $30 per haircut, barbers will work much longer hours, and the supply of haircuts will increase to 200. What is the price elasticity of supply for haircuts between $15 and $30? **[LO 4.3]**

15. Which of the following has a more elastic supply in the short run? **[LO 4.4]**
    a. Hospitals or mobile clinics?
    b. Purebred dogs or mixed-breed dogs?
    c. On-campus courses or online courses?

16. In each of the following instances, determine whether supply is elastic, inelastic, or unit-elastic. **[LO 4.4]**
    a. If price increases by 10 percent and quantity supplied increases by 15 percent, supply is _____.
    b. If price decreases by 10 percent and quantity supplied decreases by 5 percent, supply is _____.

17. In each of the following instances, determine whether quantity supplied will increase or decrease, and by how much. **[LO 4.4]**
    a. If price elasticity of supply is 1.3 and price increases by 2 percent, quantity supplied will _____ by _____ percent.
    b. If price elasticity of supply is 0.3 and price decreases by 2 percent, quantity supplied will _____ by _____ percent.

18. Suppose that the price of peanut butter rises from $2 to $3 per jar. **[LO 4.5]**
    a. The quantity of jelly purchased falls from 20 million jars to 15 million jars. What is the cross-price elasticity of demand between peanut butter and jelly? Are they complements or substitutes?
    b. The quantity of jelly purchased increases from 15 million jars to 20 million jars. What is the cross-price elasticity of demand between peanut butter and jelly? Are they complements or substitutes?

19. For each of the following pairs, predict whether the cross-price elasticity of demand will be positive or negative: **[LO 4.5]**
    a. Soap and hand sanitizer.
    b. CDs and MP3s.
    c. Sheets and pillowcases.

20. Suppose that when the average family income rises from $30,000 per year to $40,000 per year, the average family's purchases of toilet paper rise from 100 rolls to 105 rolls per year. **[LO 4.6]**
    a. Calculate the income-elasticity of demand for toilet paper.
    b. Is toilet paper a normal or an inferior good?
    c. Is the demand for toilet paper income-elastic or income-inelastic?

21. In each of the following instances, determine whether the good is normal or inferior, and whether it is income-elastic or income-inelastic. **[LO 4.6]**
    a. If income increases by 10 percent and the quantity demanded of a good then increases by 5 percent, the good is _____ and _____.
    b. If income increases by 10 percent and the quantity demanded of a good decreases by 20 percent, the good is _____ and _____.

Math Essentials: Calculating Percentage Change, Slope, and Elasticity

The math associated with the concept of elasticity covers a wide variety of topics. In order to be able to calculate elasticity, you need to be able to calculate percentage changes. In order to talk about shape of a line, and its elasticity, you need to be able to understand slope and the relationship between variables, particularly price and quantity.

Percentage Change

In Chapter 4, "Elasticity," we calculated elasticity in all its forms. If you're not entirely comfortable calculating percentage change, though, elasticity can be a daunting idea. Percentage changes represent the relative change in a variable from an old value to a new one. In the chapter, and in this appendix, we use the mid-point method to calculate percentage change. The mid-point method measures the percentage change relative to a point *midway between the two points.*

Equation C-1 shows how to calculate percentage change using the mid-point method. There, X_1 represents the original value of any variable X, and X_2 is the new value of this variable.

EQUATION C-1 $\text{Percentage change} = \left[\dfrac{(X_2 - X_1)}{\left(\dfrac{X_2 + X_1}{2} \right)} \right] \times 100$

LEARNING OBJECTIVES

LO C.1   Understand how to calculate percentage changes.

LO C.2   Use slope to calculate elasticity.

LO C.1 Understand how to calculate percentage changes.

Notice that the denominator is the *mid-point* between X_1 and X_2. In other words, it is the average of X_1 and X_2. Overall, you can use this method to calculate the percentage change in variables of various kinds. A percentage change in quantity, for example, would be expressed as:

EQUATION C-1A $\text{Percentage change in quantity} = \left[\dfrac{(Q_2 - Q_1)}{\left(\dfrac{Q_2 + Q_1}{2}\right)} \right] \times 100$

where Q_2 represents the new value of quantity demanded and Q_1 the original quantity demanded.

Similarly, a percentage change in price would be expressed as:

EQUATION C-1B $\text{Percentage change in price} = \left[\dfrac{(P_2 - P_1)}{\left(\dfrac{P_2 + P_1}{2}\right)} \right] \times 100$

Let's try an example for practice: For weeks, you have been watching the price of a new pair of shoes. They normally cost $90, but you see that the store has a sale and now offers them for $70. You find the percentage change in the price of the shoes by first subtracting the old price ($90) from the new one ($70) to find the change in price, which is −$20. To find how much of a change this is, you take this −$20 price change and divide it by the price midway between $70 and $90 ($80).

$$\frac{\$70 - \$90}{\left(\dfrac{\$70 + \$90}{2}\right)} = \frac{-\$20}{\$80} = -0.25$$

You then multiply by 100 to get the percentage change: $-0.25 \times 100 = -25\%$. In this case, the $20 price reduction was a 25 percent decrease in price. Not a bad sale!

Notice that in this case, the percentage change is negative, which indicates that the new value is less than the original. If the prices of shoes had increased instead, the associated percentage change would be a positive value.

The best way to do get comfortable with calculating percentage changes is through lots of practice. You can find a few extra problems to try on your own at the end of this appendix, and you also could challenge yourself to calculate price changes you see in your everyday life.

Slope and Elasticity

LO C.2 Use slope to calculate elasticity.

In Appendix A, "Math Essentials: Understanding Graphs and Slope," we showed that the direction of a slope tells us something meaningful about the relationship between the two variables we are representing:

- When x and y move in the *same direction*, they are said to have a *positive* relationship. Not surprisingly, this means that the slope of the line is a positive number. When the slope of a line is positive, we know that y increases as x increases, and y decreases as x decreases.
- Similarly, when x and y move in *opposite directions*, they are said to have a *negative* relationship. The slope of the line is a negative number. When the slope of a line is negative, we know that y decreases as x increases, and y increases as x decreases.

In Chapter 3, "Markets," we saw a positive relationship between price and quantity in the supply curve. We saw a negative relationship between price and quantity in the demand curve. Two variables (such as price and quantity) may have more than one relationship to each other, depending on whose choices they represent and under what circumstances.

The steepness of a slope is also important. Numerically, the closer the number representing the slope is to zero, the flatter the curve will be. Remember that both positive and negative numbers can be close to zero. So, a slope of -1 is equally steep as a slope of 1, although one slopes downward and the other upward. Correspondingly, a line with a slope of -5 is steeper than a line with a slope of -1 or one with a slope of 1.

You can tell just from looking at an equation how steep the line will be. If this idea is still a little hazy, you might want to page back to Appendix A, in the "Steepness of a slope" section, to refresh your memory. The steepness of slope is important to understanding the concept of elasticity.

Although the ideas of slope and elasticity are related, there are two basic mathematical distinctions between them:

1. Slope describes the change in y per the change in x, whereas elasticity measures are based on the change in x per the change in y.
2. We usually measure elasticity in terms of *percentage changes,* rather than absolute (unit-based) changes.

Why would we be interested in how much x changes in response to a one-unit change in y? To get at this difference, let's look at Figure C-1. It is similar to Figure A-10 (in Appendix A) but replaces the variables x and y with the quantity of a good (Q) and its price (P).

In Chapter 4, "Elasticity," you learned that *price elasticity* is a measure of the responsiveness of supply (or demand) to changes in price. In other words, it is a measure of how quantity (on the x-axis) responds to a change in price (on the y-axis). So this time, let's make the change in price (vertical distance) the same and look at how much quantity changes (horizontal distance).

Looking at Figure C-1, we can see that when price moves from P_1 to P_2, quantity supplied changes by less in panel A than it does in panel B. When price increases from P_1 to P_2 in panel A, quantity increases by 1 unit, from Q_1 to Q_2. In contrast, panel B shows an increase of 2 units from Q_1 to Q_2 for the same change in P. This means supply is less responsive to a price change in panel A compared to panel B.

FIGURE C-1

Measuring a change in Q in response to a change in P

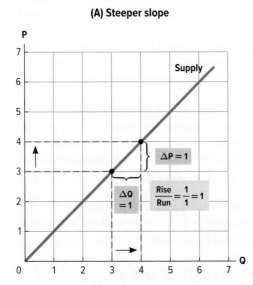

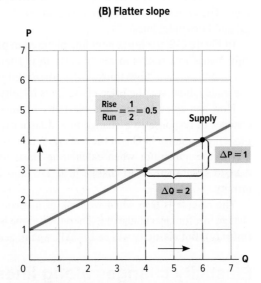

The steeper slope in panel A indicates that price changes less in panel A than in panel B in response to a change in quantity demanded.

The flatter slope in panel B indicates that price changes more in panel B than in panel A in response to a change in quantity demanded.

FIGURE C-2

Slope versus elasticity of horizontal and vertical lines

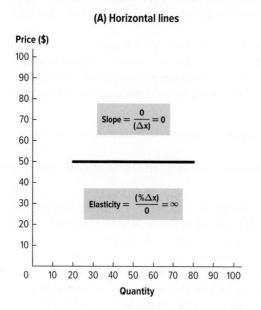

(A) Horizontal lines

(B) Vertical lines

When a line is horizontal, the slope is zero and the associated elasticity is infinite. In other words, demand or supply occurs only at a single price.

When a line is vertical, the slope is infinite and the elasticity is zero. Regardless of the price, quantity supplied or demanded is going to be the same.

X over Y, or Y over X?

We have noted that slope is indicated by $\frac{\Delta y}{\Delta x}$. In contrast, elasticity is commonly indicated by $\frac{\%\Delta Q}{\%\Delta P}$, which corresponds to $\frac{\Delta x}{\Delta y}$. In some sense, then, *elasticity is computed as the mirror image of slope.* The easiest way to picture this is to see the difference between slope and elasticity for vertical and horizontal lines.

In Figure C-2, the horizontal line pictured in panel A has a slope of zero. This is because a one-unit change in x results in zero change in y. Therefore, slope is calculated as $\frac{0}{\Delta x}$. Zero divided by any number is zero. If we think of the horizontal line as a demand curve mapping price to quantity demanded, however, the price elasticity is infinity.

How can slope be zero and elasticity infinity? Remember that slope measures how much y changes in response to a change in x. Elasticity, however, measures the sensitivity of P (on the y-axis) to a change in Q (on the x-axis). Whereas x is in the denominator when calculating slope, it is in the numerator when calculating elasticity. For a horizontal line, then, elasticity will be $\%\Delta Q/0$ since there is no change in P. Division by 0 is mathematically undefined, or known as infinity.

The reverse is true when we look at a vertical line. When a graph is vertical, there is zero change in x for any change in y. Therefore, slope is calculated as $\frac{\Delta y}{0}$. In this case, slope is undefined (infinity). But elasticity will be $0/\%\Delta P$. Again, zero divided by any number is zero.

Elasticity changes along lines with constant slope

The second important mathematical difference between slope and elasticity is that we usually measure slope in terms of absolute changes, but we measure elasticity in terms of percentage changes. This means that at different points along a straight line, slope is constant, but elasticity varies.

TABLE C-1
Demand schedule

Price ($)	Quantity
80	0
70	10
60	20
50	30
40	40
30	50
20	60
10	70
0	80

As an example, take a look at the demand schedule in Table C-1. First, let's calculate the slope between two different sets of points. Using the first two prices and quantities at the top of the demand schedule, we see that the slope between these points is −1.

$$\text{Slope \#1} = \frac{\Delta P_1}{\Delta Q_1} = \frac{(0-10)}{(80-70)} = \frac{-10}{10} = -1$$

Then, pick another two points. Using the quantities 30 and 20 and their respective prices, we can calculate that the slope is still −1.

$$\text{Slope \#2} = \frac{\Delta P_2}{\Delta Q_2} = \frac{(30-20)}{(50-60)} = \frac{10}{-10} = -1$$

No matter what two points along the demand curve we choose, the slope is the same. *Slope is constant because the demand curve is linear.*

Now let's calculate elasticity between these same two sets of points. We will use the mid-point method described in Chapter 4, "Elasticity," to calculate elasticity:

$$\text{Elasticity} = \frac{\%\Delta Q}{\%\Delta P} = \frac{\Delta Q/Q_{\text{midpoint}}}{\Delta P/P_{\text{midpoint}}}$$

Let's start with the top of the demand curve and calculate the price elasticity of demand for a price change from 80 to 70. Using the mid-point method, we have:

$$\frac{\Delta Q/Q_{\text{midpoint}}}{\Delta P/P_{\text{midpoint}}} = \frac{(0-10)/5}{(80-70)/60} = \frac{-10/5}{10/60} = \frac{-2}{0.17} = -11.8$$

Now let's calculate the price elasticity of demand at the bottom of the demand curve for a price change of 30 to 20.

$$\frac{\Delta Q/Q_{\text{midpoint}}}{\Delta P/P_{\text{midpoint}}} = \frac{(50-60)/55}{(30-20)/25} = \frac{-10/55}{10/25} = \frac{-0.18}{0.4} = -0.45$$

Even though both of these calculations represented a 10-unit change in quantity in response to a $10 change in price, along a linear demand curve, elasticity changes. Moving down along the demand curve means less elasticity. This is because the same change in Q or P is a different *percentage* of the midpoint at different points on the line.

Problems and Applications

1. Calculate the percentage change in each of the following examples using the mid-point method. [LO C.1]

    a. 8 to 12.

    b. 18 to 14.

    c. 130 to 120.

    d. 95 to 105.

2. Find the percentage change in price in each of the following examples using the mid-point method. [LO C.1]

    a. The price of a $4.50 sandwich increases to $5.50.

    b. A sale discounts the price of a sofa from $750 to $500.

3. Use the demand curve in Figure CP-1 to answer the following questions. Use the mid-point method in your calculations. [LO C.2]

FIGURE CP-1

    a. What is the price elasticity of demand for a price change from $0 to $20?

    b. What is the price elasticity of demand for a price change from $20 to $40?

    c. What is the price elasticity of demand for a price change from $40 to $60?

4. Use the demand schedule in Table CP-1 to answer the following questions. Use the mid-point method in your calculations. [LO C.2]

    a. What is the price elasticity of demand for a price change from $4 to $8?

    b. What is the price elasticity of demand for a price change from $8 to $16?

    c. What is the price elasticity of demand for a price change from $20 to $24?

TABLE CP-1

Price ($)	Quantity
0	60
4	50
8	40
12	30
16	20
20	10
24	0

5. Use the demand schedule in Table CP-2 to answer the following questions. Use the mid-point method when calculating elasticity. [LO C.2]

TABLE CP-2

Price ($)	Quantity
0	56
1	48
2	42
3	35
4	28
5	21
6	14
7	7
8	0

    a. What is the price elasticity of demand for a price change from $2 to $3? What is the slope of the demand curve for a price change from $2 to $3?

    b. What is the price elasticity of demand for a price change from $3 to $5? What is the slope of the demand curve for a price change from $3 to $5?

    c. What is the price elasticity of demand for a price change from $6 to $7? What is the slope of the demand curve for a price change from $6 to $7?

Efficiency

A Broken Laser Pointer Starts an Internet Revolution

In 1995, a young software developer named Pierre Omidyar spent his Labor Day weekend building a website he called AuctionWeb. His idea was to create a site where people could post their old stuff for sale online and auction it off to the highest bidder. Soon after, he sold the first item on AuctionWeb for $14.83. It was a broken laser pointer, which he had posted on the site as a test, never expecting anyone to bid on it. When Pierre pointed out that the pointer was broken, the bidder explained that he was "a collector of broken laser pointers."

As you might have guessed, AuctionWeb became the wildly successful company we now know as eBay. In 2017, over 20 years after the site was first conceived, the total value of items sold on eBay was $88.4 billion, and 170 million people around the world were active buyers.[1]

©bloomua/123RF

Like many creation stories, the tale of eBay's first sale gives us insight into what makes it tick. People are interested in some pretty odd things (like broken laser pointers), but given a big enough crowd, matches usually can be made between buyers and sellers. When buyers and sellers are matched up and they trade, each is made better off. The buyer gets an item he wants, and the seller gets money. Because both parties are willing participants, they benefit from engaging in such transactions. In fact, they even are willing to pay eBay to provide the marketplace where they can find one another. How else is someone with a broken laser pointer going to find an eager buyer?

eBay's success is based on one of the most fundamental ideas in economics: *Voluntary exchanges create value and can make everyone involved better off*. The importance of that idea stretches far beyond eBay. This principle drives a range of businesses—from grocery stores, to investment banks, to online retailers—that do not manufacture or grow anything themselves. Instead, they facilitate transactions between producers and consumers.

But this principle raises a question: How do we know that people are better off when they buy and sell things? Can we say anything about *how much* better off they are?

LEARNING OBJECTIVES

LO 5.1 Use willingness to pay and willingness to sell to determine supply and demand at a given price.

LO 5.2 Calculate consumer surplus based on a graph or table.

LO 5.3 Calculate producer surplus based on a graph or table.

LO 5.4 Calculate total surplus based on a graph or table.

LO 5.5 Define efficiency in terms of surplus, and identify efficient and inefficient situations.

LO 5.6 Describe the distribution of surplus, or benefits to society, that results from a policy decision.

LO 5.7 Calculate deadweight loss.

LO 5.8 Explain why correcting a missing market can make everyone better off.

To answer these questions, we need a tool to describe the *size of the benefits* that result from transactions and who receives said benefits. In this chapter we will introduce the concept of *surplus*. It can measure the benefit that people receive when they buy something for less than they would have been willing to pay. It also can measure the benefit that people receive when they sell something for more than they would have been willing to accept. *Surplus* is the best way to look at the benefits people receive from successful transactions.

Surplus also shows us why the equilibrium price and quantity in a competitive market are so special: They maximize the total well-being of those involved. Even when we care about outcomes other than total well-being (like inequality in the distribution of benefits), surplus gives us a yardstick for comparing different ideas and policies. For instance, calculations of surplus can clearly show who benefits and who loses from policies such as taxes and minimum wages. As we'll see, maximizing total surplus—an idea called *efficiency*—is one of the most powerful features of a market system. Even more remarkable is that it is achieved without centralized coordination.

Surplus also shows us how simply enabling people to trade with one another can make them better off. Often, creating a new market for goods and services (as the Grameen Bank did in Bangladesh, in the example in Chapter 1, "Economics and Life") or improving an existing market (as eBay did on the internet) can be a good way to help people. Knowing how and when to harness the power of economic exchanges to improve well-being is an important tool for businesspeople and public-minded problem solvers alike.

Willingness to Pay and Sell

LO 5.1 Use willingness to pay and willingness to sell to determine supply and demand at a given price.

eBay is an online auction platform that allows people to post items for sale that anyone else online can buy. People who want to buy the item make bids offering to pay a particular price. This decentralized marketplace supports all sorts of transactions: from real estate, to used cars, to rare books, to (in one extraordinary case) a half-eaten cheese sandwich said to look like the Virgin Mary (which sold for $28,000).[2]

Who uses eBay? What do they want? At the most basic level, they are people who want to buy or sell a particular good. We're not sure how many people want broken laser pointers or decade-old cheese sandwiches, so let's stick with something a little more typical. How about digital cameras? Just as we did in Chapter 3, "Markets," we'll make the simplifying assumption that there is just one kind of digital camera rather than thousands of slightly different models.

Imagine you see a digital camera posted for sale on eBay. Who might bid on it? What are their *wants and constraints?* Most obviously, people who bid will be those who *want* a camera. But they will also care about the price they pay: Why spend $200 for a camera if you can get it for $100 and spend the other $100 on something else? Potential buyers *want* to pay as little as possible, but on top of this general preference, each buyer has a maximum price she is willing to pay.

Economists call this maximum price the buyer's **willingness to pay** or the *reservation price.* Economists use these two terms interchangeably; in this text, we'll stick with "willingness to pay." This price is the point above which the buyer throws up her hands and says, "Never mind. I'd rather spend my money on something else." Each potential buyer wants to purchase a camera for a price that is as low as possible and no higher than her maximum *willingness to pay.*

On eBay, we can see willingness to pay in action. When the price of a product remains below a bidder's willingness to pay, he'll continue to bid on it. When the going price passes his willingness to pay, he'll drop out.

Of course, buyers are only half the story. Who posted the camera for sale on eBay in the first place? To create a functioning market for digital cameras, someone has to want to sell. Whereas buyers want to buy a camera for as low a price as possible, sellers want to sell for as high a price as possible. Why take less money if you could get more? Just as each potential buyer has a willingness to pay, each potential seller has a *willingness to sell.* **Willingness to sell** is the minimum price that a seller is willing to accept in exchange for a good or service. A seller always wants to sell for a price that is as high as possible, but never lower than his minimum.

We can see willingness to sell in action on eBay through the "reserve price" that sellers can set when they post an item. This reserve price sets a bar below which the seller will not accept any bids. If she doesn't get any higher bids, she simply keeps the item.

So far, so good: Buyers want to buy low; sellers want to sell high. What does this have to do with markets? We're about to see that willingness to pay and willingness to sell are actually the forces that drive the shape of demand and supply curves.

Willingness to pay and the demand curve

Let's return to potential camera buyers and take a closer look at how they choose to bid on the camera posted on eBay. To keep things simple, let's imagine that there are five potential buyers who are considering bidding on this particular camera.

- Bidder #1 is a bird watcher who cares passionately about having a good camera to document the rare birds she finds. She is willing to pay up to $500 for the camera.
- Bidder #2 is an amateur photographer. He has an outdated camera and is willing to pay $250 for this newer model.
- Bidder #3 is a real estate agent who will be willing to pay $200 or less to be able to take better pictures of her properties.
- Bidder #4 is a journalist. She wouldn't mind having a newer camera than the one her newspaper provided but would pay no more than $150 for it.
- Bidder #5 is a teacher who will spend no more than $100—the amount of the eBay gift certificate given to him by appreciative parents for his birthday.

We can plot on a graph each potential buyer's willingness to pay. In panel A of Figure 5-1, we've graphed possible prices for the camera against the number of buyers who would be willing to bid that price for it. Remember that each person's willingness to pay is a *maximum*—he or she would also be willing to buy the camera at any lower price. Therefore, at a price of $100, all five buyers are willing to bid; at $350, only one will bid.

If you look carefully, you might notice that the graph in panel A looks a lot like a demand curve: Price is on the *y*-axis, quantity is on the *x*-axis, and there's a line showing that quantity demanded increases as price decreases. In fact this *is* a demand curve, although it represents

willingness to pay (reservation price) the maximum price that a buyer would be willing to pay for a good or service

willingness to sell the minimum price that a seller is willing to accept in exchange for a good or service

FIGURE 5-1

Willingness to pay and the demand curve

(A) Willingness to pay with few buyers

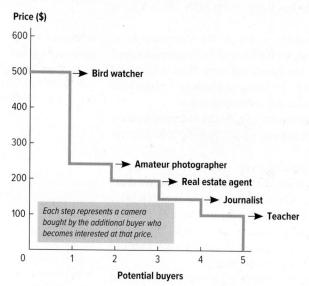

At any given price, buyers with a higher willingness to pay will buy and those with a lower willingness to pay will not. If the price were $350, only one buyer would buy. If it were $50, all five people would buy. This demand curve has a step-like shape rather than a smooth line because there are a limited number of buyers whose prices are expressed in round dollar amounts.

(B) Willingness to pay with many buyers

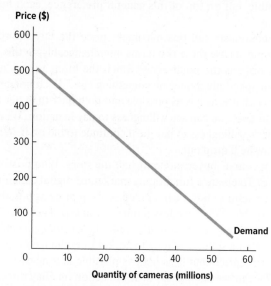

In the real market for a particular model of a digital camera, there are millions of cameras demanded at a particular price. The steps that we see in panel A get smaller and smaller until they disappear into a smooth curve.

only five potential buyers. We could conduct the same exercise in a bigger market and plot out the willingness to pay of millions of people rather than just five. In that case, we'd get a smooth demand curve, as shown in panel B of Figure 5-1. The individual steps that we see in panel A get smaller and smaller over the millions of cameras demanded, resulting in the smoothed-out curve.

Notice that although each buyer's willingness to pay is driven by different factors, we can explain the motivations behind all of their decisions by asking, *What are the trade-offs?* Money that is spent to buy a camera on eBay cannot be spent on other things. Willingness to pay is the point at which the benefit that a person will get from the camera is equal to the benefit of spending the money on another alternative—in other words, the opportunity cost. For instance, $250 is the point at which the enjoyment that the amateur photographer gets from a camera is the same as the enjoyment he would get from, say, spending $250 to upgrade his bicycle.

Since everyone has things they want other than cameras, the same opportunity cost logic applies to each of the potential buyers represented in the demand curve. At prices above the maximum willingness to pay, the opportunity cost is greater than the benefits. At lower prices, the benefits outweigh the opportunity cost.

To figure out which of our five individual buyers will actually purchase a camera, we have to know the market price. To find the market price, we have to know something about the supply of digital cameras. Therefore, we turn next to investigating the supply curve.

Willingness to sell and the supply curve

As you may have guessed, just as the shape of the demand curve was driven by potential buyers' willingness to pay, the shape of the supply curve for digital cameras is driven by potential sellers' *willingness to sell*. To simplify things, let's imagine five prospective sellers who have posted their cameras for sale on eBay.

- Seller #1 is a college student who was given a camera as a birthday present. All he really cares about is having money to see his favorite band, so he's willing to part with his camera for as little as $50.
- Seller #2 is a sales representative for a big company that makes digital cameras. She's authorized to sell a camera for $100 or higher.
- Seller #3 is a professional nature photographer who owns several cameras but won't sell for anything less than $200. At a lower price he'd rather give the camera as a gift to his nephew.
- Seller #4 is a sales representative for a small company that is just starting up in the camera industry and has much higher costs of production than the larger company; it can make money only by selling its cameras for $300 or more.
- Seller #5 is an art teacher who is sentimentally attached to her camera, given to her by a friend. She won't give it up unless she can get at least $400.

We can represent these five individuals by plotting on a graph their willingness to sell. Panel A of Figure 5-2 shows a graph of potential prices and the number of cameras that will be up for

FIGURE 5-2

Willingness to sell and the supply curve

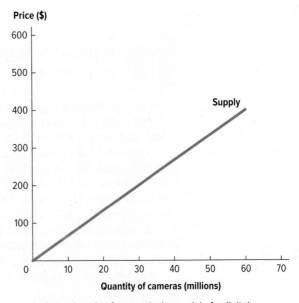

(A) Willingness to sell with few sellers

Each step represents the additional camera sold by a seller who becomes interested as the price increases.

Art teacher
Sales rep (small company)
Nature photographer
Sales rep (big company)
College student

At any given price, sellers with a lower willingness to sell will sell, while those with a higher willingness to sell will not. At a price of $400, all five people will sell their cameras, while at a price of $200, only three sell. This rough supply curve would look smooth if there were many sellers, each with a different willingness to sell.

(B) Willingness to sell with many sellers

Supply

In the real market for a particular model of a digital camera, there are millions of cameras supplied at a particular price. The steps that we see in panel A get smaller and smaller until they disappear into a smooth curve.

bid at each price. This graph is a supply curve representing only five potential sellers. As with the demand curve, if we added all of the millions of digital cameras that are actually for sale in the real world, we see the smooth supply curve we're accustomed to, as in panel B.

Sellers' willingness to sell is determined by the *trade-offs* they face, and, in particular, the opportunity cost of the sale. The opportunity cost of selling a camera for sellers #1, #3, and #5 is the use or enjoyment that the seller could get from keeping the camera. In the case of the two camera manufacturers, sellers #2 and #4, the opportunity cost is whatever else the firm would do with the money that would be required to manufacture the camera—say, marketing the camera or researching new technology. The opportunity cost of each of the five sellers will be determined by different factors—not all of them strictly monetary, as in the case of the teacher, who is sentimentally attached to her camera.

For an item that a seller just wants to get rid of (like the broken laser pointer mentioned at the start of the chapter), the starting price might be one cent. If opportunity cost is zero, anything is better than nothing!

On the other hand, in a market where manufacturers are producing and selling new products, the minimum price will have to be high enough to make it worth their while to continue making new products. This would be the case for the two camera manufacturers. If the selling price didn't cover the costs of production, the manufacturers would simply stop making the item—otherwise, they would actually lose money every time they made a sale. (Occasionally, we do see manufacturers selling below the cost of production, but only when they've made a mistake and have to get rid of already-produced goods.)

Having met five potential buyers and five potential sellers, we're now in a position to understand what happens when the two groups come together in the market to make trades.

In the real world, transactions don't always sort so neatly. Sellers may post prices well above their true willingness to sell. Buyers, on the other hand, are always looking to get a better deal. In these cases, buyers and sellers may choose to negotiate on price. Take a look at the Econ and YOU box "It pays to negotiate" to consider a common version of such trading—salary negotiations.

It pays to negotiate
Econ and YOU

No matter which way you look at the data, women earn less than men. Overall, women working full-time earn just 77 percent of what male workers earn. Controlling for the fact that women and men often work in different kinds of jobs, there still is a 4–7 percent gap in pay.

There are many explanations for this gap, and the nature of wage negotiations tells part of the story. In some jobs, you're offered a wage and you take it or leave it. But often wages are decided by negotiation: Workers argue for the wage they want, and employers respond. The trouble is that it can be hard to know exactly how much a job should pay, and different people (with different talents, bargaining skills, and backgrounds) can end up with very different pay.

Economist Marianne Bertrand points to studies that find women are far less likely to negotiate their salary. Instead, they are more likely to accept the first wage offer presented by their employer. One survey of 200 workers found that men negotiated two to four times more often than women. The problem is that simply accepting the first offer puts women at a salary disadvantage.

Why were women in the survey more likely to take the first offer? One explanation is that women fear repercussions or worry about seeming greedy. Researchers Hannah Riley Bowles, Linda Babcock, and Lei Lai showed that women who tried to negotiate were more likely to be rated negatively by male evaluators and that male evaluators were more willing to work with women who accepted the first offer. However, when the evaluator was female, women did not get "punished" for asking.

Can employees help improve outcomes? One potential solution is to invite women to negotiate. Research by economists Andres Leibbrandt and John List randomly varied whether job searchers received ambiguous salary information or were told that the salary for a position was "negotiable." While men were three times more likely to try negotiating salary with ambiguous information, women and men were equally likely to try for more money when it was explicitly stated that the salary was "negotiable."

Alternatively, some firms have gone further and ended the practice of negotiations altogether. In 2015, Ellen Pao, the CEO of Reddit, a large internet community, cited the fact that men negotiate more often than women as a major part of her decision to end salary negotiations at the company. Whether changes like these will narrow the gender pay gap remains to be seen.

What should you do? The big lesson is: It pays to negotiate.

Sources: Marianne Bertrand, "Perspectives on gender," *Handbook of Labor Economics* (2011), Vol. 4, part B, pp. 1556–1562, edited by David Card and Orley Ashenfelter, www.fiwi.uni-jena.de/wfwmedia/Lehre/GenderEconomics/Bertrand+2011+New+Perspectives+on+Gender+In+Handbook+of+Labor+Economics+4+B-p-454.pdf; Hannah Riley Bowles, Linda Babcock, and Lei Lai, "Social incentives for gender differences in the propensity to initiate negotiations: Sometimes it does hurt to ask," *Organizational Behavior and Human Decision Processes* 103 (2007), pp.84–103, www.cfa.harvard.edu/cfawis/bowles.pdf; Andreas Liebbrandt and John A. List, "Do women avoid salary negotiations? Evidence from a large-scale natural field experiment," *Management Science* (2014), http://gap.hks.harvard.edu/do-women-avoid-salary-negotiations-evidence-large-scale-natural-field-experiment#method.

✓ TEST YOURSELF

☐ How is willingness to pay determined by opportunity cost? **[LO 5.1]**

☐ What is the relationship between willingness to pay and the demand curve? **[LO 5.1]**

Measuring Surplus

Surplus is a way of measuring who benefits from transactions and by how much. Economists use this word to describe a fairly simple concept: If you get something for less than you would have been willing to pay, or sell it for more than the minimum you would have accepted, that's a good thing. Think about how nice it feels to buy something on sale that you would have been willing to pay full price for. That "bonus" value that you would have paid if necessary, but didn't have to, is *surplus*. We can talk about surplus for both buyers and sellers, individually and collectively.

surplus
a way of measuring who benefits from transactions and by how much

Surplus is the difference between the price at which a buyer or seller would be *willing* to trade and the actual price. Think about willingness to pay as the price at which someone is completely indifferent between buying an item and keeping his money. At a higher price, he would prefer to keep the money; at a lower price, he would prefer to buy. By looking at the distance between this "indifference point" and the actual price, we can describe the extra value the buyer (or the seller) gets from the transaction.

Surplus is a simple idea, but a surprisingly powerful one. It turns out that surplus is a better measure of the value that buyers and sellers get from participating in a market than price itself. To see why this is true, read the From Another Angle box "How much would you pay to keep the internet from disappearing?"

How much would you pay to keep the internet from disappearing?

Why is surplus a better measure of value than how much we pay for something? Consider the difference between what we pay for the internet versus a particular model of computer.

Most people can access the internet for very little, or even for free. You might pay a monthly fee for high-speed access at home, but almost anyone can use the internet for free at schools, libraries, or coffee shops. Once you're online there are millions of websites that will provide information, entertainment, and services at no charge.

Computer owners, on the other hand, pay a lot for particular types of computers. For instance, consumers might pay $999 for a MacBook laptop. Does this mean that we value access to the internet less than a MacBook? Probably not.

Simply measuring price falls short of capturing true value. To see why, think about how much you would pay to prevent the particular type of computer you own from disappearing from the market. You might pay something: After all, there's a reason you chose it in the first place, and you might be willing to cough up a bit extra to get your preferred combination of technical specifications, appearance, and so on. But if the price got very steep, you'd probably rather switch to another, similar type of computer instead of paying more money. That difference—the maximum extra amount you would pay over the current price to maintain the ability to buy something—is your *consumer surplus*. It is the difference between your willingness to pay and the actual price.

Now consider the same question for the internet. Imagine that the internet is going to disappear tomorrow, or, at least, that you will be unable to access it in any way. How much would you pay to keep that from happening? Remember, that means no e-mail, no Google search or maps, no Facebook, no Twitter, no YouTube, no video streaming, and no online shopping. We suspect that you might be willing to pay a lot. The amount that you're willing to pay represents the true value that you place on the internet, even though the amount that you currently spend on it might be very little. That's the magic of surplus.

Consumer surplus

LO 5.2 Calculate consumer surplus based on a graph or table.

consumer surplus
the net benefit that a consumer receives from purchasing a good or service, measured by the difference between willingness to pay and the actual price

Let's go back to our five eBay buyers and calculate the surplus they would receive from buying a camera at a given price. This part of the transaction illustrates **consumer surplus**—the net benefit that a consumer receives from purchasing a good or service, measured by the difference between willingness to pay and the actual price.

Suppose it turns out that the going rate for cameras on eBay is $160. Using that amount, we can calculate the buyers' consumer surplus:

- The bird watcher was willing to bid up to $500. Therefore, her consumer surplus from buying the camera is $340—the difference between her willingness to pay and the $160 she actually pays.

Two other potential buyers will also buy a camera if the price is $160, and two will drop out:

- The amateur photographer is willing to pay $250, and the consumer surplus he receives is $90.
- The real estate agent is willing to pay up to $200, and the consumer surplus she receives is $40.
- The other two potential buyers will have dropped out of bidding when the price rose above $100 and then above $150, so they buy nothing and pay nothing. Their consumer surplus is zero.

We can add up each individual's consumer surplus to describe the overall benefits that buyers received in a market. (Somewhat confusingly, economists use the same term for individual and collective surplus, but you should be able to tell from the context whether we mean one person's consumer surplus or total consumer surplus for all buyers in the market.) If the market for digital cameras consisted only of our five individuals, then the total consumer surplus would be:

$$\$340 + \$90 + \$40 + \$0 + \$0 = \$470$$

On a graph, we represent consumer surplus as the area underneath the demand curve and above the horizontal line of the equilibrium price. Panel A of Figure 5-3 shows consumer surplus for these five individuals when the price is $160. (Because there are only five buyers in this market, the demand curve in panel A has the step-like shape we saw earlier.)

For a refresher on the area under a linear curve, see Appendix D, "Math Essentials: The Area under a Linear Curve," which follows this chapter.

How does a change in the market price affect buyers? Since buyers would always prefer prices to be lower:

- a decrease in price makes them better off, and
- an increase in price makes them worse off.

Some people will choose not to buy at all when prices rise—which means that their surplus becomes zero. Those who do buy will have a smaller individual surplus than they had at the lower price. The opposite is true when prices fall. Measuring consumer surplus tells us *how much* better or worse off buyers are when the price changes.

FIGURE 5-3

Consumer surplus

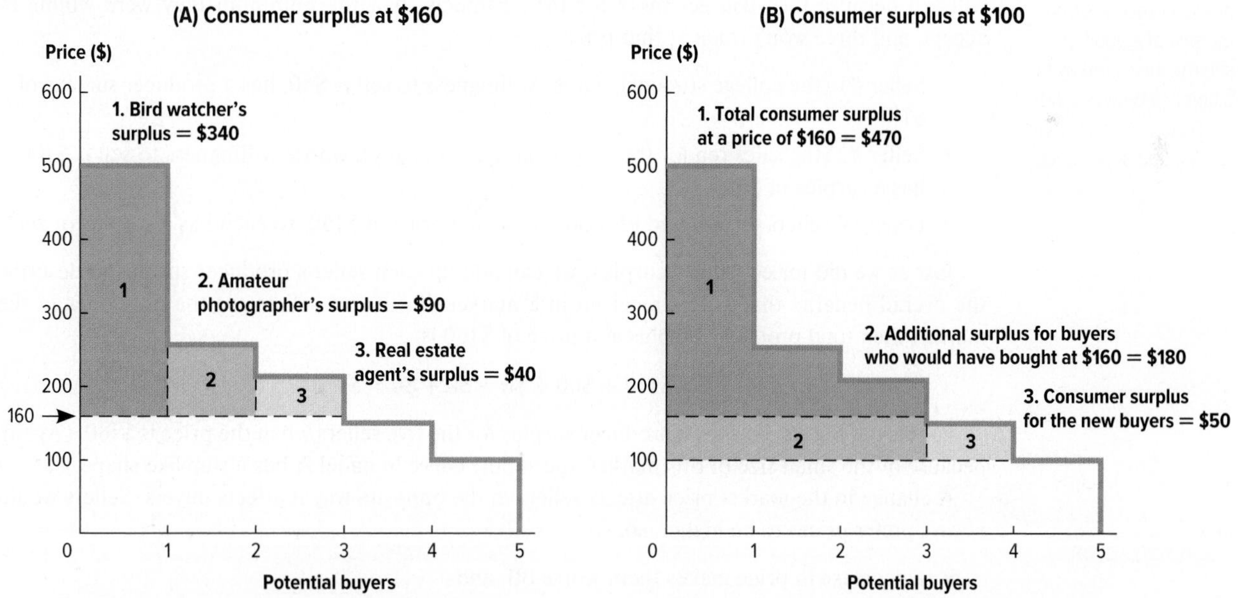

(A) Consumer surplus at $160

Price ($)

1. Bird watcher's surplus = $340
2. Amateur photographer's surplus = $90
3. Real estate agent's surplus = $40

Potential buyers

(B) Consumer surplus at $100

Price ($)

1. Total consumer surplus at a price of $160 = $470
2. Additional surplus for buyers who would have bought at $160 = $180
3. Consumer surplus for the new buyers = $50

Potential buyers

This graph shows consumer surplus in the camera market when price is $160. The shaded area is the difference between willingness to pay and the market price for each buyer. The more that a buyer would have been willing to pay, the greater the surplus at a lower price. At this price, total consumer surplus is $470, the sum of the individual surpluses shown.

When the price of cameras falls to $100, consumer surplus increases. Area 1 is consumer surplus under the old price. Area 2 is the additional surplus received by people who were willing to buy at either price. Area 3 is the surplus received by the two new buyers who enter the market when price falls. The combination of the three areas is total consumer surplus when price is $100. When the price falls, total consumer surplus increases from $470 to $700.

Panel B of Figure 5-3 shows what happens to total consumer surplus if the going price of cameras on eBay falls to $100. You can see by comparing panel A with panel B that when the price level falls, the area representing consumer surplus gets bigger. When the price falls:

- The consumer surplus of each of the three buyers who were already willing to buy increases by $60 each.

Also, two more buyers join the market:

- The journalist's willingness to pay is $150, so she gains consumer surplus of $50.
- The teacher's willingness to pay is $100; he buys a camera but gains no consumer surplus because the price is exactly equal to his willingness to pay.

When the camera's price drops to $100, total consumer surplus among our five individuals totals $700 (an increase of $230):

$$\$470 + \$60 + \$60 + \$60 + \$50 + \$0 = \$700$$

Producer surplus

LO 5.3 Calculate producer surplus based on a graph or table.

---

producer surplus
the net benefit that a producer receives from the sale of a good or service, measured by the difference between the producer's willingness to sell and the actual price

Like buyers, sellers want to increase the distance between the price at which they are willing to trade and the actual price. Sellers are better off when the market price is higher than their minimum willingness to sell. **Producer surplus** is the net benefit that a producer receives from the sale of a good or service, measured by the difference between willingness to sell and the actual price. It's called *producer* surplus regardless of whether the sellers actually produced the good themselves or—as often happens on eBay—are selling it secondhand.

If our five potential sellers find that the going price of cameras on eBay is $160, two of them will sell because they will get more for their cameras than the minimum they were willing to accept, and three won't trade at that price:

- Seller #1 (the college student), whose willingness to sell is $50, has a producer surplus of $110.
- Seller #2 (the sales rep for the bigger camera company), whose willingness to sell is $100, has a surplus of $60.
- Potential sellers #3, #4, and #5 won't trade at a price of $160, so each has a surplus of zero.

Just as we did for consumer surplus, we can add up each seller's producer surplus to describe the overall benefits that sellers received in a market. If our five sellers are the only ones in the market, then total producer surplus at a price of $160 is:

$$\$110 + \$60 + \$0 + \$0 + \$0 = \$170$$

Panel A of Figure 5-4 shows producer surplus for the five sellers when the price is $160. (Again, because of the small size of this market, the supply curve in panel A has a step-like shape.)

A change in the market price affects sellers in the opposite way it affects buyers. Sellers would always prefer prices to be higher, so:

- a decrease in price makes them worse off, and
- an increase in price makes them better off.

Some sellers will choose not to sell at all when prices fall; their surplus becomes zero. Those who do sell will have a smaller individual surplus than at the higher price. The opposite is true when the market price rises, which makes sellers better off. Measuring producer surplus tells us *how much* better or worse off sellers are when the price changes.

On a graph, we represent producer surplus as the area below the horizontal line of equilibrium price and above the supply curve. Panel B of Figure 5-4 shows what happens to producer surplus if the price drops from $160 to $100. Sellers #1 and #2 still sell, but their surplus is reduced. Total producer surplus falls to $50.

FIGURE 5-4

Producer surplus

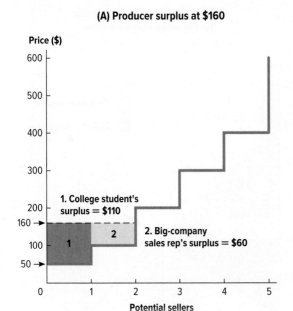

(A) Producer surplus at $160

Price ($)

1. College student's surplus = $110

2. Big-company sales rep's surplus = $60

Potential sellers

This shows the willingness to sell of all the potential sellers in our market. The shaded area (1 + 2) between the supply curve and the market prices shows total producer surplus of $170, the sum of the individual surpluses shown.

(B) Producer surplus at $100

Price ($)

2. Surplus lost by collector and big-company sales rep = $120 ($60 + $60)

1. College student's new surplus = $50

Potential sellers

Because sellers always prefer a higher price, producer surplus goes down when the price falls to $100. At $100, two sellers are still willing to sell, but are worse off because they receive less money for their cameras. Area 1 shows the new producer surplus: $50. Area 2 shows the reduction in surplus for the two sellers.

You can see by comparing panel A with panel B that when the price level falls, the area representing producer surplus gets smaller. On the other hand, the higher the price, the bigger the area, and the greater the producer surplus.

Total surplus

We now understand how to calculate consumer surplus and producer surplus at any given price. But what will the actual market price be? To find out, we have to put the demand and supply curves together and locate the point where they intersect.

Panel A of Figure 5-5 shows the demand curve for our five buyers and the supply curve for our five sellers. The two curves intersect at a price of $200. At this price, three buyers are willing to buy a camera and three sellers are willing to sell a camera. The consumer surplus of each buyer is shown as the area underneath the demand curve and above the horizontal line of the equilibrium price. Consumer surplus is:

$$\$300 + \$50 + \$0 + \$0 + \$0 = \$350$$

(Buyer #3 buys at her willingness to pay price, so she has no consumer surplus.) The producer surplus is shown as the area above the supply curve and beneath the equilibrium price.

Producer surplus is:

$$\$150 + \$100 + \$0 + \$0 + \$0 = \$250$$

(Seller #3 sells at his willingness to sell price, so he has no producer surplus.)

LO 5.4 Calculate total surplus based on a graph or table.

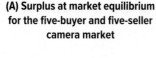

FIGURE 5-5

Surplus at market equilibrium

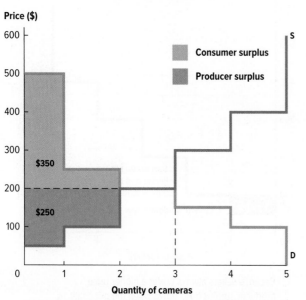

(A) Surplus at market equilibrium for the five-buyer and five-seller camera market

At the market equilibrium in our smaller market, the price of a camera is $200, and three are bought and sold. Consumer surplus is represented by the area between the demand curve and the market price, and is equal to $350. Producer surplus is represented by the area between the supply curve and the market price, and is equal to $250. Total surplus adds up to $600.

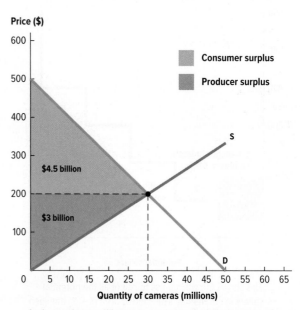

(B) Surplus at market equilibrium for the entire camera market

At the market equilibrium in our large market, the price of cameras is $200, and 30 million are bought and sold. Consumer surplus is represented by the area between the demand curve and the market price, and is equal to $4.5 billion. Producer surplus is represented by the area between the supply curve and the market price, and is equal to $3 billion. Total surplus adds up to $7.5 billion.

total surplus
a measure of the combined benefits that everyone receives from participating in an exchange of goods or services

Just as we've found total consumer surplus and total producer surplus, we can find total surplus for an entire market. **Total surplus** is a measure of the combined benefits that everyone receives from participating in an exchange of goods or services. The total surplus is the benefit received by all market participants, the sum of both consumer and producer surplus. For our camera market of five buyers and five sellers, total surplus is:

$$\$350 + \$250 = \$600$$

To better understand total surplus, let's broaden our focus beyond just five buyers and five sellers to the entire market for digital cameras on eBay. To represent this big market, we can bring back the smooth demand and supply curves from Figures 5-1 and 5-2. When we put the two together in panel B of Figure 5-5, we find that the equilibrium price is $200, and the equilibrium quantity of cameras traded is 30 million. (We're assuming a standardized model of digital camera and all the other features of a competitive market outlined in Chapter 3, "Markets.")

Total consumer surplus is represented graphically by the area underneath the demand curve and above the equilibrium price. That's the area shaded gold in panel B of Figure 5-5. Total producer surplus is represented by the area of the graph above the supply curve and below the equilibrium price—the area shaded blue.

Added together, those two areas—consumer surplus and producer surplus—make up the total surplus created by those 30 million sales of digital cameras on eBay. Graphically, total surplus is equal to the total area between the supply and demand curves, to the left of the equilibrium quantity.

We can also think of total surplus as value created by the existence of the market. Total surplus is calculated by adding up the benefits that every individual participant receives ($300 consumer surplus for the bird watcher, plus $150 producer surplus for the college student, and so on, for every one of those 30 million sales). But these benefits exist only as a result of participation in exchanges in the market.

This is an important point because sometimes people mistakenly think of the economy as a fixed quantity of money, goods, and well-being, in which the only question is how to divide it up among people. That idea is referred to as a **zero-sum game**. A zero-sum game is a situation in which whenever one person gains, another loses an equal amount, such that the net value of a transaction is zero. Playing poker is an example of a zero-sum game: Whatever one player wins, another player, logically, has to lose.

The concept of surplus shows us that the economy generally does not work like a poker game. Voluntary transactions for buyers and sellers, like buying or selling cameras on eBay, do not have a winner or loser. Rather, *both the buyer and seller are winners* since each gains surplus. Everyone ends up better off than he or she was before. Total surplus cannot be *less* than zero—if it were, people would simply stop buying and selling.

As a rule, markets generate value, but the distribution of that value is a more complicated issue. In the following sections, we will look at what surplus can tell us about the well-being generated by market transactions and by deviations from the market equilibrium. Then, in the next chapter, we'll use these tools to evaluate the effects of some common government policies when they are implemented in a competitive market. Later in the text, we will revisit some of the assumptions about how competitive markets operate, and we will discuss what happens to surplus when those assumptions don't hold true in the real world.

zero-sum game
a situation in which whenever one person gains, another loses an equal amount, such that the net value of any transaction is zero

✓ TEST YOURSELF

☐ What consumer surplus is received by someone whose willingness to pay is $20 below the market price of a good? **[LO 5.2]**

☐ What is the producer surplus earned by a seller whose willingness to sell is $40 below the market price of a good? **[LO 5.3]**

☐ Why can total surplus never fall below zero in a market for goods and services? **[LO 5.4]**

Using Surplus to Compare Alternatives

In a competitive market, buyers and sellers will naturally find their way to the equilibrium price. In our eBay example, we expect that buyers and sellers of digital cameras will bargain freely, offering different prices until the number of people who want to buy is matched with the number of people who want to sell. This is the invisible hand of market forces at work. It doesn't require any eBay manager to coordinate or set prices. But as we're about to see, the magic of the invisible hand doesn't stop there.

Market equilibrium and efficiency

The concept of surplus lets us appreciate something very important about market equilibrium. It is the point at which transactions occur between the buyers willing to pay the most and sellers able to produce at the lowest cost. It is the point at which transactions maximize total surplus.

To see why this is so, let's look at what would happen to surplus if, for some reason, the market moved away from equilibrium. Suppose an eBay manager decides to set the price of cameras so that people don't have to go to the trouble of bidding. He decides that $300 seems like a reasonable price. How will potential buyers and sellers *respond* to this situation? Figure 5-6 shows us:

LO 5.5 Define efficiency in terms of surplus, and identify efficient and inefficient situations.

- There are now 10 million fewer cameras sold (the quantity sold falls from 30 million to 20 million). Buyers who wanted 10 million cameras at the equilibrium price of $200 are no longer willing to buy at $300, reducing their consumer surplus to zero.

FIGURE 5-6

Changing the distribution of surplus

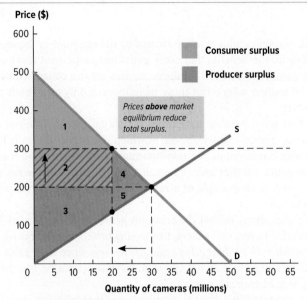

When the price rises above the market equilibrium, fewer transactions take place. The surplus shown in area 2 is transferred from consumers to producers as a result of the higher price paid for transactions that do still take place. The surplus in areas 4 and 5 is lost to both consumers and producers as a result of the reduced number of transactions.

FIGURE 5-7

Surplus when price is below equilibrium

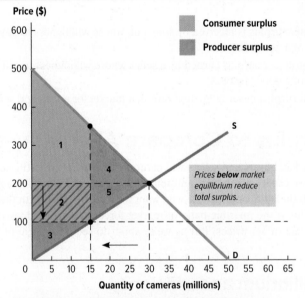

When the price of cameras drops to $100, buyers are willing to purchase 40 million, but sellers want to sell only 15 million. For those who do trade, successful buyers gain surplus of $1.5 billion (area 2) from buying at the lower price, while the sellers lose surplus of that same amount. The buyers and sellers who would have traded at equilibrium but no longer do so lose $1.875 billion of combined surplus. The surplus in areas 4 and 5 is lost to both consumers and producers as a result of the reduced number of transactions. Total surplus falls from $7.5 billion to $5.625 billion.

- That means that sellers who would have sold those 10 million cameras to buyers also miss out and get producer surplus of zero.
- For the 20 million cameras that still are sold, buyers pay a higher price and lose surplus.
- The sellers of those 20 million cameras benefit from the higher price and gain the surplus lost by consumers.

Overall, total surplus in the market is lower than it was at the equilibrium price because 10 million fewer cameras are sold.

What happens if the interfering eBay manager instead decides to sell digital cameras for $100? As Figure 5-7 shows:

- Buyers are willing to purchase 40 million cameras at a price of $100. Sellers are willing to sell only 15 million at $100.
- Since 15 million fewer cameras sell (that is, 15 million instead of 30 million at equilibrium), buyers and sellers lose the surplus that would have been gained through their sale.
- For the 15 million transactions that still take place, consumers gain surplus of $1.5 billion ($100 × 15 million) from buying at a lower price (area 2). That consumer surplus is exactly equal to the surplus the remaining sellers lose from selling at a lower price.
- The buyers and sellers who would have traded at equilibrium but no longer do so lose $1.875 billion of combined surplus. Breaking this down, we find that the 15 million buyers no longer in the market lose $1.125 billion (area 4), and sellers lose $0.75 billion (area 5) in surplus.
- This $1.875 billion total (areas 4 + 5) in lost surplus is subtracted from the amount of total surplus before the price ceiling. Overall, total surplus falls from $7.5 billion to $5.625 billion.

In both cases—when the price is $300 (above the equilibrium price) or when it is $100 (below the equilibrium price)—total surplus decreases relative to the market equilibrium. In fact, we find this same result at *any price* other than the equilibrium price. The key is that a higher or lower price causes fewer trades to take place because some people are no longer willing to buy or sell. The value that would have been gained from these voluntary trades no longer exists. As a result, *the equilibrium in a perfectly competitive, well-functioning market maximizes total surplus.*

Another way to say this is that the market is **efficient** when it is at equilibrium: There is no exchange that can make anyone better off without someone becoming worse off. Efficiency is one of the most powerful features of a market system. Even more remarkable is that it is achieved without centralized coordination.

efficient market
an arrangement such that no exchange can make anyone better off without someone becoming worse off

Changing the distribution of total surplus

A reduction in total surplus was not the only interesting thing that happened when the meddling eBay manager moved the price of digital cameras away from equilibrium. Another outcome was *reassignment of surplus* from customers to producers, or vice versa, for the transactions that did take place:

- When the price was raised, sellers gained some well-being at the expense of buyers.
- When the price was lowered, buyers gained some well-being at the expense of sellers.

LO 5.6 Describe the distribution of surplus, or benefits to society, that results from a policy decision.

In both cases, achieving this transfer of well-being from one group to the other came at the expense of *reduced total surplus.*

When an artificially high price is imposed on a market, it's bad news for consumer surplus. Consumers lose surplus due to the reduced number of transactions and the higher price buyers have to pay on the remaining transactions.

The situation for producers, though, is more complex. At the artificially high price, producers lose some surplus from the transactions that would have taken place under equilibrium and no longer do. On the other hand, they gain more surplus from the higher price on the transactions that do still take place. These two effects will compete with one another. Whichever effect "wins" will determine whether the producer surplus increases or decreases overall.

To see why, let's go back to Figure 5-6. Area 2 is surplus that is transferred from consumers to producers. Areas 4 and 5 represent surplus lost to consumers and producers, respectively, from transactions that no longer take place. Whether area 2 is bigger or smaller than area 5 will indicate whether producer surplus increases or decreases. That result depends on the shape of the demand curve and the supply curve. In this case, we can see that area 2 is bigger than area 5. The effect of the artificially high price was to make sellers better off (at the expense of making buyers even more worse off).

The opposite situation occurs when prices are lower than the market equilibrium, which you can see by looking again at Figure 5-7. Fewer transactions take place (because fewer producers are willing to sell), and so both producers and consumers lose some surplus from missed transactions. For the transactions that do still take place, consumers pay less and gain surplus at the expense of producers. Producers get paid less and lose surplus.

Thus, a price below the market equilibrium will always reduce producer surplus. That price might increase or decrease consumer surplus: The outcome depends on how much surplus is gained by those who buy at a lower price compared to what is lost to those who can no longer buy at all.

We don't expect eBay managers to start imposing their own prices any time soon—that would be contrary to the whole idea of eBay as a decentralized virtual marketplace. But there are times when governments or other organizations do decide to impose minimum or maximum prices on markets. That happens because efficiency is not the only thing we care about. Many fundamental public policy questions revolve around possible trade-offs between economic efficiency and other concerns such as fairness and equity. We'll look in much more detail at this idea in the next chapter.

Deadweight loss

LO 5.7 Calculate deadweight loss.

deadweight loss
a loss of total surplus that occurs because the quantity of a good that is bought and sold is below the market equilibrium quantity

An intervention that moves a market away from equilibrium might benefit either producers or consumers, but it always comes with a decrease in total surplus. Where does that surplus go? It disappears and becomes what is known as a **deadweight loss**. Deadweight loss is the loss of total surplus that occurs when the quantity of a good that is bought and sold is below the market equilibrium quantity. Any intervention that moves a market away from the equilibrium price and quantity creates deadweight loss. Fewer exchanges take place, so there are fewer opportunities for the generation of surplus.

We can calculate deadweight loss in two ways: One way is to subtract total surplus *after* a market intervention from total surplus at the market equilibrium *before* the intervention. Or we can calculate deadweight loss directly by determining the area of the triangle on a graph. This second method is usually the easiest.

Figure 5-8 shows what happens in the eBay camera market when the price is too low at $100. Only 15 million cameras are exchanged at this price, but the efficient quantity is 30 million. For the units between 15 million and 30 million, consumers have a willingness to pay that is higher than producers' costs. Thus, exchanging the units would create surplus, but because the units are not exchanged, this potential surplus is lost.

To calculate the exact size of this deadweight loss, we calculate the area between supply and demand for those units that aren't exchanged. The "base" of this triangle is measured along the *y*-axis from $100 to $350. The "height" is measured along the *x*-axis from 15 million to 30 million. Then, using the formula for the area of a triangle, the deadweight loss is:

$$\frac{b \times h}{2} = \frac{250 \times 15 \text{ million}}{2} = 1.875 \text{ billion}$$

We'll see in the next chapter that deadweight loss is an incredibly important concept for understanding the costs of government intervention in markets, through mechanisms such as taxes and controls on the prices of goods.

FIGURE 5-8

Deadweight loss

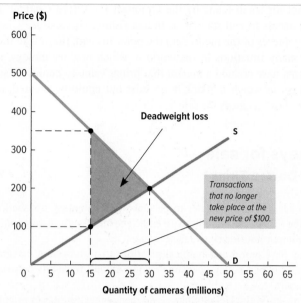

Deadweight loss represents the surplus that is lost to both producers and consumers as a result of fewer transactions taking place when the price moves away from equilibrium. Here, deadweight loss is equal to the gray shaded area.

Missing markets

When there are people who would like to make exchanges but cannot, for one reason or another, we miss opportunities for mutual benefit. In this situation, we say that a market is "missing." The term "missing" can be misleading. Sometimes a market exists, so it is not literally missing. But for some reason, some of the trades that potential buyers and sellers would *like* to make are not happening. Asking why a market is missing is important; the answer can provide guidance to policies and businesses that can allow more people to engage in trade for mutual benefit.

Markets can be missing for a variety of reasons:

- Sometimes public policy prevents the market from existing—for instance, when the production or sale of a particular good or service is banned.
- Or sometimes a particular good or service is taxed; the tax doesn't eliminate the market but does add a cost, which leads to fewer transactions.
- Markets can also be missing or shrunk due to other types of holdups: a lack of accurate information or communication between potential buyers and sellers, or a lack of technology that would make the exchanges possible.

eBay and newer companies such as Airbnb, Uber, and Lyft are examples of how technology can generate new value by creating or expanding a market. Prior to the existence of such companies, people who wanted to offer a service or product, and people who wanted to buy it, often never found each other. For example, before eBay you could hold a garage sale to get rid of your extra stuff; you could go to your local stores or post an ad in a newspaper if you were looking to buy an unusual item. But it was quite difficult to find out if someone on the other side of the country was offering a rare product or a better price. eBay allows more buyers to find sellers and vice versa, encouraging more mutually beneficial trades.

The idea that we can increase total surplus by creating new markets and improving existing ones has important implications for public policy. Policies and technologies that help people share information and do business more effectively can increase well-being. For instance, ideas

LO 5.8 Explain why correcting a missing market can make everyone better off.

like creating a market for small loans by the Grameen Bank (see Chapter 1, "Economics and Life") or expanding access to cell phones in Indian fishing villages (see Chapter 3, "Markets") don't just redistribute pieces of the pie to help the poor. Instead, they make the whole pie bigger.

Think about the many situations in the world in which new technology, new strategies, and outreach to new clients have created a market that brings value to people. Also think about some controversial situations in which markets don't exist but could be created, as described in the What Do You Think? box "Kidneys for sale."

Kidneys for sale
What Do You Think?

When buyers and sellers come together to participate in voluntary transactions, the resulting markets create value that would not otherwise exist. The idea that well-functioning markets maximize surplus is an important descriptive fact.

But people may have moral and political priorities that go beyond maximizing surplus. In fact, many important public policy questions revolve around trade-offs between economic efficiency and other goals.

For instance, the law in the United States (and many other countries) prohibits certain types of market transactions. Consider the following cases:

- It's illegal to buy or sell organs for medical transplants.
- It's illegal to buy or sell certain drugs, such as cocaine and heroin.
- It's illegal to buy or sell children for adoption.
- It's illegal to buy or sell certain types of weapons, such as nuclear devices.

Looking at it from one angle, these are all examples of missing markets. You now know that when markets are missing, we miss opportunities to create surplus by enabling voluntary transactions to take place. For instance, a market for organs could make a lot of people better off. Some healthy people would gain surplus by selling their kidneys: They would rather have money and one remaining kidney than two kidneys and no money. Meanwhile, some people with kidney disease would happily pay for the donation of a healthy kidney. Because the law prevents this transaction from happening, both miss out on surplus.

If maximizing surplus is our highest goal, it's plausible that we should allow organs and other such goods to be traded on the market. But allowing markets for organs goes against many people's moral instincts—perhaps because they hold other goals higher than maximizing surplus.

WHAT DO YOU THINK?

1. Do you agree that the law should prevent trade in organs?
2. How about drugs, children, and nuclear weapons?
3. Are there any reasons that markets for these goods might not end up maximizing surplus?
4. What values and assumptions are driving your answers?

✓ TEST YOURSELF

- ☐ What can we say about the size and distribution of total surplus in an efficient market? **[LO 5.5]**
- ☐ How do price changes affect the distribution of surplus between consumers and producers? **[LO 5.6]**
- ☐ Why does an intervention that moves a market away from the equilibrium price and quantity create a deadweight loss? **[LO 5.7]**
- ☐ What does it mean to say that a market is "missing"? **[LO 5.8]**

Conclusion

In this chapter we've introduced the concepts of willingness to pay and willingness to sell, which help explain when individual buyers and sellers will choose to make a trade. We've also discussed what it means to measure consumer and producer surplus and shown that the market equilibrium is efficient because it maximizes total surplus.

As we'll see in the next chapter, surplus and deadweight loss are powerful tools for understanding the implications of business ideas and public policies. Who will benefit from the policy? Who will be harmed by it? What effect will it have on the economy overall? The language of surplus, efficiency, and distribution of benefits is particularly helpful for getting to the bottom of controversial decisions.

Later in the text, we will describe important cases in which the efficiency rule about market equilibrium does not always hold true, and we'll see how surplus can also help us understand these cases.

Key Terms

willingness to pay (reservation price), p. 105

willingness to sell, p. 105

surplus, p. 109

consumer surplus, p. 110

producer surplus, p. 112

total surplus, p. 114

zero-sum game, p. 115

efficient market, p. 117

deadweight loss, p. 118

Summary

LO 5.1 Use willingness to pay and willingness to sell to determine supply and demand at a given price.

Willingness to pay and willingness to sell describe the value that an individual places on a particular good or service. Willingness to pay (also sometimes known as the reservation price) is the maximum price that a buyer would be willing to pay for a particular good or service. Willingness to sell is the lowest price a seller is willing to accept in exchange for a particular good or service.

Consumers will buy only if the price is lower than their willingness to pay. Producers will sell only if the price is higher than their willingness to sell.

LO 5.2 Calculate consumer surplus based on a graph or table.

Surplus is a way of measuring who benefits from transactions and how much. Consumer surplus is the net benefit that consumers receive from purchasing a good or service, measured by the difference between each consumer's willingness to pay and the actual price. Graphically, it is equal to the area below the demand curve and above the market price.

LO 5.3 Calculate producer surplus based on a graph or table.

Producer surplus is a measure of the net benefits that a producer receives from the sale of a good or service, measured by the difference between the producer's willingness to sell and the actual price. Graphically, it is equal to the area above the supply curve and below the market price.

LO 5.4 Calculate total surplus based on a graph or table.

Total surplus is a measure of the combined benefits that everyone receives from participating in an exchange of goods or services. It is calculated by adding consumer surplus and producer surplus. Graphically, it is equal to the total area between the supply and demand curves, to the left of the equilibrium quantity.

LO 5.5 Define efficiency in terms of surplus, and identify efficient and inefficient situations.

A market is *efficient* if there is no exchange that can make anyone better off without someone becoming worse off. An efficient market maximizes total surplus but doesn't tell us how the surplus is distributed between consumers and producers. In a competitive market, efficiency is achieved only at the market equilibrium price and quantity; higher prices and lower prices will both decrease the quantity bought and sold and reduce total surplus.

LO 5.6 Describe the distribution of surplus, or benefits to society, that results from a policy decision.

Prices above or below the market equilibrium reduce total surplus but also redistribute surplus between producers and consumers differently. A price above the equilibrium always decreases consumer surplus. Also, at a price above equilibrium, some producers win and others lose; the overall effect on producer surplus depends on the shape of the supply and demand curves. A price below the equilibrium always decreases producer surplus; some consumers win and others lose.

LO 5.7 Calculate deadweight loss.

Deadweight loss is the loss of total surplus that occurs when the quantity of a good that is bought and sold is below the market equilibrium quantity. Any intervention that moves a market away from the equilibrium price and quantity causes deadweight loss. Fewer exchanges take place, so there are fewer opportunities for the generation of surplus.

LO 5.8 Explain why correcting a missing market can make everyone better off.

A market is "missing" when there is a situation in which people would like to engage in mutually beneficial trades of goods and services but can't because no market for them exists. A missing market is a special case of a market in which quantity is held below the equilibrium—in this case, at or close to zero. Missing markets can occur for many reasons, including government intervention or a lack of information or technology. When missing markets are filled, people are able to trade, which generates surplus.

Review Questions

1. Sangjay is a professional photographer. His camera is broken and he needs a new one within the next hour, or he will miss an important deadline. Keiko is a high-school student who doesn't have a camera but wants to get one to take pictures at her prom next month. Who do you think would have a higher willingness to pay for a particular camera today? Why? **[LO 5.1]**

2. You are in the market for a new couch and have found two advertisements for the kind of couch you want to buy. One seller notes in her ad that she is selling because she is moving to a smaller apartment, and the couch won't fit in the new space. The other seller says he is selling because the couch doesn't match his other furniture. Which seller do you expect to buy from? Why? (*Hint:* Think who would be the more motivated seller.) **[LO 5.1]**

3. Suppose you are at a flea market and are considering buying a box of vintage records. You are trying to bargain down the price, but the seller overhears you telling a friend that you are willing to pay up to $50. Why is your consumer surplus now likely to be lower than it would have been if the seller hadn't overheard you? **[LO 5.2]**

4. Consider a market in equilibrium. Suppose supply in this market increases. How will this affect consumer surplus? Explain. **[LO 5.2]**

5. You currently have a television that you want to sell. You can either pick a price and try to sell it at a yard sale or auction it off on eBay. Which method do you think will yield a higher producer surplus? Why? **[LO 5.3]**

6. Consider a market in equilibrium. Suppose demand in this market decreases. How will this affect producer surplus? Explain. **[LO 5.3]**

7. Consider the market for plane tickets to Hawaii. A bad winter in the mainland United States increases demand for tropical vacations, shifting the demand curve to the right. The supply curve stays constant. Does total surplus increase or decrease? (*Hint:* Sketch out a generic supply and demand curve and look at what happens to the size of the triangle that represents total surplus when the demand curve shifts right.) **[LO 5.4]**

8. You need to paint your fence, but you really hate this task. You decide to hire the kid next door to do it for you. You would be willing to pay him up to $100, but you start by offering $50, expecting to negotiate. To your great surprise, he accepts your $50 offer. When you tell your friend about the great deal you got, she is shocked that you would take advantage of someone. What can you tell your friend to assure her that you did not cheat the kid next door? **[LO 5.4]**

9. New York City has a long-standing policy of controlling rents in certain parts of the city—in essence, a price ceiling on rent. Is the market for apartments likely to be efficient or inefficient? What does this imply for the size of total surplus? **[LO 5.5]**

10. Total surplus is maximized at the equilibrium price and quantity. When demand increases, price increases. Explain how total surplus is still maximized if price increases due to an increase in demand. **[LO 5.5]**

11. When the price of gasoline was very high in the summer of 2008, several U.S. presidential candidates proposed implementing a national price ceiling to keep fuel affordable. How would this policy have affected producer and consumer surplus? How would it have affected total surplus? **[LO 5.6]**

12. Consider a policy to help struggling farmers by setting a minimum trade price for wheat. Will this be an effective way to increase their surplus? Explain. **[LO 5.6]**

13. If rent control creates deadweight loss for both consumers and suppliers of housing, why are consumers often in favor of this policy? **[LO 5.7]**

14. Suppose price is 5 percent above equilibrium in two markets: a market for a necessity and a market for a luxury good. All else equal (including supply conditions), in which market do you expect deadweight loss to be greater? Explain. **[LO 5.7]**

15. Your grandmother likes old-fashioned yard sales and doesn't understand why everyone is so excited about eBay. Explain to her why the creation of a market that enables people who don't live in the same town to buy and sell used goods increases total surplus over the yard-sale market. **[LO 5.8]**

16. At Zooey's elementary school, children are not allowed to trade lunches or components of their lunches with other students. Lunchroom monitors watch closely and strictly enforce this policy. Help Zooey make an argument about the inefficiency of this policy to her principal. **[LO 5.8]**

Problems and Applications

1. Use the information in Table 5P-1 to construct a step graph of the six consumers' willingness to pay. **[LO 5.1]**

TABLE 5P-1

Buyer	Willingness to pay for one unit ($)
Fadel	8
Ann	2
Morgan	16
Andre	12
Carla	2
Hanson	4

2. Use the information in Table 5P-2 to construct a step graph of the six sellers' willingness to sell. **[LO 5.1]**

TABLE 5P-2

Seller	Willingness to sell one unit ($)
Joseph	25
Juan	20
Kristin	60
Peter	10
Candice	25
Solomon	50

3. Answer the following questions based on Tables 5P-3 and 5P-4. **[LO 5.1]**
   a. What is the quantity demanded at $10? What is the quantity supplied at $10?
   b. What is the quantity demanded at $25? What is the quantity supplied at $25?

4. Based on Table 5P-5, calculate consumer surplus for each consumer when the price is $17. What is the total consumer surplus at this price? **[LO 5.2]**

TABLE 5P-3

Buyer	A	B	C	D	E	F	G	H	I
Willingness to pay for one unit	$35	$33	$27	$22	$21	$13	$13	$12	$6

TABLE 5P-4

Seller	A	B	C	D	E	F	G	H	I
Willingness to sell for one unit	$4	$9	$12	$14	$15	$21	$23	$30	$51

TABLE 5P-5

Buyer	A	B	C	D	E	F	G	H	I
Willingness to pay for one unit	$6	$27	$13	$21	$33	$35	$12	$13	$22

5. Use the demand curve represented in Figure 5P-1 to draw the consumer surplus when the market price is $8. What is the value of consumer surplus at this price? **[LO 5.2]**

FIGURE 5P-1

6. Based on Figure 5P-2, consumer surplus is $0 when price is greater than or equal to what price? **[LO 5.2]**

7. Use the market represented in Figure 5P-2 to plot the equilibrium price and quantity and to draw the consumer surplus when the market is in equilibrium. What is the value of consumer surplus at the equilibrium price? **[LO 5.2]**

8. Use the market represented in Figure 5P-2 to draw the consumer surplus when the price is $5. What is the value of consumer surplus at this price? **[LO 5.2]**

9. Based on Figure 5P-2, producer surplus is $0 when price is less than or equal to what price? **[LO 5.3]**

10. Use the market represented in Figure 5P-2 to plot the equilibrium price and quantity and to draw the producer surplus when the market is in equilibrium. What is the value of producer surplus at the equilibrium price? **[LO 5.3]**

11. Use the market represented in Figure 5P-2 to draw the producer surplus if the price is $9. What is the value of producer surplus at this price? **[LO 5.3]**

12. Based on Table 5P-6, calculate producer surplus for each producer when the price is $20. What is total producer surplus at this price? **[LO 5.3]**

13. Use the supply curve represented in Figure 5P-3 to draw the producer surplus when the market price is $5. What is the value of producer surplus at this price? **[LO 5.3]**

FIGURE 5P-2

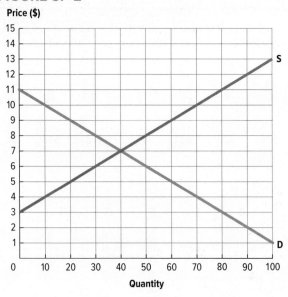

FIGURE 5P-3

TABLE 5P-6

Buyer	A	B	C	D	E	F	G	H	I
Willingness to pay for one unit	$21	$4	$30	$14	$12	$15	$51	$9	$23

14. Use the market represented in Figure 5P-4 to draw the consumer and producer surplus when the market is in equilibrium. What is the value of total surplus at equilibrium? **[LO 5.4]**

FIGURE 5P-4

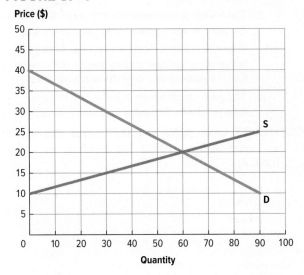

15. Consider the market represented in Figure 5P-5. **[LO 5.4]**

FIGURE 5P-5

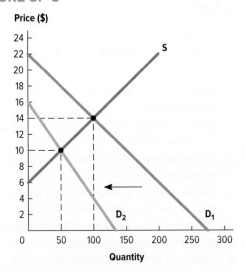

a. Calculate total surplus when demand is D_1.
b. Calculate total surplus when demand decreases to D_2.

16. Consider the market represented in Figure 5P-6. **[LO 5.4]**

FIGURE 5P-6

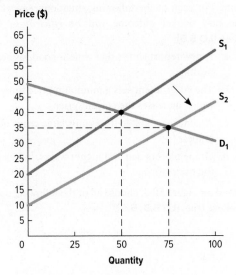

a. Calculate total surplus when supply is S_1.
b. Calculate total surplus when supply increases to S_2.

17. Consider the market represented in Figure 5P-7. **[LO 5.5]**

FIGURE 5P-7

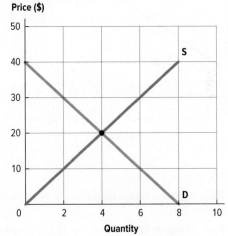

a. Draw the consumer surplus and the producer surplus at the equilibrium price and quantity. What is the value of total surplus at equilibrium?
b. Draw the consumer surplus and the producer surplus if the price is $30. What are the values of consumer surplus, producer surplus, and total surplus at this price?
c. Draw the consumer surplus and the producer surplus if the price is $10. What are the values of consumer surplus, producer surplus, and total surplus at this price?

18. Assume the market for wine is functioning at its equilibrium. For each of the following situations, say whether the new market outcome will be *efficient* or *inefficient*. **[LO 5.5]**

   a. A new report shows that wine is good for heart health.

   b. The government sets a minimum price for wine, which increases the current price.

   c. An unexpected late frost ruins large crops of grapes.

   d. Grape pickers demand higher wages, increasing the price of wine.

19. Based on Figure 5P-8, choose all of the following options that are true. **[LO 5.5, 5.6]**

20. In which of the following situations can you say, without further information, that consumer surplus decreases relative to the market equilibrium level? **[LO 5.6]**

   a. Your state passes a law that pushes the interest rate (i.e., the price) for payday loans below the equilibrium rate.

   b. The federal government enforces a law that raises the price of dairy goods above the equilibrium.

   c. Your city passes a local property tax, under which buyers of new houses have to pay an additional 5 percent on top of the purchase price.

   d. The government lowers the effective price of food purchases through a food-stamp program.

21. Use the areas labeled in the market represented in Figure 5P-9 to answer the following questions. **[LO 5.6]**

FIGURE 5P-8

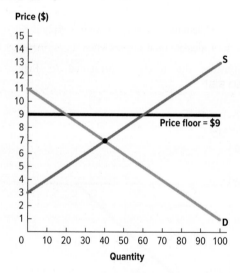

FIGURE 5P-9

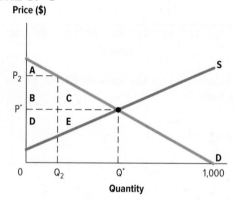

a. The market is efficient.

b. Total surplus is higher than it would be at market equilibrium.

c. Total surplus is lower than it would be at market equilibrium.

d. Producer surplus is lower than it would be at market equilibrium.

e. Consumer surplus is lower than it would be at market equilibrium.

a. What area(s) are consumer surplus at the market equilibrium price?

b. What area(s) are producer surplus at the market equilibrium price?

c. Compared to the equilibrium, what area(s) do consumers lose if price is P_2?

d. Compared to the equilibrium, what area(s) do producers lose if the price is P_2?

e. Compared to the equilibrium, what area(s) do producers gain if the price is P_2?

f. Compared to the equilibrium, total surplus decreases by what area(s) if the price is P_2?

FIGURE D-1

Measuring the area under a curve

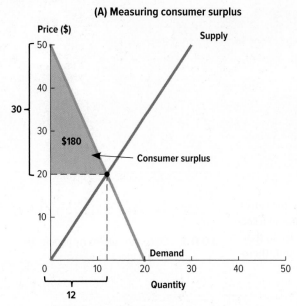

(A) Measuring consumer surplus

Consumer surplus is found by taking the area of the triangle above the market price and below the demand curve.

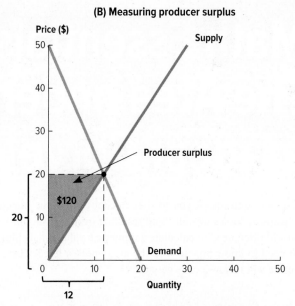

(B) Measuring producer surplus

Measuring producer surplus, on the other hand, is found by taking the area of the triangle below the market price and above the supply curve.

y-intercept of the supply curve, $(20 - 0) = 20$. Therefore the area of the triangle—and the producer surplus—is:

$$\tfrac{1}{2} \times (12 \times 20) = \$120$$

You learned in Chapter 5 that total surplus is consumer surplus plus producer surplus:

$$\text{Total surplus} = \$180 + \$120 = \$300$$

We can also calculate total surplus directly by calculating the area of the larger triangle that encompasses both. This time, the calculation of this triangle is slightly different. The base is the amount of space in between the y-intercept of the supply and demand curves. This gives a base of 50. The height of the triangle, on the other hand, is the distance from the y-axis to the equilibrium point. The area is thus $\tfrac{1}{2} \times 50 \times 12 = \$300$, the same result as before.

Occasionally, you will see oddly shaped surplus areas. You can always calculate these by breaking them down into familiar rectangles and triangles. Then calculate the area of each using length times width (for a rectangle) and $\tfrac{1}{2}$ bh (for a triangle), and add the results to find the total area.

Math Essentials: The Area under a Linear Curve

D

Chapter 5 introduced you to the concept of surplus. Surplus measures the gains or losses in well-being resulting from transactions in a market. You will often need to calculate a numerical value for surplus. To do that, you need to know how to find the area under a linear curve, and, therefore, we will review a little geometry.

The Area under a Linear Curve

Graphically, surplus is represented as the area between a supply or demand curve and the market price. The area between these curves and the market price will take the form of a triangle. In order to find surplus, you are going to need to be able to calculate the area of a triangle:

EQUATION D-1

$$\text{Area of triangle} = \frac{1}{2} \times \text{Base of triangle} \times \text{Height of triangle} = \frac{1}{2}\text{bh}$$

The key, then, is to figure which length to use as the base and which as the height.

In panel A of Figure D-1, consumer surplus is the shaded triangle below the demand curve and above the market price. The base of this triangle is the *horizontal distance* from the equilibrium point to the y-axis, $(12 - 0) = 12$. The height is the *vertical distance* from the equilibrium price to the y-intercept of the demand curve, $(50 - 20) = 30$. Therefore, the area of the triangle—and the consumer surplus—is:

$$\frac{1}{2} \times (12 \times 30) = \$180$$

Producer surplus is the shaded area below the market price and above the supply curve in panel B of Figure D-1. The base of the triangle is again the *horizontal distance* from the equilibrium point to the y-axis, $(12 - 0) = 12$. The height is the vertical distance from the equilibrium price to the

22. Figure 5P-10 shows a market for cotton, with the price held at $0.80 per pound. Draw and calculate the deadweight loss caused by this policy. **[LO 5.7]**

FIGURE 5P-10

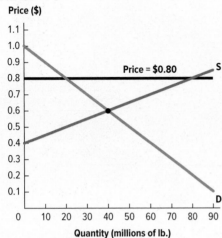

23. Consider the market represented in Figure 5P-11. **[LO 5.7]**

FIGURE 5P-11

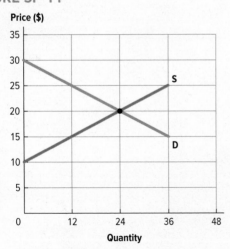

a. Suppose the government sets a minimum price of $25 in the market. Calculate the deadweight loss.

b. Suppose the government sets a maximum price of $25 in the market. Calculate the deadweight loss.

24. What is the value of the existence of the market represented in Figure 5P-12? **[LO 5.8]**

FIGURE 5P-12

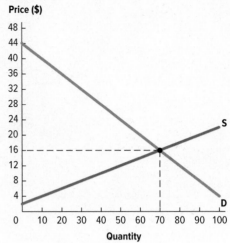

25. We can consider the market for traveling to Mars to be missing because no technology exists that allows this service to be bought and sold. Suppose that someone has invented space-travel technology that will enable this service to be provided. Figure 5P-13 shows the estimated market for trips to Mars. Calculate the surplus that could be generated by filling in this missing market. **[LO 5.8]**

FIGURE 5P-13

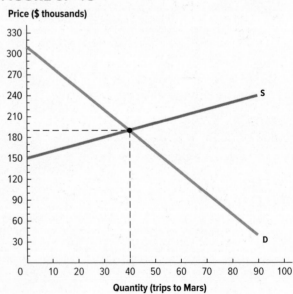

Endnotes

1. https://www.ebayinc.com/stories/news/ebay-inc-reports-fourth-quarter-and-full-year-2017-results/

2. http://news.bbc.co.uk/2/hi/4034787.stm

Problems and Applications

1. Use the graph in Figure DP-1 to answer the following questions. [**LO D.1**]

    a. What is the amount of consumer surplus?

    b. What is the amount of producer surplus?

    c. What is the amount of total surplus?

FIGURE DP-1

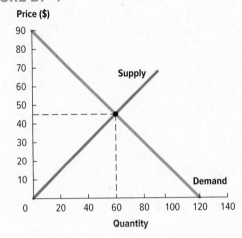

2. Use these two supply and demand equations to answer the following questions. [**LO D.1**]

    $$P = 50 - 4Q$$
    $$P = 2 + 2Q$$

    a. What is the equilibrium price? What is the equilibrium quantity?

    b. Draw a graph of supply and demand and illustrate the equilibrium.

    c. What is the amount of consumer surplus?

    d. What is the amount of producer surplus?

    e. What is the amount of total surplus?

Government Intervention

Feeding the World, One Price Control at a Time

In the spring of 2008, a worldwide food shortage caused food prices to skyrocket. In just a few months, the prices of wheat, rice, and corn shot up as much as 140 percent. In the United States, the number of people living on food stamps rose to the highest level since the 1960s. By June, low-income Americans were facing tough choices, as the prices of basics like eggs and dairy products rose. Some reported giving up meat and fresh fruit; others said they began to buy cheap food past the expiration date.[1]

Rising food prices caused trouble all over the world. The *Economist* magazine reported on the political fallout:

©Abdurashid Abdulleaf/AFP/Getty Images

[In Côte d'Ivoire,] two days of violence persuaded the government to postpone planned elections. . . . In Haiti, protesters chanting "We're hungry" forced the prime minister to resign; 24 people were killed in riots in Cameroon; Egypt's president ordered the army to start baking bread; [and] the Philippines made hoarding rice punishable by life imprisonment.[2]

Faced with hunger, hardship, and angry outbursts, many governments felt obliged to respond to the crisis. But what to do? Responses varied widely. Many countries made it illegal to charge high prices for food. Other countries subsidized the price of basic necessities. In the United States, Congress passed a farm bill that increased the amount of money low-income families received to buy food. Were these responses appropriate? What, if anything, *should* governments do in such a situation?

Food is a tricky issue for policy-makers because it's a basic necessity. If prices rise too high, people go hungry. If prices fall too low, farmers go out of business, which raises the risk of food shortages in the future. So, while policy-makers aren't too concerned if the prices of many goods—like digital cameras or lattes—jump up and down, they often do care about food prices. But attempts to lower, raise, or simply stabilize prices can backfire or create unintended side effects. Sometimes the cure ends up being worse than the problem itself.

LEARNING OBJECTIVES

LO 6.1 Calculate the effect of a price ceiling on the equilibrium price and quantity.

LO 6.2 Calculate the effect of a price floor on the equilibrium price and quantity.

LO 6.3 Calculate the effect of a tax on the equilibrium price and quantity.

LO 6.4 Calculate the effect of a subsidy on the equilibrium price and quantity.

LO 6.5 Explain how elasticity and time period influence the impact of a market intervention.

In this chapter, we'll look at the logic behind policies that governments commonly use to intervene in markets. There are often both intended and unintended consequences—and economic models and data can help think through both. We will start with *price controls*, which make it illegal to sell a good for more or less than a certain price. Then we will look at *taxes* and *subsidies*, which discourage or encourage the production of particular goods. These tools are regularly applied to a broad range of issues, from unemployment to home ownership, air pollution to education. For better or worse, they have a huge effect on our lives as workers, consumers, businesspeople, and voters.

Why Intervene?

In Chapter 3, "Markets," we saw that markets gravitate toward equilibrium. When markets work well, prices adjust until the quantity of a good that consumers demand equals the quantity that suppliers want to produce. At equilibrium, everyone gets what he or she is willing to pay for. In Chapter 5, "Efficiency," we saw that equilibrium price and quantity also maximize total surplus. At equilibrium, there is no way to make some people better off without harming others.

So, why intervene? Why not let the invisible hand of the market determine prices and allocate resources? Some would argue that's exactly what should be done. Others believe the government has to intervene sometimes—and the fact is that every single government in the world intervenes in markets in some fashion.

Three reasons to intervene

The arguments for intervention fall into three categories: changing the distribution of surplus, encouraging or discouraging consumption of certain goods, and correcting market failures. As we discuss different policy tools throughout the chapter, ask yourself which of these motivations is driving the intervention.

Changing the distribution of surplus   Efficient markets maximize total surplus, but an efficient outcome may still be seen as unfair. For example, even if the job market is efficient, wages can still drop so low that some workers fall below the poverty line while their employers make healthy profits. In such cases, some may argue for intervention in markets in order to change the distribution of surplus. The government might respond by intervening in the labor market to impose a minimum wage. This policy will change the distribution of surplus, reducing employers' profits (which may lead to higher prices) and lifting workers' incomes.

Of course, the definition of fairness is up for debate. Reasonable people can—and often do—argue about whether a policy that benefits a certain group (such as minimum-wage workers) is justified or not. Our focus will be on accurately describing the benefits and costs of such policies. Economics can help us predict whose well-being will increase, whose well-being will decrease, and who may be affected in unpredictable ways.

Encouraging or discouraging consumption   Around the world, many people judge certain products to be "good" or "bad" based on culture, health, religion, or other values. At the extreme, certain "bad" products are banned, such as many addictive drugs.

More often, governments use taxes to discourage people from consuming "bad" products, rather than simply banning them. Common examples are cigarettes and alcohol. Furthermore, in some cases consumption of a good imposes costs on others, such as second-hand smoke from cigarettes. In such cases the government may add a tax so that consumers or producers of the good have to pay more of the cost to society of consuming or producing that good. (Figuring out exactly what that cost is can be quite difficult, by the way.)

On the other hand, governments use *subsidies* to encourage people to consume "good" products or services. For instance, many governments provide public funding for schools to encourage education and for vaccinations to encourage parents to protect their children against disease.

Correcting market failures   Our model of demand and supply has so far assumed that markets work efficiently. In the real world, though, that's not always true. For example, sometimes there is only one producer of a good, who faces no competition and can charge an inefficiently high price. In other cases, one person's use of a product or service imposes costs on other people that are not captured in prices paid by the first person; an example is the pollution that others experience when smoke is ejected by your car (that is, the price you pay for the gas that is burned in your car imposes a cost on others when they must experience the pollution).

Situations in which the assumption of efficient, competitive markets fails to hold are called **market failures**. When there is a market failure, intervention can actually increase total surplus. We'll have much more to say about market failures in future chapters. In this chapter, we will stick to analyzing the effect of government interventions in efficient, competitive markets.

market failures situations in which the assumption of efficient, competitive markets fails to hold

Four real-world interventions

In this chapter we'll look at four real-world examples of how governments have intervened or could intervene in the market for food. For each, we'll consider the motives for the intervention and what its direct and indirect consequences were or could be. These four interventions are:

1. For many Mexican families, tortillas are an important food. What happened when the Mexican government set a *maximum price* for tortillas, in an effort to keep them affordable?

2. To ensure supplies of fresh milk, the U.S. government wanted to protect dairy farmers. What happened when the government set a *minimum price* for milk?

3. Many Americans struggle with health problems caused by overeating and poor nutrition. Several states have responded by banning the use of certain fats in food products; others require that restaurants post nutritional information about the foods they serve. What would happen if governments *taxed* high-fat or high-calorie foods?

4. What would happen if, instead of setting a maximum price for tortillas, the Mexican government *subsidized* tortillas?

As we walk through these examples of real policies, we want you to apply both positive and normative analysis. Remember the difference:

- *Positive analysis* is about facts: Does the policy actually accomplish the original goal?
- *Normative analysis* is a matter of values and opinions: Do you think the policy is a good idea?

Few policies are all good or all bad. The key question is, *What are the trade-offs* involved in the intervention? Do the benefits outweigh the costs?

✓ TEST YOURSELF

☐ What are three reasons that a government might want to intervene in markets?

Price Controls

price control
a regulation that sets a maximum or minimum legal price for a particular good

Suppose you are an economic policy advisor, and food prices are rising. What should you do? If you live in a region with many low-income consumers, you might want to take action to ensure that everyone gets enough to eat. One policy tool you might consider using is a **price control**—a regulation that sets a maximum or minimum legal price for a particular good. The direct effect of a price control is to hold the price of a good up or down when the market shifts, thus preventing the market from reaching a new equilibrium.

Price controls can be divided into two opposing categories: *price ceilings* and *price floors*. We met this idea already in Chapter 5, "Efficiency," when we imagined an interfering eBay manager setting prices for digital cameras. In reality, eBay would never do such a thing, but governments often do, particularly when it comes to markets for food items. What are the effects of using price controls to intervene in a well-functioning, competitive market?

Price ceilings

LO 6.1 Calculate the effect of a price ceiling on the equilibrium price and quantity.

price ceiling
a maximum legal price at which a good can be sold

A **price ceiling** is a maximum legal price at which a good can be sold. Many countries have price ceilings on staple foods, gasoline, and electricity because policy-makers try to ensure everyone can afford the basic necessities.

Here, we come to the first of the real-world interventions in the chapter: Historically, the government of Mexico has set a price ceiling for tortillas. The intent is to guarantee that this staple food will remain affordable. Panel A of Figure 6-1 illustrates a hypothetical market for tortillas without a price ceiling. The equilibrium price is $0.50 per pound and the equilibrium quantity is 50 million pounds.

Let's say that the government of Mexico responded to rising tortilla prices by setting a price ceiling of approximately $0.25 per pound, as shown in panel B of Figure 6-1. How would we expect consumers and producers to respond to this intervention?

- When the price falls, consumers will want to buy more tortillas. In this example, the price fell from $0.50 to $0.25, and as a result, quantity demanded increased from 50 million to 75 million pounds.
- Predictably, a lower price means fewer producers will be willing to supply tortillas. In this example, when the price fell to $0.25, the quantity supplied dropped from 50 million to 25 million pounds.

The lower price imposed by the price ceiling means higher quantity demanded but lower quantity supplied. Supply and demand were no longer in equilibrium. The price ceiling created a *shortage* of tortillas, equal to the 50-million-pound difference between the quantity demanded (75 million) and the quantity supplied (25 million).

FIGURE 6-1

A market with and without a price ceiling

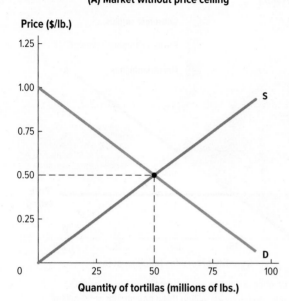

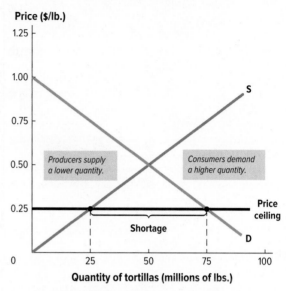

Without government intervention, the market for tortillas in Mexico would reach equilibrium at a price of $0.50 per pound and a quantity of 50 million pounds.

After government intervention, a price ceiling of $0.25 keeps the price of tortillas below the equilibrium point. At this new price, consumers want to buy more tortillas (75 million pounds) than producers want to supply (25 million pounds), resulting in a shortage of tortillas.

Did the price ceiling meet the goal of providing low-priced tortillas to consumers? Yes and no. Consumers were able to buy *some* tortillas at the low price of $0.25 a pound—but they *wanted* to buy three times as many tortillas as producers were willing to supply.

We can assess the full effect of the price ceiling by looking at what happened to consumer and producer surplus. Even without looking at the graph, we already know that a price ceiling will cause producer surplus to fall: Sellers are selling fewer tortillas at a lower price.

We also know that total surplus—that is, producer and consumer surplus combined—will fall because the market has moved away from equilibrium. Some trades that would have happened at the equilibrium price do not happen. Also, the surplus that would have been generated by those mutually beneficial trades is lost entirely. This area is known as *deadweight loss* and is represented by area 1 in Figure 6-2.

As discussed in Chapter 5, "Efficiency," **deadweight loss** represents the loss of total surplus that occurs because the quantity of a good that is bought and sold is below the market equilibrium quantity. Economists refer to changes in the economic well-being of market participants, as measured by changes in consumer surplus or producer surplus like deadweight loss, as *welfare effects*.

What we can't tell without looking at the graph is whether consumer surplus will increase or decrease; that response depends on the shape of the supply and demand curves. In this instance, consumers lose surplus from trades that no longer take place (from the 25 million pounds of tortillas no longer supplied). But for the trades that still do take place, consumers gain surplus from paying $0.25 instead of $0.50. In those trades, producers lose the same amount of surplus from receiving the lower price. This direct transfer of surplus from producers to consumers is represented by area 2 (the cross-hatched area) in Figure 6-2.

deadweight loss
a loss of total surplus that occurs because the quantity of a good that is bought and sold is below the market equilibrium quantity

FIGURE 6-2
Welfare effects of a price ceiling

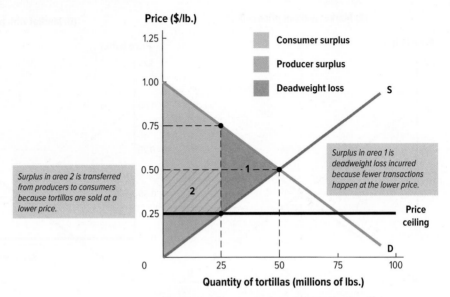

The price ceiling causes the total quantity of tortillas traded to fall by 25 million (from equilibrium at 50 million to 25 million). This results in deadweight loss. The price ceiling also causes surplus to be transferred from producers to consumers: Consumers win because they pay a lower price, and producers lose because they sell at a lower price ($0.25 instead of $0.50).

Did consumer surplus increase or decrease? Because area 2 in Figure 6-2 is larger than half of area 1 (the portion of deadweight loss that would have gone to consumers at equilibrium), we know that the intended goal of the price ceiling was achieved: a net increase in the well-being of consumers.

Was the policy worthwhile? On the one hand, consumers gained surplus. On the other hand, the surplus lost by producers was greater than that gained by consumers, meaning that total surplus decreased. Is it a price worth paying? That is a normative question about which reasonable people can disagree.

Another factor we may want to consider in our overall analysis of the price ceiling is how the scarce tortillas are allocated. Because a price ceiling causes a shortage, goods must be rationed. Rationing could be done in a number of ways:

- One possibility is for goods to be rationed equally, with each family entitled to buy the same amount of tortillas per week. This is what happened when food was rationed in the United States during World War II.
- Another possibility is to allocate goods on a first-come, first-served basis. This mode of rationing forces people to waste time standing in lines.
- In still other cases, rationed goods might go to those who are given preference by the government, or to the friends and family of sellers.
- Finally, shortages open the door for people to bribe whoever is in charge of allocating scarce supplies. Rationing via bribery results in even more deadweight loss than in the example shown in Figure 6-2. Economists call this *rent-seeking behavior*, and it is often cited as an argument against imposing price ceilings.

The What Do You Think? box "Put a cap on payday lending?" asks you to weigh the costs and benefits of a controversial price ceiling on the interest rates of payday loans.

Put a cap on payday lending?
What Do You Think?

Imagine the following scenario: You are on the way to work and your car breaks down, leaving you stranded on the side of the road. Soon, you are looking at a $300 bill for the tow truck and a new alternator. Coming up with $300 will be tough, and to make things worse, it's Monday and payday is a week away.

When faced with this type of emergency, some turn to a *payday loan,* a short-term cash loan of less than $1,000 that is intended to be repaid with the borrower's next paycheck. Many borrowers like these loans because they are quick (most centers will give you cash in 30 minutes or less) and convenient (in the United States, payday loan centers outnumber McDonald's).

Rather than charging interest rates, payday loan centers usually charge borrowers a "fee" in exchange for cash. For example, a 14-day loan of $300 might cost $35 in fees. That may not sound like a lot, but when calculated as an annual interest rate, it works out to over 300 percent. (For comparison, credit cards charge interest rates of about 20 percent.) Not only that, the loan comes due at the borrower's next paycheck, which may also be needed for food, gas, or rent. Failing to repay the $300 loan would require taking out a new loan of $335 and paying more fees. Many have a hard time finding enough money to break the cycle.

Citing these dangers, 14 states and the District of Columbia have banned payday loans altogether. Many more states have set caps on fees or the interest rate that lenders can charge. In economic terms, these caps constitute a price ceiling on payday loans. As with other price ceilings, decisions to cap interest rates and fees are controversial.

Supporters of greater regulation argue that limiting fees protects vulnerable consumers from "predatory" lenders who offer loans people can't afford. Payday lenders argue that their loans serve a real need.

Let's go back to the opening example of a broken-down car. If the car was the only way to get to work, failing to come up with $300 would mean losing your job. In that case, you might be happy to pay $35 in fees. Instead of protecting consumers, putting low caps on fees could drive some payday lenders out of business, hurting consumers who make informed decisions.

WHAT DO YOU THINK?

1. Considering that there are other ways to get money quickly, including credit cards, banks, or friends, can you think of a situation that would require visiting a payday loan center? Why might you not want to take advantage of the other ways? Can you think of "hidden" costs?
2. Price ceilings hold down interest rates and transfer surplus to consumers, but they also reduce the number of transactions that occur in a market. How would you determine whether price ceilings on payday loans are worth the cost?
3. Instead of implementing price caps, some states restrict the number of loans a borrower can take at a time or require that borrowers wait 24 hours (called a "cool-down" period) before taking out a new loan. Researchers Marianne Bertrand and Adair Morse found that providing customers with more information about the cost of loans decreased the amount and frequency of borrowing. How do you feel about these policies relative to a price ceiling?

Sources: Marianne Bertrand and Adair Morse, "Information disclosure, cognitive biases, and payday lending," *Journal of American Finance* 66, no. 6 (December 2011), pp. 1865–1863; "Payday lending state statutes," *National Conference of State Legislatures,* January 28, 2018, www.ncsl.org/research/financial-services-and-commerce/payday-lending-state-statutes.aspx

FIGURE 6-3

Nonbinding price ceiling

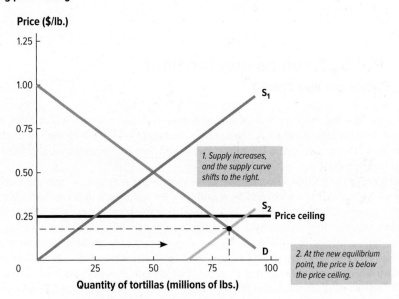

A price ceiling is intended to keep prices below the equilibrium level. However, changes in the market can reduce the equilibrium price to a level below the price ceiling. When that happens, the price ceiling no longer creates a shortage because the quantity supplied equals the quantity demanded.

Nonbinding price ceilings   A price ceiling does not always affect the market outcome. If the ceiling is set above the equilibrium price in a market, it is said to be *nonbinding*. That is, the ceiling doesn't "bind" or restrict buyers' and sellers' behavior because the current equilibrium is within the range allowed by the ceiling. In such cases, the equilibrium price and quantity will prevail.

Price ceilings are usually binding when they are first implemented. (Otherwise, why bother to create one?) Over time, though, shifts in the market can render the ceilings nonbinding. Suppose the price of corn decreases, reducing the cost of making tortillas. Figure 6-3 shows how the supply curve for tortillas would shift to the right (from S_1 to S_2) in response to this change in the market (a change in the price of inputs). This shift causes the equilibrium price to fall below the price ceiling. The new equilibrium is 80 million pounds of tortillas at $0.20 a pound, and the price ceiling becomes nonbinding.

Price floors

LO 6.2 Calculate the effect of a price floor on the equilibrium price and quantity.

A **price floor** is a minimum legal price at which a good can be sold. The United States has a long history of establishing price floors for certain agricultural goods. The rationale is that farming is a risky business—subject to bad weather, crop failure, and unreliable prices—but also an essential one, if people are to have enough to eat. A price floor is seen as a way to guarantee farmers a minimum income in the face of these difficulties, keeping them in business and ensuring a reliable supply of food.

price floor
a minimum legal price at which a good can be sold

We now come to the second of our four real-world interventions: The United States has maintained price floors for dairy products for over 65 years; the Milk Price Support Program began with the Agricultural Act of 1949. What effect has this program had on the market for milk?

FIGURE 6-4

A market with and without a price floor

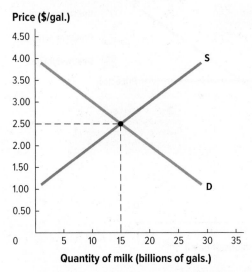

(A) Market without price floor

Without government intervention, the equilibrium point in the market for milk would be 15 billion gallons at a price of $2.50 per gallon.

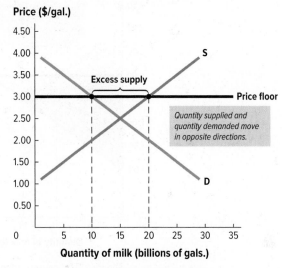

(B) Market with price floor

A price floor raises the price of milk above the equilibrium point. At the new price of $3 per gallon, consumers want to buy less than suppliers want to produce, resulting in a 10-billion-gallon surplus.

In panel A of Figure 6-4, we show a hypothetical unregulated market for milk in the United States, with an annual equilibrium quantity of 15 billion gallons and an equilibrium price of $2.50 per gallon.

Now suppose the U.S. government implements a price floor, so that the price of milk cannot fall below $3 per gallon, as shown in panel B of Figure 6-4. How will producers and consumers respond?

- At $3 per gallon, dairy farmers will want to increase milk production from 15 to 20 billion gallons, moving up along the supply curve.
- At that price, however, consumers will want to decrease their milk consumption from 15 to 10 billion gallons, moving up along the demand curve.

As a result, the price floor creates an excess supply of milk that is equal to the difference between the quantity supplied and the quantity demanded—in this case, 10 billion gallons.

Has the government accomplished its aim of supporting dairy farmers and providing them with a reliable income? As with price ceilings, the answer is yes and no. Producers who can sell all their milk will be happy: They are selling more milk at a higher price. However, producers who cannot sell all their milk, because demand no longer meets supply, will be unhappy. Consumers will be unhappy because they are getting less milk at a higher price.

Again, we can apply the concept of surplus to formally analyze how this change in total surplus is distributed between consumers and producers. Before the price floor, 15 billion gallons of milk were supplied and bought; after the price floor, this number is only 10 billion. Five billion gallons of milk that could have been traded were not, reducing total surplus. This deadweight loss is represented by area 1 in Figure 6-5.

Like price ceilings, price floors change the distribution of surplus; in this case, producers win at the expense of consumers. When the price floor is in effect, the only consumers who buy are those whose willingness to pay is above $3. Their consumer surplus falls because they are buying

FIGURE 6-5

Welfare effects of a price floor

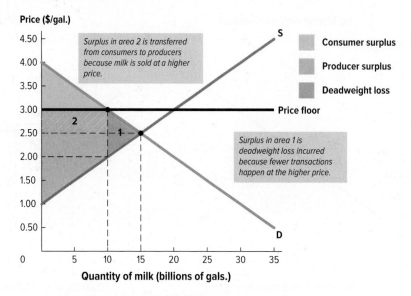

The price floor causes the total quantity of milk
traded to fall by 5 billion gallons relative to equilibrium. This results in deadweight loss. The price
floor also causes surplus to be transferred from
consumers to producers: In this example,
producers win because they sell at a higher price,
and consumers lose because they pay a higher price.

the same milk at a higher price. Consumers' lost surplus is transferred directly to the producers
who sell milk to them. This transfer of consumer surplus is represented by area 2 (the cross-
hatched area) in Figure 6-5.

Did producers gain or lose overall? The answer depends on whether the area of transferred
consumer surplus is bigger or smaller than the producers' share of the deadweight loss. Area 2
(the transfer of consumer surplus) is larger than the section of area 1 lost to producers; in this
case, the price floor policy increased well-being for producers.

Is the price of reduced total and consumer surplus worth paying to achieve increased producer
surplus? One factor to consider is how the extra surplus is distributed among producers. Producers who are able to sell all their milk at the higher price will be happy. But producers who do not
manage to sell all of their goods will be left holding an excess supply. They may be worse off than
before the imposition of the price floor. With excess supply, customers may choose to buy from
firms they like based on familiarity, political preference, or any other decision-making process
they choose.

To prevent some producers from being left with excess supply, the government may decide to
buy up all the excess supply of milk, ensuring that *all* producers benefit. In fact, that is how the
milk price support program works in the United States. The Department of Agriculture guarantees producers that it will buy milk at a certain price, regardless of the market price. Of course,
paying for the milk imposes a cost on taxpayers and is often cited as an argument against price
floors. How much milk will the government have to buy? The answer is the entire amount of the
excess supply created by the price floor. In the case of the hypothetical milk price floor, the government will have to buy 10 billion gallons at a price of $3. The cost to taxpayers of maintaining
the price floor in this example would be $30 billion each year.

FIGURE 6-6

Nonbinding price floor

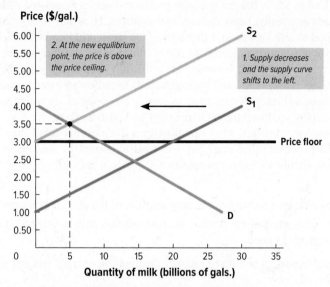

Although a price floor is usually set so as to raise prices above the equilibrium level, changes in the supply can raise the equilibrium price above the price floor. When that happens, the surplus that was created by the price floor disappears and the quantity supplied equals the quantity demanded.

Nonbinding price floors   Price floors are not always binding. In fact, in recent years, the market prices for dairy products in the United States have usually been above the price floor. The price floor may become binding, however, in response to changes in the market. Figure 6-6 shows how such a decrease in supply could render a price floor nonbinding. Consider the effect of the increased demand for ethanol in 2007 on the market for milk. Ethanol is a fuel additive made from corn. The sudden rise in demand for ethanol pushed up the price of corn, which in turn pushed up the cost of livestock feed for dairy farmers. As a result of this change in the price of inputs, the supply curve for milk shifted to the left (from S_1 to S_2 in Figure 6-6). This shift pushed the equilibrium price for milk above the $3 price floor to $3.50.

✓TEST YOURSELF

☐ Why does a price ceiling cause a shortage? **[LO 6.1]**
☐ What can cause a price ceiling to become nonbinding? **[LO 6.1]**
☐ Explain how a government can support a price floor through purchases. **[LO 6.2]**
☐ What can cause a price floor to become nonbinding? **[LO 6.2]**

Taxes and Subsidies

Taxes are the main way that governments raise revenue to pay for public programs. Taxes and subsidies can also be used to correct market failures and encourage or discourage production and consumption of particular goods. However, like price floors and price ceilings, they can have unintended consequences.

Taxes

LO 6.3 Calculate the effect of a tax on the equilibrium price and quantity.

We began this chapter by discussing hunger, which is usually a minor problem in wealthy countries. Indeed, the United States has the opposite problem: diseases associated with overeating and poor nutrition, such as obesity, heart disease, and diabetes. How can policy-makers respond to this new type of food crisis? This issue is the third of the real-world interventions in this chapter.

In 2008, the state of California banned the use of trans fats in restaurants in an effort to reduce heart disease and related problems. Trans fats are artificially produced ("partially hydrogenated") unsaturated fats. Used in many fried and packaged foods because they extend products' shelf lives, they are believed to be unhealthy if consumed in excess. For decades, trans fats have been the key to making commercially produced french fries crispy and pastries flaky.

Rather than banning trans fats, what would happen if California taxed them? When a good is taxed, either the buyer or seller must pay some extra amount to the government on top of the sale price. How should we expect people to *respond* to a tax on trans fats? Taxes have two primary effects:

- First, they discourage production and consumption of the good that is taxed.
- Second, they raise government revenue through the fees paid by those who continue buying and selling the good.

Therefore, we would expect a tax both to reduce consumption of trans fats and to provide a new source of public revenue.

Figure 6-7 illustrates this scenario by showing the impact of a trans-fat tax on the market for Chocolate Whizbangs. A delicious imaginary candy, Chocolate Whizbangs are unfortunately rather high in trans fats. Suppose that, currently, 30 million Whizbangs are sold every year, at

FIGURE 6-7

Effect of a tax paid by the seller

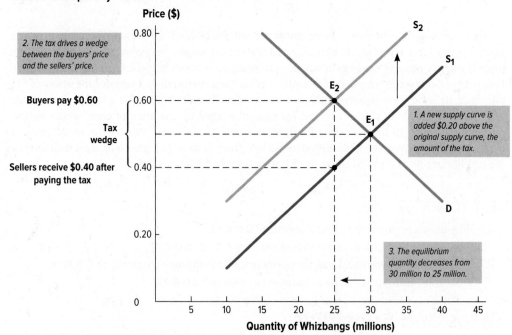

A tax levied on the seller adds a new supply curve that is $0.20 higher than the original, which is the amount of the tax. As a result, the equilibrium quantity decreases and the equilibrium price increases. At the equilibrium quantity, the price paid by buyers is now different from the amount received by sellers after the tax is paid. This "tax wedge" is equal to the amount of the tax, or $0.20.

$0.50 each. To discourage consumption, a tax on Whizbangs has been proposed; the new tax could be imposed either on sellers or on buyers. Let's look at both options.

A tax on sellers   Let's say that the government of California enacts a trans-fat tax of $0.20, which the seller must pay for every Whizbang sold. *How will buyers and sellers respond?* The impact of a tax is more complicated than the impact of a price control, so let's take it one step at a time.

1. **Does a tax on sellers affect supply?** *Yes, supply decreases.*

    When a tax is imposed on sellers (producers), they must pay the government $0.20 for each Whizbang sold. At any market price, sellers will behave as if the price they are receiving is actually $0.20 lower. Put another way, for sellers to be willing to supply any given quantity, the market price must be $0.20 higher than it was before the tax.

    Figure 6-7 shows this change in supply graphically, by adding a new supply curve (S_2). (Technically, this "shift" isn't really a shift of the curve but a way of showing the new equilibrium price; see the nearby Caution: Common Mistake box.) The new supply curve is $0.20 higher, the exact amount of the tax. At any given market price, sellers will now produce the same quantity as they would have at a price $0.20 lower before the tax: At $0.60 on curve S_2, the quantity supplied will be the same as at a price of $0.40 on curve S_1. At a price of $0.50 on curve S_2, the quantity supplied will be the same as at a price of $0.30 on curve S_1, and so on.

2. **Does a tax on sellers affect demand?** *No, demand stays the same.*

    Demand remains the same because the tax does not change any of the nonprice determinants of demand. At any given price, buyers' desire to purchase Whizbangs is unchanged. Remember, however, that the *quantity demanded* does change, although the curve itself doesn't change.

3. **How does a tax on sellers affect the market equilibrium?** *The equilibrium price rises and quantity demanded falls.*

    The new supply curve causes the equilibrium point to move up along the demand curve. At the new equilibrium point, the price paid by the buyer is $0.60. Because buyers now face a higher price, they demand fewer Whizbangs, so the quantity demanded falls from 30 million to 25 million. Notice that at the new equilibrium point, the quantity demanded is lower and the price is higher. Taxes usually reduce the quantity of a good or service that is sold, shrinking the market.

 CAUTION: COMMON MISTAKE

In Chapter 3, "Markets," we distinguished between a curve *shifting* to the left or right and *movement along* the same curve. A shift represents a fundamental change in the quantity demanded or supplied at any given price; a movement along the same curve simply shows a switch to a different quantity and price point. The question here is, does a tax cause a *shift* of the demand or supply curve or a *movement along* the curve?

The answer is neither, really. Here's why: When we add a tax, we're not really shifting the curve; rather, we are adding a second curve. We still need the original curve to understand what is happening. This is because the price that sellers receive is actually $0.20 lower than the price at which they sell Whizbangs, due to the tax. So we need one curve to represent what sellers receive and another curve to represent what buyers pay.

Notice in Figure 6-7 that the price suppliers receive is on the original supply curve, S_1, but the price buyers pay is on the new supply curve, S_2. The original curve *does not actually move,* but we add the second curve to indicate that because of the tax, buyers face a different price than what the sellers will get. In order for the market to be in equilibrium, the quantity that buyers demand at $0.60 must now equal the quantity that sellers supply at $0.40.

Now let's look at the new equilibrium price in Figure 6-7. The price paid by buyers to sellers is the new market price, $0.60. However, sellers do not get to keep all the money they receive. Instead, they must pay the tax to the government. Since the tax is $0.20, the price that sellers receive once they have paid the tax is only $0.40. Ultimately, sellers do not receive the full price that consumers pay; the tax creates what is known as a *tax wedge* between buyers and sellers. A **tax wedge** is the difference between the price paid by buyers and the price received by sellers, which equals the amount of the tax. In Figure 6-7, the tax wedge is calculated as shown in Equation 6-1.

tax wedge
the difference between the price paid by buyers and the price received by sellers in the presence of a tax

EQUATION 6-1 $\text{Tax wedge} = P_{\text{buyers}} - P_{\text{sellers}} = \text{Tax}$

For each Whizbang sold at the new equilibrium point, the government collects tax revenue, as calculated in Equation 6-2.

EQUATION 6-2 $\text{Government tax revenue} = \text{Tax} \times Q_{\text{post-tax}}$

Specifically, the government receives $0.20 for each of the 25 million Whizbangs sold, or $5 million total. Graphically, the government revenue equals the green-shaded area in Figure 6-8.

Just like a price control, a tax causes deadweight loss and redistributes surplus. We can see the deadweight loss caused by the reduced number of trades in Figure 6-8. It is surplus lost to buyers and sellers who would have been willing to make trades at the pre-tax equilibrium price.

The redistribution of surplus, however, is a little trickier to follow. Under a tax, *both* producers and consumers lose surplus. Consumers who still buy pay more for the same candy than they

FIGURE 6-8

Government revenue and deadweight loss from a tax

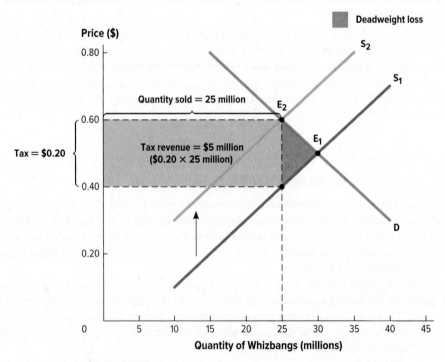

The revenue from a per-unit tax is the amount of the tax multiplied by the number of units sold at the post-tax equilibrium point. The amount of tax revenue directly corresponds to the surplus lost to consumers and producers. The trades that no longer happen under the tax represent deadweight loss.

would have under equilibrium, and producers who still sell receive less for the same candy. The difference between this lost surplus and deadweight loss, however, is that it doesn't "disappear." Instead, it becomes government revenue. In fact, the area representing government revenue in Figure 6-8 is exactly the same as the surplus lost to buyers and sellers still trading in the market after the tax has been imposed. This revenue can pay for services that might transfer surplus back to producers or consumers, or both, or to people outside of the market.

A tax on buyers   What happens if the tax is imposed on buyers instead of sellers? Surprisingly, the outcome is exactly the same. Suppose California enacts a sales tax of $0.20, which the buyer must pay for every Whizbang bought. In this case, as Figure 6-9 shows, the demand curve (rather than the supply curve) moves by the amount of the tax, but the resulting equilibrium price and quantity are the same.

To double-check this result, let's walk step by step through the effect of a tax levied on buyers.

1. **Does a tax on buyers affect the supply curve?** *No, supply stays the same.*

   The supply curve stays the same because the tax does not change the incentives producers face. None of the nonprice determinants of supply are affected.

2. **Does a tax on buyers affect the demand curve?** *Yes, demand decreases.*

   Demand decreases because the price buyers must pay per unit, including the tax, is now $0.20 higher than the original price. As Figure 6-9 shows, we take the original demand curve D_1 and factor in the amount of the tax; the result is a second demand curve D_2, which represents the price buyers pay under the tax. At any given price, buyers will now behave as if the price were actually $0.20 higher. For example, at $0.40 on curve D_2,

FIGURE 6-9

Effect of a tax paid by the buyer

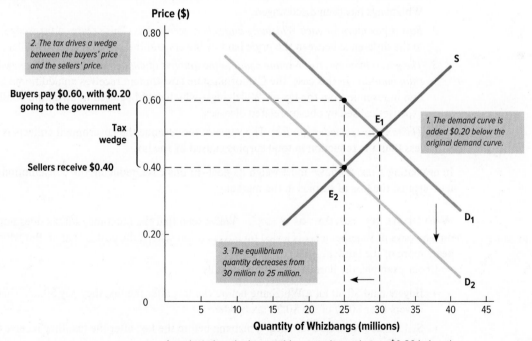

A tax levied on the buyer adds a new demand curve $0.20 below the original curve. As a result, the equilibrium quantity decreases and the equilibrium price paid by the buyer increases. These results are the same as those of a tax levied on the seller.

the quantity demanded is as if the price were $0.60 on curve D_1. At $0.30 on curve D_2, the quantity demanded is as if the price were $0.50.

3. **How does a tax on buyers affect the market equilibrium?** *The equilibrium price and quantity both fall.*

As a result, the equilibrium point with the new demand curve is further down the supply curve. The equilibrium price falls from $0.50 to $0.40 and the quantity demanded and supplied falls from 30 million to 25 million. Although the market equilibrium price goes down instead of up, as it does with a tax on sellers, the actual amount that buyers and sellers pay is the same no matter who pays the tax. When buyers pay the tax, they pay $0.40 to the seller and $0.20 to the government, or a total of $0.60. When sellers pay the tax, buyers pay $0.60 to the seller, who then pays $0.20 to the government. Either way, buyers pay $0.60 and sellers receive $0.40.

As Figure 6-9 shows, a tax on buyers creates a tax wedge just as a tax on sellers does. At the new equilibrium point, the price sellers receive is $0.40. The buyer pays $0.40 to the seller and then the $0.20 tax to the government, so that the total effective price is $0.60. Using Equation 6-1, once again the tax wedge is $0.20, exactly equal to the amount of the tax.

$$\text{Tax wedge} = \$0.60 - \$0.40 = \$0.20$$

Furthermore, the government still collects $0.20 for every Whizbang sold, just as under a tax on sellers. Again, using Equation 6-2, the post-tax equilibrium quantity is 25 million, and the government collects $5 million in tax revenue.

$$\text{Government tax revenue} = \$0.20 \times 25 \text{ million} = \$5 \text{ million}$$

What is the overall impact of the tax on Whizbangs? Regardless of whether a tax is imposed on buyers or sellers, there are four effects that result from all taxes:

1. *Equilibrium quantity falls.* The goal of the tax has thus been achieved—consumption of Whizbangs has been discouraged.

2. *Buyers pay more for each Whizbang and sellers receive less.* This creates a tax wedge, equal to the difference between the price paid by buyers and the price received by sellers.

3. *The government receives revenue equal to the amount of the tax multiplied by the new equilibrium quantity.* In this case, the California state government receives an additional $5 million in revenue from the tax on Whizbangs—which could be used to offset the public health expenses caused by obesity-related diseases.

4. *The tax causes deadweight loss.* The value of the revenue the government collects is always less than the reduction in total surplus caused by the tax.

In evaluating a tax, then, we must weigh its goal—in this case, reducing the consumption of trans fats—against the loss of surplus in the market.

Who bears the burden of a tax?   We've seen that the outcome of a tax does not depend on who pays it. Whether a tax is levied on buyers or on sellers, the cost is shared. But which group bears more of the burden?

In our example, the burden was shared equally:

- Buyers paid $0.50 for a Whizbang before the tax; after the tax, they pay $0.60. Therefore, buyers bear $0.10 of the $0.20 tax burden.

- Sellers received $0.50 for each Whizbang before the tax; after the tax, they receive $0.40. Therefore, sellers also bear $0.10 of the $0.20 tax burden.

tax incidence
the relative tax burden borne by buyers and sellers

The shaded rectangles in panel A of Figure 6-10 represent graphically this 50-50 split. The relative tax burden borne by buyers and sellers is called the **tax incidence**.

FIGURE 6-10

Tax incidence and relative elasticity

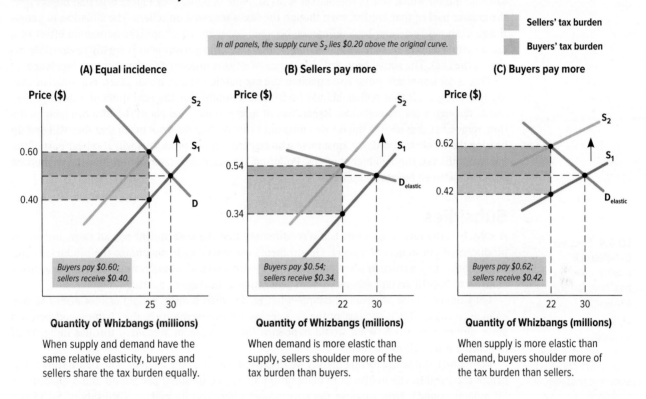

In all panels, the supply curve S_2 lies $0.20 above the original curve.

☐ Sellers' tax burden

☐ Buyers' tax burden

(A) Equal incidence

Price ($)

0.60

0.40

S_2

S_1

D

Buyers pay $0.60; sellers receive $0.40.

25 30

Quantity of Whizbangs (millions)

When supply and demand have the same relative elasticity, buyers and sellers share the tax burden equally.

(B) Sellers pay more

Price ($)

0.54

0.34

S_2

S_1

$D_{elastic}$

Buyers pay $0.54; sellers receive $0.34.

22 30

Quantity of Whizbangs (millions)

When demand is more elastic than supply, sellers shoulder more of the tax burden than buyers.

(C) Buyers pay more

Price ($)

0.62

0.42

S_2

S_1

$D_{elastic}$

Buyers pay $0.62; sellers receive $0.42.

22 30

Quantity of Whizbangs (millions)

When supply is more elastic than demand, buyers shoulder more of the tax burden than sellers.

Often, however, the tax incidence is not split equally. Sometimes one group carries much more of it than the other. Compare the example just given to another possible market for Whizbangs, represented in panel B of Figure 6-10. In this case:

- Buyers paid $0.50 before the tax. After the tax, they pay $0.54, so their tax burden is $0.04 per Whizbang.

- Sellers, on the other hand, receive only $0.34 after the tax, so their tax burden, at $0.16 per Whizbang, is four times as large as that of buyers.

Panel C of Figure 6-10 shows the opposite case, in which buyers bear more of the burden than sellers. Thus, buyers pay $0.62 and sellers receive $0.42.

What determines the incidence of a tax? The answer has to do with the relative elasticity of the supply and demand curves. Recall from Chapter 4, "Elasticity," that price elasticity describes how much the quantity supplied or demanded changes in response to a change in price. Since a tax effectively changes the price of a good to both buyers and sellers, the relative responsiveness of supply and demand will determine the tax burden. Essentially, *the side of the market that is more price elastic will be more able to adjust to price changes and will shoulder less of the tax burden.* For example:

- Panel B of Figure 6-10 imagines a market in which demand is more elastic: Many consumers easily give up their Whizbang habit and buy healthier snacks instead. In that case, Whizbang producers pay a higher share of the tax.

- Panel C of Figure 6-10 imagines a market in which demand is less elastic: Consumers are so obsessed with Whizbangs that they will buy even at the higher price. In that case, Whizbang buyers pay a higher share of the tax.

Recall that the market outcome of a tax—the new equilibrium quantity and price—is the same regardless of whether a tax is imposed on buyers or on sellers. Thus, the tax burden will be the same no matter which side of the market is taxed. Note in panel C of Figure 6-10 that buyers bear the greater part of that burden, even though the tax is imposed on sellers. The situation in panels B and C shows there can be a difference between *economic incidence* (the economic effect of a tax on either buyers or sellers) and *statutory incidence* (the person who is legally responsible for paying the tax). The actual economic incidence of a tax is unrelated to the statutory incidence.

This is an important point to remember during public debates about taxes. A politician may say that companies that pollute should be held accountable for the environmental damage they cause, through a tax on pollution. Regardless of how you may feel about the idea of taxing pollution, remember that levying the tax on companies that pollute does not mean that they will end up bearing the whole tax burden. Consumers who buy from those producers will also bear part of the burden of the tax, through higher prices. Policy-makers have little control over how the tax burden is shared between buyers and sellers.

Subsidies

LO 6.4 Calculate the effect of a subsidy on the equilibrium price and quantity.

subsidy
a requirement that the government pay an extra amount to producers or consumers of a good

A **subsidy** is the reverse of a tax: It is a requirement that the government pay an extra amount to producers or consumers of a good. Governments use subsidies to encourage the production and consumption of a particular good or service. They can also use subsidies as an alternative to price controls to benefit certain groups without generating a shortage or an excess supply.

Let's return to the Mexican dilemma—what to do when hungry people cannot afford to buy enough tortillas. This is the last of the four real-world interventions in the chapter, and here we ask a different question: What would happen if the government *subsidized* tortillas rather than imposed a price ceiling on them?

Figure 6-11 shows the tortilla market we discussed earlier in the chapter. The figure shows that before the subsidy, the market is in equilibrium at a price of $0.70 per pound and a quantity of 50 million pounds. Now suppose the government offers tortilla makers a subsidy of $0.35 per pound. *How will buyers and sellers respond to the subsidy?* They will respond in the opposite way that they respond to a tax:

- With a tax, the quantity supplied and demanded decrease, and the government collects revenue.
- With a subsidy, the quantity supplied and demanded increase, and the government spends money.

We can calculate the effect of a $0.35 tortilla subsidy by walking through the same three steps we used to examine the effect of a tax.

1. **Does a subsidy to sellers affect the supply curve?** *Yes, supply increases.*

   When producers receive a subsidy, the real price they receive for each unit sold is higher than the market price. At any market price, therefore, they will behave as if the price were $0.35 higher. Put another way, for sellers to supply a given quantity, the market price can be $0.35 lower than it would have to be without the subsidy. As a result, the new supply curve is drawn $0.35 below the original. In Figure 6-11, S_2 shows the new supply curve that is the result of the subsidy.

2. **Does a subsidy to sellers affect the demand curve?** *No, demand stays the same.*

   The demand curve stays where it is because consumers are not directly affected by the subsidy.

3. **How does a subsidy to sellers affect the market equilibrium?** *The equilibrium price decreases and the equilibrium quantity increases.*

   The equilibrium quantity with the new supply curve increases as consumers move down along the demand curve to the new equilibrium point. At the new, post-subsidy

FIGURE 6-11

Effect of a subsidy to the seller

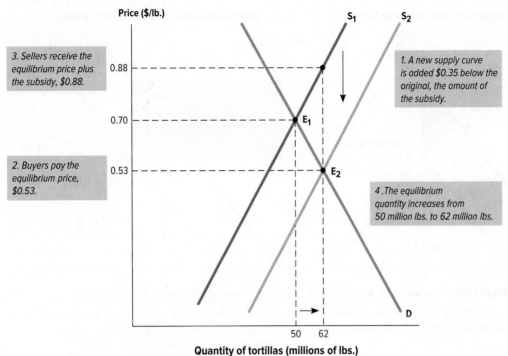

3. Sellers receive the equilibrium price plus the subsidy, $0.88.

1. A new supply curve is added $0.35 below the original, the amount of the subsidy.

2. Buyers pay the equilibrium price, $0.53.

4. The equilibrium quantity increases from 50 million lbs. to 62 million lbs.

A subsidy has the opposite effect of a tax. A new supply curve is added $0.35 below the original supply curve. This decreases the equilibrium price and increases the equilibrium quantity supplied and demanded.

equilibrium, the quantity supplied increases from 50 million pounds of tortillas to 62 million pounds. As with a tax, the price buyers pay for tortillas differs from the price sellers receive after the subsidy because the subsidy creates a wedge between the two prices. This time, however, sellers receive a *higher* price than the pre-subsidy equilibrium of $0.70, and buyers pay a *lower* one. Buyers pay $0.53 per pound and sellers receive $0.88 per pound. The government pays the $0.35 difference.

The government subsidizes each pound of tortillas sold at the new equilibrium point. To calculate the total amount of government expenditure on a subsidy, we can use Equation 6-3. The government spends $0.35 for each of the 62 million pounds of tortillas sold, or $21.7 million total.

EQUATION 6-3   Government subsidy expenditure $= \text{Subsidy} \times Q_{\text{post-subsidy}}$

Like taxes, subsidies also cause deadweight loss and redistribute surplus. Panel A of Figure 6-12 shows the deadweight loss caused by the overproduction and overconsumption of tortillas. If there is no subsidy, 50 million pounds is the equilibrium quantity. Any more, and the cost to produce them would be higher than the benefit to consumers. Thus, it would be inefficient to exchange more than 50 million pounds of tortillas. The subsidy lowers the cost to the producer, thus causing producers and consumers to exchange 12 million more pounds of tortillas than is efficient. This leads to a deadweight loss.

Panel B of Figure 6-12 shows the total government expenditure on the subsidy. You may wonder why only part of the government expenditure is counted as deadweight loss. If the government is funding 12 million more pounds of tortillas than is efficient, shouldn't the entire expenditure

FIGURE 6-12
Deadweight loss from a subsidy

(A) Deadweight loss from tortilla subsidy

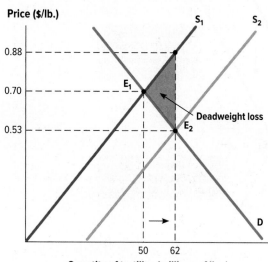

(B) Government spending on tortilla subsidy

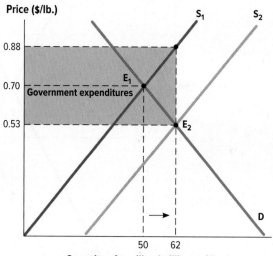

For the 12 million pounds of tortillas produced due to the subsidy, supply exceeds demand. Thus, the exchange of these tortillas causes deadweight loss.

The government subsidy expenditure is the amount of the subsidy multiplied by the post-subsidy equilibrium quantity. The subsidy increases both consumer surplus and producer surplus but imposes a cost on the government, which ultimately is paid for by taxes on consumers and producers.

be deadweight loss? The answer is no, because the government is increasing both consumer and producer surplus with its expenditures. However, the deadweight loss arises because not all of the expenditure becomes surplus.

Figure 6-13 shows the consumer surplus and producer surplus from a subsidy. Notice that both consumer surplus and producer surplus increase with a subsidy. However, recall that the increase in surplus is funded by the government, as shown in panel B of Figure 6-12. Notice that the amount of government expenditure is less than the total increase in producer and consumer surplus. Ultimately, that expenditure is passed on to taxpayers (both producers and individuals) in the form of more taxes.

Are the benefits to consumers and producers worth the cost? That depends on how much we value the increased production of tortillas and their reduced cost to consumers versus the opportunity cost of the subsidy—that is, whatever other use the government or taxpayers might have made of that $21.7 million.

In addition, as the Economics in Action box "The unintended consequences of biofuel subsidies" shows, the obvious benefits of a subsidy can sometimes be swamped by unexpected costs.

As with a tax, the effect of a subsidy is the same regardless of whether it is paid to producers or consumers. If consumers received a $0.35 subsidy for every pound of tortillas they bought, their demand curve would be $0.35 above the original, and the supply curve would remain unchanged. In that case, the equilibrium outcome would be the same as if producers received the subsidy: Quantity increases from 50 million pounds to 62 million pounds, buyers pay $0.53 per pound, and sellers receive $0.88 per pound.

Also as with a tax, the way in which the benefits of a subsidy are split between buyers and sellers depends on the relative elasticity of the demand and supply curves. *The side of the market*

FIGURE 6-13

A subsidy's effect on surplus

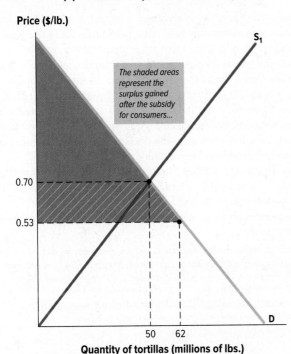

(A) Consumer surplus from tortilla subsidy

The shaded areas represent the surplus gained after the subsidy for consumers...

The post-subsidy price paid by consumers ($0.53) is lower than the initial equilibrium price ($0.70), and the post-subsidy quantity (62 million pounds) is higher than the initial equilibrium quantity (50 million pounds). This results in an increase in consumer surplus.

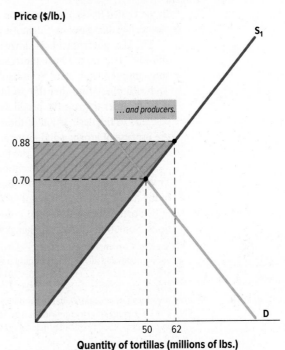

(B) Producer surplus from tortilla subsidy

...and producers.

The post-subsidy price received by sellers ($0.88) is higher than the initial equilibrium price ($0.70), and the post-subsidy quantity (62 million pounds) is higher than the initial equilibrium quantity (50 million pounds). This results in an increase in producer surplus.

that is more price inelastic receives more of the benefit. In our example, both have almost the same benefit: Buyers are better off by $0.17 per pound of tortillas, and producers by $0.18.

As with taxes, it is important to note that who gets what share of benefit from the subsidy does not depend on who receives the subsidy. Sometimes in debates about subsidies you will hear someone argue that a subsidy should be given either to buyers or sellers because they "deserve it more." This argument doesn't make much sense in a competitive market (although it might in a noncompetitive market).

In sum, a subsidy has the following effects, regardless of whether it is paid to buyers or sellers:

1. Equilibrium quantity increases, accomplishing the goal of encouraging production and consumption of the subsidized good.
2. Buyers pay less and sellers receive more for each unit sold. The amount of the subsidy forms a wedge between buyers' and sellers' prices.
3. The government has to pay for the subsidy, the cost of which equals the amount of the subsidy multiplied by the new equilibrium quantity.

✓ TEST YOURSELF

☐ What is a tax wedge? **[LO 6.3]**
☐ What determines the incidence of a tax? **[LO 6.3]**

The unintended consequences of biofuel subsidies
Economics in Action

In the United States, cars partly run on corn. "Gasoline" often contains ethanol, a "biofuel" that is a cleaner fuel than gasoline. Ethanol is fermented from starch, most often from corn in the United States.

The U.S. government subsidizes ethanol production in part to reduce pollution; as hoped, the subsidy has caused a huge increase in the production of ethanol. Unfortunately, it has also had some unintended effects. Scientists find that, indirectly, biofuels can actually increase pollution.

Researchers find that the problem is simple, and yet something policy-makers didn't anticipate. In order to grow the products that ethanol is created from, farmers need land—a need that can lead to the destruction of forests, wetlands, and grasslands. Pollution can also be created in the process of growing and fermenting corn and when distilling the ethanol. These activities can lead to the opposite effect of the hoped-for reduction in air pollution.

In addition, some organizations (including United Nations agencies, the International Monetary Fund, and the World Bank) have warned that biofuels could push food prices higher in the future (although it is not yet clear how much and when).

Unfortunately, unintended consequences aren't always just a postscript to market interventions. Sometimes, they can change the story.

Sources: Christopher W. Tessuma, Jason D. Hill, and Julian D. Marshall, "Life cycle air quality impacts of conventional and alternative light-duty transportation in the United States," *Proceedings of the National Academy of Sciences* 111, no.52 (December 30, 2014). *The New York Times* had a discussion in its environmental blog: http://green.blogs.nytimes.com/2008/11/03/the-biofuel-debate-good-bad-or-too-soon-to-tell/. Also, www.theguardian.com/global-development/poverty-matters/2011/jun/01/biofuels-driving-food-prices-higher. The US Energy Information Administration provides a perspective on ways to limit side-effects: www.eia.gov/energyexplained/index.php?page=biofuel_ethanol_environment.

☐ How does a subsidy affect the equilibrium quantity? How does it affect the price that sellers receive and the price that buyers pay? **[LO 6.4]**

☐ Does it matter whether a subsidy is paid to buyers or sellers? Why or why not? **[LO 6.4]**

Evaluating Government Interventions

LO 6.5 Explain how elasticity and time period influence the impact of a market intervention.

We began this chapter with a discussion of three reasons why policy-makers might decide to intervene in a market: to change the distribution of surplus, to encourage or discourage consumption, and to correct market failures. To decide whether policy-makers have achieved their goals by implementing a price control, tax, or subsidy, we need to assess the effects of each intervention, including its unintended consequences.

We've established a few rules about the expected outcomes of market interventions. Table 6-1 summarizes the key effects of price controls, taxes, and subsidies. In general, we can say the following:

- Price controls have opposing impacts on the quantities supplied and demanded, causing a shortage or excess supply. In contrast, taxes and subsidies move the quantities supplied and demanded in the same direction, allowing the market to reach equilibrium at the point where the quantity supplied equals the quantity demanded.

- Taxes discourage people from buying and selling a particular good, raise government revenue, and impose a cost on both buyers and sellers.

- Subsidies encourage people to buy and sell a particular good, cost the government money, and provide a benefit to both buyers and sellers.

In the following sections we will consider some of the more complicated details of market interventions. These details matter. Often the details of an intervention make the difference between a successful policy and a failed one.

TABLE 6-1

Government interventions: A summary

Intervention	Reason for using	Effect on price	Effect on quantity	Who gains and who loses?
Price floor	To protect producers' income	Price cannot go below the set minimum.	Quantity demanded decreases and quantity supplied increases, creating excess supply.	Producers who can sell all their goods earn more revenue per item; other producers are stuck with an unwanted excess supply.
Price ceiling	To keep consumer costs low	Price cannot go above the set maximum.	Quantity demanded increases and quantity supplied decreases, creating a shortage.	Consumers who can buy all the goods they want benefit; other consumers suffer from shortages.
Tax	To discourage an activity or collect money to pay for its consequences; to increase government revenue	Price increases.	Equilibrium quantity decreases.	Government receives increased revenue; society may gain if the tax decreases socially harmful behavior. Buyers and sellers of the good that is taxed share the cost. Which group bears more of the burden depends on the price elasticity of supply and demand.
Subsidy	To encourage an activity; to provide benefits to a certain group	Price decreases.	Equilibrium quantity increases.	Buyers purchase more goods at a lower price. Society may benefit if the subsidy encourages socially beneficial behavior. The government and ultimately the taxpayers bear the cost.

How big is the effect of a tax or subsidy?

Regardless of the reason for a market intervention, it's important to know exactly *how much* it will change the equilibrium quantity and price. Can the effect of a tax or subsidy on the equilibrium quantity be predicted ahead of time? The answer is yes, *if* we know the price elasticity of supply and demand.

A general rule applies: *The more elastic supply or demand is, the greater the change in quantity.* This rule follows directly from the definition of price elasticity, which measures buyers' and sellers' responsiveness to a change in price—and a tax or subsidy is effectively a change in price.

Figure 6-14 shows the effect of a $0.20 tax on the quantity demanded under four different combinations of price elasticity of supply and demand—again, for Whizbangs. It's worthwhile to walk through each combination, one by one:

- In panel A, both supply and demand are *relatively inelastic:* In this case the tax causes the equilibrium quantity to decrease, but not by much. Both buyers and sellers are willing to continue trading, even though they now must pay the tax.
- In panel B, *demand is more elastic than supply:* When the supply curve is $0.20 higher, the change in quantity is much larger than in panel A.
- In panel C, *supply is elastic but demand is relatively inelastic:* Again, because suppliers are highly responsive to the cost of the tax, the quantity changes more than in panel A.
- In panel D, *supply and demand are both elastic:* In this case, the quantity goes down even more than in the second and third examples.

To predict the size of the effect of a tax or subsidy, then, policy-makers need to know the price elasticity of both supply and demand. As we have seen, they can also use that information to determine who will bear more of the burden or receive more of the benefit.

FIGURE 6-14

Price elasticity and the effect of a $0.20 tax

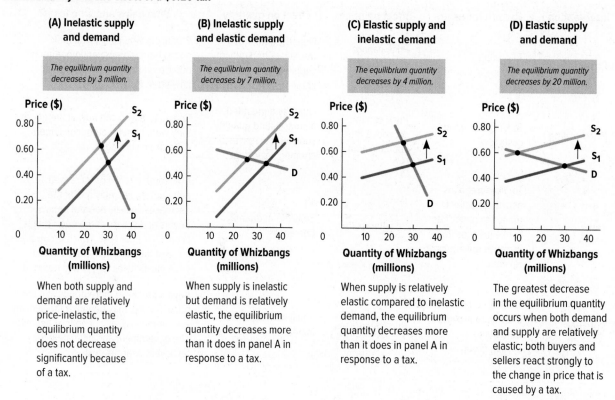

(A) Inelastic supply and demand

The equilibrium quantity decreases by 3 million.

When both supply and demand are relatively price-inelastic, the equilibrium quantity does not decrease significantly because of a tax.

(B) Inelastic supply and elastic demand

The equilibrium quantity decreases by 7 million.

When supply is inelastic but demand is relatively elastic, the equilibrium quantity decreases more than it does in panel A in response to a tax.

(C) Elastic supply and inelastic demand

The equilibrium quantity decreases by 4 million.

When supply is relatively elastic compared to inelastic demand, the equilibrium quantity decreases more than it does in panel A in response to a tax.

(D) Elastic supply and demand

The equilibrium quantity decreases by 20 million.

The greatest decrease in the equilibrium quantity occurs when both demand and supply are relatively elastic; both buyers and sellers react strongly to the change in price that is caused by a tax.

Sometimes, who pays the tax can depend on who is paying attention to true cost. The Econ and YOU box "Out of sight, out of mind" discusses research that looked into what happened when stores posted tax-inclusive prices of certain goods.

Out of sight, out of mind
Econ and YOU

Forty-five of the 50 states charge a sales tax on consumer goods. In most places, the sales tax is added on at the cash register. If the tax is 5 percent, for example, you'll be charged $21 for a book that has a $20 price tag. If you live in a place where advertised prices don't include taxes—and especially if you shop in a hurry—you might find that it's easy to focus on the number on the price tag and forget that you will end up paying more for that good.

If this happens to you, you're not alone. Economists Raj Chetty, Adam Looney, and Kory Kroft ran an experiment in a grocery store to test whether shoppers "forget" about sales tax when they look at the number on the price tag. In this experiment, price tags in some aisles listed both pre- and post-tax prices on goods. By showing both amounts, researchers would be able to compare sales of the same items at other stores that did not use the unique tags. Standard theory maintains that the different tagging shouldn't make a difference; when taxes are not posted, perfectly rational consumers should do the math on each item and make buying decisions based on the full, tax-inclusive prices.

However, the researchers found that customers weren't doing the math. So, when tax was included in the posted price of items, rather than added at the register, quantity demanded decreased by 8 percent. Clearly, something wasn't adding up.

It wasn't that people didn't know about the sales tax when it wasn't included in the posted price. When asked, most shoppers were able to correctly identify how much tax they would owe on what sort of goods. Rather, the tax simply wasn't at the top of their minds while they shopped; instead, they defaulted to thinking that the listed price was the true cost.

One result is that buying decisions were sensitive to changes in the prices on the price tags, but their decisions were not very sensitive to changes in tax rates. In terms of elasticities, demand was inelastic with respect to changes in taxes.

In this case, the quirks of human behavior—in this case, "out of sight, out of mind"—undermine our assumptions about rational, informed response to incentives. We don't expect you to start bringing a calculator to the grocery store. But stopping to spend a little more time thinking about taxes (especially on big-ticket items) can help make you make more rational decisions about what to buy.

Source: Raj Chetty, Adam Looney, and Kory Kroft, "Salience and Taxation: Theory and Evidence," *American Economic Review* 99, no. 4 (2009), p. 1145–1177.

Short-run versus long-run impact

We have seen that in addition to changing the price of a good or service, price controls cause shortages or excess supply. Because buyers and sellers take time to respond to a change in price, sometimes the full effect of price controls becomes clear only in the long run.

Suppose the U.S. government imposes a price floor on gasoline in an attempt to reduce air pollution by discouraging people from driving. Panel A of Figure 6-15 shows the short-run impact of a price floor in the market for gasoline. In the short run, the quantity of gas demanded might not change very much. Although people would cut down on unnecessary driving, the greater part of demand would still be based on driving habits that are difficult to change, such as commuting to school or work or going to the grocery store. And unless gasoline producers have a lot of unused oil wells sitting around, sellers might have trouble ramping up production quickly. In the short run, demand and supply are not very elastic, so the price floor results in only a small excess supply.

Recall that for both supply and demand, one of the determinants of price elasticity is the period over which it is measured. On both sides of the market, elasticity is often greater over a long period than over a short one:

- On the demand side, consumers might make small lifestyle changes over the medium term, such as buying a bus pass or shopping closer to home. Over the long run, they might make even bigger changes. When they need to buy a new car, for example, they will be inclined to buy a model that offers high gas mileage. If they move to a new job or home, they may place more weight than in the past on commuting distance.

- Supply will also be more elastic over the long run. Because a higher price gives suppliers an incentive to produce more, they may invest in oil exploration, dig new wells, or take steps to increase the pumping capacity of existing wells. Panel B of Figure 6-15 shows the long-run impact of a price floor in the market for gasoline. Because both supply and demand are more elastic in the long run than in the short run, the excess supply of gasoline is much larger in the long run than in the short run.

If the goal of the price floor was to reduce air pollution by giving consumers an incentive to cut down on driving, the impact might look disappointing in the short run: The quantity of gas burned

FIGURE 6-15
Government intervention in the short and long run

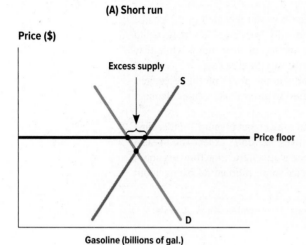

(A) Short run

In the short run, neither the supply nor the demand for gasoline is very elastic, so the effect of a price floor on the quantity supplied is relatively small.

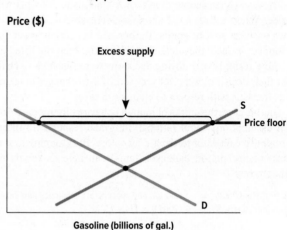

(B) Long run

In the long run, both the supply and the demand for gasoline will change in response to price controls. As a result, the long-run effect on the quantity supplied is much greater than the short-run effect.

will decrease very little. Over the long run, however, the quantity of gas burned will decrease further, and the policy will look more successful.

If, on the other hand, the reason for the price floor was to support gasoline suppliers, the short-run response would look deceptively rosy because suppliers will sell almost the same quantity of gas at a higher price. As the quantity falls over the long run, however, more producers will be stuck with an excess supply and the policy will start to look less successful.

The federal minimum wage is an example of a controversial price floor. Some advocate raising it all the way to $15 per hour. Read the full debate in the What Do You Think? box "Fight for $15."

Fight for $15
What Do You Think?

In 2013, 200 fast-food workers in New York City walked off the job, protesting low wages and poor working conditions. This walkout was the first major action of The Fight for $15 Movement, a nationwide campaign advocating for higher wages. The movement quickly gained momentum. A year later, the mayor of Seattle signed a bill to gradually increase Seattle's minimum wage to $15 per hour by 2021. Pittsburgh, Los Angeles, San Francisco, and other cities followed with similar policies. In October 2018 Amazon raised its minimum wage to $15 for all U.S. employees and challenged other companies to follow suit. Some have (such as Disney, Charter Communications), and others (such as Target) have committed to do so within a short time frame.

The biggest "Fight for $15" centers on the federal minimum wage. Raising the federal minimum wage would affect 2.6 million workers, or roughly 2 percent of the U.S. workforce who earn the minimum wage or below. Just under half are 25 or younger, and two-thirds are employed in service industries.

Advocates of the Fight for $15 argue that the current federal minimum wage of $7.25 is far too low. Working at the minimum wage 40 hours a week, 52 weeks a year, yields a yearly income of $15,080. That's above the poverty line for single people but below the $18,769 mark set for an adult supporting two children. In 2015, the National Employment Law Project reported that 42 percent of the U.S. workforce earned less than $15 per hour, a group disproportionately made up of women and workers of color. Supporters note also that in most states a worker would need to earn at least $15 an hour to afford a two-bedroom apartment. Raising the minimum wage could pull many workers and families out of poverty, allowing them to live healthier and less stressful lives.

Critics say that raising the minimum wage to $15 is a blunt tool that could actually hurt low-income workers. They cite the textbook model of supply and demand, which shows that a price floor would reduce the quantity of labor demanded by firms. A higher minimum wage would then give employers incentives to cut jobs, give workers fewer hours, and automate more operations. Critics of the $15 wage also note that living costs are not the same around the country. Money goes much further in Iowa City, Iowa, than in Seattle, for example: $15 in Iowa City is equivalent to $26 in Seattle. A minimum wage of $15 that might seem reasonable in Seattle looks unreasonably high in Iowa City.

What do the data say? Overall, most research into minimum-wage increases finds that workers benefit and the quantity of labor demanded tends to fall some, but not a lot (at least in the short run). In particular:

- A group of economists at the University of Washington found that increasing the minimum wage from $10.50 to $13 per hour in Seattle caused businesses to reduce employee hours by 9 percent, while incomes increased by 3 percent.
- Economists at the University of California, however, found no reduction in employment when focusing just on Seattle's food-service sector (a big employer of minimum-wage workers).

The answer to whether raising the minimum wage is a good policy clearly depends on who, where, and when.

WHAT DO YOU THINK?

1. Advocates argue that minimum-wage laws help give workers a fairer deal in the face of declining unions and the decreasing bargaining power of workers relative to employers. Can you think of other policies (other than raising the minimum wage by law) which could ensure that workers get a fair deal?
2. In an interview with the *Washington Post,* economist Josh Vigdor describes how he would think about the issue: "If I'm a voter, I want to ask three questions about a proposed minimum-wage increase: How far [how high a wage?], how fast [would the increase be implemented in steps?], and in what kind of economy?" How would you answer these questions in your region? How do different answers to these questions change your thoughts about the Fight for $15?
3. How might the impact of $15 initiatives affect different jobs and sectors? For example, would the owner of a farm respond the same way that a restaurant owner would? What might a manufacturing firm do in response to higher labor costs?
4. Critics argue that a higher minimum wage would surely raise the price of goods and services. Is this cost to consumers worth the benefit of higher wages to workers?

Sources: "About us," Fight for $15, https://fightfor15.org/about-us/; Christopher Ingraham, "The effects of 137 minimum wage hikes, in one chart," *The Washington Post Wonkblog,* February 5, 2018, www.washingtonpost.com/news/wonk/wp/2018/02/05/raising-the-minimum-wage-doesnt-cost-jobs-multiple-studies-suggest/?noredirect=on&utm_term=.95529f5e8896; Irene Tung, Paul K Sonn, and Yannet Lanthrop, "The growing movement for $15," *National Employment Law Project Report,* November 4, 2015, www.nelp.org/publication/growing-movement-15/.

✓ **TEST YOURSELF**

☐ If the demand for a good is inelastic, will a tax have a large or small effect on the quantity sold? Will buyers or sellers bear more of the burden of the tax? **[LO 6.5]**

☐ Would you expect a tax on cigarettes to be more effective over the long run or the short run? Explain your reasoning. **[LO 6.5]**

Conclusion

If you listen to the news, it might seem as if economics is all about business and the stock market. Business matters, but many of the most important, challenging, and useful applications of economic principles involve public policy.

This chapter gives you the basic tools you need to understand government interventions and some of the ways they can affect your everyday life. Of course, the real world is complicated, so this isn't our last word on the topic. Later, we discuss how to evaluate the benefits of both markets and government policies. We'll also discuss market failures and whether and when governments can fix them.

Key Terms

market failures, p. 131

price control, p. 132

price ceiling, p. 132

deadweight loss, p. 133

price floor, p. 136

tax wedge, p. 142

tax incidence, p. 144

subsidy, p. 146

Summary

LO 6.1 Calculate the effect of a price ceiling on the equilibrium price and quantity.

The government usually intervenes in a market for one or more of the following reasons: to change the distribution of a market's benefits, to encourage or discourage the consumption of particular goods and services, or to correct a market failure. Governments may also tax goods and services in order to raise public revenues.

A price ceiling is a maximum legal price at which a good can be sold. A binding price ceiling causes a shortage because at the legally mandated price, consumers will demand more than producers supply. This policy benefits some consumers because they are able to buy what they want at a lower price, but other consumers are unable to find the goods they want. Producers lose out because they sell less at a lower price than they would without the price ceiling.

LO 6.2 Calculate the effect of a price floor on the equilibrium price and quantity.

A price floor is a minimum legal price at which a good can be sold. A price floor causes an excess supply because at the minimum price, sellers will supply more than consumers demand. This policy benefits some producers, who

are able to sell their goods at a higher price, but leaves other producers with goods they can't sell. Consumers lose because they buy less at a higher price. Maintaining a price floor often requires the government to buy up the excess supply, costing taxpayers money.

LO 6.3 Calculate the effect of a tax on the equilibrium price and quantity.

A tax requires either buyers or sellers to pay some extra price to the government when a good is bought and sold. A tax shrinks the size of a market, discouraging the consumption and production of the good being taxed. The effect is the same regardless of whether the tax is levied on buyers or sellers. The tax burden is split between consumers and producers, and the government collects revenues equal to the amount of the tax times the quantity sold.

LO 6.4 Calculate the effect of a subsidy on the equilibrium price and quantity.

A subsidy is a payment that the government makes to buyers or sellers of a good for each unit that is sold. Subsidies increase the size of a market, encouraging the consumption and production of the good being subsidized. The effect is the same regardless of whether the subsidy is paid to buyers or sellers. Both consumers and producers benefit from a subsidy, but taxpayers must cover the cost.

LO 6.5 Explain how elasticity and time period influence the impact of a market intervention.

In evaluating the effects of a government intervention in the market, it is important to consider both the intended and unintended consequences of the policy. The size of the impact of a tax or subsidy and the distribution of the burden or benefit will depend on the price elasticities of supply and demand. Furthermore, the impact of a government intervention is likely to change over time, as consumers and producers adjust their behavior in response to the new incentives.

Review Questions

1. You are an advisor to the Egyptian government, which has placed a price ceiling on bread. Unfortunately, many families still cannot buy the bread they need. Explain to government officials why the price ceiling has not increased consumption of bread. **[LO 6.1]**

2. Suppose there has been a long-standing price ceiling on housing in your city. Recently, population has declined and demand for housing has decreased. What will the decrease in demand do to the efficiency of the price ceiling? **[LO 6.1]**

3. Suppose the United States maintains a price floor for spinach. Why might this policy decrease revenues for spinach farmers? **[LO 6.2]**

4. Suppose Colombia maintains a price floor for coffee beans. What will happen to the size of the deadweight loss if the price floor encourages new growers to enter the market and produce coffee? **[LO 6.2]**

5. Many states tax cigarette purchases. Suppose that smokers are unhappy about paying the extra charge for their cigarettes. Will it help smokers if the state imposes the tax on the stores that sell the cigarettes rather than on smokers? Why or why not? **[LO 6.3]**

6. Consider a tax on cigarettes. Do you expect the tax incidence to fall more heavily on buyers or sellers of cigarettes? Why? **[LO 6.3]**

7. In the United States, many agricultural products (such as corn, wheat, and rice) are subsidized. What are the potential benefits of subsidizing these products? What are the costs? **[LO 6.4]**

8. A subsidy will increase consumer and producer surplus in a market and will increase the quantity of trades. Why, then, might a subsidy (such as a subsidy for producing corn in the United States) be considered inefficient? **[LO 6.4]**

9. Suppose the government imposes a price ceiling on gasoline. One month after the price ceiling, there is a shortage of gasoline, but it is much smaller than critics of the policy had warned. Explain why the critics' estimates might still be correct. **[LO 6.5]**

10. A state facing a budget shortfall decides to tax soft drinks. You are a budget analyst for the state. Do you expect to collect more revenue in the first year of the tax or in the second year? Why? **[LO 6.5]**

Problems and Applications

1. Many people are concerned about the rising price of gasoline. Suppose that government officials are thinking of capping the price of gasoline below its current price. Which of the following outcomes do you predict will result from this policy? Check all that apply. **[LO 6.1]**

    a. Drivers will purchase more gasoline.

    b. Quantity demanded for gasoline will increase.

    c. Long lines will develop at gas stations.

    d. Oil companies will work to increase their pumping capacity.

2. Consider the market shown in Figure 6P-1. The government has imposed a price ceiling at $18. **[LO 6.1]**

FIGURE 6P-1

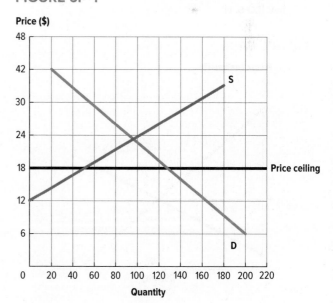

    a. At a price ceiling of $18, what is quantity demanded? Quantity supplied?

    b. At this price ceiling, is there a shortage or a surplus? By how many units?

3. Figure 6P-2 shows a market in equilibrium. **[LO 6.1]**

FIGURE 6P-2

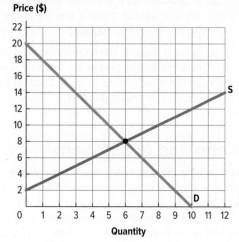

Price ($)

a. Draw a price ceiling at $12. What is the amount of shortage at this price? Draw and calculate the deadweight loss.

b. Draw a price ceiling at $4. What is the amount of shortage at this price? Draw and calculate the deadweight loss.

4. Decades of overfishing have dramatically reduced the world supply of cod (a type of whitefish). Farm-raised halibut is considered a close substitute for ocean-fished cod. Figure 6P-3 shows the market for farm-raised halibut. **[LO 6.1]**

FIGURE 6P-3

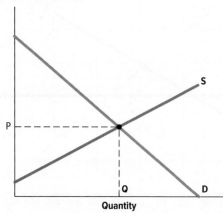

Price of halibut ($)

a. What effect will overfishing cod have on the price of cod? On the graph, show the effect of overfishing cod on the market for farmed halibut.

b. A fast-food chain purchases both cod and halibut for use in its Fish 'n' Chips meals. Already hurt by

the reduced supply of cod, the fast-food chain has lobbied aggressively for price controls on farmed halibut. As a result, Congress has considered imposing a price ceiling on halibut at the former equilibrium price—the price that prevailed before overfishing reduced the supply of cod. What will happen in the market for farmed halibut if Congress adopts the price control policy? Draw and label the price ceiling, quantity demanded, quantity supplied, and deadweight loss.

5. Consider the market shown in Figure 6P-4. The government has imposed a price floor at $36. **[LO 6.2]**

FIGURE 6P-4

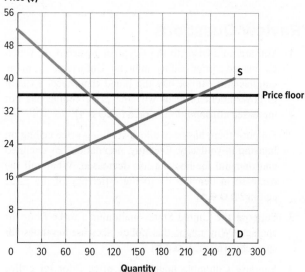

Price ($)

a. At a price floor of $36, what is quantity demanded? Quantity supplied?

b. At this price floor, is there a shortage or a surplus? By how many units?

6. The Organization for the Promotion of Brussels Sprouts has convinced the government of Ironia to institute a price floor on the sale of brussels sprouts, at $8 per bushel. Demand is given by $P = 9 - Q$ and supply by $P = 2Q$, where Q is measured in thousands of bushels. **[LO 6.2]**

a. What will be the price and quantity of brussels sprouts sold at market equilibrium?

b. What will be the price and quantity sold with the price floor?

c. How big will be the excess supply of brussels sprouts produced with the price floor?

7. The traditional diet of the citizens of the nation of Ironia includes a lot of red meat, and ranchers make up a vital part of Ironia's economy. The government of Ironia decides to support its ranchers through a price floor,

which it will maintain by buying up excess meat supplies. Table 6P-1 shows the supply and demand schedule for red meat; quantities are given in thousands of pounds. **[LO 6.2]**

TABLE 6P-1

Price ($)	Quantity demanded (thousands of lbs.)	Quantity supplied (thousands of lbs.)
6	5	80
5	20	70
4	35	60
3	50	50
2	65	40
1	80	30

   a. How many thousands of pounds of meat would you recommend that the government purchase to keep the price at $4/pound?

   b. How much money should the government budget for this program?

8. The market shown in Figure 6P-5 is in equilibrium. Suppose there is a $15 per unit tax levied on sellers.

FIGURE 6P-5

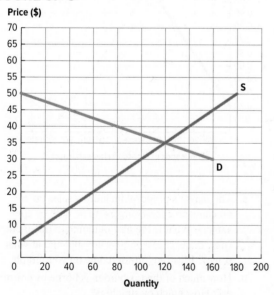

   a. Draw the after-tax supply curve.

   b. Plot the after-tax price paid by consumers and the after-tax price paid by sellers.

9. The market shown in Figure 6P-6 is in equilibrium. Suppose there is a $1.50 per unit tax levied on sellers. **[LO 6.3]**

FIGURE 6P-6

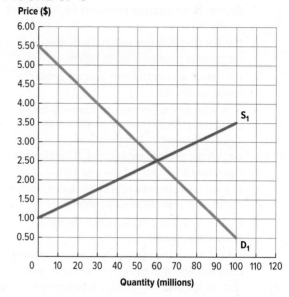

   a. Draw the after-tax supply curve.

   b. Plot the after-tax price paid by consumers and the after-tax price paid by sellers.

   c. Draw consumer surplus, producer surplus, tax revenue, and deadweight loss after the tax.

   d. Calculate deadweight loss.

   e. Calculate total surplus.

10. Suppose the government is considering taxing cigarettes. Because it is often politically more popular to tax the producers of cigarettes than the consumers of cigarettes, the government first considers the impact on the market as a result of taxing the producers of cigarettes. Figure 6P-7 shows the market in equilibrium. **[LO 6.3]**

FIGURE 6P-7

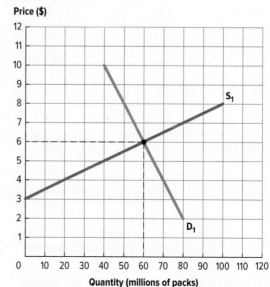

a. Draw the after-tax supply curve if the government chooses to tax cigarette producers $2.50 per pack of cigarettes.

b. Plot the after-tax price paid by consumers and the after-tax price received by sellers.

c. Do consumers or producers bear the greater burden of this tax?

d. Now suppose the government considers taxing the consumers of cigarettes instead of the producers of cigarettes. Draw the after-tax supply curve if the government chooses to tax cigarette consumers $2.50 per pack of cigarettes.

e. Plot the after-tax price paid by consumers and the after-tax price received by sellers.

f. Do consumers or producers bear the greater burden of this tax?

g. Is the price sellers receive when the government taxes consumers of cigarettes more than, less than, or the same as the price sellers receive when the government taxes producers of cigarettes?

h. Is the price buyers pay when the government taxes consumers of cigarettes more than, less than, or the same as the price buyers pay when the government taxes producers of cigarettes?

11. Suppose you have the information shown in Table 6P-2 about the quantity of a good that is supplied and demanded at various prices. **[LO 6.3]**

TABLE 6P-2

Price ($)	Quantity demanded	Quantity supplied
45	10	160
40	20	140
35	30	120
30	40	100
25	50	80
20	60	60
15	70	40
10	80	20
5	90	0

a. Plot the demand and supply curves on a graph, with price on the y-axis and quantity on the x-axis.

b. What are the equilibrium price and quantity?

c. Suppose the government imposes a $15 per unit tax on sellers of this good. Draw the new supply curve on your graph.

d. What is the new equilibrium quantity? How much will consumers pay? How much will sellers receive after the tax?

e. Calculate the price elasticity of demand over this price change.

f. If demand were less elastic (holding supply constant), would the deadweight loss be smaller or larger? **[LO 6.5]**

12. The weekly supply and demand for fast-food cheeseburgers in your city is shown in Figure 6P-8. In an effort to curb a looming budget deficit, the mayor recently proposed a tax that would be levied on sales at fast-food restaurants. **[LO 6.3]**

FIGURE 6P-8

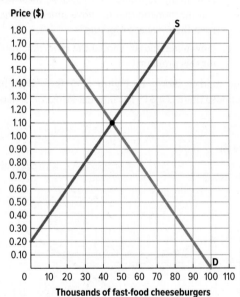

a. The mayor's proposal includes a sales tax of 60 cents on cheeseburgers, to be paid by consumers. What is the new outcome in this market (how many cheeseburgers are sold and at what price)? Illustrate this outcome on your graph.

b. How much of the tax burden is borne by consumers? How much by suppliers?

c. What is the deadweight loss associated with the proposed tax?

d. How much revenue will the government collect?

e. What is the loss of consumer surplus from this tax?

13. The market shown in Figure 6P-9 is in equilibrium. Suppose there is a $15 per unit subsidy given to buyers. **[LO 6.4]**

FIGURE 6P-9

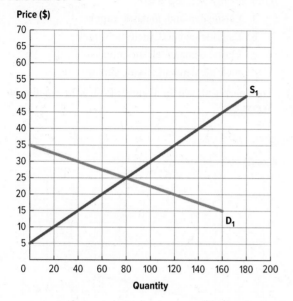

a. Draw the after-subsidy demand curve.

b. Plot the after-subsidy price paid by consumers and the after-subsidy price paid by sellers.

14. The market shown in Figure 6P-10 is in equilibrium. Suppose there is a $15 per unit subsidy given to sellers. **[LO 6.4]**

FIGURE 6P-10

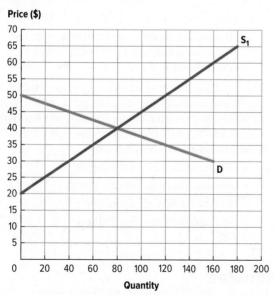

a. Draw the after-subsidy supply curve.

b. Plot the after-subsidy price paid by consumers and the after-subsidy price paid by sellers.

15. Demand and supply of laptop computers are given in Figure 6P-11. The quantity of laptops is given in thousands. Suppose the government provides a $300 subsidy for every laptop computer that consumers purchase. **[LO 6.4]**

FIGURE 6P-11

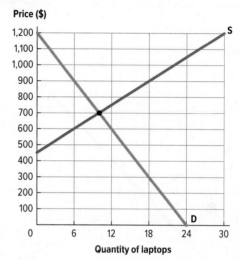

a. What will be the quantity of laptops bought and sold at the new equilibrium?

b. What will be the price consumers pay for laptops under the subsidy?

c. What will be the price that sellers receive for laptops under the subsidy?

d. How much money should the government budget for the subsidy?

16. The market shown in Figure 6P-12 is in equilibrium. Suppose there is a $1.50 per unit subsidy given to buyers. **[LO 6.4]**

FIGURE 6P-12

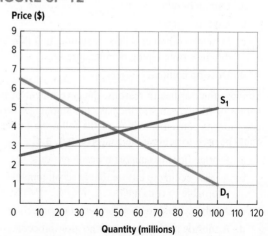

a. Draw the after-subsidy demand curve.

b. Plot the after-subsidy price paid by consumers and the after-subsidy price paid by sellers.

c. Draw government expenditures for the subsidy.

d. Calculate government expenditures.

17. The market shown in Figure 6P-13 is in equilibrium. Suppose there is a $3 per unit subsidy given to buyers. **[LO 6.4]**

FIGURE 6P-13

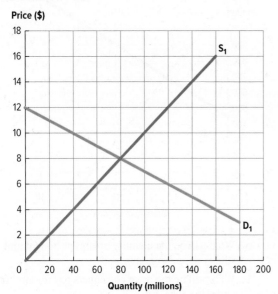

Price ($)

Quantity (millions)

a. Draw the after-subsidy demand curve.

b. Plot the after-subsidy price paid by consumers and the after-subsidy price paid by sellers.

c. Draw the deadweight loss after the subsidy.

d. Calculate deadweight loss.

18. Suppose government offers a subsidy to laptop sellers. Say whether each group of people gains or loses from this policy. **[LO 6.4]**

a. Laptop buyers.

b. Laptop sellers.

c. Desktop computer sellers (assuming that they are different from laptop manufacturers).

d. Desktop computer buyers.

19. Suppose that for health reasons, the government of the nation of Ironia wants to increase the amount of broccoli citizens consume. Which of the following policies could be used to achieve the goal? **[LO 6.1, 6.4]**

a. A price floor to support broccoli growers.

b. A price ceiling to ensure that broccoli remains affordable to consumers.

c. A subsidy paid to shoppers who buy broccoli.

d. A subsidy paid to farmers who grow broccoli.

20. The following scenarios describe the price elasticity of supply and demand for a particular good. In which scenario will a subsidy increase consumption the most? Choose only one. **[LO 6.5]**

a. Elastic demand, inelastic supply.

b. Inelastic demand, inelastic supply.

c. Elastic demand, elastic supply.

d. Inelastic demand, elastic supply.

21. The market shown in Figure 6P-14 is in equilibrium. **[LO 6.5]**

FIGURE 6P-14

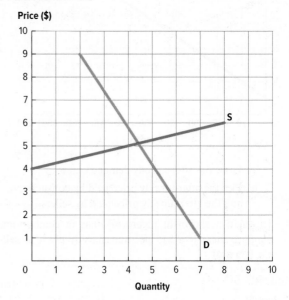

Price ($)

Quantity

a. If a tax was imposed on this market, would buyers or sellers bear more of the burden of the tax? Why?

22. The following scenarios describe the price elasticity of supply and demand for a particular good. All else equal (equilibrium price, equilibrium quantity, and size of the tax), in which scenario will government revenues be the highest? Choose only one. **[LO 6.5]**

a. Elastic demand, inelastic supply.

b. Inelastic demand, inelastic supply.

c. Elastic demand, elastic supply.

d. Inelastic demand, elastic supply.

Endnotes

1. http://www.time.com/time/magazine/article/0,9171,1727720,00.html and http://www.nytimes.com/2008/06/22/nyregion/22food.html.

2. "The new face of hunger," *The Economist*, April 17, 2008.

Individual Decisions

PART THREE

The five chapters in Part 3 will introduce you to . . .

how consumers make decisions. Every day we make lots of choices. Some are relatively small, like deciding whether to grab a bite to eat at a fast-food restaurant for lunch or to donate a dollar into a cash-register charity box. Some choices are large and important: One day you may meet with your academic advisor to discuss possible careers, you may consider buying a house, and—although it might not seem like an economic choice—you may choose someone with whom you want to spend the rest of your life.

How can we be sure of the right choices? What about the decisions of others? The five chapters in this part show how economics can help in getting a handle on these questions.

Chapter 7, "Consumer Behavior," introduces a fundamental concept that economists use to understand how people make decisions. Regardless of size or cost, decisions are made based on what is called *utility*. For the most part, the desire to maximize utility is what guides people when they make decisions.

Still, it is not always easy to translate good intentions into effective outcomes. Almost all of us make some decisions that we don't follow through on. Sometimes we make choices that may not seem completely rational. Chapter 8, "Behavioral Economics: A Closer Look at Decision Making," will explain why we sit through to the end of movies that we are not enjoying, or order a plate of fajitas instead of the healthy salad we had planned to eat. This is part of the field of behavioral economics. Behavioral economics enriches the understanding of decision making by bringing in social and psychological factors that influence decision making. It can help us turn good ideas into good outcomes—and it's as relevant to public policy and business as it is to choices you make every day.

When making decisions, in daily life or in politics and business, it is important to consider what others are doing. This is called thinking strategically. Chapter 9, "Game Theory and Strategic Thinking," introduces the tools of game theory and the advantages of thinking strategically. A winning strategy is key when running a tight political campaign, or picking a location for a new store, or handling a tricky negotiation with a boss. Making the right decisions wins elections, earns profit, and gets you the raise you deserve.

Overall, one of the most important parts of making a decision is having the relevant information—the topic of Chapter 10, "Information." If you are new in a city, how can you decide where to eat? If you are a manager, how can you make sure everyone's working hard—even when you're not around? What should you think about when you buy a used car or select an insurance plan? We'll see how information affects decisions and contracts, and how markets require good information. When information isn't available, markets can fail to deliver an efficient outcome, opening up possible ways that public policy might help.

Chapter 11, "Time and Uncertainty," considers two other elements of decision making: time and risk. Some decisions have benefits and costs that will come in the future (like saving or going to college). And some decisions also involve risk: The car you drive off the lot could strand you on the side of the road tomorrow, or it could be a champ and run perfectly for years. The successes of businesses and governments often hinge on how well they are prepared for unknowns that emerge over time. This chapter gives you conceptual tools to organize your thinking about life's uncertainties.

The problems we deal with in Part 3 are at the heart of economics. They show the power of economics to help you make better choices in everyday life, and, as a society, to help us better reach shared goals.

Consumer Behavior

The Season for Giving

Every holiday season, millions of Americans engage in a frenzy of gift-giving. Shopping malls fill with excited consumers searching for gifts that friends and family will treasure.

There is another way of telling this happy holiday story though: Every holiday season millions of Americans engage in a frenzy of inefficient spending. Gift-giving, according to this second story, is wasteful.[1] The giver spends money to buy something that the receiver may or may not want. In the best-case scenario, the gift is something the receiver would have purchased for himself had he been given money instead. In most cases, though, the gift-giver is an imperfect judge of what the receiver really wants. And if the giver is especially clueless, the gift ends up stuffed in the back of a closet, never to be seen again (or is regifted to somebody else).

Although people don't usually like to admit it, the second story might be closer to reality than the first. Economist Joel Waldfogel surveyed students in his class and found that, on average, the personal value they placed on the gifts they received was between 65 and 90 percent of the original price.[2] In other words, someone who bought a $20 gift would often have done better to hand that person $18 in cash (and keep the difference). Waldfogel wrote about

©Scott Kleinman/Getty Images

the inefficiency of gift-giving in *Scroogenomics*—a book that was, no doubt, wrapped and ironically gifted to thousands of people during the holidays.

Which holiday story is more accurate? The answer requires us to talk more carefully about a concept—utility—that is at the heart of all microeconomic thinking. *Utility* is a way of describing the value that a person places on something, like receiving a gift, eating a meal, or experiencing something fun. The tough thing about gift-giving is that it's hard to know exactly how much value another person will place on something. Some people would like an iPod; others, a pair of running shoes. (There are probably even a few people who actually want those sweaters from Aunt Mildred.) If you're going to spend $20 on a gift (or $10, or $50, or whatever amount), the recipient probably knows better than you do what will bring her the most enjoyment for that money.

It turns out that the same idea applies to weightier choices. Should billions of dollars in foreign aid and government social programs be used to subsidize things that we think are "good" like food and health care? Or should the programs instead simply distribute cash and trust families to make their own choices?

So then, why not just give people cash and let recipients decide what to do with it? If we take a broader view, cash might *not* turn out to be better than a gift. In the case of government social programs, there's a worry that when handing out cash, the money might get diverted to the wrong people or be spent on purchases that taxpayers think are not essential.

What of your own gift-giving? The receiver might derive sentimental value from your gift, precisely because you cared enough to choose it. Or a gift might be important as a signal about your relationship with the recipient and how well you know his or her likes and dislikes. In the best case of all, you might buy a gift that is better than cash, giving something the receiver didn't know about or wouldn't have thought to buy for himself. When you surprise a friend with a movie she's never heard of but that quickly becomes her favorite, it's clear that gift-giving can be utility-enhancing.

LEARNING OBJECTIVES

LO 7.1 Explain how revealed preferences indicate which goods or activities give a person the most utility.

LO 7.2 Show how the budget constraint affects utility maximization.

LO 7.3 Show how a change in income affects consumption choices.

LO 7.4 Show how a change in price affects consumption choices, and distinguish between the income and substitution effects.

LO 7.5 Outline the ways in which utility is influenced by other people.

LO 7.6 Describe how people get utility from altruism and reciprocity.

In this chapter, we will explore the full meaning of *utility* and how it drives decision making—from simple pleasures like eating and sleeping to complex social values like behaving morally or meeting others' expectations. We'll see how economists define *utility* and how they use an abstract idea about the subjective value individuals place on things to do practical economic analysis. Utility is part of what defines economics as unique from other areas of study. Although we didn't call it by name, it's at the root of most of the questions we have explored thus far. If you look back after reading this chapter, you'll see that underpinning the choices about satisfying *wants* and making *trade-offs* is the most important idea in economics: the quest to maximize utility.

The Basic Idea of Utility

The challenges of gift-giving bring up a point that is crucial to economic analysis: $20 isn't valuable in and of itself. Instead, it represents the things you could choose to buy for $20—food, music, a haircut, part of a rent payment, or savings that will let you get these things somewhere down the road. If someone gave you $20, you could probably, without too much trouble, figure out how to spend it in a way that benefits you. Most of us are pretty good at knowing our own likes and dislikes, at least when it comes to everyday things.

But it is much harder to figure out what *someone else* would want with that $20. If you could simply buy them whatever you would have wanted for yourself, that would be easy. But what makes you happiest is probably not the same as what will make them the happiest. Everyone has different likes and dislikes, situations in life, incomes, and so on. Those differences make us appreciate and prioritize different purchases and activities.

Utility and decision making

For now, let's stick with the easier scenario: Forget about what other people might like, and just think about what makes *you* happy. Imagine that it's the weekend. You have a completely free day, with no obligations. What will you do with it?

Remember the first question economists ask: What are your *wants and constraints?* Here, your *constraints* are pretty clear. You have the hours available in one day and access to however much money is available in your bank account. But what can we say about your *wants?* In this chapter, we'll look more closely at the question of what it means to "want" something.

Your possibilities for what to do on a free day are almost endless. You could spend all day watching TV. You could read a thick Russian novel. You could go to the mall and buy some new running shoes. You could study. You could work the phones for your favored candidate in the upcoming election. You could buy 300 cans of tomato soup and take a bath in them. Out of these and a million other possibilities, how do you decide what you *want* to do the most with the time and money available?

This is a surprisingly complex question. Each possible way of spending your day probably involves very different mixtures of good and bad feelings. If you spend all day watching TV, you might feel very relaxed. On the other hand, if you spend the day reading a Russian novel, you might feel proud of yourself for improving your mind and experience a little thrill every time you anticipate casually discussing *The Brothers Karamazov* with that attractive literature major.

Somehow, you need to decide what combination of activities—and what blend of emotions and sensations you get from those activities—is preferable to you, on the whole. Russian novels, TV, and tomato-soup baths are pretty different things. But since we all compare options about what to do with our time and what to buy with our money every day, we must have some sort of internal yardstick that allows us to compare the value we derive from different choices. Sometimes this evaluation is subconscious: You probably don't agonize daily over whether to bathe in soup, even though you *could* do it. Sometimes it's quite conscious and requires deep thinking or extensive research, like choosing whether to buy a car and, if so, what model.

What we need is a universal measure that allows us to compare choices like reading to TV-watching, and TV-watching to working a second job to earn a little extra money. Clearly, something like this must exist inside your mind. Otherwise you wouldn't be able to make these types of decisions, consciously or subconsciously. Economists call this measure **utility**. Utility is a measure of the amount of satisfaction a person derives from something.

utility
a measure of the amount of satisfaction a person derives from something

People get utility from the goods and services they consume and experiences they have. You can get utility from consuming a tasty snack. You can also get utility from figuratively "consuming" a pleasant sensation or experience, such as scoring a goal in a soccer game or chatting with a friend. You can get utility from things you can purchase—food, clothes, cell phones, massages—and also from things that don't usually have a dollar value, like listening to music, learning new things, or doing a good deed. In short, things you like increase your utility. If something is unpleasant and you would choose not to consume it even if it were free, we say that thing reduces your utility.

The idea of utility is fundamental to economics. Think about some of the examples discussed in earlier chapters, such as buying cell phones or Starbucks lattes. People make decisions like this by choosing to do the things they think will give them the most utility, given all of the available options. That is, if you buy a Starbucks latte, it's because you think it will give you more utility than a double espresso or a soda or anything else you could have bought with that amount of money.

Economists call this method of decision making *utility maximization.* The idea that people are *rational utility maximizers* is the baseline assumption in the way economists think about the world. Later in the text, we'll see that economists sometimes relax this assumption to account for the fact that people can be short on information or self-control when making choices. But utility maximization is always the starting point in economics for thinking about how individuals behave.

Over the course of this chapter, we hope you'll see that utility is a deep idea. It encompasses even the toughest choices we make in life and can include the ways that other people influence those choices. For instance, people do unpleasant things all the time. Is that because they are failing to maximize their utility? Not at all. If we take a broad enough view, we usually see that people are doing what they *believe* will bring them the most well-being. Often, that takes into account trade-offs between things that seem nice or feel good in the short term and things that are productive or moral or pleasant in the long term. People weigh the trade-offs between ice cream and health, personal safety and joining the armed forces to defend their country, spending now or saving for later, and so on. The idea of utility allows us to think about this internal and often instinctual calculation in all its richness and complexity.

Revealed preference

LO 7.1 Explain how revealed preferences indicate which goods or activities give a person the most utility.

Unfortunately, utility is hard to measure. If you want to know how much money you've got, you can look at your bank account and put a precise figure on it. But utility is subjective and mysterious. We can't always explain *to ourselves* why we get more utility from one thing than another. However, researchers have tried to peer inside the tricky idea of utility to understand what makes people happy. For more, read the Econ and YOU box "Spending your way to happiness?"

Spending your way to happiness?
Econ and YOU

What will make you happy? For an answer, you can turn to countless books and self-help programs. Unsurprisingly, economics has long been interested in part of the question: Can money really buy happiness?

Time and again, the answer is clear: Money buys happiness—up to a point. After basic needs are met, more money doesn't seem to increase happiness. In the United States, that point starts at an income of around $75,000 per year. (Note that psychologists take a wide view of "basic needs" to include things such as the ability to find housing in a good neighborhood, which is why the figure seems high.)

Which kind of spending produces the most happiness? Evidence has suggested spending on experiences and not just on stuff. Psychologists have found that experiencing vacations, concert tickets, and classes makes people happier on average than spending on clothes, cell phones, or cars. One reason is that the glow surrounding a new purchase fades. After a year or two, even the flashiest new gadget can start to feel dated, sending consumers back to get the latest gear.

But new research challenges the "experience over things" rule of spending by looking at the question differently. Most research had compared how happy people felt when recollecting the purchase of a recent "experience" versus a recent "thing." Instead, Tamas Hajdu and Gabor Hajdu, two professors at the Hungarian Academy of Sciences, pored over data from a survey tracking the overall life satisfaction and spending habits of 10,000 people in Hungary. When they compared the two different types of spending, they found that neither type of spending was more strongly correlated with happiness levels than the other. Both spending on experiences and spending on stuff brought similar amounts of satisfaction.

The lesson? Money *can* bring happiness, but trying to generalize lessons about spending and happiness is hard—people are different and get utility from different sources. After a certain point, it's up to you to spend money on the experiences and things that bring the most joy to your life.

Sources: Jay Cassano, "The science of why you should spend your money on experiences, not things," *Fast Company,* March 30, 2015, www.fastcompany.com/3043858/the-science-of-why-you-should-spend-your-money-on-experiences-not-thing; Hajdu Gabor and Tamas Gabor, "The association between experiential and material expenditures and subjective well-being: New evidence from Hungarian survey data," IEHAS Discussion Papers (2015), 1555, Institute of Economics, Centre for Economic and Regional Studies, Hungarian Academy of Sciences.

How can we say anything meaningful about the utility other people experience? The answer is surprisingly simple: We *observe* what people actually do, and we assume that, as rational individuals, they're doing what gives them the most utility. Their actions reveal their preferences:

- If you observe someone ordering a scoop of chocolate ice cream at the ice-cream counter, you can conclude she thought she would get more utility from the chocolate than the strawberry or chocolate-chip cookie dough flavors.

- If you observe someone buying tickets for an action movie, you can conclude that this gives him more utility than the romantic comedy he could have seen instead. This choice may not be due to the movie itself, but to his companions. For instance, maybe his companions preferred the action move, and he preferred to make his companions happy rather than see his first choice of movie. In that situation, he is maximizing his utility by agreeing to the action movie.

Economists call this idea **revealed preference**. We can tell what maximizes other people's utility by observing their behavior. The fact that someone chose to do something "reveals" that she preferred it to the other available options. Of course, this inference is specific to a particular person and situation. Different people prefer different ice-cream flavors. The same person might be in the mood for an action movie today and a romantic comedy tomorrow.

Revealed preference might sound obvious. It's actually an idea that is unique to economics, and somewhat controversial. If you're interested in understanding how economics overlaps with other disciplines such as psychology, anthropology, or political science, it's important that you understand the idea and its limitations.

Continuing our earlier example, let's say that you spent your free day watching TV instead of reading that Russian novel. Later, you tell a friend, "I really wanted to finish *The Brothers Karamazov*, but somehow I ended up spending all day watching TV." As economists, we suspect you're not being entirely honest with yourself. Observing that you spent all day in front of the TV, with *The Brothers Karamazov* lying unopened on the table next to you, revealed preference suggests that what you *really* wanted to do was watch TV. If not, why did you do it?

This is a trivial example, but it's easy to think of a more serious one. Suppose someone tells you, "I really want to stop smoking, but somehow I keep buying cigarettes." Revealed preference suggests he is getting more utility from continuing to smoke than he would get from actually quitting. If you were a policy-maker deciding how heavily to tax cigarettes, or whether to ban cigarette advertising, you'd have to think seriously about whether to give more weight to what people *say* they want or to what they actually *do*. In the case of cigarettes, there's a reasonable argument that physical addiction makes it hard for people to actually do in the moment what they know they want in the long term. There might be a role for friends or policy-makers to help by taking some options out of reach. We'll come back to this issue in a later chapter.

Despite interesting debates on tough cases like cigarettes, the idea of revealed preference can take us a long way toward understanding what people want. Notice that we're not making comparisons between people; we're looking only at what one individual prefers. In other words, we can say that two people both preferred chocolate ice cream over strawberry, but not whether one of them liked chocolate more than the other did.

Utility functions

The idea of revealed preference gives us a nice framework for evaluating people's utility. But we can't just follow people around and observe all of their behavior. (That would be impractical as well as creepy.) Instead, we need a more formal method to make revealed preferences useful in economic analysis.

In order to think systematically about how people make choices, economists construct a **utility function**. A utility function is a formula for calculating the total utility that a particular person derives from consuming a combination of goods and services. Each unique combination of goods

revealed preference
the idea that people's preferences can be determined by observing their choices and behavior

utility function
a formula for calculating the total utility that a particular person derives from consuming a combination of goods and services

bundle
a unique combination of
goods and services that
a person could choose
to consume

and services that a person could choose to consume is called a **bundle**. The utility function is a
map that connects each possible bundle to the corresponding level of utility that a person gets
from consuming it.

Earlier, we said that utility is a subjective measure that can't be readily quantified. Yet we also
said that a utility function is a way of quantitatively describing preferences. The key to understanding this apparent contradiction is that the utility measurements that go into a utility function are
relative, not absolute. The numbers we use in utility functions do not measure something concrete
like inches or pounds or dollars.

Rather, if we say that a certain activity gives a person utility of 3, what that means is that the
person values the activity more highly than an activity associated with a utility measure of 2, and
less than one with utility of 4. The numbers don't mean anything except an ordering for activities
the person likes more or less. (Because these numbers have no meaning other than *relative to each
other*, we could have said that the chosen activity has a utility of 6,000, and that the person values
that activity more highly than one with utility of 5,000, and less than one with utility of 7,000.
But the smaller the numbers—3 rather than 6,000, for example—the easier they are to work with.)

Let's apply the idea of a utility function to a simple utility-generating experience: eating dinner.
Say that Sarah is eating a dinner of macaroni and cheese, broccoli, and ice cream. We ask her to
rate the utility she gets from each part of her dinner. She responds that she gets utility of 3 from
each serving of macaroni and cheese, utility of 2 from each serving of broccoli, and utility of 8
from each scoop of ice cream. (Remember that the specific numbers we use are arbitrary. What
matters are the *relative numbers* attached to each good in the function, which help us understand
how much more utility Sarah gets from choosing one thing over another.) For dinner, she eats
one serving of mac and cheese, two servings of broccoli, and two scoops of ice cream. Her dinner
utility function is therefore:

EQUATION 7-1   Total utility = (3 × 1 mac and cheese) + (2 × 2 broccoli) + (8 × 2 ice cream)
                                    = 3 + 4 + 16 = 23

This analysis raises some questions: Does it suggest that Sarah should keep eating and eating,
with the idea that the more food, the more utility? Why stop, when every serving of broccoli, mac
and cheese, and ice cream would add positive utility? Also, since ice cream gives her far and away
the most utility, shouldn't she ditch the broccoli and mac and cheese to have an ice-cream dinner
chock full of utility? In reality, we're sure you'll agree that infinite eating of ice cream is not a good
idea and is unlikely to maximize anyone's utility. What is missing from this analysis? To find out,
keep reading.

✓ **TEST YOURSELF**

☐ What can observing people's actual choices tell us about their preferences? What is this
approach called? **[LO 7.1]**

☐ What is the word for a particular combination of goods and services that a person could
choose to consume? **[LO 7.1]**

Marginal Utility

marginal utility
the change in total
utility that comes from
consuming one additional
unit of a good or service

To understand when and why Sarah should stop eating ice cream, we need the concept of marginal utility. In Chapter 1, "Economics and Life," we introduced the idea of making decisions *at
the margin*. The change in total utility that comes from consuming one additional unit of a good
or service is called **marginal utility**.

Let's go back to ice cream. Imagine how much pleasure you'd get from a scoop of your favorite
flavor. Now imagine eating a second scoop. Is it just as enjoyable? Maybe it's a bit less yummy
than the very first taste. In other words, the marginal utility you get from a second scoop is a little

Scoops of ice cream	Marginal utility	Total utility
1	6	6
2	5	11
3	4	15
4	3	18
5	2	20
6	1	21
7	0	21
8	−1	20

TABLE 7-1
Utility from eating ice cream

lower than the marginal utility of the first scoop. Now eat a third scoop. We bet you'll enjoy this one less than the first two. A fourth scoop? You're not getting much additional enjoyment at all. A fifth, sixth, seventh, or eighth scoop? Less and less enjoyable; in fact, after eight scoops of ice cream, you likely are not feeling well.

We can assign some numbers to describe these changes in marginal utility. Let's say that, as Table 7-1 shows, the first scoop of ice cream yields 6 units of utility. But each scoop afterward yields less and less additional utility. From one scoop to two, you gain 5 units of marginal utility. Total utility increases, but the second scoop brings less marginal utility than the first scoop brought.

Sometimes, marginal utility diminishes so much that it actually becomes negative. When we offer you a seventh scoop of ice cream, you might feel indifferent between eating it or not. It adds nothing to your total utility, so it has zero marginal utility. And you'd rather not eat that eighth scoop, as it may make you sick. The eighth scoop would *reduce* your total utility. In other words, it would have *negative marginal utility*.

The principle demonstrated here is called **diminishing marginal utility**. The principle states that the additional utility gained from consuming successive units of a good or service tends to be smaller than the utility gained from the previous unit. The diminishing marginal utility of food items is particularly noticeable because our bodies have a physical reaction to additional consumption. Our stomachs start to tell us that we're full, and our sense of taste fades as the novelty of a new flavor passes.

Economists observe that the principle of diminishing marginal utility applies to most goods and services. Imagine you have recently moved to a cold climate and have no sweaters. Buying one sweater makes a huge difference in your comfort. Buying a tenth sweater isn't such a big deal.

Figure 7-1 illustrates the idea of diminishing marginal utility. Panel A of Figure 7-1 shows the total utility you get from eating more and more scoops of ice cream. The curve slopes upward to begin with, flattening out as additional scoops add less and less to your total utility. At the point marked A, the seventh scoop, your total utility peaks—and the slope of the curve is completely flat. Beyond that point, each scoop has negative marginal utility; the curve of total utility slopes downward after that point.

Panel B of Figure 7-1 shows the same idea, plotting the *marginal* utility of each scoop rather than total utility. The line in this graph slopes downward, showing that your marginal utility is diminishing with each additional scoop. Remember that even though marginal utility slopes downward, each additional scoop of ice cream still increases *total* utility as long as marginal utility is greater than zero. At point B, the marginal utility of one more scoop of ice cream is 2. Thus, consuming the fifth scoop of ice cream increases total utility, though only by a small amount. At point A, the marginal utility is zero: You get no extra enjoyment from the seventh scoop. At scoop 8, marginal utility is negative. Point A is a significant link between panel A and panel B: When the

diminishing marginal utility
the principle that the additional utility gained from consuming successive units of a good or service tends to be smaller than the utility gained from the previous unit

FIGURE 7-1

Diminishing marginal utility

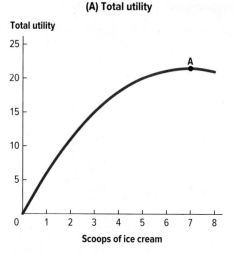

(A) Total utility

Total utility

(B) Marginal utility

Marginal utility per scoop

The first couple of scoops of ice cream cause big increases in utility. But as you eat more ice cream, the effect of each additional scoop on your total utility decreases until more ice cream will actually make you *un*happier, starting at point A.

The marginal utility, or the additional utility from each additional scoop, is always decreasing, until it actually becomes negative at point A.

marginal utility of an additional unit of a good is zero, you've maxed out the total utility you can get from consuming that good.

Although many things you can do or buy have diminishing marginal utility, not all of them will end up in *negative* marginal utility. For example, most people will never get negative utility from having more savings. If you have no savings, the marginal utility of your first $1,000 is pretty high. If you already have a million dollars, the marginal utility of having another $1,000 might be pretty small. There's probably not that much difference between your life with $1,000,000 and your life with $1,001,000. But it's hard to imagine you'd ever get *reduced* total utility from having more money appear in your savings account. If you really can't think of anything else to buy, after all, you can always give it away to someone else and enjoy being a philanthropist.

For most purchasing decisions, you wouldn't get anywhere near the point of negative marginal utility. Long before you buy a seventh scoop of ice cream, or a tenth sweater, or a fiftieth video game, you are likely to have decided you'd get higher marginal utility from spending that money on something else. After all, people don't usually offer you free, unlimited ice cream or sweaters or games. Rather, you usually have to pay or work for them. You are likely to conclude, before you reach the point of negative marginal utility, that having one more of any of those things just isn't worth it.

This brings us to the most important point in this chapter: What happens when we combine the concept of *diminishing marginal utility* with the concept of *wants and constraints?*

Maximizing utility within constraints

LO 7.2 Show how the budget constraint affects utility maximization.

Let's go back to the example of your free day. In reality, you're very unlikely to spend the entire day doing just one thing. Instead, you might do a number of different things: drive to the mall, shop for running shoes, and eat some lunch; go for a run in your new shoes; relax for a while by watching TV; make a little progress through *The Brothers Karamazov*; and go out with friends in the evening. Or there are millions of other possible combinations you could choose. How do you pick which bundle of activities to do within the time and money available?

Marginal utility helps make sense of this sort of decision by calling attention to the *trade-offs* involved. Why didn't you spend another hour at the mall? Because once you'd been there for four hours, the marginal utility of another hour was less than the marginal utility of going for an energizing run instead. Why didn't you run for a second hour? Because you were getting tired. The marginal utility of another hour of running was less than the marginal utility of watching some TV. And so on, with the rest of the day.

Of course, you don't have to make these choices consecutively, waiting until you get tired of one activity before deciding to move on. People can *think ahead* about the bundle of goods or activities that will give them the most combined utility; they can anticipate that too much of one thing isn't as good as some other option. Your choice about how to spend the day is really about selecting a *combination* of goods and activities that will maximize your utility, within the limits of time and money available to you. If you have spent your day wisely, there is no other combination of activities that could have added up to greater total utility.

Regardless of how you decide to spend your time, many other activities are available. They may be good and enjoyable, but the opportunity cost (passing up something even more enjoyable) is higher than the benefit you'd get. People have many wants, but they are constrained by the time and money available to them. If they are rational utility-maximizers, they try to optimize within those constraints by spending their resources on the bundle of goods and activities that will give them the highest possible total utility.

We can use a quantitative model to illustrate the idea of maximizing utility within constraints. Like all models, we'll have to simplify a bit. Imagine that Cody has $120 to spend each month after paying all his bills. Assume there are only two things he considers spending the money on:

- A movie ticket, which costs $15.
- A concert ticket, which costs $30.

Cody could buy several possible combinations of movie and concert tickets within his budget. He could spend $120 going to the movies and see no concerts at all. He could see four movies ($60) and two concerts ($60), and so on.

We can represent these bundle possibilities on a line called a *budget constraint*, as shown in Figure 7-2. A **budget constraint** is a line composed of all of the possible combinations of goods and services a consumer can buy with his or her income. (If this graph looks familiar to the production possibilities frontier graph of Chapter 2, "Specialization and Exchange," that's no coincidence. They express very similar ideas—the concept of choosing between different combinations of things within the constraint of limited resources.)

budget constraint
a line that is composed of all of the possible combinations of goods and services that a consumer can buy with her or his income

If Cody is a rational consumer, making choices to achieve goals in the most effective way possible, he will spend his budget on the combination of movie and concert tickets that maximizes his utility. How does he feel about going to see a movie?

- Cody feels that going to the movie theater three times in a month is very important. He'll give each of his first three movie tickets a utility score of 95. (Remember that utility is an imaginary measure. These numbers don't refer to anything, like ticket prices, that's measurable outside of Cody's mind; they're just a way of getting an insight into his relative preferences.)
- After the first three movies, seeing a fourth movie gives Cody additional utility of 80, and a fifth movie scores an additional 65 points of utility.
- Eventually, he'll become so sick of seeing movies that he'd rather not go an eighth time: The marginal utility of movie number eight would be negative, at -10.

How about concerts?

- Cody would not be happy if he went the entire month without going to a concert, so his first concert gives him utility of 100.

FIGURE 7-2
The budget constraint

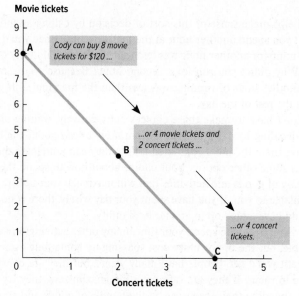

The budget constraint represents the combinations of goods that are available to Cody given his budget. Each bundle on the line costs exactly the amount of money Cody has in his budget.

TABLE 7-2

Maximizing total utility

(A) Utility from movie tickets		
Tickets	**Marginal utility**	**Total utility**
1	95	95
2	95	190
3	95	285
4	80	365
5	65	430
6	35	465
7	10	475
8	−10	465
(B) Utility from concert tickets		
Tickets	**Marginal utility**	**Total utility**
1	100	100
2	85	185
3	25	210
4	0	210

In panel A, we see that utility greatly increases as Cody buys the first few movie tickets, and peaks when he buys 7 movie tickets. After that, utility decreases. In panel B, we see that Cody gets lots of utility from the first few concert tickets. After the third ticket, he gets no further utility.

- Seeing a second concert wouldn't be as crucial, but still very enjoyable; that second concert ticket will give him utility of 85.
- After a while, Cody starts to tire of going to concerts, so the marginal utility Cody gets from each ticket decreases. By the time he's bought three tickets, he feels like that's enough, and additional tickets won't increase his total utility.

The amount of marginal and total utility Cody gets from each movie ticket is shown in panel A of Table 7-2, while the amount of marginal and total utility Cody gets from each concert ticket is shown in panel B.

By adding up the utility of each potential bundle of movie tickets and concert tickets, as shown in panel A of Figure 7-3, you can see that the optimal combination for Cody is to buy one concert ticket and six movie tickets, or bundle B. If Cody is a rational, utility-maximizing consumer, then we can expect him to do just that. Out of all the available options, that's the combination that gives him the most total utility (565).

Usually, economists don't ask people to give a utility rating to the things they could buy. Instead, they try out different utility functions and make predictions about how they expect people to behave. They might look at data about how groups of people in the real world actually did behave and compare the two. They then can assess how well they understood the wants and constraints that motivated people's choices.

As always, real life is a lot more complicated than any model. In reality, people choose between thousands of different spending possibilities rather than just two, yielding millions of possible combinations. The principle, however, is the same: Rational consumers choose to spend their budgets on the combination of goods and services that will give them the highest possible total utility.

There's another real-life complication we haven't considered in this chapter: Budgets don't fall out of the sky; they're usually determined by earlier choices about what job to apply for and how much to work. In the real world, our decisions about how to maximize utility also involve this trade-off between work and available budget: Would you get more utility from working hard and having more money to spend, or having more leisure time but less money to enjoy it with? This is an idea we'll come back to later in the book.

Appendix E, "Using Indifference Curves," which follows this chapter, presents indifference curves. Economists use indifference curves as a tool to represent utility graphically and to explain how consumers maximize utility.

✓ TEST YOURSELF

☐ If something has negative marginal utility, what happens to your total utility when you consume it? **[LO 7.2]**

☐ What is the budget constraint? **[LO 7.2]**

Responding to Changes in Income and Prices

Income changes all the time. You might get a raise for diligent work. Or, pressed by a lack of business, your boss may be forced to cut your hours, and you earn less money. Both of these changes in income are likely to change how much you decide to spend on the things you buy. The same is true for changes in prices. If lattes drop in price by $0.50 one day, you'll probably decide to buy more of them. As these examples show, rational utility maximizers will change their behavior as circumstances like income and prices change.

Changes in income

When a person's income increases, more bundles of goods and services become affordable. When income decreases, fewer bundles are affordable, and consumers will probably have to cut consumption of some things. We represent these changes by *shifting the entire budget line* to show each new range of options available to the consumer.

LO 7.3 Show how a change in income affects consumption choices.

FIGURE 7-3

Maximizing utility

(A) Maximizing total utility

Bundle	Concert tickets	Utility from concert tickets	Movie tickets	Utility from movie tickets	Total utility
A	0	0	8	465	465
B	1	100	6	465	565
C	2	185	4	365	550
D	3	210	2	190	400
E	4	210	0	0	210

This table shows all the bundles that Cody can potentially consume. The total utility he gets from each bundle depends on the number of concert tickets and the number of movie tickets in it.

(B) Utility along the budget constraint

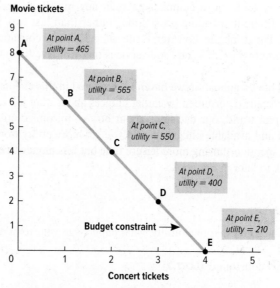

Each bundle on the budget constraint corresponds to one of the rows in the table in panel A. While each costs the same, the utility each provides varies according to Cody's preferences.

Why does this happen? Let's look at what happens when Cody gets $60 for his birthday from his grandparents. Suppose he decides to use all of his money this month—the $120 he normally would spend, plus the birthday cash. That means Cody now has a grand total of $180 to spend. Again, Cody will decide how many movie tickets to buy and how many concert tickets to buy:

- If he decides to buy only concert tickets, with the extra cash he can now buy six tickets instead of only four.
- If instead he decides to buy only movie tickets, he can now afford 12 tickets instead of eight.

With more money, Cody can buy more of both goods at every point. The entire budget line shifts out by the equivalent of $60, maintaining the same slope as it did before. As a result, Cody can buy more movie tickets or more concert tickets (or more of both) than he did before he received the birthday money. (*Note*: Don't confuse the budget constraint with the demand curve; it looks similar, but the *y*-axis here isn't price.)

Why does the slope stay the same? Even though Cody has more money, the ratio of the prices of the two goods has not changed. Movie tickets are still $15 and concert tickets, $30. The only thing that has changed is that Cody is now able to buy more tickets in whatever combination he chooses. Figure 7-4 shows the effect of this increase in income.

Changes in prices

What happens to an individual's behavior when income stays the same but the prices of goods change? Let's think about Cody again. If the price of movie tickets decreases, he can clearly afford to purchase more movie tickets. In addition, while it's not as obvious, he could also purchase more concert tickets: Now that each movie ticket is cheaper, there might be some money left over for more concert tickets.

LO 7.4 Show how a change in price affects consumption choices, and distinguish between the income and substitution effects.

In general, changes in the price of a good have two important effects, called the *income effect* and the *substitution effect*.

Before thinking about the difference between the two, observe that any price decrease causes the budget line to *rotate outward*, as shown in Figure 7-5. Why does the curve rotate outward instead of shifting right in a parallel fashion? Let's return to Cody's pre-birthday budget constraint of $120. If the price of movie tickets has decreased from $15 to $10, Cody's budget constraint changes:

- If he puts all of his money into movie tickets, he is able to afford 12 tickets at the new lower price: four more than he was originally able to buy.

- But if he puts all of his money into concert tickets, he is still able to afford only six of them since the price of concert tickets has stayed the same.

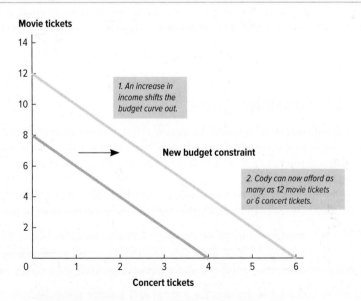

FIGURE 7-4

The effect of an increase in income

When Cody's income increases as a result of a gift, he is able to afford more goods. This shifts the budget constraint outward, and he can now buy 12 movie tickets or 6 concert tickets.

FIGURE 7-5

The effect of a price change

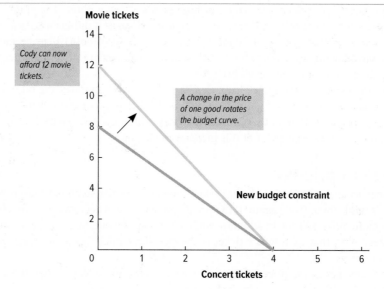

When the price of one good changes, the budget constraint rotates out to demonstrate the new consumption bundles that are available. The change in slope reflects the change in the relative prices of the two goods.

income effect
the change in consumption that results from a change in effective wealth due to higher or lower prices

Income effect   The **income effect** describes the change in consumption that results from a change in effective wealth due to higher or lower prices. If the price of movie tickets falls from $15 to $10 per ticket and Cody continues to buy his usual four movie tickets a month, he is now $5 "richer" for each ticket he buys. He now has an extra $20 in comparison to last month.

In general, consumers can buy more things when the price of a good they usually purchase decreases. When goods get cheaper, consumers' money goes farther: Cody could buy more movie tickets. He also has more money left over after buying movie tickets and could put this toward buying more concert tickets. The change in consumption as a result of Cody "feeling richer" is the *income effect*.

 CAUTION: COMMON MISTAKE

Notice that even though this effect is called the *income* effect, it is not describing the impact that a *change in income* would have on consumption. Instead, we are saying that a change in the *price* of a good effectively makes you richer or poorer. It is *as though* your income changed. However, there has been no direct change in income.

A refresher on normal goods and inferior goods is important here. After a price change causes a change in effective wealth, we need to know whether the consumer will buy more or less of each good:

- Remember that *normal goods* are those for which demand increases as income increases.
- In contrast, *inferior goods* are those for which demand decreases as income increases.
  (Instant ramen noodles, that staple of college diets everywhere, are a classic inferior good.)

The income effect impacts the demand for normal and inferior goods because the change in price mimics the effect of a change in income. If Cody chooses to increase his consumption of both movie and concert tickets when his income increases, this would imply they are both normal goods.

Substitution effect   Now let's look at the second important effect brought about by changes in the price of a good. The **substitution effect** describes the change in consumption that results from a change in the relative price of goods.

In our example, when the price of a movie ticket decreased from $15 to $10, movie tickets became cheaper *relative to* concert tickets. (We saw that relative change represented by the change in the slope of the budget line.) Said another way, concert tickets became more expensive *relative to* movie tickets, even though the price of concert tickets did not change. This relative change causes Cody to choose more movies and fewer concerts. He substitutes the good that has become cheaper in relative terms for the one that has become more expensive, which is why it's called the "substitution" effect.

Another way to say this is that the *opportunity cost* of concerts and movies has changed. When movie tickets cost $15 and concert tickets cost $30, the opportunity cost of a concert was two movies. When the price of a movie ticket decreases to $10, the opportunity cost of a concert increases to three movies. The flip-side is that the opportunity cost of movies in terms of forgone concerts has decreased (from $\frac{1}{2}$ to $\frac{1}{3}$).

Why? Think about the situation as a change in the marginal utility *per dollar* that Cody gets for each good. When the price of movie tickets decreases, the marginal utility per dollar for movie tickets goes up; the marginal utility per dollar for concert tickets stays the same. Cody now gets more utility bang for his buck from movies, so he wants to spend more of his budget on them.

Occasionally, though, people may actually choose to consume *more* of a good when its price increases. This occurs for goods known as *Veblen goods*. Veblen goods are items for which the quantity demanded is higher when prices are higher. They are something that people buy *because* they are flashy and expensive. Buyers choose them to show others that they can afford flashy and expensive goods.

The idea of Veblen goods conflicts with the idea of utility we presented earlier in this chapter; there we assumed that you would make the same choices whether you were alone or not. Would you buy a luxury watch when a basic one tells time just fine, if you were the only person who could see it? Why buy a $200 handbag when a $50 one will hold all of your stuff, if no one else will see you with it? Although you may also enjoy the high quality, durability, or design of luxury items, these goods sell at least in part because people get utility from the reaction others have to items known to be expensive or exclusive. The Veblen good suggests that utility may be far from the individual measure we have talked about so far.

This example illustrates one of the many instances in which your utility is affected by other people. The perceptions of others help explain why people buy luxury items. They also influence how we donate to charity and what gifts we give to others, and even how we interact with others in everyday situations. Such examples show the remarkable breadth of the concept of utility, and we explore this idea further in the next section.

Ultimately, both the income effect and the substitution effect influence an individual's reaction to a price change. Cody may choose to buy more movie tickets but the same number of concert tickets. Or he may choose to buy more of both goods. In unusual circumstances, he might even choose to buy fewer movie tickets and more concert tickets. After observing how his choices change after the change in price, we would then know whether he was influenced more by the income effect or the substitution effect.

substitution effect
the change in consumption that results from a change in the relative price of goods

✓TEST YOURSELF

☐ What happens to the budget constraint when income increases? **[LO 7.3]**

☐ What happens to consumption of a normal good when its price increases? **[LO 7.4]**

☐ What is the difference between the income effect and the substitution effect of a price increase for a normal good? **[LO 7.4]**

This suggests that people get utility from rewarding kindness with kindness in return, even when there's nothing in it for them.

reciprocity
responding to another's action with a similar action

We call this tendency **reciprocity**. Reciprocity means responding to another's action with a similar action. Reciprocity involves doing good things for people who did good things for us. (Note the difference from *altruism*, which involves simply wanting others to be better off.)

Reciprocity also occurs when we respond in kind to bad treatment. When people make an effort to decrease someone else's utility in response to being harmed themselves, they are engaging in *negative reciprocity*. When you steal toothpaste from that guy down the hall whose music has kept you up at night for a week, you're engaging in negative reciprocity.

People frequently engage in reciprocal actions even when they stand to lose out on some benefit. To see how this works, let's return to the game from the research experiment. Like before, you choose how much money to transfer to your partner, but now the researchers allow the partner to accept or reject the offer. If she rejects, then neither of you gets to keep *any* of the money. In theory, you might expect the partner to accept any offer: Even if you transfer only one cent, the partner is better off accepting it than rejecting it.

But that's not what happens when this experiment is played in practice. The partner regularly rejects the money if she deems the amount offered to be "too low." The partner willingly forfeits free money as a way to punish the other who has acted "unfairly." This outcome occurs despite the fact that the punishment has no future implications—the two participants don't know who the other person is and there will be no further rounds of the experiment. As the experiment shows, fairness is an ideal that people often are willing to sacrifice for, even when it's not rational to do so.

Reciprocity guides everyday interactions. When you bring over a pizza in exchange for help studying for an exam, or you buy the food that you were offered as a free sample in the store, you are engaging in reciprocity. Along with ideas such as altruism and status, reciprocity adds depth to our concept of utility, showing it as sometimes quirky and altogether human.

✓ TEST YOURSELF

☐ How can other people's opinions and impressions influence our utility? **[LO 7.5]**
☐ Name two ways that an action may provide utility, other than the direct effect of consuming a good or service. **[LO 7.6]**

Conclusion

The ideas in this chapter are at the heart of economic analysis. Everything in the following chapters (and, for that matter, the preceding chapters) is in some way based on the assumption that people attempt to maximize their utility within the limitations of their resources. As we've seen throughout the chapter, people often have preferences that extend far beyond a selfish definition of their own benefit.

With this in mind, let's revisit the question presented at the beginning of the chapter: Is holiday giving wasteful? To get a wide economic perspective on the question, the IGM Forum at the University of Chicago asked 46 prominent economists whether "giving specific presents as holiday gifts is inefficient, because recipients could satisfy their preferences more efficiently with cash." It turns out that economists hold a wide range of views. Only 17 percent of the respondents agreed that it's better to give cash. Over half disagreed. Many noted that the statement missed important parts of giving. Economist Janet Currie from Princeton University noted, "Gifts serve many functions such as signaling regard and demonstrating social ties with the recipient. Cash transfers don't do this as well." Austan Goolsbee, a professor at the University of Chicago, compared the question to another important purchase: "Instead of proposing to your wife [with a] diamond ring, you offer a gift card of equal value. Efficient—if you don't count your hospital bills."

In coming chapters, we'll enrich the picture of utility even further by looking at tough questions individuals must ask when making commonplace decisions: What is the timing of the benefits, now or later? What is the timing of the costs? What are the risks? Am I fully informed about the situation? Are others competing with me for the same goal?

Sometimes, the answers to these questions mean that people pursue their goals in unexpected or not entirely rational ways. Nonetheless, the essential idea of individuals pursuing the things they want in the face of scarcity drives economic analysis from A to Z.

Key Terms

utility, p. 167

revealed preference, p. 169

utility function, p. 169

bundle, p. 170

marginal utility, p. 170

diminishing marginal utility, p. 171

budget constraint, p. 173

income effect, p. 178

substitution effect, p. 179

altruism, p. 182

reciprocity, p. 184

Summary

LO 7.1 Explain how revealed preferences indicate which goods or activities give a person the most utility.

Utility is an imaginary measure of the amount of satisfaction a person derives from something. People get utility from things they can purchase but also from things that don't usually have a dollar value. People make decisions by choosing to do the things they think will give them the most utility, given all of the available options. Economists use the term *utility maximization* to describe this method of decision making.

Economists generally assume that individuals' preferences are demonstrated through the choices that they make, a concept known as *revealed preference*. We observe what people actually do, and assume that as rational individuals, they're doing what gives them the most utility.

LO 7.2 Show how the budget constraint affects utility maximization.

The *budget constraint* is a line that shows all the possible consumption bundles available to an individual given a fixed budget. The slope of the budget line is equivalent to the ratio of prices of the two goods. A rational individual will maximize utility given the amount of goods he or she can afford.

LO 7.3 Show how a change in income affects consumption choices.

An increase in an individual's income will cause the budget line to shift outward, allowing a consumer to buy more goods on average. A decrease in income, on the other hand, will cause a person to consume fewer goods on average.

LO 7.4 Show how a change in price affects consumption choices, and distinguish between the income and substitution effects.

A change in the price of goods can have two effects on optimal consumption. The change in consumption that results from increased effective wealth due to lower prices is called the *income effect*. When prices decrease, a consumer is able to afford larger quantities, just as if her income had increased.

The *substitution effect* describes the change in consumption that results from a change in the relative price of goods. When one good becomes relatively less expensive compared with the other good than it was before the price change, consumers will be inclined to buy more of it.

LO 7.5 Outline the ways in which utility is influenced by other people.

How much utility consumers get from a good can be influenced by how others perceive their choice. Some people choose to consume expensive goods to signal to others that they can afford these goods. Utility can also be influenced by your *frame of reference*—you're far more likely to be happy with a salary if it's in line with what everyone around you earns.

LO 7.6 Describe how people get utility from altruism and reciprocity.

Altruism is a motive for action in which a person's utility increases simply because someone else's utility increases. *Reciprocity* is the idea that some people get utility from punishing bad behavior and rewarding good, even when it comes at some cost to them.

Review Questions

1. Which of the following activities give you positive utility? **[LO 7.1]**
   a. Playing sports
   b. Receiving a prestigious scholarship
   c. Buying a new TV
   d. Eating brussels sprouts
   e. All of the above

2. Your gym offers two classes at the same time: weightlifting and yoga. Both classes are included in your membership and have space available. Your friend tells you he wants to work on his strength and take the weightlifting class, but you always see him in yoga class. Which class gives him more utility? How do you know this? **[LO 7.1]**

3. Evie has a gift pass for unlimited roller-coaster rides on her birthday. Given the information about Evie's utility in Table 7Q-1, explain why she chooses to ride only three times. **[LO 7.1]**

TABLE 7Q-1

Roller-coaster rides	Total utility
1	10
2	25
3	35
4	30

4. Dan likes to spend his allowance on two things: candy and toys. What are the three constraints that determine the possible consumption bundles of toys and candy available to Dan? **[LO 7.2]**

5. Maheet has $40 to spend at an amusement park. The roller coaster costs $10 per ride. Given the information about Maheet's utility in Table 7Q-2, explain why he chooses to ride only three times. **[LO 7.2]**

TABLE 7Q-2

Roller-coaster rides	Total utility
1	20
2	35
3	45
4	40

6. Suppose a wedge of cheese is $10 and a loaf of bread is $5. What is the opportunity cost of purchasing a wedge of cheese (in terms of bread)? Explain what happens to the opportunity cost of purchasing a wedge of cheese (in terms of bread) if your income decreases by 20 percent. **[LO 7.3]**

7. Simon spends $300 a month on voice lessons and dance lessons. He just learned that starting next month his favorite dance instructor is moving out of town and the monthly rent for his apartment is increasing. How will each of these events affect Simon's budget constraint for voice and dance lessons? **[LO 7.3]**

8. Julian buys plants and flowers every month. Both are normal goods. When the price of flowers fell, Julian purchased fewer plants. Which effect was stronger for Julian, the income effect or the substitution effect? **[LO 7.4]**

9. Sierrah spends her monthly entertainment budget on books and movies. Sierrah's initial utility-maximizing combination of books and movies is five movies and two books a month. Assume the price of books falls. Sierrah's new utility-maximizing combination of books and movies is five movies and four books. Given this information, can we say whether movies are a normal good? **[LO 7.4]**

10. Your friend says, "I'd rather be a big fish in a small pond than a small fish in a big pond." What concept does this comment illustrate? **[LO 7.5]**

11. Suppose that in addition to being a college student, you run your own business and earn $35,000 per year. Your friends are all in college, and their average annual income is $10,000 per year. When you graduate from college, you decide to continue running your business. Your friends accept jobs that pay $50,000 per year. Do you expect your utility to increase, decrease, or stay the same after graduation? Why? **[LO 7.5]**

12. You come home to discover that your roommate has left his dirty dishes in the sink (again!). Why might you be likely to leave your own dirty dishes in the sink (which you know annoys your roommate), even though you usually prefer a clean kitchen to a messy kitchen? **[LO 7.6]**

13. An organization that raises money to provide meals for seniors gives tote bags to its donors. Sami thinks it is wasteful to spend donated money on tote bags for donors because the money could be used to provide more meals. Explain to Sami why giving tote bags could make financial sense for the organization. **[LO 7.6]**

Problems and Applications

1. Total utility is maximized when marginal utility becomes (positive, zero, negative) _____. **[LO 7.1]**

2. Table 7P-1 shows the total utility that Han gets from ice cream, for each quantity he consumes. Fill in the third column showing the marginal utility he gets from each additional scoop. **[LO 7.1]**

TABLE 7P-1

Scoops of ice cream	Total utility	Marginal utility of the last scoop eaten
1	12	
2	19	
3	23	
4	25	
5	25	

3. You love going to the movies. For your birthday, your friend offers to take you to a triple feature without popcorn or a double feature with two bags of popcorn. Table 7P-2 shows your utility for movies and popcorn. Which option should you choose? **[LO 7.1]**

TABLE 7P-2

Movies	Total utility	Bags of popcorn	Total utility
1	10	1	5
2	15	2	5
3	18	3	4

4. Refer to the budget constraint for jeans and T-shirts in Figure 7P-1. Which of the following consumption bundles is attainable? **[LO 7.2]**

FIGURE 7P-1

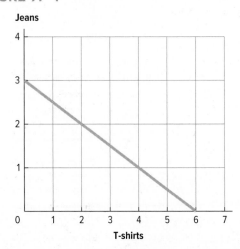

a. 3 pairs of jeans, 1 T-shirt.
b. 2 pairs of jeans, 4 T-shirts.
c. 2 pairs of jeans, 3 T-shirts.
d. 1 pair of jeans, 4 T-shirts.

5. Petra has $480 to spend on DVDs and books. A book costs $28 and a DVD costs $10. **[LO 7.2]**
   a. Write an equation for the budget constraint. Let x = books. Let y = DVDs.
   b. Use your equation to determine how many books Petra can buy if she buys 6 DVDs.

6. Jordan visits her sister several times a year. Jordan's travel budget is $600, which she uses to buy bus tickets and train tickets. The train costs $120 per trip and the bus costs $40. **[LO 7.2, 7.3]**
   a. Graph Jordan's budget constraint.
   b. How many total trips can Jordan take if she takes the train three times?
   c. Suppose Jordan's travel budget is cut to $360. Draw her new budget constraint.
   d. How many train trips can she take if she doesn't want to reduce the total number of trips she takes each year?

7. Maria has a $500 gift certificate at a spa that she can use on massages or manicures. A massage costs $100 and a manicure costs $50. **[LO 7.3, 7.4]**
   a. Write the equation for Maria's budget constraint. Let x = massages. Let y = manicures.
   b. Suppose Maria decides to split her gift certificate with a friend and transfers half of the value of her gift certificate to her friend. Write the equation for her new budget constraint.
   c. After giving away half of her gift certificate, suppose the price of massages increases by 50 percent before Maria can use her gift certificate. Write the equation for her new budget constraint.

8. Every year, Antoni hosts a holiday party for his friends. His party budget is $200. Antoni spends his budget on food platters that cost $25 each and on entertainment, which costs $50 per hour. **[LO 7.4]**
   a. Graph Antoni's budget constraint for food and entertainment.
   b. To reward his loyal business, the entertainment company Antoni hires has offered him a 50 percent discount on entertainment purchases for this year's party. On your graph, illustrate Antoni's new budget constraint for food and entertainment.
   c. Assuming that food platters and entertainment are normal goods, what can you say about the quantity of each good that Antoni will purchase

after the discount? Will the quantity of entertainment increase or decrease, or is the change
uncertain? Will the quantity of food increase or
decrease, or is the change uncertain?

9. Hideki attends baseball games and goes to movie theaters. Baseball tickets cost $15 and movie tickets cost
$10. His entertainment budget is $180. [LO 7.4]

   a. Graph Hideki's budget constraint for baseball
   and movie tickets.

   b. Suppose the home team is having a good season
   and the price of baseball tickets goes up to $20
   per game. Graph the new budget constraint.

   c. Assuming that baseball and movie tickets are
   normal goods, what can you say about the quantity of each good that Hideki will consume after
   the price of baseball tickets goes up? Will the
   quantity of baseball games he attends increase
   or decrease, or is the change uncertain? Will
   the quantity of movies he watches increase or
   decrease, or is the change uncertain?

10. For which of the following goods is the utility you get
from consuming them likely to be affected by the opinions of others? [LO 7.5]

   a. MP3s.

   b. A new car.

   c. Running shoes.

   d. A new laptop for class.

11. Davin spends his money on baseball games and concert
tickets. Baseball tickets cost $15, and concert tickets
cost $25. His entertainment budget is $150.

   a. Draw Davin's budget constraint, putting baseball
   tickets on the x-axis.

   b. Davin decides to attend three concerts and five
   baseball games. Plot this point on the budget
   constraint.

   c. Davin's best friend Jay tells Davin that his
   favorite thing to do is go to concerts. In fact,
   going to concerts is popular with a lot of Davin's
   friends. Will Davin's budget constraint increase,
   decrease, or stay the same? Will the quantity of
   concerts he attends increase, decrease, or stay
   the same? [LO 7.5]

12. Laurel's utility is influenced by reciprocity. She is likely
to respond to a surprisingly generous birthday gift from
her best friend in what way? [LO 7.6]

   a. Not giving her friend a birthday gift at all.

   b. Giving her friend the birthday gift she had
   originally planned to give.

   c. Giving her friend a more thoughtful or more generous gift than she had originally planned to give.

   d. Returning the birthday gift she received.

13. Say whether each of the following situations is an example of altruism or reciprocity. [LO 7.6]

   a. Giving a few canned goods to the local food bank
   for its annual food drive.

   b. Helping someone move her couch after she
   helped you study for an upcoming exam.

   c. The biological relationship between cleaner
   fish and large predators in the ocean, in which
   cleaner fish keep the predator free from parasites
   and the predator keeps the cleaner fish safe.

Endnotes

1. www.slate.com/articles/business/moneybox/2011/12/
scarves_no_surfing_lessons_yes_the_economist_s_guide_
to_efficient_gift_giving_.html

2. www.amherst.edu/media/view/104699/original/christmas.pdf

3. www.redcross.org/about-us/our-work/disaster-relief/
hurricane-relief/hurricane-harvey-relief-information/
long-term-recovery-program#English

Using Indifference Curves

Chapter 7, "Consumer Behavior," presented utility in all of its complexity. We learned how people maximize their utility given how much they are able to spend, how the consumption of goods is affected by the opinion of others, and how people decide how much to give to charity. In this appendix, we describe an important tool that economists use when looking at how people make such decisions—indifference curves.

Representing Preferences Graphically

Indifference curves are a way to represent utility graphically. We'll describe how they work and show that indifference curves come in many shapes and sizes. As you'll see, indifference curves can be applied to many different problems of consumer choice. These include how people maximize their utility, how they respond to changes in both income and prices, and how they relate to some fundamental concepts in economics.

Consumption bundles and indifference curves

Think back to our example from Chapter 7, "Consumer Behavior," about Cody and his decision-making process. Here, we'll look at a situation similar to Cody's, but this time we'll think about how Cody's friend, Laila, makes decisions about how to best spend her money for the month. Laila has $120 to spend on movie and concert tickets. In Laila's hometown,

LEARNING OBJECTIVES

LO E.1 Explain how the marginal rate of substitution relates to the shape of the indifference curve.

LO E.2 Outline the four properties that apply to all indifference curves.

LO E.3 Explain the shapes of indifference curves for perfect substitutes and perfect complements.

LO E.4 Describe the point at which a consumer maximizes utility.

LO E.5 Show how changes in income and prices affect utility maximization.

LO E.6 Show how to build an individual's demand curve using indifference curves.

LO E.1 Explain how the marginal rate of substitution relates to the shape of the indifference curve.

movie tickets cost $10 each and concert tickets cost $40 each. Given her budget and the costs of tickets, Laila has a lot of choices:

- She could spend most of her money on movie tickets, leaving comparatively little for concert tickets.
- She could splurge on three concert tickets and not see any movies.
- She could choose combinations of tickets in between.

Each of the possible combinations Laila could choose is called a *consumption bundle*. In Chapter 7, we put these consumption bundles into a utility function. That utility function produced a number that represented the amount of utility a person receives from a certain combination of goods. This process involved some labor, going through each consumption bundle and doing the arithmetic needed to find the utility that would be gained from each possible choice.

Fortunately, there's another way, using graphs. By representing on curves the utility from various bundles, we can easily compare the bundles visually. A curve called an **indifference curve** fulfills this need, linking all the different bundles that provide a consumer with equal levels of utility. It gets its name because it shows all of the options among which a consumer is truly indifferent. By "indifferent," economists don't mean that the consumer doesn't care about the options. Instead, "indifferent" means that the consumer experiences no real difference between one bundle of goods or services over another. In other words, any of the bundles would be equally acceptable.

Figure E-1 shows a set of indifference curves for our model consumer Laila. Each point on one of the curves represents a consumption bundle that gives Laila the same amount of satisfaction as the other bundles on that curve. If her consumption moves from point A on curve I_b to point B, she loses some movie tickets, but she gets enough extra concert tickets to compensate her so that she feels indifferent between the two options.

If Laila moved to a point on a *different* curve, though, she would not be indifferent. Specifically, moving to a point on a higher indifference curve, such as I_c, gives her higher utility. Moving to a point on a lower indifference curve, such as I_a, gives her lower utility.

indifference curve
a curve showing all the different consumption bundles that provide a consumer with equal levels of utility

FIGURE E-1
Indifference curves

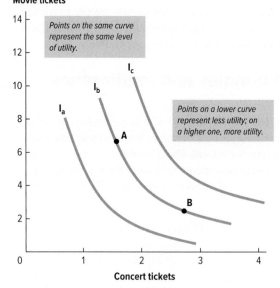

Indifference curves represent the utility provided by different combinations of goods and services. Points on the same indifference curve give the same utility. Higher indifference curves represent greater utility.

Indifference curves gain their shape from the principle of diminishing marginal utility. At each end of the curve, Laila is indifferent between bundles that trade lots of one good for very little of the other. This is due to diminishing marginal utilities. When Laila has a lot of concert tickets, she doesn't get much utility from the last few concert tickets she buys. Buying one more movie ticket, on the other hand, gives her a lot of utility because she didn't have very many movie tickets. As a result, the slope of the curve is very steep.

At the other end of the curve, the opposite is true: If Laila has a lot of movie tickets but very few concert tickets, then gaining an additional concert ticket brings her a lot of utility. In order to remain on the same indifference curve and maintain the same amount of utility, she would be willing to give up many movie tickets in exchange for the utility she gets from an extra concert ticket.

At any point, the slope of the indifference curve tells you how much more of one good Laila requires to compensate her for the loss of the other. In other words, it tells you the rate at which she would be willing to trade or substitute between the two goods. This rate is called the **marginal rate of substitution (MRS)**. Because the marginal rate of substitution is the relative satisfaction the consumer gets from two goods—in general, we'll call them X and Y—at any point, it can also be represented as the ratio of the marginal utilities of the two goods.

marginal rate of substitution (MRS) the rate at which a consumer is willing to trade or substitute between two goods

The marginal rate of substitution is also equal to the absolute value of the slope of the indifference curve at any given point:

EQUATION E-1
$$\text{Absolute value of slope} = \text{MRS} = \frac{\text{MU}_X}{\text{MU}_Y}$$

After all, the slope is just the ratio of how much the y variable changes for one unit of movement along the x-axis.

Properties of indifference curves

There are four properties of indifference curves that are essential to the way they work. Later economics classes (if you take them, which we hope you will do) will prove these rules using math; for now, we will show why they make sense intuitively.

LO E.2 Outline the four properties that apply to all indifference curves.

- *A consumer prefers a higher indifference curve to a lower one.* Since higher indifference curves contain more goods, and the average consumer gets more utility from consuming more, a higher indifference curve represents bundles of goods that provide the consumer with more utility than the bundles on lower indifference curves. Without constraints, it simply doesn't make any sense to pick a bundle on a lower indifference curve when you could pick a bundle with more goods, and more utility.

- *Indifference curves do not cross one another.* Each indifference curve represents all the bundles that provide the consumer with a certain level of utility. Suppose that one curve represents bundles with utility of 10, and a second curve represents bundles with utility of 20. If these curves crossed, the bundle at the point of intersection would simultaneously have utility of 10 and 20. That's not possible! Therefore, indifference curves do not cross each other.

- *Indifference curves usually slope downward.* Assuming that both goods are desirable, then the consumer would always prefer more of each good to less of it. A downward-sloping indifference curve—one with a negative slope—shows that when a consumer gets less of one good, her utility decreases and she requires more of the other good in order to compensate.

- *Indifference curves usually curve inward.* This inward curve, like the side of a bowl, follows from the property of diminishing marginal utility. At the top of the curve, the slope is steep because the consumer has a lot of the good on the y-axis and is willing to trade more of it for even a little of the good on the x-axis. As the curve goes downward, the consumer has less of the good represented on the *y*-axis and requires more and more of the good on the *x*-axis to compensate for the loss of that good, and the slope flattens out.

Just as utility functions are unique to a consumer and represent personal preferences, so too there is no such thing as a universal set of indifference curves for particular goods. There are only indifference curves *for a particular person*. Let's say that Cody and Laila are both trying to decide how many movie tickets to buy with the same amount of money. If Laila gets more utility from movies, she will be willing to trade many more concert tickets for movie tickets at every point along the curve.

Perfect substitutes and perfect complements

LO E.3 Explain the shapes of indifference curves for perfect substitutes and perfect complements.

In two special cases, indifference curves become straight lines. In Chapter 3, "Markets," we mentioned that many goods have substitutes and complements. Remember:

- *Substitutes* are two goods that have similar qualities and fulfill similar desires. These include tangerines and oranges, tea and coffee, or coal and natural gas, for example.
- *Complements* are goods that are consumed together, such as peanut butter and jelly, or cereal and milk.

Perfect substitutes   While many goods are general substitutes for each other, some are so similar that they can be called *perfect substitutes*. Different brands of milk are a good example. We'd wager that you can't tell the difference between any two brands in the store that are roughly the same price. Different brands of tomatoes, potatoes, and many other types of produce are also often perfect substitutes.

Since both goods are essentially the same, the rules of diminishing marginal utility simply don't apply to perfect substitutes. For example, let's say you have five cartons of Farmer John milk; a friend offers to trade you two cartons of his Happy Cow milk for two cartons of your Farmer John milk. If you can't tell the difference between the two brands, you'd have very little reason to make the trade. There'd be no benefit to giving up some of your Farmer John milk for the same amount of Happy Cow milk.

If the price is the same, you'd always be indifferent to having one brand versus the other, no matter how many cartons you already have of each brand. You are perfectly indifferent between the two. You could spend all of your milk money on each, or split it 50–50 between the two, or trade one Farmer John for one Happy Cow at any point along the curve and still get the same utility. This represents a marginal rate of substitution of 1 at every point.

As a result, the indifference curve for perfect substitutes, shown in panel A of Figure E-2, is always linear. In the case of the two milks, since you are willing to trade one carton for the other, the slope of the indifference curve is 1.

The marginal rate of substitution is not always going to be 1, though. In general, the slope of the indifference curve is going to depend on the relative value of the two goods. Take the example of money: In the vast majority of cases, you'd be indifferent toward having a $5 bill or five $1 bills; in the end you buy $5 worth of stuff with either combination. If you don't mind making the trade between the two, the marginal rate of substitution between $1 bills and $5 bills is 5 (or $\frac{1}{5}$ depending on which is on the *y*-axis), making for a much steeper indifference curve than what was the case for similarly priced milk.

Perfect complements   *Perfect complements*, unlike substitutes, are goods that *have to be consumed together*. Pairs of shoes, socks, and gloves are all perfect complements. In each of these cases, having just one of a good without its complement isn't useful at all (unless, like Michael Jackson, you favor the single-glove look). If you are having a cookout, you're generally going to want to have enough buns for your hot dogs. Having more buns than hot dogs doesn't increase your utility, as they aren't really good for much besides holding hot dogs, and they just sit around until you get more hot dogs.

FIGURE E-2

Perfect substitutes and perfect complements

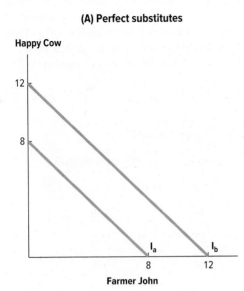

(A) Perfect substitutes

Since the two goods are perfect substitutes, a consumer is willing trade one for the other in order to maintain the same amount of utility.

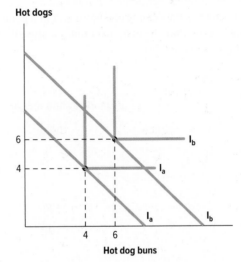

(B) Perfect complements

Once a consumer has one of each good, adding extras on either side doesn't actually add any further utility. This is because perfect complements are useless without the other good.

The relationship between complements creates an L-shaped indifference curve, part horizontal and part vertical. Let's say that you buy six hot dogs and six buns. Now imagine that you get another bun. Since you can't do anything with the extra bun, you still have the same amount of utility as when you had six hot dogs and six buns. The same is true whether you have eight buns or 12. You still get only the same amount of utility as when you had six of each. The same is also true for when you get more hot dogs. In most cases, it doesn't do you any good to have more hot dogs without buns. This relationship between perfect complements gives the L-shaped indifference curve shown in panel B of Figure E-2.

Understanding Consumer Choice

Even though indifference curves come in many different shapes, their relation to utility maximization is always the same. In Chapter 7, "Consumer Behavior," we worked through an example—movie and concert tickets—to find what bundle maximizes utility. We looked at each bundle on the budget line and added up the utility that a consumer (in that case, Cody) got from each good in the bundle. Whichever bundle resulted in the higher amount of utility was the correct choice.

This is a long and tedious process, though. The concepts of marginal rates of substitution and indifference curves presented in this appendix allow for a much clearer picture of how to find where a consumer maximizes utility. You'll find that either method leads to the optimal consumption bundle.

Equalizing the marginal utility of the last purchase

Another way to think about optimal consumption is to imagine that you are "buying utility" and trying to get the best value for your money. That is, *you want to maximize your marginal utility per dollar spent*. How would you choose a consumption bundle that fits this criterion?

Let's approach this challenge from a marginal decision-making viewpoint, once again using Laila as an example. As a rational consumer, before Laila buys anything, she has to ask herself,

LO E.4 Describe the point at which a consumer maximizes utility.

"Could I do better by spending my dollar on something else?" Suppose she starts her purchases from scratch and chooses which good to buy next based on which will bring her the greatest marginal utility per dollar. *Marginal utility per dollar spent* is calculated by taking the extra utility gained from consuming one more unit of a good and dividing it by the cost of that unit. Panel A of Table E-1 shows the marginal utility of attending concerts, and panel B shows the marginal utility of going to the movies.

TABLE E-1

Equalizing marginal utility

(A) Calculating marginal utility of concert tickets			
Tickets	Utility	$ spent	Marginal utility/$
0	0	0	—
1	70	40	1.75
2	130	80	1.5
3	185	120	1.375

(B) Calculating marginal utility of movie tickets			
Tickets	Utility	$ spent	Marginal utility/$
0	0	0	—
1	17	10	1.7
2	34	20	1.7
3	50	30	1.6
4	65	40	1.5
5	79	50	1.4

Panels A and B show the calculation of the marginal utility Laila would get from the purchase of each ticket. These numbers are used in panel C to determine the optimal amount of tickets to purchase.

(C) Purchase decisions				
Choice	Potential marginal utility/$ from next movie ticket	Potential marginal utility/$ from next concert ticket	Buy?	Total $ spent
1	1.7	1.75	Concert	40
2	1.7	1.5	Movie	50
3	1.7	1.5	Movie	60
4	1.6	1.5	Movie	70
5	1.5	1.5	Buy both!	120

Each purchase gives Laila a certain marginal utility per dollar spent. As she makes each consumption choice, she chooses the good that will bring her the highest marginal utility per dollar. At the point where the marginal utility of the next purchase of each good is equal, Laila buys one of each, and has maximized total utility.

Panel C in Table E-1 puts together the the information from panels A and B to show Laila's purchase decision-making. In panel C, you'll see that starting with nothing, Laila's best move is to buy a concert ticket. (See the highlighted box in the row for choice 1.) After that, for choices 2, 3, and 4, the good that brings her the highest marginal utility per dollar for her next purchase is a movie ticket. Laila continues to choose each purchase based on what gets her the most bang for her buck–the highest marginal utility for the next dollar she spends. When does this stop? When Laila reaches her budget limit. It's not a coincidence that, at this point, the marginal utility of the next dollar spent on each good is the same.

Suppose that instead of starting her purchases from scratch, Laila picks a random consumption bundle and then analyzes whether she could switch one of her purchases to achieve more utility. If she started with 12 movie tickets and no concert tickets, she could get more utility by switching some of her money over to buy a concert ticket. We can see that the marginal utility per dollar she would get from buying her first concert ticket is greater than the marginal utility per dollar she receives from her last $40 worth of movie tickets. She can continue to make these trades until she reaches a point where she can no longer get more marginal utility by switching her last dollar spent. At this point, the marginal utilities are the same for each of her choices.

The principle to remember is this: *Optimal consumption occurs at the point where the marginal utility gained from the dollar spent on good X equals the marginal utility gained from the last dollar spent on good Y.*

The marginal utility per dollar spent on good X can be written as the marginal utility divided by the price: $\frac{MU_X}{P_X}$. So, optimal consumption occurs where:

EQUATION E-2 $$\text{Optimal consumption} = \frac{MU_X}{P_X} = \frac{MU_Y}{P_Y}$$

In our example, Laila reaches the point where the marginal utilities per dollar for concerts and for movies are equal when she watches four movies and goes to two concerts.

Finding the highest indifference curve

You know that consumers prefer bundles on higher indifference curves to lower ones because those bundles give them greater utility. A final way to think about optimal consumption, therefore, is to find the highest possible indifference curve that still contains bundles within the budget constraint.

Figure E-3 shows Laila's budget constraint and several indifference curves. There are many bundles on curve I_1 that lie within her budget constraint, and even a few that fall on the budget line. But you can see that the highest possible indifference curve she can reach with the given budget constraint is I_2, which just grazes up against the budget line, intersecting it at only one point. She has no reason to choose a bundle on a lower curve. Bundles on higher curves like I_3 are unreachable given her budget.

At the optimal consumption bundle at point C, the slope of the budget line is the same as the slope of the indifference curve–they are tangent to one another. In order to find where the two meet, we need some math.

In general, the formula for the slope of the budget line for goods X and Y is:

EQUATION E-3 $$\text{Slope of the budget line} = \frac{P_X}{P_Y}$$

The formula for the slope of the indifference curve between those same goods is:

EQUATION E-4 $$\text{Slope of the indifference curve} = MRS = \frac{MU_X}{MU_Y}$$

FIGURE E-3
The optimal consumption bundle

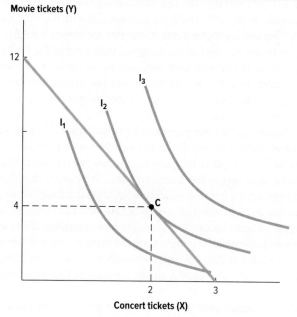

This graph shows several of Laila's indifference curves. Curves I_1 and I_2 are both within her budget. I_3 provides the most utility but will cost more than her budget allows. I_2, which just grazes the budget constraint, provides the most utility that Laila can afford.

Since the slope of the budget line is equal to the slope of the indifference curve at the optimal consumption point and they are equal at the point where they are tangent, we can put these two formulas together:

EQUATION E-5 $$\text{Optimal consumption} = \frac{P_X}{P_Y} = \frac{MU_X}{MU_Y}$$

We can reduce this equation by rearranging terms to put X on one side of the equation and Y on the other. Doing so, we can confirm that this is exactly the same formula that we earlier found in Equation E-2:

$$\text{Optimal consumption} = \frac{MU_X}{P_X} = \frac{MU_Y}{P_Y}$$

Finding the highest-possible indifference curve turns out to be the same thing as equalizing the marginal utility per dollar for each good.

In the next few sections, maximizing utility by using indifference curves will be instrumental to figuring out how consumers respond to change. In Chapter 7, "Consumer Behavior," we were able to make only very general statements about how changes in prices and income affect overall consumption. Now we'll be able to form a more complete picture of how consumers make decisions in response to change.

How Consumers Respond to Change

LO E.5 Show how changes in income and prices affect utility maximization.

Budgets change. Prices also go up and down. Consumers respond to changes in income and prices by adjusting their consumption decisions. In this section, we'll describe how to apply the optimal-choice approaches to changes in income and prices. Although in the end we will find the same results as we did in the chapter, we now do so with a more complete conception of consumer decisions using indifference curves.

Responding to a change in income

From Chapter 7, "Consumer Behavior," you'll remember that an increase in income shifts the budget constraint out, and a decrease in income has the opposite effect. We found that an increase in income leads to more consumption—as long as both goods are normal, meaning that the consumer demands more of them as income increases. This result was taken on faith that since more is better, it is only logical that a consumer would buy more when she receives more income.

Adding indifference curves to this analysis allows us to see why this is true. Although this will be similar to what happened in the body of the chapter, we'll run through another example of a change in income—this time using indifference curves. As before, we're back to Laila's decision to buy movie and concert tickets.

Suppose Laila gets $80 for her birthday. Now Laila has $200 to spend. The increase in her income means that Laila has access to higher indifference curves that contain more tickets than before. As is the case with any optimization, the goal is to find the indifference curve that is tangent to the new budget constraint. This process is shown in Figure E-4. When her income increases by $80, she ends up buying eight movie tickets and three concert tickets.

Responding to a change in prices

As you'll remember from the chapter, a change in price rotates the budget constraint. In a sense, the change in price is similar to a change in income: When the price of a good increases, for example, you can't afford the same amount of goods as before; the effect is the same as if you'd lost some income.

Although we'll go through and break the effect of a price change into its two parts, we'll first show the overall effect of a change in prices. Starting from our movie/concert ticket base, let's say

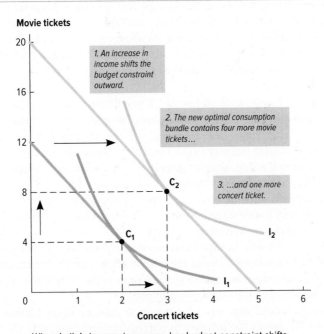

FIGURE E-4

Increases in income with normal goods

When Laila's income increases, her budget constraint shifts outward, keeping the same slope. Laila will choose to consume at the highest indifference curve possible that intersects the budget line, at point C_2. The new consumption bundle contains both more concert tickets and more movie tickets, meaning that they are both normal goods.

FIGURE E-5

Overall effect of a price decrease

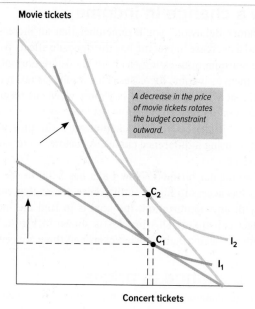

Movie tickets

A decrease in the price of movie tickets rotates the budget constraint outward.

C_2

C_1

I_2

I_1

Concert tickets

When the price of one good decreases, the budget constraint rotates outward to demonstrate the new consumption bundles that are available. The change in slope reflects the change in the relative prices of the two goods.

that the local movie theater has a special discount that decreases the price of tickets to $5, and the budget constraint rotates outward. Now Laila has higher indifference curves available to her. Figure E-5 shows this effect: Laila moves from indifference curve I_1 to I_2. Thankfully, the process of optimization is still the same, even as the budget constraint changes. All you need to do is find the indifference curve that is tangent to the new budget constraint.

The income and substitution effects   If you'll remember from the body of the chapter, the change in consumption that occurs with a change in prices can be broken into two parts, the *income effect* and the *substitution effect*. Depending on the type of good, the income and substitution effects will have different impacts on the optimal consumption bundle of the consumer when prices change. For normal goods, a price increase will lead to a larger change in the income effect versus the substitution effect, and so a consumer will consume less.

Let's see what happens when we add indifference curves: Figure E-6 shows the overall response to the price change with indifference curves, in two steps. One corresponds to the substitution effect, and the other to the income effect.

Panel A shows the first step, in which consumption responds to the changes in relative prices (substitution effect). Consumption moves along the original indifference curve to the point where the marginal rate of substitution is equal to the new slope of the budget line, which is shown by the dashed green line (parallel to the original budget line).

Panel B shows the second step, when consumption shifts up to the highest indifference curve that is now accessible due to the increase in purchasing power (income effect). This new consumption bundle is at point C_3, which includes more of both goods.

Indifference curves help make sense of the income and substitution effects. Before, we could make general statements only about the impact of a change in prices. Now, indifference curves allow us to see exactly how much the consumption changes under the income and substitution effects.

FIGURE E-6

The income and substitution effects of a price decrease

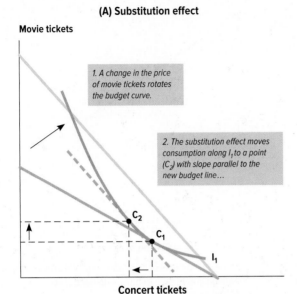

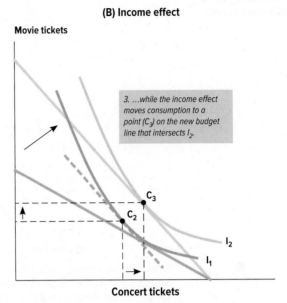

The substitution effect moves the optimal consumption point along the *same* indifference curve, increasing consumption of the good whose price has been reduced (movie tickets), and decreasing consumption of the other good (concert tickets). If the substitution effect alone were at work, consumption would move to C_2. The dashed green line reflects the new slope of the budget line.

The income effect will also increase consumption of the good with the newly reduced price (movie tickets), but it has the opposite effect on the item whose price has not changed (concert tickets). In this particular example, the income and substitution effects happen to have opposite effects on the number of concert tickets purchased. The combined impact of the income and substitution effect in this example is to increase the number of movie tickets purchased.

Deriving the demand curve using indifference curves

Indifference curves can also fill in our understanding of one of the more fundamental concepts in economics: the individual demand curve. When the demand curve was originally presented in Chapter 3, "Markets," we simply said the consumer would demand a certain quantity based on price. Did you wonder, "Where did those numbers come from?" They are actually derived from indifference curves.

Since the indifference curves show where a consumer gets the most utility, it makes sense that any consumer would demand the quantity of a good that gives the most utility. Remember that indifference curves are intrinsic to a person, and that the demand curves we are making are demand curves *for the individual*. They do not represent full-market demand. With that caveat, we'll bring back, one more time, Laila and her decision to buy concert and movie tickets.

Starting from the original $120 and $10 price for movie tickets, we know that Laila's optimal consumption bundle includes four movie tickets. That is the same as saying that at a price of $10, she demands four movie tickets. What happens if we decrease the price to $5? After the budget constraint rotates inward, her optimal consumption bundle includes five more movie tickets. At the lower price, she now demands (is willing to buy) nine tickets.

This information is all that we need to build the demand curve. Demanding four tickets when the price is $10 represents one point on the demand schedule, and demanding nine when the price

LO E.6 Show how to build an individual's demand curve using indifference curves.

FIGURE E-7

Deriving the demand curve using indifference curves

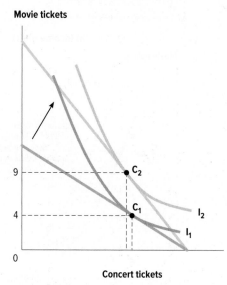

(A) Optimal consumption

When the price of movie tickets falls from $10 to $5, rotating the budget constraint, the optimal number of movie tickets Laila wants to consume increases from 4 to 9 tickets.

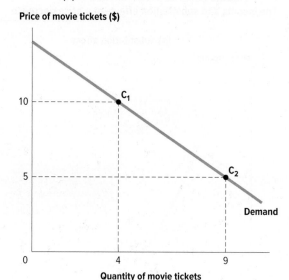

(B) The demand curve for movie tickets

These two optimal consumption bundles provide enough information to build a demand curve for movie tickets.

is $5 represents another. Finding the slope between these two points fleshes out the rest of Laila's demand curve. Figure E-7 shows how her demand curve for movie tickets is built in this way.

Conclusion

The idea that individuals maximize utility is one of the most powerful concepts in economics. Indifference curves, though they may seem complex at first, can make understanding this concept far easier. From demand curves to price changes, indifference curves can help explain how consumers decide how much to buy and how satisfied they are with their choices.

Key Terms

indifference curve, p. 188B   marginal rate of substitution (MRS), p. 188C

Summary

LO E.1 Explain how the marginal rate of substitution relates to the shape of the indifference curve.

An *indifference curve* links all the different bundles that provide a consumer with equal levels of utility. It is called an indifference curve because it shows all of the options among which a consumer is truly indifferent.

At any point, the slope of the indifference curve tells you how much more of one good a consumer requires to compensate for the loss of the other. In other words, it tells you the rate at which a consumer would be willing

to trade or substitute between the two goods. This is the *marginal rate of substitution (MRS)*. Because the marginal rate of substitution is the relative satisfaction the consumer gets from the two goods at any point, it can also be represented as the ratio of the marginal utilities of the two goods.

The marginal rate of substitution is also equal to the absolute value of the slope of the indifference curve at any given point. The slope is just the ratio of how much the y variable changes for one unit of movement along the x-axis.

LO E.2 Outline the four rules that apply to all indifference curves.

Indifference curves generally follow four rules: Consumers prefer higher indifference curves to lower ones; indifference curves do not cross; indifference curves usually slope downward; and they curve inward.

LO E.3 Explain the shapes of indifference curves for perfect substitutes and perfect complements.

Because perfect substitutes are essentially the same, the rules of diminishing marginal utility simply don't apply to them. Therefore, the indifference curve for perfect substitutes is always linear (and downward-sloping). In general, the slope of that linear indifference curve is going to depend on the relative value of the two goods.

Perfect complements are goods that have to be consumed together. You are indifferent about having an extra unit of X if you don't have an extra unit of Y. Adding an extra unit of one of them does not increase utility. This relationship between complements creates an L-shaped indifference curve, part horizontal and part vertical.

LO E.4 Describe the point at which a consumer maximizes utility.

A consumer maximizes utility at the point where the highest indifference curve is tangent to the budget constraint. That is, the utility-maximization point is where the slope of the indifference curve equals the slope of the budget constraint.

This point can also be found through two other methods: (1) Count the utility gained from each bundle on the budget constraint to see which is the greatest. (2) Find the point where the marginal utilities for the goods in the bundle are equal.

LO E.5 Show how changes in income and prices affect utility maximization.

Changes in income shift the budget constraint. Increases in income will, on average, increase the optimal consumption of goods in a bundle. The opposite is true for decreases in income.

Changes in prices rotate the budget constraint. On average, when prices decrease, the optimal consumption bundle includes more goods than before. When prices increase, the optimal consumption bundle includes fewer goods than before.

LO E.6 Show how to build an individual's demand curve using indifference curves.

An individual's demand curve can be created using that individual's indifference curves. A consumer will demand the quantity of a good that gives the most utility, and

indifference curves show precisely where that point is. Finding the optimal consumption bundle on two curves, and finding the slope between these two points, will provide the demand curve.

Review Questions

1. If an indifference curve is a vertical line, does the amount of the good on the *y*-axis influence the consumer's utility? **[LO E.1]**

2. Two friends are discussing their plans for the month. One works at a movie theater and gets 10 free movie tickets; the other works at a concert venue and gets 10 free concert tickets. What can we predict about the first person's marginal rate of substitution between movies and concerts? What can we predict about the second person's marginal rate of substitution between the two? How does this relate to the slope of each of their indifference curves? **[LO E.1]**

3. Your friend tells you that although she has a large amount of M&Ms and just a few Skittles, she would still be willing to give up the rest of her Skittles, just to get one last M&M. What characteristic of indifference curves is your friend going against? **[LO E.2]**

4. For each pair of goods listed below, state whether the indifference curves would be linear or L-shaped. **[LO E.3]**
   - Ten dollar bills and pairs of five dollar bills.
   - Coffee and tea.
   - Bagels and muffins.
   - Left shoes and right shoes.

5. Suppose that a budget constraint intersects an indifference curve at two separate points. Can either of these consumption bundles be optimal? Explain why or why not. **[LO E.4]**

6. Dan consumes two goods: peanut butter and jelly sandwiches, which are an inferior good, and chicken salad sandwiches, which are a normal good. He gets a raise at work. Will the ratio of peanut butter and jelly sandwiches to chicken salad sandwiches that he consumes increase or decrease? **[LO E.5]**

7. Haley divides her entertainment budget between movie tickets and concert tickets. Two of her indifference curves are shown in Figure EQ-1. When movie tickets are $12 and concert tickets are $20, she purchases 25 movie tickets and 45 concert tickets. This is shown on Indifference Curve 1 (IC_1). Haley finds out that she can sign up for a loyalty program with the movie theater and buy tickets at a 50 percent discount. When the price of movie tickets decreases, she buys 50 movie tickets and 50 concert tickets. This is shown on Indifference Curve 2 (IC_2). For which of these two goods can we draw Haley's demand curve? Explain. **[LO E.6]**

FIGURE EQ-1

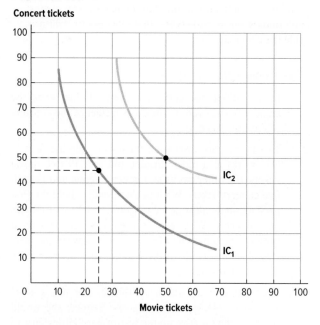

Concert tickets / Movie tickets

2. Table EP-1 shows some possible consumption bundles for a person who consumes MP3s and lattes. **[LO E.2]**

TABLE EP-1

Bundle	MP3s	Lattes	Total utility
A	13	8	20
B	3	2	12
C	13	10	23
D	6	3	15
E	9	4	17
F	6	1	12
G	17	9	23
H	4	0	11

Problems and Applications

1. Your baby cousin Hubert loves lollipops and bouncy balls. Look at the indifference curves in Figure EP-1 that represent his preferences among various bundles of the two goods. Assuming the indifference curves follow the four properties outlined in this appendix, rank bundles A through D from the highest utility to the lowest, including ties. **[LO E.1]**

FIGURE EP-1

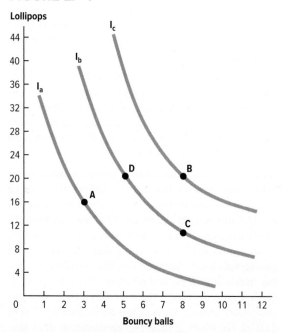

Lollipops / Bouncy balls

a. Which bundles fall on the lowest indifference curve?

b. Which bundles fall on the highest indifference curve?

3. Determine whether the preferences described below would be represented by an indifference curve that is L-shaped, bows inward, or is a straight line. **[LO E.2, LO E.3]**

a. Eliza will eat carrots only if she has hummus to go with them.

b. Andrew likes to start his day right with oatmeal, but he's just as happy starting it with steel-cut oats as he is with rolled oats.

c. Ezekiel really enjoys coffee and donuts together, but he's also happy eating just one or the other.

4. Julia is completely indifferent between eating the brand name version of her favorite cereal and eating the generic version. Her preferences would best be represented by which indifference curve in Figure EP-2: IC_a or IC_b? Are brand-name cereal and generic cereal perfect substitutes or perfect complements? **[LO E.3]**

FIGURE EP-2

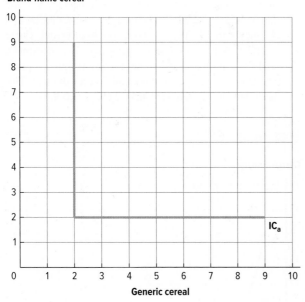

Brand-name cereal / Generic cereal / IC_a

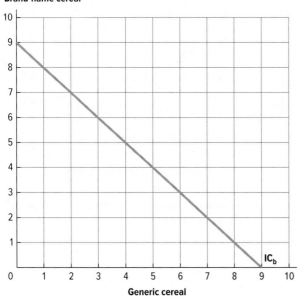

Brand-name cereal / Generic cereal / IC_b

5. A consumer is stocking up on sodas and sports drinks at the dollar store. As you might expect at a dollar store, each bottle of each drink costs $1. He has a $10 bill to spend. Based on Table EP-2 of marginal utilities, find the optimal consumption bundle. **[LO E.4]**

TABLE EP-2

Quantity of a good	Marginal utility of a soda	Marginal utility of a sports drink
1	10	8
2	8	7
3	6	6
4	5	5
5	4	4
6	3	3
7	2	2

6. A consumer is buying steaks for $4 each and potatoes for $1 per pound. She has $40. Plot her budget constraint on Figure EP-3 and find her optimal consumption bundle. **[LO E.4]**

FIGURE EP-3

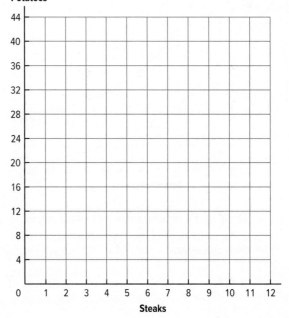

Potatoes / Steaks

7. Under utility maximization, is it possible that after an increase in income, a consumer would remain on the same indifference curve? What about after a decrease in the price of one of the goods? **[LO E.5]**

8. *True or false?* The income effect is represented by the shift in consumption of a good as the bundle moves along the old indifference curve before moving to another indifference curve tangent to the new budget line. **[LO E.5]**

9. Tyler likes to divide his entertainment between attending basketball games and attending football games. Two of his indifference curves are shown in Figure EP-4. When football games are $25 and basketball games are $20, he chooses to attend 6 football games and 7 basketball games. This is shown on Indifference Curve 1 (IC$_1$). The football team has been selling out every game, so they decide to raise the price to $45 per game. At this new price, Tyler chooses to attend 2 football games and 8 basketball games. This is shown on Indifference Curve 2 (IC$_2$). **[LO E.6]**

FIGURE EP-4

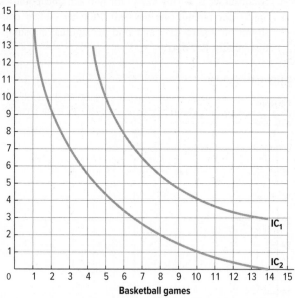

a. Draw Tyler's demand curve for football games.

b. What is the slope of the Tyler's demand curve for football games?

10. Gabriella divides her food budget between fancy dinners and casual dinners. Two of her indifference curves are shown in Figure EP-5. When casual dinners are $12 and fancy dinners are $25, she chooses 5 casual dinners and 4 fancy dinners. This is shown on Indifference Curve 1 (IC$_1$). A new restaurant opens near her apartment, and she can get a casual dinner for $6. At this new price, she chooses 8 casual dinners and 5 fancy dinners. This is shown on Indifference Curve 2 (IC$_2$). **[LO E.6]**

FIGURE EP-5

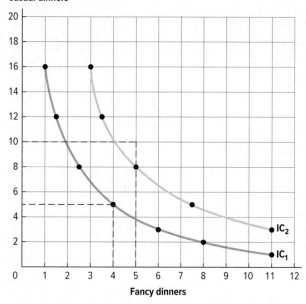

a. Draw Gabriella's demand curve for casual dinners.

b. What do we know about Gabriella's demand for fancy dinners?

Behavioral Economics: A Closer Look at Decision Making

When Is $20 Not Quite $20?

Imagine yourself in the following situation: Earlier today, you bought a ticket for a concert this evening. The ticket cost $20. You arrive at the concert venue, reach into your pocket for the ticket, and . . . it's not there. You must have dropped it somewhere on the way. How annoying! Tickets are still available at the door for $20. Which of the following is your reaction?

#1: "Oh well, never mind. These things happen. I'll just buy another ticket."

#2: "No way I'm going to spend $40 on this concert! I'd rather go do something else instead."

If you said #2, many are like you: When researchers presented a similar situation to them, 46 percent of people said they'd do something else with their evening. The other 54 percent said they'd swallow their annoyance enough to buy a replacement ticket.

©Media Union/Shutterstock

Now imagine an alternative scenario: This time you arrive at the concert venue intending to buy your ticket at the door. You reach into your pocket for the money to pay, and . . . hold on, what's this? You definitely had five $20 bills in your pocket this morning, but now you have only four. You must have lost one of them somewhere today. How annoying! Which of the following do you then say?

#1: "Oh well, never mind. These things happen. I'll get my ticket for the concert."

#2: "You know what? Forget the concert."

This time only 12 percent chose #2 and said they'd abandon their evening plans. Fully 88 percent of people said they'd buy the ticket anyway.

You may have noticed that the economics of these two situations are *exactly the same*. In both scenarios, you arrive at the venue intending to see a concert you had previously decided was worth $20 to you, only to make the unwelcome discovery that you are $20 less well off than you'd thought you were. If you are short of money for things you need in the near future, it may make sense to skip the concert in *either* case. If you're not short of money, it makes sense to go to the concert in *either* case.

What difference does it make if you lost the $20 *before* or *after* you'd converted a bill into a concert ticket? Objectively, it doesn't matter at all. Emotionally, however, it does matter. (Even if you would have bought a ticket in both scenarios, wouldn't you have felt just a little bit more annoyed about losing the ticket?) To a significant proportion of people, that emotional difference is so great it would make them abandon their plans if they had lost the ticket, but *not* if they had lost the $20 bill.

This is not rational behavior. Other examples that often indicate irrational behavior are:

- Saying you want to lose weight but ordering a high-calorie, fattening dessert.
- Being willing to pay more for something if you use a credit card than if you use cash.
- Stubbornly watching to the end of a movie you've decided you're not enjoying at all.

People who are rational (as defined in economics) wouldn't behave in these ways, but many people do. Yet, haven't we said throughout this text that economists assume people behave rationally to maximize their utility? Yes, we have. So what's going on?

The assumption that people are rational utility maximizers gets us a long way. It's true often enough to be useful. But it's not true all the time, and how much the exceptions matter is a hotly debated question in economics right now. In the past few decades, economists have been learning a lot from psychologists and biologists about how real people make everyday decisions that translate economic ideas into action. The resulting theories have developed into a branch of economics that expands our models of decision making. This field is called *behavioral economics*, the topic of this chapter.

behavioral economics
a field of economics that draws on insights from psychology to expand models of individual decision making

Irrational behavior does *not* mean "people act randomly." The interesting insights from behavioral economics come from understanding people's decision-making patterns, whether rational or not. We then can build models that make the best prediction possible for what people will actually do in a given situation.

LEARNING OBJECTIVES

LO 8.1 Explain how time inconsistency accounts for procrastination and other problems with self-control.

LO 8.2 Explain why sunk costs should not be taken into account in deciding what to do next.

LO 8.3 Identify the types of opportunity cost that people often undervalue, and recognize why undervaluing them distorts decision making.

LO 8.4 Explain why fungibility matters in financial decision making.

Behavioral economists are not just advancing our academic knowledge of how people make decisions. They also have developed some practical, easy-to-use tools that can help people enact the choices they *say* they would like to make: save more money, get healthier, give more to charity. You may even be using some of these tools without realizing it.

Formally, **behavioral economics** is a field of economics that draws on insights from psychology to expand models of individual decision making. Behavioral economics is wide-ranging, and in this chapter we'll cover just three of its more interesting applications: time inconsistency, thinking irrationally about costs, and forgetting the fungibility of money.

Dealing with Temptation and Procrastination

When we discussed utility (in Chapter 7, "Consumer Behavior"), we already provided an example of the kind of question that interests behavioral economists: You wake up one Saturday morning with great intentions to have a useful and productive day—work out, clean the apartment, study. Later, you realize that, somehow, suddenly it's Saturday evening and you're still in your pajamas watching reruns of *Game of Thrones*. Huh. How did that happen?

As we have seen, one way to look at this common experience is to use the idea of *revealed preference*—that is, no matter what you *had thought* you wanted to do, your actions reveal that what you *actually* wanted to do was to spend the day watching TV. Another way to look at it is to consider that you simply weren't acting rationally.

Neither explanation seems very satisfying. Many of us have experienced feelings of conflict when we know we *want* to do one thing but find ourselves constantly doing another. We want to study, but instead play games; we want to diet, but instead eat dessert; we want to save, but instead spend too much. Saying that our actions must reveal our true desires goes against our understanding of ourselves. On the other hand, explaining the conflict by just saying we are irrational feels like giving up; that explanation also suggests that we have no ability to predict what decisions people will make.

There *is* a third way: We can improve our models a bit, to be more accurate in predicting how we deal with the struggles against procrastination and temptation. This can be done by using the ideas of time inconsistency, competing selves, and commitment.

Time inconsistency, competing selves, and commitment

One theory of why we sometimes give in to temptation is based on the idea that people can hold two inconsistent sets of preferences:

- One set holds what we would *like to want* in the future—to study enough for exams, to lose weight, to build up a healthy savings account.
- One set holds what we *will actually want* in the future, when the future comes—to play games, to eat dessert, to go shopping.

Behavioral economists use the term **time inconsistency** to describe what is happening when we change our minds about what we want simply because of the timing of the decision.

Consider this classic example of time inconsistency: A researcher says to you, "We want to offer you a snack to thank you for taking part in a survey one week from today. Please tell us now: Which would you like after the survey—an apple or a chocolate brownie?" Most people choose the apple. However, when the following week arrives, the researcher asks the participants whether they still want the apple; most participants instead switch to the chocolate brownie. A person with time-consistent preferences would choose the same snack, regardless of whether the choice is being made ahead of time or in the moment. We are *time inconsistent* when we say that we'll prefer the apple next week and then switch to a chocolate brownie when we get to consume it immediately.

Time inconsistency helps to explain behaviors like procrastination and lack of self-control. It is as if there are two selves inhabiting our thoughts: One is a "future-oriented self," with clear-sighted preferences to get things done, eat healthily, and so on. The other is a "present-oriented self," who backslides when faced with temptation in the here-and-now. However wise the decisions your future-oriented self makes about the future, when that future becomes the present, your present-oriented self will be in charge again. If, after next week's survey, the researcher says, "We brought you an apple—but you can still have a chocolate brownie if you would prefer," our present-oriented self takes command and switches to the brownie.

It makes sense to think of time inconsistency as a battle between these two selves. In other words, a time-inconsistent individual is being neither irrational nor rational. Rather, future-oriented and present-oriented selves within the individual are each rationally pursuing their own objectives.

LO 8.1 Explain how time inconsistency accounts for procrastination and other problems with self-control.

time inconsistency a situation in which we change our minds about what we want simply because of the timing of the decision

People who are aware of their time-inconsistent preferences often seek out ways to remove temptation. If you eat too many potato chips at night, you can decide not to buy chips when at the store. If you waste too much time online, you can install a browser add-on such as Leechblock (for Firefox) or StayFocusd (for Chrome) and use it to define limits to the time you can spend on certain websites. Of course, these strategies are not foolproof. You could always make a nighttime dash to the store, or uninstall Leechblock or StayFocusd. But these actions at least put obstacles in the way of your weak-willed, present-oriented self. These are simple ways of making one's vices more expensive. By doing so, we're using the law of demand (as prices go up, quantity demanded goes down!) to coax ourselves into consuming less of our vices.

For an example of how an organization can benefit by exploiting the dynamic between future- and present-oriented selves, see the Economics in Action box "Give more tomorrow."

Give more tomorrow
Economics in Action

Do you ever intend to do something good, such as volunteering or donating money, but you keep putting it off? You're not alone. Charities know that even the best-intentioned supporters can be forgetful about sending a check. That's why so many charities encourage people to sign up for monthly contributions, which will be deducted automatically from their credit cards or bank accounts.

We can view charitable giving as another example of time inconsistency. Your future-oriented self wants to give regularly to charity, but your present-oriented self never gets around to doing so. Signing up to make monthly contributions is a winning strategy for your future-oriented self; it turns that force of inertia into an advantage. It's not surprising that, on average, monthly donors give more to charity than irregular donors.

A recent collaboration between Swedish economist Anna Breman and the charity Diakonia has taken this idea one step further. Charities, of course, would like their existing monthly contributors to give more. Would it make a difference if they were asked to increase their contribution *in the future?* Breman and Diakonia conducted an experiment to find out. They split about a thousand monthly contributors into two groups. Those in the first group were asked to consider increasing their monthly donation, starting right away. Those in the second group were asked the same thing, except that the increase would take effect in two months.

The result? The second group increased their donations by one-third more than the first group. That's a big difference for a charity that relies on funding from individual donors. It seems that Diakonia's donors, like people who ask for a brownie today but an apple next week, are more willing to give more in two months' time than to give more now.

Of course, at any time, a donor's present-oriented self could cancel the increased monthly donation, but is usually too lazy to bother. The force of inertia is a powerful one: Monthly donors tend to keep giving at their promised level for an average of seven years. Rather than simply asking donors to give more, then, it seems that charities wanting to improve their fund-raising should consider asking them to give more tomorrow.

Source: Based on Anna Breman, "Give more tomorrow," *Journal of Public Economics* 95, no. 11 (2011), pp.1349–1357, http://econpapers.repec.org/article/eeepubeco/v_3a95_3ay_3a2011_3ai_3a11_3ap_3a1349-1357.htm.

commitment device
a mechanism that allows people to voluntarily restrict their choices in order to make it easier to stick to plans

The problem of competing selves can be alleviated using what is called a **commitment device**. A commitment device is a mechanism that allows people to voluntarily restrict their choices in order to make it easier to stick to plans. A classic example of a commitment device occurs in the ancient Greek epic poem *The Odyssey*. Odysseus and his crew know that their ship is about to pass through waters populated by sirens, sea nymphs whose beautiful magic song bewitches men, causing them to jump into the sea and descend to a watery grave. Odysseus wants to hear the sirens' song, but his future-oriented self is wise enough to know that he can't trust his present-oriented self to resist the sirens' call. So Odysseus commands his men to tie him to the mast before they enter the sirens' waters. He creates a commitment device that literally binds his present-oriented self to his decision to listen but not jump.

Odysseus committed to his plan to resist the sirens by having himself tied to the mast of his ship.
©sirylok/123RF

A more everyday example of a commitment device is an arbitrary deadline. In one experiment, a professor told his business-school class they would have three assignments due for the semester and that they could set their own due dates. Failure to meet the due dates would result in a lower grade. Although students would not have been penalized for choosing the last day of the semester as a deadline for all three assignments, most did not take this option. They recognized that their present-oriented selves would be likely to procrastinate, leave all the work to the last minute, and be unable to complete everything. Most chose to space the deadlines evenly throughout the semester. By committing themselves to meet these arbitrary deadlines, they gave themselves a powerful incentive not to spend the whole semester procrastinating.[1]

For another example of a commitment device, see the Economics in Action box "Take out a contract on yourself."

Take out a contract on yourself
Economics in Action

Maybe you want to get to the gym more often, or eat better, read more books, or any number of other possible goals. But we all know that it can be hard to turn intentions into actions. The basic problem is often internal conflict. Your "future-oriented self" thinks you should work out more or skip that piece of chocolate cake. But your "present-oriented self" says, "Well, maybe later." You, like Odysseus, need some way of binding yourself.

The website stickK.com (co-founded by one of the authors of this text) is one such way. Here's how it works: You define some measurable objective—say, that on December 1 you will weigh no more than a certain weight. Then, you sign a contract that includes incentives designed to help you keep your commitment. You can nominate a trusted friend to act as your referee—someone you can rely on to dole out tough love if you fall short, instead of letting you off the hook. As a way to increase the social shame or reward, you can name a friend who will be told if you succeed or fail. You can also define an amount of money you will forfeit if you fail to reach your goal—and you enter your credit-card number, so there's no backing out. Overall, contracts with financial stakes report success 74 percent of the time.

There's an extra twist for those who choose to put money at stake. You can nominate an organization you *hate* to get your money. If you miss your target, stickK.com takes your forfeited money from your credit card and gives it to your "anti-charity."

Giving up cigarettes and losing weight are two common personal goals, but stickK.com has also inspired some creative commitments:

- "Speak more slowly to foreigners in New York City."
- "No more dating losers." (The person's best friend was assigned to judge the definition of "loser.")

(continued)

- "Study less."
- "No cutting my hair for two months."

Two important principles you should follow in order to create the most successful commitments: Be specific and be realistic. Goals that are vague do not work as well as goals that provide some detail on what one is going to do. And goals that are unrealistic are easily forgotten, overlooked, or given up.

At the time of writing, more than 395,140 contracts have been written, putting $35 million on the line. As a result, people in Stickk contracts have completed a million work outs, smoked 24 million fewer cigarettes, and, hopefully, been more patient with lost tourists in New York City.

Source: www.stickK.com, www.entrepreneur.com/article/280775.

✓TEST YOURSELF

☐ How can procrastination be explained by time inconsistency? **[LO 8.1]**

☐ What is a commitment strategy, and how can it help someone overcome time inconsistency? **[LO 8.1]**

Thinking Irrationally about Costs

In Chapter 1, "Economics and Life," we talked about how people weigh the trade-off between costs and benefits to arrive at a decision:

- If the benefits of doing something are greater than the opportunity cost, we assume that rational people will choose to do it.
- If the benefits are smaller than the opportunity cost, they won't choose to do it.

In reality, it turns out that people don't always weigh costs and benefits rationally. In this section we'll look at two common mistakes people make in thinking about costs: failing to ignore sunk costs and undervaluing opportunity costs.

These mistakes result from examples of what psychologists call *cognitive biases*. These biases are systematic patterns in how we behave that lead to consistently erroneous decisions. Cognitive biases come up a lot in behavioral economics. If you find yourself falling into the traps described below, don't be too hard on yourself—it seems that human brains simply aren't built to find it easy to think rationally in certain situations.

The sunk-cost fallacy

LO 8.2 Explain why sunk costs should not be taken into account in deciding what to do next.

Have you ever sat through to the end of a terrible movie just because you didn't want to "waste" the cost of the ticket? The logic is tempting, but it's flawed. This is an example of what economists call the *sunk-cost fallacy*. A **sunk cost** is a cost that has already been incurred and can't be refunded or recovered—such as the cost of a ticket once you've begun watching the film. It makes no sense to consider sunk costs when weighing the trade-off between opportunity costs and benefits, but people do it all the time. Why? Because we find it hard to accept our losses.

sunk cost
a cost that has already been incurred and cannot be refunded or recovered

To see why it's a fallacy to consider sunk costs in your decisions, consider the following choice: Would you like to spend the next 90 minutes watching a terrible movie that's free of charge or doing something else? You'd probably want to do something else, right? Grab a coffee, hang out with a friend, maybe even pay to see a good movie. The option of watching a terrible movie, even if it's free, is not an attractive one. Yet when you have paid to see a movie that you quickly realize is terrible, this is the situation you face. The cost of the ticket is gone—you can't get it back.

Why, then, do many people in this situation stubbornly sit through the rest of the movie? Maybe they are factoring sunk costs into their calculations: "Well, I already spent money to see this movie, so I have to watch the whole thing." They have a sense that somehow the money they spent on the ticket will have been wasted *only if* they walk out. The alternative would be to make peace with the idea that the money is *already* wasted because they're not getting pleasure from watching the movie. So to avoid feeling regret about wasting money, they stick it out. (Why not feel regret for wasting time, though? We'll come back to that question a bit later.)

A similar cognitive bias explains our chapter-opening example. Many people apparently consider that the cost of the lost ticket will be wasted *only if*

Once you've begun watching the film, the money you spent on the ticket is a sunk cost, whether you like the movie or not.
©*image100/Alamy*

they buy a replacement ticket. The rational approach is to accept that the cost of the lost ticket is wasted already and ignore it in the considerations. Doing that, the only question then is whether the *future* costs ($20 for a ticket) will outweigh the *future* benefits (the enjoyment of the concert). This trade-off is exactly the same whether you lost the ticket or a $20 bill.

Another common example of the sunk-cost fallacy is making multiple expensive repairs to a failing old car. You spend $1,000 repairing your car. The very next month it breaks down again, and the mechanic says it needs another $2,000 worth of repairs. It seems likely to keep on needing more and more repairs, totaling much more than its resale value. If you considered only *future* costs against *future* benefits, you would decide to get rid of the old car and buy another one. But many people feel that getting rid of the old car would be "wasting" the $1,000 they spent on it last month.

The sunk-cost fallacy doesn't apply only to money. Have you ever stayed in a bad relationship because you felt it would be a shame to "waste" the time and effort you'd put into it already?

Undervaluing opportunity costs

Remember that choosing one opportunity means choosing *not* to take advantage of another opportunity. Everything has an opportunity cost. Sometimes the trade-off is clear. If you are choosing between two similarly priced dishes on a restaurant menu, the opportunity cost of ordering one dish is obvious: It's the enjoyment you would have gotten from eating the other dish instead.

In many other cases, however, the trade-off is less clear. Often the benefit part of a trade-off is obvious because it is right in front of you—say, if you are trying on a $100 jacket in a store. But the opportunity cost is much harder to visualize: What else might you spend $100 on? It may be that if you thought very hard about how else you might spend that $100, you would come up with an alternative you prefer. But such alternatives can seem abstract and distant, while the jacket is concrete and immediate. As a result, you may overvalue the benefit you would get from the jacket and undervalue its opportunity cost.

People are especially prone to undervaluing opportunity costs when they are nonmonetary, such as time. In sitting through a terrible movie all the way to the end, people fall prey to the sunk-cost fallacy and also fail to recognize the opportunity cost of their time. They mistakenly put value on a nonretrievable monetary cost (the price of the ticket); they also fail to consider the value of their *nonmonetary opportunity cost* (time). Staying to the end of a bad movie means you will lose any utility you could have gained by doing something else instead.

The *implicit cost of ownership* is another nonmonetary opportunity cost that is often overlooked. The term refers to a cognitive bias, documented by behavioral economists, that leads people to value things more once they possess them. Everything you own has an opportunity cost because you could always choose to sell it. We don't tend to think in this way about the things we own.

LO 8.3 Identify the types of opportunity cost that people often undervalue, and recognize why undervaluing them distorts decision making.

But by continuing to own an item, you incur an opportunity cost equal to what someone would be willing to pay you for it.

For example, say you have a bicycle that you no longer use, and you could get $200 for it on Craigslist. If you didn't own the bicycle, you certainly wouldn't pay $200 to buy it. So why continue to own it? You are effectively "paying" $200 to keep the bike. If you thought clearly about the opportunity cost, you would sell it.

As another example, suppose you win in a raffle courtside tickets to a basketball game, and you could sell them for $400. You may well choose to use the tickets yourself, even though you would never have considered paying anything like $400 for them if you hadn't won the raffle. It's easy to remember that you are paying when money leaves your wallet. It's harder to remember that not adding money to your wallet is essentially the same thing.

Even seasoned investors often overlook the implicit cost of ownership, as they stubbornly hold onto badly performing stocks that they would never consider buying if they didn't already own them.

✓ TEST YOURSELF

☐ What is a sunk cost? Why is it *not* part of the opportunity cost of a decision? **[LO 8.2]**
☐ What is the implicit cost of ownership? **[LO 8.3]**

Forgetting about Fungibility

LO 8.4 Explain why fungibility matters in financial decision making.

fungible
easily exchangeable or substitutable

If something is **fungible**, it is easily exchangeable or substitutable. Many commonly traded commodities are fungible. Any given ton of copper can be exchanged for a different ton of copper, or a barrel of oil for another barrel of oil.

The cleanest example of a fungible object is money. A dollar is a dollar is a dollar, whether you received it as a gift, found it on the floor, or earned it by working. A dollar is also a dollar whether it's a dollar bill in your wallet, 20 nickels in a pot of loose change, or a number on the screen when you check your bank balance online. It all has the same value. Money is fungible.

This sounds like stating the obvious, but it isn't. Behavioral economists have found that people often do not behave as if money is fungible, and this leads to some odd and irrational decisions.

Creating mental categories for money

People often divide up their savings into categories, giving names to the different categories. Some people even physically label money by putting it into envelopes or jars that say "rent" or "groceries." Other people keep separate funds for special purposes, such as a vacation fund, a birthday present fund, or a rainy-day fund. Keeping separate funds helps people remember their savings goals, remain disciplined in saving toward those goals, and measure their progress toward the goals.

Consider the vacation example: You label a jar (or preferably a bank account, which is safer) "vacation money." The money you put in this fund could just as easily be spent on a whim. But if you spend that money regularly, you will likely never have the savings you need for that vacation. Putting the money in the vacation fund may help you "forget" all about it when you are looking for last-minute fun money. And even if you do remember you have money in the vacation fund, you might feel bad taking some out to go out and party, and you don't want to let down your future self. In this way, separating money into mental categories may help you organize your expenditures and stick to your plan.

However, in other cases, mentally labeling money as belonging to one category or another can be costly. Consider a college student who has amassed $1,000 in savings by working a weekend job. The student's friends are all planning a spring break trip, with a budget of $1,000. Perfect—the student "labels" the $1,000 savings as "spring break fund" and swears not to touch it. But a few months before spring break, the student, who also has a credit card, needs a bit of cash for books and school supplies. This student has a choice:

- Dip into the savings account and lose the little bit of interest the savings would earn.
- Borrow by paying for the books and supplies with the credit card. If the amount owed on the credit card isn't paid off at the end of the month, the student will pay interest on the outstanding balance.

Given this choice, many people would refuse to spend their savings and would instead borrow by using the credit card. But the credit-card debt almost certainly bears a higher interest rate than the savings account earns. The decision to hold on to savings rather than pay down debt is one that makes people poorer in the long run. The lesson is this: Sometimes having a mental label on savings helps us reach our goals, but sometimes it can be costly. Remember to think carefully about trade-offs and fungibility when making such decisions.

At least one credit-card company makes a point of enabling customers to mentally categorize debt, which may or may not be a good thing; see the What Do You Think? box "Credit-card categories: More realistic or more confusing?"

Credit-card categories: More realistic or more confusing?
What Do You Think?

In 2009, Chase Bank introduced a new credit-card product called Blueprint, designed with the help of an economist who specializes in behavioral finance. Blueprint helps customers categorize their credit-card bills so they can choose which categories to pay off right away and which to carry over. They can then create payment plans for the expenses they choose not to pay off immediately.

A series of television commercials supporting Blueprint's launch showed people choosing to pay off regular expenses such as groceries, gas, and rent, while creating special payment plans for one-time expenses such as an engagement ring. The ads appeal to a common intuition: Many people don't mind paying interest on big-ticket items but feel uncomfortable about getting into debt to cover their everyday living expenses.

The insight behind Chase's Blueprint product is to work with the way many people really think about money. The product aims to help customers put order into their finances—in the same way that it can be helpful to set aside cash for "rent" in its own envelope.

Looked at a different way, however, the product works by downplaying the fact that money is fungible. The fungibility of money means that the categories people create are meaningless in financial terms. Economic logic tells us that if you have a $500 credit-card bill and choose to pay only $300, the interest due on the remaining $200 will be identical, no matter whether you tell yourself you're paying off your monthly grocery bill or part of an engagement ring.

The risk with such products is that they nurture unclear thinking about finance by promoting a false distinction between categories of debt. Customers may be tempted to think that paying later is more acceptable for big-ticket purchases. With that mind-set, they may run up more credit-card debt on items that they could be better off saving up for instead.

WHAT DO YOU THINK?

1. Should banks design products around the way that people actually view their finances, even if the outcomes might seem irrational to outsiders?
2. Should banks design products that push customers to make choices consistent with rational economic decision making?
3. Overall, would you expect customers who use a product like Blueprint to end up with more or less debt?

Source: www.chaseblueprint.com.

People place money into categories in many different ways. Above we discussed categorizing by different spending purposes, but people also sometimes put money into mental categories depending on how they received the money. This can be helpful for organizing finances, if linked to spending. But this can also lead people to take risks they wouldn't otherwise take. For example, behavioral economists have observed that people who have recently won some money are more likely to spend it recklessly. In a casino, for example, you may hear a gambler who has just won a bet say that he is "playing with the house's money"; he may take bigger risks with that money than he would have done with the money he came in with. This is an irrational distinction: Once he had won, the money was no longer "the house's," but his own.

Irrational behavior has also been documented in investment-fund managers who are entrusted with investing people's savings. They, too, seem prone to making a false mental distinction between amounts they started out with and amounts they have just gained in the market. As a result, they make more reckless investment decisions when they have recently made a profitable trade.

For a final example of a way in which people make irrational decisions by forgetting that money is fungible, read the Econ and YOU box "Is a dollar a dollar?"

Is a dollar a dollar?
Econ and YOU

Is having a $50 bill in your pocket different from holding a stack of 50 $1 bills? In principle, it shouldn't make a difference. It's all just money. Is spending $50 in cash any different from spending $50 on a credit card? Again, apart from the fact that you can pay credit card bills over time, it shouldn't matter whether you pay with plastic or cash.

In reality, however, people often make very different purchasing decisions depending on the method of payment. Recognizing that fact can help you make more deliberate choices.

In one experiment, for example, researchers gave people $20 in cash. Some got a single $20 bill, some got 20 $1 bills, and others got various other combinations. People who received larger bills were less likely to spend the money when given a chance, compared with those who received smaller bills. People thought harder about spending when a purchase meant breaking a large bill.

In a different study, economists showed that students were willing to pay much more for the same good when using a credit card than when using cash. Two professors asked business students to bid for tickets to a sold-out basketball game between the Boston Celtics and the Miami Heat. Having first checked that students had easy access to an ATM, the professors randomly instructed half the participating students to pay in cash if they won the bidding, and the other half to pay with a credit card. Students told to pay by card bid more than twice as much, on average, as those who expected to pay in cash—$60.64 versus $28.51. The professors argued that the finding can't be fully explained by the fact that credit cards allow you to borrow and pay later.

These findings back up real-world observations that people who pay with a credit card spend more on a variety of things, including tips at restaurants. For many, spending money using a credit card seems less real than physically handing over cold, hard cash. This feeling makes the costs of buying something less significant, while the benefits are quite real (the item you are buying)—which for some leads to overspending. Reality sets in when the credit card bill arrives.

These studies point toward two strategies when you want to cut back on your spending:

1. If you have a credit card, think twice before using it instead of cash.
2. To avoid frivolous spending, carry large bills rather than lots of small ones.

Sources: Priya Raghubir and Joydeep Srivasta, "The denomination effect," *Journal of Consumer Research* 36, no. 4 (December 2009), pp. 701–713; Drazen Prelec and Duncan Simester, "Always leave home without it: A further investigation of the credit-card effect on willingness to pay," *Marketing Letters* 12, no. 1 (February 2001), pp. 5–12.

✓ TEST YOURSELF

- ☐ Why is money considered fungible? **[LO 8.4]**
- ☐ How can forgetting about money's fungibility lead to poor financial decisions? **[LO 8.4]**

Conclusion

We can go a long way in economics by assuming that people act rationally to maximize their utility. Real people, though, make economic decisions in complicated, unexpected, and sometimes nonoptimal ways. Behavioral economics shows us that, in practice, we need a broader understanding of "maximizing utility" in order to build models that predict many of the quirky things people do. Understanding these human tendencies can help us to avoid common decision-making pitfalls. It can also help us to design products and policies that allow people to make better choices.

Although the behaviors explored in this chapter can be viewed as biases or mistakes, they are the sort of mistakes that can be corrected. We've also discussed some strategies designed to help people reach their intended goals and make better choices. In a later chapter (Chapter 23, "Public Policy and Choice Architecture") we'll return to some of these issues as we think about business ideas and public policies that help people make good choices and stick to their goals.

Key Terms

behavioral economics, p. 190

time inconsistency, p. 191

commitment device, p. 192

sunk cost, p. 194

fungible, p. 196

Summary

LO 8.1 Explain how time inconsistency accounts for procrastination and other problems with self-control.

Time inconsistency occurs when we change our minds about what we want simply because of the timing of the decision. That often means wanting something now that is inconsistent with what you want for yourself in the future. Time inconsistency helps to explain behaviors like procrastination and giving in to temptation. People who are time inconsistent experience an internal battle between two selves: a "future-oriented self," who might have worthy goals such as being productive and eating healthily, and a "present-oriented self," who may be prone to slacking off and backsliding. Ideas such as *commitment devices* can help us understand and manage this battle.

LO 8.2 Explain why sunk costs should not be taken into account in deciding what to do next.

Economists usually assume that people will do something if and only if the benefits of doing it are greater than the opportunity cost. But people have an irrational tendency to place value on *sunk costs*—costs that have already been incurred, and cannot be refunded or recovered. People would make better decisions if they did not consider sunk costs, instead weighing only those costs that are still to come.

LO 8.3 Identify the types of opportunity cost that people often undervalue, and recognize why undervaluing them distorts decision making.

People frequently undervalue abstract or *nonmonetary* opportunity costs, such as the value of the time they spend on an activity or the implicit cost of owning an item. Economically, turning down an opportunity to sell an item that you already own is equivalent to buying that item at the offered price.

LO 8.4 Explain why fungibility matters in financial decision making.

A good is considered *fungible* if it is easily exchangeable or substitutable. The foremost example of a fungible good is money. Even though money is fungible, this is often not reflected in people's behavior. Instead, they may put it into various mental categories. Although this approach can help people to save money or stick to a budget, it can also lead to poor financial decisions, as when people don't use their low-interest savings to pay down high-interest debts.

Review Questions

1. Describe a situation from your own experience in which you are time inconsistent. What have you done (or might you do) to accomplish the goals of your future-oriented self? [LO 8.1]

2. You have a friend who is always resolving to improve his grades but who never seems to find time to study. Explain to him how time inconsistency might be affecting his choices and suggest some steps he might take to meet his goal. [LO 8.1]

3. You've already paid to get into an all-you-can-eat buffet and have enjoyed several plates of food. You're not really hungry anymore but feel you ought to eat more to get the full value from the buffet. Does this inclination make sense? Explain why or why not. [LO 8.2]

4. Alda is willing to pay $2,000 to visit her favorite cousin over spring break. A month ago, she booked a trip costing $1,200. Spring break has arrived, but Alda needs one day to finish an important paper before she goes. Alda could cancel her trip and get a refund of $800. Or she could pay an additional $1,000 (on top of the $1,200 she already paid) to rebook the trip for two days later. Explain what Alda should do. [LO 8.2]

5. Suppose your art history professor has a small personal art collection, including some works by a famous artist. She bought this artist's paintings at a modest price, before he became well known. One of the paintings is now worth $2 million. When you ask the professor whether she would buy it now for $2 million, she says she wouldn't. Is the professor's decision making consistent? Why or why not? [LO 8.3]

6. Isaiah received a gift certificate that covers three salsa dance lessons. After the first lesson, Isaiah decided that he doesn't like salsa, yet he still plans to go to the next lesson because it doesn't cost him anything. Evaluate Isaiah's logic. [LO 8.3]

7. You have a friend who runs up a balance on his credit card by buying new furniture to replace the furniture he has. The interest rate on the balance is 18 percent per month. The furniture store offers a layaway plan with monthly payments equivalent to an interest rate of 10 percent per month. Explain to your friend how he could manage his finances more sensibly. [LO 8.4]

8. Dora and Vicki are bartenders. Dora prefers her tips in cash because she can have the money right away. Credit-card tips don't get paid to bar staff until the payments are processed, which can take a few days. Vicki still prefers for her customers to put her tip on their credit card. Why might Vicki have this preference? [LO 8.4]

Problems and Applications

1. In which of the following cases is time inconsistency likely to be at work? [LO 8.1]

   a. A child plans to become a doctor when she grows up, but a month later reads a book about park rangers and decides to become a park ranger instead.

   b. A student keeps intending to finish reading *War and Peace*—next week.

   c. A parent plans to enroll his child in art class but enrolls her in dance class instead.

   d. A beginning piano player plans to practice three times a week but frequently practices only once a week.

2. You would like to save more money. Which of the following strategies will help you overcome time inconsistency? [LO 8.1]

   a. Deciding how much you need to save.

   b. Setting up a savings account.

   c. Putting reminders in your calendar to make deposits.

   d. Enrolling in an automatic-transfer program that will move a specified amount of money from your checking account to your savings account each month.

3. You're seated at a banquet that is beginning to become boring. Which of the following pieces of information are relevant to your decision to stay or go somewhere else? [LO 8.2]

   a. Another party is happening at the same time, and you've heard that it's fun.

   b. The dinner you were served was only so-so.

   c. You haven't eaten dessert yet, and it looks delicious.

   d. You paid $30 to attend the banquet.

   e. The other party you could attend has a cover charge of $10.

4. You just spent $40 on a new movie for your collection. You would have preferred the director's cut but discovered when you got home that you bought the theatrical version. The store you bought the movie from has an "all sales final" policy, but you could resell the movie online for $25. The director's cut sells for $50. By how much would you need to value the director's cut over the theatrical version for it to make sense for you to sell the version you bought and buy the director's cut? [LO 8.2]

5. Suppose you're bowling with friends. You've already played one game and are trying to decide whether to

play another. Each game costs $7 per person, plus a one-time rental fee of $5 for the bowling shoes. It would take another hour to play the next game, which would make you late to work. Missing an hour of work would mean that you would lose pay at a rate of $12 per hour. Based on this information, how much would you have to enjoy the next bowling game, expressed in terms of dollars, to play another game? **[LO 8.3]**

6. During a holiday party at work, you pay $5 to buy a raffle ticket for a 128-gigabyte iPad. You win the drawing. Based on a little research online, you discover that the going rate for a hardly used 128-gigabyte iPad is $300. **[LO 8.3]**

  a. What was the opportunity cost of acquiring the iPad?

  b. What is the opportunity cost of choosing to keep the iPad?

7. You are saving for a trip to Europe. You have an existing savings account that earns 2 percent interest and has a current balance of $4,200. You don't want to use your current savings for the vacation, so you decide to borrow the $1,500 you need for travel expenses. You will repay the loan in exactly one year. The annual interest rate is 5 percent. **[LO 8.4]**

  a. If you were to withdraw the $1,500 from your savings account to finance the trip, how much interest would you forgo?

  b. If you borrow the $1,500, how much will you pay in interest?

  c. How much does the trip cost you if you borrow rather than dip into your savings?

8. Suppose you have accumulated a credit card balance of $800, at an annual interest rate of 10 percent. You are also planning to open a new savings account that accumulates interest at an annual rate of 1 percent. You just got your paycheck and have $300 that you can use either to pay down your debt or open your savings account. **[LO 8.4]**

  a. If you use the full $300 to pay down your debt, what will your credit card balance be in one year? Assume no additional credit card payments during this time.

  b. If, instead, you put the full $300 into your savings account, what will be the balance in your savings account in one year, assuming you make no additional deposits during this time? What will your credit card balance be, assuming you make no additional payments during this time because your payment requirements have been deferred for one year?

  c. In one year, how much money will you have lost if you deposit the $300 in your savings account compared to paying down your credit card?

Endnote

1. http://duke.edu/~dandan/Papers/PI/deadlines.pdf.

Game Theory and Strategic Thinking

Litterbugs Beware

Litter is an eyesore, whether it's a candy bar wrapper on the sidewalk or a plastic bag caught on a fence along the highway. Most people would prefer clean streets, parks, and oceans over messy ones. So why is there litter?

Imagine it's a sunny day and you've had lunch at a table outside. You're just finishing up when the wind blows your sandwich wrapper to the ground. You could chase it, but the wind is blowing the paper even farther away. You're in a hurry, and it's unlikely that you will get caught and punished for not putting the wrapper in a trash can. Besides, there's other trash around; your wrapper is not going to make much difference to the overall environment. So, with a bit of guilt, you walk away.

©Andrew Yahin/Shutterstock

The trouble is that once others see your trash blowing about, they're more likely to decide to litter as well. That can then lead to even more litter. The result is an increasingly dirty, trash-strewn community.

That's the paradox. Everyone would like to have a clean environment, but incentives sometimes push us to make things just a little bit worse. Over time, with *everyone* making things just a little bit worse, the outcome adds up to being a lot worse. Once everyone is littering, you'll litter more too. It's not the best outcome, but somehow that's how things unwind. The problem escalates because it's impossible to get everyone to agree, voluntarily, to not litter.

How can the problem be fixed? One idea is to create strong norms against littering. One way to do that is to encourage families, schools, churches, and other civic organizations to reinforce the shared sense that it's good to keep communities clean. The now-iconic "Don't Mess With Texas" slogan was originally created at the request of the Texas Department of Transportation to try to create social norms against roadside litter.

LEARNING OBJECTIVES

LO 9.1   Understand strategic behavior, and describe the components of a strategic game.

LO 9.2   Explain why noncooperation is always the outcome in the prisoners' dilemma.

LO 9.3   Identify whether or not a player has a dominant strategy in a one-time game.

LO 9.4   Identify whether or not a Nash equilibrium will be reached in a one-time game.

LO 9.5   Explain how a commitment strategy can be used to achieve cooperation in a one-time game.

LO 9.6   Explain how repeated play can enable cooperation.

LO 9.7   Explain how backward induction can be used to make decisions.

LO 9.8   Use a decision tree to solve a sequential game.

LO 9.9   Define first-mover advantage, and identify it in practice.

LO 9.10 Explain why patient players have more bargaining power in repeated games.

LO 9.11 Explain how a commitment strategy can allow players to achieve their goals by limiting their options.

The government of Singapore in Southeast Asia took a different route; it used a strong dose of economic incentives. It chose to stop the problem before it started. If you're caught in Singapore tossing trash anywhere but in the trash can, it will cost you $1,400. In addition to the fine, the Singaporean authorities usually impose what is called a "corrective work order." This order forces you to collect trash outside in bright green vests under the full scrutiny of public humiliation. If you try to dump something a little bigger—say, by tossing a full garbage bag from your car—you face up to $35,000 in fines or a year in jail, plus the loss of your vehicle.

With these harsh punishments, it's not surprising that Singapore is generally cleaner than large cities in the United States. In New York City, for example, the fine for littering ranges from $50 to $250, which doesn't have quite the same sting as the fine in Singapore! New York City also often makes it costly (in time and effort) to be clean—you sometimes have to walk for blocks to find a trash can.

By making littering expensive, Singapore left its citizens with little choice but to put their trash in the can, solving the littering problem. Singapore's policy is tough, but authorities argue that the high fines help citizens obtain the clean outcome that they want. That outcome had been impossible to achieve because of a collective failure to voluntarily quit littering. What's more, in the end, the authorities rarely have to enforce the fines. With effective incentives in place, few people end up littering.

While Singapore has found a way to reduce litter, many other places have problems with trash that simply cannot be solved through heavy fines and rules. When trash moves across borders or floats open in the sea, it is hard to create workable international solutions. Deep within state or national parks and wilderness areas, it's hard to catch litterers. But as the Singapore example shows, taking people's motivations and incentives seriously is a helpful way to start piecing together responses.

In this chapter, we'll see that the littering problem is an example of the *prisoners' dilemma*—a game of strategy in which people make rational choices that lead to a less-than-ideal result for all. It might seem to trivialize choices to think of them as a "game," but economists use the term *game* in a broader sense than its everyday use: To economists, *games* are not just recreational pursuits like chess, *Monopoly*, or poker; instead, games are situations in which players pursue strategies designed to achieve their goals. As we'll see in this chapter, these kind of games pop up in all kinds of real-world situations, ranging from environmental protection to business to war.

LO 9.1 Understand strategic behavior, and describe the components of a strategic game.

Games and Strategic Behavior

Economists use the word **game** to refer to any situation involving at least two people that requires those involved to think strategically. The study of how people behave strategically under different circumstances is called **game theory**.

We have seen that people behave rationally when they look at the trade-offs they face and pursue their goals in the most effective way possible. When the trade-offs you face are determined by the choices someone else will make, behaving rationally involves **behaving strategically**. Behaving strategically means acting to achieve a goal by anticipating the interplay between your own and others' decisions. When your outcomes depend on another's choices, asking *How will others respond?* is the key to good decision making. (Remember, this is one of the four key questions economists consider, introduced in Chapter 1, "Economics and Life.")

Rules, strategies, and payoffs

All games share three features: rules, strategies, and payoffs. *Rules* define the actions that are allowed in a game. In chess, for example, each type of piece is allowed to move only in certain directions. In real life, people's behavior is constrained by laws both legislated and natural. For example, when two businesses are competing, the structure of costs each firm faces can be seen as a rule. In presidential elections, rules include the workings of the electoral college and the system of majority voting. In environmental games, the laws of nature could be seen as the rules that constrain and guide the decisions we humans make.

Strategies are the plans of action that players follow to achieve their goals. In the game *Monopoly*, you might decide to buy as many cheap properties as possible, to build hotels on Boardwalk and Park Place, or to become a railroads and utilities magnate. All these strategies are different approaches to the same goal: earning lots of fake money while bankrupting other players. When two businesses are competing, strategies might include producing a certain quantity of a good. One strategy in an election campaign is to use hopeful language and images to try to inspire people to vote for a certain candidate.

Payoffs are the rewards that come from particular actions. They can be monetary or nonmonetary in nature. The salary for a certain job or the profits that come from making good business decisions are monetary payoffs. In chess, the nonmonetary payoff is winning. In an election campaign, the most important payoff is usually being elected.

✓ **TEST YOURSELF**

☐ What is a strategy? **[LO 9.1]**

One-Time Games and the Prisoners' Dilemma

The name *prisoners' dilemma* comes from a situation you could imagine in an episode of *Law and Order* or other police shows: You and an accomplice have been arrested on suspicion of committing both a serious crime and a more minor one. The police hold you in separate cells. A policeman candidly explains to you that he lacks the evidence to convict either of you of the serious crime, but he does have evidence to convict you both of the minor crime. He wants to get at least one conviction for the major crime, so he offers you a deal: If you confess that you both did it, and your accomplice *doesn't* confess, you'll get let off with 1 year in prison, while your accomplice gets the maximum 20-year term for committing the major crime.

Prisoners' dilemma

The classic **prisoners' dilemma** is a game of strategy in which two people make rational choices that lead to a less-than-ideal result for both. The same ideas can be applied to situations with more than two people and also to organizations rather than individuals.

What if you confess and your accomplice *also* confesses? The policeman no longer needs your evidence to get a conviction, so the 1-year deal is off. Still, he tells you you'll get some time off the maximum sentence as a reward for cooperating—you'll both get 10 years.

---

game
a situation involving at least two people that requires those involved to think strategically

game theory
the study of how people behave strategically under different circumstances

behaving strategically
acting to achieve a goal by anticipating the interplay between your own and others' decisions

LO 9.2 Explain why noncooperation is always the outcome in the prisoners' dilemma.

prisoners' dilemma
a game of strategy in which two people make rational choices that lead to a less-than-ideal result for both

And what if neither of you confesses? The policeman sighs: Then you'll both be convicted of the minor crime only, and you'll both serve 2 years. A thought occurs to you—is the policeman offering the same deal to your accomplice? "Of course," he confirms with a smirk.

You think to yourself, "If my accomplice confesses, then I'll get 10 years if I confess and 20 years if I don't. But if my accomplice *doesn't* confess, I'll get 1 year if I confess and 2 years if I don't. Therefore, whatever my accomplice does, I'll be better off if I confess." Although you were partners in crime, you soon realize that your accomplice will be using the same logic. This means you will both confess, and you will both get 10 years. If only you and your accomplice could somehow agree to cooperate by both staying quiet, then you could avoid this outcome and each get away with serving only 2 years.

Figure 9-1 summarizes this predicament in the form of a *decision matrix*. Reading horizontally across the top row, we see that if your accomplice confesses, your choice (shown in green) is between your third-preference outcome (10 years in prison) and your fourth choice (20 years). Reading the bottom row shows that if your opponent doesn't confess, your choice is between your first-choice outcome (1 year in prison) and your second choice (2 years).

What about your accomplice? Reading vertically down the columns reveals the same set of choices for your opponent. The incentives each of you faces mean that you will both confess and end up in the top-left box, both getting your third-choice outcome. If you could have cooperated with each other, you could have ended up in the bottom-right box, both getting your second-choice outcome.

Let's see how this thinking is mirrored in a presidential election campaign between two candidates, one for Party A and the other for Party B. If you were running the Party A campaign, your thought process might have gone something like this: "If the Party B candidate goes negative, we would have to attack her back or we'd look weak. But what if she doesn't go negative? If we attack her and she doesn't attack us back, we'd destroy her chances of winning the election. So, whatever the Party B candidate does, we're better off going negative." Whoever is running the Party B campaign will be thinking the same thing. The result: Both campaigns go negative, both candidates' reputations suffer, and voters feel more and more disillusioned with the political process.

FIGURE 9-1

The prisoners' dilemma

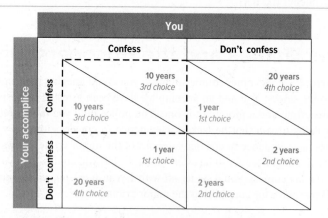

You will always choose to confess in a prisoners' dilemma because you prefer a 10-year sentence to 20 years (if your accomplice confesses) and a 1-year sentence to 2 years (if your accomplice doesn't confess). Your accomplice makes the same calculation. Both of you have a dominant strategy to confess, so you will both end up in jail for 10 years—whereas you could have both received only 2 years if you could somehow have agreed to cooperate.

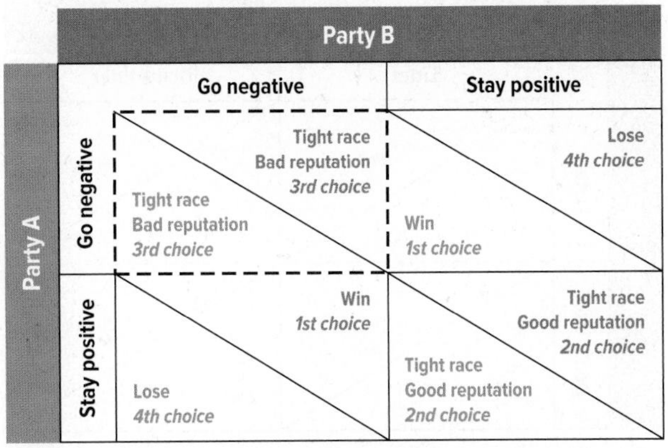

FIGURE 9-2

The prisoners' dilemma in a presidential campaign

Party B will choose to go negative because if Party A goes negative, Party B would rather keep the race tight (even if it means damaging his reputation) than lose in a landslide; if Party A stays positive, Party B would rather win in a landslide (even if it means damaging his reputation) than face a tight race. Party A makes the same calculation. As a result, both candidates will end up in a negative tight race, when they'd both have preferred a positive tight race instead.

We can analyze this situation in a decision matrix (see Figure 9-2). First we have to define the payoffs. Above all, each candidate would rather win easily than face a tight race—winning easily is their top preference. And each would rather face a tight race than lose heavily—losing heavily is their last choice. In each case, dirty campaigning is a price worth paying.

But if given the choice between a tight race in which both go negative and damage their reputations (the top-left quadrant) and a tight race in which both stay positive and enhance their reputations (the bottom-right quadrant), both candidates would prefer the positive tight race.

Just as in the original prisoners' dilemma, both candidates will look at their options and realize that whatever the other one does, they're better off going negative. As a result, they both end up with their third-choice outcome when they might both have had their second-choice outcome instead—if only they'd been able to cooperate.

The littering "game" described at the beginning of this chapter can also be shown in a decision matrix. To do so, we've assigned points to the various outcomes in order to show their pros and cons—but the exact numbers are not what's important. Instead, what matters is their relative size and whether the points are positive, negative, or zero. The people making decisions in this example—you and your neighbor—want to earn the most points they can (or lose as few points as possible). (You can think of "your neighbor" as representing all other people in the community who might litter.)

Figure 9-3 shows the payoffs in the decision you and your neighbor face when deciding if you should let your trash blow away. As you can see, littering results in the larger payoff, regardless of whether your neighbor litters or not. Again, the result is the third-choice outcome, even though potential litterers might have obtained their second-choice outcome instead—if you and your neighbor had been able to cooperate.

Finding the dominant strategy

In the original prisoners' dilemma, whatever your accomplice does, you're better off confessing. When a strategy is the best one to follow *no matter what strategy other players choose*, it is called a **dominant strategy**. Going negative is a dominant strategy for both candidates in an election campaign (and, as result, neither candidate looks good).

LO 9.3 Identify whether or not a player has a dominant strategy in a one-time game.

dominant strategy a strategy that is the best one for a player to follow no matter what strategy other players choose

FIGURE 9-3
Payoffs for littering

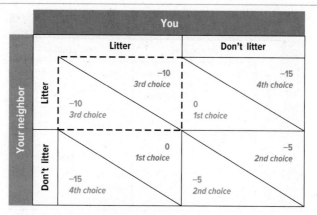

To represent the decision to litter or not, we assign points to the various outcomes (or "payoffs") of the choices that you and your neighbor make about littering. If we look at your choice to litter or not to litter, we can see that in any given situation, you'd prefer to litter—you would rather save yourself the walk to the trash can, no matter if there's litter already on the ground or not. Your neighbor faces the same trade-off; consequently, you both litter. Note that if you both had decided not to litter, you would've been better off because you would enjoy cleaner streets.

Of course, not all games feature a dominant strategy for each player. Take the familiar children's game rock-paper-scissors (Figure 9-4). As you probably know, rock beats scissors, scissors beat paper, and paper beats rock. Because both players move at the same time, predicting your opponent's choice is tough. Reading across the rows or down the columns of the decision matrix shows that there is no single strategy that will work best for you, regardless of what your opponent plays.

LO 9.4 Identify whether or not a Nash equilibrium will be reached in a one-time game.

Reaching equilibrium

Remember the concept of equilibrium from the chapters on supply and demand: The equilibrium price and quantity are reached in a market when no individual buyer has an incentive to pay more and no individual seller has an incentive to accept less, given what all the other buyers and sellers are doing.

FIGURE 9-4
A game with no dominant strategy

		Player B		
		Rock	Paper	Scissors
Player A	Rock	Tie	B wins	A wins
	Paper	A wins	Tie	B wins
	Scissors	B wins	A wins	Tie

Player B's best choice depends on what Player A plans to do. Since it's a simultaneous move, however, neither can know what the other will choose. There is no one strategy that is best every time, so there is no dominant strategy.

The concept of equilibrium is often used in game theory: In particular, a special type of equilibrium called a **Nash equilibrium** is reached when all players choose the best strategy they can, *given the choices of all other players.* In other words, this is a point in a game when no player has an incentive to change his or her strategy, given what the other players are doing. This equilibrium can also be described as the *situation of no-regrets*—that is, on discovering the decisions made by other players, you have no reason to regret your own decision. The concept is named after the famous game theorist John Nash.

In a game such as rock-paper-scissors, there is no Nash equilibrium. Let's say you play with a friend. If the friend plays scissors and you play rock, then you have no incentive to change (rock beats scissors), but the friend would have an incentive to change to paper (paper beats rock). If the friend changes to paper, though, that would give you an incentive to change to scissors (scissors beat paper). And so on. There is no stable outcome where neither of you would wish to change your strategy once you find out what the other player is doing.

In the prisoners' dilemma, there *is* a stable outcome: You both confess. If your accomplice confesses, you have no incentive to switch from confessing to not confessing. And if you are confessing, your accomplice has no incentive to switch from confessing to not confessing. Thus, there is an equilibrium where both you and your accomplice confess.

As we can see from the prisoners' dilemma, an equilibrium outcome to a game is not necessarily a good one for the participants. This negative–negative outcome is called a *noncooperative equilibrium* because the participants act independently, pursuing only their individual interests.

Some games have a stable positive–positive outcome even though everyone's acting in his or her own self-interest. Consider the "game" of driving: Suppose you are one of only two motorists on an island and you both are driving toward each other. If you decide to drive on the right and the other person drives on her left, you have a head-on collision (the least-preferred payoff for you both). This is not an equilibrium; your decision gives the other driver an incentive to drive on the right instead. When you both drive on the right, you avoid accidents (your most-preferred payoff), and neither of you has an incentive to change. Driving on the right is thus a positive–positive outcome.

Figure 9-5 shows the payoffs from this driving game. As you may have noticed from this example, games can have more than one equilibrium outcome. If both drivers drive on the right, then each receives a payoff of 5. Neither player has an incentive to change his or her strategy because doing so would result in a lower payoff. However, both of you driving on the left would also be an equilibrium. (Indeed, this is the equilibrium outcome to the driving game that has been reached by motorists in some countries outside the United States, such as the UK, Japan, and Australia.)

This example also tells us a game doesn't need to have a dominant strategy to reach an equilibrium outcome: Neither driving on the right nor driving on the left is a dominant strategy—the best decision depends on what other players do. (And to make perfectly clear: In life, driving is *not* a game.)

Staying in the correct lane is in the driver's self-interest and produces a positive-positive outcome if other drivers do the same.
©DaveAlan/Getty Images

Nash equilibrium
an equilibrium reached when all players choose the best strategy they can, given the choices of all other players. It is a situation wherein, given the consequences, the player has no regrets about his or her decision.

Avoiding competition through commitment

In our discussion of the prisoners' dilemma, we have repeatedly stressed that the players of the game would be better off if they could cooperate. So why don't they? It's not simply because they are being held in separate cells and can't talk to each other. (Opposing candidates can always pick

LO 9.5 Explain how a commitment strategy can be used to achieve cooperation in a one-time game.

FIGURE 9-5

Payoffs in a driving game

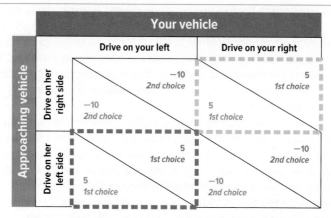

If you drive on the right side of the road and the approaching driver drives on the side to her left, you will crash. Similarly, if you choose the left side and she chooses the right, you will crash. But if you both choose to drive on the side to your right, or if you both choose to drive on the left, you avoid a crash. Neither right or left is a dominant strategy for either driver, but the game can still result in an equilibrium. In fact, there are two equilibria: one in which both drivers choose right and one in which both drivers choose left.

up the phone and agree that they both will run a positive campaign.) Nor is the problem simply one of trust: You could make a deal beforehand with your accomplice that neither of you will confess.

The problem runs much deeper: Even if you are completely sure that your accomplice can be trusted not to confess, *you* should still confess. Remember that whatever your accomplice does, you are better off confessing—that's why it's a dominant strategy. In prisoners' dilemma–type games, prearranged agreements to cooperate are tough to make work because *both* players have a strong incentive to defect.

One solution to this problem is to reduce the players' payoffs by creating a punishment for defecting. For this strategy to work, the punishment must be so bad that it outweighs the incentive not to cooperate. Is that possible? That depends on the circumstances of a particular game. In the classic prisoners' dilemma, imagine that you and your accomplice are members of an organized criminal gang in which all agree that any member who testifies against another member will be killed in retribution. This dramatically changes the payoff for confessing: a shorter prison sentence, but with the expectation of being killed at the end of it. With those options, "Don't confess" starts to look like a much more attractive option.

commitment strategy
an agreement to submit to a penalty in the future for defecting from a given strategy

Agreements like this are an example of a **commitment strategy**, in which players agree to submit to a penalty in the future if they defect from a given strategy. Changing the payoffs by agreeing to future penalties can allow players to reach a mutually beneficial equilibrium that would otherwise be difficult to maintain.

What about our example of negative election campaigns? Sadly, commitment strategies are hard to make work. Rival politicians do often make high-profile public agreements to run a clean campaign. The idea is that if one of them then goes negative, voters will be angry about the broken promise to stay positive. For this strategy to work, however, voters would have to be so angry that it would outweigh the electoral advantage of going negative. Given how many of these agreements are made and then broken, this doesn't usually appear to be the case.

Promoting competition in the public interest

Reaching a positive–positive outcome through a commitment strategy can benefit everyone. In the election game, for example, the public would benefit if politicians could somehow stay positive.

Voters would avoid the unpleasantness that comes with a negative campaign, and both voter turnout and public interest in politics might climb.

In some variations of the prisoners' dilemma game, however, *preventing* players from cooperating serves the public interest. The commitment strategy we imagined for the classic prisoners' dilemma is not so far from real-world reality: The famous code of *omertà*, which prohibits anyone in the community from ever talking with authorities, makes it difficult for prosecutors to persuade *mafiosi* to confess and testify against their mafia bosses. That's why the witness protection program was created: It attempts to increase the payoff for confessing by providing police protection before, during, and after a trial (and sometimes an entirely new identity). It nudges the players back toward an outcome in which they can pursue their self-interest.

Consider a more everyday example, from the world of business: Suppose that a town has only two gas stations, Conoco and Exxon. Each could choose to charge high prices or low prices. This gives us four possible outcomes and payoffs, visualized in the decision matrix in Figure 9-6:

- If both stations charge low prices, they both make low profits.
- If both stations charge high prices, they both make high profits.
- If Exxon charges high prices and Conoco charges low prices, everyone in town buys gas from Conoco. The Conoco station makes very high profits, and the Exxon station loses money.
- If Exxon charges low prices and Conoco charges high prices, the opposite occurs: Everyone buys gas from Exxon, which makes very high profits, while Conoco gets no customers and loses money.

By now the analysis should be familiar: This game is another application of the prisoners' dilemma, with a dominant strategy of charging low prices. Both gas stations will do so, though they would be better off if they could agree to keep prices high. This noncooperative equilibrium—both charging low prices—is bad news for the game's players, the two gas stations. But it is good news for the town's consumers, who pay lower prices for their gas.

We can expect the two gas station owners to try to think of a way they could cooperate, reaching an equilibrium in which they both make high profits. (In the next section, we'll see one way

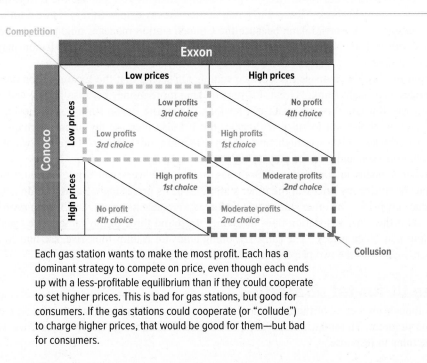

FIGURE 9-6

The prisoners' dilemma in competition between two firms

Each gas station wants to make the most profit. Each has a dominant strategy to compete on price, even though each ends up with a less-profitable equilibrium than if they could cooperate to set higher prices. This is bad for gas stations, but good for consumers. If the gas stations could cooperate (or "collude") to charge higher prices, that would be good for them—but bad for consumers.

this could happen.) But the town's consumers will want to prevent this outcome from happening because it will leave them with no choice but to pay high prices for their gas. We even have a more negative word for cooperation in this business context: *collusion*. We use a more positive word to describe the noncooperative equilibrium: *competition*.

In later chapters we will see that collusion is, in fact, a common problem: Firms often try to find ways to collude so that they all charge higher prices. Governments—working on behalf of consumers—try to find ways to stop businesses from colluding. In the language of game theory, outlawing collusion changes the rules of the price-competition game.

✓ TEST YOURSELF

- ☐ Consider the prisoners' dilemma game. If one prisoner knows for sure that the other won't confess, what should he do? Why? **[LO 9.2]**
- ☐ How do you identify whether a strategy is dominant or not? **[LO 9.3]**
- ☐ What is the distinctive characteristic of the Nash equilibrium? **[LO 9.4]**
- ☐ How can a commitment strategy help two parties in a game cooperate instead of choosing their dominant strategies? **[LO 9.5]**

Repeated Play in the Prisoners' Dilemma

LO 9.6 Explain how repeated play can enable cooperation.

So far, we have been modeling the prisoners' dilemma game as involving a one-time simultaneous decision. In the classic version of the game, with two criminal accomplices facing the prospect of a 20-year prison sentence, this is accurate—it really is a one-time decision. But in our example of a presidential campaign, that's not the case: Decisions to run positive or negative ads are not simply made once, at the start of the campaign; they are reviewed on a daily basis. Gas station owners decide on their prices on a day-to-day, or even hour-to-hour, basis. Economists call a game that is played more than once a **repeated game**.

repeated game
a game that is played more than once

Strategies and incentives often work quite differently when games are repeated. In particular, players no longer need commitment strategies to reach a mutually beneficial equilibrium. To see why, let's go back to our town with two gas stations. Imagine you manage the Exxon station. One morning you might think, "Today I'm going to increase my prices. Sure, I'll lose a little money at first, but it's a risk worth taking because the Conoco station manager might see the opportunity for us both to benefit in the longer run." In round one of the game, then, Exxon plays a "high prices" strategy.

Now imagine you manage the Conoco station. On seeing that the Exxon station has increased its prices, you might think, "Great, I'll start making more money because people will come here to buy gas. But hold on—that can't last for long. When the Exxon station starts losing money, it will have no choice but to cut prices again. But if I also increase my prices, perhaps the Exxon manager will keep his prices high, and we can *both* make more profits." In round two of the game, then, both Exxon and Conoco play a "high prices" strategy.

What happens in round three? Both gas station managers will think, "I could make more money by cutting my prices—if the other station keeps its prices high. But it wouldn't, would it? If I reduce my prices, the other station will be forced to reduce its prices. So I'll keep my prices high, and see if the other gas station does the same." In round three of the game, once again both gas stations play "high prices." The same reasoning holds for rounds four, five, six, and so on. Prices remain high, with the two players maintaining cooperation.

The tit-for-tat strategy

tit-for-tat
a strategy in which a player in a repeated game takes the same action that his or her opponent did in the preceding round

The thought processes of the Exxon and Conoco managers are an example of a type of strategy called **tit-for-tat**. Tit-for-tat is a straightforward idea: Whatever the other player does, you do the same thing in response.

It turns out that variants of tit-for-tat are very effective in repeated play of prisoners' dilemma–type games. If the other player makes a cooperative move (in the gas station example, setting high prices), then you respond with a cooperative move (also raising your prices). If the other player defects with a noncooperative move (cutting prices), you respond with a noncooperative move (also cutting prices). Two players who are both playing tit-for-tat can quickly find their way toward lasting cooperation.

Note that there is no need to enter into public commitment strategies or explicit agreements for players in a repeated-play game to achieve cooperation. For example, prices of gas in our two-station town could remain high indefinitely through nothing more than the rational game-playing of the two players. Indeed, explicit agreements to keep prices high would be illegal (collusion), and public commitments to keep prices high would not go down well with consumers. So instead, companies sometimes find subtle ways to reassure their competitors that they are committed to a tit-for-tat strategy, thereby reducing the risk that the competitor will threaten the equilibrium by lowering prices. See the Economics in Action box "What do price-matching guarantees guarantee?" to read about one common arrangement.

What do price-matching guarantees guarantee?
Economics in Action

Some companies advertise that if you can find a lower price anywhere else, they will match it. The implication is that they are confident they have the lowest prices in town. However, the real game going on here may be more subtle, and not necessarily a good one for customers. In fact, game theory suggests that price-matching guarantees guarantee higher, not lower, prices.

As of the writing of this text, the competing home-improvement giants Home Depot and Lowes had nearly identical price-matching policies. The two stores promised not only to match a competitor's advertised price, but to beat it by 10 percent. Paradoxically, these guarantees meant that neither firm had an incentive to lower prices. In fact, price-matching policies send a clear and public signal that firms are committed to a tit-for-tat strategy.

Imagine, for example, that both firms are offering the same lawnmower for $300. What happens if Lowes decides to cut the price to $250? Home Depot's price-matching offer means that customers can get the lawnmower at Home Depot for $25 less (the $250 price, less an extra 10 percent), or $225. As a result, Lowes has little to gain by lowering prices. The same logic applies to Home Depot.

We don't know of an economic study of prices at Home Depot and Lowes relative to their costs. But the example gives us insight into a surprising outcome that can happen with price-matching policies: Game theory shows us that guaranteeing a *lower price* does not necessarily guarantee *low prices*. Because explicitly cooperating to fix prices is illegal, a firm's best option is to engage in a tit-for-tat strategy. By creating and publicizing a legally binding price-match policy, the firm creates a credible threat that it will follow a tit-for-tat strategy. As a result, prices can stay high, benefiting both firms at the customers' expense.

Tit-for-tat is an extremely powerful idea. Why doesn't it also ensure that political campaigns are clean, with each campaign repeatedly rewarding the other for running only positive ads by running only positive ads itself? There are a couple of reasons:

- One is that unlike selling gas, election campaigns do not go on indefinitely—as election day draws closer, the game becomes more like a one-off game, increasing the incentive to defect.
- Another reason is that the players in the election game are primarily concerned with doing better *relative* to the other player (getting more votes than the opponent). Gas stations, in contrast, are more interested in their *absolute* payoffs (making as much profit as possible).

Even though tit-for-tat may not work in every situation, it represents an incredibly effective tool for dealing with many situations. In fact, a professor of political science, Robert Axelrod, held a tournament in which dozens of computer programs based on different strategies were run against each other. His aim was to find which strategy gave the largest payoff in a repeated prisoners' dilemma game. Out of 14 competing strategies, the most successful entry, submitted by mathematician Anatol Rapoport, was tit-for-tat.

The Econ and YOU box "Can game theory explain why you feel guilt?" describes the theory that many human emotions evolved from the tit-for-tat games played by our ancient ancestors.

Can game theory explain why you feel guilt?
Econ and YOU

Do you ever wonder where your emotions come from? Why do we feel emotions such as sympathy, gratitude, vengeance, guilt, and forgiveness? Economics is sometimes seen as a study of heartless rationalism (we disagree, but understand why it might feel like that sometimes). Some researchers, though, believe that emotions are essential to reaching efficient outcomes—certainly a topic that interests economists. Evolutionary biologists such as Robert Trivers, who developed the theory of *reciprocal altruism,* speculate that we evolved these emotions to help us achieve cooperation by playing the tit-for-tat strategy in "games" that helped our ancestors to survive.

Imagine that you are a hunter-gatherer in a prehistoric society. One day you are successful, bringing back more food than you can eat, while your neighbor returns with nothing. You could be cooperative (sharing food with your neighbor) or noncooperative (gorging on all the food yourself). The next day, perhaps your neighbor has success and you don't, and she has to make the same decision. In a situation like this, both you and your neighbor will do better if you can sustain cooperation (sharing food and both eating well every day) rather than being noncooperative (alternately starving and gorging).

What is required to achieve sustained cooperation? First, you need to feel *sympathetic* enough to give your unlucky and hungry neighbor some food. Then your neighbor needs to feel *gratitude,* prompting her to repay your favor and give you food the next day. If your neighbor one day defects with a noncooperative move, refusing to share her food with you, you need an emotion such as *vengeance* to prompt you to punish her by not sharing your food with her the next day. And if your neighbor subsequently feels *guilty* and shares with you the day after, you need an emotion such as *forgiveness* to get you back into the mutual sharing routine.

Of course, nobody knows for sure why humans have the capacity to experience the emotions that we do. But it is interesting that so many of our emotions are just what is required to successfully balance self-interest and cooperation.

Source: Robert Trivers, "The evolution of reciprocal altruism," *The Quarterly Review of Biology* 46, no. 1 (March 1971), pp. 35–57.

✓ TEST YOURSELF

☐ How does a tit-for-tat strategy help players to achieve cooperation? **[LO 9.6]**

Sequential Games

So far, we've analyzed games in which players make decisions simultaneously. In games like the prisoners' dilemma and rock-paper-scissors, each player decides which strategy to adopt before knowing what the other player will do. In many real-world situations, however, one person or company has to make a decision before the other. These are called *sequential games* because the players move sequentially rather than simultaneously.

Think forward, work backward

In sequential games, an especially important part of strategic behavior is to "think forward, work backward":

LO 9.7 Explain how backward induction can be used to make decisions.

- First you have to *think forward:* What are all the possible outcomes of the situation you are considering? Which of them do you prefer?
- Then you have to *work backward:* What choice would you need to make to achieve your preferred outcome?

This process of analyzing a problem in reverse—starting with the last choice, then the second-to-last choice, and so on, to determine the optimal strategy—is called **backward induction**. It's probably something you do naturally all the time without even realizing it.

backward induction the process of analyzing a problem in reverse, starting with the last choice, then the second-to-last choice, and so on, to determine the optimal strategy

To take a simple example, suppose you're trying to choose your courses for next semester. There are so many options—what should you do?

- First, think forward: Let's say you aspire to become a Pulitzer Prize–winning journalist.
- Now work backward: What do you need to do to win the Pulitzer? You need to get a job at a top newspaper. How do you get a job at a top newspaper? You need a graduate degree in journalism. How do you get into a graduate course in journalism? You need an undergraduate degree majoring in English or Communications. This requires that you take prerequisite courses in nonfiction writing. Therefore, you should take introductory nonfiction writing this semester.

This line of reasoning is an example of backward induction: Start with the outcome you want, then work backward in time to determine each choice you must make to achieve that outcome.

Deterring market entry: A sequential game

Backward induction can be an especially useful process in sequential games, when your aspirations are affected by decisions other players will make in response to a decision of your own. This is especially true in business; many firms have to make strategic decisions in sequential "games" including whether to open a new store or factory, whether to develop a new product.

LO 9.8 Use a decision tree to solve a sequential game.

Let's look at entry into a market for an example. Imagine that McDonald's Corporation is considering opening a restaurant in a small town that currently has no fast-food outlet. Also imagine that McDonald's will consider only locations where it expects to get at least a 10 percent rate of return on the investment because the company knows it could get 10 percent by investing the money elsewhere instead.

The company is trying to decide whether to buy land in two possible locations: It could buy in the center of town, where real estate is expensive but access for customers is more convenient. Or it could buy on the outskirts of town, where land is cheaper, but customers will have to drive out of their way to get there.

The company's calculations (which are hypothetical in this example) show that a new McDonald's on the outskirts of town will generate a 20 percent return. A new McDonald's at the central location will generate a 15 percent return. If the company stopped its analysis at this point, it would build on the outskirts.

Thinking strategically, however, McDonald's will take into account the possibility that Burger King could also be considering moving into the same town. McDonald's calculations show that the locations of the restaurants matter if there are two competing fast-food restaurants:

- If there is a fast-food restaurant at the central location, most customers won't bother driving to the restaurant on the outskirts. The restaurant in the center of town will do much better, earning a 12 percent rate of return, whereas the one on the outskirts will earn only a 2 percent rate of return.

- If there are two restaurants competing on the outskirts, each will earn an 8 percent rate of return.
- If there are two restaurants competing at the central location, each will earn a 4 percent rate of return.

What should McDonald's do, given the uncertainty about whether Burger King will enter the market?

- If McDonald's builds on the outskirts, it can expect Burger King to open in the central location, attracted by a 12 percent return. This would reduce McDonald's rate of return to only 2 percent.
- But if McDonald's builds in the central location, it can confidently predict that Burger King will not enter the market at all. With a McDonald's already existing in the central location, Burger King would receive a return of only 4 percent if it also built in the central location, or 2 percent if it built on the outskirts. It's likely that Burger King would rather invest its money for a 10 percent return elsewhere and not build at all.

We can analyze the decision McDonald's is facing using a chart called a *decision tree*, shown in Figure 9-7. Since McDonald's is ready to make a decision about entering this market, it has the first move in this game. The first decision node (on the left side of the figure) shows its choice to build on the outskirts or in the center of town. Whichever choice McDonald's makes, Burger King can then decide whether to build on the outskirts, in the center, or not at all—a decision represented at the second level of the tree (the two boxes in the center).

FIGURE 9-7

Decision tree for market entry

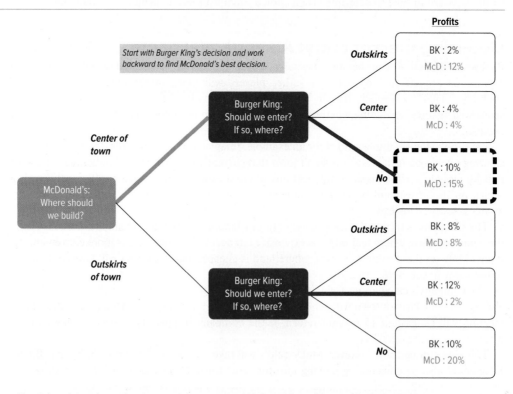

The right column shows the six potential outcomes of McDonald's and Burger King's decisions. Starting with Burger King's choices, we can narrow these six potential outcomes to two by identifying Burger King's preferred choice in each circumstance. These are the two possible outcomes that McDonald's will face, depending on what choice it makes in the first stage of the game. Then we can identify which of these outcomes McDonald's prefers.

We can use backward induction to determine the best course of action for McDonald's. First we consider Burger King's decision: Starting on the right side of the tree, we can see that Burger King will build in the center if McDonald's builds on the outskirts. (See the heavy line pointing to the "Center" option.) But if McDonald's builds in the center, Burger King will not enter the market at all.

So, the decision tree reveals that McDonald's is not facing a choice between a 15 percent return in the central location or a 20 percent return on the outskirts, as we might first have thought. Instead, the choice is between a 15 percent return in the central location or a 2 percent return on the outskirts. Even though building in the center isn't the best choice for McDonald's in the absence of competition, it *is* the best *strategic* decision because it deters competitors from entering the market.

Using strategic thinking and backward induction can even win you $1 million—if you're a contestant on the television show *Survivor*. To see how, read the What Do You Think? box "Surviving with strategic thinking."

Surviving with strategic thinking
What Do You Think?

The first season of the successful reality television show *Survivor* provides a great example of strategic thinking in a sequential game. In the final episode, three contestants remain, but only one will win $1 million. There are two rounds to pass before winning: a challenge and a vote. In the challenge, the three contestants compete to see who can stand on a stump in the water the longest. Whoever wins the challenge automatically proceeds to the next round. Also, that person gets to choose which of the two remaining contestants proceeds (and thus which one gets eliminated). The two contestants who move on to the next round are subjected to a vote by the last nine ousted contestants. Whoever wins the vote wins the $1 million.

In the first season, the remaining three contestants were Richard, Rudy, and Kelly. Rudy was quite popular among the other contestants. Kelly and Richard both knew that if Rudy made it to the final two, he would likely win. However, Richard and Rudy had previously made an agreement to protect each other. Richard knew that if he (Richard) won the challenge, he would face a tough decision:

- If he chose Kelly to go with him to the final stage, he would be breaking his pact with Rudy, which would certainly cost him Rudy's vote.
- If he chose Rudy to go with him to the final stage, he would almost definitely lose due to Rudy's popularity with the voting contestants.

However, Richard knew that if Kelly won the challenge, she would very likely choose to bring Richard with her to the final stage. Kelly would prefer to compete for votes against Richard since Rudy was so popular. Richard also knew that if Rudy won, he would likely bring Richard, keeping their pact—although Rudy would most certainly win the vote. One extra fact is helpful here: Kelly had already won a string of endurance challenges. All bets were on Kelly to beat Rudy in yet another endurance challenge.

So what did Richard do? He used backward induction and jumped off the wood stump before the other two fell. He purposefully lost the challenge because it was his best strategy to win round two. And it worked: Kelly beat Rudy and chose to go to the final stage with Richard. Because the pact hadn't (technically) been broken, Richard retained Rudy's vote and won the $1 million by a 5-4 vote.

WHAT DO YOU THINK?

1. What would you have done in this situation if you were Kelly?
2. What would you have done if you were Rudy?
3. Did either Kelly or Rudy also have a good reason to jump off early?

First-mover advantage in sequential games

LO 9.9 Define first-mover advantage, and identify it in practice.

first-mover advantage benefit enjoyed by the player who chooses first and, as a result, gets a higher payoff than those who follow

In the market-entry game, first-mover McDonald's ends up with a 15 percent return, while late-comer Burger King is forced to invest elsewhere at a 10 percent return. If Burger King had gotten to town first, it could have put itself in McDonald's situation, building in the center of town and deterring McDonald's from entering the market. In this game, whoever gets to town first gets a higher return; the company that arrives second settles for less. This is a game with a **first-mover advantage**, in which the player who chooses first gets a higher payoff than those who follow.

First-mover advantage can be extremely important in one-round sequential games. Consider a bargaining game in which a company is negotiating with its employees' labor union over wages. Effectively, the two parties are bargaining over the division of the *surplus* created by their decision to trade wages for labor. (Remember that in this context *surplus* refers to the benefits people get from transactions.) Let's say this negotiation is a one-round sequential game: If the company is the first mover, it could offer just 1 percent of the surplus, and the union would have to make a choice. The union could accept the offer, or reject it by going on strike and shutting down production. That second option leaves both the company and the union with zero surplus. Calculating that 1 percent is better than nothing, the union would begrudgingly accept the company's offer. The decision tree in Figure 9-8 represents this calculation.

However, if the *union* had the first move, it could demand 99 percent of the surplus. It could assume that the company would rather pay that amount than risk its employees going on strike (during which the company would make no money at all). This is an example of what economists call an *ultimatum game:* One player makes an offer and the other player has the simple choice of whether to accept or reject.

Of course, this is not a realistic representation of how union bargaining usually works. There are often multiple rounds of offers and counteroffers. As we will see in the next section, the ability to make counteroffers—that is, to turn a one-round game into a multiround game—dramatically changes things.

Repeated sequential games

LO 9.10 Explain why patient players have more bargaining power in repeated games.

We've seen that repeated play changes the nature of a simultaneous game such as the prisoners' dilemma by allowing cooperation to be sustained. Repeated play can also change the outcome in *sequential* games by reducing the first-mover advantage.

The ability to make counteroffers transforms bargaining from a game in which first-mover advantage trumps everything to a game in which patience is the winning strategy. Why? In almost all cases, the value of a given sum in the future is less than the value of that same sum now. Bargaining takes time; for every round of bargaining that takes place before the players reach agreement, the value of the surplus they are splitting goes down. In wage negotiations between a

---

FIGURE 9-8

Decision tree for the ultimatum game

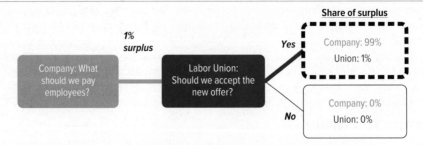

This decision tree shows the straightforward outcome when there is a very strong first-mover advantage, as seen in the ultimatum game. The company makes a "take it or leave it" offer, and the union will always accept an offer that is greater than zero. The 1% of surplus it gains may be low, but receiving nothing would be even worse.

company and a labor union, we can think of this reduction in value as the productive time that is lost while negotiations take place. In these situations, the more-patient player—the one who places more value on money in the future relative to money in the present—has an advantage. The player who is willing to hold out longer has more bargaining power, and so receives a better payoff.

In the real world most wage negotiations don't drag on for years (although some do). If each player knows how patient the other is, the two sides don't need to play all the rounds. Instead, the company can simply offer the split that *would eventually occur* if the two sides played all the rounds. In that case, the surplus will be divided in proportion to each player's patience.

Commitment in sequential games

Recall that in a commitment strategy, players agree to submit to a penalty in the future if they defect from a given strategy. In simultaneous games such as the prisoners' dilemma, making a credible commitment can change the payoffs and influence the strategy of the other players. We will see that the same is true in sequential games. Consider an example from military strategy, in which a general used a commitment strategy to improve his chances of victory—paradoxically, by limiting his own options.

In the early sixteenth century, the Spanish conquistador Hernán Cortés arrived on the coast of Mexico intending to claim the land for the king of Spain. The land was held by the powerful Aztec empire, a formidable fighting force. Figure 9-9 shows a decision tree for this game. Each opponent can choose to advance or retreat, and the Aztecs—deciding how to respond to Cortés's arrival—get the first move:

- If the Aztecs retreat, they know that Cortés will advance and take their land.
- If the Aztecs advance, then Cortés will have two choices: retreat and survive, or advance and fight to the death.

No matter how brave and committed Cortés claims his soldiers to be, the Aztecs expect that if the Spanish soldiers are faced with the prospect of a fight to the death, they would rather retreat to the safety of their boats. So the Aztecs will decide to advance. If both players behave rationally, the result of this game will be that Cortés retreats.

Anticipating the Aztecs' calculations, Cortés makes a drastic move, though: He burns his own ships, cutting off any possibility of retreat by fearful soldiers. Figure 9-10 shows how this bold

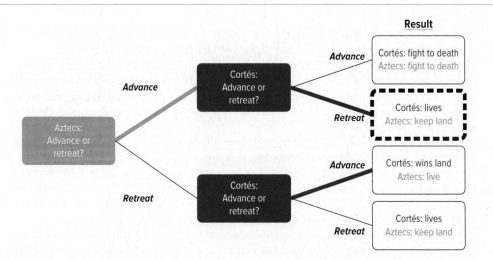

The Aztecs know that if they retreat, Cortés will advance and take their land. But if they advance, they can guess that Cortés will rather retreat and keep his troops alive. Knowing this, the Aztecs will advance to protect their land, expecting Cortés to retreat.

FIGURE 9-10

Decision tree with burning boats

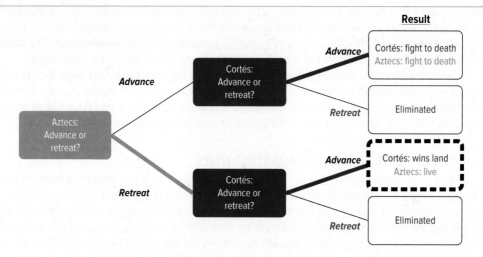

By burning his boats, Cortés removes the possibility of retreat. The Aztecs know that whatever they do, the Spanish troops have no option but to advance. Given this knowledge, the Aztecs prefer to retreat and cede their land to Cortés rather than fight to the death.

move changes the decision tree. Under the new scenario, the Aztecs now know that if they attack, Cortés will have no choice but to fight to the death. The Aztecs decide *they* would prefer to retreat and live rather than to advance and risk death.

By committing to reduce his options, Cortés forces a change in his opponents' strategy. That commitment results in a payoff that would otherwise be out of reach for Cortés. This famous historical example of a commitment strategy is sometimes referred to as "burning your boats." For other applications of commitment strategies, see the Economics in Action box "Totally MAD."

Totally MAD
Economics in Action

From the end of World War II until the fall of the Soviet Union in 1991, the United States and the Soviet Union were locked in the Cold War, a protracted struggle over which nation was the preeminent power in the world. Starting in the 1950s both sides had amassed enough weapons to completely destroy the other side many times over. Thus, any attack with a nuclear weapon would end up being mutual suicide, like a head-on car crash on a global scale. Military and political strategists believed that this tit-for-tat strategy, called *mutually assured destruction* (MAD), would prevent a full-blown conflict.

However, in September 1983, tensions between the Soviet Union and the United States reached new heights. Soviet fighter pilots had shot down Korean Air Flight 007 after mistaking the plane for an American spy mission. On September 26, 1983, the Soviet Early Warning System detected one inbound missile, followed by four more. The Soviet On-Duty Commander Stanislav Petrov had clear orders: If the system detected weapons coming from the United States, he was supposed to inform his superiors, who would likely launch a retaliatory attack.

However, Petrov had another option. He could disobey orders and wait to report the attack until he was sure the reports were true. But Petrov knew that doing so could be costly—every minute he waited put the Soviets at a larger strategic disadvantage if there was going to be a full nuclear war.

Under this intense pressure, Petrov weighed his options. The more he thought about it, the more the reports didn't make sense. First, he was told that the United States would launch an all-out attack if they moved first. It didn't make sense to send only five weapons. Doing so would allow the Soviet Union to respond with a much larger retaliatory attack, as simple game theory models tell us. Second, the message had passed through 30 levels of verification far too quickly. Finally, the reports of nuclear weapons were not verified by ground radar, which would have been required to launch a full-on nuclear attack.

A short time later, Petrov learned that his intuition was correct—the Soviet Early Warning System had malfunctioned. Although he is referred to as "the man who single-handedly saved the world," Petrov described his role simply: "I had a funny feeling in my gut. I didn't want to make a mistake. I made a decision, and that was it." Thankfully, Petrov's gut, together with a sound understanding of game theory, kept the world from going totally MAD.

Source: David Hoffman, "I had a funny feeling in my gut," *Washington Post Foreign Service,* February 10, 1999, www.washingtonpost.com/wp-srv/inatl/longterm/coldwar/shatter021099b.htm.

✓ TEST YOURSELF

- ☐ How can backward induction help you decide what courses to take next semester? **[LO 9.7]**
- ☐ Why does the possibility of Burger King's entry into the same town change McDonald's strategy? **[LO 9.8]**
- ☐ Why would Burger King have been better off if it had been the first chain to build a restaurant in the town? **[LO 9.9]**
- ☐ How can reducing your choices lead to a better outcome in a sequential game? **[LO 9.10]**
- ☐ Why does repeated play dilute the first-mover advantage in a bargaining game? **[LO 9.11]**

Conclusion

This chapter introduced the concept of strategic games. Many real-life situations can be analyzed as if they were strategic games, with associated rules, strategies, and potential payoffs.

Game theory can explain the logic behind outcomes that might not seem intuitive at first. Sometimes, for example, both players in a simultaneous game may choose to behave in a way that makes both worse off. When games are played in turns rather than simultaneously, the first mover's decision can dictate the outcome of the entire game.

With repeated play, however, the first mover's advantage weakens. Players who can communicate with each other and agree on a strategy can often secure a better outcome than if they acted alone. Such agreements may break down if one side tries to get ahead by defecting.

Backward induction is another useful analytical tool; it allows you to break down your decisions and predict how they will affect others' decisions and shape the final payoff.

When trying to solve a real-life problem, whether societal, personal, or business, it helps to think through these strategic issues. Doing so can help you see how to "play" the game given the rules and constraints. It also can help you see how to *change* the rules and constraints, if possible, to help get to a better outcome.

Much of the analysis in this chapter involved one player guessing what the other will do and acting accordingly. In the next chapter, we'll see that knowing what one player is planning to do isn't always easy, and that a lack of information can have real economic consequences.

Key Terms

game, p. 205

game theory, p. 205

behaving strategically, p. 205

prisoners' dilemma, p. 205

dominant strategy, p. 207

Nash equilibrium, p. 209

commitment strategy, p. 210

repeated game, p. 212

tit-for-tat, p. 212

backward induction, p. 215

first-mover advantage, p. 218

Summary

LO 9.1 Understand strategic behavior, and describe the components of a strategic game.

If people make the necessary choices to achieve a goal by anticipating the interaction between their own and others' decisions, we say they are *behaving strategically.* Economists use the term *game* to describe a situation that requires those involved to think strategically. Games have *rules,* which define the actions players are allowed to take; *strategies,* or plans of action that players can follow to achieve a desired goal; and *payoffs,* the rewards that come from taking particular actions.

LO 9.2 Explain why noncooperation is always the outcome in the prisoners' dilemma.

The *prisoners' dilemma* is a situation in which two people can find cooperation difficult even when it is mutually beneficial. Each player has a choice to cooperate or not to cooperate. Each prefers mutual cooperation to mutual noncooperation, but noncooperation is the best choice because its payoff is higher no matter what strategy other players choose. In this game, pursuing your own self-interest leaves everyone worse off.

LO 9.3 Identify whether or not a player has a dominant strategy in a one-time game.

When a strategy is the best one to follow no matter what strategy other players choose, it is called a *dominant strategy.* However, not all games feature a dominant strategy; in some games there is no single strategy that will work best for you.

LO 9.4 Identify whether or not a Nash equilibrium will be reached in a one-time game.

When all players choose the best strategy they can, given the choices of all other players, those players have reached a *Nash equilibrium.* Players who have reached a Nash equilibrium have no reason to regret their own decision. This doesn't necessarily mean that an equilibrium outcome to a game is a good one; we can see both negative-negative and positive-positive outcomes in equilibrium. The only condition is that there is no incentive to switch from one decision to another.

LO 9.5 Explain how a commitment strategy can be used to achieve cooperation in a one-time game.

In the prisoners' dilemma, the players of the game would be better off if they could cooperate and make a deal beforehand not to confess. However, even if you know your accomplice will not confess, you are still better off confessing. To solve this problem, players may sometimes reach a mutually beneficial equilibrium by pursuing a *commitment strategy,* in which they agree to submit to a penalty if they defect from the equilibrium.

LO 9.6 Explain how repeated play can enable cooperation.

In a *repeated game,* players can penalize each other for defecting in one round by punishing each other in the next round. As a result, players can sometimes achieve a mutually beneficial equilibrium, even when they couldn't do so in a single game.

A common strategy in repeated games is *tit-for-tat,* in which a player takes the same action as his or her opponent in the previous round. Anyone who is playing against a person with a tit-for-tat strategy has a strong incentive to cooperate because defecting would push him or her into a less profitable equilibrium in every future round of the game.

LO 9.7 Explain how backward induction can be used to make decisions.

Backward induction is the process of analyzing a problem in reverse—starting with the last choice, then the second-to-last choice, and so on—in order to determine an optimal strategy. This problem-solving tool can be used to choose between options with different consequences down the road: You first choose the goal you are trying to reach and then determine the steps you must take to reach it.

LO 9.8 Use a decision tree to solve a sequential game.

In many situations, one person or company must make a decision before the other one. These situations can be represented as games in which players move sequentially rather than simultaneously. Because the payoff each achieves still depends on the other's decision, the player who moves first must anticipate the decision the next player will make in response. These decisions can be diagrammed as the nodes in a *decision tree,* which branch off into the choices or payoffs that follow from each option. Backward induction can be used to analyze decision trees and determine the best course of action at each stage of the game.

> **LO 9.9** Define first-mover advantage, and identify it in practice.

In a game with *first-mover advantage,* the player who moves first gets a higher payoff than those who follow. The ultimate example of a first-mover advantage is a one-round bargaining game in which the person who makes the first offer gets virtually everything. The ability to bargain over multiple rounds of offers and counteroffers dilutes the first-mover advantage.

> **LO 9.10** Explain why patient players have more bargaining power in repeated games.

The ability to make counteroffers transforms bargaining from a game in which first-mover advantage trumps everything into a game of patience. Because bargaining takes time, in every round of bargaining that takes place before the players reach agreement, the value of the payoff they are splitting goes down. Thus, the more-patient player (the one who places more value on money in the future relative to money in the present) has an advantage over the less-patient player. In the end, the surplus will be divided in proportion to the patience of each player.

> **LO 9.11** Explain how a commitment strategy can allow players to achieve their goals by limiting their options.

In a sequential game, limiting your own choices can change your opponent's behavior. For example, following a commitment strategy, such as cutting off the option for retreat, turns a noncredible threat into a credible one, changing the payoffs associated with an opponent's options.

Review Questions

1. Taking an exam can be considered a game. Describe a rule, a strategy, and payoff for this game. **[LO 9.1]**

2. Why is strategic behavior required to win a presidential election? Describe some of the rules, strategies, and payoffs that define this game in the real world. **[LO 9.1]**

3. Felix and Sam are roommates. They both want the dishes to be washed, but each would prefer that the other person do it. Use the decision matrix in Figure 9Q-1 to explain why Felix and Sam are likely to end up with a sink full of dirty dishes. Their preferences are ranked from 1 (lowest) to 4 (highest). **[LO 9.2]**

FIGURE 9Q-1

4. Two neighbors share a pond they have stocked with catfish. They have agreed upon the amount of fishing each can do in order for the stock of catfish to replenish itself. If one neighbor increases the amount he fishes a little bit, the catfish stock could still replenish itself. If both neighbors increase their fishing, the stock will not be sustainable. Both neighbors would like to cheat and increase the amount they fish but want the other neighbor to stick to the agreement. **[LO 9.2]**
   a. What is the noncooperative outcome, and why does it occur?
   b. What is the cooperative outcome, and how could the neighbors achieve this outcome?

5. You have been texting with your friends trying to make plans for this evening. Your best friend Jocelyn is not sure if she will finish her homework in time to come out, but if she does, she wants to go to a new restaurant on the north end of town that you've both been wanting to try. Another group of friends is going to a restaurant on the south end of town, but you've already been to this restaurant and it was only okay. No one is returning your calls, but you need to head into town if you want to do anything this evening. You have to decide whether to head north or south. Do you have a dominant strategy? Explain why or why not. **[LO 9.3]**

6. You have just played rock, paper, scissors with your friend. You chose scissors and he chose paper, so you won. Is this a Nash equilibrium? Explain why or why not. **[LO 9.4]**

7. Two firms each have the option of polluting during production or cleaning up their production process such

that they don't pollute. Of course, polluting is cheaper than not polluting. The payoffs for each of the choice combinations are shown in the decision matrix in Figure 9Q-2. The government would like to stop pollution by making it illegal and charging a fine if a firm is found polluting. How large does the fine need to be to keep a firm from polluting? **[LO 9.5]**

FIGURE 9Q-2

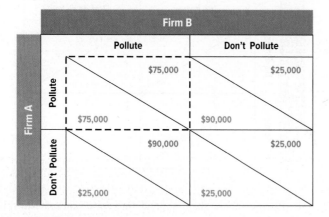

8. Explain how you could use a tit-for-tat strategy to motivate your roommate to do his share of the cleaning. **[LO 9.6]**

9. Toni and Kala are new coworkers. They make a plan to go out together every Thursday night. On their first Thursday night out, Toni buys a pitcher of beer and shares it with Kala. Kala is excited to discover that her Thursday night outings will include free beer as well as a way to have fun with her new coworker. Explain why Kala is likely to be disappointed. **[LO 9.6]**

10. Suppose your goal is to be promoted at your job. Use backward induction to determine what you should do to work toward that goal right now, and describe each step in your logic. **[LO 9.7]**

11. You are playing a game with a friend. It's your move, but you don't have a dominant strategy. Your payoff depends on what your friend does *after* your move. You consider flipping a coin to decide what to do. You are about to reach for a coin, but then you realize that your friend has a dominant strategy. Explain how using backward induction (rather than a coin toss) will now determine your next move. **[LO 9.7]**

12. Melissa let Jill cheat off her paper during a history exam last week. Now Melissa is threatening to tell on Jill unless Jill pays her $50. Use the decision tree in Figure 9Q-3 to explain whether Jill will pay Melissa to keep her quiet. **[LO 9.8]**

FIGURE 9Q-3

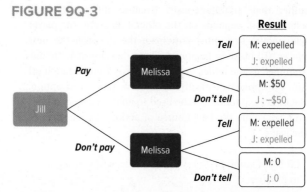

13. Nicolas has asked for a raise. His boss must decide whether to approve his request. If Nicolas doesn't get the raise, he will have to decide whether to stay at his job or quit. Construct a decision tree for these sequential decisions and choose a payoff structure where Nicolas has a dominant strategy to stay at his job even without getting the raise. **[LO 9.8]**

14. Job offers could be considered a one-round bargaining game with a first-mover advantage: The company offers you a job at a certain salary, and you can take it or leave it. Explain why the company might not capture all the surplus in this game, even if you can't make a counteroffer. **[LO 9.9]**

15. You like your job, but your boss gives lousy bonuses. You were recently offered a new job with better rewards, and your friend wants to know if you intend to take it. You say, "It depends on whether the bonus this year is generous. Let's wait and see. We'll find out next week." Explain why you are likely to be accepting the new job. How could you improve your strategy if you want to stay at your current job and be better rewarded? **[LO 9.9]**

16. Suppose you are moving out of the country and need to sell your car fast. Explain why you are likely to get lower offers from used-car dealers if they find out that you are moving away soon. **[LO 9.10]**

17. Hal is negotiating his salary for a job offer. Hal's potential employer moves first by making an offer. Hal knows he will accept the offer but asks for a couple of weeks to think it over. If the offer was acceptable to Hal, why did he do this? **[LO 9.10]**

18. Many warrior cultures have codes of conduct that make retreat from battle and other cowardly behaviors extremely dishonorable. Warriors are expected to die bravely in battle rather than surrender; if they do retreat, they face an enormous social stigma. Paradoxically, these codes could help warriors to win their battles. Explain. **[LO 9.11]**

19. A town's two gas stations are each considering lowering prices to attract more sales. How this affects the profits for each gas station depends on whether the other station also lowers prices. The decision matrix in Figure 9Q-4 shows the payoffs, depending on what each player decides to do.

FIGURE 9Q-4

		Gas Station B	
		Lower price	Higher price
Gas Station A	Lower price	$35,000 / $35,000	$65,000 / $125,000
	Higher price	$125,000 / $65,000	$95,000 / $95,000

Suppose both gas stations lower their prices, and they find themselves in the worst-case scenario in which both have also lowered their profits. Now suppose gas station A announces in an advertisement that it is committed to keeping the new low prices. Why would gas station A do this? What outcome would you expect? **[LO 9.11]**

Problems and Applications

1. Say whether each of the following is a rule, a strategy, or a payoff. **[LO 9.1]**
   a. In chess, when you capture your opponent's king, you win the game.
   b. In *Monopoly*, players frequently mortgage their existing properties to raise cash to buy new ones.
   c. In chess, the rook piece can move any number of spaces directly forward, backward, or to either side, but it cannot move diagonally.
   d. In rock-paper-scissors, you might always play rock.
2. You are going to an auction. Say whether each of the following is a rule, a strategy, or a payoff. **[LO 9.1]**
   a. Bids must increase in increments of $20.
   b. The highest bid wins the item being auctioned.
   c. You wait until the bidding is just about to close before you enter a bid.
   d. The money raised from the auction goes to charity.
3. Two families are trying to decide whether to donate to a fund to build a public park. The payoffs are shown in Figure 9P-1. **[LO 9.2]**

FIGURE 9P-1

		Family B	
		Donate	Don't Donate
Family A	Donate	$50 / $50	$75 / $10
	Don't Donate	$10 / $75	$15 / $15

   a. What is the mutually beneficial outcome?
   b. Acting in their best interests, what strategy will each family choose?
   c. Explain why this game is or is not an example of a prisoners' dilemma.
4. In Figure 9P-2, what is the dominant strategy for Player A? What is the dominant strategy for Player B? **[LO 9.3]**

FIGURE 9P-2

		Player B	
		Strategy 1	Strategy 2
Player A	Strategy 1	−2 / −2	−3 / 1
	Strategy 2	1 / −3	0 / 0

5. A town's two gas stations are each considering lowering prices to attract more sales. How this affects the profits for each gas station depends on whether the other also lowers prices. The decision matrix in Figure 9P-3 shows the payoffs, depending on what each player decides to do. Identify any Nash equilibria. **[LO 9.4]**

FIGURE 9P-3

		Gas Station B	
		Lower price	**Higher price**
Gas Station A	**Higher price**	$35,000 / $35,000	$65,000 / $125,000
	Lower price	$125,000 / $65,000	$95,000 / $95,000

6. Consider again the two families trying to decide whether to donate to a fund to build a public park. The payoffs are shown in Figure 9P-1. **[LO 9.4, LO 9.5]**

   a. What is the Nash equilibrium?

   b. Suppose Family A agrees to match the donation of Family B. Under these new circumstances, what strategy will each family choose?

7. In which of the following situations, *a* or *b*, is a tit-for-tat strategy more likely to be successful at maintaining cooperation? **[LO 9.6]**

   a. An agreement of mutual support between players on a reality television show, in which the relatively worst-off player is eliminated every episode.

   b. A peace treaty between neighboring countries.

8. Which of the following are examples of tit-for-tat strategies? **[LO 9.6]**

   a. A friend forgets to send you a birthday card this year, so you decide not to send one to her on her next birthday.

   b. Your friend let you borrow her class notes last week, so you decide to skip class again this week.

   c. You and your roommate take turns buying toilet paper, milk, and other shared items.

   d. Your book club chooses a book you don't want to read, so you decide not to go this month.

9. Using backward induction in Figure 9P-4, decide which classes a hypothetical college student should take her freshman and sophomore years, assuming that she wants to be an economics major. **[LO 9.7]**

FIGURE 9P-4

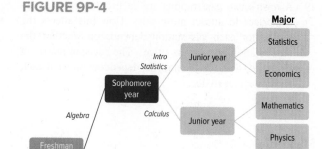

10. It's Tuesday morning and you need to travel from Minneapolis to Copenhagen. You know you need to arrive in Copenhagen no later than 4 p.m. on Wednesday. Using backward induction in Table 9P-1, choose your travel itinerary. Enter the flight numbers for each leg of your trip. **[LO 9.7]**

TABLE 9P-1

Flight Number	Departure	Arrival
13	Minneapolis 5:45pm	Chicago 7:15pm
456	Minneapolis 7:00pm	Chicago 8:35pm
1252	Minneapolis 3:45pm	New York 6:15pm
368	Minneapolis 5:50pm	New York 8:20pm
8120	Chicago 5:20pm	London 7:30am
905	Chicago 6:00pm	London 8:05am
1644	Chicago 7:10pm	London 9:45am
2004	New York 8:05pm	London 9:30am
1968	New York 10:30pm	London 11:45am
44	New York 11:10pm	London 12:30pm
952	London 9:00am	Copenhagen 11:55am
803	London 11:15am	Copenhagen 2:25pm
15	London 1:45pm	Copenhagen 4:55pm
681	London 3:05pm	Copenhagen 6:00pm

11. In the sequential game shown in Figure 9P-5, what choice should Player A make now to achieve the highest payoff at the end of the game? **[LO 9.8]**

FIGURE 9P-5

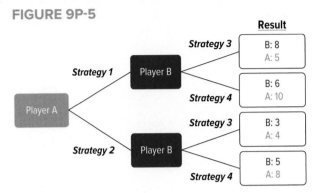

12. Company A is considering whether to invest in infrastructure that will allow it to expand into a new market. Company B is considering whether to enter the market. Assume the companies know each other's payoffs. Using Figure 9P-6, choose the outcome that will occur from the list below. **[LO 9.8]**

FIGURE 9P-6

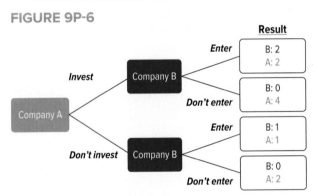

    a. A invest, B enter.

    b. A invest, B don't enter.

    c. A don't invest, B enter.

    d. A don't invest, B don't enter.

13. In the sequential game shown in Figure 9P-7, does Player A have a first-mover advantage? **[LO 9.9]**

FIGURE 9P-7

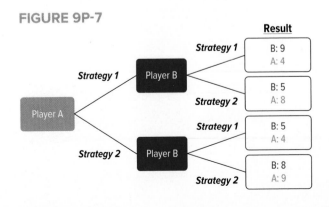

14. Which of the following are examples of first-mover advantage? **[LO 9.9]**

    a. You make an offer on a house. The seller can only accept or reject the offer.

    b. You and your roommate are dividing chores. The chores are written on slips of paper and drawn from a hat. You get to draw first.

    c. You are first in line to buy a raffle ticket.

    d. You can take vacation whenever you like, as long as no other employees are also scheduled to take vacation. You submit your vacation requests first this year.

15. Which player is likely to have higher bargaining power: a city government responding to angry citizens' demands that the trash be collected regularly or the sanitation workers' union? Explain your answer. **[LO 9.10]**

16. Which player is likely to have higher bargaining power: a large, established company shopping around for a new parts supplier or a start-up company trying to sell its parts? Explain your answer. **[LO 9.10]**

17. Figure 9P-8 shows a sequential game in which one player decides whether to injure another player. The injured player can then choose whether to sue, which involves costly legal fees. **[LO 9.11]**

FIGURE 9P-8

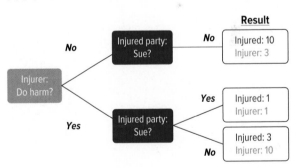

    a. What is the predicted outcome in this "game"?

    b. The injured party threatens to always sue when injured. Is this a credible threat? What is the predicted outcome if the injured party has threatened to always sue when injured?

    c. What is the predicted outcome if the injured party has made a binding commitment to always sue when injured?

18. Two companies are considering whether to enter a new market. The decision matrix in Figure 9P-9 shows each company's payoff, depending on whether one, both, or neither enters the market. Company A is in Costa Rica. Company B is in Nicaragua. **[LO 9.11]**

FIGURE 9P-9

	Company B (Nicaragua)	
	Enter	**Not Enter**
Company A (Costa Rica) — Enter	−$1M / −$3M	$0 / $2M
Company A (Costa Rica) — Not Enter	$3M / $0	$0 / $0

a. If Company A enters, what should Company B do?

b. If Company B enters, what should Company A do?

c. Suppose the Nicaraguan government releases a press statement that it will cover any profit losses for Company B. How much will this policy cost the Nicaraguan government?

Information

A Solution for Student Loans?

In the 1970s, administrators at Yale University thought they had come up with a student loan program that solved many of the problems faced by students trying to pay for an education. Here's how it worked: Students could choose to join a plan through which, instead of paying back individual loans, they would owe a small percentage of their income every year after graduation. They would stop owing payments when the debt for their *entire graduating class* was paid off.

The idea was to help students who wanted to go into public-service careers afford to do so. The university realized that these students had a harder time paying off individual loans than did students who went into better-paying careers. Under their new plan, graduates with low incomes would pay only a small amount; those with higher incomes would make up the difference. University administrators figured that every class would have some captains of industry and some social workers,

©Comstock Images/Getty Images

teachers, nonprofit staff, writers, and artists. By pooling everyone's debt, things would even out. The investment bankers and corporate lawyers would hardly miss the extra money they had to pay; teachers and artists would benefit tremendously from their lower monthly payments.

Good idea? If you said yes, you wouldn't be the only one to think so. The plan was supported by Yale economist James Tobin, who subsequently won a Nobel Prize. It drew on an idea put forward earlier by Milton Friedman, a University of Chicago economist (and another Nobel winner). Unfortunately, almost 30 years later, not a single graduating class had succeeded in paying off its collective debt. The program was deemed a total flop, and the university was pressured into canceling much of the debt.

What went wrong? There were two problems. The first was that the program was optional: Students could choose to opt out and pay off their debt individually in the usual way. Administrators had assumed that a representative cross-section of students would want to participate in the program. They overlooked the fact that many students have a fairly good sense of whether their incomes after college are likely to be high or low. Those who are drawn to banking or medicine can expect to earn a lot of money; those called to teaching or preaching can expect to earn less. To a student expecting to earn a low income, the program looked like a great deal—pay only what you can afford. For a student expecting a higher income, the prospect wasn't so attractive: She'd likely end up paying off not only her own loan, but also those of her less-wealthy peers. Not surprisingly, then, many students who anticipated a higher income chose *not* to join the program. The planned pooling of big and small contributions did not take place.

As if this wasn't bad enough, a second problem soon became apparent: The university could not automatically collect payments from alumni's paychecks. It had to rely on program participants to feel so good about their alma mater that they would willingly report their income and pay what they owed. You may not be surprised to hear that this did not work out so well. Not all participants held up their end of the deal. The university had to try to hunt down its alumni, find out how much money they had made, and force them to pay. It was not well-equipped to do this.

These two problems have a common theme—an imbalance of information. When students were deciding whether to join the program, they knew how likely it was that they would become investment bankers, but the university didn't. (Even if the university had known about students' career intentions, that wouldn't have forced the future investment bankers to participate. Alarm bells might have rung had the university noticed that the program was disproportionately packed with education and art majors, but no finance majors.) Then, as the program participants graduated and started work, the university couldn't know how much they were earning and if they were underpaying on what they owed. The problems caused by the missing information weren't just flukes or the result of lax enforcement; they were inherent in the program's design.

LEARNING OBJECTIVES

LO 10.1 Explain why information asymmetry matters for economic decision making.

LO 10.2 Explain how adverse selection is caused by asymmetric information.

LO 10.3 Explain how moral hazard is caused by asymmetric information.

LO 10.4 Differentiate between screening and signaling, and describe some applications of each.

LO 10.5 Explain how reputations can help to solve information problems.

LO 10.6 Explain how statistical discrimination might be used to solve information problems.

LO 10.7 Discuss the uses and limitations of education and regulation in overcoming information asymmetry problems.

Up to this point in the text, we have mostly assumed that economic decision makers are fully informed when they make decisions. We will see in this chapter that imbalances in information can cause problems in all kinds of transactions—between lenders and borrowers, buyers and sellers, and employers and employees. We'll see that when the parties to a deal have access to different information, markets are often inefficient; sometimes they even fall apart entirely. We'll also explore some ways that people try to find out or share information that isn't immediately observable, so they can make better decisions in the face of limited information.

Information: Knowledge Is Power

Do you want to buy a fabulous tablet? Only $50! A fantastic bargain! Now that you've given us $50, we regret to inform you that the tablet can't get on WiFi. Also, the screen is cracked. Sorry about that. And no, you can't have your money back.

Up to now, when we have asked questions like, "How much would you be willing to pay for an tablet?" we have assumed that you know exactly what you will be getting for your money. In general, to make rational economic choices, people need to know what they are choosing between.

When people are fully informed about the choices that they and other relevant economic actors face, we say they have **complete information**.

Unfortunately, people rarely have perfectly complete information. Often, they have *good enough* information to make acceptable choices. But in many cases, people are truly underinformed in ways that matter. You've probably seen people around you make decisions about which they were underinformed–decisions they later came to regret. Maybe they bought products that proved to be shoddy, lent money to an acquaintance who turned out to be a deadbeat, or moved to a new apartment with terrible plumbing or a leaky roof.

Of course, some choices are genuinely risky. When you invest in stocks or real estate, you can't have perfectly complete information about how your investment will perform. Despite this, markets can still work well. For example, let's say you are buying annual insurance against the possibility of flood damage to your house. Neither you nor the insurance company can have perfect information about exactly how much heavy rainfall there is likely to be in the next 12 months, but there still can be a market for flood insurance that works well enough for both you and the insurance company. In this chapter, we distinguish decisions that involve risk-taking from situations in which some people have better information than others and can use it to their advantage.

complete information state of being fully informed about the choices that relevant economic actors face

Information asymmetry

Problems are likely to arise when one person knows more than another, a situation that is called **information asymmetry**. Let's consider the example of taking your car to a mechanic. The mechanic knows a great deal about the condition of your car, whereas you probably know very little. He could tell you that the entire brake system needs to be replaced, and you'd probably pay for it without ever knowing if he was telling the truth.

To see why such information asymmetries create problems, consider *the wants and constraints of those involved:*

LO 10.1 Explain why information asymmetry matters for economic decision making.

information asymmetry a condition in which one participant in a transaction knows more than another participant

- You want your car fixed at the lowest possible price. You are constrained by your ignorance of exactly how your car functions or why it broke down.
- The mechanic wants to make as much money as possible. He is constrained only by his moral scruples and concern about possible damage to his reputation and his business if he turns out to have underestimated your knowledge of the workings of brake systems.

When one person knows much more than the other, that person can achieve what he wants at the other's expense–in this case, the mechanic may succeed in making more money by charging you for repairs that your car doesn't really require.

Note that this is a problem only because your wants (spend as little as possible) are opposed to the mechanic's (charge as much as possible). If both parties' incentives are *aligned*, then the information asymmetry doesn't matter. If a mechanically minded friend is fixing your car as a favor, you both want the repair to cost as little as possible. It doesn't matter that you know less than your friend about cars.

Here, we'll discuss two important types of information asymmetry–*adverse selection* and *moral hazard*. These asymmetries are common problems for the insurance industry, and we will see that they plague other markets, too.

Adverse selection and the lemons problem

As we saw in the chapter-opening example of the student loan program at Yale, rational, utility-maximizing people choose to take part in transactions from which they expect to benefit; likewise, they choose not to take part in transactions from which they do not expect to benefit.

When there are particular types of information asymmetries, the problem of *adverse selection* can result. **Adverse selection** occurs when buyers and sellers have different information about the quality of a good or the riskiness of a situation, and this asymmetric information results in failure

LO 10.2 Explain how adverse selection is caused by asymmetric information.

adverse selection
a state that occurs when buyers and sellers have different information about the quality of a good or the riskiness of a situation, and this asymmetric information results in failure to complete transactions that would have been possible if both sides had the same information.

to complete transactions that would have been possible if both sides had the same information. In Yale's student loan program, only the students who will have trouble paying off their loans (the "adverse" types) will opt into the program. But because only the bad types opt in, the loans don't get paid off.

One well-known example of adverse selection is the "lemons" problem in the used-car market. A lemon is a car that breaks down again and again. There is information asymmetry in the used-car market because sellers of used cars know a lot more about the true characteristics of their cars than potential buyers do. A test drive won't necessarily reveal how long the car will run before it breaks down. Buyers of used cars are well aware that they are on the wrong end of this asymmetry: They are always suspicious that a used car could be a lemon. They won't pay as much for a lemon as they would if they could be certain the car was in perfect shape. That means sellers of used cars that *are* in perfect shape will be underpaid.

Meanwhile, sellers of lemons will still be paid more than their cars are worth. To see why this is true, suppose the used-car market consists of just two types of cars: lemons and high-

The "lemons" problem in the used-car market is an example of information asymmetry.
©Blend Images/ SuperStock

quality cars (we'll call them "plums"). If buyers could tell which is which, they would establish one price for plums and another, lower price for lemons. But if buyers can't differentiate between plums and lemons, they will have to offer an average price that reflects the likelihood of getting one or the other. That price will be lower than they'd pay for a guaranteed plum (because there is a chance they might get a lemon); it will be higher than they'd pay for a guaranteed lemon (because there is a chance they might get a plum).

If you know the car you own is a lemon, you'll be attracted by the prospect of selling it at a high price. But if you know the car you own is a plum, you won't want to sell for less than it's worth. Sellers of lemons will be willing market participants; sellers of plums will be less willing. Over time, the result will be more lemons and fewer plums on the market. As buyers start to notice they are increasingly likely to get a lemon, they will offer even lower prices, making it even less attractive for plum sellers to enter the market. A vicious cycle ensues, in which the selection of cars on the market becomes more and more adverse from the buyer's perspective. This explains why a barely used car that works perfectly is worth a lot less than exactly the same car offered new at a dealership—the buyer of the slightly used car doesn't know whether or not to trust the seller.

Another common example of adverse selection occurs in insurance markets because of the information asymmetry between insurance companies and their customers. At any given price, drivers who know they are careless will be more eager than careful drivers to buy auto insurance; they know they will be more likely to make claims. The selection of customers is adverse from the insurance company's perspective.

To see how this problem might play out in a similar way to the lemons problem, ask, *How does the insurance company respond to this situation?* The company sets premiums according to the average risk of policyholders; as more risky drivers take out insurance, the average risk increases and so must the premiums. In turn, consumers who know they are careful drivers will respond to higher premiums by becoming even less interested in buying insurance. The average risk goes up again, so premiums must go up again: Just as in the lemons example, there is a vicious cycle. (As we'll explain later in the chapter, there is a solution to the adverse-selection problem in car insurance: mandated participation.)

Even in a best-case scenario, adverse selection reduces the efficiency of markets because some transactions that would make both sides better off fail to take place, and surplus is lost. To see why, suppose I would be willing to accept $8,000 for my used car, which I know is a plum (a good car), and you would be willing to pay $10,000 for a *guaranteed* plum. If you could be certain that my car was a plum, we could agree to trade for $9,000; each of us would enjoy $1,000 worth of surplus. But because you face the risk that my car is a lemon (a bad car), you are understandably not willing to pay $9,000. What if the car turns out to be worth only $5,000? You would have paid $4,000 too much. Given the possibility that the car might be either a plum or a lemon, you might be willing to pay only $7,000 for the used car. At that price, the deal does not take place, and we both lose out.

In a worst-case scenario, the vicious cycle caused by adverse selection can cause markets to fall apart entirely (i.e., create a market failure). That's what happened with the student loan–pooling program in the chapter-opening example. In our used-car example, it would be profitable for owners of lemons to sell their cars at a price of $7,000, but it would not be profitable for owners of plums to sell their cars for $7,000. Thus, owners of plums would not be willing to sell their used cars. The used-car market in that price range would be comprised of only lemons.

You might be wondering: If adverse selection is such a problem with used cars, then how does the used-car market continue to exist? As we will discuss later, there are some solutions to mitigate adverse selection. In the case of used cars, companies such as Carfax provide potential buyers with much more information about a used car than they could obtain on their own. This decreases the degree of information asymmetry, reduces adverse selection, and enables the market to exist.

Principal–agent problems and moral hazard

Information asymmetries can also cause problems *after* selection has occurred and the two parties have entered into an agreement. This type of problem often arises when one person entrusts a task to another person. In what is called a *principal-agent problem*, a person called a **principal** entrusts someone else, called the **agent**, with a task.

The most basic example of a principal–agent problem caused by asymmetric information is the relationship between an employer (the principal) and an employee (the agent). The asymmetry exists because each employee knows how hard he or she works, but the employer does not. Because the principal usually cannot monitor what the agent is doing all the time, the agent may be tempted to put less effort into the task than the principal would want.

In short, employees have an incentive to slack off when the boss isn't watching. Why not play games online or take a few extra coffee breaks, if no one is any the wiser? The tendency for people to behave in a riskier way or to renege on contracts when they do not face the full consequences of their actions is called **moral hazard**. With moral hazard, people engage in behavior that is considered undesirable by the person who bears the cost of the behavior.

Moral hazard can be avoided by correcting the information asymmetry through better monitoring. If the boss were able to see how much effort employees were really putting in, she could adjust their incentives to maintain steady effort. What would happen if you were inclined to play games online at work but knew someone was closely monitoring your workplace computer activity, and your wages could be docked or you could lose your job if you were caught? That knowledge would probably increase your workplace productivity significantly.

It is not always possible to correct such an information asymmetry, however. Not all types of jobs allow bosses to monitor employees closely enough to avoid moral hazard. The same is true of insurance markets, in which moral hazard is a common problem. For instance, if your car is insured against theft, you might not be as careful to park in a safe place and double-check that the door is locked; you know the insurance company would cover almost all of the cost if the car were stolen. Ironically, then, having insurance against car theft may actually make it more likely that a car will be stolen, driving up the cost to the insurance company. There is no way your insurance company can monitor where you tend to park and how careful you are about locking your doors.

LO 10.3 Explain how moral hazard is caused by asymmetric information.

principal
a person who entrusts someone with a task

agent
a person who carries out a task on someone else's behalf

moral hazard
the tendency for people to behave in a riskier way or to renege on contracts when they do not face the full consequences of their actions

There are sometimes other ingenious ways insurance companies can avoid moral hazard, such as the crop insurance described in the Economics in Action box "The weather can't cheat."

The weather can't cheat
Economics in Action

Hanumanthu, a 36-year-old farmer, lived with his mother, wife, and two children in Anantapur, India. Like a third of the world's population, they depended on agriculture for a living, growing their own crops on a small plot of land.

The year 2009 was a bad one for Hanumanthu and his family. When a prolonged drought caused their crops to fail, they did not have savings to fall back on. Hanumanthu had to borrow from the village moneylender just to cover the cost of food. As his debt grew bigger and bigger, the moneylender began harassing him to repay the loan.

This whole situation could have been helped if farmers like Hanumanthu had insurance. Their livelihoods are certainly risky; even one bad harvest can be devastating. In early attempts to offer insurance to farmers, insurers compensated farmers for low crop yields. If a farmer's fields yielded less than a certain amount of food, the insurance company would reimburse him for the difference.

This system turned out to be prone to moral hazard. Because farmers knew they could get money if their crops failed, they had less incentive to invest time and effort in farming. They might be less diligent in weeding or might skimp on expensive fertilizer. Insurers had no way to monitor the farmers to make sure they were putting in the required effort. As a result, agricultural losses actually increased with the introduction of insurance, and so did insurers' costs.

More recently, insurers have been trying a new idea: They are selling insurance that protects farmers against low rainfall levels, rather than low crop yields. The advantage of such an approach is that farmers can't control the rainfall. As long as rainfall patterns are highly correlated with crop yields, insurance will offer them protection against crop failures that are truly accidental. Insurers will not be stuck with the bill if a farmer's crop fails simply because he didn't weed or plant on time.

With rainfall insurance, farmers become less vulnerable, but they still have an incentive to invest time and effort in their fields and maximize their productivity, avoiding the pitfalls of moral hazard.

Source: Satyajit Usham, "Drought trip: Tale of a farmer's suicide told for the people of Manipur," *Shangai Times*, November 19, 2009, accessed July 13, 2018, www.e-pao.net/GP.asp?src=6..171109.nov09.

Moral hazard and adverse selection—avoiding confusion

Sometimes people confuse adverse selection with moral hazard because they often occur together. Careless drivers are more likely to buy auto insurance voluntarily (adverse selection); drivers with auto insurance may be more likely to be careless (moral hazard). To clarify, remember that:

- Adverse selection relates to *unobserved characteristics* of people or goods. It occurs *before* the parties have entered into an agreement.

- Moral hazard is about *actions* and occurs *after* the parties have voluntarily entered into an agreement.

Although adverse selection and moral hazard can be found at different stages of the same transaction, such as auto insurance, it is possible to have one without the other.

To see how, think back to our chapter-opening example of the student loan program, which involved both problems. Imagine first that the student loan–pooling scheme had been mandatory.

That would have eliminated the problem of adverse selection: Students who anticipated high earnings would not have been able to opt out. But it would have left the problem of moral hazard because it would still have been possible for all participants to evade payment.

Now consider an alternative scenario, in which participation remained optional, but the IRS agreed to help by reporting income to the university so that the university could effectively collect against its alumni with higher incomes. This plan would have lessened the moral hazard problem, but not the adverse selection. (For the record: This alternative scenario is totally hypothetical—the IRS is not legally allowed to engage in the activity described in the scenario.)

The rest of this chapter will focus on ways in which the problems arising from information asymmetries can be corrected.

✓ TEST YOURSELF

☐ Why is information asymmetry not a problem if both parties to an agreement want the same thing? **[LO 10.1]**

☐ How is the lemons problem caused by the buyer's inability to identify the true quality of a used car? **[LO 10.2]**

☐ How can better monitoring solve moral hazard problems? **[LO 10.3]**

Solving Information Problems

Before we look at ways to solve information problems, we should point out that they are not always worth solving. Sometimes, remaining uninformed is optimal. Why? Because the cost of acquiring information would be prohibitive. When you pay a mechanic for car repairs that you don't fully understand, for example, it's not as if you *couldn't* learn how brake systems work if you really wanted to. Or you could hire another mechanic to review the assessment and confirm the repairs are needed. You don't do either because it would take you a lot of time and effort to do those things. The trade-off isn't worth it. It's as if you've asked yourself, *What's the opportunity cost of acquiring more information?* For most of us, the opportunity cost of acquiring mechanical expertise is probably significantly higher than the occasional cost of unnecessary repairs.

Often, however, it *is* worth the effort to solve problems caused by information asymmetry. In this section, we'll consider some approaches that can be taken by those directly involved in a transaction: screening, signaling, building a reputation, and using statistical discrimination. Finally, we'll also consider two ways in which governments can get involved.

Screening

If you know you are on the wrong end of an information asymmetry, you could always try asking the other party for the information you want. Rather than simply hoping they tell you the truth, you could also look for clever ways to put them in a situation that forces them to reveal, perhaps without even realizing it, the information they know and you don't. Taking action to reveal private information about someone else is called **screening**. In this context, *private* doesn't necessarily mean personal or embarrassing; it simply means that the information is not public, or available to everyone.

Interviewing candidates for a job is a classic use of screening to improve hiring decisions. Employers may simply ask questions about your education, experience, and skills, and hope you're telling the truth. But because candidates have an incentive to hide negative information, many employers also use more proactive screening methods. One method is to ask for references. An applicant who cannot easily provide good references is revealing a piece of private information that any employer wants to have when hiring. Another is requiring applicants to perform certain tests of their skills, or perhaps even to take a drug test. If the applicant fails the tests, or refuses to take them, this also reveals useful private information.

LO 10.4 Differentiate between screening and signaling, and describe some applications of each.

screening
taking action to reveal private information about someone else

Ever wonder why auto insurance companies offer different deductibles? (*Deductibles* are amounts a policyholder must pay out of pocket before an insurance company settles a claim.) Offering different deductibles is not just a matter of offering different products to suit different customer needs. Instead, it's a device to force the more accident-prone drivers to reveal themselves. Reckless drivers know that their cars are likely to be involved in accidents more often than usual. A driver who expects to have frequent accidents would not choose a high-deductible plan; it could end up being very expensive. A cautious driver, however, would be willing to carry a high deductible; after all, he doesn't anticipate having frequent accidents. Offering different deductibles screens out the reckless drivers. Such screening allows the insurance company to offer lower monthly premiums to cautious customers, thus helping to avoid the problem of adverse selection.

In the next section, we'll discuss signalling, another way to overcome information problems in various situations. But first, the Econ and YOU box "Is college worth it?" asks you to think about the true value of getting a college diploma.

Is college worth it?
Econ and YOU

You probably have many reasons to be in school. Let's start with some obvious ones: Education offers you the chance to form your thinking, challenge your assumptions, and make lifelong friends. But we're guessing you're in school for financial reasons too. When you graduate, you'll have a diploma that helps to unlock all sorts of new job opportunities—the average college graduate earns 73 percent more than a high school graduate (up from 50 percent more in the 1970s).

Why do college degrees deliver such high financial returns (on average)? One answer is that you learn useful things in college and the skills and knowledge translate into higher wages.

However, Bryan Caplan, an economist at George Mason University in Virginia, argues that college degrees actually signal something entirely different. Rather than signaling hard skills like mastery of essay-writing and accounting, acquiring a college degree shows that you have the raw mental makeup, grit, social skills, and conformity to make it through college. Caplan argues that those qualities are ultimately the biggest factors that drive employers to pay more to workers with college degrees.

If college was all about acquiring hard skills, Caplan argues, each year of extra schooling beyond high school should generate a sizable boost in wages (since each year at college you acquire an important new set of skills). But Caplan shows that, on average, the wage gain from completing college is worth more than twice that from completing your freshman, sophomore, and junior years *combined*. So, *finishing* college is what generates the big reward.

As college professors ourselves, we believe that college helps you think more broadly about the world. It helps you tackle thorny problems. It offers important technical skills. In fact, those are the main goals of this text. But we also recognize that the benefits of college go well beyond the simple acquisition of knowledge.

Does Caplan's argument make sense from your own experience? Does it change how you think about college? Should it?

Source: Bryan Caplan, *The Case against Education: Why the Education System Is a Waste of Time and Money* (Princeton, NJ: Princeton University Press, 2018).

Signaling

Screening is useful when trying to correct information asymmetry by uncovering private information that people would rather not share. Sometimes, though, the party with more information would be all too happy to share it. For instance, if I am selling a used car I know is in excellent condition, I would be delighted to share this knowledge with you, the potential buyer. Both of us would prefer to eliminate the information asymmetry that afflicts us. The problem is that we lack a *credible* way to share information. After all, somebody selling a lemon also will insist that her car is top quality. Knowing this, you would have no reason to believe me.

How does the seller of a good used car prove to potential buyers that it's not a lemon, so he can ask a higher price? One way to credibly signal that a car is not a lemon is to certify it through a brand dealership. The dealership inspects the car for defects and, if it passes muster, offers it for sale with a certificate of quality and a warranty. The certificate reassures the buyer that the car is a good one and enables the seller to receive a higher price. This solution corrects an inefficiency in the market, allowing more transactions that are valuable to both buyers and sellers to take place.

When people take action, on purpose or not, to reveal their own private information, they are **signaling**. Signaling happens in many situations. The signaling theory of education argues that a college degree is like a certificate of quality for used cars: It credibly signals to potential employers that you are intelligent, hardworking, and able to complete assignments. That's why many employers prefer candidates with college degrees, even if what they learned in school has little relevance to the job in question.

signaling
taking action to reveal one's own private information

The key to a successful positive signal is that it is not easily faked. For a signal to be credible, it must carry some sort of mechanism or cost that makes it inaccessible or unappealing to those it is meant to exclude. In the case of a used-car certificate, an unbiased third party checks the car. Sellers of lemons will not apply. In the case of a college degree, both admissions screening and tuition costs discourage applicants who are not sufficiently talented and hardworking. In theory, the more selective the admissions process and the costlier the tuition, the stronger the signal a college degree sends to potential employers.

Reputation

So far we have focused on asymmetric-information problems affecting one-time interactions, such as a one-off private used-car trade. Often, however, interactions occur over and over, like the repeated games in Chapter 9, "Game Theory and Strategic Thinking." Used-car dealers, for example, sell used cars every day. This repetition can enable a new solution to the information problem, as people develop a reputation for trustworthiness (or lack thereof).

LO 10.5 Explain how reputations can help to solve information problems.

Consider a mechanic who routinely charges customers for unnecessary repairs. Once in a while, one of those customers will call on a friend who understands car repairs for a second opinion, and the mechanic will get caught overcharging. The mechanic thus risks developing a bad reputation. This risk creates an incentive for the more-informed party (in this case, the car mechanic) not to take unfair advantage of the information asymmetry. *What's the opportunity cost* of squeezing an unfair advantage out of a deal? If no one will ever find out, the answer is probably "nothing." With your reputation on the line, however, the opportunity cost is the loss of valuable business in the future.

Have you ever hesitated about buying something from eBay, but then been reassured by noticing that the seller has a good user-feedback score? If so, you will understand the power of reputation to overcome the problem of asymmetric information. A good reputation can be viewed as a special form of signaling. Just like getting a college degree, building a good reputation can be a costly and time-consuming business.

Statistical discrimination

When you don't have time to become fully informed about a specific new situation, you may find yourself relying on a rule of thumb. Suppose you're choosing between having dinner at a Mexican restaurant or the burger place next to it. You know nothing about these two restaurants, and you're too hungry to stop and ask the opinions of locals or search for reviews online. You remember hearing, though, that this neighborhood is known for great Mexican food. It makes sense to choose the Mexican restaurant. Of course, you may be unlucky and find that this *particular* Mexican restaurant happens to be terrible. Using a generalization here is perfectly rational, though: If

LO 10.6 Explain how statistical discrimination might be used to solve information problems.

the neighborhood has a reputation for great Mexican food, you have a reasonably good chance that this particular Mexican restaurant will, in fact, be great.

Filling gaps in your information by generalizing based on observable characteristics is called **statistical discrimination**. It's something most of us do all the time. Suppose you are choosing among three movies: an action movie starring Liam Neeson, a romance starring Ryan Gosling, or a psychological drama starring Jennifer Lawrence. You may know little about the particular movies but still be able to tell which you are likely to enjoy most, based on knowing which type of movie you typically like best, or which actor or actress you like the most. You've filled the gaps in your information by generalizing from what you already know.

To return to the lemons problem, you may prefer to buy one particular used car over another because you know that, in general, cars of that brand tend to age well. As with the Mexican restaurant, you may be unlucky—the particular car you buy may turn out to be a lemon. Likewise with the movie, your favorite genre or movie star does, on occasion, let you down. But generalizing in this way is a rational response to being on the wrong end of an information asymmetry.

However, statistical discrimination can be a controversial way to tackle information problems. It can often be far less benign than choosing between restaurants, movies, or used cars. The problem is that we can generalize about any observable characteristic—not just genre of food or movie or brand of car, but also a person's race, age, gender, or religion. Saying that statistical discrimination can be *rational* doesn't mean that it is always admirable, ethical, or even legal. Rational statistical discrimination can limit the opportunities of individuals just because they happen to belong to a certain group of people. See the What Do You Think? box "Should teenagers be able to buy assault rifles?" for some examples.

statistical discrimination
distinguishing between choices by generalizing based on observable characteristics in order to fill in missing information

Should teenagers be able to buy assault rifles?
What Do You Think?

In February 2018, 17 people were killed in the brutal shooting at Marjory Stoneman Douglas High School in Parkland, Florida. The killer used an AR-15 purchased legally. Immediately afterward, President Trump proposed raising the legal age for buying a rifle from 18 to 21. (He later backed away from the idea.)

Americans are divided about gun control, but many supported Trump's proposal. If the age restriction had been enacted, it would not have been the first: Under current federal law, you can't buy a handgun (as opposed to a rifle) from a licensed dealer until you're 21. And after the Parkland shooting, Florida passed legislation barring sales of rifles and shotguns to people under 21.

On the other hand, some argue, if you're 18 or older, you can vote, enlist in the U.S. armed forces, and serve on a jury. If you commit a felony, you will face strict penalties as an adult. So, why shouldn't 18-year-olds be allowed to buy rifles from licensed dealers just like other adults?

Age-related gun bans are a response to an information problem: If governments knew which customers were most likely to use a gun to harm innocent people, they could simply ban sales to those individuals. But the government doesn't have this information. Instead, age restrictions are based on a rule of thumb, banning the sale of guns to a *category* of people statistically more likely to harbor these intentions. If you were a law-abiding 19-year-old who wanted to buy a rifle to go hunting, though, you might have been pretty annoyed if Trump's original suggestion had been enacted.

The age restriction is an example of statistical discrimination. The idea goes beyond limiting the ability to purchase guns. Put yourself in the place of a successful young black male who owns a nice-looking car and keeps getting pulled over by police. Or imagine being a bearded Muslim who often gets singled out in airports for extra security checks. Both instances of statistical discrimination are highly controversial.

Some examples of statistical discrimination are so controversial, they have been banned altogether. For example, young women are statistically more likely than other employees to leave their jobs to start a family. But any employer who cites this as a reason for preferring to hire a man risks getting sued for gender discrimination.

Yet other examples of age- and gender-based statistical discrimination are hardly objected to at all. We have come across one such example already in this chapter: the cost of auto insurance. If you are an extremely careful driver who happens to be young and male, you will be charged more for your car insurance because *other* young men are statistically more likely to drive recklessly and cause accidents.

Why do we accept age- and gender-based discrimination in the auto-insurance market, but not in the jobs market? Is it fair to ban teenagers from buying rifles? Is it meaningfully different from the case of charging young men more for their car insurance?

WHAT DO YOU THINK?

1. Is banning the sale of rifles to young people an acceptable or unfair form of statistical discrimination?
2. Should statistical discrimination be used as a basis for legislation?
3. Police are sometimes accused of stopping members of some ethnic or racial groups more than others. Is racial profiling by police ever justifiable? If yes, under what conditions?

Regulation and education

When parties to a transaction can't resolve information asymmetry problems on their own and those problems have a negative effect on sufficiently large numbers of people, the government will sometimes step in.

> **LO 10.7** Discuss the uses and limitations of education and regulation in overcoming information asymmetry problems.

Governments can help to solve information asymmetry problems in two ways. One is to provide the missing information to the less-informed party, or require the more-informed party to reveal it. For example, almost every packaged-food item you can buy in the United States lists its ingredients and nutritional content. This is the result of Food and Drug Administration (FDA) regulations that force food producers to divulge otherwise-private information. These regulations correct an information asymmetry that is important (consumers want to know what they're eating) and hard to solve without government intervention.

Disclosure laws sound like a good thing, but they don't always work well. Sometimes they can replace the problem of consumers having too little information with the opposite problem—information overload. Thanks to disclosure laws, everything from cell phone plans to prescription drugs and home mortgages comes with page after page of rules, disclaimers, and technical information. Not surprisingly, many consumers don't bother to read the fine print. Instead, they base decisions on a salesperson's explanation. In the early 2000s, laws requiring banks and mortgage brokers to disclose the terms of home loans failed to prevent many Americans from entering into irresponsible mortgage agreements. In many cases, borrowers didn't read or understand the information the companies had been forced to disclose.

In Chapter 23, "Public Policy and Choice Architecture," we'll see how some organizations work to frame people's options in these situations of information overload. Their goal is to try to simplify the choices people face and help them make better decisions.

The second way governments can use public regulation to tackle information problems is to *mandate participation* in a market or program. Mandates prevent markets from failing because of adverse selection. Governments choose this option when the functioning of those markets is thought to be in the public interest. For example, we have seen how adverse selection drives up the price of auto insurance. Careful drivers might conclude that insurance is too expensive to be worth it. Those decisions could set off the vicious cycle we discussed earlier: Only reckless drivers want insurance, so premiums have to rise higher and higher, eventually leading the market to collapse.

But governments want drivers to be able to compensate innocent victims if they cause a road accident. So most states require *all* drivers to buy at least a minimum level of insurance to cover liability to third parties. This mandated participation solves the adverse-selection problem, but not the moral-hazard problem: Drivers with insurance are still more likely to drive carelessly.

One effect of the government mandating participation in the auto-insurance market is to keep premiums lower than they would be if careful drivers had a choice to opt out. This reasoning led policy-makers to make mandatory health coverage a major part of the Affordable Care Act, which became law in 2010. The idea was that mandating coverage would overcome adverse selection in the market for health insurance, allowing insurers to charge less for premiums. Critics charge that mandating coverage undermines people's freedom to choose their own insurance status.

For a health-related twist on some of the issues discussed in this chapter, see the What Do You Think? box "How much information is too much?"

How much information is too much?
What Do You Think?

So far we have focused on adverse-selection problems in the insurance industry. They arise because consumers know more than insurance companies about their risks; consumers can choose not to purchase insurance if the risk is low. But what about the opposite situation? What if insurance companies know more than their customers? What if insurers could effectively refuse insurance to certain individuals by charging prohibitively high premiums?

This worry came to the fore with advances in genetics. Your health insurance company might discover from genetic testing that you are at high risk of contracting a disease that is extremely expensive to treat. It might then want to charge you far more for your insurance than you would be able to afford or might deny you coverage entirely. Some people, worried about this possibility, were refusing to take genetic tests that would reveal the best treatment for an existing condition.

Most people think it would be unfair for insurance companies to use genetic information in this way. After all, it's not your fault if your genes are letting you down. Why should you be denied health care as a result? In 2008 Congress enacted a federal law called the Genetic Information Nondiscrimination Act. In contrast to laws that require disclosure of private information, this law prohibits insurers and employers from accessing genetic information about policyholders and employees.

However, the question is not clear-cut. If insurers can't access your genetic information, should they be allowed to ask questions about your family medical history? That's not your fault, any more than your genes are. Most people think it's fair game for health insurers to charge you more if you smoke—that's your choice. But what about charging you more if there's a history of heart disease in your family?

WHAT DO YOU THINK?

1. Should insurance companies be allowed to charge you more if you eat unhealthily and never exercise? What if you're genetically predisposed to obesity?
2. Is there any difference between insurance companies using genetics to find preexisting conditions and asking lengthy questions about family medical histories?
3. Should insurance companies be able to collect as much information as possible in order to accurately gauge the risk of their clients?

Source: Amy Harmon, "Insurance fears lead many to shun DNA tests," *New York Times*, February 24, 2008, www.nytimes.com/2008/02/24/health/24dna.html?ref=dnaage.

✓ TEST YOURSELF

☐ What is the difference between screening and signaling? **[LO 10.4]**

☐ Why does a seller with a good reputation face a different opportunity cost for offering poor-quality goods than a seller with no reputation to lose? **[LO 10.5]**

☐ What concept uses observable qualities in order to fill in missing information when making a decision? **[LO 10.6]**

☐ How can too much fine print undermine the goals of a public-disclosure law? **[LO 10.7]**

Conclusion

People make decisions based on what they know, but sometimes they don't have enough information to make good decisions. One of the key assumptions behind perfect markets is that individuals have perfect information. When this is not true, individuals are not necessarily able to make decisions that set marginal benefits equal to marginal costs.

We've seen in this chapter that in many situations information asymmetry can allow one person to take advantage of another. In other cases, markets may fall apart because people are afraid to trade with one another. Problems like adverse selection and moral hazard can derail what appear to be clever programs or business models.

Screening and signaling, if used correctly, can help to correct these inefficiencies and increase surplus. Statistical discrimination can also be helpful, but it can have unintended downsides. Sometimes government may step in to correct information problems that affect large numbers of people. The success of government regulation, however, depends on whether or not people understand and are motivated to use the information made available to them.

Key Terms

complete information, p. 231

information asymmetry, p. 231

adverse selection, p. 232

principal, p. 233

agent, p. 233

moral hazard, p. 233

screening, p. 235

signaling, p. 237

statistical discrimination, p. 238

Summary

LO 10.1 Explain why information asymmetry matters for economic decision making.

Information asymmetry means that one person knows more than another. Asymmetric information creates problems because it allows a person who is more informed to achieve goals at the expense of a person who is less informed. If the incentives of both parties are aligned, then the information asymmetry doesn't matter.

LO 10.2 Explain how adverse selection is caused by asymmetric information.

Adverse selection occurs when buyers and sellers have different information about the quality of a good or the riskiness of a situation. As a result, some buyers and sellers fail to complete transactions that would have been possible if both sides had the same information. Adverse selection relates to unobserved characteristics of people or goods, and it occurs before the two parties have entered into an agreement.

LO 10.3 Explain how moral hazard is caused by asymmetric information.

Moral hazard occurs when people behave in a riskier way or renege on a contract because they do not have to face the full consequences of their actions. In contrast to adverse selection, moral hazard has to do with actions, and it happens *after* the two parties have entered into an agreement. It generally occurs when a principal entrusts an agent with a task but cannot observe the agent's actions, as in the employer–employee relationship.

LO 10.4 Differentiate between screening and signaling, and describe some applications of each.

Screening is a method for correcting information asymmetries that involves taking action to reveal private information about someone else. Common examples include interviewing job candidates and checking references when hiring, or offering insurance products that appeal to people with different characteristics. Screening works best when there is a way to ensure that the information received is credible, since people have an incentive to keep their private information private.

Signaling is a method for correcting information asymmetries that involves taking action to reveal one's own private information. Common examples include certifying a used car, getting an advanced degree, and dressing for success. Signaling is useful in cases in which the more informed party would prefer to eliminate the information asymmetry. For a signal to be credible, it must carry some cost or mechanism that makes it inaccessible or unappealing to those it is meant to exclude; otherwise everyone will use the signal and it will lose its meaning.

LO 10.5 Explain how reputations can help to solve information problems.

The potential to develop a reputation creates an incentive for the more-informed party to an exchange to behave in a way that is fair and favorable toward the less-informed party. Because hidden information often reveals itself over time, people who consistently take advantage of a less-informed party will develop a bad reputation, and customers will begin to avoid doing business with them. A good reputation is a signal that a business or person has treated partners well in the past.

LO 10.6 Explain how statistical discrimination might be used to solve information problems.

Statistical discrimination is a method of distinguishing between choices by generalizing based on observable characteristics in order to fill in missing information. When specific information is missing, rules of thumb and inferences based on statistical averages can serve as rational decision-making tools. However, statistical averages are not necessarily accurate, nor are inferences made using statistical discrimination, even if they are the best option when full information is unavailable.

LO 10.7 Discuss the uses and limitations of education and regulation in overcoming information asymmetry problems.

When an information problem is pervasive and has a pronounced negative effect on society, government will sometimes step in to provide the missing information or require that others reveal private information. The effectiveness of these interventions depends on how well the government's requirements are enforced and how well people understand the information they receive. In a few cases, government may mandate participation in a market or program to counter a severe adverse selection problem.

Review Questions

1. Return to the description of the student loan program that opened the chapter. Suppose that all students at the university are perfectly altruistic and share the university's goal of reducing debt for graduates with low incomes. Would information asymmetry cause a problem in this situation? Why or why not? **[LO 10.1]**

2. Suppose you are in the market to purchase your first home. You found a house you like in your price range and are buying directly from the previous owner. Describe an information asymmetry in this situation. Explain who is likely to benefit from this information imbalance. **[LO 10.1]**

3. A club charges a flat fee for an open bar (all-you-can-drink). Describe the adverse-selection problem. **[LO 10.2]**

4. A course description posted during the registration period notes that homework is graded *complete* or *incomplete* rather than being corrected by the instructor. Describe the adverse-selection problem. **[LO 10.2]**

5. A club charges a flat fee for an open bar (all-you-can-drink). Describe the moral-hazard problem. **[LO 10.3]**

6. Imagine that you own a bagel shop, which you visit once a day. According to company policy, employees are supposed to pay for all the bagels they eat. Why is moral hazard likely to be a problem in this situation, and what could you do to prevent it? **[LO 10.3]**

7. The college admissions process involves both screening and signaling. Give an example of each. Who is doing the screening? Who is doing the signaling? **[LO 10.4]**

8. Explain why joining a fraternity or sorority might include elaborate or difficult rituals. **[LO 10.4]**

9. Zach wants to signal his devotion to Emily. He has $75 and is considering a bracelet for Emily or a tattoo for himself of her name. Which is the more effective signal? **[LO 10.4]**

10. Advertising often features testimonials from satisfied customers, who happily describe the characteristics of the goods or services they received. Why do advertisers use this technique rather than a direct description of the goods or services? **[LO 10.5]**

11. Two instructors are offering elective courses this semester. One instructor has been teaching at the university for several years. The other instructor is new. For which instructor will teaching evaluations be the most important this semester? Explain why. **[LO 10.5]**

12. Consider the market for life insurance. Give an example of statistical discrimination an insurer might use to set premiums. **[LO 10.6]**

13. Consider the market for auto insurance. Explain why insurers ask student drivers about their grades. **[LO 10.6]**

14. Suppose the government is thinking of requiring pharmaceutical companies to print the exact chemical formulas of medications on the label, so consumers will know exactly what they are ingesting. Is the new disclosure rule likely to benefit the average consumer? Explain your reasoning. **[LO 10.7]**

15. Some people argued that the initial mandate for health insurance coverage could reduce health-care costs. Explain this argument. What problem would mandatory coverage not solve that could undermine cost savings? **[LO 10.7]**

Problems and Applications

1. In which of the following situations is an information asymmetry likely to cause problems? **[LO 10.1]**
   a. Cab drivers know the shortest route to any destination better than their passengers do.
   b. Managers can't always supervise members of their sales staff who work on commission. (That is, staff members receive a percentage of the total value of the sales they make.)

2. In which of the following situations is an information asymmetry likely to cause problems? **[LO 10.1]**
   a. Parents know more than their children about how to write a good college application.
   b. People who book hotel rooms online know less about the quality of the room they are reserving than the hotel's management.

3. Which of the following situations are likely to involve adverse selection? **[LO 10.2]**
   a. After receiving an emergency call during class, a professor leaves students unsupervised for the rest of the period.
   b. A course has a reputation for being an easy A, even though after the term begins, students realize that it isn't.
   c. A course is a requirement for physics majors but an elective for biology majors.

4. In which of the following situations is adverse selection *not* a concern? **[LO 10.2]**
   a. A company offers employees the opportunity to purchase group health insurance.
   b. A company requires employees to purchase group health insurance.
   c. The health insurance plan does not include dental care.

5. In a town with exactly 1,000 residents, 60 percent of the residents make healthy choices, and 40 percent of the residents consistently make unhealthy choices. The health insurance company in town cannot tell, in advance, who is healthy and who is unhealthy. A healthy person has an average of $600 in medical expenses each year and is willing to pay $800 for insurance. An unhealthy person has an average of $2,100 in medical expenses each year and is willing to pay $2,400 for insurance. The health insurance provider can offer insurance at only one price. **[LO 10.2]**
   a. In equilibrium, what is the minimum price of insurance?
   b. In equilibrium, who will buy insurance?

6. Which of the following situations are likely to involve moral hazard? **[LO 10.3]**
   a. After receiving an emergency call during class, a professor leaves students unsupervised for the rest of the period.
   b. A course has a reputation for being an easy A, even though after the term begins, students realize that it isn't.
   c. A course is a requirement for physics majors but an elective for biology majors.

7. In which of the following government policies is moral hazard not a concern? **[LO 10.3]**
   a. Government provides disaster relief for homeowners who lose their homes in a flood.
   b. Government provides unemployment insurance when workers are laid off.
   c. Government raises taxes to pay for social services.
   d. Government requires hospitals to treat anyone who comes to the emergency room, regardless of insurance status.

8. Say whether each of the following situations involves screening or signaling. **[LO 10.4]**
   a. Auto shops and motels advertise that they are AAA-approved.
   b. Employers check interviewees' Facebook or Instagram profiles before hiring one of them.
   c. Applicants must pass an exam before becoming eligible for a civil service position.
   d. People wear expensive clothing with large brand names or logos.

9. Jane uses an online dating service. For each of the following activities, say whether Jane is screening or signaling. **[LO 10.4]**
   a. Jane views profiles of only nonsmokers.
   b. Jane describes her volunteer activities in her profile.

    c. Jane lists museums and foreign films among her interests.

    d. Jane looks for matches who live within 25 miles of her address.

10. Consider the effect of reputation and say whether you are likely to be treated better in scenario *a* or scenario *b*. **[LO 10.5]**

    a. You tell an auto mechanic that you have just moved to town.

    b. You tell an auto mechanic that you are moving out of town.

11. Consider the effect of reputation and say whether you are likely to be treated better in scenario *a* or scenario *b*. **[LO 10.5]**

    a. You are purchasing your car from an individual who advertised it on craigslist.

    b. You are purchasing your car from a local dealership.

12. In college admissions, which of the following are examples of statistical discrimination? Choose all that apply. **[LO 10.6]**

    a. A college has minimum required scores on standardized tests.

    b. A college is an all-women's school.

    c. A college uses high-school GPA to rank students for scholarship offers.

    d. A college requires three letters of recommendation.

13. In a market for car insurance, which of the following are examples of statistical discrimination? Choose all that apply. **[LO 10.6]**

    a. Premiums are adjusted based on the zip code of the insured.

    b. Premiums are adjusted based on the color of the car.

    c. Premiums are adjusted based on the driving record of the insured.

    d. Premiums are adjusted based on the model of the car.

14. Say which public regulation approach is likely to be more effective in providing information to consumers of pharmaceuticals. **[LO 10.7]**

    a. Requiring pharmaceutical companies to list major side effects of their medications in television advertisements.

    b. Requiring pharmaceutical companies to post online the full text of research results from medical testing done during the development of new drugs.

15. Say which public regulation approach is likely to be more effective in providing information to consumers of restaurant meals. **[LO 10.7]**

    a. Filing a notice at city hall when a restaurant fails a health and sanitation inspection.

    b. Posting a public notice on the door of a restaurant that fails a health and sanitation inspection.

Time and Uncertainty

Is College Worth It?

As the 2012 presidential campaign swung into gear, Republican Mitt Romney and Democrat Barack Obama agreed on one thing: The interest rate on federal student loans should be frozen at 3.4 percent per year.[1] Both candidates seemed to feel that the government should limit the financial burden associated with the choice to attend college.

For most students, college loans are not just political talking points. The total amount of student loan debt has now climbed to about $1.2 trillion dollars; about 40 million Americans have at least one outstanding student loan.[2] Because you pay a future fee (called *interest*) to borrow the money, you eventually pay back a lot more than the amount you borrowed. Is it worth it? In 2014, just over half of recent college graduates were working at a job that didn't require a college degree.[3]

How should you think about borrowing for college? The decision to attend college means

©Jasper White/Image Source

weighing the trade-offs involved and deciding that the costs and benefits of a college degree make it more worthwhile than other things you could be doing with your time and money. If you borrow to go to college, you have to decide that it's worth paying a future fee (the interest) to get your hands on a chunk of money right now. Whether or not you borrow, you have to believe that your time and money are better spent on college than other options, like investing an equal amount of money in a business start-up or spending more time working rather than studying.

For most people, at least part of the decision to go to college depends on anticipated future earnings. You expect a college education to pay off down the road; you anticipate it will enrich your mind and teach you skills that will increase your chances of getting a high-paying job. You're betting that your extra earnings will more than cover the interest costs of your loan. You also are betting that those earnings will be greater than what you could have accrued by investing borrowed money somewhere else and starting to work right away instead. For most people these are good bets. But there's always uncertainty, especially when the economy is shaky. Economics provides a way to think about choices like this, which have uncertain future costs and benefits.

LEARNING OBJECTIVES

LO 11.1 Explain why money is worth more now than in the future and how the interest rate represents this relationship.

LO 11.2 Calculate compounding over time with a given interest rate.

LO 11.3 Calculate the present value of a future sum.

LO 11.4 Evaluate the costs and benefits of a choice using expected value.

LO 11.5 Explain the behavior of individuals who are risk-averse or risk-seeking.

LO 11.6 Explain how risk aversion makes a market for insurance possible.

LO 11.7 Explain the importance of pooling and diversification for managing risk.

LO 11.8 Describe the challenges that adverse selection and moral hazard pose for insurance.

When you make decisions that require you to weigh uncertain future costs and benefits, you face two complications. The first is that you can't directly compare costs and benefits that show up now (such as college tuition) with those that show up in the future (such as higher salaries) because the value of money changes over time. In this chapter, we'll show how to use interest rates to make these comparisons accurately.

The second complication is that the future is uncertain. For instance, there is always the possibility that you might *not* end up earning more, despite your college degree. In the following section we look at how to account for risk when making decisions about the future. In the final part of the chapter, we'll see how some risks can be managed through diversifying and pooling.

You can put the ideas in this chapter to work to understand many important life decisions: whether to take out a loan to buy a house or a car or to start a business; whether to purchase insurance against car accidents or theft, or to provide for your children if you get too sick to work; and whether you should invest in some opportunity or other—the stock market, real estate, retirement funds—in the hope of getting income in the future.

Value over Time

In previous chapters we've talked about making decisions by weighing the benefits and opportunity cost of each option. Conveniently, many decisions involve immediate trade-offs—that is, costs and benefits that occur at the same time: You give the barista your money, and in return you get handed a coffee, right away.

In this chapter, we'll apply the question *What are the trade-offs?* to a trickier set of decisions—those that involve costs that occur at one time and benefits that occur at another time.

Timing matters

Why does it matter if the costs and benefits of a choice occur at different times? Consider the following scenario: You have won first prize in a competition. Congratulations! For your prize, you can choose one of the following options.

Option A: You can have $100,000 now.

Option B: You can have $100,000 ten years from now.

Which would you choose? We're guessing you'd take option A. If you take the $100,000 now, you can do fun or useful things with it right away—like pay for your college education, treat yourself to a brand new car, or donate tens of thousands of insecticide-treated bednets to help people living in malarial areas of Africa stay healthy. Why would you wait 10 years to do any of these things?

Even if you don't intend to do anything with the money right away, you're still better off taking option A—you can always just save it while you think about what to do with it. Pretty much everyone would rather have money now than the same amount of money later. Conversely, most people prefer *costs* that are delayed to those they have to bear immediately. That's why so many people buy things on credit.

These preferences—for immediate benefits and delayed costs—are another way of saying that money is worth more to us *now* than in the future. Because this is so, we cannot simply equate costs and benefits that occur at different times. To be able to weigh trade-offs that happen over time, we need a way of reflecting the changing value of money over time.

Interest rates

How *much* more is money worth now than in the future? Suppose that the prize options for winning the competition change to:

Option A: You can have $100,000 now.

Option B: You can have $1,000,000 ten years from now.

Which would you choose? Tempting as it would be to take $100,000 now, we bet most people would probably be willing to wait 10 years to get their hands on a million dollars.

Now ask yourself this: How much would we have to offer to convince you to take option B over option A? $105,000? $200,000? $350,000? $500,000? Not everyone will have the same answer. It depends on how much more it is worth to you to have money now, rather than 10 years from now. If you strongly prefer to have cash in hand, then we'd have to offer you a lot more money in the future in order to convince you to wait. If you're more patient, we wouldn't have to offer you so much.

Where do these individual preferences come from? Think about this question in terms of opportunity cost. *What is the opportunity cost* of waiting until the future to get your money? It's the value of whatever you could otherwise have done with the money in the meantime.

When a bank lends you money to attend college, for example, it passes up the opportunity to do something else productive with that money instead. Thus, if you want the bank to give you money now, you have to agree to pay something extra when you repay the loan in the future. The opportunity cost to the bank of lending you money is represented by the **interest rate** it charges you on the loan—the price of borrowing money for a specified period of time, expressed as a percentage per dollar borrowed and per unit of time. The interest rate tells us how much more the money is worth to the bank today than in the future. Different banks may offer loans at different interest rates, depending on how strongly they prefer to have cash in hand.

interest rate
the "price of money," typically expressed as a percentage per dollar per unit of time; for savers, it is the price received for letting a bank use money for a specified period of time; for borrowers, it is the price of using money for a specified period of time

 CAUTION: COMMON MISTAKE

In the real world, interest rates also reflect the risk that a borrower will default on a loan and the risk of inflation. For the sake of simplicity, we are ignoring inflation and are assuming that all loans are certain to be paid back. This enables us to zero in on what interest rates fundamentally represent: the *opportunity cost* of having to wait to get your money.

On the flip-side, when you save money at a bank, the bank usually pays you interest on your deposit. In essence, the bank is borrowing money from you, the depositor. You, too, have an opportunity cost—the value of whatever else you could have done with that money instead of depositing it with the bank. Again, for each individual this will be different. Some will be happy to deposit money at 1 percent interest; others would prefer to do something else with their money unless they are offered at least 5 percent. Interest rates are an important concept in macroeconomics as well as microeconomics, and we'll return to them in greater detail later in the text. For now, we'll focus on why they matter for individual decision making.

Typically, the interest rate is expressed as a percentage of the sum of money in question, over a specified time period—usually one year. For instance, if the interest rate on a loan of $1,000 is 5 percent per year, it means that after one year the borrower will owe the original $1,000 plus 5 percent of $1,000 in interest:

$$\$1,000 + (\$1,000 \times 5\%) = \$1,000 \times 1.05 = \$1,050$$

The general formula for the value of a loan of amount X at the end of one period of time with an interest rate r is:

EQUATION 11-1   Value of a loan with interest $= (X \times 1) + (X \times r) = X \times (1 + r)$

An alternate way to think of interest is as a cost per unit, just like other prices. An annual interest rate of 5 percent is the same thing as saying that the price of borrowing money is $0.05 per year for every dollar you owe. Interest is a price per dollar, *per unit of time:*

EQUATION 11-2   Interest rate: $r = \dfrac{\text{Price per \$}}{\text{Time}}$

Compounding

LO 11.2 Calculate compounding over time with a given interest rate.

An annual interest rate of 5 percent tells us that the cost of borrowing $1,000 for one year is $50. So what's the cost of borrowing $1,000 for two years, or five years, or 10 years?

Unfortunately, it's not as simple as just $50 a year. That's because interest also accumulates on interest, not just on the original sum. Let's say you deposit $1,000 in a bank account that offers 5 percent interest. (Remember, when you put your money in a bank account that pays interest, the bank is effectively borrowing the money from you.) After one year, you have $1,050. Then, in the second year, you earn 5 percent interest *on $1,050* (not the original $1,000). The interest in year 2 is $52.50. After two years you have $1,102.50, not $1,100.

$$
\begin{aligned}
\text{1st year:} \quad & \$1,000 \times 1.05 && = \$1,050.00 \\
\text{2nd year:} \quad & \$1,050 \times 1.05 && = \$1,102.50 \\
& = \$1,000 \times (1.05)^2 && = \$1,102.50
\end{aligned}
$$

This process of accumulation, as interest is paid on interest that has already been earned, is called **compounding**.

compounding
the process of accumulation that results from the additional interest paid on previously earned interest

It was relatively easy to find the amount after two years of compounded interest: We knew the amount after one year and just multiplied that amount by the 5 percent interest rate. But beyond year 2, it's far simpler to use a formula than to do year-by-year calculations. With compounding, the general formula for finding the future value of an initial deposit (PV) over a time period of n years at interest rate r is:

EQUATION 11-3   Future value of a sum $= FV = PV \times (1 + r)^n$

For discussion of the use of compounding techniques to calculate the growth of an investment over time, see Appendix F, "Math Essentials: Compounding," which follows this chapter.

Over time, compounding can have a big effect. If you were expecting your initial $1,000 deposit to grow by a steady $50 per year, then after 20 years you would expect to have $2,000 in the bank. But thanks to compounding, your 5 percent interest earnings help you accumulate $1,000 × $(1.05)^{20} = \$2,653.29$.

Compounding is welcome news for investors because it means your money grows at a greater rate than you might have expected. Instead of taking 20 years to double your money, as it would if your $1,000 grew by just $50 a year, it takes just a little over 14 years for your deposit to double in value at an interest rate of 5 percent.

See the Econ and YOU box "The rule of 70" for a quick way to estimate compounding over time.

The rule of 70
Econ and YOU

Is there a big difference between a 2 percent interest rate and a 5 percent interest rate? Finance often involves comparing different rates. The list includes interest rates, growth rates, and rates of return to investments. One handy tool for comparing rates is the "rule of 70." It provides quick and easy—and sometimes surprising—comparisons.

The "rule of 70" provides an estimate of the effects of compounding over time. It states that the amount of time it will take a quantity to double in value is roughly 70 time periods divided by the interest rate per period. So, if you are earning 2 percent interest per year on your savings account, it will take about $70 \div 2 = 35$ years for the value of your account to double (if you don't touch the account and you save the interest too). With a 5 percent interest rate, doubling would happen two decades sooner, in about $70 \div 5 = 14$ years.

The same calculation can be applied to debt. The average interest rate on credit card debt is about 16 percent per year. If you borrow at 16 percent and don't pay back the debt, letting it keep accumulating, it would take approximately $70 \div 16 = 4.4$ years for the credit card debt to double in size. Ouch. If you borrow at 20 percent, your debt would double in $70 \div 20 = 3.5$ years. That's much more ouch.

These are only rough estimates, and the rule of 70 is less precise when applied to higher rates of interest. If you do the math precisely, you will find that after 4.4 years the credit card debt would not quite have doubled yet. (In the case of $1,000 of debt, for instance: $\$1,000 \times (1.16)^{4.4} = \$1,921.39$.) But it works pretty well for most interest rates you're realistically likely to encounter.

The rule of 70 can also be applied to other rates of accumulation. For instance, when economists discuss national economic growth, they can use the same rule to estimate how many years it will take for a country's national wealth to double. For example, China's income (growing at roughly 7 percent per year) could double every 10 years, while in the United Kingdom incomes (growing at roughly 2 percent per year) may double only every 35 years.

The rule of 70 shows how seemingly small differences in interest rates and growth rates can really matter. Not bad for some back-of-the-envelope math!

As nice as compounding is for savers, it can be dangerous territory for borrowers. This is especially true when interest rates are much higher than 5 percent, as they often are for credit cards and personal loans. While federally guaranteed student loans currently top out at 6.8 percent per year, private student loans can cost as much as 18 percent. If you don't keep up with payments on your loans, unpaid interest incurs *more interest* due to compounding, and debts can rapidly spiral out of control.

Present value

The decision to go to college means accepting immediate costs—such as tuition, room and board, and time spent studying rather than earning a salary—in return for the anticipated benefit of earning higher salaries down the road. Knowing that interest rates represent the opportunity cost of delaying benefits, we can come closer to answering the question with which we started this chapter: How can you know whether the delayed benefits of college will outweigh the immediate costs?

Economists use interest rates to compare the present value and future value of a sum. Earlier, we asked how much you'd have to be offered before you'd prefer to wait 10 years than to have $100,000 right now. Let's say you think you could invest the money for an 8 percent annual return. We can calculate that the future value of $100,000 in 10 years with an 8 percent interest rate is $\$100,000 \times (1.08)^{10} = \$215,892.50$.

If we know the future value, we can also rearrange this equation to calculate **present value**. Present value is how much a certain amount of money that will be obtained in the future is worth

LO 11.3 Calculate the present value of a future sum.

present value
how much a certain amount of money that will be obtained in the future is worth today

today. So if you knew that an investment was going to pay you $215,892.50 in 10 years, and you knew that the interest rate over that time would be 8 percent, then you could calculate the present value of that investment as $215,892.50 ÷ $(1.08)^{10}$ = $100,000.

More generally, if r is the annual interest rate, then the formula for calculating the present value of a sum FV received in n years at interest rate r is as follows:

EQUATION 11-4 $$\text{Present value of a sum} = PV = \frac{FV}{(1+r)^n}$$

Notice that this formula is simply another way of writing Equation 11-3. The relationship between present value and future value is always given by the interest rate and the time period:

- If you know the present value, you can multiply by the compound interest rate to find the future value.
- If you know the future value, you can divide by the compound interest rate to find the present value.

Present value translates future costs or benefits into the equivalent amount of cash in hand today. That information enables us to compare the future amounts directly with the immediate amounts.

Let's go back to your college-loan decision. Say you expect that if you *don't* have a college degree, you'll earn a total career income of $1.2 million. (That amount equates to an average of $40,000 a year over 30 years.) If you *do* have a degree, you expect to earn an extra $20,000 a year, raising your total career income to $1.8 million. So if you go to college, you expect to have earned an extra $600,000 after working for 30 years ($20,000 × 30).

What is that future $600,000 worth in today's money? Let's say that your first job starts five years from now and that you expect to be able to invest your money at a 5 percent interest rate. We can calculate the present value of your first year of earning by entering these values into Equation 11-4:

$$PV = \frac{\$20,000}{(1.05)^5} = \$15,670.52$$

Note that $n = 5$ because you do not receive your first payment of $20,000 until five years from now (when you start your job). The way to interpret this present value is to say you could invest $15,670.52 today at an annual compounding interest rate of 5 percent, and it would yield $20,000 in five years.

The following calculation shows that the present value of the entire extra $600,000 you earn by going to college is equivalent to having $252,939 in hand right now:[4]

$$\frac{\$20,000}{(1.05)^5} + \frac{\$20,000}{(1.05)^6} + \frac{\$20,000}{(1.05)^7} + \ldots + \frac{\$20,000}{(1.05)^{34}}$$

In the above calculation, the first term is the present value of the first $20,000 payment. The second term is the present value of the second $20,000 payment, received six years from today. Similarly, we calculate the present value of the $20,000 received each year for all 30 years, with the last payment received at $n = 34$.

According to the calculation, as long as you are paying less than $252,939 to attend college, then the future benefit will exceed the present cost. In fact, a more realistic version of this calculation would show college in an even more favorable light since you don't have to pay all the tuition money at once. This is just an example, of course. With your own predictions about your likely earnings (based on your expected career, where you're going to live, and other relevant variables), you can calculate a comparison that's tailor-made for your own situation.

Knowing how to translate between present and future values can be useful in many other decisions when the benefits and opportunity cost occur at different times. For example:

- If you want a certain level of income when you retire, how much should you save into your retirement fund now?
- If you run a business, what value of future sales would be needed to make it worthwhile to invest in a new piece of machinery?

You can compare these kinds of costs and benefits as long as you know three of the four variables in Equations 11-3 and 11-4: time period, interest rate, and either the present or future value of the costs and benefits.

✓ TEST YOURSELF

☐ What does the interest rate on a loan represent to the lender? **[LO 11.1]**

☐ What is the "rule of 70"? **[LO 11.2]**

☐ What two factors determine the relationship between a future sum of money and its present value? **[LO 11.3]**

Risk and Uncertainty

If you are the worrying sort, you may have noticed a limitation of, or problem with, our analysis of the costs and benefits of college. What happens if your income doesn't increase as much as you expect it to as a result of attending college?

Just as in this example, some of the most important life decisions you will face involve weighing uncertain future costs and benefits against today's costs and benefits. We can make educated guesses about what will happen in the future, but there is always the chance that these guesses will turn out to be wrong. The changing value of money over time is only one challenge when making decisions about the future; risk is another.

What is risk?

Risk exists when the costs or benefits of an event or choice are uncertain. Everything in life involves some uncertainty. When you fly, there might be a delay that means missing an important connection. When you buy a used car, it might turn out to need expensive repairs. When you invest in a company, its stock price could tumble. When you invest in a college education, you might graduate just as the economy is tanking and well-paying jobs are hard to find. Evaluating risk requires that we think about different possible outcomes and accept that our best guess about future costs and benefits could be wrong.

risk
exists when the costs or benefits of an event or choice are uncertain

 CAUTION: **COMMON MISTAKE**

Although they may seem like similar ideas, some economists often distinguish between *risk* and *uncertainty*. They use *risk* to refer to situations in which the probabilities that different outcomes will happen *are known*. We know, for example, that a coin has a 50 percent chance of coming up heads when it's flipped. Making a bet on a coin flip thus entails risk. Or consider airline safety: Although you may not want to look at the numbers (they are actually quite reassuring), the Federal Aviation Administration collects extensive statistics on the safety of airplanes; anyone can make a reasonable guess of the chance of the next flight crashing.

Those examples contrast with situations of *uncertainty*, in which the probabilities are *not known*, and may not even be measurable. The decision to go to college, for example, involves uncertainties about your future earnings and happiness in different kinds of careers. Even the best economists can't accurately predict what the health of the economy will be 10 or 20 years down the road.

The distinction may matter when you take courses focused on risk and uncertainty. But in the rest of the chapter, we'll use the terms *risk* and *uncertainty* interchangeably to refer to choices for which the probabilities of the event occurring are known.

Expected value

Even when we can't know for *certain* how something will turn out, we can often say something about the *likelihood* that it will turn out one way versus another. If we can estimate how likely different outcomes are, and the financial implications of each outcome, then we can come up with a single cost or benefit figure that takes risk into account. That figure is called **expected value**. Expected value is the average of each possible outcome of a future event, weighted by its probability of occurring.

We can use expected value to make the analysis of the benefits of a college education a bit more realistic. In reality, of course, you could follow countless possible career paths. But for the sake of simplicity, let's say there are just two possibilities open to you *without* a college degree. Without a college degree, you have:

- A 50 percent chance of a career in which you make $1.5 million over 30 years ($50,000 a year).
- A 50 percent chance of making $900,000 over 30 years ($30,000 a year).

Then suppose that getting a college degree opens up a new range of job options. *With* a college degree, you have:

- A 50 percent chance of making $2.4 million.
- A 25 percent chance of making $1.5 million.
- A 25 percent chance of making $900,000.

Table 11-1 shows these possibilities.

We can't know for sure which of these possible career paths will come true. But since we know the probability of each, we can measure the expected value of your future income with and without college. The general formula for the expected value of a decision is found by multiplying each possible outcome of an event (which we will call S) by the probability P of it occurring, and then adding together each of these terms for n different outcomes:

EQUATION 11-5 $$\text{Expected value} = EV = (P_1 \times S_1) + (P_2 \times S_2) + \ldots + (P_n \times S_n)$$

Using this formula, the expected value of your income without a college degree is:

$$EV = (50\% \times \$1,500,000) + (50\% \times \$900,000) = \$1,200,000$$

Applying the same method to find the expected value of your income with a college degree, you get:

$$EV = (25\% \times \$1,500,000) + (25\% \times \$900,000) + (50\% \times \$2,400,000)$$
$$= \$1,800,000$$

Unlike our earlier estimates, these figures incorporate the risk that your income might actually be lower with a college degree than it would have been without. It's always a possibility—you might get unlucky. But since you cannot know ahead of time whether you will be lucky or not, you can still make a choice based on your *expected* income, which is $600,000 higher with a degree.

TABLE 11-1
Probability of outcomes

Lifetime earnings by education level	$0.9 million	$1.5 million	$2.4 million
No college degree	50%	50%	0%
College degree	25%	25%	50%

Expected value can be a useful tool for making decisions whenever future outcomes are uncertain. For example, when investing in a retirement fund, you won't know for certain how quickly that fund will grow, but calculating an expected value can help you to decide how much you need to be saving. When choosing between different options, though, you won't necessarily always want to choose the option with the highest expected value. As we will see, you will also want to consider the worst-case outcome for each option and decide whether the risk of the worst-case outcome is unacceptably high.

Propensity for risk

Some things are riskier than others. There's a very low risk of injury when playing golf, for example, and a more significant risk when skiing. Similarly, some things that you can do with your money involve a higher risk of loss than others. Putting your money in a savings account or in government bonds carries a very low risk of loss; investing in a start-up company or playing the stock market usually carries a much higher risk.

People have different levels of willingness to engage in risky activities. Those who generally have low willingness to take on risk are said to be **risk-averse**. Those who enjoy a higher level of risk are **risk-seeking**. These attitudes toward risk are an aspect of an individual's preferences—as is a preference for a certain ice-cream flavor or a preference to spend your spare income on clothes or concerts.

Although individuals have varying tastes for taking on financial risks, economists believe that people are generally risk-averse in the following sense: When faced with two options with equal expected value, they will prefer the one with lower risk. Let's say we run a competition, and you're the winner. As a prize, we offer you these options:

Option A: We flip a coin. If it comes up heads, your prize is $100,001. If it's tails, your prize is $99,999.

Option B: We flip a coin. If it comes up heads, your prize is $200,000. If it's tails, you get nothing at all.

Both options have an expected value of $100,000. (Write out this calculation using Equation 11.5 to make sure.) When economists say that people are generally risk-averse, it implies that most people prefer option A, even though both options have the same expected value. That is, people generally would prefer to forgo something in order to reduce the risk of a large loss. This is exactly why people buy insurance. (Clearly, though, not *everyone* would choose option A. If that was the case, nobody would ever go to a casino and take big chances by piling their bets on red or black on the roulette wheel.)

To put it another way, the *expected value* of option B would have to be greater before most people would accept the risk of winning nothing. If you chose option A, ask yourself *how much* would the value in option B have to rise to tempt you to switch to B? Perhaps to $250,000? (The expected value of option B would then rise to $125,000.) How about $1,000,000 (for an expected value of $500,000 for option B)? The answer depends on your personal taste for risk, and it will differ for each individual.

Although it may seem unlikely (alas) that you will ever win such a prize in a competition, this trade-off between risk and expected value is exactly the kind of choice you have to make whenever you think about investing money in stocks, retirement funds, bonds, or real estate.

LO 11.5 Explain the behavior of individuals who are risk-averse or risk-seeking.

risk-averse
having a low willingness to take on situations with risk; when faced with two options with equal expected value, the one with lower risk is preferred

risk-seeking
having a high willingness to take on situations with risk; when faced with two options with equal expected value, the one with higher risk is preferred

✓ TEST YOURSELF

☐ How is the expected value of a future event calculated? **[LO 11.4]**

☐ Why do economists say that people tend to be risk-averse? **[LO 11.5]**

Insurance and Managing Risk

People cope with uncertainty about the future in many ways. One approach is to simply avoid taking greater risks than are strictly necessary. If you don't want to risk hurting yourself while skiing, then don't go skiing! But some risks in life are unavoidable, and some risky activities—like skiing—are avoidable but fun. So people have also developed ways to *manage* the risks they face in their lives.

The market for insurance

LO 11.6 Explain how risk aversion makes a market for insurance possible.

One common way to manage risk is to buy insurance. An *insurance policy* is a product that lets people pay to reduce uncertainty in some aspect of their lives. For instance, if you enjoy skiing, you can buy insurance to cover the cost of being airlifted to a hospital if you break your leg in a fall on the slopes. Insurance products usually involve paying a regular fee in return for an agreement that the insurance company will cover any unpredictable costs that arise.

You've probably encountered many types of insurance associated with common risks that people face in life. There is auto insurance to manage the risk of having your car damaged or causing damage to someone else. Medical insurance manages the risk of becoming ill or injured. Homeowner's or renter's insurance manages the risk of having your belongings destroyed or stolen. Companies that provide these insurance products collect a fee—called a *premium*—in return for covering the costs that clients would otherwise have to pay if they experienced any of these unfortunate events.

In general, the amount people pay for insurance is higher than its *expected value*. For instance, suppose that you pay $1,000 per year for auto insurance. Suppose also that in any given year there is a 1.5 percent likelihood that you will get into an accident that costs $10,000 and a 0.2 percent likelihood of an accident that costs $200,000. If we assume that your insurance policy would cover the full cost of these accidents, then the expected value of coverage in any given year is $550:

$$EV = (1.5\% \times \$10,000) + (0.2\% \times \$200,000)$$
$$= (0.015 \times \$10,000) + (0.002 \times \$200,000) = \$150 + \$400 = \$550$$

Does paying $1,000 for something with a $550 expected value make people suckers? Not at all. Because most people are risk-averse, they are willing to incur the added cost. In the auto insurance example, the $450 buys peace of mind: That amount represents the utility that comes from knowing that if you do get into an expensive auto accident, you will not be ruined by the costs.

The reason people are generally willing to pay for insurance is that, with insurance, the upward limit of their liability in case of an unfortunate event is usually much lower than the actual cost. Without insurance, most people would have trouble finding enough money to replace their homes and all of their possessions following, say, a fire, or to cover the cost of long-term hospital care if they fell very ill. Insurance allows people to feel confident that if they are suddenly faced with these huge expenses, they won't face bankruptcy or be unable to pay for the services they need.

In fact, if the expected value of insurance policies were equal to the premiums paid, insurance companies would not stay in business very long: The insurers would be paying out approximately the same amount they received in premiums, with nothing left over. The industry exists only because it can make a profit from the extra amount that people are willing to pay for the service of managing risk.

Pooling and diversifying risk

LO 11.7 Explain the importance of pooling and diversification for managing risk.

Insurance does not reduce the risks inherent in life. Having car insurance will not make you less likely to be in an accident. (As we will see in the next section, it may actually make accidents *more* likely.) Instead, insurance works because it reallocates the costs of such an event, sparing any individual from taking the full hit. This reallocation occurs through two mechanisms.

The first mechanism for reallocating risk is called pooling. **Risk pooling** occurs when people organize themselves in a group to collectively absorb the cost of the risk faced by each individual. This is the foundational principle that makes insurance companies work. The company is able to easily absorb the cost of one person's emergency because, at any given time, it will have many other clients who are paying their premiums and not making claims.

Suppose, for example, a company has 1,000,000 clients. Putting aside the question of the company's profits, this is equivalent to every client agreeing that he or she will pay $\frac{1}{1,000,000}$ of the cost of catastrophes that happen to other clients. In return, all clients have the assurance that they won't have to pay $\frac{999,999}{1,000,000}$ of the cost if a catastrophe happens to them. Pooling doesn't reduce the risk of catastrophes happening; it just reallocates the costs when they do.

An example of risk pooling comes from the method used by the United Kingdom and other countries to pay for student loans. Rather than making individual students responsible for the costs of their education, all students get their loans from a government-backed company. That company must be repaid only if students earn enough money out of college to do so. You can read about the merits and problems of this system in the What Do You Think? box "Who should bear the risk that a college degree doesn't pay off?"

risk pooling
organizing people into a group to collectively absorb the risk faced by each individual

Who should bear the risk that a college degree doesn't pay off?
What Do You Think?

Suppose you could buy insurance against the possibility that, despite your college degree, you will never get a high-paying job: If your salary never rises above a certain level, the insurance company will pay off the loan you took out to go to college. Would you be interested in buying such an insurance product?

Actually, this is exactly the kind of student loan system in place in some countries, such as the United Kingdom. Students borrow from a government-backed company and repay their loans only once they start earning above a certain amount. If their earnings never reach that level, the loan is eventually written off.

Supporters of this system say it encourages more young people to go to college. Nobody needs to fear that by getting an education, they will incur debts that they will struggle to pay off. Critics point out that taxpayers—including people who never went to college—end up subsidizing graduates who fail to get high-paying jobs.

Some people have proposed replacing this system with a "graduate tax." Under this proposal, college education would be free; it would be paid for by levying an additional income tax on all college graduates earning above a certain sum. Instead of asking all taxpayers to foot the bill for college, only people who attend college would be on the hook.

Effectively, this is a debate about who should bear the risk that a college education doesn't pay off. In the UK, it's currently the taxpayers. Under the graduate-tax proposal, the risk would be pooled among everyone who attends college. In the United States, the responsibility usually falls on the individual student or student's family. Should others be required to pay for the education of people who decide to be social workers or poets? On the other hand, does society as a whole lose something by discouraging students from pursuing their passions for social services or the arts?

WHAT DO YOU THINK?

1. Who should bear the costs of a college education for those people who do not earn enough money to pay back their loans?
2. Should the tuition for those who go into certain majors or professions be forgiven? If you think so, how should we choose which majors or professions should be chosen for this type of program?

diversification
the process by which risks are shared across many different assets or people, reducing the impact of any particular risk on any one individual

The second mechanism for managing risk is diversification. Risk **diversification** refers to the process by which risks are shared across many different assets or people, reducing the impact of any particular risk on any one individual. Diversification is about not putting all your eggs in one basket, and it can be practiced by individuals or firms. For instance, if you invest all of your money in one company, you are completely dependent on that company's fortunes. If it goes bankrupt, so will you. Instead, many people choose to diversify by investing smaller amounts in many companies. If one company fails, they will lose some money, but not all of it. Like pooling your risks, diversifying your risks does not change the likelihood that bad things will happen. It just means that you're not going to be completely ruined by a single unfortunate event.

Suppose you are considering investing $500 in shares of stocks. Stock X is priced at $10 per share, so you can purchase 50 shares.

- There is a 20 percent chance that, in the future, the price of X will fall to $2. If it does, the value of your 50 shares would be $100.
- But there is also an 80 percent chance that, in the future, the price of X will increase to $20. If that happens, the value of your shares would be $1,000.

Thus, the expected value of your 50 shares in the future is $820:

$$EV = (0.20 \times \$100) + (0.80 \times \$1,000) = \$820$$

We can see these values in panel A of Figure 11-1. Now suppose there is a second stock available, stock Y. Stock Y is also initially priced at $10 per share and also faces the possibility of either falling to $2 per share or rising to $20 per share. However, the prices of stock X and stock Y do not necessarily rise and fall together:

- There is a 4 percent chance that the prices of both stocks will fall to $2 per share.
- There is a 16 percent chance that the price of X will rise while the price of Y falls.

FIGURE 11-1

Expected value of stock purchases with and without diversification

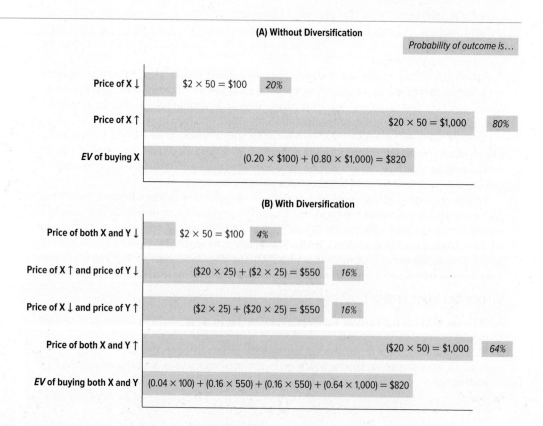

- There is a 16 percent chance that the price of X will fall while the price of Y rises.
- There is a 64 percent chance that the prices of both stocks will rise to $20.

We can see these values in panel B of Figure 11-1. Suppose you initially buy 25 shares of X and 25 shares of Y. We can again calculate the expected value of your shares in the future:

$$EV = (0.04 \times \$100) + (0.16 \times \$550) + (0.16 \times \$550) + (0.64 \times \$1,000) = \$820$$

Notice that the expected value of your shares in the future is the same whether you purchase 50 shares of only X or if you purchase 25 shares of X and 25 shares of Y. However, purchasing 25 shares of X and 25 shares of Y carries much less risk:

- There is only a 4 percent chance of ending up with $100. (In contrast, purchasing only shares of X means a 20 percent chance of having only $100 in the future.)
- Furthermore, because there is only a 4 percent chance of losing money, there is a 96 percent chance that you will have *more* money in the future than you have now.
- The potential gains from buying shares of both X and Y (64 percent) are slightly smaller than if you bought only shares of X (80 percent). However, the risk of losing any money at all is much smaller under diversification.

The key to diversification is that the risks should be as unrelated as possible. For instance, suppose an insurance company sells only one type of insurance—home insurance against earthquakes in San Francisco. This would not be a sensible way for homeowners in San Francisco to pool their risks: If one client's home is destroyed by an earthquake, that same earthquake is likely to destroy many other clients' homes as well. The insurance company could face *all* of its clients making claims at once, and would go bankrupt. In other words, the risk of earthquake damage to one home in San Francisco is *highly correlated* with the risk of earthquake damage to other homes in San Francisco. (Remember that *positive correlation* means things tend to occur together.)

To avoid this problem, the insurance company will diversify. In addition to home insurance in San Francisco, it might choose also to sell, say, car insurance in New Jersey and hurricane insurance in Florida. Earthquakes, car crashes, and hurricanes in different parts of the country are *uncorrelated:* None is more or less likely to occur if one of the others occurs. The insurance company has diversified its risk by selling different products in different places. If it has to pay out after an earthquake in San Francisco, those costs will be covered by the premiums it continues to collect in other places.

These days, you're offered insurance quite often, whether on a new tennis racquet or a cell phone. As the Econ and YOU box "Are extended warranties worth it?" describes, it can be hard to weigh the costs and benefits of these types of insurance.

Are extended warranties worth it?
Econ and YOU

You're at the store buying a new laptop or TV. You get to the cash register, and the salesperson asks if you want to protect your purchase with an extended warranty or protection plan. Should you? These plans are essentially insurance products that will pay to repair or replace your purchase if anything breaks (after the basic warranty expires). Sounds useful. The salesperson tells you horror stories of customers saddled with expensive repair bills not long after the original warranty expires.

(continued)

The economics of the decision tells a more complicated story, however. From one angle, extended warranties look like a poor investment:

- *Consumer Reports* conducted a survey on automotive extended warranties and found that fewer than half of consumers who purchased a warranty ended up using it. Those who did saved only $837 in repairs, yet they paid on average $1,214 for the extended warranty.
- Another study showed that consumers paid on average $90 for insurance on TVs but the largest repair costs were at most $400. This means that, on average, the product must completely fail about 20 to 25 percent of the time for the consumers to gain financially. That's an unrealistically high failure rate.

Research by economists Juan Miguel Abito and Yuval Salant found that consumers often overestimate failure rates. When surveyed, customers guessed that TVs fail at a rate of 13 or 14 percent; according to Consumer Reports, the true failure rate of TVs is far lower. (The actual failure rate is 5 to 7 percent on average.) Simply informing consumers about the true failure rate of products considerably decreased their willingness to pay for warranties.

Extended warranties, albeit at a high price, do provide two distinct benefits:

- First, they can provide peace of mind. Roughly 70 percent of Americans say they are unable to cover a $1,000 expense using their savings, meaning that a large uncovered bill risks putting them in real financial trouble and stress.
- Second, extended warranties also remove the where-do-I-go-to-repair-my-broken-item problem. Sometimes it can be tricky to find a repair company you trust, but with an extended warranty the store usually takes responsibility for the repairs.

As a consumer, figuring out whether extended warranties are a good deal essentially comes down to a few questions:

- First, how does the cost of the insurance compare to realistic repair costs and the actual probability that something will break down (information often available from places like *Consumer Reports*)?
- Second, how easy would it be to cover the expense of the worst outcome on your own? (Maybe you could cover the cost of a big TV repair but not a big car repair.)
- Finally, how much do you value peace of mind? That is harder to put a price on, but it matters a lot to making a good choice. The average consumer loses money on extended warranties, but that might be acceptable if you also lose stress and worry.

Sources: Jose Miguel Abito and Yuval Salant, "The effect of product misperception on the economic market: Evidence from the extended warranty market," paper submitted to *The Review of Economic Studies*, August 5, 2018, www.restud.com/paper/the-effect-of-product-misperception-on-economic-outcomes-evidence-from-the-extended-warranty-market; "Extended car warranties: An expensive gamble," *Consumer Reports*, February 28, 2014, www.consumerreports.org/extended-warranties/extended-car-warranties-an-expensive-gamble; Rafi Mohammed, "Consumer reports is wrong about extended warranties," *Harvard Business Review*, March 23, 2012, https://hbr.org/2012/03/why-consumer-reports-is-wrong.

Problems with insurance

LO 11.8 Describe the challenges that adverse selection and moral hazard pose for insurance.

Pooling and diversifying are common ways of managing risk. For example, when U.S. insurance companies insure individuals, they typically offer insurance to all employees of a particular business. In this way, they pool their risk over a large group of workers so they aren't insuring only the workers most prone to illness. In addition to mitigating risk, most insurance markets also face problems with information asymmetry. This leads to two main problems with insurance: adverse selection and moral hazard. Although we discussed these ideas at length in Chapter 10, "Information," they are particularly crucial for thinking about insurance and risk management.

The first problem insurance companies face is **adverse selection**. This concept describes a state that occurs when buyers and sellers have different information about the quality of a good or the riskiness of a situation, and this asymmetric information results in failure to complete transactions that would have been possible if both sides had the same information. In the context of insurance, adverse selection refers to the tendency for people with higher risk to be drawn toward insurance. For example, in car insurance, the hidden information is that insurers don't know who the bad drivers are, and the unattractive good is an insurance policy on a reckless driver. If you know you're a terrible driver, you'll try to buy as much car insurance as you can. If you smoke, eat mostly fast food, and do not exercise, you might be an enthusiastic customer for health insurance, and so on.

If insurance companies knew everything about their clients, adverse selection would not be a problem. The insurers would simply charge higher premiums to higher-risk clients. Insurance companies can and do ask potential clients seemingly endless questions about their driving records, smoking habits, and so on. But the clients still often know much more about their relevant risk factors than the insurance company. The result is that insurers have a hard time accurately assessing how risky a particular customer will be and charging the right price. To cover their costs, insurance companies usually end up charging higher prices to *all* customers. That decision can make insurance a much less good deal for low-risk individuals. If not kept in check, adverse selection can make it hard for less-risky individuals to find an insurance contract that's worth buying.

The second problem insurance companies face is **moral hazard**—the tendency for people to behave in a riskier way or to renege on contracts when they do not face the full consequences of their actions. If your car is insured against theft, for example, you may be more relaxed about parking it in an unsafe-looking neighborhood. This problem is especially acute with medical insurance: People who know that their medical costs are covered may demand treatments and tests that they would never purchase if they had to pay for them on their own. In these cases, insurance can actually *increase* the expected cost of risks, as discussed in the What Do You Think? box "Should health insurance include preventive care?"

adverse selection
a state that occurs when buyers and sellers have different information about the quality of a good or the riskiness of a situation, and this asymmetric information results in failure to complete transactions that would have been possible if both sides had the same information.

moral hazard
the tendency for people to behave in a riskier way or to renege on contracts when they do not face the full consequences of their actions

Should health insurance include preventive care?

What Do You Think?

One of the highest-profile political debates in America is about how to rein in the steadily increasing costs of medical care. Skyrocketing medical expenditures have been attributed to many factors, including the increased prevalence of obesity, an aging population, and steadily rising malpractice liabilities for doctors.

One strategy that many have suggested to rein in costs is to increase the incentives for people to seek preventive care. Following the passage of the Affordable Care Act of 2010, most health plans in the United States cover preventive care at no out-of-pocket cost to the patient. Examples of covered preventive care include screening for high blood pressure, screening for several types of cancers, and screening for diabetes. With many diseases—including cancer and diabetes, two of the costliest to treat—spending money on early detection and preventive care can prevent much higher costs from being incurred down the road. Preventive care can also reduce the suffering that comes with chronic illness.

On the other hand, moral hazard comes into play. If people with medical insurance are entitled to preventive care, they may demand all kinds of expensive tests and preventive treatments that they don't need. Some people worry that this increase in spending might negate the benefit of future savings.

WHAT DO YOU THINK?

1. Should government policy encourage insurance companies to cover preventive care?
2. Should insurance companies be able to choose which procedures they cover?
3. If you were asked to be a judge in a decision on this matter, what additional information would you need to answer this important question?

✓ TEST YOURSELF

- ☐ Why are people often willing to pay more for insurance than the expected value of the coverage? **[LO 11.6]**
- ☐ What's the difference between risk pooling and risk diversification? **[LO 11.7]**
- ☐ Why can moral hazard increase the costs of insurance coverage? **[LO 11.8]**

Conclusion

Some of life's most important decisions involve weighing uncertain *future* costs and benefits against costs and benefits *today*. In this chapter, we looked at tools that can help with these decisions. Interest rates enable you to compare apples to apples when you think about costs and benefits that occur at different times. Expected value can help you think about what is the best option given uncertainty. Managing risk through pooling or diversification can allow you to avoid bearing the full cost of a worst-case scenario if it happens.

Key Terms

interest rate, p. 247

compounding, p. 248

present value, p. 249

risk, p. 251

expected value, p. 252

risk-averse, p. 253

risk-seeking, p. 253

risk pooling, p. 255

diversification, p. 256

adverse selection, p. 259

moral hazard, p. 259

Summary

LO 11.1 Explain why money is worth more now than in the future and how the interest rate represents this relationship.

Money is worth more in the present than in the future because it can be immediately spent or invested in productive opportunities. The interest rate is the cost of borrowing money for a certain unit of time. It is usually expressed as a percentage per time period. The interest rate is the amount needed to compensate the lender for the opportunity cost of loaning out money—in other words, the amount of money the lender could have earned from investing in something else if he or she weren't lending it.

LO 11.2 Calculate compounding over time with a given interest rate.

Compounding is the process of accumulation that results from the additional interest paid on previously earned interest. With compound interest, the amount of interest earned increases each period, since interest payments earned in the past themselves accumulate

interest in future periods. We calculate the future value of a sum of money, including compound interest, as $FV = PV \times (1 + r)^n$.

LO 11.3 Calculate the present value of a future sum.

Present value refers to how much a certain amount of money in the future is worth today. It can be calculated by rearranging the formula for the future value of a sum, to $PV = \frac{FV}{(1 + r)^n}$. Translating cost or benefits that occur at different times into their present value gives you a common unit of value, allowing you to compare apples to apples.

LO 11.4 Evaluate the costs and benefits of a choice using expected value.

Risk exists with uncertainty about the future—the possibility that things won't turn out as you expect. In order to understand the likely value of a choice with multiple possible outcomes, we calculate its expected value. *Expected value* is the average of all possible future values, weighted by their probability of occurring. Expected value allows us to account for risk when comparing options.

LO 11.5 Explain the behavior of individuals who are risk-averse or risk-seeking.

People have varying degrees of willingness to take on risk. Those who have a low willingness to take on risk are *risk-averse;* those who have a high willingness to take on risk are *risk-seeking.* People are generally risk-averse in the limited sense that when two choices have the same expected value, they will prefer the less-risky one. People generally would prefer to gain a smaller amount than to risk losing everything. The loss of utility caused by losing a large sum is greater than the benefit of gaining the same amount.

LO 11.6 Explain how risk aversion makes a market for insurance possible.

Insurance is a common strategy for managing risk. An insurance policy lets people pay to reduce uncertainty in some aspect of their lives. Such products usually involve paying a regular fee (premium) in return for an agreement that someone else will cover any unpredictable costs that arise. Insurance does not reduce the risk of something bad happening; it simply guarantees that the cost of the event to the insured person will be low. Risk aversion makes a market for insurance profitable: People are willing to pay to shield themselves from the cost of bad things happening, above and beyond the actual expected cost of those things.

LO 11.7 Explain the importance of pooling and diversification for managing risk.

Risk pooling is a strategy for managing risk that involves many people organizing themselves in a group in order to collectively absorb the cost of the risk faced by each individual. Risk pooling doesn't decrease the risk that a bad event will occur; it only reduces the cost to a particular individual in the event that it does occur.

Diversification is another strategy for managing risk that involves replacing large risks with smaller, unrelated ones. That way, the cost of failure for any one investment is not so great, and the chance of many different investments all failing together is small, so the risk of losing a large amount is reduced. Like pooling, diversification does not change the likelihood that bad things will happen; it just reduces the costs associated with any single event.

LO 11.8 Describe the challenges that adverse selection and moral hazard pose for insurance.

One challenge faced by insurance schemes is *adverse selection*—the tendency for people with higher risk to be drawn toward insurance. If insurance companies were able to accurately identify risky clients, adverse selection would not be a problem; insurers would simply charge more for higher-risk clients. But clients often know much more about their relevant risk factors than the insurance company does.

Moral hazard is another challenge for insurance companies. *Moral hazard* means that people will behave in a riskier way when they know that their risks are covered by insurance.

Review Questions

1. Anna is indifferent between receiving $200 today and $230 in a month. What does this imply about her opportunity cost in the coming month? How much interest would Anna need to charge to lend $200 for the month in order to break even? **[LO 11.1]**

2. Cameron has a choice between $100 today and $150 in three months. Zari has a choice between $100 today and $125 in three months. Cameron chooses $100 today. Zari chooses $125 in three months. Explain why Zari is the one who delays payment even though Cameron stands to earn more by waiting. **[LO 11.1]**

3. Suppose your aunt invests $2,000 for you. You are not allowed to have the money until the original amount doubles. Your aunt's investment earns 10 percent, compounded annually. Give a rough estimate of how long it will take before you can access the money your aunt invested for you. **[LO 11.2]**

4. You are considering taking out a two-year loan of $1,000 from a bank, on which you can pay either compound yearly interest of 1 percent or a flat rate of 2 percent for the whole two-year period. Which option is a better deal, and why? **[LO 11.2]**

5. Suppose you know that an investment will earn a positive return in the future. Why is it important to know the present value of the investment? **[LO 11.3]**

6. Suppose you are selling a piece of furniture to a friend who can't afford to pay you upfront but offers to pay you in monthly installments for the next year. What information do you need to calculate the present value of this offer? (*Hint:* Think about the formula for present value.) **[LO 11.3]**

7. A pharmaceutical company is considering investing in the development of a new drug. The company stands to make a lot of profit if the drug is successful. However, there is some risk that the drug will not be approved by government regulators. If this happens, the company will lose its entire investment. Advise the company how to take this risk into account as managers evaluate whether to invest. **[LO 11.4]**

8. You have a big exam tomorrow. You were planning to study tonight, but your friend has tickets to a concert and has invited you to join her. You would be willing to accept a B on the exam in order to go to the concert. You estimate that if you don't study, you have a 35 percent chance of scoring a 90, a 35 percent chance of scoring an 80 (the score required to earn a B), a 25 percent chance of earning a 75, and a 5 percent chance of earning a 60. Will you go to the concert? Explain why or why not. **[LO 11.4]**

9. Many individuals prefer to have insurance (health insurance, car insurance, etc.) rather than not, even if the expected value of their wealth is higher without insurance. What does this imply about their willingness to take on risk? **[LO 11.5]**

10. Lenders tend to offer lower interest rates to borrowers with high credit scores and higher interest rates to borrowers with low credit scores. What does this imply about lenders' willingness to take on risk? **[LO 11.5]**

11. Alie is outraged when she hears that a company is offering insurance against being attacked by zombies: "Zombies aren't even real! This company is just taking advantage of people." Without acknowledging the possible existence of zombies, provide an alternative perspective on the insurance company's ethics. **[LO 11.6]**

12. Matek pays $1,200 for an insurance policy with an expected value of $1,000. Explain why this is a rational choice for Matek. **[LO 11.6]**

13. Suppose that the crop yield of corn farmers in Iowa depends solely on rainfall levels. Also suppose that every part of the state gets approximately the same amount of rain as every other part in any given year. Will the corn farmers of Iowa be able to effectively use pooling to reduce their exposure to risk? Why or why not? **[LO 11.7]**

14. An insurance company that faces fierce competition from other providers is considering a strategy to sell more policies by simplifying its portfolio and becoming the expert in flood insurance for the state. The company managers reason, "Everyone buys flood insurance in this state, so let's focus our efforts on becoming the preferred provider." Evaluate this strategy. **[LO 11.7]**

15. Suppose the economy is suffering and many people are afraid they will be laid off from their jobs. Workers would like to protect against this risk with insurance. Identify and explain two problems that prevent insurance companies from offering layoff insurance. **[LO 11.8]**

16. BackPedal is a bike-rental shop that rents bicycles, helmets, and other gear by the day. **[LO 11.8]**

   a. BackPedal offers an optional helmet rental for $10/day with the rental of a bicycle. To his surprise, the store manager has noticed that cycling accidents are higher among customers who rent helmets than those who do not. Explain this phenomenon using economic concepts. Assume that customers who do not rent helmets also do not own helmets.

   b. BackPedal is considering offering helmets for free with a bike rental. Explain how this new policy will affect the issues you identified in part *a*.

Problems and Applications

1. Your bank offers 4 percent annual interest on savings deposits. If you deposit $580 today, how much interest will you have earned at the end of one year? **[LO 11.1]**

2. You have $325, which a friend would like to borrow. If you don't lend it to your friend, you could invest it in an opportunity that would pay out $376 at the end of the year. What annual interest rate should your friend offer you to make you indifferent between these two options? **[LO 11.1]**

3. If you deposit $500 in a savings account that offers 3 percent interest, compounded annually, and you don't withdraw any money, how much money should you expect to have in the account at the end of three years? **[LO 11.2]**

4. Suppose you run up a debt of $400 on a credit card that charges an annual rate of 12 percent, compounded annually. How much will you owe at the end of two years? Assume no additional charges or payments are made. **[LO 11.2]**

5. Your savings account currently has a balance of $32,300. You opened the savings account two years ago and have not added to the initial amount you deposited. If your savings have been earning an annual interest rate of 2 percent, compounded annually, what was the amount of your original deposit? **[LO 11.3]**

6. You run a business and are considering offering a new service. If you offer the new service, you expect it to generate $50,000 in profits each year for your business over the next two years. In order to offer the new service, you will need to take out a loan for new equipment. Assume a 6 percent annual interest rate. **[LO 11.3]**

7. You are driving home from work and get stuck in a traffic jam. You are considering turning off from your usual route home and taking a longer route that might have less traffic. However, you know that there is some chance that the traffic on your usual, shorter route will clear up. Based on Table 11P-1, calculate the expected value (in minutes until you arrive home) of each option. **[LO 11.4]**

TABLE 11P-1

	Light traffic	Moderate traffic	Heavy traffic
Probability of encountering on Route 1	30%	20%	50%
Duration of drive on Route 1	10 minutes	30 minutes	60 minutes
Probability of encountering on Route 2	50%	50%	0%
Duration of drive on Route 2	20 minutes	40 minutes	80 minutes

8. Books for Kids is a not-for-profit organization that runs after-school reading programs in four school districts. Books for Kids is planning a fund-raiser to buy new books. Last time it held a fund-raiser, donors were allowed to specify which district program they wanted to receive their donation. Table 11P-2 shows the average donations and the percent of all donations that went to each district. Using the last fund-raiser as a projection, what is the expected value of the average donation across all four programs? **[LO 11.4]**

TABLE 11P-2

	Average donation ($)	Percent of donations (%)
Northwest district	25	20
Southeast district	40	25
West district	20	20
South district	10	35

9. Julia had two options when buying car insurance. The expected value of her wealth would be higher with Option A, but Julia chose option B. From the list below, what can we assume about these policies and Julia's willingness to take on risk? Check all that apply. **[LO 11.5]**
    a. Option B was riskier.
    b. Option A was riskier.
    c. Julia is risk-seeking.
    d. Julia is risk-averse.

10. Consider the following scenarios. For each scenario, determine whether a risk averse person will definitely choose Option A, definitely choose Option B, be indifferent between Options A and B, or might choose either Option A or B. **[LO 11.5]**
    a. *Option A:* There is a 50 percent chance of winning $1,000 and a 50 percent chance of winning $0. *Option B:* There is a 100 percent chance of receiving $500.
    b. *Option A:* There is a 40 percent chance of winning $90 and a 60 percent chance of winning $110. *Option B:* There is a 100 percent chance of winning $90.
    c. *Option A:* There is a 50 percent chance of winning $0 and a 50 percent chance of winning $100. *Option B:* There is a 50 percent chance of winning $20 and a 50 percent chance of winning $60.

11. Suppose you own a beach house on a coast that has a small chance of encountering a hurricane each year. There is a 1 percent chance that there will be a hurricane this year that would completely destroy your $350,000 home. (Assume that this home is the only store of wealth that you have.) An insurance company has offered you insurance that would reimburse you the entire value of your home in the event of a hurricane. The premium for this insurance is $4,000. **[LO 11.6]**
    a. What is the expected value of your wealth if you do not purchase insurance?
    b. What is the expected value of your wealth if you purchase the insurance at a $4,000 premium?
    c. Will a risk-averse person choose to purchase insurance?
    d. Will a risk-seeking person choose to purchase insurance?
    e. What would the premium have to be to make a risk-neutral person indifferent between buying the insurance and not buying the insurance?
    f. If the insurance company offered the premium you found in part (e), would a risk-averse person purchase insurance?

12. You are considering buying one of two types of health insurance. You guess that in the next year there is a 1 percent chance of serious illness that will cost you $67,500 in health care; a 9 percent chance of a moderate illness that will cost you $2,500; and a 90 percent chance of regular health care needs that will cost you $500. One type of health insurance is emergency-only coverage; it will cover your expenses for serious illness but not moderate illness or regular care. The other type covers moderate illness and regular expenses, but its payout is capped, so it will not cover the cost of a serious illness. **[LO 11.6]**
    a. What is the expected value of payouts from the emergency-only insurance?
    b. What is the expected value of payouts from the capped-coverage insurance?
    c. Which option is a more risk-averse person likely to choose?

13. For each of the following scenarios, say whether *pooling* or *diversification* is a more promising risk-mitigation strategy. **[LO 11.7]**

   a. Employees of a company who invest their savings in that company's stocks.

   b. Families who are worried about losing their possessions if their houses burn down.

   c. Neighboring farmers who grow the same crop, which is prone to failure in dry years.

14. You have two possessions you would like to insure against theft or damage: your new bicycle, which cost you $800, and a painting you inherited, which has been appraised at $55,000. The painting is more valuable, but your bicycle must be kept outdoors and is in much greater danger of being stolen or damaged. You can afford to insure only one item. Which should you choose? Why? **[LO 11.7]**

15. Farmer Tom is trying to decide what to produce on his farm in the upcoming season. In the past, he has usually grown Crop A. If he grows Crop A, there is a 70 percent chance that his crop will yield $15,000 in profit and a 30 percent chance that he will earn zero profit. **[LO 11.7]**

   a. What is the expected value of his profit if he grows only Crop A?

   b. Now Farmer Tom considers dividing his land between two crops: Crop A and Crop B. There is a 5 percent chance that both crops will fail, and Tom will earn zero profit. There is a 25 percent chance that only one crop will grow, and Tom will earn $6,000 in profit. There is a 60 percent chance that both crops will grow, and Tom will earn $15,000 in profit. What is the expected value of his profit if he grows both crops?

   c. Which option would a risk-averse farmer choose?

   d. Which option would a risk-seeking farmer choose?

   e. Which option would a risk-neutral farmer choose?

16. Say whether each of the following scenarios describes an insurance problem caused by *adverse selection* or by *moral hazard*. **[LO 11.8]**

   a. People who have homeowners insurance are less likely than others to replace the batteries in their smoke detectors.

   b. People who enjoy dangerous hobbies are more likely than others to buy life insurance.

   c. People whose parents died young are more likely than others to seek out health insurance with better coverage.

   d. People who have liability coverage on their car insurance take less care than others to avoid accidents.

17. As part of the Affordable Care Act of 2010, all individuals in the U.S. were required to have health insurance. Do economists expect mandatory health insurance to reduce adverse selection, moral hazard, both, or neither? **[LO 11.8]**

Endnotes

1 B. Greene, "Obama, Romney agree on extending student loan interest rate cut," *U.S. News and World Report*, April 23, 2012, http://www.usnews.com/news/articles/2012/04/23/obama-romney-agree-on-extending-stafford-interest-rate-cut.

2. K. Holland, "The high economic and social costs of student loan debt," June 15, 2015, http://www.cnbc.com/2015/06/15/the-high-economic-and-social-costs-of-student-loan-debt.html.

3. J. Weiner, "Why Sally can't get a good job with her college degree," September 5, 2014, https://www.washingtonpost.com/blogs/she-the-people/wp/2014/09/05/why-sally-cant-get-a-good-job-with-her-college-degree/.

4. The reason the superscripts in the denominators in the computation begin with 5 is that in the example, you don't start earning your salary until year 5—that is, after college is over.

Firm Decisions

The six chapters in Part 4 will introduce you to . . .

the choices and decisions that companies make. Every day, about 126.7 million Americans get up and go to work in over 7.7 million different offices, stores, factories, and other businesses.[1] These 7.7 million firms are diverse in what they do and how they do it, but there are important common threads: Most firms focus on meeting customers' needs while managing employees and physical resources. While doing that, they're usually working hard to keep up with the competition.

A lot of tough choices have to be made along the way. Imagine being a CEO at a large firm and having to decide which product to invest in, where to locate a new factory, which employees to hire, or whether to cut prices after the competition drops theirs. The next chapters explain how firms—big and small—make these kinds of choices.

We begin in Chapter 12, "The Costs of Production," with a simple look at revenues and costs. Understanding the form that costs take can give insight into the choices the firm faces. The types of costs a business has to pay drive its decisions about how much to produce to maximize profits. Those costs also drive decisions about when to stay in business or shut down.

Firms also have to know about the competition they face in the market. Some markets are a fierce battleground, with many companies trying to sell the exact same thing. Other markets are dominated by one firm that faces no competition at all. Still other markets have only a few companies. Chapters 13, 14, and 15 ("Perfect Competition," "Monopoly," and "Monopolistic Competition and Oligopoly") describe the features of these different kinds of markets, and how firms behave in each.

Regardless of what they are selling, businesses need to pay for inputs like raw materials, equipment, and workers to produce goods or services. These are called the *factors of production*, and they are the focus of Chapter 16, "The Factors of Production." Thinking about the markets for factors of production can explain why some professions earn more than others. Those markets also can explain how businesses make decisions about how much to produce and what inputs to use.

Chapter 17, "International Trade," describes what happens when businesses go global. International trade connects American consumers and businesses to people and producers all over the world. In this chapter, we take a look at why certain goods are made in one country and shipped to another. We also consider how globalization, trade, and government policies affect the well-being of workers and consumers in different countries.

Endnotes

1. Data on firms and employment are from U.S. Bureau of the Census, Statistics of U.S. Business for 2016, https://www.census.gov/quickfacts/fact/table/US/POP060210.

The Costs of Production

What Are You Paying for in That Prescription?

If you're allergic to peanuts, the threats are everywhere: birthday parties, school lunch rooms, restaurants, or even innocuous-looking snacks at the grocery store. To counter the risk, those with peanut allergies usually carry an EpiPen, a device that conveniently delivers the correct dose of a drug that stops an allergic reaction. Easy access to an EpiPen can be the difference between life and death.

EpiPens are not cheap. In 2016, the price of a two pack was about $600, up from $97 in 2007. In a campaign speech in 2016, Democratic presidential nominee Hillary Clinton called out EpiPen maker Mylan, saying the EpiPen price hikes were "just the latest example of a company taking advantage of its customers." Soon after, the Senate Special Committee on Aging asked Mylan Chief Executive Officer Heather Bresch to justify the change in EpiPen price. Insurance giant Cigna dropped brand-name EpiPens from its coverage, and CVS pharmacies started offering a competing product called Adrenaclick for $100.

After the outcry, Mylan introduced a "generic" version of the EpiPen that cost only $300. Mylan executives noted that through coupons and insurance copayments, most customers pay far less than the full price. Even with the price changes, EpiPens still cost way more than the drugs inside—a dose of epinephrine, the active drug inside the EpiPen, costs a dollar per dose. What gives?

©Steven May/Alamy

On the one hand, Mylan charges high prices for EpiPens because it has a patent on the applicator; others can't copy Mylan's design and enter the market. In addition to market power, Mylan also incurs costs in running its business. The company creates and airs ads to get people to buy its products. It also conducts expensive research and development (R&D) to find the next wonder cure and bring it to market.

Some estimates suggest that companies often spend a decade and as much as $1 billion on research to develop a new drug. Only a few of the developed drugs will be approved for sale. And only a few of those that are approved for sale will become best sellers. In fact, a research and development manager at pharmaceutical giant Pfizer has said that his team might develop 5,000 chemical compounds in a year and only a half dozen of them will make it to the clinical trials that precede approval for use.[1]

However many EpiPens Mylan makes in a year, R&D costs remain the same. Economists call this kind of cost—one that remains the same, regardless of how much is produced—a *fixed* cost. Mylan also has to hire workers, buy epinephrine to go into EpiPens, and pay for the utilities to its plants running. Since such costs depend on the number of EpiPens Mylan produces, the amount Mylan spends on these items is called *variable* cost.

LEARNING OBJECTIVES

LO 12.1 Define total revenue, total cost, and profit.

LO 12.2 Explain the difference between fixed and variable costs, and give examples of each.

LO 12.3 Explain the difference between explicit and implicit costs, and give examples of each.

LO 12.4 Calculate economic and accounting profit, and explain the importance of the difference.

LO 12.5 Define marginal product, and show why there is diminishing marginal product.

LO 12.6 Define and graph total cost, average costs, and marginal cost.

LO 12.7 Explain why firms face different costs in the long run than in the short run.

LO 12.8 Understand what economies and diseconomies of scale are and their implications for production decisions.

We'll see in this chapter that the difference between fixed and variable costs explains a lot about the way firms behave, in the pharmaceutical industry and beyond. We'll discuss different ways of measuring costs, revenue, and profits, and how they influence production decisions. We'll dig into the details that determine the supply curve we studied in earlier chapters. Understanding the details of cost and profit is critical to running a business, or deciding whether to invest in one.

The Building Blocks of Business: Revenues, Costs, and Profits

In business, people frequently say, "It's all about the bottom line." The term "bottom line" comes from accounting—profit is shown on the last line of a company's income statement. What business people mean when they say "It's all about the bottom line" is that making a profit is the central goal of a business. Everything that happens—management, engineering, marketing—is in some way directed toward generating as large a profit as possible.

Economists also assume that a firm's goal is to maximize profits. The profit motive is central to understanding firms' behavior, just as the quest for utility is the driving force behind *individual* decision making. When we ask *What are a firm's wants?*, the answer is that it wants to maximize its profits.

You've probably run into some businesses that claim to have additional goals. Some businesses refer to their "double bottom line" or "triple

bottom line." What they are saying is that they value not only dollars but also social or environmental impacts. But even a business that would sacrifice some profit to achieve social and environmental goals still has to make a profit to survive. On the whole, the profit motive does a good job of explaining the behavior of most firms.

Profit is revenue minus costs

To define profit, we have to start with two other economic concepts that may be familiar—revenue and cost:

- The amount that a firm receives from the sale of goods and services is its **total revenue**.
- The amount that a firm pays for all of the inputs that go into producing goods and services is its **total cost**. Total cost includes both *one-time expenses* (like buying a machine) and *ongoing expenses* (like rent, employee salaries, raw materials, and advertising). In other words, total cost is anything and everything that the company expends to make its products.

Together, revenue and cost determine how much profit a firm makes. In the simplest terms, **profit** is the difference between total revenue and total cost, as shown in Equation 12-1.

EQUATION 12-1 $\text{Profit} = \text{Total revenue} - \text{Total cost}$

Revenue is relatively straightforward to measure. As Equation 12-2 shows, it's equal to the quantity of each product the firm sells multiplied by the price at which it's sold. (You may have first seen this equation in Chapter 4, "Elasticity.")

EQUATION 12-2 $\text{Revenue} = \text{Quantity} \times \text{Price}$

Suppose, for simplicity's sake, that we want to calculate the revenue of Pfizer, a major pharmaceutical company, and that Pfizer makes only one drug, Lipitor. Imagine that it sells 5 billion pills of Lipitor at $2.70 each. Using Equation 12-2, we can calculate the firm's total revenue:

$$\text{Revenue} = 5 \text{ billion} \times \$2.70 = \$13.5 \text{ billion}$$

Of course, very few companies sell only one product. When multiple products are involved, revenue equals quantity times price for *all* of the products a firm sells, as Equation 12-2a shows:

EQUATION 12-2A
$$\text{Revenue} = \text{Quantity} \times \text{Price}$$
$$= (Q_1 \times P_1) + (Q_2 \times P_2) + \ldots + (Q_n \times P_n)$$

To illustrate, now suppose that Pfizer sells only two drugs—Lipitor, and an arthritis medication called Celebrex®. Imagine that it sells 5 billion pills of Lipitor at $2.70 each and 2 billion pills of Celebrex at $1.25 each. We can calculate the firm's total revenue using Equation 12-2a:

$$\text{Revenue} = (5 \text{ billion} \times \$2.70) + (2 \text{ billion} \times \$1.25)$$
$$= \$13.5 \text{ billion} + \$2.5 \text{ billion} = \$16 \text{ billion}$$

Revenue calculations are generally quite simple. *Cost* is the tricky factor when thinking about profits. We'll see in the next few sections of the chapter that measuring different types of costs—particularly opportunity costs—is complicated. The ability to measure costs accurately, though, makes a big difference for important decisions about production.

Fixed and variable costs

The first complicating factor in calculating costs is the distinction between fixed and variable costs. As noted in the chapter introduction, **fixed costs** are those that don't depend on the quantity of output produced. For Pfizer, running a research and development department is a fixed cost. The cost of office space is another example of fixed costs.

LO 12.1 Define total revenue, total cost, and profit.

total revenue
the amount that a firm receives from the sale of goods and services; calculated as the quantity sold multiplied by the price paid for each unit

total cost
the amount that a firm pays for all of the inputs that go into producing goods and services

profit
the difference between total revenue and total cost

LO 12.2 Explain the difference between fixed and variable costs, and give examples of each.

fixed costs
costs that do not depend on the quantity of output produced

Sometimes a fixed cost is a one-time, upfront payment that has to be made before production can even begin. If you are opening a take-out pizza place, for example, you will have to incur the one-time, upfront fixed cost of buying an oven before you can produce your first pizza.

Fixed costs can also be ongoing: If you lease a corner shop for your business, you have to pay the cost of the lease every month, however many pizzas you produce and sell.

variable costs
costs that depend on the quantity of output produced

Variable costs, on the other hand, depend on the quantity of output produced. These costs include the raw materials that go into production, as well as many types of labor costs. Examples:

- A drug company's variable costs would include the chemicals that go into the products, packaging materials, and wages of employees in the factories that make and package the products.

- A pizza firm's variable costs would include pizza dough and toppings, cardboard take-away containers, and the wages of employees.

In order to produce more pills or more pizzas, these firms would have to buy more raw materials and hire more employees, adding to their total variable costs.

If a firm produces nothing—if it stops production—then its variable cost is zero. But it is still stuck with its fixed costs:

- If Pfizer has developed a pill that isn't approved for sale by the Food and Drug Administration, the variable cost associated with the pill is zero once the company stops development. But Pfizer has already incurred the fixed cost of research.

- If a pizza firm decides to stop making pizzas, it no longer has to pay employees or buy ingredients. But it will still be obliged to pay for its space until the lease expires.

A firm's total cost is the combination of all of its fixed and variable costs. Table 12-1 shows how a hypothetical pharmaceutical company's total cost varies as its output increases.

TABLE 12-1

A firm's total cost

As the number of pills produced increases, so do the variable costs. The fixed costs, however, remain the same even when the number of pills produced is very large. Combining the fixed and variable costs will give us the total cost.

Quantity of pills (millions)	Fixed costs ($)	Variable costs ($)	Total cost ($)
0	1,000,000	0	1,000,000
10	1,000,000	100,000	1,100,000
20	1,000,000	200,000	1,200,000
30	1,000,000	300,000	1,300,000
40	1,000,000	400,000	1,400,000
50	1,000,000	500,000	1,500,000
60	1,000,000	600,000	1,600,000
70	1,000,000	700,000	1,700,000
80	1,000,000	800,000	1,800,000

Although we have so far been talking about variable and fixed costs in the business sense, these costs also factor into more personal decisions. For a different take on the importance of costs into decisionmaking, look at the Econ and YOU box "The quarter-million dollar kid."

The quarter-million dollar kid
Econ and YOU

You might not be thinking now about having kids. But one day you might, and, if you do, it probably won't be cheap.

Of course, deciding whether to have kids, or how many to have, isn't just about dollars and cents—as any parents reading this will attest. Your choices may have more to do with your preferences for sleep and the utility you might get from seeing your kid star in the school play. Still, raising children is one of the most important economic activities that adults undertake. It turns out that when thinking about kids, ideas like fixed and variable costs, marginal costs, and scale economies matter a lot.

Let's start with the raw numbers. The U.S. Department of Agriculture estimates that, on average, for a married-couple family with two children and a middle-income (between $59,200 and $107,400), raising a child from birth until age 17 will cost $233,610 (in 2015 dollars). The calculator that produced that estimate focuses on housing, food, childcare, and transportation. Thus, that nearly quarter-million dollar figure doesn't include the cost of college or of a parent's time.

Of course, your situation may end up differently. Costs of raising kids tend to be higher in cities and lower in rural areas. Costs tend to be higher for richer people, too, partly because housing is more expensive where richer people tend to live. Costs also tend to be higher for single parents due to extra child-care costs. Such costs, though, are lower for people lucky enough to have family nearby who can help take care of the child. The USDA has created a calculator on the internet that allows you to see what happens when you vary some of the parameters (www.cnpp.usda.gov/tools/CRC_Calculator/default.aspx).

Trying different scenarios with the USDA calculator shows important economies of scale. For example, raising two children is not, on average, twice as expensive as raising one child. The marginal cost of the second child is lower than the first. Imagine that the family described above was raising just one child. The USDA estimates that the average cost of raising a 12-year-old is $4,674 a year. But raising two 12-year-olds costs just $7,360 a year. That's not double the cost of the first, but only 1.57 as much.

While the costs of raising children are easy to put into economic terms, many parents will argue that the benefits of children are, well, priceless.

Source: M. Lino, K. Kuczynski, N. Rodriguez, and T. Schap, *Expenditures on Children by Families*, Miscellaneous Publication No. 1528-2015, U.S. Department of Agriculture, Center for Nutrition Policy and Promotion (2015).

Explicit and implicit costs

In Chapter 1, "Economics and Life," we saw that true costs are *opportunity costs*, or the value to you of what you have to give up in order to get something. When economists think about a firm's costs, therefore, they are thinking about everything the firm gives up in order to produce output. A firm's opportunity cost of operations has two components: *explicit costs* and *implicit costs*.

Explicit costs are costs that require a firm to spend money. They include just about everything we typically think of as a cost, including both fixed and variable costs. Rent on a building, employee salaries, materials, and machines—all of these require the firm to pay someone else in order to acquire them.

Implicit costs, in contrast, are costs that represent forgone opportunities. These are opportunities that *could have* generated revenue *if* the firm had invested its resources in another way.

Let's look at an example in order to understand the difference:

- Suppose Pfizer *rents* a warehouse for $4,000 a month and stores boxes of pills in it before they are shipped out to pharmacies around the country. This is an *explicit cost:* The firm has to pay cash to someone for the use of the warehouse.

LO 12.3 Explain the difference between explicit and implicit costs, and give examples of each.

explicit costs
costs that require a firm to spend money

implicit costs
costs that represent forgone opportunities

- If, however, Pfizer *owns* the warehouse and uses it for the same purpose, it incurs zero dollars in explicit costs for the use of the warehouse.
- Does that mean that using the warehouse costs nothing? No—that warehouse could instead be rented out to another company for $4,000 per month. Pfizer *could have earned* $4,000 by renting out the warehouse to someone else rather than storing pills in it. The choice to not earn money in another way is an *implicit cost.*

Once we account for implicit costs, storing pills costs Pfizer $4,000, regardless of whether it owns the warehouse or not.

One particularly notable type of cost faced by nearly all firms is the opportunity cost of the money invested in starting up the business. Suppose you need $100,000 of startup capital to get your take-out pizza place up and running. You have a few options for obtaining the startup capital:

- You can borrow the $100,000 from a bank. If you do, you will need to pay total interest of 10 percent on the loan. This would be an *explicit* cost of $10,000.
- But what if you already have $100,000 invested in your savings account? If you use that money as your start-up capital, there is no *explicit* cost; that is, you don't have to pay anyone else. But there is an *implicit* cost: You are giving up whatever interest you could have earned by placing the money in an interest-generating account or whatever you could have earned by investing it in another venture. You are also giving up the future income you could have earned by "investing" in going back to school and getting a different job.

You can see that any input used in a business—warehouses, equipment, cash—could alternatively be used to generate income some other way. To properly account for the total cost incurred by a firm, we have to think about the opportunity cost of using each of these inputs. As we are about to see, the distinction between explicit and implicit costs can have a huge impact on how we calculate a company's profits.

Economic and accounting profit

LO 12.4

Calculate economic and accounting profit, and explain the importance of the difference.

accounting profit
total revenue minus explicit costs

economic profit
total revenue minus all opportunity costs, explicit and implicit

Usually, when a company reports its profits, what you see is its **accounting profit**. This is total revenue minus explicit costs, as shown in Equation 12-3.

EQUATION 12-3   Accounting profit = Total revenue − Explicit costs

Thinking only about explicit costs, though, will mislead us about how well a business is really doing. To get a clearer picture, we need to consider implicit costs, in a measure called **economic profit**—total revenue minus all opportunity costs, both explicit and implicit—as shown in Equation 12-4.

EQUATION 12-4   Economic profit = Total revenue − Explicit costs − Implicit costs

To see why the difference matters, follow the arguments in Figure 12-1. If the CEO listens to the advice of Executive A, then the firm will have an *accounting profit* to report to investors in the company. But if she expects the investors to be happy, she will be in for an unpleasant surprise: Investors are more interested in *economic profit*. Because the shareholders are also aware of current interest rates, they will realize, like Executive B, that the company could make more money by investing in another business opportunity instead.

Knowing the distinction between economic and accounting profits is a sink-or-swim issue for most firms. However, as mentioned earlier, some investors and businesses look beyond profit when making decisions, as discussed in the From Another Angle box "Beyond the bottom line."

FIGURE 12-1

Defining profit in a business decision   The definition of profit makes a difference. Even when the *accounting profit* for an investment may be large, the *economic profit* could be small or even negative.

©Keith Brofsky/Getty Images

> **CEO:** We have the opportunity to buy a new manufacturing facility. Is this a smart move for our company?

> **Executive A:** The new facility would cost $6 million to buy and $4 million to operate over the next decade, for a total cost of $10 million. The medicines we could produce there would bring in revenue of $13 million. We could make $3 million in profits. *Buy the factory!*

> **Executive B:** But you're forgetting about all of the other things we could do with $10 million. By my calculations, we could earn $6 million in interest over the next 10 years if we invested the money. That means that the true cost of buying the facility is $16 million, and revenue would be only $13 million. *If we bought the factory, we could lose $3 million!*

Beyond the bottom line

From Another Angle

When you buy a box of rice at the store, you can't see that the rice grains were once covered by a husk (sometimes called hulls). These husks have to be removed before rice can be eaten, but there's little use for them once removed. Disposal can be a major problem. For example, farmers in Bihar, a major rice-producing state in India, produce 4 billion pounds of unwanted rice husks per year.

To tackle the problem, a group of MBA graduates created Husk Power Systems, a company that uses rice husks and a process called "biomass gasification" to generate electricity. The company then sells that electricity through mini-grids that serve 300 people each. In total, Husk Power provides electricity to 120,000 people in rice-growing regions of India and Tanzania—people who are not connected to the regional power grid. Now, the farmers produce rice and also contribute to creating a reliable electricity supply.

Husk Power Systems is an example of a *social enterprise*. The business seeks to turn a profit, but it also aims to do good. An influential business school professor, C. K. Prahalad, famously argued that some of the best untapped business opportunities lie in serving the billions of poor people at the "bottom of the pyramid" (as Muhammad Yunus, the founder of Grameen Bank, correctly realized). Many of these businesses earn accounting profit but not economic profit. Then, these low-profit businesses turn to "social investors" who are also motivated by the social

(continued)

mission. The social investors accept that they may earn less money from their investments, but they can feel good about supporting businesses that serve clients in untapped markets.

Social enterprises blur the lines between business and charity because investors effectively give up money to support a business and social cause. On one hand, social enterprises that are not making economic profit rely on the philanthropic goals of their investors, just as much as any charity. However, unlike charities, social enterprises provide investors with a financial return, which encourages investment that wouldn't happen otherwise. Thanks to social enterprises and social investors, hundreds of thousands of people now have electricity—and a way to make use of all those discarded rice husks.

Source: Tamara Chuang, "Fort Collins energy firm that uses rice husks to power remote villages earns $20 million from Shell's venture arm," *The Denver Post*, January 18, 2018, www.denverpost.com/2018/01/18/fort-collins-husk-power-systems-shell-technology-ventures/.

✓ TEST YOURSELF

- ☐ How do you calculate the revenue of a firm that produces only one good? **[LO 12.1]**
- ☐ When a firm doubles its output, how much do its fixed costs increase? **[LO 12.2]**
- ☐ When a restaurant owner works in his own restaurant waiting tables, what is the implicit cost he incurs? **[LO 12.3]**
- ☐ What is the difference between accounting profit and economic profit? **[LO 12.4]**

Production Functions

production function
the relationship between quantity of inputs and the resulting quantity of outputs

Firms create value by bringing together different ingredients to create a good or service that consumers want. The ingredients that go into the production process—raw materials, labor, machines, time, ideas—are the *inputs*. The goods and services that are produced are the *outputs*. The relationship between the quantity of inputs and the quantity of outputs is called a **production function**.

Marginal product

LO 12.5 Define marginal product, and show why there is diminishing marginal product.

The production process itself can be thought of as a sort of recipe that combines certain amounts of inputs, in a certain way, to achieve the desired output.

The analogy with cooking is not exact, however. If you've ever followed a recipe, you'll know that what matters are the *ratios* of ingredients. If the recipe serves four and you're cooking for eight, you can generally just double the amount of all ingredients. This simple scaling up or down doesn't usually work for firms. Sometimes, a firm can *more than* double its outputs by doubling its inputs. Sometimes, it has to more than double its inputs to double its outputs.

To see why, let's consider your new take-out pizza firm. For simplicity, we'll focus on just one of the inputs—labor:

- If you start out with only yourself working there, you won't be able to make many pizzas. You'll constantly have to break off to prep more ingredients, take orders, and handle payments from customers.
- If you employ a second worker to help with these jobs, doubling your labor input, you will probably be able to much more than double your pizza production; the two of you will waste less time switching between tasks.
- Adding a third worker might lead to an even bigger jump in productivity: One of you spends all your time dealing with customers, one focuses exclusively on prepping ingredients, and one does nothing but make pizzas.

There comes a point, however, when the opposite applies. Suppose you now have five workers. What happens if you employ another five?

- The kitchen gets overcrowded and people get in each other's way. You have to spend a lot more time watching over your new employees; you need to make sure they're keeping up your high standards, check that orders don't get misplaced, and see that employees are not slacking off. You'll end up producing more pizzas with 10 workers than you did with five—but probably fewer than twice as many.

The increase in the number of pizzas that can be produced by hiring an additional employee is called the marginal product of that employee. In general, the **marginal product** of any input into the production process is the increase in output that is generated by an additional unit of input.

Table 12-2 shows how this might work in a take-out pizza place. It shows the *marginal product of labor*—the increase in output that is generated by adding more workers. On your own, let's say you are able to produce 50 pizzas. Hiring another employee enables you to jump to 150 pizzas—a *marginal product* of 100 additional pizzas. Adding a third worker increases production to 330 pizzas—a marginal product of 180.

From the third worker on, however, each additional employee increases production by slightly less. When you have nine employees, adding a tenth increases production by only 40 pizzas. This illustrates a common principle of production, called **diminishing marginal product**. This principle states that, holding other inputs constant, the marginal product of a particular input decreases as the quantity of that input increases.

We can represent the production function visually on a graph like the one shown in Figure 12-2. This graph plots the data from the first two columns in Table 12-2. The number of employees appears on the *x*-axis, and the quantity of pizzas produced on the *y*-axis. Marginal product is represented by the slope of the total production curve. At low levels of output, the curve becomes steeper as workers are added. This shows that marginal product initially increases. But then the principle of diminishing marginal product kicks in and the slope of the curve gradually flattens out.

marginal product
the increase in output that is generated by an additional unit of input

diminishing marginal product
a principle stating that the marginal product of an input decreases as the quantity of the input increases

Labor (employees)	Total production (pizzas)	Marginal product of labor (pizzas)
0	0	–
1	50	50
2	150	100
3	330	180
4	500	170
5	630	130
6	730	100
7	810	80
8	875	65
9	925	50
10	965	40

TABLE 12-2

Total production and marginal product

In this pizza business, the first few workers have an increasing marginal product. Soon, however, each additional worker contributes less to total production, reflected by decreasing marginal product.

FIGURE 12-2

Production function

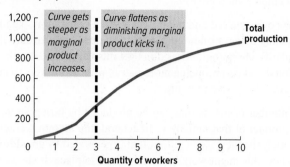

Quantity of pizzas

Curve gets steeper as marginal product increases.

Curve flattens as diminishing marginal product kicks in.

Total production

Quantity of workers

The graph of the production function shows that marginal product increases with the first few workers hired, but then begins to decrease. When output is very low, each additional worker has a higher marginal product than the previous one, represented by the increasing slope of the total production curve. As more workers are added, marginal product starts to diminish, represented by the flattening out of the curve.

Another way to visualize diminishing marginal product is to graph the number of pizzas each additional employee adds. Figure 12-3 shows that the marginal product curve initially increases as the first few workers are added; it then trends downward.

Figure 12-3 also shows *average product*—the number of pizzas produced per worker, on average. Average product is calculated by dividing total production by the number of workers. When a new employee's marginal product is greater than the existing average product, the average increases. As soon as a new worker's marginal product is less than the existing average, the average number of pizzas per worker starts to fall.

FIGURE 12-3

Average and marginal product

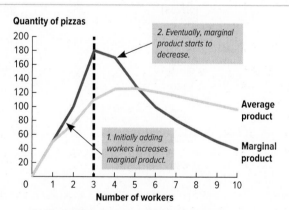

Quantity of pizzas

2. Eventually, marginal product starts to decrease.

Average product

Marginal product

1. Initially adding workers increases marginal product.

Number of workers

As the first few workers are added, marginal product increases. As the quantity of workers continues to increase, however, the principle of diminishing marginal product kicks in. When the marginal product curve crosses the average product curve, average product also starts to decrease.

Thinking about marginal product connects us to an important aspect of rational decision making first discussed in Chapter 1, "Economics and Life." We noted that people engage in marginal decision making; they weigh trade-offs, rather than seeing choices as all-or-nothing. We'll see in the coming chapters that firms also make production decisions "on the margin." That is, they compare the marginal product of an input to its marginal cost when deciding whether to employ an additional worker or build another factory.

✓ TEST YOURSELF

☐ Suppose that an accounting firm with 10 employees hires another accountant. By doing so, it goes from serving 30 customers each week to serving 32 customers each week. What is the marginal product of labor for the new accountant? **[LO 12.5]**

☐ Why might marginal product be increasing at lower levels of output and decreasing at higher levels of output? **[LO 12.5]**

Cost Curves

We've just taken a careful look at the production side of a firm. Firms decide *how much* of each input to use. These decisions, quite directly, determine the quantity of outputs the firm will produce.

Costs of inputs also matter, of course. When a firm increases its output by adjusting its use of inputs, it incurs the costs associated with that decision. In general, the cost of an input won't change simply because you've reached the point of diminishing marginal product in your firm. Your tenth employee costs as much in wages as your first, even if he adds less to your production.

In this section, we'll take a close look at how companies use the concepts of total, average, and marginal costs.

Total, average, and marginal costs

Suppose you own a pizza parlor. How will you decide how many pizzas to produce? Remember that firms want to maximize profit, calculated as total revenue minus total cost. We have already seen how firms measure their revenue. We will now look at how costs change as firms change their production quantity.

LO 12.6 Define and graph total cost, average costs, and marginal cost.

Total and average costs   Let's assume that every additional employee costs the same, regardless of how many more pizzas they help you make. Say that wages are $200 per worker. Assume that the cost of your workers is the only variable cost.

There are also fixed costs—ones you would have to pay regardless of how many pizzas you make. For simplicity's sake, we'll consider just one fixed cost: the lease on your premises. We'll say this is $300.

As defined earlier in the chapter, total cost represents all the inputs a firm uses in production. These inputs consist of fixed costs plus variable costs, as Equation 12-5 shows.

EQUATION 12-5   Total cost = Fixed costs + Variable costs

In our pizza example, if you have one worker, then your total cost is:

$300 (fixed) + $200 (variable) = $500

If you have two workers, your total cost is:

$300 + ($200 + $200) = $700

average fixed cost (AFC)
fixed cost divided by the quantity of output

average variable cost (AVC)
variable cost divided by the quantity of output

average total cost (ATC)
total cost divided by the quantity of output

And so on. You can see these data in Table 12-3.

In the example just above, we assumed simple numbers for the calculation. In a real-life situation, or a more complicated example, the numbers might not be so simple. In that case, it's useful to be able to use averages for the cost inputs:

- **Average fixed cost (AFC)** is fixed cost divided by the quantity of output.
- **Average variable cost (AVC)** is variable cost divided by the quantity of output.
- **Average total cost (ATC)** is total cost divided by the quantity of output.

Equations 12-6, 12-7, and 12-8 show that for each type of average cost, we simply divide the cost by the quantity of the output. In our example, that quantity is the number of pizzas produced.

EQUATION 12-6
$$\text{Average fixed cost (AFC)} = \frac{\text{Fixed cost}}{\text{Quantity}}$$

EQUATION 12-7
$$\text{Average variable cost (AVC)} = \frac{\text{Variable cost}}{\text{Quantity}}$$

EQUATION 12-8
$$\text{Average total cost (ATC)} = \frac{\text{Total cost}}{\text{Quantity}}$$

Table 12-3 shows the average fixed cost, average variable cost, and average total cost for our pizza example, along with a lot of other data. Let's visualize each measure in turn, with the help of some graphs.

TABLE 12-3

Costs of production

Fixed costs have to be paid, however many pizzas you produce. Pizza production depends only on your variable costs—the cost of labor. Total cost is the sum of fixed and variable costs. The marginal cost of producing one extra pizza is calculated by dividing the increase in variable cost by the increase in number of pizzas produced.

Labor (workers)	Total production (pizzas)	Marginal product (pizzas)	Fixed costs ($)	Average fixed costs ($/pizza)	Variable costs ($)	Average variable costs ($/pizza)	Total cost ($)	Average total cost ($/pizza)	Marginal cost ($/pizza)
0	0	–	300	–	0	–	300	–	–
1	50	50	300	6.00	200	4.00	500	10.00	4.00
2	150	100	300	2.00	400	2.67	700	4.67	2.00
3	330	180	300	0.91	600	1.82	900	2.73	1.11
4	500	170	300	0.60	800	1.60	1,100	2.20	1.18
5	630	130	300	0.48	1,000	1.59	1,300	2.06	1.54
6	730	100	300	0.41	1,200	1.64	1,500	2.05	2.00
7	810	80	300	0.37	1,400	1.73	1,700	2.10	2.50
8	875	65	300	0.34	1,600	1.83	1,900	2.17	3.08
9	925	55	300	0.32	1,800	1.95	2,100	2.27	4.00
10	965	45	300	0.31	2,000	2.07	2,300	2.38	5.00

Instead of these year-by-year calculations, we can use a formula. The general formula for computing the future value of money using compounding is:

EQUATION F-1   Future value $= FV = PV \times (1 + r)^n$

where PV is the amount (present value) of the initial investment, FV is the future value of the investment, r is the interest rate, and n is the number of time periods between now and the future.

Let's try the problem again using the formula for compound interest. First, remember the order of operations, which some people remember by using the acronym PEMDAS:

P: *P*arentheses, from the innermost outward

E: *E*xponents

MD: *M*ultiplication and *D*ivision from left to right

AS: *A*ddition and *S*ubtraction from left to right

Therefore, we plug in your initial investment of $100 for PV_1 and the time period of 4 years for n, and solve for FV in the following order. (*Hint:* You might want a calculator for this.)

$FV = PV \times (1 + r)^n$
$FV = 100 \times (1 + 0.1)^4$
$FV = 100 \times (1.1)^4$ (Remember to *start with the operations inside the parentheses.*)
$FV = 100 \times 1.4641$ (Now you *apply the exponent.*)
$FV = \$146.41$

After 4 years, your investment of $100 will be worth $146.41.

Let's see how the problem changes when we change the interest rate. This time, let's calculate the future value of your $100 investment if the interest rate is 5 percent. We will still invest for 4 years with interest compounded annually.

Year 1: $\$100.00 + (\$100.00 \times 0.05) = \$105.00$
Year 2: $\$105.00 + (\$105.00 \times 0.05) = \$110.25$
Year 3: $\$110.25 + (\$110.25 \times 0.05) = \$115.76$
Year 4: $\$115.76 + (\$115.76 \times 0.05) = \$121.55$

Now, let's do the problem again using the formula.

$FV = 100 \times (1 + 0.05)^4$
$FV = 100 \times (1.05)^4$
$FV = 100 \times 1.2155$
$FV = \$121.55$

After 4 years, your investment of $100 is worth $121.55.

This same method can be used to calculate the value of a borrowed sum of money, as well as an invested one. Instead of an initial investment, we can plug in the initial amount borrowed. The interest rate is the rate at which the debt increases, rather than the rate at which your investment grows; otherwise the calculations are exactly the same.

Suppose you borrow $1,000 at a monthly interest rate of 10 percent, and wait for 5 months to pay it off. Let's assume that interest is compounded monthly. How will your debt accumulate each month?

Month 1: $\$1,000.00 + (\$1,000.00 \times 0.10) = \$1,100.00$
Month 2: $\$1,100.00 + (\$1,100.00 \times 0.10) = \$1,210.00$
Month 3: $\$1,210.00 + (\$1,210.00 \times 0.10) = \$1,331.00$
Month 4: $\$1,331.00 + (\$1,331.00 \times 0.10) = \$1,464.10$
Month 5: $\$1,464.10 + (\$1,464.10 \times 0.10) = \$1,610.51$

Math Essentials: Compounding

In Chapter 11, "Time and Uncertainty," you learned how to compute the future value of money using compound interest. Compounding occurs because the interest your money earns in one time period itself earns interest in the next time period. Multiplying a single investment by an interest rate is simple enough, but calculating the growth of an investment over time is more complicated because the base keeps changing. In every period, we have to multiply the interest rate by the initial investment *plus* any interest earned in earlier time periods. This appendix will walk you through the act of compounding.

LEARNING OBJECTIVE

LO F.1 Use compounding to calculate the present and future value of money.

Compounding and Future Value

Let's say that you invest $100 right now at an interest rate of 10 percent. You plan to withdraw your money in 4 years, and the interest compounds annually. What will be the value of your investment in 4 years?

Let's first calculate the value year by year, accounting for the compounding interest. This calculation is essentially calculating percentage change. The 10 percent in interest represents how much the original amount you invest will change in one time period (in this case, one year).

LO F.1 Use compounding to calculate the present and future value of money.

Year 1:	$100.00 + ($100.00 \times 0.10) = $110.00
Year 2:	$110.00 + ($110.00 \times 0.10) = $121.00
Year 3:	$121.00 + ($121.00 \times 0.10) = $133.10
Year 4:	$133.10 + ($133.10 \times 0.10) = $143.41

Notice that each year we incorporate the interest earned in the previous year into the base investment for the next year. In other words, we multiply the interest rate not by the initial investment, but by the initial investment *plus* any previously earned interest.

Let's do the problem again using the formula.

$$FV = 1,000 \times (1 + 0.1)^5$$
$$FV = 1,000 \times (1.1)^5$$
$$FV = 1,000 \times 1.61051$$
$$FV = \$1,610.51$$

After 5 months, you will owe \$1,610.51, or more than one-and-a-half times your initial debt.

The rule of 70

You've now seen how to precisely calculate compounded amounts over time. An Econ and YOU box in Chapter 11 discussed the quick and easy tool called the "rule of 70" that will give you a more general estimate of how long it takes a figure to double in size. Remember that all you have to do is divide 70 by the annual interest rate. The rule of 70 is less precise when applied to higher rates of interest, but it works pretty well for most interest rates you're likely to encounter, so many businesspeople use it to make quick mental calculations.

Problems and Applications

1. If you invest \$250 at an annually compounded interest rate of 10 percent, how much will you have in 3 years? [**LO F.1**]

2. Suppose you invest \$500 at an annually compounded interest rate of 10 percent. [**LO F.1**]
   a. How much will you have in 10 years?
   b. How much will you have in 20 years?
   c. How much will you have in 50 years?

3. Suppose you borrow \$50 from a payday lender, who charges a monthly interest rate of 5 percent, compounded monthly. [**LO F.1**]
   a. If you pay back the loan in one month, how much will you owe?
   b. If you pay back the loan in one year, how much will you owe?
   c. If the interest rate is raised to 6 percent rather than 5 percent, how much *more* will you owe if you wait for a year to pay off the debt?

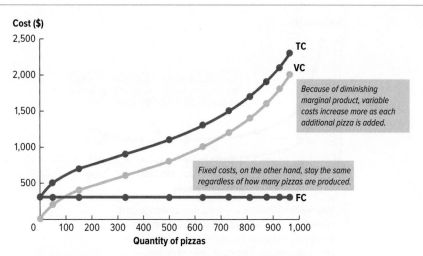

The increasing slope of the total cost curve reflects the principle of diminishing marginal product: Each additional worker costs the same as the previous worker but adds fewer additional pizzas to production. Fixed costs, of course, stay the same regardless of how many pizzas are produced. The total cost curve is the sum of variable and fixed costs.

Graphing total cost We'll start by graphing total cost; see Figure 12-4. The fixed cost of the lease, of course, stays constant at $300, regardless of how many pizzas you produce.

Looking at variable costs, notice that while the variable costs appear to increase at a constant rate in Table 12-3, this is misleading. Each *worker* costs an additional $200, but the cost to produce *each pizza* is changing (the number of pizzas made is shown on the x-axis).

Reflecting the increasing marginal product of the first few employees, the variable cost (VC) curve initially is less steep. At this point in the curve, each $200 spent for a new worker adds relatively more pizzas compared to cost. However, as the principle of diminishing marginal product kicks in, the variable cost curve in Figure 12-4 gets gradually steeper. As workers become less productive, the firm must pay the same amount of money ($200) for fewer pizzas. In other words, each pizza is becoming more costly to produce. You can see that later in the graph, each additional unit of output along the x-axis requires a bigger change in cost on the y-axis than the one before it.

This pattern of increasing marginal cost is the inevitable result of diminishing marginal product: As the productivity of each unit of input decreases, it costs more to get another unit of output.

Graphing average cost Next, let's see what happens when we graph the average cost curves, as shown in Figure 12-5. The first thing to note is that the average fixed cost (AFC) curve trends downward. The reason is that the fixed costs remain the same as quantity produced increases; as fixed costs are averaged over more units of production, the fixed cost per unit of production must decrease.

Next, note that the average variable cost (AVC) curve is U-shaped. It initially slopes downward because the first few employees have an increasing marginal product. For the first worker, the average variable cost of one pizza is $200 \div 50 = 4$. When a second, more productive worker is added, the average variable cost of one pizza declines to $400 \div 150 = \$2.67$. After the fifth worker, AVC trends upward.

What you really want to know for your pizza business are your costs *per pizza*. If you know the cost per pizza, then you can calculate the profit for each pizza by subtracting the cost per pizza

FIGURE 12-5
Average cost curves

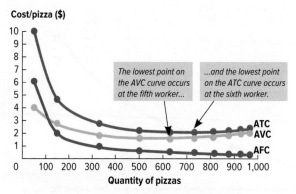

This figure shows the key features of average cost curves. Average fixed cost (the red line) always decreases as output increases because the same cost is spread out over more units of output. Average variable cost (the pink line) at first decreases and then increases, reflecting the marginal product of inputs. Average total cost (the purple line) is simply what you get when you add these two together. It's also U-shaped as the increases in average variable cost are weighed against the decreases in average fixed cost.

from the price received for each pizza. To find the cost per pizza, you have to account for both fixed and variable costs, which takes us to the average total cost.

As you can see in Figure 12-5, the shape of the ATC curve is similar to the AVC curve. The only difference is the addition of the AFC curve. Looking back at the data in Table 12-3, we can see that average *variable* costs are lowest (at $1.59 per pizza) with five employees. But average *total* cost is lowest (at $2.05 per pizza) with six employees. This shows that it would be a mistake to look only at average variable cost when considering how many workers to employ. On net, the pizzas are cheaper to make with six employees.

Marginal cost   Another important component of production and hiring decisions is *marginal cost*. Because firms make decisions on the margin, they can ask what *additional cost* they will incur by producing one additional unit of output. This is the **marginal cost (MC)** of that unit. In other words, it is the variable cost of producing the *next unit* of output.

We calculate the marginal cost of production by dividing the change in total cost by the change in the quantity of output, as Equation 12-9 shows.

marginal cost (MC)
the additional cost incurred by a firm when it produces one additional unit of output

EQUATION 12-9

$$\text{Marginal cost} = \frac{\text{Change in total cost}}{\text{Change in quantity}}$$

$$\text{MC} = \frac{\Delta \text{ total cost}}{\Delta \text{ quantity}}$$

Reading the data in Table 12-3, we can see that:

- The second worker produced an additional 100 pizzas for a cost of $200 ($700 − $500). Thus, the marginal cost of each additional pizza for the second worker is $200 ÷ 100 = $2.00.

- Employing a third worker would yield an additional 180 pizzas, but the additional variable cost remains $200. Thus, the marginal cost of each additional pizza for the third worker is only $200 ÷ 180 = $1.11.

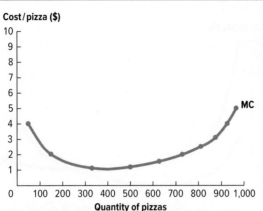

FIGURE 12-6
The marginal cost curve

The marginal cost curve has the inverse shape of the marginal product curve. This is because every additional unit of input costs the same, regardless of the contribution it makes to production. As marginal product initially increases, so marginal cost initially decreases; as the principle of diminishing marginal product kicks in, the marginal cost curve increases.

As we can see from Figure 12-6, the marginal cost curve is U-shaped. Like AVC, this U-shape is a result of an increasing and then a decreasing marginal product of labor: Marginal cost initially decreases (as marginal product increases) and then increases (as marginal product decreases).

As the data table shows, marginal cost decreases for the pizza business up through the addition of the fourth worker. Eventually, though, marginal cost increases: With the fifth worker, marginal cost begins to increase. At that point, the MC curve in Figure 12-6 begins to slope upward.

Notice in Table 12-3 that the marginal cost per pizza for the ninth worker is $4.00, and adding a tenth worker leads to a marginal cost of $5.00 per pizza. Such information is important as firms make production and hiring decisions. For example, if the marginal cost is $5.00 and your pizzas sell for $4.50, you shouldn't employ that tenth worker.

Finally, let's plot the marginal cost curve on the same graph as the ATC curve, as shown in Figure 12-7. Notice that the *marginal cost (MC) curve intersects the lowest point of the ATC curve.* Here's why:

- If the marginal cost of increasing production by one unit is *less* than your current average total cost, then producing that extra unit will *decrease* your average cost. For example, if the average total cost of producing pizzas is currently $2.20 and the marginal cost of one additional pizza is $1.54, then producing one more pizza will clearly bring the average below $2.20 per pizza. This can be seen in Table 12-3 when production increases from 500 to 630.

- If, on the other hand, the marginal cost of increasing production by one unit is *more* than your current average total cost, then producing that extra unit will *increase* your average cost. Notice that for all quantities above 730, the marginal cost is above average total cost. As a result, average total cost is pulled upward.

The concepts of marginal cost and average total cost are fundamentally important to decisions about production, as we will see in the next few chapters. To help review, Table 12-4 summarizes the various types of costs.

FIGURE 12-7

Marginal and average cost curves

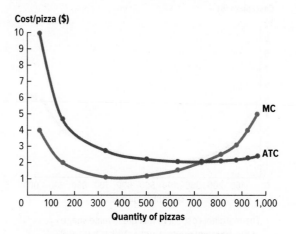

When the marginal cost of producing another pizza is less than the average total cost, producing that extra pizza will decrease the average total cost. When the marginal cost of producing another pizza is more than the average total cost, producing that extra pizza will increase the average total cost. Therefore the marginal cost curve intersects the average total cost curve at its lowest point.

TABLE 12-4

Costs in general

Cost	Description	Calculation
Total cost (TC)	The amount that a firm pays for all of the inputs (fixed and variable) that go into producing goods and services	$TC = FC + VC$
Fixed costs (FC)	Costs that don't depend on the quantity of output produced	—
Variable costs (VC)	Costs that depend on the quantity of output produced	—
Explicit costs	Costs that require a firm to spend money	—
Implicit costs	Costs that represent forgone opportunities	—
Average fixed costs (AFC)	Fixed costs divided by the quantity of output	$AFC = FC \div Q$
Average variable costs (AVC)	Variable costs divided by the quantity of output	$AVC = VC \div Q$
Average total cost (ATC)	Total cost divided by the quantity of output	$ATC = TC \div Q$
Marginal cost (MC)	The additional cost incurred by a firm when it produces one additional unit of output	$MC = \Delta TC \div \Delta Q$

✓ TEST YOURSELF

- ☐ What is the difference between average total cost and marginal cost? **[LO 12.6]**
- ☐ Why does marginal cost usually increase as output increases? Under what circumstances might marginal cost decrease? **[LO 12.6]**
- ☐ Why does the marginal cost curve intersect the average total cost curve at its lowest point? **[LO 12.6]**

Production in the Short Run and the Long Run

In Chapters 3 and 4 ("Markets" and "Elasticity"), we noted that supply is more flexible over longer periods of time. The commonsense explanation behind this fact is that some things just take time to do. For a firm to adjust its production, it may have to build new factories, purchase new properties, or hire more employees. These activities don't happen overnight. The differences between the costs that firms face in the short run and the long run reflect this need for production adjustment time.

Costs in the long run

Which costs are "fixed" depends on what timescale you're thinking in. Consider a take-out pizza firm's lease of its premises. If the firm decides to make fewer pizzas this month, it is still committed to pay the monthly cost of its lease. When the lease expires, the firm could decide to move to smaller, cheaper premises. The cost of the lease is fixed in the *short run* (whatever the length of the lease is), but not fixed in the *long run*.

We have used factory laborers and pizza take-out workers as examples of variable costs. These kinds of employees tend to operate on flexible-shift systems, working as much as—and often no more than—required. The period of notice to terminate employment tends to be short and new workers don't need much training.

In contrast, none of these things are true of research scientists. In the short run, therefore, it's pretty easy for Pfizer to reduce or increase the number of workers in its factories. But reducing or increasing the size of its R&D department is something it can do only in the long run.

How long is the *long run?* Economists don't think of the long run as being a certain number of days or months or years. Instead, the term refers to however long it would take for a firm to vary all of its costs, if it wanted to. So, the definition of long run depends on the type of firm and type of production:

- For a take-out pizza firm, the long run is probably not very long. The lease on its premises may run for a year, for example. Costs that are fixed when the firm plans for a month ahead will become variable when the firm plans for a year ahead.

- A firm such as Pfizer may need to make operational decisions over time spans of 5 or 10 years. It takes time to build new research laboratories, factories, or warehouses, or to decommission old ones.

The cost curves we have been considering so far in this chapter are short-run cost curves. We'll now turn our attention to what cost curves look like in the long run, when *all costs* are considered variable.

LO 12.7 Explain why firms face different costs in the long run than in the short run.

Economies and diseconomies of scale

Remember why the ATC curve is U-shaped? Initially, additional inputs have an increasing marginal product, which results in decreasing average total cost. Sooner or later, the principle of diminishing returns kicks in. Then marginal product decreases and average total cost starts to increase.

LO 12.8 Understand what economies and diseconomies of scale are and their implications for production decisions.

Something similar happens in the long run, too. When firms plan for the long run, they consider the *scale* at which they want to operate: Should they move to bigger or smaller premises? Should they build more factories, or close some down? *Economies of scale, diseconomies of scale,* and *constant returns to scale* describe the relationship between the quantity of output and average total cost.

Initially, a small firm may find that increasing the quantity of output enables it to lower its average total cost. When this happens, we say the firm is facing **economies of scale**. For example, if you own 10 pizza places rather than one, you may be able to negotiate bulk-purchase discounts on ingredients. The company that prints your menus will charge less per menu to print 10 times as many. You'll pay only slightly more for hosting your website, even though it's handling 10 times as much traffic.

However, bigger isn't always better. There may come a point at which increasing scale leads to *higher* average total cost. Imagine running a chain of tens of thousands of pizza places, spread across dozens of countries. It might be such a logistical nightmare to keep the spending under control that your average total cost would be higher than when you had fewer outlets in fewer countries. When a firm is in a position in which increasing its quantity of output starts to raise its average total cost, economists say it is facing **diseconomies of scale**.

In between these extremes, there may also be various quantities of output at which a firm can operate without experiencing higher or lower average total cost. In that situation, we say the firm is facing **constant returns to scale**.

Figure 12-8 illustrates the idea of economies and diseconomies of scale on a long-run ATC curve. It shows the three possibilities relating to quantity of output and average total cost:

- When a firm could achieve *economies of scale* by expanding, its long-run ATC curve slopes down. This shows that *ATC decreases as output increases.*
- When a firm would face *diseconomies of scale* by expanding, the curve slopes up. This shows that *ATC increases as output increases.*

economies of scale
returns that occur when an increase in the quantity of output decreases average total cost

diseconomies of scale
returns that occur when an increase in the quantity of output increases average total cost

constant returns to scale
returns that occur when average total cost does not depend on the quantity of output

---

FIGURE 12-8

Economies and diseconomies of scale

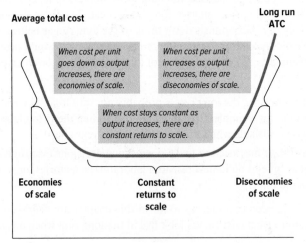

When a firm could achieve economies of scale by expanding, its long-run ATC curve slopes down, showing decreasing ATC as output increases. When it would face diseconomies of scale by expanding, the curve slopes up, showing rising ATC as output increases. The long-run ATC curve is flat in the middle, representing the various levels of output at which the firm achieves constant returns to scale.

- Often, the long-run ATC curve is shown with a flat portion in the middle. That flat portion represents *constant returns to scale*—the different levels of output the firm achieves *without increasing ATC.*

The Economics in Action box "Walmart and economies of scale" describes how one company has taken advantage of economies of scale.

Walmart and economies of scale

Economics in Action

Walmart started as a single discount store in northwest Arkansas. It now has some 5,000 stores across the United States and 11,700 worldwide. The 140 million Americans who shop at Walmart each week buy everything from car parts to groceries to prescription drugs to money transfers.

Walmart's success has come largely from its ability to offer a wide variety of products at low prices. Having so many stores means Walmart can guarantee huge purchases to vendors. As a result, it can negotiate low wholesale prices, thus lowering its average total cost—an example of an economy of scale. Smaller stores simply can't match Walmart's bargaining power.

Managing logistics at a massive scale isn't easy, and Walmart has had to be innovative. One logistical problem involves managing inventory across thousands of stores. Buying 10 million items cheaply from a wholesale supplier may not be so cost-efficient if those items are sitting in a warehouse in Oregon when a store runs out of stock in Georgia. Walmart minimized this problem by developing a sophisticated computerized inventory system. The system tracks inventories and helps to ensure that stores are stocked with the products they need.

Walmart, however, has not vanquished all competitors. Today, Walmart faces competition from large online retailers like Amazon, which has successfully taken advantage of economies of scale to cheaply deliver products to consumers' homes. The question of how well Walmart will fare against Amazon depends on which titan is able to build on its scale economies.

Sources: Walmart corporate website, http://corporate.walmart.com/newsroom/company-facts.

A firm's long-run ATC curve covers a much greater range of output than its short-run ATC curve. In the short run, all firms are constrained by the limited capacity of their fixed inputs, so can produce within only a limited range of output. However, in the long-run, firms can bring new factories online or can dramatically cut their workforce, opening much wider ranges of production. The long-run ATC curve is made up of points from the firm's short-run ATC curves at larger or smaller sizes. By increasing or decreasing their scale, firms can move along the long-run ATC curve from one short-run ATC curve to another. Figure 12-9 shows this idea.

When a firm cannot lower its average total cost by either increasing or decreasing its scale, it is said to be operating at an **efficient scale**. At that scale, it is producing the quantity of output at which average total cost is minimized.

efficient scale
the quantity of output at which average total cost is minimized

People sometimes say that a particular industry has "large economies of scale." By this, they mean that some characteristic of that industry gives an advantage to larger firms. The pharmaceutical industry is a good example: Firms such as Pfizer need to be large to sustain the research and development budget necessary to develop enough new drugs to have a chance of some of them becoming bestsellers.

Even though many companies have large research and development budgets, many diseases still wait for drugmakers to develop a treatment or cure. See the What Do You Think? box "Should drug companies care about neglected diseases?" for more about the ethics of drug development in the pharmaceutical industry.

FIGURE 12-9
Average total cost in the long run

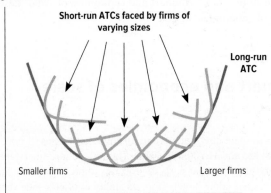

Average total cost

Short-run ATCs faced by firms of varying sizes

Long-run ATC

Smaller firms   Larger firms

Output

Short-run ATC curves cover a smaller range of output than the
long-run ATC curve. The scale of the firm limits how high production
can rise in the short run. The long-run cost curve can be thought
of as consisting of points on various short-run ATCs faced by firms
of various sizes. By increasing or decreasing their scale, firms
can move along the long-run ATC curve from one short-run
ATC curve to another.

Should drug companies care about neglected diseases?
What Do You Think?

Since 1930, the federal Food and Drug Administration (FDA) has approved 1,500 drugs, including new ways to fight cancer, arthritis, and depression. There's even a drug to prevent something
called restless leg syndrome. But many fatal diseases still await a cure, and many of them receive
nowhere near the amount of R&D investment that would be required to develop a vaccine or
treatment.

Drugs for some diseases, called "orphan diseases" because they affect only a small group of
people, are unprofitable because too few people would buy the cure. Drugs for other diseases,
like malaria or sleeping sickness, affect many more people, but these types of ailments occur
in disadvantaged parts of the globe—meaning that many wouldn't be able to afford a drug that
helps. According to the Drugs for Neglected Diseases Initiative, of the 850 products approved
between 2000 and 2011, only 4 percent were designed for these diseases, even though the need
is much greater.

Some say the market system is working exactly as it should. It is allocating scarce resources to
goods for which there is the most demand. Others think it is immoral that the system prioritizes
research into the diseases of people who can pay over research to find cures for major killers.

One approach to solving the problem of orphan diseases is called *advanced market commitment (AMC)*. In this approach, a government or private charity promises to purchase a minimum
quantity of a drug, once developed, to treat an orphan disease. The thinking is that this commitment delivers an incentive for research similar to what firms would face if the disease afflicted
large numbers of wealthy patients. For some background on the use of AMCs, look at the Gates
Foundation's efforts: www.gatesfoundation.org/vaccines/Pages/advanced-market-commitments-
vaccines.aspx.

WHAT DO YOU THINK?

1. Should pharmaceutical companies and their stockholders feel morally obligated to work on "orphan drugs"?
2. Should governments step in and pay companies to undertake research in an advanced market commitment? Should the responsibility rest with private charity?

Sources: www.nytimes.com/2012/05/02/business/pfizer-profit-declines-19-after-loss-of-lipitor-patent.html; www.statista.com/statistics/267810/expenditure-on-research-and-development-at-pfizer-since-2006; www.pfizer.com/system/files/presentation/2015_Pfizer_Financial_Report.pdf.

TEST YOURSELF

☐ Why do most fixed costs become variable costs in the long run? **[LO 12.7]**
☐ What does it imply about the shape of the average total cost curve if a firm faces constant returns to scale? **[LO 12.8]**

Conclusion

In this chapter, we've explored the costs that all firms face when they produce goods or services. Understanding the relationship between inputs, outputs, and costs is crucial because costs, along with the firm's revenues, determine profits. The pursuit of profits, of course, drives every firm's decision-making process, including how much to produce and whether to stay in business.

Over the next few chapters, we'll continue to dig into the details of firm behavior that determine the market supply curve. Hold onto your understanding of production functions, different types of costs, and ways of calculating profits. We'll build on them as we continue to describe firm choices and market structures.

Key Terms

total revenue, p. 269

total cost, p. 269

profit, p. 269

fixed costs, p. 270

variable costs, p. 270

explicit costs, p. 271

implicit costs, p. 271

accounting profit, p. 272

economic profit, p. 272

production function, p. 274

marginal product, p. 275

diminishing marginal product, p. 275

average fixed cost (AFC), p. 278

average variable cost (AVC), p. 278

average total cost (ATC), p. 278

marginal cost (MC), p. 280

economies of scale, p. 284

diseconomies of scale, p. 284

constant returns to scale, p. 284

efficient scale, p. 285

Summary

LO 12.1 Define total revenue, total cost, and profit.

The amount that a firm pays for all of the inputs that go into producing goods and services is its *total cost*. The amount that a firm receives from the sale of goods and services is its *total revenue*. *Profit* is the difference between total cost and total revenue.

LO 12.2 Explain the difference between fixed and variable costs, and give examples of each.

Fixed costs are costs that don't depend on the quantity of output produced. Often, a fixed cost is a one-time, upfront payment that has to be made before production can begin. Examples are buying a factory or hiring researchers to develop a new product. *Variable costs* are costs that depend on the quantity of output produced. Examples are the cost of raw materials and, often, workers' salaries.

LO 12.3 Explain the difference between explicit and implicit costs, and give examples of each.

Explicit costs are those that require a firm to spend money, such as paying for rent on a building, employee salaries, materials, and machines. *Implicit costs* are costs that represent forgone opportunities. They do not require a firm to spend money or take on obligations. Instead, they could have generated revenue if the firm had invested its resources in another way, such as investing money instead of spending or renting out factory space instead of producing goods.

LO 12.4 Calculate economic and accounting profit, and explain the importance of the difference.

Economists think about costs as opportunity costs, and therefore they consider both explicit and implicit costs when calculating profit. A firm's *economic profit* is total revenue minus explicit costs minus implicit costs. In contrast, accountants deal strictly with costs that involve an outlay of money. A firm's *accounting profit* is total revenue minus explicit costs.

Because economic profit subtracts explicit *and* implicit costs from revenue, it is generally smaller than accounting profit.

LO 12.5 Define marginal product, and show why there is diminishing marginal product.

The ingredients that go into the production process—raw materials, labor, machines, time, ideas—are inputs. The goods and services produced are outputs. This relationship between the quantity of inputs and the quantity of outputs is called a *production function*.

The *marginal product* of any input into the production process is the increase in output generated by an additional unit of the input. In many cases, the marginal product of an input decreases as the quantity of the input increases, a principle called *diminishing marginal product*.

LO 12.6 Define and graph total cost, average costs, and marginal cost.

Total cost is the sum of fixed costs and variable costs. Average cost is calculated by dividing cost by the total quantity of output produced.

The basic measure of average cost is *average total cost (ATC)*; it is equal to total cost divided by the quantity of output. We can also calculate *average fixed cost (AFC)* and *average variable cost (AVC)*, which are equal to fixed or variable costs, respectively, divided by quantity of output.

The *marginal cost (MC)* of production is calculated by dividing the change in total cost by the change in the quantity of output. In other words, it is the variable cost of producing the *next unit* of output.

LO 12.7 Explain why firms face different costs in the long run than in the short run.

Firms are able to adjust their property and production processes over time. Thus, costs that are fixed in the short run can become variable in the long run. A firm's long-run cost curves reflect the increased flexibility of fixed costs. In the long run, a small firm can expand its production capacity to look like that of a larger firm by changing the quantity of inputs that were fixed in the short run.

LO 12.8 Understand what economies and diseconomies of scale are and their implications for production decisions.

The average total cost curve is U-shaped. At levels of output where the curve slopes downward (i.e., ATC is decreasing as output increases), a firm faces *economies of scale*. At levels of output where the ATC slopes upward, a firm faces *diseconomies of scale*. When average total cost does not depend on the quantity of output—as in the flat middle section of the long-run curve—a firm faces *constant returns to scale*.

A firm faces an incentive to increase or decrease its production to reach its *efficient scale*, the quantity of output at which average total cost is minimized.

Review Questions

1. Economists assume that firms have a goal to maximize profits. Is this a reasonable assumption for not-for-profit organizations? **[LO 12.1]**

2. Suppose you are evaluating the profit earned by a pharmaceutical company that produces three different medicines. What information will help you determine the company's revenue? What information will help you determine the company's total cost? **[LO 12.1]**

3. Suppose that a pharmaceutical company's costs include researchers' salaries, chemicals, warehouses, and paper

and plastic packaging. Which of these costs do you expect to be fixed in the short run, and which variable? **[LO 12.2]**

4. Dustin is planning to open a catering business. Give examples of a one-time fixed cost, an ongoing fixed cost, and a variable cost his new catering business might incur. **[LO 12.2]**

5. A shopkeeper explains to you that she keeps down the cost of running her business because her husband works in the shop for free. Is her worker really free? Explain why or why not. **[LO 12.3]**

6. Dustin is planning to open a catering business. Give examples of an explicit cost and an implicit cost his new catering business might incur. **[LO 12.3]**

7. Imagine you're in a meeting with the owner of a restaurant, who is trying to decide whether to keep his restaurant open or to invest his time and money in another way. Explain to him the difference between accounting and economic profit, and why it should matter for his decision. **[LO 12.4]**

8. Explain why self-employed business owners frequently overestimate their profit levels. **[LO 12.4]**

9. Imagine a restaurant in which tables are spread over a large area, and there is only one waitperson. Explain to the manager why there might be increasing marginal product of labor associated with hiring a second waitperson. **[LO 12.5]**

10. If a firm experiences diminishing marginal product, does this mean that total output decreases? Explain. **[LO 12.5]**

11. A firm is trying to decide whether it could earn higher profits by increasing its output. Explain to the firm's manager why she needs to consider the marginal cost and the marginal revenue of the next unit of output to make this decision, rather than average costs. **[LO 12.6]**

12. A firm's output and total costs are given in Table 12Q-1. Going from a quantity of 3 to a quantity of 4, is marginal product increasing or decreasing? How can you tell? **[LO 12.6]**

13. Explain the statement, "In the long run, there are no fixed costs." **[LO 12.7]**

14. Suppose that a pharmaceutical company wants to grow in size but is constrained in the short run by its production capacity. Describe some steps that it can take in the long run to overcome these constraints. **[LO 12.7]**

15. Explain why an industry experiencing constant returns to scale is "just the right size." **[LO 12.8]**

16. Explain why the pharmaceutical industry is characterized by large economies of scale. **[LO 12.8]**

TABLE 12Q-1

Quantity	Total cost ($)
0	40
1	64
2	86
3	111
4	139
5	169

Problems and Applications

1. A hair salon offers three services: haircuts, color treatment, and styling. The salon charges $35 for a cut, $65 for color, and $30 for styling. Last month, the salon sold 68 haircuts, 34 color treatments, and 22 styling sessions. If the salon's costs for the month totaled $2,844, what was its profit? **[LO 12.1]**

2. Aisha is a self-employed physical therapist who works from a rented space. She charges $250 for a therapy session. She incurred the following costs last month: space and equipment rental, $1,400; wages, $3,500; materials, $1,800. If Aisha's profit last month was $2,800, how many clients did she see? **[LO 12.1]**

3. Isaiah runs a cake shop. His monthly expenses are listed below. For each cost, indicate whether the cost is a fixed cost or a variable cost of producing cakes in the short run. **[LO 12.2]**
   a. Ingredients (flour, butter, sugar).
   b. Bakers (cooks).
   c. Rent.
   d. Payments for equipment (ovens).
   e. Interest payments for borrowed capital.

4. An auto-repair shop faces the following weekly costs: rent, $500; labor, $400 per worker; parts and supplies, $30 per repair. Each worker can repair three cars per week. **[LO 12.2]**
   a. Fill in the costs in Table 12P-1.
   b. What are the total costs if the shop repairs 15 cars in a week?
   c. What are the total costs if the shop repairs 0 cars in a week?

TABLE 12P-1

Quantity of repairs	Fixed costs ($)	Variable costs ($)	Total cost ($)
0			
3			
6			
9			
12			
15			
18			
21			
24			

5. Paola is thinking of opening her own business. For each of the production inputs listed below, indicate whether the input incurs an implicit cost, explicit cost, or no cost. [LO 12.3]

    a. Rent.

    b. Wages.

    c. Owned equipment.

6. Paola is thinking of opening her own business. For each of the production inputs listed below, indicate whether the input incurs an implicit cost, explicit cost, or no cost. [LO 12.3]

    a. Borrowed capital.

    b. Investment from savings.

    c. Donated supplies.

7. Keri owns a landscaping business. For each of Keri's inputs given in the list below, indicate whether the associated cost is fixed or variable, whether it is explicit or implicit, and whether the cost affects accounting profit only, economic profit only, or both. [LO 12.2, 12.3, 12.4]

    a. Landscapers.

    b. Plants taken from her home garden.

    c. Truck rental.

    d. Owned lawn mowers.

8. Last year, Jarod left a job that pays $80,000 to run his own bike-repair shop. Jarod's shop charges $65 for a repair, and last year the shop performed 4,000 repairs. Jarod's production costs for the year included rent, wages, and equipment. Jarod spent $60,000 on rent and $120,000 on wages for his employees. Jarod keeps whatever profit the shop earns but does not pay himself an official wage. Jarod used $25,000 of his savings to buy a machine for the business. His savings were earning an annual interest rate of 6 percent. [LO 12.4]

    a. What is Jarod's annual accounting profit?

    b. What is Jarod's annual economic profit?

9. If adding an additional input does not produce additional output, what is the slope of the production function at this point? [LO 12.5]

10. Webby Inc. is a web development company. Webby's monthly production function for developing websites is given in Table 12P-2. [LO 12.5]

TABLE 12P-2

Programmers	Websites	Marginal product
0	0	
1	2	
2	6	
3	14	
4	20	
5	24	
6	26	

    a. Fill in the marginal product column.

    b. After which programmer does marginal product diminish?

11. Webby Inc. is a web development company. Webby's monthly production function for developing websites is given in Table 12P-3. Webby pays $4,000 a month in rent for office space and equipment. It pays each programmer $2,000 a month. There are no other production costs. Fill in the table of production costs. [LO 12.6]

TABLE 12P-3

Programmers	Websites	VC ($)	TC ($)	AFC ($)	AVC ($)	ATC ($)	MC ($)
0	0						
1	2						
2	6						
3	14						
4	20						
5	24						
6	26						

12. A firm's output, variable costs, and total costs are given in Table 12P-4. **[LO 12.6]**

TABLE 12P-4

Quantity	Variable cost ($)	Total cost ($)
0	0	100
10	50	150
20	80	180
30	120	220
40	180	280
50	260	360

a. Calculate marginal cost using the formula given in the chapter,

$$\frac{\Delta \text{ total cost}}{\Delta \text{ quantity}}.$$

b. Calculate $\frac{\Delta \text{ variable cost}}{\Delta \text{ quantity}}$.

13. The dean of a college faces the following costs: graders, faculty, classroom space, and chalk. Of these costs, which are likely to be variable in the long run? **[LO 12.7]**

14. In the pet industry, would you expect the long run to be longer for a pet store or a veterinary clinic? **[LO 12.7]**

15. Consider a firm that increases its inputs by 15 percent. For each scenario, state whether the firm experiences economies of scale, diseconomies of scale, or constant returns to scale. **[LO 12.8]**

a. Outputs increase 15 percent.

b. Outputs increase by less than 15 percent.

c. Outputs increase by greater than 15 percent.

16. A firm's long-run total costs are given in Table 12P-5. **[LO 12.8]**

TABLE 12P-5

Output	Long-run total cost ($)	Long-run average total cost ($)
0	18	
1	24	
2	28	
3	30	
4	34	
5	40	
6	48	
7	63	
8	80	

a. Fill in the long-run average total cost column.

b. Over what production range does this firm experience economies of scale?

c. Over what production range does this firm experience constant returns to scale?

d. Over what production range does this firm experience diseconomies of scale?

Endnotes

1. Bruce Roth, in http://money.cnn.com/magazines/fortune/fortune_archive/2003/01/20/335643/index.htm.

Perfect Competition

Trainside Variety

When we think about markets in action, one image that comes to mind is the bustling trading floor of the New York Stock Exchange. But let's travel for a moment to an interesting market scene that's much farther away. Imagine sitting on a long-distance train in West Africa, on a journey from Yaoundé in the south of Cameroon to Maroua in the north. Every now and then, the train grinds to a halt near a town. Not many passengers get on or off—most are simply going from one of these big cities to the other. This journey takes many, many hours, and there is no restaurant car on board the train. The travelers need food and drink, and at each stop local merchants rush toward the train, offering refreshments for sale.

There is a limited range of goods being offered. Some vendors are selling bunches of small, ripe bananas. Some sell bags of oranges,

©Tommy Trenchard/Alamy

partially skinned so you can crush them in your hand and sip the juice. Others offer bags of peanuts, which have been soaked in salty water and dried in the sun. You will be able to find corn on the cob or plantain (a less-sweet kind of banana), roasted over an open fire. Vendors jostle for position along the train as passengers take turns to hang out of the window, peruse the choice of snacks, and hand down money to the vendors.

You won't see much bargaining going on. Everyone seems to know and accept the prices as given. After all, if a vendor tries to charge more than the going rate for a roasted plantain, a passenger has many other vendors to choose from. And if a passenger tries to pay less for a roasted plantain, vendors can easily sell to someone else. Eventually, all the passengers have bought the snacks they want, the train rolls off again, and the local merchants head back home and wait for the next train to come by with a new batch of customers.

LEARNING OBJECTIVES

LO 13.1 Describe the characteristics of a perfectly competitive market.

LO 13.2 Calculate average, marginal, and total revenue.

LO 13.3 Find a firm's optimal quantity of output.

LO 13.4 Describe a firm's decision to shut down or to exit the market, and explain the difference between these choices.

LO 13.5 Draw a short-run supply curve for a competitive market with identical firms.

LO 13.6 Draw a long-run supply curve for a competitive market with identical firms, and describe its implications for profit-seeking firms.

LO 13.7 Explain why a long-run supply curve can slope upward.

LO 13.8 Calculate the effect of a shift in demand on a market in long-run equilibrium.

For reasons we will explain in this chapter, this scene is probably about as close as you will come in the real world to observing a situation that economists call *perfect competition*. Like many of the concepts we've explored in this text, a *perfectly competitive market* is a simplified model that is rarely an exact fit with messy reality. It nonetheless tells us a lot about how the real world works. It also represents one of the miracles of economics: how well-functioning markets can deliver goods and services at wide scale and at low prices—with price signals determining the appropriate supply and demand, and without the government ever stepping in.

In this chapter, we'll describe the behavior of firms in a perfectly competitive market. We'll investigate how firms in such markets make decisions about what quantity of output to produce and when to stop producing altogether. We'll see that although firms are driven to seek profits, in the long run we can expect that firms in a perfectly competitive market *won't* earn *economic* profits. Understanding the decisions made by firms takes us behind the market supply curve we've used in previous chapters, to analyze the forces that shape it in the short run and in the long run.

In showing how competition works, we'll also see why it can bring benefits to consumers. The forces of competition help make millions of products and services available and affordable to billions of people, just as competition makes cheap, refreshing snacks available to passengers on a long train journey.

A Competitive Market

In this chapter, we'll discuss how firms make production decisions. Before we can begin this analysis, we have to break down one of the most important and powerful assumptions frequently made by economists: that firms are operating in competitive markets. We can analyze the importance of competitive markets through the lens of the first economists' question, *What are firms' wants and constraints?* In the previous chapter we identified what firms *want*: to maximize their profits. Participation in a competitive market, however, places some very specific *constraints* on their ability to achieve this goal, as we're about to see.

LO 13.1 Describe the characteristics of a perfectly competitive market.

competitive market a market in which fully informed, price-taking buyers and sellers easily trade a standardized good or service

Characteristics of a competitive market

We touched on the idea of a **competitive market** in Chapter 3, "Markets," where we discussed its four defining characteristics:

1. Buyers and sellers can't affect prices—the going price is the going price.
2. Goods are standardized.
3. Buyers and sellers have full information.
4. There are no transaction costs.

There is so much competition in perfectly competitive markets that buyers and sellers cannot affect the market price, assuming that the goods offered for sale are relatively the same. Buyers can turn to the next seller if the price is too high, and as long as there are plenty of buyers, sellers have no incentive to lower prices.
©Tim Graham/Getty Images

Many markets have some degree of competitiveness but don't meet all four characteristics. Economists use the idea of *perfectly competitive markets* to refer to an idealized model of market competition in which *all four* characteristics hold true.

Let's briefly review the four main characteristics of a perfectly competitive market. We'll then add a fifth characteristic that is nonessential but important in defining competitive markets.

Individuals can't affect the going price

If you were the only seller of roasted plantains to a train full of hungry passengers, you'd be in a pretty good position: You could charge a very high price, knowing that some people would be hungry enough to pay it. Similarly, if you were the only passenger on a train and were facing dozens of roasted plantain sellers, you'd be in a great position: You could offer a very low price, confident that some seller would be desperate enough to sell you a plantain.

Most sellers and buyers in most markets are not in the happy position of being able to set their own price. Instead, most face some degree of competition. Nonetheless, they may still have some ability to decide what price to set. Say you're the only plantain seller at this train stop, but passengers know there will be many more at the next stop in half an hour's time. You may be able to charge a little bit of a premium to very hungry passengers who can't wait that long, but the presence of competition constrains your ability to charge what you like.

The first main characteristic of a *perfectly* competitive market is that buyers and sellers have *so much* competition, they have *no ability at all* to set their own price. As explained in Chapter 3, "Markets," a buyer or seller who cannot affect the market price is a *price taker*. Usually this implies that the market contains a large number of buyers and sellers. In such markets, the decisions of individual participants are so small relative to the total size of the market that they can't affect market prices. Instead, buyers and sellers have to accept the going rate. In a perfectly competitive market, buyers and sellers are price takers, who must "take" (accept) the prevailing price as they find it.

The opposite of being a price taker is having **market power**, or the ability to noticeably affect market prices.

market power
the ability to noticeably affect market prices

Goods and services are standardized

The second main characteristic of a *perfectly* competitive market is that the goods and services being traded are standardized. When goods are standardized, they are interchangeable. Buyers have no reason to prefer those sold by one producer over those sold by another, provided that they are the same price. This means that producers have to sell at the market price. They'd lose all of their business if they charged more, and they have no incentive to charge less.

Standardized goods are usually not the case in real life. Typically, goods are differentiated by quality, brand name, or characteristics that appeal to different tastes. Imagine the American equivalent of the Cameroonian train stop: turning off the interstate for a burger. Do you go to McDonald's or Burger King? Your choice is probably not determined solely by the price of the burgers, but also by your knowledge of whether you happen to prefer one over the other: A McDonald's burger is similar to a Burger King burger, but they are not the same. McDonald's fries are similar to Burger King's, but they are not the same.

When goods are not standardized, producers will be able to charge different prices. Sellers of roasted plantains to Cameroonian train passengers, though, are not in this position. There are no brand names here—one roasted plantain is the same as any other. The good is standardized, thus meeting the second defining characteristic of a perfectly competitive market.

What markets, other than plantains for Cameroonian train passengers, sell standardized goods? Many natural resources, such as metals and lumber, can be considered standardized goods. At the same price, buyers don't care whether their gold comes from a mine in the United States or Uzbekistan, or whether their crude oil comes from a well in the Saudi Arabian desert or tar sands in Canada. As long as it meets certain defined characteristics, then gold is gold, and crude oil is crude oil. Standardized goods like this are often referred to as *commodities*.

Market participants have full information   The third main characteristic of a *perfectly* competitive market is that all market participants have full information. This characteristic is closely tied to the idea that goods in a perfectly competitive market are standardized. When everyone knows exactly what is being traded, buyers and sellers have the same information; there are *no information asymmetries*.

In the Cameroonian market for roasted plantains, buyers have all the information they need to make the best decision possible. They know what price each seller is charging, and they can see the quality of the plantains for themselves. Sellers also have all the information they need to conduct transactions. From long experience, they also know the going price, where customers sit in the train, and how long they have to make a sale.

In other types of markets, some sellers may have more information than others, giving them an advantage. But in perfectly competitive markets, all sellers are able to obtain all important information.

While it may seem like this tight competition limits sellers, there are many cases in which businesses want to be right in the middle of the fray. See the Economics in Action box "Why does the 'Motor Mile' exist?" to learn why you often see many businesses of the same type right next to each other.

No transaction costs   The fourth main characteristic of a *perfectly* competitive market is that the buyers and sellers face very low or zero transaction costs. This means buyers and sellers do not incur costs (or they incur very little cost) in making an exchange of goods in a perfectly competitive market.

In the Cameroonian market for plantains, sellers can easily sell their plantains to customers. Similarly, consumers can easily purchase the plantains. Neither buyers nor sellers must pay for the right to exchange the plantains. Furthermore, the buyers and sellers are all quite near each other geographically. Together, all these things mean that there are approximately zero transaction costs in the Cameroonian market for plantains. (We say "approximately zero" because, naturally, there are some tiny costs. For example, it does take a few seconds to make a trade, and maybe one has to walk to another train car.)

Why does the "Motor Mile" exist?
Economics in Action

Why do car dealers often locate near each other? Why is the Honda dealership next to the Ford dealership and the Hyundai dealership? Why do so many places have a "Motor Mile" or an "Avenue of Autos"?

One reason is that car dealers may all be attracted to the same thing—relatively cheap parts of town with lots of land to display their cars and trucks. Zoning regulations can also limit where dealers locate.

One other big reason reason that car dealers cluster together has to do with competition. If all customers know exactly which car they want to buy, the clustering strategy makes less sense—dealers would instead find a location convenient to their customers. But a car is a big investment, and many car buyers want to see and test drive different options before making up their minds.

"We try to keep the place looking respectable," said a Dodge dealer near Spokane, Washington. "People pull in and say they were heading to Ford or another and we caught their eye." By locating near each other, the dealers increase their ability to reach customers interested in a look.

Still, locating together puts pressure on dealers—and that, too, is good news for customers. By clustering together, the dealers signal that they're going to work hard for each sale. "Your competition is right nearby," notes Dave Eadie, a sales manager at a Virginia Ford dealership. "You've got to be on your toes."

Sources: Bill Freeling, "The Motor Mile: Why Do Auto Dealers Cluster?" *fredericksburg.com*. July 14, 2007, www.fredericksburg.com/local/the-motor-mile-why-do-auto-dealers-cluster-monitoring-competition/article_92eb8fdf-461f-5801-9ec8-b485730e1fd3.html. Jennifer Plunkett, "Avenue of Autos: Cluster of Automobile Franchises along Sprague Avenue Has Grown and Changed over a Span of 70 Years," February 15, 1997, www.spokesman.com/stories/1997/feb/15/avenue-of-autos-cluster-of-automobile-franchises.

The lack of transaction costs in perfectly competitive markets is very important because this helps allow for free entry and exit—the new, fifth characteristic of perfectly competitive markets.

Firms can freely enter and exit The four characteristics described above are sufficient to define a perfectly competitive market. But another characteristic of perfectly competitive markets is important to understanding the way such markets function in the long run: *Firms are able to freely enter and exit the market*. This means that new firms can be created and begin producing goods and services if they want to, and existing firms can decide to shut down if they want to do so.

The extent to which firms can freely enter and exit explains some differences among markets. It helps us see why the market for roasted plantains at train stations comes close to a perfectly competitive market, but the market for, say, crude oil does not. It's pretty easy to set up as a plantain roaster. All you need is charcoal, a grill, and some plantains. It's a lot more difficult to set up as an oil producer. You need all kinds of expensive machinery and expertise. These entry requirements make it relatively easy for existing producers of oil to collude with each other to keep prices artificially high—causing the oil market to fail the "price-taking" requirement of perfect competition. It would be difficult for sellers of roasted plantains to do the same. New firms would enter the plantain market and undercut the colluders' prices.

In general, free entry into a market keeps existing firms on their toes. It can help drive innovation, cost-cutting, and quality improvements, as firms respond to the entry of new competitors. If entry and exit are costly, because of transactions costs, information gaps, or perhaps regulatory action, firms may collude, which would lead to a less than perfectly competitive market.

Remember that in real life, few markets meet all the assumptions of perfect competition. Nonetheless, perfect competition is a useful beginning assumption; it provides a base for describing interactions between buyers and sellers and plays a significant role in most markets. We'll work with this simplification for now, but keep in mind that the picture will become more complicated as we continue.

Revenues in a perfectly competitive market

LO 13.2 Calculate average, marginal, and total revenue.

The characteristics of perfect competition lead to a less-than-obvious conclusion: *In a perfectly competitive market, producers are able to sell as much as they want without affecting the market price.* This conclusion follows from two of the characteristics of a perfectly competitive market: (1) that individual buyers and sellers are price takers and (2) that consumers are indifferent between the standardized goods sold by different producers.

These two very important assumptions mean that when firms make decisions about the quantity they will produce, they don't have to worry about

- whether their actions will cause the market price to rise or fall or
- whether they will find buyers.

Therefore, as we analyze the revenue that firms can expect to bring in, we can assume that firms in a competitive market will be able to sell *any quantity of output at the market price.*

But remember, this doesn't mean that firms will *want* to sell an ever-increasing amount of their product. We learned in Chapter 12, "The Costs of Production," that as the quantity produced increases, average total cost first decreases but eventually increases. Because costs are not constant, firms want to find and produce *at the level of output that maximizes profits.*

 CAUTION: COMMON MISTAKE

How can every firm in a competitive market sell as much as it wants? If every firm produced more and more, wouldn't the quantity for sale outstrip the quantity demanded, pushing the price down?

In theory, yes. But there are two reasons why this doesn't interfere with our conclusion:

- First, firms will not want to produce an infinite quantity. Remember the principle of diminishing marginal product (from Chapter 12, "The Costs of Production"): As firms produce more, their costs tend to go up. As we'll see later in this chapter, that means there will come a point for every firm at which it doesn't want to produce any more.
- Second, remember that we are thinking about decisions made by individual firms. By definition, in a perfectly competitive market, each individual firm is so small relative to the size of the whole market that an increase in its output causes a negligibly small increase in the total quantity supplied. Any *individual* firm's choice about the quantity to produce has such a tiny effect on the total quantity supplied to the market that the change in price is essentially zero.

Let's imagine that you live in a Cameroonian town and you are setting up a plantain-roasting enterprise to cater to passing train travelers. What can we say about your firm's revenue? In Chapter 12, "The Costs of Production," we talked about *total revenue:* the price that a firm receives for each good, multiplied by the quantity of that good it sells, as seen in Equation 13-1. In this case, the firm sells only one good: roasted plantains. Its total revenue is therefore equal to the price of roasted plantains times the quantity it sells.

EQUATION 13-1   Total revenue = P × Q

For instance, if sellers earn a price of 1,000 CFA francs (the Cameroonian currency) for each bunch of plantains people buy, and the firm produces 5 bunches of roasted plantains, its total

TABLE 13-1

Revenue of a firm in a competitive market

The price received per plantain remains constant because the firm is a price taker in a competitive market.

(1) Quantity of plantains (bunches)	(2) Price (CFA francs)	(3) Total revenue (CFA francs)	(4) Average revenue (CFA francs/plantain bunch)	(5) Marginal revenue (CFA francs)
1	1,000	1,000	1,000	1,000
2	1,000	2,000	1,000	1,000
3	1,000	3,000	1,000	1,000
4	1,000	4,000	1,000	1,000
5	1,000	5,000	1,000	1,000

revenue will be 5,000 CFA francs. (Because firms sell quite a few plantains per day, it helps to think of revenue and costs *per bunch* of plantains produced).

Table 13-1 shows revenue for a firm in a competitive market—in this case, the plantain firm. The third column in the table shows *total revenue* at various quantities. Because the firm is a price taker in a competitive market, price remains the same regardless of the quantity that the firm produces (as shown in column 2). So, if the firm triples the quantity it produces, from 1 bunch of plantains to 3 bunches, revenue also triples, from 1,000 CFA francs to 3,000 CFA francs.

Besides total revenue, we also need to consider two other measures of revenue: average revenue and marginal revenue. **Average revenue** is the revenue generated per unit; it is calculated as total revenue divided by the quantity sold, or

average revenue
revenue generated per product, calculated as total revenue divided by the quantity sold

EQUATION 13-2
$$\text{Average revenue} = \frac{\text{Total revenue}}{\text{Quantity sold}} = \frac{P \times Q}{Q} = P$$

In other words, *for any firm selling one product, average revenue is equal to the price of the good.*

Marginal revenue is the revenue generated by selling an additional unit of a good. It is calculated as the change in total revenue divided by the change in quantity sold, or

marginal revenue
the revenue generated by selling an additional unit of a good

EQUATION 13-3
$$\text{Marginal revenue} = \frac{\text{Change in total revenue}}{\text{Change in quantity sold}}$$

In our example, when the quantity sold increases by 1 unit, what happens? The change in total revenue increases by the market price of that unit ($1,000 CFA francs). Thus, one unit of the good always generates revenue of $1 \times P = P$. So, *for a firm in a competitive market, marginal revenue is equal to the price of the good.* (If the market were not competitive, however, producing an additional unit of a good might affect the market price.)

But, wait, did we just say that average revenue is equal to the price of the good *and* that marginal revenue is equal to the price of the good? Yes—that's right: *For firms in a perfectly competitive market, average revenue and marginal revenue both equal price.*

We can check these equalities in Table 13-1 by calculating average and marginal revenue directly from quantity and price:

- Average revenue, shown in column 4, is equal to the value in column 3 (total revenue) divided by the value in column 1 (quantity).
- Marginal revenue, shown in column 5, is calculated by subtracting total revenue in one row from total revenue in the next row, as quantity increases.

We can confirm that at any quantity, average and marginal revenue are both equal to price for this price-taking firm in a competitive market.

✓ TEST YOURSELF

☐ What are the four defining characteristics of a competitive market? What is the fifth nonessential characteristic? **[LO 13.1]**

☐ What happens to the market price when a producer in a competitive market increases its output? **[LO 13.1]**

☐ What is the relationship between marginal revenue and price in a competitive market? **[LO 13.2]**

Profits and Production Decisions

The quest for profits is the most important driving force behind firms' behavior. In our analysis of competitive markets, this assumption allows us to predict how much firms will choose to produce under different circumstances. In the following section, we'll draw on our discussion from Chapter 12, "The Costs of Production," and combine it with an understanding of revenues in competitive markets.

Deciding how much to produce

LO 13.3 Find a firm's optimal quantity of output.

A plantain-roasting enterprise, like all firms, is trying to maximize its profits. Because it is a price taker in a competitive market, it cannot affect the price it receives for the roasted plantains it sells. We'll assume that the markets for its production inputs—raw plantains, charcoal, and labor—are perfectly competitive, too. At any given quantity, therefore, the firm's revenue and cost per plantain are determined by factors outside of its control.

The only choice that such a company can make to affect its profits is to decide the *quantity* of roasted plantains to produce. It is tempting to assume that since the firm can sell any quantity it wants without driving down prices, the firm should simply produce as much as possible to maximize its revenues. However, profits depend not just on revenues; costs also matter.

Table 13-2 shows (in columns 2, 3, and 4) total revenue, total cost, and the resulting profit (revenue minus cost) at each quantity of plantains that the firm might produce. It's important to realize that total cost includes both fixed and variable costs. In this case, fixed costs include the cost of the cooking equipment and monthly rent for workspace.

TABLE 13-2

Revenue, cost, and profit

As revenues increase, costs do as well. The relationship between revenues and costs determines where profits are maximized.

(1) Quantity of plantains (bunches)	(2) Total revenue (CFA francs)	(3) Total cost (CFA francs)	(4) Profit (CFA francs) [cols. (2) − (3)]	(5) Marginal revenue (CFA francs)	(6) Marginal cost (CFA francs)	(7) Marginal profit (CFA francs) [cols. (5) − (6)]
0	0	700	−700	–	–	–
1	1,000	1,200	−200	1,000	500	500
2	2,000	1,800	200	1,000	600	400
3	3,000	2,600	400	1,000	800	200
4	**4,000**	**3,600**	**400**	**1,000**	**1,000**	**0**
5	5,000	4,800	200	1,000	1,200	−200

The firm looks at the total revenue, total cost, and profit and sees that it can maximize profit by producing either 3 or 4 bunches of plantains each day. At either of those quantities, profit will be 400 CFA francs. That's useful: We now know that to maximize profit, we want to produce more than 2 bunches but not as many as 5. Can we determine whether 3 or 4 is the optimal quantity?

We have already seen (in Table 13-1) that marginal revenue stays the same in a perfectly competitive market. Column 5 of Table 13-2 shows the marginal revenue for the plantain-roasting business.

Costs matter too: As column 6 shows, the marginal cost of the first bunch is 500 CFA francs, and marginal cost increases afterwards. We can see the effect of total cost in two places in the table:

- *In column 7:* Given that marginal revenue for the first bunch is 1,000 CFA francs and marginal cost is 500 CFA francs, producing the first bunch must increase profit by 500 CFA francs.

- *In column 4:* We also see that profit increased from −700 to −200 CFA francs.

 CAUTION: COMMON MISTAKE

In case you are wondering: Yes, it's correct to say that "profit increased" when the amount of profit is a negative amount—such as when the amount in the profit column changed from −700 to −200 CFA francs. Another way to say this same thing would be to say that the "loss decreased" from −700 to −200 CFA francs.

No matter which phrasing you use, the business is coming closer to the point at which it can cover its costs and have some CFA francs in hand by the end of the business day.

As long as marginal revenue is greater than marginal cost, production of an additional unit will increase profits. When marginal revenue stays the same but marginal cost increases, this very important fact follows: *A firm should continue to increase production for as long as marginal cost is less than marginal revenue; it should stop increasing production as soon as the two are equal.*

To see how this fact can help decide how many plantains to roast, look at column 7 in Table 13-2, which shows marginal profit (marginal revenue minus marginal cost). We can confirm the decision the firm made earlier (solely on the basis of profit maximization) to increase output from 2 bunches to 3 bunches of roasted plantains:

- At an output of 2 bunches, marginal revenue is 1,000 CFA francs, marginal cost is 600 francs, and so the marginal profit is 400 francs.

- At an output of 3 bunches, marginal revenue is 1,000 CFA francs, marginal cost is 800 francs, and so the marginal profit is 200 francs.

It makes sense to increase production from 2 to 3 bunches because roasting an additional bunch will still yield positive marginal profit. This confirms the earlier decision.

What happens when the firm is producing 4 bunches of plantains? Should it increase production to 5 bunches? Marginal cost in this case is 1,200 francs, but marginal revenue remains at 1,000 francs; the marginal profit is −200 francs. The firm would *lose* 200 francs of profit by producing the extra plantains, so it should stick with 4 bunches.

These calculations lead us to a decision rule for deciding how much to produce: *The profit-maximizing quantity is the one at which the marginal revenue of the last unit was exactly equal to the marginal cost.* In Table 13-2, we find this amount at 4 bunches of plantains. If the firm produced any more than this amount, its profits would start to go down.

Figure 13-1 shows this idea graphically by plotting the values from Table 13-2 in graph form. As we discussed in Chapter 12, "The Costs of Production," the marginal cost (MC) curve slopes upward because marginal cost increases with quantity. A horizontal line at the price level represents marginal revenue (MR). The point at which the marginal revenue curve intersects the marginal cost curve shows the profit-maximizing quantity at which to produce.

A change in the going price could change a firm's decision about how much to produce. To see why, imagine that something happens to cause the market price of plantains to drop to 800 CFA francs. Let's say a rumor spreads that roasted plantains are bad for your health, making train travelers less willing to buy them. Table 13-3 shows what happens to profits at the new market price: After the change in price, the firm finds that marginal revenue equals marginal cost at a production quantity of 3 rather than 4 bunches. But the drop in price means that the business loses money at every level of production.

Despite the effect that the change in price has on profit, we can still find the optimal production level. How? By finding the quantity where marginal revenue equals marginal cost. As you can see in Table 13-3, the firm's losses are smallest when the firm cuts production from the previously optimal level of 4 bunches of plantains (at a market price of 1,000 CFA francs) to only 3 bunches (at the lower market price of 800 CFA francs).

You might be wondering at this point: Why is the firm producing at all if it loses money at every level of production? Wouldn't it be better to earn zero dollars than to lose money? Of course it would be, but firms are sometimes unable to quickly exit a market. For example, a firm that rents a space might have to continue paying rent for the remainder of its lease. Even if production drops to zero, the fixed costs remain for some time.

As we discuss below, when firms are making negative profits, they must make a decision about what to do during the time that they still owe fixed costs. Should the firm produce zero and lose all of its fixed costs? Or should the firm produce some amount and try to recoup a portion of its fixed costs?

FIGURE 13-1

Choosing the optimal production quantity

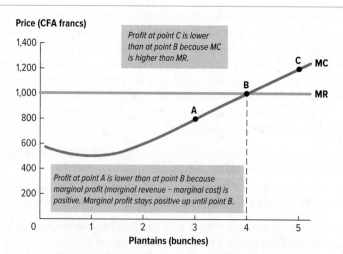

The profit-maximizing quantity is the one at which the marginal revenue of the last unit was exactly equal to its marginal cost. As long as marginal revenue remains larger than marginal cost, the firm increases its total profits by producing another unit. When marginal cost exceeds marginal revenue, however, the change in profits from producing another unit is negative.

TABLE 13-3

Revenue, cost, and profit when price falls to 800 CFA francs

When price decreases, this firm no longer earns a profit, however many bunches of plantains it sells.

(1) Quantity of plantains (bunches)	(2) Total revenue (CFA francs)	(3) Total cost (CFA francs)	(4) Profit (CFA francs) [cols. (2) − (3)]	(5) Marginal revenue (CFA francs)	(6) Marginal cost (CFA francs)	(7) Marginal profit (CFA francs) [cols. (5) − (6)]
0	0	700	−700	–	–	–
1	800	1,200	−400	800	500	300
2	1,600	1,800	−200	800	600	200
3	**2,400**	**2,600**	**−200**	**800**	**800**	**0**
4	3,200	3,600	−400	800	1,000	−200
5	4,000	4,800	−800	800	1,200	−400

Deciding when to operate

The most extreme choice that a firm can make about how much to produce is to produce nothing at all. Look again at Figure 13-1 and imagine what happens when the market price decreases: The horizontal MR line falls lower on the graph, intersecting the MC curve at lower and lower quantities. We have already seen from Table 13-3 that a price decrease lowers the profit-maximizing quantity. How low would the market price have to fall before the firm decided to produce nothing?

To answer that question, we need to break down costs even further. Remember, the difference between a firm's variable and total costs is its *fixed costs*. The firm has to pay those fixed costs regardless of how much it produces, and even if it produces nothing at all. For a plantain-roasting enterprise, fixed costs might include the purchase of roasting equipment and the lease of a place in which to set up the equipment. Variable costs—the costs that vary according to output—would include charcoal, raw plantains, and labor.

We know that in a perfectly competitive market, the market price is the same thing as the firm's average revenue. As long as average revenue (that is, the market price) remains above average total cost, total revenue will be higher than total cost, and the firm will be making positive profits. Mathematically, this leads to a new equation for calculating profits, shown in Equation 13-4:

EQUATION 13-4 $\text{Profit} = (\text{Average revenue} - \text{ATC}) \times Q$

Because average revenue is equal to the price for a competitive firm, we can rewrite this in another way, to get Equation 13-4a:

EQUATION 13-4A $\text{Profit} = (\text{Price} - \text{ATC}) \times Q$

Notice that Equation 13-4 implies that as long as the price (or average revenue) is above average total cost, the firm is making positive profits. But if the market price falls below the bottom of the firm's ATC curve, there is no level of output at which the firm can make a profit. Does that mean it should stop production?

The obvious answer is yes—at that point, the firm *wants* to exit the market. However, the decision is complicated by the fact that a firm is likely *unable* to exit the market immediately. Because of this, the answer to whether the firm will stop production depends on a concept introduced in Chapter 12, "The Costs of Production"—whether we are thinking in the *short run* or the *long run*.

LO 13.4 Describe a firm's decision to shut down or to exit the market, and explain the difference between these choices.

Short-run decisions   When a firm *shuts down* production, it stops producing for some interval of time, until market conditions change. (Note that the concept of shutting down in the short run does not mean closing the business entirely. You may have heard news reports, for example, of manufacturers shutting down operations and "furloughing" workers when they have an overabundance of certain goods; they then resume operations at the plant when inventory reaches a predetermined level.) Shutting down for some period of time avoids incurring *variable* costs because the quantity produced is zero.

However, the firm is stuck with its *fixed* costs because they do not decrease when quantity falls to zero. A cost that has already been incurred and cannot be refunded or recovered is a *sunk cost*. Fixed costs like land or large machinery are usually sunk costs in the short run. They have to be paid regardless of how much the firm produces, or whether it produces anything at all. *Fixed costs are therefore irrelevant in deciding whether to shut down production in the short run.*

The decision to stop producing depends entirely on the variable costs of production. If the market price is lower than ATC but higher than AVC, the firm should still continue to produce in the short run. Doing so yields more revenue than variable cost.

To make this idea concrete, look again at Table 13-3. As seen in column 4 of that table:

- The firm would lose 700 CFA francs if it shut down production and produced a quantity of zero. Those 700 CFA francs lost are the fixed cost incurred before producing even 1 bunch of roasted plantains.
- However, the firm will lose only 200 CFA francs if it produces 3 bunches of plantains. (That's the *smallest loss* it can incur given the fixed and variable costs at the market price of 800 per bunch.)

Thus, the firm should continue to produce 3 bunches of plantains as long as it is required to pay its fixed costs.

To generalize, the profit-maximization rule remains the same for firms whose *price is below average total cost but above average variable cost: The profit-maximizing (or in this case, the loss-minimizing) level of production is the quantity at which the market price intersects the marginal cost curve.* The firm will be losing money at that point, but it will lose less money than if it did not produce at all.

What happens if the price drops even further? In Table 13-4, we see that at a price of 400 CFA francs, losses start at 700 CFA francs and increase with each unit of production. In this

TABLE 13-4

Revenue, cost, and profit when price falls to 400 CFA francs

When price decreases still further, this firm no longer earns a profit, however many bunches of plantains it sells.

(1) Quantity of plantains (bunches)	(2) Total revenue (CFA francs)	(3) Total cost (CFA francs)	(4) Profit (CFA francs) [cols. (2) − (3)]	(5) Marginal revenue (CFA francs)	(6) Marginal cost (CFA francs)	(7) Marginal profit (CFA francs) [cols. (5) − (6)]
0	0	700	−700	–	–	–
1	400	1,200	−800	400	500	−100
2	800	1,800	−1,000	400	600	−200
3	1,200	2,600	−1,400	400	800	−400
4	1,600	3,600	−2,000	400	1,000	−600
5	2,000	4,800	−2,800	400	1,200	−800

case, the loss-minimizing level of production is zero, so it makes sense for the firm to stop production in the short run. At this level, losses due to fixed costs are unavoidable. But at least the firm won't lose even more money by roasting more plantains, each of which costs more to produce than the revenue it brings in. Another way of saying this is that *the profit-maximizing (or loss-minimizing) level of production when price is below average variable cost is to produce nothing.*

We can state the short-run shutdown rule as follows:

EQUATION 13-5   Shut down if P < AVC

Above average variable cost (AVC), a firm's short-run supply curve is the same as its marginal cost curve, as shown in Figure 13-2. At each price, the firm will supply the profit-maximizing quantity. *The profit-maximizing quantity is the one at which marginal cost equals marginal revenue.*

Since marginal revenue is the same as price in a perfectly competitive market, we can take a shortcut to finding the point at which to shut down production by simply reading the quantity corresponding to each price along the marginal cost curve. Below the shutdown price, however, the firm will not want to produce at all.

FIGURE 13-2

The short-run supply curve and the shutdown rule

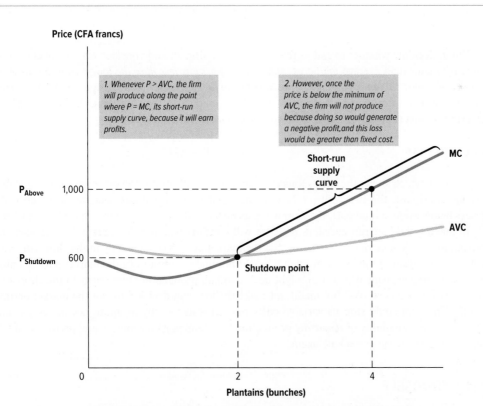

The section of the marginal cost curve that is above AVC describes the firm's short-run supply curve. At any price above that point, the firm will produce the quantity where price intersects the MC curve. At prices below the minimum of AVC, the firm produces nothing because it would generate a negative profit.

Long-run decisions   We've seen that in the *short run*, fixed costs may lead a firm to shut down production until market conditions change. When the firm makes *long-run* decisions, the reasoning is different: *In the long run, all costs become variable.* Leases can expire and not be renewed; machinery can be sold. It is only in the long run that firms are able to make the decision to completely *exit the market.*

 CAUTION: COMMON MISTAKE

The terms *shut down* and *exit* seem very similar, but to economists, each means very specific things.

- The decision to *shut down* is a decision that is made only in the *short run*. A firm that shuts down in the short run is still technically in the market, but it is not producing any units of product. The firm is still responsible for paying any fixed costs that it owes.
- The decision to *exit* is a decision that can be made only in the *long run*. When a firm exits, it closes its doors, cancels all contracts, and is no longer in the market at all.

Keep in mind that any firm that shuts down in the short run will also be exiting in the long run if it believes prices will continue to be low in the future. Additionally, even if a firm continues to produce in the short run, it will still exit in the long run if the price it can charge is less than its average total cost (that is, if the firm is making negative profits).

When deciding whether to exit in the long run, the firm should consider whether average revenue is greater than average *total* cost. *If the market price is less than the lowest point on the ATC curve, the firm should make a long-run decision to exit the market for good.* Keep in mind that firms making negative profits will always *want* to exit the market. In the short run, they are *unable* to exit. In the long run, they *are* able to do so. We can state the exit rule as:

EQUATION 13-6   Exit if P < ATC

Figure 13-3, which shows the firm's long-run supply curve, illustrates the exit rule. At prices above average total cost, the firm will produce at the point where price intersects marginal cost. At prices below average total cost, the firm will choose to produce nothing and will exit the market.

In making the long-run decision, the firm will consider whether the market price is likely to remain low *in the long run*. If it believes that the market price has fallen only in the short run, and will increase again in the long run, then it would not make sense to exit the market permanently. This reasoning explains why a firm might decide to halt production temporarily in the short run when price dips below AVC but might not make the long-run decision to exit the market permanently. The firm could stop its variable costs (lay off workers, buy no more raw materials) but keep open the possibility of restarting production by retaining its machinery and premises, in the hope that the price goes back up again.

√ **TEST YOURSELF**

☐ What is the relationship between cost and revenue at the profit-maximizing quantity of output? **[LO 13.3]**

☐ How do sunk costs affect a firm's decision to shut down? **[LO 13.4]**

☐ When should a firm exit the market in the long run? **[LO 13.4]**

FIGURE 13-3

The long-run supply curve and the exit rule

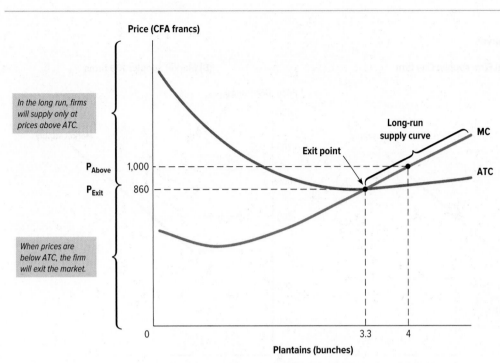

In the long run, a firm can avoid not only the variable costs of production, but also fixed costs, by exiting the market. If price is less than average total cost, the firm should exit the market. Conversely, if price is more than average total cost, a firm should enter the market.

Behind the Supply Curve

So far in this text, we've used the supply curve to describe the relationship between price and the quantity supplied on a market level. So far in this chapter, we've seen how an individual firm's costs determine its decisions about how much it is willing to supply at a given price. It's time to connect the two. By doing so, we will see how the supply curve *for the market* reflects the sum of the choices of many individual suppliers, each willing to produce a certain quantity of a good at each price.

We've seen that firms think differently about their production decisions in the short run and the long run. The choices of individual firms also generate differences between market supply curves in the short run and the long run.

Short-run supply

In the short run, we assume that the number of firms in the market is fixed. The total quantity of a good that is supplied at a given price is therefore the sum of the quantities that each individual producer is willing to supply.

To simplify things a bit, let's assume that each plantain-roasting firm currently in the market has the same cost structure. Each has the same resources, same technology, and so on, such that each is willing to supply the same quantity at a given price as all of the others. Panel A of Figure 13-4 shows the supply curve for one of these roasted-plantain firms. (Note that it's the same short-run supply curve we established in Figure 13-2: It is the firm's MC curve at points after it intersects the AVC curve.)

Now suppose that there are 100 producers currently operating in the roasted-plantain market, each with the same individual supply curve. The total quantity supplied—the market supply—is

LO 13.5 Draw a short-run supply curve for a competitive market with identical firms.

FIGURE 13-4

Firm and market supply curves

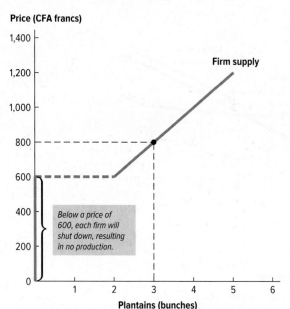

(A) Firm supply: One firm

Each firm is willing to supply a higher quantity as price increases. Price equals MR, and the optimal quantity at any price is where MR equals MC. Each optimal quantity-price pair adds a point on the supply curve.

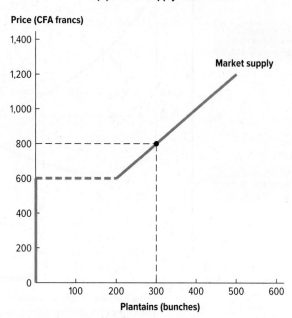

(B) Market supply: 100 firms

The total quantity supplied is the sum of the quantity that each firm supplies. If there are 100 identical firms in the market, the market supply at any price is 100 times the quantity supplied by each firm.

simply the sum of the quantities that each firm supplies. Panel B of Figure 13-4 shows the market supply curve. At every price level, the total quantity supplied in the market is 100 times the quantity supplied by each firm.

Long-run supply

LO 13.6 Draw a long-run supply curve for a competitive market with identical firms, and describe its implications for profit-seeking firms.

The key difference between supply in the short run and supply in the long run is that we assume that firms are able to enter and exit the market in the long run. The number of firms is not fixed; it changes in response to changing circumstances.

In general, the circumstances that make firms decide to exit or enter are as follows:

- We've already seen what makes a firm decide to *exit* the market—price falling below the lowest point on the ATC curve. At that point, the firm would be operating at a loss.
- Conversely, a firm would want to *enter* the market if it sees it could produce at a level of ATC that is below the market price. In other words, new firms will enter a market if the existing firms are making a profit.

Let's look more deeply at the effect on the long-run supply curve of those two decisions.

Effects of market entry on the long-run supply curve   The existence of economic profits in a market signals that there is money to be made. *How will others respond* to this signal? They will enter the market to take advantage of the profit-making opportunity. If firms supplying roasted plantains to Cameroonian train travelers are making more money than firms supplying salted peanuts or candied oranges, what would be likely to happen? We can expect orange-candying firms and peanut-salting firms to switch their resources toward plantain roasting instead, if the costs of doing so are not very large.

But as more firms enter the roasted-plantain market, what happens? Remember from Chapter 3, "Markets," that the number of firms in the market is one of the nonprice determinants of supply: *More firms means an increase in supply, and the whole market supply curve shifts to the right*. As supply increases and demand stays constant, the market equilibrium moves to a *lower price and higher quantity*.

What does the new equilibrium imply for the profits made by firms in the market? Remember that profits are revenues minus costs. As the equilibrium market price falls, revenues fall—and so do profits. As long as *economic* profit is positive, however, more firms still have an incentive to enter the market to take advantage of them.

 CAUTION: COMMON MISTAKE

At this point we need to remember the difference between *accounting profit* and *economic profit:*

Accounting profit = Total revenue − Explicit costs

Economic profit = Total revenue − Explicit costs − Implicit costs

When calculating economic profit, total costs *include opportunity costs,* such as the money a firm could have made if it had invested its resources in other business opportunities.

When a firm is making zero *economic* profit, the firm is still likely earning positive *accounting* profit. Thus, when we say that the price in the long run is such that firms earn zero economic profit, we don't mean that firms are earning no money. Instead, we simply mean that a firm is earning just as much money as it could be earning in its next-best opportunity.

In the long run, as long as *economic* profit is positive, new firms have an incentive to enter the market. As new firms enter the market, the market supply curve shifts to the right; the new market equilibrium is found at a higher quantity and a lower price.

Eventually, the price will be so low that economic profits are reduced to zero—in other words, $P = ATC$. At this point, firms are indifferent between the roasted-plantain market and other business opportunities; they no longer have an incentive to enter the market.

The fierce grappling for profit in perfectly competitive markets doesn't bode well for the entrepreneur looking to strike it rich with a new product idea. The From Another Angle box "Who wants competition?" shows that the amount of competition in a market can make or break a contestant's hopes on the ABC television show *Shark Tank*.

 ## Who wants competition?

From Another Angle

On the ABC show *Shark Tank,* entrepreneurs pitch new products to a panel of celebrity judges, referred to as "Sharks." If the Sharks like the pitch, contestants walk away with large investments and a stamp of approval from a show reaching millions of viewers. Failed contestants, on the other hand, walk away empty-handed after a round of harsh criticism from the Sharks.

Contestants pitch a diverse range of product ideas—from BBQ sauce to wine for cats to notebooks of the future. But no matter the product, judges always want to know if the product is

(continued)

The judges on *Shark Tank* often decide that the more competitive a market, the harder it is to make large profits.
©Araya Diaz/WireImage/Getty Images

unique in the market and if the entrepreneurs hold a patent for what they are selling. Judges know their economics, after all: The more competitive a market is, the harder it is to make large profits.

To see more concretely how this works, let's look at two examples. The first is Cropsticks, a set of disposable bamboo chopsticks with a built-in rest that gives users a hygienic place to put the sticks while eating. Instead of selling directly to customers, Cropsticks sells product to distributors, who then sell the product to restaurants like PF Chang's and Nobu. Cropsticks' founder wagered that higher-end chains would be interested in her innovation and could afford Cropsticks' higher cost (approximately one cent a pair), which would allow her company to scale production and bring down costs.

The other product is Seedsheet, a sheet of dissolvable pods of organic seeds. The idea is to make gardening easy. The gardener has only to lay the sheet on soil, water the sheet, and wait for the plants to grow. (It's essentially the store-bought cake mix of gardening.) The entrepreneurs even offer text-message reminders for when to water (and recipes for vegetables ready for harvest)! The founder of Seedsheet pitched his product as a solution for young people and others new to gardening.

If you were a Shark, would you have invested in either company? Here's what happened:

- After hearing the pitch, two Sharks made bids on Seedsheet, and the inventor ultimately walked away with $500,000 in exchange for 20 percent of the company's equity. One Shark called Seedsheet a "disruption" that created a new market in home and garden.
- Cropsticks didn't fare so well. Two of the Sharks noted that chopsticks are essentially a commodity, and businesses are rarely willing to spend even a faction of a cent more to buy a different commodity product. In other words, the chopsticks market is very competitive, and Cropsticks were ultimately not different enough to justify the higher cost.

Competition doesn't tell the whole story on Shark Tank; unique products do get turned down, and products in tight markets can get funding. Overall, though, when deciding whether to fund an idea, Shark Tank judges usually determine that competition isn't a winning formula.

Effects of market exit on the long-run supply curve   Now that we understand why firms might enter a market, let's consider why firms decide to make the opposite decision—to exit a market. If price falls below ATC, a firm may still be making an accounting profit. But at that point the firm is making negative economic profit. It could be making more money by pursuing other opportunities. It thus has an incentive to exit the market and invest its resources elsewhere.

What happens when some firms exit the market? *The market supply curve shifts to the left; the new market equilibrium is found at a lower quantity and a higher price.* As price increases, profits also increase. The process continues until economic profits are zero. At that point, no more firms exit the market; they are indifferent between the roasted-plantain market and other business opportunities.

Understanding the process of market entry and exit leads us to several conclusions. In the long run in a perfectly competitive market:

1. Firms earn zero economic profits.
2. Firms operate at an efficient scale.
3. Supply is perfectly elastic (in theory).

Let's consider each.

Firms earn zero economic profit   This first conclusion might sound surprising: *In the long run, firms in a perfectly competitive market earn zero economic profit.* This doesn't mean that a business is not earning *accounting* profit. It simply means that the firm could not earn greater accounting profit by choosing to operate in a different market instead.

Remember, though, that *perfectly* competitive markets do not often exist in the real world. In the next section, we'll see why this first conclusion rarely holds in reality.

Firms operate at an efficient scale   The second conclusion about firms in competitive markets is less counterintuitive than the first, but powerful nonetheless: *In the long run, firms in a competitive market operate at an efficient scale.* Remember from Chapter 12, "The Costs of Production," that a firm's *efficient scale* is the quantity that minimizes average total cost in the long run.

To reach this conclusion, we need to bring together three pieces of information discussed earlier.

- First, remember that a firm's optimal production is the point at which price (that is, marginal revenue) equals marginal cost.
- Second, remember that the marginal cost curve intersects the average total cost curve at its lowest point.
- Third, we just established that *in the long run*, economic profits are zero, meaning that price is equal to average total cost.

In equation format, these three rules for *long-run outcomes* are:

EQUATION 13-7

(1) $P = MR = MC$ at the profit-maximizing quantity
(2) $MC = ATC$ at the minimum of ATC (at its lowest point)
(3) $P = ATC$ in the long run

These identities tell us that, *in the long run,*

EQUATION 13-7A $$P = MC = ATC$$

The intersection of all three lines takes place at only one point, as shown in Figure 13-5. As we know, MC = ATC at the minimum of ATC. When a firm produces at a point that satisfies this condition, it is therefore necessarily producing the quantity that minimizes average total cost in the long run. In other words, it is operating at its *efficient scale.*

Supply is perfectly elastic   Our third conclusion about competitive markets in the long run follows directly from the first two. We have established that economic profits are zero. In order for this to be true, price must be equal to the minimum of ATC.

If anything causes the market equilibrium to move away from this price, the resulting positive or negative profits will cause firms to enter or exit the market. Such entry and exit will increase or decrease the quantity supplied, until price returns to the level that yields zero economic profits. Thus, in the long run, price is the same at any quantity. This causes the supply curve to be horizontal, as shown in Figure 13-6.

Remember from Chapter 4, "Elasticity," that a horizontal supply curve is *perfectly elastic*—producers will supply any quantity at the market price. In theory, therefore, in a competitive market, the price of a good should never change in the long run.

FIGURE 13-5

Firms operate at efficient scale in the long run

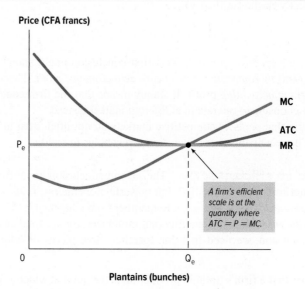

In the long run, firms in a competitive market operate at an efficient scale. A firm's efficient scale is the quantity that minimizes average total cost, which occurs where P = MC = ATC.

FIGURE 13-6

Perfectly elastic long-run supply curve

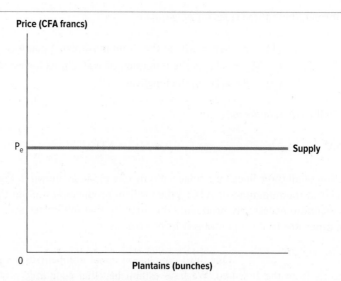

If anything causes the market to move away from the minimum-of-ATC price, the resulting positive or negative profits will cause firms to enter or exit the market, increasing or decreasing the quantity supplied until it returns to the equilibrium price. Thus, in the long run, price is the same at any quantity, and the supply curve is horizontal.

Why the long-run market supply curve shouldn't slope upward, but does

How important was our previous assumption that the price of a good or service never changes and that all firms face identical costs? It certainly enabled us to build a tidy theory. But that theory makes a few predictions that don't quite match what we actually observe to be true. Here, we'll add a few nuances to the model just discussed. You will see why price doesn't stay perfectly constant in the long run and what the effect of that fact is on the long-run market supply curve.

LO 13.7 Explain why a long-run supply curve can slope upward.

The main tweak to the model from the previous section removes the assumption that all firms have the same cost structure. In the real world, this is hardly ever true: Some firms are simply more efficient than others at converting inputs into outputs. It would not be realistic to expect new entrants to an industry to achieve the same low costs as firms that have built up expertise over the years.

The newer firms with higher costs will enter only markets with higher prices. In practice, therefore, the long-run supply curve will slope upward. Why? Because price has to rise to entice new firms to enter and increase the total quantity supplied.

In reality, price is equal to the minimum of ATC for only the least-efficient firm in the market, not for every firm currently in the market. Dropping the simplifying assumption that every firm's costs are the same also overturns the surprising conclusion we came to in the last section—that firms in a perfectly competitive market earn zero economic profit. Instead, the *last firm* to enter the market earns zero economic profit because its ATC is equal to price. But *more efficient firms, with lower ATC, are able to earn positive economic profit.*

Even if every firm in a market has the same ATC, there is a second reason why prices will still change in the long run. Over time, average total cost itself may change. Innovative firms are always searching for better production processes and new technologies that enable them to produce goods at lower cost.

For example, imagine that a new form of efficient cookstove enables plantains to be roasted using half the amount of charcoal. This innovation will reduce the variable costs of plantain-roasting firms. It will lower both the MC and the ATC curves as shown in Figure 13-7. This change, in turn, will increase profits. You can guess what will happen next: Increased profits will incentivize new firms to enter the market, which will increase the quantity supplied, which will drive down price.

For a real-world example of technological innovation driving down costs in the long run, see the Economics in Action box "How Ford changed the world."

How Ford changed the world

Economics in Action

The market for cars is not perfectly competitive; brands and styles of cars differ, so the goods are not standardized. But we can use aspects of our perfect-competition model to see how the technological innovation behind the Model T allowed Ford to lower its costs and increase its profits.

About 100 years ago, the Ford Company's pioneering use of the factory assembly line revolutionized the automobile industry. On an assembly line, each worker specializes in one small step of production, such as tightening a single bolt or welding a particular piece. The goods under production move along the line; a worker at each station completes a single step, until the product is finished. An assembly line allows each worker to learn one task very well—to specialize.

(continued)

In the early 1900s, Ford pioneered the use of assembly lines to produce its flagship automobile, the Model T. Ford spent seven years tweaking its production process to be as efficient as possible. The result was that Ford was able to produce the Model T at a dramatically lower cost than competitors' cars and to sell it at a lower price, thereby reaching a much larger market. Ford's technological innovation in the production process enabled the company to quickly become the dominant auto producer in the world.

The use of assembly lines enabled Ford to produce Model T cars, like this one, at prices affordable to middle-class buyers.
©Peter Mah/iStockphoto/Getty Images

Ford's competitors had no choice but to adopt the assembly line to stay competitive. By 1930, over 250 auto manufacturers that did *not* adopt the assembly line had gone bankrupt. Ford's surviving competitors, who adopted the assembly line themselves, were able to compete with Ford on price, creating incentives for further innovation.

The net result of this competition and innovation was that cars became cheap enough for middle-class consumers—a development that radically changed the social and geographic landscape of America.

FIGURE 13-7

Market entry due to changing production costs

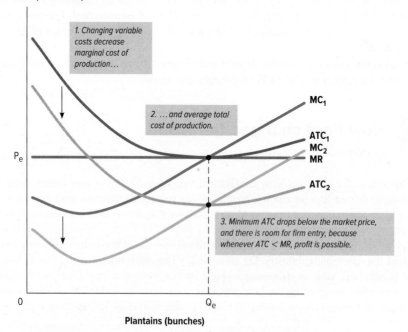

As technology and production processes improve, ATC can decrease. Since price must be equal to the minimum of ATC in the long run, price will fall as production costs fall.

Responding to shifts in demand

We have seen why the long-run supply curve will not be perfectly elastic in practice. However, we'll return to the simplified model of a perfectly elastic long-run supply curve for the final section of this chapter. This model can still tell us something about how a shift in demand affects the equilibrium of a perfectly competitive market in the long run. Although we rarely see *perfect* competition in the real world, the simplified model is helpful to understand what happens in theory. Knowing that, we are able to understand in later chapters why it matters when reality diverges from the model.

LO 13.8 Calculate the effect of a shift in demand on a market in long-run equilibrium.

Suppose, for instance, that there is a shift in demand for roasted plantains among Cameroonian train travelers. What might cause such a shift in demand? One possibility is a change in the price of a substitute good—for instance, roasted corn. Suppose there is a poor harvest of corn this year, increasing its price. Faced with more expensive corn, travelers in general will become more interested in buying plantains instead. This will shift the demand curve for plantain to the right. *How will the market respond to this shift?*

Panel A of Figure 13-8 shows the market for roasted plantains before the demand curve shifts. Notice that it shows both the short-run supply curve, which slopes upward, and the long-run supply curve, which—in theory at least—is horizontal in a perfectly competitive market.

With the increased price of corn, the short-run demand curve for plantains shifts to the right, from D_1 to D_2, as shown in panel B. The equilibrium point slides up the short-run supply curve—a higher quantity of roasted plantains is traded, at a higher price.

This higher price means that plantain-roasting firms are making economic profit. That economic profit creates an incentive for more firms to enter the market. As more firms enter the market, the short-run supply curve shifts to the right, from S_1 to S_2, as shown in panel C. The market equilibrium price slides down the new demand curve until it reaches the long-run supply curve. At that point, plantain-roasting firms are no longer making economic profit, so no new firms enter the market.

FIGURE 13-8

Responding to shifts in demand

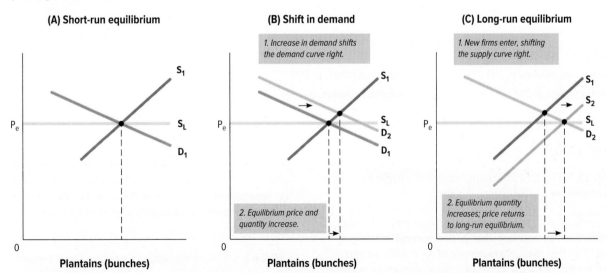

Initially, equilibrium price and quantity in a market fall at the intersection of the demand curve and the long-run supply curve (panel A). When an external change in market conditions increases demand, the price and quantity move away from the long-run equilibrium in the short term (panel B). In the long run, however, market entry increases supply, pushing price back down to the long-run equilibrium level (panel C).

In the long run, then, the end result of the demand curve shifting to the right is to *increase the quantity traded—but without any change in the price*, which remains at the minimum level of average total cost.

✓ TEST YOURSELF

☐ What induces new firms to enter a market? **[LO 13.6]**

☐ Why do firms operate at their efficient scale in the long run in a perfectly competitive market? **[LO 13.6]**

☐ Why can the long-run supply curve slope upward if firms don't have identical cost structures? **[LO 13.7]**

☐ What happens to the equilibrium price and quantity supplied in a perfectly competitive market if the market demand curve shifts to the right? **[LO 13.8]**

Conclusion

In this chapter, we examined the wants and constraints that drive firm behavior in competitive markets. Firms will choose to produce a quantity that maximizes their profits. In the short run, they will shut down if their revenues don't cover their *variable* cost of production. In the long run, they will exit the market if their revenues don't cover their *total* cost of production.

This analysis leads to some surprising conclusions about *long-run* supply in competitive markets: Firms earn zero economic profit; they operate at their efficient scale; and long-run supply is, in theory, perfectly elastic. Firms are able to enter and exit the market freely to adjust the quantity supplied at a given price.

These choices by firms benefit consumers by keeping prices low and ensuring that supply is responsive to needs. As we have noted, however, real-world markets are not guaranteed to be perfectly competitive. Firms may wield market power or offer products that are not perfectly standardized. There may be barriers that prevent firms from freely entering or exiting the market.

Understanding what perfect competition looks like, we can now spend the next few chapters looking at how firms behave when we relax the assumptions of perfect competition.

Key Terms

competitive market, p. 294

market power, p. 295

average revenue, p. 299

marginal revenue, p. 299

Summary

LO 13.1 Describe the characteristics of a perfectly competitive market.

A perfectly competitive market has four main, defining characteristics and one that is nonessential but important. The first main characteristic of a perfectly competitive market is that it contains a *large number of buyers and sellers*. The second is that sellers offer *standardized goods;* buyers have no reason to prefer one producer over

another at a given price. The third is that buyers and sellers have *perfect information*. The fourth is that there are approximately *zero transaction costs*. Finally, firms in competitive markets are usually *able to enter and exit the market freely*.

LO 13.2 Calculate average, marginal, and total revenue.

Total revenue is equal to the quantity of each good that is sold, multiplied by its price. *Average revenue* is total revenue divided by the quantity sold. In other words, average revenue is equal to the price of the good. *Marginal revenue* is the revenue generated by selling an additional unit of a good. For a firm in a competitive market, marginal revenue is also equal to the price of the good.

LO 13.3 Find a firm's optimal quantity of output.

The profit-maximizing quantity is the one at which the marginal revenue of the last unit is exactly equal to the marginal cost. Another way of putting this is that it's the *quantity at which the marginal cost (MC) curve intersects the marginal revenue (MR) curve.* Producing any more or less would decrease profits.

LO 13.4 Describe a firm's decision to shut down or to exit the market, and explain the difference between these choices.

There are two ways that a firm can choose to produce nothing. First, it can *shut down* its operations temporarily, producing a quantity of zero, but leaving open the possibility of restarting production in the future. Second, it can *exit* the market—a permanent decision in which it chooses to produce nothing in the present or in the future.

   The two decisions have different decision rules: If average revenue is less than the average variable cost of production (if P < AVC), then the firm should shut down in the short run. In the long run, if price is less than average total cost (if P < ATC), the firm should exit the market. (It's important to remember that firms cannot exit the market in the short run due to fixed costs.)

LO 13.5 Draw a short-run supply curve for a competitive market with identical firms.

In the short run, we assume that the number of firms in the market is fixed. The total quantity of goods that are supplied at a given price is therefore simply the sum of the quantity that each existing individual producer is willing to supply.

LO 13.6 Draw a long-run supply curve for a competitive market with identical firms, and describe its implications for profit-seeking firms.

The key difference between supply in the short run and supply in the long run is that we assume that firms are able to enter and exit the market in the long run. Thus, if economic profits are nonzero, firms will be induced to enter or exit the market, driving supply up or down until profits are zero.

This leads us to three conclusions about competitive markets in the long run: Firms earn zero economic profits, firms operate at their efficient scale, and supply is perfectly elastic.

LO 13.7 Explain why a long-run supply curve can slope upward.

The assumption of perfectly elastic supply is based on the idea that in the long run, price must equal the minimum of average total cost. Over time, however, average total cost itself may change. New production processes and technologies enable firms to produce goods at lower cost. Also, if firms face different costs of production due to scarce resources or skills, prices will have to be higher at higher quantities to induce higher-cost firms to enter the market.

LO 13.8 Calculate the effect of a shift in demand on a market in long-run equilibrium.

In the short run, firms in a competitive market respond to a shift in demand (in the way described in Chapter 3, "Markets"). If demand increases, price increases and quantity supplied increases. However, this pushes firms that are already in the market to earn a positive economic profit and operate at a size larger than their efficient scale. In the long run, other firms respond to the opportunity to earn economic profit by entering the market, which pushes price back down to its long-run equilibrium level.

Review Questions

1. You stop by a crafts fair and you notice consumers haggling with vendors over prices. What does this tell you about the competitiveness of this market? Suppose you plan to go to a farmers' market next. Do you expect to find more or less haggling at this market than you did at the crafts fair? Why? **[LO 13.1]**

2. In the market for gold jewelry (unlike the market for gold ore), products come in a range of designs, styles, and levels of quality. Which of the characteristics of a competitive market is violated in the jewelry market? What does this imply for consumers' willingness to buy from different producers? **[LO 13.1]**

3. Suppose that the manager of a donut shop tells you that he sold 250 donuts today, for a total revenue of $250 and average revenue of $0.90. What's wrong with this story? **[LO 13.2]**

4. Suppose an individual firm is one of many firms in a perfectly competitive market. Explain why this means the firm's marginal revenue will be equal to the market price. **[LO 13.2]**

5. The manager of the donut shop tells you that he sells donuts for $1 each, and that if he were to make additional donuts, based on his current level of output, it would cost him $0.80 per donut. Do you recommend that the manager increase or decrease the number of donuts he makes? **[LO 13.3]**

6. Suppose a firm is operating in a competitive market and is maximizing profit by producing at the point where marginal revenue = marginal cost. Now suppose that consumer wealth decreases in this market (and the good is a normal good). What might you expect to happen to the profit-maximizing output quantity for the firm? **[LO 13.3]**

7. A restaurant owner is trying to decide whether to stay open at lunchtime. She has far fewer customers at lunch than at dinner, and the revenue she brings in barely covers her expenses to buy food and pay the staff. What do you recommend that she do? Explain your reasoning to her. **[LO 13.4]**

8. In what ways are profit-maximizing and loss-minimizing the same? In what ways are they different? **[LO 13.4]**

9. Suppose that the profit-maximizing quantity of output for a firm in the competitive textile industry is 1 million yards of cloth. If this firm is representative of others in the industry, how can you describe total supply in the market, with respect to the number of firms? **[LO 13.5]**

10. What would you expect to happen to market supply if variable costs decreased for individual firms in the market? **[LO 13.5]**

11. Suppose that the airline industry is in long-run equilibrium when the price of gasoline increases, raising the cost of operating airplanes. In the long run, what do you expect to happen to the number of airlines in business? Why? **[LO 13.6]**

12. The firm in Figure 13Q-1 represents the cost structure for all firms in the industry. Describe the steps that will lead to long-run equilibrium in this market. **[LO 13.6]**

13. Corn farmers in Iowa are producers in a highly competitive global market for corn. They also have some of the most fertile, productive land in the entire world. Could Iowa's farmers be earning a positive economic profit in the long run? Why or why not? **[LO 13.7]**

14. Suppose that firms in an industry have identical cost structures and the industry is in long-run equilibrium. Explain how the profit motive could lead to *lower* market prices. **[LO 13.7]**

FIGURE 13Q-1

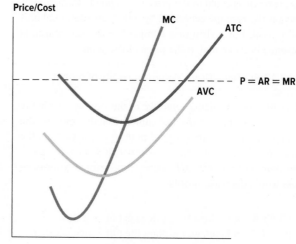

15. A market is in long-run equilibrium and firms in this market have identical cost structures. Suppose demand in this market decreases. Describe what happens to the profit-maximizing output quantity for individual firms as the market leaves and then returns to long-run equilibrium. **[LO 13.8]**

16. A market is in long-run equilibrium and firms in this market have identical cost structures. Suppose demand in this market decreases. Describe what happens to the market quantity as the market leaves and then returns to long-run equilibrium. **[LO 13.8]**

Problems and Applications

1. Suppose the market for bottled water and the market for soft drinks both have large numbers of buyers and sellers. Which of these markets is likely to be more competitive? **[LO 13.1]**

2. Suppose the market for steel and the market for cars both have large numbers of buyers and sellers. Which market is likely to be affected by information asymmetries? **[LO 13.1]**

3. Select all that apply. In a perfectly competitive market, MR equals: **[LO 13.2]**
   a. Price
   b. Average revenue
   c. Total revenue
   d. $\dfrac{\Delta \text{ in total revenue}}{\Delta \text{ in quantity}}$

4. Dani sells roses in a competitive market where the price of a rose is $8. Use this information to fill out the revenue columns in Table 13P-1. **[LO 13.2]**

TABLE 13P-1

Quantity of roses	Total revenue ($)	Average revenue ($)	Marginal revenue ($)
1			
2			
3			
4			
5			

5. On Figure 13P-1, show the profit-maximizing quantity when price is P_1. Label this point Q_{max1}. Show the profit-maximizing quantity when price is P_2. Label this point Q_{max2}. **[LO 13.3]**

6. Figure 13P-2 shows the marginal cost curve for a firm in a competitive market. The market price is $24. Plot this firm's profit-maximizing price and quantity. **[LO 13.3]**

7. Paulina sells beef in a competitive market where the price is $6 per pound. Her total revenue and total costs are given in Table 13P-2. **[LO 13.3]**

    a. Fill out the table.

    b. At what quantity does marginal revenue equal marginal cost?

    c. What is the profit-maximizing quantity?

FIGURE 13P-1

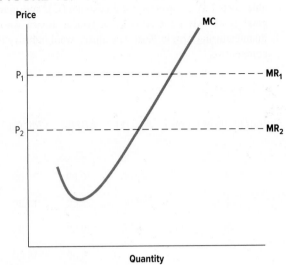

FIGURE 13P-2

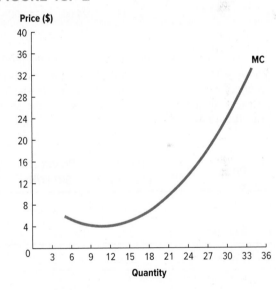

TABLE 13P-2

Quantity of beef (lb.)	Total revenue ($)	Total cost ($)	Profit ($)	Marginal revenue ($)	Marginal cost ($)	Marginal profit ($)
0	0	4		—	—	—
1	6	7				
2	12	11				
3	18	16				
4	24	22				

8. The data in Table 13P-3 are the monthly average variable costs (AVC), average total costs (ATC), and marginal costs (MC) for Alpacky, a typical alpaca wool manufacturing firm in Peru. The alpaca wool industry is competitive.

TABLE 13P-3

Output (units of wool)	AVC ($)	ATC ($)	MC ($)
0	—	—	—
1	20.00	30.00	20.00
2	17.00	22.00	14.00
3	16.70	20.00	16.00
4	17.00	19.50	18.00
5	18.00	20.00	22.00
6	22.33	24.00	44.00

For each market price given below, give the profit-maximizing output quantity and state whether Alpacky's profits are positive, negative, or zero. Also state whether Alpacky should produce or shut down in the short run. [LO 13.4]

	Price	Q_{max}	Profit (+,−, 0)	Produce in SR? (Y/N)
a.	$22.00	____	____	____
b.	$18.00	____	____	____
c.	$16.00	____	____	____

9. The marginal costs, average variable costs (AVC), and average total costs (ATC) for a firm are shown in Figure 13P-3. In the figure, mark the quantity the firm will choose to produce in the short run given this cost structure and the market price. Does the firm earn positive or negative profits? Graph the area that defines the firm's profit (or loss) at this rate of output. [LO 13.4]

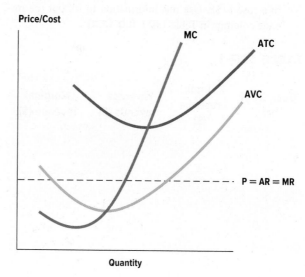

10. The marginal costs, average variable costs (AVC), and average total costs (ATC) for a firm are shown in Figure 13P-4. In the figure, mark the quantity the firm will choose to produce in the short run given this cost structure and the market price. Does the firm earn positive or negative profits? Graph the area that defines the firm's profit (or loss) at this rate of output. [LO 13.4]

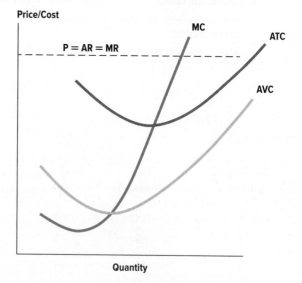

11. The cost curves for an individual firm are given in Figure 13P-5. **[LO 13.4]**

FIGURE 13P-5

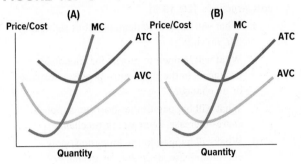

a. In panel A of Figure 13P-5, highlight the firm's short-run supply curve.

b. In panel B of Figure 13P-5, highlight the firm's long-run supply curve.

12. Suppose the quantity of apples supplied in your market is 2,400. If there are 60 apple producers, each with identical cost structures, how many apples does each producer supply to the market? **[LO 13.5]**

13. Suppose an industry consists of many firms with identical cost structures, represented by the "typical individual firm" in panel A of Figure 13P-6. Price is P_1. With the aid of panel A, draw the short-run market supply curve in panel B and show the firm and market output quantities at the equilibrium price in each panel. Label the firm output q_1 and the market output Q_1. **[LO 13.5]**

FIGURE 13P-6

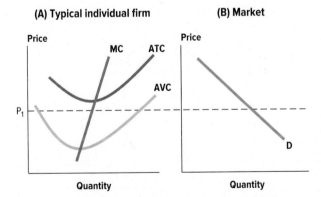

14. The monthly average variable costs, average total costs, and marginal costs for Alpacky, a typical alpaca wool manufacturing firm in Peru, are shown in Table 13P-3. All firms in the industry share the same costs as Alpacky, and the industry is in long-run equilibrium. What is the market price? **[LO 13.6]**

15. The industry in Figure 13P-7 consists of many firms with identical cost structures, and the industry experiences constant returns to scale. **[LO 13.6]**

FIGURE 13P-7

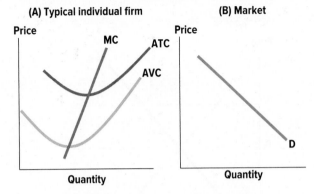

a. Draw the short-run market supply curve.

b. Draw the long-run market supply curve.

16. A firm's costs are represented in Table 13P-4. Suppose the price in the market is $110. **[LO 13.7]**

TABLE 13P-4

Quantity	VC ($)	MC ($)	AVC ($)	TC ($)	ATC ($)
0	0	—	—	1,000	—
10	500	50	50	1,500	150
20	900	40	45	1,900	95
30	1,700	80	57	2,700	90
40	4,400	270	110	5,400	135
50	8,000	360	160	9,000	180
60	14,000	600	233	15,000	250

a. Suppose all firms in the market have identical cost structures. Is the market in long-run equilibrium—yes, no, or can't determine?

b. Suppose the firms in the market may have different cost structures. Is the market in long-run equilibrium—yes, no, or can't determine?

17. Curling is a sport that involves sliding a granite stone over a patch of ice. The Winter Olympics has generated a lot of excitement about the fascinating sport of curling. As a result, demand for curling stones has increased. Curling stones are made from blue Trefor granite. There are limited deposits of blue Trefor, and other types of granite are poor substitutes. If the increase in demand for curling stones persists, do you expect the long-run equilibrium price to increase, decrease, or stay the same? **[LO 13.7]**

18. The industry in Figure 13P-8 consists of many firms with identical cost structures, and the industry experiences constant returns to scale. Consider a change in demand from D_1 to D_2, which increases price from P_1 to P_2 in the short run. **[LO 13.8]**

FIGURE 13P-8

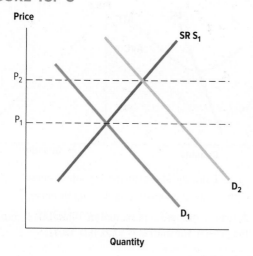

a. Draw the new short-run supply curve that will occur in response to the increase in demand and increase in price.

b. Draw the long-run supply curve.

19. Suppose the market for gourmet chocolate is in long-run equilibrium and an economic downturn has reduced consumer discretionary incomes. Assume chocolate is a normal good and the chocolate producers have identical cost structures. **[LO 13.8]**

a. What will happen to demand—shift right, shift left, no shift?

b. What will happen to profits for chocolate producers in the short run—increase, decrease, or no change?

c. What will happen to the short-run supply curve—increase, decrease, or no change?

d. What will happen to the long-run supply curve—increase, decrease, or no change?

Monopoly

Diamonds Weren't Always Forever

Diamonds are, perhaps, the ultimate symbol of luxury. For reasons we will discover in this chapter, they have become nearly synonymous with romantic commitment. More than 80 percent of brides-to-be in the United States receive a diamond engagement ring, at an average cost of around $6,000.[1] Across society, diamonds are also synonymous with conspicuous consumption. From swanky New York society to Los Angeles hip-hop stars, people use diamond jewelry to display wealth and status.

Why do diamonds carry such social cachet? They're expensive. People wearing diamonds show that they can afford the best. And why are diamonds expensive? You might assume it's because they are scarce and therefore precious. As it turns out, diamonds are not so rare. Tens of thousands of pounds of diamonds are produced every year.

©atic12/123RF

Why, then, do we pay so much for diamonds? The answer lies in the story of one of the most successful companies of all time: De Beers. For more than a century, De Beers used aggressive business tactics to control almost all of the international market for diamonds. It also used ingenious marketing methods to boost demand for its product. By controlling the production and sale of most of the world's diamonds, De Beers became the opposite of a price-taking firm in a competitive market: It had so much market power that it was effectively able to set the market price of diamonds. It did so by choosing the quantity it released into the market at any given time.

The story of De Beers starts in the 1870s, when diamonds were truly rare. Just a few diamonds were found every year, scooped out of riverbeds and jungles in India and Brazil. They were expensive; only the truly elite could afford diamond jewelry. Then, British miners discovered enormous deposits of high-quality diamonds in South Africa.[2] This must have seemed like a fabulous opportunity to make huge amounts of money. But there was also a danger: If companies flooded the market with diamonds, the quantity supplied would shoot up and the price would be forced down. Soon it would no longer be so exclusive and prestigious to own a diamond, reducing people's willingness to pay for them. This change in preferences would shift demand, which would result in even lower prices. People would buy a lot of diamonds—but the sellers wouldn't make as much money.

A businessman named Cecil Rhodes joined with other mine owners to form a single corporation, De Beers. By controlling all of the newly discovered diamond mines—and almost all of the world's diamond production—De Beers ensured that smaller amounts of diamonds came onto the market, keeping prices high. In this way, De Beers made much more money than it would have if it had produced lots of diamonds but sold them at vastly lower prices.

LO 14.1 List four barriers to entry into monopoly markets.

LO 14.2 Explain why a monopolist is constrained by demand.

LO 14.3 Calculate the profit-maximizing production price and quantity for a monopolist.

LO 14.4 Calculate the loss in total social welfare associated with a monopoly.

LO 14.5 Describe the pros and cons of common public policy responses to monopoly.

LO 14.6 Explain why a firm has an incentive to use price discrimination when possible.

In this chapter we'll see how monopolists such as De Beers calculate the optimal quantity and price to maximize their profits. We'll also see that a monopolist profits from its control of the market, but consumers lose—and, in general, total surplus decreases. Yet it can be hard to maintain this monopoly power. On the one hand, governments usually try to limit monopoly power, using a range of policies that we'll discuss. On the other, high prices in markets dominated by a monopoly create strong incentives for other firms to try to gain more market share. Even the mighty De Beers has been unable to resist these pressures. It now controls only about 30 percent of the world diamond market—still a huge share, but a far cry from its heyday.[3]

This look at monopolies takes us away from the model of perfect competition. In looking beyond markets with lots of firms competing against each other, we start to see the range and diversity of markets that make up the economy.

Why Do Monopolies Exist?

Most firms face some degree of competition. In Chapter 13, "Perfect Competition," we considered what would happen if a firm faced so much competition that it had no choice but to accept the going market price for its products. In this chapter, we'll ask what happens if a firm faces *no competition at all* and is therefore able to have total control over how much it charges for its products.

Economists call such a firm a **monopoly**. The word *monopoly* comes from a root meaning *single seller*, and it describes a firm that is the only producer of a good or service that has no close substitutes. A firm is a *perfect monopoly* if it controls 100 percent of the market in a product.

Firms can still have a large degree of *monopoly power* if they control slightly less than 100 percent of the market. For example, throughout the twentieth century, De Beers controlled 80 to 90 percent of the diamond market. It wasn't a perfect monopoly, but it wielded so much monopoly power that it was almost totally able to exert control over diamond prices.

The *lack of a close substitute* for a product is an essential part of the definition of monopoly. For example, if you are a monopoly seller of water, you can pretty much set your own price and

monopoly
a firm that is the only producer of a good or service with no close substitutes

people have no choice but to pay it. Water has no close substitutes. If you are a monopoly seller of orange juice, you don't have the same power. If you set your price too high, people will buy apple juice instead.

One of the keys to De Beers's success is that it persuaded many people that diamonds are a good with no close substitutes. This is quite an impressive feat. After all, when it comes down to it, a diamond is simply a sparkly stone that looks nice in jewelry. It can be thought to have some close substitutes, such as rubies, sapphires, and emeralds (and also synthetic diamonds, which are practically indistinguishable from ones dug out of the ground). If De Beers ensures that the price of diamonds is high, why don't people buy these other stones instead?

The answer is that De Beers has marketed diamonds very cleverly. The famous phrase "A diamond is forever" was the invention of a De Beers advertising campaign that ran in the United States from 1938 to the late 1950s. Within one generation, De Beers created the idea that the diamond is the recognized symbol of betrothal. Pursuing the same strategy in Japan, it advertised diamonds as representing modern, Western style. Between 1967 and 1981, the number of Japanese brides wearing diamond engagement rings went from 5 percent to 60 percent.[4]

Many women nowadays would feel disappointed if they received an engagement ring containing another kind of stone or an artificial diamond. Diamonds are truly beautiful, but the strength of our preference for them reflects decades of clever marketing by the people at De Beers.

Barriers to entry

It's easy to see why any firm would love to be a monopoly. But we can also see how the forces of competition are usually stacked against any one firm gaining that much market power. After all, when a firm charges high prices in a competitive market, some other enterprising firm will generally come along charging a lower price. In a monopoly situation such as the diamond market, other firms could make profits by entering the market and undercutting the monopolist's high prices. So we have to ask, *why isn't someone, or everyone, already doing it?*

The key characteristic of a monopoly market is that there are barriers that prevent firms other than the monopolist from entering the market. The barriers allow the monopolist to set prices and quantities without fear of being undercut by competitors. *Barriers to entry* contradict the *free entry and exit* feature that characterizes perfectly competitive markets.

Barriers to entry take four main forms: scarce resources, economies of scale, government intervention, and aggressive business tactics on the part of market-leading firms.

Scarce resources   The most straightforward cause of barriers to entry is scarcity in some key resource or input to the production process. This was the case, at first, in the diamond market. Diamonds come out of the ground in only a limited number of places, after all. If a firm owns all the diamond mines (as De Beers effectively did in the 1870s), it has control of the production process. A new firm cannot simply enter the market without somehow gaining control of a mine.

Economies of scale   In Chapter 13, "Perfect Competition," we discussed the idea of *economies of scale*—instances when, as a firm produces more output, its average total cost goes down. In some industries, such as power generation or pubic transport, the huge fixed cost of infrastructure creates economies of scale that help a single firm produce, at a lower cost than multiple firms, the entire quantity of output demanded.

That situation is called a **natural monopoly**. The term *natural monopoly* comes from the fact that, paradoxically, monopoly can be the "natural" outcome of competitive forces. Imagine what would be needed to create competition in the electricity-supply industry, for example: Another firm would have to build power plants and huge systems of distribution poles and wires, just to serve the same area. The two companies would have to split customers and face much higher costs as a result of the diminished economies of scale. These costs serve as a strong barrier to entry for the new firm.

LO 14.1 List four barriers to entry into monopoly markets.

natural monopoly
a market in which a single firm can produce, at a lower cost than multiple firms, the entire quantity of output demanded

Drinking-water supply and natural gas are other examples of natural monopolies; these depend on a network of pipes that would be immensely expensive for new market entrants to duplicate. Yet another example is public transport: Imagine trying to enter the railways business by constructing additional, new sets of tracks between major cities or convince a rail company to put your trains on existing tracks.

Governments often get involved in natural monopolies to try to protect the public from abuse of monopolistic power. We'll see how, later in the chapter.

Government intervention   Government intervention is another barrier to entry. Governments may create or sustain monopolies where they would not otherwise exist. In many U.S. states, for example, the government has created a monopoly on the sale of alcoholic beverages. In Iran, an elite branch of the army called the Revolutionary Guard Corps controls the construction industry as well as the oil and gas industries. Governments usually say they are creating monopolies in the public interest. Monopoly sellers of alcohol ensure that sales are tightly regulated, for example. In some cases, though, critics wonder if the real reason is to use monopoly power to benefit insiders.

Sometimes governments create monopoly power for state-owned firms. They can do this through a legal prohibition on other firms entering the market, or by subsidizing a state-owned enterprise so heavily that private companies effectively cannot compete. (Not all state-owned enterprises are monopolies, though. For instance, some governments own airlines that compete against privately owned airlines.)

Governments can also create or support private monopolies through regulation of intellectual property rights. Consider that governments grant patents and copyrights to people who invent or create something; these grants give their holders the exclusive right to produce and sell their creations for a given period of time. For example, a patent on a particular drug forbids the use of that chemical formula by other manufacturers. The patent allows the pharmaceutical company that holds it to act temporarily as a monopolist in the market for that particular drug. The patent-holder can raise prices and earn higher profits. When the patent expires, government protection of the monopoly ends; competitors can then drive down prices by producing a generic version of the same drug.

Creative works like art, movies, and music are also frequently protected by intellectual property laws. Copyright laws, for example, make it illegal to distribute unauthorized copies of movies. By granting copyright protection, governments give movie-making companies a legal monopoly over selling downloads of the movies they make. The result is that downloads of movies are more expensive than they would be if anyone could legally copy the movie and sell it.

Creating monopolies through intellectual property protection has costs and benefits for society:

- On the plus side, protection of intellectual property gives firms an incentive to invest in research and creative activities that lead to products that enrich people's lives. Movie companies wouldn't spend millions of dollars on special effects if anyone could legally copy the download of the finished movie and sell it at any price.

- On the negative side, as we will see later in this chapter, monopolies drive down consumer surplus by setting higher prices than would be charged in a competitive market. In most cases, they reduce total surplus. If the monopoly applies to a lifesaving cancer drug, the higher prices of the cure mean that some may not be able to afford it.

Whether the social costs outweigh the social benefits can be hotly debated and likely depends on the scenario at hand and the value system that people use to look at the trade-offs involved.

Aggressive tactics   A fourth barrier to entry is aggressive business tactics. As the chapter-opening story described, the limited number of diamond mines in the world was not the only explanation for how De Beers managed to exert monopoly power over the diamond industry for so long. As new deposits of diamonds were found by other companies in other countries, De Beers had to constantly protect its monopoly power from the forces of competition.

How could De Beers prevent new companies from undercutting its prices? It employed a number of tactics: It offered to buy up the companies that discovered new sources of diamonds. It entered into exclusive agreements with diamond-producing countries. And it was not afraid to employ aggressive methods of persuasion; De Beers punished anyone who did business with independent diamond producers. The punishment it meted out could be deadly for a smaller player in the diamond market.

For example, in the 1970s, Israeli diamond merchants began amassing stockpiles of diamonds as a safe way to store their wealth. De Beers didn't like this. It feared that the price of diamonds might collapse if the Israeli merchants chose to sell their stockpiles all at once. De Beers sent a representative to tell the Israeli merchants to stop stockpiling gems. If they did not do so, De Beers threatened to bar them from its "sightings," its exclusive invitation-only diamond sales. Many of the diamond merchants resisted, before eventually giving in. Those who resisted paid a high price for their rebellion: The Israeli diamond industry suffered so badly that a quarter of its employees lost their jobs.[5]

Another example of a company accused of employing aggressive tactics to gain or maintain monopoly power in local markets is Walmart. The company has been sued on several occasions for *predatory pricing*—that is, temporarily slashing prices until rival local stores are forced out of business.[6] Predatory pricing is a way for a large company, which can sustain short-term losses, to force smaller rivals out of the market. By doing so it can create monopoly power, which then enables the company to dictate its own prices.

Not all tactics to maintain monopoly power are so unwelcome to smaller competitors, however. For example, although Google controls around four-fifths of the world's internet searches,[7] it knows that a new company with a better search algorithm could overtake it. It tries to preserve its dominant position by buying promising-looking inventions in search technology. Many web entrepreneurs set up in business actively hoping that one of the giants of the industry—Google, Facebook, Microsoft, or Apple—will come along with a lucrative offer to buy them out.

✓ TEST YOURSELF

- ☐ How do scarce resources create barriers to entry? **[LO 14.1]**
- ☐ How do economies of scale create barriers to entry? **[LO 14.1]**
- ☐ How do government policies create barriers to entry? **[LO 14.1]**
- ☐ How do aggressive tactics create barriers to entry? **[LO 14.1]**

How Monopolies Work

We have to begin our analysis of a monopoly's behavior by understanding its *wants and constraints*. Just like any other firm, a monopoly *wants* to maximize its profits. As we saw in Chapter 13, "Perfect Competition," a firm in a perfectly competitive market is constrained by the fact that its production decisions cannot affect the prevailing market price. A monopoly does not face this constraint—but it *is constrained* by the market demand curve. In this section, we'll first see why this constraint exists and then how the monopolist makes production choices to maximize profits.

Monopolists and the demand curve

In a perfectly competitive market, the demand curve *for the market as a whole* slopes downward, reflecting the inverse relationship between price and quantity (as price decreases, quantity demanded increases). However, in a perfectly competitive market, each *individual firm* effectively faces a horizontal demand curve. This is because each firm is assumed to be too small for its production decisions to affect the market price. It can sell as much as it wants at the market price. But if it tries to charge more, it will be undercut by competitors and won't be able to sell anything.

LO 14.2 Explain why a monopolist is constrained by demand.

FIGURE 14-1

Competitive versus monopolistic demand curves

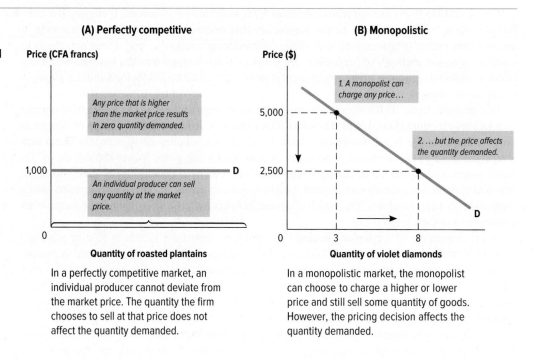

(A) Perfectly competitive

Price (CFA francs)

Any price that is higher than the market price results in zero quantity demanded.

1,000 ————————————— D

An individual producer can sell any quantity at the market price.

0

Quantity of roasted plantains

In a perfectly competitive market, an individual producer cannot deviate from the market price. The quantity the firm chooses to sell at that price does not affect the quantity demanded.

(B) Monopolistic

Price ($)

1. A monopolist can charge any price...

5,000

2. ...but the price affects the quantity demanded.

2,500

D

0   3   8

Quantity of violet diamonds

In a monopolistic market, the monopolist can choose to charge a higher or lower price and still sell some quantity of goods. However, the pricing decision affects the quantity demanded.

We can depict this relationship graphically with a horizontal line, as in panel A of Figure 14-1, which shows a horizontal demand curve for roasted plantains. (As discussed in Chapter 13, "Perfect Competition," the market for roasted plantains has many buyers and sellers, none of which can affect the price of plantains.) Panel A shows the demand faced by a seller of roasted plantains in a perfectly competitive market where the market price is 1,000 CFA francs.

To compare the demand curves in perfectly competitive and monopolistic markets, let's turn our attention from the plaintain-roasting business to violet diamonds. Violet diamonds are the rarest of colored diamonds. Each year, only a select few are mined from the Argyle diamond mine in Australia. The monopolist can choose to sell at any price it wants without fear of being undercut because there are no other firms to do the undercutting. However, it is still constrained by market demand. What, then, is the shape of the monopolist's demand curve?

As the *only* producer in the market, a monopolist faces the demand curve for the entire market, and this demand curve is downward-sloping. The demand curve faced by the monopoly seller of violet diamonds is shown in panel B of Figure 14-1. Naturally, the monopolist would love to sell a huge quantity of goods at a high price. But *how would consumers respond to a high price?* The law of demand says that, all else equal, quantity demanded falls as price rises. If the monopolist wishes to increase its price, it must accept that the increase in price will result in a decrease in quantity demanded. The monopolist may choose any price-quantity combination on the demand curve; it is unable to choose points that are not on the curve. (It can't force customers to buy more or less than the quantity they demand at any given price.) The monopolist can choose to sell at a high price of $5,000 per diamond, but at that price it will sell only a small quantity—three diamonds. Or it can choose to sell five more diamonds, reaching a total of eight, but only by lowering its price to $2,500 per diamond.

De Beers recognized the fact that its sales were limited by demand. That's why it went beyond controlling the supply side of the market and invested heavily in shifting the demand curve outward through the marketing methods we discussed earlier. Only by increasing demand would it be able to sell a higher quantity of diamonds at a higher price.

CAUTION: COMMON MISTAKE

Sometimes in this chapter we'll refer to a monopoly "picking a price." At other times, we'll say that it controls the quantity of goods available for sale. It's important to understand that these two decisions are equivalent. Each possible price corresponds to one specific quantity on the demand curve, and vice versa. So:

- The monopoly can control the market by setting a price and allowing customers to buy the quantity they demand at that price.
- Or it can control the market by restricting the quantity supplied and allowing prices to adjust so that the quantity demanded meets the quantity supplied.

Thus, the resulting price-quantity combination is the same, regardless of whether the monopoly picks a price or a quantity to supply.

Monopoly revenue

The first step in understanding a monopolist's quest for profits is to map out the revenues it can bring in. Suppose that De Beers can choose the price of the diamonds it offers for sale in the United States. To simplify our model, let's assume for now that De Beers sells diamonds of uniform quality and size (one-carat violet diamonds). What revenue can it expect to bring in at each possible price?

LO 14.3 Calculate the profit-maximizing production price and quantity for a monopolist.

Column 1 of Table 14-1 shows the range of prices De Beers is considering. Because it is constrained by demand, DeBeers has to accept the quantity that American consumers are willing to buy at a given price. Column 2 shows the quantity of diamonds demanded at various prices. When price is high, consumers demand a small quantity of diamonds. For example, if De Beers chooses to charge $6,000 per diamond, only one person would purchase a diamond. As price decreases, consumers demand higher and higher quantities. At a price of $1,500, consumers will purchase 10 violet diamonds. If we were to graph the price and corresponding quantity sold from the first two columns of the table, we would have the market demand curve (which can be seen in panel B of Figure 14-1).

The *total revenue* that De Beers could earn at each price is simply price times quantity sold, which is the amount shown in column 3. As price increases and quantity sold decreases, total revenue first rises, and then falls. Remember (from Chapter 4, "Elasticity") that total revenue increases on sections of the demand curve where demand is price-elastic; it decreases on sections of the curve where demand is price-inelastic.

Average revenue, shown in column 5, is the revenue De Beers receives per diamond sold. It is calculated by dividing total revenue by quantity sold. This is simply a rearrangement of the equation that total revenue is quantity times price. Thus, just as in a competitive market, average revenue is equal to price.

Marginal revenue (in column 4) is the revenue generated by selling each additional unit. We calculate marginal revenue by taking total revenue at a certain quantity and subtracting the total revenue when quantity is one unit lower. For instance, based on Table 14-1, total revenue from five diamonds is $20,000, and total revenue from four diamonds is $18,000. So, the marginal revenue in the interval between four and five diamonds is $20,000 − $18,000 = $2,000.

Unlike a firm in a competitive market, a monopolist's marginal revenue is not equal to price. Here are the differences:

- In a competitive market, a firm can sell as much as it wants without changing the market price. The additional revenue brought in by one unit is always simply the price of that unit. Thus, in a competitive market, marginal revenue is equal to price.
- In a market dominated by a monopoly, however, the monopoly's choice to produce an additional unit drives down the market price and thus drives down marginal revenue.

TABLE 14-1   Monopolist's revenue

The price a monopolist chooses to charge affects the quantity demanded, and therefore total revenue.

(1)	(2)	(3)	(4)	(5)
Price ($/diamond)	Quantity sold (Violet diamonds)	Total revenue ($)	Marginal revenue ($)	Average revenue ($/diamond)
6,500	0	0		—
6,000	1	6,000	6,000	6,000
5,500	2	11,000	5,000	5,500
5,000	3	15,000	4,000	5,000
4,500	4	18,000	3,000	4,500
4,000	5	20,000	2,000	4,000
3,500	6	21,000	1,000	3,500
3,000	7	21,000	0	3,000
2,500	8	20,000	−1,000	2,500
2,000	9	18,000	−2,000	2,000
1,500	10	15,000	−3,000	1,500

Because of this effect, producing an additional unit of output has two separate effects on a monopolist's total revenue:

1. *Quantity effect:* The increase in total revenue due to the money brought in by the sale of additional units.

2. *Price effect:* The decrease in total revenue that occurs because the increase in quantity requires a lower price.

Depending on which of these effects is larger, total revenue might increase or decrease when De Beers increases the quantity of diamonds it sells. If there were no price effect (as in a perfectly competitive market), then marginal revenue would be determined solely by the quantity effect; it would be equal to price. But the price effect always works in the *opposite direction* of the quantity effect—it decreases revenue. Thus, *marginal revenue in a monopoly market is always less than the price.*

Figure 14-2 shows hypothetical values for De Beers's total and marginal revenue at various prices in the U.S. market for violet diamonds. Because the demand curve is downward-sloping, the monopolist must decrease its price if it wishes to sell more diamonds. For a monopoly, the marginal revenue curve lies below the demand curve because marginal revenue is always less than price.

Table 14-1 and Figure 14-2 show that marginal revenue can sometimes be negative. This occurs in our example at quantities above the quantity at which the marginal revenue curve crosses the *x*-axis in Figure 14-2.

What does it mean when marginal revenue drops below zero in Figure 14-2? Think back to the price effect: Negative marginal revenue means that the price effect has become bigger than the quantity effect. At that point, each additional unit of output *decreases* total revenue. Thus, *the point at which the MR curve crosses the x-axis represents the revenue-maximizing quantity.* In our example, total revenue is maximized in the interval between 6 and 7.

Revenue is important, but as we know, what firms really care about is maximizing profit. So how do monopolists go about maximizing their profit?

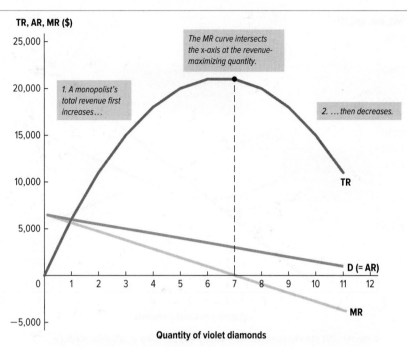

FIGURE 14-2

Monopolist's total, average, and marginal revenue

As the monopolist increases the price, total revenue (TR) first increases and then decreases. Total revenue is maximized when marginal revenue (MR—the lightest green line) equals zero. The demand curve (which equals average revenue, or price) is always above the marginal revenue curve because each additional unit sold brings less revenue than the prior unit.

Maximizing profits by picking price and quantity sold　De Beers exerted control over the diamond market through the quantity of diamonds it released for sale at any given time. The company held back stockpiles of diamonds worth billions of dollars for years at a time to maintain this control.

The purpose of this stockpiling was to ensure that the quantity of diamonds for sale was always the quantity that maximized De Beers's profits. How can a monopolist choose the price-quantity combination that maximizes its profits? Perhaps surprisingly, it can approach this problem in exactly the same way that a firm in a competitive market would.

Figure 14-3 shows hypothetical cost and revenue curves for De Beers. The general appearance of these curves should be familiar from Chapter 13, "Perfect Competition." The only relevant difference between the curves for a monopoly and the equivalent ones for a firm in a competitive market is that marginal and average revenue slope downward for the monopolist. (In a competitive market, those curves are horizontal at the market-price level.)

When determining De Beer's optimal output of violet diamonds, remember that the contribution of each additional unit of output to a firm's profit is the difference between marginal revenue and marginal cost. That relationship is key to profit:

- If the marginal revenue of a unit of output is higher than its marginal cost, then producing the unit brings in more money in sales than it costs the firm to produce it. Thus, it contributes to the firm's profit. (In Figure 14-3, that intersection is at point B, at a quantity of 4 violet diamonds.) At any quantity *less than* 4 diamonds, De Beers could earn more profits by offering an additional diamond for sale.

- What if, on the other hand, marginal revenue is lower than marginal cost? In that case, the unit costs more to produce than it brings in, and the firm loses money by producing it. At any quantity *greater than* 4 diamonds in Figure 14-3, De Beers could earn more profits by offering fewer diamonds for sale.

FIGURE 14-3

**Monopolist's cost and
revenue curves**

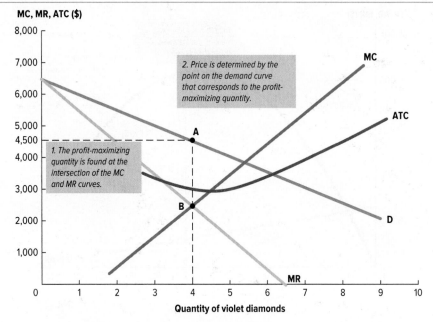

A monopolist can choose both the quantity and the price at which to produce.
To maximize profit, the monopolist will always produce that quantity at which
marginal cost equals marginal revenue. It then sets the price based on the
demand for that quantity.

Just as in a competitive market, the profit-maximizing quantity of output for a monopoly is *the point
at which the marginal revenue curve intersects the marginal cost curve*, shown as point B in Figure 14-3.

There is an important difference between a firm in a competitive market that produces at the
point where MR = MC and a monopoly that does the same thing:

- In a competitive market, marginal revenue is equal to price.
- For a monopolist, price is greater than marginal revenue; therefore, price is also greater
  than marginal cost at the optimal production point.

The profit-maximizing price for a monopolist is the price on the demand curve that corresponds to
the profit-maximizing quantity of output. This is shown as point A in Figure 14-3.

This fact—that a monopoly's profit-maximizing price is higher than its marginal costs—is key
to understanding how monopolies are able to earn positive economic profits in the long run.
Remember that a firm in a competitive market produces at the point where P = MC = ATC in the
long run. If price is higher than MC, other firms will enter the market, increasing supply and driving down the price until profits are zero and there is no longer an incentive for more firms to enter.
In a monopoly market, however, other firms can't enter the market; they face the barriers to entry
that allowed the firm to become a monopolist in the first place. The result is that a monopolist is
able to maintain a price higher than average total cost (ATC).

Remember that the formula for calculating profit is:

$$\text{Profit} = (P - ATC) \times Q$$

So, if price is greater than ATC, profits will be positive, even in the long run.

We can observe this same fact graphically, as shown in Figure 14-4. De Beers's profit is equal
to the area of the shaded box, defined as follows:

- The box's length is equal to the profit-maximizing quantity of output (4 violet diamonds).

FIGURE 14-4
Monopoly profit

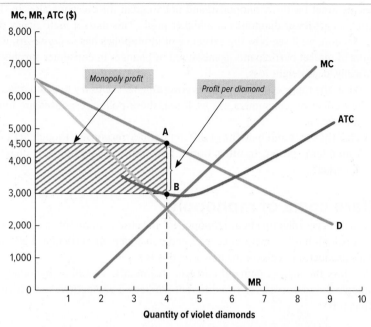

The monopolist sets the price at point A on the demand curve, which corresponds to the profit-maximizing quantity. The monopolist's profit equals the difference between the price and the average total cost (point B), multiplied by the quantity sold. Put another way, Profit = (P − ATC) × Q, or the area of the shaded box.

- The box's height is the distance between the profit-maximizing price and average total cost. We can also think of that amount—the difference between A and B in the figure, which is $1,500—as the profit earned on the average diamond sold.

This analysis shows us why De Beers had such a strong incentive to maintain its monopoly power. The fact that there were no other diamond producers to enter the market and drive down the price of diamonds gave De Beers the ability to maintain a price higher than its costs. This market power in turn allowed it to earn economic profits in the long run.

✓ TEST YOURSELF

- ☐ Why can't a monopoly choose to sell at any price-quantity combination it wants? **[LO 14.2]**
- ☐ Why is marginal revenue lower than price for a monopoly? **[LO 14.3]**
- ☐ Why are monopolies able to earn positive economic profits in the long run? **[LO 14.3]**

Problems with Monopoly and Public Policy Solutions

Since 2000, De Beers's grip on the diamond industry has lessened: Its market share has dropped from more than 80 percent of the world diamond trade to near 30 percent. This is partly due to large-scale mining of diamonds in Canada and Russia, outside of De Beers's range of control. It is also due in part to increased pressure from governments and diamond consumers to stop De Beers from exercising its monopoly power. Following a series of lawsuits in the United States and Europe, De Beers was banned from operating in certain countries and forced to pay large fees or change its practices in others.[8] Until 2004, De Beers executives weren't even allowed to travel to the United States on business.

Monopolies are great for the monopolist, and not so great for everyone else. In the De Beers example, consumers get fewer diamonds at a higher price. This market inefficiency reduces total surplus. In this section, we'll see how the existence of monopolies has *welfare costs*, which are the loss of well-being of market participants as measured by changes in consumer surplus or producer surplus—specifically, deadweight loss.

We'll also look at the range of public policies governments use to try to discourage monopolies and mitigate their effect on consumers. As we'll see, these policy responses are imperfect, and often highly controversial.

Before we weigh the costs and benefits of different policy responses, though, let's consider the welfare costs of monopoly power. In other words, how much deadweight loss does a monopoly introduce into a market?

The welfare costs of monopoly

LO 14.4 Calculate the loss in total social welfare associated with a monopoly.

Why do policy-makers get riled up about monopolies? Because a monopoly's ability to keep quantity low and prices high hurts society in general and consumers in particular. Let's dig back into the monopolist's production decision to show why this is so.

Figure 14-5 shows the market demand curve for diamonds, as well as hypothetical marginal revenue and marginal cost curves, for two different markets: a competitive market (panel A) and a monopoly (panel B).

FIGURE 14-5

Deadweight loss in a monopoly market

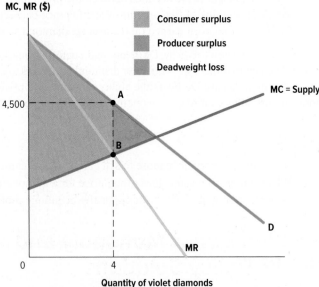

(A) Efficient market equilibrium

MC, MR ($)

Consumer surplus
Producer surplus

MC

3,500 — — — C

D

MR

0   6

Quantity of violet diamonds

A competitive market produces the equilibrium price and quantity (point C) where price equals marginal cost. When the market is in equilibrium, total surplus is maximized, and there is no deadweight loss.

(B) Inefficient monopoly market

MC, MR ($)

Consumer surplus
Producer surplus
Deadweight loss

MC = Supply

4,500 — — — A
             B

D

MR

0   4

Quantity of violet diamonds

A monopoly market produces the quantity at which marginal revenue equals marginal cost (point B). Quantity is lower than the market equilibrium quantity, and price is higher than the competitive price. As a result, consumer surplus is smaller than in the competitive case. Fewer trades take place, and society suffers a deadweight loss.

Let's look, first, at the competitive market in panel A. The equilibrium price and quantity in a competitive market maximize total surplus. In other words, *the market is efficient*. What is the efficient production level in this market? Remember from Chapter 13, "Perfect Competition," that a competitive firm's supply curve is equivalent to the section of the marginal cost curve that lies above average total cost. In the competitive market, the *efficient quantity lies at the intersection of supply (marginal cost) and demand*, at point C in panel A. What would happen at other quantities?

- At any higher quantity, total surplus is reduced because the increase in consumer surplus is less than the decrease in producer surplus.
- At any lower quantity, total surplus is also reduced—the decrease in consumer surplus is greater than the increase in producer surplus.

A monopoly, however, will produce the quantity *where marginal revenue intersects marginal cost*, at point B in panel B of Figure 14-5. This quantity is lower than the efficient quantity that would prevail in a competitive market, which tells us that total surplus is not maximized. It also tells us that producer surplus is higher than the level in a competitive market, and consumer surplus is lower. Panel B represents the loss of total surplus as a deadweight loss (exactly as we did in Chapter 5, "Efficiency," when discussing the welfare cost of taxes).

To see a list of the main differences between perfectly competitive markets and monopoly markets, see Table 14-2.

It's important to remember that this description of the costs of monopoly is a positive statement—a statement about how things *are*. That is different from a normative judgment—a statement about how things *should* be. There can be cases in which people believe that the advantages to maintaining a particular monopoly outweigh the total welfare costs due to lost surplus. This is similar to the feeling many people have that it is worth accepting some deadweight loss from taxes in order to achieve goals such as providing benefits to the poor or supporting military or police forces. There is no principle that tells us that maximizing efficiency trumps other goals.

However, voters and policy-makers in many countries have made the normative judgment that monopolies are usually a bad thing. This isn't so surprising: Maximizing total surplus means that society's resources are being used efficiently, and few people are excited to provide extra profits to monopolies. After all, voters are more likely to be consumers than owners of monopolies.

This does not mean that monopolists are always wealthy, large-scale enterprises. For an example of a monopolist toward whom we might feel more than usually sympathetic, check out the From Another Angle box "Phone ladies."

TABLE 14-2

Comparing the characteristics of market models

Characteristic	Perfect competition	Monopoly
How many firms?	Many firms	One firm
Price taker or price maker?	Price taker	Price maker
Marginal revenue?	MR = Price	MR < Price
Profit-maximizing quantity occurs where?	MR = MC	MR = MC
Can earn economic profits in the short run?	Yes	Yes
Can earn economic profits in the long run?	No	Yes
Quantity is efficient?	Yes	No

Phone ladies
From Another Angle

You might not remember when cell phones were rare, but just 20 years ago, few people had them. The cell phones available were expensive and bulky. Text messages were a cutting-edge technology. In the United States, only one in five people had a cell phone.

In Bangladesh, a country bordering India in South Asia, cell phones were even rarer. There was just one phone of any kind per 5,000 people. If you lived in rural areas, the usual way to keep up with family news or to check market prices in nearby cities was to get a firsthand account.

Muhammad Yunus (the economist, Nobel Peace Prize winner, and founder of Grameen Bank we introduced at the start of this text) had an inspiration: Why not turn the problem into a business opportunity? In 1997, Grameen Bank started recruiting long-standing clients to act as local phone operators, informally known as "phone ladies" (because nearly all were women). The bank loaned them the $420 necessary to buy a mobile phone. The phone operators then started small businesses renting out phones for a few minutes at a time. When residents needed to make a call, they could go to the local phone lady and pay a small fee to "rent" the phone.

Monopolists are not always wealthy, large-scale enterprises.
©*John van Hasselt/Sygma/Getty Images*

The demand for this phone service was tremendous, and the phone ladies' businesses flourished. Families used the phones to stay in touch with relatives who had left home to find work in the city. Farmers and traders used the phones to manage business orders and keep track of prices in local markets.

Because Grameen's phone ladies were the first to bring phone services to rural villages, they had inadvertently created a local monopoly in this previously missing market. This monopoly power turned out to be a huge windfall for the operators; they were able to earn profits often amounting to double or triple the average Bangladeshi income. Eventually, Grameen began establishing multiple phone ladies in each village, fostering healthy competition between phone ladies.

Phone ladies now provide cell phone access to about 1.75 million people in nearly every corner of the country. When you hear the word "monopolist," you might think of a massive corporation getting rich by smothering the competition, not someone in rural Bangladesh using cell phones to make a difference in her family's life. This story shows that we can't lump all monopolies together. Sometimes, monopolies are a stage on the path to greater equality of access to goods and services.

Source: www.grameentelecom.net.bd.

LO 14.5 Describe the pros and cons of common public policy responses to monopoly.

Public policy responses

Policy-makers have developed a range of policy responses to monopolies. These tools aim to break up existing monopolies, prevent new ones from forming, and ease the effect of monopoly power on consumers. Each comes with costs as well as benefits. Some economists argue that the best response is often to do nothing at all. As we discuss each type of policy, keep a critical eye on its pros and its cons.

Antitrust laws   The regulation of monopolies has been a high-profile political issue in America for quite a while. In the late nineteenth century, massive corporations called "trusts" were beginning to dominate entire industries. To check their growing power, Congress passed the Sherman Antitrust Act in 1890. The act requires the federal government to investigate and prosecute corporations that engage in anti-competitive practices. Included in such practices are price fixing and bid rigging. The early twentieth century was also a period of major antitrust activity in the United States. President Theodore Roosevelt, in particular, became known as a "trust-buster." Using the Sherman Act, he vigorously prosecuted corporations that used monopolistic practices to stifle competition. Over the years, the government has used the Sherman Act to break up monopolies in various industries, including railroads, oil, aluminum, tobacco, and telecommunications.

The Sherman Act still has an impact. As recently as the late 1990s, it was uncommon to use an internet browser other than Microsoft's Internet Explorer. In 1999, the U.S. government sued Microsoft for anti-competitive behavior. The suit alleged that by bundling Internet Explorer with Microsoft Windows, the company was unfairly pushing competing web browsers out of the market. (Microsoft eventually reached a settlement with the government and agreed to stop certain business practices perceived to be anti-competitive.) Today, there are lots of internet browsers, including Chrome, Firefox, Safari, and improved versions of Internet Explorer.

For another case concerning an area in which the antitrust law has not yet had much impact, read the Economics in Action box "Rockers vs. Ticketmaster."

Rockers vs. Ticketmaster
Economics in Action

Anyone who has been to a major concert or show in the United States has probably experienced the hefty fees and charges that come with buying a ticket through Ticketmaster. These fees can add up to between 20 and 40 percent of the face value of the tickets themselves.

Ticketmaster is a dominant player in the lucrative U.S. primary-ticket-sales business. For context, Ticketmaster has signed deals with a number of NHL and NBA teams to sell event tickets only through its site. Many of the nation's leading concert and theater venues have similar agreements. These exclusive agreements are a crucial element of Ticketmaster's business strategy. Because of them, competitors have difficulty gaining a foothold in the market. Many feel that Ticketmaster has thus become a de facto monopoly in the market for tickets.

This has infuriated many musicians who want to keep prices of tickets low for their fans' sake. Two groups have even pursued lawsuits against Ticketmaster. In 1994, Pearl Jam complained to the U.S. Justice Department about Ticketmaster's allegedly monopolistic practices and high markups. The group's lawsuit was unsuccessful. In 2003, jam band String Cheese Incident sued Ticketmaster. The suit alleged that the exclusive agreements with venues were monopolistic and violated the Sherman Antitrust Act. This case settled out of court, and the results were not publicly disclosed.

The power of Ticketmaster may not last long, though. A slew of new sites that sell concert tickets online, including StubHub, Eventbrite, and Etix, are growing steadily in the primary-ticket-sales market. While Ticketmaster is still the official ticketing partner for the NBA, several teams now have their own ticketing partners. For instance, StubHub has become the official ticketing partner for the Philadelphia 76ers, cutting directly into Ticketmaster's market share. Since competitors can offer cheaper booking fees for bands and ticket prices for fans, they may prove to be a win for everyone—except, of course, Ticketmaster.

Sources: www.rollingstone.com/music/news/string-cheese-incident-eliminate-service-charges-for-summer-tour-20120302; http://latimesblogs.latimes.com/music_blog/2010/08/ticketmaster-a-new-era-of-transparency-or-smoke-mirrors-.html; www.nba.com/sixers/news/sixers-stubhub-launch-revolutionary-new-ticketing-platform.

The U.S. government has also used the Sherman Antitrust Act and its partner, the Clayton Antitrust Act of 1914, to prevent monopolies from forming in the first place. The Justice Department can block two firms from merging if the merger would result in a company with too much market power. A few examples include a proposed merger between office-supply giants Office Depot and Staples, which the Justice Department blocked in 1997; a failed AT&T merger with T-Mobile in 2011; and a merger between Comcast and Time Warner Cable that was blocked by the Justice Department in 2015.[9]

However, in recent years the government has only infrequently used the power to block mergers outright. More often, the government investigates a potential merger and allows it to go forward. For instance, in 2017 Amazon purchased the high-end grocery chain Whole Foods. In 2018 Disney purchased many of Fox's entertainment offerings, including the 21st Century Fox movie studio and a 30 percent stake in the streaming service Hulu.[10] In both cases, the Justice Department determined there was sufficient competition from other companies (Walmart and other grocery sellers in the case of Amazon, and Viacom and Netflix in the case of Disney) to approve the sale.

People sometimes criticize antitrust actions as being politically motivated or causing more inefficiency than they create. How could antitrust action cause inefficiency in the market? It could accidentally break up a natural monopoly. Or it could break a large company into several firms that operate at a smaller-than-efficient scale. Different regulators handle these decisions differently. For instance, Microsoft still faced antitrust lawsuits in Europe long after it settled its case in the United States.

Public ownership   Natural monopolies pose a particular problem for policy-makers. On the one hand, the monopolist is able to achieve lower costs of production than multiple competing producers would. Often, the marginal cost for a natural monopolist is very low and constant. For example, the cost to an internet supplier of providing one more megabyte of data is very small. But the fixed costs of entering the market and becoming an internet provider are very high. This barrier to entry makes an internet provider a natural monopoly.

Because of the high fixed costs of entry but the low marginal costs of production, a natural monopoly is often perceived as less harmful than other monopolies. However, even a natural monopoly chooses to produce at the profit-maximizing quantity where MR = MR; this results in a price that is higher than marginal cost, causing deadweight loss.

One possible solution is for governments to run natural monopolies as public agencies. Examples of public ownership of natural monopolies include the U.S. Postal Service to deliver mail and Amtrak to provide train services. The rationale behind public ownership of natural monopolies is that governments are supposed to serve the public interest rather than maximize profit. They could choose to provide broader service than a private monopolist might. For example, a government-supported monopoly might deliver mail to any postal address in the country; a private monopolist might prefer not to deliver to remote addresses that are more expensive to reach.

Figure 14-6 shows the MC and ATC curves for a natural monopoly. Note that MC is horizontal, reflecting the near-zero cost of providing an extra kilowatt hour of energy. Panel A shows an example of how a publicly owned monopoly could set prices lower than an unregulated monopolist would. In this case, the regulated government-monopoly price is higher than average total cost but is lower than the price that an unregulated "private monopoly" would set. Even though price is lower than it would be if the monopoly were unregulated, there is still some deadweight loss, as shown in the figure.

Panel B of Figure 14-6 shows how governments often regulate prices for a natural monopoly in order to diminish deadweight loss. Recall that in a competitive market, where deadweight loss is zero, firms produce at the point where P = MC. However, a natural monopoly is defined by the fact that ATC falls as quantity increases, which means that MC must be below ATC at all possible quantities. As a result, a natural monopolist that sets price equal to marginal cost will incur losses, as shown in panel B.

FIGURE 14-6

Price regulation of a natural monopoly

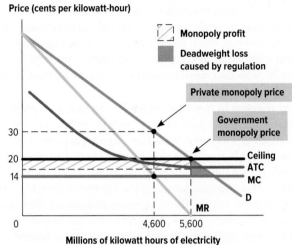

(A) Price ceiling above MC but below full monopoly pricing

When the price ceiling (20 cents) is set above the natural monopoly's average total cost, the firm will produce at the point where the price intersects the average revenue curve (which is identical to the demand curve) to maximize its profit. Some deadweight loss remains.

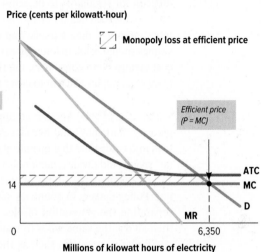

(B) Price ceiling at efficient price

In a competitive market, there is no deadweight loss, and the efficient price occurs at the point where P = MC. A publicly owned natural monopoly producing at this point loses money.

However, public ownership of a natural monopoly has its problems. Politicians may feel pressure to lower prices even further, below the level they would be in a competitive market. As we saw in Chapter 5, "Efficiency," doing so will create shortages and people will demand more than it makes sense for the producer to supply at that price. Publicly owned companies may also make business decisions—such as where to locate or what types of products to offer—on the basis of political concerns.

Perhaps the most significant problem of public ownership of a natural monopoly relates to the profit motive. The loss of the profit motive could reduce the publicly owned monopolist's motivation to improve efficiency and to provide better service or lower costs. After all, there is no rule stating that all monopolies must make a profit. (Amtrak reported an operating loss of around $194 million in fiscal year 2017, and USPS reported a loss of $540 million for the first *quarter* in 2017.[11]) If an inefficient public monopoly cannot provide a service at a price that sufficient numbers of people are willing to pay, it can remain in operation by covering its losses with revenue from taxes—as long as there is political will to do so.

These concerns explain why public ownership of monopolies has become much less common. Since the 1980s, especially in Europe, many government-operated agencies such as state airlines, telecoms, and utilities have been privatized (that is, sold to private companies) and regulated instead.

Regulation   If policy-makers don't want to go all the way to public ownership, one common intermediate step is to regulate the behavior of natural monopolies. Such regulation takes the form of controls on the prices natural monopolies are allowed to charge. This is frequently the case in utility markets. For instance, many governments allow private monopolies to exist in the supply of electricity, tap water, or natural gas but cap the price these companies can charge.

In theory, such controls could have the same effect as public ownership: By capping the price at ATC, regulators can force natural monopolies to earn zero economic profits. Doing so reduces deadweight loss as much as possible without causing the firm to incur losses and exit the market. Unfortunately, things are rarely so simple in practice: Firms have an incentive to avoid giving regulators useful information about their true costs of production. Lack of information makes it difficult for regulators to determine the appropriate price level.

Also, the idea behind privatizing natural monopolies relates to incentives: A private firm should be more motivated than a public one to increase its profits by innovating and reducing costs, and those savings should result in lower prices for consumers. But if the regulator sets a price so low that *all* of the cost savings go to consumers, the firm will have no incentive to reduce costs. If the regulator sets the price at a level insufficient to cover the monopolist's costs, it could even drive the firm out of business.

Vertical splits   Another common response to natural monopolies is to look for ways to split an industry "vertically" and introduce competition into parts of it. A "vertical" split divides the original firm into companies that operate at different points in the production process. (In contrast, a "horizontal" split would divide a monopolist into multiple companies that compete to sell the same product.)

For example, the supply of electricity is a natural monopoly, but the generation of electricity is not. Policy-makers in countries such as New Zealand have split the electricity industry vertically, separating the generation of electricity from supply. Firms compete to generate electricity, but then all use the same wires to supply the electricity to people's homes and businesses.

Similarly, countries such as the UK have split the railway industry vertically. Several competing providers of train services run their trains on the same sets of tracks. This requires active regulation to make sure that different companies do not try to run trains in different directions at the same time. Critics also say that the system enables the operators of train services and the monopoly that manages the tracks to blame each other for delays.

While it may seem like the job of regulating monopolies should fall to policy-makers in faraway government buildings, the famous board game Monopoly brings the problems created by monopolies closer to home. Read the From Another Angle box "The origins of Monopoly" to learn how the game we play today originally worked.

The origins of Monopoly

From Another Angle

You probably know the board game Monopoly. In the game, you win by building real estate empires and bankrupting friends and family members. What you may not know is that the original game had a far different intention.

About a century ago, Elizabeth J. Magie designed the game as "The Landlord's Game." At the time, the U.S. economy was dominated by monopolies such as Standard Oil and U.S. Steel, and the fear of monopoly power was a broad concern. Magie aimed to illustrate the destructive influence these monopolies had on the economy, and she wanted to nudge players toward a "fairer" system.

In the original rules, players had two options. The first was a conventional setup, which resembled the Monopoly we play today, with a similar objective (gain as much money as possible) and outcome (one monopolist who ruled the board). Magie hoped that players would see the perils of having one rich player bankrupt everyone else. She encouraged players to implement an idea, called a "single tax," adopted from the political economist Henry George.

In Magie's original game, the "single tax" taxes land and redistributes this revenue to make utilities and railroads public and give players extra wages. (In the current game of Monopoly, the money you get when you pass "Go" is the wage.) Although the objective was still to get as much cash as possible, the game ended when players felt like it, since the single tax abolished the "poorhouse" for bankrupt players.

Eventually the game was simplified and lost most of the economic message. (One key message remains, though: When you have a monopoly of a set of properties, you get to charge higher prices!) It started to resemble the cutthroat game we play today. This outcome isn't surprising—many people prefer not to get economics lessons during their family game night. But the next time you play Monopoly, you might want to, as Elizabeth Magie hoped, think about the economics behind bankrupting your friends and family.

Source: Mary Pilon, "Monopoly's Inventor: The Progressive Who Didn't Pass 'Go,'" *The New York Times*, February 13, 2015, www.nytimes.com/2015/02/15/business/behind-monopoly-an-inventor-who-didnt-pass-go.html.

No response   Looking at the pros and cons of various interventions in monopoly markets, some economists conclude that the best response to a monopoly is sometimes no response at all. When might the right solution be to do nothing? Doing nothing might be preferable if regulation is too difficult to create or manage effectively. If government interventions in the market are subject to corruption or political mishandling, it might be better not to act. This view doesn't deny that monopoly power causes inefficiency. Instead, it simply holds that sometimes the problems caused by intervention might be worse.

✓ **TEST YOURSELF**

☐ Why does monopoly cause deadweight loss? **[LO 14.4]**
☐ What are some of the potential problems with public ownership of monopolies? **[LO 14.5]**

Market Power and Price Discrimination

In any market, some consumers typically would be willing to pay more for the good than the market price. When they buy at a price lower than their willingness to pay, they enjoy consumer surplus. If you were a firm, wouldn't you like to be able to charge different individuals different prices for the same good? You could charge a higher price to customers with higher willingness to pay, transforming their consumer surplus into your producer surplus. The more monopoly power a firm has, the more able it is to do exactly this.

What is price discrimination?

The practice of charging customers different prices for the same good is called **price discrimination**. It involves "discriminating" between customers on the basis of their willingness to pay. Examples of price discrimination are all around us. Have you ever used your student ID card to claim discounts on public transport or theater tickets? That's an example of price discrimination. You are getting exactly the same product as people who are being charged full price, but you receive a discount because companies assume that for many goods, on average, students have lower willingness to pay.

How can a firm charge different customers different amounts for the same good? In a perfectly competitive market, it couldn't. Remember that firms in a perfectly competitive market sell at a price equal to their average total cost, and earn zero economic profit. They couldn't afford to offer discounted prices to students; doing so would result in *negative* profit. Nor could they choose to charge nonstudents a higher price because those customers would simply go to a competing firm instead.

As we move away from the model of perfect competition, price discrimination becomes possible. Whenever firms gain a degree of market power, they look for ways to exploit customers' varied willingness to pay. Consider why clothing stores hold periodic sales, for example. It enables them to charge two different prices: They charge one price to consumers who are willing to pay more

LO 14.6 Explain why a firm has an incentive to use price discrimination when possible.

price discrimination the practice of charging customers different prices for the same good

Price discrimination in action: Tourists who don't read Spanish pay extra.

to get the item when it first hits the market. They charge a lower price to those who don't mind waiting until the sales are on. Similarly, theaters tend to charge lower prices for matinee showings: They attract the cash-poor and time-rich during the day; people with busy work schedules will generally be both more willing and able to pay the higher prices charged for an evening showing.

The more monopoly power a firm has, the more it is able to price-discriminate. While Microsoft Office does have substitutes, such as the open source OpenOffice suite, for many people these are not close enough substitutes. If you are sharing documents with other people who all use Microsoft Office, then you probably also need to own Microsoft Office.

Consequently, Microsoft offers many different versions of Office, including different options for personal and office use. College students are often pleasantly surprised to find that they can buy computer software through their colleges for significantly lower prices than they could in a store or online. (Take a look at your school's information technology website. We bet you'll find discounts.) The Microsoft Office® suite of programs, such as Word®, Excel®, and PowerPoint®, often sells for half as much when bought through a university.

Let's break this down a little further. For simplicity, suppose Microsoft knows that there are three groups of potential Office customers:

- Students, who are willing to pay $75
- Standard computer users, who are willing to pay $150
- People who use their computers to run their businesses, who are willing to pay $225

And say there are 1 million potential customers in each group, as shown in the stylized demand curve in Figure 14-7. There is a limit to the quantity Microsoft can sell at any given price.

Of course, in reality, there is variation in people's willingness to pay within these groups. For example, some students are willing to pay more than $75, and some less. But for the sake of simplicity, let's assume for now that all students, all standard users, and all business users are the same.

Let's also assume that there is a fixed cost of $50 million to produce Office (for instance, to pay for research and development) and that the variable cost of production is essentially zero. (Zero isn't too far from reality—making a copy of software doesn't cost very much, especially now that many people download their copy of Office online.) With no variable cost, the profit that Microsoft earns is simply total revenue minus fixed costs. (Note, too, that if variable costs are zero, marginal costs also are zero.)

What price should Microsoft set for Office? If it chooses $75, all 3 million potential customers will buy a copy of Office, and the company will earn:

$$\text{Profit} = \text{Total revenue (TR)} - \text{Fixed costs (FC)}$$
$$= (3 \text{ million} \times \$75) - \$50 \text{ million}$$
$$= \$225 \text{ million} - \$50 \text{ million}$$
$$= \$175 \text{ million}$$

What if Microsoft chooses to charge $150? As the calculations in Table 14-3 show, only 2 million customers will buy at the higher price. In that case, the company will earn $250 million in profits. If it charges $225 per copy of Office, only 1 million business customers will choose to buy, and Microsoft will earn $175 million in profits.

If Microsoft can pick only one price, it should pick $150 to maximize its profits. However, by charging $150, Microsoft loses the business of students, who have a lower willingness to pay. It also misses out on the extra $75 that business customers would have been willing to pay. Microsoft

FIGURE 14-7

Demand for Microsoft Office®

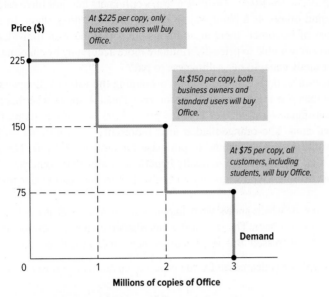

This simplified demand curve shows the demand for Office in a perfectly segmented market. In this example, all members of each group have the same willingness to pay: All business owners will pay $225 or less; all standard users will pay $150 or less; and all students will pay only $75 or less.

does best if it can find a way to charge these three groups the exact price they are willing to pay. Then, its profits are:

$$
\begin{aligned}
\text{Profit} &= \text{TR} - \text{FC} \\
&= [(1 \text{ million} \times \$225) + (1 \text{ million} \times \$150) + (1 \text{ million} \times \$75)] - \$50 \text{ million} \\
&= \$450 \text{ million} - \$50 \text{ million} \\
&= \$400 \text{ million}
\end{aligned}
$$

Microsoft can earn an additional $150 million [($400 − $250) × 1 million copies] in profits if it can charge students less and businesses more. We can see why any firm with market power would want to price-discriminate. As a student, this is good news for you too (at least if you're facing monopoly pricing).

TABLE 14-3

Profit without price discrimination

If Microsoft can charge only one price for Office, the best option is to choose $150, which will maximize profit at $250 million. That option, however, will exclude students, who are unwilling to pay more than $75.

Price ($)	Number of copies	Total revenue ($)	Fixed cost ($)	Profit ($)
75	3,000,000	225,000,000	50,000,000	175,000,000
150	2,000,000	300,000,000	50,000,000	(250,000,000)
225	1,000,000	225,000,000	50,000,000	175,000,000

Perfect price discrimination   Dividing a firm's customers into just three categories—students, business owners, and others—is a blunt way of discriminating among them. In reality, there are not just three types of customer—there are millions, all with their own individual willingness to pay. What if Microsoft was able to price-discriminate more accurately by charging every individual customer a price exactly equal to her willingness to pay?

Figure 14-8 shows a smooth demand curve representing the varied willingness to pay of many individuals (rather than just three clusters of customers). Panel A shows what happens if Microsoft does not price-discriminate—if it charges just one price, $150, for Office. Its profit is represented by the blue-shaded area. The orange-shaded area represents the consumer surplus enjoyed by customers who would have been willing to purchase for more than $150. The gray area shows deadweight loss. That represents the mutually beneficial trades that could have taken place but did not. These are customers who would have been willing to purchase Office for a price between $150 and zero.

Now look at panel B, which shows what happens when Microsoft price-discriminates among the three categories of customer. The size of the blue-shaded area, representing Microsoft's profits (producer surplus), has increased. But note the differences among the three categories of customers:

- Consumer surplus has decreased for the group of customers who were willing to pay over $150.
- Customers who were willing to pay between $75 and $150 now enjoy some consumer surplus.
- Finally, deadweight loss has been reduced to only those mutually beneficial trades that could have taken place between $75 and zero but did not.

FIGURE 14-8

Price discrimination

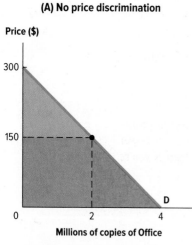

(A) No price discrimination

With no price discrimination, Microsoft charges one price, $150, to all customers.

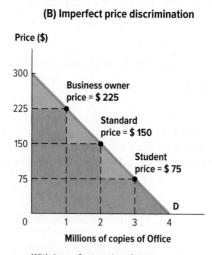

(B) Imperfect price discrimination

With imperfect or tiered price discrimination, Microsoft can earn a profit on sales to both students and other buyers. Because not all students have the same willingness to pay, however, some mutually beneficial trades (represented by the gray-shaded area) don't take place.

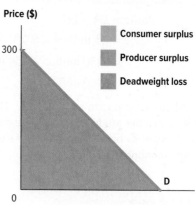

(C) Perfect price discrimination

If Microsoft could charge each customer his or her exact willingness to pay, the company would profit on all exchanges, eliminating both the deadweight loss and the consumer surplus shown in panel A.

Panel C shows what would happen if Microsoft were able to price-discriminate perfectly—if it could find each customer's willingness to pay. The area representing Microsoft's profits becomes even bigger. There is no consumer surplus at all any more. The consumer surplus that previously existed has all been transformed into producer surplus. Neither is there any deadweight loss. Instead, all possible mutually beneficial trades take place—meaning the market is *efficient*.

The more perfectly a company is able to price-discriminate, the more profit it makes, and the more efficiently the market works. Remember that efficiency doesn't say anything about the distribution of surplus—including whether it goes to consumers or producers—but only whether total surplus is maximized.

So why doesn't a monopoly charge every individual a different price? There are some obvious problems with this idea, as we will see.

Price discrimination in the real world   The first problem with price discrimination in the real world is defining categories of customers. Microsoft's price-discrimination strategy would not work very well if anyone could simply say, "I'm a student," and be charged the lower price. The company needs some way to verify who is a student. To get around this problem, Microsoft enters into agreements with colleges, which take responsibility for identifying who is a student. In general, students have to go through their colleges' websites and enter their student ID number or other verification to purchase software at the discount price. Similarly, if you turn up at the box office of a theater asking to purchase a ticket with a student discount, the cashier will ask for your student ID card.

The second problem facing the firm that tries to price-discriminate is that many products can easily be resold. If someone you know is about to pay $150 for Microsoft Office, some people might be tempted to buy student versions at a low price and illicitly resell them at a higher price. To prevent this, there needs to be some way of punishing people who cheat the system. Hence, Microsoft can use legal enforcement against anyone who uses a student version of Office for his or her business. Similarly, theaters need some way to stop students from bulk-buying tickets and selling them to nonstudents. They may, for instance, demand to see a student ID before allowing entrance into a theater with a student ticket.

Many goods do not lend themselves to this kind of tracking as easily as software or theater tickets. Imagine if Apple sold iPhones to customers under age 18 for a 50 percent discount. This might seem like a neat way to increase its profits, if there are lots of under-18s who would love to buy an iPhone but cannot afford to pay full price. However, high school students would have a thriving business buying up the iPhones at the local Apple store and reselling them to older buyers for a profit. No one over 18 would buy their iPhones directly from Apple—which therefore has no incentive to offer different prices.

For a firm that wants to practice *perfect* price discrimination, the challenges are even more forbidding. It would need to be able to read the minds of each individual customer and form an accurate impression of how much that customer would be willing to pay. Much as Microsoft would love to be able to read the minds of potential purchasers and charge them exactly what they'd be willing to pay, the task is essentially impossible.

Still, some practitioners of price discrimination are adept at sizing up their customers before quoting a price. See the From Another Angle box "Rickshaw rides: Price discrimination and asymmetric information."

✓ **TEST YOURSELF**

☐ Why do firms have an incentive to price-discriminate? **[LO 14.6]**
☐ Name several practical barriers to perfect price discrimination. **[LO 14.6]**

Rickshaw rides: Price discrimination and asymmetric information

From Another Angle

Tourist regions charge visitors notoriously inflated prices. Taxi and rickshaw drivers in India are especially famous for charging foreign-looking, wealthy-looking, or clueless-looking passengers significantly higher fares than they would charge to locals. This practice is the root of countless confrontations in which rickshaw drivers and foreign tourists try to bargain over fares, generally in a mix of broken English and improvised sign language. What are the economic forces underlying this common scene?

One explanation is that tourists are the victims of a severe information asymmetry. Tourists often don't know how far their destination is and have no idea about the standard "local" rate for going there. Since drivers invariably know more than tourists about the "fair price" of fares, they are able to exploit this information asymmetry to boost their earnings.

Another factor contributing to the difference in the prices paid by locals and tourists is their differing willingness to pay. Tourists from wealthier countries are generally willing to pay more than most Indians would for the same goods and services. Someone from

Tourists often face severe information asymmetry and also may differ from locals in their willingness to pay.
©Lissa Harrison

New York City might consider 100 rupees (about $2) for a rickshaw ride in Delhi to be an incredible bargain (a similar ride in a New York taxi could cost $25), even if 100 rupees is more than twice what locals pay.

But why doesn't competition between drivers push fares back down to competitive levels? Remember, price discrimination works only for producers with market power. One individual rickshaw driver may not have much sway in the market, but the rickshaw drivers in a particular location often operate like a cartel. Rather than competing, they have standing agreements not to undercut one another on price.

However, the days of frustrated tourists might be numbered. More and more cities across India are requiring rickshaws to start using the enemy of price-discriminating drivers everywhere: the fare meter.

Conclusion

Monopolies can use their market power to hold price above the level that would prevail in a competitive market. By doing so, they turn consumer surplus into positive economic profits and reduce total social welfare. This poses a tricky problem for policy-makers, who want to regulate or break up monopolies to increase social welfare. Practically speaking, it can be difficult to accomplish this goal without causing more inefficiency. Policies designed to address the problems associated with monopolies run the risk of setting prices at the wrong level or raising costs by breaking up a natural monopoly.

This difficult situation is complicated further by the fact that few firms are truly perfect monopolies. Instead, many markets include firms with some degree of market power, ranging on the spectrum from perfect monopoly to perfect competition. We can call markets in this range *imperfectly competitive*. It turns out that small differences in the structure of imperfectly competitive markets can make big differences in how firms behave; those differences can give policy-makers headaches. In the next chapter, we'll take a close look at two specific varieties of imperfect competition.

Key Terms

monopoly, p. 324

natural monopoly, p. 325

price discrimination, p. 341

Summary

LO 14.1 List four barriers to entry into monopoly markets.

The key characteristic of a monopoly market is that there are barriers that prevent firms other than the monopolist from entering the market. Barriers to entry take four main forms: scarce resources, economies of scale, government intervention, and aggressive business tactics on the part of market-leading firms.

Scarcity in some key resource or input into the production process means that firms may have difficulty accessing the resources they need to enter the market. When there are large economies of scale in a market, firms have no incentive to enter; they would face higher costs of production than the monopoly. Some monopolies are created or sustained by the power of government, through public ownership or protection of intellectual property. Finally, some monopolies use their size and various aggressive tactics to keep smaller firms from getting a toehold in the market.

LO 14.2 Explain why a monopolist is constrained by demand.

As the only firm in the market, a monopoly is constrained in the price-quantity combinations it can sell by the market demand curve. All else equal, quantity demanded falls as price rises. The monopoly can choose any price-quantity combination on the demand curve, but it is unable to choose points that are not on the curve because it can't force customers to buy more or less than they demand at any given price.

LO 14.3 Calculate the profit-maximizing production price and quantity for a monopolist.

A monopoly chooses the profit-maximizing quantity the same way a firm in a competitive market would: by producing at the quantity for which marginal revenue is equal to marginal cost. Price is the price that corresponds to that quantity on the demand curve.

Unlike a firm in a competitive market, however, the monopoly price is higher than marginal revenue, and therefore also higher than marginal cost at the profit-maximizing point. This means that a monopoly earns positive economic profits.

LO 14.4 Calculate the loss in total social welfare associated with a monopoly.

The equilibrium price and quantity in a competitive market maximize total surplus. A monopoly's profit-maximizing quantity, however, is lower than the efficient quantity that would prevail in a competitive market. This tells us that total surplus is not maximized, and that producer surplus is higher than competitive levels, while consumer surplus is lower. The deadweight loss caused by a monopoly is equal to total surplus under perfect competition minus total surplus under a monopoly.

LO 14.5 Describe the pros and cons of common public policy responses to monopoly.

Policy-makers have developed a range of policy tools aimed at breaking up existing monopolies, preventing new ones from forming, and mitigating the effect of monopoly power on consumers. Antitrust laws allow the government to sue firms that engage in anti-competitive practices and to block mergers that would result in too much market power. Public ownership of natural monopolies maintains the cost advantages of economies of scale but removes the profit motive that might drive quality improvements and cost reductions. Price regulation may also preserve the cost advantages of natural monopoly while holding down price, but it is practically difficult to set price at the right level. In some cases, doing nothing may actually be the best policy response to monopoly.

LO 14.6 Explain why a firm has an incentive to use price discrimination when possible.

Price discrimination is the practice of charging customers different prices for the same good. Price discrimination allows a firm to charge each customer a price closer to his willingness to pay, turning consumer surplus into producer surplus and increasing the firm's profits.

Review Questions

1. If competition places discipline on costs, motivating firms to innovate and find more cost-effective ways to produce, explain why in some markets a single firm without competitors will produce at a lower cost than if the firm faced competition. **[LO 14.1]**

2. Suppose a city has a chain of fitness centers (gyms) all owned by the same company, Fit Fun. A new company is considering opening a gym in the city. Give an example of an aggressive tactic Fit Fun might take to maintain its monopoly. **[LO 14.1]**

3. Suppose that De Beers and the local water utility are both monopolists, in the markets for diamond jewelry and water, respectively. If both monopolies decided to raise prices 15 percent, which monopoly would be more likely to see its total revenue decrease? Why? **[LO 14.2]**

4. Suppose that a producer in a previously competitive market is granted the sole right to produce in the market. Given that demand in the market is unchanged, but now all consumers must purchase from the same producer, why might the new monopolist produce less than the quantity that was produced when the market was competitive? **[LO 14.2]**

5. Suppose that an inventor discovers a new chemical compound that can change the color of people's eyes with no negative side effects. Since she holds a patent on this chemical, she has a monopoly over the sale of the new eye-color treatment. However, she's an inventor, not a businessperson. Explain to her how she should set the price for the eye-color treatment in order to maximize her profits. **[LO 14.3]**

6. Suppose a monopolist has to purchase new equipment and his fixed costs increase. Explain what will happen to the monopolist's profit-maximizing output quantity and the monopolist's profits. **[LO 14.3]**

7. Until the 1980s, AT&T held a monopoly over the national market for phone services. Suppose that AT&T argued that it was a natural monopoly because the fixed cost of creating a nationwide phone network generated huge economies of scale, and that there was therefore no welfare loss associated with its monopoly. Counter this argument by explaining how even a natural monopoly causes deadweight loss. **[LO 14.4]**

8. Suppose you are advising a mayoral candidate in your town. The candidate's platform includes strong opposition to monopoly suppliers because consumer welfare is compromised by monopoly pricing. Present your candidate with an alternative view about why it may make sense to tolerate the existence of some monopoly firms. **[LO 14.4]**

9. Suppose that your state is considering a law that would force all monopolies to charge no more than their average total costs of production. Explain to your legislator the pros and cons of this approach. **[LO 14.5]**

10. Suppose that your state is considering a law that would force all monopolies to charge the efficient price that would prevail if the market were competitive. Explain to your legislator why the state will have to subsidize natural monopolies if this law goes into effect. **[LO 14.5]**

11. Suppose a small town has one theater for live performances and several restaurants, including one Indian restaurant. Will it be easier for the theater or for the Indian restaurant to price discriminate? **[LO 14.6]**

12. Suppose a museum charges different entrance fees for children, students, adults, and seniors, but these groups all pay the same amount for souvenirs at the gift shop. Explain why the museum price discriminates on admission but not souvenirs. **[LO 14.6]**

Problems and Applications

1. The U.S. Postal Services maintains a monopoly on mail delivery in part through its exclusive right to access customer mailboxes. Which barrier to entry best describes this situation: scarce resources, economies of scale, government intervention, or aggressive tactics? **[LO 14.1]**

2. Which (if any) of the following scenarios is the result of a natural monopoly? **[LO 14.1]**

    a. Patent holders of genetically modified seeds are permitted to sue farmers who save seeds from one planting season to the next.

    b. Doctors in the United States are prohibited from practicing without a medical license.

    c. There is one train operator with service from Baltimore to Philadelphia.

    d. Coal is used as the primary energy in a country with abundant coal deposits.

3. Due to arduous certification requirements, Nature's Crunch is currently the only certified organic produce grower in a region that produces lots of nonorganic produce alternatives. From a profit-maximizing perspective, would it be better for Nature's Crunch to lobby the government to relax organic certification requirements or to require grocery stores to clearly label its produce as organic? **[LO 14.2]**

4. Nature's Crunch is currently the only certified organic produce grower in a region that produces lots of non-organic produce alternatives. To be certified organic, a producer cannot use chemical pesticides. Which of the following scenarios would increase Nature's Crunch's profits? Check all that apply. **[LO 14.2]**

   a. A tomato blight affecting chemically treated plants.

   b. An increase in the cost of chemical pesticides.

   c. A new report about the environmental dangers of chemically treated plants.

   d. Income tax cuts for all consumers.

   e. A new report showing that there is no nutritional difference between organic and nonorganic produce.

5. Table 14P-1 presents the demand schedule and marginal costs facing a monopolist producer. **[LO 14.3]**

TABLE 14P-1

Q	P ($)	TR ($)	MR ($)	MC ($)
0	12			–
1	11			3
2	10			3
3	9			3
4	8			3
5	7			3
6	6			3
7	5			3
8	4			3
9	3			3
10	2			3

a. Fill in the total revenue and marginal revenue columns.

b. What is the profit-maximizing level of output?

c. What price will the monopolist charge for the quantity in part *b*?

6. Table 14P-2 presents the demand schedule and marginal costs facing a monopolist producer. **[LO 14.3]**

   a. Fill in the total revenue and marginal revenue columns.

   b. What is the profit-maximizing level of output?

   c. What price will the monopolist charge for the quantity in part *b*?

TABLE 14P-2

Q	P ($)	TR ($)	MR ($)	MC ($)
0	8			–
1	7			1
2	6			2
3	5			3
4	4			4
5	3			5
6	2			6
7	1			7
8	0			8

7. Figure 14P-1 presents the demand curve, marginal revenue, and marginal costs facing a monopolist producer. **[LO 14.3, 14.4]**

FIGURE 14P-1

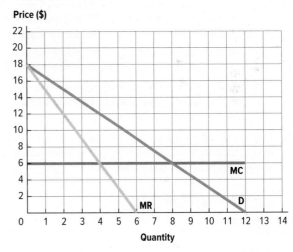

a. What is the profit-maximizing level of output?

b. What price will the monopolist charge for the quantity in part *a?*

c. Plot the profit-maximizing price and quantity from parts *a* and *b* on the graph.

d. What are the efficiency costs (deadweight loss) of monopoly output/pricing? Provide a numerical answer and illustrate this area on the graph.

e. What is consumer surplus under monopoly output/pricing? Illustrate this area on the graph.

8. Figure 14P-2 presents the demand curve, marginal revenue, and marginal costs facing a monopolist producer. [LO 14.3, 14.4]

FIGURE 14P-2

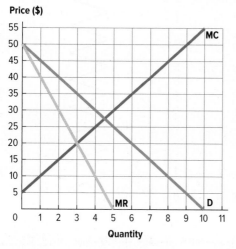

a. What is the profit-maximizing level of output?
b. What price will the monopolist charge for the quantity in part *a?*
c. What are the efficiency costs (deadweight loss) of monopoly output/pricing? Provide a numerical answer and illustrate this area on the graph.
d. What is consumer surplus under monopoly output/pricing? Illustrate this area on the graph.
e. What is the loss of consumer surplus under monopoly outcomes versus efficient outcomes? Provide a numerical answer.

9. Figure 14P-3 presents the demand curve, marginal revenue, marginal costs, and average total costs facing a monopolist producer. [LO 14.5]

FIGURE 14P-3

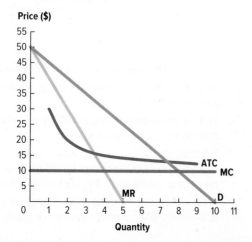

a. Plot the profit-maximizing price and quantity on the graph.
b. Under monopoly pricing, are profits positive, negative, or zero?
c. Draw the deadweight loss under monopoly pricing.
d. If government mandates P = ATC, are profits positive, negative, or zero? Compared to monopoly pricing, is deadweight loss smaller, larger, or the same size?
e. If government mandates efficient pricing, are profits positive, negative, or zero? Compared to monopoly pricing, is deadweight loss under efficient pricing smaller, larger, or the same size? Compared to a mandate where P = ATC, is deadweight loss under efficient pricing smaller, larger, or the same size?
f. Is this a natural monopoly?

10. Use Figure 14P-4 to answer the following questions. [LO 14.5]

FIGURE 14P-4

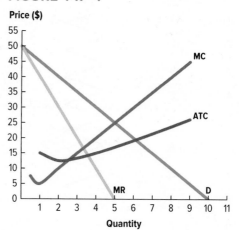

a. If this monopolist were regulated, would it prefer average total cost pricing (P = ATC) or efficient pricing?
b. Is this a natural monopoly?

11. Suppose a monopolist discovers a way to perfectly price-discriminate. What is consumer surplus under this scenario? What are the efficiency costs? [LO 14.6]

12. Suppose there are three types of consumers who attend concerts at your university's performing arts center: students, staff, and faculty. Each of these groups has a different willingness to pay for tickets; within each group, willingness to pay is identical. There is a fixed cost of $1,000 to put on a concert, but there are essentially no variable costs. [LO 14.6]

For each concert:

- There are 150 students willing to pay $20.
- There are 200 staff members willing to pay $35.
- There are 100 faculty members willing to pay $50.

   a. If the performing arts center can charge only one price, what price should it charge?

   b. What are profits at this price?

   c. If the performing arts center can price discriminate and charge two prices, one for students and another for faculty/staff, what are its profits?

   d. If the performing arts center can perfectly price discriminate and charge students, staff, and faculty three separate prices, what are its profits?

Endnotes

1. https://20somethingfinance.com/how-much-should-you-spend-on-an-engagement-ring/comment-page-2/.

2. www.theatlantic.com/magazine/archive/1982/02/have-you-ever-tried-to-sell-a-diamond/304575/.

3. www.businessinsider.com/de-beers-says-diamond-market-in-better-shape-than-2015-2016-9.

4. www.theatlantic.com/magazine/archive/1982/02/have-you-ever-tried-to-sell-a-diamond/304575/.

5. www.theatlantic.com/magazine/archive/1982/02/have-you-ever-tried-to-sell-a-diamond/304575/.

6. https://ilsr.org/walmart-charged-predatory-pricing/;https://ilsr.org/mexico-investigates-walmart-antitrust-violations/.

7. www.statista.com/statistics/216573/worldwide-market-share-of-search-engines/.

8. www.diamonds.net/News/NewsItem.aspx?ArticleID=38343.

9. www.forbes.com/sites/greatspeculations/2015/04/28/comcast-twc-merger-called-off-where-do-these-companies-stand-now/#6ce5fa9d7114.

10. www.businessinsider.com/disney-21st-century-fox-deal-approved-2018-7.

11. https://media.amtrak.com/2017/11/amtrak-sets-ridership-revenue-and-earnings-records/#_ftn1; www.govexec.com/management/2016/02/usps-records-first-profit-five-years-obama-calls-shedding-12k-postal-jobs/125825/.

Monopolistic Competition and Oligopoly

Which One of These Is Just Like the Others?

What do the musicians Taylor Swift, Katy Perry, and Kanye West have in common? We'll give you a hint. It's the same thing that Metallica has in common with Death Cab for Cutie and Dean Martin, and that Shakira shares with the winner of the 2016 Nobel Prize for Literature, Bob Dylan.

Each of these artists is on one of the three major recording labels that together account for almost 70 percent of the U.S. music market. These three labels—Universal Music Group (Universal), Sony Music Entertainment (Sony), and Warner Music Group (Warner)—each controls between 18 and 30 percent of the market.[1] If you want to be a successful recording artist, you'll have a much better chance with one of them on your side.

©Prince Williams/WireImage/Getty Images

That wasn't always the case, though. In the 1950s and 1960s, many stars were able to make their names with small record labels. An Alabama radio host named Sam Phillips started Sun Records out of a cheap storefront in Memphis. He promptly signed then-unknown artists Elvis Presley, Johnny Cash, and B.B. King. A Ford assembly-line worker, Berry Gordy, formed Motown Records in Detroit with a tiny family loan, and made stars of Marvin Gaye, Stevie Wonder, and many others.[2] In the last decade, as streaming services have revolutionized music distribution, new ways have opened up again for musicians to market themselves independently of the three major labels. But it's still not as common for an artist to break through on a small label today as it was in the early days of rock and roll.

LEARNING OBJECTIVES

LO 15.1 Name the defining features of oligopoly and monopolistic competition.

LO 15.2 Calculate the profit-maximizing price and quantity for a monopolistically competitive firm in the short run.

LO 15.3 Describe a monopolistically competitive market in the long run.

LO 15.4 Analyze the welfare costs of monopolistic competition.

LO 15.5 Explain how product differentiation motivates advertising and branding.

LO 15.6 Describe the strategic production decision of firms in an oligopoly.

LO 15.7 Explain how basic tenets of game theory apply to an oligopoly's incentive to compete or collude.

LO 15.8 Compare the welfare of producers, consumers, and society as a whole in an oligopoly to monopoly and perfect competition.

In previous chapters, we described two extreme market structures: monopoly and perfect competition. In this chapter, we'll see why neither of those two models describes the music industry—both past and present. Instead, the music industry is a market that is somewhat competitive, but not perfectly competitive. Such a market structure is quite common in the real world.

In particular, we'll discuss two types of market structures that are *imperfectly competitive:* monopolistic competition and oligopoly. These market structures aren't mutually exclusive. As we'll see, many industries, including the music industry, display characteristics of both.

Understanding market structure is key to running a successful business. A business owner needs to know the type of market in which she is engaged in order to know how much freedom she has to set prices, or how much attention to pay to the behavior of other firms. Her business strategy may differ greatly depending on how much competition she faces and of what sort. Understanding market structure can also be valuable in making good choices as a consumer or policy-maker. It can help us to interpret a firm's choice to advertise, for example, or to decide when we should favor regulators stepping in to address "anti-competitive" business practices. The concepts that we explore in this chapter will help us understand choices faced by businesses, consumers, and policy-makers.

What Sort of Market?

What sort of market is the music industry? That's the 17-billion-dollar question for everyone from record-label executives to retailers to antitrust lawyers at the Department of Justice. In answering it, we'll focus on the two characteristics that define a range of market structures: number of firms and product variety.

Let's start by looking at the number of firms. Figure 15-1 shows that the music industry is dominated by three labels; no single one of them is big enough to dominate the industry in the way that De Beers dominated the diamond market in the twentieth century. This tells us the music industry is not a monopoly.

It's also not perfectly competitive. That's not simply because the market is dominated by a few large firms. It's also because it encompasses a wide variety of products. Even if there were thousands of small recording labels competing, the market would not be perfectly competitive because music is not a standardized product. There are many similarities between, say, a Kanye West track and music by The Shins: They're both digitized versions of music, using data-compression technology with a common digital encoding format. Both emit sounds of instruments and voices when played. They're similar enough that it makes sense for us to think of them both as products of the same industry, the music industry. But they are certainly not a standardized product—at least, not to fans of either artist.

These two features of the music industry—a small number of large firms and product variety—are the defining features of two market structures that lie between the extreme models of monopoly and perfect competition. Both of those market structures—*oligopoly* and *monopolistic competition*—are common in the real world. While many industries display features of both models, understanding each model separately allows us to make powerful predictions about how firms will behave.

FIGURE 15-1

Market share in the music business   The music industry is dominated by three big firms. Their sales in 2017 represented almost 70 percent of the market. They are so big that their behavior affects the entire market for music.

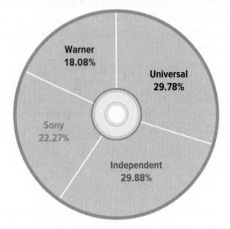

Source: Tim Ingham, www.musicbusinessworldwide.com/independents-ruled-global-market-share-in-2017-but-universal-was-king-of-streaming/.

Oligopoly and monopolistic competition

Oligopoly describes a market with only a few firms. (The word itself is derived from the Greek words for "few sellers.") These companies sell a product or service that may or may not be completely standardized but is similar enough that the firms are in competition. Examples of oligopolies are wireless network providers (the U.S. market is currently dominated by four companies—Verizon, AT&T, Sprint, and T-Mobile, with a possible merger between the latter two) and fast-food burgers (think McDonald's, Burger King, and Wendy's).

One of the defining features of an oligopoly is that strategic interactions between a firm and its rivals have a major impact on its success. In particular, we'll see that the price and quantity set by an individual firm affect the other firms' profits. This stands in contrast to firms in perfectly competitive markets or monopolists: In a perfectly competitive market, other firms' actions cannot affect the market. If you are a true monopolist, there *are* no other firms (unless another firm is trying to create a product that can substitute for yours).

If you are in charge of a company in an oligopoly, though, it is a vital part of your job to keep an eye on competitors. The shareholders of Wendy's would not be impressed if the CEO had no idea that McDonald's had just introduced a new kind of burger or that Burger King was rapidly expanding in a certain part of the country.

Oligopolies are also characterized by the existence of some barriers to entry. Remember that barriers to entry enable monopolies to exist. You couldn't set up in the diamond business to challenge De Beers without discovering a new source of diamonds. In perfect competition, by contrast, we assume there are *no* barriers to entry—it's easy for new firms to enter the market. Oligopoly is somewhere in the middle. It would be possible to set up as a wireless carrier but expensive to construct the infrastructure or gain access to existing towers. It would be possible to break into the national burger chain market but tough to overcome established brand loyalties.

Monopolistic competition describes a market with *many* firms that sell goods and services that are similar, but slightly different. Remember that a feature of *perfect competition* is that consumers are indifferent between the products of competing firms. A feature of *monopoly* is that the product has no close substitutes. Between these two extremes are *monopolistic competition* markets in which products have substitutes that are close but not perfect. Consumers might be willing to pay a bit extra, but if the price differential is too large, they will choose a substitute product instead.

Although the name *monopolistic competition* sounds like a contradiction in terms, it expresses the idea that firms in such a market have a kind of monopoly but in a limited sense. For example,

LO 15.1 Name the defining features of oligopoly and monopolistic competition.

oligopoly
a market with only a few firms, which sell a similar good or service

monopolistic competition
a market with many firms that sell goods and services that are similar, but slightly different

in the 1950s Sun Records had a monopoly on selling Elvis records. If you wanted an Elvis record, you had no choice but to buy it from Sun. Devoted fans of Elvis might be willing to pay more for an Elvis record than for records by other artists. Thus, Sun had some power to set its own price, but not much. If Sun raised the price of Elvis records too high, most people would prefer to save their money or to buy records by other artists instead.

Monopolistic competition describes a great many real-world markets. For example, Nestlé, the parent company of Häagen-Dazs, has a monopoly on selling Häagen-Dazs brand ice cream, but not a monopoly on ice cream in general. If you especially like Häagen-Dazs, you might be willing to pay a bit extra for it. But if the price differential becomes too great, you'll switch to another brand, such as Ben & Jerry's or Breyers. Similarly, you might be willing to pay a little more for a meal at your favorite restaurant, but if the price is too high, you'd be happy to settle for your second favorite.

Oligopoly and monopolistic competition are often found together, as in the music industry. In short:

- Oligopoly is about the *number of firms*.
- Monopolistic competition is about *variety of products*.

Record companies are oligopolists: There are only a few record companies, each has market power, and the basic service they provide (access and distribution of music) is roughly the same. Individual musicians are monopolistic competitors: They have a monopoly over their own music but must also compete with other musicians. Each musician, of course, is different, providing his or her own unique product.

The fact that the "music industry" can be described in both of these two ways makes it more complicated to analyze. However, there are markets that are distinctly oligopoly markets and those that are distinctly described as monopolistic competition:

- Oligopolies can exist when products are standardized. Shell, ExxonMobil, and other energy producers operate in an oligopoly market.
- Monopolistic competition can exist when there are many small firms. For example, the restaurants in your city or town likely operate in markets that are purely monopolistic competition.

To keep things clean, we will explore the two market structures separately.

✓ **TEST YOURSELF**

☐ What is the difference between oligopoly and monopolistic competition? **[LO 15.1]**

Monopolistic Competition

Remember that under the model of perfect competition, firms do not make economic profits. It's not surprising, then, that firms would rather be operating under conditions of monopolistic competition, where they *can* make economic profits.

How do monopolistically competitive firms make economic profits? By making a product that consumers perceive to be different from the products of their competitors. In other words, firms must offer goods that are similar to competitors' products but more attractive in some ways. This process is called **product differentiation**. It is an essential part of the strategy of many businesses.

product differentiation
the creation of products that are similar to competitors' products but more attractive in some ways

Sometimes product differentiation is accomplished through genuine innovation. The many record labels operating in the 1950s music business are an example. They competed to discover and shape new, exciting, *different* performers who could attract a following of loyal fans. The more enthusiastic Elvis fans were, the less interchangeable they considered Elvis's records to be with those of other artists. The less interchangeable the records, the more Sun could charge without fear of losing sales. Sam Phillips, the founder of Sun Records, discovered a wealth of previously overlooked talent in and around Memphis: He was happy to work with black musicians who were otherwise excluded from white-dominated parts of the music business in that era of segregation. In doing so, he helped to create rock and roll—not only recognizing talent, but shaping it into something new.

Regardless of whether genuine innovation is involved, firms have an interest in persuading customers that their products are unique. This is the role of advertising and branding. Even when a firm's product is not really very different from other products on the market, it may be possible to convince customers that the product *is* different, and thereby persuade them to pay more for a particular brand. We'll return to these issues later in the chapter.

Monopolistic competition in the short run

Product differentiation enables firms in monopolistically competitive markets to produce a good for which there are no exact substitutes. In the short run, this allows a firm to behave like a monopolist. In the long run, as we will see, the situation is different. This difference between the short and long run is the key to understanding monopolistic competition.

First, we'll look at the short run, when monopolistically competitive firms can behave like monopolists. Figure 15-2 shows these short-run production choices:

1. Firms face a downward-sloping demand curve. Just like a monopolist, a monopolistically competitive firm cannot adjust its price without causing a change in the quantity consumers demand.

2. Assuming that production involves both fixed and marginal costs, firms face a U-shaped average total cost (ATC) curve.

3. The profit-maximizing production quantity is at the point where the marginal revenue (MR) curve intersects the marginal cost (MC) curve. In Figure 15-2, that's at 47,000 records. The profit-maximizing price is determined by the point on the demand curve that corresponds to this quantity. In Figure 15-2, that price is $4.70.

LO 15.2 Calculate the profit-maximizing price and quantity for a monopolistically competitive firm in the short run.

FIGURE 15-2

Monopolistic competition in the short run

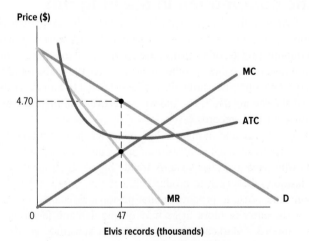

In the short run in a monopolistically competitive market, Elvis's label will produce records up to the point where marginal revenue is equal to marginal cost, and charge the corresponding price on the demand curve. At this point, we find the profit-maximizing quantity and price.

CAUTION: COMMON MISTAKE

Sun Records was a small player in a very competitive music market. So why wasn't it a *price taker*, facing a horizontal demand curve, as a small firm in a perfectly competitive market would be? Why did it face a downward-sloping demand curve in the short run?

The key here is how we define the scope of the market. Sun Records was small relative to the market for *records*. But it was large—in fact, a monopolist—in the market for *Elvis records*. Consumers who wanted Elvis records could buy them only from Sun. Because Sun was not a price taker in the market for Elvis records, it faced a downward-sloping demand curve.

The steepness of the demand curve is determined in part by the degree of substitutability between Elvis records and other records:

- What if buyers see the records as very close substitutes? In that case, if Sun raises the price even a little bit, people will switch to other artists. The demand curve will be quite flat.
- What if, on the other hand, fans are very loyal to Elvis? In that case, most won't stop buying Elvis records even when prices go up, and the demand curve will be steeper.

In other words, the less-differentiated the products are, the closer each firm's demand curve is to the horizontal curve faced by perfectly competitive firms.

By differentiating their products more—for example, finding a very distinctive artist such as Elvis and building a loyal following of devoted fans—firms can increase the steepness of the demand curve they face in the short run.

In summary, a monopolistically competitive firm can behave just like a monopolist in the short run: It will produce at the point where marginal revenue equals marginal cost and then charge a higher price according to the demand curve. In doing this, the firm can earn positive economic profits in the short run.

Monopolistic competition in the long run

LO 15.3 Describe a monopolistically competitive market in the long run.

For all of their similarities in the short run, the monopolistically competitive firm faces one huge problem that the monopolist does not: Other firms can enter the market. When existing firms are making positive economic profits, other firms have an incentive to enter the market.

Of course, it's not always possible for other firms to enter the market and produce *exactly* the same product. There's only one Elvis, after all, and he belonged to Sun Records. What other firms *can* do is look for artists who are *like* Elvis, and whose records will therefore be seen by music lovers as close substitutes for Elvis records.

This explains why, in music and in many other industries, products tend to come in waves. A new musical performer with an original style comes along and makes a splash; other record labels rush to sign artists who have a similar style. A trendy high-fashion label produces a new range of clothing; other fashion labels rush to produce clothes that look similar. Amazon releases the Echo, and other companies rush to produce similar personal assistants. And so on.

What effect does the entry of more firms have on the demand faced by each existing firm? Remember from Chapter 3, "Markets," that availability of substitute goods is one of the determinants of demand. More firms making more products that are similar to the original product means that consumers have a wider range of substitutes. With more product options from which consumers can choose, demand for the original product decreases at every price. The demand curve faced by the original firm shifts to the left.

As long as firms currently in the market are earning profits, more firms will enter the market with products that are close substitutes. As a result, the demand curve will continue to shift to the left. This process will continue until the point when potential firms no longer have an incentive to enter the market. When does that happen? At the point when existing firms are *no longer earning economic profits.*

The opposite logic holds if firms in the market are losing money in the short run: Firms will have an incentive to exit the market when they are earning negative profits. These exits will drive up demand for the existing firms and shift the demand curves they face to the right. This process will continue until, in the long run, firms are breaking even and no longer have an incentive to exit. You may have noticed something like this happening in the music industry: Sometimes so many performers are releasing similar-sounding music, the market niche becomes oversaturated.

In the long run, firms in a monopolistically competitive market face the same profit situation as firms in a perfectly competitive market: Profits are driven to zero. Remember from earlier chapters that zero profit means that total revenue is exactly equal to total cost. In per-unit terms, zero profit means that price is equal to average total cost (ATC). Figure 15-3 shows this situation; in the long run, the ATC curve is *tangent to* the demand curve at exactly one point, where ATC = Price.

Note that for the monopolistically competitive firm, ATC touches the demand curve at the same quantity where MR intersects MC. This graphic relationship is equivalent to saying that profits are zero. If ATC is not exactly tangent to the demand curve at the profit-maximizing quantity, then profits will be positive or negative, depending on the location of ATC and the demand curve:

- If the ATC is above the demand curve, this would mean that costs were higher than price, and firms would lose money and exit the market.
- If, on the other hand, ATC hit the demand curve at multiple places, costs would be below price and firms would earn profits. This situation would induce firms to enter the market.

This process of entry and exit, which moves the demand curve left or right, continues until ATC touches the demand curve at the quantity where MR intersects MC.

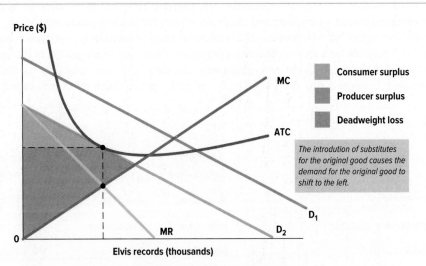

FIGURE 15-3

Monopolistic competition in the long run

Consumer surplus

Producer surplus

Deadweight loss

The introdution of substitutes for the original good causes the demand for the original good to shift to the left.

In the long run in a monopolistically competitive market, firms will enter the market, driving down demand until all market participants earn zero economic profits. Elvis's label will produce records up to the point where marginal cost equals marginal revenue. Because profits are zero, this is the same as the quantity at which the average total cost curve is tangent to the demand curve.

In the long run, monopolistic competition has some features in common with monopoly, and others in common with perfect competition. Table 15-1 summarizes some of those features. Just like a *monopoly*, a monopolistically competitive firm faces a downward-sloping demand curve. Such a curve means that marginal revenue is less than price; this in turn means that marginal cost is also less than price at the profit-maximizing quantity. But, like a firm in a *perfectly competitive* market, a monopolistically competitive firm earns zero economic profits in the long run.

These differences have two important implications:

1. **Monopolistically competitive firms operate at smaller-than-efficient scale.** As we've just described, the optimal production point for a monopolistically competitive firm in the long run will be where the ATC curve touches the demand curve. Because the demand curve is downward-sloping, this will always be on the decreasing section of the ATC curve, as panel A of Figure 15-4 shows. This contrasts with the situation in a perfectly competitive market, in which firms' optimal production is at the lowest point on the ATC curve, as shown in panel B.

   When firms produce the quantity that minimizes average total cost (as in a perfectly competitive market), we say they are operating at their *efficient scale*. In contrast, a monopolistically competitive firm maximizes profits by operating at a smaller scale than the efficient one. Another way of saying this is that the firm has *excess capacity*.

2. **Monopolistically competitive firms want to sell more.** For a firm in a perfectly competitive market, price is equal to marginal cost. If the firm sold an additional unit at that price, marginal cost would rise above price, and profit would fall.

   In contrast, a monopolistically competitive firm sells at a price that is equal to average total cost, but higher than marginal cost. (Look again at panel A of Figure 15-4.) If the firm was able to sell an additional unit without lowering the price, that unit would generate more revenue than cost, and so increase the firm's profits. In other words, when we depart from the model of perfect competition, firms have an incentive to engage in tactics for bringing in more customers, such as advertising and brand promotion.

The need for continual innovation   Our analysis of monopolistic competition in the long run has another interesting implication. Ask yourself: How will firms respond to competitors entering the market with closer and closer substitutes for existing products? Clearly, existing firms will want to step up their product differentiattion. Only by constantly finding new ways to be different is it possible for a monopolistically competitive firm to generate profits in the long run.

The need for continual innovation explains why recording labels are constantly on the lookout for new talent. It explains why firms in so many industries put so much effort into launching new

TABLE 15-1

Comparing the characteristics of market models

Characteristic	Perfect competition	Monopoly	Monopolistic competition
How many firms?	Many firms	One firm	Many firms
Price taker or price maker?	Price taker	Price maker	Price maker
Marginal revenue?	MR = Price	MR < Price	MR < Price
Profit-maximizing quantity occurs where?	MR = MC	MR = MC	MR = MC
Can earn economic profits in the short run?	Yes	Yes	Yes
Can earn economic profits in the long run?	No	Yes	No
Quantity is efficient?	Yes	No	No

FIGURE 15-4

Monopolistic competition versus perfect competition in the long run

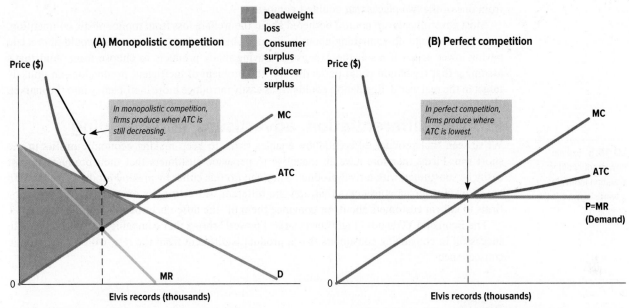

In a monopolistically competitive market, firms produce at the point where ATC is tangent to the demand curve. At this point, they could decrease ATC by producing more, but choose not to because doing so decreases profits. This results in firms producing at a smaller-than-efficient scale.

In a perfectly competitive market, firms produce at the quantity that minimizes ATC. This is the efficient choice since they cannot produce more or less without increasing costs.

products and finding new ways to advertise their products. If they don't, their competitors will catch up, and their economic profits will disappear. A truly innovative firm that manages to stay one step ahead of its competitors can continue to earn economic profit by always offering something slightly different. For this reason, economists usually believe that competition encourages innovation.

The welfare costs of monopolistic competition

Like any deviation from the equilibrium price and quantity that would prevail under perfect competition, monopolistic competition is inefficient. Firms maximize profits at a price that is higher than marginal cost, and the quantity bought and sold is smaller than it would be under perfect competition. This means that there is deadweight loss—the monopolistically competitive market does not maximize total surplus.

LO 15.4 Analyze the welfare costs of monopolistic competition.

Can anything be done about this problem? In Chapter 14, "Monopoly," we discussed ways that policy-makers try to address the welfare costs of monopolies, and noted that it is difficult to do so successfully. Unfortunately, regulating a monopolistically competitive market to increase efficiency is even harder. By definition, there are many firms in the market, and many slightly different products. Trying to assess firms' costs and regulate prices for every single one would be a gargantuan task.

Instead, the government could set a single price for all firms in the market and then let the natural forces of competition take over. Monopolistically competitive firms earn zero economic profits. With a regulated price, those firms that could not figure out how to produce at a lower cost would be forced to leave the market.

Such regulation would come with a definite cost. Although consumers would get a greater quantity of similar products at a lower price, they would also lose out on some product variety. Instead of dozens or hundreds of similar products aiming to suit consumers' different tastes, everyone would have to make do with fewer options. How would you feel if instead of having five options for fast food in town, you had only three, but the burgers were a little bit cheaper? It would be good for you if one of the three happens to be the one you like, but tough if you want a burger from one of the two places that couldn't compete.

Most governments are not too bothered about the welfare loss from monopolistic competition. Even if they could do something about it, it's not obvious whether consumers would appreciate having lower prices if it's at the expense of having many products to choose from. And that's assuming that regulation could perfectly "fix" the problem of inefficient production—an unlikely target in the real world. Regulation could just as easily introduce more inefficiency into the market.

Product differentiation, advertising, and branding

LO 15.5 Explain how product differentiation motivates advertising and branding.

We've seen that product differentiation enables firms to keep making economic profits in the short run. Firms therefore have an incentive to persuade customers that their products cannot easily be substituted with a rival product. They can do this either by making products truly different or by convincing consumers that they are different. Advertising is one strategy employed by firms to inform customers about—or convince them of—the differences between products.

The Econ and YOU box "Fight the (market) power!" shows that companies have become quite successful in convincing consumers that a product is different from the rest, with real economic consequences.

Fight the (market) power!
Econ and YOU

"Have you made the switch?" Cell phone companies often air ads pitching the many benefits of switching to a new provider—wider coverage, faster speeds, or better reliability. While this may seem like straightforward advertising, getting a customer to switch is a high-stakes campaign: the complicated fine print of device leases and contracts means that a new customer will likely stay for a while.

The result is, as economics predicts, higher prices for consumers. If a brand knows that consumers are reluctant to switch, it knows that it can increase prices and still keep customers. Cell phone providers similarly know that people locked into their contracts may be unwilling to go through the hassle of switching providers just to save a few dollars.

In economic terms, this means that cell phone providers have strong market power. Other examples of market power include companies that store billing information for online shopping accounts, cable TV and internet providers, and even food companies that market niche products to shoppers (like producers of peanut butter whose customers lock onto the particular brand and type).

Economists Brent Neiman and Joseph Vavra at the University of Chicago Booth School of Business investigated over 700 million purchases by 160,000 households over decades. Their research found that market power is increasing, and it is costing consumers money. Rather than shopping around, customers are concentrating around particular products. For example, consumers with the taste for a certain type of peanut butter are likely to buy that same brand every time they need a new jar.

How do you break the spell? The not-easy answer is to spend more time comparing across products to find the best deals (and be willing to accept a slightly different product for a lower price). For example, when you're in the grocery store and about to buy peanut better, ask yourself whether you really need the specific type of crunchy, all-natural, no-oil brand that you always get. The answer might be "yes" (you tried others already, thanks) or "not really" (maybe it's time to experiment with alternatives).

A second approach is to think twice before you hop on a hot introductory deal without investigating the true, long-term cost of the decision. This applies to both cell phone plans and the aggressive deals offered on new products at the grocery store. The deals may look good now, but they can add costs over time.

These actions can make a difference. As Austan Goolsbee, economist at the University of Chicago, wrote in *The New York Times:*

> For an individual shopper, these actions are a bit of a pain, and they may not do much to improve matters over all. But if enough people behave this way—keeping companies guessing and making them work for our business—these small acts of consumer resistance can help keep corporate market power in check.

So, maybe it's time to "fight the power" and promote competition, one peanut-butter-and-jelly sandwich at a time!

Source: Austan Goolsbee, "How Consumers Can Resist Companies' Market Power," *The New York Times*, July 20, 2018, www.nytimes.com/2018/07/20/business/how-consumers-can-resist-companies-market-power.html.

Whether advertising is a good or bad thing is a subject for debate. On the one hand, advertising can convey useful information to consumers. You may learn about a new product or technology from an ad, or find out where something you want is sold, or when it is on sale, or what styles or flavors are available. In general, advertising provides this information in a pleasant, easy-to-understand format, free of cost and inconvenience. You don't need to trudge from store to store to find out where the sales are, or search online every day to see whether that new movie has been released yet. Instead, companies will spend money to hand you all of this information.

If we believe that the main effect of advertising is to provide useful information about products and prices, then advertising serves a valuable purpose. More information will increase competition in a marketplace. Consumers will learn when a firm is offering a cheaper product that is a close substitute for higher-priced competitors. This will drive prices down, bringing the market closer to the model of perfect competition.

On the other hand, advertising rarely consists of a bullet-pointed list of straightforward facts. Instead, advertisers go to great lengths to make viewers feel good about the thing being advertised. Ads portray beautiful people having a fabulous time, or heart-warming family moments, or adrenaline-inducing stunts and special effects. Often, this portrayal has little or nothing to do with the product being advertised. Instead, it is intended to make us associate a particular image or emotion with that product. The image of happy lovers embracing in a romantic location doesn't tell us anything about the unique qualities of a particular company's jewelry. It may, though, create a strong mental association between falling in love and receiving a new pair of earrings. For evidence that this kind of advertising can and does work, see the Economics in Action box "What really sells loans?"

What if we believe that the main effect of advertising is not to convey useful information but to persuade customers that products are more different than they truly are? In this view, advertising decreases consumers' willingness to substitute between similar products. The result is that firms can charge a higher markup over marginal cost. This in turn drives prices up throughout the market.

So which *is* the main effect of advertising? There's no simple answer. Whether advertising serves mainly to provide useful information or to trigger gut-level reactions probably varies across markets and companies. Advertisements for luxury products or in highly competitive markets may highlight emotional connections rather than product features. Local businesses, on the other hand, usually stick to current sales and the tangible benefits of choosing to do business with them. Car commercials often do both, mentioning key safety features while selling the thrill of the driving experience. The next time you watch a commercial, see if you can tell which tactic a brand is using.

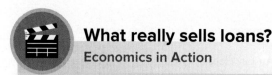

What really sells loans?
Economics in Action

Ads often aim to make the viewer feel good and to associate feeling good with the product. For example, an ad might try to associate a new car with shots of long sunny adventures with attractive friends. But how much of a difference does this really make? Don't potential customers just see through these ads? Could emotions really matter as much as something economically important, such as the price of the good? Several economists (including one of the authors of this book) designed a study to answer these questions in the context of advertising for consumer loans.

In the experiment, a lender in South Africa sent ads by mail to tens of thousands of prior clients. The ads varied in the interest rate at which the loan was offered, as well as the appearance and content of the mailer. Different mailers included different combinations of features: an image of a smiling employee, a list of possible uses for the loan, information on interest rates, or a promotional raffle for a cell phone.

Not surprisingly, customers were more likely to take out a loan in response to mailers advertising lower interest rates. But they were also more likely to borrow based on certain features of the ad's design. Mailers offering limited or no suggestions on how to use the money and (for men) showing a picture of a smiling woman did better than ads that offered many suggestions and included a picture of a person of the same race and gender of the recipient. In fact, these subtle features increased demand to the same degree as reducing the interest rate by 25 percent!

Of course, if you had asked loan customers directly whether they would rather have a 25 percent cheaper loan or look briefly at a picture of a friendly face, most would likely have opted for the cheaper loan. The fact that their responses to the mailer told a different story demonstrates that economic information is only one input into people's decision making when faced with cleverly designed advertising.

Source: Marianne Bertrand, Dean Karlan, Sendhil Mullainathan, Eldar Shafir, and Jonathan Zinman, "What's Advertising Content Worth? Evidence from a Consumer Credit Marketing Field Experiment," *Quarterly Journal of Economics* 125, no. 1 (2010), pp. 263–306.

Advertising as a signal   It's often hard to tell what real information about a product we're supposed to get from an ad. Why should we believe an actor who is well paid to say that a particular cellular network is faster than another? What does GEICO Insurance's green animated gecko know about car insurance? Sometimes, though, advertising may contain useful information for customers, even if it's not stated explicitly.

Think about the problem of *asymmetric information* (discussed in Chapter 10, "Information"). Firms know more about the true quality of their products than consumers do. Consumers would like to find the best products, and the firms who make the best products would like to make themselves known to customers. But consumers can't trust a firm that simply *says* it has high-quality products. Every firm, whether it produces high-quality or low-quality products, has an incentive to claim that its products are the best. The high-quality firms need a way *to credibly signal* the quality of their products. Advertising fits the bill because advertising costs money.

Let's think, from a firm's perspective, about the choice to advertise. Suppose that a music label has signed a brilliant new artist and is sure people will love her first album if they hear it. The company calculates that if it spends a large amount of money on a high-profile TV advertising campaign, lots of people will buy the album; they will like it so much they will tell their friends and will buy concert tickets, fan merchandise, and the artist's future albums. What are the possible outcomes?

- If the company is right about the new artist, the label will end up making $10 million in profits.

- If the company is wrong, and people don't like the album, the firm won't recover the cost of the money it spends on advertising—and will lose $5 million.

The advertising expenditure will be a great investment for the label if the quality of the product is good, and a terrible investment if the quality is bad.

On the other hand, what does this decision look like if the label is not so confident about the quality of the new album? If the firm doesn't promote the album, there's still a chance that people who buy it will love it and tell their friends. But the sales will be much lower than if there was a huge ad campaign behind it. What are the possible outcomes if the label does not advertise the album?

- If people like the unadvertised album, the label makes $2 million.
- If the people who buy the unadvertised album don't like it, the label will lose some money it spent producing the music, but only $50,000.

If the label is not so confident in the quality of the album, then it makes sense *not* to advertise. If people don't like it, at least the label will lose much less money than it would have if it had advertised it. The choice to advertise or not advertise is illustrated in the decision tree in Figure 15-5.

Now let's think from a *consumer's perspective* about the firm's choice to advertise. Consumers can observe only the final outcome—whether the firm chooses to advertise or not—and not the true quality of the product. However, consumers can view the advertising as a credible signal. If they see that a music label is spending a lot of money on high-profile TV advertising for a new singer's album, they can reasonably conclude that the label is very confident that people will like the album.

It may be perfectly reasonable, therefore, for consumers to try a product based on advertising. The important factor for consumers in assessing the usefulness of advertising as a signal is not the ad's content, but *how much it cost*. The more expensive the advertising is, the more consumers can assume the firm is confident that it has a good product that will earn repeat business from satisfied customers.

FIGURE 15-5

Advertising as a signal of quality   If the music label suspects fans will not like the album, it will actually lose money by advertising. Because rational music companies will choose to advertise an album only if they know it is good, consumers can use promotion efforts as a signal of album quality.

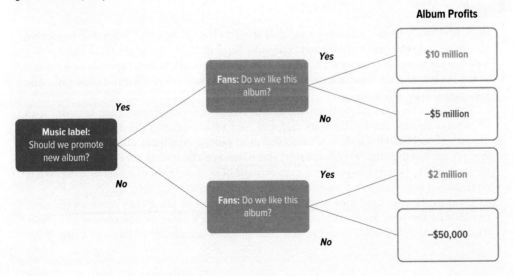

Branding   In 2009, two kitchen workers employed by Domino's Pizza uploaded videos to You-Tube showing themselves contaminating food in various ways—we'll spare you the details—before allegedly giving the food to customers. (When the story was made public, the makers of the videos insisted it was a prank and that none of the food had ever been served.) The employees responsible were immediately fired, but the damage to Domino's image had been done. Consumer surveys completed after the story broke showed a marked downturn in perception of the Domino's *brand* (the combination of characteristics that identify and differentiate a particular company or product). Consumer perceptions moved from positive to negative in a matter of days. It needed quick action and some savvy public relations work for Domino's to help its brand recover.[3]

This story illustrates why it may be rational for consumers to think of a strong brand as being an implicit guarantee of a product's quality. Firms with no reputation to protect may not be too concerned with the repercussions of selling a bad-quality product. But just one unfortunate incident can undo years of careful thought and hard work that a firm such as Domino's put into building a strong brand. Because consumers know that firms stand to lose when their brand's reputation is damaged, they can conclude that firms with strong brands probably have strong quality control in all locations and levels of the company.

For this reason, a brand may also convey useful information in a confusing situation. A traveler in a strange city may have little information about the quality of food and drink available in local stores. If she sees a Starbucks, however, she can assume with confidence that she will be able to buy a familiar drink of predictable quality. The local tea shop might actually be better than Starbucks, but the traveler doesn't know that. She may rationally choose to go for the known quantity of the Starbucks brand, rather than take a risk on the local competition.

It isn't always rational to rely on brand names to make decisions, however. Brands may also perpetuate false perceptions of quality or product differences. For instance, brand-name pharmaceuticals often command much higher prices than their generic counterparts, despite the fact that the two are made with identical active ingredients and have the same medical effect. In such cases, strong brands can even form a *barrier to entry* in a market, moving it toward a structure of oligopoly in which a few leading players have a significant amount of market power.

Before we look at how oligopolies work, see the From Another Angle box "Coke, Pepsi, and the not-so-secret formula" for an illustration of just how important it can be for firms to use branding to differentiate their products.

Coke, Pepsi, and the not-so-secret formula
From Another Angle

In its advertising, Coca-Cola makes a big deal about its "secret formula." When two employees tried to sell the company's confidential recipe to Pepsi in 2007, you might think Pepsi would have jumped at the chance to learn how its rival makes its product. In fact, Pepsi not only refused to buy the information, it participated in an FBI operation that led to the arrest of the would-be informants. What was going on here?

The market for colas can be described as monopolistically competitive: Each company tries to increase the size and loyalty of its customer base by emphasizing the differentiation of its product. Many blind taste tests have found that most people—even those who claim to be ardent fans of one brand or the other—can't distinguish between them when they don't know which they're drinking. So this seems to be a clear example of an industry in which advertising mainly serves to persuade people that products are more different than they really are.

Consider for a moment what would happen if Pepsi were to buy Coke's secret formula and publish it for the world to see. That information would make it easier for new companies to enter the cola market; they could advertise that their products are exactly identical to Coke. What would happen then? The entrance of new companies with undifferentiated products would bring the market closer to the model of perfect competition. The result would be to push down the price of Coke. This would be a disaster for Coke—but it would be bad news for Pepsi, too. The new colas would be close substitutes for Pepsi; some Pepsi customers would probably switch to the new wave of cheaper, undifferentiated colas. Under this scenario, Pepsi loses customers, and profits.

Why, then, didn't Pepsi buy the recipe, keep it secret, and use it to make its own cola taste exactly like Coke? After all, Coke is the market leader, so Coca-Cola must be doing something right. The problem for Pepsi was that since Coke has an established brand, Coke customers would have no reason to switch to Pepsi for the same taste at the same price. Pepsi would have to reduce its price to attract Coke customers to switch, and it would meanwhile lose the ability to charge a premium to loyal customers who actually claim to prefer the taste of Pepsi. If Pepsi made the move, it would not be able to earn as much economic profit.

Pepsi did the right thing in an ethical sense. But we also see why Pepsi's move may have been smart from an economic angle too. Pepsi's profit-maximizing decision was to ignore the chance to learn Coke's secret formula, and continue to differentiate its own product instead.

Sources: www.nytimes.com/ref/business/20070527_COKE_GRAPHIC.html; http://freakonomics.blogs.nytimes.com/2006/07/07/how-much-would-pepsi-pay-to-get-cokes-secret-formula; https://money.cnn.com/2018/02/20/news/companies/cola-wars-coke-pepsi/index.html; www.investopedia.com/ask/answers/060415/how-much-global-beverage-industry-controlled-coca-cola-and-pepsi.asp

✓ TEST YOURSELF

- ☐ How does product differentiation allow monopolistically competitive firms to gain market power? **[LO 15.2]**
- ☐ How does the short run differ from the long run in a monopolistically competitive market? **[LO 15.2]**
- ☐ Why are monopolistically competitive firms always willing to increase the quantity they sell? **[LO 15.3]**
- ☐ Why is it difficult to regulate a monopolistically competitive market to increase efficiency? **[LO 15.4]**
- ☐ Why might it be rational for a consumer to make purchasing decisions based on advertising? **[LO 15.5]**
- ☐ Why do firms want to develop their brands? **[LO 15.5]**

Oligopoly

Suppose you're an executive at Universal Music Group. Your day-to-day decisions hinge on how to make your company as profitable as possible. You have a lot to think about: Which new artists should we sign? How should we advertise upcoming releases? How much can we charge for albums without driving customers into illegal downloading? What should we do to get more radio play for our latest singles?

One common thread runs through these decisions: You know your competition. You know you're playing to win against Sony and Warner. You know their executives, their catalogs of artists, and at least a bit about their distribution and advertising deals. You probably also have some idea of what new releases they have coming in the pipeline. You might keep an eye on smaller, independent companies too, but your real preoccupation is with the other major players. In other words, you're playing in a game with two very identifiable competitors.

This situation contrasts sharply with the situation in a perfectly competitive market. As a price-taking firm in a perfectly competitive market, you'd be competing against dozens, hundreds, or even thousands of other firms. You probably wouldn't know the managers at those firms, and it wouldn't matter. Making business decisions with the intent of beating out any one of them would be pointless since all of the other firms would simply move in to fill the gap.

The fact that firms in an oligopoly market compete against a few identifiable rivals with market power drives our analysis. Firms in a perfectly competitive market have only one choice—what quantity to produce given the market price. Oligopolists, on the other hand, make *strategic* decisions about price and quantity that take into account the expected choices of their competitors. As we analyze oligopolies, we'll draw on our discussion of *game theory* from Chapter 9, "Game Theory and Strategic Thinking."

Oligopolies in competition

LO 15.6 Describe the strategic production decision of firms in an oligopoly.

Let's begin our analysis of oligopoly with a pared-down example from the music industry. For the sake of simplicity, suppose that there are only two big labels—Universal and Warner—rather than three. (Technically, an oligopoly with two firms is known as a *duopoly*.) Also suppose that music is a standardized good, so that consumers are indifferent between buying music released by Universal and music released by Warner. (Although we discussed earlier in the chapter why this is not entirely true, it's a reasonable simplification to clarify our analysis of oligopoly.) Each label has such a large stable of artists that fans of any particular musical genre will be likely to find close substitutes for their tastes between the two rival labels.

Figure 15-6 shows the market demand schedule for albums, and the corresponding demand and marginal revenue curves, for this two-company market. As we'd expect, the number of albums demanded increases as the price decreases. The third column of the table in panel A shows total revenue at each price-quantity combination. Remember that the quantity in the first column

FIGURE 15-6

Demand for albums

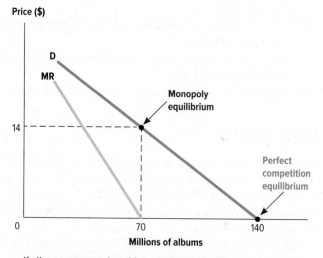

(A) Demand and revenue schedule

Albums (millions)	Price ($)	Revenue (millions of $)
40	20	800
50	18	900
60	16	960
70	14	980
80	12	960
90	10	900
100	8	800
110	6	660
120	4	480
130	2	260
140	0	0

Market equilibrium for a monopoly → 70 | 14 | 980

Market equilibrium for perfect competition → 140 | 0 | 0

(B) Demand and marginal revenue curve

If albums were produced by a monopoly, the firm would produce the profit-maximizing quantity. In perfect competition, price would be driven down to marginal cost, which in this case is zero.

represents the total quantity demanded *in the whole market*, so column 3 shows the combined revenue of the two firms.

Suppose that each firm pays a fixed cost of $100 million to sign artists and record albums. Let's also assume, for the sake of simplicity, that the marginal cost of producing each new album is zero.

Remember from Chapter 13, "Perfect Competition," that for perfectly competitive firms, marginal revenue is the same as price. The profit-maximizing quantity of output occurs where marginal revenue equals marginal cost. As a result, price is driven down until it equals marginal cost. Since we're assuming the marginal cost of production is zero, the market equilibrium under perfect competition would be 140 million albums at a price of zero. (Of course, in the long run, albums couldn't remain free because music labels would not be covering their fixed costs; firms would exit the market until the price rose to a level where fixed costs were covered.)

In contrast, what if the market were a monopoly? We know from Chapter 14, "Monopoly," that the monopolist faces a downward-sloping marginal revenue curve. The monopolist maximizes profits by producing the quantity where marginal revenue equals marginal cost and then charging a higher price according to the demand curve. Looking at the table in Figure 15-6, we can see this point would be 70 million albums at a price of $14. The monopolist's profit would be $880 million, which is its total revenue of $980 million minus its fixed cost of $100 million.

Two firms (duopoly)   What happens when there are *two* firms in the market—Universal and Warner? Since the monopoly production choice maximizes profits, the best the two firms could do would be to agree to act like a joint monopolist. If each produced 35 million albums, total quantity sold would equal 70 million, and the two labels could each earn profits of $390 million:

$$TR - TC$$
$$(35 \text{ million} \times \$14) - \$100 \text{ million} = \$390 \text{ million}$$

Sounds great, right? But let's say that Warner has a wily CEO who decides to produce another 5 million albums without letting the CEO of Universal know about her plan. The total quantity of CDs sold on the market goes up to 75 million, which pushes the price down to $13. However, rather than splitting production equally, Warner is now selling 40 million albums while Universal continues to produce 35 million. As a result, Warner's profits go up to $420 million; Universal's profits are reduced by $35 million because each of the 35 million albums it sells is now going for one dollar less than it was before:

$$\text{Warner's profits} = (40 \text{ million} \times \$13) - \$100 \text{ million} = \$420 \text{ million}$$
$$\text{Universal's profits} = (35 \text{ million} \times \$13) - \$100 \text{ million} = \$355 \text{ million}$$

The CEO of Universal won't be happy. What happens if he responds by sneaking an extra 5 million albums onto the market himself? The total quantity sold will be 80 million, which pushes the price down even further to $12. Now, each firm is selling 40 million albums, rather than 35 million, for a price that is $2 less per album:

$$\text{Profits for each of two firms} = (40 \text{ million} \times \$12) - \$100 \text{ million} = \$380 \text{ million}$$

Universal has gained some ground by retaliating, though each label is worse off than it was when it agreed to cooperate by producing 35 million albums each.

This logic continues to drive quantity sold up and price down: Now Warner's CEO decides to produce 45 million albums, which would drive price down to $11 and increase her firm's profits to $395 million. However, the Universal CEO responds with the same decision, and each firm actually sells 45 million albums at a price of $10 each, for a lower profit of $350 million. *Competition between oligopolists drives price and profits down to below the monopoly level.*

However, oligopolistic competition does not necessarily drive profits all the way down to the *efficient level*, as it does in perfect competition. Remember from Chapter 14, "Monopoly," that monopolists considering whether to produce an additional unit of output need to weigh two effects:

- *Quantity effect:* The increase in total revenue due to the money brought in by the sale of additional units.
- *Price effect:* The decrease in total revenue that occurs because the increase in quantity will push the market price down.

The oligopolist also needs to weigh the quantity and price effects. In an oligopoly:

- When the *quantity effect outweighs the price effect*, an increase in output will raise a firm's profit level. In this case, profit-maximizing firms will *increase their output*.
- But when the *price effect outweighs the quantity effect*, the firm has *no incentive to increase output*.

For example, consider the next quantity decision faced by Warner's CEO. If she produces another 5 million albums, she'll still make only $350 million in profits (50 million × $9 = 45 million × $10). The quantity effect (selling an extra 5 million units) is exactly canceled out by the price effect (the price is $1 lower). She has no incentive to increase production.

Universal faces the same decision. Thus, we can predict that both companies will choose to stay at a production level of 45 million albums. The market equilibrium in this competitive duopoly is 90 million albums at a price of $10.

Three or more firms   In reality, of course, there aren't just two big firms in the music business; there are three. But the principle remains exactly the same. Let's work through the example using three firms.

Suppose we begin again with the total profit-maximizing monopoly quantity—70 million albums at a price of $14 each—with output divided equally among the three firms. Each firm produces 23.3 million albums and brings in $326 million in revenue, minus its fixed costs of $100 million, for profit of $226 million.

$$TR - TC$$
$$(23.3 \text{ million} \times \$14) - \$100 \text{ million} = \$226 \text{ million}$$

But each firm has an incentive to raise its own profit if it can, even if it means decreasing the profits of other firms and of the market as a whole. As long as the quantity effect is greater than the price effect, each firm will keep increasing its output.

Now that there are three firms rather than two in the market, the quantity effect for each firm is larger:

- Consider the price and quantity effects for a market split between only two firms. If the two firms are each producing 35 million albums, increasing production by 5 million albums increases an individual firm's output by 5/35 = 14 percent, but it increases total market production by only 5/70 = 7 percent. When market quantity increases from 70 to 75, price falls from $14 to $13. This is a 1/14 = 7 percent decrease in price. Thus, to the individual firm, the quantity effect (14 percent) outweighs the price effect (7 percent).

- Now consider the price and quantity effects for a market split between *three* firms. If the three firms are splitting the total quantity of 70 and are each producing 22.3 million albums, increasing production by 5 million albums increases an individual firm's output by 5/23.3 = 21.5 percent, but it increases total market production by only 5/70 = 7 percent. When market quantity increases from 70 to 75, price falls from $14 to $13. This is a 1/14 = 7 percent decrease in price. Thus, to the individual firm, the quantity effect (21.5 percent) outweighs the price effect (7 percent).

It makes sense that smaller increases in total quantity in the three-firm market have a smaller downward effect on market price. Thus, each firm will increase its quantity by more before the quantity effect becomes equal to the price effect. In the three-firm market, the equilibrium quantity for each firm will be 35 million albums. This makes the total market equilibrium quantity 105 million albums and pushes the equilibrium price down to $7.

As the number of firms grows larger and larger, the oligopoly market becomes more competitive, and the equilibrium quantity comes closer to the competitive market equilibrium. This effect can be seen in Figure 15-7.

Whatever the number of firms in the market, an oligopolist will continue to increase output up to *the quantity at which the positive quantity effect of an additional unit on profits is exactly equal to the negative price effect.*

Analyzing an oligopolist's production decision in terms of the price and quantity effects highlights an important general idea: An oligopolist's production decision affects *not only its own profits, but those of other firms as well.* The profit-raising quantity effect is felt only by the individual firm that decides to produce more; the profit-lowering price effect also affects all other firms in the market. *A decision that increases profits for an individual firm lowers combined profits for the market as a whole.*

This is an example of a general economic truth: When an individual (person or firm) reaps all of the benefits and all of the costs of a decision, he (or it) will rationally make an optimal choice. But *when a decision imposes costs or benefits on others, an individual's rational choice will not necessarily be optimal for the group.* In the case of oligopoly, other firms have to bear the costs of one firm's rational decision to increase output. We'll return to this topic in much more detail in later chapters when we talk about externalities and public goods.

Compete or collude? Using game theory to analyze oligopolies

LO 15.7 Explain how basic tenets of game theory apply to an oligopoly's incentive to compete or collude.

You don't get to be CEO of Warner or Universal if you don't understand how an oligopoly works. You can bet these are smart people who know they are engaged in a strategic "game" in which one's outcomes depend on another's choices. Often, oligopolies face a *prisoners' dilemma*, a situation in which two people (or two firms) make rational choices that lead to a less-than-ideal

FIGURE 15-7

Demand for albums in different markets

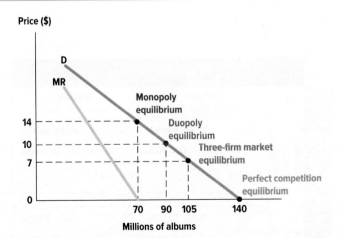

When there is only one firm in the market, the total market quantity is 70 million albums, when two firms split the market, total quantity grows to 90 million, and when three firms split the market total quantity is 105 million. As more firms are added to the market, it moves closer to the efficient quantity.

result for both. (You can review the classic prisoners' dilemma in Chapter 9, "Game Theory and Strategic Thinking.")

The best outcome of the strategic "game" in our two-firm music industry example would be for both firms to produce 35 million albums. However, both firms have an incentive to increase production to 45 million albums. But when both firms produce 45 million albums, they end up worse off than they would have been had each produced only 35 million albums. When the firms act rationally, they end up worse off.

In our example, the firms have two options: to compete with each other or to join forces and act like a monopolist. The act of working together to make decisions about price and quantity is called **collusion**. As we have seen, when Warner and Universal choose to compete with each other, they end up producing 45 million albums each and making profits of $350 million. If they agree to collude, they will each produce 35 million albums and make $390 million in profits. If collusion can enable firms to earn higher profits, *why isn't everyone doing it?*

When Universal's CEO decides how many albums to produce, he will think strategically and ask himself what Warner's CEO is thinking. What if Universal's CEO thinks that Warner will produce 35 million albums? Look at the payoff matrix in Figure 15-8. Reading across the top row of the matrix:

- We see that if Warner produces 35 million albums, Universal can make $390 million if it also produces 35 million albums.
- Alternatively, Universal can make $440 million if it produces 45 million albums when Warner is producing 35 million albums.

The right choice for Universal is clear: produce 45 million albums if it believes Warner will produce only 35 million albums.

But what if Universal's CEO thinks that Warner will produce 45 million albums? In Figure 15-8, reading across the bottom row:

- We see that if Universal makes 35 million albums, it will earn $320 million.
- Alternatively, if it produces 45 million albums, it will earn $350 million.

Again, Universal's choice is clear: produce 45 million albums if it believes that Warner will produce 45 million albums.

collusion

the act of working together to make decisions about price and quantity

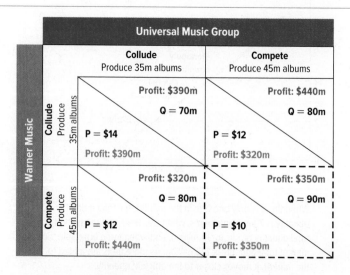

FIGURE 15-8

Oligopoly production as the prisoners' dilemma   Record labels' decision to collude can be modeled as a game called the prisoners' dilemma. Although both firms would be better off if they could agree to collude and produce a lower quantity, each has an incentive to defect from this agreement and earn more profits.

Putting this together, we can see that:

- If Universal's CEO believes Warner will produce 35 million albums, Universal should produce 45 million albums.
- If Universal's CEO believes Warner will produce 45 million albums, Universal should produce 45 million albums.

Looking at his options, the CEO of Universal will conclude that *no matter what Warner decides to do*, Universal should compete and produce 45 million albums.

When one strategy is always the best for a player to choose, regardless of what other players do, we call it a **dominant strategy**. In this example, competition (rather than collusion) is a dominant strategy for Universal.

Now, consider the decision from Warner's point of view:

- If Warner expects Universal to produce the lower, "collusion" quantity, Warner can earn $50 million more in profit by competing than by colluding. (How do we know? Compare Warner's profit in the top left square of Figure 15-8 to those in the bottom left square.)
- If Warner expects Universal to produce the higher, "competitive" quantity, Warner still earns more profit by competing than by sincerely sticking to the collusion agreement. (Compare the $350 million of the bottom right square to the $320 million of the top right square.)

We can conclude that Warner also has a dominant strategy in this game: Choosing to compete is always better for Warner *no matter what Universal chooses to do*.

Looking at the strategic decision illustrated in Figure 15-8, two things stand out:

- First, as we've already calculated, both firms do worse when they both choose to compete with each other than when they both choose to collude. By competing, they drive quantity sold above the profit-maximizing monopoly level that would be achieved by collusion.
- Second, each firm has an incentive to renege on a collusion deal and compete, regardless of what the other firm does.

In other words, *both firms have a dominant strategy, and that strategy is to compete.* As a result, both firms will choose to compete rather than collude, producing 45 million albums and making only $350 million in profits.

Oligopolies and Nash equilibriums

When all players in a game have a dominant strategy, the result is called a **Nash equilibrium**. It is an outcome in which all players choose the best strategy they can, given the choices of all other players. A Nash equilibrium is significant because when it is reached, no one has an incentive to break the equilibrium by changing his strategy. (A Nash equilibrium can be reached even when firms don't have a dominant strategy, but in the music industry example we're using, each does have a dominant strategy—to compete rather than collude.)

Not all games have a Nash equilibrium. Consider a soccer player kicking a penalty kick. He can either kick the soccer ball to the left side of the goal or to the right side of the goal. The goalie faces a similar decision; he can either defend the left side of the goal or the right side of the goal. If the player kicks the ball to the right and the goalie also defends that side of the goal, the kick is blocked. The goalie is happy with his decision, but the kicker wishes he had kicked a different direction. If he could do it again, he has an *incentive to switch his behavior*. Thus, they have not reached a Nash equilibrium.

Similarly, if the kicker kicks the ball to the right but the goalie defends the opposite side of the goal, the kicker scores a point. The kicker is happy with his decision, but the goalie would prefer to change his strategy. Because the goalie has an incentive to change his strategy, this situation is also not a Nash equilibrium. You can consider the other two possibilities, and you'll see that there is no Nash equilibrium in this game.

dominant strategy
a strategy that is the best one for a player to follow no matter what strategy other players choose

Nash equilibrium
an equilibrium reached when all players choose the best strategy they can, given the choices of all other players. It is a situation wherein, given the consequences, the player has no regrets about his or her decision.

cartel
a number of firms that collude to make collective production decisions about quantities or prices

In a Nash equilibrium, no player has an incentive to break the equilibrium by changing his or her strategy. In a prisoners' dilemma, this means that the players are stuck in a less-than-ideal outcome. In our oligopoly example, each firm would prefer that they *both* choose to collude. But Warner cannot force Universal to collude; similarly, Universal cannot force Warner to collude. Thus, once in the Nash equilibrium, there is no way for either firm to change its own strategy in a way that increases its profit.

However, as described in Chapter 9, "Game Theory and Strategic Thinking," there *is* a way out of this dilemma for the two CEOs. The key is to remember that many decisions are made not once, but over and over again between the same set of firms. Universal and Warner are not playing this game just once; the game will be repeated many times.

Once the Universal CEO considers that the interaction is a "repeated game," his incentives change. If he reneges on the deal while the CEO of Warner keeps her word, he will gain $50 million in profit for this year. But he will be sure that Warner will retaliate *next year* by going back to the competitive production levels. He therefore knows Universal will lose $40 million in profit *every year thereafter;* the firm will earn $350 million in the competitive equilibrium rather than $390 million in the collusion equilibrium. With *future* profits in mind, both companies may take an initial chance that the other will hold up its end of an initial agreement to collude. If both stand firm, they may keep cooperating, each producing 35 million albums, year after year.

This sort of strategy is often the glue that holds firms together in a **cartel**—a number of firms that collude to make collective production decisions about quantities or prices. A well-known cartel is the Organization of the Petroleum Exporting Countries (OPEC). Member countries agree to limit the amount of petroleum they produce in order to manipulate the market price and maximize their profits. Each member country knows it is in its *long-term* interest to collude rather than compete. That knowledge is enough to keep OPEC together. Interest in future profits dissuades any individual country from chasing short-term profits by producing more oil in any given year. Although OPEC does not control all of the global supply of oil, it is a powerful force in global oil prices.

If cartels are so advantageous for firms operating in an oligopoly, why don't we see more of them? There's a pretty straightforward reason: They're usually illegal. No international court has the power to force OPEC to stop colluding in the global oil market. Most countries, however, do have laws against firms making agreements about prices or quantities. If firms are caught circumventing those laws, they can be fined and punished.

Oligopoly and public policy

LO 15.8 Compare the welfare of producers, consumers, and society as a whole in an oligopoly to monopoly and perfect competition.

We saw in Chapter 14, "Monopoly," that the United States has strict laws prohibiting "anti-competitive" behavior. It is even illegal for an oligopolist to *offer* to collude, regardless of whether the collusion actually happens. The reason lawmakers are so concerned about collusion, of course, is that while it's good for the oligopolists, it's bad for the rest of us. In our hypothetical example, when Warner and Universal are colluding, the price of albums is $14. When they are competing, the price is only $10. The music-buying public is better off if Warner and Universal compete rather than collude.

Remember that in a monopoly, there is deadweight loss—a welfare loss caused by the transactions that did not take place because the market equilibrium was at a higher price and lower quantity than would be efficient. Figure 15-9 compares the producer surplus, consumer surplus, and deadweight loss under varying amounts of competition. Note that the last two graphs—collusion and monopoly—are identical. Because the market outcomes in a competitive oligopoly are between

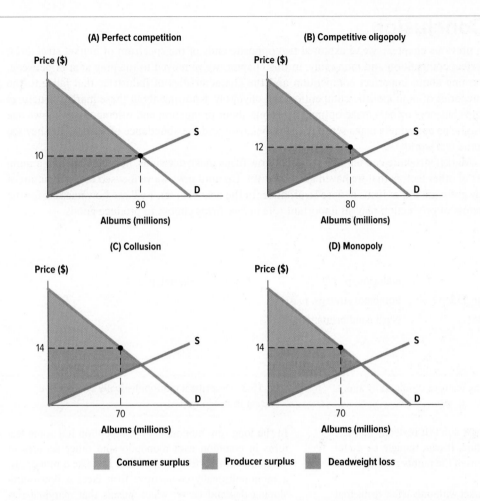

(A) Perfect competition

(B) Competitive oligopoly

(C) Collusion

(D) Monopoly

■ Consumer surplus   ■ Producer surplus   ■ Deadweight loss

FIGURE 15-9

Deadweight loss under varying amounts of competition Perfect competition represents one end of the deadweight loss spectrum, and collusion/monopoly represents the other. A competitive oligopoly falls somewhere in between. There is less deadweight loss than in the case of collusion or monopoly, but it does not eliminate deadweight loss in the way that perfect competition does.

those of a monopoly and a perfectly competitive market, deadweight loss still exists, but it is lower than when there is collusion.

It's no wonder governments are so keen to prevent firms from colluding, and no wonder firms are so keen to collude without being caught. In 1960, for example, the U.S. government reviewed its annual records for bids it had received when it invited companies to supply certain types of heavy machinery. Government agencies discovered that 47 manufacturers had submitted *identical* bids for the previous three years of bidding. This showed that the manufacturers were secretly colluding on their bids. They were taking turns to submit the lowest bid, at a price that would be much higher than if they were actually competing. It is estimated that the cartel, until it was broken up, cost U.S. taxpayers $175 million each year.

✓ **TEST YOURSELF**

☐ Why is the equilibrium in an oligopolistic market less efficient than a competitive market? **[LO 15.6]**

☐ Why would two companies in an oligopoly benefit from colluding? **[LO 15.7]**

☐ Why would it be difficult for companies to collude, even if doing so were legal? **[LO 15.7]**

☐ Why are firms more easily able to collude in a repeated game than in a game played just once? **[LO 15.7]**

☐ What happens to deadweight loss as the number of firms in an oligopolistic market increases? **[LO 15.8]**

Conclusion

In previous chapters, we've explored two opposite ends of the spectrum of market structures: perfect competition and monopoly. In this chapter, we've moved to the gray area in between, learning about imperfect competition and the characteristics of industries that fall into the categories of monopolistic competition and oligopoly. Knowing about these market structures helps business owners make optimal decisions about production and pricing. Such knowledge also helps consumers make sense of firms' behavior and the abundance of advertising they see in the real world.

Market structure can tell us a lot about how firms make decisions, but there are still a number of other factors that we haven't explored yet. Up until now, we've focused on the amount of any given good that firms choose to produce. In the next chapter, we'll see how markets for the factors of production play an important role in *how* firms choose to produce goods.

Key Terms

oligopoly, p. 355

monopolistic competition, p. 355

product differentiation, p. 356

collusion, p. 372

dominant strategy, p. 373

Nash equilibrium, p. 373

cartel, p. 374

Summary

LO 15.1 Name the defining features of oligopoly and monopolistic competition.

Most markets in the real world don't fit perfectly into any one model of market structure. It can, though, be useful to categorize markets in terms of the number of firms and product variety.

Oligopoly describes a market with only a few firms that sell a similar good or service. In this setting, firms tend to know their competition and each firm has some price-setting power, but no one has total market control.

Monopolistic competition, in contrast, describes a market with many firms that sell goods and services that are similar, but slightly different. These firms are not necessarily price takers, but they still face competition in the long run.

LO 15.2 Calculate the profit-maximizing price and quantity for a monopolistically competitive firm in the short run.

In the short run, monopolistically competitive firms behave just like monopolists. They face a downward-sloping demand curve and cannot change price without causing a change in the quantity consumers demand. The profit-maximizing production quantity is at the point where the marginal revenue (MR) curve intersects the marginal cost (MC) curve. The profit-maximizing price is determined by the point on the demand curve that corresponds to this quantity.

LO 15.3 Describe a monopolistically competitive market in the long run.

In the long run, monopolistic competition has some features in common with monopoly and other features in common with perfect competition. Just like a monopoly, a monopolistically competitive firm faces a downward-sloping demand curve, which means that marginal revenue is less than price. This in turn means that marginal cost is also less than price. Like a firm in a perfectly competitive market, however, a monopolistically competitive firm earns zero economic profit in the long run.

LO 15.4 Analyze the welfare costs of monopolistic competition.

Like any deviation from the equilibrium price and quantity that would prevail under perfect competition, monopolistic competition is inefficient. Because firms maximize profit at a price that is higher than marginal cost, some mutually beneficial trades never occur. This means that there is deadweight loss—the market does not maximize total surplus. However, regulating monopolistically competitive markets to increase efficiency is difficult, and usually comes at the expense of product variety.

LO 15.5 Explain how product differentiation motivates advertising and branding.

Producers invest in advertising to convince consumers that their products are different from other similar products. The less substitutable a good seems with other goods, the less likely consumers are to switch to other products if the price increases. Thus, producers have an incentive to differentiate their products—either by making them truly different or by convincing consumers that they are different. Through advertising and branding, firms either explicitly give the desired information to the consumer or signal the quality of their products.

> **LO 15.6** Describe the strategic production decision of firms in an oligopoly.

Oligopolists make strategic decisions about price and quantity that take into account the expected choices of their competitors. Unlike price-taking firms in a competitive market, an oligopolist produces a quantity that affects the market price.

The increase in total revenue due to the money brought in by the sale of additional units of output is called the *quantity effect*. The decrease in total revenue that occurs because the increase in quantity will push the market price down is called the *price effect*. Typically, an oligopolistic firm will increase output until the positive quantity effect outweighs the negative price effect.

> **LO 15.7** Explain how basic tenets of game theory apply to an oligopoly's incentive to compete or collude.

An oligopolist has an incentive to produce more output than is profit maximizing for the market as a whole, driving down price and imposing costs on its competitors. By colluding, firms can maximize industry profits by producing the equivalent monopoly quantity and splitting revenues. However, each firm involved always has an incentive to renege on the agreement since a firm could earn higher profits by competing.

An outcome in which all players choose the best strategy they can, given the choices of all other players, is called a *Nash equilibrium*. If all players in a game have a dominant strategy, then a Nash equilibrium will occur when they play their dominant strategies. A Nash equilibrium can also arise even if no players have a dominant strategy.

When a Nash equilibrium is reached, no one has an incentive to break the equilibrium by changing his strategy. However, if firms recognize their production decisions as a repeated game, with *future* profits in mind, a firm may take an initial chance that the other firm will hold up its end of an initial agreement to collude. This sort of strategy often holds firms together in a cartel.

> **LO 15.8** Compare the welfare of producers, consumers, and society as a whole in an oligopoly to monopoly and perfect competition.

The competitive equilibrium in an oligopoly leads to a quantity and price that are somewhere between the outcomes of a perfectly competitive market and those of a monopoly. Because the equilibrium is not the same as in a competitive market, oligopoly results in some deadweight loss and increases producer surplus at the expense of consumer surplus. When oligopolists collude, the equilibrium looks like a monopoly outcome and results in even higher deadweight loss and higher producer surplus.

Review Questions

1. Explain why an oligopolist (with few competitors) pays more attention to what its competitors are doing than a producer in a competitive market (with many competitors) does. **[LO 15.1]**

2. If a market has few barriers to entry and many firms, how might firms still have positive economic profit? Describe a strategy a firm in this type of market might use to maintain economic profits. **[LO 15.1]**

3. McDonald's, Burger King, and Wendy's all produce hamburgers, among other things. However, if you prefer burgers from McDonald's, you might consider other burgers an imperfect substitute. With this in mind, how would you expect McDonald's to set its prices in the short run? Describe the relationship between price, marginal revenue, and marginal cost. **[LO 15.2]**

4. Consider Jimmy Choo designer shoes. In what way does Jimmy Choo face many competitors? In what way does Jimmy Choo face no competitors? **[LO 15.2]**

5. Restaurants offer related but differentiated products to their consumers. In the long run, new restaurants enter the market and imitate the cuisine and atmosphere of successful competitors. How would you expect a restaurant to set its prices in the long run? Describe the relationship between price and average total cost. Does a restaurant earn economic profits? **[LO 15.3]**

6. In both perfectly competitive and monopolistically competitive markets, when firms are making positive economic profits, other firms will enter until price equals ATC and profits are zero. Despite these similarities, in a perfectly competitive market total surplus is maximized, while in a monopolistically competitive market surplus is not maximized. Explain this difference. **[LO 15.3]**

7. Suppose a perfectly competitive market for hot-dog stands in New York City becomes monopolistically competitive when gourmet, discount, and ethnic hot-dog retailers show up, making each cart slightly different. If hot dogs from different stands are now imperfect substitutes and there are numerous carts in the city, compare the producer and consumer surplus and total social welfare before and after the change. **[LO 15.4]**

8. Given that the market for smartphones is inefficient, explain why consumers of smartphones might not want the price to be regulated. **[LO 15.4]**

9. Imagine that you have a program on your cell phone that allows you to walk up to any item in the supermarket and have your phone recognize it and display all the necessary information about the product. The program tells you where and how it is made, and when it is predicted to go on sale next. Does a firm selling goods in this setting need to advertise? Why or why not? **[LO 15.5]**

10. Why might the cost of advertising be relevant to a consumer's decision about which brand of a product to purchase? **[LO 15.5]**

11. Suppose that the market for e-readers is an oligopoly controlled by Amazon, Barnes & Noble, Sony, and Apple. Barnes & Noble is considering increasing its output. How would this affect the market price? How would it affect the profits of each company? **[LO 15.6]**

12. Compare the efficiency of perfectly competitive markets, monopoly markets, and oligopoly markets. Explain why the same profit-maximizing behavior for the individual firm leads to different levels of efficiency in these three types of markets. **[LO 15.6]**

13. The Organization of the Petroleum Exporting Countries (OPEC) is a cartel of 12 countries that controls roughly two-thirds of the world's oil production. The cartel gives countries quotas for production. Why might a country be tempted to produce above quota for a year? How do you think other OPEC countries might respond if it did so? **[LO 15.7]**

14. Isabella runs an IT solutions business for her college peers and has only one competitor, Franco. Isabella and Franco have decided to collude and provide monopoly-level output. Given that they are both freshmen and intend to run their businesses for the next three years, is this agreement sustainable? Would your answer change if Franco knew he planned to transfer to another college next year? **[LO 15.7]**

15. The U.S. Postal Service (USPS) has a government monopoly on home mail delivery, but several private companies, such as FedEx, UPS, and DHL, compete with the USPS for other types of delivery service. Describe the differences in producer and consumer surplus, and in overall social welfare, that would occur in each of the following scenarios. **[LO 15.8]**

    a. The USPS has a monopoly on every type of mail or package.

    b. Consumers are allowed to choose between USPS, UPS, FedEx, and DHL for home mail delivery.

    c. There are an infinite number of local and national mail providers.

16. Explain why government is usually more concerned about regulating an oligopoly than a monopolistically competitive market. **[LO 15.8]**

Problems and Applications

1. Identify whether each of the following markets has few or many producers, and uniform or differentiated products. Which market is an oligopoly? Which market is monopolistically competitive? **[LO 15.1]**

    a. College education.

    b. Retail gas market.

2. Match the statement about goods sold in a market with the market type. **[LO 15.1]**

    a. There are imperfect substitutes for the goods.

    b. There are no substitutes for the goods.

    c. The goods may or may not be standardized.

3. Interscope sells the music of Lady Gaga, who promotes a unique public image and fashion style. Given her huge success, it is likely that by the end of the coming year, multiple performers will be imitating or borrowing heavily from her style. Suppose the current period's supply and demand for Lady Gaga MP3s is given in Figure 15P-1. **[LO 15.2, 15.3]**

FIGURE 15P-1

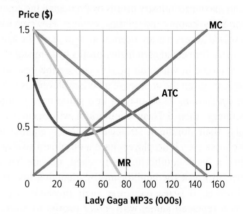

a. Identify the profit-maximizing price and quantity for Lady Gaga MP3s on the graph. What are the values for the profit-maximizing price and quantity in the short run?

b. In the long run, what happens to the demand curve?

c. In the long run, what happens to the profit-maximizing price?

4. Figure 15P-2 shows the monopolistically competitive market for smartphones. **[LO 15.3]**

FIGURE 15P-2

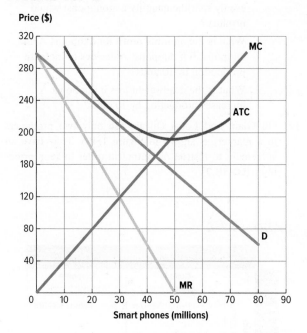

Price ($)

Smart phones (millions)

a. Plot the profit-maximizing price and quantity on the graph. Is this producer earning positive or negative profits in the short run?

b. In the long run, will supply or demand for this producer's good be affected? Will economic profits increase or decrease for this producer?

5. Figure 15P-3 shows a monopolistically competitive market for a fictional brand of shampoo called Squeaky-Kleen. **[LO 15.4]**

FIGURE 15P-3

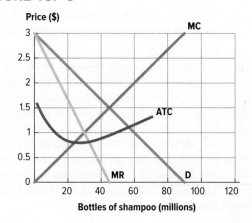

Price ($)

Bottles of shampoo (millions)

a. What are the price and quantity of SqueakyKleen in the short run?

b. What are the efficient price and quantity of SqueakyKleen?

c. Draw the deadweight loss.

6. The marginal costs (MC), average variable costs (AVC), and average total costs (ATC) for a monopolistically competitive firm are shown in Figure 15P-4. **[LO 15.4]**

FIGURE 15P-4

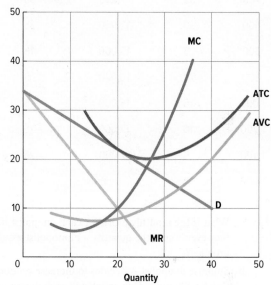

Price/Cost ($)

Quantity

a. Plot the profit-maximizing price and quantity on the graph.

b. Is this firm earning zero, positive, or negative profits? Why?

c. Is this firm in a long-run equilibrium?

7. For which good would you expect deadweight loss to be smaller relative to the total surplus in its market: Burger King hamburgers or Lady Gaga MP3s? Explain your answer. **[LO 15.4]**

8. For which product would you expect producers to have a stronger reaction to a ban on advertising: music artists or fast-food burgers? Explain your answer. **[LO 15.5]**

9. Suppose you manage a firm in a monopolistically competitive market. Which of the following strategies will do a better job of helping you maintain economic profits: obtaining a celebrity endorsement for your product or supporting the entry of firms that will compete directly with your biggest rival? Explain your answer. **[LO 15.5]**

10. Table 15P-1 shows the monthly demand schedule for a good in a duopoly market. The two producers in this market each faces $6,000 of fixed costs per month. There are no marginal costs. **[LO 15.6]**

TABLE 15P-1

Quantity	Price ($)	Total revenue ($)	Marginal revenue ($)
0	40	0	—
200	35	7,000	35
400	30	12,000	25
600	25	15,000	15
800	20	16,000	5
1,000	15	15,000	−5
1,200	10	12,000	−15
1,400	5	7,000	−25
1,600	0	0	−35

a. What is the monthly profit for each duopolist if they evenly split the quantity a monopolist would produce?

b. Suppose duopolist A decides to increase production by 200 units. How much will each duopolist produce and what price will they charge? How much profit will each duopolist earn?

11. Figure 15P-5 shows the monthly demand curve for a good in a duopoly market. There are no fixed costs. **[LO 15.6]**

FIGURE 15P-5

a. What is the monthly profit for each duopolist if they evenly split the quantity a monopolist would produce?

b. What is the deadweight loss if the duopolists evenly split the quantity a monopolist would produce?

c. What is the monthly profit for duopolist A and duopolist B if duopolist A decides to increase production by 10 units?

d. What is the deadweight loss if duopolist A increases production by 10 units?

12. Oil Giant and Local Oil are the only two producers in a market, as shown in Figure 15P-6. They have an agreement to restrict oil output in order to keep prices high. **[LO 15.7]**

FIGURE 15P-6

		Oil Giant	
		Collude 3 million barrels	Compete 4 million barrels
Local Oil	Collude 3 million barrels	Profit: $270m / Profit: $270m	Profit: $300m / Profit: $225m
	Compete 4 million barrels	Profit: $225m / Profit: $300m	Profit: $240m / Profit: $240m

a. What is the dominant strategy for each player?

b. If this game is played once, what is the Nash equilibrium?

c. Now suppose that both players know that the game will be played multiple times. What outcome would we expect?

13. Suppose Warner Music and Universal Music are in a duopoly and currently limit themselves to 10 new artists per year. One artist sells 2 million songs at $1.25 per song. However, each label is capable of signing 20 artists per year. If one label increases the number of artists to 20 and the other stays the same, the price per song drops to $0.75, and each artist sells 3 million songs. If both labels increase the number of artists to 20, the price per song drops to $0.30, and each artist sells 4 million songs. **[LO 15.7]**

FIGURE 15P-7

a. Fill in the revenue payoffs for each scenario in Figure 15P-7.

b. If this game is played once, how many artists will each producer sign, and what will be the price of a song?

c. If this game is played every year, how many artists will each producer sign, and what will be the price of a song?

14. Suppose a new product is developed and is supplied by a monopolist with a patent. Compared with the monopoly outcome, indicate whether consumer surplus, producer surplus, and total surplus increase, decrease, or remain the same under the following scenarios. **[LO 15.8]**

    a. Another producer creates a similar product and colludes with the original producer.

    b. Another producer creates a similar product and competes with the original producer.

    c. The patent expires.

15. For which of the following markets would there be a greater increase in total welfare if government were able to intervene and regulate prices: OPEC or the music industry? Explain your answer. **[LO 15.8]**

Endnotes

1. Tim Ingham, www.musicbusinessworldwide.com/independents-ruled-global-market-share-in-2017-but-universal-was-king-of-streaming.

2. http://www.peterjalexander.com/images/Market_Structure_and_Product_Variety.PDF; http://www.jstor.org/stable/2096413?seq=1#page_scan_tab_contents.

3. http://query.nytimes.com/gst/fullpage.html?res=9A04E4DD173FF935A25757C0A96F9C8B63&ref=dominos-pizza-inc.

The Factors of Production

The Fields of California

In 2018, center fielder Mike Trout earned a salary of $34.083 million a year, playing for the Los Angeles Angels. The contract extension he signed with the Angels in 2014 guaranteed him $144 million over six years, making him the highest-paid position player in Major League Baseball. In March 2019, the Angels locked the 27-year-old Trout into a 12-year contract extension worth $430 million—the largest contract in pro sports history. At the same time, another group of workers were also engaged in tough, physical work—but they earned a lot less money. California's tens of thousands of agricultural workers earned an average annual salary of just over $39,670 in 2017.[1]

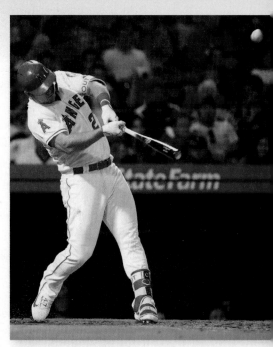

©Victor Decolongon/Getty Images

Of course, there are many, many differences between baseball and farm work. On a superficial level, though, baseball players have something in common with farm laborers. They are both mostly young men in their 20s and 30s, many of whom were born outside the United States. They do hard, physical, seasonal work, and they train on the job rather than in school.[2]

So, why does Mike Trout make about 860 times more money than someone who prunes orange trees or picks tomatoes? For that matter, why does Trout make so much more than other Major League Baseball players? (Don't feel too sorry for the others; their average salary is still over $4 million a year.) Why do baseball players make more than other professional athletes, whose average salary is about $105,000?[3]

We suspect that you intuitively know the answer to these questions. When he signed his contract extension with the Angels, Mike Trout was one of the top fielders and hitters in baseball. Of course he gets paid a lot! Not just anyone can do what he does. The same thing goes for professional baseball players in general. If there are only a thousand people in the entire country who have a particular skill, they can demand a lot of money to do what *only* they can do.

Furthermore, Americans like to watch baseball, and they're willing to pay to see it played well. We like tomatoes and oranges too, but if farm workers earned millions of dollars a year, consumers would have to be willing to pay a lot more for dinner. Similarly, the very best professional racquetball player in California makes far less money than Mike Trout. That happens not necessarily because he is less skilled or because there is a larger supply of great racquetball players, but because sports fans simply aren't willing to pay as much to watch racquetball.

The economic reasoning behind this intuition is that labor—whether slugging, fielding, or harvesting—is an ingredient in producing a good that consumers want, such as a baseball game or a tomato. The labor that goes into producing these goods is bought and sold in a way that is tied to the market for the goods themselves. The price that workers are paid depends both on the number of people who are able to supply that type of labor and on the demand for the goods that are produced with it.

LEARNING OBJECTIVES

LO 16.1 Describe how factors of production contribute to output.

LO 16.2 Graph the demand curve for a factor of production, and explain its relationship to marginal productivity.

LO 16.3 Graph the supply curve for a factor of production, and explain what determines the supply of labor.

LO 16.4 Explain how to find the equilibrium price and quantity for a factor of production.

LO 16.5 Use graphs to demonstrate the effect of a shift in labor supply or labor demand, and describe what causes these curves to shift.

LO 16.6 Explain the importance of human capital in the labor market.

LO 16.7 Describe the similarities and differences between the markets for land and capital and the market for labor.

LO 16.8 Describe two reasons why a wage might rise above the market equilibrium and how this affects the labor market.

LO 16.9 Describe several causes of imperfectly competitive labor markets and their effect on workers and employers.

In this chapter we'll discuss the markets for *factors of production*. Economists usually lump the factors of production into three categories: labor, land, and capital. We'll see how prices in the markets for factors of production are determined by markets for consumer goods as well as by public policy. Seeing how supply and demand govern factor markets enables us to understand how firms make decisions about how much of which factors to use. This choice is important for any business owner: Is it worth buying a new machine or hiring another employee? How can you know?

Understanding factor markets—particularly labor markets—is also a key to explaining people's income. We'll describe how ownership of different factors of production affects income and why people earn different amounts. This chapter is thus a building block for understanding income inequality. Since the majority of people make their living primarily by selling their labor, we'll focus on understanding the differences between the wages people earn. What differentiates Mike Trout from a farm worker, a professional racquetball player, a plumber, or you? This chapter will leave you with tools for understanding labor markets as a worker, a boss, or a voter.

The Factors of Production: Land, Labor, and Capital

When you buy a ticket to a baseball game, what are you really paying for? A baseball game requires the time and skills of players, managers, umpires, coaches, ticket collectors, food vendors, and janitors. It also requires a ballpark and a parking lot, training facilities, loudspeakers, jumbo screens, balls and gloves, and other equipment.

The ingredients that go into making a baseball game, or a tomato, or any other good or service, are called **factors of production**. We can think about three different types of factors—labor, land, and capital:

- *Labor* is the time employees spend working.
- *Land* is the place where employees work.
- **Capital** refers to manufactured goods that are used to produce new goods. The capital needed to produce a baseball game includes equipment like bats, lights, uniforms, and video screens. The capital needed to produce a tomato includes seeds, fertilizer, irrigation equipment, and trucks to transport harvested tomatoes.

LO 16.1 Describe how factors of production contribute to output.

Factors of production are bought and sold in markets, in much the same way as the goods they go into producing. The sellers in factor markets are people who own the factors of production. The buyers are firms that want to use the factors to produce goods and services. The price of each factor is determined by supply and demand.

In this section, we'll describe the production decisions that drive factor markets and make them slightly different from other markets. We'll see how factor markets are tied to markets for consumer goods, and how each factor's contribution to production is measured. These are tools that you will need to understand how businesses make production decisions, and, ultimately, to see why baseball players are paid more than farm workers.

factors of production
the ingredients that go into making a good or service

capital
manufactured goods that are used to produce new goods

Derived demand

How does a firm decide how much of each factor of production it wants to use? The Los Angeles Angels wanted—and were willing to pay for—Mike Trout's labor because it would help them win baseball games. That, in turn, would raise the value of tickets and broadcast rights to baseball games, which are then supplied to fans. (In fact, on the free agent market, baseball teams are willing to pay about $7 million for each additional win provided by a player). The demand for baseball players is "derived" from a team's choice to supply games; that demand depends on how much individual players contribute to the value of the end product. For this reason, the demand for factors of production is referred to as *derived demand*.

Likewise, consider farmers who want to produce tomatoes: They will need to decide whether to buy a field that could be used to grow tomatoes, how many workers to employ to pick tomatoes, or whether to invest in new irrigation equipment. As they make such decisions, they will consider the market for tomatoes. Like a baseball team's demand for players, farmers' demand for good tomato-growing land, tomato pickers, and irrigation equipment is *derived from* the market for tomatoes. If consumers want more tomatoes, demand for the factors of production that go into tomatoes will increase. If they want fewer tomatoes, demand for those factors of production will decrease.

Marginal productivity

In Chapter 12, "The Costs of Production," we discussed *production functions*, which describe the relationship between the quantity of inputs a firm uses and the resulting quantity of outputs. For example, a farm that hires more workers can produce more tomatoes. The increase in output that is generated by an additional unit of input is called **marginal product**.

Graphically, we can think of the marginal product of a factor as the slope of the total production curve, with output measured on the *y*-axis and the quantity of the input measured on the *x*-axis. Figure 16-1 shows the marginal product of labor in tomato production. The change in the quantity of tomatoes produced due to hiring one additional worker is the *marginal product of labor* for that worker. Marginal product also applies to the other factors of production: land and capital.

Recall that inputs usually have diminishing marginal productivity. In other words, for a given amount of land, the tenth farm worker will generally contribute less to a farm's output than the first worker. This fact will become important as we describe the demand for labor.

marginal product
the increase in output that is generated by an additional unit of input

Picking the right combination of inputs

In some cases, firms can choose what combination of factors to use, substituting one for another. For instance, picking tomatoes can be done either by hand or by machine. A farmer can choose to hire many workers and buy no machinery, or hire fewer workers and buy more machinery. (Note that this trade-off doesn't work for all goods: You can't choose to produce a baseball game by having fewer players and more bats.)

FIGURE 16-1
Marginal product of labor

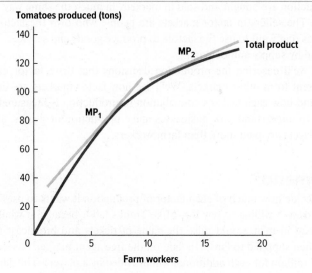

The more workers a farm employs, the more tomatoes the farm can harvest. Hiring an additional farm worker adds fewer tomatoes to the harvest than were added with the previous worker. As the number of workers increases, total production increases, but the marginal product of labor diminishes.

A profit-seeking firm will choose the combination of inputs that *maximizes profit*, based on the local price of each factor of production. The price of farm machinery is similar all over the world, but the cost of farm labor varies more widely. Thus:

- In poorer economies, labor is usually cheap, so farmers tend to hire lots of workers and buy fewer machines.
- In richer countries, labor costs more, so farmers tend to hire fewer workers and buy more machines.

Another way of saying this is that farming tends to be *labor-intensive* in poorer countries and *capital-intensive* in richer countries.

✓ **TEST YOURSELF**

☐ Give examples of each of the factors of production that are used in an auto repair shop. **[LO 16.1]**

☐ What is labor demand "derived" from? **[LO 16.1]**

☐ What is the relationship between a worker's marginal product and a firm's total output? **[LO 16.1]**

Labor Markets and Wages

We now have some concepts to use when thinking about the markets for factors of production. We'll use them to take a closer look at the markets for labor and capital. Before we start, though, there are a couple of things to mention, which will help as you learn about the market for labor:

- First, remember that individuals who work are the "suppliers" of labor. Firms that produce goods using those workers are the "buyers" of labor. This is the reverse of the usual market situation, in which we think of firms as suppliers and individual people as buyers.

- Second, the wage that workers earn is the "price" of labor. We rarely use the word *price* when talking about people and their skills. But wages play exactly the same role in labor markets as prices do in markets for goods and services. In the labor market, the terms *wage* and *price* mean exactly the same thing: Wages are simply the price of labor.

Let's start by considering the demand for labor.

Demand for labor

Let's consider how a tomato farmer decides how many workers to employ. For simplicity, we'll assume that the tomato farm is a profit-maximizing firm in a competitive market. That makes sense when there are many different tomato farms, each a price taker in the market for selling tomatoes and in the market for hiring farm workers. Let's also assume for now that all farm workers are equally productive.

What determines the number of workers the farm hires? Consider the owner's *wants and constraints*. The owner wants to maximize the farm's profit. Remember that a firm in a competitive market maximizes profits by producing *the quantity at which the revenue it earns from the last unit is equal to the cost of producing that unit.* So, a tomato farm wants to produce tomatoes up to the point where the marginal revenue from the last ton is equal to the marginal cost of producing that ton.

Since the farm is a price taker in a competitive market, the farmer cannot control the going price of tomatoes. Nor can he control the going wage of tomato pickers. Both of those factors—prices of goods and workers' wages—affect how much profit the farmer will make. Therefore, maximizing profit boils down to making the right choice about the quantity to produce.

If we leave land, tractors, and other inputs fixed at a certain level, the farm's output will be determined by the number of workers hired and each worker's marginal productivity. Table 16-1 shows relevant data for a single hypothetical farm. For any number of workers (in column 1), the table tells us the quantity of tomatoes produced (column 3) and the marginal cost of hiring the last worker (in column 6). That marginal cost of the last worker is the worker's annual wage; in this example, it is $20,000 for each worker.

Each worker hired adds something to total production—that worker's *marginal product of labor (MPL)*. In other words, the MPL is the quantity of additional output generated by the worker (shown in column 2). You can see that the marginal product of labor diminishes with each added worker. The first group of workers is able to harvest lots of tomatoes. As more and more workers come to the farm, they start to get in each other's way, and marginal productivity decreases.

The question of how much labor a firm will hire comes down to whether added workers are going to generate more revenue than what it costs to pay them. Therefore, we want to find the *marginal revenue* associated with each worker. If the worker brings in more revenue than it costs to pay him or her, the worker should be hired.

To find the marginal revenue of an additional worker, we multiply the worker's marginal product of labor (shown in column 2) by the market price of tomatoes (column 4). In doing so, we translate the worker's marginal product into a dollar value (as shown in column 5 of the table). This is shown in Equation 16-1.

EQUATION 16-1   Value of marginal product (VMP) = Marginal product × Price of output

We call this increase in revenue the **value of the marginal product**. It is calculated as the output generated by an additional unit of input times the price of the output. (The VMP is also sometimes referred to as the *marginal revenue product*.) For example, the marginal product of the eighth worker hired by the farm is 8 tons of tomatoes, and the going price for tomatoes is $2,000 per ton. The value of the marginal product of the eighth worker would be 8 × $2,000 = $16,000.

For a competitive firm, the price of the output is always going to be the same. This implies that the value of the marginal product decreases for each additional worker. Why? Because the price of the output stays constant while the marginal product of labor decreases.

LO 16.2 Graph the demand curve for a factor of production, and explain its relationship to marginal productivity.

value of the marginal product
the increase in revenue generated by the last unit of an input; calculated as the output generated by an input (marginal product) times the unit price of the output

TABLE 16-1
Labor productivity and cost

(1) # of workers (L)	(2) Marginal product of labor*	(3) Tomatoes produced (Y)	(4) Price ($) of tomatoes (P)	(5) Value ($) of marginal product†	(6) Annual wage ($) (W)	(7) Marginal profit ($)††
0	0 tons/worker	0 tons	2,000 per ton	0	20,000	—
1	15	15	2,000	30,000	20,000	10,000
2	14	29	2,000	28,000	20,000	8,000
3	13	42	2,000	26,000	20,000	6,000
4	12	54	2,000	24,000	20,000	4,000
5	11	65	2,000	22,000	20,000	2,000
6	10	75	2,000	20,000	20,000	0
7	9	84	2,000	18,000	20,000	−2,000
8	8	92	2,000	16,000	20,000	−4,000
9	7	99	2,000	14,000	20,000	−6,000

* Marginal product of labor (MPL) = Change in Y/Change in L

† Value of marginal product of labor (VMPL) = MPL × P

†† Marginal profit = VMPL − W

We stated earlier that maximizing profit boils down to making the right choice about the quantity to produce. At what number of workers will that occur for the tomato farmer? Column 7 shows the *marginal profit* for each number of workers; that amount is calculated as the value of the marginal product minus the annual wage for each worker. As you can see in the table, hiring three workers definitely makes sense for the farm. The third worker produces $26,000 of tomatoes but costs the farmer only $20,000. Therefore, hiring the third worker yields a marginal profit (column 7) of $6,000. Hiring the next two workers also makes sense for the farm: Each adds more revenue than what he or she is paid in wages.

When should the farmer stop hiring workers? A competitive firm should keep hiring *as long as the value of the marginal product is greater than or equal to the marginal cost of the worker* (the worker's wage). In our example, the tomato farmer should hire the sixth worker, whose VMP is $20,000. The farmer should not hire the seventh worker, though. That worker adds only $18,000— an amount less than the extra cost of her $20,000 wage.

Figure 16-2 shows in graph form the relationship between the value of the marginal product and the number of farm workers hired. The table in panel A shows the values of the marginal product for each worker, taken from Table 16-1. Panel B plots these numbers onto a graph. You can see that the curve formed by plotting the value of the marginal product for workers is downward-sloping, due to the diminishing marginal product of each additional worker.

What is the profit-maximizing quantity of labor that the farmer decides to hire? We find the answer by seeing where *the value of the marginal product of labor intersects the market-wage level*. At that point, the value of the last worker's marginal product is greater than or equal to the wage.

Note that at any given wage, there is only one profit-maximizing quantity of labor. As wages rise or fall, firms adjust the quantity of labor they demand. We can plot this profit-maximizing

(A) Value of the marginal product

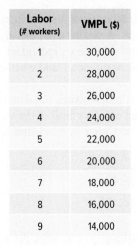

Labor (# workers)	VMPL ($)
1	30,000
2	28,000
3	26,000
4	24,000
5	22,000
6	20,000
7	18,000
8	16,000
9	14,000

(B) VMPL equals labor demand

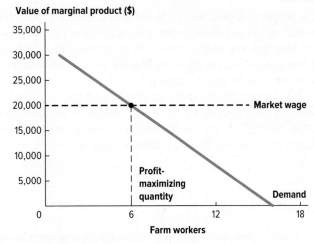

FIGURE 16-2

Value of the marginal product and the demand curve for labor

The value of the marginal product of labor decreases with the number of workers hired. The quantity of labor demanded at any given wage is the quantity at which the value of the marginal product of labor equals the wage. The result is a downward-sloping demand curve, with the quantity of labor demanded increasing as the wage decreases.

quantity for a variety of wages and generate a whole demand curve. This demand curve is the same as the value of the marginal product (VMP) curve: At each point along the demand curve, the wage is equal to the VMP of the last worker hired and therefore corresponds to a point on the VMP curve.

The curve shown in Figure 16-2 is just one demand curve—the demand curve for the tomato farmer. It's straightforward, though, to find the labor demand curve for the entire tomato market: Add up the quantities of labor demanded by all firms in the market, just as we did with the demand for consumer goods in Chapter 3, "Markets."

Supply of labor

As in all markets, the demand for labor tells only half the story. Ultimately, the equilibrium quantity and wage are determined by the interaction of demand and supply. The supply of labor is more complicated than the supply of most goods and services but is still driven by a basic trade-off between the costs and benefits of supplying labor to firms.

Consider the choice made by an individual worker—say, a farm worker in California—who is deciding how many hours to work each week. The main benefit of working is earning a certain wage for every hour of work. Workers can choose to work more hours in order to earn more money, or they could choose to work fewer hours in order to have more time off.

Now, what about the cost side of the trade-off? The "cost" to an individual of supplying her labor is more difficult to calculate than the benefit. Because the worker doesn't need to buy any inputs to "produce" an hour of labor, we can't directly compare the worker's cost of supplying labor to a firm's cost of production.

Instead, we need to *think about the opportunity cost* of supplying another hour of labor. If you work an extra hour, you give up the chance to spend that hour doing something else—such as going for a run, checking Instagram, or doing your laundry. Economists usually categorize all nonwork activities under the term *leisure*. Although they may not seem relaxing or fun, doing chores around the house or errands in town are usually classified as leisure. The cost of working is therefore the forgone opportunity to enjoy leisure.

LO 16.3 Graph the supply curve for a factor of production, and explain what determines the supply of labor.

CAUTION: COMMON MISTAKE

For simplicity's sake, we talk about people deciding to supply their labor from hour to hour. Of course, in the real world, individuals usually can't set their own hours. A worker can't usually tell the boss that she wants to work 39 or 41 hours this week instead of 40. For an individual, real labor-supply decisions are often whether to work full time, part time, or not at all, and whether to work overtime or take a second job.

It turns out, though, that over an extended period and a large group of workers, the *total* labor supply is quite flexible, and analyzing changes in average hours in fact captures most of the action. We'll continue to talk about workers choosing hours, but you should keep in mind that labor-supply decisions can involve a broader range of choices.

There is also another kind of opportunity cost associated with the choice to work for a particular employer. A person who decides to work an extra hour on a farm gives up the opportunity to spend that hour working at another paying job—say, as a construction worker or bartender. The worker has to decide whether the opportunity cost of *not* working that other job outweighs the benefits of more farm work. In making that decision, he or she will have to consider not only the wages each other job offers but also any other perks of each job. Workers value many benefits like health insurance, a pleasant work environment, and the chance to learn new skills.

The decision to supply another hour of labor depends on the trade-off between the benefits of an hour of work (the wage plus any other perks) and the opportunity cost (lost time for leisure or other kinds of work). If the benefits outweigh the costs, we would expect a person to work an additional hour. This logic holds up to the point where the benefit of another hour of work exactly equals the opportunity cost. At that point, the worker becomes indifferent between spending the next hour on work or leisure.

What happens to the quantity of labor supplied if wages go up? In most markets, when price increases, so does quantity supplied. It makes sense then that when higher wages are being offered, the benefits of work go up, people will want to work more, and the quantity of labor supplied will increase. This relationship is shown in the labor-supply curve drawn in Figure 16-3. The market labor-supply curve would be formed by adding up all of the individual labor-supply curves.

The price and income effects   One important feature of the labor-supply curve, however, makes it different from other supply curves. Although higher wages generally increase the quantity of labor supplied, this is not always true. A higher wage increases the benefit of an additional hour of work, but it also, less obviously, increases the *opportunity cost* of working.

To see why, we have to go back to the individual decision to supply labor. The key to figuring out why opportunity costs increase is the fact that leisure is usually more enjoyable when we have money to spend. If your wages go up, you have more money, so you might prefer to spend that extra hour using some of that money to enjoy your leisure time. Indeed, if you are now getting paid more per hour, you might decide that you'd rather work *fewer* hours. If this is the case, a wage increase might actually *reduce* the supply of labor.

Economists have two terms to describe the competing incentives that influence a worker's response to a change in the wage:

- The *price effect* describes the increase in labor supply in response to the higher wage that can be earned for each hour of work.

- The *income effect* describes the decrease in labor supply due to the greater demand for leisure caused by a higher income.

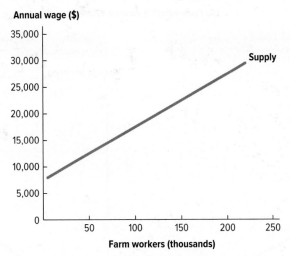

FIGURE 16-3
Supply of labor

A producer will generally supply more of a good or service as its price rises. The same rule applies to workers who supply their labor, yielding the familiar upward-sloping supply curve.

We can see in Figure 16-4 the influence of the income and price effects on labor supply decisions. (This analysis is similar to that of the income and substitution effects we saw in Chapter 7, "Consumer Behavior," when considering purchasing decisions under a budget constraint.) In this case, workers are constrained by the amount of time they have available. There are 8,760 hours in a (non-leap) year. Assuming that workers will spend some portion of that time sleeping and eating, let's say there are roughly 5,000 hours available for work per year.

Time translates into income through work and wages. At an initial wage rate of $10 per hour, workers face a budget constraint represented by the darker line in the left graphs of Figure 16-4:

- They can choose to work zero hours, earn nothing, and have 5,000 hours of leisure a year.
- They can choose to work 5,000 hours, earn $50,000, and have no leisure time.
- They could choose any point in between.

Suppose that based on personal preferences, an individual chooses to work 2,000 hours, earn $20,000, and have 3,000 hours of leisure. Now, let's say the wage increases from $10 an hour to $17 an hour (quite a raise!). When the wage increases, the budget line pivots outward. Now, the worker's choice is on the lighter line in the left graphs (which runs between no income with 5,000 hours of leisure and $85,000 with no leisure time per week).

The left graph in panel A of Figure 16-4 shows how a worker reacts to this wage increase when the *price effect* is bigger than the income effect. This worker responds to the new budget constraint by choosing to increase his hours worked from 2,000 to 3,000 hours (thus losing 1,000 hours of leisure). He earns $51,000 and has only 2,000 hours of leisure. Here, an increase in the wage has caused an increase in the amount of labor supplied. The right graph in panel A translates the leisure chosen on the left into a labor supply curve. That curve shows the hours of labor the worker supplies at any given wage rate. The fact that the price effect outweighs the income effect is reflected in the upward-sloping labor supply curve.

The left graph in panel B shows what happens when the *income effect* is bigger than the price effect. This worker responds to the same wage increase by decreasing her hours worked from 2,000 to 1,500 hours (thus gaining 500 hours of leisure). She earns $25,500 and has 3,500 hours of leisure time. Here, an increase in the wage has caused the worker to supply 500 *fewer* hours of

FIGURE 16-4

Income and price effects of a wage increase

(A) Price effect > income effect

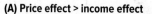
1. As the higher wage causes the budget constraint to pivot out, the optimal quantity of leisure decreases.

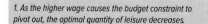

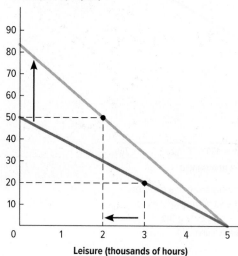

2. When the price effect dominates, the labor supply is upward-sloping.

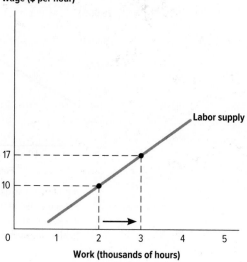

(B) Income effect > Price effect

1. As the higher wage causes the budget constraint to pivot out, the optimal quantity of leisure increases.

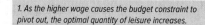

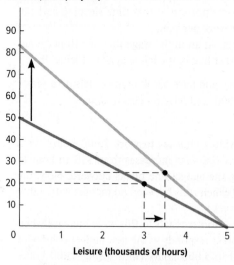

2. When the income effect dominates, the labor supply is downward-sloping.

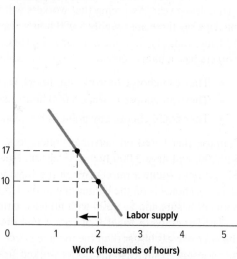

The price effect causes labor supply to increase in response to a wage increase. The income effect causes labor supply to decrease in response to the same change. Whether total labor supply goes up or down depends on which effect dominates.

labor. When the income effect outweighs the price effect, the labor supply curve slopes downward, as the right graph in panel B shows.

Either of these two situations is a rational response, depending on whether the individual in question gets more utility from additional leisure or additional money.

This analysis assumes that the marginal change in the quantity of labor supplied is the same regardless of the number of hours a person is already working. However, individual labor supply curves are not always linear—the relative size of the price and income effects depend on where an individual is on his or her labor supply curve.

Think about your own preferences. When you have a lot of spare time and little work, small increases in wages might push you to work many more hours. The price effect is larger than the income effect, and the slope of the labor supply curve will be low at that point. However, when you are already working a lot, increases in wages will likely cause smaller increases in the quantity of labor you supply. At this point in your labor supply curve, the income effect has gained ground against the price effect, causing a much steeper upward trend in the labor supply curve.

For some people, the income effect is so large at higher wages that they will actually *reduce* the quantity of hours that they want to work. That reduction in labor hours will cause the labor supply curve to appear as though it bends backward. In this special situation, rising wages lead to *less* labor supplied: The increase in wages allows some individuals to happily cut their work hours while still earning a sufficient paycheck. While possible in principle, such backward-bending labor supply curves are not the norm.

Instead, in most labor markets, labor supply curves are upward-sloping and approximately linear. So, for the rest of this chapter, we will use the standard upward-sloping supply curve for labor, indicating that the quantity of labor supplied increases as the wage increases.

Reaching equilibrium

A worker deciding how many hours to work can be represented with an individual labor-supply curve. A farm choosing the profit-maximizing number of employees can be represented with a firm-level demand curve. In order to see how the labor market works as a whole, however, we need to add up all the supply curves of individual workers and the demand curves of individual firms to find *market-level* supply and demand.

LO 16.4 Explain how to find the equilibrium price and quantity for a factor of production.

The process for identifying the equilibrium wage and quantity in the labor market should look very familiar. As in all competitive markets, the equilibrium is found at the point where the supply and demand curves intersect. Figure 16-5 shows the equilibrium in a market for tomato-farm workers in California. At this point, the quantity of labor supplied equals the quantity demanded by tomato farmers in California at the market wage. Farm workers get $20,000 per year, and farmers hire 125,000 workers.

The labor market reaches equilibrium through the same process as any other market, assuming that both wages and the quantity of labor can adjust freely in response to incentives. For instance, suppose the wage for farm workers is $11.50 per hour (roughly $23,000 per year, at 40 hours of work per week for 50 weeks per year). At that price, given the value of the marginal product of labor, farmers want to hire 100,000 workers.

However, 163,500 workers want to work at that wage, given their opportunity cost of labor. Because the quantity of labor supplied is greater than the quantity demanded, the market is out of balance. Some workers who want to work will be left without a job, or at least with fewer working hours than they want. In other words, at that price there is a surplus of farm labor.

If you were a farm owner, *how would you respond to this situation?* Knowing that there are plenty of underemployed and willing workers out there, you might offer a lower wage—say, $10 per hour instead of $11.50. ($10 per hour works out to about $20,000 per year.) If you can get the work done at a lower cost, you probably won't complain. When the wage falls from $11.50 to $10 per hour, the quantity of workers demanded by farm owners will increase.

At the lower wage, what happens to the number of workers? Some workers will be willing to work for $10 per hour. Others will find that the opportunity cost of work outweighs the benefits. The latter group will be unwilling to work for $10. Thus, the quantity of labor supplied will decrease, while the quantity demanded will increase, bringing the market into equilibrium.

FIGURE 16-5

Labor market equilibrium

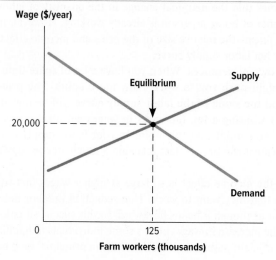

In a competitive labor market, the price of
labor (that is, the wage) is determined by the
intersection of the supply and demand curves
for labor. Here, the labor market reaches
equilibrium at a wage of $20,000 per year. At
that point 125,000 workers are hired.

If wages drop below the market equilibrium level, the opposite will happen: Farmers will demand
more labor than workers are willing to supply. Farmers will have to offer higher wages to attract the
workers they need, increasing the quantity of labor supplied and decreasing the quantity demanded.
This process will continue until the wage brings the supply of labor into balance with demand.

Shifts in labor supply and labor demand

LO 16.5 Use
graphs to demon-
strate the effect of a
shift in labor supply
or labor demand,
and describe what
causes these curves
to shift.

Just as in the supply and demand model in Chapter 3, "Markets," the supply and demand curves
for labor can shift right or left with changes in nonprice determinants. In the labor market, such
factors include technology, labor market regulations, and other external forces.

Determinants of labor demand   In thinking about the underlying determinants of the
labor demand curve, the key is to remember that *labor demand is determined by the value of the
marginal product of labor*. As a result:

- Any event that increases the value of the marginal product will increase demand, shifting
  the labor demand curve right.
- Any event that decreases the value of the marginal product will decrease demand, shifting
  the labor demand curve left.

In general, many shifts in the labor demand curve can be traced to three determinants: supply
of other factors of production, technology, and output prices. Table 16-2 summarizes the effects
of such changes.

We can see an example of a shift in labor demand resulting from technology by assuming that
the tomato farm decides to invest in more farm machinery. Adding machinery can vastly improve
the productivity of a small group of farm workers. However, with the added machinery, the marginal product of labor diminishes very quickly. Once you have the few workers you need to operate
the machines, adding more workers adds little to the quantity harvested.

Such a reduction in the marginal product of labor would decrease the quantity of labor
demanded at any given wage, shifting the entire demand curve to the left. As Figure 16-6 shows,

TABLE 16-2

Nonprice determinants of labor demand

Factors that shift labor demand	Effects on marginal product and labor demand
Technology	When technology changes are *labor-augmenting*: The MPL increases and labor demand also increases (shifts right). When technology changes are *labor-saving*: The MPL decreases and labor demand also decreases (shifts left).
Supply of other factors	If the supply of other factors causes the MPL to increase, labor demand increases (shifts right). If the supply of other factors causes the MPL to decrease, labor demand decreases (shifts left).
Output prices	If output prices decrease, the value of the marginal product of labor (VMPL) decreases and labor demand also decreases (shifts left). If output prices increase, the value of the marginal product of labor (VMPL) increases and labor demand also increases (shifts right).

FIGURE 16-6

Decrease in the demand for labor

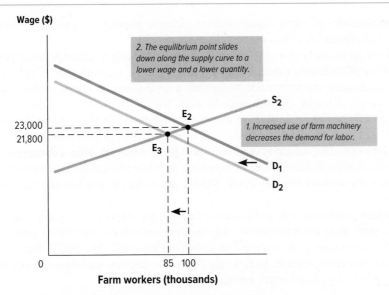

When increased use of farm machinery decreases the marginal product of labor, the labor demand curve shifts left. The equilibrium number of workers falls from 100,000 to 85,000, and the equilibrium wage falls from $23,000 to $21,800.

the equilibrium point slides down the supply curve to a new equilibrium point (E₃ in the figure) at a lower quantity and a lower wage. Note that at the new equilibrium point, there are fewer total farm workers and a lower equilibrium wage.

Determinants of labor supply   In thinking about the underlying determinants of labor supply, the key is to remember that at any given wage, *labor supply is determined by the number of workers and the opportunity cost of providing their labor*. As a result:

- Changes that increase the opportunity cost of work or decrease the number of workers will decrease the labor supply, shifting the supply curve left.
- Changes that decrease the opportunity cost of work or increase the number of workers will increase the labor supply, shifting the supply curve right.

CAUTION: COMMON MISTAKE

Popular opinion holds that technology displaces workers. This is sometimes true, as with farm machinery. However, it is not always true.

For example, consider the effect of the internet on research assistants' productivity. In pre-internet days, when a professor asked an assistant to find some data, it took days of digging at the library. Now, it takes minutes on a search engine. You might assume that when the internet came along, professors could employ fewer research assistants to do the same amount of work, just as farm machinery enables farmers to employ fewer workers to harvest the same amount of crops.

But another dynamic is at work. In the days before the internet, a professor would have had to *really* need some data before she paid a research assistant to search for it. With the internet, a professor can ask for data just on the chance that it might be interesting. As a result, professors' appetite for data has increased, and the demand for more research assistant labor has remained the same, or even increased.

The determinants of labor supply include culture, population, and other opportunities. Table 16-3 summarizes the effects of such changes.

We can see an example of a shift in labor supply by looking at changes in the population of workers. Many of California's farm workers (most, by some accounts) are in the United States illegally. Occasionally the authorities implement a crackdown on illegal immigration, increasing the strictness of border controls with Mexico. We can think of this as an external change that decreases the supply of workers at any given wage level. To see why, we first need to ask, *How should we expect Mexican prospective farm workers to respond to stricter border controls?* The greater chance of getting caught at the border and being deported, after a dangerous and expensive trip, decreases the expected value of supplying their labor to California's farmers. Faced with this choice, some workers will stay home. Others will make the trip but will be turned back at the border.

Thus, stricter border controls will cause the total supply of labor to be lower at any given wage than it was under more lax enforcement. We can represent this decrease in the supply of labor by shifting the entire supply curve to the left, as shown in Figure 16-7. The equilibrium point slides up along the demand curve, from E_1 to E_2 in the figure. At that new equilibrium point, the quantity of labor supplied is lower and wages are higher.

TABLE 16-3

Nonprice determinants of labor supply

Factors that shift labor supply	Effect on labor supply
Population	When there are more potential workers (as a result of demographic changes and/or immigration), labor supply increases (shifts right).
Culture	When cultural attitudes view work favorably, labor supply increases (shifts right). When cultural attitudes view work unfavorably, labor supply decreases (shifts left).
Other opportunities	When the next-best opportunity available to workers offers better benefits, the labor supply will move toward that better opportunity, whether that increases or decreases supply. *Examples:* Better wages in retail or service jobs might lead workers to supply less labor to farms, decreasing the labor supply for farms but increasing the labor supply for retail and service jobs. A decrease in the cost of higher education might lead workers to go back to school, decreasing the labor supply.

FIGURE 16-7

Decrease in the labor supply

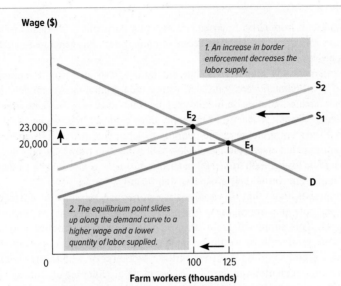

When an external change in border controls causes a
change in workers' trade-offs, the labor supply curve
shifts. In this case, stricter controls shift the curve to
the left, decreasing the equilibrium number of farm
workers supplied from 125,000 to 100,000 and increasing
the equilibrium wage from $20,000 to $23,000.

In the early 2000s, California cracked down on illegal immigration, but wages of California farm workers did not rise during this period—at least, no more than wages on average rose throughout the country. Why not? Do these real-world data mean our model is wrong? Not necessarily. There could have been another factor at work, shifting the demand curve to the left at the same time.

For instance, consider *how farm owners might respond* to an illegal immigration crackdown that was causing an increase in wages. As we saw earlier, firms can sometimes substitute one factor of production for another. Faced with a higher cost of labor, farmers might have decided they could maximize profits by employing fewer workers and investing in more farm machinery instead. That's what one farmer in Arizona did when he couldn't find enough workers to pick his jalapeño peppers— he aimed to cut the number of laborers he needed by 90 percent and hire machinists instead. Between 2007 and 2012, Arizona's population of undocumented workers dropped by 40 percent. And between 2010 and 2014, wages for Arizona farm workers rose approximately 15 percent.[4]

For a more nuanced discussion of the economic effects of immigration, read the What Do You Think? box "Should the United States be a country of immigrants?"

Should the United States be a country of immigrants?
What Do You Think?

The economy of the United States—arguably, more than any other economy in the world—has been shaped by huge waves of workers emigrating from other countries. German farmers settled the Midwest in the 1850s. Chinese workers built the transcontinental railroad in the 1880s. Immigrants from southern and eastern Europe powered northeastern factories during the early decades of the twentieth century.

(continued)

Today, immigrants from Latin America and Asia play particularly important roles in the economy (see Figure 16-8). Still, the size and scope of immigration has generated debate throughout the country's history.

The first argument you may hear is that immigrants take jobs from Americans and drive down wages. These arguments are consistent with standard labor-market models. In those models, immigration creates an increase in labor supply, which (all else the same) decreases wages. Economist George Borjas at Harvard University cites evidence that wages drop by 3 percent when there is 10 percent increase in the quantity of labor supplied at a given skill. At current rates of immigration, that means the average low-skill American worker earning $25,000 per year on average would be losing $800 to $1,500 in earnings. Borjas argues that "for many Americans, the influx of immigrants hurts their prospects significantly."

Other economists argue that this analysis is erroneously pessimistic. Instead, businesses in some sectors note that immigrants are taking jobs that Americans do not want, even at higher wages. This supply of labor allows these sectors to produce goods that would otherwise not be produced, or would be produced elsewhere and imported. For example, the agricultural sector employs 1.5 to 2 million workers, of which anywhere from 46 to 70 percent are undocumented immigrants. Many more are here legally through guest-worker programs. Americans who then eat the food produced by these farms benefit from the immigrant labor.

The problem isn't limited to agriculture—78 percent of construction companies in Texas report that they struggle to find qualified workers. Similarly, tech companies demand far more H-1B visas (which allow U.S. employers to employ foreign workers in specialty occupations) than the government is willing to provide. Relying solely on native-born workers would likely result in higher costs and slower projects in many parts of the economy.

While the exact benefits and costs of immigration are hard to measure, economists generally believe that that the lower costs of production generally outweigh the negative effects on wages and available employment. Not only that, immigrants buy food, clothes, and other services, which in turn benefits local businesses, increasing the size of the economy. Many immigrants also provide needed skills and entrepreneurial ability.

Of course, the debate on immigration stirs powerful feelings about fairness and national identity. Is it fair to withhold the ladder of opportunity that the parents and grandparents of current citizens may have climbed up? Does the worker born in Montana have a right to a job when an immigrant would do the same job for less money, thus increasing the efficiency in the market? Is the Hispanic family celebrating a *quinceanera* any less American than a family that has been living in the United States for generations? How would the fabric of the country change if we accept more or fewer immigrants?

As long as the United States continues to be a land of opportunity, attracting immigrants from around the world, this debate will surely continue.

WHAT DO YOU THINK?

1. Does the government have a responsibility to address the negative effects of immigration on native-born workers who are affected by it?
2. Should everyone who wants to work in the United States be legally allowed to do so? Where should the line be drawn, and why?

Sources: George J. Borjas, "Yes, immigration hurts American workers," *Politico*, September/October 2016, www.politico.com/magazine/story/2016/09/trump-clinton-immigration-economy-unemployment-jobs-214216; Tamar Haspel, "Illegal immigrants help fuel U.S. farms. Does affordable produce depend on them?" *The Washington Post*, March 17, 2017, www.washingtonpost.com/lifestyle/food/in-an-immigration-crackdown-who-will-pick-our-produce/2017/03/17/cc1c6df4-0a5d-11e7-93dc-00f9bdd74ed1_story.html?utm_term=.1848b75684d6.

FIGURE 16-8

U.S. immigration, 1820–2016

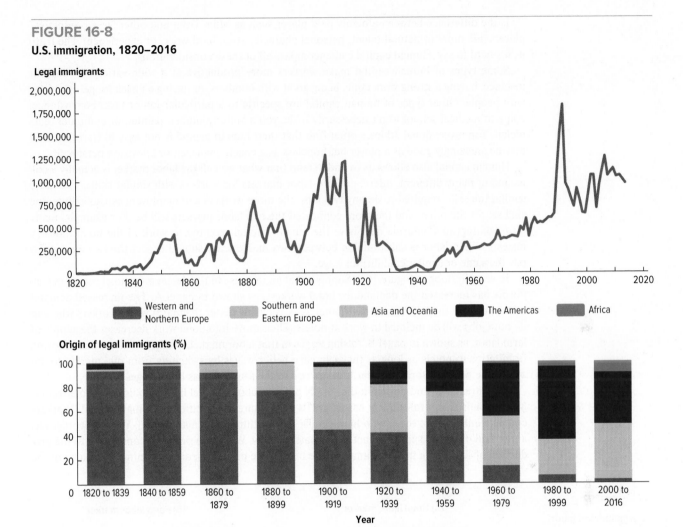

Source: www.migrationpolicy.org/programs/data-hub/us-immigration-trends#history; *DHS Handbook of Immigration Statistics 2017*, www.dhs.gov/immigration-statistics/yearbook/2017, Tables 1 and 2.

What's missing? Human capital

So far, we've described simple labor markets. What's missing? Why are professional baseball players paid more than farm workers? Why, even within specific markets like the market for baseball players, are participants paid different amounts? Mike Trout, the baseball player from the chapter opening story, in 2018 earned about four times the salary of Kole Calhoun, who played in right field next to Trout. (And Trout earned about 176 times the salary of Eric Young Jr., another center fielder for the Angels.)

What causes this difference? It's what economists call **human capital**, the set of skills, knowledge, experience, and talent that determine the productivity of workers. In taking courses at school, you are acquiring human capital. Human capital determines the productivity of workers.

Human capital is so crucial in determining how labor markets work that economists sometimes consider it the fourth, and possibly the most important, factor of production. Workers differ from one another, and are paid differently, because they have different amounts and types of human capital that allow them to be more or less productive than other workers at various tasks.

LO 16.6 Explain the importance of human capital in the labor market.

human capital
the set of skills, knowledge, experience, and talent that determine the productivity of workers

Is the difference between a highly paid player such as Mike Trout and other "less productive" players due more to natural talent, personal characteristics, hard work, or experience? The truth is, it's hard to say. Human capital can encompass all of these considerations.

Some types of human capital make workers more productive at a wide variety of jobs—for instance, having a strong work ethic, being good with numbers, or having a knack for getting along with people. Other types of human capital are specific to a particular job or task. For instance, going to medical school won't necessarily make you a better plumber, painter, or computer technician. Top professional athletes often find that their human capital is not easy to transfer: They may be amazingly good as a player but hopeless as a coach, manager, or television personality.

Human capital also allows us to understand that what we call the labor market is actually a collection of many different, interconnected labor markets for workers with similar skills. The more similar the skills required to do any two jobs, the more workers and employers can substitute one skill set for the other, and the more connected the two labor markets will be. For example, many farm laborers in California may have the human capital required to work in the hotel industry instead. When labor is substitutable between two markets, we should expect the two markets to pay the same or similar equilibrium wage.

To see why, look at Figure 16-9. Suppose that an increase in the demand for hotel rooms in California has increased the demand for hotel workers, as shown in panel A. The increased demand raises wages in the hotel industry. If hotel work is paying better than farm work, workers who can do both jobs will be inclined to work at hotels. Their move into hotel work decreases the supply of farm labor, as shown in panel B, raising wages in that labor market. Workers will continue moving from farms to hotels as long as they can earn better wages by switching from one market to the other. The process stops when farm wages rise to the same level as hotel wages.

In contrast, ups and downs in the supply of farm labor or hotel labor should have no effect on Mike Trout's salary for playing baseball. His job requires very different human capital. Workers compete only against those who have similar or substitutable human capital. When a worker has a rare skill or talent, supply in that labor market is low. When the rare skill contributes to the production of something that consumers value highly, like pitching scoreless innings, the value of the

FIGURE 16-9
Interconnected labor markets

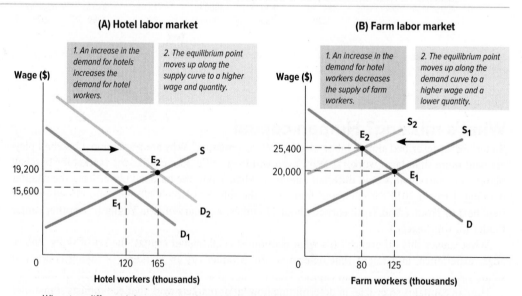

When two different jobs require workers with similar skill sets, a change in the demand for labor in one industry can affect the supply of labor in another. When the demand for hotel workers increases, as shown in panel A, workers who might have been indifferent between farm work and hotel work will shift toward hotel work. Their move to a different labor market will decrease the number of farm workers, shifting the farm labor supply curve left, as shown in panel B.

marginal product is high. Low supply and high demand leads to the equilibrium outcome we see in the Major League Baseball labor market: few workers and high wages.

✓ TEST YOURSELF

- ☐ What is the relationship between the value of the marginal product of labor, the wage, and the demand for labor? **[LO 16.2]**
- ☐ Under what circumstances might an increase in the wage decrease the labor supply? **[LO 16.3]**
- ☐ What happens to the equilibrium wage and quantity of labor when the demand for labor increases, holding all else equal? **[LO 16.4]**
- ☐ Which way does the labor supply curve shift after a population increase, holding all else equal? **[LO 16.5]**
- ☐ What are some ways that people can acquire human capital? **[LO 16.6]**

Land and Capital

We now turn from labor to the other two main factors of production: land and capital. If you were a farmer, would you be willing to pay as much for an acre of land in California's Sonoran Desert as you would for an acre of land in California's super-fertile Central Valley? If you owned a baseball team, would you pay as much for a stadium located 50 miles outside the city as you would for one in the heart of downtown? In both cases, one type of land has greater marginal productivity than the other. We can expect producers to pay more for land with higher productivity.

As these scenarios suggest, we can think about the markets for land and capital in a way that is very similar to our analysis of labor markets—with some differences. In this section, we'll examine a few features of the markets for land and capital that make them unique. We'll also look at how ownership of the different factors of production determines a person's income.

Capitalists: Who are they?

Capital is a tricky concept. Sometimes the word *capital* can mean physical capital, such as machinery. At other times it can mean financial capital, as in "She needs some start-up capital for her new business." Then, of course, there's human capital, which we discussed earlier.

These uses of the term are related. The reason the word *capital* sometimes refers to financial assets is that money can be invested in a business, which then uses the money to buy physical capital. Thus, a "capitalist" is someone who *owns physical capital.* Sometimes that ownership is direct, as in ownership of a factory. Often it is indirect, as in ownership of shares of stock, which represent partial ownership of a company and its physical capital.

In general, when people talk about investing, they mean that they have lent their money to someone who will use it to buy physical capital. Thus, anyone who puts money into the stock market, holds bonds or stocks, or opens a retirement account owns capital. This actually represents a sizable share of the population—by this definition, in the United States, just over half of Americans qualify as "capitalists."[5]

LO 16.7 Describe the similarities and differences between the markets for land and capital and the market for labor.

Markets for land and capital

Before we say anything else about the markets for land and capital, we should note one important difference from labor markets: When a firm wants to use land or capital, it has two choices—to buy or rent. When we talk about the price of land or capital, then, we need to distinguish between the rental price and the purchase price:

- The **rental price** is what a producer pays to use a factor of production for a certain period or task.
- The **purchase price** is what a producer pays to gain permanent ownership of a factor of production.

rental price
the price paid to use a factor of production for a certain period or task

purchase price
the price paid to gain permanent ownership of a factor of production

The rental price and the purchase price are both important concepts for understanding markets for land and capital.

Rental markets   The rental prices of land and capital are determined in the same way as the wage in a labor market:

- When Walmart hires a full-time cashier, Walmart is actually "renting" the cashier's labor for 40 hours a week.
- Walmart also is renting when it leases a new building or borrows money.
- When Walmart borrows money, the rental price of capital is the interest it pays on loans.

As with labor, the demand for land or capital is determined by the value of the marginal product (VMP) of each unit. No firm will rent land or machinery that contributes less to the firm's output than its rental cost.

On the other side of the market, the quantity of land or capital supplied depends on the other opportunities available for using them. The market equilibrium price and quantity in the rental market are determined by the intersection of supply and demand, just as in any other market.

economic rent
the gains that workers and owners of capital receive from supplying their labor or machinery in factor markets

In the markets for factors of production, economists use the phrase **economic rent** to describe the gains that workers and owners of capital receive from supplying their labor or machinery in factor markets. In the rental markets shown in Figure 16-10, the area above the supply curve but below the equilibrium rental price is economic rent. It represents the rental price of a factor of production minus the cost of supplying it. If Mike Trout is willing to play baseball for $30.083 million, the $4 million difference between this willingness to play and his actual salary of $34.083 million is economic rent earned by Trout.

The shaded area in Figure 16-10 may seem familiar to you: In Chapter 3, "Markets" (and elsewhere), we identified this as *producer surplus*. The concept is the same, but in the markets for factors of production, we use the term *economic rent*. Later, we'll discuss what role these gains (as part of something called the factor distribution of income) play in the economy.

Purchase markets   Renting land or capital allows a firm to use it for a certain period without worrying about its long-term value. In contrast, buying land or capital requires potential owners to think about an asset's long-run productivity.

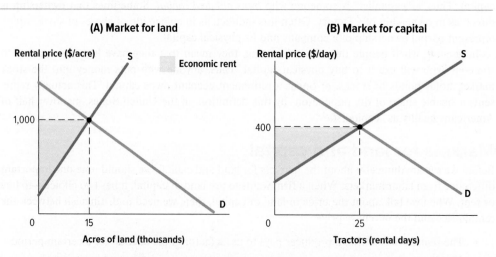

FIGURE 16-10

Economic rent in rental markets for land and capital

(A) Market for land

Rental price ($/acre)

Economic rent

1,000

S

D

0   15

Acres of land (thousands)

(B) Market for capital

Rental price ($/day)

400

S

D

0   25

Tractors (rental days)

Just as in the labor market, the rental markets for land and capital reach an equilibrium price and quantity at the point where the supply curve intersects the demand curve. The area above the supply curve and below the equilibrium rental price is called *economic rent*.

CAUTION: COMMON MISTAKE

Be careful not to confuse the term *economic rent* with the everyday usage of *rent*. The everyday use has a related but more general meaning: the money paid to landlords for the privilege of using their land or capital.

To determine the price they should pay for land or capital, potential buyers must forecast what its marginal product is likely to be over time. They can then assess the value of the expected future flows of income in order to compare them to the cost of the asset. (We explored the relevant tools in Chapter 11, "Time and Uncertainty.") Smart sellers will make similar calculations in order to calculate their own notion of a reasonable price.

The factor distribution of income

Most people own at least one factor of production. If you can work, you own your own labor, which you can rent to producers for a wage. Many people also own some capital or land. Ownership of these productive resources determines your income, which in turn determines your ability to consume goods and services. Who owns what, and how much income they receive from it, are therefore crucial questions.

Economists refer to the pattern of income that people derive from different factors of production as the *factor distribution of income*. In other words, the factor distribution of income shows how much income people get from labor compared to land and capital.

Figure 16-11 shows the U.S. factor distribution of income. In the United States, the majority of income—about 62 percent—comes from labor (shown in the figure as "compensation of employees"). Corporate profits, interest, and rent all go to owners of physical capital (including those who own physical capital by owning shares of stock). Proprietor income represents both the labor and capital factors that proprietors put into their businesses. Perhaps surprisingly, the factor distribution of income hasn't changed much in the last century, despite enormous changes in the economy and technology.

Big inequalities in earnings from the factors of production can sometimes seem unfair. Writing in the nineteenth century as new factories were transforming the economic landscape of Europe, Karl Marx unleashed his fury at the fact that workers earned so little relative to factory owners.

FIGURE 16-11

The factor distribution of income   In the United States, the majority of income comes from compensation for labor. Corporate profits, interest, and rent all go to owners of physical capital, while proprietor income goes to individual business owners for both the labor and capital put into their businesses.

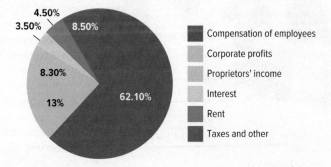

Source: Bureau of Economic Analysis, National Income and Product Accounts, www.bea.gov/iTable/iTable.cfmreqid=19&step=2#reqid=19&step=3&isuri=1&1921=survey&1903=53, Table 1.12.

To Marx, the owners of capital exploited those who earned their income through labor, and he urged workers to revolt against the capitalist system. Marx's ideas inspired some of the biggest political upheavals of the last two centuries, including revolutions in Europe, Russia, and China fought in the name of giving more power to workers. In each case, though, capitalism eventually returned as the dominant economic system.

The triumph of capitalism doesn't mean that all policy debates have ended. Marx's judgment was *normative*. His ideas differ from the *factual* analysis in this chapter of how income is determined in an efficient, competitive market—by the productivity of the land, labor, or capital that people own. That productivity, in turn, is defined by how much consumers will pay for the output the factors produce. Our aim is to describe how competitive factor markets allocate resources. Our analysis does not imply whether the existing factor distribution of income is, or is not, *fair* in a broader sense. You have to draw on your own values to answer for yourself whether it is right or wrong that Mike Trout and other professional athletes earn far more than a farm worker, or why owners of certain types of capital earn more than others.

For one example of a debate on the question of how productivity is rewarded, see the What Do You Think? box "Work, wages, and social value."

Work, wages, and social value
What Do You Think?

In most professions, people are comfortable with the idea that workers are paid according to their productivity. For example, we tend to accept that exceptionally talented professional baseball (and football, basketball, hockey, and soccer) players will earn more than their teammates, that lawyers who regularly win tough cases will charge more than other lawyers, and that salespeople who bring in lots of revenue to a firm will be rewarded accordingly. In general, we see higher pay as both a reward and an incentive for higher productivity.

In some professions, however, pay for performance may seem out of keeping with the nature of the work. For example, the idea that a pastor should be paid for each new member she brings into a congregation might strike some people as odd. That's not to say it doesn't happen, though. Looking at records from United Methodist churches in Oklahoma, researchers at the University of North Carolina found that, on average, pastors received a pay increase equal to 3 percent of the revenues generated by the new members they brought into the church. That is comparable to how much of the salary of Fortune 500 CEOs depends on their own company performance—although the typical pastor's salary is much lower.

Opinion is divided over whether teachers should be paid for how their students perform on standardized tests.
©*Monkey Business Images/Shutterstock*

Debates over performance pay are especially heated when it comes to teachers. Almost everywhere in the United States, teachers earn a salary that depends mainly on their years of experience. Proponents of performance pay say that teachers should be compensated largely in proportion to the results their students achieve, as measured through standardized tests. They argue that such a system rewards good teachers and encourages them to work hard. Opponents say that performance pay encourages teachers to focus too much on test scores, distracting them from teaching deeper concepts and helping struggling students.

A related debate focuses on the salaries of workers in nonprofit organizations, especially those that assist the poor. Some people argue that rewarding good performance with high salaries attracts the best workers; those workers make nonprofits more effective at doing good for those in need of help. Opponents counter that it is inappropriate for workers in nonprofits to earn so much more than those they serve, and that the resulting income gap can make it difficult for nonprofit workers to understand their clients' situation.

WHAT DO YOU THINK?

1. Do you think that people should accept performance pay in some professions but not in others?
2. Would performance pay for teachers be less controversial if it were easier to get a more complete picture of performance, in such areas as helping students develop rounded personalities and inspiring learning?
3. Would stronger financial incentives change the fundamental nature of social professions such as teaching and preaching? Might that be a good thing? What might be lost?

Source: www.slate.com/id/2258794.

✓ TEST YOURSELF

☐ What is the difference between the rental price and the purchase price of capital? **[LO 16.7]**
☐ How is physical capital related to financial capital? **[LO 16.7]**

Real-World Labor Markets

We've now looked at the main factors of production—labor, land, and capital, as well as human capital. For the rest of the chapter, we'll return to labor, to see how the real world looks in relation to the model of perfectly competitive labor markets we outlined above. One important dimension we consider here is the role of government policy. Another is the power of bosses or unions to influence market outcomes. Still another dimension is created by changes in population size.

The simple model of perfect competition in labor markets provides an important benchmark, and here we enrich the picture to describe realities that you'll probably encounter throughout your working life.

Minimum wages and efficiency wages

The model of labor supply and demand we outlined earlier in this chapter does a good job of explaining the most important determinants of wages. It gives a reasonably accurate picture of competitive labor markets. However, two notable exceptions to the model—minimum wages and efficiency wages—can push wage rates above the market equilibrium point.

In the United States, the federal government requires that all employers pay all workers a wage that is at or above a certain minimum rate (as of January 2018, $7.25 per hour). Some state governments impose even higher minimum wages (as of January 2018, up to $11 per hour in the state of California).[6] And some cities have pushed minimum wages up to $15 per hour.

Minimum wages are a controversial topic. Supporters usually argue that a minimum wage is needed to guarantee workers an acceptable standard of living. Opponents see a minimum wage as

LO 16.8 Describe two reasons why a wage might rise above the market equilibrium and how this affects the labor market.

a form of government interference in the free market; they contend that it raises the cost of doing business, causing unemployment in the process. As economic analysts, how can we weigh these opposing claims?

First, we need to separate positive arguments from normative arguments. Let's start by asking what effect we would expect a minimum-wage law to have on the labor market. Minimum-wage laws are examples of price floors, discussed in Chapter 6, "Government Intervention." Imposing a price floor causes the quantity demanded to decrease and the quantity supplied to increase, compared with equilibrium levels. In other words, more people are willing to work than there are jobs available, causing unemployment. This situation is shown in Figure 16-12. Imposing a price floor is good news for the people who keep their jobs, and bad news for the people who were employed at the equilibrium wage but are not employed after the minimum wage is imposed.

The evidence on how minimum wage laws affect the real world is mixed. In some cases, a minimum wage causes some unemployment. In others, the biggest impact is on *who* is employed. Since higher-skilled workers become cheaper relative to low-skilled workers when the minimum wage increases, employers might hire more skilled and experienced workers, and fewer young and unskilled workers. Whether or not you think that result is a good one is a normative question, which we will leave to your own judgment.

These impacts also depend on the local market; not all states, cities, and towns are alike in costs of living and in local market conditions. As a result, a $15 minimum wage that wins support in a high-cost city like San Francisco could create real problems for businesses and workers in low-cost small towns elsewhere.

We note that this analysis assumes that the labor market starts out being perfectly efficient, an assumption about which some economists disagree. If the market is already inefficient and the minimum wage is below the equilibrium level, a minimum wage might *not* cause unemployment. The minimum wage might instead transfer surplus from employers to workers. (For one example of inefficient labor markets, see the discussion of monopsony in the next section.)

Evaluating the impact of minimum wage policies depends on how you look at the issue, and the size and scope of the change in the market. Like so many other issues presented in the text, evaluating minimum-wage policy also depends on normative ideas of how to distribute surplus. In the end, most policy-makers have decided that some disruption in the market is worth ensuring a basic standard of living for low-wage workers.

FIGURE 16-12
The minimum wage

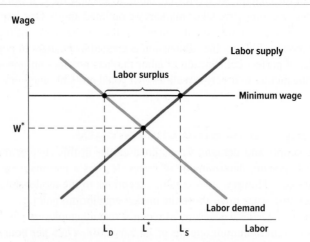

When people are willing to supply more labor than firms are willing to hire, the labor market has a surplus of workers, which is also known as unemployment.

Another reason that wages might rise above market equilibrium is that some employers may voluntarily choose to pay workers more to increase their productivity. Economists call this arrangement an **efficiency wage**. There are two ways in which an efficiency wage might increase workers' productivity. First, earning more than the market wage gives workers an incentive to stay with the firm. Thus, the firm gets to hold onto experienced, well-trained workers, rather than repeatedly having to spend time and resources to train new employees.

The second reason is an extension of the first. If workers have a lot to lose by leaving the firm, they will work hard to avoid getting fired. Efficiency wages make sense when a boss cannot constantly supervise workers—say, a shop owner who visits only a couple of times a week. If a salesperson at the shop receives the market wage, she may take the risk of slacking off since if she's caught, she can hope to get another job at an equivalent wage. But if the salesperson receives a wage sufficiently larger than the going market rate, even the small probability that the boss might catch her slacking off carries a higher potential cost. She'd be fired from an especially rewarding job.

In the end, workers respond to incentives, and when it becomes more costly to leave or get fired from a job, employees are going to work harder to stay. This is good for both sides. While businesses get more productive workers, employees also get a higher wage. This is why efficiency wages have been used from the first assembly line (Henry Ford offered his workers double the going wage in 1914) to the market for high-powered lawyers today.

That said, efficiency wages are a great deal only for workers who get them. The use of efficiency wages creates unemployment by keeping wages above the equilibrium wage level, similar to the way minimum wage laws can create unemployment. If you have a well-paying job, you'll be happy. But if you're unemployed and struggling to find a job, you will probably view the existence of efficiency wages with a wary eye.

> **efficiency wage**
> a wage that is deliberately set above the market rate to increase worker productivity

Company towns, unions, and labor laws

Just as the markets for goods and services aren't always perfectly competitive, neither are labor markets. In some real-world labor markets, *employers* have market power, pushing wages down to capture more surplus. In other labor markets, *workers* have market power, pushing wages up. In addition, government regulation of the workplace can impose costs or friction on a market.

Let's first consider the scenario in which employers have market power. Normally, we would call a firm with market power a monopolist or an oligopolist. But because firms are the buyers in this situation (remember, they are buying labor in the labor market), we need a new term. A market in which there is only one buyer but many sellers is called a **monopsony**. Whereas a monopolist can maintain a price *higher* than the price in a competitive market, a monopsonistic employer can push wages (that is, the price of labor) *lower* than the competitive level.

To see how the idea of monopsony applies in today's labor market, read the Economics in Action box "Have noncompete clauses gone too far?"

> **LO 16.9** Describe several causes of imperfectly competitive labor markets and their effect on workers and employers.

> **monopsony**
> a market in which there is only one buyer but many sellers

Have noncompete clauses gone too far?

Economics in Action

Leinani Deslandes had dreams of one day owning her own McDonald's franchise. She looked forward to flying to Illinois to attend a week at Hamburger University, the training program for McDonald's managers. Deslandes knew that attending Hamburger U. would help her advance as a manager at her local McDonald's near Orlando, Florida. But Deslandes's bosses cancelled the trip when she became pregnant.

(continued)

Deslandes was ambitious and undeterred; she tried to move to a nearby McDonald's location for a job with greater upward potential. Seems like a win-win, right? Deslandes would keep moving forward, while her new employer would get an experienced and dedicated employee. The other franchise, however, told Deslandes that it could not hire her. The problem was a legal agreement between owners of different McDonald's franchises; they were bound by a so-called "noncompete clause" that restricted hiring employees from other McDonald's locations.

Noncompete clauses are common throughout the economy. At one time, they mainly applied to CEOs and top executives who had sensitive information about companies' inner workings. Now, however, they also apply to the workers at the cash register or local store managers. Research by economists Orley Ashenfelter and Alan Krueger (a former top White House advisor) found that a quarter of the 70,000 restaurants in the United States are covered by such agreements. Companies argue that the clauses help to slow high employee turnover, limit the costs of training new employees, and protect trade secrets.

But to Deslandes, the noncompete clause didn't seem fair. She felt she had a right to work wherever she was qualified. Deslandes joined other restaurant workers in a lawsuit charging that noncompete clauses unfairly restrict their rights. The workers argued that the restrictions constrain the labor market and lock them into lower paying jobs. It is, in effect, a kind of monopsony.

Policy-makers took a deeper look. In July 2018, seven fast-food outlets in Washington State agreed to end the use of noncompete clauses, and other states took notice. McDonald's voluntarily dropped noncompete clauses from future contracts.

This story goes well beyond fast food. When unemployment is low, as it was in 2018, increased demand for labor should push wages upward. Yet in many places, wage growth has been sluggish. As a result, economists have been asking, along with Leinani Deslandes, whether markets are working as efficiently as they should. After all, when labor markets are efficient, not only is talent allocated to its best uses, but people like Leinani Deslandes get a fairer shot at their ambitions.

Sources: Rachel Abrams, "Why aren't paychecks growing? A burger-joint clause offers a clue," *The New York Times*, September 27, 2017, www.nytimes.com/2017/09/27/business/pay-growth-fast-food-hiring.html; Kyle Arnold, "Apopka McDonald's employee sues over noncompete," *Orlando Sentinel*, September 29, 2017, www.orlandosentinel.com/business/consumer/os-bz-mcdonalds-noncompete-20170929-story.html.

Sometimes, a firm that is the largest employer in a region, or one of only a few major employers, can gain market power. Historically, such situations arose when a town sprang up around the worksite for a major company. These "company towns" were common in Appalachia, where coal mines or steel plants were the main source of jobs. Often, the company literally owned everything in town, including the grocery store. More recent, less extreme examples include Detroit, with its reliance on the success of the Big Three car companies, and Redmond, Washington, home to Microsoft.

Workers also can gain market power. When they do, they can push wages higher than the market equilibrium. Gaining market power requires that workers join together to make a collective decision about when to supply their labor, much like a cartel in the market for commodities. Labor unions are the usual mechanism for organizing workers in this way. To raise wages (or improve nonwage benefits) and capture some surplus for workers, unions must have a monopoly or near-monopoly on labor in a particular market. Otherwise, competition for jobs will push wages back down to the market equilibrium level, just as in a competitive market for goods.

The 2018 Supreme Court ruling that public-sector unions can't force all employees to join the union and pay union dues hit unions hard, hurting their efforts to negotiate with a unified voice. Teachers unions across the country lost one of their most powerful weapons, and the implications remain unclear. When unions lack a monopoly or near-monopoly their threats can sound empty. One example of the importance of union monopoly was demonstrated during the 1987 NFL strike. The NFL football players union did not include all professional players (nor all

FIGURE 16-13

Major labor laws of the twentieth century

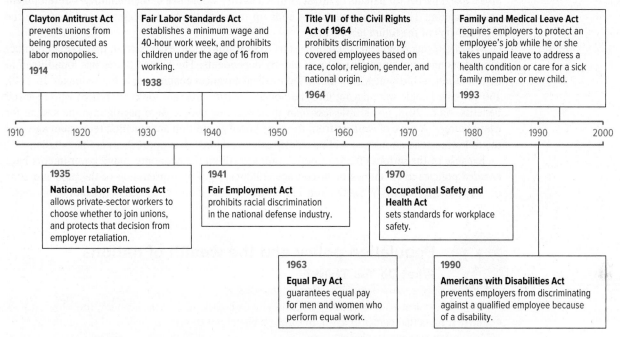

Clayton Antitrust Act
prevents unions from being prosecuted as labor monopolies.
1914

Fair Labor Standards Act
establishes a minimum wage and 40-hour work week, and prohibits children under the age of 16 from working.
1938

Title VII of the Civil Rights Act of 1964
prohibits discrimination by covered employees based on race, color, religion, gender, and national origin.
1964

Family and Medical Leave Act
requires employers to protect an employee's job while he or she takes unpaid leave to address a health condition or care for a sick family member or new child.
1993

1910   1920   1930   1940   1950   1960   1970   1980   1990   2000

1935
National Labor Relations Act
allows private-sector workers to choose whether to join unions, and protects that decision from employer retaliation.

1941
Fair Employment Act
prohibits racial discrimination in the national defense industry.

1970
Occupational Safety and Health Act
sets standards for workplace safety.

1963
Equal Pay Act
guarantees equal pay for men and women who perform equal work.

1990
Americans with Disabilities Act
prevents employers from discriminating against a qualified employee because of a disability.

Sources: www.bls.gov/opub/mlr/2015/article/labor-law-highlights-1915-2015.htm; http://library.gsu.edu/search-collections/special-collections-archives/southern-labor-archives.

potential players), so when the football players went on strike, team owners simply found replacement players to take their place. Although fans weren't entirely convinced by the new players, the games were still aired on TV; teams and owners still made money. The striking NFL players realized that if their union lacked monopoly power, the league could move on without them. That realization helped convince the players to end the strike.

In general, the larger the membership of a union, the more power it has. For this reason, unions often span multiple labor markets. The AFL-CIO, the largest union organization in the United States, is a confederation of unions that represents 12.5 million workers, ranging from pilots and bricklayers to actors and police officers. Other large union federations include AFGE (American Federation of Government Employees), the union that represents federal government workers, the NEA (National Education Association), which represents workers in many different parts of the education sector, and AFSCME (American Federation of State, County and Municipal Employees), the largest union of public-sector workers.

Finally, government intervention in the labor market can cause wages and employment to move away from the market equilibrium, much as in the markets for goods and services. We have already discussed the minimum wage. Other types of regulation, summarized in Figure 16-13, can also affect the labor market. Regulations such as standards to ensure that workers won't be injured at work are relatively uncontroversial. But they do impose some costs, moving away from the efficient equilibrium.

Changing demographics

Earlier in this chapter, we saw how immigration can affect the labor market. Rising or falling birth rates also have a profound effect on the overall supply of labor and economic growth. Countries with a declining population may have too few workers to power production and too few consumers to drive a healthy demand for goods and services.

Excessive population growth is a concern as well. Overpopulation can strain the environment and limit the government's ability to pay for education and other services. High birth rates can also make it harder for parents to invest as much as they would like in their children's development and education. This lack of investment ends up reducing the human capital (and therefore the productivity) of the future labor force.

When growing populations suddenly start to slow down, the result is often that a small number of workers ends up supporting a lot of elderly dependents. The United States has found itself in this situation, as birth rates have fallen and medical advances enable people to live longer: In 1940, 160 working people were paying into the Social Security program for every retiree who received benefits. As of 2018, just a little less than three working people were paying into the system for every retiree.[7] A wave of workers from the baby boom generation are reaching retirement age, and the following generations that will be entering the workforce to support them are far smaller.

Because of the serious effects of population growth on the economy, many governments have enacted policies to encourage or discourage childbearing. For a discussion of the pros and cons of such policies, see the What Do You Think? box "Population policy and the wealth of nations."

Population policy and the wealth of nations
What Do You Think?

When you look at a newborn baby, the child's future contribution to the economy probably is not the first thing that comes to mind. But today's birth rates determine the size of the future labor force, so many countries have adopted policies to encourage or discourage births.

Many European countries have negative population growth rates; each year more people die than babies are born. This drives European governments to encourage couples to have more children by subsidizing day care, granting generous parental leave from work, and offering tax credits for children. Russia has even created a special government award, called the "Order of Parental Glory," for parents with eight or more kids.

China faced the opposite problem: a population explosion that threatened to outstrip the country's ability to feed and house all its citizens. From 1979 to the end of 2015, China enforced a one-child policy. Under that policy, those who lived in urban areas faced heavy fees if they chose to bear more than one child. (Effective January 1, 2016, China changed to a two-child policy.)

The one-child policy was controversial, but there's little argument about its contribution to curbing the country's population growth. In 1950, the average Chinese woman had six children; under the one-child policy, the average was just under two. The country's income has grown more than 2,000 percent in two generations. Some attribute China's incredible economic growth, in part, to its population policy. (The population policy may have led to higher investments in human capital of children, and also allowed parents to work more.)

Population policies can have some serious side effects. In China and India, local government officials have reportedly used harsh means to lower birth rates, such as intimidation and forced sterilization. In places where having sons is culturally important, some women have sex-selective abortions or even practice female infanticide to ensure that their child will be male. Opponents of China's one-child policy pointed to a growing gender imbalance: By 2020, men will outnumber women in China by an estimated 24 million. Defenders of the law, on the other hand, argue that it allowed China to avoid the worst strains of overpopulation and encouraged families to invest fully in children's education.

WHAT DO YOU THINK?

1. Is it right for the government to discourage or encourage couples to bear children for economic reasons? How would you weigh the importance of lifting people out of poverty against the right to privacy and self-determination?

2. If the government is going to play a role in influencing population growth, what sort of policy might be appropriate? What kind of policy would cross the line?

3. What alternative to the one-child policy might China have had? What kind of policy would you propose for a country that has serious concerns about the economic effects of overpopulation?

Sources: http://data.un.org/Data.aspx? q=china&d=PopDiv&f=variableID%3A54%3BcrID%3A156%2C948; http://news.bbc.co.uk/2/hi/8451289.stm.

✓ TEST YOURSELF

☐ Why might an employer choose to pay an efficiency wage? **[LO 16.8]**

☐ What would you expect to happen to wages in a monopsonistic labor market? **[LO 16.9]**

☐ If birth rates go up, what happens to the size of the labor force in the future? **[LO 16.9]**

Conclusion

Why do some people earn more than others? That is one of the most fundamental questions in economics and politics. When markets are competitive, everyone earns income in proportion to the productivity of the factors of production they control. For most people, that means their income is based on their own productivity as workers. That's usually closely tied to the skills, education, and other talents that determine our human capital. For farmers, the productivity of land matters as well. For investors, income is determined by the productivity of their financial capital. Competitive markets have the remarkable ability to reward work according to what is contributed to the economy.

We've seen that we can use the familiar tools of supply and demand to put prices on the factors of production. We also examined how business owners decide how much of each factor to use in producing goods and services. Their choice is driven by both the marginal productivity and the price of each factor.

In future chapters we'll return to the markets for land, labor, and capital, to see what happens when we add public policy and collective decision making to the picture.

Key Terms

factors of production, p. 384

capital, p. 384

marginal product, p. 385

value of the marginal product, p. 387

human capital, p. 399

rental price, p. 401

purchase price, p. 401

economic rent, p. 402

efficiency wage, p. 407

monopsony, p. 407

Summary

LO 16.1 Describe how factors of production contribute to output.

The ingredients that are used to make a good or service are called factors of production. We can divide factors of production into three major categories: land, labor, and

capital (a previously produced good that can be used to produce a new good). Factors of production are rented, bought, and sold in markets, at prices and in quantities that are determined by supply and demand. Firms choose to produce using the combination of factors that will maximize their profit.

LO 16.2 Graph the demand curve for a factor of production, and explain its relationship to marginal productivity.

The demand for factors of production is determined by their contribution to the value of a firm's output. We can use the marginal product of labor (or land or capital) to measure the increase in output gained by using one more unit of a factor of production. Thus, the value of the marginal product of labor is the revenue that is generated by an additional worker.

Firms will hire workers up to the point where the wage equals the value of the marginal product of labor (where marginal revenue equals marginal cost). If we graph the value of the marginal product against the number of workers, we get a downward-sloping relationship that is the same as the demand curve for labor.

LO 16.3 Graph the supply curve for a factor of production, and explain what determines the supply of labor.

The supply of a factor of production is driven by the opportunity cost of using that factor in a given market. The opportunity cost of supplying labor in a particular labor market is the time you would otherwise have spent on leisure or working at another job.

An increase in wages has two effects on the labor supply, a price effect and an income effect. The *price effect* causes the quantity of labor supplied to increase, all else held equal. The *income effect* decreases the labor supply, as workers demand more leisure time. In general, the price effect outweighs the income effect, which means that the labor supply curve slopes upward.

LO 16.4 Explain how to find the equilibrium price and quantity for a factor of production.

Factor markets reach equilibrium at the point where the demand curve intersects the supply curve, and the quantity demanded equals the quantity supplied at a given price or wage.

LO 16.5 Use graphs to demonstrate the effect of a shift in labor supply or labor demand, and describe what causes these curves to shift.

If the underlying determinants of supply or demand change, the equilibrium point can shift. The determinants of labor demand include anything that affects the value of the marginal product, including the supply of other factors, changes in technology, and output prices. The determinants of labor supply include culture, population, and the availability of other opportunities.

LO 16.6 Explain the importance of human capital in the labor market.

In addition to the three primary factors of production, economists note a fourth critically important factor, human capital. *Human capital* is the set of skills, knowledge, experience, and talent that goes into the work people do. Workers differ from one another because they have different amounts and types of human capital to offer, which allow them to be more or less productive than others at different tasks. Some types of human capital make workers more productive at a wide range of jobs; others relate to very specific tasks. Differences in human capital are a key determinant of wages, and therefore of differences in people's incomes.

LO 16.7 Describe the similarities and differences between the markets for land and capital and the market for labor.

The markets for land and capital are similar to markets for labor, with the major difference being that land and capital can be purchased as well as rented. The *rental price* is what a producer pays to use a factor for a certain period or task; the *purchase price* is what a producer pays to gain permanent ownership.

The word *capital* is often used loosely to refer to financial capital as well as physical capital. When people invest money in the stock market or a company, they are using financial capital to purchase a share of the company's physical capital.

LO 16.8 Describe two reasons why a wage might rise above the market equilibrium and how this affects the labor market.

There are two common reasons for a wage to rise above the market equilibrium: minimum wages and efficiency wages. A *minimum wage* is a price floor on the price of labor. In an efficient labor market, a price floor causes excess supply and unemployment. An *efficiency wage* is an above-market equilibrium wage that an employer voluntarily pays to employees to increase their productivity.

LO 16.9 Describe several causes of imperfectly competitive labor markets and their effect on workers and employers.

Just as the markets for goods and services are not always perfectly competitive, neither are labor markets. When a labor market has only one employer but many workers, the employer is called a *monopsonist*. A monopsonist has the market power to push wages below market equilibrium.

Workers can also gain market power, by banding together to make joint labor supply decisions and push their wages above equilibrium. Through regulations, government can also impose costs on labor markets.

Review Questions

1. Consider the factors of production that go into a fast-food restaurant. Give an example of land, labor, and capital. **[LO 16.1]**

2. Suppose an auto manufacturer has one factory in the United States and one in Mexico. The auto manufacturer produces the same number of cars and the same models in each factory but hires more workers in Mexico than in the United States. Give an explanation for the discrepancy in the amount of labor hired in each location. **[LO 16.1]**

3. Suppose you run a flower-delivery business and employ college students to drive the vans and make deliveries. You are considering hiring an additional worker. What information would you need to know to decide whether doing so would increase or decrease your profit? **[LO 16.2]**

4. Christina runs an IT consulting firm in a competitive market. She recently determined that hiring an additional consultant would mean that she would be able to serve five more clients per week. Assuming her goal is to maximize her profits, explain why Christina did not hire another consultant. **[LO 16.2]**

5. Suppose your retired grandmother has complained of boredom and is considering taking a part-time job. Use the concept of opportunity cost to advise your grandmother how to decide whether to take the job. **[LO 16.3]**

6. Jack and Sam are both nurses at the same hospital. Jack and Sam have the same duties, experience, and performance reviews. Give an example that explains why Sam makes more than Jack for the same job. **[LO 16.3]**

7. Suppose BMW runs a great ad campaign that increases demand and drives up the price of BMWs. What do you expect will happen to the demand for the labor in auto-manufacturing plants? Explain how the equilibrium price and quantity of labor will change. **[LO 16.4]**

8. Suppose a café owner wants to switch to automatic espresso machines instead of paying baristas to pack the coffee grounds by hand. The machines are twice as effective as a human; the fixed cost per machine equals the yearly wage of one employee. Explain how the equilibrium price and quantity of labor will change. **[LO 16.4]**

9. Leo runs a bicycle repair shop. He recently examined information on wage and employment levels and noted that he employs the same number of workers today that he employed in 2012. However, wages (controlling for inflation) increased quite substantially between 2012 and 2016. Assume the supply of labor remained constant over this time period. Give two possible explanations for why Leo's workers are paid more in 2016. **[LO 16.5]**

10. Consider a labor market that traditionally discriminates against hiring women. Suppose a new law effectively prohibits this practice. What would you expect to happen to the wages of men in this industry? **[LO 16.5]**

11. Suppose your friend wants to become a doctor. Describe some of the human capital required to achieve this goal. **[LO 16.6]**

12. Madison has a full-time job, but she is considering going back to school for a master's degree. Describe how Madison might decide whether or not to continue her education. **[LO 16.6]**

13. Alexis is shopping for a space to open a new restaurant. There are two options in the target neighborhood. One space is available for lease and the other for purchase. How would you advise Alexis to think through the choice of restaurant location? What factors should be considered? **[LO 16.7]**

14. Suppose you have inherited a few acres of land from a relative and you are considering what to do with your inheritance. A farmer with land next to yours offers to buy your acres so he can expand his grazing area. How will you decide whether to sell your land to the farmer? What factors should you consider? **[LO 16.7]**

15. Large telecom companies like AT&T routinely send repair technicians to customers' homes. Although they are skilled laborers, they must usually train on the job, so it takes some time for them to reach a high standard of quality. In addition, their work cannot be constantly supervised. Explain why an efficiency wage could help telecom companies to increase the productivity of repair techs. **[LO 16.8]**

16. The Coalition of Immokalee Workers (CIW) claims that the going wage for farm labor is exploitative. The CIW supports a minimum wage for farm workers. Explain how the minimum wage would affect a farm's hiring decision. Are farm workers better off under this policy? **[LO 16.8]**

17. Suppose a new law passes requiring farms to provide health benefits to farm labor. Assume that workers value having health benefits. When the new law goes into effect, what will happen to the wage for farm labor at equilibrium? Now suppose farm workers place no value on health benefits. How does this affect your answer? **[LO 16.9]**

18. Suppose a group of high school friends work at the same fast-food restaurant. They all dislike the manager because she doesn't allow them to swap shifts with one another whenever someone has a big exam to study for or a date. One of the friends suggests that they all agree to walk out if the manager doesn't change her policy. Explain whether the manager will change her policy to avoid a walkout. **[LO 16.9]**

Problems and Applications

1. Recently, some college alumni started a moving service for students living on campus. They have three employees and are debating hiring a fourth. The hourly wage for an employee is $18 per hour. An average moving job takes four hours. The company currently does three moving jobs per week, but with one more employee, the company could manage five jobs per week. The company charges $80 for a moving job. **[LO 16.1, 16.2]**

   a. What would be the new employee's marginal product of labor?

   b. What is the value of that marginal product?

   c. Should the moving service hire a fourth worker?

2. Fresh Veggie is one of many small farms in Florida operating in a perfectly competitive market. Farm labor is also perfectly competitive, and Fresh Veggie can hire as many workers as it wants for $20 a day. The daily productivity of a tomato picker is given in Table 16P-1. If a bushel of tomatoes sells for $6, how many workers will Fresh Veggie hire? **[LO 16.1, 16.2]**

TABLE 16P-1

Labor	Bushels of tomatoes	MP of Labor	VMPL
0	0	—	—
1	12		
2	22		
3	30		
4	35		
5	38		
6	40		

3. Sasha has 60 hours a week she can work or have leisure. Wages are $8/hour. **[LO 16.3]**

   a. Graph Sasha's budget constraint for income and leisure.

   b. Suppose wages increase to $10/hour. Graph Sasha's new budget constraint.

   c. When wages increase from $8/hour to $10/hour, Sasha's leisure time decreases from 20 hours to 15 hours. Does her labor supply curve slope upward or downward over this wage increase?

4. Dalip's labor supply curve is graphed in Figure 16P-1. **[LO 16.3]**

FIGURE 16P-1

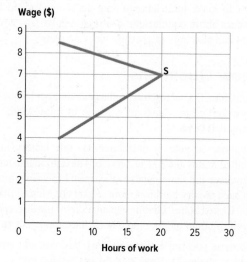

a. Consider a wage increase from $5 to $6. For Dalip, does the price effect or income effect dominate his labor supply decision?

b. Consider a wage increase from $7 to $8. For Dalip, does the price effect or income effect dominate his labor supply decision?

5. Suppose you run a business that specializes in producing graphic T-shirts, using labor as an input. Based on Table 16P-2, graph the labor supply and demand curves and identify the market equilibrium wage and quantity of labor hours. **[LO 16.4]**

TABLE 16P-2

Hourly wage ($)	Labor hours demanded	Labor hours supplied
24	0	600
22	50	550
20	100	500
18	150	450
16	200	400
14	250	350
12	300	300
10	350	250
8	400	200

6. Based on Table 16P-3, indicate what would happen in this labor market at various wage rates by selecting one of the three choices shown for each item. **[LO 16.4]**

TABLE 16P-3

Wage ($)	Quantity supplied	Quantity demanded
3	2,000	5,000
4	3,000	4,500
5	4,000	4,000
6	5,000	3,500
7	6,000	3,000
8	7,000	2,500
9	8,000	2,000

  a. At $8/hour: excess labor supply; excess labor demand; or equilibrium.

  b. At $3/hour: excess labor supply; excess labor demand; or equilibrium.

  c. At $5/hour: excess labor supply; excess labor demand; or equilibrium.

7. Identify which way the labor supply curve would shift under the following scenarios. **[LO 16.5]**

  a. A country experiences a huge influx of immigrants who are skilled in the textile industry.

  b. Wages increase in an industry that requires similar job skills.

  c. New machines require additional maintenance over time, so that the marginal productivity of labor rises.

8. Figure 16P-2 shows the supply and demand for labor in the textile industry. In each of the following scenarios, identify the direction of the shift in either the supply or demand curve and state whether the resulting equilibrium wage and quantity *increase* or *decrease*. **[LO 16.5]**

FIGURE 16P-2

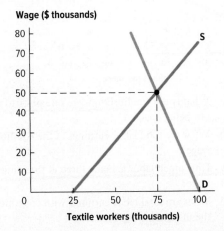

a. What are the original equilibrium wage and quantity?

b. Immigration and layoffs from other jobs increase the population of textile workers.

c. A new technology for making self-printed T-shirts reduces the marginal product of labor for textile workers.

9. Figure 16P-3 shows the supply and demand for labor in the hybrid automobile industry. In each of the following scenarios, identify the direction of the shift in either the supply or demand curve, and state whether the resulting equilibrium wage and quantity *increase* or *decrease*. **[LO 16.5]**

FIGURE 16P-3

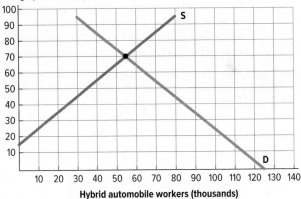

a. A new tool is invented that increases each worker's marginal product.

b. The demand for hybrid cars increases.

10. Suppose that fast-food chains start using healthier ingredients, increasing the demand for fast food and therefore for food-service workers, as shown in Figure 16P-4. **[LO 16.6]**

FIGURE 16P-4

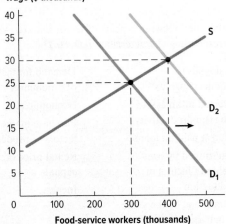

a. What are the new equilibrium wage and quantity of labor in the fast-food industry?

b. Assume that the skills required of a sales clerk at a retail store are similar to those required of workers at a fast-food restaurant. If workers are completely indifferent between fast-food jobs and retail-sales jobs, what will be the wages for sales clerks?

11. Suppose a town's largest employers are its auto manufacturing plant and its airplane manufacturing plant. Airplane manufacturing jobs require familiarity with a technology that is not currently used in auto manufacturing. Assume workers are indifferent between the two types of manufacturing work. **[LO 16.6]**

   a. All else equal, which plant will pay its workers more?

   b. Suppose the auto industry adopts the same technology used by airplane manufacturers and trains its current workers in this technology. What will happen to the pay differential between auto manufacturing and airplane manufacturing work?

12. Figure 16P-5 shows a local labor market for landscapers. What is the value of economic rent in this labor market? **[LO 16.7]**

FIGURE 16P-5

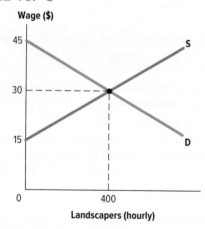

13. Match the following aspects of factor markets with the corresponding characteristics. **[LO 16.7]**

a. analogous to producer surplus

b. affected by an asset's long-run productivity

c. interest paid on loans

d. determined by ownership of factors of production

e. determined by the value of marginal product

_____Demand for factors of production

_____Economic rent

_____Purchase markets for factors of production

_____Rental price of capital

_____Income

14. Figure 16P-6 shows a local labor market for mechanics. What are the quantity supplied and quantity demanded when the minimum wage is each of the following? **[LO 16.8]**

FIGURE 16P-6

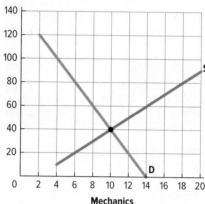

a. $20,000.

b. $40,000.

c. $60,000.

15. The market for grocery-store baggers is a competitive labor market, as shown in Figure 16P-7. Suppose a new federal law raises the minimum wage to $10 per hour. **[LO 16.8]**

FIGURE 16P-7

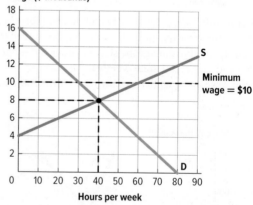

a. What is the equilibrium wage rate prior to the law being enacted?

b. What are total labor earnings at the equilibrium wage?

c. How much labor is being hired at the minimum wage?

d. What are total labor earnings with enactment of the minimum wage?

16. Imagine that, faced with budget shortfalls, a government changes its current policy of granting tax credits based on family size to a flat rate tax credit for a family with one or more children. **[LO 16.9]**

    a. Over time, what will happen to the average age in the population?

    b. Over time, what will happen to the size of the workforce?

17. In each scenario, will wages rise above the market equilibrium or fall below it? **[LO 16.9]**

    a. All but one of the factories in a town go out of business.

    b. All the software engineers in Silicon Valley organize into a union and go on strike.

    c. A major grocery store chain buys out all the other stores in the city.

Endnotes

1. https://www.spotrac.com/mlb/los-angeles-angels-of-anaheim/payroll/; https://www.bls.gov/oes/current/oes452099.htm.

2. http://www.ers.usda.gov/topics/farm-economy/farm-labor.aspx.

3. https://www.usatoday.com/story/sports/mlb/2017/12/22/players-union-end-of-year-average-mlb-salary-a-record-4m/108856114/.

4. http://www.wsj.com/articles/the-thorny-economics-of-illegal-immigration-1454984443.

5. https://news.gallup.com/poll/190883/half-americans-own-stocks-matching-record-low.aspx.

6. www.paywizard.org/main/salary/minimum-wage; www.wsj.com/articles/a-better-minimum-wage-1533682675.

7. https://www.ssa.gov/news/press/basicfact.html.

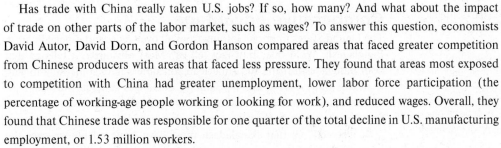

International Trade

A New Meaning to "Made in the USA"

"Made in China." That label can be found on computers, TVs, clothes, shoes, car parts, and even garlic. In 2017, the United States imported over $500 billion worth of goods from China, a volume 55 times larger than in 1985. At the same time, U.S. manufacturing has declined dramatically. In the 1950s, over 30 percent of working-age adults were employed in manufacturing. By 2015, manufacturing employed less than 10 percent.

©Feng Yu/Alamy

In a 2015 interview on *Good Morning America*, Donald Trump (before he became U.S. President) made a clear link between these two trends. He described it as "the greatest theft in the history of the world. . . . They have taken our jobs."

Has trade with China really taken U.S. jobs? If so, how many? And what about the impact of trade on other parts of the labor market, such as wages? To answer this question, economists David Autor, David Dorn, and Gordon Hanson compared areas that faced greater competition from Chinese producers with areas that faced less pressure. They found that areas most exposed to competition with China had greater unemployment, lower labor force participation (the percentage of working-age people working or looking for work), and reduced wages. Overall, they found that Chinese trade was responsible for one quarter of the total decline in U.S. manufacturing employment, or 1.53 million workers.

While increased trade with China has clearly cost jobs, the amount of pain caused by these changes depends on how easy it is to adjust to the new reality. The researchers found that adjusting has often been hard. One sign is that government transfer payments from Social Security disability, Medicare, and unemployment insurance increased in areas most exposed to Chinese trade. These payments reflect the fact that many factory workers have a hard time finding new work in their local economy. The workers most affected by the changes are those who are least likely to move to areas with more opportunity.

At the same time, American consumers benefit from a wide variety of goods imported from China. In some places, international trade has pushed regions to innovate and renew their economies. Consider Pittsburgh, Pennsylvania, a city that was once a major steel producer.

In the late 1970s, the steel industry collapsed, and the local economy suffered. By 1983, local unemployment reached 20 percent. The city focused on developing high-skilled industries, and Pittsburgh is now a hub for health care, higher education, and technology. While helping steelworkers become healthcare professionals may not be easy, for areas affected by trade, it may be one step toward revitalizing "Made in the USA."[1]

LEARNING OBJECTIVES

LO 17.1 Define comparative advantage, and list some root causes of comparative advantage on a national level.

LO 17.2 Determine whether a country will become a net-importer or net-exporter of a good when it moves from autarky to free trade.

LO 17.3 Calculate the change in surplus and the distribution of benefits within a market when a country opens up to trade.

LO 17.4 Identify when and how an economy's trade policies affect world supply of and world demand for a good.

LO 17.5 Explain the effect of a tariff on quantity, price, and the distribution of surplus.

LO 17.6 Explain the effect of an import quota on quantity, price, and the distribution of surplus.

LO 17.7 Describe the effects of trade on the factor distribution of income.

LO 17.8 Discuss the challenges of establishing environmental or labor standards in international markets.

In this chapter, we'll see how trade affects prices, workers, and consumers in different countries. We'll also see how trade provides enormous benefits to some countries and industries, but creates losers too. For a business owner, navigating this web successfully can be the difference between riches and bankruptcy. As workers and consumers, the wages we get and the prices we pay are deeply affected by trade, sometimes in ways that are hard to see at first.

Why Trade? A Review

Trade can transform economies, often (but not always) for the better. Before we get to that discussion, let's briefly review why countries would want to trade in the first place. We can draw on some basic concepts from Chapter 2, "Specialization and Exchange," to predict where different goods will be made when markets function smoothly and what the advantages of trade will be.

Comparative advantage

The United States imports clothing from all over Asia, and especially from Bangladesh. What does that fact tell us? Most obviously, it tells us that both Bangladeshi firms and American consumers have something to gain from this trade. As we know, voluntary exchanges generate surplus, leaving both participants better off than they were before. This is as true when firms or countries trade as it is when individuals do.

It also tells us that Bangladesh must have some advantage over the United States when it comes to producing clothes. If it did not, then the United States would produce its own. What kind of advantage? It might mean that Bangladeshi firms are simply more productive than those in the United States. If that were true, we would say that Bangladesh has an *absolute* advantage at clothing production. *Absolute advantage* is the ability to produce more of a good than others with a given amount of resources—for instance, to produce more T-shirts with the same number of workers.

LO 17.1 Define comparative advantage, and list some root causes of comparative advantage on a national level.

But remember that absolute advantage does not determine who produces what. Comparative advantage does. *Comparative advantage* is the ability to produce a good or service at a lower opportunity cost than others can. The fact that companies in Bangladesh sell clothing to the United States doesn't necessarily tell us that Bangladesh is more productive at making clothes, but it definitely tells us that Bangladesh's opportunity cost of making a shirt is lower than that of the United States. (For a review of absolute versus comparative advantage, look back at the "Absolute and Comparative Advantage" section in Chapter 2, "Specialization and Exchange.")

Gains from trade

If U.S. workers are at least as productive as Bangladeshi workers at making shirts, why do U.S. firms import shirts made in Bangladesh? Simply put, *both* countries can gain when each specializes in producing the good for which it has a comparative advantage. The two can then trade to get the combination of goods that people in each country want to consume. The increase in welfare in both countries that results from specialization and trade is called, straightforwardly enough, the *gains from trade*.

To see the gains from trade in action, let's compare total production and consumption with and without trade, as shown in Table 17-1. We've made up numbers to keep the example simple, but they capture the spirit of the real situation. For simplicity, we'll assume that only two goods are produced by the United States and Bangladesh: wheat and T-shirts. Let's look at what would happen, in this example, with and without trade.

Without trade, each country has to produce the combination of wheat and shirts that its people actually want to consume. This means that:

- The United States will produce 300 million shirts and 1 billion bushels of wheat.
- Bangladesh will produce 50 million shirts and 700 million bushels of wheat.

Total global production is thus 350 million shirts and 1.7 billion bushels of wheat.

When trade is possible, each country can produce the goods that it has a comparative advantage at producing, rather than the exact combination of goods its consumers want. In our simple story, that means the United States will specialize in growing wheat and Bangladesh will specialize in making shirts. Under the trade scenario:

- The United States will produce 2 billion bushels of wheat.
- Bangladesh will produce 500 million T-shirts.

The result is that global production is higher: With trade, there are 150 million more shirts and 300 million more bushels of wheat than there were before.

With trade, both countries can consume more than they were able to before, and the two countries can split this bonus in a way that makes both better off. Notice that in Table 17-1, both countries have higher consumption of both goods after specialization and trade. (To review the calculation of production specialization, look back at Chapter 2, "Specialization and Exchange," especially Table 2-1.)

TABLE 17-1

Hypothetical global production and consumption with and without trade

	Country	Wheat produced (billions)	T-shirts produced (billions)	Wheat consumed (billions)	T-shirts consumed (billions)
Without trade	United States	1.0	0.30	1.0	0.30
	Bangladesh	0.7	0.05	0.7	0.05
	Total	**1.7**	**0.35**	**1.7**	**0.35**
With trade	United States	2.0	0.0	1.2	0.3
	Bangladesh	0.0	0.5	0.8	0.2
	Total	**2.0**	**0.5**	**2.0**	**0.5**

The roots of comparative advantage

The media often describe countries trading as national entities, just as we have done above with the United States and Bangladesh. (For example: "The United States will specialize in growing wheat, and Bangladesh will specialize in making shirts.") From such wording, you might get the impression that trade requires *governments* to get together, employ an economic superplanner to crunch the numbers, and agree on who is going to specialize in what. But that's not the case at all. The reality is that the day-to-day business of trade is carried out almost entirely by firms and individuals in individual countries, not by governments.

How does a factory in Atlanta, Georgia, know what its comparative advantage is relative to a factory in Dhaka, the capital of Bangladesh? This is a case of the "invisible hand" at work. But the working of the invisible hand doesn't mean that the right decision about what to produce and who to trade with happens *automatically*. If you own a factory, it's up to you to research the cost of inputs such as labor and raw materials, and the sale prices of different goods you could produce, and calculate the most profitable option. If you get it right, you'll make profits. If you get it wrong, you'll go out of business.

Meanwhile, factory owners in Dhaka, and everywhere else in the world, are all doing the same kind of research and calculations. When everyone *responds* to the profit motives they face as individual producers, they gravitate toward producing the products in which they have a comparative advantage, and the gains from trade fall into place.

Let's get a little more concrete. We discussed in the previous chapter how the prices of *factors of production* are determined. For instance, you might want to hire workers to sew shirts in your factory in Georgia, but those workers can also choose to supply their labor to a company that makes car parts. If the workers are more productive at making car parts than shirts, the car-parts factory will be willing to offer them a higher wage. This wage difference decreases the supply of labor for making shirts, which, in turn, pushes up the wage for shirt-makers.

Now suppose that workers in Dhaka don't have such good alternatives to shirt-making. They are willing to work in a shirt factory for lower wages, so firms in Dhaka have a lower cost of producing shirts. That lower cost, in turn, makes firms in Dhaka willing to offer shirts at a lower price on the world market.

In this way, the price of each factor of production incorporates the opportunity cost of using that factor to produce other goods. You, as a would-be shirt-producer in the United States, consider the prices of all the factors of production for shirts, and the price you could get for shirts on the world market. When you compare the costs to the market price, you conclude that your factory won't be able to break even selling shirts at this lower price. This is the market telling you that your factory in Georgia doesn't have a comparative advantage at producing shirts, and you should make something else instead.

To put it another way, only a firm with a comparative advantage at producing shirts—that is, the lowest opportunity cost of production—will be able to make shirts profitably. Simply by responding to the prices of inputs and outputs and choosing to produce the good that earns it the highest profits, each firm ends up producing the good in which it has a comparative advantage.

So far, so good. But what *causes* firms in one country to have a lower opportunity cost of production for sewing shirts versus making car parts versus programming computers or anything else? Economists look to several national characteristics that affect the cost of producing goods in a particular country: natural resources and climate, endowment of factors of production, and technology.

Natural resources and climate   Why does Hawaii have a comparative advantage over Russia in growing pineapples? There's a simple reason—it's warm in Hawaii and often cold in Russia. Diversity in climate and natural resources is an important determinant of comparative advantage. Certain parts of California and France, for instance, have a complex combination of soil and weather that allows them to grow grapes that make world-class wine.

Climate and geography may also affect the costs of transporting goods to other places once they are produced. For instance, a country with great seaports will be able to trade different goods than will a landlocked country far from major consumer markets, such as Lesotho.

However, as the Economics in Action box "Made in Lesotho. But why?" shows, trade agreements can trump these natural forces. In spite of geography, a quirk in clothing trade agreements gave a unique advantage to this small country in Southern Africa.

Made in Lesotho. But why?

Economics in Action

Around the year 2000, a tiny country in southern Africa called Lesotho suddenly developed a flourishing business making T-shirts and jeans for companies including Walmart, Old Navy, Levi Strauss, and Kmart.

Lesotho is home to around 2 million citizens—smaller than the city of Houston, Texas. It doesn't grow cotton—a crop you might have expected in a country with a T-shirt and jeans industry. In fact, it doesn't grow much of anything; the mountainous country's lowest point is 4,593 feet above sea level. Common ways of earning a living in Lesotho include herding goats and working in diamond mines. It's a difficult place to get goods into or out of: It's landlocked, meaning it has no seaport, and it also lacks a major airport. All in all, Lesotho seems like a strange place in which to suddenly find a garment-export industry. Stranger yet, many of the factories that sprang up were owned by firms based in Taiwan.

Why did Taiwanese businesses go to Lesotho to make clothing to be sold thousands of miles away in the United States? What changed in 2000 that caused this unexpected trade pattern to flourish?

For over 40 years, international trade in textiles and clothing was strictly regulated through the Multifiber Arrangement. The Multifiber Arrangement was a whole group of separate treaties between individual countries that set limits on how much of what type of clothing could be traded between which countries, often on a level of detail that seems ridiculous in retrospect. How many pairs of cotton socks were Bangladeshi firms allowed to sell to American consumers? How many wool sweaters? Similar restrictions applied to most of the major clothing-producing countries in the world.

However, the African Growth and Opportunity Act (AGOA) of 2000 granted preferential trading-partner status to some very poor countries

©Peteri/Shutterstock

(continued)

in Africa, including Lesotho. Taiwanese clothing companies quickly figured out that this wrinkle in the MFA meant they couldn't sell T-shirts and jeans to American consumers if they made them in factories in Taiwan. But under AGOA they *could* reach those consumers by building factories in Lesotho. So they did.

This advantage didn't last long. By 2005, the restrictions set by the Multifiber Arrangement had been gradually phased out, freeing up trade in clothing and textiles. Lesotho clothing exports dropped substantially, from $728 million in 2004 to $438 dollars in 2012. While they don't regularly make the front page, these small changes in esoteric trade agreements can have an outsize role in where your clothes are produced.

Source: "Looming Difficulties," *The Economist*, July 17, 2007, www.economist.com/node/9516043?story_id=9516043.

Factor endowment   The relative abundance of different factors of production makes some countries better suited to produce certain goods. For instance:

- A country with a lot of land relative to its population, such as New Zealand or Argentina, may have a comparative advantage in *land-intensive* activities such as grazing cattle or sheep.
- A country with plenty of capital and little land, such as Hong Kong or Japan, might do well with more *capital-intensive* activities such as producing high-tech electronics, providing financial services, or doing biomedical research.
- A country with plenty of cheap labor, such as Bangladesh or Lesotho, will do well with *labor-intensive* activities such as clothing manufacturing, which requires relatively little capital or technology.

Factor endowment helps to explain the story we told in Chapter 2, "Specialization and Exchange," about how clothing production has moved around the world over the last few centuries. It has followed the path of cheap labor from country to country. As workforces became more educated in countries that were early leaders in the textile industry, cheap labor became less abundant relative to skilled labor and capital. As a result, comparative advantage shifted toward countries with more cheap labor relative to the other factors of production.

Technology   Lastly, technology can affect comparative advantage. Over time, technology tends to spread from country to country, equalizing opportunity costs. However, at any given time, technology or production processes developed in a particular country may give that country a temporary comparative advantage. We saw in Chapter 2, "Specialization and Exchange," that the invention of the power loom initially gave Great Britain an advantage at clothing production. However, the new technology quickly spread to the United States, erasing that advantage.

Incomplete specialization

In our analysis of international trade we have talked about comparative advantage at the country level. But, of course, not everyone in a country has the same job. Not all Americans grow wheat, not all Bangladeshis make shirts, not all New Zealanders graze sheep, and so on. If there are big gains to be had from specialization and trade, *why doesn't every country produce just one good?*

The answer has two parts. First, no national economy is a perfectly free market, and neither is trade between national economies. As we will discuss later in the chapter, specialization is often limited by trade agreements. These agreements are dependent on noneconomic considerations such as national security, tradition, and not-so-rational politicking. Those restrictions and political concerns put limits on how much specialization we can expect.

Second, even if trade were perfectly free, nations would not specialize completely. Within each country there are differences in the natural resources, climate, and relative factor endowment of different areas. For example:

- It makes sense to produce wine in California, but not in Alaska due to its cold climate.
- The opportunity cost of making cars may be low in Alabama but high in downtown Manhattan, where space for factories is hard to find.
- Land is fertile for growing corn in much of Iowa, but not in much of Nevada.

We can talk *in general* about Bangladesh having a comparative advantage in producing shirts and the United States in growing wheat. But in a super-fertile wheat-growing region of Bangladesh, the opportunity cost of growing wheat is lower than making shirts. It would make sense for Bangladesh to grow wheat in that region and import from the United States the rest of the wheat it needs.

In other words, the opportunity costs are not always constant. If the United States was producing only wheat, some farmers would probably have to work on land that isn't well-suited to producing wheat. In particular, it's very hard to grow wheat in an urban area. So in urban areas, the opportunity cost of producing wheat might be very high. Thus, the United States will produce a different good that is not wheat in areas where the opportunity cost of wheat production is very high. Because the United States is a very large country, opportunity costs vary by location, and it produces many different types of goods.

✓ TEST YOURSELF

- ☐ What is the difference between absolute and comparative advantage? Which one determines what goods countries specialize in producing? **[LO 17.1]**
- ☐ What are the major characteristics that determine comparative advantage? **[LO 17.1]**

From Autarky to Free Trade

Free, unrestricted exchanges between individual buyers and sellers maximize surplus, producing benefits for both parties. Similarly, free trade between countries maximizes surplus, producing benefits for both countries.

But simply saying "the United States gains from trade" glosses over the fact that the United States consists of many different industries, firms, and individual people. In reality, some of these will gain and some will lose from trade. However, the *total gains* will be higher than *total losses*. In order to understand the effects of trade on a more detailed level, and to see who exactly gains in what way, we need to dig deeper.

Let's start by imagining a world without any trade at all. Countries in this imaginary world neither import nor export:

- **Imports** are goods and services that are produced in other countries and consumed domestically.
- **Exports** are goods and services that are produced domestically and consumed in other countries.

We call an economy that is self-contained and does not engage in any trade with outsiders an **autarky**. Suppose that the U.S. economy is an autarky, meaning there are no imports or exports. Under autarky, nothing produced outside the country is sold inside, and nothing produced inside the country is sold outside.

What would the market for shirts in the United States look like without any trade? We can describe the domestic market with the same supply and demand curves that we've used in previous chapters. The supply curve shown in Figure 17-1 includes only *domestic* clothing manufacturers. The demand curve includes only *domestic* consumers. This situation without any trade allows

imports
goods and services that are produced in other countries and consumed domestically

exports
goods and services that are produced domestically and consumed in other countries

autarky
an economy that is self-contained and does not engage in trade with outsiders

FIGURE 17-1

Domestic supply and demand for shirts in an autarky

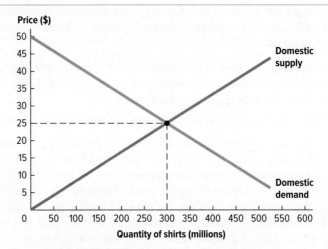

Under autarky, the domestic price and quantity of shirts are determined by the intersection of the domestic supply and domestic demand curves.

us to determine the price and quantity of shirts sold in the country by finding the intersection of the supply and demand curves, just as we've done all along. U.S. consumers and producers will buy and sell 300 million shirts per year at a price of $25.

Becoming a net-importer

LO 17.2 Determine whether a country will become a net-importer or net-exporter of a good when it moves from autarky to free trade.

LO 17.3 Calculate the change in surplus and the distribution of benefits within a market when a country opens up to trade.

In our imaginary scenario, the United States is not trading with other countries, but let's suppose that all other countries have free trade in clothing. This means that outside the United States, shirts are being bought and sold at a *world price*, which is not necessarily the same as the U.S. price (which, remember, is $25). In fact, let's say that the world price of shirts is only $15.

 CAUTION: COMMON MISTAKE

In reality, there is not a *single* world price for shirts. For a variety of reasons, a shirt in rural Mexico will have a different price than a shirt sold in New York City. However, the idea of a world price in an international market with free trade is a useful simplification that lets us describe a complicated situation. It's analogous to the market price in any other sort of market with free exchanges—any seller who tries to sell at a higher price will simply lose all of his customers to other sellers.

If you are a U.S. company trying to sell your product, you can usefully think of the world price as the amount you could get for it by exporting to a wholesaler outside of the United States.

What happens in our autarky example if the U.S. government decides to free up trade in clothing—to allow unrestricted imports and exports? The domestic price of shirts is $25, the world price is $15, and all of a sudden, shirts can be freely traded across U.S. borders. Now, U.S. consumers have no reason to pay more than $15 for a domestically produced shirt. They can instead simply buy a shirt imported from abroad.

What happens then? The market price for shirts within the United States falls to $15. At the lower price of $15, more U.S. buyers want to buy shirts. However, fewer U.S. producers are willing to produce shirts, given the lower price. Figure 17-2 illustrates the interaction between domestic

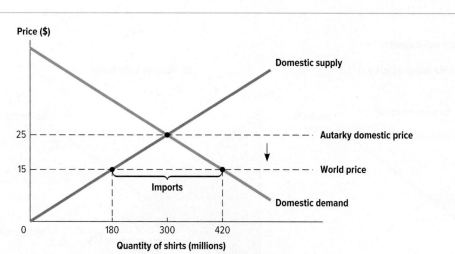

FIGURE 17-2

Becoming a net-importer

When a country opens its market to trade and the *world price is lower than the domestic price*, the domestic price will fall to meet the world price. At the lower price, domestic quantity demanded increases, but domestic quantity supplied decreases. Imports will make up the difference between the quantities domestically supplied and demanded at the world price.

supply and demand and the world price. The lower world price has pushed the quantity demanded up and the quantity supplied down. The gap between them is made up by shirts being *imported* from abroad.

Note that the domestic supply and demand curves themselves have not shifted. Trade doesn't affect the quantity that consumers demand at any given price, nor does it affect the quantity that domestic producers are willing to sell at any given price.

Trade does, however, allow consumers to buy at a price where domestic demand doesn't equal domestic supply. Of course, total quantity supplied still has to equal total quantity demanded at the equilibrium price—it's just that part of that supply can come from international producers.

In the new free-trade equilibrium, U.S. consumers buy 420 million shirts, U.S. producers sell 180 million shirts, and 240 million shirts are imported from abroad—all at a price of $15 per shirt. Because U.S. consumers demand more shirts than U.S. producers are willing to supply, the U.S. will have to import the difference—thus becoming a *net-importer* of shirts.

How does this trade affect the welfare of U.S. shirt buyers and manufacturers? Who gains from free trade and who loses? Figure 17-3 shows how consumer and producer surplus in the market for shirts change when the United States goes from autarky to free trade. Panel A shows the surplus under autarky and panel B shows what happens to the surplus after trade.

Notice that areas A, B, and D are surplus for somebody, both before and after trade:

- Area A is consumer surplus in both scenarios.
- Area D is producer surplus in both scenarios.
- Area B represents surplus that was enjoyed by U.S. producers before trade and is enjoyed by U.S. consumers after trade; that is, it is surplus that transitioned from producers to consumers.

Area C, however, is *new* surplus created by trade: It arises as trade enables consumers to buy more shirts at the lower world price. Overall, free trade increases *total* surplus by area C.

Of course, the economy is more complex than a single group of consumers and producers. In this example, we can say that *overall* the United States has gained from trade. But that doesn't mean everyone in the United States is better off. Shirt consumers have gained a lot from trade, but shirt producers have lost out. When we say that producers "lose out," we mean more than losing

FIGURE 17-3

Welfare effects of becoming a net-importer

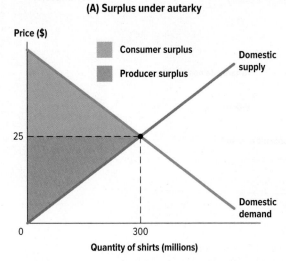

(A) Surplus under autarky

Under autarky, consumers receive the top (gold) shaded area as surplus, while producers receive the bottom (blue) shaded area.

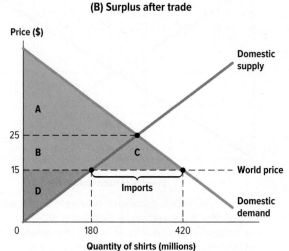

(B) Surplus after trade

When a country opens up to trade and becomes a net-importer of shirts, consumer surplus in the shirt market increases, while producer surplus decreases. In panel B, consumer surplus increases by the area B + C. Producer surplus decreases by the area B. Total surplus now equals A + B + C + D. The net increase in surplus is area C.

profit. In many cases, trade makes it hard for producers to compete on the world market. Some will have to shut their factories, forcing workers to find other jobs. Producers that are able to compete at the lower world price might have to cut wages. While this outcome is efficient, trade forces uncomfortable adjustments and real political consequences.

In principle, winners can compensate losers, but that's not always easy to do. For the rest of the chapter, when we refer to consumers or producers, be sure to think about who that refers to and what losing or gaining surplus might mean throughout the economy.

Becoming a net-exporter

Do producers always lose and consumers always win with free trade? That's the result only when the world price is *lower* than the domestic price. The opposite happens when the world price is *higher* than the domestic price. Let's look at what happens when the United States opens itself up to international trade in a good for which the world price is higher than the domestic price—say, wheat.

Figure 17-4 shows the domestic supply and demand curves for wheat in the United States. As with shirts, before trade restrictions are lifted, we can find the domestic price and quantity of wheat at the intersection of the supply and demand curves. Let's suppose U.S. consumers buy 60 million tons of wheat at a price of $200 per ton, but in the rest of the world, a ton of wheat sells for $260.

How will U.S. wheat producers *respond* to this difference in prices when trade opens up? Because they can sell as much wheat as they want to foreign consumers at $260, U.S. wheat producers have no incentive to sell it at a lower price in the United States. Therefore, if U.S. consumers want to buy wheat, they will have to pay $260, too.

At the world price of $260 per ton, U.S. farmers are willing to produce more wheat—80 million tons. However, given the higher price, U.S. consumers demand a smaller quantity, only 40 million

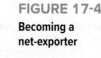

FIGURE 17-4
**Becoming a
net-exporter**

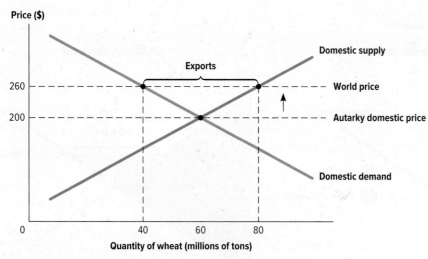

When a country opens its market to trade and the *world price is
higher than the domestic price*, the domestic price will rise to meet
the world price. At the higher price, domestic quantity supplied
increases, but domestic quantity demanded decreases. Excess
supply is exported to make up the difference between the
quantities domestically supplied and demanded at the world price.

tons. The gap between the two—40 million tons—is exported, to be sold outside the country. In this
new equilibrium, the price of wheat is higher. Because U.S. consumers demand less wheat than
U.S. producers are willing to supply, the U.S. will have to export the difference—thus becoming a
net-exporter of wheat.

How does becoming a net-exporter of wheat affect the welfare of U.S. consumers and produc-
ers? Figure 17-5 shows how consumer and producer surplus in the wheat market change when the
United States goes from autarky to free trade. Panel A shows the surplus under autarky and panel
B shows what happens to the surplus after trade.

Again, notice that areas A, B, C, E, and F were surplus for somebody both before and after trade:

- Area A is consumer surplus in both scenarios.
- Area E + F is producer surplus in both scenarios.
- Area B + C represents surplus that was enjoyed by U.S. consumers before trade and is
  enjoyed by U.S. producers after trade; that is, it is surplus that transitioned from consumers to producers.

Area D, however, is *new* surplus created by trade: It is gained by producers because trade enables
them to sell more wheat at a higher price.

On net, total surplus increases by the area of D. That means that the post-trade equilibrium is
more efficient than the pre-trade (autarky) equilibrium. In this example, we can say that overall
the United States has gained from trade. But not everyone in the United States is better off: Wheat
producers have gained from trade, but wheat consumers have lost out.

Again, let's think about what this change means more concretely. When opening to trade,
wheat producers earn more for their wheat exports, and may hire more workers or buy more
equipment to produce an extra 20 million bushels of wheat. This change is good for makers of
specialized harvesting tools, and business in towns near wheat growing regions. Conversely, wheat
is an input in a wide range of food products. An increase in the price of wheat would make these
items more expensive. Large food makers all the way down to the family buying a loaf of bread in
the store will feel the pinch.

FIGURE 17-5

Welfare effects of becoming a net-exporter

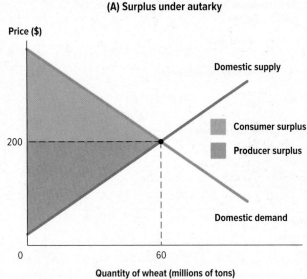

(A) Surplus under autarky

Price ($)

Domestic supply

Consumer surplus

Producer surplus

200

Domestic demand

0   60

Quantity of wheat (millions of tons)

Without trade, consumers receive the top (gold) shaded area as surplus, while producers receive the bottom (blue) shaded area.

(B) Surplus after trade

Price ($)

Domestic supply

Exports

A

260   World price

B   D

C

200

F

E

Domestic demand

0   40   60   80

Quantity of wheat (millions of tons)

When a country opens up to trade and becomes a net-exporter of wheat, consumer surplus in the wheat market decreases, while producer surplus increases. In panel B, producer surplus increases by the area B + C + D. Consumer surplus decreases by the area B + C. Total surplus now equals A + B + C + D + E + F. The net increase in surplus is area D.

Big economy, small economy

LO 17.4 Identify when and how an economy's trade policies affect world supply of and world demand for a good.

If you were paying very close attention in Chapter 3, "Markets," when we discussed the external factors that determine demand and supply, you might remember discussion of the nonprice factors that can determine the quantity of goods demanded or supplied. If you did remember that discussion as you read this chapter, then you might have come up with some questions about our analysis of what happens when we move from autarky to trade. Specifically:

- An increase in the number of buyers is one of the external factors that can move a demand curve to the right. If you remembered that, then you might have wondered, "Wouldn't free trade cause an increase in the world demand for shirts, as U.S. consumers join the world market, pushing the world price up?"

- On the supply side, an increase in the number of sellers is one of the external factors that can move a supply curve to the right. If you remembered that, then you might have wondered, "Wouldn't free trade cause an increase in the world supply of wheat as U.S. wheat farmers join the world market, pushing the world price down?"

These are good questions, and the answer to both is: It depends how big the United States is relative to the total size of the world market.

What do we mean by "big" in this context? To use the terminology of competitive markets, we assumed in our examples above that the United States is a *price taker* in the world market. That is, the decisions of its citizens about what quantity to produce or consume have no effect on the world price. Remember that buyers and sellers are *price takers* if they are too small, relative to the total size of the market, to have enough market power to influence the price.

In other words, for the United States to be a price taker in the global market for some good, the quantity it produces and consumes must be very small relative to the total amount of that good bought and sold worldwide. In some markets, the United States is probably small enough to be considered a price taker. Consider, for instance, the market for lychee—a tasty fruit that is very popular in Asia. Not many people eat lychee in the United States, and almost nobody grows lychee. Imagine that the U.S. government had banned the import and export of lychee, and then decided to end the ban and allow international trade. Would that change have much effect on the world price of lychee? Probably not, because the quantity of lychee produced and consumed in the United States is very small compared with the total quantity sold globally.

In a lot of markets, however, the United States is definitely a big economy. (In fact, depending on how you look at it, it is the biggest economy in the world.) If the United States decided to stop trading shirts or wheat, this decision almost certainly *would* affect the world price. Why? Because the quantity of these goods that the United States produces and consumes is *not* negligible relative to the total quantity sold worldwide.

This means we need to add a level of nuance to our analysis. Figure 17-6 shows supply and demand in the *world* market for shirts. (Be careful not to confuse the *world-market* supply and demand curves with the *domestic-market* supply and demand curves, shown in Figures 17-1, 17-2 and 17-3.) When the United States moves from autarky to free trade:

- The world demand curve shifts to the right because U.S. shirt consumers have entered the market.
- The world supply curve also moves a bit to the right because U.S. shirt producers have also entered the world market.

To find the new equilibrium in the world market, we need to see where the new supply and demand curves intersect. On net, because demand has increased by more than supply, we can see that the effect of the United States joining the market is that the world price of shirts increases from $15 to $17.

What does this mean for U.S. shirt producers and consumers? Figure 17-7 shows what happens when the U.S. decision to move from autarky to free trade increases the world price (now that we are considering the size of the U.S. market). The effect is the same as before: The price of shirts in the United States goes down, and the country as a whole is better off, but U.S. shirt producers lose out.

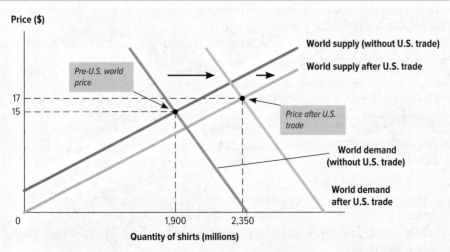

FIGURE 17-6

Impact of a big economy on world trade of shirts

When a large economy such as the United States enters the world market for shirts, it will influence both world supply and demand for that good.
Because the United States is a net-importer of shirts at the world price, the shift in world demand is greater than the shift in world supply. The result is an increase in both world price and quantity of shirts.

FIGURE 17-7

From autarky to trade in a big economy

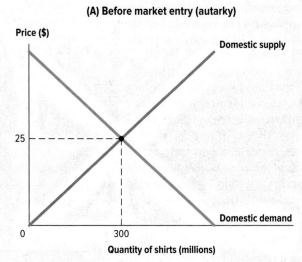

(A) Before market entry (autarky)

Under autarky, the United States produces 300 million T-shirts at a price of $25

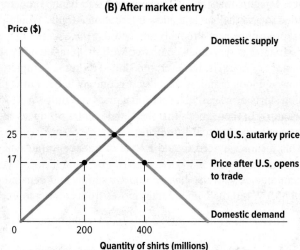

(B) After market entry

After the United States opens up to trade, the price of shirts drops from $25 to $17. The U.S. domestic price still drops relative to autarky, but by less than it would have if the United States was a price taker with no effect on the world market.

Compared with the graph in Figure 17-3, though, we can see that the quantity imported is slightly smaller than it would be if the United States were a price taker on the world market. The overall gain in surplus for the United States is smaller, and U.S. shirt producers are hurt a bit less.

Now that we've added this nuance to the analysis, we can see that the U.S. move from autarky to free trade also affects shirt producers and consumers outside the United States:

- Because the U.S. entry into the world market has increased the price of shirts, consumers in the rest of the world have to pay $17 instead of $15 for their shirts. That change reduces the surplus they enjoy.

- Foreign shirt producers, on the other hand, enjoy higher surplus due to the higher price and greater quantity they sell.

If we were to perform the same analysis for wheat, we would find that the effect of the U.S. entry into the world market would be to reduce the world price of wheat. That would be good news for foreign wheat consumers and bad news for foreign wheat producers.

✓TEST YOURSELF

☐ What is autarky? **[LO 17.2]**

☐ If the domestic price of a good is below the world price when it opens up to trade, will it become a net-importer or net-exporter of that good? **[LO 17.2]**

☐ When a country becomes a net-importer of a good, what happens to domestic consumer surplus? **[LO 17.3]**

☐ When a country becomes a net-exporter of a good, what happens to domestic producer surplus? **[LO 17.3]**

☐ When a large economy moves from restricted to unrestricted trade, what happens to world supply and world demand? **[LO 17.4]**

Restrictions on Trade

Even from our simple analysis so far, we can see how proposals to impose or lift restrictions on trade will be viewed very differently by different groups of people. A proposal for the United States to move from autarky to free trade would be opposed by U.S. shirt producers and foreign wheat farmers. But it would be welcomed by U.S. wheat farmers and foreign shirt producers. Americans who eat a lot of wheat-based food wouldn't like it, nor would foreign shirt-buyers. But Americans who buy lots of shirts would be happy, as would wheat-loving foreigners.

The big debates about international trade get more complicated because the questions are rarely about whether to completely forbid trade or to completely open it up to free global exchange. Instead, significant quantities of goods and services flow between countries, but much of that flow is heavily regulated. Understanding how prices and quantities will be affected by trade, and who wins and who loses, requires understanding trade restrictions.

Why restrict trade?

We saw in the previous section that trade is efficiency-enhancing: It *increases total surplus* regardless of whether the country becomes a net-importer or net-exporter of a particular good. Yet all countries restrict trade to some extent, and some restrict it quite heavily. Given that trade increases total welfare, why would anyone want to restrict it?

Some trade restrictions are based on global politics (as we'll discuss in the next section). But much of the rationale for restricting trade has to do with protecting those who lose surplus, or are perceived to lose surplus, as a result of free trade. For this reason, laws limiting trade are often referred to as *trade protection*, and a preference for policies that place limits on trade is called **protectionism**. In contrast, policies and actions that reduce trade restrictions and promote free trade are often referred to as **trade liberalization**.

protectionism
a preference for policies that limit trade

trade liberalization
policies and actions that reduce trade restrictions

In this section, we'll examine two common tools for restricting international trade—tariffs and quotas—and see how they affect the distribution of surplus within a country.

Tariffs

A **tariff** is a tax that applies only to imported goods. Just like any other tax, a tariff causes deadweight loss and is inefficient. It also raises public funds, but that is not usually its aim. Typically, the most important goal of a tariff is to protect the interests of domestic producers.

LO 17.5 Explain the effect of a tariff on quantity, price, and the distribution of surplus.

In 2002, for example, the United States imposed a tariff of up to 30 percent on the sale price of imported steel for a three-year period. The rationale behind the tariff was explicitly to benefit the domestic steel industry. When then-president George W. Bush announced the new tariff, he described it as:

tariff
a tax on imported goods

> . . . temporary safeguards to help give America's steel industry and its workers the chance to adapt to the large influx of foreign steel. This relief will help steel workers, communities that depend on steel, and the steel industry adjust without harming our economy.[2]

Did the steel tariff accomplish this goal? Let's take a look at what economic models say about the move. The price of a ton of steel in early 2002 was around $250. With a 30 percent tariff, foreign firms selling steel in the United States had to pay $75 to the government for the privilege of importing each ton of steel.[3]

How should we expect foreign steel producers to have responded to this new cost? They would no longer sell steel in the United States for any price lower than $325 per ton—the world price of $250 plus the $75 tariff. If they sold for less than $325 per ton in the United States, they would still have to pay the $75 tariff and the difference would be their revenue. But why accept less revenue per ton when they could sell as much as they wanted for $250 per ton in other countries?

And how should we expect domestic steel producers to have responded? Assuming that $325 is still lower than the domestic price that would prevail under autarky, they would have had no reason to sell for less than $325 either, even though they were not subject to the tariff.

FIGURE 17-8

**Effect of a tariff on
imported steel**

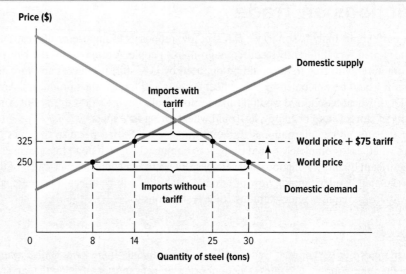

The world price before the tariff is $250. With a $75 tariff, the effective
world price increases to $325. The higher price increases domestic
supply, while it decreases domestic demand. As a result, the quantity
of imports also decreases.

The tariff thus had exactly the same effect on the U.S. steel market *as an increase in the world
price* to $325 per ton, as shown in Figure 17-8. The new, higher price pushed domestic producers
up along the supply curve. They were still not willing to produce as much as consumers wanted
to buy at that price, but they were willing to produce more than they were at a price of $250 per
ton. The difference between the quantity supplied and the quantity demanded was still made up by
imports, but that difference was smaller than it was before the tariff.

As a result of the tariff, domestic steel producers enjoyed an increase in surplus. That, after all,
was what President Bush said he wanted it to achieve. Figure 17-9 shows the surplus before the
tariff (in panel A) and after imposition of the tariff (in panel B):

- The amount producers gained in surplus from selling a larger quantity at a higher price
  is shown in area C. Notice that this gain in producer surplus comes at the expense of a
  loss in surplus for domestic consumers of steel, such as the U.S. auto and construction
  industries.
- Domestic steel consumers lost the surplus represented by area C to producers, but they
  also lost areas D, E, and F.
- Part of the loss in consumer surplus was converted into revenue for the government, which
  collects tariff payments on imports—shown as area E.
- The rest of the lost consumer surplus—areas D and F—became deadweight loss.

In other words, the combined benefits that the tariff brought to steel producers and the U.S.
government were outweighed by the loss in surplus suffered by domestic steel consumers. We can
see, then, that the steel tariff did not *exactly* achieve its goal of helping the domestic steel industry
"without harming our economy."

In the end, was imposing the tariff the right decision? That depends on how highly you value
the benefit to the U.S. steel-production industry versus the loss to steel consumers, like the auto
and construction industries. The Peterson Institute of International Economics tried to put some
numbers on this analysis and found the tariffs increased employment in the steel industry by
3,500, but at a cost of $400,000 per job.[4]

FIGURE 17-9

Domestic welfare effects of a tariff

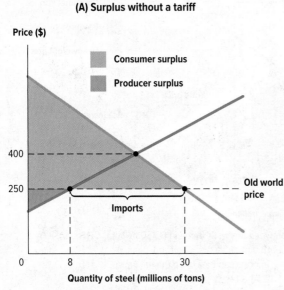

(A) Surplus without a tariff

Without a tariff the world price is $250. Consumers demand 30 million tons of steel and domestic producers are willing to sell 8 million tons.

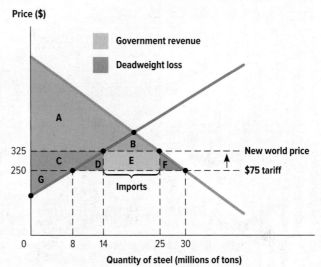

(B) Surplus with a tariff

The tariff increases producer surplus by area C, and decreases consumer surplus by area C + D + E + F. Area E is the government revenue from the imposed tariff, while area D + F is the deadweight loss. Note that the loss of consumer surplus is greater than the sum of producer surplus and government revenue gains.

In any case, the steel tariff didn't last long. In 2003, the World Trade Organization ruled that the tariffs were illegal, and President Bush withdrew them. We'll say more about the role of the World Trade Organization later in this chapter.

Quotas

The Multifiber Arrangement (MFA), which regulated trade of clothing items from the 1970s to 2005, used another type of trade restriction—the quota. An **import quota** is a limit on the amount of a particular good that can be imported. Under the MFA, different countries were subject to different quotas for different kinds of clothing goods. For instance, China could sell only so many cotton shirts in the United States, Pakistan could sell only so many, and Bangladesh, and so on.

Let's start with a simple example of a quota: a cap on the total number of pairs of blue jeans that can be imported into the United States. (For now, don't worry about how this quota is allocated between countries that produce jeans—we'll come back to that in a moment.) Figure 17-10 shows that under free trade, at the world price of $25 per pair, domestic jeans producers are willing to supply 500 million pairs of jeans. At that price, American consumers demand 1,350 million pairs of jeans. The difference—850 million pairs of jeans—is imported.

But what happens if a quota is imposed, limiting the total number of imported jeans to 500 million? The domestic price of jeans has to rise from $25 per pair to $32 per pair. That change in price shrinks the gap between domestic supply and domestic demand down to the 500 million limit imposed by the quota.

LO 17.6 Explain the effect of an import quota on quantity, price, and the distribution of surplus.

import quota
a limit on the amount of a particular good that can be imported

FIGURE 17-10

Domestic welfare effects of a quota

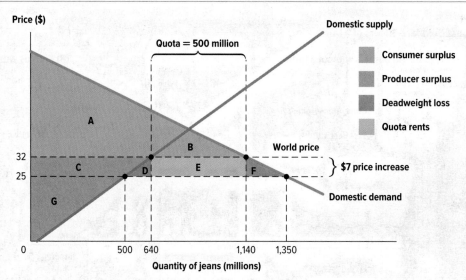

At the pre-quota price of $25, the gap between domestic demand (1,350 million) and supply (500 million) is met by an imported quantity of 850 million jeans. With an import quota of 500 million jeans, imports can't make up the full gap, pushing the domestic world price up to $32. As a result, producer surplus increases by area C, and consumer surplus decreases by area C + D + E + F. Area E is the quota rent gained by whoever holds the rights to import, while area D + F is the deadweight loss.

Notice that the effect of the quota is very similar to the effect of a tariff. The domestic (U.S.) price increases over the world price. As a result:

- domestic quantity demanded decreases,
- domestic quantity supplied increases, and
- the quantity of imports falls.

Domestic producers gain surplus from selling a higher quantity at a higher price. But domestic consumers lose even more surplus from buying a lower quantity at a higher price, resulting in deadweight loss (areas D and F).

However, there is an important distinction between the impact of tariffs and that of quotas—who *benefits* from the difference between the value of jeans in the United States and their value on the world market:

- Under a tariff, the U.S. government collects tax revenue equal to the quantity of imports multiplied by the difference between the domestic price and the world price.
- Under a quota, this value goes to whoever holds the rights to import. For instance, under a quota, if the U.S. government gives the government of Bangladesh the rights to import jeans into the United States, Bangladesh can then choose to sell those rights or hand them out to favored firms. Thus, the value of tax revenue that would have been earned in a tariff turns into profits earned by *foreign* firms or governments with a quota. These are called **quota rents**.

quota rents
profits earned by foreign firms or governments under a quota

Who will be granted the right to import how much of what goods into which countries is among the thorny issues trade negotiators grapple with when deciding on the details of trade treaties.

✓ TEST YOURSELF

- ☐ How does a tariff on an imported good affect surplus for domestic producers of that good? **[LO 17.5]**
- ☐ How does a quota on an imported good affect surplus for domestic consumers of that good? **[LO 17.6]**
- ☐ In what way are tariff revenues and quota rents similar? **[LO 17.6]**

Trade Agreements

We've described what happens when a closed economy opens up to trade and what happens when a tariff or quota is imposed or lifted. Now we can talk more about *why* these things happen.

We've touched on reasons why U.S. politicians might want to protect domestic producers by imposing tariffs, or help impoverished African economies by exempting them from quotas. In this section, we'll dig deeper into how such decisions often are motivated by political and moral ideas, and see how economic analysis can be harnessed to understand their implications.

International labor and capital

Political battles between free-traders and protectionists have always been fierce, and they continue to be so today. In the United States, protectionists accuse free-traders of shipping jobs of hard-working Americans overseas. Free-traders accuse protectionists of giving handouts to big corporations at the expense of American consumers. Why are voters and politicians unable to agree on what is best?

LO 17.7 Describe the effects of trade on the factor distribution of income.

Although the country as a whole gains from liberalizing trade, we've seen that certain segments of the population will lose out. As a general rule, free trade increases demand for factors of production that are domestically abundant. Free trade also decreases the supply of factors that are domestically scarce. In other words, free trade acts to equalize the supply of and demand for factors of production across countries.

In turn, factor prices (such as wages) then start to converge across countries. The result:

- The owners of domestically scarce factors of production lose due to increased competition.
- The owners of domestically abundant factors gain from increased demand.

As we discussed in the previous chapter, people earn income from ownership of the factors of production. Changes in factor prices as a result of international trade have a big effect on the distribution of income within a country.

Let's consider two examples of how trade has tipped the balance between owners of scarce and abundant factors of production: Bangladesh and the United States.

Bangladesh is a small country in terms of land area, but a big one in terms of population. Imagine an area the size of Illinois or Iowa, with a population equal to half of the entire United States. In the days before there was much international trade, land owners in Bangladesh benefited greatly from their control over that scarce resource, using cheap labor that was in plentiful supply. In other words, land was scarce in relation to labor.

As the country became more and more connected to international markets through trade, textile firms seeking cheap labor moved in. Bangladeshis began to earn enough from textile work to be able to import food from countries where land is less scarce. As a result, the price of labor has risen, and the price of land has fallen. The relative incomes of the owners of labor and land have changed accordingly.

In the United States, a more subtle change in the factor distribution of income has taken place. With its tech-savvy, educated population, the United States has a relative abundance of high-skilled labor—lawyers, teachers, financial planners, and so on. In comparison with other countries, the United States doesn't have so many low-skilled workers. When the country didn't engage in

The rapid growth of exports from countries like China and Bangladesh opens new opportunities—and some new debates.
©Imaginechina/AP Images

much trade, this was good for the low-skilled workers. They represented a scarce resource relative to high-skilled workers, which drove up the wages of low-skilled workers. The 1950s, for instance, were a great time to be a factory worker in the United States—the average worker earned about $41,000 in 2018 dollars.[5]

As trade has increased astronomically in recent decades, however, the balance of high-skilled and low-skilled workers has tipped. Many economists believe that this change explains part of the increase in income inequality that has occurred in the United States in recent decades. High-skilled workers are earning more as a result of the increased demand for their labor due to free trade, while low-skilled workers are earning less.

You can see why certain people in both Bangladesh and America would be upset about trade. Of course, as we have seen, trade increases efficiency and total surplus. We can therefore expect economies to grow as a result of trade—and when economies grow, they usually create jobs. Americans whose jobs have been lost to freer trade should, in theory, be able to find new jobs, given time. Nonetheless, for someone who has spent 10 or 20 years doing a particular job, the idea of moving and retraining for a different type of work is understandably daunting or unappealing.

Does this mean that we should impose trade restrictions to protect the owners of scarce factors of production, such as American factory workers? Remember that any move to liberalize or restrict trade creates losers as well as winners. In this case, the losers would be American shareholders, American consumers, and Bangladeshi factory workers—and the economy as a whole would shrink.

Arguments over trade policy are never just about protecting people in your own country from foreign competition. They're also debates about the distribution of benefits within each country.

The WTO and trade mediation

Have you heard about the great Franco-American cheese war of 2009? Probably not. No shots were fired and, as far as we know, no one was physically hurt. Nonetheless, the cheese war is an example of how trade restrictions can spiral out of control.

Paradoxically, the cheese war actually began with beef. The European Union (EU) banned imports of beef containing artificial hormones, which includes most beef raised in the United States. Not surprisingly, the United States was opposed to this trade restriction. What measures can a country take when it doesn't like another country's trade restrictions? It can appeal to the **World Trade Organization (WTO)**, an international organization designed to monitor and enforce trade agreements, while also promoting free trade. Although the WTO doesn't have an army or the power to enforce its decisions, many countries have voluntarily joined and agreed in principle to liberalize their trade policies and abide by the WTO's decisions.

That's because the WTO does have an important tool, called "most favored nation" status, for incentivizing countries to play by the rules. Most favored nation status means that members of the WTO have to offer the same trade terms to all other members of the organization. For example, without extenuating circumstances, Canada cannot place a tariff on China that it does not also place on the United States.

In the Cheese War, the WTO reviewed the evidence and the law surrounding beef imports. The WTO's rules allow such trade restrictions, but only if they protect public health and safety. The United States argued that there was no legitimate evidence that artificial beef hormones pose

World Trade Organization (WTO) an international organization designed to monitor and enforce trade agreements, while also promoting free trade

a health risk and that the EU's ban was therefore illegitimate. In 2008, the WTO ruled in favor of the United States. Although it usually abides by WTO decisions, in this case the EU felt so strongly about the issue that it refused to lift the ban.

In response, the United States slapped a 300 percent tariff on imports of French Roquefort cheese.[6] In response to that response, the French parliament debated imposing heavy import tariffs on Coca-Cola products from the United States. This tit-for-tat exchange was eventually ended, as trade negotiators reached a deal: The United States agreed to the EU keeping its ban on hormone-treated beef, and in return the EU agreed to import more nontreated beef from the United States.

Trade brinksmanship returned in 2018, this time between the United States and China. For years, various politicians in the United States had accused China of using unfair trade practices, including currency manipulation and requirements that U.S. companies share their intellectual property as a condition of doing business in China. Although these issues had been brought up before the WTO before, U.S. President Donald Trump chose to use more drastic measures, placing tariffs on Chinese steel and billions of dollars of other goods. China responded by placing tariffs on U.S. agriculture, whiskey, and other exports. The resulting "trade war" hurt farmers and businesses on both sides of the Pacific, yet both countries hoped that tariffs would resolve what the WTO had been unable to fix.

Despite these disputes, most policy-makers and politicians understand that trade brings more benefits than costs and are willing to let the WTO handle any trade issues that arise. As long as that is true, the WTO can help keep global trade fair to everyone involved.

Labor and environmental standards

The EU's resistance to artificial beef hormones is an example of a wider problem. The EU has its own set of laws and policies governing the economy, including safety policies, labor standards, environmental regulations, taxes, laws about corporate finance and governance, and much more. In fact, every country that trades on their own has a similar set of rules. These rules often vary hugely among countries, which can be a source of friction in international trade.

LO 17.8 Discuss the challenges of establishing environmental or labor standards in international markets.

For example, many clothes sold in the United States are produced in ways that would be illegal in the United States. Some of the clothes you're wearing now were probably made in a country where children work in factories, where the minimum wage is tiny or nonexistent, or where leftover chemicals and fabric dyes get dumped into the drinking water. Although these circumstances might seem unacceptable to American consumers, "unacceptable" is always in the eye of the beholder. European consumers, for instance, are often outraged by the sale of genetically modified food products, which are completely legal and relatively uncontroversial in the United States. (If you ate bread today, we bet that it was made from genetically modified grains.)

The problem of inconsistent standards can be approached in two main ways: policy-makers making explicit laws about imports and consumers making voluntary purchasing decisions.

Import standards One solution that some countries have used to address the problem of differing labor or environmental standards is simply to impose standards on imported goods. There are two main channels for this sort of policy: (1) *blanket standards* imposed on *all* imports or (2) *import standards* on *specific countries*.

Blanket standards on imports usually address issues affecting consumers, rather than workers in the countries where production takes place. In the United States, for instance, imported food products must meet certain standards to protect the health of U.S. consumers. Imports of products that violate domestic copyright or patent laws—such as pirated movies or music—are also restricted.

Import standards on specific countries are less common. Such standards typically address production issues in the country of origin, such as labor or environmental conditions. When used, they are integrated into individual trade agreements with those countries.

An example is the North American Agreement on Labor Cooperation (NAALC)—part of the North American Free Trade Agreement (NAFTA). NAALC expresses the agreement of the three countries to work in the long term toward a set of labor standards. The standards address various issues: the elimination of child labor, prevention of workplace injuries, enforcement of minimum wages, and equal pay for men and women, among others. NAALC does not, however, require each country to maintain the same standards on these issues; for instance, there is no expectation that the minimum wage in Mexico will be the same as the minimum wage in the United States. Instead, it requires only that each country enforce its own existing labor laws. Furthermore, the ability of each country to enforce compliance on the other two is quite limited. (In 2018, the United States, Mexico, and Canada agreed on a new trade agreement, called USMCA, that will replace NAFTA after all three countries pass it into law.)

In cases where the goal of regulation is to solve an international problem, such as pollution, legislating on a country-by-country basis may even worsen the problem. To see how this might happen, read the From Another Angle box "Are environmental regulations bad for the environment?"

Are environmental regulations bad for the environment?

From Another Angle

Tighter environmental regulations should improve the quality of the environment. Right? The answer seems obvious: How could laws limiting pollution *not* reduce pollution? It *is* possible, however, that regulations in one country might *increase* worldwide pollution by pushing polluting industries into countries without regulation. This idea is called *pollution displacement,* and it is enabled by international trade.

International firms decide where to operate based on the costs of production in each country. These costs include many factors, such as local wages and rents. They also include the cost of complying with regulations. In a country with strict environmental standards, companies have to pay for clean technologies, safe disposal of waste material, and so on. All else equal, the cost of production is higher in countries with stricter environmental regulations. That fact gives firms an incentive to move production to countries with less regulation and lower costs, especially when the costs of trade are low.

Worldwide emissions statistics show that this may be more than a theoretical concept. In 1997, 37 countries set pollution reduction targets through the Kyoto Protocol. Two decades later, many of these countries have reduced overall emissions.

However, was this improvement caused by a real cleaning of the air, or through pollution displacement? To answer that question, a group of researchers analyzed the emissions statistics and trade data of Kyoto Protocol countries. They found that overall imports to Kyoto Protocol countries increased over the study period and that when they added the pollution required to produce these imported goods to a country's reported emissions,

Tighter environmental regulations should reduce pollution unless pollution displacement pushes polluting industries into countries without regulation.
©Denys Bilytskyi/Alamy

their pollution *increased* overall. In other words, the pollution reduction that occurred in many countries after the Kyoto Protocol could partly be explained by companies shifting production to places with fewer environmental regulations.

Even though pollution displacement can undermine environmental regulations, that doesn't mean that countries should abandon attempts to fight pollution. Rather, it requires thinking about how trade will influence the end result.

Source: K. Kanemoto, D. Moran, M. Lenzen, and A Geschke, "International trade undermines emissions targets: New evidence from air pollution," *Global Environmental Change* 24 (2014), pp. 52–59.

Pocketbook activism   What if there are no regulations that set standards for imported goods? Individual consumers can still make choices about what they are and are not willing to buy. The *fair trade movement* attempts to inform and influence consumers' choices. It certifies and labels goods whose production meets certain standards; these include paying workers minimum wages, ensuring safe working conditions, and not causing undue harm to the environment.

Because production that meets fair-trade standards usually costs more, fair-trade-certified products cost more too. Individual consumers decide whether it is worth it to them to pay more for products that are produced in a certain way.

The fact that some consumers are willing to pay more for fair-trade goods means it is a way for producers to differentiate their products. Since the end of the Multifiber Arrangement in 2005 opened up Lesotho's garment industry to low-cost competition from Asia, one of the ways it has tried to preserve the industry is by raising standards in its factories and marketing itself as a source of fair-trade clothing.

Outside the fair-trade label, consumers can influence labor and environmental standards through boycotts and activism. For instance, in 2012, activists pressured Apple into conducting audits of Chinese factories where iPads and other popular electronics are assembled, after exposés reported dangerous working conditions. These audits now track the working hours of 1.3 million supplier employees and include guidelines on student labor and women's health.

The fair-trade movement offers consumers the opportunity to buy goods that meet certain standards. Consumers can decide whether fair-trade products, such as the bananas being harvested here, are worth the added cost.
©Simon Rawles/The Image Bank/Getty Images

Embargoes: Trade as foreign policy

Sometimes the motivations behind trade restrictions are not ultimately economic at all. Instead, countries may use trade as a tool for foreign policy. Because trade increases surplus and allows a country to access goods that it cannot manufacture itself, restricting the ability to trade can be seen as a form of punishment. The restriction or prohibition of trade in order to put political pressure on a country is an **embargo**.

For example, in 2018 the U.N. Security Council passed a resolution banning the sale of weapons to South Sudan, a country in Eastern Africa, in order to reduce violence against civilians there. Such trade restrictions can be an alternative to using military force against a country.[7]

In other cases, the goods and services covered by an embargo are not intrinsically dangerous. Between the Gulf War in 1990 and the U.S.-led invasion in 2003, the United Nations imposed a very broad embargo on Iraq. It prohibited trade of "any commodities or products" except medical supplies and food under certain conditions. Why did the United Nations want to stop ordinary

embargo
a restriction or prohibition of trade in order to put political pressure on a country

Iraqis from having cars and shirts and other consumer goods? It hoped the Iraqi people would be so annoyed about the lack of goods that the Iraqi government would fear a popular uprising and would change its policies.

✓ TEST YOURSELF

☐ What happens to the price of domestically scarce factors of production when a country opens up to trade? What happens to the price of domestically abundant factors of production? **[LO 17.7]**

☐ What does the WTO do? **[LO 17.7]**

☐ What is the purpose of an embargo? **[LO 17.8]**

Conclusion

The chapter has taken a close look at one of the most powerful economic insights: There can be big gains from specialization and exchange. This is true for countries as well as individual people and companies.

Even though the total gains from trade are usually positive on a national level, the distribution of those gains to different people and industries matters a lot in the real world. There are usually winners and losers from trade, especially in the short run. The hope is that opening up to trade eventually makes everyone better off, but getting to that point requires responsive political solutions.

Trade restrictions such as tariffs and quotas are used in varying degrees by every country in the world to protect some groups and industries from international competition. Some domestic policies, such as environmental and labor standards, can also affect trade.

Because trade takes place across countries, the role of public policy in shaping international trade is more obvious than in most of the domestic topics we've covered so far. In upcoming chapters, we'll tackle other ways that public policy drives the economy, on both the domestic and international levels.

Key Terms

imports, p. 425

exports, p. 425

autarky, p. 425

protectionism, p. 433

trade liberalization, p. 433

tariff, p. 433

import quota, p. 435

quota rents, p. 436

World Trade Organization (WTO), p. 438

embargo, p. 441

Summary

LO 17.1 Define comparative advantage, and list some root causes of comparative advantage on a national level.

Comparative advantage is the ability to produce a good or service at a lower opportunity cost than others can. *Absolute advantage* is the ability to produce more of a good than others can with a given amount of resources. It is comparative advantage, rather than absolute advantage, that determines which countries produce which goods for trade.

The most efficient economic arrangement is one in which each country specializes in the good for which it has a comparative advantage and trades with others. Characteristics such as climate, natural resources, factor endowment, and technology determine which goods and services a country will have a comparative advantage at producing. Because features like climate, population, and technology are not uniform throughout an entire country, incomplete specialization, in which a country produces some of many different kinds of goods, can also be efficient.

LO 17.2 Determine whether a country will become a net-importer or net-exporter of a good when it moves from autarky to free trade.

When a country moves from *autarky* (a self-contained economy that does not trade with others) to trade, the difference between the world price and the domestic price of a good determines whether the country becomes a net-importer or net-exporter.

If the world price is lower than the domestic price, the domestic price will drop when the country opens to trade. In that case, domestic supply will no longer be sufficient to meet domestic demand at the lower price. Imported goods will make up the difference, and the country will become a net-importer.

If the world price is higher than the domestic price, the domestic price will rise when the country opens up to trade. Domestic supply will outstrip domestic demand at the higher price, and the country will export the excess supply, becoming a net-exporter.

LO 17.3 Calculate the change in surplus and the distribution of benefits within a market when a country opens up to trade.

When markets function well, total surplus increases when a country opens up to trade. The domestic distribution of surplus depends on whether the country becomes a net-importer or net-exporter of the good being traded. In net-importing countries, consumers gain surplus from buying a larger quantity at a lower price; producers lose surplus from selling less at a lower price. When a country becomes a net-exporter, consumers lose surplus from buying a smaller quantity at a higher price; producers gain surplus. In both cases, total surplus increases, making trade more efficient than autarky.

LO 17.4 Identify when and how an economy's trade policies affect world supply of and world demand for a good.

Our previous examples hold only if the economy in question is a *price taker;* that is, the decisions of its citizens about what quantity to produce or consume have no effect on the world price.

But if we are dealing with a "big" economy, its decisions *would* affect the world price. In this case, the economy's move from autarky to free trade would shift the world demand curve to the right (because more consumers have entered the world market) and also shift the world supply curve to the right (because more producers have entered the world market).

LO 17.5 Explain the effect of a tariff on quantity, price, and the distribution of surplus.

In order to raise public funds and redistribute surplus toward domestic producers, governments use import tariffs. A *tariff* is a tax on imports, and like any tax, it causes inefficiency and deadweight loss.

A tariff raises the domestic price of a good, causing a reduction in the quantity demanded, an increase in the quantity supplied domestically, and a reduction in the quantity imported. Domestic producers will enjoy an increase in surplus as a result of selling more at a higher price, and government will receive tax revenue. However, domestic consumers lose surplus as a result of buying less at a higher price, and total surplus decreases.

LO 17.6 Explain the effect of an import quota on quantity, price, and the distribution of surplus.

Import quotas limit the amount of a particular good that can be imported. The effect of the quota on domestic price and quantity is similar to the effect of a tariff: Domestic price increases, quantity sold decreases, and the quantity imported decreases. Domestic producers gain surplus from selling at a higher price; domestic consumers lose surplus from buying a lower quantity at a higher price. Some surplus goes to whoever holds the rights to import, called *quota rents.*

LO 17.7 Describe the effects of trade on the factor distribution of income.

International trade equalizes the supply and demand of factors of production across countries. In general, trade increases demand for factors that are domestically abundant, and it increases the supply of factors that are domestically scarce.

As a result, the price of domestically scarce factors will typically drop due to increased foreign competition, and the owners of these factors lose surplus. In contrast, the price of domestically abundant factors increases due to increased demand, and owners will gain surplus.

LO 17.8 Discuss the challenges of establishing environmental or labor standards in international markets.

Each country or trading group has its own set of laws and policies governing the economy. These regulations vary among countries, which can be a source of friction when economic activity takes place across national boundaries. Policymakers and consumers approach the problem of inconsistent standards in several ways, ranging from explicit laws about imports to voluntary purchasing decisions by consumers.

Review Questions

1. Why might a country that is more productive in producing wheat than its trading partners end up importing wheat? **[LO 17.1]**

2. Imagine two nations with similar landmasses and levels of wealth that do not specialize in the same industries. What characteristics might drive differences in their comparative advantages? **[LO 17.1]**

3. Producing socks is labor-intensive, while producing satellites is capital-intensive. If India has abundant labor and the United States has abundant capital, which good will the U.S. export? Is trade beneficial to textile laborers in the United States? **[LO 17.2]**

4. Suppose Egypt wants to open its trade borders to the world market for natural gas. What will determine whether Egypt becomes a net-exporter or net-importer of natural gas? If Egypt becomes a net-exporter, will domestic supply be equal to, less than, or greater than domestic demand? **[LO 17.2]**

5. If Argentina becomes a net-exporter of beef after trade barriers are removed, how does total welfare in Argentina change compared with autarky? Are Argentine cattle ranchers better or worse off? What about Argentine consumers? **[LO 17.3]**

6. Suppose a country opens its trade borders and becomes a net-exporter of beef. Is it better for domestic consumers of beef if the country is a large player on the world market or a small player? **[LO 17.3]**

7. Suppose the United States wants to open its trade borders to the world market for coffee. What will determine whether the world price for coffee is affected? **[LO 17.4]**

8. Suppose that Japan is a net exporter of automobiles. If a large country like the United States moves from autarky to free trade in automobiles, how will the price of automobiles sold in Japan change? How will the amount of automobiles exported change? **[LO 17.4]**

9. Suppose Mexico wants to protect its domestic automobile industry from U.S. and Japanese competition. How will a tariff on imported cars help it to accomplish this task? How does the tariff affect domestic producer and consumer surplus? **[LO 17.5]**

10. Refer back to Figure 17-9. Explain why area D is a deadweight loss. What about area F? **[LO 17.5]**

11. Imagine Mexico is considering using an import quota rather than a tariff to protect its domestic automobile industry. How does the outcome differ from that of a tariff? **[LO 17.6]**

12. Explain how lifting an import quota on other countries will affect an exporting country that had been exempted from the quota restriction. **[LO 17.6]**

13. Labor is relatively abundant in Mexico compared with arable land. Explain who wins and who loses in Mexico as a result of the North American Free Trade Agreement (NAFTA), which liberalized trade between the United States, Canada, and Mexico. **[LO 17.7]**

14. If capital is domestically scarce in a country, do you expect owners of capital in that country to be free-traders or protectionists? Why? **[LO 17.7]**

15. Suppose Great Britain wants to take a stance on labor standards for imports. The prime minister imposes a blanket standard that requires all imports to meet certain labor standards. Who will benefit from this policy? What are the drawbacks for Great Britain and countries that export to Great Britain? **[LO 17.8]**

16. Suppose the United States imposes a trade embargo on North Korea in order to exert political pressure on the government. Consider how the embargo will affect U.S. producers. Under what conditions would they support the embargo? Why might they oppose it? **[LO 17.8]**

Problems and Applications

1. If a country has relatively abundant unskilled labor, with scarce land and capital, it is more likely to have a comparative advantage in which of the following industries? Check all that apply. **[LO 17.1]**
   a. Food service.
   b. Textiles.
   c. Agriculture.
   d. Financial services.

2. Suppose Ghana discovers it has lost its comparative advantage in the production of maize. Which of the following could explain the loss of comparative advantage? Check all that apply. **[LO 17.1]**
   a. Maize-processing technology developed in Ghana spreads to other maize-producing countries.
   b. Decline in global demand for maize.
   c. Immigration of cheap labor into Ghana.
   d. Growth of low-skill service jobs in Ghana.

3. Calculate the following values using Figure 17P-1, which shows domestic supply and demand for steel in the United States under autarky. **[LO 17.2]**
   a. What are the equilibrium price and quantity of steel under autarky?
   b. Suppose the United States allows trade, and the post-trade domestic quantity supplied is 150 thousand tons of steel. What are the domestic quantity demanded and the new world price?
   c. Is the United States a net-exporter or net-importer of steel?
   d. What quantity of steel is imported/exported?

FIGURE 17P-1

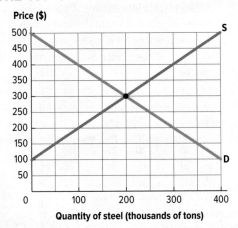

Price ($)

Quantity of steel (thousands of tons)

4. Table 17P-1 shows the domestic supply and demand schedule for rice in Thailand. **[LO 17.2]**

TABLE 17P-1

Price of rice ($/kg)	Quantity demanded (millions of kg)	Quantity supplied (millions of kg)
3.50	2,100	3,300
3.25	2,150	3,200
3.00	2,200	3,100
2.75	2,250	3,000
2.50	2,300	2,900
1.25	2,350	2,800
1.00	2,400	2,700
0.75	2,450	2,600
0.50	2,500	2,500
0.25	2,550	2,400

a. In autarky, what are the domestic quantity supplied and price?

b. The world price of rice is $1.25 per kilogram. If Thailand opens up to trade in rice, what will be the new domestic price of rice? (*Hint*: You can assume Thailand is a small producer of rice relative to the world market.)

c. What quantity of rice will be supplied by domestic producers?

d. What quantity of rice will be demanded by domestic consumers?

e. How much rice will Thailand import or export?

5. Guatemala represents a small part of the world poultry market. Based on Figure 17P-2, answer the following. **[LO 17.3]**

FIGURE 17P-2

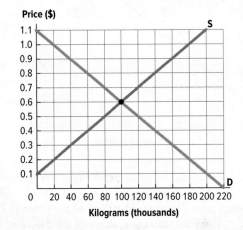

Price ($)

Kilograms (thousands)

a. Calculate producer and consumer surplus in autarky.

b. Assume that the world price of poultry is $0.30/kg. If Guatemala opens to trade, what are the domestic quantity consumed and produced? Plot these quantities on the graph. What is the quantity of imports?

c. Calculate the post-trade producer and consumer surplus, and plot these areas on the graph. Who is better off after trade: producers or consumers?

6. Guatemala represents a small part of the world poultry market, and is fully open to trade. Assume the world price of poultry is $0.30/kg. Suppose a $0.10/kg tariff is imposed on poultry imports. Based on Figure 17P-2, answer the following questions. **[LO 17.3, 17.5]**

a. What are the quantity of poultry consumed and produced in Guatemala under the tariff? Plot these quantities on the graph. What is the quantity of imports?

b. Now suppose the tariff is eliminated and instead the world price of chicken feed increases significantly. This causes the world price of poultry to rise from $0.30/kg to $0.40/kg. How much poultry is now bought and sold in Guatemala? What is the quantity of imports?

c. Compare the efficiency of the two situations. Calculate the deadweight loss under the tariff. Calculate the deadweight loss resulting from the higher price of chicken feed.

7. Suppose the United States is initially an autarky. Figure 17P-3 shows the domestic market for paper.

FIGURE 17P-3

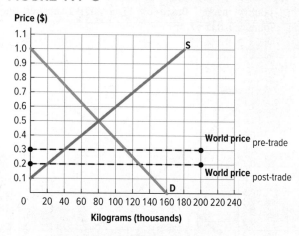

Price ($)

When the U.S. does not allow trade, the world price is $0.30. When the United States does allow trade, the world price falls to $0.20. **[LO 17.4]**

Based on the figure, which of the following statements is correct?

a. The increase in world demand for paper was larger than the increase in world supply of paper.

b. The decrease in world demand for paper was larger than the increase in world supply of paper.

c. The increase in world supply of paper was larger than the increase in world demand for paper.

d. The decrease in world supply of paper was larger than the increase in world demand for paper.

8. The world wheat market is shown in Figure 17P-4. **[LO 17.4]**

FIGURE 17P-4

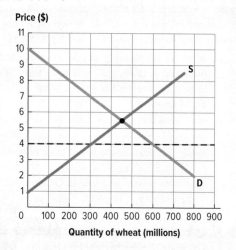

Price ($)

a. What is the initial world price?

b. Suppose a large country like the United States has been an autarky but is now going to allow

free trade. Draw the effect the entrance of the United States into the world market has on the world supply and world demand curves.

c. How will the world price be affected by the entrance of the United States into the world market?

9. The U.S. wheat market is shown in Figure 17P-5. Suppose the United States wants to protect its wheat industry by imposing a tariff of $1/bushel on foreign wheat, which currently sells at the world price of $4/bushel. **[LO 17.6]**

FIGURE 17P-5

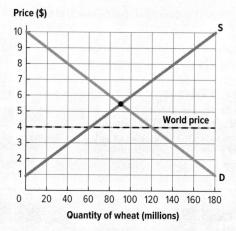

Price ($)

a. Graph consumer and producer surplus after the $1/bushel tariff is imposed.

b. How much revenue does the U.S. government collect from the tariff?

c. Graph the deadweight loss associated with the tariff below the equilibrium quantity. Then graph the deadweight loss associated with the tariff above the equilibrium quantity.

10. The U.S. wheat market is shown in Figure 17P-5. **[LO 17.6]**

a. When the world price is $4/bushel, will the United States import or export wheat? How many bushels?

b. How many bushels of wheat should be allowed under an import quota in order to increase the domestic price from $4 to $5 per bushel?

c. Graph the domestic producer surplus increase as a result of this quota.

d. Graph the deadweight loss associated with the quota below the equilibrium quantity. Then graph the deadweight loss associated with the quota above the equilibrium quantity.

11. Suppose a country imposes a tariff on coffee imports. Using the diagram of supply and demand in Figure 17P-6, identify the correct shaded areas as follows. [**LO 17.3, 17.5, 17.6**]

FIGURE 17P-6

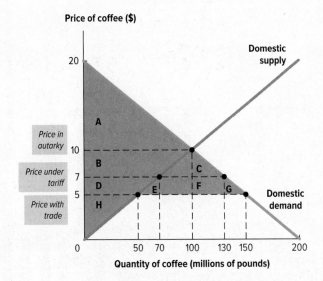

Price of coffee ($)

a. In autarky, which area(s) comprise domestic consumer surplus? Which area(s) comprise domestic producer surplus?

b. When the country opens up to trade, which area(s) do consumers gain as surplus? Which area(s) do producers lose?

c. After trade, if an import tariff is imposed, which area(s) do domestic producers gain as surplus? Which do domestic consumers lose?

d. With the tariff, which area is government revenue?

e. Which area(s) represent deadweight loss as a result of the tariff?

f. If the country uses an import quota instead of a tariff, what is the quota quantity if the quota price is $7?

12. Suppose a country where capital is scarce and most of the industry is labor-intensive with low-skilled labor moves from autarky to free trade. Which of the following do you expect to happen? Check all that apply. [**LO 17.7**]

  a. Owners of capital become wealthier.

  b. Wages for labor increase.

  c. The returns to capital (surplus) decrease.

13. Suppose two countries are considering a new agricultural trade agreement with each other. Country A has abundant low-skilled labor and scarce land. Country B has abundant arable land but little population. In which country do land owners support a trade agreement? In which country do workers support a trade agreement? [**LO 17.7**]

14. Suppose a country has abundant capital but scarce labor. Which group would be more harmed by a trade embargo: owners of capital or laborers? [**LO 17.7, 17.8**]

15. Which of the following policies is likely to cause more pollution displacement: imposing environmental standards on domestic production or a blanket environmental standard on all imports? [**LO 17.8**]

Endnotes

1. David H. Autor, David Dorn, and Gordon H. Hanson, "The China syndrome: Local labor market effects of import competition in the United States," *American Economic Review* 103, no. 6 (October 2013), pp. 2121–2168.

2. https://georgewbush-whitehouse.archives.gov/news/releases/2002/03/20020305-6.html.

3. www.fas.org/sgp/crs/misc/RL32333.pdf.

4. www.politico.eu/article/bush-trump-tariffs-why-steel-and-aluminum-failed-when-president/.

5. 1970 Current Population Survey, U.S. Department of Commerce, https://babel.hathitrust.org/cgi/pt?id=nyp.33433019 943079;view=1up;seq=9.

6. http://www.telegraph.co.uk/news/worldnews/europe/france/4306018/France-targets-Coca-Cola-in-escalating-cheese-wars.html.

7. https://news.un.org/en/story/2018/07/1014622.

Public Economics

PART FIVE

The six chapters in Part 5 will introduce you to . . .

how microeconomics might help solve important policy problems, including questions about technological innovation, the environment, inequality, and social security.

Until now, our analysis has focused on buyers and sellers in a particular market, but sometimes others have a particular stake in the outcomes. For example, many people bear the cost when a polluting factory emits smoke that contributes to climate change. Or, to take a positive example, your classmates benefit when you get a flu shot that helps prevent the spread of flu on campus. Chapter 18, "Externalities," deals with these kinds of costs and benefits, which are known as *externalities*. Externalities cause some goods and services to be overdemanded or oversupplied ("too much") or similarly, to be underdemanded or undersupplied ("too little"), relative to what might be efficient for society. This kind of inefficiency is an example of market failure.

Chapter 19, "Public Goods and Common Resources," describes two special types of goods that are undersupplied or overdemanded in free markets: *public goods* and *common-resource goods*. Public goods like national defense tend to be underprovided if left to the free market. Common resources suffer from the opposite problem: Individuals or firms will tend to use more of a common resource than is optimal socially. Overfishing in a lake is a classic example: Everyone would be better off if each person fished less in order to protect the long-term viability of the fish stock, but no individual has an incentive to cut back. We'll discuss how policy-makers might use taxes, subsidies, and quotas to get incentives right.

Few people love paying taxes, but most accept that taxes generate the revenue required by governments to build parks and highways, hire teachers and police officers, and provide other basic services for citizens. Chapter 20, "Taxation and the Public Budget," describes the role of taxes, the burden they place on taxpayers, and how some types of taxes can target certain problems better than others.

Chapter 21, "Poverty, Inequality, and Discrimination," analyzes facts and policies related to poverty and income inequality. We examine why some families are poorer and some are richer, and we describe what new research suggests about reducing income gaps. At the end of the chapter, we look at insights from economics into the problem of discrimination.

No matter what the particular topic is, making policy choices involves both economics and politics. With that in mind, Chapter 22, "Political Choices," looks at the political system through an economic lens. We show how economic analysis provides insight into fundamental political questions like why people vote, how politicians become corrupt, and how the president can influence the economy.

Chapter 23, "Public Policy and Choice Architecture," describes a new set of ideas that are shaping policy discussions. The idea of "choice architecture" builds on the simple insight that *how you frame a choice* can shape the decision that's made. We show how policy-makers are using "nudges" designed to help people achieve goals like saving for retirement and conserving energy.

Together, these chapters show how microeconomics gives us insight and possible ways to address policy problems, big and small.

Externalities

The Costs of Car Culture

California's culture centers around cars. In 1904, Los Angeles was home to just 1,600 cars. (Back then, the speed limit was 6 miles per hour downtown.) Today, nearly 35 million vehicles drive on the state's roads. Californians drive from the state's beaches to its mountains, and everywhere in between.[1]

But all of that driving has a downside as well. Los Angeles is notorious for its gridlocked freeways full of commuters. It's also one of the smoggiest cities in the country. If you're stuck in L.A. traffic, you won't need much persuading that the presence of all those other cars on the road is imposing a cost on you. (Of course, *your* presence on the road is also contributing to congestion that imposes a cost on everyone else.) Likewise, if you're an L.A. resident breathing in exhaust fumes every day, you're paying a price for the city's car culture.

©Getty Images

In previous chapters, we saw that when people make individual decisions to maximize their own welfare or well-being, competitive markets are typically efficient. Or, as some economists would say, the magic of the invisible hand maximizes total surplus. That's an important result, but it is true only when one person's choice does not affect the well-being of others. In many cases, that's a fair assumption. There are some situations, however—such as driving on congested highways—in which one person's decision has real implications for others.

In this chapter, we'll look at transactions that affect people other than the buyers and sellers directly involved. We'll see that in these cases, markets may no longer work efficiently. That is, *markets fail to maximize total surplus when individual choices impose uncompensated costs or benefits on others.*

LEARNING OBJECTIVES

LO 18.1 Explain how external costs and benefits affect the trade-offs faced by economic decision makers.

LO 18.2 Calculate the effect of a negative externality on market price and quantity.

LO 18.3 Calculate the effect of a positive externality on market price and quantity.

LO 18.4 Describe how individuals could reach a private solution to an externality, and explain why this doesn't always occur.

LO 18.5 Show how a tax or subsidy can be used to counteract an externality, and discuss the pros and cons of such solutions.

LO 18.6 Show how quantity regulations and tradable allowances can be used to counteract an externality, and discuss the pros and cons of such solutions.

We'll also look at some ways in which we can try to correct these market failures and restore efficiency. California's gasoline taxes—58.3 cents per gallon, one of the top-ten highest of U.S. states—are one example.[2] As we will see, such taxes are partly an attempt to force drivers to consider the costs they impose on others when they get behind the wheel. There is much debate over the right way to design policies to control congestion and pollution. Yet most economists agree that controlling pollution is an area in which government should be part of the solution.

In this chapter, we'll see how government intervention, taxes, and other regulations might actually *increase* efficiency in the presence of externalities, by changing prices to reflect the true cost of individuals' decisions. That's right—in the presence of certain types of market failure, taxes can make everyone better off.

What Are Externalities?

Think about the decision to drive a car. Although you probably don't make a conscious calculation every time you sit in the driver's seat, there is an underlying *trade-off* that you consider, at least subconsciously. On the one hand, you get the benefit of driving: getting from one place to another quickly and easily. On the other hand, you incur the costs of driving: paying for gasoline and some wear and tear on the car, and maybe also toll fees and the cost of parking.

When you make the decision to purchase or drive a car you are considering only your private costs and private benefits. We can model these decisions using supply and demand curves for a market with only private costs and private benefits, as shown in Figure 18-1, which illustrates the market for gasoline. The price and quantity at

---

FIGURE 18-1

Market with only private costs and private benefits   In a market with only private costs and benefits associated with the transaction, the market will reach an equilibrium at the intersection of supply and demand. The equilibrium quantity of gasoline traded will set marginal benefit equal to marginal cost for the last unit traded.

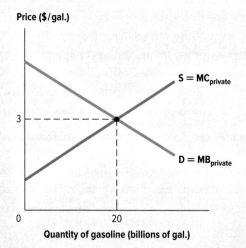

which buyers and sellers trade goods and services reflect their *private* costs and benefits. Recall the discussion from Chapter 5, "Efficiency," to see this relationship.

Now let's consider other types of costs that you might not typically think about. Every mile you drive burns gasoline, which emits pollutants into the air. If you're the only one on the road, the costs are negligible. When there are lots of drivers, the costs add up. The pollutants have two kinds of costs, one local and one global:

- Locally, if pollution levels get high, they can create regional smog and health problems. The situation in and around Los Angeles, California, is an example.
- Globally, the cost of burning gas comes from the production of carbon dioxide. Carbon dioxide is a greenhouse gas, which traps heat from the sun in the atmosphere and contributes to global warming, the gradual warming of the earth's atmosphere. Rising temperatures contribute to higher sea levels and melting of glaciers and ice caps, as well as changed precipitation patterns around the world.[3] Although global temperatures have fluctuated throughout history, most scientists today agree that human production of greenhouse gases contributes to climate change.

Do you consider these costs every time you weigh whether to go somewhere in your car? We don't know many people who do. The pollution caused by burning gasoline imposes costs on people *other than* the driver. In the case of vehicle emissions, any single driver has a tiny impact on the costs borne by others, so they're often easily ignored. The problem is that millions of small external costs, incurred every day, can add up to create big concerns.

So, let's imagine that drivers *did* take into account these kinds of costs, on top of the costs to themselves. Their cost-benefit trade-offs would shift slightly, and they would, on net, drive a bit less since total costs of driving would now be higher compared to just private costs. This suggests that failure to recognize the external costs is causing people to drive more than is optimal from the perspective of society as a whole.

Similarly, when you purchase a new car, you are buying a car that had to be manufactured. That manufacturing process emitted carbon dioxide (among other potential emissions).[4] If buyers considered all the costs associated with manufacturing a new car, their trade-offs would change by a small amount and likely fewer people would buy a car.

These kinds of issues are common in economics. We'll see that expanding upon the basic supply and demand framework shown in Figure 18-1 gives us a simple way to think about these external costs and benefits.

LO 18.1 Explain how external costs and benefits affect the trade-offs faced by economic decision makers.

External costs and benefits

To think clearly about the issues of external costs and benefits, we need to introduce some new terminology. The first piece of new terminology involves costs:

- In the car example, when we've talked about costs, we've been talking about costs borne by a driver herself—such as gasoline, wear and tear on a car, road tolls, and parking fees. To be specific, we call costs that fall directly on an economic decision maker **private costs**.
- But we've seen that there are other costs as well, such as the cost of pollution. Individual drivers don't personally bear all—or even most—of the costs of the pollution they produce. Pollution, and any other uncompensated costs that are imposed on someone other than the person who caused them, are called **external costs**.
- When we add private costs to external costs, we call the sum **social cost**.

For example, suppose you decide to host a noisy party. The *private costs* might include food, drink, and any cleanup costs the next day. The *external costs* would include annoyance felt by neighbors who can't sleep or study because of the noise your party is creating; your neighbors are not compensated for the discomfort caused by your party. The *social cost* would be the sum of these two types of costs.

private costs
costs that fall directly on an economic decision maker

external costs
costs imposed without compensation on someone other than the person who caused them

social cost
the entire cost of a decision, including both private costs and any external costs

TAKE NOTE... 🖉

Why don't we call the sum of private costs plus external costs "total cost" instead of *social cost?* Because *total cost* is the term used in another context in economics—to describe costs of production. Also, the term *social cost* helps make it clear that we are thinking about this idea from society's perspective.

Another piece of new terminology involves benefits. There also are lots of situations in which a person's behavior helps, rather than hurts, others. Like costs, benefits can be private or external:

- Imagine that you have decided to tidy up your messy front yard and paint your house. Clearly, you benefit from this decision: You have the aesthetic pleasure of a tidy yard and a prettier house, and the value of your property might even increase. These are benefits that accrue directly to the decision maker. We call them (as you might have guessed) **private benefits**.

private benefits
benefits that accrue directly to the decision maker

- Your neighbors, too, benefit from your decision to fix up your house. They get the pleasure of living in a nicer-looking neighborhood, and the value of their properties may also increase a bit—all at no cost to them. Benefits that accrue without compensation to someone other than the person who caused them are called **external benefits**.
- When we add private benefits to external benefits, we call the sum **social benefit**.

external benefits
benefits that accrue without compensation to someone other than the person who caused it

As another example, suppose you decide to get vaccinated against the flu and to wash your hands frequently. The private benefit is that you are less likely to get the flu. The external benefit is that you are less likely to transmit the flu to other people. The social benefit is the sum of these two effects—the overall reduction in likelihood of the flu spreading, both to yourself and to others.

We use the term **externality** to refer to an external cost or an external benefit. We typically call an external cost a *negative externality* and an external benefit a *positive externality:*

social benefit
the entire benefits of a decision, including both private benefits and external benefits

- External cost = a negative externality
- External benefit = a positive externality

Externalities are an incredibly important concept in economics. They are one of the most common causes of market failure. From this point on, we will use the terms learned in this section to distinguish between two types of choices:

externality
a cost or benefit imposed without compensation on someone other than the person who caused it

- choices that are optimal from the perspective of an *individual decision maker* (those based only on private costs and private benefits)
- choices that are optimal from the perspective of *society as a whole* (those that account for social costs and social benefits).

The size of the external cost or benefit caused by a particular action may vary based on location, timing, quantity, or many other factors. For instance, driving during the middle of the day in the summer usually contributes more to smog than driving at night or driving during winter (because sunlight is a key ingredient in the formation of smog). Painting the one run-down house in a nice neighborhood is likely to boost neighbors' property values more than painting one house in a neighborhood full of run-down homes. However, for the sake of simplicity, in this chapter we mostly assume that externalities involve a *constant, predictable* external cost or benefit.

Finally, there is one special type of externality that doesn't neatly fit into the categories we just laid out. A **network externality** is the effect that an additional user of a good or participant in an activity has on the value of that good or activity for others. Network externalities imply that people can help or harm others simply by virtue of their participation in a group. Network externalities can be positive or negative.

network externality
the effect that an additional user of a good or participant in an activity has on the value of that good or activity for others

We've already described one example of a negative network externality—driving in L.A. rush hour. Every additional person who decides to use the L.A. road network imposes a *negative network externality* on other road users. You may have also experienced negative network externalities on wireless internet networks, when each additional user draws down bandwidth, slowing the connection for other users.

Positive network externalities are frequently associated with technology, especially communication technology. An important historical example is the telephone. Telephones, like most communication devices, are useful only if other people have them too. In the early days, when very few people had telephones, having one let you contact only a limited number of people. Now, most people have phones, and in seconds you can reach people across town or across the world. The more common telephones became, the more people they allowed you to contact, and the more useful they got. Each person who joined the telephone network made telephones more useful for everyone else—a positive network externality. More recently, Snapchat and Instagram are perfect examples of services that have positive network externalities: If more of your friends use them, you get more benefit from using them yourself.

Negative externalities and the problem of "too much"

We can separate externalities by whether they impose an external cost or an external benefit on others:

- A negative externality is one that *imposes a cost* on another.
- A positive externality is one that *creates a benefit* for another.

We can also think about when the externality occurs: during the production or the consumption of the good or service:

- An externality that occurs when a good or service is being produced is a **production externality**.
- An externality that occurs when a good or service is being consumed is a **consumption externality**.

In this section, we will look at negative production and consumption externalities.

Negative production externality

A *negative production externality* is an external cost that occurs when a good or service is being produced. For example: When a car company considers whether to make a new car, it takes into account how much the car costs to manufacture by adding up the cost of labor and the cost of material. But without regulations or taxes, the company does not have to take into account any external, third-party costs that are generated by the manufacturing process, such as pollution. Society as a whole incurs those negative production costs. From the perspective of the car company, the car seems "cheaper" to manufacture than it seems to society as a whole. The private cost to the car company is less than the cost to society as a whole.

Imagine that car sales are completely unregulated in California. At any given price, there are some suppliers who consider that price to be greater than the costs of producing the car and thus are willing to sell the car at that price. This relationship between price and quantity supplied is the car company's supply curve in the market.

To add in the external cost associated with car production, we need to quantify how much damage is being imposed on everyone each time a car is manufactured. This external cost represents the size of the negative production externality. Because the negative production externality adds an external cost to society, we show this externality using the supply side of the market, as seen in Figure 18-2. The external cost is the vertical distance between the private supply curve ($S = MC_{private}$) and the social cost curve. (The social cost curve is sometimes called the "marginal social cost" curve, but we use the simpler term.)

What are the equilibrium price and quantity of cars traded in an unregulated market? It occurs where the private supply curve ($S = MC_{private}$) and the market demand curve ($D = MB_{private}$) intersect. In Figure 18-2, that is the point at which 10 million cars are produced and each is sold for $20,000.

But when the negative external cost is accounted for by producers, we see that the efficient quantity of new cars produced falls—to the point where social cost and the market demand curve intersect.

LO 18.2 Calculate the effect of a negative externality on market price and quantity.

production externality
an externality that occurs when a good or service is being produced

consumption externality
an externality that occurs when a good or service is being consumed

FIGURE 18-2

Market with a negative production externality   At the private equilibrium, 10 million cars are manufactured at a price of $20,000 each. At the private equilibrium the market creates a deadweight loss by not accounting for the external costs. Once those external costs associated with car manufacturing are accounted for, the efficient equilibrium falls to 8 million cars, while the efficient price rises to $22,000.

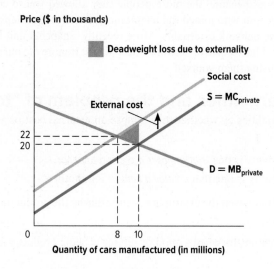

As a result, the efficient price for a new car rises. The true, or social, cost of manufacturing a car is higher than the private cost. The socially efficient equilibrium in the market reflects the external costs in addition to the benefits and costs to the buyers and sellers.

The cost to society of manufacturing too many cars is shown via the deadweight loss triangle in Figure 18-2. For every car manufactured beyond the socially efficient quantity (at 8 million), the cost to society is more than the benefit to buyers from acquiring the car. Remember from Chapter 5, "Efficiency," that producing where marginal costs exceed marginal benefits creates a *deadweight loss* to society. This deadweight loss reduces economic surplus to society. The negative production externality results in "too much" car production.

Negative consumption externality   A *negative consumption externality* is a cost imposed on others when a good or service is being consumed. As an example, let's consider cars again, and this time think about how much someone drives. (Naturally, this logic also applies to the decision to buy a car at all versus using public transportation, biking, or walking.)

Because air pollution and environmental damage are external costs, the costs of driving a car look smaller from the perspective of an individual driver than from the perspective of society as a whole. Because drivers don't take the external cost into account, they will decide to drive more than they would if they themselves had to bear the full cost of driving (which mostly includes the cost caused by any pollution, and which people may value differently depending on their views).

Why is that a problem? It means people drive "too much"—that is, more than they would if they faced the social costs of their actions. Where there are externalities, the free market no longer allocates resources in a way that maximizes total surplus for society as a whole.

Just like in the case of a negative production externality, buyers and sellers in the market don't consider the external costs, and the market outcome occurs at "too much production." Every gallon of gas consumed beyond the efficient quantity costs society more than buyers value the gasoline. *The overconsumption produces a deadweight loss and decreases overall economic surplus.* The negative consumption externality results in "too much" gasoline production.

Positive externalities and the problem of "too little"

Externalities can also occur when a benefit for others is created. These are *positive* externalities. As was the case for negative externalities, there can be positive production and positive consumption externalities. We'll look at both types of positive externalities in this section.

It is tempting to think that a positive externality must be a good thing. A negative externality decreases surplus, so a positive externality must do the opposite, right? Sadly, that is not the case. A positive externality also pushes quantity away from the efficient equilibrium level, reducing total surplus.

Positive consumption externality   A *positive consumption externality* is a third-party benefit that occurs when a good or service is being consumed. Consider the decision to paint the outside of your house. A homeowner will paint her house if the private benefits (such as increased property value, a nicer-looking home) outweigh the private costs (such as the time and money required to paint the house or pay someone else to do it). But this personal decision doesn't take into account benefits that accrue to neighbors, who also enjoy increased property values and a tidier-looking neighborhood. As a result, houses get painted "too little"—that is, less than the amount that would maximize total surplus, once we also consider the surplus of people other than the homeowner and house painter.

Although the external benefits of house painting probably vary a lot, let's make a rough estimate. Suppose that the external benefits are worth $500 per paint job. In other words, $500 is the combined amount your neighbors would be willing to pay you to *avoid* having your shabby-looking house lowering the tone of the neighborhood. Let's imagine that somehow it were possible to turn the external benefit into private benefit—by some magic, every time a homeowner paints her house, $500 is transferred from her neighbors' bank accounts into her own.

If this $500 transfer happened, the homeowner's trade-off would look different: The benefits of painting would increase and the costs would stay the same. *How would she respond* to this change? We can represent the difference between the private trade-off and the social trade-off (including the external benefit) by adding the external benefits to the private benefit or demand curve, creating a new social benefit curve. At any given market price, homeowners will behave as if the price were reduced by the amount of the external benefit.

Maintaining the outside of one's house creates both private benefits for the homeowner and external, social benefits for the neighborhood. ©Jupiterimages/Getty Images

Because the positive consumption externality adds an external benefit to society, we show this externality using the demand side of the market. We can show the case of painting our homeowner's house by modeling the social benefit curve $500 above the private demand curve, as shown in Figure 18-3. (The social benefit curve is sometimes called the "marginal social benefit" curve, but we stick with the simpler language.)

We can find the equilibrium price and quantity of painted houses in an unregulated market by looking at the intersection of the private supply curve ($S = MC_{private}$) and private demand curve ($D = MB_{private}$). In the unregulated market, 300 houses get painted. When the external benefit is accounted for, we see that the efficient quantity of painted houses increases to 360 houses. The social demand (social benefit) curve intersects the private supply curve at a higher quantity. This means that the social benefit of painting your house is higher than the private benefit. The socially efficient equilibrium in the market incorporates the external benefits in addition to the benefits that accrue to the buyers and sellers.

Here again, the net cost to society is shown in Figure 18-3 via the deadweight loss triangle. For every house painted below the efficient quantity, it would benefit society more than it costs the seller, thus producing a deadweight loss and decreasing overall economic surplus. Again, recall

FIGURE 18-3

Market with a positive consumption externality At the private equilibrium, 300 houses are painted at a price of $1,500 each. At the private equilibrium, the market creates a deadweight loss by underproducing house painting and not accounting for the external benefits. Once the $500 external benefits associated with painting your house are accounted for (given by the vertical distance between the private demand curve and the social benefit curve), the efficient equilibrium rises to 360 houses, while the efficient price rises to $1,750.

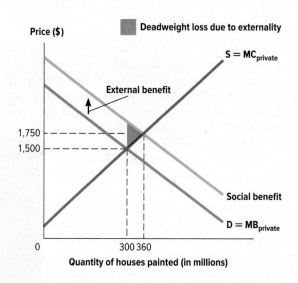

the discussion of deadweight loss from Chapter 5, "Efficiency." *Underproducing a good or service will reduce economic surplus and generate a deadweight loss.* The positive consumption externality results in "too little" house painting.

Positive production externality A *positive production externality* is a third-party benefit that occurs when a good or service is being produced. Consider a power company producing electricity. We often think of power plants as creating negative externalities (along with lots of private benefits, of course). But along the coast of Florida, power plants produce an unexpected positive externality. Power plants in Florida use ocean water in their cooling systems, drawing in the cold water and then releasing the warmed water back into the ocean. This warmed water turns out to be an ideal manatee habitat. Warm water emissions from Florida power plants have helped the manatee population to increase from fewer than 1,000 manatees in 1967 to over 6,620 manatees in 2017.[5] Manatees are an important part of ecosystems and help maintain healthy sea grass beds.

The increased number of manatees (and habitats for them) is an external benefit to a power plant's decision to produce electricity. In an unregulated market, the power plant will not consider the effects on the manatee population when making production decisions.

But if regulations force the power plant to improve the manatee habitat, then the question to be considered is how much power the plant should produce. To consider how much power to produce, we need to measure the value to society of the manatee habitat. We can then use this value to measure the positive production externality of the Florida power plants.

In the same way we might measure how much people would pay to avoid pollution, we can measure how much people would pay to preserve manatee populations. If, hypothetically, the value of supporting the manatee population (and thus helping to sustain marine ecosystems) is $1 per kilowatt hour of electricity produced by the power plant, we can find the social benefit of the electricity production. The social benefit is then worth the private benefit plus the $1 per kilowatt hour of external benefits.

But in an unregulated market, power plants and consumers do not consider the external benefit when making the production decision, and the market will produce "too little." Just as we saw with our positive consumption example, producing an amount of output different from the socially efficient quantity produces a deadweight loss. In this case, the market is underproducing electricity by failing to take into account the full social benefits of the activity. For every kilowatt hour of electricity not produced between the market equilibrium and the socially efficient equilibrium, society is missing out on a net benefit. *This underproduction produces a deadweight loss and decreases overall economic surplus.* The positive production externality results in "too little" electricity production.

The manatee population along the coast of Florida has flourished in part due to warm water being released by nearby power plants.
©James R.D. Scott/Getty Images

✓ TEST YOURSELF

☐ What is the difference between a positive and negative externality? **[LO 18.1]**
☐ How is a network externality different from other externalities? **[LO 18.1]**
☐ How does a negative externality affect the supply curve? How does this change the equilibrium price and quantity relative to the same market in which the externality is faced? **[LO 18.2]**
☐ How does a positive externality affect the demand curve? How does this change the equilibrium price and quantity relative to the same market without the externality? **[LO 18.3]**
☐ Does an externality cause total surplus to increase or decrease? **[LO 18.2, 18.3]**

Private Solutions to Externalities

We've learned that externalities reduce total surplus by creating a deadweight loss for society. In theory, however, it is possible to address this problem by *transforming external costs and benefits into private costs and benefits.* Efficiency could be restored if drivers give money to pollution sufferers or if neighbors join together to subsidize the painting of rundown houses on their block. Under certain circumstances, private individuals may be able to deal with externalities, restoring efficiency to the market on their own. This section details the conditions necessary for private solutions to externalities to be successful and discusses why it is often the case that those necessary conditions don't exist in the market.

Suppose a friend is enjoying his lunch, but his tuna sandwich is giving off a really strong odor. Unless you like the smell of tuna, he would be causing a negative externality by eating the tuna in front of you. What can you do? You could ask him to eat it later, but he might object. If you felt strongly enough, you could consider paying him to not eat the sandwich. In practice, that would probably seem weird, but in principle it's a legitimate option for eliminating the externality. After

LO 18.4 Describe how individuals could reach a private solution to an externality, and explain why this doesn't always occur.

all, not every conflict involving externalities requires a regulatory solution. Sometimes, people can find solutions to conflicts surrounding externalities on their own.

A basic idea in economics is that individuals will pursue mutually beneficial trades. No mutually beneficial trade should go unexploited because someone always has something to gain from pursuing it. The result is that when we add up all of the actions of self-interested individuals, every opportunity to gain surplus should have been exploited, and total surplus should be maximized.

But we've just seen that an externality reduces surplus. Therefore—somewhere, somehow—there are mutually beneficial trades *waiting to be exploited*. For instance, the Californians who bear the cost of air pollution lose more surplus than is gained by drivers who don't have to pay for it. Here's a crazy idea: Why don't those who suffer from pollution *pay* drivers to drive less? Since there is surplus to be gained from decreasing the quantity of gas burned, a mutually beneficial trade exists. If a given reduction in driving would cause drivers to lose \$9.4 billion in surplus and other Californians to gain \$10 billion in surplus, why don't those other Californians agree to pay drivers, say, \$9.7 billion to drive less? Both groups will be better off. The quantity of driving—and, hence, of pollution—would fall to the efficient equilibrium level, and total surplus in society as a whole would be maximized.

The idea that individuals can reach an efficient equilibrium through private trades, even in the presence of an externality, is called the **Coase theorem**. The Coase theorem is named for economist Ronald Coase, a British economist whose work focused on property rights and transaction costs. He won the Nobel Prize in Economics in 1991.[6] A couple of key assumptions must hold for the Coase theorem to work:

Coase theorem
the idea that even in the presence of an externality, individuals can reach an efficient equilibrium through private trades, assuming zero transaction costs

1. People can make enforceable agreements (also known as contracts) to pay one another.
2. There are no transaction costs in coordinating and enforcing agreements.

The trouble is that these two assumptions almost never hold true. What kind of elaborate organization would be required to bring together all 39 million citizens of California, get each of them to agree to pay the amount that avoiding pollution is worth to them personally, redistribute that money to drivers who agreed to drive less, and then monitor those drivers to make sure they actually followed through? Whew! The costs of coordination and enforcement would surely be much higher than the surplus lost to the externality. It wouldn't be worth the effort even to try.

The idea of having people in California pay drivers to reduce their driving illustrates a second drawback of the Coase theorem. The private solution yields an *efficient* outcome—the surplus-maximizing quantity of gas is bought and sold. But the *distribution* of that surplus (who gets the benefit of the surplus) is often quite different from solutions reached through government intervention:

- In the private solution, the *citizens of California* have to pay drivers not to drive. The citizens are still better off paying the drivers (because pollution decreases), but they are not as well off as they would be if drivers had to pay for the right to pollute.
- In a solution reached by government intervention (for example, adding a tax to the market and using the revenue to compensate pollution sufferers), it is likely that the *drivers* would have to pay all California citizens \$1 per gallon to compensate for pollution.

Notice that either solution is efficient, but the assumptions about what is "fair" and who has the "rights" to do what are different:

- In one case (the private solution), it's assumed that drivers have a right to pollute and have to be paid not to.
- In the other case (the government intervention), it's assumed citizens have a right to live free of pollution and have to be paid to accept pollution.

The Coase theorem reminds us that efficiency is all about maximizing total surplus. It says nothing about achieving a "fair" distribution of that surplus. Whoever starts with the property rights, if the conditions of the Coase theorem hold, should not affect who ends up with them. But it does affect who pays whom to compensate for trading the rights.

But what happens when property rights are unclear and transacting is not costless? See the What Do You Think? box "Reclining transactions" for an interesting debate regarding the transaction of reclining your airline seat.

Reclining transactions
What Do You Think?

On a United Airlines flight from New Jersey to Denver, two passengers seated near each other got into such an intense fight that the pilot had to divert the plane to Chicago. The passengers were arguing over whether the one in the front seat could recline his seat. If they had thought like economists, they might have averted the conflict.

This is a simple example of a consumption externality:

- The person in the front seat "consumes" the reclining function of the seat; doing so has a negative impact on the person in the back seat.
- If the person in the back seat "consumes" the space in front of him (he prevents the person in the front seat from reclining), this has a negative impact on the person in front.

How might an economist approach this problem? Simple:

- First, we must understand who starts with the *property right*. Does the person in front have the right to recline "his" chair? Or does the person behind have the right to fly without the passenger in front leaning back into "his" space?
- Next, we should give the two passengers an opportunity to make a trade in which the party with the property right could sell it to the other.

This logic is essentially the Coase theorem: The efficient solution can be found, as long as parties can easily transact with each other.

To solve the externality problem of reclining airline seats, you must first understand who has the property rights to the seat—the person in the seat or the person behind the seat.
©Ingram Publishing/SuperStock

(continued)

This situation is not merely hypothetical. Economist Erik Snowberg likes to recline his seat when flying. If the passenger seated behind Snowberg asks him not to recline, Snowberg politely asks that passenger, "How much is it worth to you for me not to recline my seat?" So far, nobody has offered Snowberg more than $5. He values reclining his seat more than $5, so he has yet to accept an offer. But by monetizing the transaction, Snowberg has avoided conflicts (or befuddled people into silence).

Why is this solution not more common? There are two complicating factors.

- First, the property rights need to be clearly assigned. In this case, consumers sign a contract with the airline when they buy plane tickets. This contract gives them the right to use their chair and its functions (one of which is to recline), subject to safety rules. But not everyone knows this. When you don't know who is holding the rights—in this case, that passengers have the right to recline their own seats—it's hard even to consider, much less complete, a trade.
- Second, the Coase theorem requires that transacting is costless. In the case of the airline seat, social norms make it awkward for many to shift the conversation to "How much can I pay you not to put your seat back?" Not everybody is willing to start up a negotiation with a stranger or to put a price on something that's not commonly assigned a value. Because of social norms, transaction costs may not be zero. (Feeling weird and awkward counts as a transaction cost!) Some individuals, like Erik Snowberg, may find it easy to start a negotiation, and for these people, the transaction costs are near zero. But for others, the perceived personal costs of opening negotiation may be high enough that they are not willing to speak up.

Still, think about how a market for seatback space could benefit both parties: The business traveler in back who wants to open her large laptop to make last-minute changes to a presentation might be more than willing to offer a few dollars to the teenager in front, who in turn might be thrilled to have some extra money to spend when the plane lands. So, the next time you're on a plane and the person sitting in front of you starts to reach for the recline button, perhaps think about what it's worth to you and make an offer.

WHAT DO YOU THINK?

1. Would a world with more bargaining be a better one?
2. Could you imagine bargaining with a stranger on an airplane over reclining your seat? Why or why not?
3. Can you think of another way to solve this problem?

Sources: "United Flight Diverts over 'Knee Defender' Fight," *USA Today*, August 26, 2014; United Airlines' aircraft seating FAQs: www.united.com/web/en-US/content/help/seating.aspx.

In practice, deciding who pays whom in order to solve the externality problem is often less a question of economics than of politics, law, and philosophy. Even when it would make people better off to pay someone else to do, or stop doing, something that affects them, they often feel it is not "fair" or "just" to do so. For example, the 2000 movie *Erin Brockovich* is based on the true story of a woman who discovered that a big company was polluting the groundwater in her community, allegedly causing high rates of cancer and other health conditions. She started a legal campaign to force the company to stop polluting and compensate the families. Can you imagine if Erin Brockovich instead organized her community under the Coase theorem to *pay the company* to stop polluting? We very much doubt that moviegoers would have found it such a heartwarming, feel-good story.

Given the challenges described above, people usually care not only about reaching an efficient equilibrium, but also about how we get there and who benefits. If you go knocking on your neighbors' doors to explain positive externalities and propose that they contribute toward the cost of painting your house, you'll probably get doors slammed in your face. For a somewhat unlikely application of the Coase theorem, look at the From Another Angle box "Does no-fault divorce law increase the divorce rate?"

Does no-fault divorce law increase the divorce rate?
From Another Angle

In 1969, California became the first state in the country to legalize "no-fault" divorce. Prior to no-fault laws, a divorce could be granted only if a person showed that his or her spouse was "at fault" for committing some wrongdoing, such as adultery, abandonment, or abuse. If both partners wanted out, they could agree to lie in court, pretending that one of them was at fault. But if only one partner wanted out, he or she was stuck. Under no-fault divorce laws, either partner could obtain a divorce, without agreement or having to show evidence of wrongdoing.

Should we expect this change in the law to increase the divorce rate? At first glance, the answer might be yes: Before, it was extremely difficult to get divorced if your partner didn't agree. After, it is relatively easy.

However, the Coase theorem gives us a different perspective. It predicts that the number of divorces will stay the same, but the *distribution of surplus between marriage partners* will change.

To see how this works, imagine a situation in which one partner wants to get divorced and the other doesn't. Under the old law, the partner who wanted the divorce would have to make concessions to persuade his or her spouse to lie in court—say, offering more alimony or greater visitation rights to the children. The partner who wanted to stay married needed to offer no concessions at all.

Once no-fault divorce came in, this situation was reversed: The partner who wanted to stay married would have to offer something that would improve the value of the marriage to the partner who wanted out. For example, maybe he or she would offer to dramatically change behavior or make amends for a serious failing.

The Coase theorem predicts that roughly the same number of couples will eventually agree to divorce or stay married under no-fault divorce law as before—but the partner who wanted out will now get the better end of the bargain. The partner who wants to keep the marriage together will make the concessions.

As it happens, divorce rates *didn't* go up much after no-fault laws. A short flurry of divorces was followed by a return to pre-no-fault levels. In this instance at least, the Coase theorem made the right prediction.

Source: J. Wolfers, "Did Unilateral Divorce Laws Raise Divorce Rates? A Reconciliation and New Results," *American Economic Review* 96, no. 5 (2006).

✓ TEST YOURSELF

☐ What conditions are required in order for people to be able to privately solve externalities under the Coase theorem? **[LO 18.4]**

Public Solutions to Externalities

Because of the cost and difficulty of designing and coordinating private solutions, people often turn to public policy for solutions to externalities. The most common public policy remedies to externality problems involve taxes and subsidies or quotas and tradable allowances.

It sounds relatively straightforward to impose a tax on a good that creates a negative externality, right? However, solutions to the externality problems are often easier to describe than to implement. External costs and benefits can be diffuse, complex, and hard to control. Solutions must try to ensure that economic decision makers experience costs and benefits that are *equal in value* to the true social costs and benefits of their choices. If everyone affected has to be involved in the process, that could mean coordinating across millions—or even billions—of people. This is a tricky problem to solve, even for the most committed policy-makers.

We will also see that there can be a tension between efficiency and fairness in finding solutions to externalities. Saying a market "works efficiently" means only that *it maximizes surplus*. Increasing surplus *for society* may decrease surplus for some groups while increasing it for other groups. Thus, efficiency doesn't say anything at all about the *distribution* of that surplus—who gets the benefits of the surplus. For example, if people who commute are poorer than those who live downtown, transferring surplus from "polluters" to "nonpolluters" means transferring from poor to wealthy. Also, some technically sound solutions might seem unfair (like rewarding people for *not* polluting, rather than taxing people who do pollute) and thus also might not get far in the political arena.

In this section we will look at public solutions to externalities in detail and discuss the successes and challenges of such solutions.

Taxes and subsidies

LO 18.5 Show how a tax or subsidy can be used to counteract an externality, and discuss the pros and cons of such solutions.

At points in the chapter, we've said that the most basic public policy remedy to an externality problem involves counterbalancing the externality with a tax or a subsidy. Here, we look more deeply at two options: countering a negative externality with a tax and countering a positive externality with a subsidy.

Countering a negative externality with a tax   Let's return to the negative externality created by cars. Imagine that the city government in Los Angeles decides to solve the problem of too much car driving by taxing car dealers at a rate of $4,000 per car. The city then will use that money to compensate those affected by any environmental damage created.

Pigovian tax
a tax meant to counterbalance a negative externality

A tax meant to counter the effect of a negative externality is called a **Pigovian tax**, named for economist Arthur Pigou. Pigou was an English economist at the University of Cambridge; his work focused primarily on welfare economics.[7] Other Pigovian taxes include so-called sin taxes on alcohol and cigarettes as well as carbon taxes.

As panel A of Figure 18-4 shows, the effect of a negative externality is that the supply curve $(S = MC_{private})$ is lower than it would be if car dealers had to account for social costs. The effect of a Pigovian tax—like the effect of any tax—is that it *increases the effective price* that is paid for a good. As shown in panel B of Figure 18-4, this creates a new supply curve (S + tax) above the private supply curve $(S = MC_{private})$. If the supply curve (S + tax) is pushed up far enough, it will move the equilibrium quantity back to the efficient level—that is, the level at which the market maximizes total surplus.

With a production tax, car dealers face the full social costs of producing and selling the car, represented by the new supply curve (social cost). When a production tax is introduced, the equilibrium point moves up along the demand curve to its intersection with the social supply curve, resulting in a higher price–lower quantity combination. The example demonstrates a very important conclusion: *If car dealers had to pay the full cost of producing and selling vehicles, including the external cost of pollution, they would choose to sell fewer vehicles.*

However, Pigovian taxes are not a perfect solution to externalities. There are two problems. The first is *setting the tax at the right level*. As we have seen, it is not always easy to put an exact dollar-and-cents value on external costs. In our example, we estimated the external cost associated with selling a car to be $4,000, so we chose an optimal Pigovian tax of $4,000 per vehicle. What will happen if the estimate is wrong?

FIGURE 18-4

A tax counteracts the effect of a negative externality

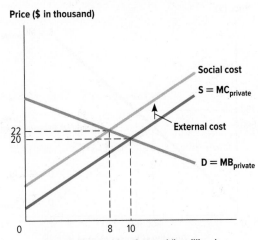

(A) The effect of a negative externality

Price ($ in thousand)

Quantity of cars manufactured (in millions)

Under a negative externality, the private supply curve is below the social marginal cost curve by the amount of the external cost. This causes the equilibrium quantity to be higher than the efficient level.

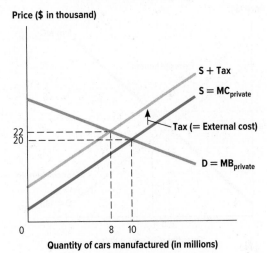

(B) The effect of a Pigovian tax

Price ($ in thousand)

Quantity of cars manufactured (in millions)

A Pigovian tax counteracts a negative externality. If the tax is set equal to the external cost, the tax raises the private marginal cost to the social marginal cost, and the resulting equilibrium quantity is efficient.

- If the estimate is too low, then the tax is set too low. In that case, the market will move closer to the efficient equilibrium, but it will remain somewhat inefficient.
- If our estimate is too high, then the tax is set too high. In that case, the market will overshoot—the new equilibrium quantity will be inefficient because it is too low, rather than too high.

The second problem with Pigovian taxes involves *distribution of the surplus*. Taxes are effective at transferring surplus away from consumers and producers and toward the government. But there is no guarantee that the government can or will then do anything to help the people who are bearing the external cost. The revenue collected from a Pigovian tax is sometimes used as compensation, but often it is not.

Yet, whether or not the revenue is redistributed to address the impacts of climate change, the tax still maximizes total surplus *in society as a whole* by moving the car market to the efficient equilibrium. Remember, the *distribution of surplus* is an entirely separate question from *maximizing total surplus*.

Capturing a positive externality with a subsidy   Just as a tax can counterbalance an external cost, a subsidy can help consumers or producers capture the benefits of positive externalities. If the government calculates that painting houses creates $500 worth of external benefits for neighbors, it might offer $500 subsidies to people who want to paint their houses.

As panel A of Figure 18-5 shows, the effect of a positive externality is that the demand curve ($D = MB_{private}$) is lower than it would be if consumers accounted for social benefits. The effect of a subsidy is that it *decreases the effective price* that is paid for a good by the buyer. As panel B of Figure 18-5 shows, this creates a new demand curve ($D + subsidy$) above the private demand

FIGURE 18-5

A subsidy counteracts the effect of a positive externality

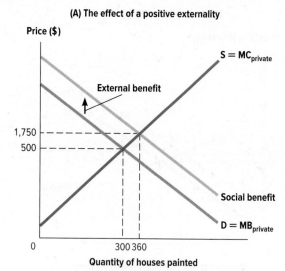

(A) The effect of a positive externality

Under a positive externality, the private demand curve is below the social marginal benefit curve by the amount of the external benefit. This causes the equilibrium quantity to be lower than the efficient level.

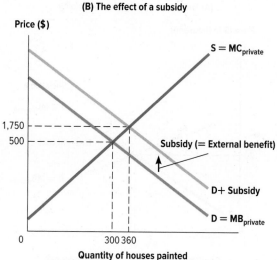

(B) The effect of a subsidy

A subsidy counteracts a positive externality. If the subsidy is set equal to the external benefit, the subsidy raises the private marginal benefit to the social marginal benefit, and the resulting equilibrium quantity is efficient.

curve ($D = MB_{private}$). If the demand curve (D + subsidy) is pushed up far enough, it will move the equilibrium quantity up to the efficient level—that is, the level at which the market maximizes total surplus.

Remember that, as with a Pigovian tax, using a subsidy to increase efficiency does not necessarily equal fairness. Such a subsidy would maximize total surplus in society. But the *distribution of that surplus* depends on where the government gets the money to pay for the subsidies. It might seem more "fair" if the subsidies were paid for out of property taxes because property owners have the most to gain from nicer neighborhoods. But even if the money was collected from general taxation, total surplus would still be maximized.

Public policies that use subsidies to solve externality problems are sometimes less noticeable than taxes. Once you begin to look for them, you'll see they are extremely widespread.

One example that's a lot less trivial than painting houses is elementary and secondary education. If parents had to pay to send their children to school, many might decide the trade-off wasn't worth it; more kids might drop out before finishing high school. Yet educating children has all sorts of external benefits: With education, children are more likely to become economically productive members of society and engaged citizens. That's why most governments offer public schools, which subsidize the cost of education.

You may also have seen how universities often subsidize small services in the campus community. Examples include free immunization shots to keep students from passing the flu around and antivirus software to keep viruses and malware out of the university computer network. In both of these cases, the thinking is that if it were left entirely to the market, students would consume "too little" of these goods or services. That is, fewer students would pay for immunizations and antivirus software than the amount that would maximize total surplus on the campus as a whole.

As with taxes, solving a positive externality through subsidies requires quantifying the external cost or benefit accurately. What will happen if the estimate is wrong?

- If the subsidy is set too low—say, a $50 subsidy for painting your house—then the number of houses painted will remain inefficiently low.
- If the subsidy is set too high—say, a $5,000 subsidy—then total surplus will not be maximized either. The increase in social benefits from the additional house painting will be less than the cost of the subsidy.

Other policy options: Quotas and tradable allowances

Another set of policy options is to set regulations or quotas on the amount of a good or service that can be produced or consumed. Sometimes these quotas can be designed to be traded among interested parties.

LO 18.6 Show how quantity regulations and tradable allowances can be used to counteract an externality, and discuss the pros and cons of such solutions.

Quotas   If we know the socially optimal quantity of something—for instance, how much pollution we are willing to tolerate—why not simply regulate quantity (set a *quota*) rather than impose taxes? For example, California could calculate the efficient quantity of cars on the road and limit each producer's sales to its share of that amount. This approach would reduce car sales by the same amount as a tax and also would reduce pollution by the same amount.

However, perhaps surprisingly, limiting total consumption to the efficient quantity *does not* make the market efficient. The real magic of the invisible hand in a market is not just that it pushes price and quantity to the efficient level. Rather, it does so by allocating resources to those with the greatest willingness to pay for them. Maximizing surplus depends not only on how many cars are sold but also on *who* manufactures and sells them. Some car manufacturers will find it easy to reduce emissions. Others may use old technology and find it difficult to reduce their emissions. A tax allows the market to sort itself out in this way; a quota does not.

Tradable allowances   You may have spotted an obvious way to improve a quota system. The fact that different manufacturers have a different ability to reduce emissions implies that there is a missed opportunity for a mutually beneficial trade: A high-emissions manufacturer could pay a low-emissions manufacturer some amount in exchange for the rights to emit one more ton of carbon. In that trade, both would end up better off.

Why not set a quota but then allow firms to buy and sell their quota allowances? This solution allows policy-makers to choose a quantity rather than set a tax rate, while still ensuring that the quota is allocated to the people with the highest willingness to pay. A production or consumption quota that can be bought and sold is called a **tradable allowance**.

Just as with a quota, a system of tradable allowances will result in the efficient quantity of a good being bought and sold (as long as the total quota is set at the right quantity, of course). Like a tax, tradable allowances maximize surplus.

There is one important difference, though, between a Pigovian tax and a tradable allowance:

tradable allowance a production or consumption quota that can be bought and sold

- The Pigovian tax results in revenue collected by the *government*.
- In contrast, the tradable allowance creates a market in which quota rights are bought and sold among *private parties*.

The government could collect revenue by selling the initial quotas. But in cases where such programs have been implemented, they are more commonly allocated for free to consumers or producers, who then trade among themselves.

For more on the recent policy debate over whether to institute a carbon tax or a system of tradable carbon allowances in the United States, read the Economics in Action box "Why not tax ourselves?"

Why not tax ourselves?
Economics in Action

The stadium at the University of Michigan is the biggest in the United States. With a capacity of 107,601 people, the stadium can hold a small city. Thanks to the stadium lights and the massive electronic scoreboard, it also uses a lot of energy.

To reduce external costs, the University of Michigan proposed taxing different parts of the university, including the athletic program, in proportion to their energy use.
©Steven Pepple/123RF

Like factories, big universities contribute to the greenhouse-gas emissions that have been linked to climate change. It's not only university stadiums that burn lots of energy, but also research labs, university hospitals, offices, classrooms, and dorms.

In 2015, the University of Michigan decided to try to reduce its contribution to greenhouse-gas emissions. A committee of staff and students considered proposals. One student knew that economists argue that the best solution is often to impose taxes on external costs like contributions to greenhouse-gas emissions. In fact, the 2018 Nobel Prize in Economics was awarded to William Nordhaus who has long championed this idea (often known as carbon taxes). The student thought, "Why not try that here at Michigan? Why not tax ourselves?" The committee proposed that the university consider imposing a small "tax" on different parts of the university in proportion to their energy use.

"Wait a minute," said the scientists. "If the university charges us more for the electricity we use in our labs, our costs will go up. Then we'll have a much harder time winning competitive grants. And why should *we* pay extra but not the economists or anthropologists who have fewer energy needs?"

"Wait," said the hospital administrators. "Why impose so much hardship on *us?* It's already hard to provide quality service to the community."

And so it went. Eventually, the tax idea died, and the university found other ways to cut its energy use.

Versions of what happened at the University of Michigan happen in other contexts. Economists continue to argue that taxes on external costs make sense, but the idea is seldom greeted enthusiastically. Despite attempts, the United States has failed to enact a national tax on greenhouse-gas emissions.

Part of the challenge is that people don't usually want to pay more taxes. But there's another part that's even trickier: The main beneficiaries of efforts to combat climate change include people who are not yet born—the future children and grandchildren of today's younger generation. Those future residents of the planet may be profoundly affected by the decisions of today's voters—and they would likely wish that we impose taxes on greenhouse emissions *today.* The hard part is that future generations can't vote in today's elections. In the end, no matter how compelling are the economic equations, the political equation still doesn't quite add up.

Source: Barry Rabe, *Can We Price Carbon?* (Cambridge, MA: MIT Press, 2018).

Targeting externalities with public policy

When economists propose taxes or tradable allowances as a way to tackle externalities, they try to propose taxes based on the externality itself, rather than on the action that generates it. But this is often quite hard to do. In this chapter, we've discussed gas taxes, which are targeted at a good that generates pollution, rather than at pollution itself. Ideally, environmental policy would target the end product—carbon emissions—directly. That way, the policy would apply to all the thousands of different activities that generate an external cost through carbon emissions—from raising livestock, to operating a power plant, to lighting a wood fire in a fireplace. However, measuring emissions from all these different sources is extremely difficult, logistically speaking. Taxing gasoline, rather than pollution, is a second-best solution; the first-best solution may simply be unattainable.

Because of the difficulty of measuring pollution directly, many policies do target individual goods and processes. For instance:

- Cars are generally required to have catalytic converters, which reduce emissions of nitrous oxides, carbon monoxide, and unburnt hydrocarbons.
- Governments often subsidize recycling or energy-saving appliances and light bulbs.
- Local governments ban wood fires during smoggy times of the year or when dry conditions make fires especially dangerous.

The downside of targeting individual activities is that such policies risk misaligning the incentives that consumers and producers face with the goal of minimizing the externality.

For example, in 1975 the U.S. government imposed fuel-efficiency standards, called the *CAFE standards*, on cars. The goal was to reduce pollution. But the regulations were designed in such a way that "light trucks" were subject to looser standards than cars. The result? Auto manufacturers started producing cars that were big and heavy enough to be classed as a light truck; those vehicles didn't have to meet the standards for cars. Average fuel efficiency of cars actually *fell* rather than increased. The CAFE standards were updated in 2012 with new regulations requiring automakers to raise the *average* fuel efficiency to 54.5 miles per gallon for cars and light trucks by 2025.[8]

A policy that directly targets pollution encourages the development of cleaner technology and processes; it doesn't give clever companies the chance to find ways around the policy. In fact, such policies give consumers and producers an incentive to find new ways of doing things that *don't* generate pollution. They want to avoid having to pay a tax or pay for the rights to an allowance—and that desire aligns their incentives with the end goal of the policy. Of course, policy-makers have many goals, and in 2017 the Trump administration took another look and advocated reducing fuel-efficiency standards in order to promote jobs and manufacturing.

✓ TEST YOURSELF

- ☐ Are subsidies used to correct for positive or negative externalities? **[LO 18.5]**
- ☐ Which is a more efficient way of correcting a negative externality—a quota or a tax? **[LO 18.6]**
- ☐ What is the difference between a normal quota and a tradable quota? Which is more efficient and why? **[LO 18.6]**

Conclusion

Typically, we rely on the invisible hand of markets to maximize total surplus by allocating the right quantity of goods to the right people. But what happens when one person's choices impose costs or benefits on others? Free-market outcomes can be less than ideal. They sometimes result in too much or too little of the good or activity in question.

As the examples in this chapter show, positive or negative externalities (for both production and consumption) are a common part of economic life. They're the context for discussions of issues like climate change, pollution, blighted neighborhoods, and education policy. Sometimes, individuals can find private solutions, by paying others to do (or to not do) things that affect them. However, the difficulty of coordinating or enforcing these private agreements often overwhelms the benefits.

In these cases, we've seen that government policies like taxes and subsidies can actually *increase* efficiency, even though we typically think of taxes as creating distortions. This is because taxes and subsidies can counterbalance an externality by forcing buyers or sellers to take into account the value of the external cost or benefit. At first glance, quotas look like a simple way to counter the "too much" problem of negative externalities, but they fail to maximize surplus unless people are allowed to buy and sell the quotas.

In the next chapter, we'll examine other challenges that are closely related to the idea of externalities. When goods are collectively owned, individuals have limited incentive to take into account the impact of their actions on the publicly held resources. As we are about to see, the resulting market failures and corresponding policy solutions look very similar to those we've discussed in this chapter.

Key Terms

private costs, p. 453

external costs, p. 453

social cost, p. 453

private benefits, p. 454

external benefits, p. 454

social benefit, p. 454

externality, p. 454

network externality, p. 454

production externality, p. 455

consumption externality, p. 455

Coase theorem, p. 460

Pigovian tax, p. 464

tradable allowance, p. 467

Summary

LO 18.1 Explain how external costs and benefits affect the trade-offs faced by economic decision makers.

Any cost that is imposed without compensation on someone other than the person who caused it is an *external cost*. A benefit that accrues without compensation to someone other than the person who caused it is called an *external benefit*. External costs and benefits are collectively referred to as *externalities*. We call external costs *negative externalities* and external benefits *positive externalities*.

Costs and benefits that fall directly on an economic decision maker are *private costs/benefits*, while the total cost of the decision including any externalities is referred to as the *social cost/benefit*.

LO 18.2 Calculate the effect of a negative externality on market price and quantity.

A negative externality makes the private cost of a decision lower than the social cost, which causes the individuals who bear only the private cost to demand or supply an inefficiently high quantity at any given price.

In the presence of a negative externality (production or consumption), the market equilibrium yields a higher quantity than the efficient level, failing to maximize total surplus. The market price is too low relative to the social cost. The loss of surplus falls on those outside the market who bear the external cost of the decision.

LO 18.3 Calculate the effect of a positive externality on market price and quantity.

A positive externality makes the private benefit of a decision lower than the social benefit, which causes individuals who enjoy only the private benefit to demand or supply an inefficiently low quantity at any given price.

In the presence of a positive externality (production or consumption), the market equilibrium yields a lower quantity than the efficient level, failing to maximize total surplus. The market price is too low relative to social benefit. The loss of surplus falls on those outside the market who would gain from a larger quantity transacted.

LO 18.4 Describe how individuals could reach a private solution to an externality, and explain why this doesn't always occur.

The idea that individuals reach an efficient equilibrium through private trades, even in the presence of an externality, is called the *Coase theorem*. Because an externality fails to maximize surplus, in theory, everyone could be made better off if those who are burdened with external costs or benefits pay others to buy or sell the efficient quantity. The theorem makes two big assumptions, however: that people can make enforceable agreements and that there are no costs involved in the transaction.

> **LO 18.5** Show how a tax or subsidy can be used to counteract an externality, and discuss the pros and cons of such solutions.

A tax meant to counterbalance the effect of a negative externality is known as a *Pigovian tax*. In order to exactly counterbalance a negative externality, policy-makers want to set the tax equal to the value of the external cost, thus reducing the equilibrium quantity. Similarly, a subsidy can counterbalance a positive externality by moving the equilibrium to a higher quantity.

When the tax or subsidy is set at the right level, the externality is exactly counterbalanced, and the market becomes efficient.

> **LO 18.6** Show how quantity regulations and tradable allowances can be used to counteract an externality, and discuss the pros and cons of such solutions.

Setting a *quota* (a quantity regulation) to counteract inefficiently high consumption due to a negative externality can bring quantity down to the efficient level, but it does not actually maximize surplus. Maximizing surplus and achieving efficiency depends not only on how much of a good is bought and sold, but also on *who* buys and sells it.

A production or consumption quota that can be bought and sold is called a *tradable allowance*. Just as with a quota, a system of tradable allowances will result in the efficient quantity of a good being bought and sold, as long as the total number of allowances is set at the right quantity. Like a tax, tradable allowances maximize surplus by allocating sales to those with the highest willingness to pay. The government can collect revenue by selling the initial quotas, but more often, they are allocated for free to consumers or producers, who then trade among themselves.

Review Questions

1. Describe an externality not listed in the chapter. Is it positive or negative? Who is the economic decision maker, and who bears the external cost or benefit? **[LO 18.1]**

2. Consider the decision to adopt a dog. Describe a private cost, a private benefit, an external cost, and an external benefit that might result from your decision to adopt a dog. **[LO 18.1]**

3. What are the private costs and benefits associated with smoking cigarettes? What are the external costs? If smokers paid the social cost of cigarettes, what would happen to the quantity demanded? **[LO 18.2]**

4. When U.S. farmers in the Southwest irrigate their land, salt in the ground soil leaks into the Colorado River. The Colorado River has become so salty that Mexican farmers further down the river cannot irrigate their own land, and Mexican crops have suffered. Explain why this situation constitutes a negative production externality, how it leads to too much irrigation, and what it would mean for U.S. farmers to face the externality. **[LO 18.2]**

5. If education has private benefits to an individual as well as external benefits to society, explain why a less-than-optimal amount of education occurs. **[LO 18.3]**

6. Hand washing has external health benefits, helping prevent the spread of communicable diseases. If a program were somehow devised so that people got paid a small reward every time they washed their hands, how would it affect the number of people who are sick at any given time? **[LO 18.3]**

7. Joan loves turning up her electric guitar amp all the way, but her next-door neighbor hates listening to her. How might Joan and her neighbor reach a private solution to their problem? Describe potential problems that might make it hard for a private solution to occur. **[LO 18.4]**

8. Felix and Oscar are roommates. Oscar is messy, and Felix is planning to move out unless they can come to an agreement. For the roommates to reach a private solution, does it matter whether Oscar compensates Felix for being messy or Felix pays Oscar to clean up? **[LO 18.4]**

9. Suppose that you are an economic policy advisor. Environmental groups are pressuring you to implement the highest-possible carbon tax, while industry groups are pressuring you to implement no carbon tax at all. Both argue that their position makes more sense economically. Explain to them what the most efficient tax level will be and why there are costs to setting the tax too high or too low. **[LO 18.5]**

10. In what circumstances will a tax make a market less efficient? In what circumstances will a tax make a market more efficient? **[LO 18.5]**

11. The city of Seattle limits each household to one can of free garbage collection per week. There are fees for any extra garbage collected from the curb. Is this policy the most efficient way of reducing waste? Why or why not? **[LO 18.6]**

12. Suppose an environmental impact study shows that the coral reef near Port Douglas, Australia, can sustain 18 scuba diving tours per week. Explain why a quota might have an advantage over a tax in this situation. **[LO 18.6]**

13. The city of Seattle limits each household to one can of free garbage collection per week. There are fees for any extra garbage collected from the curb. Suppose that a neighborhood group in Seattle organizes a group of families so that those who plan to go over their one-can garbage quota can find households that are under their quota and pay them to put out the extra trash. Does this change the efficiency of the policy? **[LO 18.6]**

14. Suppose the government is considering two policies to limit factory air pollution: taxing all producers, or providing each producer with an allotment of tradable permits. If both policies lead to the same amount of pollution reduction, why might producers prefer the tradable-permit option? **[LO 18.6]**

Problems and Applications

1. State whether each of the following primarily causes an external cost or an external benefit. **[LO 18.1]**
   a. Fishing at a popular lakeside vacation spot.
   b. Buying a fax machine.
   c. Conducting research to find an AIDS vaccine.
   d. Occupying a seat on a bench in a crowded park.
   e. Littering.
   f. Spaying or neutering your pet.

2. You are considering whether to enter a holiday lights display contest that pays $1,000 to the winner. State whether each of the following constitutes private costs, private benefits, external costs, or external benefits. Check all that apply. **[LO 18.1]**
   a. Increased traffic congestion.
   b. Neighbors have difficulty parking on your street.
   c. Increased electric bill from the holiday lights.
   d. Winning the holiday lights display contest.

3. Figure 18P-1 shows the demand curve for a U.S. farmer for irrigating his land. It costs the farmer $100 per acre to irrigate the land. Each acre of land irrigation generates salty runoff that winds up in the Colorado River. It costs $50 to desalinate this river water so Mexican farmers can irrigate their crops. **[LO 18.2]**
   a. Draw the marginal private cost of irrigation on the graph.
   b. Draw the marginal social cost of irrigation on the graph.
   c. How many acres will the U.S. farmer irrigate?
   d. What is the efficient level of irrigation?

4. The weekly supply and demand for packs of cigarettes in the United States is given in Figure 18P-2. **[LO 18.2]**

FIGURE 18P-2

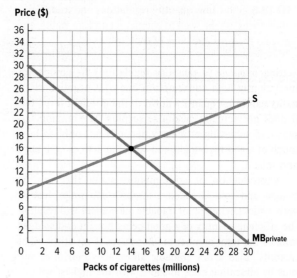

   a. Suppose cigarette smoking causes a $6/pack external cost on nonsmokers. Draw the social benefit curve that accounts for the external cost associated with smoking.
   b. Assuming the externality associated with smoking is not faced by consumers, how many packs of cigarettes are consumed per week?
   c. What is the efficient number of cigarette packs?

5. Figure 18P-3 shows supply and demand for first-aid training, based on private costs and benefits. **[LO 18.3]**

FIGURE 18P-3

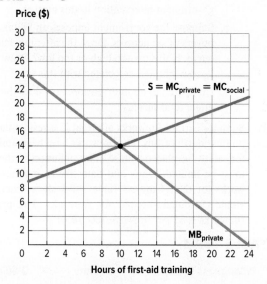

a. Suppose that the external benefit from first-aid training is worth $6. Graph the social benefit curve for first-aid training that accounts for the external benefit.

b. Ignoring the social benefits of training, how many hours of first-aid training will occur?

c. What is the socially optimal quantity of first-aid training?

d. What is the deadweight loss to society when consumers are unable to capture the $6 external benefit they provide from first-aid training? Graph the deadweight loss.

6. Figure 18P-4 shows supply and demand for planting trees, based on private costs and benefits. Trees sequester carbon, meaning that they help counteract pollutants that contribute to climate change. **[LO 18.3]**

FIGURE 18P-4

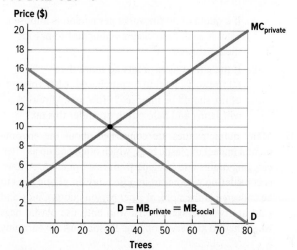

a. Suppose that the carbon sequestration that results from planting a tree is worth $4. Graph the social cost curve for tree planting that accounts for the positive externality of trees.

b. Ignoring the positive externality, how many trees will be planted?

c. What is the socially optimal quantity of trees?

d. What is the deadweight loss that occurs when suppliers are unable to capture the $4 external benefit they provide from planting trees? Graph the deadweight loss.

7. Your neighbor never mows his lawn. You don't have any legal right to force him to mow, but the mess in his front yard is making your neighborhood unsightly and reducing the value of your house. The reduction in the value of your house is $5,000, and the value of his time to mow the lawn once a week is $1,500. Suppose you offer him a deal in which you pay him $3,000 to mow. How does this deal affect surplus? **[LO 18.4]**

   a. The deal increases only your surplus.

   b. The deal increases only your neighbor's surplus.

   c. The deal increases both your surplus and your neighbor's.

   d. The deal increases your surplus but decreases your neighbor's.

   e. The deal increases your neighbor's surplus but decreases yours.

   f. The deal does not affect surplus.

8. Johnston Forest in Rhode Island has a cave that houses thousands of fruit bats. Bat droppings are highly acidic and have ruined the paint on many cars. The flying radius of the Johnston Forest bats encompasses two towns, Johnston and Foster. The residents of Johnston collectively value bat removal at $400,000. Foster residents collectively value bat removal at $500,000. Pest control experts estimate that the cost of bat removal would be $450,000. Which of the following scenarios would lead to removal of the bats? Check all that apply. **[LO 18.4]**

   a. Foster pays Johnston $50,000 to contribute to bat removal.

   b. Foster and Johnston evenly split the cost of bat removal.

   c. Johnston contributes nothing toward bat removal.

9. The local government has decided that because children's health has large external benefits, it will offer a subsidy to help families pay for visits to the pediatrician. However, the government isn't sure at what level to set the subsidy. Figure 18P-5 shows the current demand curve for pediatricians' visits ($MB_{private}$) and three alternative subsidies, represented by curves $D_{subsidy=$30}$, $D_{subsidy=$60}$, and $D_{subsidy=$90}$. **[LO 18.5]**

FIGURE 18P-5

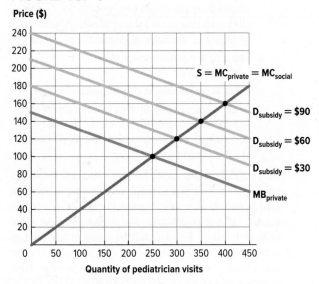

Price ($)

a. Assume that the correct level of subsidy is $60. What is the socially optimal level of pediatrician visits?

b. Compared to the efficient outcome, graph the deadweight loss that would result from subsidies of $30 or $90.

10. Figure 18P-6 shows the daily market for water skiing permits on El Dorado Lake. Suppose each skier (each permit) causes $4 of damage to the lake. **[LO 18.5]**

FIGURE 18P-6

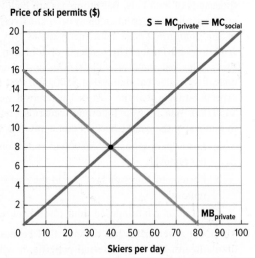

Price of ski permits ($)

a. Draw the social benefit curve that accounts for the external cost of skiers, and draw the deadweight loss that occurs at the market equilibrium. What is the socially optimal level of water skiing?

Calculate the deadweight loss if there is no government intervention in this market.

b. Suppose the government imposes an $8 tax on buyers of ski permits. Draw the after-tax demand curve. Is this tax too high or too low? Draw the deadweight loss associated with this tax.

c. Compared to no intervention, how does the tax affect total surplus?

11. Suppose certain fireworks are legal in a residential area on the Fourth of July. The fireworks have been approved for safety, but they do cause noise pollution so their use must be limited. Jenny and Salo like to purchase fireworks for their families; Table 18P-1 shows each individual's willingness-to-pay for fireworks. The price of fireworks is $2 per firework. **[LO 18.6]**

TABLE 18P-1

Willingness to pay ($)	Q Jenny	Q Salo
10	0	0
9	10	5
8	20	10
7	30	15
6	40	20
5	50	25
4	60	30
3	70	35
2	80	40
1	90	45
0	100	50

a. If a quota of 30 fireworks per person is imposed, what is each individual's willingness-to-pay for their last firework?

b. If the government wants no more than 60 fireworks total to be purchased, what amount of tax should be imposed? How many fireworks will Jenny and Salo purchase under this tax?

12. Many municipalities are concerned about the environmental impact of plastic bags, which often end up as litter, clogging drains and hanging from tree branches. A town is considering whether to impose a tax on plastic bags to be collected at the store, or a per person quota. Cindy and Carl are two average citizens who both use plastic bags when they go grocery shopping. Plastic bags are currently

free when they shop. Figure 18P-7 shows each individual's demand curve for plastic bags. **[LO 18.6]**

FIGURE 18P-7

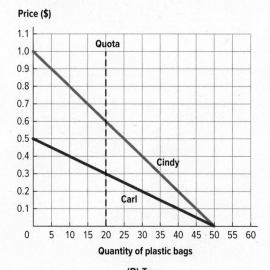

(A) Quota

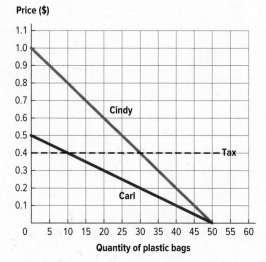

(B) Tax

a. Under the quota, what is each individual's willingness-to-pay for the last bag used?

b. How many bags will each shopper use under the tax? What is each individual's willingness-to-pay for the last bag used under the tax?

c. Would you recommend that the town adopt a plastic-bag quota or tax?

Endnotes

1. http://www.laalmanac.com/transport/tr10.htm; https://www.dmv.ca.gov/portal/wcm/connect/5aa16cd3-39a5-402f-9453-0d353706cc9a/official.pdf?MOD=AJPERES.

2. http://www.sandiegouniontribune.com/business/energy-green/sd-fi-california-gastax-20170413-story.html.

3. National Research Council, *Advancing the Science of Climate Change* (Washington, DC: The National Academies Press, 2010).

4. http://www.theguardian.com/environment/green-living-blog/2010/sep/23/carbon-footprint-new-car.

5. www.eenews.net/stories/1060031090.

6. https://coase.org/aboutronaldcoase.htm.

7. https://www.britannica.com/biography/Arthur-Cecil-Pigou.

8. http://www.nhtsa.gov/About+NHTSA/Press+Releases/2012/Obama+Administration+Finalizes+Historic+54.5+mpg+Fuel+Efficiency+Standards.

Public Goods and Common Resources

A New Tragedy of the Commons

In 1910, there were roughly 300,000 rhinoceroses roaming the savannas of East Africa. A century later, rhino populations are dwindling in alarming numbers: There are no more than 5,500 black rhinos on the African continent, with several other species near extinction.[1] A growing human population encroaching on the rhinos' habitat is part of the explanation. The bigger cause of the rhinos' downfall has been their own value to hunters.

In the early 1900s, thousands of big-game hunters traveled from Europe and America to shoot rhinos for sport, including U.S. president Theodore Roosevelt. These days, it's mostly illegal to hunt rhinos, but a flourishing illegal trade in ivory from rhino horns continues. In

©Spaces Images/Blend Images

parts of Asia, ivory is an ingredient in traditional medicines and is worth more per ounce than gold. As a result, some species of rhino—such as the northern white—are on the verge of extinction.

Why are poachers killing rhinos so fast that they're becoming extinct? As soon as they become extinct, after all, that's the end of the profits for poachers. Wouldn't poachers want to carefully manage the rhino population so that it can produce ivory for many years to come? The problem, as we'll see in this chapter, is that the rhinos don't "belong" to anyone in particular. As a result, no one has a big enough financial incentive to maintain their value. Instead, everyone wants to get in quickly and take what they can before the rhinos are gone.

LO 19.1 Define different types of goods in terms of rivalry and excludability.

LO 19.2 Describe the free-rider problem and its consequences.

LO 19.3 Explain how and when problems with public goods can be effectively solved by social norms, government provision, and expansion of property rights.

LO 19.4 Describe the tragedy of the commons and its consequences.

LO 19.5 Explain how and when problems with common resources can be effectively solved by social norms, government regulation, and expansion of property rights.

The near-extinction of black rhinos in Africa isn't just a problem for biologists and nature-lovers; it's also an example of an important type of economic inefficiency. Not all goods are allocated efficiently by competitive markets, and in this chapter, we'll discuss two major types of goods that are subject to market failure. The first category is *public goods*, such as national defense, public health, roads, education, and research. Public goods could end up *undersupplied* if left to competitive markets. The second category is *common resources* such as rhinos and other wildlife. As the rhino example shows, common resources could end up *overconsumed* and depleted if left to competitive markets.

In both cases, we'll see that the root of the problem is the difficulty of forcing people who consume the goods to pay for what they take. Both the problems this causes and the corresponding solutions are related to the concept of external costs and external benefits we discussed in the previous chapter.

In the end, rhinos aren't doomed. Some policies for protecting common resources and providing public goods are extremely effective. As a result, the population of white rhinos in southern Africa has taken the opposite path from that of the black rhinos. Although there were only 50 remaining white rhinos in the wild in the early 1900s, there are now approximately 20,000. What made this difference? Paradoxically, part of the solution was to encourage people to hunt rhinos—but only on their own private land. The government of South Africa also established well-protected national parks.[2]

In this chapter, we'll see why these and other examples of government action and thoughtfully designed public policies can go a long way toward allocating both public goods and common resources more efficiently.

Characteristics of Goods

What types of goods tend to go the way of the rhino, suffering from overuse? River water, but not orange juice. Fish in the sea, but not chickens on the farm. Computers at the public library, but not personal laptops. What is the common thread?

The first thing to notice is that river water, fish in the sea, and public-library computers are not usually owned by a private individual. Instead, they are *held collectively* by a community or country.

We can go further and specify two important characteristics that determine how goods are used and whether they are allocated efficiently by markets:

- When a good is **excludable**, sellers can prevent its use by those who have not paid for it.
- When a good is **rival in consumption** (or just **rival**), one person's consumption prevents or decreases others' ability to consume it.

Most of the goods we've discussed in this text are *private goods*, which are *both* excludable and rival in consumption. Many goods, however, lack one or both of these characteristics. Before describing these types of goods, we'll explore the ideas of excludability and "rivalness" a bit further.

excludable
a characteristic of a good or service that allows owners to prevent its use by people who have not paid for it

rival in consumption (rival)
the characteristic of a good for which one person's consumption prevents or decreases others' ability to consume it

Excludable goods

Excludability matters because it allows owners to set an enforceable price on a good. If you can't prevent people from consuming something, then they have little reason to pay for using it.

For instance, street lights are a nonexcludable good. Once they are put up in a neighborhood, everyone who comes through gets the benefit, regardless of whether they've paid to put up the lights. How would you prevent people who didn't pay from getting the benefit of the lamps? Have a police officer standing by to make them wear special dark sunglasses? Make them close their eyes? Wall off the neighborhood? Most of the time, it's hard to imagine that you could allow some people but not others to enjoy the benefit of street lights.

Excludability can be a matter of degree, though. Take roads: It *is* possible to make bridges, tunnels, and major highways excludable by setting up toll booths at every entrance. For most roads, though, this is not a practical option. You can't have a toll booth at the end of every small street. (Although with new technological advances, we are starting to see strategies approaching this. For example, in London driving in the city center incurs congestion charges during peak times; cameras set up throughout the city help enforce these payments.)

Rival-in-consumption goods

Rivalry has to do with whether one person's consumption of a good prevents or decreases others' ability to consume it. Most goods are rival goods. Some particularly obvious examples:

- Rhino horns: When someone shoots a rhino and cuts off its horn, the next person to come along can't also use the rhino for that purpose.
- Fish: Once a fish is caught by one fishing boat, it's no longer out in the water to be caught by the next boat.
- Jeans: If one person is wearing a pair of jeans, someone else cannot also be wearing that same exact pair of jeans.
- Food: After you eat your lunch, nobody else can eat that same exact plate of food.

So, what types of goods are *nonrival?* Here are some examples:

Sunlight is a public good—both nonrival and nonexcludable. Shade, on the other hand, can be offered at a premium.
©LiliGraphie/Shutterstock

- Streetlights: Two people walking down a lit-up street are able to enjoy the light just as much as one person. (This is a good that is both nonexcludable and nonrival.)
- A song on the radio: One person listening doesn't "use it up" and doesn't prevent others from listening as well.

In general, knowledge and technology are nonrival because once something has been thought up or invented, everyone can take advantage of it.

Often, rivalry is a matter of degree. Again, think of roads. A rarely used country road is probably not rival in consumption. If one more person drives on the road, it has a negligible effect on the ability of other drivers to use it. A heavily congested highway, however, has elements of a rival good. Every car that gets on the highway increases the amount of traffic, slowing down other cars and reducing the value of the highway for other drivers.

The same applies to streetlights: One other person walking along will likely not get in your way. But if 100 people are crowded onto the sidewalk, and you're trying

FIGURE 19-1
Four categories of goods

	Excludable	Nonexcludable
Rival	**Private goods** Plane tickets, pizza, minivans	**Common resources** Forests, fisheries, wildlife
Nonrival	**Artificially scarce goods** Pay-per-view movies, subscription-only websites	**Public goods** Open-source software, traffic lights, national defense

to use the streetlight to find something you dropped, you might have trouble. But this is an extreme situation; for the most part we think of streetlights as nonrival goods.

Four categories of goods

Whether a good is excludable and rival in consumption has important implications for how it is allocated through a market system. By combining the concepts of excludability and rivalry, we can define four categories of goods, as shown in Figure 19-1.

private good
a good that is both excludable and rival

public good
a good that is neither excludable nor rival

common resource
a good that is not excludable but is rival

artificially scarce good
a good that is excludable but not rival.

- **Private goods** are goods that are both excludable and rival. They are usually allocated efficiently by competitive markets, as we've discussed throughout the text.
- **Public goods** are the opposite of private goods, as the name suggests. They are neither excludable nor rival.
- **Common resources** are not excludable but are rival.
- **Artificially scarce goods** are excludable but not rival.

We have already discussed the economic issues surrounding artificially scarce goods, in Chapter 14, "Monopoly," and Chapter 15, "Monopolistic Competition and Oligopoly." Essentially, the markets for artificially scarce goods function just like natural monopolies, and it is the ability of a business to prevent consumers from access to the good that makes it artificially scarce. This scarcity allows the sellers of these goods some power to charge a price above marginal cost. To see an example of how this works, see the Economics in Action box "Artificially scarce music."

Artificially scarce music
Economics in Action

Companies like Apple, Amazon, and Spotify are building big businesses based on streaming music, driven by their belief that customers will be willing to pay for access to a far wider variety of music—anytime, anywhere—and that customers will pay to avoid ads. To do that, the companies had to rethink the economics of selling music. Before streaming, music came in two forms:

albums and airtime on the radio. Albums are a private good, since the format of a record, tape, or digitally protected download make music both rival and excludable. Music on the radio, on the other hand, is traditionally a public good—both nonrival and nonexcludable. Anyone with a radio can listen.

Streaming services are like radio with one important difference: Because customers have to log in to music platforms with a password, listening is now excludable—no password, no music. Streaming is still nonrival; like radio, listening to a song on Spotify or Pandora won't diminish anyone else's ability to listen to that same song at the same time. Economists call goods or services that are excludable but nonrival "artificially scarce." Subscription services, such as Amazon Prime videos, Netflix, and Hulu also create artificially scarce goods.

Let's take a quick look at the economics of artificially scarce goods using streaming services as an example. The nonrivalness of artificially scarce goods tells us something important about the costs of producing streaming services—the marginal cost of producing these goods is (essentially) zero. To give one example, once Spotify has paid artists, built its user interface, and set up server space, it does not incur much extra cost for each new subscriber. Since the efficient point for consumption happens where price equals marginal cost, efficiency in the market for streaming music happens when the price for subscriptions is zero too. Looking solely at efficiency implies that streamed music should be costless and freely available to all; otherwise, too few people will listen (relative to the efficient level of music consumption).

You can probably see the problem. Spotify and other streaming services incur costs in providing music to the world. Setting a price of zero wouldn't cover these costs. Instead, the companies need to set the subscription price to at least cover their average total cost, reducing total surplus. Although the price of subscriptions will then always be higher than the marginal cost of the service and fewer people subscribe than is efficient, at least a market exists—and tens of millions of people are now happily listening to their favorite tunes.

The remainder of the chapter will focus on public goods and common resources.

✓TEST YOURSELF

☐ What does it mean for a good to be excludable? **[LO 19.1]**
☐ What does it mean for a good to be rival in consumption? **[LO 19.1]**
☐ What is the difference between public goods and common resources? **[LO 19.1]**

Public Goods

Markets work well for allocating private goods efficiently. They do not always work so well for allocating public goods and common resources. The reason is that the price charged by competitive firms does not capture the true costs and benefits of consumption. In this way, the problems with public goods and common resources are closely tied to the problems of externalities discussed in the previous chapter.

Although public goods and common resources are both inefficiently allocated, the problem with public goods is fundamentally different from the problem with common resources. For public goods, that problem is called the *free-rider problem*.

The free-rider problem

Think about a public, city bus. It costs something to run the bus along its route—to pay the driver, buy gasoline, make repairs, and so on. To support these costs, the city requires the bus driver to charge riders a fare as they enter the bus. But suppose someone decides he doesn't want to pay the

LO 19.2 Describe the free-rider problem and its consequences.

fare and slips in the back door when the driver's not looking? This person gets to ride the bus for free. In fact, we might even call him a "free rider."

If this free rider is alone, then no great harm is done. He takes up a seat on the bus but doesn't fundamentally detract anything from others. Also, there are still enough paying riders to cover the cost of operating the bus.

However, imagine a bus with a back door that is always open. Riders can choose to get on through the front door and pay the fare, or they can choose the back door and not pay anything. Under these circumstances, we'll likely see a lot of free riders.

As more people choose to ride for free, the city will have less revenue to cover the costs of operating buses. If too many people ride for free, the city will no longer be able to afford to run as many buses as before. The reduced bus services don't reflect reduced demand or a lower value to riders, though. There are still many people who have a willingness to pay that is at least as high as the price of a bus ticket, but no individual person has an incentive to *voluntarily* pay the fare.

free-rider problem
a problem that occurs when the nonexcludability of a public good leads to undersupply

In technical terms, the **free-rider problem** we've just described is caused by nonexcludability leading to *undersupply* of a public good. When a good is not easily excludable, what people pay for it will not necessarily reflect the real value they place on it. After all, even if you value the bus ride highly and would willingly pay for a ticket if you had to, you might still hop on for free if given the chance. The problem is that when a good is nonexcludable, it is difficult for firms to make any profit from the production and sale of the good. If firms cannot earn a profit, there is no incentive to produce the good. As a result, the good will be undersupplied (as compared to the efficient quantity).

Note that the free-rider problem *does not* have to do with whether nonpaying riders are taking up seats on the bus. Imagine a bus that could fit an infinite number of riders: Seats would not be in short supply, but not enough riders would pay the fare to cover the cost of running the bus. Even J. K. Rowling's Knight Bus, which can defy the laws of physics, charges Harry Potter 11 sickles to ride.

Since public goods are, by definition, nonexcludable, the free-rider problem occurs with *all public goods*. Public transportation is the classic example for which the problem is named, but there are many other cases in which people metaphorically "ride" for free. All sorts of services end up undersupplied as a result:

- Imagine a public bathroom with a sign reading, "Please clean the sink when you're finished." How many people would do that? Surely not everyone, even if everyone places some value on having a clean public bathroom.

- Or suppose if, after a big snowfall, everyone was expected to get a shovel and clear part of the road. If everyone pitched in, the road would get cleared in no time. But this is not usually what happens.

If given the opportunity, people will free-ride: They will walk out of the bathroom without cleaning up, and they will choose not to go out to shovel the road.

One way to think about the free-rider problem is that free riders enjoy positive externalities from others' choices to pay for bus rides, clean public bathrooms, or shovel roads. As we saw in Chapter 18, "Externalities," when positive externalities exist, the equilibrium quantity of the good or service is less than the level that would maximize total surplus in society as a whole. The result is that public transportation, clean public bathrooms, and clear roads after a snowstorm are *undersupplied* if left solely to the market. To combat the problem of free-riding, cities and states with frequent snowstorms require property owners to shovel their sidewalks or face fines.

Some important public goods are more abstract than buses or bathrooms. Health, cleanliness, general knowledge, and safety are all public goods that have a huge impact on everyday life. Consider an example from public health: If 99 percent of the population is vaccinated against a disease—such as polio or measles—the remaining 1 percent can probably remain unvaccinated without fear of getting sick.

But if everyone tried to be a free rider by remaining unvaccinated, the risk of disease would quickly increase. It's not possible to exclude the unvaccinated from the benefits of living around others who are vaccinated. When there are too many free riders and an undersupply of vaccination, the result is that everyone is more likely to get sick. Similarly, an army, police force, and "neighborhood watch" are all ways of providing public safety. It is not possible to easily exclude free-riding residents who don't contribute from enjoying the benefits.

One of the most abstract public goods is general knowledge or information. For a case in which the free-rider problems surrounding these public goods seem to have been overcome to everyone's benefit, look at the From Another Angle box "Why does Wikipedia work?"

Why does Wikipedia work?

From Another Angle

Wikipedia is a classic public good. It is nonexcludable because anyone can use it for free. It is nonrival because, generally speaking, one person reading a web page doesn't diminish others' ability to do so.

Given what we know about public goods, it's easy to think of ways that Wikipedia might have failed. At best, we might expect articles to be undersupplied. After all, how many people will want to spend their time writing encyclopedia articles for free? At worst, we can imagine contributors filling Wikipedia with self-serving or misleading information. Stephen Colbert, formerly the host of the satiric news-commentary show *The Colbert Report,* was once banned from Wikipedia for asking his viewers to edit the page on elephants to say that their population had tripled in three months. Colbert's point, of course, was that "facts" on Wikipedia are sometimes subject to the whims and biases of contributors.

In Wikipedia's early days, it seemed as if these predictions might cripple the project. Articles were short, riddled with errors, and much more likely to be about *Star Trek* than Friedrich Nietzsche. Eighteen years later, however, Wikipedia has around 5.7 million articles—more than 60 times the number in the online version of *Encyclopedia Britannica.* A spot-check of 45 articles on general science topics found that Wikipedia is just as accurate as traditional peer-reviewed encyclopedias. How does Wikipedia overcome the problems of undersupply and misuse that generally plague public goods?

To rephrase the question: What sort of benefits could outweigh the costs of time and effort involved in editing Wikipedia? When asked directly in a survey, the vast majority of contributors listed altruistic-sounding reasons, such as: to "fix an error" or "contribute to the share of knowledge." Only 2 percent of all contributors listed fame or recognition as a motivation for editing. We might be somewhat skeptical about this modesty, though. After all, many contributors register a user name and page that provides a history of their edits for others to view.

Whatever the exact motivation of contributors, Wikipedia is designed in a way that is conducive to overcoming the challenges it faces as a public good. Since the costs of contributing are relatively low (just click "edit," type the changes, and click "submit"), it is easy to correct abuses. As a result, fewer than 5,000 dedicated editors (those who make over 100 edits a month) in the English version at last count do a remarkably good job of correcting incidences of vandalism and misuse. In addition, the project capitalizes on the idea that sharing knowledge is good for society. This motivates users to contribute and police one another on their own.

As free, open-source resources like Wikipedia grow in popularity, economists are adapting their ideas about the provision of public goods, and the motivations that drive people to contribute to them.

Sources: Denise Anthony et al., "Reputation and Reliability in Collective Goods: The Case of the Online Encyclopedia Wikipedia," *Rationality and Society* 21, no. 3 (2009), pp. 283–306; https://en.wikipedia.org/wiki/Wikipedia:Size_comparisons.

Solutions to the free-rider problem

The free-rider problem leads to a market failure: *Markets typically undersupply public goods.* Fortunately, this undersupply problem can be solved in a variety of ways:

- Change social norms relating to the good or service.
- Make somebody responsible for the provision of a certain quantity of the good or service (such as municipal snow plowing on public roads).
- Make the good or service more excludable by assigning property rights (such as the pay-per-use public toilets found in some big cities).

The many possible solutions generally fall under three categories: social norms, government provision, and private property rights. We'll consider each of these solutions in this section, starting
with social norms.

Social norms   For some public goods, society tries to get people to act in the interest of society by shifting social norms. For example, campaigns to shame those who try to sneak on the back
of the bus or suggested donations at a museum's entrance may change people's opinions on what
is individually optimal.

Suggested-donation boxes
attempt to change social
norms in order to address
the free-rider problem
which leads to the under-
supply of public goods.
©Matthew Ferris/Alamy

The free-rider problem is a problem of *trade-offs*—people
are able to enjoy the benefits of something without paying the corresponding costs. Strong social norms can help
rebalance the trade-off by imposing "costs" on people who
litter, sneak through the back door of the bus, fail to do
their bit of snow shoveling, and so on. Remember, costs
don't have to be financial. Social disapproval, guilt, or
conflict with those in your community can also be costs.

As you would expect, social disapproval carries a
higher cost in places where you know the people around
you, care about their opinions, and expect to interact with
them again in the future. For example, we might expect
social norms to be more effective at deterring free riders
on a small-town bus system than on the subway in New
York City.

While changing social norms works for some public
goods, in other cases, the government tries to fix the market failure through regulation or direct
government provision.

Government provision   To combat the undersupply of public goods, the more typical solution is for government to step in and provide a good directly. In the United States and many other
wealthy countries, we see government provision of public goods everywhere: in national defense,
transportation systems, education and research, parks, safety, and much more.

Well-intentioned people can argue about when it makes sense for government to provide these
services directly and when it should contract with a private company to provide them or force
individuals to pay a private provider. Whichever method a government chooses to supply a public
good, two common issues arise: First, what is the right amount of the public good to supply? Second, who will pay for it?

In a functioning market, people will buy a good up to the point where the marginal benefit
they enjoy from the last unit is equal to the marginal cost of that unit. If the marginal benefit were
greater than the cost, they could increase their utility by buying more. If the cost were greater than
the marginal benefit, they could increase their utility by buying less. This same analysis applies to
public goods: If the government is supplying a public good, such as road maintenance, *the efficient
quantity is the one at which the marginal social benefit equals the cost.*

What is the marginal social benefit of a public good? Each individual who uses the road network gains some marginal benefit from increased road maintenance (more potholes filled, more frequent repaving). When roads are in good repair, everyone who uses them enjoys the benefits. Therefore, the marginal social benefit is actually the sum of the marginal benefit gained by each individual user. So, the government should calculate the cost of increased road maintenance, add up the marginal benefit to every user, and supply the quantity of road maintenance at which the two are equal—right?

Unfortunately, this cost-benefit analysis is simpler in theory than it is in practice. How can the government find out the true value that each citizen places on an additional unit of road maintenance? You might think one way would be to simply ask everyone how much they value well-maintained roads. Unfortunately, each individual has an incentive to overstate the marginal benefit she will receive because she expects the government to pay for it. Since no individual driver pays the cost, each might as well petition for perfectly maintained roads. This is another example of individually rational behavior being socially inefficient.

In reality, governments try to conduct a cost-benefit analysis when deciding how much of a public good to supply, whether it is road maintenance, schools, the military, or cancer research. This means making a best guess at what the marginal social benefit of an additional unit will be. Sometimes economic research can help with this problem. It can, for example, attempt to quantify the dif-

Local governments usually repair roads. Why doesn't the private sector do it instead?
©Andy Carpenean/Laramie Boomerang/AP Images

fuse benefits that people get from better schools, reduced disease, or safer neighborhoods. But we usually have to accept that our best guess will be an imperfect one.

The second issue is figuring out how to pay for government provision of public goods. Determining who will pay depends in part on how easy it is to exclude people who don't pay. In some cases, it is possible to make the good excludable: The government can use its power to monitor use and enforce payments among those who actually use them. Examples are the tolls that drivers pay to use toll roads, the fares that riders pay on buses and trains, and the tuition that students pay at public universities.

In other cases, it is either difficult or undesirable to charge user fees. For services that are "used" by almost all citizens—sewer systems, police and fire protection, and military defense—it may be more costly to try to exclude nonusers than it is worth. Instead, these services are usually funded through general tax revenue, usually in a way that is not directly connected to the services themselves (as we'll see in Chapter 20, "Taxation and the Public Budget").

Assigning property rights The defining characteristics of a *public good* are nonexcludability and nonrivalry. *Private goods* are both excludable and rival. Thus, one solution to the free-rider problem is to make a public good more like a private good. This can be achieved by making a public good excludable.

As discussed above, one way to make a good more excludable is to use the government to monitor use and enforce payments. Another way to achieve excludability is to give individuals or firms the right to use or sell a public good, by assigning property rights. (Remember the example of reclining airline-seats in the What Do You Think? box "Reclining transactions" in Chapter 18 on "Externalities.")

For public goods like knowledge and ideas, a public good can be made excludable through patents and copyrights. Without patent or copyright protection, the profits from a new idea could be claimed by anyone, not just the inventor of a new idea. As we saw with the examples of Mylan's EpiPens and Pfizer's drug Lipitor in Chapter 12, "The Costs of Production," the idea behind intellectual property rights is to assure corporations that others will not be able to free-ride on their innovations. Such protection increases their incentives to undertake research that will create new knowledge. Giving firms an incentive to conduct research solves the undersupply problem.

✓**TEST YOURSELF**

☐ How does the free-rider problem affect the supply of public goods? What is the resulting effect on equilibrium quantity? **[LO 19.2]**

☐ How can social norms change the trade-offs faced by potential free riders? **[LO 19.3]**

Common Resources

Like public goods, common resources are inefficiently allocated. However, public goods and common resources suffer from different problems:

- The problem with public goods is that they are undersupplied.
- In contrast, the problem with common resources is that they are overconsumed.

This overconsumption problem is called the *tragedy of the commons*.

The tragedy of the commons

LO 19.4 Describe the tragedy of the commons and its consequences.

Remember that public goods are nonrival—they are not used up when people consume them. As we have seen, rhinos are not a public good because they *are* rival—if someone shoots a rhino, it is definitely *not* there for the next person to enjoy.

Usually, when you consume a rival good, you have to compensate the person who owns it. When you want to eat chicken, you pay the grocery store, or the restaurant, or the chicken farmer. But historically, before land was divided into private pieces, when you hunted a wild animal such as a rhino, buffalo, or elephant, you didn't have to pay anyone. No one owned the wildlife, so it was not excludable.

Goods and services that are not excludable but are rival, such as wildlife, are called *common resources*. Common resources face two problems: Nonexcludability causes people to demand a higher quantity than they would if they had to pay for what they consumed. At the same time, no one has an incentive to provide the good because they cannot control who consumes it. Because a common resource is also rival, it gets "used up" every time someone accesses it. This combination leads to what is often called the **tragedy of the commons**—the depletion of a common resource due to individually rational but collectively inefficient overconsumption.

tragedy of the commons
the depletion of a common resource due to individually rational but collectively inefficient overconsumption

Notice the contrast between the free-rider problem and the tragedy of the commons:

- The free-rider problem is triggered by nonexcludability alone.
- The tragedy of the commons arises from the combination of rivalry and nonexcludability.

How can equilibrium quantity be both individually rational and collectively inefficient? Let's start with the *individually rational* part: Think about the consumption decision from the perspective of rhino hunters. On the benefit side, they get the high value of rhino ivory on the black market. On the cost side, they face the cost of hunting equipment, the time spent hunting rhinos, and the risk of getting in trouble with the law. They do not, however, have to pay anyone for the rhino horn they take. As a result, hunters will hunt more than they would if they had to pay someone for the rhino horn.

Why is this *collectively inefficient*? Because we don't typically think of rhinos as having market value, it may be difficult to see that unrestricted hunting does not maximize total surplus. However, using a common resource imposes a *negative externality* on others: When the rhino population is depleted through poaching, the people of Africa lose a key part of the local ecosystem. Anyone who wants to go on safari to see rhinos will lose surplus. So too will local communities that get a boost from safari tourism. Lastly, if rhinos go extinct, there is a loss to the world's biodiversity.

Applying the reasoning we used in the previous chapter, if rhino hunters could be forced to consider the external costs of their activities, their demand curve would shift downward. The equilibrium quantity of rhinos poached would fall to the efficient level—the level that would maximize surplus in society as a whole.

Solutions to the tragedy of the commons

We've seen that overdemand for common resources leads to an inefficient quantity of production and consumption. In other words, common resources are subject to market failures. There are many possible solutions, which generally fall under three categories: social norms, government regulation, and private property rights.

As we discuss each solution, think about how it changes the *trade-off* between costs and benefits that people face when supplying or consuming a common resource. We'll see that the range of solutions to the tragedy of the commons is related to externalities.

Social norms   Dirty public spaces arise because littering is easy. Littering saves you the trouble of finding a garbage can and is very unlikely to incur any real punishment or cost. There is little incentive to take into account the negative externality imposed on others. In spite of this potential problem, lots of public spaces manage to stay clean and pleasant and relatively free of litter. How does this happen?

Sometimes, especially in big cities, public spaces stay clean because the government pays janitors or public-works employees to clean them. But there are many public spaces, especially in close-knit neighborhoods, that stay clean through a simpler mechanism: the expectations and potential disapproval of the community. If you don't litter, we're guessing that it's *not* primarily because you're afraid of being caught and fined by the police. Rather, it's simply because you've learned that it's not a *nice* thing to do.

Elinor Ostrom, winner of the Nobel Prize in Economics in 2009, showed that social norms can sometimes be powerful enough for commonly held property to be managed extremely well, as described in the Economics in Action box "It's not necessarily a tragedy."[3]

LO 19.5 Explain how and when problems with common resources can be effectively solved by social norms, government regulation, and expansion of property rights.

It's not necessarily a tragedy

Economics in Action

In 1968, environmentalist Garrett Hardin wrote an article in the magazine *Science* called "The Tragedy of the Commons." Hardin argued that since no one person has an incentive to curb use of a common resource, everyone overconsumes, leaving tragedies of overfished fisheries, polluted water, and overhunted wildlife. The phrase stuck, and the article influenced decades of discussion about common resource management.

However, a group of researchers, including a young political scientist named Elinor Ostrom, pushed back at the idea. Ostrom's early research focused on local groups managing groundwater near Los Angeles, California. The situation had seemed destined for Hardin's tragedy—in a dry climate, property owners were pumping large amounts of water to maintain thirsty green lawns and crops. Recognizing the challenge, voters had created the West Basin Water Management District in 1948 to help control groundwater in unincorporated Los Angeles County. The agency charged a heavy fee to users to limit overall use of water and used the proceeds to manage the

(continued)

overall health of the basin, including pumping fresh water back into the basin to keep out sea-water. The West Basin Water Management District was so successful that the basin contains more water today than when it was first created.

Ostrom later studied forestry conservation and irrigation water management in Nepal. Like in the West Basin of Los Angeles County, local groups in Nepal were able to overcome the tragedy of the commons through careful local stewardship of the resource. Ostrom noted one especially vivid example from her fieldwork to illustrate why: A farmer had cut an unauthorized irrigation canal down a hill to his farm. Other farmers responsible for managing the irrigation canals started running down the hill, shouting at him for the transgression while others patched up the breach, restoring the flow of water back to what the group had originally agreed upon. The picture highlighted the investment that farmers had in their system and the importance of quick action to right wrongdoing.

Through her work, Ostrom settled on eight principles key to successful management of common resources. At the heart of the eight principles is trust, as she outlined in an interview after receiving the Nobel Prize: "When people have trust that others are going to reciprocate and be trustworthy, including their officials, they will be highly cooperative. When there's no trust, no matter how much force is threatened, people won't cooperate unless immediately facing a gun."

Facing the evidence, Garrett Hardin eventually admitted that the "tragedy" he wrote of applied only to unmanaged commons. Elinor Ostrom's work clearly showed that working together in management of common resources produces a much happier ending.

Sources: http://newsroom.ucla.edu/stories/10-questions-for-nobel-prize-winning-200205; https://news.mongabay.com/2014/05/tipping-the-scale-how-a-political-economist-could-save-the-worlds-forests.

Some specific "design principles" make informal, community-based solutions to common-resource problems more effective. These principles include:

- Clear distinctions between who is and is not allowed to access the resource.
- The participation of resource users in setting the rules for use.
- The ability of users to monitor one another.

Application of such principles in support of social norms is one possible solution to the tragedy of the commons.

Government regulation: Bans and quotas

What happens when informal institutions and rules are not enough? The management of common resources is one case in which government regulation can be productive and efficiency-enhancing. The reason for this is simple: Often, government bodies have the power to impose limits on how much of a resource is consumed when individuals and informal associations do not. Have a problem with keeping public spaces clean? Make littering illegal. Worried about rhinos and other endangered species becoming extinct? Make hunting them illegal, or impose a quota on how many rhinos each poacher is legally allowed to hunt.

Of course, littering usually is illegal, and bans or quotas apply to hunters in many countries. Yet the problems persist, so it's clear that implementing bans and quotas is not a perfect solution. To see why, we have to understand that making something illegal is simply one way of changing the *trade-offs* that people face; it does so by creating costs for breaking the ban or exceeding the quotas. The cost that rule-breakers expect to face depends both on the punishment associated with rule breaking *and* on the likelihood of being caught and punished. If the punishment is not severe, or the likelihood of getting caught is low, the cost may not be high enough to change the trade-off.

Bans and quotas therefore often fail in situations where it is difficult or costly for authorities to monitor and punish rule-breakers. For instance, poor countries find it difficult to enforce laws against poaching and habitat destruction. Most governments in East Africa, for instance, typically lack the funds to hire enough park rangers, build enough fences, and take other measures needed to fully protect wildlife. Bans on poaching rhinos thus have limited impact.

In contrast, the United States and other wealthy countries tend to have relatively well-funded, well-policed national parks and conservation areas. Bans and quotas in these areas effectively protect endangered species. More than 90 percent of species listed as endangered in the United States are still in existence since being declared endangered.[4] Similarly, South Africa has several large and well-managed national parks that protect rhinos and elephants effectively. As a result, the ban on hunting rhinos has proved to be effective.

In countries that have the resources to enforce them, bans or quotas that limit the use of common resources are straightforward public-policy approaches to solving the problem of overuse. Especially when the optimal quantity of consumption is zero—for instance, with an endangered species on the brink of extinction—it may be the best approach.

In conservation, tough moral and practical questions come into play. In particular, policy-makers argue over both the principle and the pragmatism of setting total bans on use of endangered species and habitats versus allowing people to earn money from limited use. For a deeper consideration of these questions, read the What Do You Think? box "Should conservationists be principled or pragmatic?"

Should conservationists be principled or pragmatic?
What Do You Think?

Can you put a dollar value on the existence of tigers? How about elephants? How about the Devil's Hole pupfish, a tiny fish less than one-inch long that is native to a single pool in a limestone cavern in Death Valley National Park in California? What about unique habitats such as the Grand Canyon or the Amazon rain forest? How much would you be willing to pay to preserve these natural wonders?

Some conservationists argue, on principle, against efforts to place a monetary value on the existence of beautiful, unique creatures and landscapes. Such things are beyond value, they argue, and even trying to put a price tag on them demeans and undermines conservation efforts.

Other conservationists feel that putting a price on endangered land and animals is the only practical way to save them in the long run. When something has no monetary value, they argue, no one has an incentive to protect and sustain it. Saying that something is "beyond" financial value sounds great, but functionally, they argue, it is the same as saying that it has *zero* financial value.

Those who take the latter approach promote programs that allow people to earn money from controlled use of endangered resources. These pragmatists favor use of private incentives to improve excludability and conservation. They point out that locals often face a steep opportunity cost of conserving land or endangered species by forgoing hunting, farming, or logging.

A prime example of this pragmatic strategy is ecotourism. It offers locals an alternative way to earn money by showing interesting flora or fauna to travelers, and it gives them an incentive to conserve natural areas.

In a related strategy, some nonprofit groups in the United States are paying ranchers and other landowners to set aside parts of their land. These agreements—known as *easements*—allow landowners to enter voluntarily into legal contracts that restrict what they can do with their land. For instance, a conservation group might pay someone who owns sensitive marshland in a suburban area to agree not to build on that land. The owner earns money from leaving the land undeveloped. Similar ideas are being tried in East Africa: Conservation groups directly pay locals to maintain endangered plants and habitats, and governments give locals the rights to earn money through tourism or controlled hunting or harvesting.

(continued)

Even conservationists who believe it is possible to put a price on conservation, though, sometimes criticize such pragmatic approaches. Their concerns relate to difficulties in monitoring and enforcement. The United States may have a well-functioning legal system, but many endangered species and landscapes are located in countries that do not. Without effective monitoring mechanisms, it can be difficult to distinguish legitimate activities from illegitimate activities. An outright ban may therefore be easier to enforce.

WHAT DO YOU THINK?

1. Should we try to put a dollar value on the existence of endangered species? If so, how could we go about calculating it?
2. If the existence of a place or species is a public good, how could we get individuals to contribute the real value they put on it, rather than free riding?
3. Is it always better to hold a hard line and stick to a pure preservation, zero-use approach to avoiding the tragedy of the commons? Or are there situations in which limited-use approaches are more likely to succeed?

Property rights: Privatization   Common resources are not allocated efficiently by markets, but private goods are. Wouldn't the most convenient solution be to turn everything into a private good? In some cases, the answer is, yes!

The classic case of turning a common resource into a private good is the one that gave the "tragedy of the commons" problem its name. Hundreds of years ago, most villages in Europe and America had town "commons"—open, grassy areas in the middle of town that were used by everyone and owned by no one. Farmers could graze their livestock on the common. You know the end of this story: The town common was a common resource, and each farmer had an incentive to graze more and more animals. Individual farmers had no incentive to limit their own usage in order to preserve the value of the common for everyone. The grazing land was ruined, and everyone was left worse off.

In the end, the solution to this original tragedy of the commons was surprisingly simple. The first step was to institute rules about who got to graze where and when. The ultimate step was to break up the town common into private lots. Each farmer had to graze his livestock on his own land. In New England, many towns still have a small "green," which is the descendant of the town common, but you are unlikely to see sheep or cows grazing there. When each farmer had to bear all the costs and all the benefits of his choices about how many animals to graze, each made the most efficient decision for his own land. Privatization solved the nonexcludability problem.

One policy credited with contributing to rhinos' recovery in South Africa allowed farmers to own wild animals on their land. Landowners are eligible for tax breaks if they keep and protect endangered species (such as rhinos). They also can earn money by selling the animals or admitting tourists to see them. This law essentially "privatizes" rhinos and other large animals like elephants; it allows individuals to capture the benefits of protecting the animals. This policy gives people an incentive to keep out poachers and increase the population of rhinos.

Increasingly, many governments are taking this sort of combined public-private approach to wildlife and other resource management. The privatization aspect helps introduce excludability and assign responsibility for costs and benefits; the public aspect helps counteract remaining externalities.

Assigning property rights over common resources is often far from simple, though. Especially in cases in which many people are already using a resource, it can be very difficult to decide who owns what. Not surprisingly, no one wants to be the person who has to reduce her consumption.

For a case that illustrates some mistakes in the management of a very important common resource, see the Economics in Action box "Why the Colorado River no longer reaches the ocean."

Why the Colorado River no longer reaches the ocean

Economics in Action

The mighty Colorado River once carved out the Grand Canyon. Now, it barely trickles into Mexico, and it vanishes altogether before even reaching the Gulf of California. The reason? As the river passes through five U.S. states and six dams, vast amounts of water get diverted to grow thirsty crops in arid dusty fields and to supply drinking water to the booming cities in the Southwest.

The story starts in 1922, when seven states formed the Colorado River Compact. This compact was a well-intentioned effort to divide up the waters of the Colorado in a way that was as fair as possible to all of the states along the river. This compact had two problems, though:

- Calculations of how much water was available were based on abnormally high recent flows. This overstated the amount of available water by over a trillion gallons.
- The compact assigned property rights over river water but didn't make them easily tradable. All applications to transfer water rights have to go through a bureaucratic review process. That process often involves court cases or public hearings that can drag on for months. This second problem was even greater than the first.

Since individual water rights were assigned on a "first-come, first-served" basis, most of the water rights were given to farmers. The difficulty of transferring water rights means that 80 to 90 percent of the water in the Colorado is still deeded to farmers. Holders of water rights are allowed to keep their shares as long as they can show that the water is being put to good use. This gives farmers a perverse incentive to creatively waste water in years when their needs are lower, to ensure that they can hold on to their shares. Meanwhile, cities in the region have to scramble to find more water for their growing populations.

We might expect that farmers and cities would reach the obvious solution predicted by the Coase theorem: Farmers would grow hardier crops or get out of farming, and would sell any excess water to city dwellers at high prices. The city of San Diego has tried to use the coordinating power of government to implement the solution suggested by the Coase theorem. In order to meet the growing demands of

The legal complexities of transferring water rights have hampered management of water use between farmers and cities in the arid Southwest.
©Pixtal/age fotostock

(continued)

thirsty citizens, the city water authority pays farmers for their water. In most cases, it is able to offer prices to farmers that are higher than what they would have earned from crops, making the transfer a good deal for both parties. Although many farmers are happy with the payments they receive and the city of San Diego now has a secure source of water, the process has been beset by the legal complexities of transferring water rights ever since it went into effect in 2003.

Until the system of property rights surrounding the Colorado River is changed, it seems likely that legal battles over water will continue to plague the arid Southwest.

Sources: https://wrrc.arizona.edu/publications/arroyo-newsletter/sharing-colorado-river-water-history-public-policy-and-colorado-river; http://ron-griffin.tamu.edu/x677/readings/BurnessQuirk.pdf; www.sdcwa.org/water-transfer

Property rights: Tradable allowances   One common way that governments can institute private property rights is through the use of tradable allowances or permits. Remember that quotas can control total quantity, but they don't necessarily allocate supplies in the most efficient way. They can result in undesirable side effects, such as damaging extraction methods or rushes to get as much of a resource as possible before hitting the quota.

The method of using tradable allowances works the same way for solving a common-resource problem as it does for solving an externality problem: A cap is set on the total quantity of the resource that can be used, and shares of that total are allocated to individuals or firms. After the initial allocation, people can buy and sell their shares. Trading ensures that the resource is allocated to those with the highest willingness to pay, while still limiting overall quantity to an efficient level. The people who own shares now have private property rights—and an incentive, as owners, to make sure that the common resource does not get overused.

This may sound familiar. In Chapter 18, "Externalities," we discussed tradable allowances and permits as a way to tackle negative externalities. Since the depletion of common resources imposes a negative externality, tradable permits are also useful in allocating common resources.

There is a whole field dedicated to the study of the economics of the environment. Appropriately named *environmental economics*, this field applies many of the tools you have learned so far in this course to problems that were once thought to be the responsibility of government officials and environmentalists. If this is something that interests you, you may want to see if your school offers a class in environmental or resource economics.

✓TEST YOURSELF

- ☐ How does the tragedy of the commons affect the demand for common resources? What is the resulting effect on equilibrium quantity? **[LO 19.4]**
- ☐ Why is a tradable quota more efficient than a traditional quota? **[LO 19.5]**
- ☐ How can turning a common resource into private property solve the tragedy of the commons? **[LO 19.5]**

Conclusion

Public goods and common resources are a significant source of market failure. Generally speaking, unregulated public goods will encounter the free-rider problem, in which nonexcludability leads to undersupply. On the other hand, unregulated common-resource goods will fall prey to the tragedy of the commons, which occurs when nonexcludability and rivalry combine to cause overconsumption and depletion of the resource.

These challenges can be overcome through a variety of solutions. In some cases, strong social norms or local organizations can improve excludability and increase the cost of free riding or overconsumption enough to avoid market failure. In other cases, government can step in, enforcing bans or quotas to limit the use of a common resource. In general, limits like bans and quotas work only when they are backed by sufficiently strong monitoring and enforcement. Sometimes, it makes sense for government to simply provide a public good to counteract undersupply.

In places where these solutions are not workable, the solution may involve property right. Privatization, tradable allowances, or combined public-private solutions can harness individual incentives to manage use and improve excludability.

In the next chapter, we'll look into the practical details of how governments fund the provision of public goods and other services.

Key Terms

excludable, p. 478

rival in consumption (rival), p. 478

private good, p. 480

public good, p. 480

common resource, p. 480

artificially scarce good, p. 480

free-rider problem, p. 482

tragedy of the commons, p. 486

Summary

LO 19.1 Define different types of goods in terms of rivalry and excludability.

When a good is *excludable,* those who haven't paid for it can be prevented from using it. When a good is *rival,* one person's consumption prevents or decreases others' ability to consume it. Most of the goods discussed in this text are *private goods,* which are both excludable and rival.

Public goods are the opposite of private goods: They are neither excludable nor rival. *Common resources* are rival, but not excludable. *Artificially scarce goods* are excludable, but not rival.

LO 19.2 Describe the free-rider problem and its consequences.

The *free-rider problem* is caused by nonexcludability leading to undersupply of a public good. When a good is not easily excludable, individuals have no incentive to pay for it. Therefore, supplying a public good involves a significant positive externality to free riders who receive the benefits without paying for them. The result is undersupply of a good.

LO 19.3 Explain how and when problems with public goods can be effectively solved by social norms, government provision, and expansion of property rights.

Strong social norms can help rebalance the trade-offs involved in consuming public goods by imposing social costs on those who break the "rules" of good behavior. Imposing costs on free riding can help bring the quantity consumed closer to the efficient level.

Another way to solve the undersupply problem inherent in public goods is for the government to directly provide the public goods, or to force individuals to pay a private provider. Just as in a functioning market, the government must find the efficient quantity at which the marginal social benefit equals the cost. Oftentimes, governments must guess at what the marginal social benefit of an additional unit will be. They must also solve the issue of figuring out who will pay for the supply of the public good.

Alternatively, the government can make the public good more like a private good by giving some individuals or firms the right to produce and sell a good; this often is accomplished through patents and copyrights.

LO 19.4 Describe the tragedy of the commons and its consequences.

A *tragedy of the commons* is the depletion of a common resource due to individually rational but collectively inefficient overconsumption. The ability to access the benefits of a common resource without paying any costs increases demand. Because the resource is rival in consumption, it imposes a negative externality on those whose ability to consume the resource is reduced.

LO 19.5 Explain how and when problems with common resources can be effectively solved by social norms, government regulation, and expansion of property rights.

Strong social norms can help rebalance the trade-offs involved in consuming common resources by imposing social costs on those who break the "rules" of good behavior. Imposing costs on overconsumption can help bring the quantity consumed closer to the efficient level.

Often, government bodies have the power to solve the nonexcludability problem, while individuals do not. Banning or limiting use of common resources is a straightforward public-policy approach to solving the problem of overuse. However, such bans and limits often fail in situations where it is difficult or costly for authorities to monitor and punish rule breakers, and it is not necessarily efficient.

Sometimes the best way to solve the tragedy of the commons is to convert a common resource into a private good. Privatization works when it is possible to divide up a resource and make it excludable by giving a private owner control over its use. The owner has the right incentives to ensure an efficient level of use—bearing all of the costs and reaping all of the benefits.

Another common way that governments can institute private property rights is through the use of tradable allowances or permits. Tradable allowances create a market for the rights to consume a common resource, ensuring that it is allocated to those with the highest willingness to pay.

Review Questions

1. Popular software can cost thousands of dollars even though the marginal cost of producing another copy on a thumb drive or via download is near zero. What kind of good are these programs? **[LO 19.1]**

2. Suppose a popular band decides to hold a free concert in its hometown. Admission is available on a first-come, first-served basis. Is the concert a public good? **[LO 19.1]**

3. A talented musician plays for tips on the street but never seems to make very much money. Explain why his tip jar is never very full. **[LO 19.2, 19.4]**

4. Suppose a community garden in your neighborhood has both individually owned plots and a large, common plot. If soil and sunlight conditions are the same everywhere in the garden, explain why tomatoes grown in individually owned plots are so much better than tomatoes grown in the common plot. **[LO 19.2, 19.4]**

5. Why is it difficult for private markets to provide the optimal quantity of a public good? Why is it difficult for government to provide the optimal quantity of a public good? **[LO 19.3]**

6. Consider a fund-raising campaign for your school's library. What is the free-rider problem in this situation? How might publicly listing the names of donors to the library fund affect this problem? **[LO 19.3]**

7. Aquifers are underground sources of clean water that stretch over thousands of square miles. People who own land over the aquifer are free to take as much as they want. What is likely to happen to water supplies in an aquifer? Is this efficient? **[LO 19.4]**

8. Which do you expect to be more sustainable: grazing on public land or grazing on privately owned pastures? Why? **[LO 19.4]**

9. Even though many school zones don't have much traffic and aren't regularly monitored by the police for speed, most drivers are very careful to drive at or below speed limits when near schools. Why might this be the case even in the absence of strong government intervention? **[LO 19.3, 19.5]**

10. Consider a proposal to privatize street lighting. Would this be feasible? Why or why not? Does street lighting suffer from a tragedy of the commons problem? **[LO 19.3, 19.5]**

11. The government of India has made killing Bengal tigers illegal, but poaching of the endangered animal continues. List some possible reasons that the ban hasn't been very successful, and suggest an alternative approach. **[LO 19.5]**

12. The U.S. government is concerned about the huge numbers of people converging on Yellowstone Park every year. Government officials are worried that the park might be getting overused and the natural beauty will be ruined as a result. Suppose someone suggests dividing the park into private lots and selling it to individuals. How might this solution address the tragedy of the commons that is occurring? **[LO 19.5]**

Problems and Applications

1. Identify whether each of the following goods is usually excludable or nonexcludable. **[LO 19.1]**
   a. AM/FM radio.
   b. A round of golf on a course.
   c. Street art.
   d. A museum exhibition.
   e. Toll roads.

2. Identify whether each of the following goods is rival or nonrival. **[LO 19.1]**
   a. Cable TV.
   b. A pair of jeans.
   c. Street signs.
   d. Attending a baseball game.

3. Consider community safety or defense, meaning freedom from crime and threats, to answer the following questions. **[LO 19.2]**
   a. What sort of good is community safety?
   b. If you lived in a place with no government-funded police force, would you expect community safety to be *oversupplied* or *undersupplied*?

c. Suppose that some neighbors get together and organize a block watch group. What term do economists use to describe someone who lives in the neighborhood but chooses not to volunteer as part of the block watch?

4. From the list below, which of the following do you expect to suffer from a free-rider problem? Check all that apply. **[LO 19.2]**
    a. Pay-what-you-can yoga classes.
    b. Unlimited yoga classes with monthly membership dues.
    c. Fund-raiser for public television.
    d. Neighborhood park cleanup day.
    e. Housecleaning business operating in your neighborhood.
    f. Suggested museum-admission donation.

5. Which of the following subway announcements are attempts to establish or enforce a social norm? **[LO 19.3]**
    a. "Loud music and phone conversations are discourteous to fellow riders. Please keep the noise down."
    b. "If you see something, say something."
    c. "Please watch your step as you exit. Be careful of the gap between the train and the platform edge."
    d. "Please be patient and allow others to exit the train before you attempt to enter."
    e. "The train is being held at the station due to traffic ahead. We apologize for the inconvenience."

6. Would you expect tourists or locals to be more likely to give up their seat on a bus to an elderly person? **[LO 19.3]**

7. Consider the following government-provided goods. Which of these goods necessarily require funding via general taxation (as opposed to direct user fees)? **[LO 19.3]**
    a. Street lights.
    b. A park.
    c. A fireworks display.
    d. Public radio.
    e. A library.

8. In much of the United States and Canada, logging takes place in both privately owned and government-owned forests. **[LO 19.4]**
    a. Are privately owned forests excludable? Are they rival? What type of good are they?
    b. Suppose that anyone is legally allowed to enter a government-owned forest and start logging. What type of good are these forests?

c. Do you expect the rate of logging in government-owned forests to be faster, slower, or equal to the efficient level?

9. Suppose that the government decides to start regulating use of its forests, charging anyone who wants to log. Which of the following ways of calculating the price to charge for each acre will lead to an efficient quantity of logging? **[LO 19.4]**
    a. The sum of the marginal social value of each acre to all logging companies.
    b. The average price citizens say they would be willing to pay for an acre.
    c. The external cost that logging an acre imposes on all citizens.

10. Determine whether each of the following policy interventions is designed to increase supply or decrease demand for a public good or common resource. **[LO 19.3, 19.5]**
    a. A city government increases the frequency of street sweeping.
    b. London begins charging a toll to all vehicles that drive within the city limits.
    c. A gated community passes a bylaw requiring all homeowners to mow their lawns once a week during the summer.
    d. The National Park Service increases the cost of a pass to enter the Everglades.

11. Public-opinion polls in a small city have revealed that citizens want more resources spent on public safety, an annual fireworks display, and more community swimming pools. Which of these three citizen requests could be privatized by assigning property rights? **[LO 19.5]**

12. For each of the following examples, state which of these approaches is being taken to manage a common resource or supply a public good: social norms, quota, tradable allowance, government provision, or property rights. **[LO 19.3, 19.5]**
    a. A nonprofit organization spray-paints signs on storm drains reminding everyone that it "drains to the ocean" with a picture of a fish.
    b. A city starts a free program that collects recyclable glass, paper, and plastic from residents' doorsteps.
    c. In England, municipal-waste authorities are given a percentage of an overall limit that can be put in the landfill each year. These percentages can be traded among municipalities.
    d. American bison, which once roamed freely across the Great Plains, are now raised on ranches for commercial purposes.

13. There is a road between the suburbs and downtown. The road becomes congested at rush hour. As long as fewer than 100 people use the road at rush hour, the trip takes 30 minutes. When the 101st person enters the road, everyone has to slow down and the trip now takes 31 minutes. People value their time at $6 per hour (i.e., $0.10 per minute) and so a 30 minute trip costs $3.

[LO 19.5]

a. What is the private cost of one of the 100 individuals using the road? What is the total private cost of 100 people using the road? What is the total social cost of 100 people using the road?

b. What is the total social cost of 101 people using the road? What is the private cost of using the road for the 101st individual? What is the external social cost of the 101st person using the road?

Endnotes

1. www.savetherhino.org/rhino_info/ rhino_population_figures.

2. www.economist.com/node/16941705?story_id$16941705; https://rhinos.org/2018-state-of-the-rhino/.

3. Elinor Ostrom, *Governing the Commons: The Evolution of Institutions for Common Action* (New York: Cambridge University Press, 1990).

4. www.biologicaldiversity.org/campaigns/esa_wild_success/.

Taxation and the Public Budget

Chapter 20

Happy to Pay Taxes?

Lawn signs are a common sight during election season. With bright colors and catchy slogans, they try to draw the attention of passersby to the name of a favored political candidate. In 2003, however, a new and unusual sign appeared on the lawns of some Minnesota voters. In place of a politician's name, the bright orange signs simply read, "Happy to pay for a better Minnesota."

The Minnesota couple behind the "happy to pay" campaign told reporters that they weren't promoting any particular candidate or party. They simply wanted to share their opinion that a tax increase was not necessarily a bad thing. In their view, a tax increase would allow Minnesota to have a balanced budget *and* maintain public services.[1]

The "happy to pay" campaign raised eyebrows because it bucked the usual trend of voters demanding lower taxes. Sometimes, as with the "Tea Party" movement that swept U.S. politics in 2009–2010, voters demand cuts in *both* government programs *and* taxes. Other voters express a desire for functional roads, good schools, and other services, while also wanting lower taxes.

Governments can, and often do, borrow money, rather than raise taxes, to pay for public spending. But the borrowed money comes due eventually. Sooner or later, somehow or other, government will always need to collect tax revenues to pay for what it spends.

©Joe Imel/Daily News/AP Images

LEARNING OBJECTIVES

LO 20.1 Describe the major public policy goals of taxation.

LO 20.2 Explain how deadweight loss and administrative costs contribute to the inefficiency of a tax.

LO 20.3 Calculate the effect of a tax increase on revenue, taking into account price and quantity effects.

LO 20.4 Identify proportional, progressive, and regressive taxes.

LO 20.5 Describe the sources of tax revenue in the United States, and discuss the role played by different types of taxes.

LO 20.6 Discuss the important features of the public budget and the relationship between revenues and expenditures.

Each time you vote, whether for your mayor or a national candidate, you're likely to face choices between candidates with different views on taxes. In this chapter we describe general principles of taxation and spending that can help you disentangle the debates. In earlier chapters we saw that when externalities exist, taxes can correct market failures, and thus increase total surplus. But we also saw that when markets are already efficient, taxes reduce total surplus.

Here we investigate the effects of a variety of taxes: how much money they raise, how much inefficiency they cause, and who bears the burden. We'll explore arguments for and against each kind of taxation, and give you the tools to weigh the issues and make informed choices when casting your vote.

Why Tax?

Taxpayers often dread April 15th—the day when federal income tax returns are due. Unlike the "happy to pay" tax supporters in Minnesota, many citizens grumble about the bite that taxes take out of their paychecks. Why do voters continue to support governments that tax them? What's the gain that balances the pain? We saw in earlier chapters that taxes do two things: raise revenue and change the behavior of buyers and sellers.

LO 20.1 Describe the major public policy goals of taxation.

- **Raising revenue:** The most obvious use of taxes is to raise public revenue. This revenue allows governments to provide goods and services to citizens, from national defense to highway building. Many tax-funded programs, such as public schools and roads, are intended to increase surplus and stimulate economic growth. Others are intended to provide basic human needs such as food, health care, or housing to people in need. People may disagree about which services should be funded through tax dollars, but most agree that at least some services are necessary.
- **Changing behavior:** Taxes change behavior because they alter the incentives faced by market participants. Taxes drive a wedge between the price paid by buyers and the price received by sellers. That wedge results in a lower equilibrium quantity of the good or service being consumed. In some cases, this effect on incentives is just a side effect of a tax designed to raise revenue; in others, it is the explicit purpose of the policy. Taxes on alcohol, tobacco, and gasoline are examples of policies *designed* partly to reduce demand.

Figure 20-1 summarizes these two effects of taxes.

We saw in Chapter 18, "Externalities," that when a market involves negative externalities, such as air pollution, the effect of a tax can be to *increase* total surplus in society as a whole by moving the market to a lower equilibrium quantity.

However, we also saw in Chapter 6, "Government Intervention," that when a tax is implemented in an already-efficient market, it causes *deadweight loss*. Deadweight loss is usually considered a *cost of taxation*.

Sometimes, though, even when markets are functioning efficiently, governments use taxes to discourage certain purchases. For a discussion of whether such taxes increase or decrease total surplus, see the From Another Angle box "Can some taxes make people happier?."

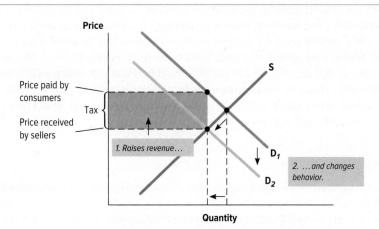

FIGURE 20-1

A tax raises revenue and changes behavior

A tax shrinks the market, moving equilibrium to a lower quantity and driving a wedge between the price paid by buyers and the price received by sellers. A tax also raises revenue, equal to the tax rate multiplied by the quantity traded under the new equilibrium.

Can some taxes make people happier?

From Another Angle

Smoking and drinking are not like other economic activities. Some people *want* to stop smoking and drinking (or at least cut back) but have a tough time following through, due to problems with self-control or addiction. Under these circumstances, what people do (i.e., what economists call "revealed preference") doesn't always tell the whole story about what people really *want*.

Society has a stake in some of these choices. The public health costs of smoking and excessive drinking are astronomical. Smoking-related disease kills 480,000 people per year in the United States and costs $320 billion in health care costs and lost productivity per year. Excessive drinking costs an extra $250 billion.

These statistics are the major motivations for "sin taxes" on cigarettes and alcohol. (We're not being judgmental with that term; "sin tax" is the phrase used by policy-makers.) Since sin taxes reduce consumption of these goods, taxes combat negative externalities—the costs to others associated with breathing secondhand smoke or encountering drunk drivers on the road—while also reducing these overall health costs. "Sin taxes" are clearly beneficial for those who don't smoke or drink. But what if "sin taxes" could also be good for some smokers and drinkers?

Economists Jonathan Gruber and Sendhil Mullainathan looked at how the self-reported happiness of people in the United States and Canada changed as cigarette taxes rose. They found that increases in cigarette taxes actually made people who were likely to smoke happier. Why? The research suggests that sin taxes can act as a sort of commitment device for people who truly want to change their behavior but have problems with self-control. Making cigarettes and alcohol more expensive through taxes changes the cost-benefit calculation, giving smokers an extra incentive to quit.

As economists gain a better understanding of behavioral and psychological responses to public policy, we are learning more about the nuances and versatility of taxes. For the smokers who are able to quit, sin taxes can be a win-win policy.

Source: Jonathan Gruber and Sendhil Mullainathan, "Do cigarette taxes make smokers happier?" *Advances in Economic Policy and Analysis* 5, no. 1 (2005).

Throughout the chapter, keep in mind the two goals of taxation: raising revenue and changing behavior. People may disagree about when it is appropriate to use taxes to accomplish them, but the goals provide a starting point for discussion about the costs and benefits of taxation.

Even when people have agreed on a goal, some types of taxes may be more effective than others in achieving it. In this chapter, we will evaluate the effects and side effects of different methods of taxation. We hope that you will combine this factual understanding of taxes with your moral and political beliefs about which public services should be funded and what types of behavior ought to be discouraged, and vote accordingly.

✓ TEST YOURSELF

- ☐ Does a tax increase or decrease the quantity of the taxed good that is consumed? **[LO 20.1]**
- ☐ Why does a tax in an efficient market decrease total surplus, while a tax in a market with a negative externality increases total surplus? **[LO 20.1]**

Principles of Taxation

If you live in the United States, your state constitution (unless you live in Vermont) requires that the state budget be balanced. So, if your governor has ambitious ideas to offer new state services, keep in mind that the legislature and governor almost surely have to raise fees or taxes to make it happen. Even if your governor is working to reduce taxes, he or she has to decide which kinds of taxes to cut and how fast. The economic question is how to tax in a way that keeps the economy healthiest.

Not all taxes are alike, and there are different ways to design a tax to raise a certain amount of revenue. In this section, we focus on the impact of different types of taxes. Three concepts are particularly useful in evaluating the costs and benefits of alternative types of taxes: *efficiency, revenue*, and *incidence*. We'll discuss each of these concepts as a framework for evaluating the costs and benefits of a particular tax.

Efficiency: How much (extra) will the tax cost?

LO 20.2 Explain how deadweight loss and administrative costs contribute to the inefficiency of a tax.

When considering the costs and benefits of a tax, it is tempting to assume that the cost is the amount that taxpayers have to pay and the benefit is whatever services are provided using those funds.

However, we know from the analysis of taxes in earlier chapters that it's not quite that simple. Taxes cause changes in economic behavior, potentially shifting supply and demand away from their optimal levels. We need to take that effect into account. In addition, collecting taxes takes up resources in itself.

Just because a tax creates inefficiency does not necessarily mean that the tax is bad. While the tax itself may create an inefficiency, the revenue it generates may be used to fix another one. For example, revenues raised by tariffs can be used to fund job-training programs for displaced factory workers. In each case, the net effect of the tax is specific to each tax and to each use of government proceeds from the tax.

Here we will discuss two types of inefficiencies that taxes can create:

- The first kind of inefficiency we consider is one we have described already: *deadweight loss*. This is the difference between the loss of surplus to taxpayers and the tax revenue collected.
- The second form of inefficiency is *administrative burden*, which comes from the costs involved in collecting the tax.

We'll discuss these two costs and how to calculate their size.

Deadweight loss   Remember from Chapter 6, "Government Intervention," that a tax in an efficient market decreases total surplus. This loss of surplus is called **deadweight loss**. It occurs because the quantity of a good that is bought and sold is below the market equilibrium quantity.

It's important to distinguish deadweight loss from the total amount of surplus lost to those in the market as the result of a tax:

- The surplus that is lost to buyers and sellers but converted into tax revenue is not considered a cost because the tax revenue funds public services. Those services provide surplus to citizens who benefit from them. Sometimes these are the same people who paid the taxes, and sometimes not. The value of that surplus may be *transferred* to someone else through government policies, but *it is not lost*.

- In contrast, deadweight loss is value that simply *disappears* as the result of a tax. Neither buyers nor sellers nor recipients of government services benefit from it. It is lost altogether.

Let's briefly review how to calculate the value of deadweight loss that results from a tax in an efficient market—say, the market for jeans. Suppose that the market equilibrium for jeans is 4 million pairs at a price of $50 per pair. For the sake of simplicity, let's imagine that the sales tax on clothes is a flat dollar amount (rather than a percent of the sale price). Figure 20-2 demonstrates the effect of a $20 per pair tax on jeans. (We admit that's a pretty large tax, but it helps clarify the example.)

What happens? The tax causes the demand curve to shift down by the amount of the tax. The reason: The effective price paid by consumers is now $20 higher at any given market price. Thus, the amount consumers are willing to pay to suppliers (before the tax) is $20 less. The tax drives a wedge between the price received by sellers (the market price—in this case, $40) and the price paid by buyers (the market price plus the $20 tax—in this case, $60). The shift in the demand curve causes the equilibrium point to slide down the supply curve to a lower market (pre-tax) price ($40) and a lower quantity (3 million pairs of jeans). Under the tax, 1 million fewer pairs of jeans are sold. The consumer and producer surplus that is no longer generated by those sales is deadweight loss.

deadweight loss
a loss of total surplus that occurs because the quantity of a good that is bought and sold is below the market equilibrium quantity

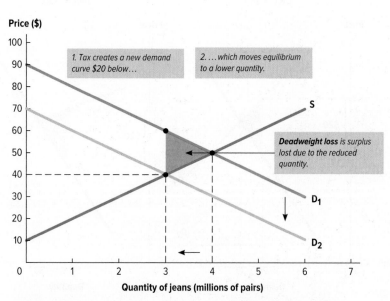

FIGURE 20-2

A tax causes deadweight loss

A tax of $20 on jeans adds a new demand curve, sliding the equilibrium point along the supply curve from 4 million to 3 million pairs. The surplus lost to people who would have bought and sold those 1 million pairs of jeans but no longer do so under the tax is deadweight loss.

How much deadweight loss a tax causes depends on how *responsive* buyers and sellers are to a price change. In other words, the size of deadweight loss is determined by the price elasticity of supply and demand: The more price-elastic the demand or supply curve, the larger the drop in equilibrium quantity caused by a given increase in price, and the larger the deadweight loss will be.

Figure 20-3 shows graphically that the area of the triangle representing deadweight loss is larger in a market with higher price elasticity of demand, given a tax of the same size. This leads to a general principle of taxation: Deadweight loss is minimized when a tax is levied on something for which people are *not likely to change their behavior much in response to a price change*.

It is worth bearing in mind that this discussion also applies to the markets for factors of production. In general, a tax discourages people from engaging in whatever behavior is taxed. For example, a tax on income discourages people from working extra hours. How much inefficiency is caused by income tax, and how much revenue is raised by it, depends on *how price-sensitive* people are. In other words, how much will workers reduce the quantity of labor they supply in response to a tax on wages? (Not surprisingly, policy-makers are particularly interested in the answer to this question.)

lump-sum tax (head tax)
a tax that charges the same amount to each taxpayer, regardless of their economic behavior or circumstances

If deadweight loss is minimized when we tax activities that people will continue to do anyway, why not push this idea to its logical conclusion and simply tax people for existing? This idea—of taxing everyone the same amount, regardless of their economic behavior—is called a **lump-sum tax**, or **head tax**. To understand why a lump-sum tax is very efficient, think about *how taxpayers*

FIGURE 20-3

Deadweight loss increases with price elasticity

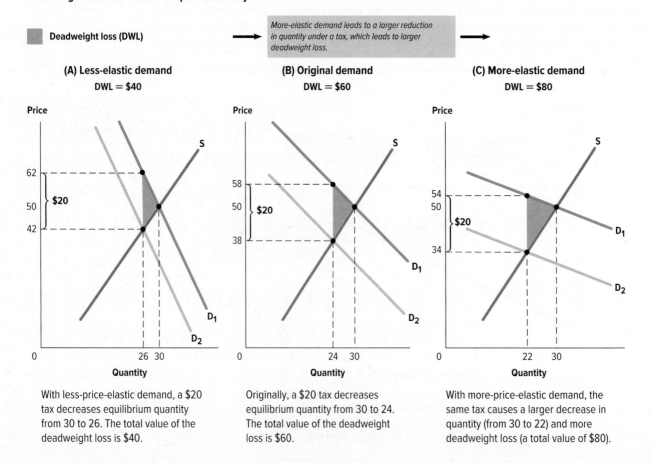

■ Deadweight loss (DWL)

More-elastic demand leads to a larger reduction in quantity under a tax, which leads to larger deadweight loss.

(A) Less-elastic demand
DWL = $40

(B) Original demand
DWL = $60

(C) More-elastic demand
DWL = $80

With less-price-elastic demand, a $20 tax decreases equilibrium quantity from 30 to 26. The total value of the deadweight loss is $40.

Originally, a $20 tax decreases equilibrium quantity from 30 to 24. The total value of the deadweight loss is $60.

With more-price-elastic demand, the same tax causes a larger decrease in quantity (from 30 to 22) and more deadweight loss (a total value of $80).

will respond to the tax. If everyone is required to pay $1,000 to the government each year no matter what they do, or how much they earn, or what they buy, there is no incentive to change such behaviors.

If our only goal in implementing a tax was to maximize efficiency and minimize deadweight loss, a head tax might be the way to go. But while head taxes may be highly efficient, many people do not think it's fair to have everyone, both rich and poor, pay the exact same dollar amount in taxes. A lump-sum tax also reduces the total amount of revenue that can be raised, because the size of the tax is limited by the poorest citizens' ability to pay. For these reasons, we rarely see lump-sum taxes.

Administrative burden   Administering and collecting taxes carries costs. Someone has to create procedures for collecting revenues, enforcing tax payments, and handling the collected funds. These logistical costs associated with implementing a tax are called the **administrative burden**. It includes the time and money spent by the government agencies that track and follow up on tax bills. It also includes taxpayers' time and expense of filing their returns and hiring accountants and lawyers to give them tax advice. For instance, in 2018 the federal government spent $11.43 billion to run the Internal Revenue Service (IRS), the government agency tasked with collecting around $3.33 trillion (or $3,330 billion) in tax revenue.[2] Administrative burden is the second form of tax inefficiency.

administrative burden the logistical costs associated with implementing a tax

In general, the more complex the tax, the higher the administrative burden will be. Consider, for instance, the difference between the federal income tax and a local sales tax:

- The federal income tax requires people to fill out pages and pages of forms, calculate types of income from different sources, and account for deductions and exclusions. Record-keeping takes time and sometimes involves hiring a tax preparer or an accountant. On the government side, the income tax involves an entire government agency (the IRS) devoted to calculating and processing tax returns and tracking down people who fail to pay.

- In contrast, a sales tax, while certainly not costless, is much easier to process. Merchants calculate and collect the tax with each purchase, and they send this tax revenue to the local government. The sales tax doesn't require as much extra time or effort to process.

If maximizing efficiency was our only goal, simpler taxes would certainly be more efficient than more complicated ones.

Revenue: How much money will the tax raise?

Calculating the revenue raised by a tax is simple: Multiply the tax rate per unit by the number of units of the thing being taxed:

LO 20.3 Calculate the effect of a tax increase on revenue, taking into account price and quantity effects.

EQUATION 20-1   Tax revenue = Tax per unit × Number of units

If it's a tax on a toll road, for example, multiply the fee per car by the number of cars. If it's a general sales tax, then you multiply the tax per dollar of sales by the number of dollars in sales. If it's an income tax, multiply the tax per dollar of income by the number of dollars of income.

The catch is to not forget that the tax shrinks the market before you get to collect revenue. Remember that *when you tax something, you get less of it*. So, don't multiply the tax rate by the *pre-tax* quantity of units. Instead, you have to figure out how taxpayers will *respond* to the tax and predict the *post-tax* quantity.

Look again at Figure 20-3. It shows that the rectangle representing tax revenue is smaller in the market with more-price-elastic demand (panel C) because the equilibrium quantity shrinks further (from 30 to 22).

All else equal, imposing taxes in markets where demand and supply are price-inelastic not only causes less inefficiency but also raises more revenue. This may be another reason—beyond negative externalities and "sin"—why governments like to tax cigarettes and alcohol: The demand for these goods is highly price-inelastic. This inelastic demand ensures that the tax collects a large amount of revenue. In New York State, a $1.60 tax on cigarettes imposed in 2010 raised over $500 million.

To see why it is so important to understand elasticity, suppose that you are a state legislator considering whether to increase a gasoline tax from $1 per gallon to $2. You know that 5 million gallons of gasoline are currently sold in your state every day. The current tax brings in $5 million in tax revenue. If you raise the tax by a dollar, can you expect to bring in *another* $5 million of revenue? No—remember that the tax will increase the price of gasoline; the higher price will drive down demand, reducing the equilibrium quantity bought and sold. In an extreme case, the net effect of a tax increase could even be to *reduce* total tax revenue. For example, if the tax increase reduces the equilibrium quantity to 2 million gallons, your $2 gas tax would bring in only $4 million in revenue.

In other words, we have to consider two opposing effects of a tax increase:

- Raising taxes means that the government gets more revenue per units sold—the *price effect*.
- But the higher tax rate causes fewer units to be sold—the *quantity effect*.

This idea, shown in Figure 20-4, is parallel to the discussion in Chapter 4, "Elasticity," of the relationship between price elasticity and revenue for a private firm.

We can generalize this point to see that raising taxes has diminishing returns to revenue, as shown in Figure 20-5:

- As tax rates get higher, we can expect revenue to increase at a slower and slower rate. This occurs as the quantity effect catches up with the price effect.
- At some point, taxes can get so high that the quantity effect dominates. At that point, raising taxes reduces total revenue.

The point at which the revenue-maximizing tax level is reached depends on the elasticity of supply and demand: The more elastic, the quicker the revenue-maximizing point will be reached.

After the revenue-maximizing point, *lowering* taxes *increases* total revenue. The graph shown in Figure 20-5 is sometimes referred to as the *Laffer curve*, after economics professor Arthur Laffer.

FIGURE 20-4

Raising taxes has both price and quantity effects on revenue

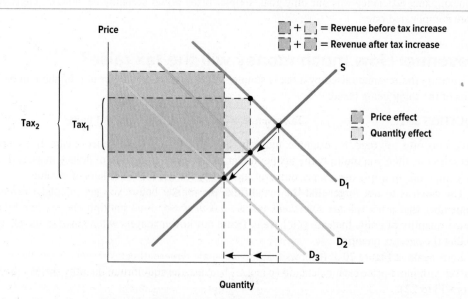

An increase in the tax rate increases the amount of revenue earned per unit, but the higher "price" of taxes means that quantity decreases. The net effect on revenue depends on whether the quantity effect outweighs the price effect.

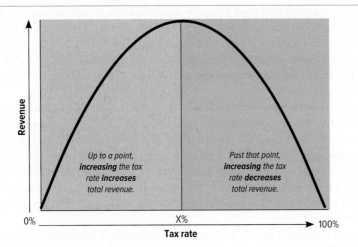

FIGURE 20-5

Raising income taxes first increases and then decreases revenue

In the beginning, raising the income tax rate increases revenue. After a certain point, further increases in the tax rate decrease the amount of revenue collected. At this point, maximum revenue is collected.

As an advisor to President Ronald Reagan in the 1980s, Laffer argued that U.S. income tax rates had become so high (especially on the wealthiest Americans, who paid 70 percent of their income in taxes in 1980) that Reagan could achieve a politician's dream: He could lower income tax rates and simultaneously increase government revenue. Reagan took this advice and signed large-scale tax cuts into law in 1981.

The idea that people change their behavior in response to taxes is uncontroversial among economists. But the question about *how much* and *in what ways* they change their behavior is the subject of much research. Most of that research suggests that the elasticity of the labor supply with respect to taxes is very low for most people: In contrast to Laffer's prediction, people hardly increase the amount they work when tax rates fall. Evidence shows that tax revenue usually drops when taxes are cut. In other words, the economy is usually on the left side of Figure 20-5.

However, research shows that people *do* rearrange their income from different sources to reduce their tax burden, especially higher-income people who face the highest tax rates. In the end, we can't say for sure at what point the Laffer curve reaches its maximum. Estimates range from 40 percent to near 80 percent. This may seem high, but remember, what we're considering here is the tax rate that maximizes the government's revenues, not the level that is "best" for the economy.

As we'll discuss later in the chapter, knowing the price and quantity effects of taxation is critical when weighing political arguments about who should be taxed and by how much.

Incidence: Who ultimately pays the tax?

We have seen that, in theory, a head tax would be more efficient than other types of taxes. That's because a head tax is levied equally on everyone, no matter how much they earn or what they buy. As a result, a head tax won't distort economic behavior and thus it minimizes deadweight loss. So, why don't governments simply collect all of their tax revenue using a head tax?

LO 20.4 Identify proportional, progressive, and regressive taxes.

Let's use some real numbers to draw a rough sketch of what a head-tax-only system would look like in the United States. Say the goal is to collect $3.33 trillion in taxes—which was the approximate federal tax revenue in 2018. (For this thought experiment, individuals would pick up the tab currently paid by corporations and foreign producers.) With approximately 55 percent of America's population (or about 181 million people) paying taxes in the country, to raise the needed amount, a head tax would have to be about $18,400 per taxpayer. Even if this thought experiment narrowed to focus only on personal income taxes, the average taxpayer would still have to hand over $9,400 and *still* pay their share of payroll taxes. Given that roughly 40 percent of Americans earn less than $25,000 per year, any head tax would be a very big percentage of many people's income.[3]

incidence
a description of who bears the burden of a tax

The larger lesson here is that policy-makers—and taxpayers, of course—are concerned not only with what a tax does, but also with who pays it. In Chapter 6, "Government Intervention," we introduced the idea of incidence as the relative burden of an excise tax on buyers versus sellers. We can now generalize the concept of **incidence** as a description of who bears the burden of any sort of tax. This means not just buyers and sellers, but also old people or young people, rich people or poor people, and so on.

In Chapter 6, "Government Intervention," we also described an important insight that's not immediately obvious. We observed that the burden a tax places on buyers versus sellers is independent of which side is charged for the tax. This idea says that the *statutory incidence* of the tax (that is, who is legally obligated to pay the tax to the government) has no effect on the *economic incidence* of the tax (that is, who actually loses surplus as a result of the tax). Instead, the side of the market that is more inelastic—the side that responds less to changes in prices—will bear more of the tax burden. This means that policy-makers do not have much power in shifting the tax burden between buyers and sellers.

The distinction between statutory and economic incidence is important. For instance, the statutory incidence of a sales tax may fall entirely on consumers; they're the ones actually paying the tax at the cash register. But if consumers respond by buying less, the tax will clearly also affect the stores where they shop. If the stores respond by reducing prices, the stores are effectively sharing part of the tax burden. The economic incidence of the tax thus falls in part on the stores, even though they don't literally pay the tax.

Similarly, an income tax that employees are legally obliged to pay will also affect the corporations that employ them. If the tax reduces employees' willingness to supply labor at any given price level, corporations may have to raise wages in response in order to attract workers. The higher wages could lead corporations to reduce the dividends they pay to shareholders. Or corporations might increase the prices charged to customers. Both would represent a loss of surplus. In short, the people who pay the tax can be very different from those who ultimately feel the pinch.

Behavioral economists are adding another layer to our understanding of ways in which statutory incidence *can* actually affect people's behavior. Refer back to the Real Life box "Who really pays the sales tax?" in Chapter 6 for a discussion of how an understanding of behavioral responses to taxes can affect our analysis of taxes.

We generally assume that policy-makers do not have the power to redistribute the tax burden between consumers and producers. But they *do* have the ability to affect the relative economic incidence of the tax burden on the rich and the poor. Economists and policy-makers classify taxes in one of three categories: proportional, regressive, or progressive.

proportional/flat tax
a tax that takes the same percentage of income from all taxpayers

Proportional taxation   A tax that is **proportional** takes the same *percentage* of income (as opposed to the same dollar amount) from all taxpayers. In other words, people are taxed *in proportion* to their income. In a political context, a proportional income tax is sometimes called a "flat tax."

Under a 25 percent flat tax on income, for instance, someone with an income of $20,000 would pay the same *proportion* of his or her income as someone with an income of $200,000. The absolute amount paid by each of the two taxpayers would be $5,000 ($0.25 \times \$20,000$) versus $50,000 ($0.25 \times \$200,000$), as shown in panel A of Figure 20-6.

progressive tax
a tax that charges low-income people a smaller percentage of their income than high-income people

Progressive taxation   The current income tax in the United States is not a proportional tax—instead, it is **progressive**. A tax is considered progressive if people with low incomes owe not only a smaller absolute amount but also a smaller *percentage* of their income than high-income people.

The U.S. personal income tax has different "brackets" for people with different levels of income; the percentage of income owed increases with each bracket. Panel B of Figure 20-6 shows an example of a progressive income tax: The person earning $20,000 pays at a 20 percent tax

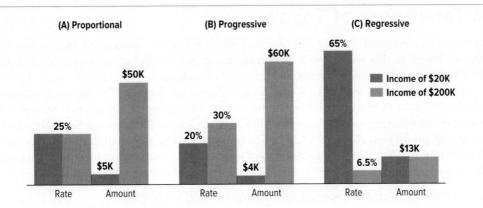

FIGURE 20-6

Proportional, progressive, and regressive taxes

Under a proportional tax, everyone pays the same percentage of their income in taxes. With a progressive tax, lower incomes are taxed less both as a percentage of their incomes and in total amount paid. A regressive tax charges the poor a higher percentage of their income than the rich, even though everyone is taxed the same dollar amount.

rate—for an absolute amount of $4,000 (0.20 × $20,000). The person earning $200,000 pays at a 30 percent tax rate—for an absolute amount of $60,000 (0.30 × $200,000).

Regressive taxation   The final category of tax incidence is regressive. A **regressive tax** is levied in such a way that low-income taxpayers pay a greater proportion of their income toward taxes than do high-income taxpayers. Most countries avoid explicitly regressive income taxes. That is, they structure their tax systems so that people in lower brackets do not pay a higher percentage of income in taxes.

regressive tax
a tax that charges low-income people a larger percentage of their income than it charges high-income people

However, other taxes can still be regressive. The lump-sum tax is an example, as shown in panel C of Figure 20-6. Assume that both taxpayers must pay the same absolute lump-sum tax of $13,000. That amount equates to a much higher proportion of the poorer taxpayer's income—65 percent ($13,000 ÷ $20,000) compared with only 6.5 percent ($13,000 ÷ $200,000) for the high earner.

As we consider different types of taxes, it is important to keep in mind the relationship between efficiency and incidence. For example, some politicians propose replacing all *income* taxes with a single *sales* tax. The beauty of the idea is that it would be much simpler and more efficient than the current system. On the other hand, it would be regressive: On average, people with lower incomes spend a higher proportion of their income, rather than saving or investing it. Thus, a higher proportion of their income would be affected by a sales tax.

In contrast, an income tax system like the one currently in place in the United States is more progressive, but is also probably less efficient due to the higher administrative burden and incentive effect on richer households.

We can see some of the challenges faced by politicians and economists as they try to find taxes that are fair and efficient and that raise enough money. Finding a tax system that pleases everyone is seldom possible. As a voter, you can expect to have to weigh both *positive* judgments about the efficiency of a proposed tax and *normative* judgments about the "fairness" of its incidence.

✓ TEST YOURSELF

☐ Which is likely to be more efficient: a tax on a good with highly price-elastic demand or a tax on a good with inelastic demand? **[LO 20.2]**

☐ What is the difference between the price effect and the quantity effect of a tax increase on tax revenue? **[LO 20.3]**

☐ Is a tax that charges $100 to every citizen for garbage collection regressive, proportional, or progressive? **[LO 20.4]**

A Taxonomy of Taxes

LO 20.5 Describe the sources of tax revenue in the United States, and discuss the role played by different types of taxes.

So far, we've mentioned several types of taxes without going into much detail on how and why they are levied. In this section, we'll explain the important features of different kinds of taxes. We'll focus on the revenue, efficiency, and incidence of each tax.

Let's start first with an overview of U.S. government tax revenue. The federal government calculates taxes by *fiscal year*, which begins in October of one calendar year and runs through September of the following year. In fiscal year 2018 (that is, October 2017 through September 2018), the federal government collected $3.33 trillion in revenue. Where does all this tax money come from? Figure 20-7 lists the various categories of taxes and the percentage of total tax revenue that they contribute. Approximately 90 percent of tax revenue comes from three sources:

- Personal income taxes account for 50 percent of total tax revenue.
- Payroll taxes account for 35 percent of total tax revenue.
- Corporate income taxes account for 6 percent of total tax revenue.

In this section, we'll discuss each of these three major federal taxes, as well as other, smaller ones. States also levy taxes, but because state-level taxes vary a lot, we'll focus mainly on federal taxes. (In many states, sales taxes provide the most revenue, followed by a personal income tax if the state has one.)

Personal income tax

income tax
a tax charged on the earnings of individuals and corporations

An **income tax** is exactly what it sounds like: a tax charged on the earnings of individuals and corporations. The largest source of income for most people is wages earned at work. Other sources may include income from interest in savings accounts, rental income from properties you own, investment income, or even lottery and game-show winnings.

Calculating personal income tax The higher your income, the higher your income tax "bracket." Each bracket is taxed at a different tax rate, and those in higher tax brackets pay a higher percentage of their income. The relationship between tax rates and brackets is somewhat

FIGURE 20-7

Federal tax receipts in the united states

The U.S. government earns most of its revenue from individual income taxes and payroll taxes (social insurance and retirement contributions). The vast majority of social insurance and retirement contributions come from Medicare and Social Security payments.

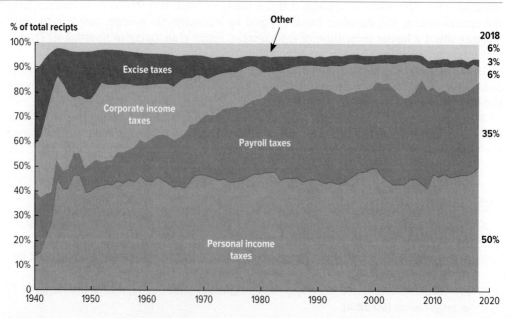

Single tax bracket ($)	Marginal tax rate (%)
1–9,525	10.0
9,526–38,700	12.0
38,701–82,500	22.0
82,501–157,500	24.0
157,501–200,000	32.0
200,001–500,000	35.0
500,000+	37.0

TABLE 20-1

U.S. personal income tax brackets in 2018

Source: https://taxfoundation.org/2018-tax-brackets/.

complicated—not every dollar is treated equally. Instead, the tax rate corresponding to each tax bracket is a **marginal tax rate**, or the tax rate charged on the last dollar a taxpayer earns.

marginal tax rate
the tax rate charged on the last dollar a taxpayer earns

To see how this works, let's look at an example. Table 20-1 illustrates the tax brackets for a single person for the tax year 2018. The lowest tax bracket applies to incomes from $1 to $9,525 and has a marginal rate of 10 percent. The second bracket applies to incomes from $9,526 to $38,700 and has a marginal rate of 12 percent.

Let's say that you are a single person who earned $50,000 in 2018. How much federal income tax would you owe?

- On the first $9,525, you would owe 10 percent, or $952.50.
- On the income above $9,525 but below $38,700 ($38,700 – $9,525 = $29,175), you would owe 12 percent, or $3,501.
- On the remaining income over $38,700 ($50,000 – $38,700 = $11,300), you would owe 22 percent, or $2,486.

In calculating the amount of personal income tax you owe, you would round the amounts to the nearest dollar:

$$\begin{aligned} \$9,525 \times 0.10 &= \$\ \ 953 \\ +29,175 \times 0.12 &=\ \ 3,501 \\ +11,300 \times 0.22 &=\ \ 2,486 \\ \text{Total tax} &= \$6,940 \end{aligned}$$

Your *marginal* tax rate is 22 percent—that's the rate you pay on the last dollar you earned. But notice that your *average* tax rate is only about 14 percent:

$$\frac{\$6,940}{\$50,000} = 13.9\%$$

Note that if you earn any amount less than $9,525, your average tax rate is 10 percent. Once you earn above that amount, the more you earn, the higher your average tax rate will be. In other words, the American individual income tax is *progressive:* The more you earn, the higher the percentage of your total income you pay.

Economists debate the extent to which income taxes discourage people from supplying their labor. One argument in favor of a progressive income tax rests on the idea that the supply of labor becomes more price-inelastic as people earn more. In other words, high earners tend to be highly educated people in jobs they like for reasons beyond the paycheck. They tend to be motivated by enjoyment of their work and the social status of their positions, not just the salary. If this is the case, we could expect that increasing the marginal tax rates on high earners would not cause them to work significantly fewer hours. Thus, progressive tax rates should bring in tax revenue without causing much deadweight loss. Note that this is a *positive* argument about the efficiency of progressive income tax rates (not a *normative* or philosophical one).

Many other countries around the world also use a progressive income tax system. However, the marginal tax rates can vary a great deal across countries. Table 20-2 shows the top marginal tax rate for several different countries. This table also shows how high one's income must be before one faces the highest marginal tax rate. Notice that in Sweden, The Netherlands, and Belgium the top marginal tax rate is higher than in the United States *and* more individuals face the top marginal rate in those countries than in the United States (because the highest rate kicks in at a lower income). Both the tax rate as well as the income threshold required to meet this rate can affect a tax system's progressivity.

Many complicating factors can make the amount you owe in income taxes different from what would be suggested by your tax bracket alone. For instance, people who live in a household with a spouse or dependent children or a disabled relative will be charged less for the same level of income. Certain types of expenses, such as charitable donations, college tuition, and business expenses can be deducted from your taxable income. In reality, therefore, you might earn $50,000, but your *adjusted (or taxable) income* would probably be lower than that.

It might be useful to say a few words about the mechanics of tax collection: In the United States, the federal government withholds federal personal income tax from your paycheck based on your *expected* annual income. (You'll see later that income from certain sources is subject to additional or lower taxes.) Many states also withhold a state personal income tax, also based on your *expected* annual income. When you file taxes for the year, you report your *actual* earnings:

- If actual earnings are lower than the expected earnings, you overpaid the amount you owe. The government returns some of the taxes it withheld: You get a tax refund.

- If actual earnings are higher than expected earnings, you have to write a check to the government for the additional money you owe.

Withholding income taxes from your paycheck makes collecting the taxes easier. People don't have to remember to put the money aside. Imagine if the government didn't withhold money for

TABLE 20-2

International comparison of tax rates, tax year 2018

Country	Top marginal tax rate (%)	Income threshold for top marginal tax rate (USD)
Sweden	60.1	71,486
Japan	55.8	450,041
Israel	50.0	168,625
The Netherlands	49.7	88,173
Germany	47.5	343,175
Belgium	46.0	58,545
United States	37.0*	500,000
New Zealand	33.0	47,792

*In 2018, the United States implemented tax legislation that both decreased the top marginal tax rate and increased the income threshold for the top tax rate. The data in Table 20-2 reflect these changes.

Source: Organisation for Economic Co-Operation and Development, https://stats.oecd.org/index.aspx?DataSetCode=TABLE_I7.

taxes, and people had not put money aside: April 15th would come around and many would find themselves unable to pay their tax bill.

Capital gains tax

Although the personal income tax doesn't generally distinguish between income from different sources, there is one important exception: capital gains. People often buy real estate, shares on the stock market, or other financial assets as investments. They hope, eventually, to earn a "return" by selling those capital assets at a higher price in the future.

While they own these assets, investors may earn income from them—dividends on shares or rent on real estate—that is taxed as normal income. However, the profit earned by buying investments and selling them at a higher price is called a *capital gain*. Capital gains are taxed separately from other types of income, under the appropriately named **capital gains tax**.

Taxes on capital gains in the United States are somewhat complicated and the subject of much debate. The relevant fact, however, is that income from capital gains is taxed at a lower rate than most other income. Congress lowered the tax on long-term capital gains in 2003 and raised it again in 2013. The intent of the lower rate was to give individuals and corporations greater incentives to invest in capital and, by doing so, to encourage entrepreneurship. Critics contend that because higher-income people earn more through capital gains, the benefits of this tax cut go mostly to the wealthy.

The tax law has special provisions meant to reward some kinds of investment. For instance, assets that are owned for longer than one year are taxed at a lower rate than those held for a short time. Also, the sale of a house that was used as a primary residence is taxed at a lower rate than other real estate. In both cases, policy-makers have decided to offer people incentives to maintain long-term home ownership because they believe it is beneficial for the overall economy. While people may disagree about what to tax and how much, policy-makers frequently use the tax code to incentivize some behaviors and discourage others.

capital gains tax
a tax on income earned by buying investments and selling them at a higher price

Payroll tax

In the United States (and many other countries), specific programs are funded by taxing payroll; this type of tax is thus often referred to as a **payroll tax**. Payroll taxes are different from income taxes (although the taxation may feel the same).

In the United States, payroll taxes are charged and accumulated to pay for Social Security and Medicare. Payroll taxes are charged to *both* employees and employers, each paying half. (In 2018, the employer and the employee both pay a rate of 6.2 percent.) If you are self-employed, you pay both parts of the tax (the employee and the employer parts plus an additional Medicare tax, for a rate of 15.3 percent).

The employee's portion shows up on your paystub as *FICA withholding* (*FICA* stands for Federal Insurance Contribution Act). Your employer withholds that amount and sends it to the federal government on your behalf. (This is in addition to the amount held for personal income taxes discussed above.) As Figure 20-7 showed, FICA makes up a huge portion of federal government revenue.

Employers pay their half of payroll taxes directly to the government when they send the employee's amount. If you are self-employed, you typically send a check to the government every three months for the FICA amount you owe.

The payroll tax in the United States is different from the personal income tax in several critical ways. The most important difference is that income taxes go into general government revenue, to be allocated through the public budget. The FICA payroll tax is a direct contribution to Social Security and Medicare, programs that provide income and medical benefits to retired people. Since people who pay FICA during their working years are eligible for Social Security and Medicare benefits when they retire, the payroll tax is considered to be forced saving for retirement.

payroll tax
a tax on the wages paid to an employee

However, the connection between what you pay and what you later receive in Social Security and Medicare benefits is indirect. The government doesn't just hold your money until you retire and then pay it back to you. Instead, the Social Security system is based on a pay-as-you-go model, under which people who are currently working pay taxes that are then spent to provide benefits for people who are currently retired. When you retire, your benefits will be paid for by the next generation. The benefits that the elderly receive are determined through a complex formula based on earnings (and therefore FICA tax payments) during their working years. As the number of retired people relative to the number of working people grows, this system has run into problems, which we discuss later in the chapter.

Two more differences between the U.S. payroll tax and personal income tax are important. First, the payroll tax is charged only on "earned" income, such as wages or income from self-employment. Thus, the payroll tax is not paid on other sources of income such as investments or gifts. Because people with higher overall income also tend to receive a higher percentage of income from these other sources, they end up paying less in payroll taxes *as a percentage* of their total income.

Second, the Social Security component of the payroll tax applies only to income up to $128,400 in 2018 (the cap typically increases a little bit each year). People who make more than $128,400 pay, in payroll tax, a *lower percentage* of their total earnings the more they earn. Thus, households with higher income typically pay less in payroll tax as a percentage of their income.[4]

These two factors imply that the payroll tax is a regressive tax, but this is not inherent to the nature of a payroll tax. One could design a payroll tax that has no cap, or one that charges higher marginal rates for people with higher wages. The benefits people receive from Social Security are progressive: Those who had higher income during their working years receive higher benefits in absolute dollar amounts, but lower benefits as a percentage of their earnings.

Corporate income tax

Like individuals, corporations also pay taxes, the most prominent of which is the *corporate income tax*. In the United States, the corporate income tax is progressive: Corporations that earn less income pay a lower percentage of their income than those that earn more income). In 2018, the Tax Cuts and Jobs Act instituted a flat corporate tax rate that requires all companies to pay taxes on 21 percent of corporate income. Most states, although not all, also charge a corporate income tax; most top out with the highest bracket somewhere between 3 and 12 percent.[5] The 2018 tax cut for corporations makes U.S. corporate taxes more competitive with those in other countries.

Although corporations are legally responsible for paying the corporate income tax, the burden of the tax could be borne in varying degrees by shareholders (through lower dividends), employees (through lower wages), or customers (through higher prices).

Other taxes

sales tax
a tax that is charged on the value of a good or service being purchased

excise tax
a sales tax on a specific good or service

Even if you've yet to pay income tax, you have often paid sales tax. Sales tax is charged based on the value of a good or service being purchased. Many states have a general sales tax but exempt certain classes of items considered to be necessities, such as food or clothing. Often, states also charge separate sales taxes, called excise taxes, that are targeted at specific goods, such as gasoline or cigarettes.

In the United States, there is no *federal* sales tax, but sales taxes are a major source of revenue for state governments. In fact, in 2016 sales taxes made up almost half of state tax revenue, with about two-thirds of that generated by general sales taxes and one-third by excise taxes on goods such as alcohol, insurance premiums, gasoline, and cigarettes.[6] This average conceals wide variation across states. For instance, California's sales tax is the highest at 7.25 percent, while five states—Alaska, Delaware, Montana, New Hampshire, and Oregon—have no sales tax at all.

Online shopping has created a gray area for sales tax collection. Originally, online retailers were required to collect sales taxes only if they had a physical presence in the state where the buyer lived. States complained that they were losing revenue that they would collect if the transaction occurred in a brick-and-mortar store. The dispute traveled all the way to the Supreme Court, which ruled in 2018 that avoiding sales taxes provided online retailers with an unfair advantage. As part of the decision, the court allowed states to collect sales taxes from larger retailers with an "economic interest" in their state.

Although there is no federal sales tax at this time, every so often politicians propose a form of national sales tax, called a *value-added tax (VAT)*, common in Europe. There are, as with any tax, arguments pro and con that have to do with tax incidence. Like any sales tax, VATs are regressive, as people with less income spend a greater share of what they earn on taxed goods.

For many people, a house is the most valuable item they own. **Property tax** is a tax on the estimated value of a home or any property owned by a taxpayer. Property taxes are an important source of revenue for local governments in many parts of the country. For instance, property taxes often fund public schools. The local taxing authority assesses property values every few years and charges a fraction of the value as the tax. (Property taxes are not collected at the federal or state levels in the United States.)

property tax
a tax on the estimated value of a home or other property

The categories we've just discussed cover the major types of taxes and bring in the majority of federal and state government revenue. There are also many minor taxes, which make up only a small part of the federal budget but sometimes pack an outsized political punch. These include taxes on certain types of imports, taxes on large financial gifts (unless they are donations to a recognized nonprofit group), and taxes on money and assets that are left to heirs when you die. This last tax—the *estate tax*, also sometimes known as the inheritance or "death" tax—has been a particularly divisive issue in recent years. Read up on it in the What Do You Think? box "Death and taxes."

Death and taxes
What Do You Think?

People often argue about taxes. Those arguments are often about the ideas behind taxes, rather than about particular facts. In other words, debates over taxation are often driven by underlying *normative* disagreements.

One of the most politically divisive arguments over U.S. tax policy has centered on the estate tax. This tax is charged when a person dies and passes money or assets on to his or her heirs. Opponents of the estate tax sometimes refer to it as the "death tax."

Here's how the estate tax works: After a person dies, his or her estate is valued, and the value determines the tax rate. No tax is due if the value of the estate is less than a certain sum—$11.2 million in 2018. Estates worth more than that are charged a 40 percent tax on the amount above $11.2 million. There are exemptions for widows and widowers and for people in specific circumstances, such as inheriting family-owned farms. However, only a very small number of wealthy people pay the tax at all. It is estimated that only 1,700 estates would be subject to the federal estate tax in 2018, equal to less than 0.1 percent of all deaths.

So, why the big fuss about a tax that affects only a tiny minority of Americans? One possibility is confusion caused by the success of its opponents in popularizing the term "death tax." After all, everyone dies, so you might assume that everyone must be subject to a "death tax," right? There is, in fact, some evidence that such confusion does exist: One survey found that almost half of the voters surveyed wrongly thought that the estate tax applied to "most" American families. If it were popularly referred to as, say, the "inherited-wealth tax" instead, such popular confusion might be reduced.

(continued)

Beyond this possibility, the estate tax hits a nerve because it addresses underlying political and moral disagreements over the role of taxes in redistributing wealth. Opponents argue that people should have a right to do what they want with their money. That includes saving it and passing it on to their children. The estate tax, some argue, is an unfair double tax. First, people are taxed when they earn their income, and then they're taxed again when they give it to heirs at the end of life. (Of course, if the estate tax is a double tax, then we are all being taxed four or five times already: Payroll taxes, income taxes, sales taxes, excise taxes, and property taxes all cut into our earnings at some point.)

Supporters of the estate tax, including the billionaire Warren Buffett, counter that it's healthier for the economy and for society to give each generation incentives to work their way up on their own merits, rather than living off inherited wealth.

WHAT DO YOU THINK?

1. Which of the arguments—for or against the estate tax—do you find more convincing? Should there be any limits on people's ability to pass down wealth across generations?
2. If you were in charge, what, if anything, would you change about the estate tax? Would you abolish it? Or, alternatively, would you make it even more progressive by increasing the marginal rates or expanding the number of people it applies to?

Sources: www.irs.gov/businesses/small/article/0,,id=98968,00.html; www.irs.gov/businesses/small-businesses-self-employed/estate-tax; www.taxpolicycenter.org/taxvox/only-1700-estates-would-owe-estate-tax-2018-under-tcja.

✓ TEST YOURSELF

☐ Why is there a difference between the marginal tax rate associated with an income tax bracket and the average tax rate that people in that bracket end up paying? **[LO 20.5]**

☐ Why is FICA a regressive tax? **[LO 20.5]**

☐ What is the difference between a general sales tax and an excise tax? **[LO 20.5]**

The Public Budget

LO 20.6 Discuss the important features of the public budget and the relationship between revenues and expenditures.

The U.S. federal government collected almost $3.33 trillion in revenue in 2018. That's a big sum of money—so big that it's a bit difficult to visualize what it means in real terms. There are a number of ways to consider tax revenue that make it easier to grasp. In our flat-tax thought experiment earlier in the chapter, we estimated total tax revenue as an average amount paid per taxpayer—approximately $18,400.

However, the flat-tax thought experiment misses the fact that the figures include many sources of revenue beyond traditional income taxes. While 51 percent of all tax revenue comes from personal income taxes, the rest is broken down between Social Security contributions (35 percent roughly split between employers and employees), corporate income tax (6.2 percent). If we were to break down the flat-tax to collect only federal personal income tax, the average taxpayer would be on the hook for only $9,400.

Another, more common approach is to look at tax revenue in comparison to the size of the total economy. The *gross domestic product (GDP)* is one way to measure the size of a country's economy. It is the sum of the market values of all final goods and services produced within a country in a given period of time. In 2017, the United States federal government received tax revenue equivalent to 17 percent of GDP. If we also include taxes collected by states and localities, total tax revenue in the United States (for 2016) was approximately 26 percent of the country's GDP.[7]

Comparing the quantity of tax revenue collected in other countries to tax receipts in the United States is another way to better understand the quantity of taxes collected by the government. As Figure 20-8 shows, low-income countries tend to collect less in taxes as a percentage of GDP.

FIGURE 20-8

Taxes around the world

Looking at tax revenue as a percentage of GDP is one way to compare taxes across countries. Wealthy countries that provide many social services to their citizens tend to collect a greater share of GDP in taxes in order to pay for those services.

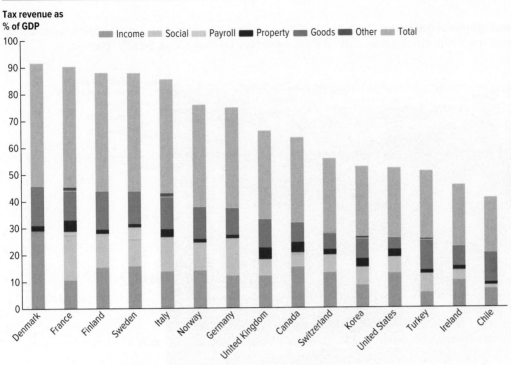

Tax revenue as % of GDP

Income   Social   Payroll   Property   Goods   Other   Total

Source: https://read.oecd-ilibrary.org/taxation/revenue-statistics-1965-2016_9789264283183-en#page1.

High-income countries, especially those with extensive government-provided social benefits, tend to collect taxes that represent a greater share of their GDP. (The United States is an extreme exception to this rule.) Denmark, for example, collects taxes equal to 46 percent of its GDP. In contrast, the taxes collected by the government of Chile represent only 20 percent of the country's total GDP.

The relationship between public revenue and public expenditure is messy. On one hand, spending eventually has to be covered by revenue. Even the government can't go on forever spending more than it earns. On the other hand, most public spending is not tied directly to government revenue, let alone to particular taxes. Revenue collected at a certain time or place can be stockpiled or moved around to pay for expenditures in a different time or place. Or, more commonly, governments borrow against future revenue to finance spending today.

Figure 20-9 shows how the U.S. government spends tax revenue:

- Social Security is the largest percentage of government spending for a stand-alone program. This program is funded by proceeds from the payroll tax and provides income to people aged 62 years and older. (People who wait until age 66 to receive Social Security will receive the full percentage of benefits; the age for full benefits is set to increase slowly over time.)
- In recent years, the amount of spending on health expenditures has grown substantially, making it currently the second-largest category of outlays.
- National defense represents the third largest category of government expenditures.
- The fourth-largest category of expenditure includes programs to support people with low income, such as welfare, public and subsidized housing, and food stamps.

One interesting feature of federal government spending in the United States is that less than half of it is discretionary. **Discretionary spending** involves public expenditures that have to be approved each year, such as the military, public construction and road building, and scientific and medical research.

discretionary spending public expenditures that have to be approved each year

FIGURE 20-9

Federal government spending in the united states   The allocation of the U.S. budget has shifted in response to national events. During World War II, national defense took priority. In recent years, as the U.S. population ages, health and Social Security have risen.

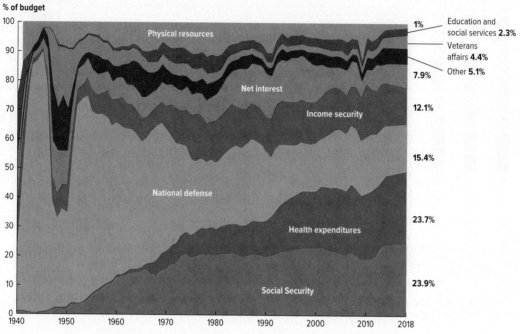

Source: Budget of the U.S. Government, Historical Tables, FY 2018, https://www.whitehouse.gov/omb/historical-tables/.

mandatory spending
public expenditure that "entitles" people to benefits by virtue of age, income, or some other factor

In contrast, the majority of federal expenditures is **mandatory spending**. This spending is mandatory because existing legislation requires the government to fund certain programs, including Social Security, Medicare, and some welfare programs. These programs are also called *entitlement programs* because people are "entitled" to benefits by virtue of age, income, or some other factor.

Spending on entitlement programs automatically rises and falls with the number of people who are eligible according to the legal criteria. Therefore, expenditures on these programs cannot be decreased without changing the eligibility requirements and benefits set in the laws on which the programs are based.

You may be surprised by some of the things that are *not* included in Figure 20-9. Many of the public services that touch people's daily lives in the most noticeable ways are funded by state and local budgets:

- Public education is largely (although not entirely) supported at the state and local levels.
- Services such as police and fire protection, motor vehicle registration, and garbage collection also come out of state or local budgets.
- Many of the most visible federally funded services—such as subsidized student loans and national parks—actually make up a very small proportion of the federal budget.

budget deficit
an amount of money a government spends beyond the revenue it brings in

budget surplus
an amount of revenue a government brings in beyond what it spends

Balancing the budget

In many years, the federal government spends more than it brings in. When a government spends more than it earns in revenue, we say that it has a **budget deficit**. When it earns more than it spends, we say it has a **budget surplus**.

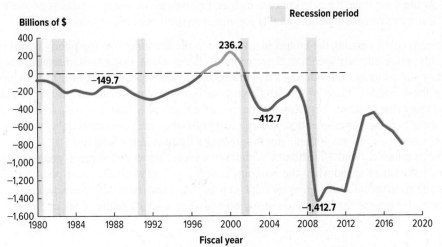

Billions of $

236.2

−149.7

−412.7

−1,412.7

Recession period

1980 1984 1988 1992 1996 2000 2004 2008 2012 2016 2020

Fiscal year

Source: *Office of Budget and Management*, Table 1.3, column D, www.whitehouse.gov/omb/historical-tables; and https://home.treasury.gov/news/press-releases/sm522.

FIGURE 20-10

Surpluses and deficits in recent U.S. history

For most of the past three decades, the U.S. government has run a budget deficit. Although deficits have not been correlated with recession historically, the most recent large budget deficit occurred during a deep recession.

Deficits and surpluses are commonly calculated as a percentage of national GDP. So:

- If the federal government brings in $3.33 trillion in tax revenues and spends $4.11 trillion, as it did in 2018, the budget deficit *in absolute terms* is $0.78 trillion.

- The budget deficit is usually stated as a *percentage relative to GDP*. For example, the 2017 deficit was approximately 3.8 percent of GDP ($0.78 trillion ÷ U.S. GDP of $20.5 trillion = 3.8 percent).[8]

Historically, the United States has gone back and forth between surplus and deficit, as shown in Figure 20-10.

You may notice that there have been a lot more deficits than surpluses in recent years. Many people are concerned about the growing *debt*—which is the cumulative sum of all deficits and surpluses. People are concerned about the debt for the same reasons you'd be worried about a family sinking deeper and deeper into debt: Debts have to be paid at some point, and the longer you stay in debt, the more you owe in interest. (The U.S. government paid $310 billion on FY 2018 debt!) For this reason, some people favor balanced-budget laws, which require the government to spend no more than it owes in any given year. In fact, most state governments have a balanced-budget requirement of some sort, although some are stricter than others.

(Remember from the beginning of the chapter the Minnesota voters who were "happy to pay" more taxes? The U.S. Treasury has a program by which people who are concerned about the federal debt and are "happy to pay" more taxes can do so. Any taxpayer can give a voluntary gift to the U.S. Treasury to reduce the public debt. In 2017, such gifts totaled a little over $2.6 million, which is not much given the nearly $21.8 billion debt.)

On the surface, balancing the budget seems like an unarguably great idea. It forces policymakers to adopt responsible spending policies that prevent the government from going into debt over the long run. So *why don't all governments balance the budget every year?*

The short answer is that a government doesn't follow the same financial rules as a family. To start, governments are often considered trustworthy borrowers and have access to relatively cheap credit. In addition, it can be difficult to balance a public budget every year. Even with the best planning, it is unlikely that revenues will exactly equal planned expenditures in any given year. For instance, think about what happens during an unexpected economic downturn:

- If people lose their jobs and companies earn lower profits, the government gets less individual and corporate income tax revenue than it was expecting. It also may collect less sales tax revenue as people cut back on purchases.

- At the same time, it has to increase its spending on entitlement programs as people's incomes decrease and more qualify for unemployment benefits or food stamps.

This means that balancing the budget in a year when the economy is doing poorly would require deep cuts in discretionary spending. Some economists argue that, by contrast, discretionary public spending should be *increased* during a downturn, to help stimulate the economy back to growth.

For these reasons, many economists argue that governments should not try to balance the budget every year. Instead, they advocate that public budgets be balanced *over the business cycle*. In brief, the idea is that governments should run surpluses when the economy is doing well and allow deficits when the economy is doing poorly—striking a balance in the long run.

Sounds sensible, right? Unfortunately, policy-makers are under just as much pressure from voters and lobbyists to spend when the economy is doing well as when it's doing poorly. The result is that the government sometimes gets stuck in patterns of unsustainable spending. For an important case in point, see the Economics in Action box "The insecure future of Social Security."

The insecure future of Social Security
Economics in Action

Most Americans get their paychecks only after part of their earnings have been taxed to pay for Social Security and Medicare. These two programs provide pension and medical insurance benefits to retired and disabled people and their families. Social Security is a hugely popular program. Without it, almost 40 percent of Americans over the age of 66 would fall below the poverty line.

So far, the Social Security system has worked well, but recent demographic shifts are creating challenges. The system is funded through a pay-as-you-go strategy: Current workers' taxes fund benefits for current retirees. The strategy works well when there are a lot of people of working age relative to the number of retirees. The trouble is that over the last half century, Americans began to live much longer and have fewer children. As a result, the number of working-age people relative to retired people has decreased. In 1950, there were 16 workers for every retiree. By 2035, there will be only two.

This means that Social Security has to support more and more retirees with tax revenue from fewer and fewer workers. As Figure 20-11 shows, the outlay for Social Security is projected to increase over the coming decades, while the revenues stay steady. The figure also shows that in past decades, revenues have exceeded outlays. The good news is that this money is being saved up in the Social Security Trust Fund. The bad news is that this fund is projected to run dry by 2034—well before most of today's college students reach retirement age.

Many proposals have been floated to fix the Social Security problem. Some solutions focus on reining in spending by making retirement benefits less generous—for example, by raising the retirement age. When the retirement age is increased, presumably people would work and pay into the system for longer. When the Social Security Act was first implemented, the full retirement age was 65, and was so for many years. However, a 1983 amendment raised the retirement age to 66 for people born after 1938 and to 67 for people born after 1959. This move is projected to save the system an average of $30,000 per worker.

Other proposed solutions focus on increasing tax revenues. As of 2018, the Social Security payroll tax applies only to earnings up to $128,400. Anything you earn beyond that cap isn't taxed for Social Security. (It is, of course, taxed as part of your personal income tax.) So one idea is to eliminate the Social Security cap. Doing so would effectively increase the payroll taxes paid by some workers.

Another option would be to increase the rate of payroll taxes that fund Social Security for all workers (currently 15.3 percent of earnings, split equally between employers and employees).

FIGURE 20-11

The future of Social Security   Presently, the revenue stream for Social Security is greater than the outlays paid in benefits. Funds can be withdrawn from the Social Security Trust Fund to make up the difference between revenue and outlays for several more decades, but the trust fund is projected to run out in 2034.

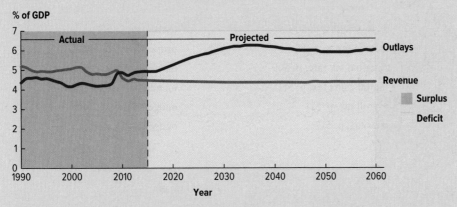

Source: Congressional Budget Office, www.cbo.gov/publication/51047.

Because Social Security is an entitlement program, with benefits defined and mandated by law, making changes requires action by Congress. Neither raising taxes nor dropping benefits is popular with constituents, so legislators have been slow to act. This issue no doubt will remain a hot debate for years to come.

Sources: www.ssa.gov/pressoffice/basicfact.htm; http://www.cbo.gov/doc. cfm?index=11943&zzz=41347; www.irs.gov/taxtopics/tc751.html; www.ssa.gov/history/1983amend. html; www.cbo.gov/publication/51047; www.ssa.gov/oact/trsum; www.cbpp.org/research/social-security/social-security-keeps-22-million-americans-out-of-poverty-a-state-by-state.

✓ TEST YOURSELF

☐ What is the difference among discretionary, nondiscretionary, and entitlement spending in the public budget? **[LO 20.6]**

☐ Why is maintaining a balanced budget every year more difficult than it might at first seem? **[LO 20.6]**

Conclusion

The fine points of tax law are complex, but the basics are fairly straightforward. The ideas and evidence in this chapter show what's at stake in political debates. Understanding the implications of taxes can also help you make better personal financial choices, such as buying a new house.

When it comes to taxes, economists focus on trade-offs between revenue, efficiency, and incidence. In other words, we're concerned with how much money is raised, how costly it is to raise it, and who ultimately shoulders the burden. We've seen why governments need to balance revenues and expenditures in the long run, but also why they might not want to do so in the short run.

Public support for taxation depends on whether citizens like how governments spend their tax dollars. If voters think that governments misuse money or spend too much, they'll want to reduce taxes. When voters think that governments are helping to create stronger communities and better opportunities for citizens, they won't mind the tax bite as much.

We'll dig deeper into some of these questions in the next chapter, as we address issues around poverty, inequality, and the uses of public funds.

Key Terms

deadweight loss, p. 501

lump-sum tax (head tax), p. 502

administrative burden, p. 503

incidence, p. 506

proportional/flat tax, p. 506

progressive tax, p. 506

regressive tax, p. 507

income tax, p. 508

marginal tax rate, p. 509

capital gains tax, p. 511

payroll tax, p. 511

sales tax, p. 512

excise tax, p. 512

property tax, p. 513

discretionary spending, p. 515

mandatory spending, p.516

budget deficit, p. 516

budget surplus, p. 516

Summary

LO 20.1 Describe the major public policy goals of taxation.

The most important goal of taxation is to raise public revenue. This allows governments to provide goods and services such as education, highways, and national defense.

A second use of taxation is to change the behavior of market participants by driving a wedge between the prices faced by buyers and sellers. This function of a tax can counterbalance a negative externality, bringing consumption down to an efficient level.

Taxes may also be used to discourage specific behaviors, such as smoking or drinking, for reasons that are not necessarily related to negative externalities.

LO 20.2 Explain how deadweight loss and administrative costs contribute to the inefficiency of a tax.

There are two sources of inefficiency associated with taxation: administrative burden and deadweight loss. *Administrative burden* includes the time and money spent by the government to collect and monitor tax payments, as well as the time and money spent by individuals on filing tax returns or hiring accountants. *Deadweight loss* is the reduction in total surplus that results from the decrease in the number of trades that occur due to the tax.

LO 20.3 Calculate the effect of a tax increase on revenue, taking into account price and quantity effects.

Two forces are at play in the relationship between tax rates and revenue. Raising taxes means that the government gets more revenue per units sold, which increases total revenue. But the shrinking effect of a higher tax rate causes fewer units to be sold, which decreases total revenue. In other words, a change in the tax rate has both a *price effect* (the government collects more tax for every unit) and a *quantity effect* (the government collects taxes on fewer units).

Raising taxes has diminishing returns to revenue because the quantity effect gradually overtakes the price effect. At some point, taxes can be so high that the price effect dominates, and raising taxes actually reduces total revenue.

LO 20.4 Identify proportional, progressive, and regressive taxes.

Incidence describes who bears the burden of paying a tax. Incidence can describe whether the tax burden falls on buyers or sellers but also on how much is paid by the rich versus the poor.

Proportional taxes take the same percentage of income from everyone. *Progressive* taxes take a higher percentage of income from those with higher income. *Regressive* taxes do the opposite, charging a higher percentage of income to those with lower income.

The economic incidence of the tax describes who ultimately bears the burden of the tax and is not necessarily the same as the statutory incidence of the tax, which describes who is legally obligated to pay it.

LO 20.5 Describe the sources of tax revenue in the United States, and discuss the role played by different types of taxes.

The vast majority of tax revenue the United States collects comes from personal income and payroll taxes; a significant minority comes from the corporate income tax.

Personal income taxes are charged on income from all sources, with increasing marginal rates for higher income levels. *Payroll taxes* are charged at a flat rate on earned income and are tied directly to Social Security and Medicare expenditures. The personal income tax and corporate income tax are progressive; the payroll tax is generally considered to be regressive.

In contrast to the federal government, many state governments bring in most of their revenue through general sales and excise taxes.

> **LO 20.6** Discuss the important features of the public budget and the relationship between revenues and expenditures.

The United States takes in tax revenue equal to about 17 percent of its GDP. However, spending is not tied directly to government revenue. Revenue collected at a certain time and place can pay for expenditures in a different time or place, and the federal government can and does borrow money to pay for current expenses.

The majority of federal government spending goes to *nondiscretionary* budget items. These include entitlement programs like Social Security and Medicare, for which benefits are mandated by law. Both tax revenue and spending fluctuate from year to year as the economy goes up and down, resulting in *budget deficits* or *surpluses*.

Review Questions

1. Both a payroll tax and an excise tax on alcohol raise revenue and, respectively, shrink the markets for labor and alcohol. Although both have some functions in common, governments may have different goals when levying them. What goals do you think motivate a payroll tax? What goals motivate an alcohol tax? **[LO 20.1]**

2. The demand for cigarettes, which create negative externalities through secondhand smoke, is often relatively inelastic. That is, when the price of cigarettes changes, the quantity demanded changes by a smaller portion. Using this fact, explain to what extent you think a tax on cigarettes would fulfill each of the goals of taxation. **[LO 20.1]**

3. Which would you expect to be less efficient, a flat tax on all income or a property tax (charged based on the assessed value of real estate)? Explain why, in terms of both deadweight loss and administrative costs. **[LO 20.2]**

4. A local government is considering ways to raise taxes to pay for making sidewalks. One prominent citizen suggests taxing people based on how much they walk on the sidewalk, measured in yards each day. Explain why, despite its apparent fairness, this tax is likely very inefficient. **[LO 20.2]**

5. In an election debate, two candidates for governor are debating about whether to raise the general sales tax from 5 to 7 percent. Candidate A argues that this would increase tax revenues, enabling the state to maintain essential services. Candidate B argues that the tax would hurt retailers and consumers, and would actually slow down the economy so much that it would decrease tax revenues too. Restate these candidates' positions in economic terminology and explain what assumptions they must be making in order to justify their different positions, in terms of price and quantity effects. **[LO 20.3]**

6. Explain, with reference to the price and quantity effects, why all else equal, taxing several goods at a modest rate is better than taxing one good at a very high rate. **[LO 20.3]**

7. People with low income spend more, as a share of their overall income, on food and clothing than wealthier people. As a result, they tend to spend a higher proportion of their income relative to people with high income. Given this trend, explain how a general sales tax of 8 percent could be regressive. Now, suppose that food and children's clothing are exempted from the sales tax. Is this likely to make the tax more or less regressive? **[LO 20.4]**

8. Suppose you turn on the television to find an ad by a local politician accusing car dealers of making too much money off consumers. As a remedy for this abuse, the official proposes to tax the dealers at a higher rate and reward car buyers with the proceeds of the tax. Drawing on the idea of economic incidence and administrative cost, explain why this tax may not benefit consumers after all. **[LO 20.4]**

9. Your friend Edgar has just finished his first year working full time and comes home beaming, carrying an envelope from the IRS, which has sent him a check for $650 after he sent in his tax forms. Explain to Edgar why this does not mean that he didn't pay taxes. **[LO 20.5]**

10. Explain why most people's marginal tax rate is higher than their average tax rate. Is a system in which average tax rates are higher than marginal tax rates regressive, proportional, or progressive? **[LO 20.5]**

11. A challenger presidential candidate vows to cut entitlement spending by 20 percent in the first few weeks that she is in office. Why is it unlikely the candidate could achieve this reduction? **[LO 20.6]**

12. When the federal government borrows money, it can fund higher expenditures in the short term but incurs a debt that accrues interest and has to be paid off in the long term. What does this imply about the trade-off between current and future taxes? How might this trade-off change if the overall size of the economy grows over time? **[LO 20.6]**

Problems and Applications

1. Consider each of the following tax policies. Decide for each whether the primary public policy goal is most likely raising revenue or changing behavior (with or without a market failure). **[LO 20.1]**

   a. Income tax.

   b. Cigarette tax.

   c. Payroll tax.

   d. Income tax exemption for charity donations.

2. Governments throughout history have levied some very interesting taxes. Each of the following taxes changed citizens' behavior. Determine whether it's likely that the tax also addressed a market failure. **[LO 20.1]**

   a. *The Hat Tax:* Adopted by the British government, requiring every hat to bear a stamp on the inside showing it was legal.

   b. *The "Flatulence Tax":* Proposed, but ultimately not adopted, in New Zealand to help reduce methane emissions from livestock.

   c. *The Window Tax:* Levied by English King William III on the number of windows in a house, which tended to be more numerous in wealthier homes.

   d. *The Cowardice Tax:* Introduced in medieval England and applied to people who refused to defend the country at the request of the king.

3. Suppose the government wants to levy a new excise tax. For each of the following goods, determine whether you would expect an excise tax to result in high or low deadweight loss. **[LO 20.2]**

   a. Alcohol.

   b. Milk.

   c. Diamonds.

   d. Tropical vacations.

   e. Socks.

4. Table 20P-1 shows supply and demand in the market for sub sandwiches in Wheretown, where the local government wants to raise revenue via a $1 tax on all sandwiches, collected from sandwich shops. **[LO 20.2]**

   a. Graph the initial supply and demand curves, before the tax. Then graph the after-tax supply curve. Before and after the tax: What is the equilibrium quantity? What is the equilibrium price? What price is paid by consumers? What price is received by suppliers?

   b. Calculate consumer and producer surplus before and after the tax.

   c. How much tax revenue does Wheretown receive? Draw this tax revenue on the graph.

   d. How much deadweight loss is caused by the tax?

TABLE 20P-1

Price of sub sandwich ($)	Quantity demanded	Quantity supplied
8.00	0	100
7.50	10	90
7.00	20	80
6.50	30	70
6.00	40	60
5.50	50	50
5.00	60	40
4.50	70	30
4.00	80	20
3.50	90	10
3.00	100	0
2.50	110	0
2.00	120	0

   e. Suppose it costs Wheretown $35 to collect the tax revenue from sandwich shops. In the end, how much revenue from the sub tax is actually available to spend on public services?

5. Figure 20P-1 shows a hypothetical market for gasoline. **[LO 20.3]**

FIGURE 20P-1

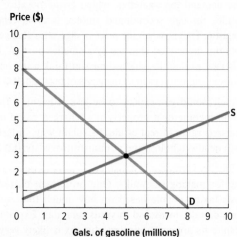

a. Suppose an excise tax of $1.50 per gallon is levied on gasoline suppliers. Draw the after-tax supply curve. What price will consumers pay? What price will sellers receive?

b. How much government revenue will result from the tax?

c. Suppose the tax is raised to $3 per gallon. Draw the new after-tax supply curve. How much additional revenue will this raise compared to the $1.50 tax?

d. Suppose the tax is raised again to $4.50 per gallon. Draw the new after-tax supply curve. Does this newest tax increase cause tax revenue to increase, decrease, or remain the same as compared to the $3 per gallon tax?

6. In each of the following examples, determine whether the price effect or the quantity effect dominates when the tax is applied. **[LO 20.3]**

a. The government raises taxes on iPads from $10 per iPad to $20 per iPad. Prior to the tax increase, 10 million iPads were sold each year. The new equilibrium quantity is 9 million iPads.

b. In response to concerns about chewing gum in schools, the government raises the tax on packs of gum from $0.20 per pack to $0.30 per pack. Before the tax increase, 50 million packs were sold each year. After the tax increase, 40 million packs are sold each year.

c. Worried that Americans are addicted to coffee, the government raises the $0.05 tax on a cup of coffee to $0.10. Before the tax increase, 10 billion cups were sold each year. Afterward, 5 billion cups are sold each year.

7. Determine whether each of the following taxes is proportional, regressive, or progressive. **[LO 20.4]**

a. An income tax of 25 percent on income from all sources.

b. An income tax with three brackets and corresponding marginal tax rates: 10 percent for income up to $50,000; 20 percent for income up to $100,000; and 30 percent for income over $100,000.

c. A fee of $500 per year for municipal services, charged to everyone who lives within the city limits.

d. A capital gains tax that charges a flat rate of 40 percent, but only on capital gains over $1 million.

e. A payroll tax of 10 percent on income under $200,000.

8. Table 20P-2 shows an income tax schedule for the imaginary country of Independence. Connor is a citizen of Independence who earns $94,000 per year at his job. Assume Connor is not eligible for any deductions or exemptions. **[LO 20.4, 20.5]**

TABLE 20P-2

Taxable income ($)	Marginal tax rate (%)
0–5,000	5
5,001–15,000	7
15,001–30,000	9
30,001–50,000	11
50,001–75,000	13
75,001–100,000	15
100,001–130,000	20
130,001–175,000	21
175,001+	22

a. How much does Connor pay in income tax?

b. What is Connor's marginal tax rate? What is his overall tax rate?

c. Connor isn't crazy about his job and wants to move to a job in a related industry that pays $100,000. How much will Connor have to pay in taxes in the new job?

d. Is the income tax in Independence regressive, proportional, or progressive?

9. Evangeline is a citizen of Independence, whose income and expenditures are shown in Table 20P-3. Table 20P-2 showed Independence's personal income tax schedule. In answering the questions that follow, you may assume the following. **[LO 20.5]**

(1) All income other than capital gains falls under the personal income tax.

(2) Deductible expenses are subtracted from income before income tax is calculated.

(3) Charitable donations and money paid in payroll taxes are tax-deductible.

(4) Payroll tax is 5 percent of earned income up to $50,000.

(5) Capital gains tax is 3 percent on capital gains over $10,000.

(6) Sales tax is 6 percent.

TABLE 20P-3

Category	Amount ($)
Income earned in wages	92,000
Income from capital gains	22,000
Spending on consumer goods subject to sales tax	12,000
Spending on charitable donations	4,000

    a. How much does Evangeline pay in payroll taxes?

    b. How much does Evangeline pay in capital gains taxes?

    c. What is Evangeline's adjusted income subject to the personal income tax? How much does she pay in personal income tax?

    d. How much does Evangeline pay in sales taxes?

    e. How much does Evangeline pay in taxes, in total? What percentage of her income does this represent?

10. Table 20P-4 shows an economy's GDP, current expenditures, and tax revenue for 2015–2018. **[LO 20.6]**

TABLE 20P-4

Year	GDP ($)	Prior-year debt ($)	Current expenditures ($)	Tax revenue ($)
2015	8,500	5,100	1,200	950
2016	8,650		1,400	1,525
2017	9,000		1,800	1,500
2018	9,200		2,100	1,600

    a. Complete the table by filling in the prior-year debt for each year listed.

    b. For each year, is this economy experiencing a budget surplus or budget deficit?

    c. Debt is what percentage of GDP in 2015?

    d. Between 2015 and 2018, by what percentage has GDP changed? By what percentage has the debt changed? Is debt as a percentage of GDP growing, constant, or shrinking between 2015 and 2018?

11. Table 20P-5 shows an economy's GDP, population, debt, and GDP per capita for 2017 and 2018. **[LO 20.6]**

    a. Complete the table by filling in the debt per capita for both years.

    b. What is the percentage change from 2017 to 2018 in each of the following?

      i. GDP.

      ii. Population.

      iii. Debt.

      iv. GDP per capita.

      v. Debt per capita.

    c. Which is growing faster—GDP per capita or debt per capita? Why?

Endnotes

1. http://news.minnesota.publicradio.org/features/2003/04/28_helmsm_happytopay.

2. https://www.irs.gov/statistics/irs-budget-and-workforce.

3. https://www.ssa.gov/cgi-bin/netcomp.cgi?year=2017.

4. Beginning in 2013, an additional Medicare tax of 0.9 percent applies for individual wages of more than $200,000 ($250,000 for married couples filing jointly).

5. https://taxfoundation.org/final-tax-cuts-and-jobs-act-details-analysis; and www.northwesternmutual.com/life-and-money/tax-law-changes-that-will-impact-business-owners-in-2018.

6. www.census.gov/programs-surveys/gov-finances.html.

7. www.oecd.org/tax/tax-policy/global-revenue-statistics-database.htm.

8. www.marketwatch.com/story/us-ends-fiscal-2017-with-666-billion-budget-deficit-2017-10-20.

TABLE 20P-5

Year	GDP (millions of $)	Population (millions)	Debt (millions of $)	GDP per capita ($)	Debt per capita ($)
2017	10,675,000	305.0	7,472,500	35,000	
2018	10,995,250	311.1	7,920,850	35,343	

Poverty, Inequality, and Discrimination

Striking It Richer

How rich is super-rich? In 1915—the era of the Rockefellers, Vanderbilts, and Carnegies, whose names are synonymous with extraordinary wealth—people worried that the wealthiest 1 percent of the population held 15 percent of the nation's income. Today, the richest 5 percent of the U.S. population holds almost *22 percent* of the income, and the richest 20 percent together earns over 51 percent. To be part of the richest 5 percent of the U.S. population in 2016, your family had to earn over $214,462. That's around half of what an average Wall Street worker in New York City took home in 2016; it's almost the same as the annual wage a typical surgeon earns, and four times the average salary of elementary school teachers.[1]

While the rich have gotten richer, the poor have gotten richer too. Fifty years ago, almost a quarter of Americans lived in poverty. Over just a few decades, the national poverty rate fell by half. How can poverty be falling and

©Kick Images/Getty Images

inequality be rising at the same time? The answer is that the poor have gotten richer, but the rich have gotten richer at an even faster rate. Economic growth has increased incomes throughout the population, but a disproportionate amount has stayed with the wealthy.

Internationally, the picture looks similar. Hundreds of millions of people have been lifted out of poverty by economic growth in recent decades, but global inequality is also high. A lot of this has to do with differences between countries: Being born into a poorer family in the United States places you at about the same income level as the upper class in India or China.

Does inequality matter? The more equal a society is, the more that everyone will gain when the economy improves. But it doesn't necessarily follow that the most equal society is the best society, or even that it provides the most resources for its disadvantaged members. One view is that inequality gives people an incentive to work hard and take risks. In that view, work and risk-taking create jobs and contribute to economic growth that can benefit everyone, including the poorest.

Thinking about the "right" level of inequality is one of the hardest economic questions we face. Does success at the top trickle down to benefit the poor? To what extent do taxes and programs that equalize income also create a disincentive for hard work and entrepreneurship?

LEARNING OBJECTIVES

LO 21.1 Understand how to measure poverty, and describe the difference between absolute and relative measures of poverty.

LO 21.2 Understand how different factors contribute to poverty.

LO 21.3 Explain and interpret different methods of measuring income inequality.

LO 21.4 Describe how income mobility differs from income equality.

LO 21.5 Identify the public policies that are used to reduce poverty and inequality and understand their goals.

LO 21.6 Explain the trade-off between equity and efficiency in poverty-reduction policy.

LO 21.7 Explain why economists differentiate between correlation and causation when studying discrimination and why markets do not always eliminate discrimination.

In this chapter, we will explore tough issues surrounding poverty and inequality—how they can be measured, how they affect people's lives and choices, and how governments design public policy in response. What can economics say about these big questions? We'll show examples of how innovative economic problem solving has provided new approaches to fighting poverty. We will also explore the economics of discrimination, an issue that is tied to longstanding patterns of poverty and inequality in many countries.

As we weigh ideas and evidence in this chapter, we ask you to remember the distinction between positive and normative analysis. We will use *positive* analysis to understand what poverty, inequality, and discrimination look like and how they affect the economy. That's a separate question from the big *normative* issue: Should governments try to reduce poverty, inequality, and discrimination in the name of social justice and fairness?

Poverty

Economics is the study of how people manage their resources. Poverty, which we can think about as a lack of material resources, is of particular interest to economists, who ask: Do people with few resources make different decisions than the wealthy? Do they approach those decisions in a different way? Why are they poor in the first place?

Of course, poverty is of concern for less-intellectual reasons as well. It can be upsetting to see people struggling to support themselves or even to stay alive. Without financial resources, it's difficult to access many of the basic goods that make life livable—food, shelter, health—and certainly those that make life comfortable. Economic thinking can suggest ways to make life better for those in need, both at home and around the world.

Several ideas will come up over and over again in this chapter:

- Is poverty a problem only when it represents an absolute deprivation, such as not having enough to eat?
- Or is poverty best defined in relative terms?
- Should people be considered to be "poor" when they have enough to live on, but still have much less than others in society?

Another theme to follow is that the causes of poverty may not always be obvious. For instance, around the world, being poor often comes along with having less education.

- Does a lack of education make people poor, or are poor people less able or willing to access education?

The patterns of poverty over decades or generations are also critical:

- How hard is it to start out poor and become rich, or vice versa?
- If your parents are poor, how does that affect you and your chances in life?

Keep these underlying questions in mind as we discuss the measurement of, causes of, and solutions to poverty.

Measuring poverty

At first glance, defining and measuring poverty might seem like a simple task. You know it when you see it, right? But there are important disagreements about how to measure poverty on a national level. As it turns out, different definitions of poverty paint different pictures of who is poor and how they live.

LO 21.1 Understand how to measure poverty, and describe the difference between absolute and relative measures of poverty.

Absolute and relative measures   Imagine two families:

- One lives in the United States and has an income of $15,000 per year. This family of four lives in an apartment with running water, electricity, heat, and four rooms.
- The other family lives in India and earns $1,500 per year. This family of six lives in a one-room house with no water or electricity.

Both families earn less money than the majority of the people living in their countries. One, however, makes ten times as much money as the other. Which family is "poor"? Are both families "poor"?

When defining poverty, the first important distinction to make is between absolute and relative measures. An **absolute poverty line** defines poverty as income below a certain amount, fixed at a given point in time. An absolute poverty line is usually set based on the cost of certain essential goods. In the United States, for instance, a married couple with two children who earned $23,263 per year in 2017 was below the poverty line, which was $24,858 for a family of four that year. We can see this in Table 21-1. So the first family in our example above, the one from the United States with earnings of $15,000, is indeed considered poor.

In the United States, the official poverty line is an *absolute poverty line* based on the price of food. In the 1960s, officials calculated the cost of what they considered to be a reasonable diet for households of different sizes. They calculated that middle-class people at the time tended to spend about one-third of their income on food. So they set the poverty line by taking the cost of food for a family of a given size and multiplying it by three. Recognizing that the price of food and

absolute poverty line
a measure that defines poverty as income below a certain amount, fixed at a given point in time

Poverty line ($)	Family size
12,752	1
16,414	2
19,730	3
24,858	4
29,253	5
33,753	6
36,685	7

TABLE 21-1

U.S. poverty line for different family sizes

Poverty lines are determined every year by the U.S. Census Bureau to measure the number of Americans living in poverty. Larger families need more money to keep themselves out of poverty.

Source: Data for 2017. Family sizes with more than two people are families with two adults plus children. A full set of poverty lines is available at www.census.gov/data/tables/time-series/demo/income-poverty/historical-poverty-thresholds.html.

other goods increases over time, the government adjusts the poverty line each year based on the *Consumer Price Index (CPI)*, which we'll discuss at length in another chapter. The CPI measures increases in the price of a set of common consumer goods.

Critics of the U.S. definition of poverty note that it fails to account accurately for expenditures other than food. This is a real worry because most families today devote a smaller share of their income to food than they did in the 1960s. If the price of food has gone down relative to the prices of other things such as rent, transportation, and utilities (including phone service), then basing the poverty level on the price of food will not account for those other necessary costs. Because of this change, a reasonable standard of living may now cost *more than* three times the price of food.

Critics also point out that the U.S. poverty definition does not account for regional differences in the cost of living. The federal government currently has only one "official" poverty line, even though the same income buys much more in some parts of the country than in others.

Recently, the U.S. government has begun to address these methodological challenges. In 2011, the Census Bureau introduced an "alternate" poverty measure, called the *Supplemental Poverty Measure (SPM)*. This alternate measure bases the poverty line on the prices of food, clothing, shelter, and utilities, and it adjusts for geographic differences in the cost of living. When thinking about issues relating to poverty, it's helpful to track absolute poverty as measured by both the official and the alternate measures.

A different approach to measuring poverty is based on a *relative poverty line*. Rather than measuring absolute deprivations, the **relative poverty line** defines poverty in relation to the income of the *rest* of the population. In the United Kingdom, for instance, the poverty line is set at 60 percent of the median income. The *median income* is the level earned by the household exactly in the middle of the national income distribution. (In other words, compared to that household, half of the population earns less and half earns more.)

Both absolute and relative poverty measures have merits:

- An absolute poverty line captures a family's ability to consume essential goods like food, shelter, and clothing. It defines as poor someone who can't afford basic necessities, regardless of how well off the rest of society is.

- In contrast, a relative poverty line captures the fact that people tend to measure themselves against the people around them, rather than against an absolute standard. (For a review of this idea, turn back to Chapter 7, "Consumer Behavior.") It defines poverty as not whether you're starving, but whether you're keeping up with the rest of society.

The difference in one's focus has important implications for policies that help the poor, specifically for deciding who should receive support and how much:

- If someone is more concerned with inequality, the relative poverty line is more relevant.

- For someone more interested in the ability to buy a basic bundle of food, education, health care, and housing, the absolute poverty line will be more relevant.

Who is poor?   For now, we'll focus on the absolute poverty level of U.S. households, using the official federal poverty line. In 2017, 43.1 million people—12.3 percent of the population—lived under the official poverty line in the United States. This number was up from a near all-time low of 11.3 percent in 2000.[2]

A common measure of the distribution of income is the **poverty rate**—the percentage of the population that falls below the absolute poverty line. Today, poverty in the United States looks remarkably different than it did when the government began tracking it in the late 1950s. As Figure 21-1 shows, almost a quarter of the population lived in poverty in 1959. That number plummeted throughout the 1960s and early 1970s. Since then, the poverty rate has fluctuated between 11 and 15 percent of the population.

relative poverty line
a measure that defines poverty in terms of the income of the rest of the population

poverty rate
the percentage of the population that falls below the absolute poverty line

FIGURE 21-1

U.S. poverty over time   Since the 1960s, the poverty rate has decreased by about 10 percent through economic growth and government assistance. After 1970, the poverty rate has largely fluctuated between 10 and 15 percent. Even though the U.S. population has nearly doubled since 1960, the number of people in poverty has increased by only a few million, and there are actually fewer children in poverty today than there were in 1960.

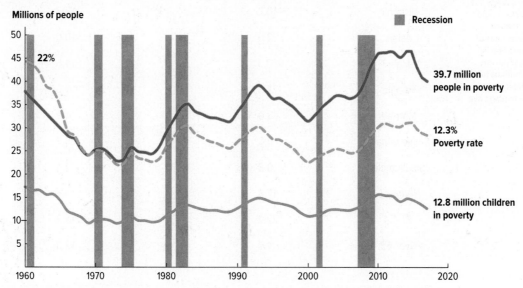

Source: U.S. Census Bureau, *Income and Poverty in the United States (2017)*, Table 3, www.census.gov/library/publications/2018/demo/p60-263.html.

What changed in the 1960s? One important factor was economic growth. Between 1959 and 1973, the total size of the U.S. economy grew at an average rate of 4.4 percent per year. (In contrast, it grew at an average rate of only 2.6 percent from 1974 to 2017.) The development in the 1960s of new government programs to assist the poor also made a big difference. Between 1960 and 1995, for example, increases in Social Security benefits helped reduce the poverty rate among older Americans, from 35 percent down to 10 percent.[3]

Poverty rates may have improved for older people, but they remain high for other parts of the population. Table 21-2 shows that today black and Hispanic Americans have poverty rates twice as high as white Americans—roughly 18 to 21 percent versus about 9 percent. Note, however, that more white people live in poverty *in total*, even though the poverty *rate* is lower, because there are more white people than black or Hispanic people in the United States. One other notable fact is that households headed by single women are especially likely to be poor.

Not all experiences of poverty are the same. The most fundamental distinction is between *chronic* and *transient* poverty. The difference between the two is essentially the difference between always being poor and being poor for a short time:

- *Chronic poverty* is usually defined as spending three or more years in poverty.
- *Transient poverty* is usually measured as a spell of poverty that lasts at least two consecutive months within a year.

Research from the United States found that only about 3.5 percent of people living under the poverty line in any given year were chronically poor. More than a quarter of the U.S. population experienced transient poverty at some point in their lives, perhaps due to losing a job or experiencing sickness or injury.[4]

The difference between transient and chronic poverty matters when evaluating anti-poverty policies. Later in the chapter we'll discuss programs like unemployment insurance, disability or

TABLE 21-2

The face of U.S. poverty (2017 and 2018)

A diverse group of people live below the poverty line. Hispanics, blacks, single women, and children have the highest rates of poverty. Married families have the lowest poverty rates; single mothers have the highest. Nearly one-third of single mothers live in poverty.

Demographic	Number in poverty (millions)	Proportion of demographic in poverty (%)
White*	17.0	8.7
Black	9.0	21.2
Hispanic	10.8	18.3
Asian	2.0	10.0
Male	17.3	11.0
Female	22.3	13.6
Married	3.0	4.9
Single female	4.0	25.7
Single male	0.8	12.4
Under 18	12.8	17.5
18–64	22.2	11.2
Over 65	4.7	12.3

* White, non-Hispanic

Source: U.S. Census Bureau poverty data, 2017 and 2018, Tables 3 and 7 https://www.census.gov/data/tables/time-series/demo/income-poverty/historical-poverty-people.html.

health insurance, and job training. Those programs can be helpful in tackling transient poverty but are unlikely to make a big dent in chronic poverty. Addressing long-lasting poverty requires digging deeper to understand what causes a person to be poor over many years or a family to be poor over many generations.

Measuring international poverty   Measuring poverty on an international scale is similar to measuring it on a national one. The same concerns about differences in the cost of living and relative standards of wealth apply—only more so, since these differences are much more dramatic on a global scale than a national one.

The most common international poverty measure is the number of people living on less than $1.90 per day. That's much lower than the official U.S. poverty line. Still, according to most estimates, 736 million people lived on less than $1.90 per day in 2015, or roughly 10 percent of the world's population.[5] Over 77 percent of those (309 million) lived in South Asia, 388 million lived in sub-Saharan Africa, and nearly 147 million lived in East Asia and the Pacific.

As always, however, we have to be careful about the difference between the *absolute numbers* of people in poverty and the *percentage* of people in poverty (the poverty rate): Only about 9 percent of East Asians lived on less than $1.90 per day, compared to about 33 percent of South Asians and 43 percent of people living in sub-Saharan Africa. Figure 21-2 shows the *percentage* of the population living on less than $1.90 per day in each country.

Calculating the $1.90 per person per day international poverty line involves a series of steps. Most importantly, poverty lines have to be adjusted to account for differences in prices across countries. Fortunately, there's a useful tool, called the **purchasing power parity (PPP) index**, to make those adjustments. It describes the overall difference in prices of goods between countries. With the index, you can translate the equivalent cost of a basket of goods in various countries.

To create the PPP index, economists collect data on prices in every country and develop an index that describes the overall difference in prices between countries. The aim is to capture the

purchasing power parity (PPP) index index that describes the overall difference in prices of goods between countries

FIGURE 21-2

Percentage of people living on less than $1.90 per day, by country   This map shows the percentage of people living on less than $1.90 per day, adjusted for purchasing power in each country. That level of income is the World Bank's measurement of extreme poverty. Most extreme poverty is clustered in sub-Saharan Africa. The majority of countries in the Northern Hemisphere have very low levels of poverty.

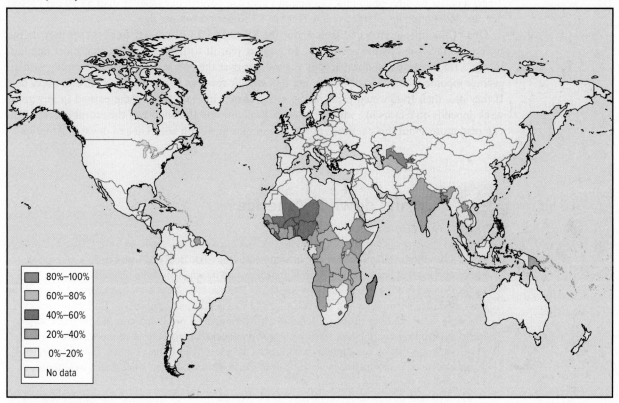

Source: World Bank Poverty & Equity Data (2014), Poverty headcount ratio, $1.90 per day, http://povertydata.worldbank.org/poverty/home.

differences in prices among countries. For example, the PPP would show that most goods are cheaper in India than they are in the United States, cheaper in the United States than they are in Sweden, and so on. The process is not perfect since we don't all consume exactly the same things. (For example, Americans eat a lot of beef, while Indians eat relatively little beef.) Nevertheless, the PPP index captures key price differences.

The international poverty line is actually $1.90 per day at purchasing power parity. That means that in each country the poverty line is the amount that will allow you to buy a basket of goods equivalent to what $1.90 would buy in the United States. The $1.90 (PPP) per day line was chosen by averaging the national poverty lines of 15 poor countries. The idea is that this low poverty line represents *absolute* (not relative) poverty by some globally comparable standard. The $1.90 line is so low that it's not very relevant for the United States, but it gives a useful global snapshot.

Using the $1.90 standard, we can see significant changes in the pattern of global poverty over the last 25 years. Overall, rapid economic growth has reduced the global poverty rate from 36 percent in 1990 to 10 percent in 2015. This change is a pretty incredible reduction. When we dig further, we see:

- The reduction in poverty has been heavily concentrated in China, whose poverty rate dropped from 67 percent in 1990 to under 1 percent in 2015.

- South Asia and the Middle East saw significant reductions as well, and Latin America achieved smaller reductions.
- The poverty rate in sub-Saharan Africa has recently started to fall more quickly, dropping from 58 percent in 2000 to 41 percent in 2015.[6]

To get a better picture, economists sometimes also use poverty lines higher than $1.90 per person per day. Most often an alternative line is set at $3.10 per person per day.

One of the little-appreciated facts about the $1.90 and $3.10 poverty lines is that they define poverty as measured by *average income* in a given year. It turns out, though, that most families' incomes fluctuate up and down around the average over the course of the year. No family with an average income of, say, $2 per person per day *literally* receives $2 per person each and every day. If they did, their lives would probably be much easier. Instead, the income earned in any given week depends on factors like whether jobs are available and the bounty of the recent harvest. You can read more about this challenge in the Economics in Action box "Up and down in America."

Up and down in America
Economics in Action

It was a beautiful, sunny October day in southwest Ohio, but Becky Moore was in a bad mood. Becky worried that her husband's next paycheck would be small, and she had bills to pay.

Becky lived in the same small town where she had grown up, but a lot had changed. Factory work used to be plentiful in that part of Ohio, and steady jobs had been easy to find. Now factory jobs were fewer, and her husband, Jeremy, was working as a mechanic at a nearby truck stop. Jeremy worked on commission, earning bigger paychecks when there were more trucks to fix. The trouble was that on beautiful fall days, trucks were less likely to break down. Jeremy's biggest paychecks came, instead, in deep winter and in the height of summer, when harsh weather took a heavy toll on the big rigs.

The ups and downs of Jeremy's paychecks created financial stress for the family. A good month might bring home $3,400, a livable paycheck. Bad months bought in closer to $1,800, not nearly enough to support their family of six.

Jeremy's experience shows that having a steady job does not guarantee a steady paycheck. Unstable pay is also a challenge experienced by workers who depend on tips, bonuses, and side-jobs, and those whose weekly hours fluctuate. One national study of low-income households showed that for an average of five months of the year, households' monthly income was either 25 percent above or 25 percent below their monthly average. When monthly income spikes and dips, it is harder to always pay rent and bills, and it is harder to consistently budget and save.

Becky and Jeremy's story is part of a book called *The Financial Diaries: How American Families Cope in a World of Uncertainty* (jointly written by one of the authors of this text). The "financial diaries" are records of family expenses, income, and financial transactions kept for a year. The records reveal that for a lot of households, financial challenges

The timing and amount of paychecks matters; unstable pay makes it hard to budget and save.
©Peter Scholey/Alamy

are not just determined by how much they earn in total during the year. The timing and amount of paychecks matters too.

A few years after that beautiful October day in Ohio, Becky had news to share. Jeremy had finally had enough of the ups and downs at his job. He had quit and moved to a new job with a longer commute and with a lower annual income. But the new job provided guaranteed pay from month to month, and the family was doing better. For Becky and Jeremy, and many other Americans, the path to financial security starts with a steady paycheck.

Source: Jonathan Morduch and Rachel Schneider, *The Financial Diaries: How American Families Cope in a World of Uncertainty* (Princeton, NJ: Princeton University Press, 2017).

Why are people poor?

Economists and policy-makers want to design policies that can attack poverty at its roots, rather than just deal with its consequences. To do so, we need to understand not only *who* is poor but also *why* they are poor.

LO 21.2 Understand how different factors contribute to poverty.

Of course, the real world is an incredibly complex place and so the reasons for poverty are varied. Poverty can be a matter of bad circumstances, bad choices, bad luck, or a combination of these. But we know from observation that some common factors make falling into poverty more likely and climbing out of it harder.

Poverty from generation to generation   People who grow up in poor families are more likely to be poor themselves. One reason is straightforward: Poor parents tend to have limited money to bequeath to the next generation. Two other economic ideas—*human capital* and *social networks*—capture somewhat more subtle, but also critical, mechanisms.

Human capital is the set of skills, knowledge, experience, and talent that determine people's productivity as workers. Workers have different amounts and types of human capital that allow them to be more or less productive at different tasks and therefore earn more or less money. You acquire human capital by being healthy, getting a good education, and gaining experience in jobs. You also benefit from watching and learning from your peers, your neighbors, and others around you.

human capital
the set of skills, knowledge, experience, and talent that determine the productivity of workers

You probably know (or know of) well-educated and successful professionals who came from humble backgrounds. But evidence shows that children in poor communities typically have reduced opportunities to acquire human capital, for many reasons. Think about all of the ways your skills and abilities are influenced by the environment in which you grew up. How good were the schools in your neighborhood? Did you have regular check-ups with a doctor, to minimize health problems that might have kept you away from school? Was a family member able to help you with your homework? Were you actively encouraged to go to college? Can you afford to take unpaid internships to learn new skills rather than working during the summer?

As you can see, it is often difficult to tell cause from effect:

- Does low human capital cause poverty—because people with low human capital are less productive in jobs and therefore likely to earn less money?
- Or does poverty cause low human capital—because growing up in a poor community can reduce access to health care, education, and informal learning opportunities?

Likely, the causality runs both ways, creating a negative cycle of poverty and low human capital. To the extent that low human capital causes poverty, policies that break this cycle—such as improving schools, offering training in job skills, and providing health care—can help.

Family and community poverty may also pass from generation to generation through more subtle channels. Economic research shows that people at all income levels find jobs and other opportunities through their *social networks*. In this context, we don't mean social media networks like Facebook and Snapchat. Rather, we mean the real-world ways in which friends of your parents, neighbors, and others in your community can alert you to employment opportunities. The problem is that if the people around you are unemployed, or not employed in the kind of job you seek, how likely is it that they can help you find a job? If they don't have much money themselves, how can they help you finance a new business?

The Economics in Action box "Getting out of the neighborhood" describes a program that tried to help people break into new, higher-resource social networks by helping families move out of areas with high levels of poverty. The results are very interesting, and have strong implications for policy.

 ## Getting out of the neighborhood

Economics in Action

Housing is one of the biggest expenses faced by families, so a common way that governments try to help poor families is to offer them inexpensive apartments to rent. Those apartments are usually in large housing complexes, where poor families are clustered with other poor families, typically in poorer neighborhoods. But does that create problems of its own? Would residents of public housing be better off if they moved somewhere else instead?

To find out, the U.S. Department of Health and Human Services launched a program called Moving to Opportunity (MTO). MTO created a lottery for residents of public housing in high-poverty areas of five U.S. cities. The lottery offered three outcomes:

1. Families could move to any area where the poverty rate was low (under 10 percent), and they got a voucher to help pay for rent and utilities in private housing in these richer neighborhoods.
2. Families could move to any neighborhood outside of public housing (it could be richer or poorer), and they got a voucher to help to pay for rent and utilities in private housing.
3. Families received no voucher, but residents were free to move or stay in public housing.

The design of the program allowed researchers to isolate the effects of moving to a new, less-poor neighborhood. They hypothesized that moving to the new, richer neighborhoods would offer better social networks for finding jobs, with more support for searching for and keeping jobs. Researchers also expected that the new neighborhoods would pose fewer of the dangers and stresses that led to mental and physical health problems in public housing. Researchers thus expected increased income, employment, and health among people who moved into private housing in richer neighborhoods.

Fifteen years later, the results were clear and mostly positive. The focus was on how the children in the families fared as they became adults. The program was disruptive for older kids who were already teenagers at the time of the move. Moving to richer neighborhoods made them slightly worse off by their twenties.

But kids who were younger when they moved (who thus spent their teenage years in the new, richer neighborhoods) did a lot better. College attendance rates went up. They were less likely to become single parents and more likely to live in better neighborhoods as adults. By their mid-twenties, their annual income was, on average, $3,477 higher (31 percent) than the families who received no vouchers and were free to move or stay in public housing (group 3 above) and about $1,700 more than those who were given housing vouchers but no restrictions on where to live (group 2 above).

Intuitively, this makes sense—younger children were able to make new friends, integrate into new social circles, and adopt new perspectives more easily than older children and adults. The longer the exposure to the new community, the better the results: College attendance rates and adult earnings both increased more for each year spent in the better-off neighborhood.

The findings show that success in life is determined not just by your parents and your own qualities. Where you grow up matters a lot too.

Source: Raj Chetty, Nathaniel Hendren, and Lawrence Katz, "The Effects of Exposure to Better Neighborhoods on Children: New Evidence from the Moving to Opportunity Project," *American Economic Review* 106, no. 4 (April 2016), pp. 855–902.

Poverty creates poverty   You may have heard the saying, "the rich get richer and the poor get poorer." We've just described how difficulties in acquiring human capital or finding job opportunities might cause this to be true. But there can also be self-reinforcing mechanisms that make it hard for individuals to break out of poverty once they are already poor, regardless of family background. These mechanisms are called **poverty traps**, and they can help illuminate why the poor often stay poor.

poverty trap
a self-reinforcing mechanism that causes the poor to stay poor

Bad health is a straightforward example of a poverty trap. This trap is more relevant in very-low-income countries than it is in the United States. Suppose you live in a poor, rural area and you farm or work on other people's farms for your living. This is hard, physical work. For some reason—a bad harvest, low crop prices, illness, or injury—you may fall into poverty and not be able to afford enough food to eat. Malnutrition makes your body weak and you are not able to do physical work as effectively. This in turn decreases your ability to earn income, which means you have less to eat, which makes you even weaker, and so on. The fact of being poor makes it hard to stay healthy and productive, and the resulting vicious cycle may be hard to escape.

There are also many poverty traps that affect people in rich countries. Suppose you lose your job, can't pay your rent, and suddenly become homeless. You want to apply for new jobs. What should you put down as your contact address? Where will you shower and change before interviews? This is the same sort of vicious cycle as malnutrition, although a nonphysical one: Not having a job to begin with actually makes it harder to find a job.

A different kind of poverty trap was presented at the beginning of this text. We discussed a case in which poor Bangladeshis with potentially profitable business opportunities were unable to borrow the money needed to take advantage of them. Banks would lend money only if the borrower could pledge a valuable asset as collateral (in case the investment turns out badly). The problem for poor borrowers is that they often lack the assets to pledge as collateral. So, even if they have great ideas, they can't get a loan to put their ideas into action. This poverty trap is called a **credit constraint**—the inability to get a loan even though a person expects to be able to repay the loan plus interest. Credit constraints are one reason why a lack of human capital isn't a simple problem to fix.

credit constraint
inability to get a loan even though a person expects to be able to repay the loan plus interest

Even in the United States, where the financial sector is much more developed, it can be difficult for people without collateral or with bad credit histories to get loans. Sometimes these potential borrowers are genuinely risky or have bad investment ideas. But even if you have in mind a low-risk, profitable opportunity, you will have trouble getting a loan if you don't have the collateral or the credit history to back it up. As a result, credit constraints can limit the ability of talented but poor individuals to make profitable investments that will help them climb up the income ladder. A talented kid may not be able to borrow money to invest in education or internships, even if those opportunities would more than pay for themselves later in life in the form of better jobs and higher wages.

Poverty in the community   In some places in the world, there are opportunities to earn more money and live in greater comfort, even if they may be difficult to come by. In others, these opportunities may not exist, at least not for the majority of the population. What is it like to live in a society where a third or a half of the population is poor and most of the people you know struggle to find jobs?

Consider the difference, for instance, between having trouble paying your electric bill and living in a place where there is *no* electrical grid, even if you could afford it. Or what would it be like to search for a job in a place where very few formal jobs exist? What if you lived in a country where even if you had a good business idea, it takes two years and a fortune in bribes to get a business permit? This is the case in many developing countries around the world.

Even in wealthy countries, community-wide poverty creates problems beyond those faced by individuals. In these communities, transportation may be limited, jobs scarce, and schools below average. When most of the region is poor, it's hard for local governments to raise money through taxes; that makes it harder in turn for the region as a whole to invest in infrastructure, jobs, and schools.

Long-term solutions to poverty must, then, involve ways to grow the economy and expand the range of opportunities available to the population.

✓ TEST YOURSELF

- ☐ What is the difference between an absolute and a relative poverty threshold? **[LO 21.1]**
- ☐ What is the international poverty line most commonly used, and why is it adjusted for purchasing power parity? **[LO 21.1]**
- ☐ What is a credit constraint, and how is it an example of a poverty trap? **[LO 21.2]**

Inequality

Poverty rates in the United States have changed little over the last few decades. However, income inequality has increased, mostly as a result of gains by the rich.

Does inequality matter?

- Some argue that overall *economic growth* is more important than the distribution of income. Those who hold this view note that if everyone is getting richer, the relative speed of these gains isn't as important.
- Others care about *inequality for its own sake*, believing that it is fundamentally unjust for some people to have much when others have little.

The degree of inequality can be an important factor that signals or causes other things going on in the economy, such as the incentive people at the top have to work hard or the resources available to people at the bottom to invest in human capital.

In this section, we'll discuss how inequality can be measured and how it can relate to economic growth and stability. We'll also see some evidence of how unequal different countries actually are and how easy or difficult it is to go from being poor to rich or vice versa.

Measuring inequality

LO 21.3 Explain and interpret different methods of measuring income inequality.

Imagine that we could line up every adult in the United States in order of the amount of income they earn. We make their heights proportional to their incomes: People with average income are of average height, and the more money someone makes, the taller he or she is. Now, we ask them all to march down Main Street in that order, over the course of one hour. As bystanders watching this parade, what would we see?

- The first marchers would be invisible, with their heads underground. These are people who own businesses or farms that are losing money.
- Next we would see tiny people walking by, only inches high. These people earn very small amounts of money; they may be unemployed or on a small fixed income.
- As we pass the half-hour mark, halfway through the parade, the people going by are still only waist-high. These marchers in the middle represent minimum-wage workers, retail sales people, unskilled clerical workers, and the like.

- Even as skilled tradespeople and office workers start to stroll by, they are still below average size.
- Finally, at about 40 minutes, the people going by are of average adult height. They include high school teachers, accountants, and managers.
- In the parade's last 10 minutes, we start to see giants, more than 10 feet tall. These are specialist doctors, lawyers, scientists, and so on.
- Then, corporate executives go by, hundreds of feet tall.
- Next come movie stars and professional athletes, thousands of feet tall.
- In the last seconds of the parade, some of the richest people in the country go by (hello, Jeff Bezos, Bill Gates, and Warren Buffett), with their heads towering several *miles* above the ground.

This parade—first imagined by economist Jan Pen—is a visual representation of the income distribution in the United States.[7] It uses the marchers' heights as an analogy that allows us to visualize the relative income of people throughout the population. The parade image emphasizes some notable features of the income distribution: People of average height and income don't show up until well after halfway through the parade. The rich are *really* rich, compared not only with the poorest but even with highly paid professionals.

Measuring by quintiles   However visually striking the parade analogy may be, economists need more precise ways of summarizing the income distribution. The simplest method divides those marchers into five equally sized groups. We call each group a *quintile*, or 20 percent of the population. In a country of just over 300 million people, the approximate population of the United States, the first quintile is the 60 million poorest people, the second is the next 60 million, and so on, until the fifth quintile is the 60 million richest people.

We can use our quintiles to organize different types of statistics that describe income inequality. Table 21-3 shows two ways of looking at income inequality in the United States:

- First, we could find the *average income* within each quintile (column 2).
- Second, we could add up everyone's income and find out what percentage of income earned in the whole country is earned by people within each quintile (column 3). If income were distributed completely equally—that is, if every person in the country made the same amount of money—each quintile representing 20 percent of the population would also earn 20 percent of the income.

Income is not distributed perfectly equally anywhere in the world, though. Thus, we always see that the top quintiles earn a disproportionately high share of income (more than 20 percent),

Quintile	Average pre-tax income ($)	Share of pre-tax income (%)
Lowest 20 percent	13,258	3.1
Second 20 percent	35,401	8.2
Third 20 percent	61,564	14.3
Fourth 20 percent	99,030	23.0
Highest 20 percent	221,846	51.5
Top 5 percent	385,289	22.3

Source: U.S. Census Bureau, Historical Income, www.census.gov/data/tables/time-series/demo/income-poverty/historical-income-households.htmlUS, Tables H-2 and H-3.

TABLE 21-3

Income distribution by quintile

Income in the United States is not equally distributed. The gap between the average incomes of the richest 20 percent and the poorest 20 percent is approximately $210,000. The richest 20 percent hold more than half of the income earned in the United States, while the top 5 percent earn about a fifth of pre-tax income.

and the lower quintiles earn a disproportionately low share (less than 20 percent). In the United States, the top 20 percent earns around 51 percent of total income, while the poorest 20 percent earns only 3.2 percent of total income.

Cross-country comparisons: The Lorenz curve and Gini coefficient If we want to compare income inequality across countries, income quintiles are less useful. Just as we need absolute and relative measures of poverty, we need measures of income inequality that allow us to compare the United States to other countries, like India. Households in India earn much less money in an absolute sense than households in the United States, so it doesn't make sense to compare the income quintiles in India to the U.S. income quintiles. Two measures of income inequality that do allow cross-country comparisons are the *Lorenz curve* and the *Gini coefficient*.

Lorenz curve

a graphic representation of income distribution that maps percentage of the population against cumulative percentage of income earned by those people

We can summarize income inequality visually, using a graph called the **Lorenz curve**. The Lorenz curve maps the percentage of the population against the cumulative percentage of income earned by those people. It shows the cumulative percentage of the population on the *y*-axis and the cumulative percentage of income those people earn on the *x*-axis.

The best way to understand the Lorenz curve is to see that if every person earned the exact same amount, the curve would be a straight, diagonal line with a slope of 1, as shown in panel A of Figure 21-3. That is, 20 percent of the population would earn 20 percent of the income, and 73 percent of the population would earn 73 percent of the income, and so on. However, if income is unequally distributed, the Lorenz curve will be bowed out in a U-shape: The poorest 1 percent of

FIGURE 21-3

The Lorenz curve

(A) Perfectly equal income distribution

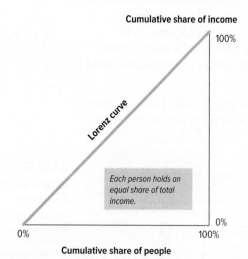

With a perfectly equal income distribution, each extra 1 percent of the population earns another 1 percent of income. In that case, the Lorenz curve forms at a 45-degree angle.

(B) Unequal income distribution

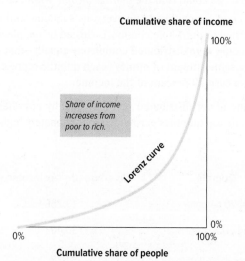

When income is not distributed equally, each extra percent of poorer segments of the population earn less than 1 percent of the total income. Among the richer part of the population, each extra 1 percent of the population adds more than 1 percent of their income. This distribution gives the Lorenz curve a concave shape.

FIGURE 21-4
The Gini coefficient

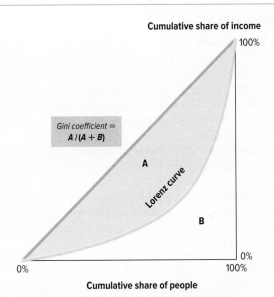

The Gini coefficient is calculated by measuring the area between the line of perfect equality and the Lorenz curve. This is represented by $A/(A + B)$. The greater the inequality, the deeper the U-shape in the Lorenz curve. The greater the area of A, the higher the Gini coefficient.

people will earn less than 1 percent of income, and the richest 1 percent will earn more than 1 percent of the income, as shown in panel B.

The Lorenz curve allows us to calculate an even more concise inequality metric—the **Gini coefficient**. The Gini coefficient describes inequality by putting a single number on the shape of the Lorenz curve. Specifically, the Gini coefficient is equal to the area between the Lorenz curve and the line of perfect equality (area A in Figure 21-4) divided by the total area under the line of perfect equality (area A plus area B in the figure). This calculation gives us a single number to describe income inequality. (Since Gini coefficients are supposed to reflect percentages, the final calculation is usually multiplied by 100 to get a whole number.)

Think about the two possible Gini coefficient extremes:

- If everyone earned the same amount and the income distribution were perfectly equal, the Gini coefficient would be zero: The Lorenz curve would *be* the line of perfect equality, and so the area between them would be 0.

- If one person earned all of the income and no one else earned anything, the Gini coefficient would be 100.

In reality, the distribution is always somewhere between these extremes. *The closer the Gini coefficient is to 100, the more unequal the income distribution.*

Now that we have a better sense of what inequality means and how to measure it, we can go back to the initial question: Does inequality matter?

The popular media regularly present us with stories about the unbelievably large incomes of professional athletes, famous entertainers, and high-profile businesspeople, but many super-wealthy people stay out of the public eye. This group has accrued massive wealth in the past few decades. Is that the sign of a strong economy or a sign of problems? To understand more, see the What Do You Think? box "The super-wealthy."

Gini coefficient
a single-number measure of income inequality; ranges from 0 to 1, with higher numbers meaning greater inequality

The super-wealthy
What Do You Think?

When people reap the rewards of their efforts, they are more likely to work hard and innovate. But when people are rewarded for their efforts, we typically end up with some inequality. From this angle, inequality is a by-product of a well-functioning market system, a system that ought to help everyone. Someone may get very rich by building a new website that millions use, but the millions of users also benefit by gaining access to the new website.

Wealth inequality is greater today than it has been for nearly a century. Historical data show that the increase in wealth inequality in the United States is almost entirely due to the growing fortunes of the top 0.1 percent of wealthiest people. In 2014, this group included a mere 160,000 individuals and families with net wealth over $100 million. That's not just the top 1 percent—*it's the top 10 percent of the top 1 percent*. This super-wealthy sliver now holds more wealth than the bottom 90 percent of the country. Almost half of the entire increase in U.S. wealth between 1986 and 2012 went to the top 0.1 percent alone.

WHAT DO YOU THINK?

1. Should these economic divides be embraced as part of the normal and desirable working of the economy? After all, the wealth has been accrued legally.
2. Can there be a level of inequality that is so high that citizens should be concerned? If so, are the most pressing concerns political, social, or economic?
3. What extra pieces of evidence would give a more informed view?

Sources: Emmanuel Saez and Gabriel Zucman, "Wealth Inequality in the United States Since 1913: Evidence from Capitalized Income Tax Data," *Quarterly Journal of Economics* 131, no. 2 (2016), pp. 519–578, http://gabriel-zucman.eu/files/SaezZucman2016QJE.pdf; www.cnbc.com/2014/03/31/the-other-wealth-gapthe-1-vs-the-001.html; www.washingtonpost.com/news/wonk/wp/2015/11/19/bernie-sanders-is-right-the-top-0-1-have-as-much-as-the-bottom-90/?noredirect=on&utm_term=.555e299ba084.

Inequality in the United States and around the world   Now that we have some tools for measuring inequality, what can we say about how income distribution differs between countries and over time? Lorenz curves and Gini coefficients can be particularly helpful:

- For visualizing how inequality changes over time for a particular country, or how countries around the world differ, we use the Lorenz curve.
- For quantifying inequality differences, we use the Gini coefficient.

Most countries in the world have Gini coefficients ranging from 25 to 60. As you can see in Figure 21-5, there are significant geographic clusters. Most of Europe has relatively low inequality. Much of Latin America and southern Africa has relatively high inequality.

The global pattern of inequality has been changing in recent decades:

- Inequality *between* countries, in terms of differences in their average national incomes, has been decreasing. Economic growth has lifted billions of people out of poverty, especially in China and India. Nonetheless, the poorest 5 percent of people in the United States are still richer on average than 70 percent of the rest of the world.
- Inequality *within* countries has largely been on the rise. This is true for both rich countries and poor ones, for countries with large amounts of growth and those that are barely growing at all.

For example, Gini coefficients in China have risen significantly since the 1980s as the country has experienced strong economic growth. In India and other Asian countries, though, which have

FIGURE 21-5

Gini coefficients around the world   The Gini coefficient is one way to measure inequality. A coefficient of zero indicates perfect equality; a coefficient of 100 indicates perfect inequality. Geographical areas in this figure are identified by color: Europe in (purple); the Americas in (green); the Middle East and Far East in (blue); and Africa in (orange).

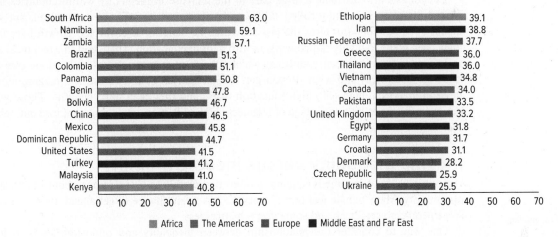

Sources: Data are from the World Bank, https://data.worldbank.org/indicator/SI.POV.GINI, for 2015 unless otherwise noted. Data for South Africa, Mexico, Turkey, Iran, and Vietnam are for 2014. The number for Canada is for 2013. The number for China is an estimate for 2016, from the *CIA World Factbook*, https://www.cia.gov/library/publications/the-world-factbook/rankorder/2172rank.html. The number for the United States is for 2016, from FRED.stlouisfed.org/series/SIPOVGINI/USA.

experienced similar amounts of growth, income inequality has not changed much at all: Gini coefficients are essentially the same as they were three decades ago.

To paint a more specific picture of inequality within a sample of countries, Table 21-4 shows income distribution, measured in quintiles, in four countries. Here we can see how the United States compares with Sweden (a rich European country), Uganda (a poor African country), and Brazil (a middle-income Latin American country). Uganda's income *distribution* is the one the most similar to the United States, although, of course, the total *amount* of income being distributed is much lower. *Average income* in Sweden is much closer to that in the United States. But the distribution of that income is very different, with about two-and-a-half times as much held by those in the bottom quintile in Sweden.

What causes such big differences in income distribution among countries? One factor is the extent to which governments redistribute income through the public budget. In many European

	% of total national income			
	United States	**Sweden**	**Uganda**	**Brazil**
Top quintile	51.5	37.6	49.8	56.1
Fourth quintile	23.0	22.8	20.4	19.7
Middle quintile	14.3	17.6	13.8	12.7
Second quintile	8.2	13.9	9.8	7.9
Bottom quintile	3.1	8.2	6.1	3.6

TABLE 21-4

Income distribution comparison, four countries

The amount of income held by different levels of the population in various countries is one way to measure inequality. Among the countries in this table, Sweden is the most equal; Brazil is the most unequal.

Sources: https://data.worldbank.org/indicator/SI.DST.FRST.20. Figures are from the latest available data (U.S. 2017, Sweden 2015, Uganda 2016, and Brazil 2015).

countries, for instance, taxes on the rich are higher than in the United States; public services and income support to the poor are also higher. The result is that the after-tax income distribution is more equal than the income distribution before taxes were paid and public services provided.

Economists also attribute a large part of the increase in inequality within countries like the United States to something called *skill-biased technical change*. That's a mouthful, but what it means is straightforward: Over the last 50 years, the benefits of economic growth have increasingly been going to highly skilled workers with a lot of education. Then, add this technical change to increased trade between countries (which allows more manual jobs to be done overseas in low-wage countries) and what do you get? People in rich countries are specializing more and more in high-tech, high-skill, high-education work, and they reap huge benefits. Those who are not in a position to take advantage of high-tech, high-skill, high-education work lose out, relatively speaking.

Income inequality versus income mobility

LO 21.4 Describe how income mobility differs from income equality.

income mobility
the ability to improve one's economic circumstances over time

How we feel about income inequality is often tied closely to assumptions about the equality of opportunity. Many people feel that if everyone has a fair chance to get ahead, then the fact that some people do get ahead and some don't, matters less.

One way to consider the relationship between inequality and opportunities is to look at **income mobility**–the ability to improve one's economic circumstances over time. Measuring income mobility tells us how likely a person is to end up rich if he or she starts out poor, or vice versa.

A standard way to measure mobility is to compare people's income to their parents' income. The idea is that if opportunities are truly equal, it should not matter much if your parents are rich or poor. Just as with poverty, we can measure income mobility in both absolute and relative terms:

- In *absolute* terms, we can look at whether a person's income is higher than her parents'.
- In *relative* terms, we can look at whether a person's income places her higher up in the income distribution than her parents.

Both measures are important. The United States has had high absolute income mobility in the last century. This is not surprising considering it has had relatively high economic growth. Until recently, every generation has, on average, earned more and lived longer than their parents.

In relative terms, however, the United States has much less income mobility. Almost 43 percent of those whose fathers were in the lowest income bracket end up in the lowest bracket themselves. Only 4 percent makes the "rags to riches" jump to the highest quintile.[8] (In contrast, "perfect" income mobility would imply that there is a 20 percent chance of ending up in each income quintile, regardless of one's parents' income.)

On the other end of the income distribution, it takes an average of six generations for the benefits of being born into a wealthy family to disappear. In other words, we have to go back six generations before your ancestors' place in the income distribution ceases to have any predictive power for what your own will be. In contrast, in Norway it takes only three generations. Figure 21-6 shows how relative mobility in the United States stacks up against that for a selection of other wealthy countries.

✓ TEST YOURSELF

- ☐ What variables are on the *x*- and *y*-axes when we graph the Lorenz curve? **[LO 21.3]**
- ☐ What does it mean if a country's Gini coefficient is 0? What does it mean if the Gini coefficient is 100? **[LO 21.3]**
- ☐ What is income mobility? **[LO 21.4]**

FIGURE 21-6

Income mobility in rich countries   This mobility measure shows the amount of intergenerational income elasticity (the relationship between parents' and children's incomes) around the world. Note that income mobility decreases as the intergenerational elasticity measure increases. Many European countries have high-income mobility, while countries in other parts of the world have less.

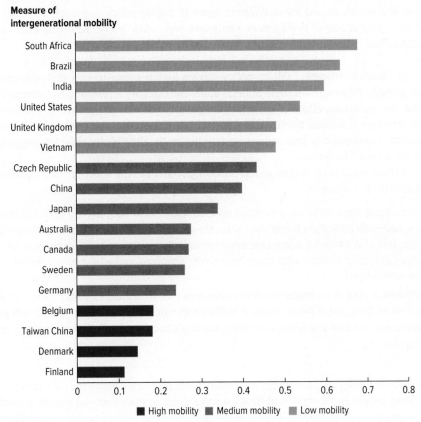

Sources: https://equalchances.org.

Policies to Reduce Poverty and Inequality

Most governments, in both rich and poor countries, aim to limit poverty and inequality to some extent. Yet views differ about how to do so. It's also a difficult and controversial area of policy-making. Some people feel that taking from the rich to give to the poor is justice. Others feel it's theft. Some focus on equalizing opportunities rather than outcomes. Others focus on creating a safety net for people who lose their jobs or get sick. Even when people can agree on policy goals, they may disagree about how to design the best policies to accomplish those goals. In this section, we'll discuss both motivations and design issues surrounding poverty-fighting policies.

Public policy goals

Before we talk about the "how" of policy-making, we have to talk about what policy-makers are trying to accomplish. Why might it be desirable to reduce poverty or inequality?

- Some people cite humanitarian reasons—concern for others suffering from hunger or homelessness.

LO 21.5 Identify the public policies that are used to reduce poverty and inequality and understand their goals.

- Some focus on the harm to the economy and social disadvantages that may result when much of the population lacks access to quality health care, education, and basic services like banking.
- Still others take a strictly pragmatic approach: A country with too much poverty or glaring inequalities is prone to violence, political unrest, or economic instability.

We can distinguish among three different types of public policy approaches related to poverty and inequality: *economic development, safety nets*, and *redistribution*. Knowing which goals are being pursued has important implications for designing public policies.

Economic development

Often, policy-makers look for investments that will spur future economic growth. We can group these policies under the category *economic development:* The goal is not only the immediate effect of the policy on poverty but also the growth it will produce for the entire economy. Common examples include public investments in education, job training, and infrastructure. These policies help reduce poverty indirectly, through increased economic growth and opportunities in the future.

Many of these policies serve dual goals—providing services in the short run and contributing to long-run growth. For instance:

- Education is considered an important good in itself. Most people want their children to have access to education for its own sake. However, from the perspective of the government, it is also a tool for economic development: Better-educated children grow up to be more productive workers who contribute to the economy and who are less likely to be poor and unemployed.
- Similarly, a plan to revitalize the downtown area of a struggling city may have dual goals: It may make living there more pleasant in the short run. The hope is also that it will attract businesses and new residents, improving the city's economy and reducing poverty in the long run.

Safety nets

Earlier in the chapter, we looked at the difference between transient and chronic poverty. Most people go through hard times at some point in their lives—an illness, a death in the family, the loss of a job, and so on. For those living close to the edge of poverty, one bad event can be enough to tip the scales.

social insurance
government programs under which people pay into a common pool and are eligible to draw on benefits under certain circumstances

Many policies are designed to protect against the temporary hard times that can lead to transient poverty. We can broadly categorize these as **social insurance** programs. Under these government programs, people pay into a common pool and are in turn eligible to draw on benefits under certain circumstances. Important examples in the United States include unemployment insurance, Social Security, and Medicare.

Such programs are referred to as "social insurance" because, like private insurance programs, they pool risks across a large population. (For a more general discussion of insurance, turn back to Chapter 11, "Time and Uncertainty.") Unemployment insurance, for example, pools risk across the labor force. Since a large majority of people in the labor force have jobs and pay taxes, the system is able to provide benefits for the minority who lose their jobs. The same is true for Social Security and Medicare, but the risks in these programs are spread across time. In both of these programs, benefits are provided by younger workers, who pay into the system under the promise that they'll get benefits when they retire.

One difference from private insurance programs is that social insurance programs usually serve everyone who meets baseline eligibility requirements. For instance, people who paid payroll taxes during their working years can draw on Social Security and Medicare when they retire or suffer a disability; those who live longer or have higher health care costs don't have to pay higher premiums in order to receive benefits.

Redistribution　Some policies explicitly seek to redistribute resources with the aim of alleviating the effects of poverty or income inequality. For instance:

- Homeless shelters and food banks don't have much to do with long-run economic development. Instead, they are meant to provide comfort and security to people who face an immediate lack of food and shelter.
- Similarly, government-subsidized housing, food stamps, Medicaid (health insurance for low-income households), and many other programs offer resources to the poor over the long term.

Most people see the primary purpose of such programs as using resources from society's wealthier members to ensure a basic minimum standard of living for its poorer members.

The welfare state

The term "welfare state" describes the idea that government has a responsibility to promote the economic well-being (the welfare) of its citizens. The basics of the welfare state in the United States started as part of the New Deal legislation that responded to the Great Depression in the 1930s. The government rolled out a variety of programs, including Social Security and the Civilian Conservation Corps, intended to help the growing number of poor and unemployed workers.

From those beginnings, the United States created a variety of programs to help guarantee a minimum standard of living for all. These programs range from assistance to help the poor buy food (Supplemental Nutrition Assistance Program, SNAP) to Head Start, an early-childhood education program. In this section, we discuss some of the more important economic welfare policies.

Progressive taxation　Governments can address poverty and inequality in two ways: how public money is spent and how people are taxed. As discussed in Chapter 20, "Taxation and the Public Budget," the design of the U.S. federal income tax system is *progressive*–the government charges lower tax rates to those with lower incomes. This design has the effect of reducing income inequality: Those with high income tend to pay a larger proportion of their income as taxes than those with low incomes. The result is that the after-tax gap between rich and poor is smaller than the pre-tax gap. Other types of taxation–such as sales and payroll taxes–can be *regressive*. The overall burden of federal taxation in the United States, though, is progressive.

One tax policy, the *Earned Income Tax Credit (EITC)*, has a particularly large effect on the poor. The EITC is exactly what it sounds like: Those with low income are eligible for a tax credit, proportional to the amount of income they earn and the size of their families. The more the family earns, the higher the credit; that credit is then subtracted from the amount of federal tax the family owes. For those with very low incomes, the tax credit may be larger than the amount owed in taxes, in which case the balance is paid to the family as a tax "refund." The EITC is a way to encourage work while still providing income support to families with very low income.

Income support　Government programs that give money to the poor are commonly referred to as "welfare." In fact, there is no single program in the United States called "welfare." Rather, the term *welfare* is used to refer broadly to the various income-support programs for the poor run by each state and the federal government. (Note that it differs from the term *welfare effects* that we first used in the context of deadweight loss calculations in Chapter 6, "Government Intervention.")

In 1996, Congress passed and President Clinton signed into law an act that greatly changed the role of the federal government in providing welfare. Until then, the federal government administered a program called Aid to Families with Dependent Children (AFDC). As the name suggests, this program gave money to poor households with children. To be eligible, the children had to be "deprived of parental support" in some way, usually by having a single or divorced parent. Each state set the level of income at which families of different sizes were eligible, as well as the amount of benefits received. Anyone who met the eligibility criteria was entitled to benefits. Under the program, each state received unlimited reimbursement from the federal government to cover the cost.

We can think of AFDC as an "unconditional" cash-transfer program; it provided financial support to any eligible person, without any restrictions on how the money could be used. In contrast, the program that replaced AFDC in 1996—called Temporary Assistance to Needy Families (TANF)—is a **conditional cash-transfer** program. Under this program, financial support is given only to people who engage in certain actions. The exact requirements vary from state to state. Generally, welfare recipients

conditional cash transfer

a program in which financial support is given only to people who engage in certain actions

- are eligible for benefits for a maximum of five years,
- must start working within two years of joining the program, and
- must work a minimum number of hours per week.

These conditions have shifted the nature of welfare away from a redistribution program toward a social insurance program. They are designed to help people through temporary hard times rather than provide long-term income support.

Conditional cash-transfer programs are an increasingly popular antipoverty strategy, especially outside the United States. Often, the conditions attached to financial transfers require recipients to invest in health and education for their children. Such conditional cash-transfer programs combine redistributive goals with economic-development goals.

To learn more about programs that promote investment in human capital, look at the From Another Angle box "Just give money."

"Just give money"
From Another Angle

What do former union leader Andy Stern, technology titan Mark Zuckerberg, conservative economist Milton Friedman, and Martin Luther King Jr. have in common? (No, this is not the premise for a bad joke). All have supported the idea of *universal basic income (UBI)*. Although universal basic income has many different proposed forms, the core idea is the same: pay a large *(universal)* group of people a set amount *(income)* that lets them afford the essential *(basic)* requirements of life. The "big idea" is to just give people money.

In some designs, UBI would pay working-age adults a fixed sum of money that covers most living essentials—say, $1,000 each month. In other designs, universal basic income would be limited to those who would otherwise normally receive government benefits. One key to all UBI designs is that there would be no conditions and no work requirements.

Some see UBI as a response to the disruption in the economy caused by automation. Oxford University researchers Carl Frey and Michael Osborne calculate that 45 percent of jobs could be automated using current technologies, with millions more jobs at risk in the future. What then? As the writer Annie Lowrey says, "crummy jobs" (and disappearing jobs) could be replaced in part by UBI. Facebook CEO Mark Zuckerberg argues that people could then spend their time in other ways, maybe pursuing entrepreneurial or artistic ideas. Similarly, Andy Stern, a former president of the Service Employees International Union, argues that UBI is a dignified way to avoid high unemployment and poverty among those whose jobs will inevitably be replaced by machines.

Some conservative economists and policy-makers approach UBI from a slightly different angle. Currently, the federal government offers 83 means-tested programs (meaning that recipients have to prove that they earn below certain income levels to qualify). They range from Section 8 housing vouchers to SNAP (food stamp) benefits. These programs have separate sets of qualifying requirements and often require recipients to work through complicated procedures to demonstrate their need. Replacing those programs with a single UBI payment, paid to everyone, would be simpler, and it could help shrink government bureaucracy.

Others see UBI as a way to provide people with steady financial flows. The greater stability, it's hoped, would help people to save, invest, and build their own financial security.

Of course, not everyone is a fan of the idea. If people get cash hand-outs, wouldn't UBI take away the incentive to work? Others argue that targeted job training and more education funding would better train workers for the economy of the future. And of course, there is the raw cost of such a program. Depending on scope and scale, a national UBI in the United States could cost anywhere from $1.5 to $3.9 *trillion*.

UBI hasn't yet been implemented at large scale, but governments and organizations around the world have experimented with smaller UBI offerings. Finland offered 2,000 unemployed adults a monthly stipend of about $600. Similar programs have also been rolled out in Canada, Kenya, India, and Brazil. In Alaska, cash grants are made to all qualifying citizens using oil revenues accrued by the Alaska Permanent Fund. The Eastern Band of Cherokee Indians similarly disburses to its tribal members revenues from gaming and hotel operations, amounting to thousands of dollars each.

So far, the results have been mostly positive. Evaluations of the different programs have found improvements in various metrics of well-being, with little negative effect on labor force participation. In Alaska, financial stability improved. For members of the Cherokee nation, intergenerational poverty fell.

Still, it's not clear how UBI would work across larger populations. And it's expensive. However, as long as the idea has such wide support, expect to see experiments continue well into the future.

Sources: Patrick Gillespie, "Mark Zuckerburg Supports Universal Basic Income. What Is It?" *CNN Money*, May 26, 2017, https://money.cnn.com/2017/05/26/news/economy/mark-zuckerberg-universal-basic-income/index.html; Annie Lowrey, *Give People Money: How a Universal Basic Income Would End Poverty, Revolutionize Work, and Remake the World* (New York: Crown, 2018); Ioana Marinescu, "No Strings Attached: The Behavioral Effects of U.S. Unconditional Cash Transfer Programs," Roosevelt Institute report, May 2017; Karl Wilderquist, "Current UBI Experiments: An Update for July 2018," Basic Income Earth Network. July 1, 2018, https://basicincome.org/news/2018/07/current-ubi-experiments-an-update-for-july-2018/.

In-kind transfers   In contrast to cash-transfer programs, many government programs involve **in-kind transfers**. These programs provide goods or services, rather than cash, directly to needy individuals or households.

In the United States, common in-kind transfers include public housing, free school breakfasts and lunches, and the medical treatment benefits provided by Medicaid. Often, in-kind transfers take the form of vouchers that are redeemable only for certain items. For example, the Supplemental Nutrition Assistance Program (SNAP, formerly known as the Food Stamp Program) provides vouchers that can be used to purchase only approved food items.

In-kind transfer programs are, by design, more restrictive than cash-transfer programs. When a poor household receives income support, it can use the money to buy whatever goods and services it wishes. When that same household receives an in-kind transfer, the choice of how to spend the money has already been made. If we believe that people make considered choices to maximize their own well-being, then in-kind transfers are inefficient. After all, cash provides recipients with the flexibility to choose the goods that will do them the most good.

Why might a government prefer in-kind transfers? One reason is that it prevents recipients from spending cash on luxury items or on socially disapproved goods such as alcohol or drugs.

in-kind transfer
a program that provides specific goods or services, rather than cash, directly to needy recipients

Social insurance   Social-insurance programs are designed to help people weather temporary bad periods. They also help people survive old age, disability, or other long-term conditions.

As we noted above, in these programs, the government plays a role similar to that of a private insurance company: It collects contributions from working people in a common pool, defines the circumstances under which people are eligible to draw benefits, and administers and monitors the allocation of those benefits.

In the United States, the largest social insurance programs are

- *Social Security*, which provides pensions to retired and disabled people.
- *Medicare*, which provides medical insurance to retired and disabled people.
- *Unemployment insurance*, which gives short-term income support to the unemployed.

Unemployment benefits are examples of social insurance in a straightforward sense. If you lose your job or have an injury or medical condition that prevents you from working, the government will step in to provide a small stipend to help cover everyday living expenses.

Retirement benefits are less like private insurance (which is generally used to protect against unexpected events) and more like a collective saving program. Nevertheless, because there is an uncertainty about the circumstances the elderly face—when they will retire, what medical problems they will face, how high the cost of living will be, and how long they will need to live on retirement income—retirement benefits are widely seen as an example of social insurance. They play an important role in reducing poverty among the elderly, as we showed earlier in the chapter.

Trade-offs between equity and efficiency

LO 21.6 Explain the trade-off between equity and efficiency in poverty-reduction policy.

All of the programs we just discussed are paid for by taxes. This is true for programs that target everyone, such as Social Security and public schools, and for programs that target the poor, such as Medicaid and food stamps. Of course, the amount of money required for each program can vary dramatically.

Figure 21-7 shows the annual spending on several different types of welfare programs in the United States. As we saw in Chapter 20, "Taxation and the Public Budget," higher taxes often mean larger deadweight loss. Pursuing equity—that is, greater income equality—thus means accepting some inefficiency due to increased taxation.

FIGURE 21-7

Federal expenditure on welfare programs

This figure shows federal expenditure on large welfare programs in the United States in 2017.

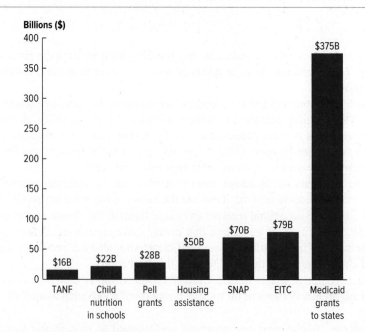

Source: http://federalsafetynet.com/welfare-budget.html.

Some social welfare programs are *means-tested*. **Means-tested** programs define eligibility for benefits based on recipients' income. The goal of means-testing is to target resources toward those who need them the most. Often, means-testing is more complex than a simple eligible/not-eligible distinction, and welfare programs that are means-tested can be problematic when not designed carefully. For instance, under the EITC described earlier, the size of the credit at first increases with earned income at very low income levels; it then begins to decrease as income rises past the poverty line. The thinking is that a family with income *just* under the poverty threshold requires less support to access basic goods and services than a family very far below the line.

But means-testing can create perverse incentives. Imagine a simple means-test: If your income is under the poverty line, you are eligible for a cash transfer of $5,000 per year. If your income is over the poverty line, you are not. Now imagine you are working part time and living just under the poverty line. Your boss offers you the opportunity to pick up an extra five hours of work each week. Here's the choice you face:

- If you accept the added hours, your income will increase by $3,000 over the course of the year.
- That $3,000 more in pay will push you over the poverty line.
- As a result, you will lose your government transfer of $5,000. On net, you will end up $2,000 poorer.

How would you respond to this situation? Would you accept the extra hours? Unless there is some sort of extra benefit we're not considering (such as gaining experience or favor with your boss that will improve your job opportunities down the road), most people would say no to working longer hours for lower income.

It is possible to fix this sort of perverse incentive by designing more nuanced means-tests. For instance, a program could phase out benefits as income increases (like the EITC) rather than use a strict cutoff. That way, there will be no point at which a large amount of benefits are lost from a small increase in income.

In general, the more narrowly targeted support is to those with low income, the greater the potential inefficiency caused. These examples show why economists often see a trade-off between equity and efficiency in poverty policy.

This is not to say that poverty policy is always inefficient. Some policies, like those that alleviate credit constraints or those that promote equal opportunities, can improve both equity *and* efficiency. In this case, a market failure is being solved, so there is no trade-off. Understanding the potential for trade-offs and unintended consequences is an important consideration when designing poverty policy.

means-tested
the characteristic of a program that defines eligibility for benefits based on recipients' income

✓ TEST YOURSELF

- ☐ What is social insurance? **[LO 21.5]**
- ☐ What's the difference between a conditional and an unconditional cash-transfer program? **[LO 21.5]**
- ☐ What is means-testing? **[LO 21.6]**

Discrimination

You may be wondering why we discuss discrimination in this chapter. In many ways it's a separate topic from poverty and income inequality: Not everyone who is poor is discriminated against, and not everyone who is discriminated against is poor. We chose to discuss these topics in the same chapter because, historically, they have often gone hand in hand. It's important to understand when discrimination, poverty, and inequality are connected; when they are not; and how to tell the difference.

LO 21.7 Explain why economists differentiate between correlation and causation when studying discrimination and why markets do not always eliminate discrimination.

discrimination
making choices by using generalizations based on people's observable characteristics like race, gender, and age

Economists think about **discrimination** as the practice of making choices using generalizations based on observable characteristics like race, gender, or age. But people can also discriminate based on ethnic origin, appearance, sexual orientation, what type of music you listen to, or any other observable characteristic that allows them to generalize about what type of person you might be. In Chapter 10, "Information," we said that discrimination can be a useful tool for making decisions when we don't have access to full information. In common language, however, when people say "discrimination," they usually mean "unfair or illegal discrimination."

Economists recognize that *statistical discrimination*—making a choice based on the difference in average characteristics between two groups—can sometimes be rational. For instance, imagine that an employer has to make a quick decision on which of two candidates to employ, a younger candidate versus an older one. She decides to hire the younger one as she believes that the younger candidate would be healthier and miss work less frequently. When forced to make a decision without full information, the employer is making a *rational guess* based on her knowledge of the average differences between middle-aged people and young people. It's an understandable strategy if she doesn't have good information about the health of the two candidates as individuals, but that doesn't make it fair or efficient for society. (In fact, making a hiring decision based on a worker's age or health is generally illegal.)

Society loses when talented individuals who face discrimination are discouraged from acquiring the skills, education, and positions that they otherwise might get. In 1960, 94 percent American doctors and lawyers were white men. By 2010, only 62 percent were. The changes are due not just to reductions in discrimination, though they play an important role. Economists estimate that in the 50 years between 1960 and 2010, the improved allocation of talent (due to expanded opportunities for women and members of minority groups) explains about one quarter of the growth in aggregate output per person in the United States.[9] In short, discrimination might sometimes seem "rational" for an individual employer, but that doesn't necessarily make it right, socially efficient, or even legal.

Measuring discrimination in the labor market

There's little doubt that discrimination has played a major role in U.S. history. Does it still matter today? It's surprisingly hard to say how big an effect discrimination now has on people's economic opportunities and success.

We can start to answer this question by looking at the outcomes achieved by people in different demographic groups. Table 21-5 shows that average income for adults still varies widely across gender and racial groups. It's possible that these differences are due to discrimination in the labor market, but there are also plenty of other possible explanations. For instance, historically more men have had college degrees than women, and to the extent that being more educated is a signal or a cause of higher productivity as a worker, this could explain higher male wages. (However, based on data collected in 2015, women are now more likely to have a bachelor's degree than

TABLE 21-5

Income by race and gender in the United States

Median personal income distribution varies by race and gender in the United States.

Group	Male ($)	Female ($)
Asian	47,213	28,324
White	41,578	25,793
All	40,396	25,486
Black	30,112	23,639
Hispanic	30,691	20,312

Source: U.S. Census Bureau, 2015 data, Table P2: Race and Hispanic Origin of People by Median Income and Sex, www.census.gov/data/tables/time-series/demo/income-poverty/historical-income-people.html.

men, so wages should even out if they are based mainly on completion of a bachelor's degree.[10] Fields of study, though—such as engineering, economics, or finance versus traditional liberal arts disciplines—might still explain wage differences.) Similarly, women are more likely than men to choose to leave the labor force when they have children, and therefore have less work experience on average.

We should be careful about confusing *correlation* with *causation*. In this case, income is *correlated* with race and gender. That doesn't necessarily mean that discrimination based on race and gender is *causing* the difference in wages. To draw on a concept from all the way back in Chapter 1, "Economics and Life," it's possible that *omitted variables* are causing the correlation. Other factors that are related to both earnings and race or gender but that we are not observing could include education, work experience, and choice of occupation.

It's also important to remember that we don't know what might be causing differences in those other factors. Suppose that a large part of the difference in wages between men and women can be explained by differences in occupational choice. For instance, men are more likely to be doctors and women are more likely to be nurses.[11] Since doctors earn more on average than nurses, the gender difference in occupational choices contributes to the difference in earnings between men and women. This doesn't tell us *why* women are more likely to be nurses—maybe it's a response to social pressures, or a need for flexibility in work hours, or maybe it has to do with differences in how girls and boys are brought up. These explanations may also be partly a function of a kind of discrimination.

To read about an innovative way researchers tested one of the factors that could be causing a discrepancy in wages in the labor market, read the Economics in Action box "Are Emily and Greg more employable than Lakisha and Jamal?"

Are Emily and Greg more employable than Lakisha and Jamal?

Economics in Action

Many companies go out of their way to advertise their support for diversity in the workplace or to note they are an "equal opportunity employer." Title VII of the Civil Rights Act of 1964 made it unlawful to discriminate on the basis of race, color, religion, gender, or national origin when hiring employees.

Yet in spite of the good intentions of many companies and legal prohibitions against racial discrimination in the workplace, people of different races still have very different rates of employment and levels of earnings. How much of this, if any, is due to lingering discrimination by employers?

To answer this question, economists Marianne Bertrand and Sendhil Mullainathan conducted a now-classic study to test for racial discrimination in the job-application process. They created résumés for fictitious applicants and sent the résumés in response to help-wanted ads. Some résumés represented a fake applicant with a "white-sounding" name, such as Emily Walsh or Greg Baker. Others were given traditionally "black-sounding" names like Lakisha Washington or Jamal Jones. Aside from the difference in names, the actual qualifications and job experience were the same on average across "white" and "black" résumés.

The researchers found that "white" names—with otherwise-identical qualifications—were 50 percent more likely to receive callbacks in response to a job application. On average, Emily and Greg had to send out 10 résumés in order to receive a response from an employer. Lakisha and Jamal had to send out 15.

(continued)

Furthermore, résumés with "black" names got less benefit from increased qualifications. An "Emily" résumé with more education or job experience got 27 percent more callbacks than an "Emily" with a lower-quality résumé. In contrast, résumés with "black" names and higher qualifications got only 8 percent more callbacks than those with lower qualifications. In other words, applicants with "black-sounding" names received fewer rewards in their job search for the same increase in accomplishments.

Recent research that follows up on the original 2004 study finds that this kind of discrimination is also partly based on the perceived socioeconomic status of applicants, not just race. Whether based on "class" or race, from the perspective of real young people of different races and backgrounds, discrimination reduces the incentives to invest time and money in education and skill-building. That could, ultimately, be the biggest cost for society.

Sources: www.eeoc.gov/laws/statutes/titlevii.cfm; Title VII of the 1964 Civil Rights Act; Marianne Bertrand and Sendhil Mullainathan, "Are Emily and Greg More Employable than Lakisha and Jamal? A Field Experiment on Labor Market Discrimination," *American Economic Review* 94, no. 4 (September 2004), pp. 991–1013.

Do free markets reduce discrimination?

How does the idea of discrimination fit into a model of efficient, well-functioning markets? Under some conditions, markets may help to eliminate discrimination. For instance, imagine a shop owner who has a unique prejudice against people over six feet tall. He refuses to hire tall employees or to serve tall customers. Since no one else in the market has this strange bias against tall people, the shop owner's competitors will take advantage of his discrimination: They will hire good workers who happen to be tall and will get business from the tall customers he refuses to serve. If the market is competitive, the discriminatory shop owner will get pushed out of the market; his competitors will benefit from his inefficient choices.

Under other circumstances, however, discrimination can be consistent with an efficient market. For a large part of the twentieth century, for instance, shopkeepers who discriminated against black customers were the norm rather than the exception. As long as their competitors and their white customers agreed with and supported this discrimination, it was unfortunately often in their interest to maintain it. For instance, a shopkeeper in the 1940s who allowed black people to sit at the same counter as white people risked losing business from prejudiced white customers. In situations where businesses discriminate in response to the preferences of consumers, discrimination is consistent with efficient markets—which, of course, doesn't make it morally right or acceptable.

Long-term effects of discrimination

Even though the passage of the Civil Rights Act in 1964 made many forms of discrimination illegal, it couldn't undo the effects of discrimination that took place in earlier decades. Discrimination can have long-lasting effects on people and markets, even after the active discrimination itself ends.

We noted earlier that differences in educational attainment explain part of the difference in earnings between racial groups. We have to ask ourselves: Why do people of different races have more or less education on average? Although there are many complicated social, cultural, and economic reasons, some part of it is certainly the lingering result of discrimination decades ago.

On the most basic level, a black person who was born in the United States in the 1940s probably completed most of his or her education in segregated schools. But the lingering effects of historical discrimination can affect new generations, even if they didn't grow up under discriminatory policies.

One important example is segregated communities. Earlier in the chapter, we discussed the idea that people's chances in life are affected by the human capital of those around them. Imagine that, at one time, people of a certain race, national origin, or religion experienced discrimination that made it harder for them to get a good education or acquire job experience or productive skills. Even after that active discrimination ends, imagine that they still tend to cluster together in neighborhoods. The kids who grow up in these neighborhoods are surrounded by adults who have low education or job experience, affecting the development of the kids' human capital.

Correcting such lingering effects of discrimination is one reason often put forward for "affirmative action" programs that ensure people of other races gain access in college admissions or hiring decisions, as described in the What Do You Think? box "Affirmative action in college admissions."

Affirmative action in college admissions
What Do You Think?

In 1961, President John F. Kennedy required government contractors to "take affirmative action to ensure that applicants are employed [. . .] without regard to their race, creed, color, or national origin." That original use of the term "affirmative action" meant taking steps to avoid racial discrimination. Over time, the term evolved to refer to the general practice of giving preference to members of underrepresented groups.

One of the most hotly debated areas of affirmative-action policy is in university admissions. Since the 1970s, many universities have practiced "positive discrimination" to increase the number of women and racial minorities they admit. Early on, many of these policies took the form of specific racial quotas, such as reserving 15 percent of available spots for nonwhite students. The Supreme Court ruled quotas unconstitutional (in the 1978 case *Regents of the University of California v. Bakke*) but allowed less-explicit forms of racial affirmative action. In a hard-fought case involving the University of Michigan (*Gratz v. Bollinger* in 2003), the Court ruled that considering race as a "plus" in a multifactor admissions decision is acceptable if it helps achieve diversity among students. However, the Court noted that it viewed this as a short-term solution that would be unnecessary in 25 years.

Proponents of affirmative action in university admissions commonly base their support on one of two ideas:

- First, having a diverse student body is inherently valuable and serves educational purposes.
- Second, "positive discrimination" is a temporary measure to counteract the lingering, intergenerational effects of historical "negative discrimination."

Opponents often argue that there is no such thing as "positive discrimination." They feel that preference on the basis of race is simply wrong, regardless of who is harmed or helped by it. "Two wrongs don't make a right," they say.

Still others argue that if affirmative action is intended to address historical disadvantages, it should take a wider view than race. For example, who has been more disadvantaged by his family background: the son of a poor white coal miner or the son of a wealthy black neurosurgeon?

WHAT DO YOU THINK?

1. In what ways, if any, do you think that students applying to U.S. colleges today might be affected by past racial and gender discrimination? Think about human capital investments, social networks, and economic mobility.
2. If some students are adversely affected by historical discrimination, are college admissions an effective way to correct that disadvantage before graduates enter the labor market? How should we think about the benefits and costs of such a policy, including the opportunity cost? Can actions be taken to counter these disadvantages elsewhere in society or the economy?

✓ TEST YOURSELF

☐ How do economists define discrimination? [LO 21.7]

☐ Why don't differences in income between demographic groups necessarily imply discrimination? [LO 21.7]

Conclusion

Understanding the roots of poverty, inequality, and discrimination matters for economists and policy-makers alike. From an intellectual perspective, these topics push us to understand how markets and institutions really work. They also take us below the surface of statistics such as average income and GDP to understand who gets how much and why. From the perspective of a policy-maker or a concerned citizen, they may raise challenging economic and social issues. What does a fair society look like? How much poverty is acceptable? Does equality of opportunity matter more than the distribution of income itself?

We've seen in this chapter that even the measurement of poverty, inequality, mobility, and discrimination can be tricky. We have to decide whether we care more about absolute or relative measures, adjust for differences across regions, and pick out the causal factors we care about.

In the next chapter, we turn to the question of how these and other policy issues are dealt with in the political world. We'll see that arriving at policy choices is even more complicated than simply finding the facts and establishing goals. The workings of the political system itself have a huge influence on the shape of the economic policies that are created.

Key Terms

absolute poverty line, p. 527

relative poverty line, p. 528

poverty rate, p. 528

purchasing power parity (PPP) index, p. 530

human capital, p. 533

poverty trap, p. 535

credit constraint, p. 535

Lorenz curve, p. 538

Gini coefficient, p. 539

income mobility, p. 542

social insurance, p. 544

conditional cash transfer, p. 546

in-kind transfer, p. 547

means-tested, p. 549

discrimination, p. 550

Summary

LO 21.1 Understand how to measure poverty, and describe the difference between absolute and relative measures of poverty.

An *absolute poverty line* defines poverty as income below a certain amount. The poverty line is fixed at a certain dollar amount at a given point in time; it is usually set based on the cost of certain essential goods. In contrast, a *relative poverty line* defines poverty in terms of the income of the rest of the population.

The official U.S. poverty line is an absolute amount based on the price of food in the 1960s; poverty rates in the United States have fluctuated between 10 and 15 percent of the population in recent decades. The most commonly used international poverty measure is also an absolute poverty line, $1.90 per person per day at

purchasing power parity. According to this metric, roughly one-quarter of the world's population lives in poverty.

Absolute poverty lines measure people's access to concrete goods and services; relative poverty lines do a better job of capturing the importance of economic conditions relative to those of others.

LO 21.2 Understand how different factors contribute to poverty.

Some common factors help explain why poverty continues to exist. We tend to see poverty continue from generation to generation, although we cannot say for sure whether this is because low *human capital* causes poverty or because poverty causes low human capital. There are also *poverty traps* that tend to make the poor stay poor—things like poor health, *credit constraints*, and imperfect markets for making investments. And for some societies, community-wide problems hinder the poor—problems such as drought and war.

LO 21.3 Explain and interpret different methods of measuring income inequality.

Income inequality is commonly summarized by measuring the average income in each *quintile* of the population, or the percentage of total income held by people in each quintile. We can also represent income inequality using a graph called the *Lorenz curve*. It maps the cumulative percent of the population against the cumulative percent of income those people earn. The *Gini coefficient* summarizes inequality in a single number by dividing the area between the Lorenz curve and the line of perfect equality by the total area under the line of perfect equality. A gini coefficient of zero indicates perfect equality; a Gini coefficient of 100 indicates perfect inequality.

LO 21.4 Describe how income mobility differs from income equality.

Income mobility is the ability to improve your economic circumstances over time. Measuring income mobility in a country tells us how likely you are to end up rich if you start out poor, or vice versa. We can measure income mobility in both absolute and relative terms. In absolute terms, we can look at whether a person's income is higher than her parents'. In relative terms, we can look at whether a person's income places her higher up in the income distribution than her parents.

LO 21.5 Identify the public policies that are used to reduce poverty and inequality and understand their goals.

Four main policies are used to reduce poverty and inequality. Progressive taxation reduces inequality, as it taxes the rich at a higher rate than the poor, narrowing the gap between these two groups. Income support comes in two forms, *conditional cash transfers* and direct cash transfers. In both, families receive cash from the government. *In-kind transfers* give goods and services (most commonly, food stamps and housing vouchers) to the poor instead of cash. *Social insurance* programs, including Social Security and Medicare, pool risks across the population by providing income support and health care, respectively, for the elderly.

LO 21.6 Explain the trade-off between equity and efficiency in poverty-reduction policy.

Means-tested programs define eligibility for benefits based on recipients' income. Often, means-testing involves not just a simple eligible/not-eligible distinction, but also a determination of how much recipients are eligible to receive. However, anytime benefits decrease as income increases, the motivation to earn additional income is reduced. There is no way to prevent everyone from falling through the cracks without loss of efficiency. Thus, economists see a trade-off between equity and efficiency in poverty policy. Trade-offs are also created due to the inefficiencies created by taxes levied to pay for anti-poverty programs.

LO 21.7 Explain why economists differentiate between correlation and causation when studying discrimination and why markets do not always eliminate discrimination.

Income for adults varies widely by race and gender in the United States. These differences could be the result of discrimination in the labor market. They also could be the result of other factors that are related to both earnings and race or gender, such as education, work experience, and choice of occupation. It is difficult to distinguish the causal effect of discrimination from these other unobserved factors.

Under some conditions, markets may help to eliminate discrimination. When consumer preferences are not in agreement with the discrimination (or when the discrimination is irrelevant to consumers' preferences), markets will cause those who discriminate to lose profitable opportunities. However, when consumer preferences support discrimination, discrimination and efficient markets can coexist.

Review Questions

1. In season three of the TV show *The West Wing*, the federal government considers redefining the national poverty measure in a way that would classify an additional 4 million people as poor. The president worries that his administration will be criticized for leading the country into greater poverty. Explain whether this change would have reflected a shift in an absolute measure of poverty or a relative measure of poverty, or whether it cannot be known. Finally, explain why, all else equal, the president is not responsible for causing greater poverty. **[LO 21.1]**

2. Poverty in Decilia is measured relatively, with people in the bottom 10 percent of the income distribution being defined as poor. Suppose a politician in Decilia promises to halve the poverty rate in five years. Explain why this could never be achieved given the poverty statistic Decilia uses. Propose an alternative measure of poverty that would allow the politician to achieve that goal. **[LO 21.1]**

3. Explain why it might be difficult for low-income individuals to receive a college education and why the government may need to subsidize student loans for a college education. **[LO 21.2]**

4. Some people argue that unpaid internships should be illegal. In what ways is an unpaid internship part of a poverty trap? **[LO 21.2]**

5. Is it possible for two countries to have the same Gini coefficient but different distributions of income? Explain how you came to your conclusion. **[LO 21.3]**

6. Explain why it's possible for income inequality to decrease globally while increasing in every country at the same time. **[LO 21.3]**

7. In which of the following countries is income mobility likely higher? Explain your answer. **[LO 21.4]**

    a. A country with a poverty rate of 25 percent, of which 80 percent represents chronic poverty.

    b. A country with a poverty rate of 30 percent, of which 20 percent represents chronic poverty.

8. Suppose there is an economy where 80 percent of people earn more than their parents and 40 percent end up in a different income quintile than their parents. What measure of the income distribution does the first statistic tell you about? What about the second? **[LO 21.4]**

9. In March 2010, President Barack Obama signed into law the Patient Protection and Affordable Care Act, which required insurance companies to accept patients with preexisting conditions. Classify this provision into one of the approaches to alleviating poverty discussed in the chapter and explain your reasoning. **[LO 21.5]**

10. If unconditional cash transfers have the same effect as conditional cash transfers, which one allows the government to alleviate poverty more effectively? In answering the question, draw on your knowledge of administrative costs. **[LO 21.5]**

11. John Rawls is a philosopher famous for his "maximin" principle, which states that society should maximize the position of the people with the minimum amount of goods, and not focus only on the level of inequality. For instance, Rawls would favor a society in which the bottom 10 percent earn $30,000 per year and the top 10 percent earn $2 million over a society in which the bottom 10 percent earn $28,000 per year and the top 10 percent earn $40,000 per year. Drawing on the trade-off between equity and efficiency, explain whether Rawls would favor (a) redistribution that limits growth but creates equality or (b) economic development that encourages growth but creates inequality. **[LO 21.6]**

12. Your professor has decided that, from now on, students who receive less than a 60 percent grade on any exam will be eligible to go to a review session. If they attend the session, they will receive an extra 10 percent on their grade. You see a problem with this policy, and instead propose to your professor that people who go to the review session should receive 50 percent of the difference between their grade and 60 percent. Explain why this situation represents a trade-off between equity and efficiency. **[LO 21.6]**

13. Is it possible that even though men make more than women in a particular industry, there could be gender discrimination *against* men in that industry? If no, explain why not. If yes, explain why and give an example. **[LO 21.7]**

14. For each of the scenarios below, determine whether you think it is likely that an employer could be discriminating against a person because of his or her age. Explain why or why not. **[LO 21.7]**

    a. A young lawyer who just finished work on a multimillion-dollar development deal downtown is hired by an economic development firm in lieu of an older lawyer who works on litigation.

    b. A large retail outlet hires an 80-year-old woman to greet customers instead of a 30-year-old woman who has been greeting customers in other stores for a decade.

    c. The owner of a local, hip smoothie bar in a university town just fired a graduate student who had worked at the bar for three years and instead hired a college sophomore.

15. Jackie Robinson broke baseball's color barrier in 1947, which precipitated integration in all major league teams after 12 years. Explain why the market might have acted to eliminate discrimination in this example. **[LO 21.7]**

16. Some economists have studied the effects of "lookism," or discrimination based on how attractive a person is. Give an example of a case in which the market might encourage lookism and an example of a case in which the market might combat lookism. **[LO 21.7]**

Problems and Applications

1. Table 21P-1 shows a data set that contains the annual income of 20 households, each with a household size of four people. **[LO 21.1]**

    a. What percent of these households are below the national poverty line of $25,100 for a household of four people?

    b. What is the average income of the bottom 20 percent of the households?

TABLE 21P-1

Income of households 1–10 ($)	Income of households 11–20 ($)
30,000	10,000
11,000	41,000
88,000	21,500
17,000	78,000
21,000	25,000
75,000	13,000
24,000	103,000
81,000	149,000
52,000	76,000
44,000	27,000

2. Table 21P-2 shows the incomes of 10 households in two different years, 2020 and 2021. Assume that the government is considering two different measures of poverty, an absolute level of below $10,000 and a relative measure of being in the bottom 40 percent of income earners. **[LO 21.1]**

   a. What is the poverty rate using the *absolute* measure of poverty in 2020? In 2021? Does it go up, down, or stay the same between the two years?

TABLE 21P-2

Household	Income in 2020 ($)	Income in 2021 ($)
1	20,000	20,050
2	8,000	9,000
3	13,000	13,000
4	33,000	34,000
5	2,000	2,500
6	7,500	8,000
7	9,050	10,100
8	80,000	85,000
9	40,000	42,000
10	3,000	3,100

   b. What is the poverty rate using the *relative* measure of poverty in 2020? In 2021? Does it go up, down, or stay the same between the two years?

   c. Which yields a higher rate, the absolute measure of poverty or the relative measure of poverty in 2020? In 2021?

   d. Now assume that the government decides to index the poverty rate to inflation. Suppose inflation was 5 percent from 2020 to 2021. Now what is the poverty rate according to the absolute measure in 2021? Is it higher than the relative rate in 2021?

3. In the United States, public schools are often funded by property taxes levied on the property in surrounding areas. Which of the following statements explains how this can result in a poverty trap? Select all that apply. **[LO 21.2]**

   a. Individuals must buy a higher-priced home in order to attend a school that receives more property taxes.

   b. Renters do not have to pay property taxes.

   c. Schools in areas with cheaper housing will receive less funding.

   d. Low-income families are able to receive the same quality schooling for less money.

4. Table 21P-3 shows the incomes of 10 households in two different years, 2020 and 2030. Each household makes a choice in 2020 about how many years of education they will acquire. Suppose each year of education costs $2,000 and households can acquire a maximum of six years of education. For the sake of simplicity, suppose that there is no risk in education. Each year of education will increase your 2030 income by $3,000. Otherwise, your 2030 income will be the same as your 2020 income. Finally, suppose you need at least $2,000 to survive. **[LO 21.2]**

   a. Fill in the three remaining columns in the table.

   b. What is the percentage of total societal income held by the lowest quintile in 2020?

   c. What is the percentage of total societal income held by the lowest quintile in 2030?

   d. How is this an example of a poverty trap?

5. Using the data for income distribution found in Table 21-4, determine the following. (The data are provided by the World Bank.) **[LO 21.3]**

   a. Does Sweden or Brazil have a higher Gini coefficient?

   b. From the bottom quintile to the middle quintile, is the Lorenz curve for Brazil above or below Sweden's?

TABLE 21P-3

Household	Income in 2020 ($)	Income quintile in 2020	Income in 2030 ($)	Income quintile in 2030
1	20,000			
2	8,000			
3	13,000			
4	33,000			
5	2,000			
6	7,500			
7	9,050			
8	80,000			
9	40,000			
10	3,000			

6. Look at the various measures of poverty in 2015 for several countries in Table 21P-4. (The data are provided by the World Bank.) **[LO 21.3]**

   a. Rank the countries from the country with the highest inequality to the lowest using the Gini coefficient. (Remember that higher Gini coefficients represent higher inequality.)

   b. Rank the countries from the country with the highest inequality to the lowest using the ratio of the top decile to the bottom decile.

   c. Rank the countries from the country with the highest inequality to the lowest inequality using the share of total income held by the top 10 percent.

7. Determine whether each of the scenarios is possible. **[LO 21.4]**

   a. A poverty rate based on a relative measure is high, income mobility is low, and there is perfect income equality.

   b. A poverty rate based on an absolute measure is high, income mobility is zero, and there is perfect income equality.

   c. A poverty rate based on an absolute measure is high, income mobility is high, and there is high income equality.

   d. There is no poverty based on a relative measure, income mobility is high, and there is perfect income equality.

TABLE 21P-4

Country	Gini coefficient	% of income held by bottom 10%	% of income held by top 10%
Brazil	51.3	3.6	40.4
Chile	47.7	4.8	38.0
El Salvador	40.6	6.1	31.8
Honduras	49.6	3.6	37.0
Panama	50.8	3.4	39.0
Paraguay	48.0	4.3	36.7
Peru	43.5	4.7	32.8
Uruguay	40.2	5.6	29.9

8. The left column of Table 21P-5 shows the income data for 10 people at age 40. The right column shows the income for one of their children at the same age (adjusted for inflation). **[LO 21.4]**

TABLE 21P-5

Income for 1st generation (at age 40) ($)	Income for 2nd generation (at age 40) ($)
800	2,225
9,120	2,105
12,830	1,380
1,275	1,140
6,260	10,200
1,600	11,880
4,150	1,250
2,200	15,000
975	420
3,590	5,630

a. How many people in the second generation are in a higher income quintile than their parents?
b. How many people in the second generation are in a lower income quintile than their parents?
c. How many people are in the highest income quintile who had parents who were in the lowest quintile?

9. Classify the following social policies based on the approach taken to alleviating poverty: economic development, safety nets, or redistribution. **[LO 21.5]**

a. The government of Zimbabwe reorganizes property rights, giving traditionally marginalized black Zimbabweans access to land owned by white Zimbabweans.
b. As part of a package called the GI Bill, the United States offered to pay the college tuition of newly returned veterans of World War II.
c. The government of Chile privatizes its social security system. The new system sets up private accounts that require contributions of at least 10 percent of income. This money is invested by private actors and then returned to each person at retirement.

10. Imagine a person who makes $480 per week working 40 hours per week for 50 weeks of the year. He is currently eligible for a welfare program, available to people with income below $24,000, which gives him $800 a year. No such program is available to people with income above $24,000 per year. His boss offers him a promotion that would increase his wage by 50 cents per hour. **[LO 21.5]**

a. What is his total income before the promotion?
b. What is his total income if he accepts the promotion?
c. Should he accept the promotion if he wants to have higher income?

11. President Monique Naomitall just published a report for her country, laying out various scenarios for the economy in the next year. Table 21P-6 shows her report, with various levels of GDP growth, income equality, and tax rates. **[LO 21.6]**

a. Rank the scenarios from the most equal to the most unequal income distribution (defined as the average income of the top decile of earners divided by the average income of the bottom decile of earners).
b. Rank each scenario in terms of the level of GDP growth between 2020 and 2021.
c. Between which scenarios is there no trade-off between GDP growth and income equality?

TABLE 21P-6

Scenario	GDP in 2020 (trillions of $)	Average tax rate (%)	Average total income for the bottom 10% of earners ($)	Average total income for the top 10% of earners ($)	GDP in 2021 (trillions of $)
A	14.1	16	25,000	100,000	14.6
B	13.0	40	35,000	80,000	13.2
C	16.5	30	27,000	90,000	17.2
D	18.0	45	40,000	95,000	18.1

12. Which of the following are means-tested programs? **[LO 21.6]**

    a. A local public university starts to give financial aid to individuals who score above the 98th percentile on the SAT.

    b. The United Kingdom decides to start giving out pension benefits based on individuals' prior amount of savings.

    c. A government decides to give tax credits to anyone who purchases computers made domestically.

    d. Canada begins to pay half of the cost of public transportation for people who do not own a car.

13. Table 21P-7 shows hypothetical salaries for three pairs of men and women who share the same position. It also shows the average increase in income associated with having certain qualities as a worker; assume these represent the only qualities that are relevant for doing the job well. Using these averages, determine for each male-female pair (A, B, and C) whether there is gender discrimination. If so, say who it is against and how large the gap is in dollar terms. **[LO 21.7]**

14. Working women in the United States earn only around 80 percent of what men earn. Consider each of the following explanations for this statistic, and say whether each *could be true* or *must not be true* in order to explain this fact. **[LO 21.7]**

    a. Women choose lower-paying professions (e.g., becoming a nurse rather than a doctor).

    b. Women are discriminated against when being considered for promotions or raises.

    c. Women are more educated and have more work experience than men, on average.

    d. Women are discriminated against in the hiring process.

    e. Women benefit from affirmative action in the hiring process.

15. Are the workings of the free market likely to encourage or discourage discrimination in the following examples? **[LO 21.7]**

    a. The musical director of a symphony orchestra that records but never performs in front of an audience refuses to hire female musicians.

    b. In apartheid South Africa (where racial discrimination was legal and popular among white voters for many decades), a white business owner refuses to hire black candidates to work in management positions dealing with white customers.

    c. In a Martian culture in which blue hair is considered the most beautiful, a Martian modeling agency preferentially hires blue-haired models.

16. Consider Table 21P-8, which shows several different types of goods sold in a hypothetical town. Imagine a new competitor enters who refuses to discriminate between locals and foreigners in hiring employees. Determine whether the new competitor will do well in the town, given market conditions for each market (pajama pants, bow ties, and yo-yos). **[LO 21.7]**

TABLE 21P-7

Industry-average compensation	Gender	Years of schooling $1,000 per year of schooling	Years of experience $2,000 per year of experience	Salary ($) A base salary of $50,000
A	Male	5	10	75,000
	Female	3	8	69,000
B	Male	0	5	60,000
	Female	2	7	70,000
C	Male	3	5	63,000
	Female	3	7	63,000

TABLE 21P-8

Good	% of customers who will buy the good only from companies that hire only locals	% of stores that hire only local employees
Pajama pants	50	70
Bow ties	70	50
Yo-yos	10	5

Endnotes

1. www.investopedia.com/news/how-much-income-puts-you-top-1-5-10/; www.washingtonpost.com/news/business/wp/2018/03/26/wall-streets-average-bonus-in-2017-three-times-what-most-u-s-households-made-all-year/?noredirect=on&utm_term=.3542968592e6; https://money.usnews.com/careers/best-jobs/elementary-school-teacher/salary; https://work.chron.com/much-money-general-surgeons-earn-9471.html.

2. www.census.gov/library/publications/2018/demo/p60-263.html.

3. www.nber.org/aginghealth/summer04/w10466.html.

4. www.washingtonpost.com/news/wonk/wp/2014/01/08/one-in-three-americans-slipped-below-the-poverty-line-between-2009-and-2011/?noredirect=on&utm_term=.87c579675021; www.irp.wisc.edu/publications/focus/pdfs/foc262g.pdf.

5. www.worldbank.org/en/topic/poverty/overview.

6. www.worldbank.org/en/topic/poverty/overview.

7. www.theatlantic.com/magazine/archive/2006/09/the-height-of-inequality/5089/.

8. www.pewtrusts.org/~/media/legacy/uploadedfiles/pcs_assets/2012/pursuingamericandreampdf.pdf.

9. Chang-Tai Hsieh, Erik Hurst, Charles I. Jones, and Peter J. Klenow, "The Allocation of Talent and U.S. Economic Growth," Working paper, April 6, 2018.

10. http://time.com/4064665/women-college-degree.

11. http://kff.org/other/state-indicator/physicians-by-gender.

Political Choices

Global Warming Hot Potato

Since the turn of the 21st century, debate over climate change has been a fixture of American politics. Scientists and economists have been drawn into this debate to provide their expert opinions on the factual questions involved. The consensus of scientists is clear. An October 2018 report on global warming conducted by the Intergovernmental Panel on Climate Change predicted that if current trends continue the earth will warm by 2.7 degrees Fahrenheit over pre-industrial levels, sinking coastlines and causing widespread drought and coral reef die-offs.[1]

The economics of the issue are less clear. Although the changing climate and worldwide consequences are stark negative externalities of burning fossil fuels, the practical applications of policy are far more complicated. The 2018 Nobel Memorial Prize in Economics, awarded to Yale's William Nordhaus, recognized the contribution that economists can have in addressing the complexities of climate change.

©tdelcastillo photo/Moment/Getty Images

Two economic solutions to counter the externalities associated with carbon emissions have been widely debated. The first is a carbon tax levied on businesses, which provides an incentive to reduce emissions. The second approach is a "cap-and-trade" policy that grants businesses the right to emit a certain amount of carbon and then allows them to buy or sell those allowances as needed. Both policies would reduce the total quantity of pollution by raising the price of burning carbon-based fuels.

However, both cap-and-trade and carbon tax legislation has died in U.S. Congress. Why? It is possible for reasonable and informed people to disagree about the merits of a carbon tax versus a cap-and-trade policy, and the necessity of either. But the failure of the proposals appeared to have little to do with science and a lot to do with old-fashioned politics.

Most economists, regardless of political philosophy, believe that a carbon tax is a simpler and more transparent and efficient solution than cap-and-trade. But many policy-makers viewed backing any sort of "tax" as political suicide. Some policy-makers and electric companies instead favored a cap-and-trade proposal that granted companies some free carbon allowances. In the end, however, politicians rejected even the cap-and-trade proposal, worried that the resulting increase in consumer heating and gas prices would anger voters.[2]

In the previous few chapters, we've seen how government action can correct market failures and increase total surplus. The fight over a carbon tax versus cap-and-trade is just one illustration of how difficult it can be to translate economic theory into government action. Students of economics, therefore, have an interest in understanding how policy is formed through the political process. Economics is, after all, the study of how resources are managed, and governments play a major role in resource allocation.

The most basic economic model for understanding electoral politics starts from standard assumptions of economics—that people are rational and fully informed. The model assumes that voters have preferences regarding policy, have full information about candidates, and vote for the one whose policy platform most nearly resembles their preferences. Once those candidates are in office, the expectation is that they will simply implement the platforms on which they were elected. In this way, rational voters directly determine the shape of public policy.

You may have noticed, however, that the real world is much more complicated. Voters are not necessarily well informed, politicians often pursue their own interests rather than those of voters, and small groups with large stakes in a policy proposal (such as electric companies in the case of a carbon tax) can have a big influence on the outcome.

LEARNING OBJECTIVES

LO 22.1 Explain the predictions and assumptions of the median-voter theorem.

LO 22.2 List the characteristics of an "ideal" voting system, and identify which criteria are met by real systems.

LO 22.3 Discuss problems with the idea of the "rational voter," and define the idea of rational ignorance.

LO 22.4 Explain the persistence of policies that provide concentrated benefits to a few while imposing diffuse costs on the majority.

LO 22.5 Explain why corruption and rent-seeking can persist in a democratic system.

LO 22.6 List three major features of political structure, and identify how they can affect policy choices.

To help account for these real-world observations, in this chapter we'll build an economic model of political choices. We'll talk about why it's not so simple to arrive at policy conclusions by just adding up the votes. We'll question the assumptions that voters are rational and informed and that they vote according to their preferences. We'll look at post-election policy choices and talk about why voter preferences won't necessarily translate directly into policy. Finally, we'll see how political structure affects policy outcomes; we will zoom in on some specific features of the U.S. political structure that affect the national economy.

Our goal here isn't to take a stand, but rather to provide you with the tools to understand how politics and voting work locally, nationally, and even for international issues like climate change.

The Economics of Elections

To start, imagine that the typical voter has clear opinions on a broad range of policy issues and knows the positions held by every candidate in every election. To assess the realism of this assumption, take a quick quiz: Do you know your senators' and representative's positions on the death penalty or foreign policy? Very few of us, sometimes including politicians themselves, can actually answer questions like these with confidence.

Even if these assumptions held true, how do you think that elections would play out? We'll start by thinking about a simplified model, and then get more realistic in two important ways.

Stick to the middle: Median-voter theorem

Does it ever seem to you that political candidates in the United States stake out extreme positions in primary debates but start to shift their rhetoric toward the "middle" before the general election? If so, a basic theory of political decision making in economics can help explain why.

Imagine a one-dimensional policy question, such as how much money to spend on the military. Now, suppose that all voters have a preference along this one dimension (more spending or less spending on the military). Each person will vote for the politician whose policy platform is closer to his or her own preferences. To simplify the math, let's also imagine there are only seven voters. (You can think of each of the seven as representing one-seventh of all the real voters.) In this simple model, how should two candidates running for election choose their policy positions?

Suppose the two candidates start by saying what they really think. One candidate, Mr. Dove, advocates relatively low military spending. As shown in panel A of Figure 22-1, his position falls between the beliefs of the third and fourth voters. The other candidate, Ms. Hawk, favors very high military spending. Her position falls at the other end of the scale. The result? Ms. Hawk will get only two of the seven votes; the other five voters are closer to Mr. Dove's position.

LO 22.1 Explain the predictions and assumptions of the median-voter theorem.

FIGURE 22-1

Candidates win by catering to the median voter

(A) An extreme position loses the election: Seven voters are ranked on a one-dimensional scale. Each voter votes for the candidate who is closest to his own preferences. Opinion polls show that, by taking an extreme position, Ms. Hawk is set to attract the votes of only two out of seven voters.

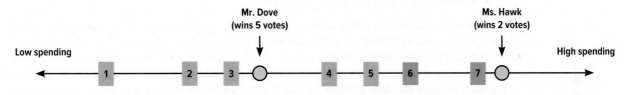

(B) Moving to the center wins more votes: Ms. Hawk looks at the polls and decides to moderate her position. New opinion polls show she will now win the election with four votes, against three for Mr. Dove.

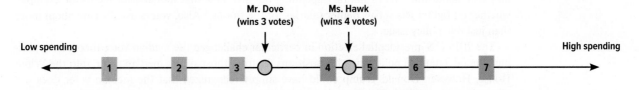

(C) Candidates end up catering to the median voter: Mr. Dove now looks at the opinion polls and decides to moderate his position, too. By moving closer to the median voter, he now wins 4-3. This process of moderating positions continues until both candidates are advocating the position held by the median voter.

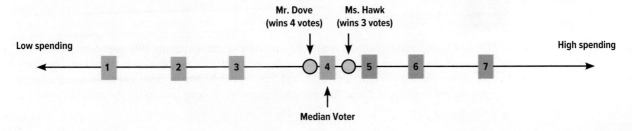

Now suppose you are employed by Ms. Hawk's campaign. What would you advise? If she moves her position toward the center (in other words, toward lower proposed military spending), she can grab voters #4 and #5 from Mr. Dove and win the election, as panel B shows.

How can Mr. Dove *respond* to this strategy to regain the lead? He can also move toward the center, recapturing the vote of voter #4, as shown in panel C.

If we take this electoral game to its logical conclusion, the only way for either candidate to maximize votes is to take the exact same position as voter #4—the median, or middle, voter. If either candidate moves away from this position, he or she loses the middle voter and thus loses the election. So, regardless of what they really think, if the candidates want to maximize their chances of winning, we would expect both candidates to end up advocating the *exact same position.*

median-voter theorem
a model stating that under certain conditions, politicians maximize their votes by taking the policy position preferred by the median voter

This simple model is called the **median-voter theorem**. It suggests that politicians maximize their votes by taking the policy position preferred by the median voter, under certain conditions. The conditions are:

- There is a single, one-dimensional policy question (such as more or less spending).
- Voters always vote for the candidate whose position is closest to their own.
- There are only two candidates.
- A candidate wins by majority vote.

Note that under this model, the chosen policy will be the one preferred by the *median* voter, rather than the average voter or the largest number of voters. We can imagine a situation, for instance, in which

- Three voters want zero spending on the military.
- Three voters want to spend 50 percent of the budget.
- Only one voter wants to spend 20 percent.

Median-voter theorem says that military spending will end up being 20 percent of the budget (which is the middle ground), even though only one voter actually preferred that solution.

The median-voter theorem also casts light on why we often see presidential candidates change their positions over the course of a campaign. They may advocate relatively extreme positions during party primary elections because the goal is to appeal to the median *of voters in their own party.* In the general election, they want to appeal to the median *of all voters,* so they adopt positions closer to the center.

Of course, real elections aren't this simple. Many policy issues are not one-dimensional. (You may care about the level of military spending but also how that money gets spent—for example, whether on fighter jets versus higher salaries for the troops.) Also, voters usually care about more than just one policy issue.

The 2016 U.S. presidential election in particular challenged the median voter theorem by placing Donald Trump, a politician with positions far from those of the median voter, into the White House. However, Donald Trump could have simply recognized that the median voter does not neatly fit in the middle. The Economics in Action box "The rise of Donald Trump" looks at the median voter theorem and the political rise of a unique politician.

The rise of Donald Trump
Economics in Action

Donald Trump accomplished a series of astonishing upsets during the 2016 presidential election campaign. In the Republican primary, he bested numerous establishment candidates, including former Florida Governor Jeb Bush and Senator Marco Rubio. Both had name recognition, government experience, strong funding, and conservative voting records. In the general election,

Trump then beat Democratic candidate Hillary Clinton, who had extensive political experience (including time as First Lady, U.S. Senator, and Secretary of State), a centrist platform, and deep establishment support.

How did Trumpism become the identity of Republican Party politics and bring a unique candidate into the presidency? Many believe that Donald Trump's unique blend of conservative policy and unconventional style built a lot of his support.

In 2016, voters were not looking for an established politician. Before the 2016 election, only 19 percent of Americans reported trusting the government most or all of the time, and only 9 percent of Americans said they trusted Congress. Trump's status as businessman and Washington outsider, and his calls to "drain the swamp" (meaning the corruption in Washington, DC), resonated with many of these voters. So did Trump's "tell it like it is" style.

Trump's policy started with the economy. In one exit poll, 90 percent of Republican voters cited the economy as a very important issue in the 2016 election. Although by 2016 many economic metrics had improved since the "Great Recession" of 2007–2009, the recovery hadn't reached everyone. Rural areas were hit hard by unemployment caused by globalization and the shift to a more service-driven economy. Wages had not risen for many workers, and the labor force participation rate (the measure of how many people able to work are actively employed or looking) had yet to recover.

During his campaign, Donald Trump promised to reduce the number of undocumented immigrants in the country. At the same time, he bucked Republican support of free trade agreements, promising to tear up and renegotiate NAFTA (the trade deal between the U.S., Canada, and Mexico) if he became president.

Median voter theory says that it's smart for politicians to take positions in the center of the ideological spectrum, thus appealing to the most voters. But Trump's positions were decidedly on the right of the spectrum, not close to the median voter in the United States. If the theory was correct, Trump would have surely lost the election to Hillary Clinton. So, how did he win?

The basic theory ignores an important truth that Trump understood well: You also need to energize your supporters and make sure they get out to vote for you. Trump took the political gamble that it can be better to take more extreme political positions, moving away from the center, but to build a base of voters who are really excited about your candidacy and who will be motivated to vote in large numbers.

The Pew Research Center found that over the past two decades, politically engaged voters of both parties have pulled away from the center. Donald Trump correctly sensed that shift and took advantage of it. If politicians follow Trump's strategy, expect to see more extreme positions taken by politicians of both the left and right.

Sources: Chris Cilliza, "The 13 Most Amazing Findings of the 2016 Exit Poll," *The Washington Post,* November 10, 2016, www.washingtonpost.com/news/the-fix/wp/2016/11/10/the-13-most-amazing-things-in-the-2016-exit-poll/?utm_term=.3e9803b58564; Pew Research Center, "The Partisan Divide on Political Values Grows Even Wider," October 5, 2017, www.people-press.org/2017/10/05/the-partisan-divide-on-political-values-grows-even-wider/; Mark Schmitt, "Trump Did Not Break Politics," *The New York Times,* January 6, 2016, www.nytimes.com/2016/01/04/opinion/campaign-stops/trump-did-not-break-politics.html; Jane C. Timm, "The 141 Stances Donald Trump Took During His White House Bid," *NBC News,* November 18, 2016, www.nbcnews.com/politics/2016-election/full-list-donald-trump-s-rapidly-changing-policy-positions-n547801.

The elusive perfect voting system

Now, let's get more realistic. What happens if voters care about more than one policy (say, military policy *and* the budget deficit), or if they have more than two candidates to consider? Once voting becomes more complicated, the way in which votes are cast becomes important.

How do we take the preferences of all voters and add them up in a fair and consistent way, so that the opinion held by the most voters carries the day? Imagine that voters were directly voting

LO 22.2 List the characteristics of an "ideal" voting system, and identify which criteria are met by real systems.

on the issues, rather than for a candidate. In his book *Social Choice and Individual Values*, economist Kenneth Arrow proposed four criteria for an "ideal" voting system:

1. **Unanimity.** If everyone in the group prefers option X to option Y, then X beats Y. In other words, if every voter would rather spend more on education than on national parks, then the ideal voting system would be structured so that education spending wins.

2. **No dictator.** There is no person who has the power to single-handedly enact his or her own preferences. A voting system would not be ideal if someone has the power to put all funds into national parks, even if most would rather spend the money on schools.

3. **Transitivity.** If option X beats Y, and Y beats Z, then transitivity says that X also beats Z. In other words, if voters would rather spend on schools than parks, and they would rather spend on parks than alternative energy, then any voting system that could result in alternative energy winning out over schools would not be considered ideal.

4. **Independence of irrelevant alternatives.** If a group is voting on option X versus option Y, this decision should not depend on any information or preference about another unconnected option, Z. In other words, whether or not spending on alternative energy also happens to be an option shouldn't affect whether voters prefer spending on schools versus parks.

These all sound reasonable enough. You might think it should be straightforward enough to create a voting system that meets these four criteria. To see why it isn't, let's look at how a couple of existing voting systems measure up.

First-past-the-post   In most elections in the United States (and in many other countries), the voting system is simple:

- All candidates go up against each other at once.
- Each voter can choose one and only one candidate.
- The candidate who receives the most votes wins.

This voting system is often referred to as *first-past-the-post*, or *plurality voting*.

First-past-the-post has merits, notably simplicity. Voters have to think about only one thing—which candidate is their favorite—and then check the box next to that candidate's name.

But plurality voting is not an ideal system: It fails the "independence of irrelevant alternatives" criterion, also known as the "third-party problem." In most national elections in the United States, the major candidates represent the two major parties: the Republican Party and the Democratic Party. Every once in a while, which of them wins depends on whether an additional candidate from a minor "third party" is also on the ballot.

Consider the 2000 presidential election between Governor George W. Bush and Vice President Al Gore. Consumer advocate Ralph Nader also ran, as the candidate of the Green Party. In total, Nader received less than 3 percent of the vote, yet many commentators believe Nader's presence on the ballot swung the election for Bush over Gore in a tight race, especially in the pivotal state of Florida. In the end, the state of Florida was decided by only 537 votes, while about 97,000 people voted for Nader.

The election hinged on the workings of the Electoral College system, and Florida was the deciding state in that election: Whoever won the popular vote in Florida won the presidency. Panel A of Figure 22-2 shows a theoretical distribution of voters' preferences between the two major-party candidates in Florida. If the choice is between only these two, our theoretical figures show that Gore will win Florida and the election 51 percent to 49 percent.

What happens when we add Nader into the mix, in panel B? Notice that Nader's presence doesn't change any voters' preferences between Bush and Gore. Any Floridian who wants Bush over Gore or vice versa still feels the same way. But because in this example the 3 percent of voters who now vote for Nader would have favored Gore, the effect is that Gore's share drops to 48 percent, and Bush now wins Florida, and the election, by 49 percent to 48 percent. The addition

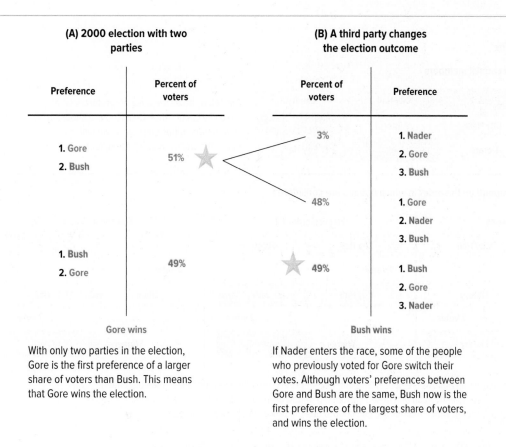

FIGURE 22-2

The third-party-candidate problem

With only two parties in the election, Gore is the first preference of a larger share of voters than Bush. This means that Gore wins the election.

If Nader enters the race, some of the people who previously voted for Gore switch their votes. Although voters' preferences between Gore and Bush are the same, Bush now is the first preference of the largest share of voters, and wins the election.

of an "irrelevant alternative"—Nader—flips the outcome of the election. Plurality voting fails one of the ideal voting-system criteria.

Condorcet paradox   How might we avoid the third-party problem? One possible answer could be to use a system called *pair-wise majority voting*. It gets its name because options are taken in pairs, and the majority vote wins. When all options have been put to a "head-to-head" match between a pair of opponents, you might expect the most popular option to win. Likewise, we might expect the best tennis player to win a tournament consisting of a series of head-to-head matches.

To see how this might work, imagine that in the 2000 election, voters had first been asked to choose between Bush and Nader. It turns out that more voters would prefer Bush to be president, so Bush wins round one. He then goes on to face Gore in round two. More voters prefer Gore, so Gore becomes president. This result holds true regardless of the order of the vote. Gore would defeat both Bush and Nader in any round in which they were pitted against each other.

However, it turns out that this system fails another of our criteria—transitivity. To see why, imagine a city council with three members, voting on how to spend the city's construction budget for public buildings. The council has three choices: a new jail, a new city hall, or a new library. Each council member has his or her own order of preference, as shown in panel A of Figure 22-3.

If the council members take a simple vote, the result is a three-way tie. Suppose that they instead decide to use pair-wise majority voting to narrow their choices:

- They decide to vote first on the jail versus the city hall. As shown in panel B of Figure 22-3, under the first election order, the jail wins this matchup, with two votes to one for the city hall.
- As the winner of the first round, the jail goes up against the library and loses, with one vote for the jail versus two for the library.

FIGURE 22-3
Condorcet voting paradox

(A) Preferences of 3 city council members

This table shows the ordered preferences of three city council members who are choosing among three different projects on which to spend the city's construction budget.

Member 1:	Jail	>	City Hall	> Library
Member 2:	City Hall	>	Library	> Jail
Member 3:	Library	>	Jail	> City Hall

(B) Election outcomes depend on the order in which options are considered

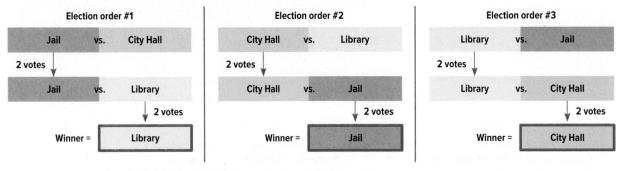

When pairs of the three construction options are considered in different orders, the ultimate outcome of the vote changes. This chart shows that any of the three buildings can be chosen depending on the order of votes. As a result, the person who "sets the agenda" by choosing the order in which options are considered has the power to affect the outcome.

Therefore, the council decides to build the library. Tie broken, right?

Not so fast. What if the council changes the order in which they vote on each pair? Let's look at panel B again, this time with the second election order presented. Suppose they vote first on the city hall versus the library, and then the library versus the jail. In this case:

- The city hall beats the library in the first round.
- The jail beats the city hall in the second round.

In this second election order, the jail ends up as the overall winner.

Furthermore, we can look at the third election order. In this case:

- If the council starts with the library versus the jail, the library wins.
- If it then votes on the library versus city hall, the city hall wins.

In other words, it's possible for *any* of the three building plans to be chosen, depending on the order in which they vote on the pairs. Even though each individual's preferences are transitive, this method of aggregating the group's preferences is not transitive. (Remember that transitivity means that if an option X is preferred to another option Y, and Y to a third option Z, then X must be preferred to Z.) This is called the **Condorcet paradox**.

Condorcet paradox
a situation in which the preferences of each individual member of a group are transitive, but the collective preferences of the group are not

When voting systems fall short of the ideal by violating the principle of transitivity, the power to set the agenda is sometimes crucial in shaping the final outcomes. The person who decides on the order in which issues are brought to a vote for the city council, for example, wields considerable power.

Arrow's impossibility theorem   We've looked at two ways of holding elections. There are many more possible systems, devised over the years by political scientists, social scientists, and economists. Here are several, for example:

- Variations on first-past-the-post, such as holding a runoff election between the top two candidates at a later date if neither receives 50 percent of the initial vote. A few states and cities currently use these runoffs to decide the winner of party-only primary elections.

- "Instant-runoff" systems, in which voters rank all of the candidates by *order* of preference rather than casting a vote for their single most preferred candidate. If no candidate receives a majority of the vote in the initial count, election officials use these preferences to reallocate the votes for less popular candidates to the frontrunners until one candidate gains a majority.

- The Borda count, commonly used to rank sports teams in national polls. For example, in the college football AP Poll, voters rank teams 1-25. The top team gets 25 points, the next 24, and so on. The "votes" for each team get added up to build the rankings.

Recognizing some of the challenges of a first-past-the-post voting system, the voters of Maine decided to try ranked-choice or "instant-runoff" voting in statewide elections starting in 2018. In one congressional race in particular, the new system came under close scrutiny, as the leader on election night ended up losing the election when all votes were reallocated. Read the Economics in Action box "Ranked-choice takes the Golden ticket to Washington" for more about this unique election.

Ranked-choice takes the Golden ticket to Washington
Economics in Action

As election night 2018 ended, over 30 races for the U.S. House of Representatives were too close to call. In one of those, with all votes counted, the race for Maine's 2nd Congressional District, the incumbent Republican Bruce Poliquin held a narrow 2,632 vote lead over the Democratic challenger Jared Golden. In most other elections, that vote margin would be enough to win. But this was not an ordinary election. In July 2018 Maine voters approved a switch to "ranked-choice voting" from the traditional system in which the candidate with the most votes wins. This change meant that on the November 2018 ballot in Maine, all voters were asked to vote for their first choice *and their second choice* in the elections.

Counting the first votes gave the following results:

- Bruce Poliquin (Republican): 46.1 percent
- Jared Golden (Democrat): 45.9 percent
- Tiffany Bond (Independent): 5.7 percent
- Will Hoar (Independent): 2.4 percent

Since Poliquin did not win more than 50 percent of the votes, second-choice votes came into play. First, election officials looked at second-choice preferences of voters who chose fourth-place candidate Will Hoar and reassigned those votes to the remaining three candidates in the race. Even then, no candidate topped 50 percent.

Next, the 5.7 percent of the votes won by third-place candidate Tiffany Bond was also split according to second-choice preferences. This time, Jared Golden just crossed the finish line, with 50.5 percent of the vote to Poliquin's 49.5 percent. Nine days after the election, the Maine Supervisor of Elections confirmed Jared Golden as the winner of the election for Maine's 2nd Congressional District.

The ranked-choice system meant that voters supporting independent candidates Bond and Hoar didn't "waste" their votes on someone who wasn't likely to win; their second-choice preferences still counted. And Bond and Hoar could run without worrying that they would be cast as

(continued)

spoilers (candidates whose presence on the ballot tips outcomes, even though they're not predicted to come close to winning).

In Maine, a state notorious for its independent streak, ranked-choice voting gives voters a way to register their broad preferences, something particularly valuable for voters who are not crazy about the Republican or Democratic options.

Ranked-choice voting was a win for Democrats, who gained an extra seat in the U.S. House of Representatives, and for independents, who got a chance to register their preferences in an election. Yet some people are not fans of the new system. Bruce Poliquin, the election night winner, filed a lawsuit to restore the original results (and head back to Washington, DC). However, thanks to ranked-choice voting, we know that outcome would not be the preference of most voters in his district.

Source: Kate Taylor and Liam Stack, "Maine's Bruce Poliquin, Lone Republican in House from New England, Loses Re-election," *New York Times,* November 15, 2018, www.nytimes.com/2018/11/15/us/politics/poliquin-maine-loses.html.

Arrow's impossibility theorem
a theorem showing that no voting system can aggregate the preferences of voters over three or more options while satisfying the criteria of an ideal voting system

In *Social Choice and Individual Values*, economist Kenneth Arrow proved that no voting system can aggregate the preferences of voters (assuming they are choosing among three or more options) while meeting all four of the criteria for an "ideal" voting system. This idea is called **Arrow's impossibility theorem**. Although the proof of Arrow's theorem is well beyond the scope of this text, his takeaway message is worth remembering: No voting process is perfect, but some are better than others. Arrow's impossibility theorem helps us understand the trade-offs we face between different voting systems.

Political participation and the myth of the "rational voter"

So far, we've assumed that voters are rational and fully informed. What if they're not?

LO 22.3 Discuss problems with the idea of the "rational voter," and define the idea of rational ignorance.

Politicians do not behave as if they believe most voters are influenced only by policy issues. Instead, politicians often use tactics that have little to do with policy positions—handshaking, baby-kissing, mudslinging, eating food at state fairs, and so on. Research demonstrates that elections can be swayed by factors *other than the rational policy considerations* of well-informed voters.

rational ignorance
choosing to remain ignorant when the opportunity costs of gathering information outweigh the benefits

Let's not be too hard on voters for not being fully informed. After all, it takes time to learn about the issues and the candidates, and that time could be spent doing something else. The trade-off may simply not be worth it. Economists call this idea **rational ignorance**. It means choosing to remain ignorant when the opportunity costs of gathering information outweigh the benefits. We saw in Chapter 19, "Public Goods and Common Resources," that what is individually rational is not necessarily *socially optimal*. If we think of good governance as a public good created by well-informed voters, we can predict that it will be undersupplied.

Even voting *itself* is not costless. The time you spend getting to a polling place, waiting in line, and marking your ballot (or marking your mail-in ballot and mailing it) could be spent on other things. What are the benefits of voting that outweigh these opportunity costs? The most obvious answer is to influence the outcome of the election and have your preferences represented in government.

However, the odds of one vote actually making the difference in any given election are extremely low. In all of the U.S. congressional elections in the past 100 years, only one has been decided by one vote. In over 40,000 elections for state legislators, with 1 billion votes cast, only seven have been decided by a single vote. In the end, only 1 out of 100,000 votes cast in U.S. elections was pivotal in changing the outcome of an election.[3] In other words, your vote has a 99.999 percent chance of being pointless. Would a rational person find a better use for his or her time?

Research has shown that voters are, indeed, more likely to turn out in elections with small electorates and when the election is likely to be very competitive. These results suggest that the likelihood of casting a pivotal vote may influence the choice to vote. However, by looking at voting only in terms of time costs and likelihood of casting the pivotal ballot, we may be missing the point. Perhaps voters gain "expressive benefits" from voting. In other words, they get utility from participating in a civic event, regardless of whether their votes are likely to be decisive. Alternatively, voters may altruistically decide to contribute to the democratic process by voting, even when it is not personally beneficial to do so.

Another theory suggests that people may vote partly in response to social pressure to "do their duty" as citizens. For example, when Switzerland—which has famously high levels of voting—started allowing people to mail in their ballots rather than go to a polling place, voting decreased in small towns. On the face of it, this is a baffling result. Mail-in ballots, after all, represent a significant reduction in the time costs associated with voting. One explanation is that people in small Swiss communities went out to vote because they wanted to be seen carrying out their civic duty. Once voting wasn't visible to the rest of the community, people had less incentive to do it at all.[4] The social benefit of voting may be the idea behind the "I voted" stickers that many polling places hand out.

Returning to the idea of rational ignorance, although many voters talk about policy issues when deciding who to vote for, the decision may be about how the politician makes them feel, rather than, say, the specific nuts and bolts of an education plan. See the Economics in Action box "Face value—May the best-looking politician win" for more about these factors.

Face value—May the best-looking politician win
Economics in Action

The opening debate of the 1960 election was the first presidential debate ever to be aired on television. Before then, debates had been broadcast only on radio. One of the candidates, Senator John F. Kennedy, understood the difference. He arrived looking tanned, fresh, and well rested. His opponent, Vice President Richard Nixon, did not.

Nixon was out campaigning until just hours before the debate. He arrived tired and unshaven, refused the attention of make-up artists, and went on the air looking pale and sweaty and sporting a five o'clock shadow. Supposedly, his own mother called him after the debate to ask if he was sick.

This dramatic difference in appearance had a remarkable influence on voters: Those who had watched the debate on television overwhelmingly reported that Kennedy had won the debate. Those who listened on the radio—and therefore only heard the candidates but didn't see them—thought Nixon carried the day. The television opinion won out, and shortly after the debates, John F. Kennedy pulled ahead in polling and eventually won the election.

If voters were rational and based their voting decisions purely on the policy statements of the candidates, these results would be hard to explain. No one seriously thought that Nixon was too sick to function as president. Nor is a tan usually considered to be a meaningful indicator of political ability. But looks are an important part of electoral politics.

This finding has been backed up by formal studies around the world. In a study of Australian elections, attractive candidates consistently did about 1.5 to 2 percent better in the vote than plainer-looking competitors. Studies of Finnish national elections and German state-level elections found similar results.

(continued)

Why does physical appearance influence voters? One explanation is the *halo effect*. The halo effect is a psychological bias in which the perception of one trait in a person is influenced by the perception of their other traits. This means, for instance, that voters might assume that more-attractive candidates are also more intelligent or more competent.

Research has found appearance to be more influential in "low information" elections, in which voters know little about the candidates. The halo effect fades as voters gain more substantive information about the people they are evaluating.

Appearance can influence voters' opinions of candidates, as it did in the 1960 Kennedy-Nixon debate.
©*AP Images*

Sources: http://people.anu.edu.au/andrew.leigh/pdf/BeautifulPoliticians.pdf; http://courses.washington.edu/pbaf-hall/514/514%20Readings/todorov%20science.pdf; http://www.ifo.de/portal/page/portal/DocBase_Content/WP/WP-CESifo_Working_Papers/wp-cesifo-2007/wp-cesifo-2007-05/cesifo1_wp2002.pdf.

✓ **TEST YOURSELF**

☐ Can the median-voter theorem be applied to multidimensional policy questions? **[LO 22.1]**

☐ What does it mean for a voting system to satisfy the independence of irrelevant alternatives? **[LO 22.2]**

☐ Why might it be rational for voters to remain uninformed? **[LO 22.3]**

The Economics of Policy-Making

Now that we've looked at who gets elected, we'll turn to how policies get made. In this section we'll see why a minority of voters who feel strongly about an issue can often win out over a larger group with a different opinion. We'll also look at how the interests and incentives of policy-makers help predict their behavior.

Diffuse costs, concentrated benefits

LO 22.4 Explain the persistence of policies that provide concentrated benefits to a few while imposing diffuse costs on the majority.

In Chapter 19, "Public Goods and Common Resources," we saw that markets won't necessarily allocate public goods (like national parks and police protection) efficiently. The problem is that people are often reluctant to voluntarily pay for goods and services that provide benefits for everyone, including those who don't pay. This is the "free-rider" problem, and it happens when people think, "Why pay if I don't have to?" If enough people think like that, valuable goods and services are undersupplied because everyone hopes that someone else will pay for them.

The same idea can apply to political advocacy and engagement. Inefficiencies can happen when people think, "Why get personally involved if I can spare myself the hassle but still benefit from the solutions that others create?" The problem is that the best ideas might not win out if lots of people fail to lend their support.

We refer to situations in which individuals need to act collectively to reach solutions that will make everyone better off as **collective-action problems**. In these situations, a group of people stand to gain from an action that is not rational for any of the members to undertake individually.

However, engaging in collective action has costs. It takes time and money to organize a group or a campaign and to get the attention of lots of busy people. As a rule, the larger the group that needs to be organized, the more difficult and costly it is to coordinate successful collective action. Even if the total benefit to coordinating is big, each individual member may stand to gain only a small amount.

Combining these two ideas, we find that organizing larger groups often involves higher costs and lower benefits per person. The likelihood of successful collective action can therefore be lower for large groups. This leads to an interesting prediction: If two groups disagree about a policy, a smaller group that experiences higher benefits per person can be the one more likely to get its way.

collective-action problem
a situation in which a group of people stands to gain from an action that it is not rational for any of the members to undertake individually

Imagine, for instance, there is a national park where private companies run tour buses. Many people who visit the park find the tour buses to be disruptive and also harmful to the wildlife. Some organize a campaign to tighten regulations on tours in the park. Alarmed by this proposal, the tour-bus companies work together to contest the proposed new regulations. Whichever group is more effective in organizing and influencing the opinion of park management will get its way.

We can imagine that there are only a few owners of tour-bus companies. It will be easy for them to coordinate. We can also imagine that each one gains a lot from unrestricted use of the park. Thus, all of the tour-bus owners will be willing to devote a lot of resources to fighting the proposals.

When the costs of collective action—such as keeping buses out of national parks—are diffuse and the benefits per person are relatively low, collective action is less likely to succeed.
©Santiparp Wattanaporn/ Shutterstock

What about the organizing efforts of the park visitors? Even if restricting bus use would deliver higher *total* benefits to the many people who visit the park occasionally, those benefits are much lower *per person*. The park visitors may be willing to sign a petition or write an e-mail, but most will not feel strongly enough to fight as determinedly as the tour-bus operators.

There are collective-action differences:

- The benefits of pro-bus policy are *concentrated* for tour-bus company owners.
- The costs of anti-bus policy are *diffuse* for private park users.

From this difference, we can predict that the tour-bus owners will care more and will likely get their way.

The theory that groups with concentrated benefits tend to win out in policy battles over those with diffuse costs has many applications. Economists use it to explain the persistence of policies that don't appear to be in the interest of the majority of voters. For instance, observers are sometimes puzzled by the staying power of large farm subsidies and trade protections for agricultural goods. These policies push up the costs of food and taxes for the majority of voters. Why don't voters elect officials who will end these policies?

One theory is that the typical voter experiences only small costs—a few extra cents in the price of milk and sugar, a few dollars in taxes. At the same time, a small number of commercial farms and agricultural businesses experience high benefits. The members of the small group find it easier and individually worthwhile to organize themselves for lobbying and public relations efforts to capture those large benefits. Organizing a whole nation of voters for a comparable effort to fight the small increase in the price of groceries would be extremely difficult.

Corruption and rent-seeking

An economic analysis of politics needs to account for the fact that policy-makers have their own interests, biases, and priorities. In other words, they have their own *wants and constraints*. Of course, we would like to think that all policy-makers *want* to do what their best judgment tells them is in the public good. But some may, instead, *want* to promote their own personal gain or that of their friends and family. In such cases, they will be constrained only by the capacity of their opponents and of watchdog organizations to find out what they are doing and make voters care about it. At its extreme, the use of the powers of government by public officials to achieve personal gains is *corruption*.

rent-seeking
the act of pursuing privileges that increase the surplus of a person or group without increasing total surplus

More generally, government can create waste and inefficiency by contributing to **rent-seeking**. Rent-seeking is the act of pursuing privileges that increase the surplus of a person or group without increasing total surplus. Often, this activity involves lobbying by groups that receive exclusive benefits or contracts to keep others from getting access. On the flip side, it can involve lobbying by those who don't yet have access to such benefits but want to have it.

Some lobbying shapes trade regulations—say, domestic-steel producers trying to keep imports out. Others shape licensing policy—for instance, protecting doctors who want to strictly limit who gets to call themselves a doctor. Big campaign contributions usually come alongside the lobbying efforts, all in an attempt to get extra clout for groups that benefit from particular regulations and licenses. Such rent-seeking and lobbying are perfectly legal, but can be wasteful.

Why doesn't the process of electing officials prevent rent-seeking and corruption? If politicians start making policies that hurt their constituents or promote themselves at constituents' expense, why don't they get kicked out of office by angry voters in the next election? Why don't corrupt bureaucrats always get fired? The reality is that it is costly to acquire information about what public officials are and should be doing. What voter has time to study public expenditures looking for corrupt behavior? How many voters care enough to analyze whether a particular firm wins a government contract because it is the most qualified or because it is owned by the mayor's buddy?

Of course, political opponents have every incentive to dig up dirt on incumbents before an election and to inform voters about anything bad they find. But such revelations can get lost in the noise of campaigning. Also, voters might not be sure that the opponents will end up being more trustworthy than the incumbents.

The news media—blogs, television, radio, newspapers—can play an important role in uncovering corruption. But even in a relatively free society, the media may face mixed incentives: Reporters rely to some extent on public officials' willingness to give them information about what's happening in government. If reporters blow the whistle on minor offenses, they may suddenly find that their sources are no longer so friendly.

Bureaucratic capture is a specific avenue through which corruption and rent-seeking can occur. This involves filling government positions with people who have close ties to the group they are supposed to regulate. Of course, there are sensible reasons for appointing people with practical experience in a certain area of policy. But having close ties between regulators and those they are regulating can introduce biases or personal sympathies. In the aftermath of the 2008 financial crisis, for instance, some accused the SEC of failing to enforce capital market regulations that might have mitigated the crisis. They say this was because the SEC was staffed by people with close ties to the financial industry.

Corruption goes one step further than the types of rent-seeking described above. Since it is illegal, corruption is by nature hidden. As a result, it can be difficult to find out how much of it really goes on. It also can be difficult to determine what methods are most effective at reducing it. This is why attempts to reform government actions believed to be corrupt center on *transparency*. The more the public knows about the actions of government, the theory goes, the more they will be able to see and oust corrupt actions and politicians.

The system matters: How political structure affects outcomes

During the eighteenth century, the Polish legislature used the *liberum veto* (Latin for "I freely forbid"). At any time, a member of parliament had the right to shout *Nie pozwala!* ("I do not allow"). This move forced an end to the current session and voided any legislation that had been passed. The intent was to make sure that there was complete consensus about new laws.[5]

As you might expect, the system often led to chaos. Eventually, foreign powers took advantage of this system and bribed Polish legislators to oppose unwanted legislation with a cry of *Nie pozwala*, grinding the Polish political system to a halt. Not surprisingly, the *liberum veto* went out of fashion. Still, the lesson remains relevant: The rules of the game can have a big effect on outcomes.

There are too many aspects of political structure to discuss all of them here. (We'll leave that to political science professors.) There are, though, three worth singling out: the *number of political parties*, *term limits*, and *increasing the right to vote*. These three have a particularly big impact on how voters' preferences are translated into policy choices.

Number of political parties The first is the number of viable political parties. Few countries—with the exception of single-party dictatorships—have explicit requirements about the number of parties. In general, first-past-the-post voting, like that used in the United States, leads to a two-party system. Since candidates have to obtain a plurality of votes to win an election, a third party could consistently win 20 percent of the votes and still win zero elections. As a result, if smaller parties want to have a say in policy-making, they have an incentive to consolidate with larger ones. Doing so will increase their chance of gaining enough vote share to win elections and have a say in policy-making.

In contrast, many countries use a *proportional-representation* system. In such systems, a party that receives 20 percent of the votes nationwide will receive about 20 percent of the seats in the legislature. Under such a system, small parties can carve out niches. From these, they are able to influence policy-making by forming coalitions with others after being elected.

Compared to proportional-representation systems, two-party systems are thought to lead to more centrist politics. (Remember the median-voter theorem.) In addition, since both parties have to represent large portions of the population, they sometimes lead to unwieldy combinations of policies within one platform. For instance, supporters of less government spending often vote Republican. But these voters may have a wide range of opinions about social issues. As a result, people with different policy preferences may have to make compromises when voting. If, for instance, you support both low taxes and abortion rights, you might have to decide which of those issues is more important to you when choosing which party will get your vote.

Proportional-representation systems, on the other hand, are thought to bring more diverse views into the policy process and offer a wider variety of platforms among which voters can choose. One criticism of this system, however, is that small extremist parties can wield disproportionate power. When a big party doesn't get an outright majority, it has to ask small parties to join with it in a governing coalition in order to form a majority. In bargaining for political support, the smaller party will often insist that some of its policies be enacted, even if those policies don't represent the preferences of most people.

Term limits A second feature of political structure that's worth mentioning is *term limits*. Term limits prevent officials from holding office for longer than a certain amount of time. For instance, U.S. presidents can't be elected to office more than twice or hold office for more than 10 years. These laws are typically thought to discourage corruption by ensuring that one person isn't allowed to hold onto power for too long. At the same time, term limits would allow politicians to "do the right thing" in their last term without fear of retribution at the ballot box.

However, some have speculated that the opposite might be true under certain circumstances. Politicians who know they will be out of office at the end of their term, regardless of their behavior, have less of an incentive for good behavior.

LO 22.6 List three major features of political structure, and identify how they can affect policy choices.

In Brazil, for example, mayors are limited to two terms. While first-term mayors who are up for reelection have an interest to stay relatively clean, mayors who know they will be out of office at the end of their term regardless of their behavior have less of an incentive to do so. A recent study by two economists found that misappropriation of funds was 27 percent lower among mayors who had to face reelection than among second-termers.[6] If this is right, then getting rid of term limits could reduce losses due to corruption by $160 million, equal to about half of the amount spent on *Bolsa Familia*, Brazil's largest social program to help poor families.

Increased enfranchisement   The final important part of political structure comes from *enfranchisement*, or who has the right to vote. Historically, controlling who was able to vote was an important tool for those who wanted to keep other groups out of power, especially women, ethnic and religious minorities, and the poor. Even when the right to vote is universal, poll taxes, literacy requirements, or other such obstacles to voting can keep the poor or uneducated from being able to vote. Such rules resulted in political systems that represented the interests of those who could vote at the expense of others.

But voters can also be disenfranchised by circumstance. Voters who cannot get to the polls or who cannot read the ballots when they get there are, for all intents and purposes, disenfranchised as well. For an example of how a simple change can promote enfranchisement, see the Economics in Action box "Enfranchising the poor helps the poor."

Enfranchising the poor helps the poor
Economics in Action

It stands to reason that politicians are more interested in helping people who are likely to vote. But in most of the world, the poor are much *less likely* to vote than the wealthy. The result is that politicians may be less concerned with catering to the needs and interests of the poor.

Brazil first approached this problem with a straightforward solution: The government simply required all citizens to vote. Unfortunately, 23 percent of the population could not read or write. They struggled to understand the paper ballots, which often contained thousands of eligible candidates. As a result, about a quarter of all ballots were filled out incorrectly and thus disqualified. In effect, many of the poorest voters were still disenfranchised, even when they had voted.

Next, officials in Brazil looked for ways to make voting easier for the illiterate poor. They created electronic voting machines that closely resembled the interface of a telephone. Each candidate has a number; before confirming their votes, voters are presented with the name and pictures of the candidate corresponding to the number code they put into the machine.

The introduction of this new technology increased the number of votes cast correctly by 11 percent. This change was particularly pronounced in poorer districts and in the votes for parties that are traditionally supported by the poor. Millions of poor people whose votes would previously not have been counted were suddenly enfranchised in fact as well as in theory.

How did this sudden enfranchisement affect policies? Since the poor were able to vote for the politicians they wanted, they were able to put officials in office who worked to implement policies that helped them. Research by Thomas Fujiwara shows that shortly after the electronic voting machines went into use, the amount of state budgets spent on public health increased by 50 percent. Fujiwara shows that this increase in spending on public health translated into improved health outcomes, such as improved birth weight of infants.

Brazil's experience shows that enfranchising the poor doesn't always need complex government initiatives or changes to the political structure. A simple change in technology can be all it takes.

Source: Thomas Fujiwara, "Voting Technology, Political Responsiveness, and Infant Health: Evidence from Brazil," *Econometrica* 83, no. 2 (March 2015), www.princeton.edu/~fujiwara/papers/elecvote_site.pdf.

✓ TEST YOURSELF

- ☐ Given the same amount of total benefits, why is it harder for a large group to overcome a collective-action problem than a small one? **[LO 22.4]**
- ☐ How does rent-seeking differ from corruption? **[LO 22.5]**
- ☐ Why is it difficult for small third parties to survive under a first-past-the-post voting system? **[LO 22.6]**

Conclusion

As students of economics, we are interested in how policy is formed—both for its own sake as an important realm of human decision making and for the effect it has on the economy. In this chapter, we began with a simplified model of political choices: Voters are fully informed and rational, they pick the candidate that best fits their views, and that candidate then faithfully carries out the policy platform on which he or she was elected.

We then moved to a more nuanced model of political choices. First, we saw that even if voters are informed and rational, aggregating their opinions through elections is not as simple as just tallying the votes. In fact, no process exists that can meet even a fairly basic set of criteria we'd hope for in an ideal voting system.

Second, we questioned just how rational and informed voters really are—and whether a rational person would even choose to vote. Then, we looked at government officials as fallible humans with their own biases and interests. Many of these biases are shaped by the rules of the political system, and we showed how these rules affect policy outcomes.

In the next chapter, we'll take a look at how policy-makers can influence outcomes, sometimes without even changing the underlying policies. Sometimes the way policies are presented can lead to important changes in the choices people make, on topics as important as retirement savings and as simple as what to eat for breakfast.

Key Terms

median-voter theorem, p. 566

Condorcet paradox, p. 570

Arrow's impossibility theorem, p. 572

rational ignorance, p. 572

collective-action problem, p. 575

rent-seeking, p. 576

Summary

LO 22.1 Explain the predictions and assumptions of the median-voter theorem.

The *median-voter theorem* suggests that politicians maximize their votes by taking the policy position preferred by the median voter. The theorem relies on several assumptions: that there is a one-dimensional policy question, voters always vote for the candidate whose position is closest to their own, there are only two candidates, and the winner is determined by majority vote.

Given these conditions, the median-voter theorem suggests that candidates in a two-party system should take similar policy positions in order to maximize their

chances of winning. Second, it predicts that the chosen policy will be the one preferred by the median voter, rather than the average voter or the largest number of voters. The median-voter theorem falls apart when voters care about multiple issues or issues that can't be measured on a single spectrum.

LO 22.2 List the characteristics of an "ideal" voting system, and identify which criteria are met by real systems.

Arrow's impossibility theorem states that no system can aggregate the preferences of voters among three or more discrete options while satisfying four basic criteria for an ideal voting system: unanimity, transitivity, irrelevance of independent alternatives, and no dictator. The plurality system used in the United States, for example, violates the independence of irrelevant alternatives; the presence of a third-party candidate can alter the outcomes of an election between the two leading candidates. Pair-wise majority voting violates the principle of transitivity, which causes the ultimate outcome of an election to depend on the order in which the choices are considered.

LO 22.3 Discuss problems with the idea of the "rational voter," and define the idea of rational ignorance.

The simplest economic models of political decision making treat voters as fully informed, rational agents. However, voting incurs costs, in both time spent to inform oneself about policy issues and time spent actually casting a ballot. The likelihood that any one vote changes the outcome of an election is very low; the benefits of voting are low as well. We should not be surprised if many people choose to vote ill-informed, or not to vote at all. Uninformed voting is an example of *rational ignorance,* when the costs of gathering information outweigh the benefits. Since people are not typically perfectly rational, we should expect voters to sometimes be biased and influenced by less-than-rational factors when choosing candidates.

LO 22.4 Explain the persistence of policies that provide concentrated benefits to a few while imposing diffuse costs on the majority.

Often, government is the coordinating force that allows people to work together to overcome the free-rider problem or the tragedy of the commons. These are *collective-action problems,* in which a group of people stands to gain from an action that it is not rational for any of the group members to undertake individually.

Collective action is easier when the benefits are concentrated among members of a small group and is harder when the benefits are spread out over a large group because the cost of organizing is higher with a lower potential gain for each participant. As a result, when two groups stand to benefit from contradictory policy choices, we should expect the one that experiences more concentrated costs or benefits to prevail. The theory that groups that experience concentrated benefits tend to win out over those with diffuse costs in policy battles is often used to explain the persistence of policies that don't appear to be in the interest of the majority of voters.

LO 22.5 Explain why corruption and rent-seeking can persist in a democratic system.

Corruption is the use by public officials of the powers of their position to achieve personal gains. *Rent-seeking* is the act of pursuing arrangements that increase one's own surplus without increasing total surplus. It can encompass corruption by politicians but also actions by any political actors to shape policy to their own benefit.

In a simplistic model of politics, we might expect that the process of electing officials would prevent rent-seeking and corruption. But voters have trouble tracking all of the details of policies and the actions of elected officials. This lack of transparency may make it difficult for them to monitor and punish corruption in reality.

Bureaucratic capture is a specific avenue through which corruption and rent-seeking can occur. Through it, government positions are filled by people with close ties to the industry or other group that they are intended to regulate.

LO 22.6 List three major features of political structure, and identify how they can affect policy choices.

Certain features of political structures can affect voters' preferences and thus policy choices. Three major features are the number of political parties, term limits, and increasing the right to vote.

First, countries vary widely with respect to the number of political parties. Few countries have explicit requirements about the number of political parties. Some implement a proportional-representation system, thought to offer more diverse views, whereas others hold two-party systems, thought to lead to more centrist politics.

Second, term limits are meant to discourage corruption by ensuring one person can't hold power for too long, although in some cases they may remove the incentive for good behavior.

Third, controlling who is able or likely to vote keeps certain groups out of power and results in political systems that represent the interests of those who do vote. Voters who do not vote due either to law or the costs of voting can become disenfranchised.

Review Questions

1. Assume there's an election coming up in which voters need to decide between two candidates on the question of taxes. Polls indicate the attitudes about taxes among likely voters as shown in Table 22Q-1. Candidate A proposes a 20 percent tax, and Candidate B, a 15 percent tax. According to the median-voter theorem, which candidate will win? **[LO 22.1]**

TABLE 22Q-1

Level of taxation (%)	Percent of voters in favor (%)
No taxes	10
10	20
20	40
25	30

2. Suppose we are trying to predict the positions that three candidates will take on who should be eligible for public-housing subsidies (e.g., poor families, the elderly, poor families with children, and so on). Can we use the median-voter theorem to analyze this problem? Explain why or why not, based on which of the assumptions of the median-voter theorem are met by this situation. **[LO 22.1]**

3. In researching a voting system, you discover that it obeys three of the four criteria of an ideal voting system: transitivity, irrelevance of independent alternatives, and unanimity. With this information, what else do you know about this system? How can you be sure? **[LO 22.2]**

4. Every year the residents of a historical town gather to determine how much to spend on their park, 10 percent or 15 percent of the budget. If everyone votes for the same percentage, they will spend that amount, unless the year before everyone voted for the opposite percentage, in which case they spend the average of the two. What characteristic of the ideal voting system is violated in this example? **[LO 22.2]**

5. Compare a national presidential election that receives around-the-clock media coverage with an obscure local race for a state house seat. Which imposes higher costs on people seeking to become informed voters, and why? Which carries higher benefits to voting, and why? **[LO 22.3]**

6. Explain whether you think the following changes in a voting system would increase or decrease the number of votes cast. **[LO 22.3]**

    a. Before casting their ballot, voters are required to watch a 30-minute video with facts about the issues at hand, greatly increasing the information they have about the issues.

    b. A new cellphone app allows you to vote by sending a text to your local Board of Elections.

    c. After voting, voters can elect to receive a small pin that allows everyone to know that they voted.

7. Chapter 17, "International Trade," discussed the trade restrictions that limit imports of clothing into the United States and Europe from certain clothing-manufacturing companies. Explain why a policy like this might persist even if it was unpopular with the majority of voters. **[LO 22.4]**

8. As part of a plan to subsidize avocado production, farmers suggest that the costs of a subsidy should be paid by grocery-store owners (who will presumably benefit from higher sales of avocados). Are there concentrated benefits in this situation? Are there diffuse costs? Is there a collective-action problem? Explain your answer. **[LO 22.4]**

9. Do collective-action problems contribute to or discourage rent-seeking? Explain your answer. **[LO 22.5]**

10. Explain why having a minimum voting age may cause rent-seeking. **[LO 22.5]**

11. Explain why voters are more likely to share beliefs with candidates in a proportional-representation system than a two-party system. **[LO 22.6]**

12. Explain why political candidates in the United States often have unusual and also persistent combinations of policy preferences. (For example, a candidate who supports abortion rights is usually also for gun control and supports higher taxes.) **[LO 22.6]**

Problems and Applications

1. Suppose that two candidates in a local election are trying to develop their policy positions regarding how much their town should spend on education. The numbers break down as shown in Table 22P-1.

TABLE 22P-1

Percent of budget to spend on education (%)	Number of voters in favor
1	40
5	80
8	220
15	150
17	110
21	180
25	90

According to the median-voter theorem, how much will the town spend on education? **[LO 22.1]**

2. A soccer team is voting for a captain based on how many times the captain would have the team practice per week. Table 22P-2 shows the number of team members in favor of various numbers of practices per week. **[LO 22.1]**

TABLE 22P-2

Number of practices per week	Team members in favor
2	10
4	11
6	10
8	10

a. If the team is choosing between three captains—Ainsley, Bailey, and Jenna—can we use the median-voter theorem?

b. Assume that at the last minute, Ainsley decides to withdraw from the race. Can we use the median-voter theorem for the race as it stands now?

c. If you can use the median-voter theorem to predict the result without Ainsley, how many times will the team practice? If you cannot use the theorem, what two answers can you rule out?

d. Assume that two more players join the team before the vote. They both prefer to practice 10 times a week. If you can use the median-voter theorem to predict the result without Ainsley, how many times will the team practice? If you cannot use the theorem, what two answers can you rule out?

3. Three friends are trying to decide where to go to dinner. There are four restaurants nearby: Thai, Italian, Tex-Mex, and sushi. Assume the friends have the following preferences: **[LO 22.2]**

Gabe: Thai > Italian > Sushi > Tex-Mex
Arnold: Italian > Tex-Mex > Sushi > Thai
Julie: Sushi > Tex-Mex > Thai > Italian

a. The friends decide to hold a majority vote that pits the Thai place against the Italian; the winner of that vote against the Tex-Mex; and then the next winner against the sushi. Which restaurant do they end up going to?

b. If they vote on sushi versus Tex-Mex, the winner against Italian, and then the winner against Thai, which restaurant will they choose?

c. Which of the criteria for an ideal voting system is violated in this example?

4. In a runoff election, if no candidate receives a majority of votes in the first round of voting, the top two candidates face each other in a second round. Let's say that people voting on Candidates A, B, C, and D in a runoff election have the following preferences. **[LO 22.2]**

12 voters: A > B > C > D
8 voters: C > B > D > A
10 voters: D > B > C > A
4 voters: B > D > A > C

a. Does anyone receive an outright majority in the first round? If so, which candidate? If not, which two candidates move on to the second round, and which of them wins?

b. Suppose Candidate A drops out of the race. Does any candidate now receive an outright majority in the first round? If so, which candidate? If not, which two candidates move on to the second round, and which of them wins?

c. Does this situation violate the independence of irrelevant alternatives?

5. According to the rational voter theory, will the following increase or decrease voter turnout? **[LO 22.3]**

a. Electronic voting machines make the process of casting a ballot faster and less complicated.

b. 24-hour news networks emphasize how close they expect the election to be, with only a few thousand votes deciding the outcome.

c. The number of polling stations increases.

d. Pollsters predict a landslide victory for the incumbent candidate a few days before the election.

6. Determine whether each of the following represents rational ignorance. **[LO 22.3]**

a. Doug doesn't know the return on his retirement account in the last quarter or the types of investments that comprise the account.

b. Sally doesn't know about a new provision in nuclear energy regulation, which is decided by a national panel overseen by nuclear physicists.

c. Mateo doesn't know whether to support new requirements for licensing among city contractors.

d. Jin doesn't know the average price of a parking ticket, despite parking on the street every day.

7. For each of the following, state who benefits and who bears the costs, and whether the costs and benefits are concentrated or diffuse. Based on this assessment, predict which side is likely to get its way. **[LO 22.4]**

   a. A rubber producer lobbies the government to prohibit the import of cheaper foreign rubber, driving up the cost of consumer goods.

   b. The government increases federal gas taxes by 1 cent per gallon to finance building high-speed train routes between major East Coast cities.

8. For each of the following conditions, determine whether a collective-action problem exists. **[LO 22.4]**

   a. Diffuse benefits, diffuse costs.

   b. Diffuse benefits, concentrated costs.

   c. Concentrated benefits, diffuse costs.

   d. Concentrated benefits, concentrated costs.

9. Decide which of these labels best fits each of the following situations: *rent-seeking, corruption,* or *bureaucratic capture.* (If more than one is potentially applicable, pick the one that is the most narrowly tailored to the scenario.) **[LO 22.5]**

   a. A contract manager at a government department is bribed to ensure that her friend's company gets a construction contract even though it was not the lowest bidder.

   b. A senior-citizens group lobbies the city government to spend more on special public-transit shuttles for the elderly.

   c. The president appoints a former head of an investment bank to the Securities and Exchange Commission (which oversees capital markets and enforces financial regulations).

   d. The head of a local teachers' union offers support to a political candidate in exchange for his promise to spend more of the state budget on teacher salaries.

10. Determine whether each of the following shifts is likely to increase or decrease the prevalence of rent-seeking. **[LO 22.5]**

    a. The spread of smartphones enables more widespread access to information.

    b. Judges strike down a law that forces politicians to report when they receive a gift worth over $500.

    c. Congress passes a law requiring lobbyists to spend at least two years in another unrelated position before getting hired in government to regulate the industries they were advocating for as lobbyists.

11. Suppose that political candidates in an election are trying to develop their policy positions regarding how high to set the top marginal tax rate. The numbers break down as shown in Table 22P-3.

TABLE 22P-3

Top marginal tax rate (%)	Number of voters in favor
5	60
10	70
15	110
20	170
25	200
30	110
35	90

If the political system is a two-party system, will a candidate who believes the top marginal tax rate should be 30 percent be more likely to announce support for a marginal tax rate below 30 percent, above 30 percent, or exactly 30 percent? **[LO 22.6]**

12. Suppose that a country currently does not allow its political leaders to be in office for more than one term. The country is considering moving from a policy of no reelection to allowing one reelection (i.e., two terms in office). Figure 22P-1 shows a governor's options while serving as governor. She can either act honestly or dishonestly. If she acts honestly, the voters will vote to reelect her. If she acts dishonestly, the voters will not vote for her reelection. Assume that the governor would prefer to be reelected. How will moving from a policy of no reelection to allowing one reelection affect the governor's honesty in her first (and potentially second) terms? **[LO 22.6]**

FIGURE 22P-1

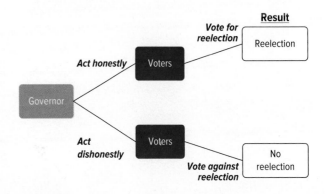

Endnotes

1. https://www.nytimes.com/2018/10/07/climate/ipcc-climate-report-2040.html?action=click&module=Top%20Stories&pgtype=Homepage.

2. www.washingtonpost.com/wp-dyn/content/article/2007/03/31/AR2007033101040.html.

3. www.nytimes.com/2005/11/06/magazine/why-vote.html.

4. www.nytimes.com/2005/11/06/magazine/why-vote.html; http://papers.ssrn.com/sol3/papers.cfm?abstract_id=917770.

5. www.britannica.com/topic/liberum-veto.

6. http://eml.berkeley.edu/~ffinan/Finan_Termlimits.pdf.

Public Policy and Choice Architecture

Saving More for Tomorrow

Many Americans save little for retirement outside of the "forced" savings of contributions to Social Security made through payroll taxes. Taken alone, this fact isn't necessarily puzzling; maybe most people don't want to save more than that. What makes it strange, though, is that most Americans *say* that they want to be saving more.

If people want to save more, why don't they do it? Typically, economists assume that people make rational, purposeful decisions about saving. They save up when income is high and spend down savings when income is low or gone, such as in retirement. Based on the idea of *revealed preference*, economists often infer that whatever choices people are making must be "right" for them and their situations in life. If someone occasionally doesn't save as much as planned one month, we assume that he or she will simply adjust to put a little more in the bank in the future. Over the long term, we expect to see people's actions matching up with their intentions.

©ever/Shutterstock

But suppose that some people are consistently letting current temptations get in the way of long-term saving goals. They're not just miscalculating for a month here and there, but are saving much less than they'd like to over years and years. They may find themselves with less than they want to have in the bank to support their kids' education or to live on in retirement. Can anything be done, in their moments of reflection and planning, to help them make decisions they would feel better about? Economists Shlomo Benartzi and Richard Thaler designed a program to help people overcome their own limitations and save more.[1]

This approach, called Save More Tomorrow (or SMarT™), offers employees the option to commit a fraction of future pay raises to a tax-free retirement savings account. Benartzi and Thaler realized that most of us dislike the feeling of giving up what we already have—such as having to accept a cut in our current pay in order to save more. By tying increases in saving to *future* pay raises, SMarT helps people save without feeling they are "giving up" something in order to save more. (To be as flexible as possible, the program allows people to change their minds later on and, if they want, back out of their commitment and lower their saving rate back down.)

If people are already making optimal choices about saving, then a program like SMarT will have no effect. But it turns out that people who participated in SMarT almost quadrupled their saving rate over a few years. That rate went from 3.5 percent of income to 13.6 percent. This increase suggests that people really *were* saving less than they wanted to but needed a little nudge to get them on track.

SMarT is designed to help employees overcome at least two different types of mental barriers to saving:

- First, SMarT takes advantage of a *status-quo bias:* We often are reluctant to make active decisions to change something, even if it is fairly easy to do so. SMarT is designed so that an increase in future savings occurs if the participant takes *no action*. If you want to change your mind about the amount committed to future savings, you can do so easily. It turns out, though, that with saving as the default option, people are more likely to go through with it.

- Second, SMarT can overcome *time inconsistency:* Many people are unwilling to forgo current consumption to save now but *are* willing to cut back future consumption to save for the even farther-off future. Why? Saving more right now means giving up things that are immediately tempting to us. It's often hard to do that. Saving *later* doesn't feel as painful right now, so we are more willing to agree to do it. However, if one must wait until the future to make the saving decision, then you might find yourself unwilling to save when the future finally arrives. By committing *now* to saving in the future, you can maintain the saving decision that you want.

The SMarT program shows that simply changing the way we present options can affect people's behavior and help them overcome mental biases and avoid regret. Thaler and his collaborator Cass Sunstein have come up with a term for this idea: *choice architecture*. When we think critically about how to design the environment in which people make choices, we are engaging in *choice architecture*. In their book *Nudge: Improving Decisions About Health, Wealth, and Happiness*, Thaler and Sunstein promote the idea that the structure of policies and products affects the outcomes of individuals' decisions. They argue that it is possible to design policies and products in a way that gently "nudges" people toward choices that will make them happier in the long run.

What makes people happier in the long run can be hotly debated. Thaler and Sunstein don't want to dictate what people *should* do. Instead, they want to make it easier to make better choices, while leaving people free to make those choices themselves. Even if policy-makers do not want to engage in "nudging," they still have to choose how to present choices to people. Each presentation approach will lead to certain predictable choices. So the mantra of Thaler and Sunstein is to recognize this responsibility and nudge toward good outcomes. In 2017, Richard Thaler was awarded the Nobel Prize in Economics for these insights.

In this chapter, we'll describe how choice architecture works. We'll start by describing some of the psychological biases that can shape economic choices. Then we'll explore how policy-makers, private companies, and choice architects of all sorts are putting the ideas into action to help guide people toward decisions that they say they want to make.

LEARNING OBJECTIVES

LO 23.1 Define choice architecture, and identify how nudges can influence individual decision making.

LO 23.2 Explain several ways in which human decision making does not conform to the model of full information and rational choices.

LO 23.3 Explain how demand for commitment devices can be rational.

LO 23.4 Explain how information, when presented well, can help people make decisions that are good for them.

LO 23.5 Describe how default rules affect people's choices and the implications for policy.

LO 23.6 Describe how framing affects the way people process information and its implications for policy.

Choice Architecture and Nudges

Sometimes people do things that they themselves would agree are not the right decisions. They might *say* they want to save money but never get around to opening a savings account. They might agree that they'd be better off dieting, but they keep eating junk food.

We first approached this idea in Chapter 8, "Behavioral Economics: A Closer Look at Decision Making." Here, we'll apply some of the insights of behavioral economics to see how policy-makers can design products and policies that nudge people toward making better decisions.

Why nudge?

A growing pile of evidence indicates that people's decisions can be influenced by how options are presented to them. **Choice architecture**—the organization of the context and process in which people make decisions—can alter actual decisions and thus the ultimate outcomes. Choice architecture focuses on such factors as the timing of choices and how different options are described.

"Choice architects" are people who are in a position to shape the decision-making environment. Because they can influence the outcomes of people's choices, we have to ask how they ought to exercise this influence. As Uncle Ben told Peter Parker (aka Spiderman), "with great power comes great responsibility." Some might say choice architects should aim to use their power as lightly as possible, by being "neutral."

On closer inspection, though, it's not clear what a neutral policy means in most situations. For instance, research shows that supermarket shoppers are more likely to purchase items placed in noticeable locations, such as at eye level on the shelf. No matter how you arrange things, some products are going to be located at eye level and others aren't. There's no such thing as "neutral" shelving. But we *can* make a choice about which items end up at eye level. This is where the power of choice architecture comes into play.

If policy can't be neutral, what should it be? For the supermarket manager, the answer is easy enough. She wants to put at eye-level items that will maximize profits. What if the choice architect has in mind goals other than maximizing profit? In that case, the decision is a tougher one:

- Should choice architects aim to encourage choices that *they* think will be better for society?
- Or should choice architects try to push people toward things that *people themselves* would agree are better for them?

In this chapter, we focus mainly on describing *how* policy can influence people's decisions. We leave open the question of the appropriate use of these tools.

Thaler and Sunstein use the term **nudge** to describe an implementation of choice architecture that alters people's behavior in a deliberate and predictable way without changing economic

LO 23.1 Define choice architecture, and identify how nudges can influence individual decision making.

choice architecture
the organization of the context and process in which people make decisions

nudge
an implementation of choice architecture that alters people's behavior in a deliberate and predictable way without changing economic incentives much

incentives much.[2] In other words, a nudge is a gentle push in a particular direction, but anyone who wants to go in a different direction is still able to do so. The SMarT program, for example, nudges people toward higher saving, but people still have the freedom to change their minds and lower their saving rate. In the grocery store, placing an item at eye level nudges shoppers toward selecting it, but they can still choose items from higher or lower shelves instead.

Nudges can sometimes accomplish public policy goals in a less expensive and less coercive way than more traditional methods. Why set tough quotas, crank up taxes, or make something illegal if you can nudge people in the socially desired direction? Below, we'll see numerous examples of successful, cost-effective nudges. These nudges help people make the choices that they would actually prefer to make for themselves. Most importantly, unlike strict rules, they still preserve freedom of choice for others who don't want to go in the direction they're being nudged in. Read the Economics in Action box "It's all about timing" for one example of a nudge from the developing world.

It's all about timing

Economics in Action

Retirement is not a surprise. Yet, despite anticipating it for decades, many Americans reach retirement age without sufficient savings. The problem is that saving is hard, given the costs of housing, kids, and the rest of life. The chapter opened with the example of a nudge to help Americans prepare for retirement.

A similar problem—but in a very different place and context—engaged three economists working in Kenya. The saving problem involved difficulty saving for just a few months during the year, but it turned out to be costly for those involved.

Researchers found that a nudge in the form of fertilizer vouchers encouraged Kenyan farmers to commit to use fertilizer by paying for it when they had money available.
©boezie/Getty Images

In Western Kenya, subsistence farmers typically earn the equivalent of a dollar a day, mainly because the soil is very poor. Studies show that by applying fertilizer to the soil, farmers can increase their harvest by about 50 percent. The return on this investment is well worth the cost of the fertilizer, and farmers are well aware of these benefits. But still, 55 percent of farmers in this region have never used fertilizer. Why not?

The answer isn't just about a lack of money. It is also about a lack of money *at the right time*. The farmers have trouble saving after the harvest (when they have enough money) to pay for fertilizer at planting time (when money is usually tight).

As with retirement, the need for money at planting time is no surprise. Moreover, most farmers say that they *intend* to use fertilizer and that they earn enough *at harvest time* to be able to afford it. But when the time comes to plant their crops, they no longer have enough money to afford fertilizer.

In response to this problem, the three economists working with a nonprofit organization, Innovations for Poverty Action, created a nudge to help farmers follow through on their intention to use fertilizer. Field workers sold vouchers that let farmers pay for the fertilizer at harvest-time, with a guarantee that fertilizer would be delivered to them at the next planting season.

Sure enough, when the workers visited farmers shortly after a harvest, fertilizer purchases increased by 60 percent. The fertilizer vouchers enabled the farmers to *commit* to use fertilizer by paying for it when they had money available. Of course, they could have saved the money for those three months, but without the commitment, that often didn't happen.

The evidence suggests that timing was everything. Choice architecture—in this case, altering the *timing* of the farmers' decision about fertilizer purchases—made a real difference, even to people who are among the poorest in the world. The farmers already knew it was in their best interests to buy fertilizer. All they needed was the right nudge.

Source: Esther Duflo, Michael Kremer, and Jonathan Robinson, "Nudging Farmers to Use Fertilizer: Theory and Experimental Evidence from Kenya," *American Economic Review* 101, no. 6 (2011), pp. 2350–90, DOI:10.1257/ aer.101.6.2350.

What is a "bad" choice?   When we talk about a "mistake" or a "bad" choice in this chapter, we're not imposing our own views about the merits of a choice in question. Instead, we're defining "mistake" from the perspective of the person doing the choosing. A mistake is a choice that the chooser later regrets.

It's worth a short side trip to consider how economists think about good and bad choices. Economics allows for the idea that people have diverse preferences. As a result, it's difficult to say what constitutes a good choice for other people. For some, the frustration of sticking to a diet is worth the weight loss. For others, it might not be. As a rule, economics assumes that people weigh trade-offs and make choices that maximize their utility. In a traditional economic view (as seen in the idea of *revealed preference* described in Chapter 7, "Consumer Behavior"), there is no such thing as a "bad" choice. That's because we assume, by definition, that people choose what is best for themselves.

Consider a person who runs up huge debts by taking out expensive loans. A psychologist might conclude that he is a compulsive shopper with a self-control problem. But economists usually start with the assumption that the shopper's decision can be explained by his preferences. If he has a strong preference for current consumption, for example, then he is rationally maximizing his utility by taking on heavy future repayment obligations to buy more stuff now.

This traditional economic approach is at the core of this text for good reason. For one thing, it's based on a reasonable simplifying assumption: People do tend to *try* to act in their own self-interest. It also gives people the benefit of the doubt that they often know what's best for themselves, at least better than others do.

Studying behavioral economics, choice architecture, and nudges allows us to integrate some lessons from psychology into this core economic approach; we can go beyond the simplifying assumption that people *always* make the choices that are best for themselves.

However, this leaves us in a tough spot. When people make choices that look funny to others, is it simply because they have different preferences? Or are they actually making mistakes? A behavioral economics approach suggests that it could be either. Who gets to decide what constitutes a "bad" choice? Friends? Neighbors? Parents? Policy-makers? How and when should their opinions be put into action? Answering these questions could take up entire texts, and we don't attempt to address them here. Instead, we use the words "bad" choice and "mistake" only when *the decision makers themselves* would later agree that they have made a bad choice or mistake.

Mistakes people make

LO 23.2 Explain several ways in which human decision making does not conform to the model of full information and rational choices.

Once we accept that people try to maximize their well-being but sometimes make mistakes, we start to find that those mistakes happen in common and predictable ways. Here, we consider some important categories of biases in human decision making. In the next section, we'll see more examples of how choice architects can put these insights to work.

Temptation   In Chapter 8, "Behavioral Economics: A Closer Look at Decision Making," we talked about how people struggle with temptation and procrastination. How can we as economists and policy-makers understand people who say they want one thing–to save money, or stay on a diet, or quit smoking–but then do something else? Our economic model described temptation as sort of a split-personality problem: We have one set of preferences about what to do today and another about what to do in the future.

time inconsistency

a situation in which we change our minds about what we want simply because of the timing of the decision

We use the term **time inconsistency** to describe a situation in which we change our minds about what we want simply because of the timing of the decision. People's preferences about the present are inconsistent with their preferences about the future, simply because the future choices are more distant.

Note that it's not time inconsistency if your preferences are different because the circumstances are different in some important way. For instance:

- If you want to eat junk food now because you're on vacation and you will start a diet next week when the vacation is over, that's not time-inconsistent.
- When you want to start your diet one week from today, but when that time comes, you want to start it in yet one more week, and so on, it *is* time-inconsistent. In this case, your preferences changed simply because time passed.

Sometimes temptation is just temptation, and we might rationally choose to give in to the temptation. But sometimes recognizing time inconsistency in temptations can help people avoid undesirable choices. When we recognize the problem, we can use appropriate solutions.

As we saw in Chapter 8, "Behavioral Economics: A Closer Look at Decision Making," a common solution to time inconsistency is a commitment device. If you can commit your future self to making the decision you want, then it is impossible to give in to the temptation of changing your behavior in the future. As we saw in the chapter-opening story, time inconsistency is one of the common biases that the SMarT program helps to tackle.

Limited processing power   We learned in Chapter 22, "Political Choices," why it can be rational to choose to not be fully informed about a political issue. We used the term *rational ignorance* to explain that people might choose to remain ignorant when the opportunity costs of gathering information outweigh the benefits.

For example, you would probably do a bit of comparative shopping before buying a new computer, but few people become world experts on computing technology. Is it possible that you're making the wrong decision about which machine is best for you? Sure. But is it really worth spending a whole year researching computers in order to be more sure that you're picking the exactly right model? Probably not. Think about all of the other things you could be doing during that year that are worth more to you than the risk of having a less-than-ideal computer.

Sometimes, though, our ignorance isn't so carefully considered, and the consequences of bad choices are big. We might simply get overwhelmed by the complicated information involved in a choice. For example, the question of how much you should be saving at any given time in your life to achieve a comfortable retirement is challenging to answer, even for economics professors. Psychological research shows that choices that involve processing lots of complicated information are, unsurprisingly, likely to turn out worse than those involving simple information.

Practice can make perfect, even when making hard decisions. But unfortunately, lots of important choices in life don't come with practice rounds. Familiar choices–like what to eat for dinner—are easy. They are easier than choices that we make only infrequently, such as how to invest retirement funds or choosing between different types of surgery. In part, this is because we have all eaten enough dinners to understand the utility we are likely to get from different choices. We're more likely to make mistakes with situations we face infrequently, such as how to invest our retirement funds, how different types of surgery are likely to affect us five years down the road, or which college we should go to.

Avoiding mistakes when making infrequent decisions is especially hard when it's not clear how to translate available information into something personally meaningful. When deciding which college to go to, you may have been bombarded with statistics and stories—average SAT scores, how many students graduate on time, professor-to-student ratios, and so on. This information was useful to you only insofar as you could translate it into a prediction for how enjoyable and productive your life as a student at that college would be. This problem gets even worse in situations where you're not sure what will ultimately matter to you. If you've never been to college before, how can you know whether you care about how big your classes will be?

Reluctance to change   People go with the flow. They tend to stick with the current situation over other options, even when it is cheap to switch. Economists call this **status-quo bias**. It is one of the common mistakes we saw in the chapter-opening story about SMarT.

In the arena of decision making, status-quo bias means that the "default" option—the one that will automatically take place if the chooser fails to make an active decision—has a lot of power. For an example of status-quo bias at work, consider what happens when you sign up for a free trial of an online product. Most of the time, if you don't go back and cancel, you'll be signed up for the full program automatically at the end of the free trial. Many of us plan to cancel but then just forget and end up paying for something we didn't really want.

An interesting twist on status-quo bias is the **endowment effect**. This is the tendency to place a higher value on something you already own simply because you own it. In a well-known experiment, psychologist Daniel Kahneman and economists Jack Knetsch and Richard Thaler doled out plain coffee mugs to one group of students. They then asked another group who didn't get mugs how much they'd be willing to pay to get one. (Everyone could see the mug and assess its quality.) They also asked students with mugs how much they'd have to be paid to give up their mugs. If the students had similar tastes on average (which is reasonable to assume, given that they were randomly split into groups), we'd expect that the values for the mugs would be roughly the same. But in the experiment, students who had been given mugs placed a higher value on them than students who hadn't—more than twice as much, in fact.[3] This experiment was cited by the Nobel Committee when awarding Daniel Kahneman the Nobel Prize in Economics in 2002.

The endowment effect is related to **loss aversion**, a general tendency for people to put more effort into avoiding losses than achieving gains. Loss aversion is not to be confused with *risk aversion*, which we described in Chapter 11, "Time and Uncertainty." Risk aversion is about preferring certain outcomes over uncertain ones. Instead, the insight behind loss aversion is that people will typically put out more effort to avoid *losing* $100 than they would to *gain* $100.

Framing matters   Choice architects know that whether something *feels* like a loss or gain often depends on how it is *framed*. For instance, suppose you are a shopkeeper who charges a slightly higher price for credit-card transactions than for cash purchases. We could describe this price difference in two ways:

- As a "discount" for paying in cash.
- As a "fee" for paying with a credit card.

Evidence shows that people care more about avoiding a fee than they care about getting a discount. So as a shopkeeper, you can expect a greater tilt toward cash-paying when you advertise a "credit-card fee" than if you advertise an equivalent "discount" for paying cash.

status quo bias
the tendency to stick with the current situation over other options, even when it is cheap to switch

endowment effect
the tendency of people to place more value on something simply because they own it

loss aversion
the tendency for people to put more effort into avoiding losses than achieving gains

There are many other situations in which people respond to the way choices are framed. This is true even when that framing does not change the substance of the available options. Imagine you're deciding which of two universities to attend:

- University A sends you a brochure saying, "Within three months after graduation, 80 percent of our students have found jobs!"
- University B's brochure says, "Three months after graduation, 20 percent of our students have failed to find jobs."

Which school do you want to choose?

As we're sure you noticed, universities A and B actually have identical job-placement rates—but university A clearly has a better public relations department. On a purely rational level, a reader should see that 80 percent of graduates from both schools have jobs and 20 percent don't. But our subconscious processing system interprets the information differently. We respond better to the positive framing (emphasizing the successful graduates) than to the negative (emphasizing the failures).

✓ **TEST YOURSELF**

☐ Does a nudge force people to make a better choice? **[LO 23.1]**

☐ Explain how time inconsistency accounts for procrastination. **[LO 23.2]**

☐ What is the endowment effect? **[LO 23.2]**

Tools of Choice Architecture

In this section we explore techniques that choice architects use to structure the decisions that people face. Remember that we're discussing methods—not necessarily endorsing the outcomes.

Commitment devices

LO 23.3 Explain how demand for commitment devices can be rational.

In a simple world, we usually assume that having more options is a good thing. Typically, there is no cost to ignoring options you don't like. In the best-case scenario, you gain new, good options. In the worst-case scenario, you ignore all the new, bad options and are in the exact same spot you were before.

However, understanding time inconsistency shows us why someone might rationally want to limit her own options. Assume you want to start a diet in a week, but you know that your future self will be tempted to keep putting off the diet. You don't quite trust yourself to make the right choice. So, you might want to take actions now to make sure there won't be any junk food in the house next week. By limiting your food options, you make it harder for your future self to make bad choices.

In Chapter 8, "Behavioral Economics: A Closer Look at Decision Making," we saw some examples of tools that allow people to voluntarily restrict later choices so they can make better decisions in the future: setting personal deadlines for long-term assignments, signing up for a savings account that requires regular deposits, or installing a browser extension that limits your access to time-sink websites.

commitment device a mechanism that allows people to voluntarily restrict their choices in order to make it easier to stick to plans

These voluntary mechanisms are **commitment devices**. They allow people to voluntarily restrict their choices in order to make it easier to stick to plans. Some commitment devices are completely informal—such as not buying junk food this week so that you won't have ready access to it next week when you intend to start your diet. Other commitment devices are formal policies and products. For instance, salaried workers can sign up to have their employers automatically deduct pension contributions from future paychecks.

Commitment devices are an example of using choice architecture to help people overcome temptation. Some commitment devices have strong commitments that are hard to get out of. Other devices have weak commitments that are easier to change. Neither is inherently better than the other. Specific people and situations call for different types of commitment. SMarT is a weak commitment device; it commits you to a savings plan, but it's easy to reverse the decision later. One way of understanding the economic insight behind commitment devices is to think about them as methods either to increase the price of your vices or to lower the price of your virtues.

Three important rules help create good commitment devices:

1. Make goals realistic.
2. Be specific about what you will do and how you will do it.
3. Set the right stakes, whether financial or peer pressure, that will keep you on track to fulfill your goal.

Information campaigns and disclosure rules

Because choices are hard and people have limited processing capacity, we often rely on rules of thumb. Rules of thumb help us translate complicated information into a simpler and more familiar framework. A rule of thumb is an example of a **heuristic**—a mental shortcut that helps us make decisions (sometimes in good ways, but sometimes not). Some such rules of thumb can be entirely personal. For example, one person we know always goes with the spicier option when facing unknown food choices in a new restaurant.

Another popular heuristic is **anchoring**—estimating unknown quantities by starting from a known "anchor" point. Suppose you were asked to estimate the cost of a flight from Omaha to New Orleans for Thanksgiving vacation. You might start by thinking of a figure you happen to know that is somewhat related—say, the cost of a flight from Chicago to Houston. You then would do something to that figure—say, add a bit because you're not sure how far apart Omaha and New Orleans actually are and you know that flights are generally more expensive around Thanksgiving. It's a rough way of making a guess, but you'll probably be closer than someone who has no idea what any plane tickets cost, and so has no anchor point.

However, research shows that people also tend to latch onto any nearby number as an anchor point, without even realizing it. Suppose we asked, "Guess how much an Omaha to New Orleans flight costs. Is it more than $200?" You might think, "Surely it's got to be more than that . . . say, $300?" But if we asked, "Guess how much an Omaha to New Orleans flight costs. Is it less than $600?" you might think, "Gee, that does sound like a lot. . . . Is it $500, perhaps?" The question hasn't changed, but suggesting an anchor has changed your guess.

Anchoring can bias choices in some predictable ways. Think of how charities solicit donations. Nonprofits often send fund-raising requests in the mail, with suggestions of amounts to contribute. People who get a solicitation with boxes suggesting donations of $50, $100, or $500 will tend to give more than if the boxes suggested $1, $5, or $10—even though the donors are also given the option to write in any amount they want instead of checking a box. A clever choice architect at a charitable organization can nudge people to give more simply by suggesting different amounts on a web page or a mail flyer. (Of course, there is a balance to be struck. If you set the anchor points too high, you risk scaring people away from donating at all.)

Choice architects can also affect the choices that people make by nudging them toward the use of specific choices in particular situations. For example, the Environmental Protection Agency (EPA) has for decades required car manufacturers to use a standard-format sticker disclosing the city and highway gas mileage of each car model. However, the average person may not be able to translate gas mileage into facts that really matter to them: How much might I spend on gas each year? How much gas will I need to drive 100 miles? Recognizing the importance of translating this into helpful information, the EPA updated the formatting of the stickers to try to help people make better choices.

Can presenting information differently also help people stay out of debt? In the 2007–2009 recession, for example, many families got into trouble

LO 23.4 Explain how information, when presented well, can help people make decisions that are good for them.

heuristic
a mental shortcut for making decisions (sometimes in good ways, but sometimes not)

anchoring
estimating unknown quantities by starting from a known "anchor" point.

The newest EPA stickers (bottom sticker) give estimated annual fuel costs in comparison to the average new vehicle, plus emission ratings, to nudge consumers toward vehicles that have better fuel efficiency.
Source: fueleconomy/EPA.gov

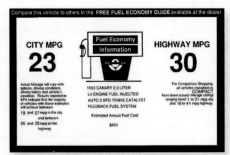

Source: fueleconomy/EPA.gov

from having run up too much debt on their credit cards. The federal government already required lenders to disclose detailed information about fees, interest rates, and so on. But many people do not read in detail, or do not understand, the lengthy sections of small print on the credit-card application and monthly statements.

Recognizing this problem, Congress passed the Credit Card Accountability, Responsibility, and Disclosure Act (CARD Act), which went into effect in 2010.[4] It requires credit-card bills to state the interest rate and other terms of the card. It also requires them to translate that information in ways that customers will understand. For example, all credit-card bills must now tell you how long it will take to pay off the full balance if you pay only the minimum amount. They also must tell you how much you would have to pay each month to pay off your balance within three years.

Even more than credit-card companies, "payday lenders" are often accused of not providing the information that would help their clients make informed choices about whether to use their services. Payday lenders provide high-fee, high-interest, short-term loans meant to help people pay for expenses until their next paycheck arrives. If these loans aren't paid off quickly, the costs add up fast.

Recently, researchers have tried to figure out whether borrowers really understand what they're getting into when they take out payday loans. To find out what happened, see the Econ and YOU box "Is payday lending predatory?"

Is payday lending predatory?
Econ and YOU

You've run out of money, and it's only halfway through the month. What can you do? If you have a steady job with a paycheck, you can visit a "payday lender" who will give you a cash loan that you agree to repay when payday rolls around in a couple of weeks.

Payday lenders commonly charge fees on the order of $15 for every $100 borrowed. If you think $15 doesn't sound like a lot of money, you may be falling prey to a psychological bias known as the *peanuts effect*—the tendency to discount small sums, even when they are large relative to the total amount in question. In fact, that $15 fee translates into an annual interest rate of about 400 percent APR, about 20 times a typical credit-card rate.

The fact that payday lenders charge such high rates has led some critics to conclude that uninformed borrowers are being suckered into making poor financial decisions. Payday rates *are* high, but that doesn't necessarily mean that borrowers are making a bad or irrational choice. It's possible they have concluded that payday loans are the best, or only, option available to them. If payday borrowers are making a bad choice, why do they do it? This question is central to the policy debate about whether payday lending should be allowed, and if so, how and to what extent it should be regulated by the government.

Two economists, Marianne Bertrand and Adair Morse of the University of Chicago, worked with one of the largest payday lenders in the United States to get the facts straight. They found that more than half of payday-loan customers thought that keeping a loan out for three months cost $30 to $60; the actual cost is many times that amount. Most also believed that they would be able to repay the loans within two weeks. In reality, however, customers tended to take five to six weeks to fully repay the debt (and racked up extra interest due to the delays).

Bertrand and Morse devised an experiment to try to understand what would happen if customers were given information about loan terms in easily understandable formats. The researchers split current payday-loan customers into three groups:

- The first group was told the interest rate on a payday loan (roughly 400 percent). They also were told, as an anchor, the rate for other forms of credit such as credit cards and car loans (often below 20 percent).
- The second group was shown the cost of borrowing $300 for two weeks ($45), one month, two months, or three months ($270). They also were given the comparable costs

for putting that same amount on a credit card (about $2.50 for two weeks up to $45 for three months).

- The third group was told how long it took the average customer to repay a loan—aiming to correct their overoptimistic expectations about how quickly they were likely to pay off.

Each of these information interventions affected the frequency and amount of borrowing from payday lenders. Across the three groups, 11 percent fewer customers took out loans. Those who did take out loans borrowed from 12 to 23 percent less money, depending on which sort of information they received.

Clearly, the new ways of presenting information changed customers' decisions. That said, the majority of customers continued to take out loans, and the amounts they borrowed didn't decrease by all that much. This suggests that if the decision to borrow is in fact a bad one, the causes are more complicated than simple ignorance or misunderstanding of the terms.

Source: Marianne Bertand and Adair Morse, "Information Disclosure, Cognitive Biases and Payday Borrowing." *Journal of Finance* 66, no. 6 (November 2011), pp. 1865–1893.

Default rules

Earlier we noted that people tend to stick with the current or starting option in many choice situations. Even if they're completely free to change things, they often don't. If your employer starts you off with a basic retirement plan, for example, you're more likely to stick with it than you would be to choose it yourself from a whole set of options. We call this starting option a **default rule**; it defines what will automatically occur if someone fails to make an active decision otherwise.

For example, many workers have retirement savings accounts called 401(k) accounts. As part of an employment-benefits package, some employers offer to match their employees' contributions to the accounts (up to a specified percentage). Commonly, companies will add an amount equal to half of what an employee adds, up to some percent of their salary. It's usually a good deal: The matching contribution from the company is "free money" for the employee, who can defer paying taxes on it until he or she withdraws from the account later in a career or at retirement. However, signing up for a 401(k) retirement account usually requires filling out some paperwork, and a large fraction of people who are eligible for such a plan simply fail to enroll. At many companies, the default rule for a 401(k) account is "no contribution," and many people stick with this default.

Choice architects suggest a simple solution: Change the default option so that all new employees are automatically enrolled. Those who don't want to put money into a 401(k) account can still opt out. Those who do want to put money into a 401(k) won't have to bother filling out forms, and they also will capture the employer's matching contribution.

The idea of changing behavior by changing default rules has been applied in unexpected places. For an example, see the Economics in Action box "Who doesn't want to be an organ donor?"

LO 23.5 Describe how default rules affect people's choices and the implications for policy.

default rule
a rule defining what will automatically occur if a chooser fails to make an active decision otherwise

Who doesn't want to be an organ donor?
Economics in Action

Over 114,000 people in the United States are currently waiting to receive a donated organ, like a healthy kidney or lung. Many transplants do take place (about 34,000 each year), but about 73,00 people die each year while waiting for an organ. On the face of things, it's hard to see why there is such a mismatch between supply and demand. The vast majority of Americans say they support organ donation. Since many people die with healthy organs every year, the supply of organs for transplants should be plentiful. But it's not.

(continued)

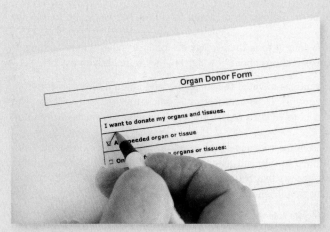

A change in the default rule—to opt out rather than in—increases organ donation.
©Robert Kirk/Getty Images

A big part of the reason lies in how people are asked about organ donation. The rules governing organ donation differ from state to state. In most cases, when people receive or renew their driver's licenses, they are asked if they would like to be a donor. In other words, people have to actively *opt in* to being an organ donor; the default is *to not be* a donor. The result is that about 54 percent of adults are registered donors, in contrast with the 95 percent who say they support organ donation.

Some policy-makers have suggested a different system. Why not simply require people who *don't* want to be organ donors to opt out? This system, often called *presumed consent*, sets donation as the default option.

We can see some startling differences in rates of organ donation between countries that do and do not have an opt-out system:

- Germany has an opt-in system, and only about 12 percent of its population registers to donate.
- Germany's neighbor Austria has an opt-out system, and 99 percent of the population is registered to donate.
- In Belgium, kidney donation doubled within three years after presumed-consent legislation passed.

Researchers have found similar results in studies in the United States. They divided people into two groups. Each group was told to imagine they had moved to a different state and needed to make a decision about whether to be an organ donor. The default rule changed behaviors:

- For one group, the default was *to not be* an organ donor. Only 50 percent stayed with that default.
- For the other group, the default was *to be* a donor. Over 80 percent of people in this group stayed with the default.

A simple change of the default rule was enough to cause a 30-percentage-point difference in the number of (hypothetical) registered donors.

Even without changing the default rule, subtle differences in the way people are asked about organ donation are correlated with big differences in outcomes. In the states with the highest donation rates, at the time when you receive or renew your driver's license, employees of the Department of Motor Vehicles are required to ask whether you want to be an organ donor. In the states with the lowest rates, applicants have to volunteer that they want to be an organ donor or find a checkbox deep in the driver's license renewal forms.

When it comes to figuring out who wants to be an organ donor, the answer depends on how you ask the question.

Sources: www.econlib.org/library/Columns/y2009/Tabarroklifesaving.html; http://optn.transplant.hrsa.gov; http://nudges.org/2010/10/10/how-required-choice-for-organ-donation-actually-works-in-practice; www.dangoldstein.com/papers/DefaultsScience.pdf; www.hks.harvard.edu/fs/aabadie/pconsent.pdf; www.organdonor.gov/statistics-stories/statistics.html.

Framing choices

We have seen already in this chapter some examples of how the *framing* of choices can affect people's decisions. In fact, marketers in private companies knew this long before behavioral economists started talking about "nudges" and "choice architecture." As we saw in Chapter 15, "Monopolistic Competition and Oligopoly," advertisers know that *framing* a product matters: Associating the product with young, beautiful people partying on a tropical island will cause more people to buy it, even if the product has nothing to do with being young, beautiful, or on a tropical island. The ways that framing can be used to influence people's choices are diverse. Here we'll look at two that are particularly relevant for public policy-makers: social norms and loss aversion.

If you were a policy-maker in charge of persuading people to pay their taxes, how would you go about it? You could run a campaign informing them about fines for nonpayment. But it turns out there's an even more powerful way to persuade them: Inform them that almost everyone else pays their taxes. Researchers have found that when you frame choices in terms of *social norms*—that is, what others do—people tend to go along with the majority. Most of us don't like to feel that we are outliers.

Pressure to conform to social norms can be a double-edged sword for choice architects, though. If you were charged with increasing voter turnout among the young, you might want to raise awareness of the problem by talking about how "only about 20 percent of young people voted in the last election." Unfortunately, this approach might actually make the problem worse. Hearing this, young people may conclude, "So it's no big deal if I don't vote—no one else is doing it either."

We have already seen a couple of examples of how choice architects can use the idea of loss aversion: the SMarT program's tying of saving to future pay raises, and the difference between a "cash discount" and a "credit-card fee."

Some creative researchers wrestled with framing decisions as they tried to harness the power of social norms to reduce home-energy consumption. The results, described in the From Another Angle box "Turn down the AC for a smiley face," might surprise you.

LO 23.6 Describe how framing affects the way people process information and its implications for policy.

Turn down the AC for a smiley face

From Another Angle

Americans spend a lot on energy to heat and cool their homes. This isn't necessarily a "bad" choice. Still, many people say they want to use less energy, and energy companies have tried many techniques to encourage them to follow through. They may increase prices during periods of peak energy use or ask people to commit to reducing their consumption. One study found that simply asking people to set goals for their own energy use caused a reduction of 4 to 7.5 percent. Providing people with feedback on how well they did increased the reduction to 12 percent.

A group of researchers wondered if there might be an easier, cheaper way. What if we harnessed the power of social norms to frame people's choice about how high to crank up the air conditioning? What if we simply tell people if they're using more electricity than their neighbors?

One such experiment was conducted in San Marco, California. Hundreds of households received notices telling them how much energy they had consumed in the past two weeks relative to the average energy consumption in their neighborhood. Sure enough, in response to this information, households that had been consuming more than average reduced their usage. Unfortunately, though, households that discovered they had been consuming less than average actually *increased* their usage! In other words, both high- and low-use consumers moved toward the middle, an outcome that researchers refer to as the "boomerang effect." Maybe customers who discovered they were low-use felt able to indulge themselves a bit more by turning up the AC. Or maybe people simply like to do whatever everyone else is doing, for better or worse.

(continued)

Adding a smiley face to the bills of customers who used less electricity than average nudged them to use even less in subsequent months.

This was a head-scratcher. How could the energy company nudge high-use customers to use less electricity without inadvertently also nudging low-use customers to use more? The answer turned out to be very, very easy: The researchers added a smiley face to the notice for households consuming less than average. It added a frowny face for households consuming more than average. The reduction by high-use customers increased, and the boomerang effect among low-use customers disappeared.

While people's most basic impulse is to be average, you can overcome that impulse. You just have to find a way of signaling to them that it's good to be better than average.

Sources: Hunt Allcott, "Social Norms and Energy Conservation," *Journal of Public Economics*, 2011, DOI:10.1016/j.jpubeco.2011.03.003; P. W. Schultz, J. Nolan, R. Cialdini, N. Goldstein, and V. Griskevicius, "The Constructive, Destructive, and Reconstructive Power of Social Norms," *Psychological Science* 18 (2007), pp. 429–434.

✓ TEST YOURSELF

- ☐ How can a commitment device help overcome time-inconsistent preferences? **[LO 23.3]**
- ☐ What is a heuristic? **[LO 23.4]**
- ☐ Why does status-quo bias imply that default rules are important? **[LO 23.5]**
- ☐ How do choice architects use social norms to frame choices? **[LO 23.6]**

Conclusion

Advertisers know that sales depend on more than delivering an appealing economic proposition. Clinching the deal often depends on hitting the right psychological buttons. Recently economists have also started bringing psychology into their problem-solving approach, and it's delivering practical ways to help people make choices that they are less likely to regret.

Choices are often influenced by the way that options are presented. Almost any presentation subtly pushes people toward one option or another, so it's difficult for choice frameworks to be truly neutral. In this chapter, we described how "choice architects" can present options in a way that helps people overcome biases and voluntarily make choices they are happier with.

We've walked through some of the tools that choice architects can use to "nudge" people toward better decisions. Often, these nudges are simple and inexpensive: changing the wording or increasing the clarity of information provided to people, redefining default options, or offering people ways to commit to a desired course of action. Used thoughtfully, nudges can help companies earn more profit and can help policy-makers achieve economic and social goals. One of the most striking lessons from behavioral economics is that small changes in choice architecture can sometimes lead to big changes in behavior.

Key Terms

choice architecture, p. 587

nudge, p. 587

time inconsistency, p. 590

status-quo bias, p. 591

endowment effect, p. 591

loss aversion, p. 591

commitment device, p. 592

heuristic, p. 593

anchoring, p. 593

default rule, p. 595

Summary

LO 23.1 Define choice architecture, and identify how nudges can influence individual decision making.

Choice architecture is the design of the environment in which people make decisions. It matters because evidence shows that people's decisions are influenced by the way in which options are presented to them. Although the idea that people are rational utility-maximizers is a useful simplifying assumption, we know that people also make mistakes in their efforts to increase their own well-being. They choose options that they themselves would agree were not the right ones to pick.

A *nudge* is an aspect of choice architecture that affects people's behavior without coercing them or fundamentally changing the economic incentives they face. Nudges can be used to help people bypass their own shortcomings to make better choices.

LO 23.2 Explain several ways in which human decision making does not conform to the model of full information and rational choices.

People make mistakes in some common and predictable ways. *Time inconsistency*—a situation when we change our minds about what we want simply because of the timing of the decision—helps us explain procrastination and temptation. People also have limited ability to process information. They are more likely to make mistakes when the decisions they face are complicated or unfamiliar, or for which the relationship between available information and the outcomes that actually matter is unclear.

In general, people have trouble with change, tending to prefer the *status quo*, avoiding losses, and ascribing more value to things they own than things they don't. Finally, decisions are influenced by the way in which options are *framed*, including minor details like phrasing.

LO 23.3 Explain how demand for commitment devices can be rational.

Commitment devices are strategies and tools that allow people to commit to make good choices in the future by voluntarily restricting their own options. If a person is aware of her own time inconsistency, she might prefer to have fewer options to choose from (or to make bad options more expensive); these strategies might help reduce the chance that she'll give in to temptation in the future. As a result, allowing people to voluntarily opt in to a commitment device can actually help them increase their own well-being.

LO 23.4 Explain how information, when presented well, can help people make decisions that are good for them.

People often rely on *heuristics*, which are mental shortcuts to help them make decisions. This suggests that information presented well, and at the right time, can help people make good decisions. People often also use *anchoring*, starting from a known "anchor" point in order to estimate unknown quantities. Choice architects try to figure out what information people need to make good decisions and give that information to them in a usable and timely way.

LO 23.5 Describe how default rules affect people's choices and the implications for policy.

People tend to stick with what they're given—whether that is a mug or a default option for investing their retirement funds. This fact means that *default rules* in products and policies, which define the option that will automatically occur if someone fails to make an active decision, have a power to influence people's choices. Default rules can nudge people toward particular outcomes.

LO 23.6 Describe how framing affects the way people process information and its implications for policy.

People respond to the way in which the choices are framed, even when that framing does not change the substance of the options available to them. Choice architects can encourage people to make certain choices through the context or way in which they present information. For instance, people are more likely to do something if they think everyone around them is also doing it; giving people information on how they compare to their peers can encourage or discourage behaviors.

Review Questions

1. Is instituting a $100 fine for anyone caught littering a nudge? Why or why not? **[LO 23.1]**

2. Suppose parents present their 16-year-old with a list of the cars that they will allow him to buy. If the parents decide to add another vehicle to the list, is that affecting the choice architecture for their son? Why or why not? **[LO 23.1]**

3. Suppose you have plans to save 5 percent of your salary next year. Then your company goes bankrupt, your pay

gets slashed by 20 percent, and you end up not saving at all. Is this an example of time inconsistency? Why or why not? **[LO 23.2]**

4. With her first paycheck, Hailey decides to buy a car. After spending hours researching the many specifications each car has—from gas mileage to horsepower—she decides to give up trying to find the perfect car based on these metrics and buys the best-looking one on the first lot she visits. Explain one aspect of bounded rationality discussed in the text that this example exhibits. **[LO 23.2]**

5. At the website stickK.com (started by one of the authors of this text), you can sign up for a contract in which you promise to meet certain weight-loss targets each week and forfeit money that you put up as stakes if you fail to meet those targets. Describe why a rational person might be willing to pay money if he does not lose weight, and how this constitutes a commitment strategy. **[LO 23.3]**

6. One contributor to the rational demand for commitment devices is the time-inconsistency problem. Explain how limited processing capacity might also contribute to the demand. **[LO 23.3]**

7. Suppose you need to estimate the cost of your texts for the upcoming semester. What would be a good "anchor" to use in your estimate? **[LO 23.4]**

8. Barry sees a sweater that he likes in a store. The price is $25. He wouldn't usually purchase the sweater at this price. But then he notices a sign that says the sweater is marked down from $50 and decides to buy the sweater. Is Barry's decision an example of a commitment device, the endowment effect, a nudge, or anchoring bias? Explain. **[LO 23.4]**

9. Many online subscription services have "automatic renewal" policies, in which they will automatically bill you for another year's subscription when your current one runs out. Why is this default rule a savvy business strategy on the part of the online company? **[LO 23.5]**

10. Explain the psychological bias that causes people's decisions to be affected by default rules or the endowment effect. **[LO 23.5]**

11. Imagine a public service announcement on television that is intended to scare kids away from using drugs. A big focus of the PSA is that a *lot* of teens are already on drugs. The directors of the PSA intend this statement to emphasize the size of the problem. Explain why this strategy for framing the anti-drugs message to teenagers could backfire. **[LO 23.6]**

12. Suppose you're trying to get your friends to go to dinner with you. Which of the following statements is more likely to convince your friends to go out to dinner? **[LO 23.6]**

Statement 1: "The dinner would cost only $5 more than the food we would make ourselves."

Statement 2: "Dinner at our favorite restaurant will cost $5 less than a meal at every other restaurant around town."

Problems and Applications

1. In each of the following scenarios, determine whether the change in people's behavior is the result of a nudge or a substantive change in economic incentives. **[LO 23.1]**

   a. A country with a low birth rate decides to offer free public child care for kids under the age of five.

   b. A nonprofit organization runs a highly publicized campaign offering teenage girls a very small symbolic reward (say, $5) for each week that they stay in school, come to support group meetings, and avoid pregnancy.

   c. A country with a rapidly growing population levies steep fines on any family that has more than two children.

   d. A government agency runs an ad on television informing women about low-cost birth-control options.

2. Determine whether each of the following changes represents a shift in the choice architecture of a decision. **[LO 23.1]**

   a. After presenting the dessert menu to patrons, the waiter at a restaurant mentions that there's an additional option for dessert not on the menu.

   b. A restaurant presents dessert menus to patrons before they have eaten.

   c. A waiter shows patrons a menu without prices.

   d. A waiter asks patrons whether they would like to order more fries after telling the couple that the plate of fries is very small.

3. Label each of the following examples as a case of *time inconsistency, limited processing capacity, status-quo bias,* or *framing.* **[LO 23.2]**

   a. A person buys a nice bottle of wine for $50 and leaves it in the pantry for 20 years. At that point, the wine has aged and the value has appreciated to $250. Although he would never be willing to buy a bottle of the same wine for $250, the person plans to drink his old bottle rather than sell it.

   b. Every night, a person sets her alarm for 7 a.m. the next morning, and every morning, she hits the snooze button at least four times.

c. People who are told the survival rate for a surgical procedure are more likely to undergo it than people who are told the death rate (even though the death rate is actually the same in both cases).

4. Determine whether each of the following represents loss aversion. **[LO 23.2]**

   a. Nearing retirement, an investor chooses investments with lower return and lower risk because she wants to make sure she has a certain amount of money available in five years.

   b. A gambler refuses to play a game in which if heads shows up after a coin toss he will win $40, but if tails shows up he will lose $50.

   c. Offered a brand-new blanket that is twice as comfortable and cute as her old one—the only two criteria she cares about in a blanket—a toddler refuses to give up her old blanket.

The following information applies to Problems 5, 6, and 7: Clocky™ is an alarm clock that rolls off your bedside table and runs away when you hit the snooze button. When the alarm goes off again, Clocky will be hiding somewhere on the opposite side of your bedroom so that you are forced to get out of bed to turn off the alarm.

5. Clocky is a commitment device to help overcome time inconsistency. Which of the following are the time periods over which someone might have inconsistent preferences and need Clocky's help? **[LO 23.3]**

   a. Between the time the person hits the snooze button and the time the alarm goes off again.

   b. Between the time the person sets the alarm the previous night and the time the alarm goes off.

   c. Between the time the person actually gets out of bed one morning and the time he sets his alarm for the next morning.

6. Which of the following are relevant areas of preference inconsistency that Clocky is able to help with? **[LO 23.3]**

   a. The optimal volume for an alarm.

   b. What time to go to bed at night.

   c. What time to wake up in the morning.

   d. Whether an alarm should be placed on the bedside table or across the room.

7. How much should someone with time-inconsistent preferences be willing to pay for Clocky? **[LO 23.3]**

   a. Nothing because a regular alarm will work just as well.

   b. Something because Clocky increases his utility by getting him up at the right time.

   c. You'd have to pay him to use Clocky because his utility is decreased by having to get out of bed and search around to shut off the alarm.

8. Which of the following is not a strictly rational reason for someone to be interested in a commitment device? **[LO 23.3]**

   a. The device can eliminate the time-inconsistency problem.

   b. By making the decision to restrict choices now, the person saves future effort in deciding among more, but undesirable, choices.

   c. Restricting choice now eliminates the possibility of considering other, potentially better choices that can't be foreseen right now.

   d. The device helps the person make the choice that she wants to make right now but might not make in the future.

9. When it comes to making decisions, which of the following statements are true? Select all that apply. **[LO 23.4]**

   a. Individuals will make the same choices no matter how information is presented.

   b. Anchoring is always helpful when making decisions.

   c. Anchoring can mislead individuals into making suboptimal choices.

   d. Anchoring can help individuals make better decisions.

10. Suppose you want to buy your significant other tickets to see his or her favorite musical on Broadway in New York City, but you have never purchased tickets to a Broadway musical before and don't know how much they cost. What would be a good "anchor" to use in your estimate? **[LO 23.4]**

    a. The cost of movie tickets.

    b. The cost of the soundtrack to the musical.

    c. The cost of tickets to a musical performed by your local community theater group.

    d. The cost of tickets to a Broadway production touring in your hometown.

11. Which of the following are true statements about default rules? (You can choose more than one.) **[LO 23.5]**

    a. Defaults have staying power because opting out of them is typically very costly, requiring people to hire lawyers or prove to authorities that they have sufficient reason for choosing another option.

    b. The more difficult it is to opt out of the default option, the more likely people are to stick with it.

    c. One reason default options might have staying power is that people often equate "default option" with "recommended option."

    d. Default rules work to influence choices only if people are aware of the default option.

12. In which of the following examples would we see the influence of a default option? (You can choose more than one.) **[LO 23.5]**

    a. A doctor recommends continuing treatment, but the ultimate decision of whether to continue treatment is left up to the patient.

    b. A website automatically checks the option "share my activity with my friends on Facebook" when users sign up.

    c. Pets from an animal shelter are automatically spayed or neutered unless the owner would prefer them not to be.

    d. A mobile phone user has to enter a choice at start-up between installing a special feature or not. The user is informed that most people choose to install the special feature.

13. A group of people is offered two scenarios and asked which they would prefer: (A) a 3 percent wage decrease in a world with no inflation or (B) a 3 percent wage increase in a world with 6 percent inflation. **[LO 23.6]**

    a. What is the increase or decrease in the real wage in option A? What about in option B?

    b. Knowing what you know about framing and loss aversion, which option do you expect more people to prefer?

    c. In light of your answer to b, if you were an employer trying to cut real labor costs, would you prefer to have some inflation or no inflation in the economy?

14. Choose the statement that people are more likely to choose based on the framing of the choice. **[LO 23.6]**

    a. Stock investment:

        i. Invest in a stock with low uncertainty of return.

        ii. Invest in a stock with high certainty of return.

    b. Car purchase:

        i. Buy a car that costs $20,000, which is $5,000 cheaper than the next level for that maker.

        ii. Buy a car that costs $20,000, which is $5,000 more expensive than the lower level for that maker.

    c. Movie choice:

        i. Go to the movie to which 100 out of 150 people give a five-star rating.

        ii. Go to the move to which 50 out of 150 people give less than a five-star rating.

    d. Choice of college class:

        i. Take a class in which 50 percent of students get an A.

        ii. Take a class in which 50 percent of students don't get an A.

Endnotes

1. http://www.anderson.ucla.edu/faculty/shlomo.benartzi/smartjpe226.pdf.

2. Cass Sunstein and Richard Thaler, *Nudge* (New Haven: Yale University Press, 2008).

3. https://www.princeton.edu/~kahneman/docs/Publications/Anomalies_DK_JLK_RHT_1991.pdf.

4. http://bucks.blogs.nytimes.com/2010/02/22/what-the-credit-card-act-means-for-you/?_r=0.

Guide to Data Sources

Throughout this text . . . we've used data from a wide variety of sources to present theories on phenomena ranging from international aid to financial crises. Without accurate and timely data, we couldn't reliably say nearly as much about these issues.

Before recent advances in information technology, gathering data was much more cumbersome—and data sources were far less prevalent. Today, we have the opposite problem. The amount of data already collected is astounding. With so much data available, finding the right sources can seem like a challenge.

To help you dive into the real world of economics, we provide this guide to some of the most useful and widely used data sources for the economy. Since the quality of your data will have a big impact on the quality of any investigation in economics, you'll want to be sure you have the best data out there—and, more importantly, the correct data. Going to the right source can help you ensure that your data are from a trusted organization and up to date. (In the United States, the government is often the most reliable source.)

This short guide will introduce you to the sources that many economists use to answer thousands of different questions. In the sections that follow, we provide an overview of each source, including the organization's purpose and the data it hosts, and then we look at an example of how those data have been used. To gain experience using these sources, you'll need to explore each source on your own and learn how to manipulate the data as they appear on the site. To that end, we ask you to answer a few questions using the data you find.

National (United States) Data

Bureau of Economic Analysis (BEA)

http://bea.gov

Interactive database can be found at www.bea.gov/itable/index.cfm

The Bureau of Economic Analysis (BEA) is an agency within the U.S. Department of Commerce. Its mission is to promote "a better understanding of the U.S. economy by providing the most timely, relevant, and accurate economic accounts data in an objective and cost effective manner."

The BEA is one of the most widely cited sources for current economic news. Partly that's because it's responsible for publishing the granddaddy of all economic indicators, GDP. GDP is part of the National Income and Product Accounts, which give a broad overview of economic activity in the United States. The BEA publishes this information quarterly and houses historical data dating back to 1929.

A sample of the indicators you can find . . .

- GDP and its components
- Personal income and outlays
- Consumer spending
- Balance of payments
- Corporate profits
- Foreign direct investment

Note: When looking for information from the BEA (and other sources), be sure to look at the databases and not just the news releases. Only the databases will provide comprehensive information about the indicator over time.

TRY IT YOURSELF

✓APPLICATIONS

Suppose you're an economic advisor to the president and are trying to gauge how well the economy is performing now in comparison to the last few years.

1. Find the historical database for seasonally adjusted real GDP and report the seasonally adjusted real GDP for the latest quarter available.
2. Use this same database to retrieve the quarterly data for GDP for the three most recent years in the database. Which quarter had the highest rate of GDP growth? Which quarter had the lowest? Graph these data over time.

✓PROBLEMS

1. Does consumer spending in the United States tend to stay at the same levels throughout the year, or are there certain months in which it's higher than others?
2. Which countries have the most foreign direct investment in the United States? Where does the United States have the most foreign direct investment?

Federal Reserve Economic Data (FRED), Federal Reserve Bank of St. Louis

http://fred.stlouisfed.org

The Federal Reserve Bank of St. Louis hosts FRED, a database of more than 570,000 U.S. and international economic indicators (time series) from 87 sources. It's the most inclusive, "one-stop shop" data source available for the U.S. economy.

The FRED website allows you to download, graph, track, and compare vast amounts of data covering a wide array of categories. Those include banking, business/fiscal, employment and population, exchange rates, financial data, foreign exchange intervention, GDP, interest rates, international data, monetary aggregates, prices, reserves and monetary base, U.S. regional data, and U.S. Trade and International Transaction data.

In addition, the Atlanta Federal Reserve bank publishes a real-time estimate of GDP growth at www.frbatlanta.org/cqer/research/gdpnow.aspx.

A sample of the indicators you can find . . .

- The federal funds rate
- Yield on Treasury bills
- Money supply
- GDP data

TRY IT YOURSELF

✓ APPLICATIONS

Suppose you're an economist trying to examine how the Federal Reserve responds to various GDP growth rates in the economy.

1. Find the series for the monthly effective federal funds rate. (*Tip:* Use the search bar on the FRED home page.) What is the latest value for the effective federal funds rate? What was the value for the effective federal funds rate two years ago?
2. Now find the series for GDP growth. What is the average growth rate of annual GDP in the last two years?
3. Based on your answers to questions 1 and 2 (and lessons you learned from the macroeconomic chapters), do you think there's a relationship between the federal funds rate and GDP growth? If so, how would you describe that relationship?

✓ PROBLEMS

1. What was the average personal savings rate in 1950? What is it today?
2. How much money is in circulation in the United States today, using M2?

U.S. Bureau of Labor Statistics (BLS)

www.bls.gov

The U.S. Bureau of Labor Statistics (BLS) is a government agency that is the primary source of statistics on employment and prices. Each month, it publishes an "Employment Situation Summary," which, among other statistics, gives an account of the number of unemployed people and the unemployment rate.

Labor statistics are of interest to a diverse crowd: from labor economists trying to understand the relationship between minimum wage and employment, to college graduates attempting to predict their employment prospects.

A sample of the indicators you can find . . .

- Unemployment rate
- Consumer Price Index (CPI)
- Consumer spending
- Wages
- Worker productivity, workplace injuries, illnesses, and fatalities

TRY IT YOURSELF

✓ APPLICATION

Imagine you're advising a presidential candidate running against the incumbent. The candidate wants you to tell her about the employment situation, including specific information about whether certain parts of the population face higher unemployment rates than others do.

1. Find the latest Employment Situation Summary. When was it issued?
2. What was the unemployment rate for the last month? How did it compare to the unemployment rate for the month before that? Was it higher or lower?
3. Finally, look at the site's Table A-4, "Employment status of the civilian population 25 years and over by educational attainment." For the latest month available, what is the difference in the unemployment rate between those with a bachelor's degree and those without a high school diploma?

✓PROBLEMS

1. What is the highest rate of unemployment the United States has experienced in the past 20 years?
2. In the past 20 years, when did the Consumer Price Index have the fastest rate of annual increase?

Congressional Budget Office (CBO)

www.cbo.gov

The Congressional Budget Office (CBO) is a federal agency responsible for providing objective, nonpartisan analysis to assist Congress with budgetary decisions. Whenever you hear politicians argue over whose plan to improve the economy will cost more, it's a good bet that they'll mention a projection from the CBO. The CBO is responsible for projecting the costs of government programs at the request of Congress. The CBO also provides regular reports to Congress on fiscal policy through the *Budget and Economic Outlook* and cost estimates of the president's budget through its *Analysis of the President's Budget.*

A sample of the indicators you can find . . .

- The federal deficit
- Federal spending
- Federal revenue

TRY IT YOURSELF

✓APPLICATIONS

Imagine your professor has announced that the subject for a class debate is "Should the United States balance the budget?" You want to find the statistics that will back up your position.

1. Find the latest version of the *Budget and Economic Outlook* and navigate to the full document. Find the table titled "CBO's Baseline Budget Projections." What is the total deficit projected for this year in billions of dollars? What percentage of GDP does that represent?
2. According to the CBO's economic outlook, will the budget deficit increase, decrease, or remain the same over the next five years?

✓PROBLEMS

1. What is the projected shortfall in Social Security in 2050?
2. What is the projected budget deficit/surplus in 2025 as a percentage of GDP?

U.S. Census Bureau

www.census.gov

Interactive database can be found at http://factfinder2.census.gov/faces/nav/jsf/pages/index.xhtml

The U.S. Census Bureau is an agency within the Department of Commerce. The Bureau is responsible for conducting the United States Census, which attempts to collect very detailed information about all households in the United States every 10 years. These data provide a very clear picture of the changes and trends happening throughout America. In addition to the Census, the Bureau collects data every year through the American Community Survey and other sources.

A sample of the indicators you can find . . .

- Population
- Demographic information about households (age, sex, ethnicity)
- School enrollment
- Poverty
- Health insurance
- The number of businesses in a region
- The number of houses in a region

TRY IT YOURSELF

✓APPLICATIONS

Suppose you're a governor trying to determine whether your state's tax base will increase or decrease. As part of that effort, you want to know about population trends.

1. Find the two most recent population numbers for your state. How much did the population increase or decrease in the last decade?
2. Compare your state's population growth rate to the rate of population growth in the entire United States. Is the United States gaining population faster or slower than your state?

PROBLEMS

1. What is the state with the highest percentage of people living in poverty? With the lowest?
2. How many businesses are operating in your county?

International Data

The World Bank

http://databank.worldbank.org/data/home.aspx

The World Bank is an international financial institution that seeks to reduce poverty. As part of its efforts, it collects and analyzes statistics about economies around the world. Its World Development Indicators (WDI) are a widely cited source of statistics about development; its Global Development Finance indicators provide external debt and financial flows statistics for several countries. The bank publishes these two sources in an online database called the "World DataBank." The World DataBank catalogs indicators about a wide array of topics including income, education, health, gender, and the environment.

A sample of the indicators you can find . . .

- Government expenditure per student
- Urban population growth
- Real interest rate
- Net migration

- Gini coefficients
- Official development assistance

TRY IT YOURSELF

✓ APPLICATIONS

Imagine you're an entrepreneur trying to start a global company and are looking for the best country in which to start it.

1. Navigate to the "Doing Business" database and select it. Under the "Economy" section, click to "Select all." Under the "Series" drop-down, scroll down to the data series called "Ease of doing business index." Select that series, and click on the small icon at the left to see metadata about the series, including a "Long definition" of the series. In your *own* words, what does the ease of doing business index represent?
2. Close the metadata window and open the "Time" drop-down, then choose "Select all." You should now have selected variables for Country, Series, and Time. Click on "Table" (at the top of the screen) to see your choices in table view. On the left-hand side of the page, switch to the "Layout" tab and set the options that will format your table with Country in rows, Series on the page, and Time in columns. Based on the latest available year in the table, what country has the highest ease of doing business? What country has the lowest?
3. What country made the most progress in the index from the earliest year available to the latest year available?

✓ PROBLEMS

1. What country has the lowest literacy rate? What is that rate?
2. Which region in the world has the highest GDP per capita? The lowest?

CIA World Factbook

https://www.cia.gov/library/publications/the-world-factbook

Despite the sound of its title, the CIA's World Factbook is not a book for spies, filled with hidden facts about the inner workings of foreign governments. Rather, the World Factbook provides information on the history, people, government, economy, geography, communications, transportation, military, and transnational issues for 267 world entities. (Of course, spies could use it if they wanted to know any of that information.) If you're looking for the population of Armenia, or the percentage of people working in the agricultural sector in Vietnam, the World Factbook is the place to go.

The main advantage of the World Factbook is its ease of navigation. Whereas finding statistics on other sites is an exercise in sleuthing and patience, the World Factbook divides statistics by country and navigates like any other website—no databases to query here.

A sample of the indicators you can find . . .

- Maps of the major world regions
- Trade statistics
- Miles of paved roads

TRY IT YOURSELF

✓ APPLICATIONS

Suppose your boss is looking at a few countries to invest in and wants you to put together a general country brief for each. Find and state the information detailed below for four countries: Bulgaria, Moldova, Romania, and Poland.

1. People and society
   a. Age structure
   b. Life expectancy at birth
2. Economy
   a. Labor force—by occupation
   b. GDP (purchasing power parity)
   c. GDP—per capita
   d. GDP—real growth rate
   e. GDP—composition, by sector of origin
   f. Exports ($ value)
   g. Exports—partners
   h. Imports ($ value)
   i. Imports—partners

✓PROBLEMS

1. What is the size, in square miles, of Eritrea? Of Ethiopia?
2. How many miles of paved roads are in Poland?

The United Nations Statistics Division

http://data.un.org

Human Development Index can be found at http://hdr.undp.org/en/data/trends

UNdata is an initiative by the United Nations Statistics Division (UNSD) that brings together several data sources hosted by the United Nations. The United Nations collects statistics from its member states on a wide variety of topics. These include crime, education, energy, environment, population, and health, among others. Among its most popular indicators is the Human Development Index, a measure of general well-being calculated across countries. The Human Development Report Office within the United Nations Development Program hosts a site devoted specifically to this indicator. In addition to providing data on HDI, the site allows users to graph the data in simple and compelling ways, distilling complex data into concise graphs.

A sample of the indicators you can find . . .

- Quantity traded of commodity goods
- Gender inequality
- CO_2 emissions
- Foreign direct investment
- Prevalence of HIV

TRY IT YOURSELF

✓APPLICATIONS

Suppose you're the head of a foundation with the mission to support governments and organizations trying to improve primary-school enrollment around the world. You want to know where to start your efforts.

1. Go to data.un.org, navigate to "The State of the World's Children" database, and view the data for "Net attendance ratio in primary education (NAR)." Over what years are the observations given? What are the subgroups for the observations?
2. What country has the lowest attendance rate for males? What is it?
3. What country has the highest attendance rate for females? What is it?

✓ PROBLEMS

1. What is the most populous country?
2. What country receives the most development assistance?

Other Directories of Data

Google's Public Data

www.google.com/publicdata/directory

Google's Public Data site publishes several publicly available datasets in an easy-to-use way. The site continues to add sources; current sources include the U.S. Bureau of Economic Analysis, World Bank, World Economic Forum, International Monetary Fund, and the U.S. Bureau of Labor Statistics, among others.

The U.S. Government

www.data.gov

The U.S. government has combined several government data sources into one site. This can be a good place to start if you know what category of data you need but aren't sure where to look for it.

Williams College Economics Department

http://econ.williams.edu/students/online-resources

The Economics Department at Williams College has provided links to many different data sources on one web page to help students like you conduct research in several areas.

glossary

A

absolute advantage the ability to produce more of a good or service than others can with a given amount of resources

absolute poverty line a measure that defines poverty as income below a certain amount, fixed at a given point in time

accounting profit total revenue minus explicit costs

administrative burden the logistical costs associated with implementing a tax

adverse selection a state that occurs when buyers and sellers have different information about the quality of a good or the riskiness of a situation, and this asymmetric information results in failure to complete transactions that would have been possible if both sides had the same information

agent a person who carries out a task on someone else's behalf

aggregate demand curve a curve that shows the relationship between the overall price level in the economy and total demand

aggregate expenditure (Y) the level of aggregate expenditure that consists of consumption, government spending, net exports, and actual investment by firms

aggregate price level a measure of the average price level for GDP; in practice, the CPI or GDP price deflator

aggregate supply curve a curve that shows the relationship between the overall price level in the economy and total production by firms

altruism a motive for action in which a person's utility increases simply because someone else's utility increases

anchoring estimating unknown quantities by starting from a known "anchor" point

arbitrage the process of taking advantage of market inefficiencies to earn profits

Arrow's impossibility theorem a theorem showing that no voting system can aggregate the preferences of voters over three or more options while satisfying the criteria of an ideal voting system

artificially scarce good a good that is excludable but not rival

autarky an economy that is self-contained and does not engage in trade with outsiders

automatic stabilizers taxes and government spending that affect fiscal policy without specific action from policy-makers

autonomous expenditure spending that is not directly influenced by income; it is instead independent of the current level of aggregate income in the economy

average fixed cost (AFC) fixed cost divided by the quantity of output

average revenue revenue generated per product, calculated as total revenue divided by the quantity sold

average total cost (ATC) total cost divided by the quantity of output

average variable cost (AVC) variable cost divided by the quantity of output

B

backward induction the process of analyzing a problem in reverse, starting with the last choice, then the second-to-last choice, and so on, to determine the optimal strategy

balance of trade the value of exports minus the value of imports

balance-of-payments identity an equation that shows that the value of net exports equals net capital outflow

barter directly offering a good or service in exchange for some good or service you want

behaving strategically acting to achieve a goal by anticipating the interplay between your own and others' decisions

behavioral economics a field of economics that draws on insights from psychology to expand models of individual decision making

bond a form of debt that represents a promise by the bond issuer to repay the face value of the loan, at a specified maturity date, and to pay periodic interest at a specific percentage rate

bubble trade in an asset whose price has risen unsustainably far above historically justified levels

budget constraint a line that is composed of all of the possible combinations of goods and services that a consumer can buy with her or his income

budget deficit an amount of money a government spends beyond the revenue it brings in

budget surplus an amount of revenue a government brings in beyond what it spends

bundle a unique combination of goods and services that a person could choose to consume

business cycle fluctuations of output around the level of potential output in the economy

C

capability something a person is able to be or do, such as to engage fully in life, including having economic and political freedoms

capital manufactured goods that are used to produce new goods

capital gains tax a tax on income earned by buying investments and selling them at a higher price

cartel a number of firms that collude to make collective production decisions about quantities or prices

causation a relationship between two events in which one brings about the other

central bank the institution ultimately responsible for managing the nation's money supply and coordinating the banking system to ensure a sound economy

choice architecture the organization of the context and process in which people make decisions

circular flow model a simplified representation of how the economy's transactions work together

closed economy an economy that does not interact with other countries' economies

clusters networks of interdependent firms, universities, and businesses that focus on the production of a specific type of good

Coase theorem the idea that even in the presence of an externality, individuals can reach an efficient equilibrium through private trades, assuming zero transaction costs

collective-action problem a situation in which a group of people stands to gain from an action that it is not rational for any of the members to undertake individually

collusion the act of working together to make decisions about price and quantity

commitment device a mechanism that allows people to voluntarily restrict their choices in order to make it easier to stick to plans

commitment strategy an agreement to submit to a penalty in the future for defecting from a given strategy

commodity-backed money any form of money that can be legally exchanged into a fixed amount of an underlying commodity

common resource a good that is not excludable but is rival

comparative advantage the ability to produce a good or service at a lower opportunity cost than others

competitive market a market in which fully informed, price-taking buyers and sellers easily trade a standardized good or service

complements goods that are consumed together, so that purchasing one will

make consumers more likely to purchase the other

complete information state of being fully informed about the choices that relevant economic actors face

compounding the process of accumulation that results from the additional interest paid on previously earned interest

conditional cash transfer a program in which financial support is given only to people who engage in certain actions

Condorcet paradox a situation in which the preferences of each individual member of a group are transitive, but the collective preferences of the group are not

constant returns to scale returns that occur when average total cost does not depend on the quantity of output

Consumer Price Index (CPI) a measure that tracks changes in the cost of a basket of goods and services purchased by a typical U.S. household

consumer surplus the net benefit that a consumer receives from purchasing a good or service, measured by the difference between willingness to pay and the actual price

consumption (C) spending on goods and services by private individuals and households

consumption externality an externality that occurs when a good or service is being consumed

contractionary fiscal policy decisions about government spending and taxation intended to decrease aggregate demand

contractionary monetary policy actions that reduce the money supply in order to decrease aggregate demand

convergence theory the theory that countries that start out poor will initially grow faster than rich ones but will eventually converge to the same growth rate

core inflation measure of inflation that measures price changes minus food and energy costs, which are traditionally volatile

correlation a consistently observed relationship between two variables

credit constraint inability to get a loan even though a person expects to be able to repay the loan plus interest

cross-price elasticity of demand a measure of how the demand for one good changes when the price of a different good changes

crowding out the reduction in private borrowing caused by an increase in government borrowing

cyclical unemployment unemployment caused by short-term economic fluctuations

D

deadweight loss a loss of total surplus that occurs because the quantity of a good that is bought and sold is below the market equilibrium quantity

debt service the amount that consumers have to spend to pay their debts, often expressed as a percentage of disposable income

default the failure of a borrower to pay back a loan according to the agreed-upon terms

default rule a rule defining what will automatically occur if a chooser fails to make an active decision otherwise

deflation an overall fall in prices in the economy

demand curve a graph that shows the quantities of a particular good or service that consumers will demand at various prices

demand deposits funds held in bank accounts that can be withdrawn ("demanded") by depositors at any time without advance notice

demand schedule a table that shows the quantities of a particular good or service that consumers are willing and able to purchase (demand) at various prices

depression a particularly severe or extended recession

derivative an asset whose value is based on the value of another asset

diminishing marginal product a principle stating that the marginal product of an input decreases as the quantity of the input increases

diminishing marginal utility the principle that the additional utility gained from consuming successive units of a good or service tends to be smaller than the utility gained from the previous unit

discount rate the interest rate charged by the Fed for loans of reserves through the discount window

discount window the lending facility run by the Fed that allows any bank to borrow reserves

discouraged workers people who have looked for work in the past year but have given up looking because of the condition of the labor market

discretionary spending public expenditures that have to be approved each year

discrimination making choices by using generalizations based on people's observable characteristics like race, gender, and age

diseconomies of scale returns that occur when an increase in the quantity of output increases average total cost

disinflation a period in which inflation rates are falling, but still positive

diversification the process by which risks are shared across many different assets or people, reducing the impact of any particular risk on any one individual

dividend a payment made periodically, typically annually or quarterly, to all shareholders of a company

domestic savings savings for capital investment that come from within a country; equal to domestic income minus consumption spending

dominant strategy a strategy that is the best one for a player to follow no matter what strategy other players choose

dual mandate the twin responsibilities of the Federal Reserve, to use monetary policy to ensure price stability and to maintain full employment

E

economic profit total revenue minus all opportunity costs, explicit and implicit

economic rent the gains that workers and owners of capital receive from supplying their labor or machinery in factor markets

economics the study of how people, individually and collectively, manage resources

economies of scale returns that occur when an increase in the quantity of output decreases average total cost

efficiency use of resources to ensure that people get what they most want and need given the available resources

efficiency wage a wage that is deliberately set above the market rate to increase worker productivity

efficient market an arrangement such that no exchange can make anyone better off without someone becoming worse off

efficient points combinations of production possibilities that squeeze the most output possible from all available resources

efficient scale the quantity of output at which average total cost is minimized

efficient-market hypothesis (EMH) the idea that market prices always incorporate all available information and therefore represent true value as correctly as is possible

elastic demand that has an absolute value of elasticity greater than 1

elasticity a measure of how much consumers and producers will respond to a change in market conditions

embargo a restriction or prohibition of trade in order to put political pressure on a country

endowment effect the tendency of people to place more value on something simply because they own it

equilibrium the situation in a market when the quantity supplied equals the quantity demanded; graphically, this convergence happens where the demand curve intersects the supply curve

equilibrium aggregate expenditure the level of aggregate expenditure where unplanned investment is equal to zero, or, equivalently, where planned aggregate expenditure is equal to actual aggregate expenditure

equilibrium price the price at which the quantity supplied equals the quantity demanded

equilibrium quantity the quantity that is supplied and demanded at the equilibrium price

excess reserves any additional amount, beyond the required reserves, that a bank chooses to keep in reserve

exchange rate the value of one currency expressed in terms of another currency

exchange-rate appreciation an increase in the value of a currency relative to the value of another currency

exchange-rate depreciation a decrease in the value of a currency relative to other currencies

excise tax a sales tax on a specific good or service

excludable a characteristic of a good or service that allows owners to prevent its use by people who have not paid for it

expansionary fiscal policy decisions about government spending and taxation intended to increase aggregate demand

expansionary monetary policy actions that increase the money supply in order to increase aggregate demand

expected value the average of each possible outcome of a future event, weighted by its probability of occurring

expenditure multiplier the factor by which output increases in response to an initial change in aggregate expenditure

explicit costs costs that require a firm to spend money

exports goods and services that are produced domestically and consumed in other countries

external benefits benefits that accrue without compensation to someone other than the person who caused it

external costs costs imposed without compensation on someone other than the person who caused them

externality a cost or benefit imposed without compensation on someone other than the person who caused it

F

factors of production the ingredients that go into making a good or service

federal funds rate the interest rate at which banks choose to lend reserves held at the Fed to one another

Federal Reserve ("the Fed") the system consisting of a seven-member Board of Governors and 12 regional banks that act as the central bank of the United States

fiat money money created by rule, without any commodity to back it

financial intermediaries institutions that channel funds from people who have them to people who want them

financial market a market in which people trade future claims on funds or goods

financial system the group of institutions that bring together savers, borrowers, investors, and insurers in a set of interconnected markets where people trade financial products

financing gap the difference between the savings rate within an economy and the amount of investment needed to achieve sustainable growth

first-mover advantage benefit enjoyed by the player who chooses first and, as a result, gets a higher payoff than those who follow

fiscal policy government decisions about the level of taxation and public spending

fixed costs costs that do not depend on the quantity of output produced

fixed exchange rate an exchange rate that is set by the government, instead of determined by the market

floating exchange rate an exchange rate whose value is determined by the market

foreign direct investment (FDI) investment that occurs when a firm runs part of its operation abroad or owns all or part of another company abroad

foreign portfolio investment investment in domestic financial assets, funded by foreign sources

fractional-reserve banking a banking system in which banks keep on reserve less than 100 percent of their deposits

free-rider problem a problem that occurs when the nonexcludability of a public good leads to undersupply

frictional unemployment unemployment caused by workers who are changing location, job, or career

fungible easily exchangeable or substitutable

G

gains from trade the improvement in outcomes that occurs when producers specialize and exchange goods and services

game a situation involving at least two people that requires those involved to think strategically

game theory the study of how people behave strategically under different circumstances

GDP deflator a measure of the overall change in prices in an economy, using the ratio between real and nominal GDP

GDP per capita a country's GDP divided by its population

Gini coefficient a single-number measure of income inequality; ranges from 0 to 1, with higher numbers meaning greater inequality

government purchases (G) spending on goods and services by all levels of government

Green GDP an alternative measure of GDP that subtracts the environmental costs of production from the positive outputs normally counted in GDP

gross domestic product (GDP) the sum of the market values of all final goods and services produced within a country in a given period of time

gross national product (GNP) the sum of the market values of all final goods and services produced by citizens of a country within a given period of time

H

headline inflation measure of inflation that measures price changes for all of the goods in the market basket of the average urban consumer

heuristic a mental shortcut for making decisions (sometimes in good ways, but sometimes not)

human capital the set of skills, knowledge, experience, and talent that determine the productivity of workers

hyperinflation extremely long-lasting and painful increases in the price level

I

idiosyncratic risk any risk that is unique to a particular company or asset

impact investing investing money in firms to generate both financial and social returns

implicit costs costs that represent forgone opportunities

import quota a limit on the amount of a particular good that can be imported

imports goods and services that are produced in other countries and consumed domestically

in-kind transfer a program that provides specific goods or services, rather than cash, directly to needy recipients

incentive something that causes people to behave in a certain way by changing the trade-offs they face

incidence a description of who bears the burden of a tax

income effect the change in consumption that results from a change in effective wealth due to higher or lower prices

income elasticity of demand a measure of how much the demand for a good changes in response to a change in consumers' incomes

income mobility the ability to improve one's economic circumstances over time

income tax a tax charged on the earnings of individuals and corporations

indexing the practice of automatically increasing payments in proportion to the cost of living

indifference curve a curve showing all the different consumption bundles that provide a consumer with equal levels of utility

industrial policy effort by a government to favor some industries over others

inelastic demand that has an absolute value of elasticity less than 1

inferior goods goods for which demand decreases as income increases

inflation an overall rise in prices in the economy

inflation rate the size of the change in the overall price level; the percent change in a price index such as the CPI from year to year

inflationary output gap an output gap that occurs when equilibrium aggregate expenditure is above the level needed for full employment

information asymmetry a condition in which one participant in a transaction knows more than another participant

institutions the humanly devised constraints that shape human interactions

interest rate the "price of money," typically expressed as a percentage per dollar per unit of time; for savers, it is the price received for letting a bank use money for a specified period of time; for borrowers, it is the price of using money for a specified period of time

inventory the stock of goods that a company produces now but does not sell immediately

investment (I) spending on productive inputs, such as factories, machinery, and inventories

investment trade-off a reduction in current consumption to pay for investment in capital intended to increase future production

K

Keynesian equilibrium a situation in which planned aggregate expenditure is equal to actual aggregate expenditure

L

labor demand curve a graph showing the relationship between the total quantity of labor demanded by all the firms in the economy and the wage rate

labor force people who are in the working-age population and are either employed or unemployed; people who are currently working or who are actively trying to find a job

labor supply curve a graph showing the relationship between the total labor supplied in the economy and the wage rate

labor unions groups of employees who join together to bargain with their employer(s) over salaries and work conditions

labor-force participation rate the number of people in the labor force divided by the working-age population

law of demand a fundamental characteristic of demand that states that, all else equal, quantity demanded rises as price falls

law of supply a fundamental characteristic of supply that states that, all else equal, quantity supplied rises as price rises

leverage the practice of using borrowed money to pay for investments

leverage ratio the ratio of a company's assets to its equity, where equity is defined as the firm's assets minus its liabilities

liquidity a measure of how easily a particular asset can be converted quickly to cash without much loss of value

liquidity-preference model idea that the quantity of money people want to hold is a function of the interest rate

loan an agreement in which a lender gives money to a borrower in exchange for a promise to repay the amount loaned plus an agreed-upon amount of interest

long-run aggregate supply (LRAS) curve a curve that shows the relationship between the overall price level in the economy and total production by firms in the long run

Lorenz curve a graphic representation of income distribution that maps percentage of the population against cumulative percentage of income earned by those people

loss aversion the tendency for people to put more effort into avoiding losses than achieving gains

lump-sum tax (head tax) a tax that charges the same amount to each taxpayer, regardless of their economic behavior or circumstances

M

M1 definition of money that includes cash plus checking account balances

M2 definition of money that includes everything in M1 plus savings accounts and other financial instruments where money is locked away for a specified amount of time; less liquid than M1

macroeconomics the study of the economy as a whole, and how policymakers manage the growth and behavior of the overall economy

mandatory spending public expenditure that "entitles" people to benefits by virtue of age, income, or some other factor

marginal cost (MC) the additional cost incurred by a firm when it produces one additional unit of output

marginal decision making comparison of additional benefits of a choice against the additional costs it would bring, without considering related benefits and costs of past choices

marginal product the increase in output that is generated by an additional unit of input

marginal propensity to consume (MPC) the amount that consumption increases when after-tax income increases by $1

marginal rate of substitution (MRS) the rate at which a consumer is willing to trade or substitute between two goods

marginal revenue the revenue generated by selling an additional unit of a good

marginal tax rate the tax rate charged on the last dollar a taxpayer earns

marginal utility the change in total utility that comes from consuming one additional unit of a good or service

market buyers and sellers who trade a particular good or service

market basket a list of specific goods and services in fixed quantities

market economy an economy in which private individuals, rather than a centralized planning authority, make the decisions

market failures situations in which the assumption of efficient, competitive markets fails to hold

market for loanable funds a market in which savers supply funds to those who want to borrow

market power the ability to noticeably affect market prices

market (systemic) risk any risk that is broadly shared by the entire market or economy; also called systemic risk

means-tested the characteristic of a program that defines eligibility for benefits based on recipients' income

median-voter theorem a model stating that under certain conditions, politicians maximize their votes by taking the policy position preferred by the median voter

medium of exchange the ability to use money to purchase goods and services

menu costs the costs (measured in money, time, and opportunity) of changing prices to keep pace with inflation

microeconomics the study of how individuals and firms manage resources

mid-point method method that measures percentage change in quantity demanded (or quantity supplied) relative to a point midway between two points on a curve; used to estimate elasticity

model a simplified representation of the important parts of a complicated situation

monetary base the sum of currency in circulation and reserves held by banks at the Federal Reserve

monetary policy actions by the central bank to manage the money supply, in pursuit of certain macroeconomic goals

money the set of all assets that are regularly used to directly purchase goods and services

money multiplier the ratio of money created by the lending activities of the banking system to the money created by the government's central bank

money supply the amount of money available in the economy

monopolistic competition a market with many firms that sell goods and services that are similar, but slightly different

monopoly a firm that is the only producer of a good or service with no close substitutes

monopsony a market in which there is only one buyer but many sellers

moral hazard the tendency for people to behave in a riskier way or to renege on contracts when they do not face the full consequences of their actions

multiplier effect the increase in consumer spending that occurs when spending by one person causes others to spend more too, increasing the impact on the economy of the initial spending

mutual fund a portfolio of stocks, bonds, and other assets managed by a professional who makes decisions on behalf of clients

N

Nash equilibrium an equilibrium reached when all players choose the best strategy they can, given the choices of all other players. It is a situation wherein, given the consequences, the player has no regrets about his or her decision

national savings the sum of the private savings of individuals and corporations plus the public savings of the government

natural monopoly a market in which a single firm can produce, at a lower cost than multiple firms, the entire quantity of output demanded

natural rate of unemployment the normal level of unemployment that persists in an economy in the long run

net capital flow the net flow of funds invested outside of a country; specifically, the difference between capital inflows (investment financed by savings from another country) and capital outflows (domestic savings invested abroad)

net exports (NX) exports minus imports; the value of goods and services produced domestically and consumed abroad minus the value of goods and services produced abroad and consumed domestically

net present value (NPV) a measure of the current value of a stream of cash flows expected in the future

network externality the effect that an additional user of a good or participant in an activity has on the value of that good or activity for others

neutrality of money the idea that, in the long run, changes in the money supply affect nominal variables, such as prices and wages, but do not affect real outcomes in the economy

nominal exchange rate the stated rate at which one country's currency can be traded for another country's currency

nominal GDP GDP calculation in which goods and services are valued at current prices

nominal interest rate the reported interest rate, not adjusted for the effects of inflation

non-accelerating inflation rate of unemployment (NAIRU) the lowest possible unemployment rate that will not cause the inflation rate to increase

normal goods goods for which demand increases as income increases

normative statement a claim about how the world should be

nudge an implementation of choice architecture that alters people's behavior in a deliberate and predictable way without changing economic incentives much

O

oligopoly a market with only a few firms, which sell a similar good or service

open economy an economy that interacts with other countries' economies

open-market operations sales or purchases of government bonds by the Fed, to or from banks, on the open market

opportunity cost the value to you of what you have to give up in order to get something; the value you could have gained by choosing the next-best alternative

output gap the difference between actual and potential output in an economy

P

payroll tax a tax on the wages paid to an employee

pension fund a professionally managed portfolio of assets intended to provide income to retirees

perfectly elastic demand demand for which any increase in price will cause quantity demanded to drop to zero; represented by a perfectly horizontal line

perfectly inelastic demand demand for which quantity demanded remains the same regardless of price; represented by a perfectly vertical line

Phillips curve a model that shows the connection between inflation and unemployment in the short run

physical capital the stock of equipment and structures that allow for production of goods and services

Pigovian tax a tax meant to counterbalance a negative externality

planned aggregate expenditure (PAE) the amount of spending and production that businesses, households, and others are planning to make, consisting of planned consumption, investment, government spending, and net exports

planned aggregate expenditure curve planned aggregate expenditure as a function of actual aggregate expenditure, holding all other factors constant

positive statement a factual claim about how the world actually works

potential output the total amount of output a country could produce if all of its resources were fully engaged

poverty rate the percentage of the population that falls below the absolute poverty line

poverty trap a self-reinforcing mechanism that causes the poor to stay poor

PPP-adjustment recalculating economic statistics to account for differences in price levels across countries

present value how much a certain amount of money that will be obtained in the future is worth today

price ceiling a maximum legal price at which a good can be sold

price control a regulation that sets a maximum or minimum legal price for a particular good

price discrimination the practice of charging customers different prices for the same good

price elasticity of demand the size of the change in the quantity demanded of a good or service when its price changes

price elasticity of supply the size of the change in the quantity supplied of a good or service when its price changes

price floor a minimum legal price at which a good can be sold

price index a measure showing how much the cost of a market basket has risen or fallen relative to the cost in a base time period or location

price taker a buyer or seller who cannot affect the market price. In a perfectly competitive market, firms are price takers as a consequence of many sellers selling standardized goods.

principal a person who entrusts someone with a task

prisoners' dilemma a game of strategy in which two people make rational choices that lead to a less-than-ideal result for both

private benefits benefits that accrue directly to the decision maker

private costs costs that fall directly on an economic decision maker

private goods goods that are both excludable and rival

private savings the savings of individuals or corporations within a country

producer surplus the net benefit that a producer receives from the sale of a good or service, measured by the difference between the producer's willingness to sell and the actual price

product differentiation the creation of products that are similar to competitors' products but more attractive in some ways

production externality an externality that occurs when a good or service is being produced

production function the relationship between quantity of inputs and the resulting quantity of outputs

production possibilities frontier (PPF) a line or curve that shows all the possible combinations of two outputs that can be produced using all available resources

productivity output produced per worker

profit the difference between total revenue and total cost

progressive tax a tax that charges low-income people a smaller percentage of their income than high-income people

property tax a tax on the estimated value of a home or other property

proportional/flat tax a tax that takes the same percentage of income from all taxpayers

protectionism a preference for policies that limit trade

public debt the total amount of money that a government owes at a point in time; the cumulative sum of all deficits and surpluses

public good a good that is neither excludable nor rival

public savings the difference between government tax revenue and government spending

purchase price the price paid to gain permanent ownership of a factor of production

purchasing power parity (PPP) the theory that purchasing power in different countries should be the same when stated in a common currency

purchasing power parity (PPP) index index that describes the overall difference in prices of goods between countries

Q

quantitative easing policies that are designed to directly increase the money supply by a certain amount

quantity demanded the amount of a particular good that buyers will purchase at a given price during a specified period

quantity equation the equation $M \times V = P \times Y$, which relates the money supply and velocity of money to the price value of real output

quantity supplied the amount of a particular good or service that producers will offer for sale at a given price during a specified period

quantity theory of money theory that the value of money (and thus the aggregate price level) is determined by the overall quantity of money in existence (the money supply); it states that changes in the price level (inflation or deflation) are primarily the result of changes in the quantity of money

quota rents profits earned by foreign firms or governments under a quota

R

randomized controlled trial (RCT) a method that randomly assigns subjects into control and treatment groups in order to assess the causal link from an intervention to specific outcomes

rational behavior making choices to achieve goals in the most effective way possible

rational ignorance choosing to remain ignorant when the opportunity costs of gathering information outweigh the benefits

real exchange rate the value of goods in one country expressed in terms of the same goods in another country

real GDP GDP calculation in which goods and services are valued at constant prices

real interest rate the interest rate adjusted for the effects of inflation

real-wage or classical unemployment unemployment that results from wages being higher than the market-clearing level

recession a period of significant economic decline

recessionary output gap an output gap that occurs when equilibrium aggregate expenditure is below the level needed for full employment

reciprocity responding to another's action with a similar action

regressive tax a tax that charges low-income people a larger percentage of their income than it charges high-income people

relative poverty line a measure that defines poverty in terms of the income of the rest of the population

rent-seeking the act of pursuing privileges that increase the surplus of a person or group without increasing total surplus

rental price the price paid to use a factor of production for a certain period or task

repeated game a game that is played more than once

required reserves the minimum fraction of deposits that banks are legally required (by the Federal Reserve) to keep on hand

reserve ratio the fraction of deposits a bank must hold as reserves; calculated as the amount of cash kept as reserves divided by the total amount of demand deposits

reserve requirement the regulation that sets the minimum fraction of deposits banks must hold in reserve

reserves the money that a bank keeps on hand, either in cash or in deposits at the Federal Reserve

revealed preference the idea that people's preferences can be determined by observing their choices and behavior

rise vertical distance; calculated as the change in y

risk exists when the costs or benefits of an event or choice are uncertain

risk pooling organizing people into a group to collectively absorb the risk faced by each individual

risk-averse having a low willingness to take on situations with risk; when faced with two options with equal expected value, the one with lower risk is preferred

risk-free rate the interest rate at which one would lend if there were no risk of default; usually approximated by interest rates on U.S. government debt

risk-seeking having a high willingness to take on situations with risk; when faced with two options with equal expected value, the one with higher risk is preferred

rival in consumption (rival) the characteristic of a good for which one person's consumption prevents or decreases others' ability to consume it

run horizontal distance; calculated as the change in x

S

sales tax a tax that is charged on the value of a good or service being purchased

savings the portion of income that is not immediately spent on consumption of goods and services

scarcity the condition of wanting more than we can get with available resources

screening taking action to reveal private information about someone else

securitization the practice of packaging individual debts into a single uniform asset

shoe-leather costs the costs (measured in time, money, and effort) of managing cash in the face of inflation

short-run aggregate supply (SRAS) curve a curve that shows the relationship between the overall price level in the economy and total production by firms in the short run

shortage (excess demand) a situation in which the quantity of a good that is demanded is higher than the quantity supplied

signaling taking action to reveal one's own private information

slope the ratio of vertical distance (change in y) to horizontal distance (change in x)

social benefit the entire benefits of a decision, including both private benefits and external benefits

social cost the entire cost of a decision, including both private costs and any external costs

social insurance government programs under which people pay into a common pool and are eligible to draw on benefits under certain circumstances

specialization spending all of your time producing a particular good

standard deviation a measurement of the amount of variation in a set of numbers

standardized good a good for which any two units have the same features and are interchangeable

statistical discrimination distinguishing between choices by generalizing based on observable characteristics in order to fill in missing information

status-quo bias the tendency to stick with the current situation over other options, even when it is cheap to switch

stock a financial asset that represents partial ownership of a company

store of value a certain amount of purchasing power that money retains over time

structural unemployment unemployment that results from a mismatch between the skills workers can offer and the skills in demand

subsidy a requirement that the government pay an extra amount to producers or consumers of a good

substitutes goods that serve a similar-enough purpose that a consumer might purchase one in place of the other

substitution effect the change in consumption that results from a change in the relative price of goods

sunk cost a cost that has already been incurred and cannot be recovered or refunded

supply curve a graph that shows the quantities of a particular good or service that producers will supply at various prices

supply schedule a table that shows the quantities of a particular good or service that producers will supply at various prices

supply shocks significant events that directly affect production and the aggregate supply curve in the short run

surplus (excess supply) a situation in which the quantity of a good that is supplied is higher than the quantity demanded

surplus a way of measuring who benefits from transactions and by how much

T

tariff a tax on imported goods

tax incidence the relative tax burden borne by buyers and sellers

tax wedge the difference between the price paid by buyers and the price received by sellers in the presence of a tax

time inconsistency a situation in which we change our minds about what we want simply because of the timing of the decision

tit-for-tat a strategy in which a player in a repeated game takes the same action that his or her opponent did in the preceding round

"too big to fail" so large in terms of assets or customers or so historically important that banking regulators allow the bank to keep operating despite insolvency

total cost the amount that a firm pays for all of the inputs that go into producing goods and services

total revenue the amount that a firm receives from the sale of goods and services; calculated as the quantity sold multiplied by the price paid for each unit

total surplus a measure of the combined benefits that everyone receives from participating in an exchange of goods or services

tradable allowance a production or consumption quota that can be bought and sold

trade deficit a negative balance of trade; a greater amount of imports than exports

trade liberalization policies and actions that reduce trade restrictions

trade surplus a positive balance of trade; a greater amount of exports than imports

tragedy of the commons the depletion of a common resource due to individually rational but collectively inefficient overconsumption

transaction costs the costs incurred by buyer and seller in agreeing to and executing a sale of goods or services

Treasury securities debt-financing arrangements made by the U.S. government

U

underemployed workers who are either working less than they would like to or are working in jobs below their skill level

unemployment situation in which someone wants to work but cannot find a job in the current market

unemployment insurance money paid by the government to people who are unemployed

unemployment rate the number of unemployed people divided by the number of people in the labor force

unit of account a standard unit of comparison

unit-elastic demand that has an absolute value of elasticity exactly equal to 1

United Nations Development Program (UNDP) a global United Nations network that provides knowledge and resources to developing countries

utility a measure of the amount of satisfaction a person derives from something

utility function a formula for calculating the total utility that a particular person derives from consuming a combination of goods and services

V

value of the marginal product the increase in revenue generated by the last unit of an input; calculated as the output generated by an input (marginal product) times the unit price of the output

variable costs costs that depend on the quantity of output produced

velocity of money the number of times the entire money supply turns over in a given period

W

willingness to pay (reservation price) the maximum price that a buyer would be willing to pay for a good or service

willingness to sell the minimum price that a seller is willing to accept in exchange for a good or service

World Bank a multinational organization dedicated to providing financial and technical assistance to developing countries

World Trade Organization (WTO) an international organization designed to monitor and enforce trade agreements, while also promoting free trade

Z

zero lower bound the natural lower limit on interest rates

zero-sum game a situation in which whenever one person gains, another loses an equal amount, such that the net value of any transaction is zero

index

Note: **Boldface** entries indicate key terms and the page numbers where they are defined.

A

Abito, Juan Miguel, 258
Abrams, Rachel, 408
Absolute advantage, 33-35, 420
Absolute change in quantity, 83
Absolute payoffs, 213
Absolute poverty line, 527-528, 531
Absolute value, defined, 83
Absolute value of slope, 188C
Accounting profit, 272-274, 309, 310
Acquisitions, 338
Adjusted (taxable) income, 510
Adjustment time, 84-85, 94
Administrative burden, 500, **503**
Advanced market commitment (AMC), 286
Adverse selection
  defined, **231-232, 259**
  information asymmetry and, 231-235, 237-240, 259
  in insurance market, 232, 239-240, 259
  lemons problem and, 232-233, 237, 238
  moral hazard vs., 234-235
  reduction of market efficiency by, 232-233
  student loan programs and, 234-235
  in used-car market, 232-233
Advertising, 362-365
AFC (average fixed cost), 278-280, 282
AFDC (Aid to Families with Dependent Children), 545-546
Affirmative action, 553
Affordable Care Act (2010), 240, 259
AFGE (American Federation of Government Employees), 409
AFL-CIO, 409
Africa. *See also specific regions and countries*
  immigration to U.S. from, 399
  income inequality in, 540, 541
  poverty in, 530, 532
African Americans
  comparative income for, 550
  job-application discrimination and, 551-552
  poverty rate for, 529, 530
African Growth and Opportunity Act of 2000 (AGOA), 423-424
AFSCME (American Federation of State, County and Municipal Employees), 409
Age discrimination, 238, 239, 550
Agent, 233
Aggressive tactics, 326-327
Agricultural Act (1949), 136
Agriculture
  crop insurance, 234
  fertilizer use in, 588-589
  price floors in, 136-139

Aid to Families with Dependent Children (AFDC), 545-546
Airbnb, 119
Air conditioning use, 597-598
Airline prices, 97
Alaska
  cash grants in, 547
  lack of sales tax in, 512
Alcohol taxes, 464, 499, 503-504
Alessi, S. M., 87
Allcott, Hunt, 598
Altruism, 182-184, 214
Amazon, 154, 285, 338, 358, 480, 481
AMC (advanced market commitment), 286
American Federation of Government Employees (AFGE), 409
American Federation of State, County and Municipal Employees (AFSCME), 409
Americans with Disabilities Act (1990), 409
Amtrak, 338, 339
Anchoring, 593
Andreyeva, T., 87
Anthony, Denise, 483
Antitrust laws, 337-338, 409
Appelbaum, Binyamim, 40
Apple Inc., 327, 345, 441, 480
Area under linear curve, 128A-128B
Arnold, Kyle, 408
Arrow, Kenneth, 568, 572
Arrow's impossibility theorem, 572
Artificially scarce goods, 480, 481
Ashenfelter, Orley, 408
Asia. *See also specific regions and countries*
  immigration to U.S. from, 397-399
  income inequality in, 540-541
  poverty in, 530, 531
Asian Americans
  comparative income for, 550
  poverty rate for, 530
Assault rifles, 238, 239
Assembly lines, 37, 313-314, 407
Assumptions, in models, 16
Asymmetric information. *See* Information asymmetry
AT&T, 338, 355
ATC. *See* Average total cost
AuctionWeb, 103
Australia
  elections in, 573
  income mobility in, 543
Austria, organ donation in, 596
Autarky, 425-432
Automobile industry
  assembly line in, 37, 313-314

CAFE standards for, 469
car culture, 451-456
company towns in, 408
competition in, 297, 313-314
lemons problem in, 232-233, 237, 238
market share of domestic and imported vehicle types, 46B, 46C
mileage sticker requirements, 593
"motor mile" in, 297
new car purchases, 180-181
used-car market, 232-233, 236-238
Automobile insurance, 233, 236, 239-240, 254
Autor, David, 40, 419
AVC (average variable cost), 278-280, 282, 304-306
Average fixed cost (AFC), 278-280, 282
Average fixed cost curve, 278-280
Average product, 276
Average revenue, 299, 329, 331
Average total cost (ATC)
  defined, **278**
  description and calculation, 282
  diseconomies of scale and, 284-285
  economies of scale and, 284-285
  graphing, 280
  for monopolies, 332, 333
  in perfectly competitive markets, 304, 306, 308, 310
  price and, 311, 313, 340
Average total cost curve
  diseconomies of scale and, 284-285
  economies of scale and, 284-285
  long run, 283-286
  for monopolistic competition, 357, 359, 360
  for natural monopolies, 338, 339
  in perfectly competitive markets, 311
Average variable cost (AVC), 278-280, 282, 304-306
Average variable cost curve, 278-280
Axelrod, Robert, 214
Axes, in Cartesian coordinate system, 46C-46D
Aztecs, 219-220

B

Babcock, Linda, 108-109
Baby boom generation, 410
Backward induction, 215, 217
"Bad" choices, 589
Bangladesh
  factor distribution of income in, 437
  Grameen Bank in, 3-4, 9, 10, 12, 104, 120, 336
  lack of access to loans in, 5-6

Bangladesh—*Cont.*
 microloans in, 3-4, 8-10, 12, 120
 poverty trap in, 535
 textile industry in, 420-422, 425
Banks, opportunity cost of lending by, 247
Bans, 488-489
Bar charts, 46A-46B
Bargaining game, 218
Barnhart, C., 87
Barriers to entry
 aggressive tactics, 326-327
 branding, 366
 economies of scale, 325-326
 government intervention, 326
 natural monopoly, 325-326
 in oligopolies, 355
 scarce resources, 325
Baseball, 34-35, 383-385, 399-402, 404
Basketball, 337
Behaving strategically, 205
Behavioral economics, 189-199. *See also*
 Consumer behavior; Rational behavior
 choice architecture and, 589
 cognitive biases, 194-196
 commitment devices, 193-194, 589, 592-593
 decision making in, 189-190
 defined, **190**
 fungibility and, 196-198
 implicit cost of ownership and, 195-196
 irrational behavior, 189-190, 194-198
 mental categories for money, 196-198
 procrastination and, 191, 193
 sunk-cost fallacy in, 194-195
 taxes to change behavior, 498-500, 505
 tax incidence and, 506
 temptation and, 191, 192, 590
 time inconsistency and, 191-193
 undervaluing opportunity costs and,
  195-196
Belgium
 comparison of 2017 tax rates, 510
 income mobility in, 543
 organ donation in, 596
Belobaba, P., 87
Ben & Jerry's, 356
Benartzi, Shlomo, 585-586
Berry, Dan, 66
Bertrand, Marianne, 108, 364, 551, 552,
  594-595
Bezos, Jeff, 537
Biases
 cognitive, 194-196
 status-quo, 586
Bid rigging, 337, 375
Bill and Melinda Gates Foundation, 286
Biofuel subsidies, 148-149
Blacks. *See* African Americans
Blanket standards on imports, 439
Blueprint credit card, 197
Bond, Tiffany, 571-572
Boomerang effect, 597-598
Borda count, 571

Borjas, George, 398
Bottom line, 268-269
Bowles, Hannah Riley, 108-109
Brackets, tax, 506-510
Branding, 296, 366-367
Brazil
 enfranchisement in, 578
 income distribution in, 541
 income mobility in, 543
 term limits in, 578
 universal basic income in, 547
Breman, Anna, 192
Bresch, Heather, 267
Breyers, 356
Brockovich, Erin, 462
Brownell, K. D., 87
Brown-Philpot, Stacy, 39
Budget constraint, 173-176, 188G-188L
Budget deficit
 defined, **516**
 as percentage of GDP, 517
 in U.S. (1980-2018), 517
Budget surplus, 516-517
Buffett, Warren, 514, 537
Bundles, 170, 173-175. *See also* Consumption
  bundles
Bureaucratic capture, 576
Burger King, 215-218, 296, 355
Bush, George W., 433-435, 568-569
Bush, Jeb, 566
Business cycle, 518
Business firms
 bottom line and, 268-269
 in circular flow model, 15-16
 constraints on, 294
 corporations, 508, 512
 cost curves for, 277-282
 cost structure, 313
 efficiency in, 11-12
 entry and exit of, 297
 income tax for, 508, 512
 long-run average total cost curve for,
  283-286
 opportunity costs for, 271-272
 production functions in, 274-277
 profits for, 300-307
 promoting competition in public interest,
  211-212
 revenue for, 298-300
 social enterprises, 273-274
 startup costs for, 272
 supply curve and, 307-316
 total cost for, 269, 270
 total revenue for, 88-91
 wants of, 268-269, 294
Buyers
 adverse selection and, 231-233
 consumer surplus, 110-112
 demand and number of, 57
 as demand determinant, 57
 in factor markets, 385
 of labor, 386

 lemons problem and, 232-233, 237, 238
 market equilibrium and, 65
 missing markets and, 119-120
 in perfectly competitive markets, 295, 296
 response to price changes, 502
 subsidies to, 149
 tax burden on, 506
 taxes on, 143-144, 149
 willingness to buy, 53, 80
 willingness to pay, 105-106, 110

C

CAFE standards, 469
Calhoun, Kole, 399
California
 ban on trans fats in, 140-141
 car culture in, 451
 crackdown on immigration, 396, 397
 energy use in, 597-598
 gasoline taxes in, 452
 no-fault divorce laws in, 463
 sales tax in, 512
 West Basin Water Management District,
  487-488
Cameroon trainside market, 293-294, 296,
  308-309, 315
Canada
 income mobility in, 543
 in NAFTA, 567
 tax revenue as percentage of GDP, 515
 universal basic income in, 547
Candidates. *See* Elections
Cap-and-trade policy, 563-564
Capital
 defined, **384**
 factor distribution of income and, 403-404
 factor endowment for comparative
  advantage, 424
 human (*See* Human capital)
 international, 437-438
 markets for, 401-403
 use of term, 401
Capital gains tax, 511
Capital-intensive production, 386, 424
Capitalists and capitalism, 401, 404
Caplan, Bryan, 236
Carbon dioxide, 453
Carbon taxes, 464, 468, 563-564
Car culture, 451-456. *See also* Automobile
  industry
CARD (Credit Card Accountability,
  Responsibility, and Disclosure) Act of
  2010, 594
Careers in economics, 97, 492
Cars. *See* Automobile industry
Cartels, 374, 375
Cartesian coordinate system, 46C-46F
Cash, Johnny, 353
Causation, 13-16, 551
Celebrex, 269
Cell phones
 advertisements for, 362-363

Grameen Bank "phone ladies," 336
market for, 49-72
use by Indian fishermen, 71-72, 120
Ceteris paribus concept, 52
Charitable donations, 180, 182-183, 192
Chase Bank, 197
Cherokee Indians, 547
Chetty, Raj, 152-153, 535
Children, costs of raising, 271
Chile, tax revenue as percentage of GDP, 515
China
    Gini coefficients in, 540
    income mobility in, 543
    population policy in, 410
    poverty in, 531
    trade with U.S., 419, 439
Choice architecture, 585-598. *See also* Choices
    "bad" choices and, 589
    commitment devices and, 589, 592-593
    default rules and, 595
    defined, **587**
    disclosure rules and, 593-594
    endowment effect and, 591
    framing and, 591-592, 597
    information campaigns and, 593-594
    limited processing power and, 590-591
    loss aversion and, 591
    mistakes and, 590-592
    nudges and, 586-589, 593
    organ donation and, 595-596
    reluctance to change, 591
    savings programs and, 585-586
    status-quo bias and, 586, 591
    temptation and, 590
    time inconsistency and, 586, 590, 592
    tools of, 592-598
Choices. *See also* Choice architecture; Political choices
    "bad" choices, 589
    biased by anchoring, 593
    comparison of, 167
    framing, 591-592, 597
    restricting, 592-593
Chrome, 337
Chronic poverty, 529-530
Chuang, Tamara, 274
Cialdini, R., 598
Cigarette taxes, 131, 464, 499, 503-504
Cilliza, Chris, 567
Circular flow model, 15-16
Civilian Conservation Corps, 545
Civil Rights Act (1964), 409, 551, 552
Clayton Antitrust Act (1914), 338, 409
Climate, comparative advantage and, 422-423
Climate change, 453, 468, 563-564
Clinton, Bill, 545
Clinton, Hillary, 267, 567
Close substitutes, 55, 324-325, 358
Coase, Ronald, 460
Coase theorem, 460-463, 491
Coca-Cola Company, 366-367, 439
Coefficient of *x*, 78A

Cognitive biases, 194-196
Cohen, Jessica, 87-88
Coincidence, 13-14
Colbert, Stephen, 483
Cold War, 220-221
Collateral, 10
Collective-action problems, 575
College education. *See also* Student loans
    affirmative action in admissions, 553
    completion rates, 17
    cost-benefit analysis of, 245-246
    cost of, 18, 249
    expected value from, 252
    income and, 17, 236, 245-246, 250
    trade-offs in, 245-246
Collusion
    cooperation as, 212
    defined, **372**
    oligopolies and, 371-375
Colorado River, 491-492
Comcast, 338
Commitment devices, 192-194, 589, **592**-593
Commitment strategy, 209-210, 219-221
Commodities, 296
Common resources, 486-492
    bans and quotas for, 488-489
    conservation efforts, 489-490
    defined, **480**
    examples of, 478
    government regulation of, 488-489
    overconsumption of, 478, 486
    privatization of, 490
    property rights and, 490-492
    social norms and, 487-488
    tradable allowances and, 492
    tragedy of the commons and, 486-492
Community poverty, 533, 535-536
Company towns, 408
Comparative advantage
    absolute advantage vs., 420
    in baseball, 35
    defined, **33**
    factor endowment and, 424
    factors of production for, 422, 424
    gains from trade and, 421
    incomplete specialization and, 425-426
    invisible hand and, 422
    natural resources and climate, 422-423
    over time, 40-41
    in production, 33-34
    roots of, 422-424
    technology and, 424
Competing selves (present vs. future orientation), 191-193
Competition. *See also* Monopolistic competition
    in automobile industry, 297, 313-314
    avoidance through commitment strategy, 209-210
    in oligopolies, 368-374
    promoting in public interest, 210-212

Competitive markets. *See also* Perfectly competitive markets
    characteristics of, 50-52, 294-298
    defined, **50, 294**
    equilibrium price in, 335
    equilibrium quantity in, 335
    failure of, 131
    price in, 71-72, 79-80, 298-300
Complements, 55-56, 188D-188E
Complete information, 231
Compounding
    defined, **248**
    future value calculation, 248-249, 264A-264C
    of interest, 248-249, 264A-264C
    for savers vs. borrowers, 249
Conditional cash transfers, 546
Condorcet paradox, 569-570
Conoco, 211-212
Consent, presumed, 596
Conservation, 489-490
Conspicuous consumption, 181, 323
Constant returns to scale, 284-285
Constraints
    budget, 173-175, 176, 188G-188L
    on business firms, 294
    credit, 535
    decision making and, 167
    information asymmetry and, 231
    on labor demand, 387
    on monopolies, 327
    on policy-makers, 576
    in production possibilities frontier, 27
    utility maximization within, 172-176
    on wants, 5-6
    in willingness to pay or sell, 105
Consumer behavior, 165-185. *See also* Behavioral economics; Decision making
    advertising and, 363-364, 365
    boomerang effect and, 597-598
    branding and, 366
    budget constraint and, 173-176, 188G-188L
    diminishing marginal utility and, 171-172
    equalizing marginal utility and, 188E-188G
    gift-giving, 165, 166, 180
    income changes and, 175-177, 188I
    income effect and, 178, 188J-188K
    indifference curves and, 188A-188L
    price changes and, 177-179, 188I-188K
    price elasticity of demand and, 81-91
    rational utility maximization, 167
    response to change, 188H-188L
    substitution effect and, 179, 188J-188K
    utility function and, 169-170
Consumer expectations. *See* Expectations
Consumer preferences. *See* Preferences
Consumer Price Index (CPI), 528
Consumer surplus
    calculation of, 110-111, 128A, 128B
    deadweight loss and, 118-119
    defined, **110**
    market structure comparison, 374, 375

Consumer surplus—*Cont.*
   in monopolistic competition, 359, 361
   with net-exporters, 429, 430
   with net-importers, 427, 428
   price ceilings and, 133–134
   price changes and, 110–112
   price discrimination and, 344
   price floors and, 137–138
   subsidies and, 148–149
   total, 113–115
Consumption
   conspicuous, 181, 323
   diminishing marginal utility and, 171–172
   income effect and, 178, 188J–188K
   optimal, 188E–188G
   overconsumption of common resources, 478
   policies to encourage or discourage, 131,
      140–141, 143–144, 146
   substitution effect and, 179, 188J–188K
   with and without trade, 421
Consumption bundles, 188A–188C,
      188G–188L
Consumption externalities, 455–458
Contracts, as commitment devices, 193–194
Cooperation, 211, 214
Copyrights, 326, 485–486
Corporations, 508, 512. *See also* Business firms
Correlation, 13–15, 551
Corruption, 576–578
Cortés, Hernán, 219–220
Cost-benefit analysis
   of car culture, 452–454
   of college attendance, 245–246
   expected value and, 252–253
   external costs and benefits, 454
   of intellectual property protection, 326
   of policy-making, 575
   for public goods, 485
   risk factor in, 251
   of supplying labor, 389–393
   time preferences and, 246–247
Cost curves, 277–286
   average fixed, 278–280
   average total (*See* Average total cost curve)
   average variable, 278–280
   in long run, 283–286
   marginal (*See* Marginal cost curve)
   for monopolies, 331, 332, 334
   for monopolistic competition, 357, 359–361
   in perfectly competitive markets, 302,
      304, 305
   in short run, 305
   total, 277, 279
Costs
   of collective action, 575
   college education, 18, 249
   explicit, 271–272, 282
   external, 453–456
   fixed (*See* Fixed costs)
   implicit, 195–196, 271–272, 282
   of living, 528, 530
   marginal (*See* Marginal cost)

   opportunity (*See* Opportunity cost)
   private, 453, 457
   production (*See* Production costs)
   of raising children, 271
   relative to income, 84
   research and development, 268
   social, 453–456
   startup, 272
   sunk, 8, 194–195, 304
   of taxation, 498
   thinking irrationally about, 194–196
   total (*See* Total cost)
   transaction, 51, 296
   variable (*See* Variable costs)
Cost structure, 307, 313
CPI (Consumer Price Index), 528
Credit Card Accountability, Responsibility, and
      Disclosure (CARD) Act of 2010, 594
Credit cards, 197, 198, 249, 594
Credit constraint, 535
Credit crisis, 594
Crop insurance, 234
Cross-price elasticity of demand, 81, 94–96
Cultural attitudes, 396
Cultural differences. *See* Race and ethnicity
Czech Republic, income mobility in, 543

D

Dalai Lama, 3
Deadlines, 193
Deadweight loss
   calculation of, 118
   defined, **118, 133, 501**
   externalities and, 456–458
   government intervention and, 118, 338
   import quotas and, 436
   monopolies and, 334, 338, 374–375
   in monopolistic competition, 359, 361
   oligopolies and, 374–375
   perfectly competitive markets and, 375
   price ceilings and, 133
   price changes and, 118–119
   price floors and, 137, 138
   subsidies and, 147–148
   taxes and, 142, 144, 498, 500–503
Death Cab for Cutie, 353
Death (estate) tax, 513–514
De Beers, 323–334, 354, 355
Debt and debt market. *See* Loans
Decision making. *See also* Choice
      architecture; Choices; Cost-benefit
      analysis
   backward induction and, 215, 217
   in behavioral economics, 189–190
   with complete information, 231
   expected value in, 252–253
   hiring decisions, 235
   littering and, 204–205, 207, 208
   long run, 306–307
   marginal, 8–9, 188E
   new car purchases, 180–181
   risk in, 251

   short run, 304–305
   utility and, 167–168
Decision matrix, in prisoners' dilemma,
      206–208, 210, 211
Decision trees, 216–220
Deductibles, 236
Default rules, 595
Delaware, lack of sales tax in, 512
Demand, 52–59
   cross-price elasticity of, 81, 94–96
   defined, 52
   derived, 385
   determinants of, 53–59, 394–395
   elastic, 85–86, 88–90, 151–152
   for ethanol, 139
   income elasticity of, 81, 95–96
   inelastic, 85–86, 88–90, 151–152
   for labor (*See* Labor demand)
   for land, 402
   law of, 52–53, 328
   market demand, 52
   nonprice determinants of, 53–59, 394–395
   perfectly elastic, 85
   perfectly inelastic, 85
   price elasticity of, 79–92, 96
   price influences on, 52–53
   quantity (*See* Quantity demanded)
   supply and (*See* Supply and demand)
   taxes and, 140–141
   trade-offs and, 59
   unit-elastic, 86, 91
Demand curve
   deadweight loss of taxes, 501
   defined, **53**
   for domestic markets, 428, 429
   elasticity along, 88, 90–91
   elasticity of, 145
   entry and exit effects on, 359
   example of, 54
   indifference curves for derivation of,
      188K–188L
   for labor, 389
   market equilibrium and, 64
   for monopolies, 327–328
   for monopolistic competition, 357–360
   movement along, 58, 141
   number of buyers and, 57
   for oligopolies, 368
   for perfectly competitive markets, 327
   shifts in, 57–59, 66–71, 141, 315–316
   slope of, 46I
   subsidies and, 146, 149
   taxes and, 141, 143–144
   willingness to buy and, 53
   willingness to pay and, 105–106
   for world market, 431
Demand schedule, 53, 54
Demographics
   future of Social Security and, 518
   labor market and, 409–411
   of population policy, 410–411
   of poverty, 528–530

Denmark
    income mobility in, 543
    tax revenue as percentage of GDP, 515
Dependent variables, 46D
Derived demand, 385
Deslandes, Leinani, 407-408
Developing countries, cell phones in, 55,
    71-72
Development economics, 544
Diakonia, 192
Diamond market, 323-334, 354, 355
Dictators, 568
Diehl, M. A., 87
Differentiation. *See* Product differentiation
Diminishing marginal product, 275-276, 298
Diminishing marginal utility, 171-172,
    188C-188D
Diminishing returns, 283
Direction of slope, 46H-46I
Disability benefits, 544, 547, 548
Disclosure laws, 239
Disclosure rules, 593-594
Discretionary spending, 515
Discrimination, 549-553
    affirmative action to combat, 553
    age-based, 238, 239, 550
    defined, **550**
    free markets in reduction of, 552
    gender-based, 238, 239, 551
    in labor market, 239, 550-552
    legislation on, 409
    long-term effects of, 552-553
    positive, 553
    racial, 238, 551-553
    statistical, 237-239, 550
Diseconomies of scale, 284-285
Disenfranchisement, 578-579
Disincentives, 9
Disneyland, 94
Diversification, 256-257
Diversity. *See* Race and ethnicity
Dollars, 16. *See also* Money
Domestic markets
    net-exporters and, 428-430
    net-importers and, 426-428
    supply and demand curves for, 428, 429
    world market vs., 430-432
Dominant strategy
    defined, **207, 373**
    in pricing decisions, 211
    in prisoners' dilemma, 207-208, 373
Domino's Pizza, 366
Dorn, David, 40, 419
Double bottom line, 268-269
Drayer, J., 87
Driving game, 209, 210
Drugs for Neglected Diseases Initiative, 286
Duflo, Esther, 589
Dunkin' Donuts, 51, 79, 94-95
Duopolies, 368-370
Dupas, Pascaline, 87-88
Dylan, Bob, 353

E

Eadie, Dave, 297
Earned Income Tax Credit (EITC), 545, 549
Earnings. *See* Income; Wages
Earthquake insurance, 257
Easements, 489
East Africa, rhinoceros poaching in, 477,
    488-489
East Asia, poverty in, 530
eBay, 103-108, 110-119, 132, 237
Economic analysis, 12-19
    correlation and causation in, 13-15
    models for, 15-17
    overview, 12
    positive and normative, 17-19, 132
Economic development, 544
Economic growth
    income and, 525
    poverty and, 525, 529, 531
    skill-biased technical change and, 542
    in United States, 529
Economic incidence, 146, 506
Economic profit
    defined, **272**
    equation for, 272
    in monopolistic competition, 356, 358,
        359-361
    perfectly competitive markets and, 294,
        308-311, 313
    social enterprises and, 273-274
    zero, 309, 311, 313, 360, 361
Economic rent, 402, 403
Economics
    analysis in (*See* Economic analysis)
    basic insights of, 4-12
    behavioral (*See* Behavioral economics)
    careers in, 97, 492
    of climate change, 563
    defined, **4**
    development, 544
    of elections, 564-574
    environmental, 492
    macroeconomics, 4
    microeconomics, 4
    of policy-making, 574-579
    questions for problem solving in, 5
Economies of scale, 284-285, 325-326
The Economist, 129
Economy
    circular flow model of, 15-16
    efficiency of, 11
    lack of recovery from Great Recession, 567
    size relative to world market, 430-432
    as zero-sum game, 115
Ecotourism, 489
Education. *See also* College education
    gender differences in, 550-551
    as solution to information asymmetry
        problems, 239-240
Efficiency, 103-121. *See also* Surplus
    (efficiency)
    adverse selection in reduction of, 232-233

    defined, **10**
    equity-efficiency trade-off, 548-549
    government intervention and, 11
    innovation and, 11
    market failures and, 11
    as maximization of total surplus, 104
    practical implications of, 11-12
    in production possibilities frontier, 30-31
    profit and, 12
    of taxation, 500-503, 507, 510
Efficiency wage, 407
Efficient markets, 117, 501
Efficient points, 30-31
Efficient scale, 285, 311, 312, 360
EITC (Earned Income Tax Credit), 545, 549
Elastic demand
    cross-price elasticity of demand, 81, 94-96
    defined, **86**
    income elasticity of demand, 81, 95-96
    perfectly elastic, 85
    price changes and, 90
    price elasticity of demand, 79-92, 96
    taxes and, 145, 151-152
    total revenue and, 88-89
Elasticity, 79-98. *See also* Price elasticity of
        demand; Price elasticity of supply
    airline prices and, 97
    calculation of, 102E
    defined, **80**
    measures of, 80-81, 96
    slope and, 102B-102E
    of supply and demand curves, 145
    variations along demand curve, 88, 90-91
Elastic supply, 93, 151-152, 311-312
Elections. *See also* Presidential election
        campaigns; Voting
    Borda count and, 571
    economics of, 564-574
    instant-runoff systems, 571
    median-voter theorem and, 565-567, 577
    number of political parties in, 577
    perfect voting system, 567-572
    political participation in, 572-574
    ranked-choice voting, 571-572
    rational voter myth, 572-574
    term limits, 577-578
    third-party candidate problem in, 568-569
Electronic voting machines, 578
Embargoes, 441-442
Employees. *See also* Labor
    high-skilled workers, 438
    labor-supply decisions for, 390
    low-skilled workers, 437-438
    marginal product and, 275-276
    market power of, 407
    in principal-agent problems, 233
    response to higher wages, 390-393
    savings plans for, 585-586
    screening, 235
    tax effects on, 502
Employers. *See also* Business firms
    hiring decisions by, 235, 239

Employers—*Cont.*
  market power of, 407, 408
  in principal–agent problems, 233
Employment. *See also* Labor market
  affirmative action in, 553
  careers in economics, 97, 492
  interviews for, 235
  job-application discrimination, 551–552
  opportunities for, 533–534
Endangered species, 489, 490
Endowment effect, 591
Enfranchisement, 578–579. *See also* Voting
Entitlement programs, 516, 518, 519
Entry
  barriers to, 325–327, 355, 366
  demand curve effects, 359
  long-run supply curve and, 308–309
  in perfectly competitive markets, 297
  price and supply effects, 311
  production cost changes as motivation for, 313, 314
Environmental economics, 492
Environmental issues. *See also* Pollution
  air conditioning use, 597–598
  biofuels and, 149
  climate change, 453, 468, 563–564
  fair trade movement and, 441
  import standards, 439
  littering, 203–204, 207, 208
EPA (U.S. Environmental Protection Agency), 593
EpiPens, 267–268
Equal Pay Act (1963), 409
Equations. *See also* Linear equations
  absolute value of slope, 188C
  accounting profit, 272
  area of triangle, 128A
  average fixed cost, 278
  average revenue, 299
  average total cost, 278
  average variable cost, 278
  cross-price elasticity of demand, 95
  economic profit, 272
  exit rule, 306
  expected value, 252
  future value, 248, 264B
  government subsidy expenditure, 147
  government tax revenue, 142
  graphs turned into, 78B, 78C
  horizontal distance, 46G
  income elasticity of demand, 95
  interest rates, 248
  line, 78A
  long-run outcomes, 311
  marginal cost, 280
  marginal revenue, 299
  optimal consumption, 188G
  percentage change, 102A–102B
  present value, 250
  price elasticity of demand, 81–82
  price elasticity of supply, 92–93
  profit, 269, 303, 332

revenue, 269
shutdown rule, 305
slope, 46G
slope of budget line, 188G
slope of indifference curve, 188G
tax wedge, 142
total cost, 277
total revenue, 298, 503
total utility, 170
turning graphs into, 78B–78D
value of marginal product, 387
vertical distance, 46G
with *x* and *y* reversed, 78D–78E
Equilibrium
  Coase theorem and, 460
  defined, **63**
  free-trade, 427
  linear equations to solve for, 78H–78I
  market (*See* Market equilibrium)
  Nash equilibrium, 209, 373–374
  noncooperative, 209, 211, 212
  in prisoners' dilemma, 208–209
Equilibrium price
  in competitive markets, 335
  defined, **63**
  demand shifts and, 66–71
  in labor supply, 393–394
  in rental market, 402
  subsidies and, 146–147, 151
  supply shifts and, 67–71
  taxes and, 140–144, 146, 151–152
Equilibrium quantity
  in competitive markets, 335
  defined, **63**
  in labor supply, 393–394
  in rental market, 402
  subsidies and, 146–147, 149, 151
  taxes and, 140–144, 146, 151–152
Equilibrium wage, 393–394, 406, 407
Equity-efficiency trade-off, 548–549
Erin Brockovich (film), 462
Estate tax, 513–514
Ethanol, 139, 148–149
Ethnicity. *See* Race and ethnicity
Etix, 337
Europe. *See also* specific countries
  ban on beef imports, 438–439
  immigration to U.S. from, 397, 399
  income distribution in, 541–542
  income inequality in, 540, 541
  negative population growth in, 410
Eventbrite, 337
Excess demand. *See* Shortage
Excess supply. *See* Surplus (excess supply)
Excise tax, 506, 508, **512**
Excludable goods, 478, 479, 481, 485
Exit
  demand curve effects, 359
  long-run supply curve and, 310–311
  in perfectly competitive markets, 297, 306–307
  price and supply effects, 311

Expectations
  as demand determinant, 57
  future income, 252
  of future prices, 57, 62
  as supply determinant, 62
Expected future income, 252
Expected value, 252–254
Expenditures, government. *See* Government expenditures
Explicit costs, 271–272, 282
Exports, 425, 428–430. *See also* International trade
Extended warranties, 257–258
External benefits, 454, 455, 457
External costs, 453–456
Externalities, 451–470
  of carbon emissions, 563
  from car culture, 451–456
  deadweight loss and, 456–458
  defined, **454**
  negative (*See* Negative externalities)
  network, 454–455
  positive (*See* Positive externalities)
  private solutions to, 459–463
  problems in dealing with, 455–459
  public policies for targeting, 469
  public solutions to, 463–469
  quotas and, 467
  taxes and subsidies to deal with, 464–467
  technology and, 455
  tradable allowances and, 467, 469
ExxonMobil, 211–212, 356

F
Facebook, 46B, 327
Factor distribution of income, 403–405, 437–438
Factor endowment, 424
Factor markets, 384, 385, 404
Factors of production, 383–411
  capital (*See* Capital)
  in circular flow model, 15–16
  in company towns, 408
  for comparative advantage, 422, 424
  defined, **384**
  demographic changes and, 409–411
  derived demand for, 385
  economic rent and, 402, 403
  input combinations, 385–386
  labor (*See* Labor)
  land, 384, 401–404
  marginal productivity and, 385
  market for, 16, 385
  reaching equilibrium, 393–394
  in real-world labor markets, 405–410
  supply and demand for, 437
  taxes and effects on, 502
Fair Employment Act (1941), 409
Fair Labor Standards Act (1938), 409
Fair trade movement, 441
Fajgelbaum, Pablo D., 40
Family and Medical Leave Act (1993), 409

Family poverty, 533
Farming. *See* Agriculture
FBI (U.S. Federal Bureau of Investigation), 366
FC. *See* Fixed costs
FDA (U.S. Food and Drug Administration), 239, 270, 286
Fears, Darryl, 92
Federal Insurance Contribution Act (FICA), 511, 512
Female infanticide, 410
Fertilizer use, 588-589
Fight for $15 Movement, 154-155
Financial crisis of 2008, 576
The Financial Diaries: How American Families Cope in a World of Uncertainty (Morduch & Schneider), 532-533
Financial markets, 576
Finland
  elections in, 573
  income mobility in, 543
  tax revenue as percentage of GDP, 515
  universal basic income in, 547
Firefox, 337
Firms. *See* Business firms
First-mover advantage, 218
First-past-the-post voting, 568-569, 571, 577
Fiscal year, 508
Fixed costs (FC)
  average, 278-280, 282
  defined, **269**
  description of, 282
  examples of, 269-270
  as explicit costs, 271
  in perfectly competitive markets, 303-305
  prescription drugs and, 268
Flat/proportional tax, 506, 507
Florida, in presidential election (2000), 568-569
Food prices, 129-130, 527-528
Food stamps, 129, 545-548
Football, 13-14, 408-409, 571
Ford, Henry, 407
Ford Motor Company, 313-314
Fox, 338
Frame of reference, 181-182
Framing choices, 591-592, 597
France
  Franco-American cheese war, 438-439
  tariffs on Coca-Cola products, 439
  tax revenue as percentage of GDP, 515
Franco-American cheese war (2009), 438-439
Freeling, Bill, 297
Free-rider problem, 481-486
  defined, **482**
  nonexcludability and, 482, 485
  in policy-making, 574-575
  positive externalities and, 482
  solutions to, 484-486
  Wikipedia example, 483
Free trade
  benefits of, 425
  debates regarding, 433
  incomplete specialization and, 424-425

net-exporters and, 428-430
net-importers and, 426, 427
North American Free Trade Agreement, 440
protectionism vs., 437
world market and, 430-432
Free-trade equilibrium, 427
Frey, Carl, 546
Friedman, Milton, 229, 546
Frontier Airlines, 97
Fuel-efficiency standards, 469
Fujiwara, Thomas, 578
Full information, 51, 296
Fungibility, 196-198
Future orientation, 191-193
Future value, 248, 264A-264C

G
Gains, relative, 17
Gains from trade, 26, **37**-40, 421, 427
Games. *See also* Game theory; Strategies
  bargaining, 218
  defined, **204**
  driving game, 209, 210
  littering, 203-204, 207, 208
  market entry, 215-217
  Monopoly, 340-341
  one-time games, 205-212
  repeated, 212-214, 218-219, 374
  sequential, 214-221
  ultimatum, 218
Game theory, 203-221. *See also* Strategies
  bargaining games, 218
  defined, **204**
  Nash equilibrium in, 209, 373-374
  negative-negative outcomes in, 209-211
  noncooperative equilibrium in, 209, 211, 212
  oligopolies and, 371-374
  one-time games, 205-212
  positive-positive outcomes in, 209-211
  prisoners' dilemma, 203-214, 371-374
  repeated games, 212-214, 218-219, 374
  rules, strategies, and payoffs in, 205
  sequential games, 214-221
  ultimatum games, 218
  zero-sum game, 115
Garment industry. *See* Textile industry
Gasoline taxes, 452, 504
Gates, Bill, 537
Gates Foundation, 286
Gaye, Marvin, 353
GDP. *See* Gross domestic product
GEICO Insurance, 364
Gender
  affirmative action and, 553
  discrimination based on, 238, 239, 551
  education and, 550-551
  female infanticide, 410
  income differences and, 108, 550
  wage negotiations and, 108-109
Generational poverty, 533-535
Genetic Information Nondiscrimination Act (2008), 240

Genetic testing, 240
George, Henry, 340
Germany
  comparison of 2017 tax rates, 510
  elections in, 573
  income mobility in, 543
  organ donation in, 596
  tax revenue as percentage of GDP, 515
Geschke, A., 441
Gift-giving, 165, 166, 180
Gillespie, Patrick, 547
Gini coefficient, 539-541
GiveWell, 183
Global warming. *See* Climate change
Golden, Jared, 571
Goldin, Claudia, 17
Goldstein, N., 598
Goods and services
  artificially scarce, 480, 481
  bundles, 170, 173-175
  characteristics of, 478-480
  in circular flow model, 15-16
  common resources, 478, 480, 486-492
  differentiation of (*See* Product differentiation)
  diminishing marginal utility, 171-172, 188C-188D
  excludable, 478, 479, 481, 485
  inferior, 56, 178
  market for, 16
  normal, 56, 178
  private, 478, 480, 481, 485
  production of (*See* Production)
  public, 478, 480-486
  quantity demanded (*See* Quantity demanded)
  quantity supplied (*See* Quantity supplied)
  rationing, 134
  related, 55-56, 61
  rival-in-consumption, 478-481, 485, 486
  specialization in, 36-37
  standardized, 51, 295-296, 356
  subsidies to encourage consumption of, 131
  substitutes (*See* Substitutes)
  utility from, 167
  Veblen, 179
Google, 327
Goolsbee, Austan, 363
Gordy, Berry, 353
Gore, Al, 568-569
Gosling, Ryan, 238
Government
  expenditures (*See* Government expenditures)
  intervention by (*See* Government intervention)
  political structure of, 577-579
  provision of public goods, 484-485
  purchase of excess supply by, 138
  regulation by (*See* Government regulation)
  revenue (*See* Government revenue)
  subsidy costs for, 150

Government expenditures
   discretionary, 515
   entitlements, 516
   for Internal Revenue Service, 503
   mandatory, 516
   national defense, 516
   Social Security, 516, 518-519
   welfare, 516, 548
Government intervention, 129-156
   as barrier to entry, 326
   deadweight loss and, 118, 338
   efficiency and, 11
   evaluation of, 150-155
   food prices and, 129-130
   information asymmetry problems and,
     239-240
   in labor market, 131, 407
   long-run vs. short-run impact of, 153-154
   normative analysis of, 132
   population policy, 410-411
   positive analysis of, 132
   price ceilings and, 132-136
   price floors and, 136-139
   real-world examples, 131-132
   reasons for, 130-131
   subsidies, 131, 146-151
   summary of, 151
Government regulation. *See also* Public policy
   of common resources, 488-489
   of deadweight loss, 338
   information asymmetry problems and,
     239-240
   labor laws, 409
   of minimum wage, 131, 406
   of monopolies, 337-340
   of monopolistic competition, 361-362
Government revenue
   calculation of, 503-505
   capital gains tax, 511
   corporate income tax, 508, 512
   estate tax, 513-514
   excise tax, 506, 508, 512
   fiscal year for, 508
   international comparisons, 514-515
   Laffer curve and, 504-505
   payroll tax, 508, 511-512
   personal income tax, 502, 506-511
   revenue-maximizing point, 504
   sources of, 498, 508-513
   taxes for increasing, 498-500, 503-505
   tax receipts (1940-2018), 508
   U.S. collection of (2018), 514
Graduate tax, 255
Grameen Bank, 3-4, 9, 10, 12, 104, 120, 336
Graphs
   bar charts, 46A-46B
   Cartesian coordinate system, 46C-46F
   creating, 46A-46F
   equations turned into, 78B-78D
   line, 46B, 46C
   of one variable, 46A-46C
   pie charts, 46B, 46C

   time-series, 46B, 46C
   turning into equations, 78B, 78C
   of two variables, 46C-46F
Gratz v. Bollinger (2003), 553
Great Britain. *See* United Kingdom
Great Depression, 545
Great Recession (2007-2009), 567, 594
Greenhouse gases, 453, 468
Griskevicius, V., 598
Gross domestic product (GDP)
   deficits and surpluses as percentage of, 517
   of Mexico, 46B, 46C
   tax revenue as percentage of, 514-515
Group responsibility, 10
Growth. *See* Economic growth
Gruber, Jonathan, 499
GuideStar, 183
Gun control, 238, 239

H

Häagen-Dazs, 356
Haiti earthquake (2010), 182
Hajdu, Tamas and Gabor, 168
Halo effect, 574
Hanson, Gordon, 40, 419
Happiness, 168
"Happy to pay" campaign, 497
Hardin, Garrett, 487, 488
Harmon, Amy, 240
Haspel, Tamar, 398
Head Start, 545
Head tax. *See* Lump-sum tax
Health and health care
   insurance for, 240, 254, 259
   malaria prevention, 87-88
   percent of government expenditures, 516
   poverty trap and, 535
   preventive, 259
Health insurance, 240, 254, 259
Helbling, T., 87
Hendren, Nathaniel, 535
Hershbein, Brad, 17
Heuristics, 593
High-skilled workers, 438
Hill, Jason D., 149
Hiring decisions, 235, 239
Hispanic Americans
   comparative income for, 550
   poverty rate for, 529, 530
Hoar, Will, 571-572
Hockey, 337
Hoffman, David, 221
Holiday season gift-giving, 165, 166
Home Depot, 213
Homelessness, 535
Homeowner's insurance, 254
Horizontal splits, 340
Households, in circular flow model, 15-16
Housing, public, 534-535
Huffman, E.S., 66
Huggins, Miller, 34-35
Hulu, 481

Human capital
   acquisition of, 533
   defined, **399, 533**
   labor market and, 399-401
   population policy and, 410
   poverty in relation to, 533
Husk Power Systems, 273-274

I

Ideal voting system. *See* Perfect voting system
Illegal immigrants, 396-398, 567
Immigration, 396-399, 567
ImpactMatters, 183
Implicit costs, 195-196, **271-272,** 282
Import quotas, 435-436
Imports. *See also* International trade
   defined, **425**
   European Union ban on beef, 438-439
   net-importers, 426-428
   quotas on, 435-436
   standards for, 439-440
   tariffs on, 433-435, 439
Import standards, 439-440
Impossibility theorem (Arrow), 572
Incentives, 9-10
Incidence, 504. *See also* Tax incidence
Income. *See also* Wages
   college education and, 17, 236, 245-246, 250
   consumer response to changes in, 175-
     177, 188I
   cost relative to, 84
   as demand determinant, 56
   distribution of (*See* Income distribution)
   economic growth and, 525
   expected future value of, 252
   factor distribution of, 403-405, 437-438
   gender differences in, 108, 550
   inequality in (*See* Income inequality)
   median, 528
   of professional athletes, 383, 399
   racial and ethnic differences in, 550
   redistribution of, 541-542, 545
   taxable, 510 (*See also* Income tax)
   universal basic income, 546-547
   unstable, 532-533
Income distribution. *See also* Income inequality
   budget constraint and, 173-176, 188G-188L
   factor distribution, 403-405, 437-438
   international comparisons, 540-542
   by quintiles, 537-538, 541
   by race and gender, 550
   wealthiest Americans, 525, 537, 540
Income effect, 178, 188J-188K, 390-393
Income elasticity of demand, 81, **95-96**
Income inequality, 536-553
   among professional athletes, 383, 399
   cross-country comparisons, 538-542
   discrimination and, 549-553
   economic development and, 544
   equity-efficiency trade-off and, 548-549
   growth of, 536
   income mobility vs., 542-543

measurement of, 536–542
public policy goals and, 543–545
redistribution and, 541–542, 545
relevance of, 525–526, 536
rich vs. poor, 525
skill-biased technical change and, 542
strategies for reduction of, 543–549
in United States, 540–542
welfare state and, 545–548
Income mobility, 542–543
Income redistribution, 541–542, 545
Income-support programs, 545–546
Income tax
corporate, 508, 512
defined, **508**
Earned Income Tax Credit, 545, 549
personal, 502, 506–511
Incomplete specialization, 424–425
Independence of irrelevant alternatives, 568, 569
Independent variables, 46D
India
cell phone use by fishermen in, 71–72, 120
income inequality in, 540–541
income mobility in, 543
population policy in, 410
rickshaw rides in, 346
universal basic income in, 547
Indifference curves
complements and, 188D–188E
consumer behavior and, 188A–188L
consumption bundles and, 188A–188C, 188G–188L
defined, **188B**
demand curve derived using, 188K–188L
finding the highest, 188G–188H
income changes and, 188I
price changes and, 188I–188K
properties of, 188C–188D
slope of, 188G
substitutes and, 188D, 188E
utility maximization and, 188E
Industrial Revolution, 40
Inefficiency
created by taxes, 500, 502, 503
deadweight loss and, 500, 502
market failures and, 11
of monopolies, 334
of personal income tax, 502
from rent-seeking, 576
of resource allocation, 478
Inelastic demand, 85–86, 88–90, 151–152
Inelastic supply, 93, 151–152
Inequality. *See* Income inequality
Inferior goods, 56, 178
Information, 229–241. *See also* Information asymmetry
advertising for conveyance of, 362–365
branding for conveyance of, 366–367
complete, 231
full information, 51, 296
importance of, 230

opportunity cost of acquiring, 235
solving information problems, 235–240
Information asymmetry, 231–240
adverse selection and, 231–235, 237–240, 259
advertising and, 364
defined, **231**
education solution for, 239–240
government intervention and, 239–240
in insurance market, 232, 259
lemons problem and, 232–233, 237, 238
moral hazard and, 233–235, 259
perfectly competitive markets and, 296
price discrimination and, 346
principal-agent problems and, 233
problems created by, 231
regulatory solution for, 239–240
reputation solution for, 237
screening solution for, 235–236
signaling solution for, 236–237
statistical discrimination and, 237–238, 550
in used-car market, 232–233
Information campaigns, 593–594
Information overload, 239
Ingraham, Christopher, 155
Inheritance (estate) tax, 513–514
In-kind transfers, 547
Innovation
efficiency and, 11
in monopolistic competition, 360–361
product differentiation and, 356–357, 360
Innovations for Poverty Action (IPA), 589
Inputs
availability of, 94
in circular flow model, 16
fixed costs for, 269–270
marginal product of, 275–277, 385
opportunity cost of using, 272
picking right combination of, 385–386
price elasticity of supply and availability of, 94
prices of, 62
principle of diminishing returns and, 283
in production functions, 274–277
total cost of, 269
Instagram, 455
Instant-noodle sales, 56–57
Instant-runoff systems, 571
Insurance
adverse selection and, 232, 239–240, 259
automobile, 233, 236, 239–240, 254
crop, 234
deductibles, 236
expected value from, 254
health, 240, 254, 259
homeowner's, 254
mandate for, 239–240
market for, 254
moral hazard and, 233–234, 259
pooling and diversifying risk, 254–257
premiums, 254
problems with, 258–259

renter's, 254
risk management and, 254–259
social, 544, 547–548
statistical discrimination and, 239
unemployment, 544, 548
Intellectual property rights, 326, 485–486
Interest rates
caps on payday loans, 135
comparison of, 249
compounding, 248–249, 264A–264C
defined, **247**
equation for, 248
future value calculation, 248, 264A–264C
present value calculation, 249–251
price ceiling on, 135
rule of 70 and, 249, 264C
on student loans, 245
student loans and, 245
value over time and, 247–248
Intergovernmental Panel on Climate Change, 563
Internal Revenue Service (IRS), 235, 503
International poverty, 530–532
International trade, 419–442
absolute advantage in, 33, 34, 420
agreements and treaties, 423–424, 437–442
autarky vs., 425–432
capital and, 437–438
comparative advantage in, 33–34, 40–41, 420–426
embargoes and, 441–442
exports, 425, 428–430
free trade, 424–433, 437
gains from trade, 26, 37–40, 421, 427
impact on society, 419–420
imports (*See* Imports)
labor and, 437–438
labor and environmental standards, 439–441
liberalization of, 433, 437, 438
"most favored nation" status in, 438
net-exporters, 428–430
net-importers, 426–428
production and consumption with and without, 421
protectionism and, 433–437, 439
restrictions on, 433–436
size of economy relative to world market and, 430–432
specialization and, 35–37, 425–426
tit-for-tat strategy in, 439
winners and losers in, 39–40
World Trade Organization in, 435, 438–439
Internet, 110, 337
Intervention. *See* Government intervention
Interviews, 235
Inventory management, 285
Invisible hand, 26, 42, 50, 422, 451
IPA (Innovations for Poverty Action), 589
Iraq, embargo on, 441–442
Ireland, tax revenue as percentage of GDP, 515
Irrational behavior
from cognitive biases, 194–196

Irrational behavior—*Cont.*
    in decision making, 189–190
    with money, 196–198
IRS (Internal Revenue Service), 235, 503
Israel
    comparison of 2017 tax rates, 510
    diamond industry in, 327
Italy, tax revenue as percentage of GDP, 515

J

Japan
    comparison of 2017 tax rates, 510
    income mobility in, 543
Jensen, Robert, 71–72
JetBlue, 97
Jobs. *See* Employment

K

Kahneman, Daniel, 591
Kanemoto, K., 441
Karlan, Dean, 183, 364
Katz, Lawrence, 17, 535
Kearney, Melissa, 17
Kennedy, John F., 553, 573–574
Kenya
    fertilizer use in, 588–589
    universal basic income in, 547
Khandelwal, Amit K., 40
King, B. B., 353
King, Martin Luther, Jr., 3, 546
Kline, B., 87
Kmart, 423
Knetsch, Jack, 591
Kremer, Michael, 589
Kroft, Kory, 152–153
Krueger, Alan, 408
Krugman, P., 87
Kyoto Protocol, 440–441

L

Labor. *See also* Employees; Income; Wages
    buyers and sellers of, 386
    defined, 384
    demand for (*See* Labor demand)
    factor distribution of income and, 403–404
    factor endowment for comparative
        advantage, 424
    international, 437–438
    marginal product of, 275, 385–389, 394–395
    market for (*See* Labor market)
    profit-maximizing quantity of, 388–389
    supply of (*See* Labor supply)
Labor-augmenting technology, 395
Labor demand
    determinants of, 387–389, 394–395
    output price effects and, 394
    shifts in, 394–399
    technology effects and, 394–396
    value of the marginal product and, 387–389
Labor demand curve, 389
Labor-intensive production, 386, 424

Labor market. *See also* Employment
    demand (*See* Labor demand)
    demographic changes and, 409–411
    determinants of supply and demand,
        394–397
    discrimination in, 239, 550–552
    efficiency wage in, 407
    government intervention in, 131, 407
    human capital component of, 399–401
    immigration and, 396–399
    interconnected, 400
    labor laws, 409, 439–441
    minimum wage in, 131, 405–407
    monopsony and, 407
    population policies, 410
    real world, 405–410
    shifts in supply and demand, 394–399
    supply (*See* Labor supply)
Labor-saving technology, 395
Labor standards, 409, 439–441
Labor supply
    cost-benefit analysis and, 389–393
    cultural attitudes and, 396
    determinants of, 395–397
    immigration, 396–399
    opportunity cost and, 389–390, 395
    population and, 396
    price and income effects, 390–393
    shifts in, 394–399
    taxation and, 509–510
    wage rates and, 390–393
Labor supply curve, 390, 391
Labor unions, 218, 408–409
Laffer, Arthur, 504–505
Laffer curve, 504–505
Lai, Lei, 108–109
Land
    defined, 384
    demand for, 402
    factor distribution of income and, 403–404
    factor endowment for comparative
        advantage, 424
    markets for, 401–403
Land-intensive activities, 424
Landry, Craig, 183
Lanthrop, Yannet, 155
Latin America. *See also specific countries*
    immigration to U.S. from, 398
    income inequality in, 540, 541
    poverty in, 531
Latinos/Latinas. *See* Hispanic Americans
Law of demand, 52–53, 328
Law of supply, 59, 60
Lawrence, Jennifer, 238
Leapfrog technology, 55
Leibbrandt, Andres, 109
Leisure, 389–392
Lemons problem, 232–233, 237, 238
Lenzen, M., 441
Lesotho, 423–424, 441
Levin, L., 87
Levi Strauss, 423

Lewis, M. S., 87
Liberum veto, 577
Life, opportunity cost of, 7–8
Limited processing power, 590–591
Linear curve, area under, 128A–128B
Linear equations
    examples of, 78B
    graphs turned into, 78B, 78C
    to interpret equation of a line, 78A–78E
    shifts and pivots, 78E–78H
    solving for equilibrium, 78H–78I
    turning graphs into, 78B–78D
    with x and y reversed, 78D–78E
Line graphs, 46B, 46C
Lines, slope of, 46F
Lipitor, 269
List, John, 109, 183
Littering, 203–204, 207, 208
Loans. *See also* Student loans
    advertisements for, 363–364
    collateral for, 10
    credit constraint, 535
    group responsibility for, 10
    lack of access to, 5–6
    microloans, 3–4, 8–10, 12, 120
    payday, 135, 594–595
Lobbying, 576
Local taxes. *See* State and local taxes
Lohr, Steve, 14
Long, M. W., 87
Long run
    cost curves in, 283–286
    monopolistic competition in, 358–361
    in perfectly competitive markets, 306–314
    shifts in demand, 315–316
Long-run average total cost curve, 283–286
Long-run production costs, 283–286
Long-run supply curve, 306–314
    efficient scale and, 311, 312
    exit rule and, 306–307
    market entry and, 308–309
    market exit and, 310–311
    perfectly elastic, 311–312
    upward slope of, 313–314
Looney, Adam, 152–153
Lorenz curve, 538–540
Los Angeles Angels, 383, 385
Loss aversion, 591
Lowell, Francis Cabot, 32
Lowes, 213
Lowrey, Annie, 546, 547
Low-skilled workers, 437–438
Lump-sum tax (head tax), 502–503, 505, 507
Lyft, 119

M

Macroeconomics, 4
MAD (mutually assured destruction),
    220–221
Mafia, 211
Magie, Elizabeth J., 340–341
Mail-in ballots, 573

Maine, 2nd Congressional District election (2018), 571-572
Major League Baseball (MLB), 34-35, 383-385, 399-402, 404
Malaria prevention, 87-88
Mama Noodles Index, 56
Mandatory spending, 516
Marginal cost curve
    for monopolies, 332, 334, 338, 339
    for monopolistic competition, 357, 359-361
    in perfectly competitive markets, 302, 304, 305
    production costs and, 280-282
Marginal cost (MC)
    defined, **280**
    description and calculation, 282
    equation for, 280
    opportunity cost and, 8
    in perfectly competitive markets, 300-302, 305, 306
    in production costs, 280-282
Marginal decision making, 8-9, 188E
Marginal product
    average product and, 276
    defined, **275, 385**
    diminishing, 275-276, 298
    of inputs, 275-277, 385
    of labor, 275, 385-389, 394-395
    total production and, 275
    value of, 387-389
Marginal productivity, 385, 387
Marginal profit, 300, 301, 388
Marginal rate of substitution (MRS), 188C
Marginal revenue
    defined, **299**
    demand for labor and, 387
    of monopolies, 329-331
    in perfectly competitive markets, 299-302, 305
Marginal revenue curve
    for monopolies, 330, 332, 334
    for monopolistic competition, 357, 359-361
    in oligopolies, 368
    in perfect competition, 302
Marginal revenue product, 387
Marginal social benefit of public goods, 484-485
Marginal tax rate, 509, 510
Marginal utility, 170-176
    budget constraint and, 173-176, 188G-188L
    defined, **170**
    diminishing, 171-172, 188C-188D
    equalizing, 188E-188G
    negative, 171-172
    per dollar spent, 188E
    substitution effect and, 179
    trade-offs and, 173
Marinescu, Ioana, 547
Marjory Stoneman Douglas High School shooting (2018), 238
Market-clearing price, 64
Market demand, 52

Market economy, 50
Market-entry games, 215-217
Market equilibrium
    changes in, 65-71
    convergence of supply and demand at, 63-64
    demand shifts and, 66-71, 315-316
    in perfectly competitive markets, 117
    prices below, 118-119
    reaching, 64-65
    subsidies and, 146-147, 151
    supply shifts and, 67-71
    surplus (efficiency) and, 115-117
    taxes and, 140-144, 151-152
    technology and, 72
Market failures, 11, **131,** 139, 454, 484
Market for factors of production, 16
Market for goods and services, 16
Market power
    of cell phone providers, 362
    defined, **295**
    of labor unions, 408-409
    of monopsony, 407
    price discrimination and, 341-345
    price setting and, 323
Market price
    exit rule and, 306
    net-importers and, 426
    in perfectly competitive markets, 303, 304, 306
    shutdown decisions and, 304
    world price and, 426
Markets, 49-72
    advanced market commitment, 286
    for cell phones, 49-72
    competitive (*See* Competitive markets)
    creating or improving, 119-120
    defined, **50**
    demand and (*See* Demand)
    diamond, 323-334, 354, 355
    in discrimination elimination, 552
    domestic (*See* Domestic markets)
    efficient, 117, 501
    equilibrium (*See* Market equilibrium)
    factor, 384, 385, 404
    financial, 576
    for insurance, 254
    labor (*See* Labor market)
    for land and capital, 401-403
    missing, 119-120
    for organ transplants, 120
    purchase, 402-403
    rental, 402
    scope of, 85
    supply and (*See* Supply)
    world, 430-432
Market share, 46B, 46C, 355
Market structure. *See* Competitive markets; Monopolies; Oligopolies
Market supply, 59
Market supply curve, 308-310, 313-314
Marshall, Julian D., 149
Martin, Dean, 353

Marx, Karl, 403-404
Mass shootings, 238
Maxcy, J. G., 87
MC. *See* Marginal cost
McDonald's, 37, 79, 215-218, 296, 355, 407-408
Means-tested programs, 549
Median income, 528
Median-voter theorem, 565-567, **566,** 577
Medicaid, 545, 547, 548
Medical insurance. *See* Health insurance
Medicare, 511-512, 516, 518, 544, 548
Men. *See* Gender
Mergers, 338
Metallica, 353
Mexico
    Aztecs of, 219-220
    farm workers from, 396
    GDP growth in, 46B, 46C
    in NAFTA, 567
    price ceilings in, 132-134, 136
    subsidies in, 146-149
MFA (Multifiber Arrangement), 423-424, 435-436, 441
Microeconomics, 5
Microloans, 3-4, 8-10, 12, 120
Microsoft Corporation, 327, 337, 338, 342-345, 408
Middle class, 527
Middle East, poverty in, 531
Mid-point method, 81-82, 93
Migration. *See* Immigration
Milk Price Support Program, 136-139
Minimum wage
    advantages and disadvantages, 405-406
    Fight for $15 Movement, 154-155
    government intervention and, 131
    as price floor, 406
Minorities. *See* Race and ethnicity
Mistakes, 590-592
MLB. *See* Major League Baseball
Models
    assumptions clearly stated by, 16
    circular flow, 15-16
    defined, **15**
    economic analysis, 15-17
    policy-making, 574-579
    political choice, 564-574
    prediction of cause and effect by, 16
    production possibilities frontier, 27-32
    real world descriptions in, 17
    utility maximization within constraints, 172-176
Model T Ford, 313-314
Mohammed, Rafi, 258
Money
    creating mental categories for, 196-198
    fungibililty of, 196-198
    future value of, 248-249, 264A-264C
    irrational behavior with, 196-198
    present value of, 249-251
    time preferences, 246-247
    value over time, 246-249

Monopolies, 323–347. *See also* Monopolistic
    competition
    aggressive tactics in, 326–327
    antitrust laws and, 337–338
    barriers to entry and, 325–327
    characteristics of, 335, 360
    control of scarce resources in, 325
    cost curves for, 331, 332, 334
    deadweight loss and, 334, 338, 374–375
    defined, **324**
    demand curve for, 327–328
    diamond market, 323–334, 354, 355
    economies of scale in, 325–326
    government intervention and, 326
    Grameen Bank "phone ladies," 336
    inefficiency of, 334
    labor unions as, 408
    from lack of substitutes, 324–325, 342–343
    monopolistic competition vs., 355, 360
    natural, 325–326, 338–340
    no response to, 340–341
    oligopolies vs., 355
    perfect, 324
    price discrimination and, 341–346
    pricing decisions in, 327–329, 331–333
    problems associated with, 334–335
    profit maximization in, 324, 331–333
    public ownership of, 338–339
    public policy on, 336–341
    regulation of, 337–340
    revenue of, 329–333
    vertical splits, 340
    wants and constraints for, 327
    welfare costs of, 334–335
Monopolistic competition, 355–367
    advertising and, 362–365
    branding and, 366–367
    characteristics of, 355–356, 360
    in cola market, 366–367
    consumer surplus and, 359, 361
    cost curves for, 357, 359–361
    deadweight loss and, 359, 361
    defined, **355**
    demand curve for, 357–360
    desire to sell more in, 360
    economic profit and, 356, 358, 359–361
    innovation in, 360–361
    in long run, 358–361
    marginal revenue curve for, 357, 359–361
    monopolies vs., 355, 360
    in music industry, 354, 356
    perfectly competitive markets vs., 355, 360
    producer surplus and, 359, 361
    product differentiation and, 356–357, 362–365
    profit maximization in, 360
    regulation of, 361–362
    in short run, 357–358
    welfare costs of, 361–362
Monopoly (game), 340–341
Monopsony, 407
Montana, lack of sales tax in, 512
Moore, Becky and Jeremy, 532–533

Moral hazard
    adverse selection vs., 234–235
    defined, **233, 259**
    information asymmetry and, 233–235, 259
    in insurance market, 233–234, 259
    student loan programs and, 235
Moran, D., 441
Morduch, Jonathan, 533
Morse, Adair, 594–595
"Most favored nation" status, 438
Mother Teresa, 3
Motor vehicles. *See* Automobile industry
Motown Records, 353
Movement along demand curve, 58, 141
Movement along supply curve, 62–63, 141
Moving to Opportunity (MTO) program,
    534–535
MRS (marginal rate of substitution), 188C
Mullainathan, Sendhil, 364, 499, 551, 552
Multiculturalism. *See* Race and ethnicity
Multifiber Arrangement (MFA), 423–424,
    435–436, 441
Music industry, 353–361, 367–374, 480–481
Mutually assured destruction (MAD), 220–221
Mylan, 267–268

N

NAALC (North American Agreement on
    Labor Cooperation), 440
Nader, Ralph, 568–569
NAFTA (North American Free Trade
    Agreement), 440, 567
Nash, John, 209
Nash equilibrium, 209, 373–374
National Basketball Association (NBA), 337
National defense spending, 516
National Education Association (NEA), 409
National Employment Law Project, 155
National Football League (NFL), 13–14, 408–409
National Hockey League (NHL), 337
National Labor Relations Act (1935), 409
National Park Service, 91–92
Natural monopolies, 325–326, 338–340
Natural resources, 422–423. *See also*
    Environmental issues
NBA (National Basketball Association), 337
NEA (National Education Association), 409
Necessity, price elasticity of demand and, 84
Neeson, Liam, 238
Negative consumption externalities, 455, 456
Negative correlation, 13
Negative externalities
    of carbon emissions, 563
    consumption, 455, 456
    defined, 454
    effect on surplus, 456
    network, 454
    problem of "too much" and, 455–456
    production, 455–456
    quantifying external costs, 455–456
    supply and demand analysis for, 455, 456
    taxes for countering, 464–465, 499

Negative incentives, 9
Negative marginal utility, 171–172
Negative-negative outcomes, 209–211
Negative production externalities, 455–456
Negative reciprocity, 184
Negative slope, 46I, 102B
Negotiation for wages, 108–109
Neiman, Brent, 362
Nestlé, 356
Net-exporters, 428–430
Netflix, 338, 481
Netherlands, comparison of 2017 tax rates, 510
Net-importers, 426–428
Network externalities, 454–455
Neutral policies, 587
New Deal legislation, 545
New Hampshire, lack of sales tax in, 512
New York City, littering fine in, 204
New York Stock Exchange, 293
New York Yankees, 34–35
New Zealand
    comparison of 2017 tax rates, 510
    vertical splits in, 340
NFL (National Football League), 13–14,
    408–409
NHL (National Hockey League), 337
Nixon, Richard M., 573–574
No-fault divorce laws, 463
Nolan, J., 598
Nonbinding price ceilings, 136
Nonbinding price floors, 139
Noncompete clauses, 408
Noncooperative equilibrium, 209, 211, 212
Nonexcludable goods. *See also* Public goods
    examples of, 479, 481
    free-rider problem and, 482, 485
    privatization solution for, 485–486
Nonmonetary opportunity cost, 195–196
Nonprice determinants of demand
    consumer preferences, 54–55
    defined, 53
    expectations, 57
    income, 56
    labor market, 394–395
    number of buyers, 57
    prices of related goods, 55–56
    shifts in demand curve and, 57–59
Nonprice determinants of supply
    defined, 60
    expectations, 62
    labor market, 395–397
    number of sellers, 62
    prices of inputs, 62
    prices of related goods, 61
    shifts in supply curve and, 62–63
    technology, 61
Nordhaus, William, 468, 563
Normal goods, 56, 178
Normative analysis, 17–19, 132
Normative statements
    defined, **18**
    by Marx, 404

on monopolies, 335
on taxes, 507, 510
Norms, social, 484, 487–488, 597
North American Agreement on Labor
    Cooperation (NAALC), 440
North American Free Trade Agreement
    (NAFTA), 440, 567
Norway
    income mobility in, 542
    tax revenue as percentage of GDP, 515
*Nudge: Improving Decisions About Health, Wealth,
    and Happiness* (Thaler & Sunstein), 586
Nudges, 586–589, **587,** 593
Number of buyers, demand and, 57
Number of sellers, supply and, 62

O

Obama, Barack, 245
Occupational Safety and Health Act
    (1970), 409
Odoni, A., 87
O'Donnell, Rosie, 66
Office Depot, 338
Old Navy, 423
Oligopolies, 367–375
    barriers to entry and, 355
    characteristics of, 355
    collusion and, 371–375
    competition in, 368–374
    deadweight loss and, 374–375
    defined, **355**
    demand curve for, 368
    dominant strategy for, 373
    duopoly type, 368–370
    game theory and, 371–374
    monopolies vs., 355
    in music industry, 354, 367–374
    Nash equilibrium and, 373–374
    perfectly competitive markets vs., 355,
        367–368
    price effect and, 370–371
    public policy on, 374–375
    quantity effect and, 370–371
Olmstead, S. M., 87
Olmstead, T. A., 87
Omertà, 211
Omidyar, Pierre, 103
Omitted variables, 14, 551
One-time games, 205–212
OPEC (Organization of Petroleum Exporting
    Countries), 374
Opportunity cost. *See also* Trade-offs
    of acquiring information, 235
    of bank lending, 247
    in comparative advantage, 424
    defined, **6**
    explicit cost and, 271–272
    gains from trade and, 38–39
    implicit cost and, 271–272
    of input use, 272
    labor supply and, 389–390, 395
    of life, 7–8

marginal cost and, 8
nonmonetary, 195–196
of production, 61
in production possibilities frontier, 29–30
of related goods, 55
in startup costs, 272
substitution effect and, 179
trade-offs and, 6–7, 53, 59, 195
undervaluing, 195–196
of unfair advantage, 237
of voting, 572
of waiting for money, 247
in willingness to pay, 106
in willingness to sell, 108
of working, 390
Optimal consumption, 188E–188G
Optimal production quantity, 302, 360
Oregon, lack of sales tax in, 512
Organ donors, 595–596
Organization of Petroleum Exporting Countries
    (OPEC), 374
Organ transplants, 120, 595–596
Origin, 46D
Orphan drugs, 286
Osborne, Michael, 546
Ostrom, Elinor, 487–488
Outputs. *See also* Production
    in circular flow model, 16
    in production functions, 274–277
    in production possibilities frontier, 27
    variable costs for, 270
Overconsumption of common resources,
    478, 486
Overpopulation, 410

P

Pacula, R. L., 87
Pair-wise majority voting, 569–570
Pandora, 481
Pao, Ellen, 109
Patents, 326, 485–486
Payday loans, 135, 594–595
Pay-for-performance, 404–405
Payoffs
    absolute, 213
    defined, 205
    in driving game, 209, 210
    for littering, 207, 208
    monetary vs. nonmonetary, 205
    in price competition, 211
    in prisoners' dilemma, 207–211
Payroll tax, 508, **511**–512
Peanuts effect, 594
Pearl Jam, 337
Pen, Jan, 537
PepsiCo, 366–367
Percentage change
    calculation of, 102A–102B
    mid-point method for, 81–82, 93
    price elasticity of demand and, 81–83
    price elasticity of supply and, 93
    in quantity, 83

Perfect complements, 188D–188E
Perfectly competitive markets, 293–316
    accounting profit and, 309, 310
    buyers in, 295, 296
    Cameroon trainside market, 293–294, 296,
        308–309, 315
    characteristics of, 50–52, 294–298, 335, 360
    deadweight loss and, 375
    demand curve for, 327
    economic profit and, 294, 308–311, 313
    efficient scale of operations in, 311, 312
    entry and exit in, 297, 306–307
    equilibrium in, 117
    full information in, 51, 296
    long run in, 306–314
    monopolistic competition vs., 355, 360
    oligopolies vs., 355, 367–368
    operating decisions in, 303–307
    price changes in, 302, 303
    price discrimination and, 341
    pricing decisions in, 295
    production decisions in, 300–307
    profit in, 300–306
    quantity supplied vs. quantity demanded
        in, 298
    rarity of, 51
    revenue in, 298–306
    sellers in, 295, 296
    shifts in demand, 315–316
    short run in, 304–305, 307–308
    shutdown decisions in, 304–306
    standardized goods and services in, 51,
        295–296
    supply curve in, 305–316
    transaction costs and, 51, 296
Perfectly elastic demand, 85
Perfectly elastic supply, 93, 311–312
Perfectly inelastic demand, 85
Perfectly inelastic supply, 93
Perfect monopolies, 324
Perfect price discrimination, 344–345
Perfect substitutes, 188D, 188E
Perfect voting system, 567–572
    Arrow's impossibility theorem on, 572
    Condorcet paradox and, 569–570
    criteria for, 568
    first-past-the-post, 568–569, 571, 577
    pair-wise majority voting and, 569–570
    third-party candidate problem in, 568–569
Performance pay, 404–405
Perry, Katy, 353
Personal income tax, 502, 506–511
Peterson Institute of International
    Economics, 434
Petrov, Stanislav, 220–221
Petry, N. M., 87
Pew Research Center, 567
Pfizer, 268–272, 285
Phillips, Sam, 353, 357
Pie charts, 46B, 46C
Pigou, Arthur, 464
Pigovian taxes, **464**–465, 467

Pilon, Mary, 341
Pivots, 78E-78H
Plunkett, Jennifer, 297
Plurality voting. *See* First-past-the-post voting
Pocketbook activism, 441
Poland, *liberum veto* in, 577
Policy-making. *See also* Public policy
    collective-action problems and, 575
    corruption and, 576-578
    diffuse costs and concentrated benefits in, 574-576
    economics of, 574-579
    free-rider problem in, 574-575
    lobbying and, 576
    political structure and, 577-579
    rent-seeking and, 576
    tax incidence and, 506
    wants and constraints in, 576
Polio, 14
Poliquin, Bruce, 571, 572
Political choices, 563-579. *See also* Elections; Voting
    climate change and, 563-564
    economic models of, 564-574
    median-voter theorem and, 565-567, 577
    perfect voting system and, 567-572
    rational voter myth and, 572-574
Political participation, 572-574, 578
Political structure
    enfranchisement and, 578-579
    liberum veto in Poland, 577
    number of political parties in, 577
    policy-making outcomes and, 577-579
    proportional-representation system, 577
    term limits, 577-578
    two-party system, 577
Pollution
    biofuels and, 149
    cap-and-trade policy and, 563-564
    carbon taxes and, 464, 468, 563-564
    costs of, 453
    displacement of, 440
    Kyoto Protocol on, 440-441
    public policies for targeting, 469
    taxes for, 146
Pollution displacement, 440
Pollution taxes, 146
Population. *See also* Demographics
    labor supply and, 396
    overpopulation, 410
Population policy, 410-411
Positive analysis, 17-19, 132
Positive consumption externalities, 457-458
Positive correlation, 13
Positive discrimination, 553
Positive externalities
    consumption, 457-458
    defined, 454
    effect on surplus, 457-459
    free-rider problem and, 482
    network, 455
    problem of "too little" and, 457-459

production, 458-459
    subsidies for capturing, 465-467
    supply and demand analysis for, 457
Positive incentives, 9
Positive-positive outcomes, 209-211
Positive production externalities, 458-459
Positive slope, 46I, 102B
Positive statements
    defined, 18
    on monopolies, 335
    on taxes, 507, 510
Poverty, 526-536. *See also* Poverty line; Poverty rate
    absolute and relative measures, 527-528, 531
    chronic, 529-530
    community-wide, 533, 535-536
    defining, 527, 528
    demographics of, 528-530
    discrimination and, 549-553
    disenfranchisement and, 578
    economic development and, 544
    economic growth and, 525, 529, 531
    equity-efficiency trade-off and, 548-549
    extreme, 531
    generational, 533-535
    income redistribution and, 545
    income-support programs and, 545-546
    international, 530-532
    measurement of, 527-532
    patterns of, 527
    progressive taxes and, 545
    public housing and, 534-535
    public policy goals and, 543-545
    reasons for, 533-536
    safety nets and, 544
    social enterprises and, 273-274
    social insurance programs and, 544, 547-548
    strategies for reduction of, 543-549
    transient, 529-530
    in U.S. (1960-2018), 529
    welfare state and, 545-548
Poverty line
    absolute, 527, 531
    alternative measures, 528
    by family size, 527
    international, 530-532
    means-testing and, 549
    purchasing power parity index and, 530-531
    relative, 528
    in United Kingdom, 528
    in United States, 527-528
Poverty rate
    for African Americans, 529, 530
    decline with rising inequality, 525
    defined, **528**
    economic growth and, 529, 531
    for Hispanic Americans, 529, 530
    in U.S. (1960-2018), 529
Poverty traps, 535
PPF. *See* Production possibilities frontier
Prahalad, C. K., 273
Predatory lending, 135, 594-595

Predatory pricing, 327
Preferences
    "bad" choices and, 589
    as demand determinant, 54-55
    graphical representation of, 188A-188E
    over time, 55
    revealed, 168-169, 191, 499, 585, 589
    time inconsistency and, 191, 192, 590
    of voters, 564
Prelec, Drazen, 198
Premiums (insurance), 254
Prescription drugs, 267-268, 285, 286, 326
Present orientation, 191-193
Present value, 249-251
Presidential election campaigns
    Bush vs. Gore (2000), 568-569
    Kennedy vs. Nixon (1960), 573-574
    Obama vs. Romney (2012), 245
    prisoners' dilemma in, 206-207, 212
    tit-for-tat strategy in, 213
    Trump vs. Clinton (2016), 566-567
Presley, Elvis, 353, 356, 358
Presumed consent, 596
Preventive care, 259
Price ceilings, 132-136
    consumer surplus and, 133-134
    deadweight loss and, 133
    defined, **132**
    in natural monopolies, 339
    nonbinding, 136
    on payday loans, 135
    producer surplus and, 133-134
    shortages caused by, 132, 134
    welfare effects of, 133, 134
Price changes
    consumer response to, 177-179, 188I-188K
    consumer surplus and, 110-112
    deadweight loss and, 118-119
    expectations regarding, 57, 62
    income effect and, 178, 188J-188K
    indifference curves and, 188I-188K
    in perfectly competitive markets, 302, 303
    producer surplus and, 112-113
    quantity demanded and, 52-53, 81-84
    quantity supplied and, 59
    response of buyers and sellers to, 502
    substitution effect and, 179, 188J-188K
    total revenue and, 88-89
    total surplus and, 114
Price controls, 132-139
    defined, **132**
    long- vs. short-run impact, 153-154
    in natural monopolies, 339
    price ceilings, 132-136
    price floors, 136-139, 153-154
    quantity supplied/demanded and, 132, 150
Price discrimination, 341-346
    defined, **341**
    imperfect, 344
    information asymmetry and, 346
    lack of substitutes and, 342-343
    perfect, 344-345

real-world, 345
willingness to pay and, 344–346
Price effect
labor supply and, 390–393
in oligopolies, 370–371
of tax increases, 504
total revenue and, 88–89, 330
Price elasticity of demand, 79–92
calculation of, 81–83
cross-price elasticity of demand, 81, 94–95
deadweight loss of taxes, 502
defined, **81**
determinants of, 84–85
estimated, 87
extremes of, 85–86
for gourmet coffee, 79–82, 94–96
malaria prevention and, 87–88
mid-point method and, 81–82
national park entrance fees and, 91–92
nature of, 80
summary of, 96
tax increases and, 151–152
utilization of, 85–92
Price elasticity of supply
calculation of, 92–93
defined, **92**
determinants of, 93–94
mid-point method and, 93
nature of, 80
summary of, 96
tax increases and, 151–152
Price fixing, 337
Price floors, 136–139
in agriculture, 136–139
consumer surplus and, 137–138
deadweight loss and, 137, 138
defined, **136**
long- vs. short-run impact, 153–154
minimum wage, 406
nonbinding, 139
producer surplus and, 137–138
welfare effects of, 138
Price level
quota effects, 436
steel tariff, 433–435
tax effects and, 498, 499
Price-matching guarantees, 213
Prices
average total cost and, 311, 313, 340
below market equilibrium, 118–119
changes in (*See* Price changes)
in competitive markets, 71–72, 79–80, 298–300
demand curve shifts and, 57–59
demand schedule and, 53, 54
equilibrium (*See* Equilibrium price)
food prices, 129–130, 527–528
of inputs, 62
of labor, 387
market (*See* Market price)
market-clearing price, 64
net-importers and, 426, 427

of output and labor demand, 394
of prescription drugs, 267–268
purchase price, 401–402
of related goods, 55–56, 61
rental price, 401–402
supply curve shifts and, 62–63
supply schedule and, 60
tax wedge and, 142
Veblen goods and, 179
willingness to pay and, 105–106
willingness to sale and, 105, 107–108
world (*See* World price)
Prices of related goods, 55–56, 61
Price takers
defined, **51**
demand for labor and, 387
monopolistic competition and, 358
in perfectly competitive markets, 51, 295, 298
in world market, 430–432
Pricing analysts, 97
Pricing decisions
dominant strategy in, 211
in monopolies, 327–329, 331–333
in oligopolies, 368–369
in perfectly competitive markets, 295
predatory pricing, 327
price-matching guarantees, 213
in repeated games, 212
by Starbucks, 79–80
Principal, 233
Principal–agent problems, 233
Prisoners' dilemma, 203–214
commitment strategy in, 209–210
competition between firms, 211–212
decision matrix in, 206–208, 210, 211
defined, **205**
dominant strategy in, 207–208, 211, 373
littering problem and, 203–204, 207, 208
oligopolies and, 371–374
payoffs in, 207–211
in presidential campaigns, 206–207, 212
preventing cooperation in, 211
reaching equilibrium in, 208–209
repeated play in, 212–214
tit-for-tat strategy in, 212–214
without dominant strategy, 208
Private benefits, 454, 457, 458
Private costs, 453, 457
Private goods, 478, 480, 481, 485
Private solutions to externalities, 459–463
Privatization of goods and resources, 485–486, 490
Processing power, limited, 590–591
Procrastination, 191, 193
Producer surplus
calculation of, 112, 128A–128B
deadweight loss and, 118–119
defined, **112**
economic rent and, 402
market structure comparison, 374, 375
in monopolistic competition, 359, 361

with net-exporters, 429, 430
with net-importers, 427, 428
price ceilings and, 133–134
price changes and, 112–113
price discrimination and, 344
price floors and, 137–138
subsidies and, 148–150
total, 113–115
Product differentiation
advertising and, 362–365
branding and, 296, 366–367
Coke vs. Pepsi, 366–367
defined, **356**
demand curve and, 358
innovation and, 356–357, 360
in monopolistic competition, 356–357, 362–365
quality and, 296
Production. *See also* Outputs
absolute advantage in, 33, 34
assembly lines in, 37, 313–314
capital-intensive, 386, 424
comparative advantage in, 33–34, 40–41
constant returns to scale and, 284–285
coordination in, 26
costs of (*See* Production costs)
decisions in (*See* Production decisions)
diseconomies of scale and, 284–285
economies of scale and, 284–285
factors of (*See* Factors of production)
flexibility in, 94
labor-intensive, 386, 424
opportunity cost of, 61
policies to encourage or discourage, 131, 140–143, 146
possibilities for, 27–32
specialization in, 26, 35–36
of T-shirts, 25–39
with and without trade, 421
Production costs, 267–287
cost curves for, 277–282
explicit costs, 271–272, 282
fixed costs, 269–270, 278–280, 282
implicit costs, 271–272, 282
labor productivity and, 387–388
in long run, 283–286
marginal cost, 280–282
market entry due to changes in, 313, 314
for monopolies, 338
for prescription drugs, 267–268
production functions and, 274–277
returns to scale, 284–285
in short run, 283, 285
summary of, 282
as supply determinant, 62
total cost, 269, 278, 280, 282
variable costs, 270, 278–280, 282
Production decisions
factors of production in, 385–386
in monopolistic competition, 357, 360
in oligopolies, 368–371
in perfectly competitive markets, 300–307

Production decisions—*Cont.*
　pollution displacement and, 440
　profit maximization and, 388
Production externalities, 455–456, 458–459
Production functions, 274–277, 385
Production possibilities frontier (PPF)
　constraints in, 27
　defined, **27**
　efficient points in, 30–31
　gains from trade and, 38
　opportunity cost in, 29–30
　shifting, 31–32
　technology and, 32
　trade-offs in, 29
　wants in, 27
　wheat vs. T-shirt production example, 27–32
Production taxes, 464
Profit. *See also* Economic profit; Profit
　　maximization
　accounting profit, 272–274, 309, 310
　calculation of, 269, 303, 332
　defined, **269**
　efficiency and, 12
　labor and, 388–389
　marginal, 300, 301, 388
　in oligopolies, 369–371
　in perfectly competitive markets, 300–306
Profit maximization
　factors of production in, 386
　as goal of firms, 268–269
　input combinations and, 386
　in monopolies, 324, 331–333
　in monopolistic competition, 360
　in perfectly competitive markets, 300–305
　production decisions and, 388
Profit-maximizing quantity of labor, 388–389
Profit motive, 268–269, 339
Progressive tax
　brackets for, 506–507
　corporate income tax, 512
　defined, **506**
　efficiency of, 510
　personal income tax, 506–507, 509
　welfare state and, 545
Property rights
　in airline seating, 461–462
　common resources and, 490–492
　intellectual, 326, 485–486
　public goods and, 485–486
　tradable allowances and, 492
Property tax, 513
Proportional/flat tax, 506, 507
Proportional-representation system, 577
Protectionism
　defined, **433**
　free trade vs., 437
　quotas and, 435–436
　reasons for, 433
　tariffs and, 433–436, 439
Public budget, 514–519. *See also* Taxes and
　　taxation
　balancing, 516–518

business cycle and, 518
deficits and surpluses, 516–517
expenditures, 515–516
future of Social Security and, 518–519
income redistribution through, 541–542
revenue for, 514–515
Public goods, 481–486
　cost-benefit analysis for, 485
　defined, **480**
　determining right amount of, 485
　examples of, 478, 481
　free-rider problem and, 481–486
　government provision of, 484–485
　marginal social benefit of, 484–485
　nonexcludable, 482, 485
　paying for, 485
　privatization of, 485–486
　property rights and, 485–486
　social norms and, 484
　undersupplied, 478, 482–484, 486, 574
Public housing, 534–535
Public interest, promoting competition in,
　　210–212
Public ownership of natural monopolies,
　　338–339
Public policy. *See also* Government regulation;
　　Policy-making
　cap-and-trade policy, 563–564
　carbon taxes and, 563–564
　on climate change, 563–564
　during Great Depression, 545
　income inequality and, 543–545
　on monopolies, 336–341
　nudges and, 588
　on oligopolies, 374–375
　poverty reduction and, 543–545
　targeting externalities with, 469
Public solutions to externalities, 463–469
Purchase markets, 402–403
Purchase price, 401–402
Purchasing power parity index, 530–531

Q

Quadrants, 46D–46F
Quality
　branding and, 366
　in differentiation of goods and services, 296
　of environment, 440
Quantity, absolute vs. percentage change in, 83
Quantity demanded
　cross-price elasticity of demand and, 95
　defined, **52**
　determinants of, 53–57
　income elasticity of demand and, 95–96
　linear equations and, 78H–78I
　in perfectly competitive markets, 298
　perfectly elastic demand and, 85
　perfectly inelastic demand and, 85
　price changes and, 52–53, 81–84
　price controls and, 132, 150
　price elasticity and, 151–152
　quotas and, 436

shifts in demand curve and, 57–59
shortage and, 65
surplus and, 64–65
tax increases and, 151
Veblen goods and, 179
Quantity effect
　in oligopolies, 370–371
　of tax increases, 504
　total revenue and, 88–89, 330
Quantity supplied
　defined, **59**
　determinants of, 60–62
　linear equations and, 78H–78I
　in perfectly competitive markets, 298
　price changes and, 59
　price controls and, 132, 150
　quotas and, 436
　shortage and, 65
　surplus and, 64–65
Quintiles of income distribution, 537–538, 541
Quota rents, 436
Quotas
　in affirmative action, 553
　for common resources, 488–489
　to deal with externalities, 467
　import, 435–436
　tradable allowances, 467, 469

R

Rabe, Barry, 468
Race and ethnicity
　affirmative action and, 553
　discrimination based on, 238, 551–553
　income differences and, 550
　poverty rate by, 529, 530
Raghubir, Priya, 198
R&D (research and development), 268,
　285, 286
Ranked-choice voting, 571–572
Rational behavior
　in decision making, 189–190
　defined, **4**
　marginal decision making and, 8
　opportunity cost and, 6
　trade-offs and, 205
　in utility maximization, 167, 173
　of voters, 572–574
Rational ignorance, 572, 573
Rational utility maximization, 167, 173
Rational voter myth, 572–574
Rationing of goods, 134
Reagan, Ronald W., 505
Real world descriptions, in models, 17
Real-world labor markets, 405–410
　demographic changes in, 409–411
　efficiency wage in, 407
　labor unions in, 408–409
　minimum wage in, 405–407
　monopsony and, 407
Real-world price discrimination, 345
Recession
　financial crisis of 2008, 576

Great Recession, 567, 594
  prediction of, 56
Reciprocal altruism, 214
Reciprocity, 183-184
Regents of the University of California v. Bakke (1978), 553
Regressive tax, 507, 513
Regulation. *See* Government regulation
Related goods, 55-56, 61
Relative gain, 17
Relative poverty line, 528
Relative status, 182
Reluctance to change, 591
Rent
  economic rent vs., 403
  quota rents, 436
Rental markets, 402
Rental price, 401-402
Renter's insurance, 254
Rent-seeking, 134, **576**
Repeated games
  defined, **212**
  in oligopolies, 374
  prisoners' dilemma, 212-214
  sequential, 218-219
  strategies in, 212-214
Reputation, 237
Research and development (R&D), 268, 285, 286
Reservation price. *See* Willingness to pay
Resources. *See also* Common resources
  allocation of, 11, 404, 478
  defined, 11
  intangible, 4
  natural, 422-423
Retirement benefits. *See also* Social Security
  age of eligibility for, 518
  Medicare, 511-512, 516, 518, 544, 548
Retirement savings, 585-586, 588
Returns to scale, 284-285
Revealed preferences
  "bad" choices and, 589
  in behavioral economics, 191, 499
  defined, **169**
  savings and, 585
  utility and, 168-169
Revenue
  average, 299, 329, 331
  calculation of, 269
  government (*See* Government revenue)
  marginal (*See* Marginal revenue)
  of monopolies, 329-333
  in perfectly competitive markets, 298-306
  for public budget, 514-515
  from taxes, 498-500, 503-505, 514-515
  total (*See* Total revenue)
Reverse causation, 14-15
Rhinoceros poaching, 477, 487-490
Rhodes, Cecil, 324
Rickshaw rides, 346
Rise, 46G

Risk
  defined, **251**
  diversifying, 256-257
  management of, 254-259
  pooling, 255
  propensity for, 253
  uncertainty vs., 251
Risk aversion, 253, 591
Risk management, 254-259
Risk pooling, 255
Risk-seeking, 253
Rival-in-consumption goods, 478-481, 485, 486
Robinson, Jonathan, 589
Romney, Mitt, 245
Roosevelt, Theodore, 337, 477
Ros, A. J., 87
Rossen, Jake, 66
Rowling, J. K., 482
Rubio, Marco, 566
Rule of 70, 249, 264C
Rules for games, 205
Rules of thumb, 237, 238, 593
Run, 46G
Rungfapaisarn, Kwanchai, 57
Russia, population policy in, 410
Ruth, Babe, 34-35

S

Saez, Emmanuel, 540
Safari, 337
Safety nets, 544
Salant, Yuval, 258
Salary. *See* Income; Wages
Sales tax, 152-153, 503, 506-508, **512-**513
Salk, Jonas, 14
Save More Tomorrow (SMarT) program, 585-586, 588, 590-593, 597
Savings programs, 585-586, 588, 597
Scarce resources, as barrier to entry, 325
Scarcity, 6-7
Schlosser, Eric, 37
Schmitt, Mark, 567
Schneider, Rachel, 533
School. *See* Education
School shootings, 238
Schultz, P. W., 598
Scope of market, 85
Screening, 235-236
Scroogenomics (Waldfogel), 165
SEC (U.S. Securities and Exchange Commission), 576
Sellers
  adverse selection and, 231-233
  in factor markets, 385
  of labor, 386
  market equilibrium and, 64
  missing markets and, 119-120
  number of, 62
  in perfectly competitive markets, 295, 296
  producer surplus, 112-113
  response to price changes, 502
  subsidies to, 146-147, 149

  tax burden on, 506
  taxes on, 140-143, 149
  willingness to sell, 60, 105, 107-108
Sequential games, 214-221
  backward induction in, 215, 217
  commitment strategy in, 219-221
  decision trees in, 216-217
  first-mover advantage in, 218
  market entry, 215-217
  repeated, 218-219
Services. *See* Goods and services
Shafir, Eldar, 364
Shakira, 353
Shark Tank (television show), 309-310
Shell, 356
Sherman Antitrust Act (1890), 337, 338
Shifts, 78E-78H
Shifts in demand curve
  equilibrium changes and, 66-71
  nonprice determinants of demand and, 57-59
  in perfectly competitive markets, 315-316
  taxes and, 141
Shifts in supply curve
  equilibrium change and, 67-71
  nonprice determinants of supply and, 62-63
  taxes and, 141
The Shins, 354
Shortage (excess demand), 65-66, 132, 134
Short run
  cost curves in, 283, 285
  monopolistic competition in, 357-358
  in perfectly competitive markets, 304-305, 307-308
  shifts in demand, 315
Short-run production costs, 283, 285
Short-run supply curve, 305, 307-308
Shutdown decisions, 304-306
Signaling, 236-237, 364-365
Simester, Duncan, 198
Singapore, littering fine in, 204
Singer, Peter, 7, 8
Single tax, 340-341
Single-variable graphs, 46A-46C
Sin taxes, 464, 499, 503-504
Situation of no regrets, 209
Skill-biased technical change, 542
Slope
  absolute value of, 188C
  of budget line, 188G
  calculation of, 46G-46H, 102E
  defined, **46G**
  of demand curve, 46I
  direction of, 46H-46I
  elasticity and, 102B-102E
  of indifference curve, 188G
  of lines, 46F
  of long-run supply curve, 313-314
  negative, 46I, 102B
  positive, 46I, 102B
  of production possibilities frontier, 29-30
  rise, 46G

Slope—*Cont.*
  run, 46G
  steepness of, 46I-46J, 102C
  of supply curve, 46I
Slope intercept form, 78A
Small loans. *See* Microloans
SMarT. *See* Save More Tomorrow program
Smith, Adam, 26, 42
Smoking. *See* Cigarette taxes
Snapchat, 455
SNAP (Supplemental Nutrition Assistance
    Program), 545-547
Snowberg, Erik, 462
Social benefits, 454, 457-459, 573
Social Choice and Individual Values (Arrow),
    568, 572
Social costs, 453-456
Social enterprises, 273-274
Social insurance, 544, 547-548
Social media platforms, monthly average users
    of, 46A-46B
Social networks, 533, 534
Social norms, 484, 487-488, 597
Social Security
  contributions to, 585
  FICA tax for, 511, 512
  function of, 548
  future of, 518-519
  in New Deal legislation, 545
  pay-as-you-go model, 512
  payroll tax for, 511-512
  percent of government expenditures, 516
  population decline and, 410
  in poverty reduction, 529
  as safety net, 544
Social Security Act (1935), 518
Social Security Trust Fund, 518
Social value, 404-405
Sonn, Paul K., 155
Sony Music Entertainment, 353, 355, 367
South Africa
  diamonds from, 324
  income mobility in, 543
  national parks in, 478
  privatization of animals in, 490
South Asia, poverty in, 530, 531
South Korea, tax revenue as percentage of
    GDP, 515
South Sudan, embargo on, 441
Southwest, 97
Soviet Union, in Cold War, 220-221
Specialization
  defined, **36**
  gains from trade and, 37-40
  in goods and services, 36-37
  incomplete, 424-425
  international trade and, 35-37
  in production, 26, 35-36
Specific-country import standards, 439
Spending. *See* Government expenditures
Spirit Airlines, 97
SPM (Supplemental Poverty Measure), 528

Spotify, 480, 481
Sprint, 355
Srivasta, Joydeep, 198
Stack, Liam, 572
Standardized goods and services, 51,
    295-296, 356
Standard Oil, 340
Staples, 338
Starbucks, 79-81, 94-96, 167, 366
Startup costs, 272
State and local taxes, 503, 504, 508, 510, 512-514
State-owned enterprises, 326
Statistical discrimination, 237-239, **238,** 550
Status, 180-182
Status-quo bias, 586, **591**
Statutory incidence, 146, 506
Stavins, R. N., 87
Steel tariff, 433-435
Steepness of slope, 46I-46J, 102C
Stern, Andy, 546
StickK.com, 193-194
Stock market, 13-14
Strategies (game)
  commitment, 209-210, 219-221
  decision trees, 216-220
  defined, 205
  dominant, 207-208, 211, 373
  first-mover advantage, 218
  in market-entry games, 215-217
  pricing decisions, 211-212
  in prisoners' dilemma, 207-208, 211, 373
  in repeated games, 212-214, 218-219, 374
  in sequential games, 214-221
  tit-for-tat, 212-214, 439
Strikes, 409
String Cheese Incident, 337
StubHub, 337
Student loans
  adverse selection and, 234-235
  interest rates on, 245
  moral hazard and, 235
  present value calculation, 250
  regulation of, 18-19
  risk pooling and, 255
  at Yale University, 229-232
Sub-Saharan Africa, poverty in, 530, 532
Subsidies, 146-151
  for biofuels, 148-149
  buyer response to, 149
  for capturing positive externalities, 465-467
  deadweight loss and, 147-148
  defined, **146**
  effects of, 151
  to encourage consumption, 131
  seller response to, 146-147, 149
Substitutes
  availability of, 84
  close substitutes, 55, 324-325, 358
  defined, **55**
  indifference curves and, 188D, 188E
  monopolies due to lack of, 324-325,
    342-343

  in monopolistic competition, 358
  perfect, 188D, 188E
  price elasticity of demand and, 84
Substitution effect, 179, 188J-188K
Sunk cost, 8, 194-195, 304
Sunk-cost fallacy, 194-195
Sun Records, 353, 356-358
Sunstein, Cass, 586, 587
Super Bowl, 13-14
Supplemental Nutrition Assistance Program
    (SNAP), 545-547
Supplemental Poverty Measure (SPM), 528
Supply, 59-63
  defined, 59
  demand and (*See* Supply and demand)
  determinants of, 60-63, 395-397
  elastic, 93, 151-152, 311-312
  entry and exit impacted by, 311
  inelastic, 93, 151-152
  of labor (*See* Labor supply)
  law of, 59, 60
  market supply, 59
  nonprice determinants of, 60-63, 395-397
  perfectly elastic, 93, 311-312
  perfectly inelastic, 93
  price elasticity of, 80, 92-94, 96
  quantity (*See* Quantity supplied)
  taxes and, 140, 141
  trade-offs and, 59
  unit-elastic, 93
Supply and demand
  in autarky, 425-426
  cell phones, 49-72
  convergence at equilibrium, 63-64
  externalities and, 455-457
  for factors of production, 437
  in gasoline market, 452
  interaction in markets, 63
  net-exporters, 428-430
  net-importers and, 427, 428
  shifts in, 68-71, 394-399
  in world market, 431
Supply curve
  defined, **60**
  for domestic markets, 428, 429
  elasticity of, 145
  for labor, 390, 391
  long run, 306-314
  market, 308-310, 313-314
  market equilibrium and, 64
  movement along, 62-63, 141
  in perfectly competitive markets, 305-316
  shifts in, 62-63, 67-71, 141
  short run, 305, 307-308
  slope of, 46I
  subsidies and, 146, 149
  taxes and, 141, 143
  willingness to sell and, 60, 107-108
  for world market, 431
Supply schedule, 60
Surplus (budget), 516-517
Surplus (efficiency), 109-120

in bargaining game, 218
changing distribution of, 130–131
consumer (*See* Consumer surplus)
deadweight loss and, 118–119
defined, **109**
government intervention and, 130–131
market equilibrium and, 115–117
measurement of, 109–115
missing markets and, 119–120
producer (*See* Producer surplus)
reassignment of, 117–118
total (*See* Total surplus)
uses for, 104, 115–120
Surplus (excess supply)
as area under linear curve, 128A–128B
defined, **64**
externalities and, 456–459
government purchase of, 138
price ceilings and, 133–134
price floors and, 137–138, 153–154
redistribution by taxes, 142–143
steel tariff and, 434, 435
subsidies and, 148–149
Survivor (television program), 217
Sweden
comparison of 2017 tax rates, 510
income distribution in, 541
income mobility in, 543
tax revenue as percentage of GDP, 515
Swift, Taylor, 353
Switzerland
political participation in, 573
tax revenue as percentage of GDP, 515

T
Taiwan, income mobility in, 543
TANF (Temporary Assistance to Needy
    Families), 546
Tariffs, 433–436, 439
TaskRabbit, 39
Tax brackets, 506–510
Taxes and taxation, 497–520
    administrative burden, 500, 503
    bearing burden of, 144–146
    behavioral changes from, 498–500, 505
    on buyers, 143–144, 149
    capital gains tax, 511
    carbon tax, 464, 468, 563–564
    corporate income tax, 508, 512
    costs of, 498
    for countering negative externalities,
        464–465, 499
    deadweight loss and, 142, 144, 498, 500–503
    to discourage production and consumption,
        131, 140–146
    effects of, 151–152
    efficiency of, 500–503, 507, 510
    estate tax, 513–514
    excise tax, 506, 508, 512
    federal receipts (1940–2018), 508
    fiscal year for, 508
    gasoline tax, 452, 504

goals of, 498–500
graduate tax, 255
"happy to pay" campaign, 497
income tax, 502, 506–512
increases in, 151–152, 504–505
inefficiency created by, 500, 502, 503
international comparisons, 510, 514–515
lump-sum (head tax), 502–503, 505, 507
marginal rate tax, 509, 510
overall impact of, 144
payroll tax, 508, 511–512
personal income tax, 502, 506–511
Pigovian, 464–465, 467
pollution tax, 146
principles of, 500–507
production tax, 464
progressive tax, 506–507, 509–510,
    512, 545
property tax, 513
proportional/flat tax, 506, 507
regressive tax, 507, 513
revenue from, 498–500, 503–505, 514–515
sales tax, 152–153, 503, 506–508, 512–513
on sellers, 140–143, 149
single tax, 340–341
sin tax, 464, 499, 503–504
state and local, 503, 504, 508, 510, 512–514
tariffs and, 433–435
taxonomy of, 508–513
tradable allowances vs., 467
value-added tax, 513
for welfare and social insurance
    programs, 548
Tax incidence, 144–146, 505–507, 513
Tax rates, 503–505, 509, 510
Tax revenue, 498–500, 503–505, 514–515
Tax wedge, 142, 144
Taylor, Kate, 572
TC. *See* Total cost
Tea Party movement, 497
Technology. *See also* Cell phones
    for comparative advantage, 424
    Internet, 110, 337
    labor-augmenting, 395
    labor demand and, 394–396
    labor-saving, 395
    leapfrog, 55
    market equilibrium and, 72
    as positive network externality, 455
    productive capacity and, 32
    skill-biased technical change, 542
    as supply determinant, 61
Temporary Assistance to Needy Families
    (TANF), 546
Temptation, 191, 192, 590
Term limits, 577–578
Tessuma, Christopher W., 149
Texas Department of Transportation, 203
Textile industry
    autarky and, 425–426
    in Bangladesh, 420–422, 425
    in Lesotho, 423–424, 441

Multifiber Arrangement, 423–424,
    435–436, 441
net-importers, 426–428
T-shirt production, 25–39
world market, 431–432
Thailand, Mama Noodles Index in, 56
Thaler, Richard, 585–587, 591
Third-party candidate problem, 568–569
Ticketmaster, 337
"Tickle Me Elmo" shortage, 66
Time. *See also* Value over time
    adjustment time, 84–85, 94
    comparative advantage over, 40–41
    opportunity cost of, 195
Time inconsistency
    charitable donations and, 192
    choice architecture and, 586, 590, 592
    defined, **191, 590**
    future vs. present orientation and, 191–193
    limiting options and, 592
    procrastination and, 191, 193
    temptation and, 191, 192
Time-series graphs, 46B, 46C
Time Warner Cable, 338
Timm, Jane C., 567
Tit-for-tat strategy, 212–214, 439
Title VII of the Civil Rights Act (1964),
    409, 551
T-Mobile, 338, 355
Tobacco use. *See* Cigarette taxes
Tobin, James, 229
Total cost curve, 277, 279
Total cost (TC). *See also* Average total cost
    (ATC)
    components of, 270
    defined, **269**
    description and calculation, 282
    equation for, 277
    graphing, 279
    in perfectly competitive markets, 300–301
Total revenue
    defined, **88, 269**
    elasticity and changes in, 88–91
    of monopolies, 329–331
    in perfectly competitive markets, 298–301
    price changes and, 88–91
    price effect and, 88–89, 330
    quantity effect and, 88–89, 330
Total surplus
    calculation of, 114–115, 128B
    changing distribution of, 117–118
    creation of new markets and, 119–120
    deadweight loss of, 118–119
    defined, **114**
    efficiency and, 104
    from free trade, 427
    maximization of, 104, 451
    price ceilings and, 133
    price changes and, 114
    taxation in decrease of, 501
Toyota Motor Corporation, 94
Toyota Prius, 180–181

Tradable allowances, 467, 469, 492, 563

Trade, international. *See* International trade

Trade agreements, 437-442

  African Growth and Opportunity Act, 423-424

  Multifiber Arrangement, 423-424, 435-436, 441

  North American Free Trade Agreement, 440, 567

Trade liberalization, 433, 437, 438

Trade-offs

  assumptions regarding, 9-10

  in car culture, 452-453

  in college attendance, 245-246

  in cost-benefit analysis, 245

  demand curve and, 53

  equity-efficiency, 548-549

  free-rider problem and, 484

  incentives and, 9-10

  income inequality and, 548-549

  in law of demand, 53

  in law of supply, 59

  in marginal decision making, 8

  marginal utility and, 173

  microloans and, 8-9

  opportunity cost and, 6-7, 53, 59, 195

  in production possibilities frontier, 29

  rational behavior and, 205

  sunk cost and, 194, 195

  utility and, 166, 168

  in willingness to pay, 106

  in willingness to sell, 108

Trade restrictions. *See* Protectionism

Trade unions. *See* Labor unions

Tragedy of the commons, 477, 486-492

Transaction costs, 51, 296

Transient poverty, 529-530

Transitivity, in perfect voting system, 568-570

Transparency, 576

Triple bottom line, 268-269

Trivers, Robert, 214

Trout, Mike, 383, 385, 399, 400, 402, 404

Trump, Donald, 238, 419, 439, 566-567

Trusts, 337

T-shirt production, 25-39

Tung, Irene, 155

Turkewitz, Julie, 92

Turkey, tax revenue as percentage of GDP, 515

Two-party system, 577

Tyco, 66

U

Uber, 119

UBI (universal basic income), 546-547

Uganda, income distribution in, 541

Ultimatum games, 218

Unanimity, in perfect voting system, 568

Uncertainty, 246, 251

Uncorrelated variables, 13

Undersupplied goods, 478, 482-484, 486, 574

Unemployment insurance, 544, 548

Unions. *See* Labor unions

United Airlines, 461-462

United Kingdom

  income mobility in, 543

  Industrial Revolution in, 40

  poverty line basis in, 528

  student loans in, 255

  tax revenue as percentage of GDP, 515

  vertical splits in, 340

United Methodist churches, 404

United Nations, 441-442

United States

  agricultural policies in, 136-139

  biofuel subsidies in, 148-149

  budget deficits and surpluses (1980-2018), 517

  in Cold War, 220-221

  college completion rates in, 17

  comparative advantage in, 41, 420-421

  comparison of 2017 tax rates, 510

  demographics of poverty in, 528-530

  domestic and imported vehicle types in, 46B, 46C

  economic growth in, 529

  factor distribution of income in, 403, 437-438

  federal expenditures (1940-2018), 516

  Franco-American cheese war, 438-439

  Great Depression in, 545

  immigrant populations in, 396-399, 567

  imports from China, 419, 439

  income by race and gender and, 550

  income distribution in, 536-537, 541

  income inequality in, 540-542

  income mobility in, 542, 543

  income tax brackets (2018), 509

  labor laws in, 409

  labor unions in, 408-409

  minimum wage in, 405-406

  in North American Free Trade Agreement, 567

  organ donation in, 595-596

  packaged food regulation in, 239

  poverty line basis in, 527-528

  poverty line by family size, 527

  poverty rate over time (1960-2018), 529

  public budget, 514-518

  revenue collection (2018), 514

  size of economy relative to world market, 430-432

  social insurance programs in, 548

  tax revenue as percentage of GDP, 515

  term limits in, 577

  wealthiest Americans, 525, 537, 540

Unit-elastic demand, 86, 91

Unit-elastic supply, 93

Universal basic income (UBI), 546-547

Universal Music Group, 353, 355, 367-374

University of Michigan, 468, 553

U.S. Census Bureau, 528

U.S. Department of Agriculture (USDA), 138, 271

U.S. Department of Health and Human Services, 534

U.S. Department of Justice, 337, 338, 354

U.S. Environmental Protection Agency (EPA), 593

U.S. Federal Bureau of Investigation (FBI), 366

U.S. Food and Drug Administration (FDA), 239, 270, 286

U.S. Postal Service (USPS), 338, 339

U.S. Securities and Exchange Commission (SEC), 576

U.S. Steel, 340

U.S. Supreme Court, 553

Used car market, 232-233, 236-238

Usham, Satyajit, 234

Utility, 165-184. *See also* Marginal utility

  altruism and, 182-184

  basic idea of, 166-170

  decision making and, 167-168

  defined, **167**

  frame of reference and, 181-182

  in gift-giving, 165

  indifference curves for representation of, 188A

  reciprocity and, 183-184

  revealed preference and, 168-169

  society and, 180-184

  status and, 180-182

  Veblen goods and, 179

Utility function

  calculation of, 170

  consumption bundles in, 188A-188C, 188G-188L

  defined, **169**

  in predicting behavior, 175

Utility maximization

  within constraints, 172-176

  defined, 167

  indifference curves and, 188E

  rational, 167, 173

V

Value

  absolute, 83

  expected, 252-254

  resources in creation of, 11

  taxation in loss of, 501

Value-added tax (VAT), 513

Value of the marginal product (VMP), 387-389

Value over time

  compounding, 248-249, 264A-264C

  future value, 248, 264A-264C

  interest rates and, 247-248

  present value, 249-251

  time preferences and, 246-247

Variable costs (VC)

  average, 278-280, 282, 304-306

  defined, **270**

  description of, 282

  examples of, 270

  as explicit costs, 271

  in perfectly competitive markets, 303-306

  prescription drugs and, 268

Variables

correlation of, 13–14
dependent, 46D
independent, 46D
linear relationship of, 78A, 78B
omitted, 14, 551
one variable graphs, 46A–46C
two variable graphs, 46C–46F
VAT (value-added tax), 513
Vavra, Joseph, 362
VC. *See* Variable costs
Veblen, Thorstein, 181
Veblen goods, 179
Vehicles. *See* Automobile industry
Verizon, 355
Vertical splits, 340
Viacom, 338
Vietnam, income mobility in, 543
VMP (value of the marginal product), 387–389
Voluntary transactions, 103–104, 115, 120
Voting
    electronic voting machines, 578
    first-past-the-post, 568–569, 571, 577
    halo effect and, 574
    increased enfranchisement, 578–579
    mail-in ballots, 573
    median-voter theorem, 565–567, 577
    opportunity cost of, 572
    pair-wise majority voting, 569–570
    perfect voting system, 567–572
    preferences of voters, 564
    ranked-choice voting, 571–572
    rational voter myth, 572–574
    social benefit of, 573
Vouchers, 589

W

Wages. *See also* Income; Minimum wage
    efficiency, 407
    equilibrium, 393–394, 406, 407
    Fight for $15 Movement, 154–155
    labor supply and wage rates, 390–393
    labor unions and, 408
    negotiation for, 108–109
    performance pay, 404–405
    as price of labor, 387

profit-maximizing quantity of labor and, 388–389
    social value and, 404–405
Waldfogel, Joel, 165
Walmart, 285, 327, 402, 423
Walt Disney Company, 338
Wants
    of business firms, 268–269, 294
    constraints on, 5–6
    decision making and, 167
    information asymmetry and, 231
    in labor demand, 387
    of monopolies, 327
    of policy-makers, 576
    in production possibilities frontier, 27
    utility and, 166, 167
    in willingness to pay or sell, 105
Warner, Tracy, 39, 40
Warner Music Group, 353, 355, 367–374
Warranties, 257–258
Wealth, 525, 537, 540
WeChat, 46B
Welfare effects
    of monopolies, 334–335
    of monopolistic competition, 361–362
    from net-exporters, 429, 430
    from net-importers, 427, 428
    of price ceilings, 133, 134
    of price floors, 138
    of quotas, 436
    of tariffs, 435
Welfare programs, 516, 545–549
Welfare state, 545–548
Wendy's, 355
West, Kanye, 353, 354
West Basin Water Management District, 487–488
WhatsApp, 46B
Whole Foods, 338
Wikipedia, 483
Wilderquist, Karl, 547
Willingness to buy, 53, 80
Willingness to pay (reservation price)
    defined, **105**
    demand curve and, 105–106

for Internet, 110
    price discrimination and, 344–346
    tourists and, 346
Willingness to sell, 60, **105,** 107–108
Witness protection program, 211
Wolak, F. A., 87
Wolfers, J., 463
Women. *See* Gender
Wonder, Stevie, 353
Work. *See* Employment; Labor market
Workers. *See* Employees; Labor
World Bank, 531
World market, 430–432
World price
    higher than domestic price, 428–429
    lower than domestic price, 426–428
    net-exporters and, 428–430
    net-importers and, 426–428
    quota effect on, 436
    size of economy and, 430–432
    steel tariff and effect on, 434
World Trade Organization (WTO), 435, **438**–439
World War II (1939–1945), 134, 516

X

X-axis, 46C–46D
X-coordinates, 46D

Y

Yale University, 229–232
Y-axis, 46C–46D
Y-coordinates, 46D
Y-intercept, 78A
Young, Eric, Jr., 399
YouTube, 46B
Yunus, Muhammad, 3–5, 9, 10, 12, 273, 336

Z

Zero economic profit, 309, 311, 313, 360, 361
Zero-sum game, 115
Zinke, Ryan, 91
Zinman, Jonathan, 364
Zuckerberg, Mark, 546
Zucman, Gabriel, 540